Foreword

By Evan Silva and Dan Pizzuta

Jimmy Haslam's purchase of the Cleveland Browns finalized on October 25, 2012. From that point through the start of the 2018 season, the Browns went 19-70 (.213). Yet according to *Forbes*, the value of the Browns' franchise appreciated by *one billion dollars* since Haslam's purchase. If an owner is treating his pro football organization as a moneymaking business enterprise, where, exactly, is the incentive to finish first out of 32?

Finishing first out of 32 isn't easy, especially in a salary-capped league designed to promote parity. Finishing first out of 32 in any competitive endeavor is hard. And it's *supposed* to be hard. It's *supposed* to be hard to win the Super Bowl.

But in any competitive endeavor where the goal is to finish first, some competitors try harder than others. Groups at the top pour more resources into finishing first. They outwork their competition. They *want it more*.

In the NFL, every team is successful. Because the NFL is a business first and foremost, and it is run by 32 business owners who are all extremely profitable. Fantasy football, sports betting, TV contracts, ticket sales, and merchandise ensure these business owners stay rich. They are so profitable that the owner of the NFL's losingest franchise got *one billion dollars* richer in a five-year span.

And these cash cows are just hitting their stride. Dallas Mavericks owner **Mark Cuban** recently estimated the value of pro sports franchises will *double* once sports betting is legalized throughout the United States.

Everyone in the NFL *prefers* to win games. But *preferring* to win games should not be conflated with prioritizing a first-place finish out of 32. A small handful of teams go above and beyond to find competitive advantages and exploit market inefficiencies, and they tend to be the same teams in the hunt for first.

Identifying ways teams can gain edges on their competition is what this book is all about.

The Patriots most obviously prioritize finishing first

Over the last 20 years, no team has discovered more competitive edges than the Patriots, and they've so pushed the envelope that they've been accused of cheating. Albeit reprehensible, videotaping Jets defensive coaches' signals in 2007 was done in the interest of gaining an edge. In January of 2015, Ravens coach **John Harbaugh** (falsely) accused the Patriots of using illegal substitutions and deceptively declaring players eligible and ineligible pass catchers to fool Baltimore's defense. (Harbaugh's Ravens used similar tactics in a game against the Raiders the very next year.) If the Patriots really did deflate footballs, as the Colts accused them of doing, it was done to create potential advantages ranging from improving **Tom Brady**'s grip to lowering New England's fumble rate.

Winning off the field

But New England's greatest recent market-inefficiency discovery involves trading late-round picks for proven veterans and, better yet, pick-swap trades that simultaneously exploit the NFL's compensatory draft-pick process. Last year, the Patriots acquired CB **Jason McCourty** from the Browns in exchange for moving down just 14 slots in the seventh round of the draft. Pro Football Focus graded McCourty No. 13 among 123 cornerbacks last season, and McCourty's end-zone pass breakup against **Brandin Cooks** was the biggest defensive play of Super Bowl 53. The Pats' best defensive player in the AFC Championship was LB **Kyle Van Noy**, who New England acquired from Detroit in exchange for dropping just 24 slots on day three of the 2017 draft. The Lions used their "improved" late-round pick on the great **Brad Kaaya**.

Highway robberies

Yet no recent Patriots trade exploited cracks in the system more than their acquisition of LT **Trent Brown**. In doing so, New England dropped from the No. 95 pick in the 2018 draft to No. 143, where they selected Week 1 starting middle linebacker **Ja'Whaun Bentley**. Brown started all 19 games on Brady's blind side and earned the biggest free agent contract for an offensive lineman in NFL history after the season, which will net the Patriots a third-round compensatory pick in the 2020 draft.

In sum, New England parlayed 2018's No. 95 overall pick into a full year of quality left tackle play, their potential middle linebacker of the future, and a likely top-100 pick next year. That is highway robbery.

Rulebook mastery

Harbaugh was wrong to accuse the Patriots of cheating. He simply didn't understand the ins and outs of the rulebook as well as New England did. Although famed-but-mysterious Patriots research director **Ernie Adams** is sometimes credited with being an analytics guru, Adams' actual primary contribution is identifying every possible competitive advantage in the pages of the rulebook.

And the Patriots gained a competitive advantage over Harbaugh with uncommon substitution practices in that playoff game. "It's a substitution trick type of a thing," Harbaugh claimed at the time. "So they don't give you the opportunity, they don't give you a chance to make the proper (counter) substitutions."

"Maybe these guys gotta study the rulebook and figure it out," Brady responded. "We obviously knew what we were doing and we made some pretty important plays. It was a real good weapon for us."

Down by two touchdowns, the Patriots came back to beat the Ravens 35-31.

The Colts are coming, and the Eagles have already arrived

But the Patriots aren't the only team that prioritizes finishing first. Eagles owner **Jeffrey Lurie** is hellbent on winning, and members of his organization have spoken more publicly than any team in football about Philadelphia's use of analytics. An analytics expert relays win probabilities and Success Rates into coach **Doug Pederson**'s headset before play calls on the field. The Eagles became even more analytically driven by hiring ex-**Sashi Brown** lieutenant **Andrew Berry** as VP of Football Operations and promoting analytics wiz kid **Alec Halaby**, a Harvard graduate like Berry. GM **Howie Roseman** acquired **DeSean Jackson** in the equivalent of a pick-swap trade, surrendering the Eagles' 2019 sixth-round pick for Jackson and the Bucs' 2020 seventh-rounder. Roseman has also begun hammering the compensatory market, adding fourth- and sixth-round selections in 2019 with additional third- and fourth-round picks on the way in 2020.

The Colts have become the league's fastest-rising team on savvy GM **Chris Ballard**'s watch. Ballard's market-inefficiency exploitation has involved stockpiling second-round picks, making a league-high *seven* round-two selections over the last two drafts and acquiring Washington's second-round pick next year. Many NFL commentators cite first-round picks as preferred assets because they carry fifth-year options, but the option years aren't priced all that favorably for teams. Second-round picks generate extreme expected-net surplus relative to contract value. As the Redskins are one of the worst teams in the league and will likely be starting a rookie quarterback, the second-rounder Ballard acquired should be near the top of the round.

Perhaps most importantly, Ballard hired **Frank Reich** away from the analytically-minded Eagles, and that imprint was immediately evident in Reich's play calling. As you'll read in Warren's Colts chapter, Reich passed at the NFL's third-highest rate (60%) on first downs in first halves of games. The trickle-down effect allowed Indianapolis to face the league's second-fewest average yards to go on third downs (6.3).

2019 Football Preview

By: Warren Sharp
@SharpFootball

of

SharpFootballAnalysis.com
SharpFootballStats.com
sharp@sharpfootballanalysis.com

Evan Silva
Executive Editor

Associate Editors:
Julie Rone
Matt Kelley
Adam Hardstad

Most of the league is still far behind

Teams that *prefer* to win but don't *prioritize* it encompass the majority of the league. The Bengals barely invest in their scouting infrastructure and embrace mediocrity to an egregious degree. The Chargers don't even have an analytics department. In Washington, seemingly no amount of losing is enough to get **Bruce Allen** fired. His record as Redskins GM is 52-75-1 (.410). It pays to be **Dan Snyder**'s crony. Allen has unbelievably outlasted **Mike Shanahan**, **Kyle Shanahan**, **Sean McVay**, **Scot McCloughan**, and **Matt LaFleur** in D.C. The Giants literally drafted a running back at No. 2 overall. Hilariously paying **Eli Manning** $23.2 million this season, what was once one of the NFL's proudest franchises has become a laughingstock under owner **John Mara**.

Teams that fall into this behind-the-times bucket need to read this book. And they need to read the following data-backed tenets identified by Big Blue View's Dan Pizzuta using statistics from Sports Info Solutions and Next Gen Stats.

Third-down backs should be first-down backs

First down has long been perceived as a running down. In 2017, the league-wide average pass-run split on first down was 47-53. It was 50-50 last season, but that was still well below the 59-41 league-wide split on all downs. Yet passing to running backs on first down is *significantly* more effective.

In 2018, there were 6,248 running back rushing attempts on first down. They averaged 4.5 yards per carry, minus-0.01 Expected Points Added per attempt, and a positive play rate of 41.3%. When teams threw to running backs on first down, they averaged 6.02 yards per target, 7.8 yards per reception, 0.08 EPA per attempt — slightly more efficient than the average of all passes regardless of down at 0.05 EPA — and a positive play rate of 52.3%.

Throwing to running backs has typically been reserved for third downs given the idea of a third-down back. But since receiving skills are now more necessity than luxury, the ball is getting thrown to running backs more often on early downs. But even while there were more running back targets on first down (1,454) than third down (718) in 2018, they weren't exactly treated the same way. Running back targets on first down were caught 0.17 yards behind the line of scrimmage on average, while the average running back reception on third down was caught beyond the line. This indicates that while passes to running backs have increased on first down, they're still often used as a last-resort check down and are not fully schemed.

The Panthers and Patriots were the best at getting the ball to backs on first down, and both got their backs the ball beyond the line of scrimmage. **Christian McCaffery** led all running backs in first-down targets (59) and receptions (54). He only had two fewer first downs (17) on those receptions than he did on 128 first-down carries. If the goal is to gain yards and move the chains, the Panthers were far more successful with McCaffery catching the ball on early downs than running it.

New England's **James White** – often labeled a third-down back – was second in first-down targets among running backs with 44.

If teams treated throws to running backs on first down more like they do on third down — and increase their volume compared to rushing attempts — teams could set themselves up better for second and third downs or just face third downs less frequently.

Play action is a cheat code

Play action remains one of the most efficient and underused offensive strategies in football. In 2016, only one team used play action on at least 25% of drop backs. That increased to seven teams in 2017 and doubled to 14 in 2018. Still, only 24% of drop backs featured play action in 2018 despite the significant improvement a passing game sees with a play fake.

Last season on non-play-action drop backs, teams averaged 7.01 yards per attempt, 0.00 EPA per attempt, and a positive play rate of 49.5%. On play-action passes, teams averaged 8.49 yards per attempt, 0.12 EPA per attempt, and a positive play rate of 50.4%.

2018	Attempts	YPA	TD%	INT%	Sack%	EPA/Att	Positve Play %
Non-PA	13383	7.01	4.6%	2.4%	7.3%	0.00	46.6%
PA	4288	8.49	5.5%	2.2%	5.3%	0.12	50.4%

While teams are starting to catch onto the impact of play action, there are additional layers to exploit to gain an even bigger advantage.

Going deep off play action

Deep passes (traveling 20 or more yards in the air) increase expected points but lower Success Rate. It's a clear payoff for the chance at a bigger play, but it's also a part of the game that has seen a bit of a decline as many teams move to shorter passes to up completion rates.

Non-play-action deep throws averaged 11.6 yards per attempt, 0.23 EPA per attempt, and a positive play rate of 34.2% last season. Add a fake handoff before the throw and those numbers improved to 15.5 yards per attempt, 0.52 EPA per attempt, and a positive play rate of 41.3%.

Deep passes were thrown off play action at a rate slightly higher than all passes (28%). But because of the relatively low volume of deep passes, only 15 teams averaged at least one deep shot off play action per game. The Falcons and Rams – two of the top offenses in the league – were the only teams to average at least two.

Seattle might have been the league's best team with this combining the Seahawks' overall success with play action, **Russell Wilson**'s deep arm, and **Tyler Lockett**'s efficiency deep downfield. Seattle had the seventh-most deep attempts off play action and a league-high 1.48 EPA per attempt.

Taking advantage of 12 personnel

As passing has increased around the league, teams have embraced 11 personnel (three wide receivers, one running back, and one tight end). In 2018, teams lined up in 11 personnel 66% of the time. That shift has forced defenses to change to a nickel package (five defensive backs) as its primary formation.

Throwing from 12 personnel (two receivers, one back, two tight ends) happens less frequently yet is more efficient. A heavier personnel package with more tight ends invites defenses' base personnel with more linebackers and fewer defensive backs. 12 personnel also serves as pseudo play action because defenses are expecting the run from that package. Whereas teams threw the ball 66% of the time in 11 personnel in 2018, they passed just 48% of the time in 12.

From 11, teams averaged 7.16 yards per attempt, 0.03 EPA per attempt, and a positive play rate of 49.5%. Efficiency increased to 8.08 yards per attempt and 0.15 EPA with a positive play rate of 54% of out 12. Now add a play fake and teams averaged 9.19 yards per attempt and 0.15 EPA. 14 teams averaged at least 9.0 yards per attempt off play action from 12 personnel in 2018. That was only true for eight teams out of 11 personnel.

By EPA and Success Rate, throwing from 12 without play action is slightly more efficient than throwing from 11 with it.

2018	YPA	EPA/Att	Positve Play %
11 non-PA	6.96	-0.02	46.0%
11 PA	8.12	0.11	49.6%
12 non-PA	7.15	0.12	50.6%
12 PA	9.19	0.15	51.6%

No team passed from 12 personnel more than the Eagles in 2018 by both overall passes and play action attempts. With **Zach Ertz** and **Dallas Goedert**, Philadelphia passed 61% of the time in 12 personnel. Because of the passing threat, defenses didn't know whether to use base or nickel against that package. The heavier personnel didn't impact Philly's ability to run the ball; they still had the third-most rushing attempts against a nickel defense.

The NFL's percentage of plays in 12 personnel dropped from 25% in 2017 to just 16% in 2018. That's part of the league's continuing passing explosion, but teams that can still embrace a pass-heavy approach with personnel packages that indicate run find themselves with a schematic advantage.

Throw deep to slot receivers

The NFL is shifting to shorter passes. Over the past three seasons, average target depth dropped from 8.8 yards in 2016 to 8.3 in 2017 to 8.1 in 2018. It's a subtle shift, but one that has been apparent in many NFL schemes that value safe completions to move the offense.

Last season, 70.6% of NFL passes were thrown within ten yards of the line of scrimmage. But nearly 200% of the league's passing value by EPA came on throws that went more than ten yards downfield. Despite over 70% of throws coming within ten yards, teams totaled minus-897.7 Expected Points Added on them. Only nine teams finished with positive EPA on throws within ten yards. The real value — and where teams separate themselves — comes in the intermediate and deep areas of the field.

Deep passes give teams the highest EPA per attempt but with the tradeoff of a lower Success Rate. While deep throws off play action are most efficient, there is another way teams can exploit deep passes for higher EPA and Success Rate. Throwing deep to a slot receiver.

The typical deep threat lines up outside. There's nothing wrong with that. There were 925 deep passes thrown to receivers lined up out wide in 2018 to the tune of 0.22 EPA per attempt and a positive play rate of 31.6%. Only slightly fewer passes were thrown deep to receivers who lined up in the slot (852) but the production was better: 0.35 EPA per attempt with a positive play rate of 38.1%.

What can make this a competitive advantage for teams is not just having a player who can win deep from the slot, but having a player who can play outside and then rotate in to win deep from the slot. The two players with the most deep targets from the slot in 2018 were **Tyreek Hill** (25) and **Brandin Cooks** (18), two receivers from great offenses who spent most of their time lined up wide. Other star receivers like **T.Y. Hilton**, **Julio Jones**, and **DeAndre Hopkins** were among the leaders in targets, each with at least ten deep passes from the slot.

Leaving the Dumb Teams Behind

By The Ringer's Kevin Clark

It is not much of a surprise that professional football was the last major sport to embrace analytics. The NFL is *still* a league in which a solid chunk of coaches believe in establishing the run for the sake of establishing the run, it's a league in which "that's the way we've always done it" is viewed as an acceptable answer, it's a league in which **Eli Manning** has made more money than any player in history.

That is what makes this era of football so fascinating: we are watching the most stubborn major sports league go through a radical change in front of our eyes. Every team has invested in analytics, but only the smartest teams have made major decisions based on those investments. The Eagles and Patriots use analytics as much as anyone, and they've won Super Bowls because of it.

The bottom line of modern football is that smart teams beat dumb teams. It is about teams finding the tiniest edges and exploiting them until they become huge advantages. These edges can come in many forms. There's more data about football than ever before and there's more access to plays and playbooks on the internet than coaches have ever had at their disposal. This is an era of unlimited information and innovation, and if you are not using all of it you're probably going to get fired.

Over the last year, I've reported heavily on these changes in the sport. I've seen a handful of teams' analytics databases and had long talks with some of the smartest general managers in the sport about where the game is headed. The answers vary greatly but all have the same theme: it's innovating at an unprecedented rate.

Just a few years ago, NFL coaches wouldn't dare look to the lower level of football for ideas. Now, coaches have told me they scour YouTube in search of high school plays they might be able to borrow. Teams that aren't borrowing heavily from the college game on a weekly basis are offensively stagnant. General managers monitor Twitter looking for analytic breakdowns of their team. Coaches are going for it on fourth down at historic rates. Teams use GPS player tracking, available league wide for the first time in 2018, to help play-calling or evaluate prospects.

Competitive advantages are not supposed to exist in the NFL. This is a sport that legislates fairness to the point that every team should hover around 8-8 every year. This is why the league has a draft, free agency, a hard salary cap, limits on practice time and a schedule based on where teams finished the year before. Teams are *supposed* to be even. That is why the teams that reliably find those edges should be studied and celebrated.

It is not a surprise that the Patriots, whose entire model is based on winning on the margins and being *slightly* better than the next-best team, have dominated this era. Their innovations (like their usage of the slot receiver) and mastery of the salary cap have led to the most impressive run in league history. The sport can now change in a year more than it did in entire decades, and a team like the Patriots changes with it constantly.

We know what smart teams are doing now: a heavy dose of play-action, a skillful use of the rookie wage cap, passing out of heavy formations, and aggressive play calling that eliminates the need for third downs. We also know what comes next: Smart teams using 2019 to find more edges and building a franchise around those edges. And then leaving the dumb teams behind.

www.sharp football analysis.com

The Forefront of Inventing & Incorporating Custom Advanced Analytics & Metrics into Football Handicapping

Winning 60% on NFL totals. For more than a decade.

Warren Sharp and Sharp Football Analysis offer the level of examination, insight, and actionable recommendations found in NFL meeting rooms and front offices throughout the league. That's why professional betting groups and NFL teams hire him—to find the edges to exploit and the advantages to accelerate wins.

Now it's accessible to you: the most valuable edge in betting, fantasy, DFS, and prop recommendations, with statistical analysis you won't find anywhere else.

Transparent Record Keeping
All client plays publicly displayed minutes after the start of the game

NFL's Most Consistent Results
Delivering winning seasons annually since 2006. Emphasizing sound money management, +EV betting opportunities & beating the market

Lifetime NFL Record
Totals: 497-326 (60%)
Sides (Personal Plays): 626-488 (56%)

Lifetime NFL Playoffs Record: 134-77 (64%)
Lifetime Super Bowl Record: 18-9 (67%)

Lifetime College Football Record
Totals: 716-594 (55%)

Respected Analysis
Numerous betting syndicates acquire recommendations & Warren's work is well known by current and former linemakers

Line Value
Using timed release system, when Warren releases a play to clients, the market reacts giving clients consistent, significant & measurable line value

SHARP
FOOTBALL ANALYSIS

SharpFootballAnalysis.com is Relaunching July 8, 2019!

Join for the 2019 season starting July 8!

"I noticed Warren was moving some lines around on Wednesdays after he put his stuff up on his site, and he was winning. Instantly, when Warren gives out his play, the books move toward his line. Very rarely will you get a better number than his. He's a consistent winner."
- Professional Bettor & Las Vegas Legend
Bill "Krackman" Krackomberger

Warren Sharp of sharpfootballanalysis.com is an industry pioneer at the forefront of incorporating advanced analytics and metrics into football handicapping after spending years constructing, testing, betting and perfecting computer models written to beat NFL and college football totals.

"Warren's synopsis on game totals is vastly superior utilizing his mathematical formulas, to any preview I have ever seen. His success is two-fold, beating the closing number by up to 3 pts and winning at a clip needed to secure a hefty profit. Getting in early ensures some fantastic middling opportunities."
- **Richie Baccellieri**, former Director of Race and Sports in Las Vegas at Caesars Palace, MGM Grand and The Palms

A licensed Professional Engineer by trade, Warren now works as a quantitative analyst for multiple professional sports betting syndicates in Las Vegas and has parlayed a long-term winning record into selections for clients which move the Vegas line and beat the closing number with regularity.

Hear Pro Bettor "Krackman"

Results NOW, Pay LATER:
Get all the 2019 recommendations now but defer the majority of the season package cost until after the season! Details at www . sharp football analysis . com

SHARP
FOOTBALL ANALYSIS

iii FOREWORD, BY EVAN SILVA, DAN PIZZUTA and KEVIN CLARK

COLUMNS

01 YOU ARE WHAT YOUR RECORD SAYS YOU ARE

09 **32** ANALYTICAL OBSERVATIONS

13 **2019** INJURY PREVIEW

16 FANTASY STOCK: FIVE FANTASY BREAKOUTS FOR **2019**

18 NFL TEAMS TURNED TO THE PASS IN **2018** AND TURNED THE CORNER

DEDICATION

TO my wife & children – I love you so much TO the NFL teams that consulted with me in the past and those looking to do so in the future TO the decision makers in NFL front offices who exhaust every means to gain an edge because they care about winning TO anyone who spreads the word about this book, my websites and my passion for analyzing football and TO all who join in as 2019 clients of Sharp Football Analysis

ACKNOWLEDGMENTS

TO Evan Silva, thank you for editing this year's preview – you exceeded my expectations as usual. Thank you for coming through on the foreword! And TO Kevin Clark and Dan Pizzuta for their contributions in the foreword

TEAM CHAPTERS

24 LAYOUT AND DEFINITIONS

25 CHAPTERS
    25 ARIZONA CARDINALS
    32 ATLANTA FALCONS
    39 BALTIMORE RAVENS
    46 BUFFALO BILLS
    53 CAROLINA PANTHERS
    60 CHICAGO BEARS
    67 CINCINNATTI BENGALS
    74 CLEVELAND BROWNS
    81 DALLAS COWBOYS
    88 DENVER BRONCOS
    95 DETROIT LIONS
    102 GREEN BAY PACKERS
    109 HOUSTON TEXANS
    116 INDIANAPOLIS COLTS
    123 JACKSONVILLE JAGUARS
    130 KANSAS CITY CHIEFS
    137 LOS ANGELES CHARGERS
    144 LOS ANGELES RAMS
    151 MIAMI DOLPHINS
    158 MINNESOTA VIKINGS
    165 NEW ENGLAND PATRIOTS
    172 NEW ORLEANS SAINTS
    179 NEW YORK GIANTS
    186 NEW YORK JETS
    193 OAKLAND RAIDERS
    200 PHILADELPHIA EAGLES
    207 PITTSBURGH STEELERS
    214 SAN FRANCISCO 49ERS
    221 SEATTLE SEAHAWKS
    228 TAMPA BAY BUCCANEERS
    235 TENNESSEE TITANS
    242 WASHINGTON REDSKINS

You Are What Your Record Says You Are

By Warren Sharp

I remember not being able to say these things:

I consult for multiple NFL teams. I have a visualized-data website, Sharp Football Stats, that is free-to-use and allows the public a means to better understand the game. I run an NFL analysis website, Sharp Football Analysis, that shares cutting-edge content, via written, video and audio delivery, and provides weekly recommendations on game outcomes. Upon release, my recommendations on NFL totals move betting lines because my win rate is 60.3%, with a track record spanning an over 800-game sample that was over a decade in the making. I work privately for betting "groups" because of my longstanding record of success on NFL betting recommendations.

It wasn't easy to get to this point. You must pay your dues and show strong work for years upon years. It's been a journey. And I took a circuitous route in some respects.

But I'm where I'm meant to be. I'm happy knowing I am doing what I was born to do. What I excel at doing. What I love doing.

Where does the story end? It's far too soon to tell. I'm not focused on the ending. I'm focused on making every day the best day possible. Learning the most I can, sharing the most I can, working as hard as I can and being as successful as I can. If I stack as many of those days together as possible, I know that I'll end up where I'm meant to be.

My story started probably quite like many of you reading this right now. I was a huge fan of football growing up. I loved to watch the strategy and the action. I remember my brain sparking when John Madden shared the secret to knowing whether it was a pass or a run based on how the offensive linemen reacted at the snap. As a kid in elementary school watching football on TV, I always felt I was a second behind because I couldn't tell if the quarterback was going to hand off to his running back or not. Once I knew the cues to look for, my brain had that extra second to process the routes or the run blocking, rather than wondering if it was a run or a pass.

My dad was a passionate fan. He had two teams he pulled for. Our home team that played closest to us and his home team where he grew up. This was way before the days of Direct Ticket. So we rarely watched his home team except when they were on in a primetime slot. Mainly we watched our home team. I'd venture to say that at least 40 percent of the time that we watched a game, we turned it on just prior to the opening kickoff, and the TV would be off by the start of the fourth quarter. He hated watching bad football.

He played Division I basketball and baseball in college, but not football. I don't know if he had a deep understanding for why the team was losing, but he sure as hell didn't like it. After we bought a TV with a remote control, when the team was losing in the second half and turned the ball over, or allowed a touchdown, he would take the remote and mash the power button. <ZOMMPF> Power off. There goes the game. He would set the remote neatly in its proper spot, shake his head and storm out of the room. He was a busy man, and I think he felt as if he wasted his time watching bad football. "If they're going to play like this, I've got more important things to do with my time." He was a typical fan. He'd get frustrated. His most common refrain was to yell a question to the players from his couch, as if they could hear him through the TV while wearing helmets surrounded by thousands of screaming fans hundreds of miles away. "What are you doing??!!" Typically, that was followed by a pause, and often a frustrated "Stupid!"

I thought his anger was semi-humorous, but what I didn't like was how it seemed to affect the rest of his afternoon. He'd be more than bummed, and as an elementary school kid, I didn't like how a group of players in another city, having nothing to do with my family, affected his joy after he turned off the game. "What is wrong with this team?" I thought. "Why can't they get it together?"

The one thing I noticed that I still remember, was he never seemed to get mad at the coaches. It was always the players. He didn't watch SportsCenter. He didn't listen to sports talk radio. He didn't know exactly what the team should be doing to win. He just watched the game on Sunday and hoped they knew what to do. And if a guy threw an interception, or dropped a touchdown, or didn't run for a first down, it was that guy's fault. The assumption was that appropriate amounts of strategy and coaching came baked-in, and if it wasn't perfect, it was on the player. Rarely was it about the coach, the game plan, the strategy, the preparation. It was always a player.

I played sports throughout high school. I was on the State team for the Olympic Development Program before breaking my leg in a game my freshman year. (I turned my tibia fracture into a science fair project which won awards and ultimately landed me in the International Science & Engineering Fair.) I was recruited for college during my junior year, but then tore my knee up that spring and needed surgery. I was invited to summer tryouts to walk on, but wearing a bulky knee brace, it was never going to work. I was put on the practice squad and quit before ever practicing. I knew my playing career was over and wanted to focus on school.

But one thing I loved about playing was the strategy. I was that on-field coach whose brain never shut off. Constantly picturing angles and vectors in my mind. Always trying to anticipate plays. I focused on positioning and accuracy. I was ultracompetitive and hated losing. And I simply loved removing myself from the real world, and in between those lines, trying to solve the puzzle of winning that singular game, using a combination of performance and strategy.

You can fast forward through most of college and early professional life. I studied Civil Engineering at a Top-10 Engineering school. Highlights after graduation included working first for a Big Five accounting firm, then a Big Four accounting firm and getting my Professional Engineering license. During college and immediately after college, one of my passions was building a computer program that would accurately predict outcomes of NFL games and thus, the ability to spot "value" in the lines released by linemakers.

I already had a knack for looking at two teams and predicting which team would cover the spread. After years of back testing and then using it in-season, I finally perfected the computer model. Combining its precision with my own abilities to use my intuition from watching games and side-research, I had something I knew could be special.

The first thing was to validate it, so I entered a handicapping contest. It was the 2005 NFL Playoff competition. The rules were simple: pick sides and/or totals for as many or as few playoff games as you would like. You start with $0 in your balance and place virtual wagers on the playoff games in $100 increments, from between $100 and $500. Winner at the end is the contestant with the largest final bankroll. Heading to the Super Bowl, I was 15-1 and in first place. But this was a 6,000-contestant field, so there were a few people within shooting range. I finished 16-2 and my bankroll stood at $6,630. First place. I didn't care as much about the cash prize as I did the thrill of winning.

I started posting my recommendations for free on message boards. First, a public fantasy football message board. Then, public NFL betting message boards. The recommendations were doing really well. As in, attention-grabbing. After years of documented winning on public message boards, in the middle of the 2008 season, in which I was 23-9 (72%) through week 9, I was contacted by an anonymous guy from Las Vegas. He worked for a betting "group". We began talking and continued over the rest of that year. That summer, after the season, I went to Vegas to meet with this "group". We formed a relationship and I began providing them with my recommendations.

Fast forward again. Many successful years passed. I was still working professionally as a licensed PE and was still moonlighting with my sports betting and handicapping career. I was becoming more well known, joining radio shows for betting segments and getting invited to speak at the Las Vegas Hilton (and then Westgate) Supercontest seminar multiple times. I was vacationing with the guys from Vegas-based betting "group" because we had become really close friends over the years. Life was good.

Eventually, I maxed out in the information I could incorporate into my models. I yearned for data, not just to model, but to study and research. I made my first purchase of play-by-play data. <BOOM> Mentally cue the clip of an atomic bomb exploding and a mushroom cloud forming inside someone's brain. I could do almost anything with this information.

After researching for weeks, the first thing I wanted to do was to share some of the information. I wrote a 2015 Preview book that was available only in PDF. It wasn't too similar to what you see today in my season previews, but it was a start. I spent the 2015 season viewing the data and modeling. Prior to the 2016 season, I created the first real genesis-edition of my current Preview series. And I launched Sharp Football Stats.com.

I created a visualized data website with access to play-by-play data broken down and put together in pictorial form. The goal was to showcase this information in an easier-to-digest manner for the public. So that they could view the NFL in a different prism than they do when they watch the broadcast angle of the games on Sunday afternoon. And to provide valuable context to general stats.

One offseason, a team reached out via email. We exchanged emails. I was "on their radar" but nothing happened beyond that.

The next offseason, in early 2018, I had multiple teams reach out to me. The most memorable was on the Fourth of July. My season preview was being sold on Amazon and in PDF. Some copies of the PDF got stuck in the queue and I needed to email them out. I sat down at my computer after cooking out with my family, to process requests before we headed out to a fireworks show. As I'm sending out the PDF copy to several people, I realized that one of the people I sent it to worked in an NFL front office. In my rush to process them, at first, I didn't even notice his email's signature and logo.

I consulted for one team last season. It was a successful and amazing season. During the season, a great article on NFL analytics was written by Kevin Clark of the Ringer. He wrote: "[Warren] is among the top minds in football not working full time for a team. In fact, when you talk to people inside the league, some think he might be the top mind, period."

Getting notes back after that season from the team I worked for, saying how much they enjoyed my contributions and wanted to do it again next year was a great feeling. I received an invitation to speak at the prestigious MIT Sloan Sports Analytics Conference held in early March in Boston. I was on the NFL panel, along with the Rams Executive VP/COO and the head of analytics for the Steelers. I shared my view of where we were and where we could go from an analytics perspective to advance the sport. It was a blast. My only regret was not getting enough time to spend in Boston, as I flew directly there from the Combine.

Since early 2019, I've had nine different teams reach out for discussions and/or interviews for various roles. Some were full time, some were as a consultant. I met with some teams at the Super Bowl in Atlanta and at the NFL Combine in Indianapolis. I was flown in for other interviews at the team facilities.

I realized right away that the time had come for a permanent transition to NFL analysis. I no longer worked in the engineering world. I am a full-time NFL analyst.

One of my favorite types of research is uncovering something that either brings about change upon sharing it, or my awareness of it gets me in on the ground level of what is about to occur. Several years ago, I loved researching running back passes and uncovering the edges that exist when quarterbacks target running backs on early downs. I didn't understand why more teams weren't utilizing them for their efficiency edges. I spoke openly on podcasts and Twitter about the efficiency gain.

Since then, several of the best teams ramped up their early down running back targets tremendously. Which teams adopted them? Only those led by two of the smartest coaches in the NFL—Bill Belichick and Sean Payton. What quarterbacks do they have? Only two sure-fire, first-ballot Hall of Famers—Tom Brady and Drew Brees.

Of all passing attempts in 2015, the Patriots targeted backs 22% of the time on early downs. That rate increased to 25% in 2016, 29% in 2017 and a league-leading 33% in 2018.

In 2015, the Saints targeted their backs 20% of the time. That rate increased to 26% in 2016, 34% in 2017 and 29% in 2018.

Why are two of the smartest coaches calling for more early-down RB passes, when these passes seem so basic and they have two insanely great quarterbacks at their disposal? Because these passes work.

I didn't come up with this idea through data. I came up with it simply by watching the game evolve.

I've watched football my entire life, but just over ten years ago, I started watching every single game of the season. All 256 plus 11 playoff games. I have a theater with a massive 12-foot projector screen and multiple side-monitors so I can watch everything unfold in real time.

This is vital for processing the game, for live betting and simply for understanding the elements—players, coaches, schemes, decision making, etc. Often, I double back and watch the all-22 film of certain elements I noted in my first watching that required further study. On rare occasions I go back and rewatch the condensed broadcast versions. Even more rare but still done at times is going back and rewatching the uncut broadcast version. That is primarily for identifying injury aftermath or getting better context surrounding the players off the field.

While I can't speak for anyone else, I know that without having watched these 267 games a year for over 10 years, I would not be where I am today. Having play-by-play data is great, but when you combine it with watching games upon games for years upon years, you pick up on nuances and ideas. Ideas you can research for the future. Theories to test.

The other thing that undoubtedly helped my development was betting on games for years. By having actual skin in the game and risk on the line, you absolutely watch the game through a totally different prism. All plays "seem" more meaningful. More life-and-death. It's feels more important that coaches call smart plays more frequently. Time management is more vital.

Packaging those two elements (substantial volume of game-viewing and having critical interest in the outcome) and combining them with statistical research and deep analysis brought me to this point.

Why the Professionals Use & Trust Warren Sharp

He is among the top minds in football not working full time for a team. In fact, when you talk to people inside the league, some think he might be the top mind, period.
    - Kevin Clark, The Ringer

When I was told about and introduced to Warren Sharp I was beyond skeptical. After working with some of the most successful syndicate groups for 15+ years I knew the NFL was practically unbeatable. After all, I worked 60+ hour work weeks breaking down and analyzing lines and looked forward to my Sunday's off. Needless to say that's not the way it is anymore on Sundays due to Warren. His NFL and especially his totals are second to none. Also, nobody can break down a NFL game like Warren and I don't know how anyone bets without his analysis and selections. I am now proud to say he is now one of my best friends and I do not fail to mention him when I am a guest on a radio or tv show. I also give him a live podcast each and every Sunday live from Las Vegas which is available free to his customers. He has proved to me and the gambling public that you CAN beat the NFL.
    - Bill Krackomberger, winning professional gambler, seen on ESPN, CNN, Fox Sports and dozens of publications and newspapers around
      the country

Warren's dedication and acumen for analyzing football is clearly evident in the work he produces. This book is completely unlike anything I've read in a preview before, but that's what I've come to expect from Warren. His ability to approach the game logically, analytically and in a predictive manner sets him apart from the crowd. Between the narratives, articles and graphics, I have no doubt after reading this preview you will be far more prepared for your fantasy drafts and just football in general. If you're a NFL fan of any kind, I cannot recommend this preview enough.
    - Evan Silva, Establish The Run

A truly indispensable resource to kick off your handicapping process for the upcoming NFL season, Warren Sharp's analytics-based Football Preview makes up for mainstream media's shortcomings by providing smart and advanced schedule analysis, insightful context to roster construction, and team and player projections, all certain to give you a leg up on both sportsbooks and your fantasy competition alike.
    - Gill Alexander, Host of "A Numbers Game" - Vegas Stats & Information Network (VSiN)

Been at this for 38 years in print, and have enjoyed every minute, win or lose. The NFL has given me problems forever. A few games over .500, a few games under .500, nothing exceptional, and mostly paying my guy every week. Until last season when one of the most INFLUENTIAL whales in the wagering world put me on to Warren Sharp. Read Sharp's 2016 Football Preview from cover to cover, and wound up posting a Ridiculous 137-110-8 record picking every game in the NFL. And even tastier, 12-3-1 in my weekly best bets Coincidence? NAH. It was Sharp's amazing angles and deep dives into stats I didn't even know existed. And when you see his records, it's STRAIGHT UP HONEST. How do I know? I had access to Sharp's picks every week, and his percentages tickled and exceeded the 60% range. As most know who have read my columns for the past 37 years, I have NEVER recommended any handicapper. Most are SCAMDICAPPERS that get you to pay for recycled GARBAGE. Sharp's stats, amazing graphics and advanced metrics are FREAKIN' GROUND BREAKING. Get Sharp, stay Sharp, live Sharp. You will be AMAZED!!!
    - Benjamin Eckstein, Americas Line nationally syndicated sportswriter in the New York Daily News and part of Ecks & Bacon

Analytics plays a bigger role in sports betting than ever before. Information travels at a speed nobody would have thought possible a decade ago. With so many analytical options available to both the bettor and the odds maker the choices we make for analytics have never been more important. When it comes to the NFL there is no one I trust and use more than Warren Sharp. Warren has an amazing grasp of the analytics that matter in the sports betting world and how to implement those in a practical and easy to read format. I would highly recommend that anyone involved in the sports betting industry try implementing Warren's analyses into their NFL work.
    - Matthew Holt, COO of CG Analytics

Warren's synopsis on game totals is vastly superior utilizing his mathematical formulas, to any preview I have ever seen.   His success is two-fold, beating the closing number by up to 3 pts and winning at a clip needed to secure a hefty profit. Getting in early ensures some fantastic middling opportunities.
    - Richie Baccellieri, former Director of Race and Sports in Las Vegas at Caesars Palace, MGM Grand and The Palms

I can't speak highly enough about Warren to give him the credit he deserves. He's the hardest working guy I know in the business, more importantly, his attention to detail is unparalleled. I don't think we've ever had a phone conversation less than an hour due to the amazing wealth of knowledge he rolls off with ease. I hold him in great regard. I appreciate his dedication and talent.
    - "Las Vegas Cris" - winning professional gambler

Sharp Football Analysis.com is <u>RELAUNCHING</u> JULY 8TH!!
NEW content covering Fantasy, Prop Betting & Film Study!

To a point where I have become extremely prepared to isolate the key elements a team needs in order to win a particular game against a particular opponent given their particular injuries and other weekly circumstances.

Imagine taking five analysts and letting them share what they believe are the five most important elements a team should account for in order to win a particular game. Do you think you'd wind up with 25 recommendations? Likely not. More often than not, multiple analysts would have quite similar lists. For me, it's not simply churning through data and finding the largest statistical mismatches. Some of those are too obvious. I'm looking to add depth and specificity. My background has allowed me to have intimate knowledge of all 32 teams from watching their coaches and key players every single game for years. I have a good idea what they will try to do, and whether it will or won't work. And I have a good idea of what they "should" try to do.

If I'm consulting for that team, I share that with them. And often several of my suggestions are going to be so unique that in a group of four other analysts, I'd be the only one to think them up.

Over the years, I've shared research on very basic principles. Many of these you've read before. Some are unique to me, some are refrains that the analytics community have pounded the table for in the past. These are all testable and verifiable using data. They are factual. Some teams may choose to ignore them, some teams may use them on a limited basis, other teams may think they don't matter that much. But they all are +EV and factually optimal:

- Pass more on first down, especially with a young quarterback
- Don't run on 2nd-and-10 after an incompletion
- Target the middle of the field more often
- Optimize the psyche of expensive running backs without destroying their bodies
- Pass more from 2-WR sets and target TEs more
- Run the ball more often on 3rd-and-short
- Run the ball more often in the red zone
- Optimize goal line play-calling through personnel groupings
- Use receiving backs as rushers in the red zone
- Run the ball often on 2nd-and-short and do so using tempo
- Stop huddling and get to the line of scrimmage faster
- Use cadence and pre-snap motion to gather free information on the defense
- Use post-snap motion (via play action) to disguise intent and confuse the defense
- Play less prevent defense in one-score games
- Practice defensive touchdown returns and encourage intelligence and aggression
- Use more creative route concepts to create conflict
- Incorporate RPOs and force the defense to adjust
- Design more offensive plays to look similar
- Be multiple from plays, be creative and ever-evolving
- Attempt to be ultra-aggressive offensively early in games to build leads & force a tactical adjustment from your opponent
- Be more adaptable if something isn't working, and adapt quickly
- Prepare multiple backup plans
- Devote more time to studying your own tendencies and break them in the second half
- Avoid play caller fatigue
- Improve decision making in "crisis" mode

There is no point in dwelling on these. They're in the rearview mirror. We've pretty much proved all of those ideas are important. I'm onto the next frontiers. What keeps my brain fired is trying to "solve" football.

Unlike basketball or baseball, I don't think we will "solve" the NFL anytime soon. What makes it unique? For starters, 22 players on the field for every play, with most of them intimately involved in the activity. Plays themselves, in that there is a stoppage before each one to adjust, rotate in personnel and regroup. It's very different in that respect than other professional sports. Then there's the salary cap, roster size and the varying degrees of competency. Things that become "acceptably +EV behavior" in the future, thanks to analytics, will still have large tweaks due to the strengths or weaknesses of each roster. Great advice to one team might be poor advice to another.

No, I don't envision the NFL will be "solved" anytime soon, but it's the pursuit that makes it the challenge.

What are the next things that research is showing us? Aside from those items outlined above, what are the most important things that teams are still getting "wrong" from a strategy and play-calling perspective? What items have the highest leverage, such that if they got them "right" they would have the most impact?

These are the things I take pleasure in analyzing and uncovering. Some of those things I've incorporated into the team chapters in this 2019 Preview.

I am tough on decision makers when studying optimal strategy and coaching. This is because I believe the impact of scheme and coaching is far more beneficial or harmful than any single player, with extremely rare exceptions.

We've seen it for years. I won't list the stats or the improved records. But you've seen it too: Jared Goff with Sean McVay as opposed to Rob Boras… Carson Palmer with Bruce Arians as opposed to Greg Knapp or Bob Bratkowski. We saw it last year: Mitchell Trubisky with Matt Nagy as opposed to Dowell Loggains… Baker Mayfield with Freddie Kitchens as opposed to Todd Haley/Hue Jackson… Ryan Fitzpatrick with Todd Monken as opposed to Dirk Koetter or Chan Gailey.

The difference is night and day, and it's from one year to the next. In some cases, it's from one week to the next. This isn't mere "development" or "taking time to mature" or "becoming a better professional" – this is the impact of good coaching and superior scheme.

It's important to identify the suboptimal, to bring it to the surface and then to eradicate it.

Coaching matters, and as you review this preview, I hope you'll see I'm sharing the underlying reasons as to why teams failed to meet or may have exceeded their expectations. I identify what they could do better and improve on in the future. I compile where coaches may have missed something that they could correct for next year.

This book takes months to research, layout and write. It starts after the Super Bowl, and ends in late June. It's a labor of love. But I get to work with my great friend and awesome editor Evan Silva. Putting the finishing touches on this book gets me so ready for the season. I can't wait to analyze it!

But we're not done yet. I hope you come with me for my next journey.

I'm expanding Sharp Football Analysis to include more writers and more subject areas. We will be covering fantasy football and prop betting in a deeper manner and with a more analytical eye than you've likely seen before. We'll be breaking down film and sharing videos and articles. We'll be giving you a more advanced view into the process of winning or losing games than you've ever seen. Our hope is to educate and enlighten, and help you win some money in the process.

We'll be pulling back the curtain as we examine the next frontiers of efficiency in the NFL.

Over the last couple of years, I can't count the number of people who reached out, looking for internships or opportunities. Now, I'll finally be able to provide those breaks for the best and brightest individuals who are interested.

I may no longer be working in the engineering field, but I'll continue to apply that same problem-solving mentality to attacking the NFL as I've done in the past. Only now, I'll have more hours to do that, and I hope they pay off in the form of building a compelling website that you come to love as much as I do.

In between the lines on the football field, I don't believe that you are what your record says you are. In fact, I despise that saying. There is so much more to a team than it's wins and losses. The metrics of that team and the context in which they recorded those metrics cannot be summarized into wins and losses. I capitalize on the general public having a sentiment about a particular team based on its record and where they sit in the standings.

But outside the lines, you are what your record says you are. You build that record through how you live—your passion, the work you put in, and the achievements you earn. I've been fortunate to earn my actual record of 60.3% on NFL totals, but I know I've put in the hard work each day for years upon years to get there. I'm working to earn other accolades. Working for NFL teams was certainly something I envisioned at some point, because I wanted to improve the on-field product and felt I had certain edges that would assist in that capacity. Now I want to continue to excel in both areas while building a great website to allow us to share more analytical thoughts with you in a more immersive, personal and meaningful way.

I don't know where my story ends, but I know that right now, I'm exactly where I'm meant to be.

QR Code Audio and Video

Download any QR Reader or QR Scanner as an app on your phone and scan the below codes on the dates listed for either audio or video that will give you up-to-the-minute analysis leading up to the start of the 2019 NFL season!

NEW Website Re-Design!

◄ **Scan on July 8th**

Training Camp Updates

◄ **Scan on August 7th**

Beach Week Recap Video

Scan on July 15th ►

Final Season Preview

Scan on August 28th ►

Walking Through the NFL with 32 Analytical Observations

By Warren Sharp

Arizona Cardinals – Kliff Kingsbury's "4 Verts" offense has been discussed often, but an interesting talking point should be quarterback runs. Last year, the most successful QB-runs were those from 10 personnel (1 RB, 0 TEs and 4 WRs). They produced a 62 percent success rate and a gain of 5.8 YPC. Only two offenses had more than two QB-runs from 10 personnel: Cleveland (**Baker Mayfield** and **Tyrod Taylor**) averaged a 75 percent success rate and 10 YPC. Carolina (**Cam Newton**) posted a 67 percent success rate and 7 YPC. Running from 3+ WR groupings produced a 59 percent success rate and 6.6 YPC (no kneels or sneaks), a full yard better than running from 2- WR groupings.

Atlanta Falcons – Running in short yardage situations is optimal. The Falcons ran the ball at an above average rate in both 2016 and 2017 in these short yardage situations on second and third down. But in 2018, they became the sixth-most pass-heavy team. Ignoring fourth quarter game theory situations, Atlanta produced a 76 percent success rate when running, fourth best in the NFL. When they passed the ball, their success rate dropped to 58 percent and those passes averaged only 5.8 YPA, eighth-worst in the NFL.

Baltimore Ravens – Lamar Jackson ranked as QB8 over the final seven weeks of the season despite his 17 percent red zone passing touchdown rate, which ranked 35th out of 39 qualifying quarterbacks. If he can improve that ranking, his overall fantasy value certainly will improve.

Buffalo Bills – The Bills called the most runs on second and 10+ yards to go in the NFL, running the ball on 45 percent of their play calls. These runs produced a successful gain just 21 percent of the time. Because of their early down play calling, the Bills faced 3rd and 8.3 yards to go on average, the longest distance to go in the NFL.

Carolina Panthers – In 2016, on early downs, **Cam Newton** passed the ball the sixth-least in the NFL (51 percent). Neither early down passes nor rushes exceeded a 46 percent success rate. On early downs in 2017, Newton passed the ball the fourth-least in the NFL (46 percent). Neither early down passes nor rushes exceeded a 48 percent success rate. On early

downs last year, Newton passed the ball the 11th most (56 percent). Both early down passes and rushes produced a 53 percent success rate or better.

Chicago Bears - In 2017, Chicago ranked dead last in the league, needing 8.4 yards-to-go on third down. The Bears were much more efficient on early downs in 2018 under **Matt Nagy**, leaving **Mitchell Trubisky** with an average of only 6.9 yards-to-go on third down, the fourth best mark in the league behind only the Patriots, Saints and Colts.

Cincinnati Bengals – After a 10+ yard explosive run, the only RB in the league who was given the ball for a second straight run play more than **Joe Mixon** was **Sony Michel**. Mixon averaged 2.5 YPC and produced a 10 percent success rate after these explosive runs. On all other first-and-ten runs, Mixon averaged 5.8 YPC and produced a 53 percent success rate. Let him catch his breath.

Cleveland Browns – Turnover margin decides games more than any other metric. Teams win approximately 80 percent of games over the last 30 years when winning the turnover margin. In **Hue Jackson's** 8 games in 2018 the Browns were +11 in turnover margin but had a 2-5-1 record. Since 2006 there were 38 teams with a +8 turnover margin or better through 8 weeks and none had a losing record, except the 2018 Browns. Since 1975 there were 71 teams with a +11 turnover margin or better thru 8 weeks and none had a losing record, except the 2018 Browns. Since 2016, when Hue Jackson took over the Browns, their record when winning the turnover battle was 37.5 percent. Another Hue oddity: games that end in regulation as a tie and go to overtime should mean the two teams are very even. With coin tosses deciding possession, it would be hard for one team to have a really high or really low win rate in overtime. But under Hue Jackson, the Browns went 1-6-1 (14.3 percent) in overtime.

Dallas Cowboys – Dallas finished 2018 with a bottom-5 red zone offense. They were successful on just 38 percent of their red zone plays (fourth worst). They scored touchdowns on just 48 percent of their trips to the red zone, also fourth worst. Their red zone play success rate did not improve with **Amari Cooper**, as they still were only successful on 35 percent of their red zone plays (second worst in the league over the second half of the season). The struggles came from the passing attack. It produced a 28 percent success rate in the red zone, worst in the NFL.

Denver Broncos – Arm strength does not equate to efficient deep passing. In 2018, **Joe Flacco** ranked 32nd of 33 quarterbacks on deep passes. His 34 percent completion rate was also 32nd. In 2017, Flacco ranked 31st of 32 quarterbacks on deep passes. His 32 percent completion rate was also 31st. In 2016, Flacco ranked 29th of 31 quarterbacks on deep passes. His 29 percent completion rate ranked 30th. Over the last three years combined, of 27 qualifying quarterbacks with enough deep attempts, Flacco's deep passing ranks dead last in the NFL. Joe Flacco may have a big arm. But it hasn't helped at all with his ability to make deep throws.

Detroit Lions – In 2016 the Lions passed the ball on 53 percent of first downs in the first half, tenth most in the league (7.0 YPA, 58 percent success rate). In 2017, the Lions passed the ball on first half first downs at the ninth highest rate (7.1 YPA, 51 percent success rate). In 2018, the Lions completely shifted to the NFL's ninth most run-heavy team on first downs in the first half. Rushes gained only 4.1 YPC, sixth worst in the NFL. Passes were not more effective either, gaining just 6.1 YPA, worst in the NFL. **Matt Patricia's** mandate to go run-heavy torpedoed the Lions offense.

Green Bay Packers – On third and short (1-4 yards-to-go), it is more efficient to throw the ball short of the sticks and run for the first down rather than throw beyond the sticks. (As the distance to-go increases, it becomes more efficient to target receivers beyond the sticks.) The league average was a 58 percent conversion rate when thrown short of the sticks but a 47 percent conversion rate when thrown beyond the sticks. Naturally, 100 percent of completions past the sticks are first downs. But a large 79 percent of passes caught short are conversions. And the problem is that on third and short, only 47 percent of passes thrown beyond the sticks are caught. Whereas 74 percent of passes thrown short of the sticks are caught. Last year the Packers threw 53 passes on third and 1-4 yards to go. A whopping 81 percent were beyond the sticks, the highest rate in the league. Those passes averaged 15 air yards, even though the yardage to go was, at most, four yards. The Packers converted only 42 percent of those passes for first downs, whereas they converted 70 percent of passes thrown short of the sticks into first downs.

Houston Texans – After a first and ten incompletion, the three-year league average is 59 percent pass on second and ten. But **Bill O'Brien** is 47 percent pass (53 percent run), the number one most run-heavy team

in the league. The Texans average 4.2 YPC (4th worst) and record a 21 percent success rate (dead last). Meanwhile, their passes on these second and ten record 8.8 YPA (2nd best) and record a 48 percent success rate (8th best).

Indianapolis Colts – The six weeks when **Jack Doyle** was healthy in 2018, the Colts used the third-most 12 personnel (34 percent) and the third-least 11 personnel on early downs. But when Doyle was out, the Colts 11 personnel rate rocketed from third-least to second-most (from 57 percent to 79 percent) when passing on early downs. **Frank Reich** knows how to adapt his offense. He also knows what works best for quarterbacks: despite **Andrew Luck** not throwing a football for over 500 days and not getting a full offseason program in, Reich's Colts were the fourth-most pass-heavy team on early downs last year (59 percent pass). Reich knew that you don't protect a quarterback by avoiding him on early downs and forcing him into predictable third down passing situations. You protect him by providing him with many short passing opportunities on early downs.

Jacksonville Jaguars – Last year **Leonard** Fournette's 1.9 YPC average with a second-half lead ranked 68th of 69 qualifying backs. Out of 66 backs with 50+ rushes the last three years with second half leads, Fournette ranks 60th with a 35 percent success rate. Out of 49 backs with over 35 rushes on first down with a second half lead, Fournette ranks dead last, both in success rate (34 percent) as well as YPC (2.5).

Kansas City Chiefs – **Patrick Mahomes** led the league in deep passing completions (59) and deep passing yards (1,804), yet he ranked 28th of 35 quarterbacks in percentage of his total passing yards on the season came through the air. That's amazing and seems impossible. The only reason it can occur is because of how much of a genius **Andy Reid** is with short, high completion percentage running-back passes. In 2018, Chiefs first down running back passes in standard situations (1-10 yards to go) produced a 69 percent success rate and averaged an insane 10.1 YPA. Mahomes 69 percent success rate on these passes led the NFL (min 30 att), as did his 10.1 YPA and his 148.4 passer rating. The reason these are such money makers is Reid's design, and the fact that the quarterback is completing 83 percent of them.

Los Angeles Rams – The Rams used the highest rate of first down play action. Their splits: with play action, they gained 9.9 YPA, a 56 percent success rate and a 105.2 rating. Without play action, they gained 7.0 YPA, a 56 percent success and a 91.6 rating. One of the most interesting ways they used play action was to target their running back. On first downs league-wide, teams only used play action and passed to their backs

26.5 percent of the time. No team used it more than the Rams, who threw to their backs after play action on nearly 50 percent of their total first down RB-targets. They improved from a 45 percent success rate and 4.6 YPA to a 67 percent success rate and 7.3 YPA by using play action to target their running back on first down.

Los Angeles Chargers – In 2016, the Chargers targeted backs on early downs only 21 percent of attempts, approximately league average. In 2017, they increased to 25 percent, two percent above the 2017 league average. But in 2018, they rocketed up to 32 percent, nine percent above the 2018 league average. And they were incredible on these passes. The Chargers posted a 58 percent success rate (#2 behind the Chiefs) and a 7.7 YPA average (#3 behind the Chiefs and Bears). This efficiency helped the Chargers rank as the third-most efficient offense despite facing the tenth-toughest schedule of defenses.

Miami Dolphins – Through the Dolphins bye week (week 11), they had a mere 45 percent success rate when passing from 11 personnel and averaged 6.7 YPA. But from 12 personnel, the offense had a 61 percent success rate and averaged 13.6 YPA. However, OC **Dowell Loggains** used the second highest rate of 11 personnel (86 percent, behind of only the Rams) and the second lowest rate of 12 personnel (5 percent, ahead of only the Rams).

Minnesota Vikings – Through seven weeks, the Vikings were 4-2-1. They won because they had a solid passing offense and emphasized it, while deemphasizing their bad run offense. Minnesota was tied for the NFL's most pass-heavy offense on first half first downs. On these downs, their passing offense ranked second in the league, producing a 64 percent success rate with 8.2 YPA. It was way more efficient than the Vikings first down rushing attack, which produced a 42 percent success rate (25th) with only 3.7 YPA. But **Mike Zimmer** wanted to go run-heavy, and so the Vikings shifted their strategy – and ran themselves right out of the playoff hunt.

New England Patriots – Writing last year's Preview, I noticed the Patriots had shifted too pass-heavy near the goal line. Inside the five-yard line in 2017, the Patriots went 60 percent pass (67 percent run in 2016). Their passes were far less successful (51 percent as compared to 59 percent from runs). I urged the Patriots to shift to a more run-heavy approach in 2018. They did that. They replicated their 2016 run rate of 67 percent. And runs were tremendously more productive. Run plays averaged a 65 percent success rate compared to passes which produced a mere 30 percent success rate. It was wise for the Patriots to go more run-heavy. **Sony Michel's** 67 percent success rate and seven rushing touchdowns led the way.

New Orleans Saints – Over the last two years, the only team to target running backs more on early downs than the Patriots were the Saints. Why would two of the most creative offensive minds (**Sean Payton, Josh McDaniels/Bill Belichick**) with two first ballot Hall of Fame quarterbacks and solid run games decide to, of all things, throw the ball to running backs at a rate exceeding everyone else in the NFL? Because it's highly efficient. The last three years, early down RB-runs in standard "to-go" situations of 1-10 yards gain 4.2 YPC with a 47 percent success rate league-wide. Passes to RBs gain 6.1 YPC with a 54 percent success rate. The Saints and Patriots passes to WRs are both top-five in success and YPA, but they realize the floor of the RB-passes compared to other passes. Their QBs complete roughly 75 percent of these passes. And their ceiling is much higher than RB-runs. When the best teams in the league are now using this successful strategy, you can either get on board or get left behind.

New York Giants – last year the Giants attempted only one fourth down when tied or leading in a game. Only the 49ers attempted fewer. They kicked the ball (punt or FG) 48 times, but made only one attempt (vs the Bears, which was a touchdown). Outside two-minute drills and fourth quarter deficits, the Giants only attempted eight fourth downs all season long. The Giants need to optimize their fourth down decision making. They must get more aggressive. Making matters even more discouraging is the Giants drafted what they expect to be the best running back in the NFL second overall. If any back should be entrusted to convert a short yardage run on fourth down, you have to believe **Saquon Barkley** is at the top of the list. Why spend massive draft capital on him and yet never use him? In all fourth downs last year, the Giants gave Barkley only one rushing attempt.

New York Jets – In **Sam Darnold's** starts, no team called as high a percentage of runs on second and 10+ yards-to-go in the first half as the Jets. Fifty-one percent of their plays were runs. These generated 3.3 YPC and posted a 13 percent success rate. Over the entire game, the Jets runs on second and 10+ gained 2.9 YPC (worst in the league) and produced a 15 percent success rate (second worst in the league). But the only reason that percentage wasn't lower was because Darnold ran on 8 plays, and his runs produced a 50 percent success rate. On non-Darnold runs, the Jets were successful on just 8 percent of their second and long rushes, and these plays gained a pathetic 1.9 YPC. Both were worst in the NFL, yet the Jets were one of the top-five most run-heavy teams in this situation. It set up disaster. In Sam Darnold's starts, the Jets faced an average of 7.9 yards-to-go on third down, tied for the third-worst in the NFL.

Oakland Raiders – Tom Cable is an Offensive line coach. His line's rank in pass protection in his NFL career:

06 ATL: 31
07 OAK: 27
08 OAK: 30
09 OAK: 31
10 OAK: 26
11 SEA: 24*
12 SEA: 20
13 SEA: 32
14 SEA: 24
15 SEA: 30
16 SEA: 25
17 SEA: 25
18 OAK: 25**

* #14 the year prior to Tom Cable
** #3, 4, 1 & 7 the 4 years prior to Tom Cable

Philadelphia Eagles – In 2018, **Carson Wentz** took major strides in early down passing. And he did so with no wide receiver catching over 65 passes and no running back averaging over 4.3 YPC. He did so coming off a torn ACL and LCL, and ending the year with a stress fracture in his back. Wentz delivered a 105.3 rating on early downs (6th of 50 quarterbacks) and his 55 percent success rate ranked second best in the league behind only **Drew Brees**. These marks were dramatically better than his marks in 2017 (90.3 rating and 44 percent success). Entering 2018, only nine teams in the last 30 years lost two games in the same season after holding a 14-point lead in a game, including at least a 7-point lead heading into the fourth quarter. The 2018 Eagles became the tenth team.

Pittsburgh Steelers – League-wide, using play action on passes increases your YPA from 6.8 to 8.0 and your passer rating from 88.3 to 95.9. No team used play action less often than the Steelers. It's particularly useful when targeting wide receivers or tight ends in the slot. They increase their YPA from 7.8 to 10.3 and the passer rating from 95.6 to 107.8. It's especially useful on curl routes to these slot receivers. They increase their YPA from 6.9 to 11.2 and their success rate from 64 percent to 75 percent. It won't be shocking to hear the Steelers threw the fewest slot targets from play action, even though their performance improved from 7.3 YPA and an 89.7 rating without it to 10.3 YPA and a 125.3 rating with it. The Steelers didn't target a single slot curl route using play action.

San Francisco 49ers – There were only two teams to rank top-10 both offensively and defensively in EDSR (Early Down Success Rate) over the full 16-game season in 2018. Only two teams pulled off the "double" in 2017. And somehow, the 49ers were able to achieve it without a starting quarterback, against a top-10 schedule of defenses, with the fourth-most injured roster.

Seattle Seahawks – Seattle was the most run-heavy team in the NFL. Last year they passed on only 48 percent of plays, the only team in the league to pass on fewer than 52 percent of all plays. On first half first downs, the NFL average was to pass the ball on 51 percent of attempts. Seattle was at 40 percent. On early downs (both first and second), Seattle was the only team in the league to pass less than 45 percent. Seattle was at 40 percent pass, by far the lowest in the league (average was 54 percent). Seattle ranked #32, and the teams that ranked #31, #30 and #29? The Bills, Titans and Jaguars. Three teams with quarterbacks that vary from terrible, to inexperienced, to inaccurate, to injured, to historically unproductive. The exact opposite of Super Bowl Champion, 6x Pro Bowler, former Rookie of the Year **Russell Wilson**, who leads the NFL in various passing stats on an annual basis and to whom the team just gave a four-year, $140 M contract.

Tampa Bay Buccaneers – On early down deep passes, **Jameis Winston's** 9.5 YPA ranks 28th of 30 qualifying quarterbacks the last three years, ahead of only **Brock Osweiler** and **Joe Flacco**. Now he'll be coached by one of the most aggressive, downfield offensive masterminds in the league. Entering 2017, then Head coach **Dirk Koetter** told Winston that the passing offense needed to "cut our risk a bit." Current Head coach **Bruce Arians** motto is "no risk it, no biscuit." It should be an interesting contrast in styles.

Tennessee Titans – The **Matt LeFleur** Titans ran the ball on early downs more often and less successfully than **Mike Mularkey** did in each season of the "Exotic Smashmouth" offense:

2018: 56 percent run with a 44 percent success rate
2017: 51 percent run with a 45 percent success rate
2016: 54 percent run with a 52 percent success rate

Washington Redskins – Last year's fifth-worst offense (in both efficiency and EDSR) will be the most expensive in the NFL in 2019. The 2018 Redskins averaged second-and-8.6 yards-to-go, the second-longest yardage-to-go on second down of any team in the league last year. Only the Buffalo Bills, with an extremely inaccurate rookie quarterback (Josh Allen) were worse. They put themselves in that position because they have one of the most run-heavy offenses on first down and were so unsuccessful when running. Also note: they have the most expensive TE group, but last year despite terrible wide receiving talent, they involved their top-2 TEs (**Jordan Reed** and **Vernon Davis**) on only 8 of 109 red zone plays.

2019 Injury Preview

by ProFootballDoc (Dr. David Chao)

I am pleased to contribute this small chapter to Sharp Football Analysis. In doing the podcast with Warren last year, I found his analysis to be very insightful. The hope here is to add the injury element to the equation.

Here are some of the top injury stories leading into the season.

Quarterbacks

• **Jimmy Garoppolo** - The 49ers QB is progressing nicely from his ACL tear. He should be ready to go and have a successful 2019 season. Admittedly, his knee will get better as the season goes along but it should not affect his throwing. Garoppolo has hopefully learned to run out of necessity only and to get out of bounds when he can to avoid injury.

• **Carson Wentz** - Coming off back to back season-ending injuries with his knee ACL/LCL and now his back stress fracture can make anyone nervous but the Eagles do not seem to be, having given their QB the big extension before they had to do it. The knee was never ready when Wentz missed the start of the season and then started Week 3. That likely led to modified mechanics and unmasked his high school low back stress fracture. The knee issue should be behind him and the back should be as well but I am sure it will be monitored. I still believe the Eagles have learned their lesson and will only run Wentz to keep the defense honest because if they run him routinely as part of the offense, they will be playing Russian Roulette.

• **Cam Newton** – After his second surgery, his surgeon spoke of cartilage damage. This is something to watch as it means there is some arthritis. Wear and tear in the shoulder is less of a big deal than in the knees, but this is his throwing shoulder. I believe Newton will be ready and fully healthy for the start of the 2019 season but the tweaks to his mechanics worry me. Is that because of the shoulder issues? It is hard enough to change a rookie QB's throwing mechanics, altering veteran habits as he enters his ninth NFL season is a tall task. Maybe a full season with offensive guru Norv Turner can offset those issues.

• **Marcus Mariota** – 2018 was a rough season as the Titans QB had multiple injury issues. The biggest concern was his ulnar nerve injury on his throwing side that affected his grip. The team did a good job managing that and keeping him going, but it clearly affected his play. Barring disaster where it is re-injured with new trauma, expect the elbow nerve to be a non-issue this season.

• **Alex Smith** – With his external fixator still on his leg as of this writing, Smith is a non-story for 2019 and possibly beyond. There is no way for him to recover and get back this season. He likely has more surgery to come for his broken leg which became infected. The hope is that he has an outside chance to eventually return but if news finally confirms the need for flap surgery where muscle is taken to cover exposed bone, that would officially signal the end of a nice career.

Running Backs

• **Todd Gurley** – With knee arthritis confirmed, this is not the end of a productive Gurley but it is the end of his being a "bell cow" RB. The days of 300+ carry seasons or 20+ games are likely over. The Rams are taking the right approach limiting his offseason work and even loosing five pounds can take pressure off the knee. The knee will need to be managed but he can still be productive. He could be at the top of the league in yards per carry, but will not be in the season long rushing title race.

• **Sony Michel** – The Patriots did a good job of managing their first round draft pick's knee arthritis last year, but it will be more of the same. My suspicion is this former Georgia RB's knee is actually worse than the previous one discussed immediately above. Expect more of the same with somewhat spotty production out of Michel, but do not expect him to make it to his second contract.

• **Jerick McKinnon** – The one advantage of a preseason ACL tear is more time to recover. With the full calendar year, I expect the 49ers to have their guy ready to go for week one, but he will get stronger as the season comes along.

• **Derrius Guice** – Here is another preseason ACL tear that I am less optimistic about. After his ACL surgery, there was an infection, which resulted in several other procedures. Video of Guice shows him working hard but I still detected he was favoring the knee. He could play and contribute this season, but do not be shocked if he starts on PUP or is slow to produce in the early going.

Wide Receivers

• **Emmanuel Sanders** – The Broncos did pick up his option but he is in recovery from a December Achilles repair surgery. Recent video had him looking good while aggressively running routes but in analyzing the film, it was easy for me to see him still favoring his left side where he was still somewhat weak on push off. He may avoid PUP but I do not expect a banner year, especially not in the early going.

• **Cooper Kupp** – Coming off a week 10 ACL tear, I expect Kupp to be ready to contribute this year but feel it will be hard for him to start. That could change in the latter half of the season.

• **Will Fuller** - The Texans WR is coming off of a Week 8 ACL tear. Fuller should regain his speed and return to being a downfield threat. Given the type of player he is and how one recovers from ACL surgery, I am cautiously optimistic to his upside this year.

• **Albert Wilson** – While his "significant" hip injury has not been detailed yet (I suspect a hip labral repair), Wilson says he should be ready for Week 1 but has not been allowed on the field yet. I expect he will start training camp on PUP and we will see from there.

• **Anthony Miller** – The Bear's rookie played through a labral tear which intermittently dislocated. The brace he wore limited his catch radius. Offseason surgery will fix this. I expect an even better sophomore campaign.

• **Cole Beasley** – Core muscle surgery is minor and has reliably good recovery. The change of scenery to Buffalo will be the bigger factor.

Tight Ends

• **Greg Olsen** – Recurrent foot injuries sidelined Olsen for most of 2018. Given his age of 34, he will play but is on the decline. Coupled with a chance of recurrent foot stress fracture injury, I would preach caution in what to expect.

• **Delanie Walker** – The Titans TE is in recovery from a Week 1 ankle fracture dislocation and was limited in minicamp. Even with the advanced age of 34, I expect a reasonable bounce back year. Given the way he plays and the team's reliance on his steady hands, I expect him to be a fantasy draftable TE in the mid to late rounds.

Offensive Line

• **Travis Frederick** – As expected he missed all of last season with Guillain-Barre syndrome, a nerve disorder. However, the anticipation was always a full recovery for 2019. The rust and his shoulder surgery are the bigger worry than the nerve condition which is behind him and should be a non-factor.

Defense

• **Earl Thomas** – Will he be elite with the Ravens? I understand the worry after his second tibia fracture; however, I expect a fully recovered and dominant safety to return to his old form with no limitations.

• **DeMarcus Lawrence** - The Cowboy's star got his new contract in April and then had shoulder labral repair surgery. I expect a start of training camp on PUP and hope (but do not guarantee) a return for Week 1. The leverage of delaying shoulder surgery got the deal done, but it may cost him and the team on the back end.

• **Ezekiel Ansah** – The new Seahawk had similar labral repair surgery, but months earlier. Ansah projects to be ready to go and have a big year in Seattle.

• **Jason Pierre-Paul** – The initial news had him done for the year. Now he could be back in October or November. I suspect it was an odontoid fracture high up in his neck that will heal. Expect a strong late season return.

• **Kwon Alexander** – The new 49er's LB is trying to work his way back after an October ACL tear. Even if he is cleared for training camp, he will have to learn a new system. Do not judge this acquisition based on the start of this season.

Here is wishing all these players well for 2019.

A message from Warren Sharp

We're finally here – the finish line! A true labor of love that I undertake starting in February each offseason, this season preview you are reading is the culmination of months of research, analysis, writing, full of new discoveries, exciting findings and much more. I truly think this year's book tops all others in the past, and I hope you feel that way too!

It's with extreme happiness I'm able to share that I'm expanding Sharp Football Analysis for the 2019 football season!

As you can tell by this book, I've been completely dedicated to analyzing the game of football and sharing my findings with you for years now.

You've helped my Twitter following @SharpFootball grow and that has helped spread the word even further.

Last season was my first working as a consultant for a NFL team and I have multiple teams I'll be consulting for in 2019. I wanted to continue to grow the information I'm sharing publicly, so this offseason, for the first time ever, I hired someone to work for my website and assist me in continuing to share and spread cutting edge, insightful analysis.

We'll be tackling fantasy football using the talents of Rich Hribar and several other writers. Our sports betting content will expand to a heavy analysis of the football prop marketplace using multiple established and winning sports bettors. And we'll be delivering analysis from current and former coaches, complete with film study and written content. I couldn't be happier or looking more forward to a season than I am the 2019 season!

Here's where we can continue to use your help in supporting these efforts to deliver deeper and better analysis:

1. Please rate and review this book on Amazon, even if you bought the PDF

2. If you bought this book on Amazon, consider purchasing the PDF starting July 8th on our relaunched website. We literally make a few pennies per copy to deliver these 250+ pages in stunning full-color.

3. Follow us on Twitter @SharpFootball

4. Tweet a copy of your book and share your feedback on Twitter!

5. Starting July 8th, purchase a 2019 subscription to Sharp Football Analysis. Your subscriptions will allow us to continue to build and add more written, video and podcast content!

6. Check out the interactive stats website SharpFootballStats.com

7. Join the mailing list at Sharp Football Analysis or Sharp Football Stats to ensure you catch all our updates and announcements.

Thank you for everything, and I hope you enjoy the 2019 Football Preview! - Warren

SHARP
FOOTBALL ANALYSIS

Check us out the Relaunched Sharp Football Analysis.com on July 8th!

Fantasy Stock: Five Fantasy Breakouts for 2019

By Rich Hribar

Hello, Sharp Football fans! I hope you're all enjoying the most thorough 2019 NFL preview you can find anywhere. Taking a break from the top-shelf football analysis you've combed through so far; we're focusing solely on things from a fantasy perspective here. You may be wondering if Warren called me in for this short piece solely as a favor, but that's not just the case. This is the formal announcement that I have joined Warren and Sharp Football Analysis team this season as their primary fantasy contributor. If you're looking for **The Worksheet** and all of my other fantasy content this season, the one place to find it all will be at Sharp Football Analysis.

While that introduction was used as an announcement, there's still a fantasy article to get to. Player values will fluctuate all summer long prior to your actual fantasy draft through OTAs, training camp and the preseason. When it comes to the players garnering the most fantasy hype prior to training camps opening at the end of July, these are the five that I am buying the most as still being potentially undervalued despite their increased industry appeal.

Jameis Winston

Through four seasons, Winston has yet to finish a season at a top-12 overall scorer at his position while finishing as the QB15 or lower in points per game in each of those seasons. His 2018 season began with a three-game suspension and had a nightmarish in-game benching. Despite that, Winston has now been a top-12 scoring quarterback in nine of his past 16 regular-season starts while finishing as the QB11 in points per game (19.3 points) in his games started in 2018, which included that debacle against the Bengals. Winston's completion rate (64.6 percent) and passing yardage per game (272 yards) also rose again, just as they have in each season of his career thus far. His 7.9 yards per attempt ranked 10th for all qualifying passers.

Winston also found a way to counter his high-turnover propensity in fantasy – he also had a career-worst 3.7 interception rate- as he rushed for a career-high 281 yards during his partial season. Winston now has a longer leash in a make-or-break season with Fitzpatrick gone behind him while the change over to a **Bruce Arians**-led offense will still allow Winston to attack defenses vertically as he did under **Todd Monken** the past three seasons. The Tampa Bay defense has strong potential to be porous once again in 2019 and their potential lack of a rushing attack leaves plenty of passing volume on the bone for a Buccaneers offense that has the easiest passing efficiency outlook for opponents per Sharp Football and the second-lightest outlook against opponent's passing play success rates for the season.

Chris Godwin

Godwin is a chalky breakout, but one that makes too much sense to just run away from the inflation he's received because the hype is warranted. Godwin caught 59-of-95 targets a year ago for 842 yards and seven touchdowns at age 22 while often times operating as the third or fourth option in the passing game. In 18 career games in which he's played at least 50 percent of the Tampa Bay offensive snaps, Godwin has averaged 12.2 PPR points per game. In six career games without **DeSean Jackson** on the field, Godwin has averaged 7.7 targets, 72.8 receiving yards and 14.9 points per game.

Now, not only did the Buccaneers lose Jackson via trade this offseason, but they also lost **Adam Humphries** through free agency. Both Jackson and Humphries accounted for 29 percent of the Tampa Bay receptions and receiving yards while Tampa Bay brought in marginal depth at the position, leaving a runway for Godwin to break out in his third NFL season.

Christian Kirk

Kirk led all rookie receivers in target market share per game (20.2 percent) in 2018 and was second in air yardage percentage (24 percent). In a beyond terrible offensive climate, Kirk lead the Cardinals in receiving yardage (590 yards) prior to having his season end in Week 13 due to a broken foot. Kirk proved that he can be used downfield as well, catching 9-of-13 targets on throws 15-plus yards downfield. He also averaged 5.3 yards after the catch, something surely to be accentuated more in the **Kliff Kingsbury's** Air Raid scheme with quick hitters at the line of scrimmage.

Kirk was a 5-Star recruit entering Texas A&M in 2015 and as a true freshman, he started for the Aggies, leading the team with 80 receptions for 1,009 yards and seven touchdowns at the age 19. That A&M team also had this year's number one overall pick **Kyler Murray** on it as a true freshman. Although Murray played behind starter Kyle Allen that season, Murray threw two of his five touchdowns that season to Kirk while Kirk managed to catch 22 passes for 203 yards and two touchdowns over the three games that Murray attempted 20 or more passes that season.

Marquez Valdes-Scantling

Valdes-Scantling is in line to build off a rookie season in which he posted the most PPR fantasy points by Packers rookie wide receiver since **Aaron Rodgers** became the starting quarterback in 2008. In the 10 games in which he played at least half of the team snaps, Valdes-Scantling averaged 6.4 targets and 10.2 fantasy points per game. He averaged 5.7 yards after the catch (18th) to have ability thriving in the slot role vacated by **Randall Cobb** and also led all rookie wide receivers with 311 receiving yards on targets 20-plus yards downfield. Valdes-Scantling averaged 3.3 yards of separation per route, which led all Green Bay pass catchers.

With the Packers looking for someone to step up behind **Davante Adams**, Valdes-Scantling has an opportunity to garner more opportunities to go along with the explosive-play upside he showed as a rookie.

Vance McDonald

McDonald posted career-highs in targets (72), receptions (50), yards (610) and catch rate (69.4 percent) to go along with four touchdowns in 2018. He also led all qualifying tight ends in expected points added per target. McDonald is a threat to make a real jump on that target opportunity this season with the Steelers missing 33.4 percent of their team targets (fifth highest) from a year ago.

The Steelers also lost **Jesse James**, who played 562 snaps last year compared to the 563 that McDonald played. The only other Steeler tight end to run a passing route in the NFL is **Xavier Grimble**, who has tallied just 22 career receptions through four NFL seasons. McDonald has yet to play a full season in six years and is not your traditional breakout candidate from a career perspective, but the 29-year old has his best opportunity ahead of him in 2019.

NFL Offenses Turned to the Pass in 2018 and Turned the Corner

By Warren Sharp

We will look back on the 2018 NFL season as one that broke many offensive records. There were a lot to discuss.

- Most touchdowns (1,371)
- Most passing touchdowns (847)
- Highest passer rating (92.9)
- Highest completion rate (64.9)

The 2018 season saw the second-most points in history scored as well. But we didn't just luck into this happening.

It happened because offenses got more aggressive than ever before and finally opened their eyes to three of the most seductive words for any fan of offensive production: *first-down passing*.

Last summer, after the Rams signed **Todd Gurley** to a $60 million extension with $45 million in guarantees, some thought this was a turning point. After all, in 2017 teams ran the ball on first down in the first half of games 52.8% of the time (avg. over the last 20 years was 51.8%).

I argued strongly against that logic. I argued in favor of taking things to the extreme in the opposite direction. Last **summer I wrote:**

My contention is that teams are actually running the football too often. And they haven't learned their lesson over the last two decades. Teams are stuck in the past. They feel it's of-value to establish the run. This is -EV strategy. Teams should not run on first down in the first half to "establish the run". We need to change the philosophy of "establish the run" to "establish the lead," and that comes by passing early and allowing teams to run late. First-and-10 pass plays are more successful, they gain more yardage and will have a higher floor in 2018 than they did in years past… First-and-10 in the first half needs to become more of a passing down.

Despite a high-water mark in first-and-10 run rate in 2017 league-wide, and the bank being broken for the most expensive running back signing in history, play callers around the NFL listened.

Historical Pass Rates on First-and-10

In 2018, the NFL saw a record 51.5% pass rate on first-and-10 in the first half. These plays averaged 8.2 yards per attempt, another league record. And they averaged 67.6% completions, a third record.

Last year I created the graphic below from 1997-2017, studying play calls and production on first-and-10 play calls in the first half. I've updated the graphic to insert the 2018 season for comparison:

First & 10 Play Calls & Production in the First Half
(Historical vs 2018)

Year	Pass	Rush	YPA	YPC	YPP Var	Comp %
2018	51.5%	48.5%	8.2	4.79	3.41	67.6%
2015-2017	48.8%	51.2%	7.7	4.33	3.37	65.2%
2012-2014	48.6%	51.4%	7.6	4.39	3.21	63.8%
2009-2011	48.1%	51.9%	7.9	4.52	3.38	63.6%
2006-2008	47.8%	52.2%	7.6	4.25	3.35	62.7%
2003-2005	47.0%	53.0%	7.8	4.27	3.53	62.5%
2000-2002	49.0%	51.0%	7.3	4.25	3.05	61.1%
1997-1999	48.0%	52.0%	7.1	4.14	2.96	58.0%

During the 2010 NFL season, the league modified penalties on passing plays to keep quarterbacks and receivers safer. This allowed easier pass-to-pass efficiency. Looking at every year since the midseason rule changes of 2010, it's evident how the 2018 season stands out:

First & 10 Play Calls & Production in the First Half
(By year, since new passing rules implemented)

Year	Pass	Rush	YPA	YPC	YPP Var	Comp %
2018	51.5%	48.5%	8.2	4.79	3.41	67.6%
2017	47.2%	52.8%	7.8	4.18	3.62	64.5%
2016	50.2%	49.8%	7.6	4.55	3.05	65.2%
2015	49.0%	51.0%	7.7	4.26	3.44	65.9%
2014	47.9%	52.1%	7.6	4.34	3.26	65.3%
2013	49.1%	50.9%	7.8	4.35	3.45	63.1%
2012	48.6%	51.4%	7.5	4.49	3.01	62.9%
2011	47.9%	52.1%	7.7	4.48	3.22	62.1%

Offenses became more aggressive with their first-and-10 play calls. They intelligently opted to shift to the pass in a very strong manner. Aggressive passing on first downs early in the game opened up the run game for many teams as well. As a result, the run game was more productive.

Smarter Rushing Using Personnel Groupings

In 2018, 55% of plays on first downs in the first half were called from 11 personnel (1 RB, 1 TD and 3 WRs). Compare that to 48% in 2017 and 52% in 2016. First-down runs from 11 personnel are extremely efficient. In the first half, they can paint the picture of a pass play, with three receivers on the field, and create a lighter box to run into.

Compare the efficiency of first-down runs in the first half based on personnel (citing the five most-common groupings used):

- 11 personnel (3 WRs): 52% success, 4.8 YPC
- 12 personnel (2 WRs): 48% success, 4.3 YPC
- 21 personnel (2 WRs): 54% success, 5.3 YPC*
- 22 personnel (1 WR): 34% success, 2.5 YPC
- 13 personnel (1 WR): 41% success, 4.6 YPC

*21 personnel numbers are heavily skewed by the Patriots, 49ers and Saints. These three offenses combined to total 37% of rushes from 21 personnel, and all three were extremely strong when running from 21 (NE: 55% success, 5.4 YPC, NO: 68% success, 6.8 YPC, SF: 47% success, 6.1 YPC).

Running from one-receiver sets on first down was extremely unproductive, as the defense was very likely playing run. Running from two-receiver sets had more success, but for most teams around the league, running from three-wide 11 personnel was most productive.

And in 2018, on first downs in the first half, more runs occurred from 11 personnel than in any of the last three years:

- 2018: 49% of all runs from 11 personnel on first down in the first half
- 2017: 41%
- 2016: 44%

First-down passing is more efficient than first-down rushing, but when teams run the ball, they need to do so intelligently. We saw more of that in 2018, which produced much more successful rushing numbers league-wide.

Still Room for Improvement

The efficiency created by more first-and-10 passing in the first half was not a fluke. But the league still must increase its usage. In addition, teams can improve their personnel grouping deployment for even better success.

The most visually stunning & artistic yet data-intensive experience available for NFL analytics...

a 100% interactive experience featuring customizable NFL information & stats, supported with data on proprietary dashboards and visualizations

- **Customize** – Every visualization is customizable and can be manipulated for efficiency in data discovery, providing the best user experience possible.
- **Visualize** – As society trends to more visual learning, Sharp Football Stats allows the user to see the stats to help better understand them.
- **Process** – The user will better make sense of these visualized metrics than most other delivery platforms. Understanding the "why" is as important as knowing the "why".
- **Retain** – A fleeting "aha" moment is worthless if not retained. Through the visual learning method, users will remember what they learned and carry it forward, opening more doors to new ideas along the way.

- Aerial Passing Distance
- Yards thrown short of sticks
- Snap rates
- Toxicity
- Explosive Play Rankings
- Personnel Grouping Frequency and Success Rates
- Strength of Schedule
- Advanced Metrics, such as Success Rate, Missed YPA, YAS% and TOARS

- Positional Target Rates
- Shotgun vs Under Center Rates
- Red Zone Metrics
- Efficiency Metrics
- Advanced Stat Box Scores for Every Game
- Highly detailed and filterable play-by-play data to find specific plays and team trends
- Updated weekly on Monday and Tuesday in-season
- And MUCH MORE

for best results, view on a computer (not mobile devices)

www . SharpFootballStats . com

Much like rushing from passing looks is +EV, passing from run looks is +EV as well. Compare passing efficiency by personnel grouping on first downs in the first half last year:

- 11 personnel (3 WRs): 54% success, 7.5 YPA
- 12 personnel (2 WRs): 54% success, 8.5 YPA
- 21 personnel (2 WRs): 57% success, 8.4 YPA
- 13 personnel (1 WR): 54% success, 8.8 YPA
- 22 personnel (1 WR): 57% success, 9.5 YPA

Last year, 62% of all first-down passes in the first half came from 11 personnel, with just 21% coming from 12 and 9% coming from 21.

Offenses need to look to pass more from 12 or 21 personnel on first downs.

Additionally, if we examine the way in which plays are called from these groupings, it's clear that there is room for improvement:

- 11 personnel sees a 57% pass rate and a 43% run rate
- 12 personnel sees a 53% run rate and a 47% pass rate
- 21 personnel sees a 58% run rate and a 42% pass rate

While these numbers seem logical, I would argue the NFL needs to investigate flipping them on their heads. I'd be in favor of 12 and 21 personnel being used as pass groupings on first down.

Examine some of the teams that bucked the trends the most in 2018 by passing from 12 personnel (NFL average was 47% pass from 12 personnel):

- 67% – Denver: 64% success, 9.8 YPA
- 62% – Indianapolis: 66% success, 9.8 YPA
- 61% – Oakland: 65% success, 7.7 YPA
- 59% – Kansas City: 43% success, 7.7 YPA (12.8 air YPA)*
- 57% – New England: 88% success, 9.6 YPA
- 57% – Atlanta: 50% success, 9.2 YPA
- 56% – New Orleans: 66% success, 9.7 YPA

* KC often used 12 personnel for shot plays on first downs in the first half. Their air yards per attempt of 12.8 was substantially higher than the NFL average, as well as their own passes from 11 personnel (8.0 air YPA) or 21 personnel (6.7 air YPA). As such, their success rate was much lower on these plays.

Which Teams Called the Most Passes on First Half First Downs?

Many teams with great quarterbacks called passes early and often, but even teams with mediocre QB situations were passing early and often and seeing a lot more success in doing so than they did when they ran the ball.

Teams like the Broncos (**Case Keenum**) and Buccaneers (**Jameis Winston** or **Ryan Fitzpatrick**) took to the air on first downs in the first half at well above-average rates and had substantially more success when doing so as compared to when they ran. When the Buccaneers passed on first-and-10 in the first half, they averaged 10.3 YPA and a 61% success rate, as compared to first-and-10 runs which averaged just 4.7 YPC and a 53% success rate.

The biggest surprise team was the Seahawks. Despite having **Russell Wilson** in his prime, the Seahawks chose to run the ball 10% above average, at a 59% clip, second highest in the NFL. While their Success Rates were similar, passes averaged a full 4.0 YPA more than run plays (8.7 YPA vs 4.7 YPC). Expect the Seahawks to continue their run-first ways since it led them to the playoffs last year with OC **Brian Schottenheimer** and defensive-minded HC **Pete Carroll** still calling shots. But their offense would have a substantial upside if they let Wilson pass the ball more on first down.

What team was balanced but blew it by not being more pass heavy? The Chargers.

Despite my pleas with the team to go much more pass heavy **last summer**, the Chargers still passed the ball at a below-average rate (50%). These passes averaged 10.8 YPA and a 58% Success Rate, whereas runs averaged 4.8

YPA (league average) and a mere 44% Success Rate (7th worst). If the Chargers went more pass heavy on first-and-10 in the first half, they would be much more dangerous offensively.

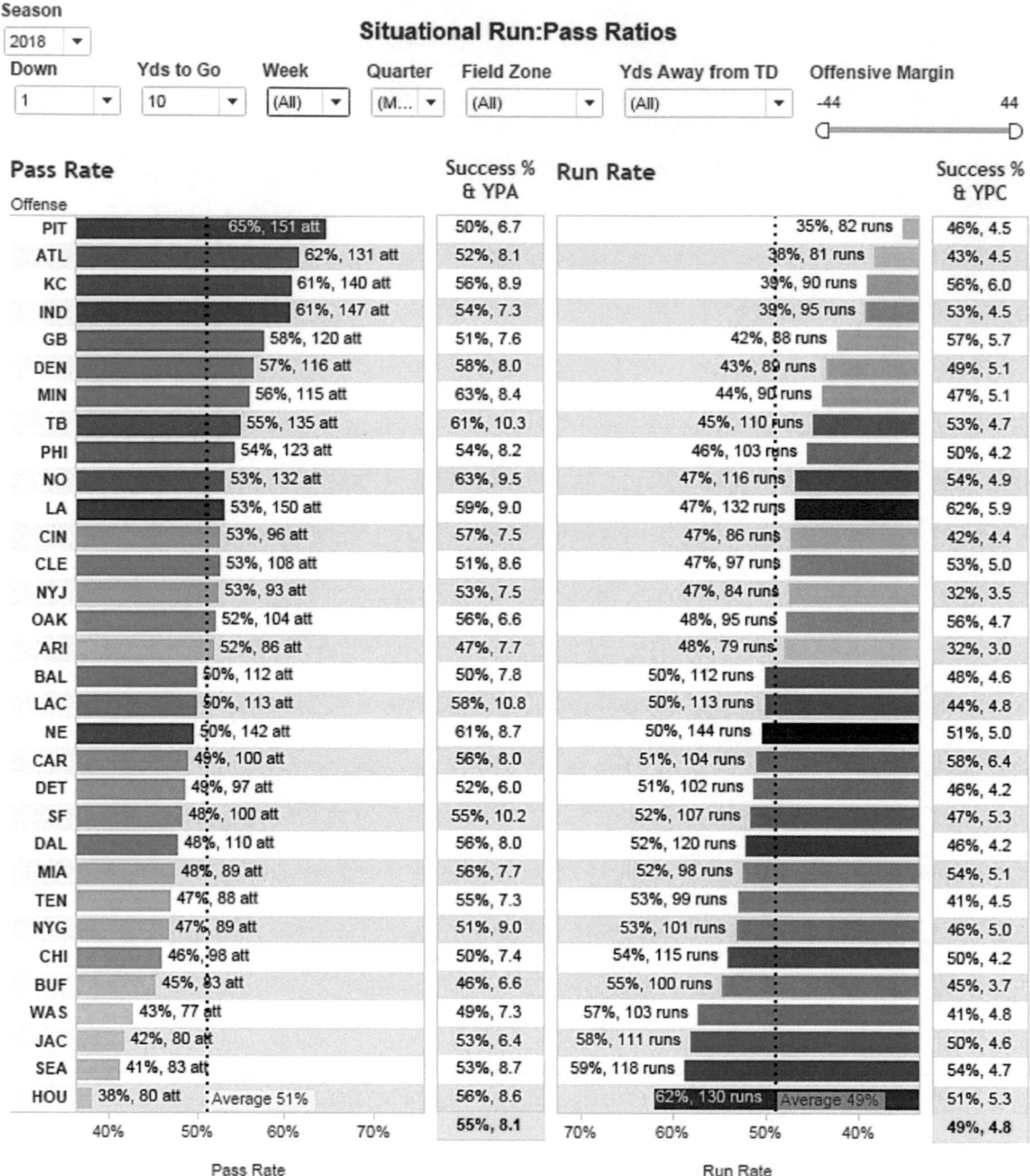

Will Teams Continue to "Pass" on First Down Rushing in 2019?

Yes. It should be a no-brainer, but nothing smart seems to be a no-brainer in the NFL. That said, I believe it will continue. More intelligent offensive minds are being hired or promoted to positions of importance around the league. Better analytics are being made available and coaches are unable to deny the information, and the people with these analytics have more influence on teams and league-wide thought processes.

Coaches should look to pass *even more* on first down in the first half than they did in 2018. Coaches should spend time this offseason devising more pass plays with high completion rates for use on first down. Coaches should look to 21 personnel in particular as an edge in the passing game. The extra tight end provides a huge mismatch, creates less predictability pre-snap, and can provide situations where there are more max-protection passes or better downfield blocking with TEs releasing to become blockers after high percentage passes to WRs. And coaches should look to run more from 11 personnel rather than 2 or 1 WR groupings.

Teams can try to establish the run and make the playoffs, like Chicago, Dallas, Seattle and Houston did last year. These teams went 1-4 in the playoffs, with the lone win when Dallas beat Seattle (solely because Seattle ran the ball so often). But don't mistake correlation as causation - these four teams didn't make the playoffs because they established the run. They were good teams with good rosters. They would have made the playoffs regardless of whether they went *over-the-top run heavy* or not. The ceiling is much higher for the Dallas offense if they pass more on first downs (56% success, 8.0 YPA) rather than run more (46% success, 4.2 YPC), and the same is true with the other run-heavy teams.

Running as often as some of these teams did is like fighting against the tide. It will work when the tide is low and you're playing an opponent who is beatable with any style, so it convinces you to continue with this -EV strategy. But at high tide, fighting against the rules and modern-day efficiencies which favor the passing game when taking on a tough opponent won't often end well. These teams would be well served to reassess their 2018 tactics.

Have you heard?

Sharp Football Analysis.com is RELAUNCHING July 8th!

...and we're expanding our analysis:

- **Betting** – All of the successful, consistent football betting analysis you've come to expect from Warren Sharp, with even more written weekly content planned for 2019, as well as integrating interactive video and more podcasts!

- **Prop Betting** – We've added new prop specialists who will be tackling NFL props, starting with the season-long props and sharing weekly prop recommendations and analysis backed by the best analytics and delivering the most reliable results.

- **Fantasy Football** – We've hired Rich Hribar and several other fantasy writers to deliver cutting-edge analysis on a daily basis throughout the season. Rich's premier Wednesday article, "The Worksheet" will get your weekly analysis started on the right foot, and we'll have other articles, rankings, analysis and multiple weekly chats to get you the more connected with our recommendations than ever before.

- **Analysis** – We'll be delivering more insight and content than you thought possible, including diving into coaching and play breakdowns from multiple current and former coaches. You'll read insight you won't see anywhere else.

- **Stats** – We're building out Sharp Football Stats.com to add more visualizations and analysis than you ever thought possible.

Check us out on July 8th!

Layout and Definitions

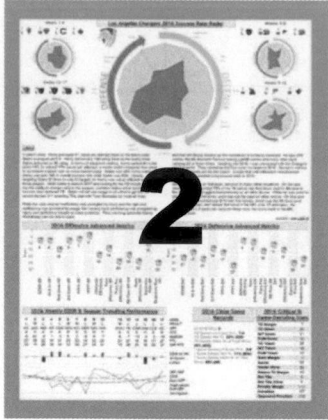
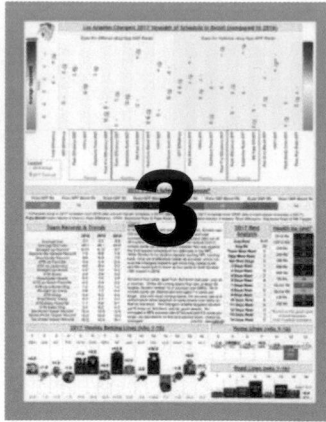

PAGE 1: Schedule listed according to strength of opponent based on win totals // Asterisk next to draft round indicates compensatory selection // Projected starting roster shaded based on current year (2017) cap hit to see where team is spending for its starters // Positional spending shows 2017 rank as "Rank" and 2016 rank as "2016 Rk" // Average line listed is based on weeks 1-16 lines which were opened by CG Technology

PAGE 2: Radars posted based on success rates only. These radars will be posted on Sharp Football Stats and updated in-season for 2017 on a weekly basis // Weekly EDSR and Season Trending Performance measures total EDSR per week, combining offense and defense together. A green vertical bar indicates the team "won" the EDSR battle that week. A red vertical bar indicates they lost. The longer the bar, the more lopsided the result. The trend chart represents offense (blue) and defense (red). When blue is high, the offense was efficient in EDSR. When the red bar is low, the defense was efficient in EDSR. EDSR stands for Early Down Success Rate, and measures efficiency on early downs only and ability to bypass 3rd down on offense, or force opponent into 3rd downs on defense.

PAGE 3: Strength of Schedule in Detail – the red "dot" is the true final result in 2016 based on the real schedule played. The logo is the 2017 forecast rank based on the real schedule the team will play // Schedule Variances indicate if the schedule became easier or harder than last year's schedule, and by how much. Extremes are most notable (a team ranking 31st or 32nd saw their schedule become much easier. A team ranking 1st or 2nd saw their schedule become much harder this year // Health by Unit are league rankings (1-32) based on Football Outsiders (Scott Kacsmar's) work.

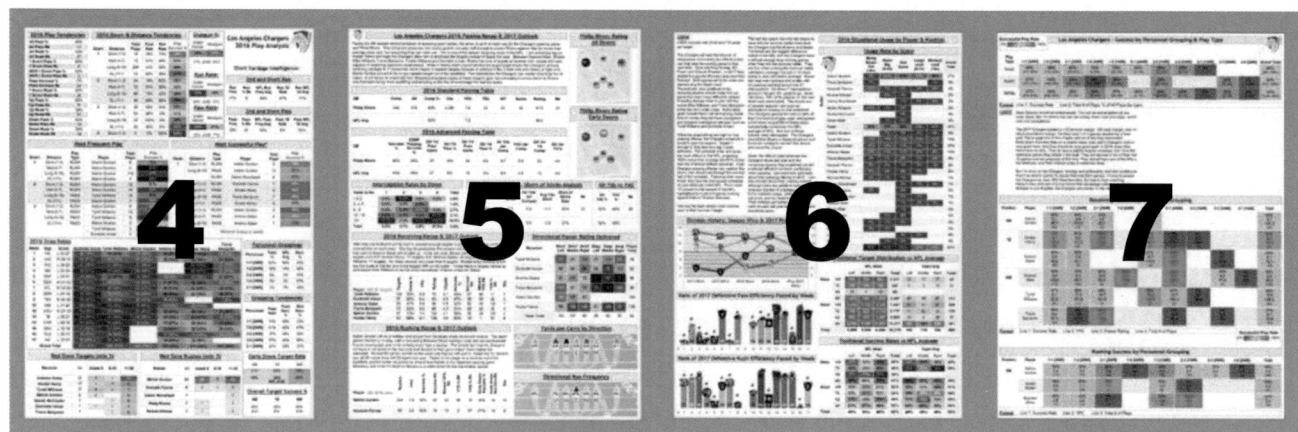

PAGE 4: Most metrics should be self explanatory // Frequent play vs successful play looks at play frequency and compares to when a team saw the most success for a particular down & distance // Snap rates include players who recorded 300+ snaps, with cutoff if too many on a certain team hit that mark // Target rates are only for early downs, target success looks at every down

PAGE 5: YPA = yards per attempt // Success rate is defined as a play which gained the minimum required yardage based on down and distance. Cutoffs are 40% of yards to go on 1st down, 60% of yards to go on 2nd down and 100% of yards to go on 3rd or 4th down // 20+ and 30+ yard pass gains are not air yards, but pass plays which totaled gains of 20 or 30 yards // Air Yds = distance ball traveled in the air per attempt // YAC = yards gained after the catch // TOARS = Target and Output-Adjusted Receiving Success – the higher the number the better the performance delivered // Missed YPA = yardage on unsuccessful plays which fell short of that required yardage cutoff. The fewer Missed YPA, the closer a player was to turning the unsuccessful play into a successful one.

PAGE 6: Usage Rate By Score examines percentage of a team's total plays in that given score margin are delivered to that player // Positional target distribution and success rates look at where a team was throwing and how successful they were, based on field location (left/mid/right) and depth (short = within 15 yards of line of scrimmage, deep = greater than that) and position // Weekly schedule for offensive players based on defensive strengths for the run and pass is found in the bottom left.

PAGE 7: Team success rate by personnel grouping and play type. Shares success rate & personnel grouping usage (frequency) // Also lists individual players, first receiving, then rushing, and lists data including success rate, yards per play, passer rating and total number of plays

Arizona Cardinals

Head Coach:
Kliff Kingsbury (Texas Tech HC, Calls Plays) (new)
Offensive Coordinator:
Tom Clements (GB OC) (new)
Defensive Coordinator:
Vance Joseph (DEN HC) (new)

EASY HARD

2019 Forecast

Wins	Div Rank
5	#4

Past Records

2018: 3-13
2017: 8-8
2016: 7-8-1

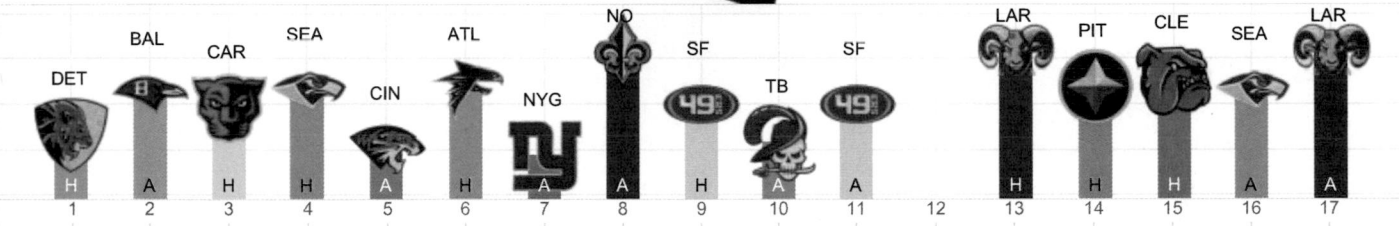

DET	BAL	CAR	SEA	CIN	ATL	NYG	NO	SF	TB	SF		LAR	PIT	CLE	SEA	LAR
H	A	H	H	A	H	A	A	H	A	A		H	H	H	A	A
1	2	3	4	5	6	7	8	9	10	11	12	13	14	15	16	17

TNF

Key Players Lost

Player	New
Antoine Bethea (FS)	NYG
Arthur Moats (OLB)	Retired
Benson Mayowa (DE)	OAK
Deone Bucannon (ILB)	TB
Gerald Hodges (ILB)	Retired
J.J. Nelson (WR)	OAK
John Wetzel (G)	ATL
Josh Rosen (QB)	MIA
Markus Golden (DE)	NYG
Mike Glennon (QB)	OAK
Mike Iupati (G)	SEA
Oday Aboushi (G)	DET
Olsen Pierre (DT)	NYG

Average Line	# Games Favored	# Games Underdog
5.7	0	15

2019 Arizona Cardinals Overview

The last time a college coach jumped to the pros with this much hype, **Chip Kelly** left Oregon for the Eagles to coach another athletic quarterback who offset his height deficiency with quickness and mobility. That quarterback was **Michael Vick**. And while Kelly elevated a previously 4-12 Eagles team to 10-6, only a portion of that turnaround resulted from Kelly's strategies.

More came from a flipped turnover ratio, **Lane Johnson** and **Zach Ertz**'s rookie talent infusions, and some good old-fashioned luck.

The 2012 Eagles' turnover margin was -24. Vick and **Nick Foles** threw a combined 15 interceptions and fumbled 19 times. The 2012 Eagles fumbled *37 times* as a team.

All of those totals were all bound to regress. And regress they did.

Kelly's Eagles cut their fumble total from 37 to 19. Foles relieved an injured Vick for a sterling 27:2 TD-to-INT ratio and 8-2 record in ten starts. Kelly's Eagles finished +12 in turnover margin, a 36-takeaway flip representing the franchise's second-largest one-year improvement since 1991.

Kelly's Eagles were also the NFL's second-healthiest team after Philly fielded 2012's most-injured offense. Massive win-loss improvement is entirely possible when a team rights the turnover ship and keeps its best players on the field.

Similarities are many between Kelly's debut season and what **Kliff Kingsbury** walks into with Arizona. Last year's Cardinals fielded the NFL's second most-injured offense after Arizona experienced the league's most injury depletion in 2017. This year's Cardinals should be destined for better injury luck.

(cont'd - see ARI2)

Key Free Agents/ Trades Added

Player	AAV (MM)
Charles Clay (TE)	$2
Darius Philon (DT)	$5
J.R. Sweezy (G)	$4.5
Jordan Hicks (ILB)	$8.5
Marcus Gilbert (RT)	Trade
Robert Alford (CB)	$7.5
Terrell Suggs (OLB)	$5
Tramaine Brock (CB)	$1.3

Drafted Players

Rd	Pk	Player (College)
1	1	QB - Kyler Murray (Oklahoma)
2	33	CB - Byron Murphy (Washing..
	62	WR - Andy Isabella (UMass)
3	65	DE - Zach Allen (Boston Coll..
4	103	WR - Hakeem Butler (Iowa S..
5	139	S - Deionte Thompson (Alab..
6	174	WR - KeeSean Johnson (Fre..
	179	C - Lamont Gaillard (Georgia)
7*	248	OT - Joshua Miles (Morgan S..
	249	DE - Michael Dogbe (Temple)
	254	TE - Caleb Wilson (UCLA)

Regular Season Wins: Past & Current Proj

Forecast 2019 Wins	5
2018 Wins	3
Forecast 2018 Wins	5.5
2017 Wins	8
2016 Wins	7
2015 Wins	13

1 3 5 7 9 11 13 15

Lineup & Cap Hits

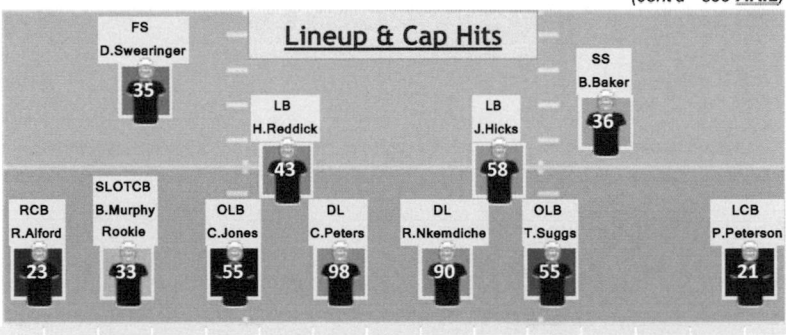

FS D.Swearinger 35

SS B.Baker 36

LB H.Reddick 43

LB J.Hicks 58

RCB R.Alford 23

SLOTCB B.Murphy Rookie 33

OLB C.Jones 55

DL C.Peters 98

DL R.Nkemdiche 90

OLB T.Suggs 55

LCB P.Peterson 21

LWR A.Isabella Rookie 89

LT D.Humphries 74

LG J.Sweezy 64

C M.Cole 64

RG J.Pugh 67

RT M.Gilbert 77

TE C.Clay 85

RWR C.Kirksey 13

SLOTWR L.Fitzgerald 11

QB K.Murray Rookie 1

RB D.Johnson 31

WR2 H.Butler Rookie 17

WR3 C.Williams 10

RB2 C.Edmonds 29

QB2 B.Hundley 7

2019 Cap Dollars

2019 Unit Spending

All OFF
All DEF

Positional Spending

	Rank	Total	2017 Rk
All OFF	27	$82.81M	31
QB	27	$9.26M	29
OL	19	$36.13M	30
RB	4	$12.76M	17
WR	19	$19.80M	9
TE	28	$4.85M	14
All DEF	14	$89.13M	20
DL	9	$41.04M	16
LB	25	$15.37M	19
CB	13	$24.01M	17
S	18	$8.71M	18

Also like the 2013 Eagles, the 2019 Cardinals received major talent infusions. DE **Terrell Suggs**, MLB **Jordan Hicks**, OG **J.R. Sweezy**, and RT **Marcus Gilbert** arrived via free agency and trade. No. 1 overall pick **Kyler Murray** – a longtime Kingsbury crush – and second-round WR **Andy Isabella** added playmaking ability in the draft.

While the 2013 Eagles' six-win improvement will be tough for the Cardinals to mimic, steps forward are likely. Arizona's -12 turnover margin ranked third worst in the league last season, and their 23 fumbles were in large part caused by predictable passing situations behind a bad offensive line.

Quarterbacks getting the ball out quickly is a calling card of Kingsbury's offense, which is designed to deliver the football to playmakers before pressure arrives. 2018 Cardinals starter **Josh Rosen** faced pressure on 40% of his dropbacks, the second-highest rate in the league.

To fully appreciate Kingsbury's plan, we must first examine how much his approach will differ from last year's **Mike McCoy**- and **Byron Leftwich**-coordinated disaster. Passing efficiency is significantly more correlated to wins than rushing efficiency, and any philosophies that hurt a quarterback's ability to perform are red flags. Rosen played his first NFL season in a red-flag sea.

The 2018 Cardinals offensive line finished dead last in pass protection. Facing relentless pressure with pass catchers who didn't separate, Rosen's 59% expected completion rate ranked last among quarterbacks.

Arizona's run game likewise finished dead last in efficiency. The Cardinals lacked offensive elements to instill trepidation into defensive coordinators, who fearlessly blitzed Rosen and persistently knifed into Arizona's backfield on run plays.

The offensive scheme was so bad the Cardinals fired McCoy midyear. Switching coordinators at midseason added further burden onto Rosen, who also faced the toughest pass-defense schedule among rookie quarterbacks. Behind 35-year-old **Larry Fitzgerald**, Rosen's next three most-targeted wide receivers were 22, 22, and 24 years old.

And one-and-done coach **Steve Wilks**' run defense got wrecked. The 2017 Cardinals finished No. 1 in run defense, only to plummet to 29th in Wilks' lone year. Losing teams tend to face more rushing attempts, shortening games and lessening comeback opportunities. Especially when those theoretical

comebacks are staged behind the NFL's worst pass-blocking offensive line with a poor receiving corps. Because the Cardinals consistently played from behind and Wilks' defense couldn't stop the run, they faced a league-high 31.9 rushing attempts per game.

The Cardinals weren't bad because of Rosen, who we'll discuss in the Dolphins' chapter. Arizona's *coaching* deserved more blame. McCoy's backs ran the ball directly behind center on 66% of attempts, over double the NFL average. **David Johnson** averaged 1.8 yards per carry with a 10% Success Rate on first-down runs. McCoy's last three NFL offenses all ranked bottom ten in rushing, and all three ran behind center at rates 10-20% above league average.

*(cont'd - see **ARI-3**)*

2018 Passing Performance

QB	1st Dwn	2nd Dwn	3rd Dwn	
Josh Rosen	47%	31%	28%	Success Rate
	7.7	4.4	5.0	YPA
	84.6	55.2	60.6	Rating
Pass Rate	56%	60%	84%	
NFL AVG	53%	47%	36%	Success Rate
	7.7	7.3	6.9	YPA
	95.1	93.7	87.1	Rating
Pass Rate	53%	62%	80%	

2018 Rushing Performance

Offense	1st Dwn	2nd Dwn	3rd Dwn	
ARI	37%	43%	39%	Success Rate
	3.8	3.7	3.6	YPC
Run Rate	44%	40%	16%	
NFL AVG	48%	46%	51%	Success Rate
	4.5	4.4	4.3	YPC
Run Rate	47%	38%	20%	

2018 Offensive Advanced Metrics

Rank (y-axis: 1, 5, 10, 15, 20, 25, 30)

Data points by category:
- EDSR Off: ~32
- 30 & In Off: 30
- Red Zone Off: 29
- 3rd Down Off: ~32
- YPPA Off: 28
- YPPT Off: ~32
- Offensive Efficiency: ~32
- Pass Efficiency Off: ~32
- Pass Pro Efficiency Off: 26
- RB Pass Eff Off: ~32
- Rush Efficiency Off: ~32
- Explosive Pass Off: ~32
- Explosive Run Off: 2

2018 Defensive Advanced Metrics

Rank (y-axis: 1, 5, 10, 15, 20, 25, 30)

Data points by category:
- EDSR Def: 18
- 30 & In Def: 1
- Red Zone Def: 19
- 3rd Down Def: 9
- YPPA Def: 7
- YPPT Def: 29
- Defensive Efficiency: 3
- Pass Efficiency Def: 17
- Pass Pro Efficiency Def: 8
- RB Pass Eff Def: 29
- Rush Efficiency Def: 29
- Explosive Pass Def: ~32
- Explosive Run Def: 26

2018 Weekly EDSR & Season Trending Performance

	1	2	3	4	5	6	7	8	10	11	12	13	14	15	16	17	WEEK
	L	L	L	L	W	L	L	W	L	L	L	W	L	L	L	L	RESULT
	WAS	LA	CHI	SEA	SF	MIN	DEN	SF	KC	OAK	LAC	GB	DET	ATL	LA	SEA	OPP
	H	A	H	H	A	A	H	H	A	H	A	H	A	H	A	A	SITE
	-18	-34	-2	-3	10	-10	-35	3	-12	-2	-35	3	-14	-26	-22	-3	MARGIN
	6	0	14	17	28	17	10	18	14	21	10	20	3	14	9	24	PTS
	24	34	16	20	18	27	45	15	26	23	45	17	17	40	31	27	OPP PTS

EDSR by Wk
W=Green
L=Red

OFF/DEF
EDSR
Blue=OFF
(high=good)
Red=DEF
(low=good)

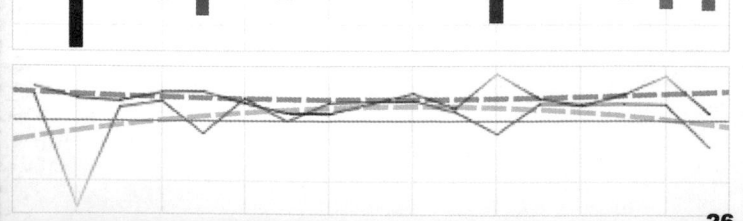

2018 Close Game Records

All 2018 Wins: **3**
FG Games (<=3 pts) W-L: **2-4**
FG Games Win %: **33% (#22)**
FG Games Wins (% of Total Wins): **67% (#2)**

1 Score Games (<=8 pts) W-L: **2-4**
1 Score Games Win %: **33% (#24)**
1 Score Games Wins (% of Total Wins): **67% (#8)**

2018 Critical & Game-Deciding Stats

TO Margin	-12
TO Given	28
INT Given	18
FUM Given	10
TO Taken	16
INT Taken	7
FUM Taken	9
Sack Margin	-3
Sacks	49
Sacks Allow	52
Return TD Margin	-1
Ret TDs	3
Ret TDs Allow	4
Penalty Margin	-1
Penalties	101
Opponent Penalties	100

Arizona Cardinals 2019 Strength of Schedule In Detail (compared to 2018)

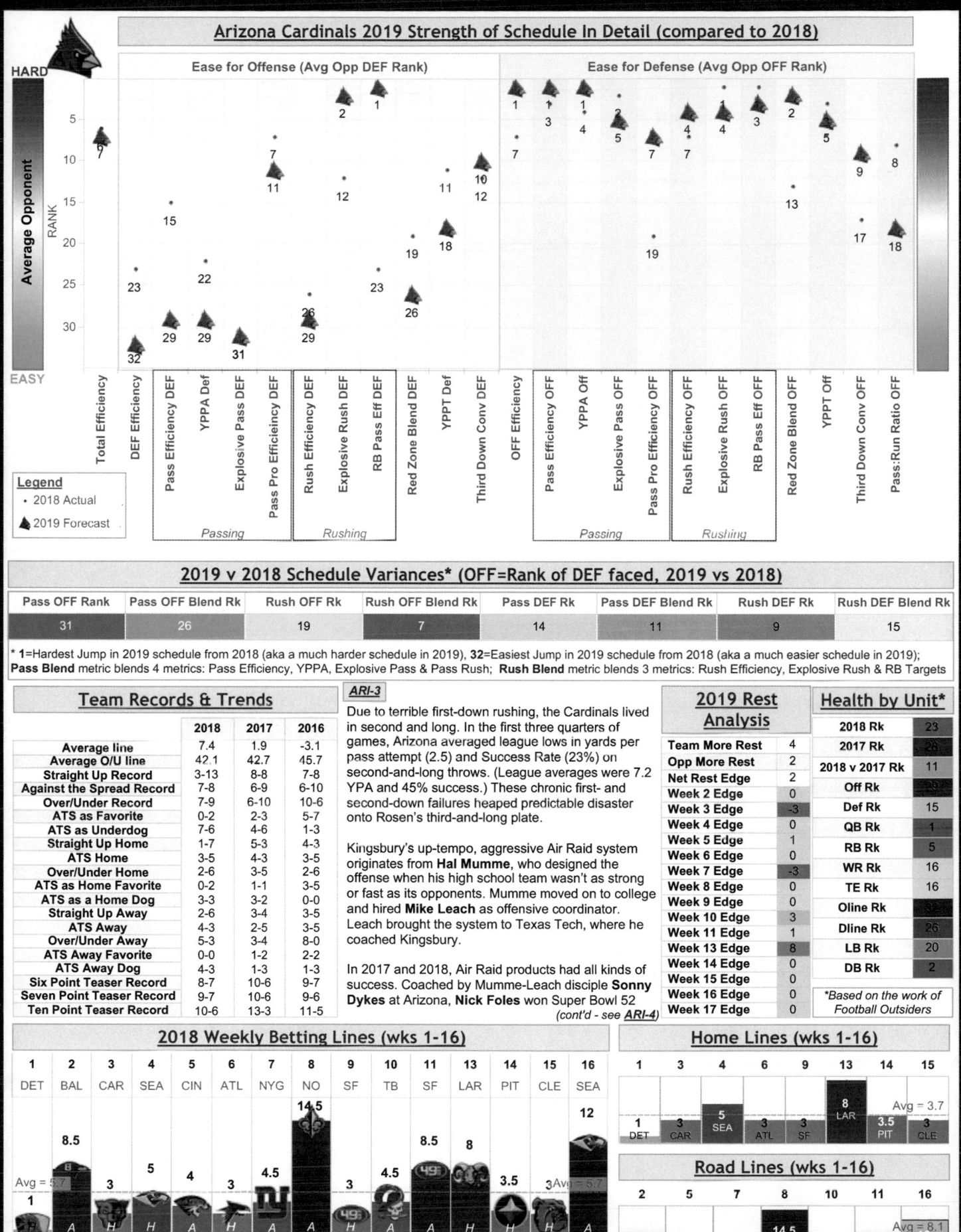

Ease for Offense (Avg Opp DEF Rank) / Ease for Defense (Avg Opp OFF Rank)

Legend
- 2018 Actual
- 2019 Forecast

2019 v 2018 Schedule Variances* (OFF=Rank of DEF faced, 2019 vs 2018)

Pass OFF Rank	Pass OFF Blend Rk	Rush OFF Rk	Rush OFF Blend Rk	Pass DEF Rk	Pass DEF Blend Rk	Rush DEF Rk	Rush DEF Blend Rk
31	26	19	7	14	11	9	15

* **1**=Hardest Jump in 2019 schedule from 2018 (aka a much harder schedule in 2019), **32**=Easiest Jump in 2019 schedule from 2018 (aka a much easier schedule in 2019);
Pass Blend metric blends 4 metrics: Pass Efficiency, YPPA, Explosive Pass & Pass Rush; **Rush Blend** metric blends 3 metrics: Rush Efficiency, Explosive Rush & RB Targets

Team Records & Trends

	2018	2017	2016
Average line	7.4	1.9	-3.1
Average O/U line	42.1	42.7	45.7
Straight Up Record	3-13	8-8	7-8
Against the Spread Record	7-8	6-9	6-10
Over/Under Record	7-9	6-10	10-6
ATS as Favorite	0-2	2-3	5-7
ATS as Underdog	7-6	4-6	1-3
Straight Up Home	1-7	5-3	4-3
ATS Home	3-5	4-3	3-5
Over/Under Home	2-6	3-5	2-6
ATS as Home Favorite	0-2	1-1	3-5
ATS as a Home Dog	3-3	3-2	0-0
Straight Up Away	2-6	3-4	3-5
ATS Away	4-3	2-5	3-5
Over/Under Away	5-3	3-4	8-0
ATS Away Favorite	0-0	1-2	2-2
ATS Away Dog	4-3	1-3	1-3
Six Point Teaser Record	8-7	10-6	9-7
Seven Point Teaser Record	9-7	10-6	9-6
Ten Point Teaser Record	10-6	13-3	11-5

ARI-3

Due to terrible first-down rushing, the Cardinals lived in second and long. In the first three quarters of games, Arizona averaged league lows in yards per pass attempt (2.5) and Success Rate (23%) on second-and-long throws. (League averages were 7.2 YPA and 45% success.) These chronic first- and second-down failures heaped predictable disaster onto Rosen's third-and-long plate.

Kingsbury's up-tempo, aggressive Air Raid system originates from **Hal Mumme**, who designed the offense when his high school team wasn't as strong or fast as its opponents. Mumme moved on to college and hired **Mike Leach** as offensive coordinator. Leach brought the system to Texas Tech, where he coached Kingsbury.

In 2017 and 2018, Air Raid products had all kinds of success. Coached by Mumme-Leach disciple **Sonny Dykes** at Arizona, **Nick Foles** won Super Bowl 52
(cont'd - see ARI-4)

2019 Rest Analysis

Team More Rest	4
Opp More Rest	2
Net Rest Edge	2
Week 2 Edge	0
Week 3 Edge	-3
Week 4 Edge	0
Week 5 Edge	1
Week 6 Edge	0
Week 7 Edge	-3
Week 8 Edge	0
Week 9 Edge	0
Week 10 Edge	3
Week 11 Edge	1
Week 13 Edge	8
Week 14 Edge	0
Week 15 Edge	0
Week 16 Edge	0
Week 17 Edge	0

Health by Unit*

2018 Rk	23
2017 Rk	28
2018 v 2017 Rk	11
Off Rk	20
Def Rk	15
QB Rk	1
RB Rk	5
WR Rk	16
TE Rk	16
Oline Rk	32
Dline Rk	26
LB Rk	20
DB Rk	2

*Based on the work of Football Outsiders

2018 Weekly Betting Lines (wks 1-16)

1	2	3	4	5	6	7	8	9	10	11	13	14	15	16
DET	BAL	CAR	SEA	CIN	ATL	NYG	NO	SF	TB	SF	LAR	PIT	CLE	SEA

Avg = 5.7

| 1 | 8.5 | 3 | 5 | 4 | 3 | 4.5 | 14.5 | 3 | 4.5 | 8.5 | 8 | 3.5 | 3 | 12 |
| A | H | H | A | H | A | H | H | A | H | A | H | H | A | A |

Home Lines (wks 1-16)

1	3	4	6	9	13	14	15
DET	CAR	SEA	ATL	SF	LAR	PIT	CLE
1	3	5	3	3	8	3.5	3

Avg = 3.7

Road Lines (wks 1-16)

2	5	7	8	10	11	16
BAL	CIN	NYG	NO	TB	SF	SEA
8.5	4	4.5	14.5	4.5	8.5	12

Avg = 8.1

2018 Play Tendencies

All Pass %	60%
All Pass Rk	14
All Rush %	40%
All Rush Rk	19
1 Score Pass %	55%
1 Score Pass Rk	25
2017 1 Score Pass %	60%
2017 1 Score Pass Rk	5
2018 Pass Increase %	-5%
Pass Increase Rk	29
1 Score Rush %	45%
1 Score Rush Rk	8
Up Pass %	50%
Up Pass Rk	17
Up Rush %	50%
Up Rush Rk	16
Down Pass %	65%
Down Pass Rk	24
Down Rush %	35%
Down Rush Rk	9

2018 Down & Distance Tendencies

Down	Distance	Total Plays	Pass Rate	Run Rate	Play Success %
1	Short (1-3)	2	0%	100%	100%
	Med (4-7)	6	17%	83%	67%
	Long (8-10)	243	49%	51%	39%
	XL (11+)	13	54%	46%	46%
2	Short (1-3)	22	14%	86%	73%
	Med (4-7)	57	54%	46%	37%
	Long (8-10)	85	49%	51%	26%
	XL (11+)	36	78%	22%	19%
3	Short (1-3)	27	67%	33%	41%
	Med (4-7)	52	96%	4%	33%
	Long (8-10)	35	83%	17%	17%
	XL (11+)	30	80%	20%	13%
4	Short (1-3)	3	33%	67%	33%

Shotgun %:

Under Center	Shotgun
46%	54%

37% AVG 63%

Run Rate:

Under Center	Shotgun
69%	18%

68% AVG 23%

Pass Rate:

Under Center	Shotgun
31%	82%

32% AVG 77%

Arizona Cardinals
2018 Play Analysis

Short Yardage Intelligence:

2nd and Short Run

Run Freq	Run Rk	NFL Run Freq Avg	Run 1D Rate	Run NFL 1D Avg
82%	3	65%	91%	68%

2nd and Short Pass

Pass Freq	Pass Rk	NFL Pass Freq Avg	Pass 1D Rate	Pass NFL 1D Avg
18%	30	35%	40%	56%

Most Frequent Play

Down	Distance	Play Type	Player	Total Plays	Play Success %
1	Short (1-3)	RUSH	David Johnson	2	100%
	Med (4-7)	RUSH	David Johnson	3	33%
	Long (8-10)	RUSH	David Johnson	91	27%
	XL (11+)	RUSH	David Johnson	5	40%
2	Short (1-3)	RUSH	David Johnson	14	93%
	Med (4-7)	RUSH	David Johnson	18	44%
	Long (8-10)	RUSH	David Johnson	35	31%
	XL (11+)	RUSH	David Johnson	6	0%
3	Short (1-3)	RUSH	David Johnson	7	57%
	Med (4-7)	PASS	Christian Kirk	9	56%
	Long (8-10)	PASS	Larry Fitzgerald	8	0%
	XL (11+)	PASS	Larry Fitzgerald	5	40%

Most Successful Play*

Down	Distance	Play Type	Player	Total Plays	Play Success %
1	Long (8-10)	PASS	David Johnson	13	69%
	XL (11+)	RUSH	David Johnson	5	40%
2	Short (1-3)	RUSH	David Johnson	14	93%
	Med (4-7)	RUSH	David Johnson	18	44%
	Long (8-10)	PASS	Larry Fitzgerald	7	43%
	XL (11+)	PASS	Christian Kirk	5	0%
		RUSH	David Johnson	6	0%
3	Short (1-3)	RUSH	David Johnson	7	57%
	Med (4-7)	PASS	Larry Fitzgerald	8	63%
	Long (8-10)	PASS	Larry Fitzgerald	8	0%
	XL (11+)	PASS	Larry Fitzgerald	5	40%

*Minimum 5 plays to qualify

2018 Weekly Snap Rates

Wk	Opp	Score	Larry Fitzgerald	David Johnson	Christian Kirk	Ricky Seals-Jones	Chad Williams	Jermaine Gresham	Trent Sherfield
1	WAS	L 24-6	52 (98%)	36 (68%)	45 (85%)	49 (92%)	50 (94%)		
2	LA	L 34-0	26 (58%)	35 (78%)	31 (69%)	44 (98%)	34 (76%)		
3	CHI	L 16-14	48 (96%)	43 (86%)	37 (74%)	42 (84%)	43 (86%)	17 (34%)	
4	SEA	L 20-17	52 (87%)	55 (92%)	40 (67%)	39 (65%)	51 (85%)	33 (55%)	
5	SF	W 28-18	42 (82%)	48 (94%)	32 (63%)	34 (67%)	41 (80%)	28 (55%)	3 (6%)
6	MIN	L 27-17	49 (84%)	55 (95%)	46 (79%)	39 (67%)	39 (67%)	30 (52%)	
7	DEN	L 45-10	64 (97%)	48 (73%)	52 (79%)	29 (44%)	45 (68%)	39 (59%)	
8	SF	W 18-15	66 (100%)	53 (80%)	50 (76%)	48 (73%)	47 (71%)	31 (47%)	
10	KC	L 26-14	70 (96%)	56 (77%)	65 (89%)	46 (63%)		29 (40%)	39 (53%)
11	OAK	L 23-21	50 (93%)	43 (80%)	48 (89%)	21 (39%)		39 (72%)	20 (37%)
12	LAC	L 45-10	43 (91%)	37 (79%)	43 (91%)	19 (40%)		31 (66%)	20 (43%)
13	GB	W 20-17	60 (97%)	52 (84%)	53 (85%)	22 (35%)		44 (71%)	31 (50%)
14	DET	L 17-3	67 (96%)	62 (89%)		44 (63%)		30 (43%)	65 (93%)
15	ATL	L 40-14	65 (96%)	34 (50%)		55 (81%)		20 (29%)	64 (94%)
16	LA	L 31-9	52 (98%)	40 (75%)		5 (9%)	29 (55%)	46 (87%)	45 (85%)
17	SEA	L 27-24	66 (100%)	52 (79%)			51 (77%)		56 (85%)
	Grand Total		872 (92%)	749 (80%)	542 (79%)	536 (61%)	430 (76%)	417 (55%)	343 (61%)

Personnel Groupings

Personnel	Team %	NFL Avg	Succ. %
1-1 [3WR]	71%	65%	36%
1-2 [2WR]	18%	17%	43%
2-1 [2WR]	5%	8%	40%
2-2 [1WR]	4%	3%	28%
1-3 [1WR]	2%	3%	37%

Grouping Tendencies

Personnel	Pass Rate	Pass Succ. %	Run Succ. %
1-1 [3WR]	70%	35%	39%
1-2 [2WR]	44%	39%	46%
2-1 [2WR]	31%	50%	35%
2-2 [1WR]	9%	0%	31%
1-3 [1WR]	42%	63%	18%

Red Zone Targets (min 3)

Receiver	All	Inside 5	6-10	11-20
Larry Fitzgerald	13	4	1	8
David Johnson	9		7	2
Chad Williams	5	1	1	3
Christian Kirk	5		2	3
Ricky Seals-Jones	4	1	2	1

Red Zone Rushes (min 3)

Rusher	All	Inside 5	6-10	11-20
David Johnson	29	9	7	13
Chase Edmonds	8		5	3
Sam Bradford	1			1

Early Down Target Rate

RB	TE	WR
25%	18%	57%
23%	21%	56%
	NFL AVG	

Overall Target Success %

RB	TE	WR
35%	40%	45%
#32	#32	#30

28

Arizona Cardinals 2018 Passing Recap & 2019 Outlook

In spite of **Josh Rosen**'s struggles, all of his key passing metrics were superior to **Jared Goff**'s rookie year. Upgrading from **Jeff Fisher** to **Sean McVay**, Goff took a massive sophomore leap and made the Super Bowl in year three. I believe Rosen would have performed adequately in Arizona with coaching and roster improvements. And I believe **Kyler Murray** will perform even better. Kingsbury's deployment of personnel and use of tempo should cause confusion for defenses, especially early in the year. Last season, the division-rival 49ers, Seahawks, and Rams faced four-plus-receiver sets on just 43 combined snaps over 48 games. That's less than one play per game on average. Kingsbury's four-verts package has potential to put defenses in binds. Teams like the Patriots (21 personnel), Rams (11 personnel), and Eagles (12 personnel) that stay true to specific groupings make themselves tougher to defend. And Murray's dual threat is an enormous X-factor on a spread-out field.

2018 Standard Passing Table

QB	Comp	Att	Comp %	Yds	YPA	TDs	INT	Sacks	Rating	Rk
Josh Rosen	217	393	55%	2,278	5.8	11	14	45	67	48
Sam Bradford	50	80	63%	400	5.0	2	4	6	63	50
NFL Avg			62%		7.0				87.5	

2018 Advanced Passing Table

QB	Success %	EDSR Passing Success %	20+ Yd Pass Gains	20+ Yd Pass %	30+ Yd Pass Gains	30+ Yd Pass %	Avg. Air Yds per Comp	Avg. YAC per Comp	20+ Air Yd Comp	20+ Air Yd %
Josh Rosen	36%	40%	23	6.0%	10	3.0%	5.9	4.6	14	4%
Sam Bradford	33%	36%	6	8.0%	3	4.0%	4.0	4.0	3	4%
NFL Avg	44%	48%	29.5	8.4%	12.5	3.7%	5.8	5.1	14.5	6%

Interception Rates by Down

Yards to Go	1st Dwn	2nd Dwn	3rd Dwn	4th Dwn	Total
1 & 2		33.3%	11.1%	0.0%	14.3%
3, 4, 5	0.0%	0.0%	0.0%	50.0%	1.9%
6 - 9	0.0%	3.9%	4.0%	0.0%	3.8%
10 - 14	2.0%	6.5%	3.8%		3.2%
15+	0.0%	0.0%	0.0%	0.0%	0.0%
Total	1.8%	4.6%	2.9%	12.5%	3.2%

3rd Down Passing - Short of Sticks Analysis

QB	Avg. Yds to Go	Avg. YIA (of Comp)	Avg Yds Short	Short of Sticks Rate	Short Rk
Josh Rosen	8.4	5.7	-2.7	64%	35
NFL Avg	7.8	6.4	-1.4	60%	

Air Yds vs YAC

Air Yds %	YAC %	Rk
55%	45%	18
53%	48%	

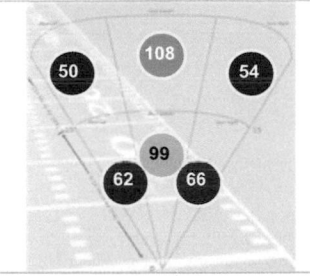
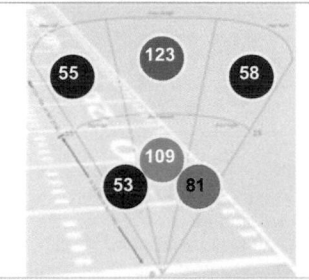
2018 Receiving Recap & 2019 Outlook

Last year's Cardinals pass-catcher corps featured a running back and tight end among its top-three target shares with **Larry Fitzgerald** dominating targets. Expect a much more diverse 2019 attack that emphasizes wide receivers and a more-even target distribution where **Christian Kirk** can be a primary beneficiary. Arizona faces the NFL's fourth-easiest pass-defense schedule.

Player *Min 50 Targets	Targ	Comp %	YPA	Rating	Success %	Success Rk	Missed YPA Rk	YAS % Rk	YTS % Rk	TDs
Larry Fitzgerald	112	62%	6.6	87.4	51%	64	121	102	4	6
David Johnson	76	66%	5.9	83.6	34%	128	153	43	87	3
Ricky Seals-Jones	70	49%	4.9	49.9	37%	127	178	75	26	1
Christian Kirk	68	63%	8.7	81.1	44%	110	123	67	87	2

Directional Passer Rating Delivered

Receiver	Short Left	Short Middle	Short Right	Deep Left	Deep Middle	Deep Right	Player Total
Larry Fitzgerald	83	102	95	54	88	91	87
David Johnson	64	99	65	119		158	84
Ricky Seals-Jones	24	79	52	96	40	58	50
Christian Kirk	72	70	62	56	158	117	81
Chad Williams	66	100	2	79	1	40	38
Trent Sherfield	108	119	85	59	81	0	72
Chase Edmonds	84	90	86				85
J.J. Nelson	83		25	13	40	40	7
Jermaine Gresham	117	98	83				97
Team Total	68	95	65	57	75	90	71

2018 Rushing Recap & 2019 Outlook

The 2017 Cardinals resorted to washed-up **Adrian Peterson** in place of injured **David Johnson**. Johnson's 2018 comeback didn't go as planned, finishing with a worse Success Rate, explosive run rate, and similar yards per carry to 2017 Peterson. The 2017 Cardinals were the league's 12th-most successful team targeting running backs out of the backfield. In 2018, the Cardinals ranked dead last. Kingsbury's offense may mix in read option, which would raise Johnson's ceiling because most backs that play with dual-threat quarterbacks log better rushing efficiency. Johnson is also dangerous in the slot, where Kingsbury could explore using him if Arizona's young slot prospects don't come along fast. Either way, expect improvement on **Mike McCoy**'s egregious 2018 usage of the Cardinals' best offensive player.

Player *Min 50 Rushes	Rushes	YPC	Success %	Success Rk	Missed YPA Rk	YTS % Rk	YAS % Rk	Early Down Success %	Early Down Success Rk	TDs
David Johnson	258	3.6	38%	67	59	57	69	38%	65	7
Chase Edmonds	60	3.5	45%	48	66	29	26	45%	46	2

Yards per Carry by Direction

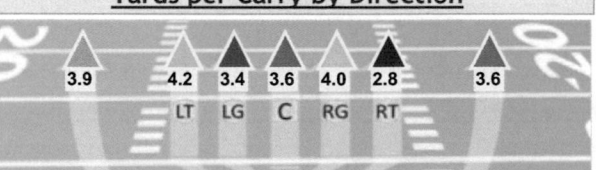

LT	LG	C	RG	RT		
3.9	4.2	3.4	3.6	4.0	2.8	3.6

Directional Run Frequency

LT	LG	C	RG	RT		
5%	7%	5%	60%	6%	11%	6%

MVP. **Jared Goff**, coached by Dykes at Cal, took the 2018 Rams to the Super Bowl. **Baker Mayfield**, recruited by Kingsbury to Texas Tech before resurfacing under Leach-learned **Lincoln Riley** at Oklahoma, became the No. 1 pick and turned in one of the best rookie quarterback seasons of all time. Kingsbury-coached **Patrick Mahomes** threw 50 touchdowns in his first year as an NFL starter.

Leach tweaked the Air Raid when he parted with Mumme, whose offenses often used two backs. Leach evolved to fewer backs and more four-wideout formations, increased split spacing between offensive linemen to aid in pass protection, and directed his receivers to run four verticals but with ample freedom to read cornerbacks and make route adjustments. In the Air Raid, a receiver's goal is to find unoccupied space and present a high-percentage target. Leach, smartly, only runs the ball when the number of defenders in the box favors the offense.

Although **Andy Reid**'s Chiefs and **Todd Monken**'s Bucs offense incorporate elements of Leach and Mumme's brainchild, no NFL team has fully adopted Air Raid yet. In 2018, NFL teams passed on 59% of offensive plays. Kingsbury's Red Raiders passed at a 65% clip. In 2018, NFL offenses aligned in 10 personnel (1 running back, 0 tight ends, 4 wide receivers) on only 2% of snaps. Kingsbury used 10 personnel at a 60% rate.

(cont'd - see ARI-5)

Arizona Cardinals Fantasy Corner

Christian Kirk shook off a slow rookie-year start to clear 75 yards and/or score a touchdown in five of his final ten games before breaking his foot in Week 13. Even as his skill set coming out of college best projected to the slot, Kirk deferred to HOF slot man **Larry Fitzgerald** and ran 70% of his routes outside. Kirk did dominate his interior opportunities, securing 15-of-20 slot targets for 196 yards and a touchdown with 1.90 yards per slot route run versus Fitz's sluggish 1.36 clip. At Texas Tech, **Kliff Kingsbury** used smaller **Jakeem Grant**, **Keke Coutee**, **Bradley Marquez**, and **Jonathan Giles** inside with larger **Antoine Wesley** and **Dylan Cantrell** outside, suggesting 5-foot-10, 201-pound Kirk's slot usage will rise. At minicamp, Kingsbury praised Kirk for his advanced understanding of the offense after playing in a similar scheme at Texas A&M. Assuming rational coaching, Kirk will pass Fitzgerald as Arizona's top wideout this year.
\- Evan Silva

2018 Situational Usage by Player & Position

Usage Rate by Score

		Being Blown Out (14+)	Down Big (9-13)	One Score	Large Lead (9-13)	Blowout Lead (14+)
RUSH	David Johnson	17%	10%	70%	2%	
	Chase Edmonds	35%	7%	52%		7%
	Christian Kirk			67%	33%	
	Chad Williams		100%			
	J.J. Nelson	25%	25%	50%		
	Total	21%	10%	66%	2%	1%
PASS	David Johnson	32%	17%	48%	3%	
	Larry Fitzgerald	30%	23%	47%		
	Chase Edmonds	64%	5%	32%		
	Christian Kirk	16%	13%	69%		3%
	Ricky Seals-Jones	31%	17%	53%		
	Chad Williams	33%	10%	55%	3%	
	J.J. Nelson	50%	17%	25%	8%	
	Jermaine Gresham	20%	30%	40%	10%	
	Total	31%	17%	51%	1%	1%

Share of Offensive Plays by Type

	David Johnson	Larry Fitzgerald	Chase Edmonds	Christian Kirk	Ricky Seals-Jones	Chad Williams	J.J. Nelson	Jermaine Gresham
RUSH	79%		18%	1%		0%	1%	
PASS	17%	27%	6%	17%	16%	11%	3%	3%
ALL	46%	14%	12%	10%	8%	6%	2%	1%

Positional Target Distribution vs NFL Average

		NFL Wide				Team Only			
		Left	Middle	Right	Total	Left	Middle	Right	Total
Deep	WR	33%	17%	31%	**81%**	35%	21%	22%	**79%**
	TE	5%	4%	7%	**16%**	7%	2%	8%	**17%**
	RB	1%	0%	2%	**3%**	1%		3%	**4%**
	All	**39%**	**22%**	**40%**	**100%**	**43%**	**24%**	**34%**	**100%**
Short	WR	20%	14%	21%	**55%**	19%	14%	23%	**56%**
	TE	6%	6%	8%	**20%**	7%	4%	7%	**18%**
	RB	10%	5%	10%	**25%**	12%	3%	12%	**26%**
	All	**36%**	**25%**	**39%**	**100%**	**37%**	**21%**	**42%**	**100%**
Total		**37%**	**24%**	**39%**	**100%**	**38%**	**22%**	**40%**	**100%**

Positional Success Rates vs NFL Average

		NFL Wide				Team Only			
		Left	Middle	Right	Total	Left	Middle	Right	Total
Deep	WR	40%	50%	40%	**42%**	32%	32%	35%	**33%**
	TE	43%	54%	42%	**46%**	50%	0%	29%	**33%**
	RB	36%	33%	40%	**38%**	100%		100%	**100%**
	All	**40%**	**51%**	**40%**	**43%**	**37%**	**29%**	**40%**	**36%**
Short	WR	55%	61%	53%	**56%**	46%	55%	48%	**49%**
	TE	56%	62%	55%	**57%**	40%	63%	27%	**40%**
	RB	46%	54%	46%	**48%**	49%	40%	14%	**33%**
	All	**53%**	**60%**	**51%**	**54%**	**46%**	**55%**	**35%**	**43%**
Total		**51%**	**58%**	**49%**	**52%**	**44%**	**49%**	**36%**	**42%**

Division History: Season Wins & 2019 Projection

2015 Wins	2016 Wins	2017 Wins	2018 Wins	Forecast 2019 Wins

Rank of 2019 Defensive Pass Efficiency Faced by Week

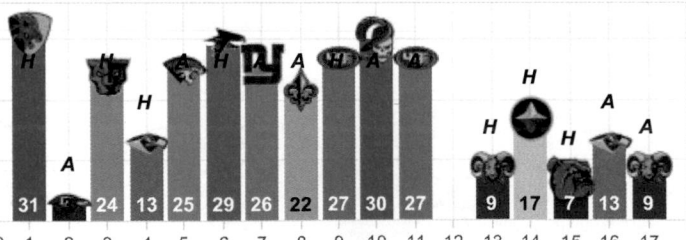

31	24	13	25	29	26	22	27	30	27		9	17	7	13	9
1	2	3	4	5	6	7	8	9	10	11	12	13	14	15	16	17

Rank of 2019 Defensive Rush Efficiency Faced by Week

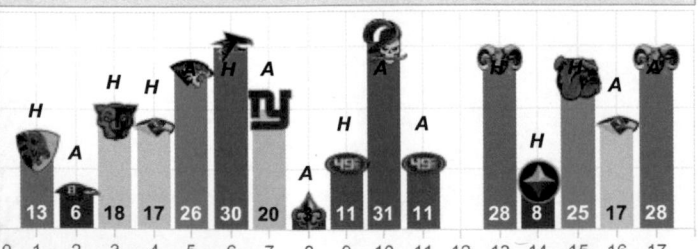

13	6	18	17	26	30	20		11	31	11		28	8	25	17	28
1	2	3	4	5	6	7	8	9	10	11	12	13	14	15	16	17

2018 Detailed Analytics Summary
Success by Play Type & Primary Personnel Groupings

Type	1-1 [3WR]	1-2 [2WR]	2-1 [2WR]	2-2 [1WR]	1-3 [1WR]	2-0 [3WR]	0-0 [5WR]	1-0 [4WR]	2-3 [0WR]	ALL
PASS	35% (444)	39% (70)	50% (14)	0% (3)	63% (8)	25% (4)		0% (1)	0% (1)	36% (545)
RUSH	39% (193)	46% (80)	35% (31)	31% (29)	18% (11)		50% (2)			39% (355)
All	36% (637)	43% (159)	40% (45)	28% (32)	37% (19)	25% (4)	50% (2)	0% (1)	0% (1)	37% (900)

Format   Success Rate (Total # of Plays)

Receiving Success by Top-4 Personnel Groupings
(Min 50 targets)

POS	Player	1-1 [3WR]	1-2 [2WR]	2-1 [2WR]	1-0 [4WR]	4 Grp Total
RB	David Johnson	30% (63) 5.0, 77.0	57% (7) 10.1, 148.5	0% (3) 0.3, 42.4		32% (73) 5.3, 83.4
TE	Ricky Seals-Jones	38% (55) 3.8, 45.1	25% (12) 5.0, 47.9			36% (67) 4.0, 44.9
WR	Larry Fitzgerald	51% (94) 6.4, 82.7	57% (14) 8.7, 101.8	50% (2) 6.5, 70.8		52% (110) 6.7, 89.0
	Christian Kirk	45% (60) 8.1, 78.8	50% (6) 17.7, 158.3	0% (1) 0.0, 0.0	0% (1) 0.0, 39.6	44% (68) 8.7, 81.1

Format   Line 1: Success Rate (Total # of Plays)   Line 2: YPA, Passer Rating

Rushing Success by Top-4 Personnel Groupings
(Min 25 carries)

Rusher (Last, First)	1-1 [3WR]	1-2 [2WR]	2-1 [2WR]	2-2 [1WR]	4 Grp Total
Johnson David	36% (140) 3.9	43% (69) 3.3	36% (22) 3.5	41% (17) 3.8	38% (248) 3.7
Edmonds Chase	41% (32) 2.1	50% (14) 2.9	33% (9) 6.4	67% (3) 5.0	43% (58) 3.1

Format   Line 1: Success Rate (Total # of Plays)   Line 2: YPC

Passing by Coverage Scheme

M2M	40% (186) 5.9, 67.5
Zone	46% (185) 6.0, 73.0
Screen	31% (67) 5.3, 84.9
Combo	63% (16) 11.4, 115.4

Passing by Route

Out	42% (73) 4.9, 56.8
Curl	57% (70) 6.0, 60.6
Screen	35% (68) 5.5, 91.4
Dig	50% (24) 7.0, 76.4
Flat	25% (24) 2.3, 59.7
Slant	68% (22) 9.4, 116.9

Throw Types

Level 1	47% (262) 5.9, 84.7
Level 2	38% (157) 5.7, 61.0
Level 3	23% (39) 8.8, 59.5
Shovel	60% (5) 4.0, 83.3
Sidearm	20% (5) 2.8, 79.2

QB Drop Types

3 Step	44% (196) 5.9, 70.0
5 Step	38% (91) 7.0, 57.7
0/1 Step	45% (88) 4.6, 81.0
Basic Screen	30% (46) 5.1, 81.4
7 Step	54% (26) 12.8, 109.8
Designed Rollout Right	25% (16) 2.5, 77.1

QB State at Pass

Planted	44% (326) 6.0, 75.8
Shuffling	29% (65) 4.3, 52.2
Moving	40% (47) 6.5, 77.2

Play Action

	Play Action	No P/A
Under Center	44% (75) 8.8, 99.9	35% (34) 5.5, 81.4
Shotgun	42% (19) 3.7, 70.3	41% (340) 5.6, 68.5
ALL	44% (94) 7.8, 93.9	41% (374) 5.6, 60.6

Run Types

Outside Zone	47% (102) 3.8
Inside Zone	40% (94) 3.6
Lead	28% (29) 3.0
Power	32% (28) 4.1
Pitch	21% (14) 2.1
Stretch	18% (11) 1.5

ARI-5

The Seahawks, Lions, and Bucs used 10 personnel most among NFL teams last year. Seattle used it to run – 78% of the Seahawks' 10-personnel plays were carries – and it produced a 58% rushing Success Rate, well above Seattle's primary 11-personnel grouping's 47% rate of success. The Lions and Bucs used 10 personnel to pass and produced better efficiency, Success Rates, and yards per attempt than they did in their preferred 11-personnel grouping.

If Kingsbury becomes the first NFL coach to successfully implement Air Raid, it will be because **Kyler Murray** is the perfect Air Raid fit. At this year's MIT Sloan Analytics Conference, Leach outlined to me his five ideal quarterback traits. In order, they are accuracy, decision making, foot quickness, speed, and then arm strength fifth. Leach told me most Hall of Fame quarterbacks possess only three of those traits. Neither **Tom Brady** nor **Drew Brees** is fast, and both excel without elite foot quickness and power arms. Above all, Leach stressed the importance of a quarterback elevating his teammates. Murray has at least four of Leach's preferred traits.

Kingsbury's personnel deployment stood out at Texas Tech. He tended to align short, quick receivers inside and plus-sized pass catchers closer to the boundaries. If Kingsbury follows suit in the pros, 5-foot-10 **Christian Kirk** and 5-foot-9 **Andy Isabella** look like ideal slot candidates with 6-foot-3 **Larry Fitzgerald** and 6-foot-6 **Hakeem Butler** outside in four-wide sets. Although Murray's pass-catcher corps isn't among the NFL's most talented or proven, keep in mind the Air Raid originated from Mumme's need to score points with lesser players.

In six years as Texas Tech's coach, just one of Kingsbury's receivers was drafted in the first five rounds. Just one Red Raiders offensive lineman was drafted at all. Even as Texas Tech lacked big-league talent during Kingsbury's time there, his teams *never* struggled to score points.

And it just so happens that this year's schedule sets up nicely for Kingsbury's Cardinals to score points.

My projections show the Cardinals will face the NFL's easiest schedule of defenses, beginning with four home games in the first six weeks and three bottom-ten opponents in the first seven. Through their Week 12 bye, Arizona draws just two pass defenses that finished above average in 2018, and nine opponents that ranked bottom ten in the league. The Cardinals' pass-defense schedule closes in difficult fashion, however, with the NFL's toughest five-week finish to the year. An additional downside to facing these tough teams late is that they'll catch the Cardinals with nearly a full season to study Kingsbury's Air Raid and expose any of its flaws.

The Cardinals' defensive talent is largely underrated but lacks depth, and **Patrick Peterson**'s six-game PEDs suspension makes the unit look much worse. Offenses intentionally avoid Peterson, who was the nearest defender to targeted pass catchers on just 10% of his 2018 coverage snaps, the fourth-lowest rate among NFL corners.

Coaches (Prior Yrs)

Head Coach:
Dan Quinn (5 yrs)
Offensive Coordinator:
Dirk Koetter (TB HC) (new)
Defensive Coordinator:
Quinn calls plays (new)

EASY   HARD

2019 Forecast

Wins	Div Rank
9	#2

Past Records

2018: 7-9
2017: 10-6
2016: 11-5

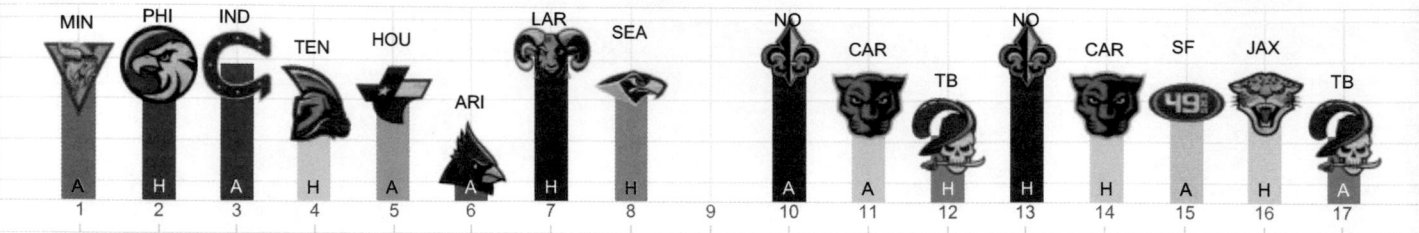

MIN	PHI	IND	TEN	HOU	ARI	LAR	SEA		NO	CAR	TB	NO	CAR	SF	JAX	TB
A	H	A	H	A	A	H	H		A	A	H	H	H	A	H	A
1	2	3	4	5	6	7	8	9	10	11	12	13	14	15	16	17
	SNF											TNF				

Key Players Lost

Player	New
Andy Levitre (G)	Retired
Ben Garland (G)	SF
Brian Poole (CB)	NYJ
Brooks Reed (DE)	ARI
Bruce Irvin (DE)	CAR
Jordan Richards (SS)	OAK
Justin Bethel (CB)	BAL
Marvin Hall (WR)	CHI
Robert Alford (CB)	ARI
Terrell McClain (DT)	ARI
Tevin Coleman (RB)	SF

Average Line	# Games Favored	# Games Underdog
0.2	6	9

Regular Season Wins: Past & Current Proj

Forecast 2019 Wins	9
2018 Wins	7
Forecast 2018 Wins	9
2017 Wins	10
2016 Wins	11
2015 Wins	8

1 3 5 7 9 11 13 15

2019 Atlanta Falcons Overview

National stage. Primetime game. NFL season kickoff. And **Steve Sarkisian** blew it.

The Falcons lost to the defending Super Bowl champion Eagles by six points last Week 1 despite driving to Philadelphia's 1-, 5-, and 15-yard lines. Those drives resulted in *zero points*. Among 16 red-zone plays against the Eagles, the Falcons were successful on just three (19%). **Matt Ryan** averaged 0.9 yards per red-zone attempt with just one successful pass among 11, one interception, and a sack taken. Atlanta ran multiple times from jumbo personnel with *zero success* on four plays inside the five-yard line, recording a net loss of one yard.

My 2018 Falcons chapter ended with this exact statement: "Atlanta figures to find itself back in the playoffs if Sarkisian solves his red-zone woes."

He didn't.

If you can't execute in the red zone, you aren't likely to succeed in modern football. The 2018 Falcons ranked top ten in offense but 28th inside the ten-yard line and 31st inside the five. A big reason was their inability to connect with **Julio Jones** in scoring position. On 73 snaps inside opponents' ten-yard line last season, Jones drew just seven targets and caught only three.

The last time new Falcons OC **Dirk Koetter** held a full-time playcalling role, he was coaching the 2017 Bucs, who ranked 24th in red-zone offense. Coach **Dan Quinn** cannot afford a lateral move for Atlanta's scoring-position execution.

A defensive mind by trade, Quinn's side of the ball wasn't what led the Falcons on their Super Bowl 51 run. They ranked 27th in both defensive efficiency and

(cont'd - see __ATL2__)

Key Free Agents/ Trades Added

Player	AAV (MM)
Adrian Clayborn (DE)	$2
J.J. Wilcox (FS)	$0.9
James Carpenter (G)	$5.2
Jamon Brown (G)	$6.2
Kenjon Barner (RB)	$0.9
Luke Stocker (TE)	$2.7
Tyeler Davison (DT)	$0.9

Drafted Players

Rd	Pk	Player (College)
1	14	G - Chris Lindstrom (Boston College)
1	31	OT - Kaleb McGary (Washington)
4	111	CB - Kendall Sheffield (Ohio State)
4*	135	DE - John Cominsky (Charleston)
5	152	RB - Qadree Ollison (Pittsburgh)
5*	172	CB - Jordan Miller (Washington)
6	203	WR - Marcus Green (Louisiana-Monroe)

Lineup & Cap Hits

FS R.Allen 37
LB D.Campbell 59
LB D.Jones 45
SS K.Neal 22
RCB I.Oliver 20
SLOTCB D.Kazee 27
DE T.McKinley 98
DE G.Jarrett 99
DE V.Beasley 44
DT A.Clayborn 94
LCB D.Trufant 21
LWR J.Jones 11
LT J.Matthews 70
LG J.Carpenter 77
C A.Mack 51
RG C.Lindstrom Rookie 63
RT C.McGary Rookie 76
TE A.Hooper 81
RWR C.Ridley Rookie 18
SLOTWR M.Sanu 12
QB M.Ryan 2
RB D.Freeman 24
WR2 R.Gage 83
WR3 C.Blake 16
RB2 I.Smith 25
QB2 M.Schaub 8

2019 Cap Dollars

2019 Unit Spending

All DEF / All OFF

Positional Spending

	Rank	Total	2017 Rk
All OFF	3	$116.81M	3
QB	19	$17.70M	15
OL	2	$52.56M	2
RB	11	$9.84M	13
WR	8	$28.44M	6
TE	15	$8.27M	31
All DEF	19	$81.96M	24
DL	17	$29.37M	23
LB	16	$21.17M	29
CB	20	$18.88M	20
S	13	$12.54M	19

Early Down Success Rate allowed. Quinn's team won double-digit games in 2017 but ranked 22nd in defensive efficiency and 30th in EDSR allowed. One of the architects of Seattle's Legion of Boom has delivered nothing remotely close in Atlanta.

Quinn will call the Falcons' 2019 defensive plays after 2017-2018 defensive coordinator **Marquand Manuel**'s contract wasn't renewed. Quinn's defense should benefit from positive health regression after fielding last year's eighth most-injured defense and fifth most-injured secondary. The value of pass defense is greatly enhanced in today's pass-heavy NFL. Both Falcons safeties suffered year-ending injuries in the opening month of last season, and difference-making MLB **Deion Jones** missed over half the year.

Unfortunately, Atlanta can't soften its schedule. The Falcons face rock-solid NFC South rivals Carolina and New Orleans twice, and draw a major influx of quality non-division quarterbacks. Six of Atlanta's ten non-division foes field passing games projected as above average in efficiency, including four probable top-ten units in the Rams, Colts, Eagles, and Seahawks with the Texans and Vikings not far behind.

Atlanta draws three other passing offenses that ranked bottom ten last year but are likely to improve. The Cardinals are dangerous with a new dual-threat quarterback and aggressive play caller. The 49ers get back **Jimmy Garoppolo**, and the Jaguars finally turned the page on **Blake Bortles**. The Falcons' final non-division opponent is the Titans, who have more wins than losses in three straight years.

The 2019 Falcons face just three teams classified as bottom ten in overall strength and only one bottom-five opponent. No NFL team draws fewer "easy" foes. Among their five road games outside the division, the Falcons do face four teams indoors (Vikings, Colts, Texans, Cardinals), although all are in the first six weeks of the year. Atlanta played just four games combined in non-division domes over the last six seasons.

The Falcons' win totals have been boosted by success inside the NFC South, going 6-1 in their last seven games against the Panthers with five straight wins over the Bucs.

Even when Quinn's roster was healthy in pre-2018 years, his defense was bad. Last year's unit collapsed due to a shortage of depth, and this year's schedule of opposing passing games will leave Quinn minimal margin for error.

2018 Passing Performance

QB	1st Dwn	2nd Dwn	3rd Dwn	
Matt Ryan	55%	53%	43%	Success Rate
	8.5	7.7	7.7	YPA
	106.3	110.9	100.8	Rating
Pass Rate	64%	62%	86%	
NFL AVG	53%	47%	36%	Success Rate
	7.7	7.3	6.9	YPA
	95.1	93.7	87.1	Rating
Pass Rate	53%	62%	80%	

2018 Rushing Performance

Offense	1st Dwn	2nd Dwn	3rd Dwn	
ATL	46%	43%	61%	Success Rate
	4.4	4.4	5.4	YPC
Run Rate	36%	38%	14%	
NFL AVG	48%	46%	51%	Success Rate
	4.5	4.4	4.3	YPC
Run Rate	47%	38%	20%	

Atlanta's 2018 defensive decimation forced the offense to put up lofty point totals to stay competitive. With the exception of their Week 16 win against Carolina's backup quarterback, the Falcons went 5-2 when scoring over 30 points but 1-7 when scoring below 30. Atlanta is 0-13 when scoring less than 20 over the past two years; only the Raiders (0-19) have been worse. But the Falcons are 17-2 over the last two seasons when scoring over 20; only the Vikings and Rams have been better. As no team in the NFL was more sensitive to the 20-point inflection point during Sarkisian's two years as coordinator, his red-zone deficiencies were especially detrimental to Atlanta's win-loss success.

One concerning element about Atlanta's offense is health, where they've experienced great fortune. **Matt Ryan** and his wide receiver group have

(cont'd - see **ATL-3**)

2018 Offensive Advanced Metrics

Rank values by category:
- EDSR Off: 12
- 30 & In Off: 12
- Red Zone Off: 16
- 3rd Down Off: 5
- YPPA Off: 6
- YPPT Off: 12
- Offensive Efficiency: 8
- Pass Efficiency Off: 7
- Pass Pro Efficiency Off: 14
- RB Pass Eff Off: 18
- Rush Efficiency Off: 21
- Explosive Pass Off: 15
- Explosive Run Off: 7

2018 Defensive Advanced Metrics

Rank values by category:
- EDSR Def: 29
- 30 & In Def: 9
- Red Zone Def: 26
- 3rd Down Def: 31
- YPPA Def: 24
- YPPT Def: 20
- Defensive Efficiency: 31
- Pass Efficiency Def: 29
- Pass Pro Efficiency Def: 25
- RB Pass Eff Def: 24
- Rush Efficiency Def: 30
- Explosive Pass Def: 11
- Explosive Run Def: 21

2018 Weekly EDSR & Season Trending Performance

WEEK	1	2	3	4	5	6	7	9	10	11	12	13	14	15	16	17
RESULT	L	W	L	L	L	W	W	W	L	L	L	L	L	W	W	W
OPP	PHI	CAR	NO	CIN	PIT	TB	NYG	WAS	CLE	DAL	NO	BAL	GB	ARI	CAR	TB
SITE	A	H	H	H	A	H	H	A	A	H	A	H	A	H	A	A
MARGIN	-6	7	-6	-1	-24	5	3	24	-12	-3	-14	-10	-14	26	14	2
PTS	12	31	37	36	17	34	23	38	16	19	17	16	20	40	24	34
OPP PTS	18	24	43	37	41	29	20	14	28	22	31	26	34	14	10	32

EDSR by Wk
W=Green
L=Red

OFF / DEF
EDSR
Blue=OFF
(high=good)
Red=DEF
(low=good)

2018 Close Game Records

All 2018 Wins: **7**
FG Games (<=3 pts) W-L: **2-2**
FG Games Win %: **50% (#13)**
FG Games Wins (% of Total Wins): **29% (#17)**
1 Score Games (<=8 pts) W-L: **4-4**
1 Score Games Win %: **50% (#15)**
1 Score Games Wins (% of Total Wins): **57% (#12)**

2018 Critical & Game-Deciding Stats

TO Margin	+1
TO Given	18
INT Given	7
FUM Given	11
TO Taken	19
INT Taken	15
FUM Taken	4
Sack Margin	-5
Sacks	37
Sacks Allow	42
Return TD Margin	-1
Ret TDs	2
Ret TDs Allow	3
Penalty Margin	+7
Penalties	101
Opponent Penalties	108

Ease for Offense (Avg Opp DEF Rank) | Ease for Defense (Avg Opp OFF Rank)

HARD

Average Opponent RANK

EASY

Legend
- 2018 Actual
- 🦅 2019 Forecast

Ease for Offense categories: Total Efficiency, DEF Efficiency, Pass Efficiency DEF, YPPA Def, Explosive Pass DEF, Pass Pro Efficiency DEF, Rush Efficiency DEF, Explosive Rush DEF, RB Pass Eff DEF, Red Zone Blend DEF, YPPT Def, Third Down Conv DEF (*Passing*, *Rushing*)

Ease for Defense categories: OFF Efficiency, Pass Efficiency OFF, YPPA Off, Explosive Pass OFF, Pass Pro Efficiency OFF, Rush Efficiency OFF, Explosive Rush OFF, RB Pass Eff OFF, Red Zone Blend OFF, YPPT Off, Third Down Conv OFF, Pass:Run Ratio OFF (*Passing*, *Rushing*)

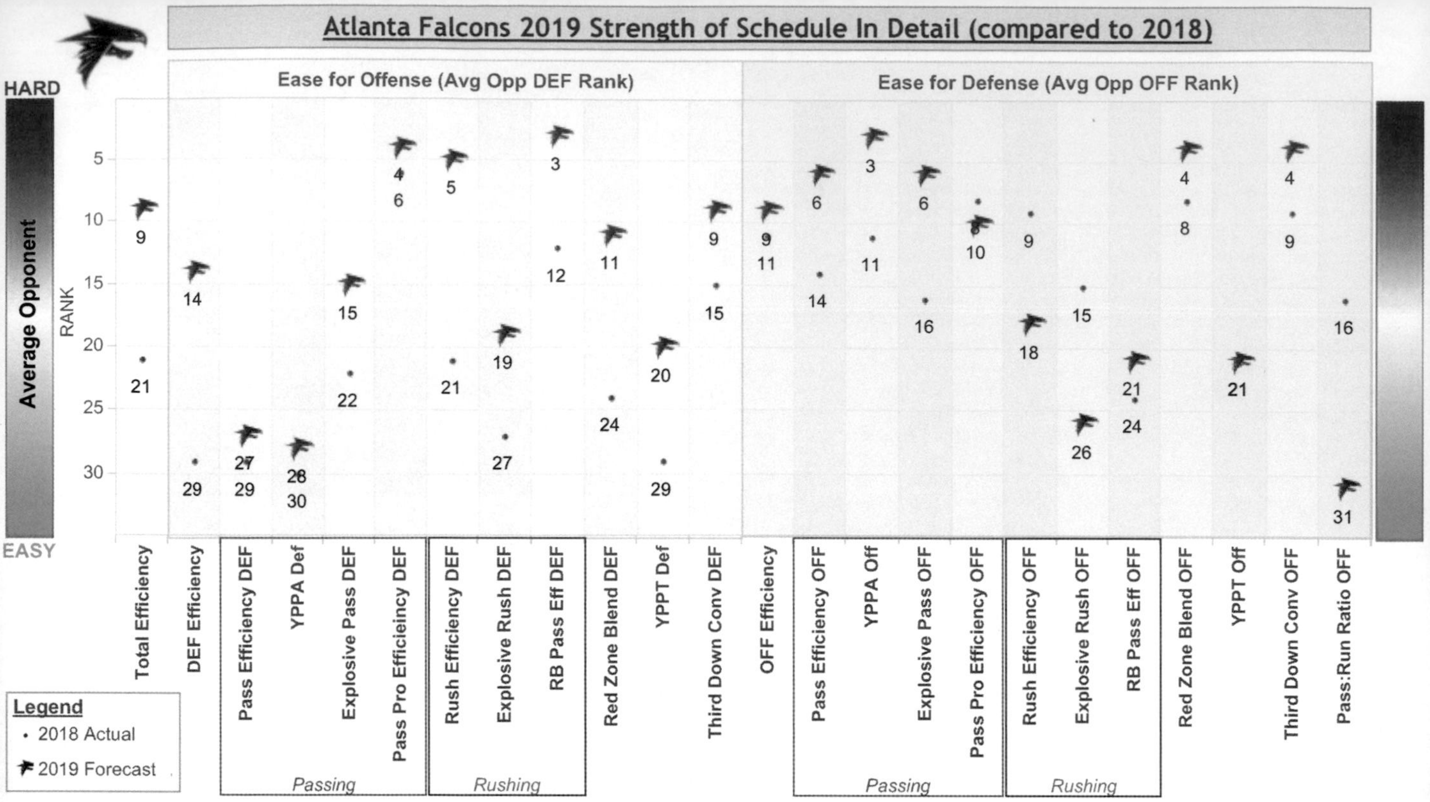

2019 v 2018 Schedule Variances* (OFF=Rank of DEF faced, 2019 vs 2018)

Pass OFF Rank	Pass OFF Blend Rk	Rush OFF Rk	Rush OFF Blend Rk	Pass DEF Rk	Pass DEF Blend Rk	Rush DEF Rk	Rush DEF Blend Rk
10	11	6	5	6	8	26	24

* **1**=Hardest Jump in 2019 schedule from 2018 (aka a much harder schedule in 2019), **32**=Easiest Jump in 2019 schedule from 2018 (aka a much easier schedule in 2019);
Pass Blend metric blends 4 metrics: Pass Efficiency, YPPA, Explosive Pass & Pass Rush; **Rush Blend** metric blends 3 metrics: Rush Efficiency, Explosive Rush & RB Targets

Team Records & Trends

	2018	2017	2016
Average line	-1.0	-3.7	-2.1
Average O/U line	50.4	48.6	49.8
Straight Up Record	7-9	10-6	11-5
Against the Spread Record	5-10	7-9	10-6
Over/Under Record	9-7	4-11	13-3
ATS as Favorite	4-6	6-7	5-5
ATS as Underdog	1-4	1-2	5-1
Straight Up Home	4-4	5-3	5-3
ATS Home	3-5	5-3	3-5
Over/Under Home	5-3	2-6	8-0
ATS as Home Favorite	3-5	5-3	2-5
ATS as a Home Dog	0-0	0-0	1-0
Straight Up Away	3-5	5-3	6-2
ATS Away	2-5	2-6	7-1
Over/Under Away	4-4	2-5	5-3
ATS Away Favorite	1-1	1-4	3-0
ATS Away Dog	1-4	1-2	4-1
Six Point Teaser Record	10-6	12-4	13-3
Seven Point Teaser Record	11-5	12-3	13-3
Ten Point Teaser Record	13-3	13-3	16-0

ATL-3

both ranked top six in roster health over the last two years. Ryan has started 16 games in *nine* straight seasons. The Falcons emphasized keeping him clean by adding two first-round offensive linemen to a position group that is now the NFL's second-most expensive behind the Cowboys.

Ryan signed a five-year, $150 million extension last offseason and paid it forward with incredible production that wasn't widely recognized due to Atlanta's struggles as a team. Ryan's numbers were nearly identical to his 2016 MVP year in passing yards (4,924 vs. 4,944), TD-to-INT ratio (35:7 vs. 38:7), and completion rate (69.4% vs. 69.9%). Ryan's 2018 efficiency was lower than 2016 but substantially better than 2017. His rate of 30-plus-yard explosive pass plays doubled that from the previous year. And he was tremendous throwing deep directionally, where his passer rating to the deep right and deep left both topped 100 after Ryan finished below 70

(cont'd - see **ATL-4**)

2019 Rest Analysis

Team More Rest	1
Opp More Rest	1
Net Rest Edge	0
Week 2 Edge	0
Week 3 Edge	0
Week 4 Edge	-3
Week 5 Edge	0
Week 6 Edge	0
Week 7 Edge	0
Week 8 Edge	0
Week 10 Edge	0
Week 11 Edge	0
Week 12 Edge	0
Week 13 Edge	0
Week 14 Edge	3
Week 15 Edge	0
Week 16 Edge	0
Week 17 Edge	0

Health by Unit*

2018 Rk	16
2017 Rk	2
2018 v 2017 Rk	
Off Rk	12
Def Rk	25
QB Rk	1
RB Rk	
WR Rk	4
TE Rk	10
Oline Rk	17
Dline Rk	16
LB Rk	22
DB Rk	

*Based on the work of Football Outsiders

2018 Weekly Betting Lines (wks 1-16)

1	2	3	4	5	6	7	8	9	10	11	12	13	14	15	16
MIN	PHI	IND	TEN	HOU	ARI	LAR	SEA	NO	NO	CAR	TB	NO	CAR	SF	JAX
4	-1.5	4	-4	3.5	-3	2	1.5	7	7	2	-7	2.5	-4.5	1.5	-5

Avg = 0.2 ... Avg = 0.2

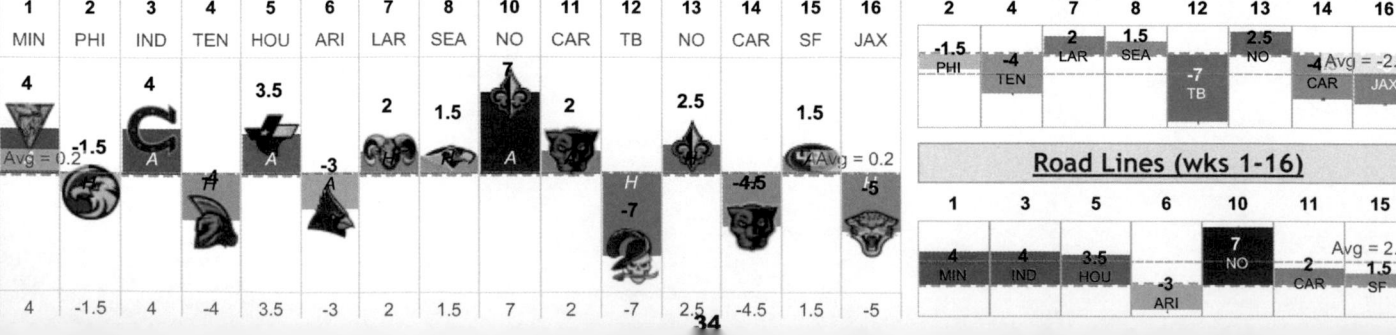

Home Lines (wks 1-16)

2	4	7	8	12	13	14	16
-1.5 PHI	-4 TEN	2 LAR	1.5 SEA	-7 TB	2.5 NO	-4 CAR	JAX

Avg = -2.0

Road Lines (wks 1-16)

1	3	5	6	10	11	15
4 MIN	4 IND	3.5 HOU	-3 ARI	7 NO	2 CAR	1.5 SF

Avg = 2.7

2018 Play Tendencies

All Pass %	65%
All Pass Rk	3
All Rush %	35%
All Rush Rk	30
1 Score Pass %	64%
1 Score Pass Rk	5
2017 1 Score Pass %	55%
2017 1 Score Pass Rk	21
2018 Pass Increase %	9%
Pass Increase Rk	3
1 Score Rush %	36%
1 Score Rush Rk	28
Up Pass %	60%
Up Pass Rk	2
Up Rush %	40%
Up Rush Rk	31
Down Pass %	69%
Down Pass Rk	9
Down Rush %	31%
Down Rush Rk	24

2018 Down & Distance Tendencies

Down	Distance	Total Plays	Pass Rate	Run Rate	Play Success %
1	Short (1-3)	3	67%	33%	33%
	Med (4-7)	7	14%	86%	43%
	Long (8-10)	314	60%	40%	49%
	XL (11+)	12	92%	8%	75%
2	Short (1-3)	37	35%	65%	78%
	Med (4-7)	64	52%	48%	59%
	Long (8-10)	97	54%	46%	37%
	XL (11+)	44	84%	16%	39%
3	Short (1-3)	40	68%	33%	55%
	Med (4-7)	44	98%	2%	48%
	Long (8-10)	37	95%	5%	49%
	XL (11+)	26	100%	0%	15%
4	Short (1-3)	6	50%	50%	50%
	Med (4-7)	2	50%	50%	50%

Shotgun %:

Under Center	Shotgun
50%	50%

37% AVG 63%

Run Rate:

Under Center	Shotgun
57%	12%

68% AVG 23%

Pass Rate:

Under Center	Shotgun
43%	88%

32% AVG 77%

Short Yardage Intelligence:

2nd and Short Run

Run Freq	Run Rk	NFL Run Freq Avg	Run 1D Rate	Run NFL 1D Avg
54%	27	65%	65%	68%

2nd and Short Pass

Pass Freq	Pass Rk	NFL Pass Freq Avg	Pass 1D Rate	Pass NFL 1D Avg
46%	5	35%	53%	56%

Most Frequent Play

Down	Distance	Play Type	Player	Total Plays	Play Success %
1	Med (4-7)	RUSH	Tevin Coleman	4	50%
	Long (8-10)	RUSH	Tevin Coleman	73	40%
	XL (11+)	PASS	Julio Jones	3	100%
2	Short (1-3)	RUSH	Tevin Coleman	14	71%
	Med (4-7)	RUSH	Tevin Coleman	11	64%
			Ito Smith	11	64%
	Long (8-10)	RUSH	Tevin Coleman	28	25%
	XL (11+)	PASS	Julio Jones	8	50%
3	Short (1-3)	PASS	Julio Jones	9	67%
	Med (4-7)	PASS	Calvin Ridley	7	43%
			Mohamed Sanu	7	43%
			Austin Hooper	7	43%
	Long (8-10)	PASS	Julio Jones	10	60%
	XL (11+)	PASS	Julio Jones	7	0%

Most Successful Play*

Down	Distance	Play Type	Player	Total Plays	Play Success %
1	Long (8-10)	PASS	Justin Hardy	7	71%
2	Short (1-3)	RUSH	Tevin Coleman	14	71%
	Med (4-7)	PASS	Calvin Ridley	6	83%
	Long (8-10)	PASS	Julio Jones	9	67%
	XL (11+)	PASS	Julio Jones	8	50%
			Austin Hooper	6	50%
3	Short (1-3)	PASS	Julio Jones	9	67%
	Med (4-7)	PASS	Julio Jones	6	83%
	Long (8-10)	PASS	Calvin Ridley	6	67%
	XL (11+)	PASS	Julio Jones	7	0%

*Minimum 5 plays to qualify

2018 Weekly Snap Rates

Wk	Opp	Score	Mohamed Sanu	Julio Jones	Austin Hooper	Calvin Ridley	Tevin Coleman	Logan Paulsen	Ito Smith	Devonta Freeman
1	PHI	L 18-12	56 (80%)	57 (81%)	59 (84%)	45 (64%)	36 (51%)	19 (27%)		39 (56%)
2	CAR	W 31-24	48 (76%)	48 (76%)	53 (84%)	35 (56%)	40 (63%)	29 (46%)	19 (30%)	
3	NO	L 43-37	59 (87%)	54 (79%)	58 (85%)	42 (62%)	53 (78%)	21 (31%)	10 (15%)	
4	CIN	L 37-36	55 (79%)	54 (77%)	57 (81%)	38 (54%)	40 (57%)	29 (41%)	30 (43%)	
5	PIT	L 41-17	59 (82%)	53 (74%)	55 (70%)	40 (67%)	27 (38%)	19 (26%)	12 (17%)	28 (39%)
6	TB	W 34-29	33 (49%)	51 (76%)	54 (81%)	7 (10%)	38 (57%)	37 (55%)	31 (46%)	
7	NYG	W 23-20	40 (62%)	49 (75%)	56 (86%)	41 (63%)	37 (57%)	27 (42%)	28 (43%)	
9	WAS	W 38-14	47 (69%)	55 (81%)	54 (79%)	47 (69%)	39 (57%)	30 (44%)	28 (41%)	
10	CLE	L 28-16	70 (93%)	73 (97%)	61 (81%)	53 (71%)	49 (65%)	27 (36%)	22 (29%)	
11	DAL	L 22-19	51 (91%)	51 (91%)	47 (84%)	40 (71%)	34 (61%)	17 (30%)	20 (36%)	
12	NO	L 31-17	57 (81%)	62 (89%)	48 (69%)	52 (74%)	35 (50%)	20 (29%)	26 (37%)	
13	BAL	L 26-16	44 (83%)	41 (77%)	38 (72%)	34 (64%)	29 (55%)	18 (34%)	24 (45%)	
14	GB	L 34-20	57 (80%)	63 (89%)	55 (77%)	44 (62%)	33 (46%)		32 (45%)	
15	ARI	W 40-14	61 (91%)	32 (48%)	34 (51%)	43 (64%)	34 (51%)	15 (22%)	29 (43%)	
16	CAR	W 24-10	32 (67%)	24 (50%)	31 (65%)	29 (60%)	31 (65%)	25 (52%)		
17	TB	W 34-32	61 (79%)	51 (66%)	49 (64%)	46 (60%)	25 (32%)	29 (38%)		
	Grand Total		830 (78%)	818 (77%)	809 (76%)	644 (61%)	580 (55%)	362 (37%)	311 (36%)	67 (47%)

Personnel Groupings

Personnel	Team %	NFL Avg	Succ. %
1-1 [3WR]	60%	65%	51%
1-2 [2WR]	17%	17%	53%
2-1 [2WR]	10%	8%	48%
1-3 [1WR]	4%	3%	45%
2-2 [1WR]	3%	3%	31%
0-1 [4WR]	2%	1%	33%

Grouping Tendencies

Personnel	Pass Rate	Pass Succ. %	Run Succ. %
1-1 [3WR]	74%	50%	53%
1-2 [2WR]	53%	58%	46%
2-1 [2WR]	59%	50%	45%
1-3 [1WR]	38%	63%	35%
2-2 [1WR]	20%	43%	29%
0-1 [4WR]	83%	35%	25%

Red Zone Targets (min 3)

Receiver	All	Inside 5	6-10	11-20
Julio Jones	15	5	2	8
Austin Hooper	13	5	5	3
Tevin Coleman	10	2	2	6
Calvin Ridley	9	2	2	5
Mohamed Sanu	5	3		2
Ito Smith	4		2	2
Justin Hardy	3	2		1
Marvin Hall	2	1		1

Red Zone Rushes (min 3)

Rusher	All	Inside 5	6-10	11-20
Ito Smith	21	4	4	13
Tevin Coleman	17	6	4	7
Matt Ryan	8	2	2	4
Devonta Freeman	3	2	1	
Brian Hill	2	1		1

Early Down Target Rate

RB	TE	WR
16%	16%	69%
23%	21%	56%
	NFL AVG	

Overall Target Success %

RB	TE	WR
46%	58%	57%
#17	#9	#3

Atlanta Falcons 2018 Passing Recap & 2019 Outlook

Matt Ryan was not to blame for Atlanta's 2018 regression, and he was especially effective in crunch time. When trailing in the fourth quarter, Ryan finished top three in the league in yards per attempt (8.6), Success Rate (56%), and passer rating (115). Ryan's 2017 to 2018 ascent combined with his elite supporting cast and soft schedule bode promisingly for another big year, considering the strength of his offensive line and the easy pass defenses he is projected to face in 2019, particularly after the bye week. The Falcons also offer ample room for improvement in red-zone efficiency.

Matt Ryan Rating All Downs

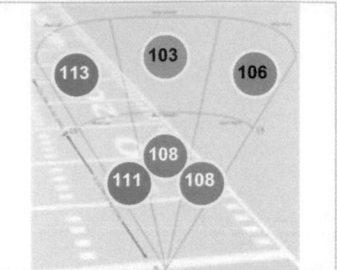

2018 Standard Passing Table

QB	Comp	Att	Comp %	Yds	YPA	TDs	INT	Sacks	Rating	Rk
Matt Ryan	422	609	69%	4,907	8.1	35	7	41	108	7
NFL Avg			62%		7.0				87.5	

2018 Advanced Passing Table

QB	Success %	EDSR Passing Success %	20+ Yd Pass Gains	20+ Yd Pass %	30+ Yd Pass Gains	30+ Yd Pass %	Avg. Air Yds per Comp	Avg. YAC per Comp	20+ Air Yd Comp	20+ Air Yd %
Matt Ryan	51%	54%	56	9.0%	30	5.0%	6.6	5.1	28	5%
NFL Avg	44%	48%	29.5	8.4%	12.5	3.7%	5.8	5.1	14.5	6%

Matt Ryan Rating Early Downs

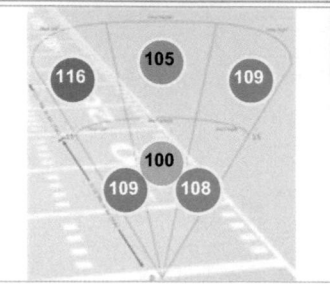

Interception Rates by Down

Yards to Go	1st Dwn	2nd Dwn	3rd Dwn	4th Dwn	Total
1 & 2	0.0%	0.0%	0.0%	0.0%	0.0%
3, 4, 5	0.0%	0.0%	5.4%	0.0%	2.6%
6 - 9	0.0%	0.0%	0.0%	0.0%	0.0%
10 - 14	2.0%	0.0%	0.0%	0.0%	1.4%
15+	0.0%	0.0%	0.0%		0.0%
Total	**1.8%**	**0.0%**	**1.2%**	**0.0%**	**1.1%**

3rd Down Passing - Short of Sticks Analysis

QB	Avg. Yds to Go	Avg. YIA (of Comp)	Avg Yds Short	Short of Sticks Rate	Short Rk
Matt Ryan	7.7	6.5	-1.2	61%	16
NFL Avg	7.8	6.4	-1.4	60%	

Air Yds vs YAC

Air Yds %	YAC %	Rk
56%	44%	13
53%	48%	

2018 Receiving Recap & 2019 Outlook

Julio Jones, **Calvin Ridley,** and **Mohamed Sanu** were all highly efficient in Atlanta's primary 11-personnel grouping. Only six of Ridley's 92 targets came in two-tight end 12 personnel, and his 17% target share on 11-personnel passes was second highest on the team. OC **Dirk Koetter**'s 2017 Bucs used 11 personnel on 74% of pass plays – 12th most in the NFL – and last year's Bucs did so at an even-higher 77% clip. Ridley's target shares ranked third in 21 personnel and fourth on the team in 12-personnel formations.

Player *Min 50 Targets	Targ	Comp %	YPA	Rating	Success %	Success Rk	Missed YPA Rk	YAS % Rk	YTS % Rk	TDs
Julio Jones	170	66%	9.9	106.9	58%	27	43	26	97	6
Mohamed Sanu	94	70%	8.9	111.9	62%	7	22	80	13	3
Calvin Ridley	92	70%	8.9	124.4	50%	78	54	59	87	10
Austin Hooper	88	81%	7.5	108.3	59%	21	24	113	26	4

Directional Passer Rating Delivered

Receiver	Short Left	Short Middle	Short Right	Deep Left	Deep Middle	Deep Right	Player Total
Julio Jones	114	86	121	103	84	108	107
Mohamed Sanu	112	130	98	109	75	74	112
Calvin Ridley	120	107	122	135	94	75	124
Austin Hooper	101	115	105	114		40	108
Tevin Coleman	123	92	121	40		96	127
Ito Smith	82	95	86				86
Justin Hardy	130	135	32			40	92
Devonta Freeman	77	104	58				75
Team Total	112	109	112	112	88	99	111

2018 Rushing Recap & 2019 Outlook

Devonta Freeman returns from an injury-ruined year to face the NFL's fifth-toughest run-defense schedule after Atlanta drew last year's 11th-softest slate. **Tevin Coleman** and **Ito Smith** failed to capitalize in Freeman's absence; Coleman's explosive run rate was third highest in the league, but he ranked 55th in both Success Rate (43%) and early-down success. Three of Coleman's four rushing TDs came outside the red zone. Smith shined on inside-zone runs by averaging 4.8 yards per carry with a 67% Success Rate, yet Sarkisian sub-optimally sent Smith on more outside-zone runs, which were Coleman's forte.

Player *Min 50 Rushes	Rushes	YPC	Success %	Success Rk	Missed YPA Rk	YTS % Rk	YAS % Rk	Early Down Success %	Early Down Success Rk	TDs
Tevin Coleman	167	4.8	43%	55	60	61	3	43%	55	4
Ito Smith	90	3.5	48%	35	47	2	49	49%	26	4

Yards per Carry by Direction

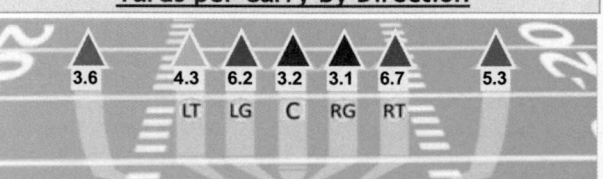

3.6	4.3	6.2	3.2	3.1	6.7	5.3
	LT	LG	C	RG	RT	

Directional Run Frequency

23%	17%	12%	8%	11%	11%	18%
	LT	LG	C	RG	RT	

in each category in 2017.

2018 first-round pick **Calvin Ridley** played a critical role in Atlanta's offensive resurgence, leading all rookie receivers in touchdowns (10) and opening up the field for others. In 2017 when **Julio Jones** was targeted in three-receiver 11 personnel, his Success Rate was just 44% with 8.2 yards per target and a 78 rating. In 2018, those numbers spiked to 53% success, 9.5 yards per target, and a 103 passer rating.

The Falcons' offense does return almost everyone, and their offensive line is improved. Top to bottom, Koetter inherits a top-five group that will benefit from drawing one of the NFL's ten softest pass-defense slates. Their toughest stretch is Weeks 1-8, where Atlanta faces multiple top-ten returning pass defenses, including the Vikings and Cardinals on the road. But **Patrick Peterson**'s PEDs suspension will greatly damage Arizona's defense, and after the Falcons' Week 9 bye, they draw just one pass defense that ranked better than 22nd in efficiency last year. It's the third-easiest second half of the season for any passing offense.

Last year's Falcons passed the ball third-most often in the league and fifth-most often (64%) when games were within one score.

(cont'd - see ATL-5)

Atlanta Falcons Fantasy Corner

With **Tevin Coleman** in San Francisco, **Devonta Freeman**'s volume projection is the highest of his career on a team that invested two first-round picks on offensive linemen and signed three in free agency. Yet it's fair to wonder if Freeman's best days are behind him. He sprained multiple knee ligaments in 2017, missed three 2018 games after reinjuring the knee last Week 1, sprained his foot in Week 6, wound up needing groin surgery, and was shut down for the year. Freeman was fully cleared for OTAs, however, and he totaled 1,447 yards with nine touchdowns and 49 receptions over his previous 16 games entering last season. If Freeman's injuries are truly behind him, that kind of production would make him a value pick at his third-round ADP.

— Evan Silva

2018 Situational Usage by Player & Position

Usage Rate by Score

		Being Blown Out (14+)	Down Big (9-13)	One Score	Large Lead (9-13)	Blowout Lead (14+)
RUSH	Tevin Coleman	7%	6%	74%	2%	11%
	Julio Jones			100%		
	Ito Smith	14%	6%	62%	3%	14%
	Calvin Ridley			60%		40%
	Mohamed Sanu	14%		57%		29%
	Brian Hill	5%		55%		40%
	Devonta Freeman		7%	93%		
	Jeremy Langford		33%	67%		
	Total	9%	6%	69%	2%	14%
PASS	Tevin Coleman	12%	5%	68%	2%	12%
	Julio Jones	11%	5%	75%	5%	4%
	Ito Smith	15%	4%	74%	4%	4%
	Calvin Ridley	18%	2%	69%	5%	6%
	Mohamed Sanu	11%	4%	72%		13%
	Austin Hooper	17%	4%	76%	1%	1%
	Brian Hill		50%	50%		
	Devonta Freeman			100%		
	Justin Hardy	11%	11%	44%	11%	22%
	Total	13%	4%	72%	4%	7%

Share of Offensive Plays by Type

	Tevin Coleman	Julio Jones	Ito Smith	Calvin Ridley	Mohamed Sanu	Austin Hooper	Brian Hill	Devonta Freeman	Justin Hardy	Jeremy Langford
RUSH	53%	1%	29%	2%	2%		6%	4%		3%
PASS	9%	32%	6%	17%	17%	15%	0%		1%	4%
ALL	26%	19%	15%	11%	11%	9%	3%	2%	2%	1%

Positional Target Distribution vs NFL Average

		NFL Wide				Team Only			
		Left	Middle	Right	Total	Left	Middle	Right	Total
Deep	WR	33%	17%	31%	81%	44%	16%	28%	88%
	TE	5%	4%	7%	16%	6%		3%	9%
	RB	1%	0%	2%	3%	1%		2%	3%
	All	38%	22%	40%	100%	51%	16%	33%	100%
Short	WR	20%	13%	21%	55%	23%	18%	23%	64%
	TE	6%	6%	8%	20%	6%	5%	7%	18%
	RB	10%	5%	10%	25%	9%	3%	5%	18%
	All	36%	25%	39%	100%	39%	26%	35%	100%
Total		37%	24%	39%	100%	41%	24%	35%	100%

Positional Success Rates vs NFL Average

		NFL Wide				Team Only			
		Left	Middle	Right	Total	Left	Middle	Right	Total
Deep	WR	40%	50%	40%	42%	46%	41%	32%	41%
	TE	42%	53%	42%	45%	71%		0%	50%
	RB	39%	33%	42%	41%	0%		50%	33%
	All	40%	50%	41%	42%	48%	41%	31%	41%
Short	WR	55%	60%	52%	55%	62%	65%	61%	63%
	TE	55%	62%	54%	57%	44%	75%	65%	60%
	RB	47%	54%	45%	48%	41%	53%	54%	48%
	All	53%	59%	51%	54%	54%	65%	61%	60%
Total		50%	58%	49%	51%	53%	62%	55%	56%

Division History: Season Wins & 2019 Projection

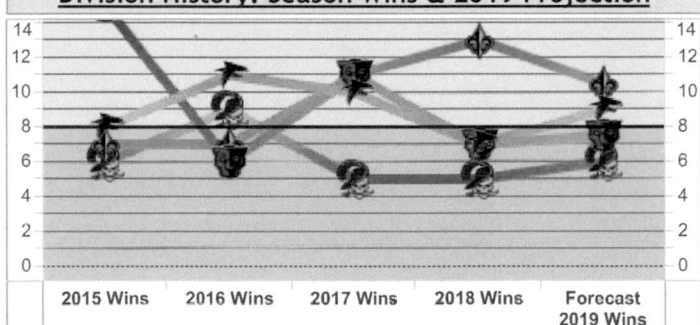

2015 Wins | 2016 Wins | 2017 Wins | 2018 Wins | Forecast 2019 Wins

Rank of 2019 Defensive Pass Efficiency Faced by Week

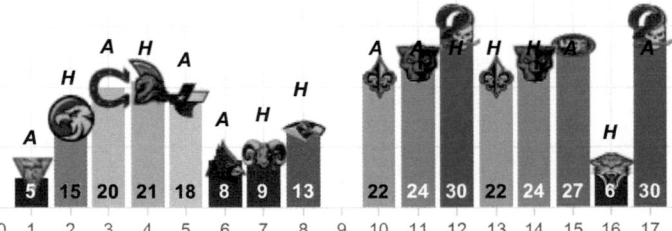

5 | 15 | 20 | 21 | 18 | 8 | 9 | 13 | | 22 | 24 | 30 | 22 | 24 | 27 | 6 | 30

Rank of 2019 Defensive Rush Efficiency Faced by Week

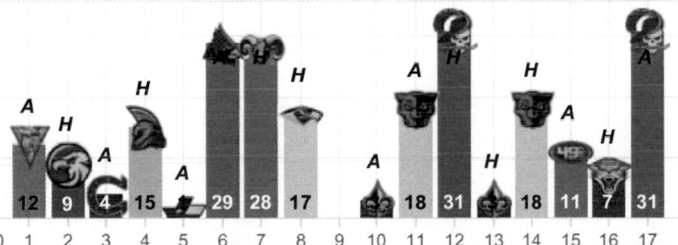

12 | 9 | 4 | 15 | | 29 | 28 | 17 | | 18 | 31 | | 18 | 11 | 7 | 31

2018 Detailed Analytics Summary
Success by Play Type & Primary Personnel Groupings

Successful Play Rate 0% ▓▓▓ 100%

Type	1-1 [3WR]	1-2 [2WR]	2-1 [2WR]	1-3 [1WR]	2-2 [1WR]	0-1 [4WR]	1-0 [4WR]	2-0 [3WR]	2-3 [0WR]	0-0 [5WR]	ALL
PASS	50% (449)	58% (89)	50% (58)	63% (16)	43% (7)	35% (20)	40% (15)	50% (2)	0% (1)		51% (657)
RUSH	53% (160)	46% (80)	45% (40)	35% (26)	29% (28)	25% (4)	40% (5)	0% (3)	0% (2)	100% (1)	46% (349)
All	51% (609)	53% (169)	48% (98)	45% (42)	31% (35)	33% (24)	40% (20)	20% (5)	0% (3)	100% (1)	49% (1,006)

Format   Success Rate (Total # of Plays)

Receiving Success by Top-4 Personnel Groupings
(Min 50 targets)

POS	Player	1-1 [3WR]	1-2 [2WR]	2-1 [2WR]	1-0 [4WR]	4 Grp Total
TE	Austin Hooper	65% (60) 7.9, 109.1	50% (18) 5.8, 128.0	67% (3) 3.7, 72.9		62% (81) 7.2, 112.3
WR	Julio Jones	53% (105) 9.5, 102.6	71% (28) 9.4, 97.9	56% (18) 7.9, 86.1	25% (4) 4.8, 63.5	56% (155) 9.2, 98.9
	Mohamed Sanu	70% (66) 9.4, 126.2	50% (8) 11.9, 93.2	67% (9) 10.7, 102.1	40% (5) 3.4, 49.6	66% (88) 9.4, 117.2
	Calvin Ridley	50% (70) 8.1, 123.0	67% (6) 11.5, 114.6	57% (7) 7.3, 80.1	50% (4) 7.3, 94.8	52% (87) 8.2, 124.5

Format   Line 1: Success Rate (Total # of Plays)   Line 2: YPA, Passer Rating

Rushing Success by Top-4 Personnel Groupings
(Min 25 carries)

Rusher (Last, First)	1-1 [3WR]	1-2 [2WR]	2-1 [2WR]	2-2 [1WR]	4 Grp Total
Coleman Tevin	50% (78) 5.1	38% (39) 4.4	33% (18) 6.3	43% (14) 3.4	44% (149) 4.9
Smith Ito	46% (41) 3.0	55% (29) 4.1	44% (9) 5.1	0% (2) 0.5	48% (81) 3.5
Ryan Matt	81% (16) 5.3		33% (3) 5.0	0% (6) -1.0	56% (25) 3.8

Format   Line 1: Success Rate (Total # of Plays)   Line 2: YPC

Passing by Coverage Scheme

Zone	62% (255) 9.1, 118.0
M2M	53% (236) 7.1, 103.8
Screen	34% (53) 4.8, 105.7
Combo	63% (16) 8.4, 94.5

Passing by Route

Out	57% (82) 6.2, 86.0
Curl	71% (73) 9.1, 113.8
Slant	57% (63) 7.4, 97.7
Dig	59% (46) 7.1, 84.3
Screen	33% (46) 5.1, 108.3
Flat	49% (41) 5.0, 120.0

Throw Types

Level 1	59% (390) 7.2, 107.8
Level 2	58% (146) 8.8, 112.9
Level 3	32% (53) 12.4, 112.1
Sidearm	17% (6) 1.0, 39.6
Shovel	67% (3) 3.3, 80.6

QB Drop Types

3 Step	56% (272) 7.9, 113.9
0/1 Step	56% (149) 7.2, 102.6
5 Step	53% (59) 9.9, 109.6
7 Step	49% (45) 8.0, 87.4
Designed Rollout Right	74% (35) 9.7, 133.5
Basic Screen	24% (21) 4.7, 112.8

QB State at Pass

Planted	57% (404) 8.6, 113.7
Shuffling	44% (82) 5.0, 95.2
Moving	62% (58) 6.8, 112.4

Play Action

	Play Action	No P/A
Under Center	55% (123) 9.2, 103.6	64% (75) 7.2, 115.3
Shotgun	68% (31) 12.5, 132.1	53% (371) 7.3, 109.5
ALL	58% (154) 9.9, 109.4	55% (446) 7.3, 110.5

Run Types

Outside Zone	47% (87) 4.0
Pitch	44% (66) 4.5
Inside Zone	48% (58) 3.9
Stretch	34% (29) 4.2
Lead	46% (24) 6.6
Power	59% (17) 6.5

ATL-5

Atlanta needs more punch from its running game, which fell to 21st without injured **Devonta Freeman**. But improvements can also be made in the Falcons' run-play design.

Sarkisian should have run the ball more in short-yardage situations. On both second and third and short, Sarkisian called pass plays well above league average. Atlanta's Success Rate was nearly 20% higher when running than passing on second and short, and their Success Rate on third and short was over 10% higher when running.

By design, the Falcons are a zone-run team that features outside-stretch plays and pitches. Whereas last year's NFL average was 31% of all run plays behind center, Atlanta ran behind center at just an 8% clip. They ran outside off left tackle 23% of the time, and 18% off the right side. On a league-high 40% of run plays, the Falcons did not run behind the shadow of their offensive line at all. But they were ineffective on such runs.

In **Kyle Shanahan**'s final year running Atlanta's offense, the Falcons' first-and-ten rushing attack recorded a 52% Success Rate up the middle. In 2017, it improved to 55%. Last year's first-and-ten rushing Success Rate fell to 44%, sixth worst in the league. Hopefully, this year's run game will rebound from offensive line upgrades and schematic modifications.

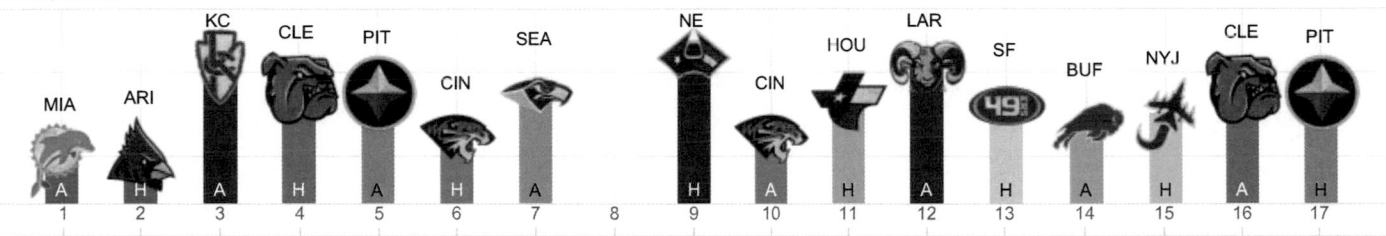

Coaches (Prior Yrs)

Head Coach:
John Harbaugh (11 yrs)
Offensive Coordinator:
Greg Roman (BAL TE) (new)
Defensive Coordinator:
Don Martingale (1 yr)

EASY   HARD

2019 Forecast

Wins	Div Rank
8.5	#3

Past Records
2018: 10-6
2017: 9-7
2016: 8-8

Schedule: MIA(A) ARI(H) KC(A) CLE(H) PIT(A) CIN(H) SEA(A) — NE(H) CIN(A) HOU(H) LAR(A) SF(H) BUF(A) NYJ(H) CLE(A) PIT(H)
1 2 3 4 5 6 7 8 9 10 11 12 13 14 15 16 17
SNF   MNF   TNF

Key Players Lost

Player	New
Brent Urban (DT)	TEN
C.J. Mosley (ILB)	NYJ
Eric Weddle (FS)	LAR
Javorius Allen (RB)	NO
Jeremy Maclin (WR)	Retired
Joe Flacco (QB)	DEN
John Brown (WR)	BUF
Maxx Williams (TE)	ARI
Terrell Suggs (OLB)	ARI
Ty Montgomery (RB)	NYJ
Za'Darius Smith (OLB)	GB

Average Line	# Games Favored	# Games Underdog
-0.6	9	6

2019 Baltimore Ravens Overview

In my 2018 NFL preview, I forecast the Ravens to exceed their eight-game Win Total. I wanted Baltimore to transition to **Lamar Jackson** quickly rather than use the year as **Joe Flacco**'s farewell tour.

They did. Later than I had hoped, but better late than never. And it was fun to watch, if you're into coaching that maximizes player strengths. If you're into reinventing a team. If you're into teams that zig while the rest of the league zags to give itself the best chance to win. If you're into a team *doing something different*.

Do something different, and do it well. When it comes to NFL offenses, that mantra works. Defenses have a tough time adjusting to things they don't see regularly, and that's been amplified by the CBA's reduction of padded practices. Most teams are similar. But each of the four teams to make the Championship Games last year performed extremely well in a particular personnel usage.

Over the first nine weeks of last season, the Ravens were Flacco's team. Apart from mop-up duty, Jackson played sparingly with a few rushes per week. Flacco's Ravens were the NFL's pass-heaviest team in one-score games (66%), fourth pass heaviest in first halves, and ninth pass heaviest on all plays. The NFL average was 58% pass in one-score games.

But Flacco's passes weren't successful. In one-score games, Flacco's Ravens produced a 44% passing Success Rate – three points below the league's 47% average – and Flacco ranked 27th among 34 qualified quarterbacks in passer rating. His yards per attempt was 6.5, fourth worst. Shockingly, Flacco's 2018 numbers were better than 2017, which speaks to how little he was contributing to Baltimore's offense.

(cont'd - see BAL2)

Key Free Agents/ Trades Added

Player	AAV (MM)
Earl Thomas (FS)	$13.
Justin Bethel (CB)	$2
Mark Ingram (RB)	$5
Michael Floyd (WR)	$0.9
Pernell McPhee (OLB)	$1
Shane Ray (OLB)	$1.2

Drafted Players

Rd	Pk	Player (College)
1	25	WR - Marquise Brown (Oklahoma)
3	85	DE - Jaylon Ferguson (Louisiana Tech)
3	93	WR - Miles Boykin (Notre Dame)
	113	RB - Justice Hill (Oklahoma State)
4	123	G - Ben Powers (Oklahoma)
	127	CB - Iman Marshall (USC)
5	160	DT - Daylon Mack (Texas A&M)
6	197	QB - Trace McSorley (Penn State)

Regular Season Wins: Past & Current Proj

Forecast 2019 Wins — 8.5
2018 Wins — 10
Forecast 2018 Wins — 8
2017 Wins — 9
2016 Wins — 8
2015 Wins — 5

1 3 5 7 9 11 13 15

Lineup & Cap Hits

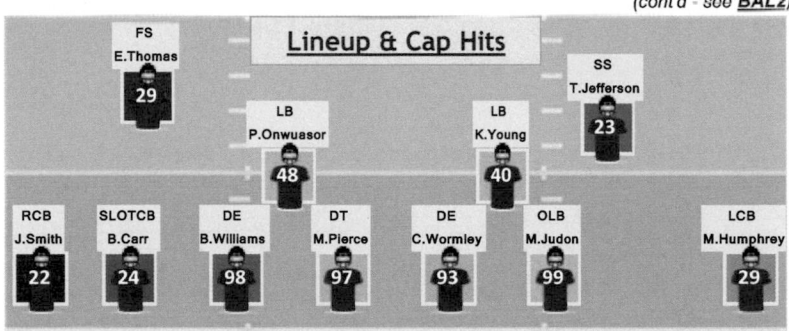

FS E.Thomas 29
SS T.Jefferson 23
LB P.Onwuasor 48
LB K.Young 40
RCB J.Smith 22
SLOTCB B.Carr 24
DE B.Williams 98
DT M.Pierce 97
DE C.Wormley 93
OLB M.Judon 99
LCB M.Humphrey 29

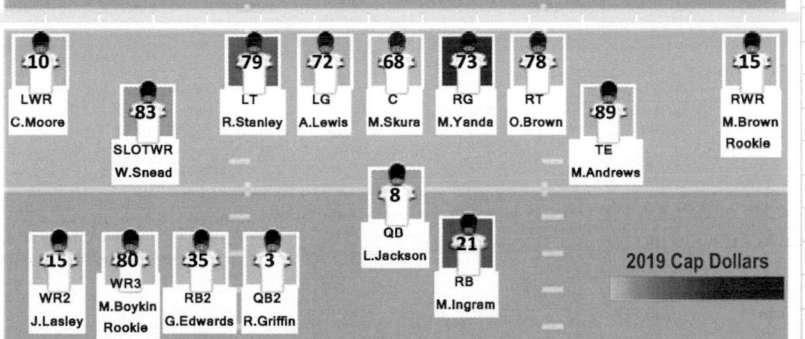

LWR C.Moore 10
SLOTWR W.Snead 83
LT R.Stanley 79
LG A.Lewis 72
C M.Skura 68
RG M.Yanda 73
RT O.Brown 78
TE M.Andrews 89
RWR M.Brown Rookie 15
QB L.Jackson 8
RB M.Ingram 21
WR2 J.Lasley 15
WR3 M.Boykin Rookie 80
RB2 G.Edwards 35
QB2 R.Griffin 3

2019 Cap Dollars

2019 Unit Spending

All OFF
All DEF

Positional Spending

	Rank	Total	2017 Rk
All OFF	31	$62.52M	27
QB	31	$4.19M	2
OL	28	$29.10M	28
RB	20	$6.68M	27
WR	30	$14.39M	25
TE	16	$8.16M	23
All DEF	11	$94.49M	12
DL	22	$23.33M	31
LB	31	$11.96M	11
CB	1	$36.51M	5
S	4	$22.69M	5

The Ravens went 1-4 over Flacco's final five starts entering their Week 10 bye.

During the off week, **John Harbaugh** made the correct decision to turn to Lamar.

And the Ravens did a 180. Baltimore immediately morphed from the NFL's pass-heaviest team to its run heaviest, chopping its league-high 66% pass rate in one-score games to a league-low 37%. And they were *great* running the ball, leading the league in yards per carry (5.4) and finishing No. 6 in rushing Success Rate from Week 11 on.

It was impressive to see how smoothly Harbaugh and Jackson were able to execute the transition from pass-heavy to run-heavy.

Baltimore's offensive efficiency spiked, joining the group of teams that "do something different and do it well" while propelling Jackson's Ravens to a 6-1 finish and Wild Card playoff berth.

Another benefit of Flacco's departure is his salary. Since signing his 2013 contract immediately after winning the Super Bowl through 2018, no quarterback was paid more money than Flacco. Flacco thereafter ranked dead last in yards per attempt, touchdown rate, and TD-to-INT ratio among qualified quarterbacks. His record was 45-46. Flacco's trade to Denver took Baltimore from the NFL's second-highest salary allocation to the quarterback position to its second lowest.

So the Ravens made noise in free agency, signing **Earl Thomas**, **Mark Ingram**, **Shane Ray**, and **Pernell McPhee** while extending **Nick Boyle** and **Tavon Young**. And they emphasized speed and athleticism in the draft, swapping out **Michael Crabtree** and **John Brown** for field stretcher **Marquise Brown** and third-round athletic phenom **Miles Boykin**. 4.4 speedster **Justice Hill** joins Ingram in the backfield. Fourth-round pick **Ben Powers** will push **Alex Lewis** at left guard.

Baltimore's in-season offensive shift included eradicating first-half primary backs **Alex Collins** and **Buck Allen** in a Thanos-like disintegration. **Gus Edwards**, **Kenneth Dixon**, and **Ty Montgomery** were installed as the Lamar-unit backs. Flacco's Ravens used 11 personnel at a 39% clip, 12 personnel at 28%, 22 personnel at 16%, and 13 at an 11% rate. They exceeded 4.0 yards per carry in none of those groups. Jackson's Ravens ran 11 personnel on 50% of run plays and dominated with 6.3 yards per carry and a 58% Success Rate. Ingram and Hill are more talented than any of last year's Lamar-unit backs.

2018 Passing Performance

QB	1st Dwn	2nd Dwn	3rd Dwn	
Lamar Jackson	56%	33%	31%	Success Rate
	8.5	6.6	5.5	YPA
	98.6	65.4	74.8	Rating
Pass Rate	49%	59%	68%	
NFL AVG	53%	47%	36%	Success Rate
	7.7	7.3	6.9	YPA
	95.1	93.7	87.1	Rating
Pass Rate	53%	62%	80%	

2018 Rushing Performance

Offense	1st Dwn	2nd Dwn	3rd Dwn	
BAL	49%	52%	63%	Success Rate
	4.2	5.0	5.3	YPC
Run Rate	51%	41%	32%	
NFL AVG	48%	46%	51%	Success Rate
	4.5	4.4	4.3	YPC
Run Rate	47%	38%	20%	

Public perception of Jackson is unfairly skewed because his rookie-year passes weren't always pretty. His season needs context. 21-year-old Jackson spent his first NFL offseason working with the second-team offense, yet delivered more yards per attempt, a better TD-to-INT ratio, and a superior QBR to Flacco's 23-year-old rookie season. And Jackson's 7.1 YPA, 3.5% TD Rate, and 84.5 passer rating were all higher than Flacco's in any of the last four years.

Flacco "looks" the part, standing as a prototypical quarterback with a big arm. Jackson isn't the typical prototype, so he may be judged more critically, especially moving from Flacco to Jackson. But Jackson delivered more on the field than Flacco, and that is what matters most. Adding the context of Jackson playing with the second team and Flacco being a seasoned

*(cont'd - see **BAL-3**)*

2018 Offensive Advanced Metrics

2018 Defensive Advanced Metrics

2018 Weekly EDSR & Season Trending Performance

	1	2	3	4	5	6	7	8	9		11	12	13	14	15	16	17
RESULT	W	L	W	W	L	W	L	L	L		W	W	W	L	W	W	W
OPP	BUF	CIN	DEN	PIT	CLE	TEN	NO	CAR	PIT		CIN	OAK	ATL	KC	TB	LAC	CLE
SITE	H	A	H	A	A	H	A	H	H		H	H	A	A	H	A	H
MARGIN	44	-11	13	12	-3	21	-1	-15	-7		3	17	10	-3	8	12	2
PTS	47	23	27	26	9	21	23	21	16		24	34	26	24	20	22	26
OPP PTS	3	34	14	14	12	0	24	36	23		21	17	16	27	12	10	24

WEEK / RESULT / OPP / SITE / MARGIN / PTS / OPP PTS

EDSR by Wk
W=Green
L=Red

OFF/DEF
EDSR
Blue=OFF
(high=good)
Red=DEF
(low=good)

2018 Close Game Records

All 2018 Wins: **10**

FG Games (<=3 pts) W-L: **2-3**
FG Games Win %: **40% (#18)**
FG Games Wins (% of Total Wins): **20% (#23)**

1 Score Games (<=8 pts) W-L: **3-4**
1 Score Games Win %: **43% (#21)**
1 Score Games Wins (% of Total Wins): **30% (#31)**

2018 Critical & Game-Deciding Stats

TO Margin	-3
TO Given	20
INT Given	9
FUM Given	11
TO Taken	17
INT Taken	12
FUM Taken	5
Sack Margin	+11
Sacks	43
Sacks Allow	32
Return TD Margin	+3
Ret TDs	4
Ret TDs Allow	1
Penalty Margin	-3
Penalties	116
Opponent Penalties	113

Baltimore Ravens 2019 Strength of Schedule In Detail (compared to 2018)

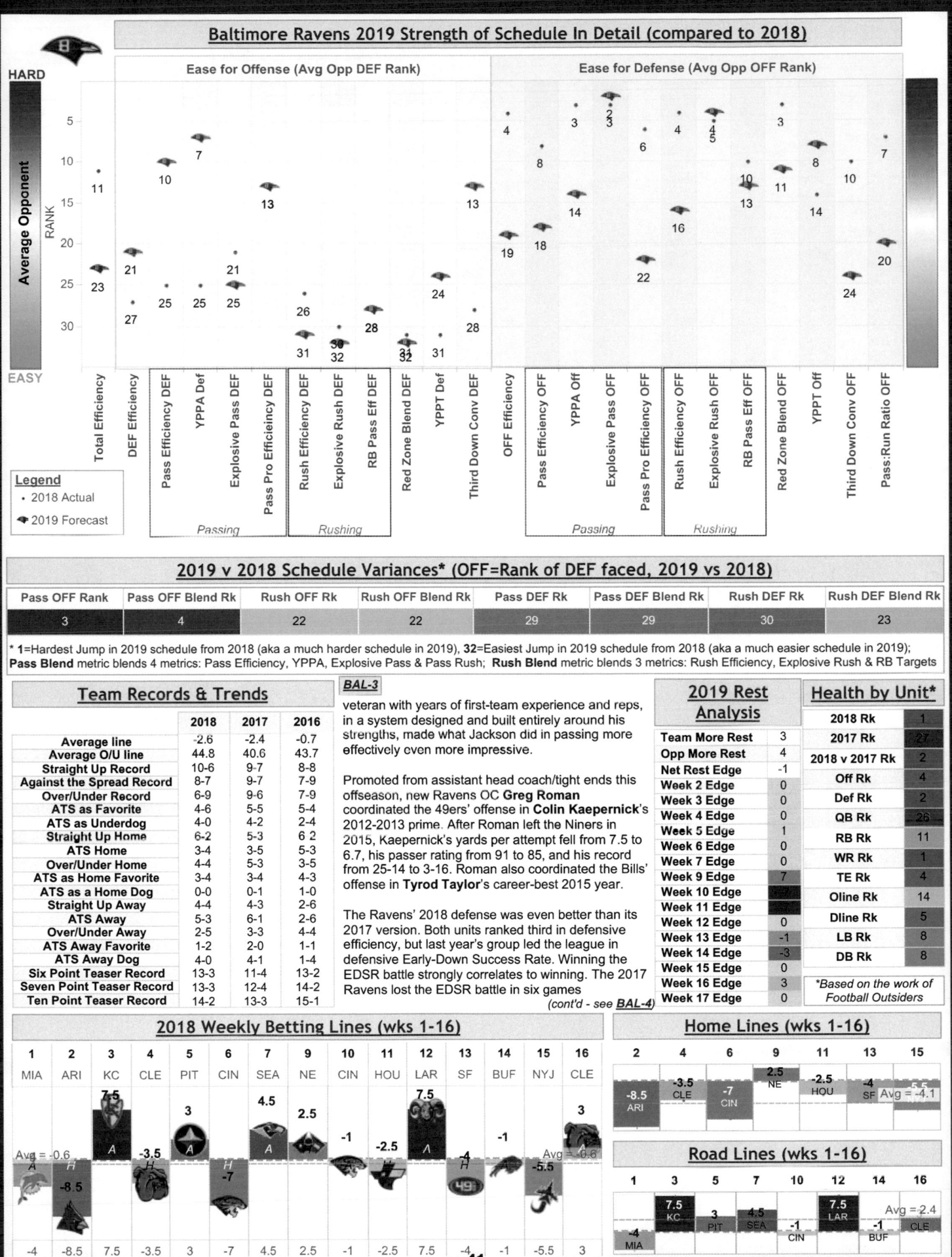

Ease for Offense (Avg Opp DEF Rank)

Ease for Defense (Avg Opp OFF Rank)

Legend
- 2018 Actual
- 2019 Forecast

2019 v 2018 Schedule Variances* (OFF=Rank of DEF faced, 2019 vs 2018)

Pass OFF Rank	Pass OFF Blend Rk	Rush OFF Rk	Rush OFF Blend Rk	Pass DEF Rk	Pass DEF Blend Rk	Rush DEF Rk	Rush DEF Blend Rk
3	4	22	22	29	29	30	23

* **1**=Hardest Jump in 2019 schedule from 2018 (aka a much harder schedule in 2019), **32**=Easiest Jump in 2019 schedule from 2018 (aka a much easier schedule in 2019);
Pass Blend metric blends 4 metrics: Pass Efficiency, YPPA, Explosive Pass & Pass Rush; **Rush Blend** metric blends 3 metrics: Rush Efficiency, Explosive Rush & RB Targets

Team Records & Trends

BAL-3

	2018	2017	2016
Average line	-2.6	-2.4	-0.7
Average O/U line	44.8	40.6	43.7
Straight Up Record	10-6	9-7	8-8
Against the Spread Record	8-7	9-7	7-9
Over/Under Record	6-9	9-6	7-9
ATS as Favorite	4-6	5-5	5-4
ATS as Underdog	4-0	4-2	2-4
Straight Up Home	6-2	5-3	6-2
ATS Home	3-4	3-5	5-3
Over/Under Home	4-4	5-3	3-5
ATS as Home Favorite	3-4	3-4	4-3
ATS as a Home Dog	0-0	0-1	1-0
Straight Up Away	4-4	4-3	2-6
ATS Away	5-3	6-1	2-6
Over/Under Away	2-5	3-3	4-4
ATS Away Favorite	1-2	2-0	1-1
ATS Away Dog	4-0	4-1	1-4
Six Point Teaser Record	13-3	11-4	13-2
Seven Point Teaser Record	13-3	12-4	14-2
Ten Point Teaser Record	14-2	13-3	15-1

veteran with years of first-team experience and reps, in a system designed and built entirely around his strengths, made what Jackson did in passing more effectively even more impressive.

Promoted from assistant head coach/tight ends this offseason, new Ravens OC **Greg Roman** coordinated the 49ers' offense in **Colin Kaepernick**'s 2012-2013 prime. After Roman left the Niners in 2015, Kaepernick's yards per attempt fell from 7.5 to 6.7, his passer rating from 91 to 85, and his record from 25-14 to 3-16. Roman also coordinated the Bills' offense in **Tyrod Taylor**'s career-best 2015 year.

The Ravens' 2018 defense was even better than its 2017 version. Both units ranked third in defensive efficiency, but last year's group led the league in defensive Early-Down Success Rate. Winning the EDSR battle strongly correlates to winning. The 2017 Ravens lost the EDSR battle in six games

*(cont'd - see **BAL-4**)*

2019 Rest Analysis

Team More Rest	3
Opp More Rest	4
Net Rest Edge	-1
Week 2 Edge	0
Week 3 Edge	0
Week 4 Edge	0
Week 5 Edge	1
Week 6 Edge	0
Week 7 Edge	0
Week 9 Edge	7
Week 10 Edge	
Week 11 Edge	
Week 12 Edge	0
Week 13 Edge	-1
Week 14 Edge	-3
Week 15 Edge	0
Week 16 Edge	3
Week 17 Edge	0

Health by Unit*

2018 Rk	1
2017 Rk	27
2018 v 2017 Rk	2
Off Rk	4
Def Rk	2
QB Rk	26
RB Rk	11
WR Rk	1
TE Rk	4
Oline Rk	14
Dline Rk	5
LB Rk	8
DB Rk	8

*Based on the work of Football Outsiders

2018 Weekly Betting Lines (wks 1-16)

1	2	3	4	5	6	7	9	10	11	12	13	14	15	16
MIA	ARI	KC	CLE	PIT	CIN	SEA	NE	CIN	HOU	LAR	SF	BUF	NYJ	CLE

Avg = -0.6 ... Avg = -0.6

| -4 | -8.5 | 7.5 | -3.5 | 3 | -7 | 4.5 | 2.5 | -1 | -2.5 | 7.5 | -4 | -1 | -5.5 | 3 |

Home Lines (wks 1-16)

2	4	6	9	11	13	15
-8.5 ARI	-3.5 CLE	-7 CIN	2.5 NE	-2.5 HOU	-4 SF	-5.5

Avg = -4.1

Road Lines (wks 1-16)

1	3	5	7	10	12	14	16
-4 MIA	7.5 KC	3 PIT	4.5 SEA	-1 CIN	7.5 LAR	-1 BUF	CLE

Avg = -2.4

Baltimore Ravens 2018 Play Analysis

2018 Play Tendencies

All Pass %	52%
All Pass Rk	30
All Rush %	48%
All Rush Rk	3
1 Score Pass %	50%
1 Score Pass Rk	29
2017 1 Score Pass %	58%
2017 1 Score Pass Rk	15
2018 Pass Increase %	-7%
Pass Increase Rk	31
1 Score Rush %	50%
1 Score Rush Rk	4
Up Pass %	42%
Up Pass Rk	28
Up Rush %	58%
Up Rush Rk	5
Down Pass %	65%
Down Pass Rk	23
Down Rush %	35%
Down Rush Rk	10

2018 Down & Distance Tendencies

Down	Distance	Total Plays	Pass Rate	Run Rate	Play Success %
1	Short (1-3)	12	17%	83%	42%
	Med (4-7)	8	38%	63%	38%
	Long (8-10)	360	44%	56%	53%
	XL (11+)	19	53%	47%	37%
2	Short (1-3)	49	43%	57%	65%
	Med (4-7)	106	65%	35%	47%
	Long (8-10)	110	53%	47%	43%
	XL (11+)	38	68%	32%	26%
3	Short (1-3)	50	34%	66%	74%
	Med (4-7)	66	76%	24%	48%
	Long (8-10)	37	95%	5%	35%
	XL (11+)	27	93%	7%	11%
4	Short (1-3)	11	36%	64%	55%
	Med (4-7)	3	100%	0%	67%
	XL (11+)	1	100%	0%	0%

Shotgun %:

Under Center	Shotgun
22%	78%

37% *AVG* 63%

Run Rate:

Under Center	Shotgun
63%	35%

68% *AVG* 23%

Pass Rate:

Under Center	Shotgun
37%	65%

32% *AVG* 77%

Short Yardage Intelligence:

2nd and Short Run

Run Freq	Run Rk	NFL Run Freq Avg	Run 1D Rate	Run NFL 1D Avg
61%	22	65%	64%	68%

2nd and Short Pass

Pass Freq	Pass Rk	NFL Pass Freq Avg	Pass 1D Rate	Pass NFL 1D Avg
39%	11	35%	44%	56%

Most Frequent Play

Down	Distance	Play Type	Player	Total Plays	Play Success %
1	Short (1-3)	RUSH	Alex Collins	4	50%
			Javorius Allen	4	50%
	Med (4-7)	RUSH	Alex Collins	2	0%
			Lamar Jackson	2	50%
	Long (8-10)	RUSH	Gus Edwards	59	69%
	XL (11+)	RUSH	Lamar Jackson	3	0%
2	Short (1-3)	RUSH	Lamar Jackson	9	89%
			Gus Edwards	9	89%
	Med (4-7)	RUSH	Gus Edwards	12	42%
	Long (8-10)	RUSH	Alex Collins	18	28%
	XL (11+)	PASS	John Brown	8	25%
3	Short (1-3)	RUSH	Lamar Jackson	11	82%
	Med (4-7)	PASS	Michael Crabtree	11	27%
		RUSH	Lamar Jackson	11	64%
	Long (8-10)	PASS	John Brown	7	0%
	XL (11+)	PASS	John Brown	4	25%

Most Successful Play*

Down	Distance	Play Type	Player	Total Plays	Play Success %
1	Long (8-10)	PASS	Nick Boyle	9	78%
2	Short (1-3)	RUSH	Gus Edwards	9	89%
			Lamar Jackson	9	89%
	Med (4-7)	PASS	Mark Andrews	6	83%
		RUSH	Alex Collins	6	83%
	Long (8-10)	RUSH	Lamar Jackson	11	82%
	XL (11+)	RUSH	Lamar Jackson	5	40%
3	Short (1-3)	RUSH	Joe Flacco	5	100%
	Med (4-7)	PASS	John Brown	6	67%
	Long (8-10)	PASS	Michael Crabtree	6	50%

Minimum 5 plays to qualify

2018 Weekly Snap Rates

Wk	Opp	Score	Willie Snead	Michael Crabtree	John Brown	Nick Boyle	Chris Moore	Maxx Williams	Alex Collins	Javorius Allen	Gus Edwards	Kenneth Dixon
1	BUF	W 47-3	42 (53%)	53 (66%)	48 (60%)	54 (68%)	19 (24%)	44 (55%)	27 (34%)	30 (38%)		22 (28%)
2	CIN	L 34-23	57 (67%)	73 (86%)	68 (80%)	43 (51%)	26 (31%)	28 (33%)	42 (49%)	42 (49%)		
3	DEN	W 27-14	40 (56%)	52 (72%)	55 (76%)	38 (53%)	22 (31%)	37 (51%)	35 (49%)	39 (54%)		
4	PIT	W 26-14	39 (51%)	48 (63%)	44 (58%)	55 (72%)	33 (43%)	40 (53%)	36 (47%)	33 (43%)		
5	CLE	L 12-9	67 (77%)	72 (83%)	59 (68%)	39 (45%)	23 (26%)	27 (31%)	27 (31%)	50 (57%)		
6	TEN	W 21-0	55 (72%)	41 (54%)	41 (54%)	48 (63%)	39 (51%)	34 (45%)	35 (46%)	28 (37%)	14 (18%)	
7	NO	L 24-23	44 (65%)	48 (71%)	50 (74%)	32 (47%)	30 (44%)	20 (29%)	28 (41%)	30 (44%)	7 (10%)	
8	CAR	L 36-21	52 (76%)	45 (66%)	46 (68%)	31 (46%)	38 (56%)		33 (49%)	23 (34%)	8 (12%)	
9	PIT	L 23-16	43 (70%)	43 (70%)	39 (64%)	21 (34%)	24 (39%)		31 (51%)	26 (43%)	2 (3%)	
11	CIN	W 24-21	53 (67%)	53 (67%)	51 (65%)	53 (67%)	28 (35%)		17 (22%)	5 (6%)	49 (62%)	
12	OAK	W 34-17	49 (70%)	47 (67%)	45 (64%)	51 (73%)	25 (36%)	8 (11%)		1 (1%)	43 (61%)	
13	ATL	W 26-16	66 (81%)	36 (44%)	43 (53%)	50 (62%)	51 (63%)	21 (26%)			40 (49%)	17 (21%)
14	KC	L 27-24	51 (72%)	51 (72%)	50 (70%)	39 (55%)	23 (32%)	22 (31%)			31 (44%)	23 (32%)
15	TB	W 20-12	58 (76%)	44 (58%)	47 (62%)	21 (28%)	26 (34%)	43 (57%)		3 (4%)	33 (43%)	39 (51%)
16	LAC	W 22-10	42 (68%)	43 (69%)	34 (55%)	39 (63%)	27 (44%)	20 (32%)			23 (37%)	29 (47%)
17	CLE	W 26-24	63 (82%)	56 (73%)	37 (48%)	37 (48%)	33 (43%)	30 (39%)			36 (47%)	22 (29%)
	Grand Total		821 (69%)	805 (68%)	757 (64%)	651 (55%)	467 (40%)	374 (38%)	311 (42%)	310 (34%)	286 (35%)	152 (35%)

Personnel Groupings

Personnel	Team %	NFL Avg	Succ. %
1-1 [3WR]	53%	65%	49%
1-2 [2WR]	25%	17%	52%
1-3 [1WR]	8%	3%	38%
2-2 [1WR]	6%	3%	54%
1-0 [4WR]	3%	2%	35%
2-1 [2WR]	2%	8%	48%

Grouping Tendencies

Personnel	Pass Rate	Pass Succ. %	Run Succ. %
1-1 [3WR]	57%	44%	56%
1-2 [2WR]	44%	52%	52%
1-3 [1WR]	33%	38%	37%
2-2 [1WR]	14%	56%	54%
1-0 [4WR]	94%	34%	50%
2-1 [2WR]	44%	36%	57%

Red Zone Targets (min 3)

Receiver	All	Inside 5	6-10	11-20
John Brown	12	2	3	7
Mark Andrews	8	1	2	5
Michael Crabtree	8	2	3	3
Willie Snead	6			6
Javorius Allen	5		1	4
Nick Boyle	5	3		2
Alex Collins	3		1	2

Red Zone Rushes (min 3)

Rusher	All	Inside 5	6-10	11-20
Lamar Jackson	39	6	10	23
Alex Collins	21	6	6	9
Gus Edwards	17	2	5	10
Javorius Allen	11	6	1	4
Kenneth Dixon	5	3	1	1
Joe Flacco	3			3
Ty Montgomery	3			3

Early Down Target Rate

RB	TE	WR
18%	25%	57%
23%	21%	56%
	NFL AVG	

Overall Target Success %

RB	TE	WR
48%	53%	46%
#13	#22	#29

Baltimore Ravens 2018 Passing Recap & 2019 Outlook

Lamar Jackson has a shot at a huge 2019 in both real life and fantasy football. He recorded 37 red-zone carries in just seven regular season starts last year – eighth most in the NFL – and averaged 5.3 red-zone rushes per game, nearly one more per week than league leader **Todd Gurley**. If Jackson can improve his 17% red-zone passing touchdown rate – which ranked 35th out of 39 qualifying quarterbacks – his box-score production will further improve.

But there is a fine balance between Jackson's rushing upside and injury avoidance. Arguably the best times for Jackson to run are in high-leverage situations, but 216-pound Jackson must get down before taking big hits. In the first month of the season, Jackson will face three defenses that finished 2018 ranked 12th or better versus the pass. Although all three ranked bottom ten against run.

Lamar Jackson Rating All Downs

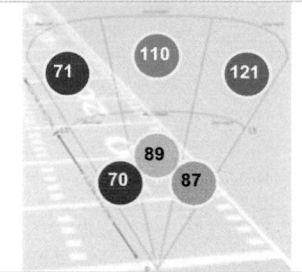

2018 Standard Passing Table

QB	Comp	Att	Comp %	Yds	YPA	TDs	INT	Sacks	Rating	Rk
Joe Flacco	232	379	61%	2,470	6.5	12	6	16	84	35
Lamar Jackson	113	199	57%	1,395	7.0	8	4	23	84	36
NFL Avg			62%		7.0				87.5	

Lamar Jackson Rating Early Downs

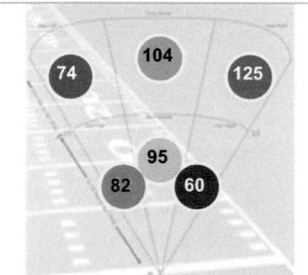

2018 Advanced Passing Table

QB	Success %	EDSR Passing Success %	20+ Yd Pass Gains	20+ Yd Pass %	30+ Yd Pass Gains	30+ Yd Pass %	Avg. Air Yds per Comp	Avg. YAC per Comp	20+ Air Yd Comp	20+ Air Yd %
Joe Flacco	45%	47%	29	8.0%	7	2.0%	6.1	4.5	11	3%
Lamar Jackson	41%	44%	16	8.0%	5	3.0%	6.8	5.5	6	3%
NFL Avg	44%	48%	29.5	8.4%	12.5	3.7%	5.8	5.1	14.5	6%

Interception Rates by Down

Yards to Go	1st Dwn	2nd Dwn	3rd Dwn	4th Dwn	Total
1 & 2	0.0%	0.0%	0.0%	0.0%	0.0%
3, 4, 5		5.9%	0.0%		3.3%
6 - 9	0.0%	3.4%	0.0%	0.0%	1.7%
10 - 14	1.5%	0.0%	8.3%	0.0%	2.1%
15+	0.0%	0.0%	0.0%		0.0%
Total	1.4%	2.5%	1.6%	0.0%	1.8%

3rd Down Passing - Short of Sticks Analysis

QB	Avg. Yds to Go	Avg. YIA (of Comp)	Avg Yds Short	Short of Sticks Rate	Short Rk
Lamar Jackson	8.5	6.2	-2.3	67%	30
NFL Avg	7.8	6.4	-1.4	60%	

Air Yds vs YAC

Air Yds %	YAC %	Rk
55%	45%	17
53%	48%	

2018 Receiving Recap & 2019 Outlook

Moving on from **Michael Crabtree** and **John Brown**, the Ravens got much younger and more athletic at wide receiver. First-round pick **Marquise Brown**'s speed and quickness make him a threat to score from any part of the field, and **Miles Boykin** was the most athletic player in the entire 2019 draft. The Ravens' offense still relies heavily on its tight ends, last year averaging an otherworldly 14.6 yards per pass attempt with a 65% Success Rate when targeting the position in 12 personnel in Jackson's starts.

Player *Min 50 Targets	Targ	Ccmp %	YPA	Rating	Success %	Success Rk	Missed YPA Rk	YAS % Rk	YTS % Rk	TDs
Michael Crabtree	104	54%	6.2	80.6	47%	95	133	67	38	5
Willie Snead	101	64%	6.9	75.6	50%	78	109	97	13	1
John Brown	100	44%	7.3	77.5	38%	124	173	67	59	3
Mark Andrews	57	65%	10.2	116.3	60%	14	9	9	110	3

Directional Passer Rating Delivered

Receiver	Short Left	Short Middle	Short Right	Deep Left	Deep Middle	Deep Right	Player Total
Michael Crabtree	109	69	108	24	119	50	81
Willie Snead	69	101	54	40	104	0	76
John Brown	85	69	88	47	50	104	78
Mark Andrews	40	112	137	127	104	117	116
Javorius Allen	85	89	118			0	92
Nick Boyle	99	76	50		40		67
Chris Moore	92	89	93	40	119	40	91
Alex Collins	58	96	112				98
Maxx Williams	81	119	137	119			120
Ty Montgomery	42	94	63			40	67
Kenneth Dixon	94	119	97				110
Team Total	81	91	98	56	84	56	86

2018 Rushing Recap & 2019 Outlook

The Ravens are flush with functional running backs, not a bad thing given how they are built. Last year's team especially impressed with its ability to improve rushing efficiency on later downs. They averaged 4.2 yards per carry on first-down carries, 5.0 YPC on second downs, and 5.3 YPC on third-down runs. As this year's Ravens face the NFL's second-softest run-defense slate, the ground game should remain highly efficient. But with a deep stable of backs and Jackson's propensity for stealing scoring-position carries, fantasy confidence in individual members of Baltimore's backfield may waver week to week.

Player *Min 50 Rushes	Rushes	YPC	Success %	Success Rk	Missed YPA Rk	YTS % Rk	YAS % Rk	Early Down Success %	Early Down Success Rk	TDs
Gus Edwards	145	5.1	61%	3	2	26	47	59%	2	2
Alex Collins	114	3.6	47%	37	51	1	58	45%	46	7
Kenneth Dixon	66	5.3	52%	19	42	42	39	53%	12	2

Yards per Carry by Direction

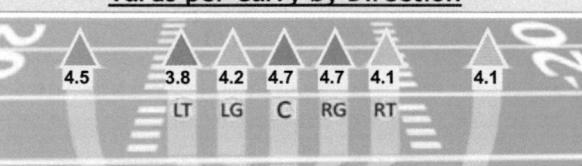

Directional Run Frequency

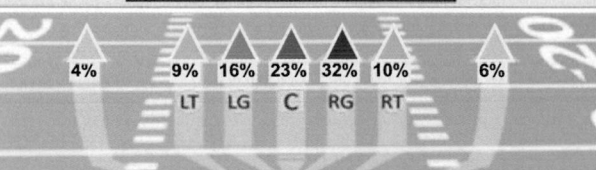

and went 1-5 in them. Last year's Ravens lost the EDSR battle twice, losing both. They were Flacco's final two starts in Baltimore.

There are many reasons for optimism about this year's Ravens. The 2017 version went 9-7 with a +17 turnover margin and +6 return-TD margin. Both stats massively determine wins and losses. Last year's Ravens went 10-6 but were -3 in turnover margin and +3 in return TDs. Only three other teams since 2013 have won double-digit games with a -3 turnover margin or worse. The 2018 Ravens only went 3-4 in one-score games while experiencing terrible fumble luck, all positive signs in mean-regression terms.

The style in which the Ravens' 2018 season ended may prove a best-case scenario for this year's club. In the Wild Card Round, the Chargers held Baltimore to a 29% Success Rate and only 3.6 yards per carry on runs through three quarters while taking a commanding 12-3 fourth-quarter lead.

(cont'd - see BAL-5)

Baltimore Ravens Fantasy Corner

2018 third-round pick **Mark Andrews** stepped forward as the Ravens' lead tight end as a rookie, finishing fifth at the position in yards per route run (2.01) and establishing the best rapport with **Lamar Jackson** among Baltimore's pass catchers. Andrews' 552 yards were fifth most by any rookie tight end in the last decade, and his 16.2 yards per catch ranked second behind only **O.J. Howard**'s 16.6 last year. Andrews also led the Ravens in targets (7) in their playoff loss to the Chargers. 2018 first-round pick **Hayden Hurst**'s role will expand after an injury-plagued rookie campaign, but Andrews is the preferred late-round fantasy dart. With 4.67 speed at 6-foot-5, 256, Andrews is a field stretcher with big-play ability in the seams.

- Evan Silva

2018 Situational Usage by Player & Position

Usage Rate by Score

		Being Blown Out (14+)	Down Big (9-13)	One Score	Large Lead (9-13)	Blowout Lead (14+)
RUSH	Gus Edwards	1%	2%	86%	4%	6%
	Alex Collins	8%	4%	70%	4%	14%
	Willie Snead			100%		
	John Brown			100%		
	Kenneth Dixon		3%	68%	9%	20%
	Javorius Allen	7%	7%	61%	15%	10%
	Ty Montgomery			67%	7%	27%
	Chris Moore	20%		80%		
	Maxx Williams		33%	33%	33%	
	Total	4%	3%	75%	6%	12%
PASS	Gus Edwards	50%		50%		
	Alex Collins	31%	6%	50%	6%	6%
	Willie Snead	25%	8%	51%	3%	14%
	Michael Crabtree	10%	6%	70%	3%	11%
	John Brown	15%	7%	70%	4%	4%
	Kenneth Dixon		33%	56%	11%	
	Javorius Allen	15%	27%	39%		18%
	Mark Andrews	14%	18%	54%	2%	12%
	Nick Boyle	13%	10%	60%		17%
	Ty Montgomery			79%	21%	
	Chris Moore	10%	14%	48%	14%	14%
	Maxx Williams	10%	30%	40%		20%
	Total	15%	11%	59%	4%	11%

Share of Offensive Plays by Type

	Gus Edwards	Alex Collins	Willie Snead	Michael Crabtree	John Brown	Kenneth Dixon	Javorius Allen	Mark Andrews	Nick Boyle	Ty Montgomery	Chris Moore	Maxx Williams
RUSH	37%	29%	0%		1%	17%	10%			4%	1%	1%
PASS	0%	4%	19%	19%	17%	2%	8%	12%	7%	3%	5%	2%
ALL	18%	16%	10%	10%	9%	9%	9%	6%	4%	4%	3%	2%

Positional Target Distribution vs NFL Average

		NFL Wide				Team Only			
		Left	Middle	Right	Total	Left	Middle	Right	Total
Deep	WR	33%	17%	30%	81%	27%	16%	38%	82%
	TE	5%	4%	7%	16%	6%	6%	4%	16%
	RB	1%	0%	2%	4%			2%	2%
	All	39%	22%	39%	100%	33%	22%	44%	100%
Short	WR	21%	13%	21%	55%	14%	28%	16%	57%
	TE	6%	6%	8%	20%	5%	7%	10%	22%
	RB	10%	5%	10%	25%	5%	6%	9%	20%
	All	37%	24%	39%	100%	24%	41%	35%	100%
Total		37%	24%	39%	100%	26%	38%	37%	100%

Positional Success Rates vs NFL Average

		NFL Wide				Team Only			
		Left	Middle	Right	Total	Left	Middle	Right	Total
Deep	WR	40%	49%	40%	42%	22%	63%	26%	32%
	TE	43%	54%	41%	45%	50%	50%	75%	56%
	RB	38%	33%	44%	41%			0%	0%
	All	41%	50%	41%	43%	27%	59%	30%	35%
Short	WR	55%	61%	53%	56%	54%	53%	42%	50%
	TE	56%	62%	54%	57%	30%	61%	67%	56%
	RB	47%	53%	45%	48%	40%	61%	41%	47%
	All	53%	60%	51%	54%	46%	55%	49%	51%
Total		51%	58%	49%	52%	42%	56%	44%	48%

Division History: Season Wins & 2019 Projection

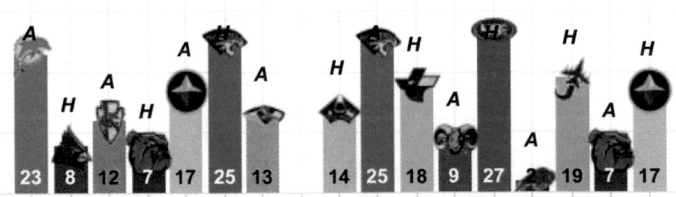

| 2015 Wins | 2016 Wins | 2017 Wins | 2018 Wins | Forecast 2019 Wins |

Rank of 2019 Defensive Pass Efficiency Faced by Week

| 23 | 8 | 12 | 7 | 17 | 25 | 13 | | 14 | 25 | 18 | 9 | 27 | 2 | 19 | 7 | 17 |

0 1 2 3 4 5 6 7 8 9 10 11 12 13 14 15 16 17

Rank of 2019 Defensive Rush Efficiency Faced by Week

| 24 | 29 | 32 | 25 | 8 | 26 | 17 | | 19 | 26 | 4 | 28 | 11 | 14 | 21 | 25 | 8 |

0 1 2 3 4 5 6 7 8 9 10 11 12 13 14 15 16 17

2018 Detailed Analytics Summary
Success by Play Type & Primary Personnel Groupings

Type	1-1 [3WR]	1-2 [2WR]	1-3 [1WR]	2-2 [1WR]	1-0 [4WR]	2-1 [2WR]	0-1 [4WR]	2-3 [0WR]	0-0 [5WR]	2-0 [3WR]	ALL
PASS	43% (344)	49% (122)	38% (26)	56% (9)	33% (30)	36% (11)	44% (9)		100% (1)	33% (3)	44% (555)
RUSH	55% (253)	51% (152)	36% (55)	54% (54)	50% (2)	60% (15)		57% (7)	0% (3)		52% (541)
All	48% (597)	50% (274)	37% (81)	54% (63)	34% (32)	50% (26)	44% (9)	57% (7)	25% (4)	33% (3)	48% (1,096)

Format   Success Rate (Total # of Plays)

Receiving Success by Top-4 Personnel Groupings
(Min 50 targets)

POS	Player	1-1 [3WR]	1-2 [2WR]	1-0 [4WR]	2-1 [2WR]	4 Grp Total
TE	Mark Andrews	66% (29) 9.0, 111.6	53% (19) 12.9, 120.0			60% (48) 10.6, 115.5
WR	Willie Snead	53% (81) 7.3, 81.8	40% (5) 4.6, 15.0	25% (4) 5.5, 66.7		51% (90) 7.1, 75.0
	Michael Crabtree	49% (55) 6.5, 91.3	53% (19) 6.4, 77.1	40% (10) 4.9, 72.5	0% (2) 0.0, 0.0	48% (86) 6.1, 79.0
	John Brown	37% (51) 7.7, 75.0	57% (23) 10.7, 140.8	20% (5) 5.8, 59.6	50% (2) 2.5, 16.7	42% (81) 8.3, 88.1

Format   Line 1: Success Rate (Total # of Plays)   Line 2: YPA, Passer Rating

Rushing Success by Top-4 Personnel Groupings
(Min 25 carries)

Rusher (Last, First)	1-1 [3WR]	1-2 [2WR]	2-2 [1WR]	2-1 [2WR]	4 Grp Total
Jackson Lamar	55% (66) 5.6	60% (45) 5.1	29% (14) 4.6	75% (4) 6.3	54% (129) 5.3
Collins Alex	51% (37) 5.1	37% (38) 2.9	62% (13) 2.7	0% (1) 0.0	46% (89) 3.7
Dixon Kenneth	45% (40) 5.5	56% (16) 4.6	100% (5) 5.2	100% (1) 13.0	53% (62) 5.4
Allen Javorius	27% (11) 2.3	17% (6) 3.2	30% (10) 2.3	100% (1) 2.0	29% (28) 2.5
Montgomery Ty	60% (10) 5.2		100% (4) 5.8	0% (1) 3.0	67% (15) 5.2

Format   Line 1: Success Rate (Total # of Plays)   Line 2: YPC

Passing by Coverage Scheme

Zone	50% (232) 8.0, 97.9
M2M	50% (187) 6.6, 77.3
Screen	26% (27) 3.3, 92.7
Combo	64% (14) 7.0, 108.6

Passing by Route

Curl	56% (52) 7.0, 88.0
Out	57% (49) 6.0, 83.3
Slant	60% (48) 9.0, 102.2
Dig	50% (34) 7.6, 65.6
Screen	26% (27) 2.9, 76.3
Flat	43% (23) 3.0, 90.7

Throw Types

Level 1	53% (321) 6.5, 90.3
Level 2	50% (111) 8.8, 105.7
Level 3	25% (48) 8.6, 57.9
Sidearm	38% (8) 8.5, 100.0
Shovel	29% (7) 2.9, 79.2

QB Drop Types

3 Step	50% (236) 6.9, 93.9
0/1 Step	47% (115) 6.9, 82.2
5 Step	40% (68) 8.3, 81.9
Designed Rollout Right	50% (30) 5.9, 71.0
7 Step	67% (18) 12.3, 94.9
Basic Screen	25% (12) 2.2, 77.1

QB State at Pass

Planted	50% (342) 7.6, 93.9
Moving	55% (56) 7.0, 87.8
Shuffling	31% (48) 3.9, 58.2

Play Action

	Play Action	No P/A
Under Center	62% (34) 10.8, 105.8	57% (21) 5.0, 70.3
Shotgun	48% (91) 7.8, 87.8	47% (352) 6.8, 89.6
ALL	52% (125) 8.6, 92.7	47% (373) 6.7, 88.6

Run Types

Power	50% (58) 5.3
Inside Zone	43% (47) 3.7
Outside Zone	42% (31) 3.7
Lead	54% (24) 2.9
Stretch	50% (14) 3.6
Pitch	40% (10) 1.8

BAL-5

The Ravens leaned on Jackson for a season-high 29 pass attempts against the NFL's No. 10 pass defense. In a fourth-quarter flurry, Jackson averaged 8.5 yards per attempt with a 117 rating while significantly increasing his depth of target downfield.

The Ravens should know teams have studied their offense intently this offseason, and seeing the Chargers stop their rushing attack may give Baltimore a blueprint for how opponents will defend them in 2019. And Jackson's fourth-quarter passing success against Los Angeles should increase the Ravens' confidence in his ability to throw the ball efficiently.

It helps that Baltimore's 2019 schedule is favorable. They're a run-first team facing the NFL's second-softest schedule of run defenses, which last year combined to allow the league's highest explosive run rate. The Ravens' pass-defense schedule does toughen considerably from last year, but Jackson will finally get a full offseason of first-team reps and preparation.

The Ravens open 2019 facing the NFL's two likeliest candidates for 2020's No. 1 overall pick in the Dolphins and Cardinals. They next face the Chiefs, a team Jackson nearly knocked off in Kansas City last season and may be without **Tyreek Hill**. Baltimore doesn't play the Steelers in primetime this year. They have a midseason bye, and get to face the Patriots after that off week. They host a late-season Thursday Night Football game, results of which have skewed heavily in favor of home teams. The Ravens don't have any back-to-back road stands. And they play six games against quarterbacks with just one year of experience as full-time starters. They get **Kyler Murray** in the second start of his career. The Ravens are 8-4 over the last three seasons when facing quarterbacks in their first two seasons. They're 19-17 in all other games.

Coaches (Prior Yrs)

Head Coach:
  Sean McDermott (2 yrs)
Offensive Coordinator:
  Brian Daboll (1 yr)
Defensive Coordinator:
  Leslie Frazier (1 yr)

EASY   HARD

Buffalo Bills

2019 Forecast

Wins	Div Rank
7	#3

Past Records
2018: 6-10
2017: 9-7
2016: 7-9

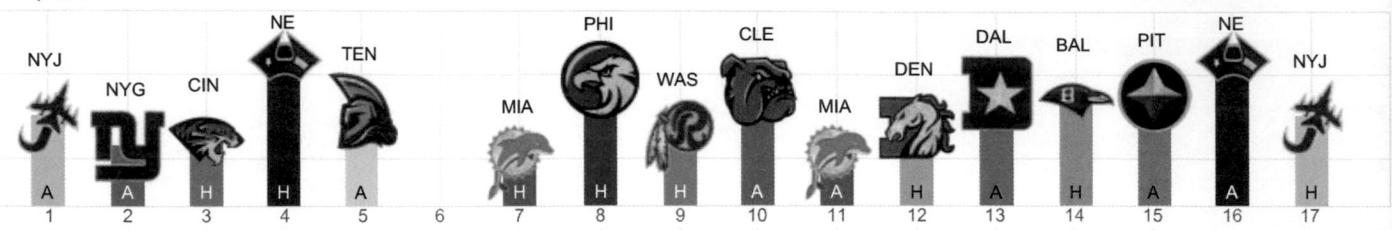

NYJ	NYG	CIN	NE	TEN		MIA	PHI	WAS	CLE	MIA	DEN	DAL	BAL	PIT	NE	NYJ
A	A	H	H	A		H	H	H	A	A	H	A	H	A	A	H
1	2	3	4	5	6	7	8	9	10	11	12	13	14	15	16	17

TNF

Key Players Lost

Player	New
Charles Clay (TE)	ARI
Deonte Thompson (WR)	NYJ
Derek Anderson (QB)	Retired
John Miller (G)	CIN
Logan Thomas (TE)	DET
Matt Darr (P)	NYJ
Taiwan Jones (RB)	HOU
Vontae Davis (CB)	Retired

Average Line	# Games Favored	# Games Underdog
2.9	4	11

Regular Season Wins: Past & Current Proj

Forecast 2019 Wins	7
2018 Wins	6
Forecast 2018 Wins	6.5
2017 Wins	9
2016 Wins	7
2015 Wins	8

1 3 5 7 9 11 13 15

2019 Buffalo Bills Overview

The Bills were my priciest team Win Total bet last season, and my partners and I found a book dealing seven wins. This book respects our group and was willing to take our business to find out where the sharp money is. They gave us 67% higher limits than usual, and we max bet the under on Buffalo at seven wins.

I *knew* the Bills would stumble early. My metrics forecast Buffalo to face the NFL's toughest schedule in Weeks 1-6. I also forecast the Bills to draw the league's hardest run-defense slate, forcing more onto raw rookie **Josh Allen**'s plate.

My end-of-season metrics showed Buffalo played the NFL's second-toughest schedule in Weeks 1-6, and the league's most difficult through the first nine weeks. They also faced the league's third-toughest schedule of run defenses. We *nailed* this team.

Buffalo was 2-7 through nine weeks. And then, they got started to get lucky.

The Bills drew the NFL's second-easiest schedule from Week 10 on, featuring the Dolphins and Jets twice, and the underachieving Jaguars and Lions. After logging a passing Success Rate of 36% or worse in six of its first nine games, Buffalo exceeded 36% in each of its final seven. The Bills' explosive pass rate exceeded 12% in zero of their opening nine games but four of their final seven.

Buffalo won four times in those final seven weeks to finish 6-10. Although we were fortunate to squeak out our wager, the Bills should maintain positivity about the long-term projection of **Sean McDermott**'s team.

Allen fell in line with my low rookie-year expectations, but he got better late in the year. He completed just 22% of his early-down deep passes in his first six games,

*(cont'd - see **BUF2**)*

Key Free Agents/ Trades Added

Player	AAV (MM)
Andre Roberts (WR)	$2.2
Cole Beasley (WR)	$7.2
John Brown (WR)	$9
Kevin Johnson (CB)	$3
Mitch Morse (C)	$11.
Spencer Long (C)	$4.2
Ty Nsekhe (RT)	$5
Tyler Kroft (TE)	$6.2

Drafted Players

Rd	Pk	Player (College)
1	9	DT - Ed Oliver (Houston)
2	38	OT - Cody Ford (Oklahoma)
3	74	RB - Devin Singletary (Florida Atlantic)
3*	96	TE - Dawson Knox (Ole Miss)
5	147	LB - Vosean Joseph (Florida)
6	181	CB - Jaquan Johnson (Miami)
7	225	DE - Darryl Johnson Jr. (North Carolina A&T)
7	228	TE - Tommy Sweeney (Boston College)

Lineup & Cap Hits

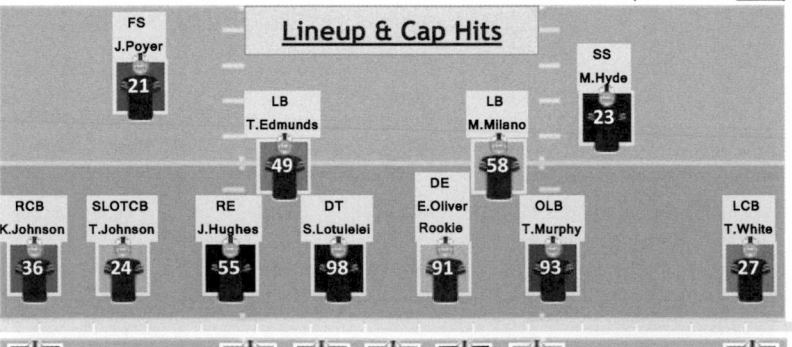

FS J.Poyer 21
SS M.Hyde 23
LB T.Edmunds 49
LB M.Milano 58
DE E.Oliver Rookie 91
RCB K.Johnson 36
SLOTCB T.Johnson 24
RE J.Hughes 55
DT S.Lotulelei 98
OLB T.Murphy 93
LCB T.White 27

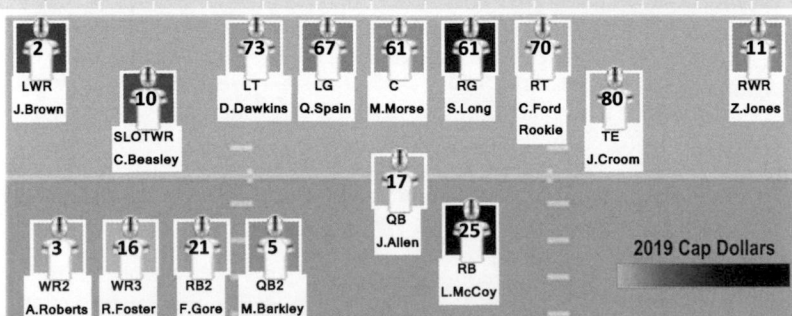

LWR J.Brown 2
SLOTWR C.Beasley 10
LT D.Dawkins 73
LG Q.Spain 67
C M.Morse 61
RG S.Long 61
RT C.Ford Rookie 70
TE J.Croom 80
RWR Z.Jones 11
QB J.Allen 17
RB L.McCoy 25
WR2 A.Roberts 3
WR3 R.Foster 16
RB2 F.Gore 21
QB2 M.Barkley 5

2019 Cap Dollars

2019 Unit Spending

All DEF | All OFF

Positional Spending

	Rank	Total	2017 Rk
All OFF	25	$89.35M	32
QB	30	$7.05M	30
OL	18	$36.69M	32
RB	1	$15.13M	1
WR	15	$23.94M	32
TE	23	$6.54M	9
All DEF	18	$84.79M	26
DL	4	$45.86M	11
LB	30	$12.30M	28
CB	27	$11.06M	27
S	10	$15.57M	8

then more than doubled that (47%) over his final six starts.

The Bills' installation of **Robert Foster** coincided with winning. Over the NFL's final eight weeks among 96 qualified receivers, Foster's 14.2 yards per target ranked No. 2 behind only **Tyler Lockett**. Foster's 128 passer rating when targeted ranked fifth. Although he was a deep threat, Foster efficiently caught 13-of-16 passes thrown inside 15 Air Yards downfield and notched a 63% Success Rate.

The Bills won my customized Early-Down Success Rate metric battle in only one of their first eight games. (A one-point win over the Titans.) McDermott's team won EDSR in five of its final seven, however, and went 5-0 in those games.

Allen threw 12 interceptions with eight fumbles in 12 games. Only one of Allen's 12 picks came on passes delivered within 10 Air Yards. Seven came at depths between 18 and 23 yards. Allen struggled with accuracy at Wyoming and last year ranked 39th among 39 qualified quarterbacks in adjusted completion rate. Under pressure, he ranked dead last in completions (28%).

The Bills' attempted to deal with Allen's 2018 accuracy struggles by surrounding him with big receivers with large catch radiuses. 6-foot-5 **Kelvin Benjamin** – who has a 99th-percentile catch radius – was the Bills' most-targeted receiver before they cut him in November. 6-foot-2 second-round pick **Zay Jones** has a 93rd-percentile catch radius. But Jones' 42% Success Rate ranked 114th at the position, and his explosiveness quotient (YAS) ranked 94th.

The Bills went in a different direction this offseason, scrapping their size and catch radius fetish in favor of speed and quickness. Even if smaller, faster receivers can't outjump or outreach defensive backs, they tend to be more adept at creating separation. Smaller, quicker receivers also win more at the line of scrimmage. As the Panthers' defensive coordinator, McDermott witnessed how much 5-foot-9 **Steve Smith Sr.** helped **Cam Newton** early in his career. Newton won league MVP when **Kelvin Benjamin** tore his ACL and 5-foot-10 **Ted Ginn** caught ten touchdowns.

Last season, Benjamin ranked dead last in separation at time of the catch. **Robert Foster** is below the 50th percentile in catch radius but has a 91st-percentile 40-yard dash. **John Brown**'s arm length is in the 17th percentile, but he runs 4.34. **Cole Beasley** is tiny with short arms but has an 82nd-percentile burst score at PlayerProfiler.com. In an ideal configuration, Brown would play outside across from Foster with Beasley in the slot and Jones spelling them.

2018 Passing Performance

QB	1st Dwn	2nd Dwn	3rd Dwn	
Josh Allen	45%	37%	27%	Success Rate
	6.8	7.2	5.5	YPA
	77.2	75.0	49.0	Rating
Pass Rate	53%	50%	79%	
NFL AVG	53%	47%	36%	Success Rate
	7.7	7.3	6.9	YPA
	95.1	93.7	87.1	Rating
Pass Rate	53%	62%	80%	

2018 Rushing Performance

Offense	1st Dwn	2nd Dwn	3rd Dwn	
BUF	47%	41%	41%	Success Rate
	4.2	4.4	4.4	YPC
Run Rate	47%	50%	21%	
NFL AVG	48%	46%	51%	Success Rate
	4.5	4.4	4.3	YPC
Run Rate	47%	38%	20%	

One of the best things going for the 2019 Bills is their schedule of opposing run defenses. My projections show they face the seventh-softest run-defense slate, including the second easiest through Week 11. I was down on last year's Bills partly because they were indoctrinating a rookie quarterback while facing the league's toughest run-defense schedule. They indeed ranked 24th in rushing efficiency. This offseason, Buffalo upgraded its backfield depth with **Frank Gore**, **T.J. Yeldon**, and rookie **Devin Singletary**.

The 2016 Bills ranked 16th in Success Rate when targeting running backs on early downs, then dipped to 23rd in 2017. Last year, they ranked 32nd. Allen's Bills targeted running backs at the NFL's second-lowest rate on early-down plays. Buffalo's running backs also struggled on the ground, averaging 3.0 YPC with a 38% Success Rate that ranked 30th in the NFL.

(cont'd - see BUF-3)

2018 Offensive Advanced Metrics

Rank (from top: 1, 5, 10, 15, 20, 25, 30)

Metric	Rank
EDSR Off	27
30 & In Off	24
Red Zone Off	25
3rd Down Off	30
YPPA Off	30
YPPT Off	30
Offensive Efficiency	31
Pass Efficiency Off	31
Pass Pro Efficiency Off	23
RB Pass Eff Off	31
Rush Efficiency Off	24
Explosive Pass Off	20
Explosive Run Off	3

2018 Defensive Advanced Metrics

Rank (from top: 1, 5, 10, 15, 20, 25, 30)

Metric	Rank
EDSR Def	8
30 & In Def	15
Red Zone Def	27
3rd Down Def	3
YPPA Def	12
YPPT Def	23
Defensive Efficiency	2
Pass Efficiency Def	2
Pass Pro Efficiency Def	18
RB Pass Eff Def	16
Rush Efficiency Def	14
Explosive Pass Def	25
Explosive Run Def	25

2018 Weekly EDSR & Season Trending Performance

	1	2	3	4	5	6	7	8	9	10		12	13	14	15	16	17
RESULT	L	L	W	L	W	L	L	L	L	W		W	L	L	W	L	W
OPP	BAL	LAC	MIN	GB	TEN	HOU	IND	NE	CHI	NYJ		JAC	MIA	NYJ	DET	NE	MIA
SITE	A	H	A	A	H	A	A	H	H	A		H	A	H	H	A	H
MARGIN	-44	-11	21	-22	1	-7	-32	-19	-32	31		3	-4	-4	1	-12	25
PTS	3	20	27	0	13	13	5	6	9	41		24	17	23	14	12	42
OPP PTS	47	31	6	22	12	20	37	25	41	10		21	21	27	13	24	17

WEEK

EDSR by Wk
W=Green
L=Red

OFF/DEF
EDSR
Blue=OFF
(high=good)
Red=DEF
(low=good)

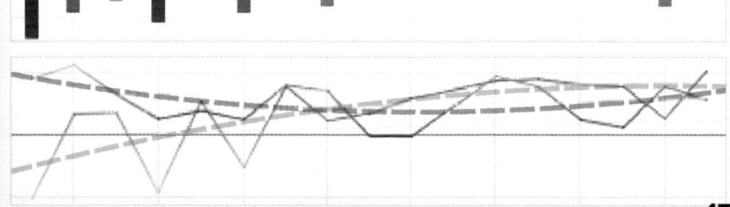

2018 Close Game Records

All 2018 Wins: **6**
FG Games (<=3 pts) W-L: **3-0**
FG Games Win %: **100% (#1)**
FG Games Wins (% of Total Wins): **50% (#3)**
1 Score Games (<=8 pts) W-L: **3-3**
1 Score Games Win %: **50% (#15)**
1 Score Games Wins (% of Total Wins): **50% (#15)**

2018 Critical & Game-Deciding Stats

TO Margin	-5
TO Given	32
INT Given	23
FUM Given	9
TO Taken	27
INT Taken	16
FUM Taken	11
Sack Margin	-5
Sacks	36
Sacks Allow	41
Return TD Margin	-4
Ret TDs	1
Ret TDs Allow	5
Penalty Margin	-17
Penalties	116
Opponent Penalties	99

Buffalo Bills 2019 Strength of Schedule In Detail (compared to 2018)

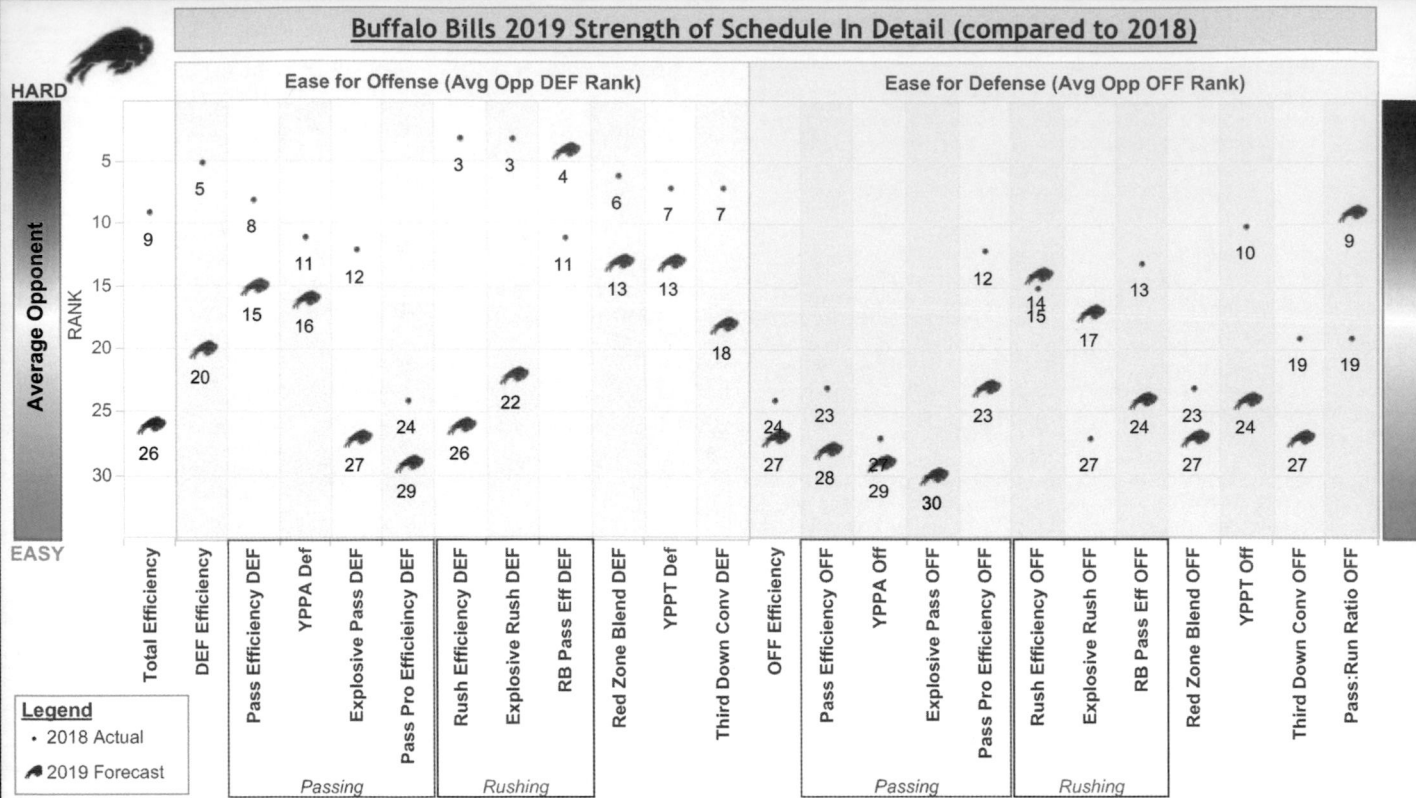

Ease for Offense (Avg Opp DEF Rank) — **Ease for Defense (Avg Opp OFF Rank)**

Average Opponent RANK — HARD (top) / EASY (bottom)

Legend
- • 2018 Actual
- 🏈 2019 Forecast

Offense categories (left to right): Total Efficiency, DEF Efficiency, Pass Efficiency DEF, YPPA Def, Explosive Pass DEF, Pass Pro Efficiency DEF *(Passing)*, Rush Efficiency DEF, Explosive Rush DEF, RB Pass Eff DEF *(Rushing)*, Red Zone Blend DEF, YPPT Def, Third Down Conv DEF

Defense categories (left to right): OFF Efficiency, Pass Efficiency OFF, YPPA Off, Explosive Pass OFF, Pass Pro Efficiency OFF *(Passing)*, Rush Efficiency OFF, Explosive Rush OFF, RB Pass Eff OFF *(Rushing)*, Red Zone Blend OFF, YPPT Off, Third Down Conv OFF, Pass:Run Ratio OFF

2019 v 2018 Schedule Variances* (OFF=Rank of DEF faced, 2019 vs 2018)

Pass OFF Rank	Pass OFF Blend Rk	Rush OFF Rk	Rush OFF Blend Rk	Pass DEF Rk	Pass DEF Blend Rk	Rush DEF Rk	Rush DEF Blend Rk
24	30	32	30	21	22	12	12

* **1**=Hardest Jump in 2019 schedule from 2018 (aka a much harder schedule in 2019), **32**=Easiest Jump in 2019 schedule from 2018 (aka a much easier schedule in 2019);
Pass Blend metric blends 4 metrics: Pass Efficiency, YPPA, Explosive Pass & Pass Rush; **Rush Blend** metric blends 3 metrics: Rush Efficiency, Explosive Rush & RB Targets

Team Records & Trends

BUF-3

	2018	2017	2016
Average line	6.5	2.0	-0.4
Average O/U line	40.7	43.4	44.7
Straight Up Record	6-10	9-7	7-9
Against the Spread Record	8-8	9-6	6-9
Over/Under Record	7-9	8-8	12-4
ATS as Favorite	1-2	5-1	2-4
ATS as Underdog	7-6	4-5	3-4
Straight Up Home	4-4	6-2	4-4
ATS Home	3-5	5-2	3-5
Over/Under Home	5-3	5-3	8-0
ATS as Home Favorite	1-2	4-0	2-2
ATS as a Home Dog	2-3	1-2	1-2
Straight Up Away	2-6	3-5	3-5
ATS Away	5-3	4-4	3-4
Over/Under Away	2-6	3-5	4-4
ATS Away Favorite	0-0	1-1	0-2
ATS Away Dog	5-3	3-3	2-2
Six Point Teaser Record	11-5	11-5	11-4
Seven Point Teaser Record	11-5	11-5	12-4
Ten Point Teaser Record	12-4	12-4	13-3

As a team, the Bills averaged 4.9 yards per carry on early downs with a 46% Success Rate. But that was in large part thanks to Allen's rushing prowess. The 2019 Bills' running backs were flat-out terrible.

Allen's wheels brought an entirely new dimension to Buffalo's rushing attack following the team's Week 11 bye. Unleashed on the ground by OC **Brian Daboll**, Allen went from never rushing for 40-plus yards in Buffalo's first six games to rushing for 90 or more in four of his final six. He also logged individual runs of 30-plus yards in four of those six. And Allen's rushing Success Rate was a dominant 74% at 11.3 yards per carry on 35 early-down runs.

As team, the Bills' most successful first-and-ten play occurred when Allen ran the ball (79%). Their most successful second-and-long plays were Allen runs. Their most successful second-and-medium plays were Allen runs.

*(cont'd - see **BUF-4**)*

2019 Rest Analysis

Team More Rest	2
Opp More Rest	1
Net Rest Edge	1
Week 2 Edge	0
Week 3 Edge	0
Week 4 Edge	0
Week 5 Edge	0
Week 7 Edge	7
Week 8 Edge	0
Week 9 Edge	-3
Week 10 Edge	0
Week 11 Edge	0
Week 12 Edge	0
Week 13 Edge	0
Week 14 Edge	3
Week 15 Edge	0
Week 16 Edge	0
Week 17 Edge	0

Health by Unit*

2018 Rk	2
2017 Rk	9
2018 v 2017 Rk	10
Off Rk	3
Def Rk	6
QB Rk	
RB Rk	17
WR Rk	2
TE Rk	15
Oline Rk	6
Dline Rk	17
LB Rk	12
DB Rk	4

Based on the work of Football Outsiders

2018 Weekly Betting Lines (wks 1-16)

1	2	3	4	5	7	8	9	10	11	12	13	14	15	16
NYJ	NYG	CIN	NE	TEN	MIA	PHI	WAS	CLE	MIA	DEN	DAL	BAL	PIT	NE
3	3	-4	6.5	5	-4.5	3	-3.5	7	2.5	-3	7.5	1	7	13

Avg = 2.9

Home Lines (wks 1-16)

3	4	7	8	9	12	14
-4 CIN	6.5 NE / -4.5 MIA	3 PHI	-3.5 WAS	-3 DEN		Avg = -1.0.6 BAL

Road Lines (wks 1-16)

1	2	5	10	11	13	15	16
3 NYJ	3 NYG	5 TEN	7 CLE	2.5 MIA	7.5 DAL	7 PIT	Avg = 6.0 NE

2018 Play Tendencies

All Pass %	54%
All Pass Rk	28
All Rush %	46%
All Rush Rk	5
1 Score Pass %	49%
1 Score Pass Rk	31
2017 1 Score Pass %	50%
2017 1 Score Pass Rk	31
2018 Pass Increase %	-1%
Pass Increase Rk	19
1 Score Rush %	51%
1 Score Rush Rk	2
Up Pass %	39%
Up Pass Rk	32
Up Rush %	61%
Up Rush Rk	1
Down Pass %	62%
Down Pass Rk	28
Down Rush %	38%
Down Rush Rk	5

2018 Down & Distance Tendencies

Down	Distance	Total Plays	Pass Rate	Run Rate	Play Success %
1	Short (1-3)	3	0%	100%	67%
	Med (4-7)	12	50%	50%	25%
	Long (8-10)	280	43%	57%	40%
	XL (11+)	13	62%	38%	31%
2	Short (1-3)	26	4%	96%	73%
	Med (4-7)	74	39%	61%	41%
	Long (8-10)	97	51%	49%	29%
	XL (11+)	47	57%	43%	19%
3	Short (1-3)	30	50%	50%	60%
	Med (4-7)	56	95%	5%	29%
	Long (8-10)	37	76%	24%	32%
	XL (11+)	38	74%	26%	11%
4	Short (1-3)	7	14%	86%	71%
	Med (4-7)	2	100%	0%	50%
	Long (8-10)	2	50%	50%	0%

Shotgun %:

Under Center	Shotgun
44%	56%

37% *AVG* 63%

Run Rate:

Under Center	Shotgun
70%	22%

68% *AVG* 23%

Pass Rate:

Under Center	Shotgun
30%	78%

32% *AVG* 77%

Buffalo Bills
2018 Play Analysis

Short Yardage Intelligence:

2nd and Short Run

Run Freq	Run Rk	NFL Run Freq Avg	Run 1D Rate	Run NFL 1D Avg
94%	1	65%	65%	68%

2nd and Short Pass

Pass Freq	Pass Rk	NFL Pass Freq Avg	Pass 1D Rate	Pass NFL 1D Avg
6%	32	35%	100%	56%

Most Frequent Play

Down	Distance	Play Type	Player	Total Plays	Play Success %
1	Short (1-3)	RUSH	Josh Allen	2	50%
	Med (4-7)	PASS	Kelvin Benjamin	2	0%
		RUSH	LeSean McCoy	2	0%
			Josh Allen	2	50%
	Long (8-10)	RUSH	LeSean McCoy	69	42%
	XL (11+)	PASS	Chris Ivory	2	0%
			Kelvin Benjamin	2	50%
		RUSH	LeSean McCoy	2	50%
			Josh Allen	2	50%
2	Short (1-3)	RUSH	LeSean McCoy	10	60%
	Med (4-7)	RUSH	LeSean McCoy	19	32%
	Long (8-10)	RUSH	LeSean McCoy	23	17%
	XL (11+)	RUSH	LeSean McCoy	8	25%
3	Short (1-3)	RUSH	Josh Allen	8	88%
	Med (4-7)	PASS	Kelvin Benjamin	5	40%
	Long (8-10)	PASS	Kelvin Benjamin	6	17%
	XL (11+)	PASS	Kelvin Benjamin	9	0%

Most Successful Play*

Down	Distance	Play Type	Player	Total Plays	Play Success %
1	Long (8-10)	RUSH	Josh Allen	19	79%
2	Short (1-3)	RUSH	Chris Ivory	6	83%
	Med (4-7)	RUSH	Josh Allen	6	83%
			Marcus Murphy	6	83%
	Long (8-10)	RUSH	Josh Allen	7	57%
	XL (11+)	RUSH	LeSean McCoy	8	25%
3	Short (1-3)	RUSH	Josh Allen	8	88%
	Med (4-7)	PASS	Kelvin Benjamin	5	40%
	Long (8-10)	PASS	Kelvin Benjamin	6	17%
	XL (11+)	PASS	Kelvin Benjamin	9	0%

Minimum 5 plays to qualify

2018 Weekly Snap Rates

Wk	Opp	Score	Zay Jones	Kelvin Benjamin	Charles Clay	LeSean McCoy	Robert Foster	Jason Croom	Chris Ivory	Logan Thomas	Andre Holmes	Isaiah McKenzie
1	BAL	L 47-3	60 (94%)	47 (73%)	40 (63%)	34 (53%)	16 (25%)	18 (28%)	7 (11%)	18 (28%)	11 (17%)	
2	LAC	L 31-20	51 (82%)	40 (65%)	43 (69%)	30 (48%)	29 (47%)	16 (26%)	9 (15%)	19 (31%)	36 (58%)	
3	MIN	W 27-6	42 (63%)	41 (61%)	40 (60%)		22 (33%)	25 (37%)	54 (81%)		31 (46%)	
4	GB	L 22-0	53 (91%)	35 (60%)	43 (74%)	36 (62%)	23 (40%)	12 (21%)	22 (38%)		27 (47%)	
5	TEN	W 13-12	50 (77%)	42 (65%)	49 (75%)	47 (72%)	8 (12%)	21 (32%)	18 (28%)	24 (37%)	33 (51%)	
6	HOU	L 20-13	58 (94%)	44 (71%)	44 (71%)	47 (76%)	2 (3%)	16 (26%)	16 (26%)	18 (29%)	33 (53%)	
7	IND	L 37-5	51 (91%)	44 (79%)	39 (70%)	2 (4%)		16 (29%)	36 (64%)	10 (18%)	38 (68%)	
8	NE	L 25-6	60 (94%)	49 (77%)	41 (64%)	46 (72%)		17 (27%)	19 (30%)	18 (28%)	35 (55%)	
9	CHI	L 41-9	79 (87%)	67 (74%)	8 (9%)	37 (41%)		42 (46%)	30 (33%)	47 (52%)	24 (26%)	
10	NYJ	W 41-10	62 (85%)	37 (51%)		49 (67%)	33 (45%)	44 (60%)		30 (41%)	5 (7%)	7 (10%)
12	JAC	W 24-21	55 (95%)	23 (40%)		37 (64%)	34 (59%)	29 (50%)	19 (33%)	31 (53%)	4 (7%)	33 (57%)
13	MIA	L 21-17	66 (92%)	42 (58%)	45 (63%)	54 (75%)	36 (50%)	25 (35%)	12 (17%)		1 (1%)	36 (50%)
14	NYJ	L 27-23	69 (91%)		42 (55%)	9 (12%)	73 (96%)		27 (36%)	36 (47%)		59 (78%)
15	DET	W 14-13	66 (97%)	41 (60%)			57 (84%)	32 (47%)			35 (51%)	
16	NE	L 24-12	61 (100%)		31 (51%)	59 (97%)	44 (72%)		26 (43%)		39 (64%)	
17	MIA	W 42-17	58 (94%)	29 (47%)	31 (50%)	58 (94%)	30 (48%)	31 (50%)	7 (11%)		13 (21%)	
	Grand Total		941 (89%)	511 (64%)	504 (60%)	490 (53%)	450 (53%)	387 (39%)	300 (35%)	284 (35%)	278 (36%)	222 (47%)

Personnel Groupings

Personnel	Team %	NFL Avg	Succ. %
1-1 [3WR]	70%	65%	39%
1-2 [2WR]	12%	17%	42%
2-1 [2WR]	12%	8%	48%
2-2 [1WR]	2%	3%	33%

Grouping Tendencies

Personnel	Pass Rate	Pass Succ. %	Run Succ. %
1-1 [3WR]	62%	36%	44%
1-2 [2WR]	39%	37%	46%
2-1 [2WR]	32%	47%	48%
2-2 [1WR]	10%	50%	32%

Red Zone Targets (min 3)

Receiver	All	Inside 5	6-10	11-20
Zay Jones	14	2	2	10
Kelvin Benjamin	6	2		4
Robert Foster	3	1		2
Andre Holmes	2	1		1
Charles Clay	2	1		1
LeSean McCoy	2			2

Red Zone Rushes (min 3)

Rusher	All	Inside 5	6-10	11-20
LeSean McCoy	22	4	6	12
Josh Allen	21	5	6	10
Chris Ivory	10	3	2	5
Marcus Murphy	8	1		7
Isaiah McKenzie	4		1	3

Early Down Target Rate

	RB	TE	WR
	24%	20%	56%
NFL AVG	*23%*	*21%*	*56%*

Overall Target Success %

	RB	TE	WR
	38%	43%	41%
	#31	#31	#32

Buffalo Bills 2018 Passing Recap & 2019 Outlook

I touched on **Josh Allen**'s positives, but he still needs substantial work. **Mike Leach** told me accuracy was the single-greatest quarterback skill, mainly because it can't be taught. Allen was a wild passer throughout college and was the league's least-accurate thrower in 2018. The Bills' hope is their rebuilt line and infusion of quickness and separation skills at receiver will keep Allen calm in the pocket to sit and deliver to spots where his receivers wind up rather than target moving players in tight coverage. If the Bills improve their target efficiency on running back passes, they will raise Allen's floor on passing plays. They should also incorporate more of what Allen does well and limit where he struggles. For example, Allen had his most 2018 success on stick-nod routes in the slot, delivering 15.1 yards per attempt and a 61% Success Rate. Allen's most-targeted route was the curl, however, where he managed 5.7 YPA and 45% success.

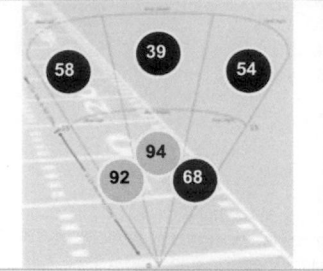

Josh Allen Rating All Downs

2018 Standard Passing Table

QB	Comp	Att	Comp %	Yds	YPA	TDs	INT	Sacks	Rating	Rk
Josh Allen	168	319	53%	2,065	6.5	10	12	28	68	47
Nathan Peterman	44	81	54%	297	3.7	1	7	7	31	55
NFL Avg			62%		7.0				87.5	

2018 Advanced Passing Table

QB	Success %	EDSR Passing Success %	20+ Yd Pass Gains	20+ Yd Pass %	30+ Yd Pass Gains	30+ Yd Pass %	Avg. Air Yds per Comp	Avg. YAC per Comp	20+ Air Yd Comp	20+ Air Yd %
Josh Allen	37%	41%	30	9.0%	13	4.0%	6.7	5.6	17	5%
Nathan Peterman	30%	31%	3	4.0%			3.0	3.8		0%
NFL Avg	44%	48%	29.5	8.4%	12.5	3.7%	5.8	5.1	14.5	6%

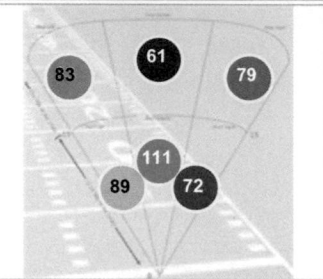

Josh Allen Rating Early Downs

Interception Rates by Down

Yards to Go	1st Dwn	2nd Dwn	3rd Dwn	4th Dwn	Total
1 & 2			0.0%		0.0%
3, 4, 5	0.0%	0.0%	7.1%	0.0%	4.0%
6 - 9		2.9%	0.0%		1.4%
10 - 14	2.4%	7.7%	4.8%	0.0%	3.8%
15+	14.3%	0.0%	6.7%		5.6%
Total	3.0%	3.8%	3.8%	0.0%	3.4%

3rd Down Passing - Short of Sticks Analysis

QB	Avg. Yds to Go	Avg. YIA (of Comp)	Avg Yds Short	Short of Sticks Rate	Short Rk
Josh Allen	8.6	6.8	-1.8	60%	24
NFL Avg	7.8	6.4	-1.4	60%	

Air Yds vs YAC

Air Yds %	YAC %	Rk
51%	49%	26
53%	48%	

2018 Receiving Recap & 2019 Outlook

The majority of Allen's 2018 targets went to slot receivers, primarily **Zay Jones** (55). Jones is likely to play more outside with **Cole Beasley** in Buffalo. Capitalizing on Allen's connection with **Robert Foster** is critical after Foster produced a 60% Success Rate and 15.8 yards per target on 2018 slot routes despite predominately running deep routes out wide.

Player *Min 50 Targets	Targ	Comp %	YPA	Rating	Success %	Success Rk	Missed YPA Rk	YAS % Rk	YTS % Rk	TDs
Zay Jones	102	55%	6.4	80.2	42%	114	169	94	38	8
Kelvin Benjamin	62	37%	5.7	22.6	32%	129	185	28	122	1

Directional Passer Rating Delivered

Receiver	Short Left	Short Middle	Short Right	Deep Left	Deep Middle	Deep Right	Player Total
Zay Jones	91	52	94	128	48	36	80
Kelvin Benjamin	37	48	77	38	29	0	23
LeSean McCoy	90	3	79			119	76
Robert Foster	114	104	99	81	39	149	114
Charles Clay	93	98	25	119	40	40	60
Jason Croom	67	114	57	0		135	71
Isaiah McKenzie	97	64	15	83	77	110	63
Andre Holmes	94	119	85	47	83	4	43
Chris Ivory	104	83	92				95
Logan Thomas	94	56	81		40	94	80
Deonte Thompson	73		90	0	40		3
Terrelle Pryor		17	40	40		40	0
Jeremy Kerley	56	40	83				56
Team Total	86	60	71	57	31	57	65

2018 Rushing Recap & 2019 Outlook

Buffalo's running back picture is significantly muddled given the additions of **Frank Gore**, **T.J. Yeldon**, and third-round pick **Devin Singletary**. **LeSean McCoy** is on his last legs and probably won't be a Bill in 2020. 36-year-old Gore outproduced McCoy in 2018, finishing top six among 50 qualified running backs in percentage of carries that gained five or more yards. Gore also produced the fourth-lowest rate of carries that produced three yards or less.

Yards per Carry by Direction

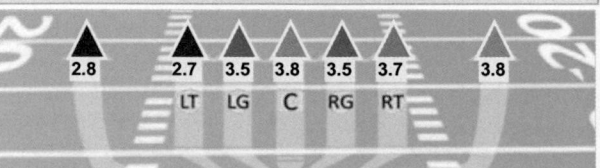

	LT	LG	C	RG	RT	
2.8	2.7	3.5	3.8	3.5	3.7	3.8

Directional Run Frequency

	LT	LG	C	RG	RT	
7%	8%	16%	31%	21%	11%	6%

Player *Min 50 Rushes	Rushes	YPC	Success %	Success Rk	Missed YPA Rk	YTS % Rk	YAS % Rk	Early Down Success %	Early Down Success Rk	TDs
LeSean McCoy	161	3.2	37%	70	65	12	60	37%	67	3
Chris Ivory	115	3.3	44%	51	55	4	63	43%	55	1
Marcus Murphy	52	4.8	42%	57	69	65	71	46%	41	0

BUF-4

And their most successful third-and-short plays were Allen runs. At 6-foot-5, 237, Allen presents a large target to hit, and rushing him with such frequency is a risky proposition going forward. But his dual-threat ability is a difference-making weapon.

Daboll still has fundamental play-calling problems to fix. Daboll did the best he could to hide Allen's erratic arm as a rookie, instead relying on **LeSean McCoy** and **Chris Ivory**. But McCoy and Ivory were two of the least successful runners in the league, and no real in-season adjustment was ever made.

On early downs in one-score games, the Bills ran the ball on a league-high 60% of play calls. League average is a 48% early-down, one-score run rate. When handing off to running backs on such plays, Buffalo averaged a measly 3.2 yards per carry with a 40% Success Rate, fifth worst in the NFL.

(cont'd - see BUF-5)

Buffalo Bills Fantasy Corner

2018 third-round pick **Mark Andrews** stepped forward as the Ravens' lead tight end as a rookie, finishing fifth at the position in yards per route run (2.01) and establishing the best rapport with **Lamar Jackson** among Baltimore's pass catchers. Andrews' 552 yards were fifth most by any rookie tight end in the last decade, and his 16.2 yards per catch ranked second behind only **O.J. Howard**'s 16.6 last year. Andrews also led the Ravens in targets (7) in their playoff loss to the Chargers. 2018 first-round pick **Hayden Hurst**'s role will expand after an injury-plagued rookie campaign, but Andrews is the preferred late-round fantasy dart. With 4.67 speed at 6-foot-5, 256, Andrews is a field stretcher with big-play ability in the seams.

- Evan Silva

Division History: Season Wins & 2019 Projection

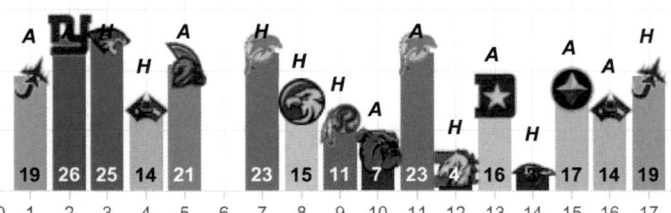

Rank of 2019 Defensive Pass Efficiency Faced by Week

| 19 | 26 | 25 | 14 | 21 | | 23 | 15 | 11 | 7 | 23 | 4 | 16 | 3 | 17 | 14 | 19 |

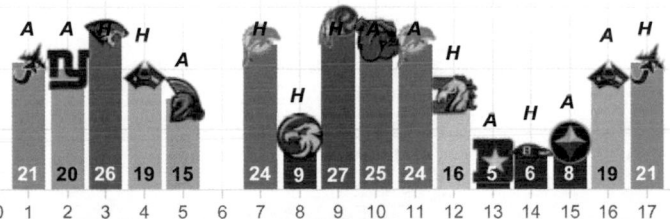

Rank of 2019 Defensive Rush Efficiency Faced by Week

| 21 | 20 | 26 | 19 | 15 | | 24 | 9 | 27 | 25 | 24 | 16 | 5 | 6 | 8 | 19 | 21 |

2018 Situational Usage by Player & Position

Usage Rate by Score

		Being Blown Out (14+)	Down Big (9-13)	One Score	Large Lead (9-13)	Blowout Lead (14+)
RUSH	LeSean McCoy	14%	6%	66%		14%
	Chris Ivory	19%	2%	55%	3%	22%
	Zay Jones	100%				
	Marcus Murphy	27%		38%		35%
	Isaiah McKenzie			80%		20%
	Terrelle Pryor	100%				
	Total	**18%**	**4%**	**58%**	**1%**	**20%**
PASS	LeSean McCoy	31%	12%	52%		5%
	Chris Ivory	55%		35%		10%
	Zay Jones	36%	8%	42%	2%	12%
	Marcus Murphy	94%				6%
	Kelvin Benjamin	35%	9%	49%		7%
	Robert Foster	22%	6%	56%	3%	14%
	Charles Clay	33%	9%	55%		3%
	Isaiah McKenzie	13%	9%	74%		4%
	Jason Croom	52%	6%	36%	3%	3%
	Andre Holmes	50%	14%	14%		23%
	Terrelle Pryor	50%		25%		25%
	Deonte Thompson	25%		75%		
	Jeremy Kerley	50%		50%		
	Total	**38%**	**8%**	**44%**	**1%**	**9%**

Share of Offensive Plays by Type

	LeSean McCoy	Chris Ivory	Zay Jones	Marcus Murphy	Kelvin Benjamin	Robert Foster	Charles Clay	Isaiah McKenzie	Jason Croom	Andre Holmes	Terrelle Pryor	Deonte Thompson	Jeremy Kerley	Patrick DiMarco
RUSH	47%	34%	0%	15%			3%				0%			0%
PASS	11%	5%	22%	5%	14%	9%	8%	6%	8%	6%	2%	2%	1%	1%
ALL	28%	18%	12%	9%	8%	5%	4%	4%	4%	3%	1%	1%	1%	1%

Positional Target Distribution vs NFL Average

		NFL Wide				Team Only			
		Left	Middle	Right	Total	Left	Middle	Right	Total
Deep	WR	33%	17%	31%	**81%**	40%	17%	26%	**83%**
	TE	5%	4%	7%	**16%**	4%	2%	9%	**15%**
	RB	1%	0%	2%	**4%**			2%	**2%**
	All	**39%**	**22%**	**39%**	**100%**	**44%**	**19%**	**37%**	**100%**
Short	WR	20%	14%	21%	**55%**	18%	7%	17%	**42%**
	TE	6%	6%	8%	**20%**	6%	7%	16%	**30%**
	RB	10%	5%	10%	**25%**	14%	3%	11%	**28%**
	All	**36%**	**25%**	**39%**	**100%**	**38%**	**17%**	**44%**	**100%**
Total		**37%**	**24%**	**39%**	**100%**	**40%**	**18%**	**42%**	**100%**

Positional Success Rates vs NFL Average

		NFL Wide				Team Only			
		Left	Middle	Right	Total	Left	Middle	Right	Total
Deep	WR	40%	50%	40%	**42%**	33%	35%	28%	**32%**
	TE	43%	54%	42%	**46%**	50%	0%	33%	**33%**
	RB	38%	33%	41%	**39%**			100%	**100%**
	All	**40%**	**50%**	**40%**	**43%**	**35%**	**32%**	**33%**	**34%**
Short	WR	55%	61%	53%	**56%**	44%	56%	43%	**46%**
	TE	55%	62%	55%	**57%**	47%	72%	33%	**45%**
	RB	46%	54%	46%	**48%**	49%	38%	31%	**41%**
	All	**53%**	**59%**	**51%**	**54%**	**46%**	**60%**	**36%**	**44%**
Total		**50%**	**58%**	**49%**	**52%**	**43%**	**51%**	**35%**	**41%**

2018 Detailed Analytics Summary
Success by Play Type & Primary Personnel Groupings

Type	1-1 [3WR]	1-2 [2WR]	2-1 [2WR]	2-2 [1WR]	2-0 [3WR]	1-3 [1WR]	0-0 [5WR]	1-0 [4WR]	0-1 [4WR]	2-3 [0WR]	ALL
PASS	36% (433)	37% (49)	47% (38)	50% (2)	33% (6)	0% (1)	20% (5)	0% (2)	100% (1)		36% (537)
RUSH	44% (270)	46% (76)	48% (79)	32% (19)	50% (8)	50% (6)	0% (1)	0% (1)		0% (1)	44% (461)
All	39% (703)	42% (125)	48% (117)	33% (21)	43% (14)	43% (7)	17% (6)	0% (3)	100% (1)	0% (1)	40% (998)

Format Success Rate (Total # of Plays)

Receiving Success by Top-4 Personnel Groupings
(Min 50 targets)

POS	Player	1-1 [3WR]	2-1 [2WR]	1-2 [2WR]	4 Grp Total
WR	Zay Jones	40% (84) 6.5, 82.7	62% (13) 7.8, 111.7	0% (2) 0.0, 39.6	42% (99) 6.5, 84.9
	Kelvin Benjamin	29% (49) 5.0, 24.3	25% (4) 2.0, 39.6	71% (7) 12.0, 72.0	33% (60) 5.7, 27.7

Format Line 1: Success Rate (Total # of Plays) Line 2: YPA, Passer Rating

Rushing Success by Top-4 Personnel Groupings
(Min 25 carries)

Rusher (Last, First)	1-1 [3WR]	2-1 [2WR]	1-2 [2WR]	2-2 [1WR]	4 Grp Total
McCoy LeSean	35% (97) 3.2	33% (27) 2.3	41% (27) 4.5	33% (6) 0.7	36% (157) 3.2
Ivory Chris	45% (53) 3.8	46% (24) 3.1	46% (24) 3.6	50% (2) -0.5	46% (103) 3.5
Allen Josh	55% (56) 7.2	67% (18) 4.8	88% (8) 14.1	50% (4) 1.8	60% (86) 7.1
Murphy Marcus	36% (33) 5.0	63% (8) 4.0	43% (7) 5.3	100% (1) 5.0	43% (49) 4.9

Format Line 1: Success Rate (Total # of Plays) Line 2: YPC

Passing by Coverage Scheme

M2M	40% (213) 6.1, 69.5
Zone	41% (188) 7.5, 64.5
Screen	42% (43) 3.9, 82.8
Combo	20% (10) 2.1, 0.0

Passing by Route

Curl	45% (71) 5.7, 71.7
Out	48% (42) 4.8, 77.6
Screen	36% (39) 3.6, 81.6
Dig	41% (34) 8.6, 44.7
Flat	46% (24) 4.2, 89.1
Slant	35% (20) 3.7, 46.7

Throw Types

Level 1	43% (293) 5.6, 74.9
Level 2	40% (124) 7.4, 53.0
Level 3	28% (43) 10.7, 83.3
Shovel	80% (5) 6.4, 93.3
Sidearm	60% (5) 4.8, 86.7

QB Drop Types

3 Step	38% (218) 6.3, 63.9
5 Step	43% (91) 7.5, 47.2
0/1 Step	45% (80) 4.8, 96.9
7 Step	48% (31) 11.4, 87.2
Basic Screen	43% (23) 4.7, 86.4
Designed Rollout Right	33% (18) 5.0, 46.1

QB State at Pass

Planted	43% (345) 7.0, 72.8
Moving	29% (55) 5.6, 46.6
Shuffling	39% (44) 3.8, 71.1

Play Action

	Play Action	No P/A
Under Center	45% (69) 9.2, 76.7	54% (41) 8.4, 106.0
Shotgun	33% (36) 3.3, 71.4	40% (329) 6.0, 62.0
ALL	41% (105) 7.2, 74.9	41% (370) 6.3, 66.9

Run Types

Outside Zone	39% (94) 3.0
Inside Zone	51% (76) 4.4
Lead	33% (45) 2.4
Power	32% (38) 3.6
Stretch	25% (28) 2.0
Pitch	60% (10) 3.9

BUF-5

Due to their lack of early-down success, the Bills faced a league-high average of 8.3 yards to go on third-down plays. They called the league's most second-down runs with ten or more yards to go (45%), producing just a 21% Success Rate. Their passes on second and long were over 57% more successful and averaged 7.6 yards per attempt, nearly three more yards than the Bills averaged on second-and-long runs.

Daboll's notion of "hiding" or "protecting" his quarterback with conservative early-down play calling resulted only in inefficiency. And Buffalo's decision to run so frequently became even more inexplicable when you consider how tough their run-defense schedule was.

Perhaps Daboll will feel more confident calling pass plays with Allen in his second year and more receiving talent. The Bills also made major upgrades on the offensive line. **Mitch Morse** is a colossal upgrade on **Russell Bodine** at center. They also landed versatile T/G **Ty Nsekhe**, G/C **Spencer Long**, G/C **Jon Feliciano**, and second-round RT **Cody Ford**. On paper, the Bills now have two solid tackles and are strong at center.

Defensively, Buffalo is still probably one edge rusher from reaching true dominance after finishing 18th in pass-rush efficiency in 2018. Underrated RE **Jerry Hughes** returns, but last year's club ranked 21st in quarterback hits and 26th in sacks. Still an ascending unit, McDermott has turned Buffalo from the bottom-ten defense he inherited to 2017's No. 15 unit and 2018's No. 2 group. The defense should take another step forward in 2019 against the league's sixth-softest schedule of opposing offenses.

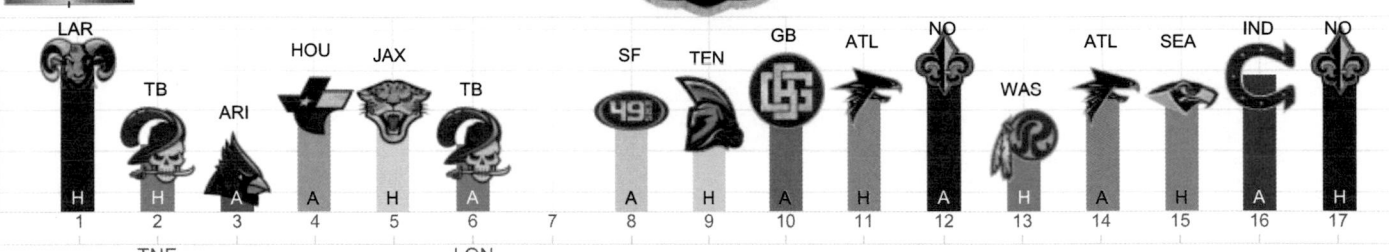

Carolina Panthers

Coaches (Prior Yrs)

Head Coach:
Ron Rivera (7 yrs)
Offensive Coordinator:
Norv Turner (1 yr)
Defensive Coordinator:
Eric Washington (1 yr)

2019 Forecast

Wins	Div Rank
7.5	**#3**

Past Records

2018: 7-9
2017: 11-5
2016: 6-10

EASY   HARD

LAR	TB	ARI	HOU	JAX	TB		SF	TEN	GB	ATL	NO	WAS	ATL	SEA	IND	NO
H	H	A	A	H	A	A	A	H	A	H	A	H	A	H	A	H
1	2	3	4	5	6	7	8	9	10	11	12	13	14	15	16	17

TNF   LON

Key Players Lost

Player	New
Chandler Catanzaro (K)	NYJ
Damiere Byrd (WR)	ARI
David Mayo (ILB)	SF
Devin Funchess (WR)	IND
Garrett Gilbert (QB)	CLE
Jonathan Stewart (RB)	Retired
Julius Peppers (DE)	Retired
Kenjon Barner (RB)	ATL
Matt Kalil (LT)	HOU
Thomas Davis (OLD)	LAC

Average Line	# Games Favored	# Games Underdog
0.6	8	7

2019 Carolina Panthers Overview

Sometimes, teams have seasons that seem bigger than others. 2019 is a *huge* season for the Panthers. Coach **Ron Rivera** particularly needs a big year. Since their 2015 Super Bowl appearance, Rivera's Panthers have zero playoff wins. Defensive-minded Rivera has eight years under his belt in a world of offensive-minded head coaches under a new owner with a quarterback on the back nine of his prime.

And you know a defensive-minded head coach is feeling heat when he takes over play calling as Rivera did from **Eric Washington** following Carolina's Week 13 loss to Tampa Bay, his team's fourth loss in a row. 6-6 at the time, the Panthers went on to lose their next three games.

Although Washington remains on staff, Rivera will continue calling Carolina's defensive plays. New owner **David Tepper** put the Panthers' play calling on the spot when stating, "We have one of the best offensive coaches (**Norv Turner**) and defensive coaches (Rivera) that there are. Hopefully, the team together calling plays will result in a pretty successful year."

It's also a huge season for **Cam Newton**, the Panthers' only-ever franchise quarterback coming off a superb season in Norv's first year. Cam's contract initially had detrimental salary cap implications in the first four years, but the Panthers would carry only $2 million in dead cap by moving on after this season. And Newton's contract is up in 2021.

Newton's recurring shoulder problems necessitated the Panthers invest more into their backup quarterback. Enter third-round pick **Will Grier** out of West Virginia. Carolina's willingness to spend top-100 draft capital at quarterback suggests they're at least beginning to think about their post-Cam future. Prior to Greer, Carolina hadn't drafted a quarterback in any round since 2011. And that was Cam himself.

(cont'd - see CAR2)

Key Free Agents/ Trades Added

Player	AAV (MM)
Bruce Irvin (DE)	$4
Gerald McCoy (DT)	$8
Matt Paradis (C)	$9.6

Drafted Players

Rd	Pk	Player (College)
1	16	DE - Brian Burns (Florida State)
2	37	OT - Greg Little (Ole Miss)
3*	100	QB - Will Grier (West Virginia)
4	115	LB - Christian Miller (Alabama)
5	154	RB - Jordan Scarlett (Florida)
6*	212	OT - Dennis Daley (South Carolina)
7	237	WR - Terry Godwin (Georgia)

Regular Season Wins: Past & Current Proj

Forecast 2019 Wins	7.5
2018 Wins	7
Forecast 2018 Wins	9
2017 Wins	11
2016 Wins	6
2015 Wins	15

1 3 5 7 9 11 13 15

Lineup & Cap Hits

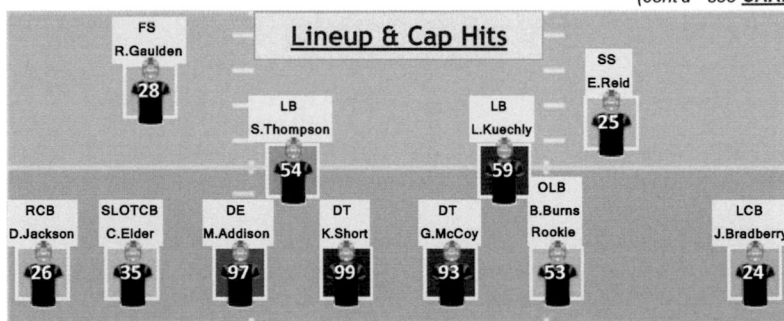

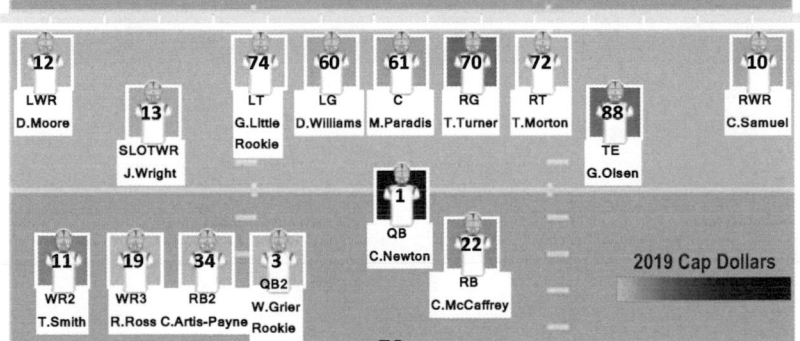

2019 Cap Dollars

2019 Unit Spending

All DEF   All OFF

Positional Spending

	Rank	Total	2017 Rk
All OFF	15	$98.96M	14
QB	13	$25.20M	16
OL	11	$39.49M	14
RB	17	$7.49M	16
WR	26	$16.57M	27
TE	11	$10.20M	12
All DEF	13	$91.73M	9
DL	1	$49.32M	4
LB	9	$24.64M	13
CB	30	$9.18M	23
S	20	$8.59M	20

After drafting Grier, GM **Marty Hurney** explained the quarterback position is so valuable that if you find a guy you like, you have to pull the trigger. He said Grier had "it" factor and was extremely talented with plenty of arm strength. Grier is an older prospect – 24, three years older than **Kyler Murray** – and the theoretical time to maximize Grier would be during his cheap four-year rookie deal, which converges with the end of Newton's contract. Hurney nevertheless insisted Grier was purely a depth pick.

Newton can put to bed any concerns about his Carolina future and earn a pricey third contract if his ascension continues under Norv. The Panthers improved their offensive Early Down Success Rate from 21st in 2017 to 9th last year, largely because of Cam's strong passing performance despite a shoulder injury that plagued him in the second half of the year. He was shut down after 14 starts and required offseason surgery. Newton admitted he was "weak, vulnerable, scared, and afraid" because of his shoulder discomfort.

"I couldn't throw the ball further than 30 years, no lie. So I was trying to keep up with it as much as possible until the wheels fell off. I felt like defenses were exposing me because they knew I couldn't throw the ball downfield."

Newton first landed on the injury report after the Panthers' thrilling Week 7 comeback win over the Eagles. Down 17-0, Cam led Carolina to 21 fourth-quarter points. In Week 8, backup **Taylor Heinicke** was inserted for a Hail Mary at the end of the first half. In Weeks 9-10, Cam attempted only two passes traveling 20-plus Air Yards downfield.

The Panthers were on a 5-1 run entering Week 10 against the Steelers, in which Newton took a brutal hit to his throwing shoulder. Carolina didn't win another game started by Cam. They began the season 6-2 with Newton at the controls, and finished 0-6.

Newton did attempt more 20-plus-yard passes from Week 10 onward (18) than in the season's initial eight weeks (15). But his downfield passing efficiency in both timeframes was terrible with a 20% Success Rate and 5.6 yards per attempt in Carolina's opening eight games, and a 28% Success Rate at 7.5 YPA over Newton's final six starts.

Film review confirmed Newton was correct saying defenses began to sit on his routes because they knew he couldn't go deep. His Success Rate on passes traveling 15-plus yards in the air was 10% lower with 2.2 fewer yards per attempt than on Newton's shorter throws. Defenses geared up to stop his short passes and dared Cam to go long more and more as the year progressed.

2018 Passing Performance

QB	1st Dwn	2nd Dwn	3rd Dwn	
Cam Newton	54%	53%	38%	Success Rate
	7.1	8.1	5.9	YPA
	96.0	97.7	87.3	Rating
Pass Rate	57%	63%	72%	
NFL AVG	53%	47%	36%	Success Rate
	7.7	7.3	6.9	YPA
	95.1	93.7	87.1	Rating
Pass Rate	53%	62%	80%	

2018 Rushing Performance

Offense	1st Dwn	2nd Dwn	3rd Dwn	
CAR	54%	53%	51%	Success Rate
	5.7	4.6	3.5	YPC
Run Rate	43%	37%	28%	
NFL AVG	48%	46%	51%	Success Rate
	4.5	4.4	4.3	YPC
Run Rate	47%	38%	20%	

Cam's passes 1-9 yards downfield dropped in Success Rate from 66% in his first eight starts to 54% in the final six.

Under Norv and QBs coach **Scott Turner**'s tutelage, Newton nevertheless made improvements in early-down passing efficiency. 2017 Cam posted a 50% Success Rate on first-down throws and 45% on second-down passes. The pre-Turner Panthers tried to protect Cam by running on 54% of first-down plays and ran at a league-high 53% rate on second downs, over 10% above league average.

Last year's strategy changed, with some of my own personal offseason influence. After the Panthers passed on 56% of their first-half first downs in a Week 1 win over Dallas, Tepper publicly confirmed they were proactively

(cont'd - see CAR-3)

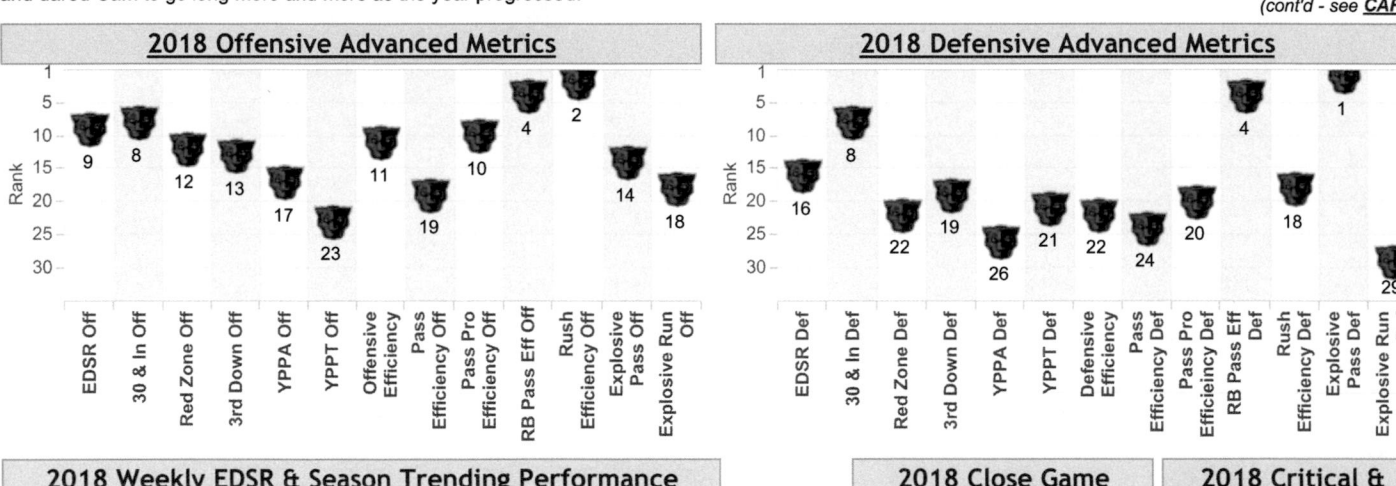

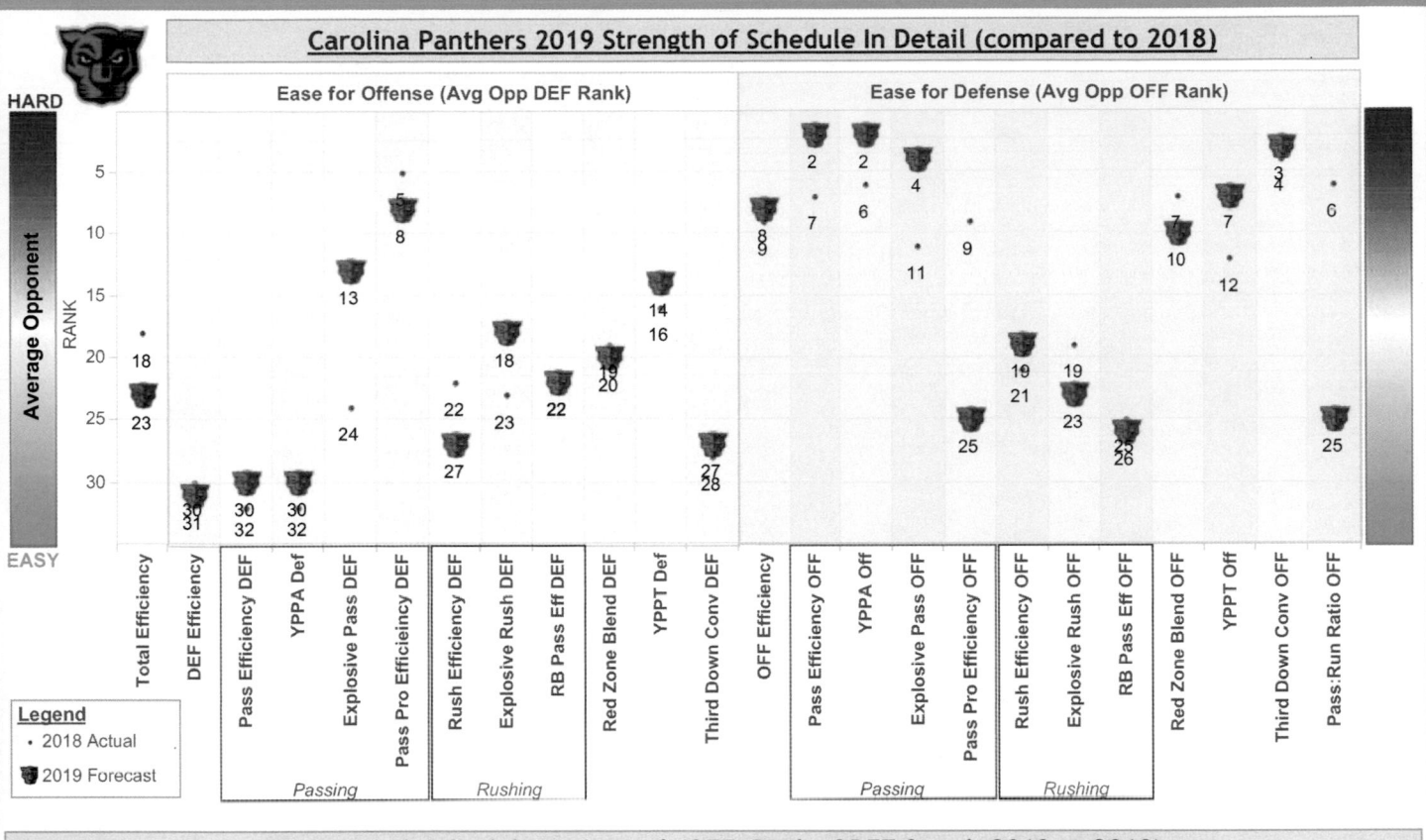

Carolina Panthers 2019 Strength of Schedule In Detail (compared to 2018)

HARD ... **EASY**

Average Opponent — RANK

Ease for Offense (Avg Opp DEF Rank)

Category	2019 Forecast	2018 Actual
Total Efficiency	23	18
DEF Efficiency	30	31
Pass Efficiency DEF	30	32
YPPA Def	30	32
Explosive Pass DEF	13	24
Pass Pro Efficiency DEF	8	5
Rush Efficiency DEF	27	22
Explosive Rush DEF	18	23
RB Pass Eff DEF	22	
Red Zone Blend DEF	19/20	
YPPT Def	14/16	
Third Down Conv DEF	27/28	

Ease for Defense (Avg Opp OFF Rank)

Category	2019 Forecast	2018 Actual
OFF Efficiency	8/9	
Pass Efficiency OFF	2	7
YPPA Off	2	6
Explosive Pass OFF	4	11
Pass Pro Efficiency OFF	9	
Rush Efficiency OFF	19/21	
Explosive Rush OFF	19/23	
RB Pass Eff OFF	25/26	
Red Zone Blend OFF	7	10
YPPT Off	7	12
Third Down Conv OFF	3/4	
Pass:Run Ratio OFF	25	6

Passing / Rushing

Legend
- • 2018 Actual
- 🛡 2019 Forecast

2019 v 2018 Schedule Variances* (OFF=Rank of DEF faced, 2019 vs 2018)

Pass OFF Rank	Pass OFF Blend Rk	Rush OFF Rk	Rush OFF Blend Rk	Pass DEF Rk	Pass DEF Blend Rk	Rush DEF Rk	Rush DEF Blend Rk
10	12	22	14	10	14	11	16

* **1**=Hardest Jump in 2019 schedule from 2018 (aka a much harder schedule in 2019), **32**=Easiest Jump in 2019 schedule from 2018 (aka a much easier schedule in 2019);
Pass Blend metric blends 4 metrics: Pass Efficiency, YPPA, Explosive Pass & Pass Rush;   **Rush Blend** metric blends 3 metrics: Rush Efficiency, Explosive Rush & RB Targets

Team Records & Trends

CAR-3

	2018	2017	2016
Average line	0.3	-1.5	-1.4
Average O/U line	46.9	44.2	47.0
Straight Up Record	7-9	11-5	6-10
Against the Spread Record	7-9	9-7	6-9
Over/Under Record	8-8	8-7	6-9
ATS as Favorite	3-5	4-5	3-7
ATS as Underdog	4-3	5-2	3-2
Straight Up Home	5-3	6-2	4-4
ATS Home	5-3	4-4	3-5
Over/Under Home	5-3	4-3	2-6
ATS as Home Favorite	3-2	2-4	3-4
ATS as a Home Dog	2-1	2-0	0-1
Straight Up Away	2-6	5-3	2-6
ATS Away	2-6	5-3	3-4
Over/Under Away	3-5	4-4	4-3
ATS Away Favorite	0-3	2-1	0-3
ATS Away Dog	2-2	3-2	3-1
Six Point Teaser Record	10-4	11-5	9-5
Seven Point Teaser Record	12-3	12-3	11-5
Ten Point Teaser Record	13-1	14-2	12-4

trying to be more aggressive on such plays. Newton went on to pass on 57% of his first-down plays in 2018, a huge increase on his 2017 rate. Newton passed on 63% of second downs, a 47% hike over his 2017 percentage. And it worked.

Increased early-down passing not only allowed Newton to attack defenses that were in run-pass conflict, it benefited Carolina's rushing attack. Cam also targeted higher-percentage routes on early downs. His deep target rate on first downs dropped from 19% to 17%, and on second downs from 19% to 14%. The shorter depths of target went beyond simply checking down to **Christian McCaffrey**, however. Panthers wide receivers saw their first-down deep target rate drop from 30% to 23%. On second down, it fell from 24% to 15%.

The Panthers did well to get the ball out of Cam's hands at the quickest rate of his career, and he

*(cont'd - see **CAR-4**)*

2019 Rest Analysis

Team More Rest	3
Opp More Rest	1
Net Rest Edge	2
Week 2 Edge	0
Week 3 Edge	3
Week 4 Edge	0
Week 5 Edge	0
Week 6 Edge	0
Week 8 Edge	7
Week 9 Edge	0
Week 10 Edge	0
Week 11 Edge	0
Week 12 Edge	0
Week 13 Edge	0
Week 14 Edge	-3
Week 15 Edge	0
Week 16 Edge	1
Week 17 Edge	0

Health by Unit*

2018 Rk	26
2017 Rk	7
2018 v 2017 Rk	
Off Rk	25
Def Rk	27
QB Rk	22
RB Rk	8
WR Rk	11
TE Rk	25
Oline Rk	
Dline Rk	10
LB Rk	6
DB Rk	

Based on the work of Football Outsiders

2018 Weekly Betting Lines (wks 1-16)

1	2	3	4	5	6	8	9	10	11	12	13	14	15	16
LAR	TB	ARI	HOU	JAX	TB	SF	TEN	GB	ATL	NO	WAS	ATL	SEA	IND
3	-6	-3	4.5	-3.5	-2.5	2.5	-3	5.5	-2	9	-5	4.5	-1.5	6

Avg = 0.6

Home Lines (wks 1-16)

1	2	5	9	11	13	15
3 LAR	-6 TB	-3.5 JAX	-3 TEN	-2 ATL	-5 WAS	-1.5

Avg = -2.6

Road Lines (wks 1-16)

3	4	6	8	10	12	14	16
-3 ARI	4.5 HOU	-2.5 TB	2.5 SF	5.5 GB	9 NO	4 ATL	IND

Avg = 3.3

Carolina Panthers 2018 Play Analysis

2018 Play Tendencies

All Pass %	59%
All Pass Rk	16
All Rush %	41%
All Rush Rk	17
1 Score Pass %	57%
1 Score Pass Rk	18
2017 1 Score Pass %	53%
2017 1 Score Pass Rk	27
2018 Pass Increase %	5%
Pass Increase Rk	9
1 Score Rush %	43%
1 Score Rush Rk	15
Up Pass %	45%
Up Pass Rk	24
Up Rush %	55%
Up Rush Rk	9
Down Pass %	74%
Down Pass Rk	3
Down Rush %	26%
Down Rush Rk	30

2018 Down & Distance Tendencies

Down	Distance	Total Plays	Pass Rate	Run Rate	Play Success %
1	Short (1-3)	4	0%	100%	75%
	Med (4-7)	13	54%	46%	54%
	Long (8-10)	303	50%	50%	55%
	XL (11+)	11	73%	27%	18%
2	Short (1-3)	40	35%	65%	73%
	Med (4-7)	69	51%	49%	57%
	Long (8-10)	79	66%	34%	44%
	XL (11+)	40	68%	33%	33%
3	Short (1-3)	37	41%	59%	65%
	Med (4-7)	43	77%	23%	42%
	Long (8-10)	27	85%	15%	33%
	XL (11+)	26	81%	19%	4%
4	Short (1-3)	4	50%	50%	75%
	Med (4-7)	5	80%	20%	80%

Shotgun %:

Under Center	Shotgun
24%	76%

37% AVG 63%

Run Rate:

Under Center	Shotgun
68%	26%

68% AVG 23%

Pass Rate:

Under Center	Shotgun
32%	74%

32% AVG 77%

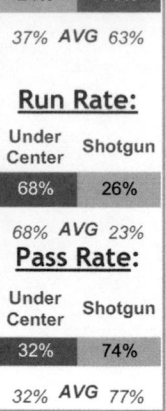

Short Yardage Intelligence:

2nd and Short Run

Run Freq	Run Rk	NFL Run Freq Avg	Run 1D Rate	Run NFL 1D Avg
54%	27	65%	85%	68%

2nd and Short Pass

Pass Freq	Pass Rk	NFL Pass Freq Avg	Pass 1D Rate	Pass NFL 1D Avg
46%	5	35%	65%	56%

Most Frequent Play

Down	Distance	Play Type	Player	Total Plays	Play Success %
1	Short (1-3)	RUSH	Christian McCaffrey	2	100%
	Med (4-7)	RUSH	Christian McCaffrey	5	60%
	Long (8-10)	RUSH	Christian McCaffrey	92	57%
	XL (11+)	PASS	Christian McCaffrey	3	33%
2	Short (1-3)	RUSH	Christian McCaffrey	15	73%
	Med (4-7)	RUSH	Christian McCaffrey	19	68%
	Long (8-10)	RUSH	Christian McCaffrey	18	44%
	XL (11+)	PASS	Christian McCaffrey	6	17%
		RUSH	Christian McCaffrey	6	33%
3	Short (1-3)	RUSH	Christian McCaffrey	12	58%
	Med (4-7)	PASS	Jarius Wright	10	80%
	Long (8-10)	PASS	D.J. Moore	5	40%
	XL (11+)	PASS	Christian McCaffrey	5	0%

Most Successful Play*

Down	Distance	Play Type	Player	Total Plays	Play Success %
1	Med (4-7)	RUSH	Christian McCaffrey	5	60%
	Long (8-10)	RUSH	D.J. Moore	8	88%
2	Short (1-3)	RUSH	Cam Newton	5	80%
	Med (4-7)	PASS	Devin Funchess	7	71%
	Long (8-10)	PASS	D.J. Moore	10	70%
	XL (11+)	RUSH	Christian McCaffrey	6	33%
3	Short (1-3)	RUSH	Cam Newton	8	88%
	Med (4-7)	PASS	Jarius Wright	10	80%
	Long (8-10)	PASS	D.J. Moore	5	40%
	XL (11+)	PASS	Christian McCaffrey	5	0%

*Minimum 5 plays to qualify

2018 Weekly Snap Rates

Wk	Opp	Score	Christian McCaffrey	D.J. Moore	Devin Funchess	Jarius Wright	Ian Thomas	Curtis Samuel	Greg Olsen	Chris Manhertz	Torrey Smith
1	DAL	W 16-8	57 (85%)	17 (25%)	57 (85%)	31 (46%)	37 (55%)		16 (24%)	34 (51%)	51 (76%)
2	ATL	L 31-24	63 (94%)	17 (25%)	66 (99%)	44 (66%)	63 (94%)			13 (19%)	58 (87%)
3	CIN	W 31-21	67 (100%)	33 (49%)	52 (78%)	26 (39%)	52 (78%)			39 (58%)	44 (66%)
5	NYG	W 33-31	69 (97%)	29 (41%)	51 (72%)	30 (42%)	49 (69%)	12 (17%)		37 (52%)	46 (65%)
6	WAS	L 23-17	60 (100%)	27 (45%)	58 (97%)	37 (62%)	1 (2%)	3 (5%)	59 (98%)	10 (17%)	42 (70%)
7	PHI	W 21-17	59 (100%)	27 (46%)	54 (92%)	32 (54%)		19 (32%)	59 (100%)	6 (10%)	30 (51%)
8	BAL	W 36-21	64 (98%)	46 (71%)	48 (74%)	17 (26%)	8 (12%)	26 (40%)	63 (97%)	22 (34%)	
9	TB	W 42-28	61 (98%)	53 (85%)	45 (73%)	22 (35%)	2 (3%)	17 (27%)	60 (97%)	25 (40%)	
10	PIT	L 52-21	54 (95%)	49 (86%)	49 (86%)	29 (51%)	9 (16%)	19 (33%)	45 (79%)	15 (26%)	
11	DET	L 20-19	58 (100%)	45 (78%)	48 (83%)	41 (71%)	2 (3%)	16 (28%)	56 (97%)	12 (21%)	
12	SEA	L 30-27	59 (100%)	54 (92%)		27 (46%)	2 (3%)	54 (92%)	58 (98%)	18 (31%)	13 (22%)
13	TB	L 24-17	70 (100%)	66 (94%)	32 (46%)	39 (56%)	53 (76%)	58 (83%)	13 (19%)	8 (11%)	9 (13%)
14	CLE	L 26-20	74 (100%)	67 (91%)	29 (39%)	38 (51%)	61 (82%)	69 (93%)		21 (28%)	2 (3%)
15	NO	L 12-9	58 (100%)	57 (98%)	11 (19%)	36 (62%)	54 (93%)	55 (95%)		15 (26%)	
16	ATL	L 24-10	82 (90%)	86 (95%)	22 (24%)	57 (63%)	76 (84%)	78 (86%)		25 (27%)	9 (10%)
17	NO	W 33-14	10 (14%)	59 (82%)		22 (31%)	56 (78%)	40 (56%)		44 (61%)	20 (28%)
	Grand Total		965 (92%)	732 (69%)	622 (69%)	528 (50%)	525 (50%)	466 (53%)	429 (79%)	344 (32%)	324 (44%)

Personnel Groupings

Personnel	Team %	NFL Avg	Succ. %
1-1 [3WR]	69%	65%	52%
1-2 [2WR]	13%	17%	52%
2-2 [1WR]	7%	3%	44%
2-1 [2WR]	6%	8%	57%

Grouping Tendencies

Personnel	Pass Rate	Pass Succ. %	Run Succ. %
1-1 [3WR]	69%	49%	58%
1-2 [2WR]	41%	44%	57%
2-2 [1WR]	15%	82%	37%
2-1 [2WR]	37%	52%	60%

Red Zone Targets (min 3)

Receiver	All	Inside 5	6-10	11-20
Christian McCaffrey	15	1	5	9
Devin Funchess	12	4	3	5
Curtis Samuel	8	1	3	4
Greg Olsen	6	3		3
D.J. Moore	5		2	3
Ian Thomas	5	1	1	3
Jarius Wright	4	1		3
Torrey Smith	3	2		1

Red Zone Rushes (min 3)

Rusher	All	Inside 5	6-10	11-20
Christian McCaffrey	46	16	13	17
Cam Newton	16	5	5	6
Cameron Artis-Pay..	5			5
Alex Armah	4	4		
C.J. Anderson	3		1	2

Early Down Target Rate

	RB	TE	WR
	27%	16%	57%
	23%	21%	56%
		NFL AVG	

Overall Target Success %

	RB	TE	WR
	53%	57%	52%
	#4	#12	#13

Carolina Panthers 2018 Passing Recap & 2019 Outlook

Cam Newton's 2018 season was an overwhelming success – particularly given context – but he can still improve, especially as a deep passer and on plays where he needs more than 2.5 seconds to throw. In fantasy, Newton was 2018's QB12 despite a shoulder injury that affected him at least from Week 10 onward and cost him two full games. Beyond Cam's health, it's concerning that **Norv Turner** appeared to make a conscious decision to reduce Newton's red-zone rushing. Cam logged 28 red-zone carries in 2017, but only 16 last year.

Cam Newton Rating All Downs

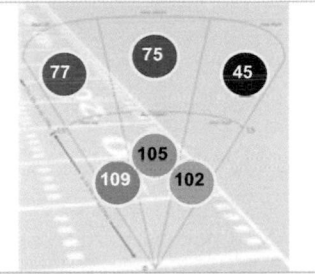

2018 Standard Passing Table

QB	Comp	Att	Comp %	Yds	YPA	TDs	INT	Sacks	Rating	Rk
Cam Newton	320	471	68%	3,395	7.2	24	13	29	94	19
Taylor Heinicke	35	57	61%	320	5.6	1	3	2	61	51
NFL Avg			62%		7.0				87.5	

2018 Advanced Passing Table

QB	Success %	EDSR Passing Success %	20+ Yd Pass Gains	20+ Yd Pass %	30+ Yd Pass Gains	30+ Yd Pass %	Avg. Air Yds per Comp	Avg. YAC per Comp	20+ Air Yd Comp	20+ Air Yd %
Cam Newton	50%	53%	44	9.0%	10	2.0%	5.1	5.5	8	2%
Taylor Heinicke	41%	41%	2	4.0%	1	2.0%	4.5	4.7	2	4%
NFL Avg	44%	48%	29.5	8.4%	12.5	3.7%	5.8	5.1	14.5	6%

Cam Newton Rating Early Downs

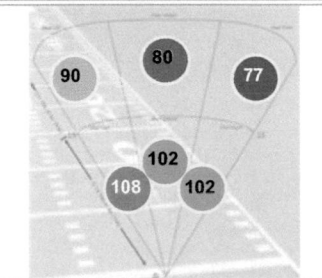

Interception Rates by Down

Yards to Go	1st Dwn	2nd Dwn	3rd Dwn	4th Dwn	Total
1 & 2		0.0%	0.0%	0.0%	0.0%
3, 4, 5	0.0%	6.3%	0.0%	0.0%	2.8%
6 - 9	0.0%	0.0%	2.9%	0.0%	1.0%
10 - 14	2.6%	1.9%	0.0%	0.0%	2.3%
15+	12.5%	7.7%	16.7%		12.1%
Total	2.8%	2.4%	2.7%	0.0%	2.6%

3rd Down Passing - Short of Sticks Analysis

QB	Avg. Yds to Go	Avg. YIA (of Comp)	Avg Yds Short	Short of Sticks Rate	Short Rk
Cam Newton	7.5	4.5	-3.0	67%	36
NFL Avg	7.8	6.4	-1.4	60%	

Air Yds vs YAC

Air Yds %	YAC %	Rk
48%	52%	41
53%	48%	

2018 Receiving Recap & 2019 Outlook

With **Devin Funchess** gone to Indianapolis, 79 targets open up for Carolina's passing attack. Turner dramatically increased 11-personnel usage from 47% to 69%, committing to keeping three receivers on the field. Funchess was Carolina's least-productive receiver in 11 personnel with just 6.6 yards per target, a 49% Success Rate, and 68 passer rating. As **D.J. Moore** and **Curtis Samuel**'s roles will increase, it's notable that the Panthers face three top-ten pass defenses in the first five weeks but draw the NFL's easiest pass-defense schedule thereafter.

Player *Min 50 Targets	Targ	Comp %	YPA	Rating	Success %	Success Rk	Missed YPA Rk	YAS % Rk	YTS % Rk	TDs
Christian McCaffrey	124	86%	7.0	111.9	56%	37	56	88	67	5
D.J. Moore	82	67%	9.6	90.9	52%	59	87	18	113	2
Devin Funchess	79	56%	6.9	68.0	51%	64	101	28	67	4
Curtis Samuel	65	60%	7.6	90.2	49%	85	85	59	26	4
Jarius Wright	60	72%	7.5	91.5	57%	32	55	80	18	1

Directional Passer Rating Delivered

Receiver	Short Left	Short Middle	Short Right	Deep Left	Deep Middle	Deep Right	Player Total
Christian McCaffrey	122	108	103	40		96	112
D.J. Moore	53	119	97	96	117	40	91
Devin Funchess	90	71	51	85	40	3	68
Curtis Samuel	83	90	101	76	82	96	90
Jarius Wright	49	118	100	40	110	110	91
Ian Thomas	90	85	107	81	0	104	88
Greg Olsen	133	111	116	40	158	83	128
Torrey Smith	125	96	102	56		40	98
C.J. Anderson	158	0					63
Team Total	103	104	100	69	94	52	97

2018 Rushing Recap & 2019 Outlook

Christian McCaffrey was insanely good operating as Norv's newest version of **LaDainian Tomlinson**, and there's little reason to believe he'll have a worse 2019. McCaffrey's versatility is obvious, but he also excels in situations that many running backs do not. On first-and-ten carries, McCaffrey posted a 53% Success Rate and 5.7 yards per carry, the best combination of any running back in the league. On second-and-long runs (10-15 yards), McCaffrey recorded a 43% Success Rate and averaged 5.7 yards per carry, the second-best combination in the league. Buoyed by 46 red-zone carries including 16 inside the five-yard line and facing the NFL's sixth-easiest run-defense schedule this year, the arrow is still pointing up on McCaffrey.

Player *Min 50 Rushes	Rushes	YPC	Success %	Success Rk	Missed YPA Rk	YTS % Rk	YAS % Rk	Early Down Success %	Early Down Success Rk	TDs
Christian McCaffrey	219	5.0	55%	9	16	30	24	56%	6	7

Yards per Carry by Direction

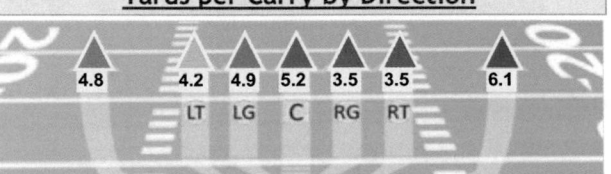

Directional Run Frequency

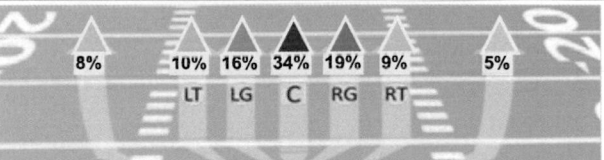

read defenses better than ever. When releasing the ball in less than 2.5 seconds, Newton's completion rate was 77% with a 112 passer rating, up from 2017's 66% completions and 87 rating. Cam still struggled when defenses forced him to hold the ball longer than 2.5 seconds, however, managing to complete just 59% of his throws with a 75 rating. When pressured, Newton managed 5.0 yards per attempt and a 48 passer rating, which ranked 34th among 37 qualified quarterbacks. Nos. 35-37 were rookies **Josh Allen**, **Sam Darnold**, and **Josh Rosen**.

Although Newton shined in the Turners' short passing game, Cam's downfield numbers were atrocious, both before and after his injury. His Success Rate on 15-plus-yard passes was 39% with a 56 passer rating that ranked 29th among 31 qualified QBs. On 5-7 step drops, his efficiency was especially atrocious.

The Turners also need to improve Cam's aggressiveness on pushing the ball beyond the sticks on third-down passes. 53% of Newton's third-down completions were tackled short of the sticks. Only 43% of his third-down passes went for first downs, and his first-down conversion rate on third downs decreased over the course of the season.

Even as Cam's 2018 was an improvement on the year prior, it should be noted Carolina faced the NFL's easiest schedule of pass defenses. Fortunately, the 2019 Panthers are scheduled to face the league's third-softest pass-defense slate.

(cont'd - see CAR-5)

Carolina Panthers Fantasy Corner

D.J. Moore flashed his lofty ceiling and then some as a first-round rookie, averaging only 24.8 snaps in Carolina's initial six games before popping to 56.3 the rest of the way with WR20 fantasy PPR results in Weeks 8-17. Moore led all rookies with 50-plus targets in yards per route run and showed afterburners on a league-high 7.9 yards after catch per reception. 2018's No. 2 SPARQ receiver and first wideout drafted, Moore checks virtually every box as sophomore breakout and WR2 pick with WR1 upside.

- Evan Silva

2018 Situational Usage by Player & Position

Usage Rate by Score

		Being Blown Out (14+)	Down Big (9-13)	One Score	Large Lead (9-13)	Blowout Lead (14+)
RUSH	Christian McCaffrey	8%	5%	76%	3%	9%
	D.J. Moore	8%	17%	75%		
	Curtis Samuel	38%		63%		
	Jarius Wright		50%	50%		
	C.J. Anderson	8%		63%	17%	13%
	Cameron Artis-Payne	5%		37%	32%	26%
	Travaris Cadet					100%
	Total	8%	4%	69%	5%	13%
PASS	Christian McCaffrey	17%	5%	72%	2%	4%
	D.J. Moore	21%	6%	59%	3%	11%
	Devin Funchess	26%	12%	54%	3%	6%
	Curtis Samuel	23%	6%	60%	2%	9%
	Jarius Wright	20%	6%	63%	6%	4%
	Greg Olsen	24%	8%	50%	5%	13%
	Ian Thomas	19%		63%	9%	9%
	Torrey Smith	17%	21%	59%		3%
	C.J. Anderson	67%		33%		
	Cameron Artis-Payne	50%				50%
	Travaris Cadet					100%
	Kenjon Barner	100%				
	Total	22%	7%	60%	3%	8%

Share of Offensive Plays by Type

	Christian McCaffrey	D.J. Moore	Devin Funchess	Curtis Samuel	Jarius Wright	Greg Olsen	Ian Thomas	Torrey Smith	C.J. Anderson	Cameron Artis-Payne	Travaris Cadet	Kenjon Barner
RUSH	74%	4%		3%	1%				8%	6%	4%	
PASS	24%	15%	15%	12%	11%	8%	7%	6%	1%	1%	0%	0%
ALL	44%	11%	9%	8%	7%	5%	4%	4%	4%	3%	2%	0%

Positional Target Distribution vs NFL Average

		NFL Wide				Team Only			
		Left	Middle	Right	Total	Left	Middle	Right	Total
Deep	WR	33%	17%	31%	81%	39%	17%	22%	79%
	TE	5%	4%	7%	16%	6%	4%	8%	18%
	RB	1%	0%	2%	3%	1%		2%	3%
	All	39%	22%	40%	100%	46%	21%	33%	100%
Short	WR	20%	14%	21%	55%	21%	10%	24%	56%
	TE	6%	6%	8%	20%	6%	4%	6%	16%
	RB	10%	5%	10%	25%	11%	6%	11%	28%
	All	36%	25%	39%	100%	38%	20%	42%	100%
Total		37%	24%	39%	100%	39%	20%	40%	100%

Positional Success Rates vs NFL Average

		NFL Wide				Team Only			
		Left	Middle	Right	Total	Left	Middle	Right	Total
Deep	WR	40%	49%	40%	42%	46%	47%	25%	40%
	TE	44%	54%	41%	45%	20%	50%	57%	44%
	RB	39%	33%	42%	41%	0%		50%	33%
	All	40%	50%	40%	42%	41%	47%	34%	40%
Short	WR	55%	60%	52%	55%	46%	74%	56%	55%
	TE	55%	62%	54%	57%	65%	72%	52%	62%
	RB	46%	53%	45%	47%	58%	68%	46%	55%
	All	53%	59%	51%	54%	52%	72%	52%	56%
Total		50%	58%	49%	52%	50%	68%	50%	54%

Division History: Season Wins & 2019 Projection

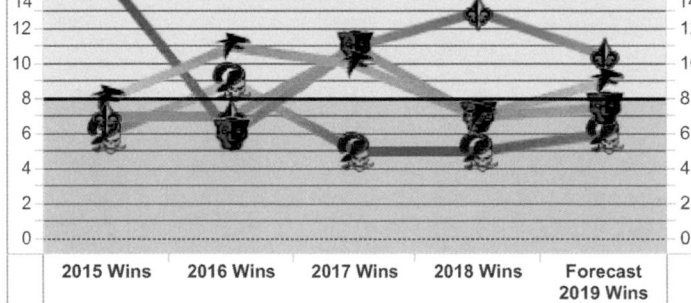

2015 Wins · 2016 Wins · 2017 Wins · 2018 Wins · Forecast 2019 Wins

Rank of 2019 Defensive Pass Efficiency Faced by Week

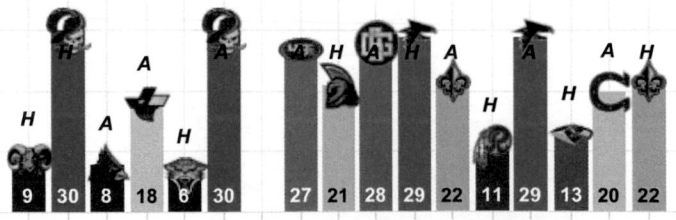

9 · 30 · 8 · 18 · 6 · 30 · 27 · 21 · 28 · 29 · 22 · 11 · 29 · 13 · 20 · 22

Rank of 2019 Defensive Rush Efficiency Faced by Week

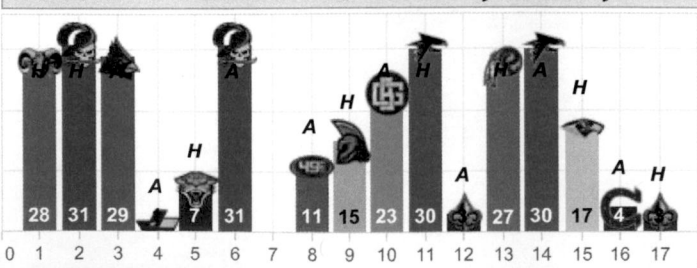

28 · 31 · 29 · 7 · 31 · 11 · 15 · 23 · 30 · 27 · 30 · 17 · 4

2018 Detailed Analytics Summary
Success by Play Type & Primary Personnel Groupings

Type	1-1 [3WR]	1-2 [2WR]	2-2 [1WR]	2-1 [2WR]	1-0 [4WR]	1-3 [1WR]	0-0 [5WR]	0-1 [4WR]	2-3 [0WR]	2-0 [3WR]	ALL
PASS	49% (477)	44% (52)	82% (11)	52% (23)	43% (14)	83% (6)	0% (3)	33% (3)		0% (1)	49% (590)
RUSH	58% (216)	57% (74)	37% (62)	60% (40)	60% (5)	17% (12)	0% (1)		50% (2)		54% (412)
All	52% (693)	52% (126)	44% (73)	57% (63)	47% (19)	39% (18)	0% (4)	33% (3)	50% (2)	0% (1)	51% (1,002)

Format Success Rate (Total # of Plays)

Receiving Success by Top-4 Personnel Groupings
(Min 50 targets)

POS	Player	1-1 [3WR]	1-2 [2WR]	2-1 [2WR]	1-0 [4WR]	4 Grp Total
RB	Christian McCaffrey	55% (98) 6.9, 109.0	67% (9) 8.1, 100.5	25% (4) 5.0, 64.6	67% (3) 5.7, 81.3	55% (114) 6.9, 107.1
WR	DJ Moore	52% (73) 9.6, 90.2	80% (5) 11.0, 112.5	33% (3) 6.0, 54.9		53% (81) 9.6, 90.4
	Devin Funchess	49% (61) 6.6, 67.8	56% (9) 8.3, 129.4	83% (6) 10.0, 108.3	0% (2) 0.0, 39.6	51% (78) 6.9, 76.7
	Curtis Samuel	50% (58) 7.7, 93.2	33% (3) 8.3, 104.2	67% (3) 7.0, 95.8		50% (64) 7.7, 98.0
	Jarius Wright	56% (55) 7.7, 85.7			60% (5) 4.6, 71.3	57% (60) 7.5, 84.5

Format Line 1: Success Rate (Total # of Plays) Line 2: YPA, Passer Rating

Rushing Success by Top-4 Personnel Groupings
(Min 25 carries)

Rusher (Last, First)	1-1 [3WR]	1-2 [2WR]	2-2 [1WR]	2-1 [2WR]	4 Grp Total
McCaffrey Christian	59% (121) 6.2	53% (47) 3.8	36% (25) 2.0	71% (17) 6.5	56% (210) 5.2
Newton Cam	53% (53) 6.2	58% (12) 6.6	40% (20) 2.3	50% (4) 1.3	51% (89) 5.2
Anderson C.J.	67% (3) 4.0	50% (6) 3.2	0% (1) -1.0	54% (13) 5.6	52% (23) 4.5

Format Line 1: Success Rate (Total # of Plays) Line 2: YPC

Passing by Coverage Scheme

M2M	57% (247) 7.9, 106.0
Zone	54% (200) 7.6, 86.7
Screen	40% (57) 5.2, 99.9
Combo	57% (7) 5.9, 91.1

Passing by Route

Curl	60% (52) 7.3, 74.1
Out	57% (49) 6.5, 104.0
Screen	36% (47) 5.3, 102.9
Dig	62% (37) 9.5, 73.1
Slant	73% (37) 8.5, 126.7
Flat	57% (35) 6.0, 110.8

Throw Types

Level 1	56% (370) 6.9, 94.6
Level 2	53% (129) 9.1, 109.0
Level 3	27% (33) 9.6, 94.2
Shovel	67% (6) 1.8, 79.2
Touch	0% (1) -3.0, 79.2

QB Drop Types

3 Step	56% (197) 8.4, 96.4
0/1 Step	57% (148) 6.5, 106.3
5 Step	44% (104) 7.7, 78.2
Basic Screen	37% (27) 4.5, 85.5
7 Step	48% (23) 6.5, 76.2
Designed Rollout Right	65% (20) 7.0, 89.6

QB State at Pass

Planted	55% (405) 7.7, 98.2
Shuffling	47% (51) 5.8, 88.4
Moving	50% (48) 7.4, 112.6

Play Action

	Play Action	No P/A
Under Center	63% (52) 7.1, 118.2	57% (7) 13.0, 153.3
Shotgun	52% (103) 7.8, 112.4	52% (379) 7.3, 88.5
ALL	56% (155) 7.6, 114.4	52% (386) 7.5, 90.8

Run Types

Inside Zone	52% (83) 5.2
Power	50% (72) 3.9
Outside Zone	55% (47) 5.0
Lead	50% (16) 2.5
Pitch	64% (14) 5.4
Stretch	0% (2) -3.5

CAR-5

Last year's Panthers also more creatively incorporated **Christian McCaffrey** into the passing game. McCaffrey's target total didn't change much, but his catch rate spiked from 71% to 86% in the Turners' first year. McCaffrey also dominated on the ground, increasing his yards per carry from 3.7 to 5.0 and his Early Down Success Rate from 43% to 56%.

This year's Panthers can improve their personnel packaging on run plays. Last year's club spiked its Success Rate in 11 and 12 personnel by nearly 10% from the season prior, but the Turners' 22-personnel usage was questionable. In these two-back, two-tight end bunch formations, the Panthers predictably ran on 85% of snaps. They earned just a 37% Success Rate and averaged 1.7 yards per carry. Yet the Panthers ran 22 personnel at the second-highest rate in the league.

Working in the Panthers' favor should be a 2019 return to health. After finishing as 2017's seventh-healthiest team, Carolina was the league's seventh most-injured in 2018. And last year's injuries occurred at positions that impact wins and losses the most. The Panthers' secondary was the league's most-injured unit. Their offensive line was third-most injured. Cam's shoulder injury caused his season to fall apart down the stretch.

The Panthers' salary cap is built around their offensive and defensive lines, where they've devoted the second-most monetary resources in the NFL. So when a costly offensive line sustains injuries, it manifests itself in offensive production as a whole. The Panthers bolstered both lines in the draft with DE/OLB **Brian Burns** and LT **Greg Little** in the first and second rounds.

Although the Panthers' 2018 offense took a big jump in Early Down Success Rate, their defense couldn't say the same. Rivera's unit dropped from 2017's second-best defense in EDSR allowed to 16th last year. In overall defensive efficiency, Carolina dipped from No. 7 to No. 22. Thus, last year's Panthers didn't win many EDSR battles. Rivera must turn his defense around to keep the Panthers competitive and retain his job.

But this year's schedule won't do him any favors. I project the Panthers to face a slightly tougher schedule of opposing offenses than last year, including the NFL's second-toughest schedule of passing games. Last year's Panthers ranked 20th in pass-rush efficiency and 31st in quarterback hits. That's where Rivera needs **Bruce Irvin**, two pass-rusher draft picks, and DT **Gerald McCoy** to chip in. Carolina's secondary is still lacking and will be exploited if enemy quarterbacks have time to throw.

Coaches (Prior Yrs)

Head Coach:
Matt Nagy (1 yr)
Offensive Coordinator:
Mark Helfrich (1 yr)
Defensive Coordinator:
Chuck Pagano (IND HC 2017) (new)

Chicago Bears

2019 Forecast

Wins	Div Rank
9.5	#1

Past Records

2018: 12-4
2017: 5-11
2016: 3-13

EASY   HARD

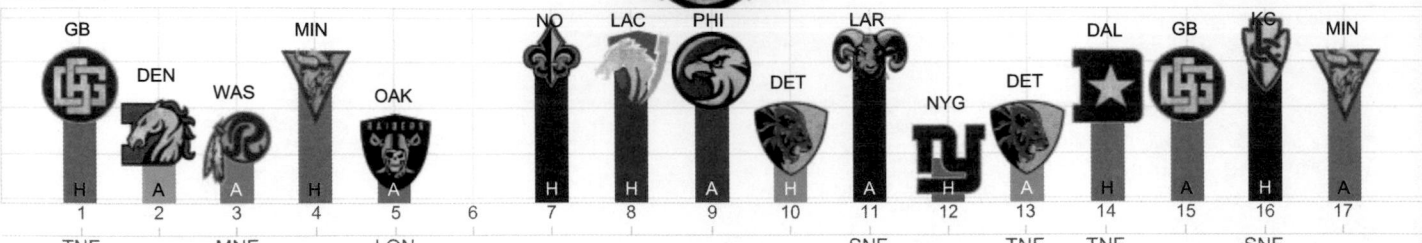

	GB	DEN	WAS	MIN	OAK		NO	LAC	PHI	DET	LAR	NYG	DET	DAL	GB	KC	MIN
	H	A	A	H	A		H	H	A	H	A	H	A	H	A	H	A
	1	2	3	4	5	6	7	8	9	10	11	12	13	14	15	16	17

TNF   MNF   LON   SNF   TNF   TNF   SNF

Key Players Lost

Player	New
Adrian Amos (FS)	GB
Benny Cunningham (RB)	JAC
Bryan Witzmann (G)	CLE
Bryce Callahan (CB)	DEN
Daniel Brown (TE)	NYJ
Eric Kush (G)	CLE
Jordan Howard (RB)	PHI
Josh Bellamy (WR)	NYJ
Kevin White (WR)	ARI
Zach Miller (TE)	Retired

Average Line	# Games Favored	# Games Underdog
-2.3	11	4

Regular Season Wins: Past & Current Proj

Forecast 2019 Wins — 9.5
2018 Wins — 12
Forecast 2018 Wins — 6.5
2017 Wins — 5
2016 Wins — 3
2015 Wins — 6

1 3 5 7 9 11 13 15

2019 Chicago Bears Overview

As noted in last year's football preview, a commonality among the eight quarterbacks drafted within the top-15 picks between 2012 and 2016 was their tendency to take gargantuan second-year leaps. Aside from **Robert Griffin III** – who sustained a major knee injury – seven of those eight quarterbacks posted better win-loss records in year two, and all told they went from 37-59 (39%) as rookies to 63-44 (59%) as sophomores. The individual quarterbacks' passing efficiency spiked, fueling their teams' improved results.

Mitchell Trubisky followed suit in his second year. Pegged for 6.5 wins and fourth place in the NFC North, Trubisky's Bears instead went 12-4 and won the division. Trubisky's record jumped from 4-8 to 11-3 as a starter, and his completion rate from 59% to 67%. His yards per attempt leapt from 6.6 to 7.4. His TD Rate more than doubled from 2.1% to 5.5%. But Trubisky wasn't alone.

Fellow sophomore signal caller **Deshaun Watson** went from 3-3 as a rookie to 11-5. **Patrick Mahomes'** inclusion is less meaningful because he started only one game as a rookie, but he was another year-two quarterback making a huge leap with 50 touchdown passes and a 12-4 record. All told, quarterbacks drafted in the top-15 picks since 2012 now carry a combined 45-70 (39%) record as rookies but a 97-56 (63%) clip as sophomores. We should see this trend extend to **Baker Mayfield**, **Sam Darnold**, and **Josh Allen** among others in 2019.

First-year coach **Matt Nagy** did have a major impact on his team's improvement. But the ease of the Bears' schedule can't be overlooked. Opponent strength is especially critical in a small-sample sport with only 16 games where teams play 63% of their schedule against unfamiliar teams outside their division. Chicago's schedule variance has been as stark as I've ever seen.

(cont'd - see CHI2)

Lineup & Cap Hits

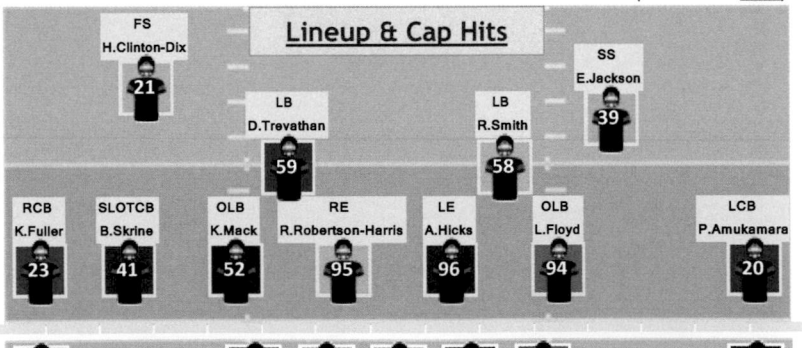

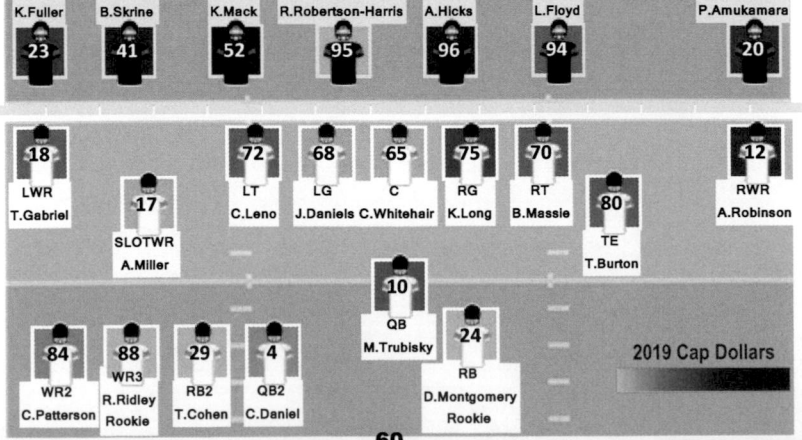

2019 Cap Dollars

Key Free Agents/ Trades Added

Player	AAV (MM)
Buster Skrine (CB)	$5.5
Cordarrelle Patterson (WR)	$5
HaHa Clinton-Dix (FS)	$3
Mike Davis (RB)	$3
Ted Larsen (G)	$1.02

Drafted Players

Rd	Pk	Player (College)
3	73	RB - David Montgomery (Iowa State)
4	126	WR - Riley Ridley (Georgia)
6*	205	CB - Duke Shelley (Kansas State)
7	222	RB - Kerrith Whyte Jr. (Florida Atlantic)
	238	CB - Stephen Denmark (Valdosta State)

2019 Unit Spending

All DEF   All OFF

Positional Spending

	Rank	Total	2017 Rk
All OFF	24	$90.70M	15
QB	20	$14.58M	24
OL	30	$27.54M	20
RB	25	$4.96M	28
WR	5	$30.91M	3
TE	4	$12.70M	3
All DEF	7	$95.40M	11
DL	23	$22.38M	26
LB	3	$34.92M	1
CB	3	$31.42M	14
S	30	$6.67M	32

By my metrics, the 2017 Bears faced the NFL's toughest schedule. They faced the league's second-softest slate in 2018. They went from facing the NFL's seventh-toughest slate of defenses in 2017 to the league's easiest defensive schedule in 2018. On defense, the Bears went from facing the league's toughest schedule of offenses in 2017 to last year's 12th-softest slate. Strength of schedule ratings are most useful when involving extremes. Moving from 12th to 19th, for instance, isn't that big a swing. But moving from the top to bottom or bottom to top can make a huge difference.

Just how easy was the Bears' 2018 schedule early in the season? Of their first five opponents, *four* went on to fire their head coach (Packers, Cardinals, Bucs, Dolphins).

The 2017 Bears played nine games against top-12 teams and only three against bottom-12 opponents. Nagy's Bears played five games against top-12 foes and eight against bottom-12 teams. Opening point spreads released before the season favored Chicago in only three games all year. Closing spreads at kickoff favored the Bears in 12 contests.

In addition to the most-favorable schedule shift I've ever measured from one season to the next, the Bears experienced one of the largest year-to-year improvements in player health. **John Fox**'s 2017 club was the second most-injured team in the NFL. In fact, Fox's three Bears teams never finished higher than 28th in roster health. Nagy's Bears were the league's third healthiest.

The Bears also experienced a major 2018 talent influx. The biggest difference maker was **Khalil Mack**, but **Allen Robinson**, **Taylor Gabriel**, and **Trey Burton** were all new faces and wound up being three of Chicago's four most-targeted players.

The 2017 Bears faced the NFL's toughest schedule with a rookie quarterback, over-the-hill **John Fox** as coach, and fielded the league's second most-injured team. In hindsight, we shouldn't even be the least bit surprised last year's club took a quantum leap.

But where does that leave the 2019 Bears? To get there, we must first examine their roster construction and some problems they haven't faced yet, but will in the near future. Perhaps as soon as this year.

2018 Passing Performance

QB	1st Dwn	2nd Dwn	3rd Dwn	
Mitchell Trubisky	51%	51%	39%	Success Rate
	7.6	7.9	6.4	YPA
	96.6	96.6	90.1	Rating
Pass Rate	49%	58%	71%	
NFL AVG	53%	47%	36%	Success Rate
	7.7	7.3	6.9	YPA
	95.1	93.7	87.1	Rating
Pass Rate	53%	62%	80%	

2018 Rushing Performance

Offense	1st Dwn	2nd Dwn	3rd Dwn	
CHI	49%	46%	49%	Success Rate
	3.9	4.5	4.5	YPC
Run Rate	51%	42%	29%	
NFL AVG	48%	46%	51%	Success Rate
	4.5	4.4	4.3	YPC
Run Rate	47%	38%	20%	

The 2019 season gives the Bears potentially their final window to assemble an optimal roster based on future salary cap allocation. **Khalil Mack**'s cap hit more than doubles from $11.9 million this year to $26.6 million in 2020. **Leonard Floyd** costs $5 million this year and $13.2 million in 2020. **Eddie Goldman** goes from $5.3 million to $10.8 million. **Kyle Fuller** from $13.5 million to $17.5 million. **Bobby Massie**, $3.8 million to $8.3 million. Trubisky is still on his rookie contract but will be hunting for an extension soon.

As their roster stands today, the Bears have the NFL's second-highest total cap allocations for 2020 and are nearly $25 million over the projected 2020 salary cap. Their cap commitments for 2020 are $53 million above league average.

(cont'd - see CHI-3)

2018 Offensive Advanced Metrics

Rank (lower = better), by category:

Category	Rank
EDSR Off	16
30 & In Off	27
Red Zone Off	8
3rd Down Off	15
YPPA Off	15
YPPT Off	5
Offensive Efficiency	20
Pass Efficiency Off	20
Pass Pro Efficiency Off	7
RB Pass Eff Off	5
Rush Efficiency Off	16
Explosive Pass Off	16
Explosive Run Off	1

2018 Defensive Advanced Metrics

Category	Rank
EDSR Def	2
30 & In Def	10
Red Zone Def	2
3rd Down Def	4
YPPA Def	2
YPPT Def	9
Defensive Efficiency	2
Pass Efficiency Def	1
Pass Pro Efficiency Def	12
RB Pass Eff Def	19
Rush Efficiency Def	2
Explosive Pass Def	28
Explosive Run Def	2

2018 Weekly EDSR & Season Trending Performance

	1	2	3	4	6	7	8	9	10	11	12	13	14	15	16	17	
RESULT	W	W	W	W	L	L	W	W	W	W	W	L	W	W	W	W	WEEK
OPP	GB	SEA	ARI	TB	MIA	NE	NYJ	BUF	DET	MIN	DET	NYG	LA	GB	SF	MIN	
SITE	A	H	A	H	A	H	H	A	H	H	A	A	H	H	A	A	
MARGIN	-1	7	2	38	-3	-7	14	32	12	5	7	-3	9	7	5	14	
PTS	23	24	16	48	28	31	24	41	34	25	23	27	15	24	14	24	
OPP PTS	24	17	14	10	31	38	10	9	22	20	16	30	6	17	9	10	

EDSR by Wk
W=Green
L=Red

OFF/DEF
EDSR
Blue=OFF
(high=good)
Red=DEF
(low=good)

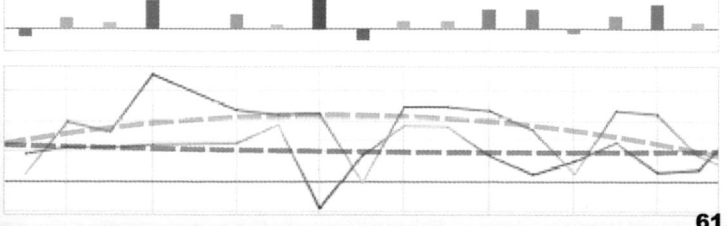

2018 Close Game Records

All 2018 Wins: **12**
FG Games (<=3 pts) W-L: **1-3**
FG Games Win %: **25% (#25)**
FG Games Wins (% of Total Wins): **8% (#29)**
1 Score Games (<=8 pts) W-L: **6-4**
1 Score Games Win %: **60% (#7)**
1 Score Games Wins (% of Total Wins): **50% (#15)**

2018 Critical & Game-Deciding Stats

TO Margin	+12
TO Given	24
INT Given	14
FUM Given	10
TO Taken	36
INT Taken	27
FUM Taken	9
Sack Margin	+17
Sacks	50
Sacks Allow	33
Return TD Margin	+3
Ret TDs	6
Ret TDs Allow	3
Penalty Margin	+17
Penalties	97
Opponent Penalties	114

Chicago Bears 2019 Strength of Schedule In Detail (compared to 2018)

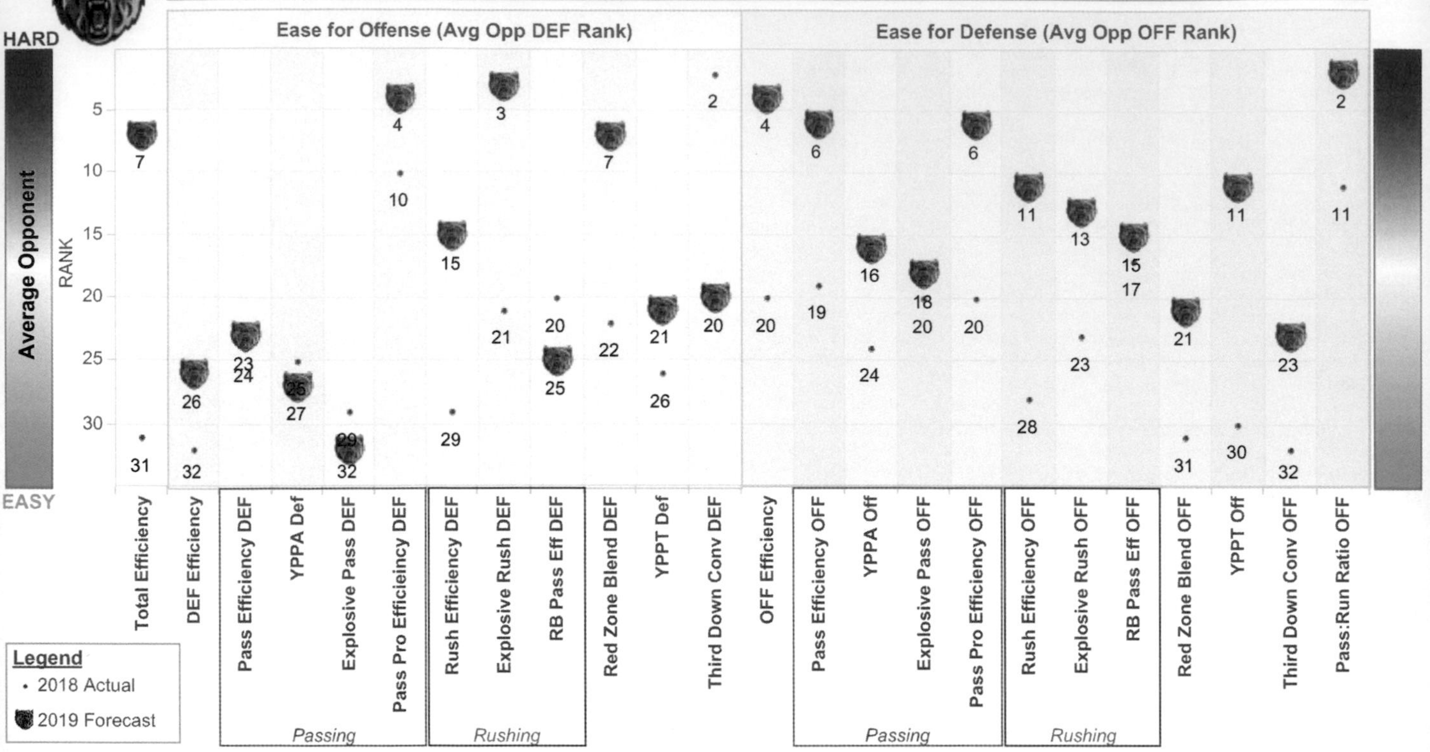

HARD

Average Opponent

RANK

Ease for Offense (Avg Opp DEF Rank)

Category	2019 Forecast	2018 Actual
Total Efficiency	7	31
DEF Efficiency	26	32
Pass Efficiency DEF	23	24
YPPA Def	27	26
Explosive Pass DEF	29	32
Pass Pro Efficiency DEF	4	10
Rush Efficiency DEF	15	29
Explosive Rush DEF	3	21
RB Pass Eff DEF	20	25
Red Zone Blend DEF	7	22
YPPT Def	2	21/26
Third Down Conv DEF	20	20

Passing | Rushing

Ease for Defense (Avg Opp OFF Rank)

Category	2019 Forecast	2018 Actual
OFF Efficiency	4	20
Pass Efficiency OFF	6	19
YPPA Off	16	24
Explosive Pass OFF	18	20
Pass Pro Efficiency OFF	6	20
Rush Efficiency OFF	11	28
Explosive Rush OFF	13	23
RB Pass Eff OFF	15	17
Red Zone Blend OFF	21	31
YPPT Off	11	30
Third Down Conv OFF	23	32
Pass:Run Ratio OFF	2	11

Passing | Rushing

EASY

Legend
- 2018 Actual
- 2019 Forecast

2019 v 2018 Schedule Variances* (OFF=Rank of DEF faced, 2019 vs 2018)

Pass OFF Rank	Pass OFF Blend Rk	Rush OFF Rk	Rush OFF Blend Rk	Pass DEF Rk	Pass DEF Blend Rk	Rush DEF Rk	Rush DEF Blend Rk
13	17	7	8	5	5	2	6

* **1**=Hardest Jump in 2019 schedule from 2018 (aka a much harder schedule in 2019), **32**=Easiest Jump in 2019 schedule from 2018 (aka a much easier schedule in 2019);
Pass Blend metric blends 4 metrics: Pass Efficiency, YPPA, Explosive Pass & Pass Rush; **Rush Blend** metric blends 3 metrics: Rush Efficiency, Explosive Rush & RB Targets

---

Team Records & Trends

	2018	2017	2016
Average line	-2.9	4.8	3.8
Average O/U line	44.2	41.7	44.0
Straight Up Record	12-4	5-11	3-13
Against the Spread Record	12-4	7-6	6-10
Over/Under Record	8-8	5-11	7-8
ATS as Favorite	9-3	1-2	0-3
ATS as Underdog	3-1	6-4	5-7
Straight Up Home	7-1	3-5	3-5
ATS Home	7-1	4-2	4-4
Over/Under Home	4-4	2-6	3-4
ATS as Home Favorite	6-0	1-2	0-2
ATS as a Home Dog	1-1	3-0	3-2
Straight Up Away	5-3	2-6	0-8
ATS Away	5-3	3-4	2-6
Over/Under Away	4-4	3-5	4-4
ATS Away Favorite	3-3	0-0	0-1
ATS Away Dog	2-0	3-4	2-5
Six Point Teaser Record	14-2	12-4	10-6
Seven Point Teaser Record	15-0	12-4	10-5
Ten Point Teaser Record	16-0	12-4	12-4

CHI-3

So the Bears probably won't have as talented a roster in 2020, and their young talent has been depleted by trades. GM **Ryan Pace** made just five picks in this year's draft, including zero in the first two rounds. The Bears walked away with two running backs, two cornerbacks, and a fourth-round receiver. In the 2020 draft, the Bears are again missing their first- and third-round picks. And they traded their 2020 fourth-round pick to the Patriots. Over the past three drafts, the Bears have selected the fewest players in the league. And they've drafted a league-low six players in the first three rounds.

When a team trades up in the draft, this naturally inhibits their ability to accumulate younger talent on cheap rookie deals. But the NFL provides a workaround called the compensatory process, which gives teams free picks in exchange for letting unrestricted free agents walk. Pace's Bears haven't dipped their toes into that pool and are one of just
(cont'd - see CHI-4)

2019 Rest Analysis

Team More Rest	4
Opp More Rest	2
Net Rest Edge	2
Week 2 Edge	4
Week 3 Edge	0
Week 4 Edge	-1
Week 5 Edge	0
Week 7 Edge	7
Week 8 Edge	0
Week 9 Edge	0
Week 10 Edge	0
Week 11 Edge	0
Week 12 Edge	
Week 13 Edge	0
Week 14 Edge	0
Week 15 Edge	3
Week 16 Edge	0
Week 17 Edge	1

Health by Unit*

2018 Rk	3
2017 Rk	
2018 v 2017 Rk	1
Off Rk	6
Def Rk	4
QB Rk	24
RB Rk	1
WR Rk	7
TE Rk	20
Oline Rk	10
Dline Rk	10
LB Rk	14
DB Rk	7

Based on the work of Football Outsiders

2018 Weekly Betting Lines (wks 1-16)

1	2	3	4	5	7	8	9	10	11	12	13	14	15	16
GB	DEN	WAS	MIN	OAK	NO	LAC	PHI	DET	LAR	NYG	DET	DAL	GB	KC
-4	1	-2.5	-3.5	-6	-1	-3	3	-8	5.5	-10	-3.5	-4	3	-1

Avg = -2.3

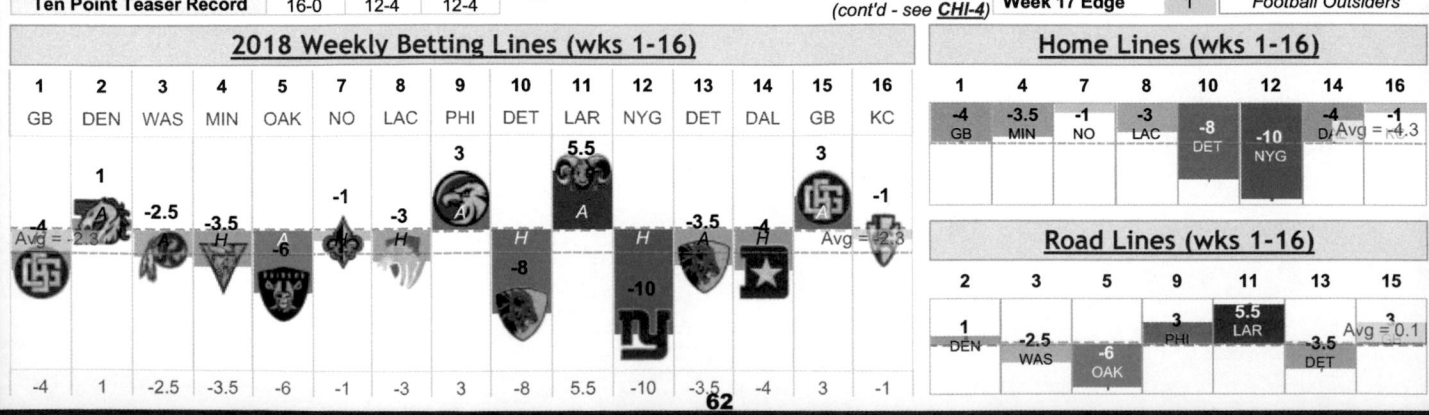

Home Lines (wks 1-16)

1	4	7	8	10	12	14	16
-4	-3.5	-1	-3	-8	-10	-4	-1
GB	MIN	NO	LAC	DET	NYG	DAL	KC

Avg = -4.3

Road Lines (wks 1-16)

2	3	5	9	11	13	15
1	-2.5	-6	3	5.5	-3.5	3
DEN	WAS	OAK	PHI	LAR	DET	

Avg = 0.1

2018 Play Tendencies

All Pass %	54%
All Pass Rk	27
All Rush %	46%
All Rush Rk	6
1 Score Pass %	55%
1 Score Pass Rk	24
2017 1 Score Pass %	50%
2017 1 Score Pass Rk	32
2018 Pass Increase %	5%
Pass Increase Rk	8
1 Score Rush %	45%
1 Score Rush Rk	9
Up Pass %	49%
Up Pass Rk	20
Up Rush %	51%
Up Rush Rk	13
Down Pass %	65%
Down Pass Rk	20
Down Rush %	35%
Down Rush Rk	13

2018 Down & Distance Tendencies

Down	Distance	Total Plays	Pass Rate	Run Rate	Play Success %
1	Short (1-3)	10	40%	60%	70%
	Med (4-7)	10	30%	70%	70%
	Long (8-10)	335	49%	51%	51%
	XL (11+)	12	92%	8%	42%
2	Short (1-3)	57	35%	65%	65%
	Med (4-7)	79	63%	37%	54%
	Long (8-10)	92	60%	40%	48%
	XL (11+)	47	72%	28%	32%
3	Short (1-3)	51	45%	55%	53%
	Med (4-7)	56	80%	20%	48%
	Long (8-10)	29	76%	24%	24%
	XL (11+)	24	88%	13%	17%
4	Short (1-3)	7	14%	86%	71%
	Med (4-7)	3	100%	0%	67%
	Long (8-10)	1	100%	0%	0%

Shotgun %:

Under Center	Shotgun
21%	79%

37% *AVG* 63%

Run Rate:

Under Center	Shotgun
76%	33%

68% *AVG* 23%

Pass Rate:

Under Center	Shotgun
24%	67%

32% *AVG* 77%

Short Yardage Intelligence:

2nd and Short Run

Run Freq	Run Rk	NFL Run Freq Avg	Run 1D Rate	Run NFL 1D Avg
65%	16	65%	77%	68%

2nd and Short Pass

Pass Freq	Pass Rk	NFL Pass Freq Avg	Pass 1D Rate	Pass NFL 1D Avg
35%	17	35%	57%	56%

Most Frequent Play

Down	Distance	Play Type	Player	Total Plays	Play Success %
1	Short (1-3)	RUSH	Jordan Howard	4	75%
	Med (4-7)	RUSH	Tarik Cohen	4	75%
	Long (8-10)	RUSH	Jordan Howard	92	47%
	XL (11+)	PASS	Taylor Gabriel	2	100%
			Anthony Miller	2	50%
2	Short (1-3)	RUSH	Jordan Howard	23	78%
	Med (4-7)	RUSH	Jordan Howard	20	55%
	Long (8-10)	RUSH	Jordan Howard	17	24%
	XL (11+)	PASS	Allen Robinson	10	30%
3	Short (1-3)	RUSH	Jordan Howard	13	54%
	Med (4-7)	RUSH	Mitchell Trubisky	8	75%
	Long (8-10)	PASS	Anthony Miller	5	20%
	XL (11+)	PASS	Tarik Cohen	4	0%
			Taylor Gabriel	4	0%

Most Successful Play*

Down	Distance	Play Type	Player	Total Plays	Play Success %
1	Long (8-10)	RUSH	Taylor Gabriel	6	83%
2	Short (1-3)	RUSH	Tarik Cohen	7	86%
	Med (4-7)	PASS	Tarik Cohen	8	88%
	Long (8-10)	PASS	Allen Robinson	14	64%
	XL (11+)	RUSH	Tarik Cohen	5	40%
3	Short (1-3)	PASS	Taylor Gabriel	5	80%
			Trey Burton	5	80%
	Med (4-7)	RUSH	Mitchell Trubisky	8	75%
	Long (8-10)	PASS	Anthony Miller	5	20%

Minimum 5 plays to qualify

2018 Weekly Snap Rates

Wk	Opp	Score	Trey Burton	Taylor Gabriel	Allen Robinson	Jordan Howard	Anthony Miller	Tarik Cohen	Josh Bellamy	Dion Sims	Kevin White	Adam Shaheen
1	GB	L 24-23	61 (87%)	60 (86%)	67 (96%)	50 (71%)	39 (56%)	28 (40%)	2 (3%)	20 (29%)	12 (17%)	
2	SEA	W 24-17	57 (86%)	63 (95%)	63 (95%)	48 (73%)	37 (56%)	21 (32%)	2 (3%)	35 (53%)	2 (3%)	
3	ARI	W 16-14	63 (85%)	55 (74%)	69 (93%)	46 (62%)	36 (49%)	30 (41%)	18 (24%)	28 (38%)	12 (16%)	
4	TB	W 48-10	45 (74%)	48 (79%)	53 (87%)	33 (54%)		29 (48%)	9 (15%)	31 (51%)	28 (46%)	
6	MIA	L 31-28	51 (73%)	46 (66%)	59 (84%)	36 (51%)	41 (59%)	34 (49%)	16 (23%)	31 (44%)	16 (23%)	
7	NE	L 38-31	70 (85%)	64 (78%)	61 (74%)	46 (56%)	52 (63%)	42 (51%)	18 (22%)	16 (20%)	20 (24%)	
8	NYJ	W 24-10	48 (73%)	44 (67%)		38 (58%)	48 (73%)	38 (58%)	55 (83%)	20 (30%)	29 (44%)	
9	BUF	W 41-9	40 (78%)	44 (86%)		26 (51%)	36 (71%)	28 (55%)	32 (63%)	14 (27%)		
10	DET	W 34-22	43 (75%)	46 (81%)	54 (95%)	30 (53%)	42 (74%)	31 (54%)	6 (11%)			
11	MIN	W 25-20	59 (80%)	55 (74%)	67 (91%)	48 (65%)	60 (81%)	30 (41%)	13 (18%)		19 (26%)	
12	DET	W 23-16	55 (95%)	47 (81%)	51 (88%)	35 (60%)	33 (57%)	22 (38%)	18 (31%)	5 (9%)		
13	NYG	L 30-27	68 (82%)	76 (92%)	70 (84%)	34 (41%)	58 (70%)	42 (51%)	20 (24%)		24 (29%)	
14	LA	W 15-6	57 (80%)	57 (80%)	61 (86%)	39 (55%)	37 (52%)	30 (42%)	19 (27%)		22 (31%)	
15	GB	W 24-17	46 (77%)	46 (77%)	46 (77%)	34 (57%)	26 (43%)	38 (63%)	14 (23%)		27 (45%)	
16	SF	W 14-9	50 (78%)	51 (80%)	44 (69%)	40 (63%)	29 (45%)	33 (52%)	22 (34%)		29 (45%)	
17	MIN	W 24-10	47 (69%)	28 (41%)		41 (60%)	2 (3%)	19 (28%)	57 (84%)		46 (68%)	39 (57%)
	Grand Total		860 (80%)	830 (77%)	765 (86%)	624 (58%)	576 (57%)	495 (46%)	321 (30%)	195 (36%)	170 (28%)	160 (39%)

Personnel Groupings

Personnel	Team %	NFL Avg	Succ. %
1-1 [3WR]	64%	65%	48%
1-2 [2WR]	17%	17%	51%
2-1 [2WR]	12%	8%	50%
2-2 [1WR]	2%	3%	18%

Grouping Tendencies

Personnel	Pass Rate	Pass Succ. %	Run Succ. %
1-1 [3WR]	59%	47%	49%
1-2 [2WR]	48%	49%	53%
2-1 [2WR]	50%	56%	43%
2-2 [1WR]	14%	33%	16%

Red Zone Targets (min 3)

Receiver	All	Inside 5	6-10	11-20
Tarik Cohen	14	1	6	7
Trey Burton	14	3	4	7
Anthony Miller	11	3	3	5
Allen Robinson	10	2	2	6
Taylor Gabriel	6	3	2	1
Jordan Howard	5	1	1	3

Red Zone Rushes (min 3)

Rusher	All	Inside 5	6-10	11-20
Jordan Howard	34	12	7	15
Tarik Cohen	12	2	2	8
Mitchell Trubisky	7	2	2	3
Taylor Gabriel	2		2	

Early Down Target Rate

	RB	TE	WR
	25%	19%	56%
	23%	*21%*	*56%*
		NFL AVG	

Overall Target Success %

RB	TE	WR
51%	53%	51%
#6	#21	#15

Chicago Bears 2018 Passing Recap & 2019 Outlook

Mitchell Trubisky benefited greatly from **Matt Nagy**'s scheme, a soft pass-defense slate, and an influx of receiving talent in his sophomore season. He'll have all three on his side again. Nagy perfectly masked Trubisky's weaknesses with simplicity that generated explosive plays. Will defenses figure out Nagy's coaching intricacies and make Trubisky less comfortable going forward? Trubisky's dual-threat ability does enhance his difficulty to defend. He ranked No. 4 among qualified quarterbacks in yards per carry (6.2) and No. 6 in rushing Success Rate (56%).

Mitchell Trubisky Rating All Downs

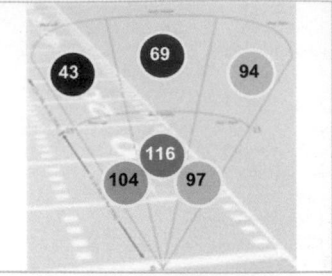

2018 Standard Passing Table

QB	Comp	Att	Comp %	Yds	YPA	TDs	INT	Sacks	Rating	Rk
Mitchell Trubisky	314	476	66%	3,515	7.4	24	12	25	94	20
Chase Daniel	53	76	70%	515	6.8	3	2	9	91	27
NFL Avg			62%		7.0				87.5	

Mitchell Trubisky Rating Early Downs

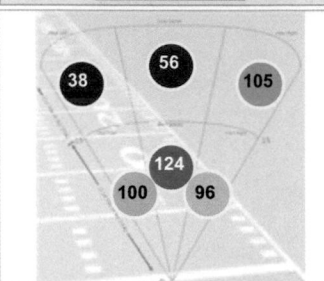

2018 Advanced Passing Table

QB	Success %	EDSR Passing Success %	20+ Yd Pass Gains	20+ Yd Pass %	30+ Yd Pass Gains	30+ Yd Pass %	Avg. Air Yds per Comp	Avg. YAC per Comp	20+ Air Yd Comp	20+ Air Yd %
Mitchell Trubisky	48%	51%	45	9.0%	23	5.0%	6.4	4.8	27	6%
Chase Daniel	45%	53%	6	8.0%	3	4.0%	6.3	3.4	5	7%
NFL Avg	44%	48%	29.5	8.4%	12.5	3.7%	5.8	5.1	14.5	6%

Interception Rates by Down

Yards to Go	1st Dwn	2nd Dwn	3rd Dwn	4th Dwn	Total
1 & 2	0.0%	0.0%	0.0%	0.0%	0.0%
3, 4, 5	0.0%	3.6%	0.0%	0.0%	1.4%
6 - 9	0.0%	1.7%	1.9%		1.7%
10 - 14	3.5%	0.0%	8.7%	0.0%	3.1%
15+	0.0%	9.1%	0.0%		3.4%
Total	3.1%	1.7%	2.3%	0.0%	2.4%

3rd Down Passing - Short of Sticks Analysis

QB	Avg. Yds to Go	Avg. YIA (of Comp)	Avg Yds Short	Short of Sticks Rate	Short Rk
Mitchell Trubisky	6.9	6.4	-0.6	53%	13
NFL Avg	7.8	6.4	-1.4	60%	

Air Yds vs YAC

Air Yds %	YAC %	Rk
57%	43%	11
53%	48%	

2018 Receiving Recap & 2019 Outlook

All of Trubisky's key pass catchers return, preserving continuity and enhancing his ceiling if Trubisky takes another step in year two with Nagy. Trubisky threw to slot routes on 50% of last year's non-running back attempts, but Nagy used diverse personnel on the receiving end of those targets. **Allen Robinson**, **Taylor Gabriel**, **Anthony Miller**, and **Trey Burton** were each targeted between 43 and 46 times in the slot. Robinson was by far Trubisky's most successful slot option and is also the likeliest Bear to benefit if Trubisky's deep ball improves.

Player *Min 50 Targets	Targ	Comp %	YPA	Rating	Success %	Success Rk	Missed YPA Rk	YAS % Rk	YTS % Rk	TDs
Allen Robinson	107	61%	8.4	91.5	53%	52	61	36	67	5
Taylor Gabriel	102	70%	7.1	88.1	51%	64	80	84	38	2
Tarik Cohen	94	79%	8.0	108.9	54%	47	100	36	110	5
Trey Burton	77	70%	7.4	106.5	57%	32	42	43	51	6
Anthony Miller	59	61%	7.7	117.7	49%	85	81	59	51	7

Directional Passer Rating Delivered

Receiver	Short Left	Short Middle	Short Right	Deep Left	Deep Middle	Deep Right	Player Total
Allen Robinson	107	116	84	14	40	104	92
Taylor Gabriel	92	127	85	100	3	43	88
Tarik Cohen	70	152	109	110	83	96	109
Trey Burton	97	113	130	9	117	110	106
Anthony Miller	141	79	110	1	141	120	118
Jordan Howard	77	104	81				83
Josh Bellamy	74	75	93	58	40	16	53
Adam Shaheen	92	99	119	119	40		125
Kevin White	56		108	40	119	90	92
Dion Sims	79	40	104	40			56
Team Total	94	114	102	44	87	91	96

2018 Rushing Recap & 2019 Outlook

With **Jordan Howard** shipped to Philadelphia, the Bears acquired **David Montgomery** and **Mike Davis** to team with **Tarik Cohen** in the backfield. Montgomery was excessively prized by GM **Ryan Pace**, who sent a 2019 fifth-round pick and 2020 fourth-rounder to move up just 14 spots for Montgomery in the third round. Montgomery projects as the Bears' lead runner with Cohen in the change-of-pace/receiving role.

Player *Min 50 Rushes	Rushes	YPC	Success %	Success Rk	Missed YPA Rk	YTS % Rk	YAS % Rk	Early Down Success %	Early Down Success Rk	TDs
Jordan Howard	260	3.7	50%	24	23	11	55	50%	24	9
Tarik Cohen	100	4.4	44%	52	64	46	13	45%	46	3

Yards per Carry by Direction

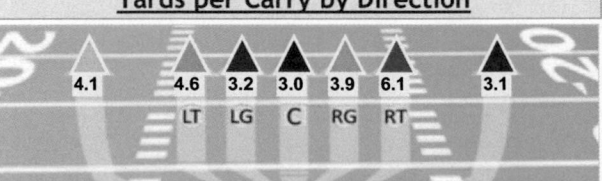

4.1	4.6	3.2	3.0	3.9	6.1	3.1
	LT	LG	C	RG	RT	

Directional Run Frequency

10%	10%	23%	19%	18%	10%	9%
	LT	LG	C	RG	RT	

five teams to *not earn a single compensatory pick* in the last five years. That's astonishing.

Fellow Super Bowl contenders New England and Kansas City earned 12 and 10 compensatory picks over the last five years, respectively. Fellow NFC title contenders Green Bay, Seattle, and Dallas each earned nine. The Bears have *none*.

Although the 2019 Bears will field a considerably talented roster, they haven't assembled nearly the depth many of their top competitors have due to trades up and trading picks for veterans. The 2020 Bears may be forced to make many difficult roster cuts, especially if Pace decides to sign Trubisky to a high-priced extension.

Matt Nagy's first year saw the Bears dramatically increase their use of three-receiver 11 personnel, hiking it from 42% under Fox to 64% last season. League averages were 71% 11 personnel when trailing and 59% when ahead. Fox's 2017 Bears ran 34% 11 personnel when leading, but Nagy's offense nearly doubled that rate (60%) when ahead. As this year's Bears are unlikely to repeat a 12-4 record, they will likely use 11 personnel even more. **Allen Robinson** projects as the primary beneficiary after delivering team highs in Success Rate (55%) and yards per target (9.1) in 11 last season. **Taylor Gabriel** and **Trey Burton** were better in 12.

(cont'd - see CHI-5)

Chicago Bears Fantasy Corner

Allen Robinson is one of my favorite 2019 season-long buys at his affordable Average Draft Position after a predictably up-and-down 2018 campaign where Robinson switched teams and learned a new offense with a new quarterback following Robinson's ACL-ruined 2017. Including his 10/143/1 Wild Card eruption against the Eagles in the playoffs, Robinson logged a rock-solid 74 / 1,025 / 6 full-season pace in 14 appearances, missing three games with hip and rib injuries. Targeted by Trubisky more than any other Bears pass catcher, Robinson is talented enough in an opportune enough situation to flirt with low-end WR1 production at a fringe WR3 cost.

- Evan Silva

2018 Situational Usage by Player & Position

Usage Rate by Score

		Being Blown Out (14+)	Down Big (9-13)	One Score	Large Lead (9-13)	Blowout Lead (14+)
RUSH	Jordan Howard	2%	2%	69%	15%	13%
	Tarik Cohen	2%	1%	72%	9%	16%
	Taylor Gabriel			91%	9%	
	Allen Robinson			100%		
	Trey Burton			100%		
	Anthony Miller			100%		
	Benny Cunningham			42%	25%	33%
	Total	2%	2%	70%	13%	14%
PASS	Jordan Howard			74%	7%	19%
	Tarik Cohen	2%	7%	71%	7%	13%
	Taylor Gabriel	8%	4%	71%	5%	12%
	Allen Robinson	2%	6%	82%	2%	8%
	Trey Burton	4%	3%	75%	6%	13%
	Anthony Miller	5%	3%	74%	3%	14%
	Josh Bellamy		4%	73%	8%	15%
	Benny Cunningham	50%	50%			
	Kevin White	13%		75%		13%
	Dion Sims			25%	75%	
	Total	4%	5%	74%	5%	12%

Share of Offensive Plays by Type

	Jordan Howard	Tarik Cohen	Taylor Gabriel	Allen Robinson	Trey Burton	Anthony Miller	Josh Bellamy	Benny Cunningham	Kevin White	Dion Sims
RUSH	66%	26%	3%	0%	0%	2%		3%		
PASS	6%	19%	20%	21%	15%	12%	5%	0%	2%	1%
ALL	33%	22%	12%	11%	8%	0%	7%	3%	2%	1%	0%

Positional Target Distribution vs NFL Average

		NFL Wide				Team Only			
		Left	Middle	Right	Total	Left	Middle	Right	Total
Deep	WR	33%	17%	30%	**81%**	27%	13%	38%	**77%**
	TE	5%	4%	7%	**16%**	6%	5%	3%	**13%**
	RB	1%	0%	2%	**3%**	3%	2%	5%	**9%**
	All	**39%**	**22%**	**39%**	**100%**	**35%**	**19%**	**45%**	**100%**
Short	WR	20%	14%	21%	**55%**	18%	14%	21%	**53%**
	TE	6%	6%	8%	**20%**	4%	9%	6%	**19%**
	RB	10%	5%	10%	**25%**	9%	5%	14%	**28%**
	All	**36%**	**25%**	**39%**	**100%**	**32%**	**28%**	**41%**	**100%**
Total		**37%**	**24%**	**39%**	**100%**	**32%**	**26%**	**42%**	**100%**

Positional Success Rates vs NFL Average

		NFL Wide				Team Only			
		Left	Middle	Right	Total	Left	Middle	Right	Total
Deep	WR	40%	50%	40%	**42%**	31%	40%	36%	**35%**
	TE	44%	54%	41%	**45%**	29%	50%	67%	**44%**
	RB	35%	25%	42%	**39%**	67%	50%	50%	**55%**
	All	**41%**	**50%**	**40%**	**43%**	**33%**	**43%**	**39%**	**38%**
Short	WR	55%	61%	52%	**55%**	61%	61%	54%	**58%**
	TE	55%	62%	54%	**57%**	41%	54%	61%	**53%**
	RB	46%	54%	45%	**47%**	49%	48%	53%	**50%**
	All	**53%**	**60%**	**51%**	**54%**	**55%**	**56%**	**55%**	**55%**
Total		**50%**	**58%**	**49%**	**52%**	**49%**	**54%**	**51%**	**51%**

Division History: Season Wins & 2019 Projection

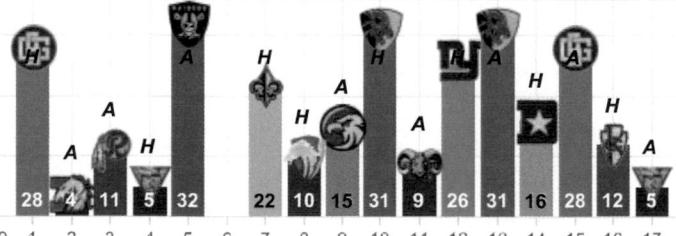

2015 Wins	2016 Wins	2017 Wins	2018 Wins	Forecast 2019 Wins

Rank of 2019 Defensive Pass Efficiency Faced by Week

| 28 | 4 | 11 | 5 | 32 | | 22 | 10 | 15 | 31 | 9 | 26 | 31 | 16 | 28 | 12 | 5 |

0 1 2 3 4 5 6 7 8 9 10 11 12 13 14 15 16 17

Rank of 2019 Defensive Rush Efficiency Faced by Week

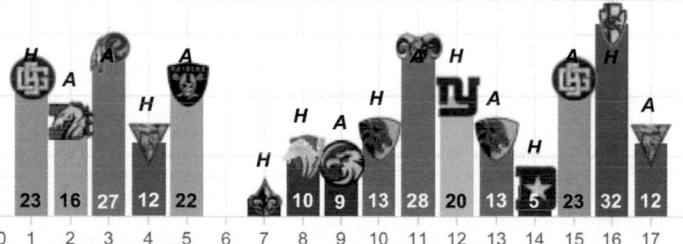

| 23 | 16 | 27 | 12 | 22 | | 10 | 9 | 13 | 28 | 20 | 13 | 5 | 23 | 32 | 12 |

0 1 2 3 4 5 6 7 8 9 10 11 12 13 14 15 16 17

2018 Detailed Analytics Summary
Success by Play Type & Primary Personnel Groupings

Type	1-1 [3WR]	1-2 [2WR]	2-1 [2WR]	2-2 [1WR]	1-3 [1WR]	1-0 [4WR]	2-0 [3WR]	2-3 [0WR]	0-0 [5WR]	0-1 [4WR]	ALL
PASS	46% (415)	49% (88)	55% (64)	33% (3)	60% (5)	40% (5)		100% (1)	100% (1)	100% (1)	48% (583)
RUSH	48% (277)	54% (93)	42% (64)	16% (19)	23% (13)	100% (2)	50% (6)	50% (2)	0% (1)		47% (477)
All	47% (692)	51% (181)	48% (128)	18% (22)	33% (18)	57% (7)	50% (6)	67% (3)	50% (2)	100% (1)	47% (1,060)

Format Success Rate (Total # of Plays)

Receiving Success by Top-4 Personnel Groupings
(Min 50 targets)

POS	Player	1-1 [3WR]	1-2 [2WR]	2-1 [2WR]	1-0 [4WR]	4 Grp Total
RB	Tarik Cohen	49% (65) 7.7, 107.4	56% (9) 7.0, 95.8	65% (20) 7.8, 115.6		53% (94) 7.7, 110.3
TE	Trey Burton	55% (53) 6.2, 90.8	64% (14) 9.6, 111.6	60% (5) 6.8, 95.0		57% (72) 6.9, 101.5
WR	Allen Robinson	55% (75) 9.1, 98.0	50% (20) 6.1, 56.5	78% (9) 10.0, 145.4	0% (1) 0.0, 39.6	55% (105) 8.5, 93.2
WR	Taylor Gabriel	49% (78) 6.9, 83.0	56% (16) 4.9, 69.3	67% (6) 11.5, 114.6		51% (100) 6.8, 83.0
WR	Anthony Miller	48% (52) 7.2, 105.6	50% (4) 3.0, 116.7	50% (2) 9.0, 120.8	100% (1) 55.0, 118.8	49% (59) 7.7, 117.7

Format Line 1: Success Rate (Total # of Plays)   Line 2: YPA, Passer Rating

Rushing Success by Top-4 Personnel Groupings
(Min 25 carries)

Rusher (Last, First)	1-1 [3WR]	1-2 [2WR]	2-1 [2WR]	2-2 [1WR]	4 Grp Total
Howard Jordan	48% (145) 4.0	52% (54) 3.0	40% (42) 3.9	29% (7) 0.9	47% (248) 3.7
Cohen Tarik	40% (72) 4.5	53% (15) 3.4	60% (5) 7.6		43% (92) 4.5
Trubisky Mitch	68% (37) 7.8	64% (14) 5.0	50% (6) 8.3	17% (6) -0.2	60% (63) 6.5

Format Line 1: Success Rate (Total # of Plays)   Line 2: YPC

Passing by Coverage Scheme

M2M	49% (228) 7.1, 89.9
Zone	58% (188) 8.9, 99.0
Screen	47% (72) 4.8, 110.0
Combo	53% (15) 7.1, 115.6

Passing by Route

Curl	68% (81) 7.7, 93.7
Screen	48% (67) 5.4, 103.9
Out	63% (65) 6.9, 111.6
Flat	35% (31) 3.3, 85.1
Slant	58% (19) 9.7, 99.5
Dig	56% (16) 7.4, 53.9

Throw Types

Level 1	58% (340) 6.5, 99.1
Level 2	44% (108) 9.3, 77.1
Level 3	33% (57) 11.1, 97.9
Sidearm	38% (21) 3.1, 86.6
Shovel	57% (14) 3.0, 118.8

QB Drop Types

3 Step	49% (268) 8.0, 86.9
0/1 Step	58% (110) 6.5, 102.0
5 Step	40% (57) 7.8, 80.1
Basic Screen	40% (30) 6.2, 103.5
Designed Rollout Right	59% (29) 5.8, 112.3
7 Step	43% (14) 11.1, 114.0

QB State at Pass

Planted	53% (361) 8.1, 95.0
Moving	52% (66) 5.3, 102.5
Shuffling	48% (61) 6.4, 107.9

Play Action

	Play Action	No P/A
Under Center	62% (26) 9.1, 110.4	50% (22) 5.6, 82.2
Shotgun	59% (70) 6.7, 103.7	50% (423) 7.5, 95.5
ALL	59% (96) 7.3, 105.5	50% (445) 7.4, 94.8

Run Types

Inside Zone	50% (160) 3.7
Outside Zone	41% (68) 4.0
Power	48% (50) 4.7
Stretch	35% (26) 2.4
Pitch	43% (14) 4.3
Lead	23% (13) 1.6

CHI-5

Nagy's 2018 passing attack was built on curls, outs, and screens. Trubisky's task was to master these three specific routes, and it was all Chicago needed. 32% of Trubisky's passes were curls or outs, and he recorded a 64% Success Rate with 7.2 yards per attempt on such plays. On passes that weren't screens, curls, or outs, Trubisky's Success Rate was 43% with 6.9 yards per attempt. His curl-route throws averaged just 6.9 yards in target depth, and his out-route passes averaged 7.2.

Trubisky was much less effective on deeper throws, including goes and flies (29% success, 12.0 YPA, 74 rating), fades (8% success, 2.5 YPA, 39.6 rating), posts (20% success, 4.4 YPA, 5.8 rating), and seam balls (47% success, 8.4 YPA, 56 rating). On all passes attempted 15-plus yards downfield, Trubisky's 69.7 rating came in 25th among qualified quarterbacks with a measly 39% Success Rate, seven touchdowns, and nine picks. The Bears still moved the ball thanks to Trubisky's short-pass success and occasional deep connections. Chicago's passing offense still ranked just 20th in efficiency despite facing the NFL's ninth-softest schedule of pass defenses.

It's hard to say exactly how much of Trubisky's year-two jump should be credited directly to him rather than Nagy's scheming, an improved supporting cast, and Chicago's weak opponents. Nagy also improved the Bears' early-down efficiency, leaving Trubisky with an average of just 6.9 yards to go on third-down plays. It was the fourth-best mark in the league behind only the Patriots, Saints, and Colts. The 2017 Bears averaged a league-high 8.4 yards to go on third downs.

Nagy also took a page from mentor **Andy Reid**'s book by designing explosive plays on high-percentage completions. In 2017, Trubisky managed just seven completions of 30-plus yards. That number spiked to 23 in 2018 with a jump of 36% to 48% in overall Success Rate. And Trubisky's adjusted completion rate on red-zone passes rose from 64% to 73% with an improvement of 81 to 106 in red-zone passer rating.

I again project the Bears to face a soft schedule of pass defenses. But their run-defense slate will take one of the biggest jumps in difficulty across the league. Chicago's defense will face much tougher offensive opponents and figures to miss **Vic Fangio**'s genius.

Last year's Bears defense was fortunate to face many poor quarterbacks, but it did get exposed by quality passers. **Tom Brady** averaged 7.9 yards per attempt with a 111 rating versus Chicago. **Aaron Rodgers** (8.0 YPA, 97 rating) and **Russell Wilson** (6.8 YPA, 94 rating) were also successful against Fangio's group. Even **Brock Osweiler** put up 9.5 yards per attempt and a 104 rating. Fangio's defense dominated **Nathan Peterman**, **Eli Manning**, Nick Mullens, **Nick Foles**, **Sam Darnold**, and **Sam Bradford**. **Jared Goff** (4.4 YPA, 21 rating) was a quality passer against whom Fangio's defense had success, albeit without **Cooper Kupp** in a weather-affected game.

This year's Bears are projected for 9.5 wins and first place in the NFC North. They have a brutal midseason stretch facing the Saints, Chargers, Eagles, and Rams in a five-week span. They close out against the Cowboys, Packers, Chiefs, and Vikings all in a row. Things aren't going to be nearly as easy as they were last season.

Cincinnati Bengals

Coaches (Prior Yrs)

Head Coach:
Zac Taylor (LAR QB, Calls Plays) (new)
Offensive Coordinator:
Brian Callahan (OAK QB) (new)
Defensive Coordinator:
Lou Anarumo (NYG DB) (new)

EASY   HARD

2019 Forecast

Wins	Div Rank
6	#4

Past Records

2018: 6-10
2017: 7-9
2016: 6-9-1

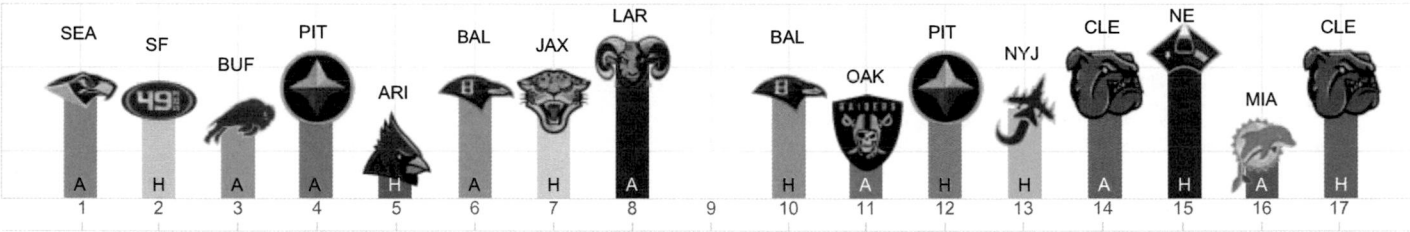

SEA	SF	BUF	PIT	ARI	BAL	JAX	LAR		BAL	OAK	PIT	NYJ	CLE	NE	MIA	CLE
A	H	A	A	H	A	H	A		H	A	H	H	A	H	A	H
1	2	3	4	5	6	7	8	9	10	11	12	13	14	15	16	17

MNF (under 4) — LON (under 8)

Key Players Lost

Player	New
Adolphus Washington (DT)	MIA
Cedric Ogbuehi (LT)	JAC
Jake Fisher (TE)	BUF
Tom Savage (QB)	DET
Tyler Kroft (TE)	BUF
Vontaze Burfict (OLB)	OAK

Average Line	# Games Favored	# Games Underdog
4.0	2	11

Regular Season Wins: Past & Current Proj

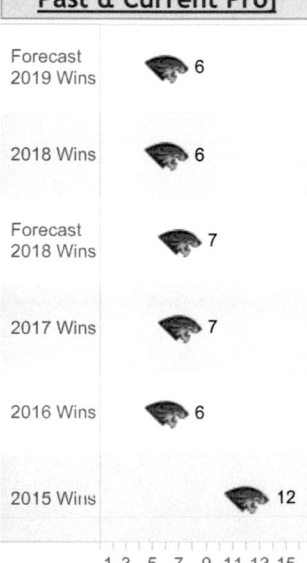

Forecast 2019 Wins		6
2018 Wins		6
Forecast 2018 Wins		7
2017 Wins		7
2016 Wins		6
2015 Wins		12

1 3 5 7 9 11 13 15

2019 Cincinnati Bengals Overview

In the NFL, you either get fired, or you quit. If you refuse to quit, you *will* get fired.

Yet **Marvin Lewis** brilliantly survived in Cincinnati for 16 years. Whether quarterbacked by **Carson Palmer** or **Andy Dalton**, finishing 12-4 and atop the AFC North, or 9-7 for third place in the division, Lewis' teams never advanced in the playoffs. He had no patience for **Ken Zampese**, who Lewis fired two games into his second year as Bengals offensive coordinator in 2017. But owner **Mike Brown** had plenty of patience for Lewis, until finally blinking and replacing him with the about-face hire of wide-eyed 36-year-old Rams QBs coach **Zac Taylor**.

Lewis' 2018 Bengals were frustrating to watch. OC **Bill Lazor** isn't from **Sean McVay**'s coaching tree, but Lazor was virtually forced to emulate it when determining personnel deployment. Frustrated by Lazor's 2017 personnel packaging, I wrote in last year's preview that he needed to use fewer three-receiver 11 sets in 2018.

The 2018 Bengals used 11 personnel at a league-average clip in the first month, deploying it on 71% of pass plays. Their use of two-tight end 12 personnel increased, and their 12-personnel passes generated 9.8 yards per attempt compared to 7.1 YPA in 11 with a 65% to 48% disparity in Success Rate. In first halves of games, Cincinnati ran 12 personnel on 28% of passes – the highest rate in the league. They started 3-1 and fielded the NFL's No. 7 passing offense. They were No. 4 in passing efficiency on non-wide receiver targets.

The Bengals lost TE **Tyler Eifert** in Week 4. The very next game, No. 2 TE **Tyler Kroft** broke his foot. Third-stringer **C.J. Uzomah** spent the final three months as Cincy's every-down tight end.

(cont'd - see CIN2)

Key Free Agents/ Trades Added

Player	AAV (MM)
B.W. Webb (CB)	$3.5
John Miller (G)	$5.5

Drafted Players

Rd	Pk	Player (College)
1	11	OT - Jonah Williams (Alabama)
2	52	TE - Drew Sample (Washington)
3	72	LB - Germaine Pratt (NC State)
4	104	QB - Ryan Finley (NC State)
4	125	DT - Renell Wren (Arizona State)
4*	136	G - Michael Jordan (Ohio State)
6	182	RB - Trayveon Williams (Texas A&M)
6*	210	LB - Deshaun Davis (Auburn)
6*	211	RB - Rodney Anderson (Oklahoma)
7	223	CB - Jordan Brown (South Dakota State)

Lineup & Cap Hits

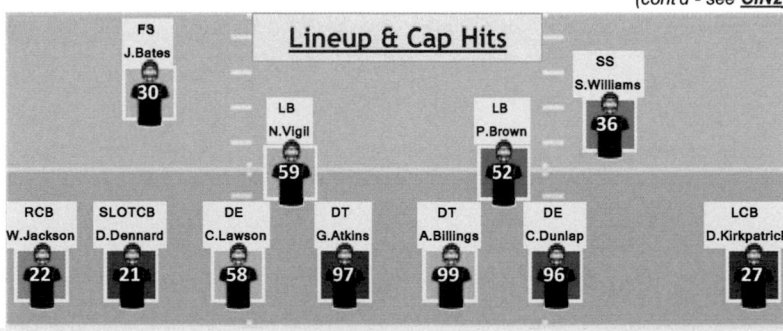

2019 Cap Dollars

2019 Unit Spending

All DEF / All OFF

Positional Spending

	Rank	Total	2017 Rk
All OFF	9	$103.49M	16
QB	18	$17.91M	19
OL	17	$37.00M	21
RB	15	$8.54M	19
WR	12	$27.63M	8
TE	6	$12.41M	13
All DEF	24	$78.53M	7
DL	14	$33.70M	6
LB	32	$11.15M	15
CB	9	$25.17M	7
S	22	$8.52M	23

The Bengals went 2-2 in Weeks 5-8, forgivably losing to the Chiefs and Steelers. But their 12-personnel usage on passes dropped from 23% to 9%. Cincinnati used 11 personnel on 86% of pass plays. And they lost **A.J. Green** in Week 8.

Lazor went 11-personnel heavy after his top-two tight ends went down. After Green's injury, Lazor maintained his 11-heavy usage (84%). Yet the Bengals produced a 64% Success Rate from 12 personnel versus a 41% Success Rate in 11. **Andy Dalton**'s passer rating was 108 in 12 versus 68 in 11, and Uzomah averaged just 4.0 yards per target with an anemic 32% Success Rate in 11 personnel. The Bengals went 0-3 without Green.

Dalton was lost for the season in Week 12. **Jeff Driskel** went 1-4 thereafter, and Cincinnati was a mess from all groupings.

There were still positive takeaways from the Bengals' 2018 season.

Dalton averaged 7.2 yards per attempt with a 49% Success Rate and 93 rating with Green in the lineup. Dalton's deep-ball performance improved from 2017 despite playing less with Green. **Tyler Boyd** emerged as an elite slot receiver, posting a 63% Success Rate to finish third among 88 qualified receivers and ranking sixth in passer rating when targeted (122). And Boyd excelled despite playing five games with Driskel's inept quarterbacking.

Joe Mixon was similarly impressive. After the 2017 Bengals faced the NFL's second-toughest run-defense schedule, I forecast last year's team would improve based on losing liability C **Russell Bodine** and facing a much softer slate. I noted an interesting Bodine-related anomaly with the Bengals' offensive line.

Teams typically run directly behind center on roughly 30% of carries. Under Zampese in 2016, the Bengals ran behind center only 9% of the time. That number remained low (15%) in 2017. They avoided running behind center in large part because Bodine stunk.

Bodine headed to Buffalo last offseason, and the Bengals drafted Ohio State C **Billy Price** in the first round. Cincinnati's behind-center runs spiked to 25% and were highly productive, delivering 4.8 yards per carry with a 53% Success Rate on first-down carries. Mixon produced a 57% Success Rate behind center on first downs – 9% above league average – and averaged 5.8 yards per attempt.

The best time to run behind center is generally in short-yardage situations. In 2016 with Bodine at center, Bengals running backs rushed just once behind center on third-down plays out of 25 attempts. In 2017 with Mixon as their

primary ball carrier, he didn't have a single behind-center rush on third down. But Mixon ran behind center on third downs on 8-of-19 attempts last season, producing a 63% Success Rate – 16% above league average. Cincinnati spiked from 3% of third-down runs behind center with Bodine to 42% with Price.

Mixon's 2017-to-2018 improvement wasn't limited to behind center. Out of 32 NFL backs with at least 125 early-down carries, only Mixon and **Nick Chubb** ranked both top five in explosiveness and top 15 in Success Rate. The NFL's most-explosive early-down runner was **Saquon Barkley**, but his Success Rate (41%) ranked 27th among 32. Mixon's early-down Success Rate rose from 40% in 2017 to 48% last year, and his yards per carry leapt from 3.5 to 4.9. All of that despite a depleted supporting cast.

(cont'd - see CIN-3)

2018 Passing Performance

QB	1st Dwn	2nd Dwn	3rd Dwn	
Andy Dalton	57%	46%	35%	Success Rate
	7.3	7.7	5.7	YPA
	96.5	90.2	76.1	Rating
Pass Rate	57%	67%	82%	
NFL AVG	53%	47%	36%	Success Rate
	7.7	7.3	6.9	YPA
	95.1	93.7	87.1	Rating
Pass Rate	53%	62%	80%	

2018 Rushing Performance

Offense	1st Dwn	2nd Dwn	3rd Dwn	
CIN	46%	43%	55%	Success Rate
	4.7	4.6	5.1	YPC
Run Rate	43%	33%	18%	
NFL AVG	48%	46%	51%	Success Rate
	4.5	4.4	4.3	YPC
Run Rate	47%	38%	20%	

2018 Offensive Advanced Metrics

Rank

EDSR Off	30 & In Off	Red Zone Off	3rd Down Off	YPPA Off	YPPT Off	Offensive Efficiency	Pass Efficiency Off	Pass Pro Efficiency Off	RB Pass Eff Off	Rush Efficiency Off	Explosive Pass Off	Explosive Run Off
20	19	13	16	29	9	19	18	19	22	14	11	25

2018 Defensive Advanced Metrics

Rank

EDSR Def	30 & In Def	Red Zone Def	3rd Down Def	YPPA Def	YPPT Def	Defensive Efficiency	Pass Efficiency Def	Pass Pro Efficiency Def	RB Pass Eff Def	Rush Efficiency Def	Explosive Pass Def	Explosive Run Def
10	14	25	32	28	26	27	25	31	26	4	20	

2018 Weekly EDSR & Season Trending Performance

	1	2	3	4	5	6	7	8	10	11	12	13	14	15	16	17	
RESULT	W	W	L	W	W	L	L	W	L	L	L	L	L	L	W	L	WEEK
OPP	IND	BAL	CAR	ATL	MIA	PIT	KC	TB	NO	BAL	CLE	DEN	LAC	OAK	CLE	PIT	
SITE	A	H	A	A	H	H	A	H	H	A	H	A	H	A	H	A	
MARGIN	11	11	-10	1	10	-7	-35	3	-37	-3	-15	-14	-5	14	-8	-3	
PTS	34	34	21	37	27	21	10	37	14	21	20	10	21	30	18	13	
OPP PTS	23	23	31	36	17	28	45	34	51	24	35	24	26	16	26	16	

EDSR by Wk
W=Green
L=Red

OFF/DEF
EDSR
Blue=OFF
(high=good)
Red=DEF
(low=good)

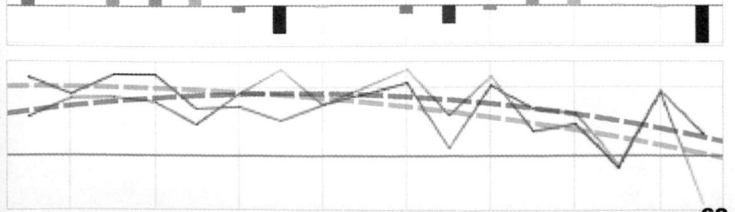

2018 Close Game Records

All 2018 Wins: **6**

FG Games (<=3 pts) W-L: **2-2**
FG Games Win %: **50% (#13)**
FG Games Wins (% of Total Wins): **33% (#11)**

1 Score Games (<=8 pts) W-L: **2-5**
1 Score Games Win %: **29% (#30)**
1 Score Games Wins (% of Total Wins): **33% (#29)**

2018 Critical & Game-Deciding Stats

TO Margin	+1
TO Given	17
INT Given	13
FUM Given	4
TO Taken	18
INT Taken	12
FUM Taken	6
Sack Margin	-4
Sacks	33
Sacks Allow	37
Return TD Margin	+3
Ret TDs	5
Ret TDs Allow	2
Penalty Margin	-1
Penalties	114
Opponent Penalties	113

Cincinnati Bengals 2019 Strength of Schedule In Detail (compared to 2018)

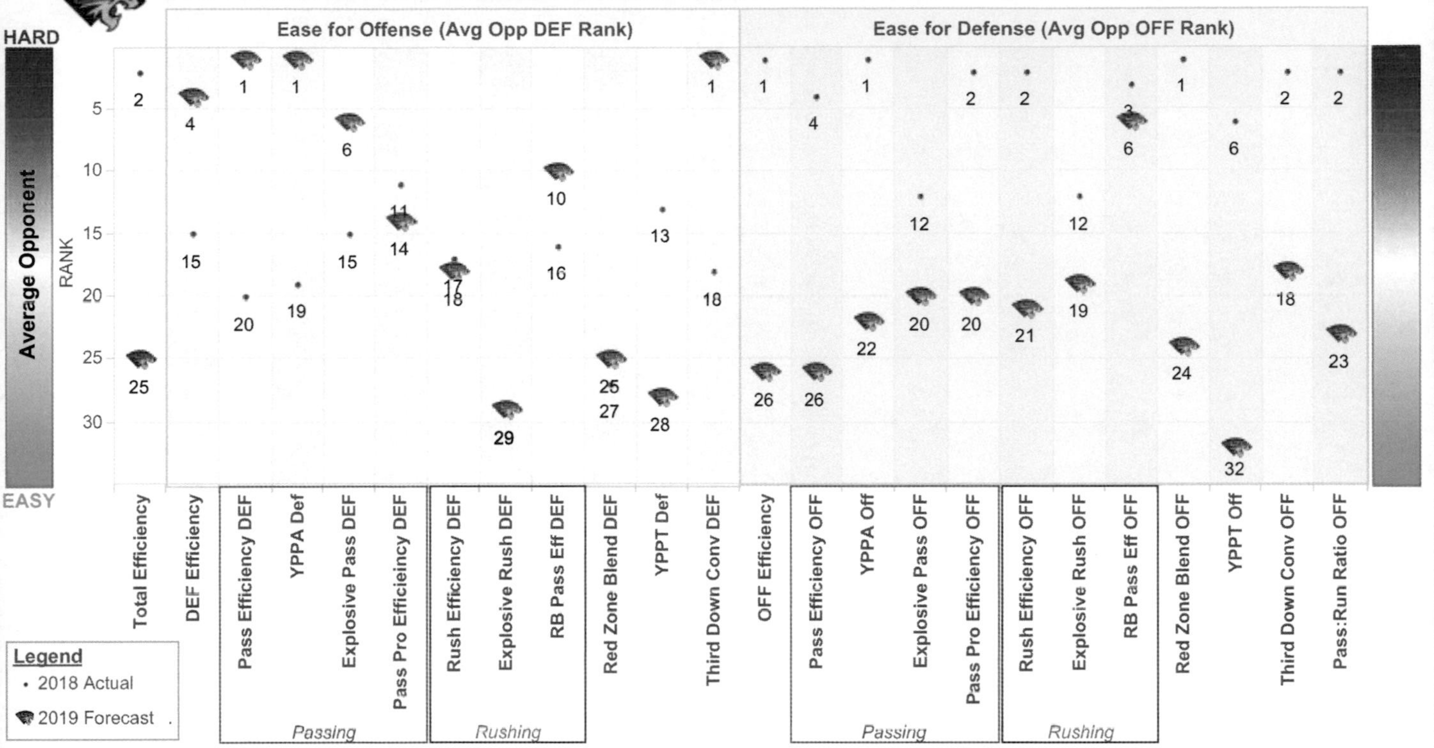
Ease for Offense (Avg Opp DEF Rank)
Ease for Defense (Avg Opp OFF Rank)
HARD
EASY
Average Opponent
RANK
Total Efficiency
DEF Efficiency
Pass Efficiency DEF
YPPA Def
Explosive Pass DEF
Pass Pro Efficieincy DEF
Rush Efficiency DEF
Explosive Rush DEF
RB Pass Eff DEF
Red Zone Blend DEF
YPPT Def
Third Down Conv DEF
OFF Efficiency
Pass Efficiency OFF
YPPA Off
Explosive Pass OFF
Pass Pro Efficiency OFF
Rush Efficiency OFF
Explosive Rush OFF
RB Pass Eff OFF
Red Zone Blend OFF
YPPT Off
Third Down Conv OFF
Pass:Run Ratio OFF
Passing
Rushing
Passing
Rushing
Legend
• 2018 Actual
2019 Forecast

2019 v 2018 Schedule Variances* (OFF=Rank of DEF faced, 2019 vs 2018)

Pass OFF Rank	Pass OFF Blend Rk	Rush OFF Rk	Rush OFF Blend Rk	Pass DEF Rk	Pass DEF Blend Rk	Rush DEF Rk	Rush DEF Blend Rk
2	2	16	11	31	31	32	32

* **1**=Hardest Jump in 2019 schedule from 2018 (aka a much harder schedule in 2019), **32**=Easiest Jump in 2019 schedule from 2018 (aka a much easier schedule in 2019); **Pass Blend** metric blends 4 metrics: Pass Efficiency, YPPA, Explosive Pass & Pass Rush; **Rush Blend** metric blends 3 metrics: Rush Efficiency, Explosive Rush & RB Targets

Team Records & Trends

	2018	2017	2016
Average line	3.2	1.0	-1.0
Average O/U line	48.3	40.9	44.7
Straight Up Record	6-10	7-9	6-9
Against the Spread Record	9-7	9-7	5-9
Over/Under Record	8-6	7-8	6-10
ATS as Favorite	2-2	3-4	4-4
ATS as Underdog	6-4	6-3	0-4
Straight Up Home	4-4	4-4	4-3
ATS Home	3-5	4-4	4-3
Over/Under Home	4-3	3-4	3-4
ATS as Home Favorite	2-2	2-4	3-2
ATS as a Home Dog	0-2	2-0	0-1
Straight Up Away	2-6	3-5	2-6
ATS Away	6-2	5-3	1-5
Over/Under Away	4-3	4-4	2-6
ATS Away Favorite	0-0	1-0	1-1
ATS Away Dog	6-2	4-3	0-3
Six Point Teaser Record	10-6	9-7	12-4
Seven Point Teaser Record	10-5	9-7	13-3
Ten Point Teaser Record	13-3	12-3	13-2

CIN-3

The Bengals were tremendous on first-down passes with Dalton despite the absence of his top-two tight ends and Green later on. On first downs in first halves of games, Cincinnati passed at a 59% rate, fifth highest in the league. Dalton delivered 8.0 yards per attempt with a 115 passer rating and 57% Success Rate. Among 27 quarterbacks with at least 75 pass attempts, Dalton's Success Rate and passer rating both ranked top five.

If Taylor takes after McVay, the Bengals are unlikely to pass as often on first down. But McVay has been exceedingly successful on first-down play calls regardless of run or pass.

Defensively, I anticipated last year's Bengals facing a tough schedule of opposing offenses. But I underestimated just how difficult it would be.

(cont'd - see CIN-4)

2019 Rest Analysis

Team More Rest	1
Opp More Rest	3
Net Rest Edge	-2
Week 2 Edge	0
Week 3 Edge	0
Week 4 Edge	0
Week 5 Edge	-1
Week 6 Edge	0
Week 7 Edge	0
Week 8 Edge	0
Week 10 Edge	7
Week 11 Edge	-3
Week 12 Edge	-3
Week 13 Edge	0
Week 14 Edge	0
Week 15 Edge	0
Week 16 Edge	0
Week 17 Edge	0

Health by Unit*

2018 Rk	28
2017 Rk	20
2018 v 2017 Rk	21
Off Rk	27
Def Rk	23
QB Rk	30
RB Rk	23
WR Rk	20
TE Rk	31
Oline Rk	12
Dline Rk	29
LB Rk	25
DB Rk	6

**Based on the work of Football Outsiders*

2018 Weekly Betting Lines (wks 1-16)

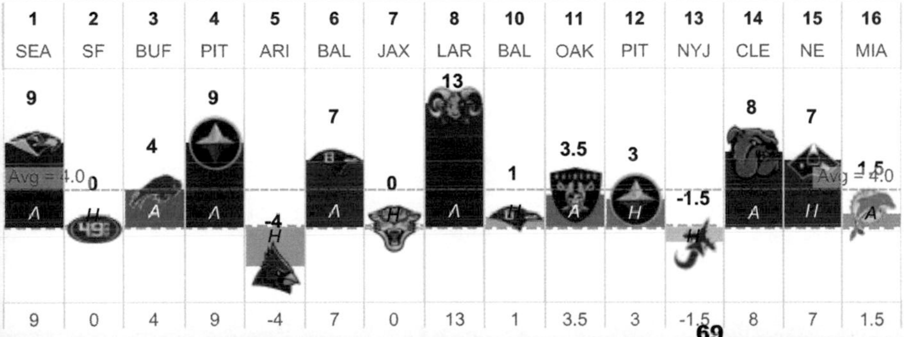
1 SEA 9 A
2 SF 0 H
3 BUF 4 A
4 PIT 9 A
5 ARI -4 H
6 BAL 7 A
7 JAX 0 H
8 LAR 13 A
10 BAL 1 H
11 OAK 3.5 A
12 PIT 3 H
13 NYJ -1.5 H
14 CLE 8 A
15 NE 7 H
16 MIA 1.5 A
Avg = 4.0
9 0 4 9 -4 7 0 13 1 3.5 3 -1.5 8 7 1.5

Home Lines (wks 1-16)

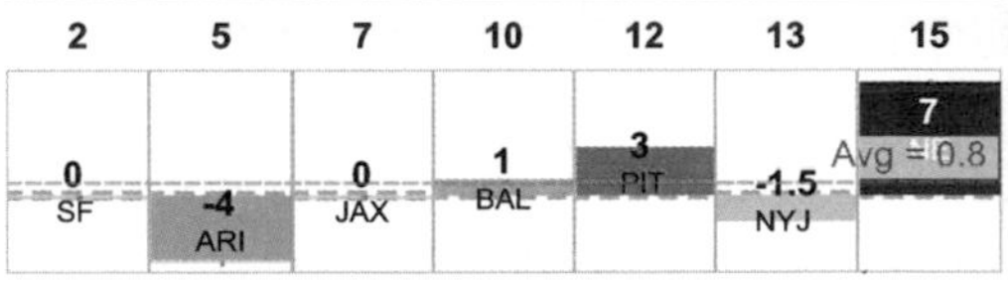
2 5 7 10 12 13 15
0 SF
-4 ARI
0 JAX
1 BAL
3 PIT
-1.5 NYJ
7
Avg = 0.8

Road Lines (wks 1-16)

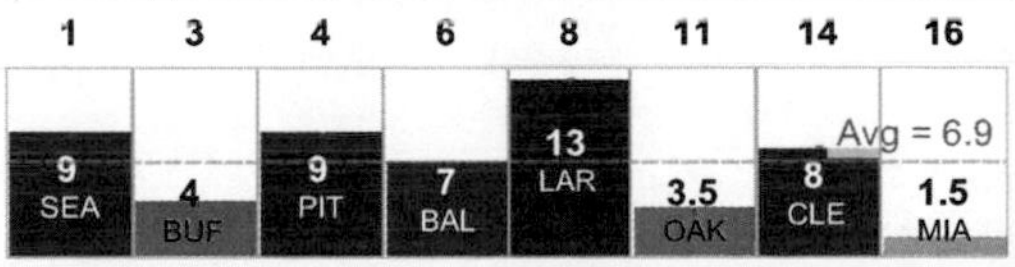
1 3 4 6 8 11 14 16
9 SEA
4 BUF
9 PIT
7 BAL
13 LAR
3.5 OAK
8 CLE
1.5 MIA
Avg = 6.9

2018 Play Tendencies

All Pass %	62%
All Pass Rk	8
All Rush %	38%
All Rush Rk	25
1 Score Pass %	61%
1 Score Pass Rk	8
2017 1 Score Pass %	57%
2017 1 Score Pass Rk	16
2018 Pass Increase %	4%
Pass Increase Rk	11
1 Score Rush %	39%
1 Score Rush Rk	25
Up Pass %	55%
Up Pass Rk	6
Up Rush %	45%
Up Rush Rk	27
Down Pass %	66%
Down Pass Rk	17
Down Rush %	34%
Down Rush Rk	16

2018 Down & Distance Tendencies

Down	Distance	Total Plays	Pass Rate	Run Rate	Play Success %
1	Short (1-3)	11	36%	64%	64%
	Med (4-7)	10	60%	40%	60%
	Long (8-10)	278	53%	47%	50%
	XL (11+)	11	73%	27%	27%
2	Short (1-3)	40	40%	60%	53%
	Med (4-7)	61	69%	31%	54%
	Long (8-10)	84	61%	39%	32%
	XL (11+)	33	79%	21%	30%
3	Short (1-3)	31	42%	58%	65%
	Med (4-7)	44	84%	16%	45%
	Long (8-10)	31	87%	13%	32%
	XL (11+)	34	97%	3%	12%
		35	1	0%	100%	0%
4	Short (1-3)	7	43%	57%	71%
	Long (8-10)	1	0%	100%	0%
	XL (11+)	1	100%	0%	0%

Shotgun %:

Under Center	Shotgun
35%	65%

37% AVG 63%

Run Rate:

Under Center	Shotgun
67%	21%

68% AVG 23%

Pass Rate:

Under Center	Shotgun
33%	79%

32% AVG 77%

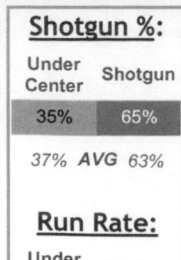

Cincinnati Bengals
2018 Play Analysis

Short Yardage Intelligence:

2nd and Short Run

Run Freq	Run Rk	NFL Run Freq Avg	Run 1D Rate	Run NFL 1D Avg
63%	20	65%	55%	68%

2nd and Short Pass

Pass Freq	Pass Rk	NFL Pass Freq Avg	Pass 1D Rate	Pass NFL 1D Avg
38%	13	35%	25%	56%

Most Frequent Play

Down	Distance	Play Type	Player	Total Plays	Play Success %
1	Short (1-3)	RUSH	Joe Mixon	4	75%
	Med (4-7)	RUSH	Joe Mixon	3	67%
	Long (8-10)	RUSH	Joe Mixon	94	47%
	XL (11+)	PASS	Tyler Boyd	3	0%
2	Short (1-3)	RUSH	Joe Mixon	18	56%
	Med (4-7)	RUSH	Joe Mixon	16	50%
	Long (8-10)	RUSH	Joe Mixon	21	33%
	XL (11+)	PASS	A.J. Green	4	50%
3	Short (1-3)	RUSH	Joe Mixon	16	69%
	Med (4-7)	PASS	Tyler Boyd	10	60%
	Long (8-10)	PASS	Tyler Boyd	5	80%
	XL (11+)	PASS	Giovani Bernard	8	0%

Most Successful Play*

Down	Distance	Play Type	Player	Total Plays	Play Success %
1	Long (8-10)	PASS	Tyler Eifert	8	88%
2	Short (1-3)	RUSH	Giovani Bernard	6	67%
	Med (4-7)	PASS	Tyler Boyd	6	83%
	Long (8-10)	PASS	C.J. Uzomah	5	60%
3	Short (1-3)	RUSH	Joe Mixon	16	69%
	Med (4-7)	PASS	Tyler Boyd	10	60%
	Long (8-10)	PASS	Tyler Boyd	5	80%
	XL (11+)	PASS	Tyler Boyd	7	14%

*Minimum 5 plays to qualify

2018 Weekly Snap Rates

Wk	Opp	Score	C.J. Uzomah	Tyler Boyd	Joe Mixon	A.J. Green	Alex Erickson	Giovani Bernard	Cody Core	Tyler Eifert	Josh Malone
1	IND	W 34-23	36 (64%)	49 (88%)	44 (79%)	53 (95%)	1 (2%)	12 (21%)		23 (41%)	2 (4%)
2	BAL	W 34-23	37 (49%)	58 (76%)	39 (51%)	69 (91%)		39 (51%)		49 (64%)	6 (8%)
3	CAR	L 31-21	35 (54%)	51 (78%)		33 (51%)	7 (11%)	57 (88%)	6 (9%)	42 (65%)	29 (45%)
4	ATL	W 37-36	51 (70%)	62 (85%)		69 (95%)	36 (49%)	44 (60%)	11 (15%)	19 (26%)	4 (5%)
5	MIA	W 27-17	55 (92%)	45 (75%)	47 (78%)	51 (85%)	36 (60%)		8 (13%)		10 (17%)
6	PIT	L 28-21	56 (92%)	57 (93%)	42 (69%)	57 (93%)	46 (75%)		9 (15%)		4 (7%)
7	KC	L 45-10	55 (96%)	56 (98%)	44 (77%)	46 (81%)	20 (35%)		14 (25%)		
8	TB	W 37-34	64 (97%)	61 (92%)	55 (83%)	62 (94%)	51 (77%)		6 (9%)		4 (6%)
10	NO	L 51-14	42 (98%)	41 (95%)	29 (67%)		16 (37%)	12 (28%)	20 (47%)		
11	BAL	L 24-21	55 (100%)	52 (95%)	34 (62%)		9 (16%)	26 (47%)	34 (62%)		
12	CLE	L 35-20	74 (100%)	72 (97%)	53 (72%)		7 (9%)	23 (31%)	30 (41%)		
13	DEN	L 24-10	67 (99%)	66 (97%)	39 (57%)	17 (25%)	5 (7%)	28 (41%)	35 (51%)		
14	LAC	L 26-21	58 (87%)	64 (96%)	47 (70%)		21 (31%)	25 (37%)	33 (49%)		
15	OAK	W 30-16	69 (86%)	39 (49%)	52 (65%)		36 (45%)	30 (38%)	51 (64%)		
16	CLE	L 26-18	41 (87%)		38 (81%)		32 (68%)	14 (30%)	43 (91%)	1 (2%)	
17	PIT	L 16-13	45 (92%)		33 (67%)		41 (84%)	19 (39%)	11 (22%)	8 (16%)	
	Grand Total		840 (85%)	773 (87%)	596 (70%)	457 (79%)	364 (41%)	329 (43%)	311 (37%)	133 (49%)	68 (12%)

Personnel Groupings

Personnel	Team %	NFL Avg	Succ. %
1-1 [3WR]	75%	65%	45%
1-2 [2WR]	18%	17%	48%
1-3 [1WR]	3%	3%	36%

Grouping Tendencies

Personnel	Pass Rate	Pass Succ. %	Run Succ. %
1-1 [3WR]	65%	43%	48%
1-2 [2WR]	52%	53%	41%
1-3 [1WR]	20%	40%	35%

Red Zone Targets (min 3)

Receiver	All	Inside 5	6-10	11-20
A.J. Green	12	4	1	7
John Ross	10	5	1	4
Tyler Boyd	10	1	2	7
Joe Mixon	7	1	3	3
C.J. Uzomah	6	2	1	3
Alex Erickson	3		1	2

Red Zone Rushes (min 3)

Rusher	All	Inside 5	6-10	11-20
Joe Mixon	32	13	8	11
Giovani Bernard	9	3	3	3
Andy Dalton	1			1

Early Down Target Rate

RB	TE	WR
22%	22%	57%
23%	21%	56%
	NFL AVG	

Overall Target Success %

RB	TE	WR
44%	56%	49%
#23	#15	#25

Cincinnati Bengals 2018 Passing Recap & 2019 Outlook

Andy Dalton is one of the NFL's least-entertaining quarterbacks. He is productive enough to keep a team in purgatory but unlikely to propel it to any level of consequence, or to play poorly enough to land a top-five pick. This year's Bengals are slated to face the NFL's most-difficult schedule of pass defenses based on my 2019 metrics. In their first nine games, Cincinnati draws six opponents that finished top five in pass defense in 2018, by far most in the NFL.

2018 Standard Passing Table

QB	Comp	Att	Comp %	Yds	YPA	TDs	INT	Sacks	Rating	Rk
Andy Dalton	226	365	62%	2,566	7.0	21	11	21	90	30
Jeff Driskel	105	176	60%	1,003	5.7	6	2	16	82	37
NFL Avg			62%		7.0				87.5	

2018 Advanced Passing Table

QB	Success %	EDSR Passing Success %	20+ Yd Pass Gains	20+ Yd Pass %	30+ Yd Pass Gains	30+ Yd Pass %	Avg. Air Yds per Comp	Avg. YAC per Comp	20+ Air Yd Comp	20+ Air Yd %
Andy Dalton	48%	52%	38	10.0%	12	3.0%	6.2	5.1	14	4%
Jeff Driskel	39%	43%	15	9.0%	2	1.0%	5.0	4.6	8	5%
NFL Avg	44%	48%	29.5	8.4%	12.5	3.7%	5.8	5.1	14.5	6%

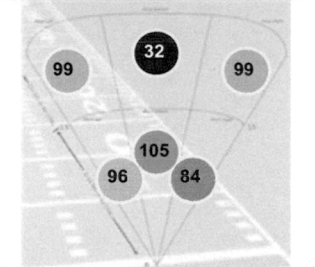

Andy Dalton Rating All Downs

99 32 99
105
96 84

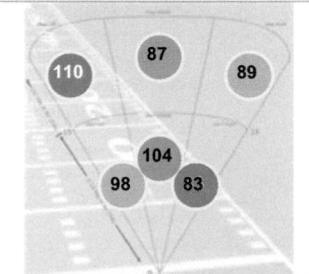

Andy Dalton Rating Early Downs

87
110 89
104
98 83

Interception Rates by Down

Yards to Go	1st Dwn	2nd Dwn	3rd Dwn	4th Dwn	Total
1 & 2	0.0%	0.0%	10.0%	0.0%	4.3%
3, 4, 5	0.0%	3.7%	0.0%	0.0%	1.9%
6 - 9		0.0%	0.0%	0.0%	0.0%
10 - 14	2.9%	4.7%	0.0%	0.0%	2.9%
15+	0.0%	7.7%	25.0%		10.0%
Total	2.6%	3.0%	3.3%	0.0%	2.8%

3rd Down Passing - Short of Sticks Analysis

QB	Avg. Yds to Go	Avg. YIA (of Comp)	Avg Yds Short	Short of Sticks Rate	Short Rk
Andy Dalton	7.9	6.3	-1.6	55%	20
NFL Avg	7.8	6.4	-1.4	60%	

Air Yds vs YAC

Air Yds %	YAC %	Rk
54%	46%	19
53%	48%	

2018 Receiving Recap & 2019 Outlook

My belief is Taylor will use ample amounts of 11 personnel to get **Tyler Boyd**, **A.J. Green**, and **John Ross** on the field together. When all were healthy last season and aligned in 11, Green was targeted nearly as often in the slot (29) as he was outside (31), and he dominated with 11.9 yards per target, a 72% Success Rate, and three touchdowns on interior routes. Boyd drew 50 targets in the slot in those games, and only 3 targets out wide.

Player *Min 50 Targets	Targ	Comp %	YPA	Rating	Success %	Success Rk	Missed YPA Rk	YAS % Rk	YTS % Rk	TDs
Tyler Boyd	108	70%	9.5	122.0	63%	3	67	59	38	7
A.J. Green	77	60%	9.0	104.6	56%	37	52	18	87	6
C.J. Uzomah	66	65%	6.7	99.2	56%	37	69	117	4	3
John Ross	58	36%	3.6	51.0	26%	130	183	28	122	6
Joe Mixon	55	78%	5.4	87.6	51%	64	75	88	18	0

Directional Passer Rating Delivered

Receiver	Short Left	Short Middle	Short Right	Deep Left	Deep Middle	Deep Right	Player Total
Tyler Boyd	123	109	110	115	146	114	122
A.J. Green	56	110	91	140	104	119	105
C.J. Uzomah	90	111	117	40	85	63	99
John Ross	122	104	21	0	2	48	51
Joe Mixon	56	90	88			121	88
Giovani Bernard	77	83	81				82
Alex Erickson	85	93	91		40	40	84
Cody Core	75	158	55	40	96	0	62
Tyler Eifert	149	86	114	119	0		102
Tyler Kroft	90	0	92				43
Team Total	99	106	91	81	62	66	93

2018 Rushing Recap & 2019 Outlook

As this year's Bengals face the league's toughest pass-defense schedule but No. 17 run-defense slate, **Joe Mixon** is an enticing fantasy pick. He played in only 14 games last season but ranked RB9 and has clear control of Cincinnati's ground attack in the red zone, where Mixon logged 32 carries with 21 inside the ten-yard line compared to Bernard's six last year. Taylor comes from the Rams, where they have a similarly mediocre quarterback and ran **Todd Gurley** until the wheels literally came off.

Player *Min 50 Rushes	Rushes	YPC	Success %	Success Rk	Missed YPA Rk	YTS % Rk	YAS % Rk	Early Down Success %	Early Down Success Rk	TDs
Joe Mixon	237	4.9	49%	31	36	62	4	48%	29	8
Giovani Bernard	56	3.8	41%	60	71	60	42	44%	52	3

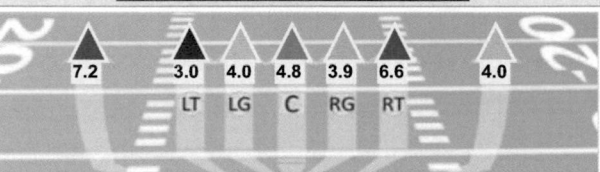

Yards per Carry by Direction

7.2 (LT) 3.0 (LG) 4.0 (C) 4.8 (RG) 3.9 (RT) 6.6 | 4.0

Directional Run Frequency

8% (LT) 10% (LG) 21% (C) 25% (RG) 18% (RT) 11% | 7%

They wound up facing the toughest schedule of offenses in the entire league, playing just two teams that ranked bottom half in offensive efficiency (Dolphins, Raiders). Cincinnati was also unfortunate to catch Cleveland late in the season, after incompetent **Hue Jackson** got fired and **Baker Mayfield** caught fire. The Bengals wound up facing five top-five offenses (Chiefs, Saints, Chargers, Steelers twice) and dropped to No. 27 in defensive efficiency after ranking 17th in 2017. Despite those struggles, the Bengals' Early-Down Success Rate defense ranked top ten, identical to their previous-year mark.

The Bengals' biggest 2018 problem wasn't their early-down defense. It was their third-down defense, where Cincinnati allowed the NFL's highest third-down conversion rate, and the highest mark in the entire league since 2011. The Bengals' defense also spent more time on the field than any other team.

Lewis' Bengals still didn't give up. They went 4-1 against the spread in Driskel's five starts, keeping one-score pace with the Chargers, Steelers, and Browns.

The 2018 Bengals unfortunately went 2-5 in one-score games after going 4-4 in 2017. They were near neutral in turnover ratio, penalty margin, and sack differential. They've sustained horrendous injury luck in two straight years. A top-three team in terms of health in both 2015 and 2016, the Bengals fell to 20th and 28th the past two seasons.

(cont'd - see CIN-5)

Cincinnati Bengals Fantasy Corner

Tyler Boyd was 2018's premier third-year receiver breakout, parlaying **Tyler Eifert**'s early-season injury and **John Ross**' virtual nonexistence into No. 2 target status in Cincinnati. Even as he lost the final two games to an MCL sprain, Boyd's 733 yards gained on slot routes ranked third in the NFL behind **Tyreek Hill** (857) and **JuJu Smith-Schuster** (771), and Boyd ranked 21st among 96 qualified receivers in yards per route run (2.06). Boyd figures to be used similarly to **Cooper Kupp** under ex-Rams assistant **Zac Taylor**. Not yet 25 years old, Boyd's arrow is pointing up entering his contract season.

- Evan Silva

2018 Situational Usage by Player & Position

Usage Rate by Score

		Being Blown Out (14+)	Down Big (9-13)	One Score	Large Lead (9-13)	Blowout Lead (14+)
RUSH	Joe Mixon	18%	5%	63%	5%	8%
	Giovani Bernard	9%	5%	75%	9%	2%
	Tyler Boyd			100%		
	John Ross		25%	25%		50%
	Alex Erickson		33%	67%		
	Total	16%	6%	65%	6%	8%
PASS	Joe Mixon	22%	7%	64%	4%	2%
	Giovani Bernard	13%	11%	63%	7%	7%
	Tyler Boyd	15%	3%	67%	5%	9%
	A.J. Green	16%	4%	70%	1%	7%
	C.J. Uzomah	36%	3%	51%	5%	5%
	John Ross	26%	7%	59%	4%	4%
	Alex Erickson	12%		65%	12%	12%
	Cody Core	42%	8%	42%	8%	
	Tyler Eifert	5%	11%	63%	11%	11%
	Tyler Kroft			60%	20%	20%
	Total	21%	5%	62%	5%	7%

Share of Offensive Plays by Type

	Joe Mixon	Giovani Bernard	Tyler Boyd	A.J. Green	C.J. Uzomah	John Ross	Alex Erickson	Cody Core	Tyler Eifert	Tyler Kroft
RUSH	78%	19%	1%			1%	1%			
PASS	10%	10%	21%	15%	14%	12%	6%	5%	4%	1%
ALL	38%	14%	13%	9%	8%	8%	4%	3%	3%	1%

Positional Target Distribution vs NFL Average

		NFL Wide				Team Only			
		Left	Middle	Right	Total	Left	Middle	Right	Total
Deep	WR	33%	17%	31%	81%	30%	24%	34%	88%
	TE	5%	4%	7%	16%	3%	3%	3%	10%
	RB	1%	0%	2%	4%			2%	2%
	All	39%	22%	39%	100%	34%	27%	39%	100%
Short	WR	20%	14%	21%	55%	18%	15%	21%	55%
	TE	6%	6%	8%	20%	8%	4%	8%	20%
	RB	10%	5%	10%	25%	7%	7%	11%	25%
	All	36%	25%	39%	100%	34%	26%	40%	100%
Total		37%	24%	39%	100%	34%	26%	40%	100%

Positional Success Rates vs NFL Average

		NFL Wide				Team Only			
		Left	Middle	Right	Total	Left	Middle	Right	Total
Deep	WR	40%	49%	40%	42%	30%	48%	37%	37%
	TE	44%	54%	42%	46%	33%	33%	33%	33%
	RB	38%	33%	42%	40%			50%	50%
	All	41%	50%	40%	43%		46%	37%	37%
Short	WR	55%	61%	53%	55%	55%	63%	49%	55%
	TE	55%	62%	54%	57%	67%	56%	58%	61%
	RB	47%	54%	45%	48%	38%	52%	49%	47%
	All	53%	59%	51%	54%	54%	59%	51%	54%
Total		50%	58%	49%	52%	50%	57%	48%	51%

Division History: Season Wins & 2019 Projection

(chart: vertical axis 0–14)

2015 Wins | 2016 Wins | 2017 Wins | 2018 Wins | Forecast 2019 Wins

Rank of 2019 Defensive Pass Efficiency Faced by Week

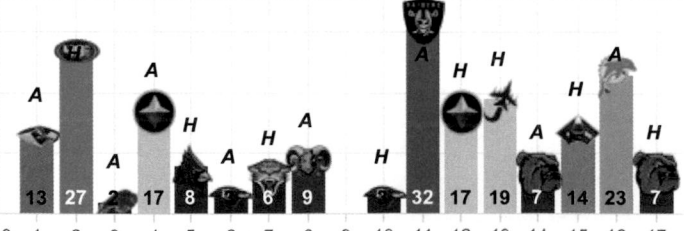

13 | 27 | 2 | 17 | 8 | | 6 | 9 | | 32 | 17 | 19 | 7 | 14 | 23 | 7

0 1 2 3 4 5 6 7 8 9 10 11 12 13 14 15 16 17

Rank of 2019 Defensive Rush Efficiency Faced by Week

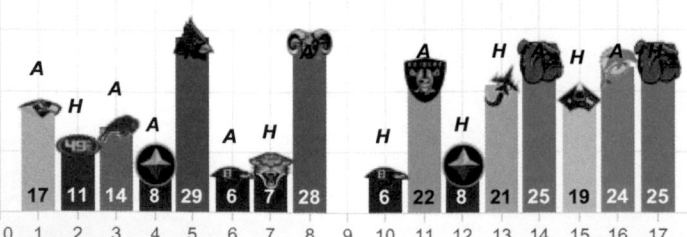

17 | 11 | 14 | 8 | 29 | 6 | 7 | 28 | | 6 | 22 | 8 | 21 | 25 | 19 | 24 | 25

0 1 2 3 4 5 6 7 8 9 10 11 12 13 14 15 16 17

2018 Detailed Analytics Summary
Success by Play Type & Primary Personnel Groupings

Successful Play Rate 0% — 100%

Type	1-1 [3WR]	1-2 [2WR]	1-3 [1WR]	2-1 [2WR]	2-2 [1WR]	1-0 [4WR]	0-0 [5WR]	2-0 [3WR]	2-3 [0WR]	ALL
PASS	43% (457)	53% (86)	40% (5)	64% (14)	50% (2)	67% (6)	50% (2)	0% (4)		45% (576)
RUSH	48% (242)	41% (78)	35% (20)	25% (4)	30% (10)			50% (2)	100% (3)	45% (359)
All	45% (699)	48% (164)	36% (25)	56% (18)	33% (12)	67% (6)	50% (4)	0% (4)	100% (3)	45% (935)

Format Success Rate (Total # of Plays)

Receiving Success by Top-4 Personnel Groupings
(Min 50 targets)

POS	Player	1-1 [3WR]	1-2 [2WR]	2-1 [2WR]	1-0 [4WR]	4 Grp Total
RB	Joe Mixon	49% (37) 4.8, 80.7	55% (11) 6.7, 94.7	75% (4) 3.8, 82.3	0% (1) 6.0, 91.7	51% (53) 5.2, 86.4
TE	C.J. Uzomah	52% (50) 6.1, 92.4	58% (12) 7.4, 88.5	100% (2) 12.5, 118.8	100% (1) 20.0, 118.8	55% (65) 6.7, 94.3
WR	Tyler Boyd	64% (86) 9.8, 130.1	63% (16) 10.2, 101.8		100% (3) 7.7, 98.6	65% (105) 9.8, 125.4
	A.J. Green	62% (61) 9.2, 112.7	43% (14) 8.4, 96.7			59% (75) 9.0, 109.8
	John Ross	26% (53) 3.8, 48.2	25% (4) 1.8, 56.3			26% (57) 3.7, 51.2

Format Line 1: Success Rate (Total # of Plays) Line 2: YPA, Passer Rating

Rushing Success by Top-4 Personnel Groupings
(Min 25 carries)

Rusher (Last, First)	1-1 [3WR]	1-2 [2WR]	2-2 [1WR]	2-1 [2WR]	4 Grp Total
Mixon Joe	51% (159) 5.4	43% (53) 4.1	43% (7) 0.7	33% (3) 0.7	49% (222) 4.9
Bernard Giovani	34% (35) 3.1	43% (14) 5.7			37% (49) 3.9
Driskel Jeff	58% (19) 6.9	0% (3) 0.7	0% (3) -1.0		44% (25) 5.2

Format Line 1: Success Rate (Total # of Plays) Line 2: YPC

Passing by Coverage Scheme

M2M	51% (247) 7.0, 87.5
Zone	52% (165) 7.4, 93.6
Screen	45% (55) 5.4, 89.3
Combo	75% (12) 4.8, 126.4

Passing by Route

Out	53% (77) 5.1, 88.3
Screen	47% (55) 5.9, 91.3
Curl	55% (51) 5.7, 91.4
Slant	57% (42) 7.8, 86.1
Dig	54% (28) 7.6, 66.7
Flat	29% (24) 4.2, 54.3

Throw Types

Level 1	55% (303) 6.5, 95.1
Level 2	48% (168) 7.6, 95.7
Level 3	23% (35) 6.4, 57.5
Sidearm	67% (6) 4.8, 86.8
Shovel	0% (1) -1.0, 79.2

QB Drop Types

3 Step	51% (213) 7.5, 91.3
0/1 Step	53% (146) 6.1, 98.7
5 Step	45% (73) 7.3, 82.8
Basic Screen	40% (30) 5.4, 89.3
Designed Rollout Right	59% (27) 5.6, 102.5
7 Step	53% (17) 7.4, 91.5

QB State at Pass

Planted	51% (363) 7.2, 90.1
Moving	56% (57) 6.8, 113.6
Shuffling	43% (47) 5.5, 74.7

Play Action

	Play Action	No P/A
Under Center	55% (62) 7.1, 92.2	66% (38) 9.4, 128.8
Shotgun	56% (59) 8.3, 110.1	47% (361) 6.2, 84.1
ALL	55% (121) 7.7, 100.9	48% (399) 6.5, 88.4

Run Types

Inside Zone	49% (134) 4.5
Outside Zone	43% (95) 5.3
Pitch	55% (22) 5.1
Stretch	15% (13) 4.2
Lead	62% (13) 3.9
Power	40% (10) 1.6

CIN-5

Fortunately, my schedule analytics forecast this year's Bengals will face the NFL's largest decrease in opponent offensive strength. Outside of the AFC North, they draw the Cardinals, Bills, Jaguars, Jets, Dolphins, Raiders, and 49ers. All ranked bottom ten in offensive efficiency last year. Last year's Cincinnati schedule included **Patrick Mahomes**, **Drew Brees**, **Philip Rivers**, **Matt Ryan**, **Andrew Luck**, and **Cam Newton**.

Transitioning from Bodine to Price paid 2018 dividends, and this year's first-round investment on Alabama LT **Jonah Williams** should also pay off. Their second-round reach for blocking TE **Drew Sample** seemed overly reactionary given last year's tight end injuries, however, and fourth-round QB **Ryan Finley** won't upgrade on Dalton. Dalton's 2020 cap hit of $17.7 million ranks only 16th among quarterbacks signed for the next two years, and **Giovani Bernard**'s return behind Mixon made Cincinnati's two running back picks seem unnecessary.

I'm still not as down on the Bengals as most are. If they do catch better injury luck and Williams comes along quickly, Taylor's debut season can surprise. They should have better fortune in one-score games, and the schedule softens considerably. But it's still no cakewalk. In Weeks 11-12, for instance, the Bengals face the Raiders and Steelers with both teams on extra rest coming off Thursday night games. And Cincinnati's schedule of opposing pass defenses projects as hardest in the league.

The 2019 Bengals' outlook hinges on how well equipped Taylor is for his first head-coaching job and whether he can minimize the weaknesses of Dalton. Will Taylor successfully implement a McVay-like scheme? Will he make on-the-fly adjustments to enhance his underrated toolbox of players and exploit opponent deficiencies? If so, Cincinnati can rebound as a competitive team and exceed its Win Total. If not, this team's floor is low.

Cleveland Browns

Coaches (Prior Yrs)

Head Coach:
Freddie Kitchens (CLE OC, Calls Plays) (new)
Offensive Coordinator:
Todd Monken (TB OC) (new)
Defensive Coordinator:
Steve Wilks (ARI HC) (new)

EASY　HARD

2019 Forecast

Wins	Div Rank
9	#1

Past Records

2018: 7-9
2017: 0-16
2016: 1-15

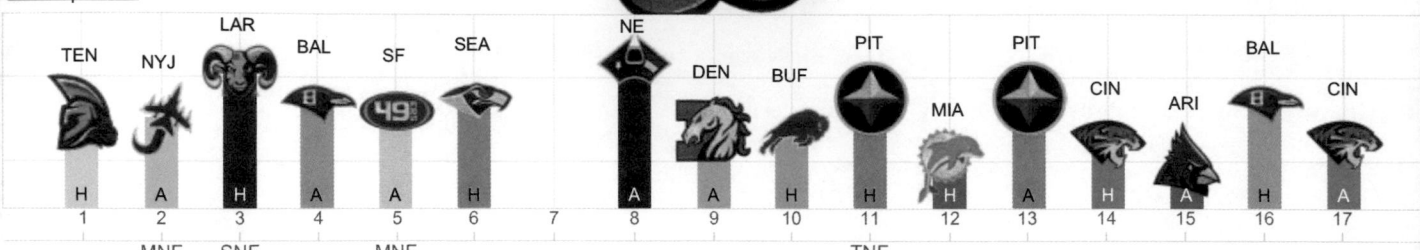

	TEN	NYJ	LAR	BAL	SF	SEA		NE	DEN	BUF	PIT	MIA	PIT	CIN	ARI	BAL	CIN
	H	A	H	A	A	H		A	A	H	H	H	A	H	A	H	A
	1	2	3	4	5	6	7	8	9	10	11	12	13	14	15	16	17
		MNF	SNF		MNF								TNF				

Key Players Lost

Player	New
Breshad Perriman (WR)	TB
Brian Boddy-Calhoun (S)	HOU
Darren Fells (TE)	HOU
Dwayne Bowe (WR)	Retired
E.J. Gaines (CB)	BUF
Emmanuel Ogbah (DE)	KC
Jabrill Peppers (FS)	NYG
Jamie Collins (OLB)	NE
Kevin Zeitler (OG)	NYG
Ricardo Louis (WR)	MIA
Tyrod Taylor (QB)	LAC

Average Line	# Games Favored	# Games Underdog
-1.1	8	6

2019 Cleveland Browns Overview

What a difference a year makes.

I began last year's Browns preview discussing an 0-6 season, the Factory of Sadness, and **Hue Jackson**'s dip into the lake. I discussed how Hue's 2017 Browns trailed at halftime by more than one score in just 5-of-16 games. Yet they *lost all of them* due to terrible coaching. While I don't actively root for teams – I root for efficiency – it was so painful to watch a team and city suffer as Cleveland did for years.

And I'm glad to not have to write about Hue's record or **Gregg Williams**' silly "Angel" defense. I closed out last year's Browns chapter asking, "Where is the accountability? (Hue and Gregg) had more influence on Cleveland's 2017 results than any individual players. After a busy 2018 offseason, the Browns have a rejuvenated roster with upside. But coaching matters in the NFL," and I hoped for the sake of the players and fans that those coaches would improve.

Better late than never: we *got* the accountability. The Browns fired Jackson and OC **Todd Haley** following a 33-18 Week 8 loss to Pittsburgh. Although most didn't know much about then-interim OC **Freddie Kitchens**, I had been a follower of his since 2013 when Kitchens encountered health issues during an Arizona Cardinals minicamp practice. Kitchens was diagnosed with a heart attack, and his spirited attitude following hours of surgery grabbed my attention. Kitchens never called plays in Arizona but learned under **Bruce Arians** as the Cardinals' quarterbacks coach. Kitchens took the Browns' offensive reigns at midseason, and he was a maestro.

But to truly appreciate the greatness of Kitchens and **Baker Mayfield**'s immediate bond and success, we must first understand the struggle. The **Hue Jackson**'s circus.

(cont'd - see CLE2)

Key Free Agents/ Trades Added

Player	AAV (MM)
Demetrius Harris (TE)	$3
Eric Murray (CB)	Trade
Kareem Hunt (RB)	$1.1
Morgan Burnett (SS)	$3.7
Odell Beckham Jr. (WR)	Trade
Oliver Vernon (OLB)	Trade
Sheldon Richardson (DT)	$12.

Drafted Players

Rd	Pk	Player (College)
2	46	CB - Greedy Williams (LSU)
3	80	LB - Sione Takitaki (BYU)
4	119	S - Sheldrick Redwine (Miami)
5	155	LB - Mack Wilson (Alabama)
5	170	K - Austin Seibert (Oklahoma)
6	189	OT - Drew Forbes (Southeast Missouri State)
7	221	CB - Donnie Lewis Jr. (Tulane)

Regular Season Wins: Past & Current Proj

Forecast 2019 Wins	9
2018 Wins	7
Forecast 2018 Wins	5.5
2017 Wins	0
2016 Wins	1
2015 Wins	3

1 3 5 7 9 11 13 15

Lineup & Cap Hits

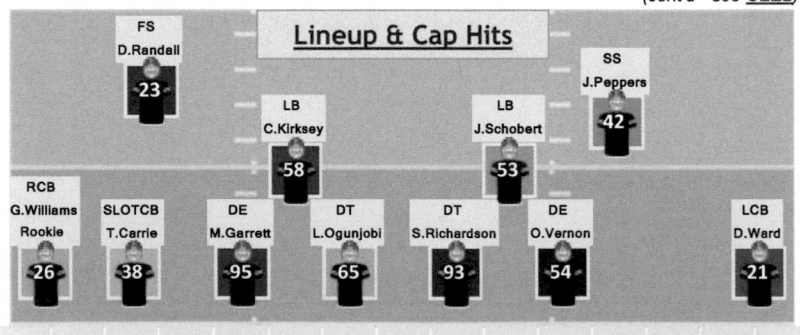

FS D.Randall -23-

SS J.Peppers -42-

LB C.Kirksey -58-
LB J.Schobert -53-

RCB G.Williams Rookie -26-
SLOTCB T.Carrie -38-
DE M.Garrett -95-
DT L.Ogunjobi -65-
DT S.Richardson -93-
DE O.Vernon -54-
LCB D.Ward -21-

LWR A.Callaway -11-
SLOTWR J.Landry -80-
LT G.Robinson -78-
LG J.Bitonio -75-
C J.Tretter -64-
RG A.Corbett -63-
RT C.Hubbard -74-
TE D.Njoku -85-
RWR O.Beckham Jr. -13-

QB B.Mayfield -6-
RB N.Chubb -24-

WR2 D.Ratley -18-
WR3 R.Higgins -81-
RB2 D.Johnson -29-
QB2 D.Stanton -9-

2019 Cap Dollars

2019 Unit Spending

All DEF / All OFF

Positional Spending

	Rank	Total	2017 Rk
All OFF	10	$103.05M	6
QB	22	$12.33M	10
OL	15	$38.14M	9
RB	19	$6.77M	20
WR	1	$38.21M	12
TE	20	$7.61M	16
All DEF	2	$105.26M	25
DL	3	$47.92M	25
LB	22	$17.17M	12
CB	11	$24.17M	13
S	9	$16.00M	27

In August of 2017, Jackson named **DeShone Kizer** the Browns' starting quarterback. Hue cited Kizer's "it" factor after pounding the table for Cleveland to draft Kizer in the second round. Hue trained Kizer and praised him, and started him in Week 1 as a 21-year-old rookie. Jackson then yanked Kizer out of the lineup repeatedly, and traded him after one season in the league.

Last August, Jackson claimed he knew Mayfield was a born leader and nicknamed him "The Pied Piper" after Baker – in Hue's words – cupped his hands and hollered "Hee Hee" to teammates during a pre-draft private workout for the Browns. The teammates echoed "Hee Hee" back to Baker and jogged over to him in unison. Hue called this "the most unbelievable thing I've ever seen." But there was more to the story.

Mayfield tore up Browns training camp, but Jackson refused to give him any first-team reps. And unlike Kizer, Jackson didn't start Baker in Week 1. Whereas Kizer was a 21-year-old second-round rookie, Mayfield was a 23-year-old first overall pick. But Hue declined to start Mayfield until **Tyrod Taylor** got hurt. Only in **Hue Jackson**'s mind could this possibly make sense.

In the preseason, Jackson never relented that Tyrod was unquestionably Cleveland's starter, even as Mayfield outplayed Taylor in camp. Jackson ripped Mayfield on HBO's Hard Knocks, knowing it would gain publicity. So it was no wonder Mayfield held and continues to hold a grudge against Hue. From Kizer to **Cody** "Trust Me" **Kessler**, **Robert** "The Earth Shook" **Griffin III**, Mayfield, and Tyrod, Jackson's quarterback evaluations as Browns coach could not possibly have gone worse.

Ironically, Jackson's first win in well over a year occurred because Mayfield was *forced to play* due to Tyrod's injury. After Taylor ran into pressure and got knocked out of the Browns' Week 3 game, Mayfield led a 14-point comeback to beat the Jets. Mayfield went 17-of-23 and averaged 8.7 yards per attempt with a 100 passer rating.

Asked by reporters after the game who would start in Week 4, Jackson dumbfoundingly replied, "*I need to watch the tape.*"

Last summer, second-year TE **David Njoku** was struggling to catch passes in practice. Jackson "punished" Njoku by requiring him to catch thirty balls from the JUGS machine afterwards. Browns coaches and GM **John Dorsey** literally brought out folding chairs to watch as Njoku counted to 30. Meanwhile, around the rest of the NFL, receivers and tight ends voluntarily catch hundreds of balls per day from JUGS machines.

2018 Passing Performance

QB	1st Dwn	2nd Dwn	3rd Dwn	
Baker Mayfield	54%	44%	36%	Success Rate
	8.4	6.7	7.9	YPA
	95.0	94.4	93.6	Rating
Pass Rate	56%	59%	84%	
NFL AVG	53%	47%	36%	Success Rate
	7.7	7.3	6.9	YPA
	95.1	93.7	87.1	Rating
Pass Rate	53%	62%	80%	

2018 Rushing Performance

Offense	1st Dwn	2nd Dwn	3rd Dwn	
CLE	50%	41%	47%	Success Rate
	4.3	4.9	5.7	YPC
Run Rate	44%	41%	16%	
NFL AVG	48%	46%	51%	Success Rate
	4.5	4.4	4.3	YPC
Run Rate	47%	38%	20%	

Jackson treated second-round RB phenom **Nick Chubb** similarly to Mayfield. Jackson sat Chubb behind journeyman **Carlos Hyde** to start the season. Week after week, Hyde proved highly inefficient on his carries, and Chubb was brilliant off the bench. Hue let Weeks 1-6 go by as Hyde averaged 3.4 yards per carry with a 38% Success Rate. Chubb averaged 10.8 YPC with 56% success. Dorsey finally took the decision away from Jackson by trading Hyde to the Jaguars after Week 6, *forcing* Hue to play Chubb.

In eight games under Hue, the 2018 Browns went +11 in turnover margin but managed a 2-5-1 record. Since 2006, there have been 38 NFL teams with a +8 turnover margin or better through eight weeks.

None of them had a losing record, except Hue's Browns.

(cont'd - see CLE-3)

2018 Offensive Advanced Metrics

2018 Defensive Advanced Metrics

2018 Weekly EDSR & Season Trending Performance

1	2	3	4	5	6	7	8	9	10		12	13	14	15	16	17	WEEK
T	L	W	L	W	L	L	L	L	L		W	L	W	W	W	L	RESULT
PIT	NO	NYJ	OAK	BAL	LAC	TB	PIT	KC	ATL		CIN	HOU	CAR	DEN	CIN	BAL	OPP
H	A	H	A	H	H	A	H	H	H		A	A	H	A	H	A	SITE
0	-3	4	-3	3	-24	-3	-15	-16	12		15	-16	6	1	8	-2	MARGIN
21	18	21	42	12	14	23	18	21	28		35	13	26	17	26	24	PTS
21	21	17	45	9	38	26	33	37	16		20	29	20	16	18	26	OPP PTS

EDSR by Wk
W=Green
L=Red

OFF / DEF
EDSR
Blue=OFF
(high=good)
Red=DEF
(low=good)

2018 Close Game Records

All 2018 Wins: **7**

FG Games (<=3 pts) W-L: **2-4**
FG Games Win %: **33%** (#22)
FG Games Wins (% of Total Wins): **29%** (#17)

1 Score Games (<=8 pts) W-L: **5-4**
1 Score Games Win %: **56%** (#11)
1 Score Games Wins (% of Total Wins): **71%** (#7)

2018 Critical & Game-Deciding Stats

TO Margin	+7
TO Given	24
INT Given	17
FUM Given	7
TO Taken	31
INT Taken	17
FUM Taken	14
Sack Margin	-1
Sacks	37
Sacks Allow	38
Return TD Margin	-2
Ret TDs	0
Ret TDs Allow	2
Penalty Margin	+7
Penalties	112
Opponent Penalties	119

Cleveland Browns 2019 Strength of Schedule In Detail (compared to 2018)

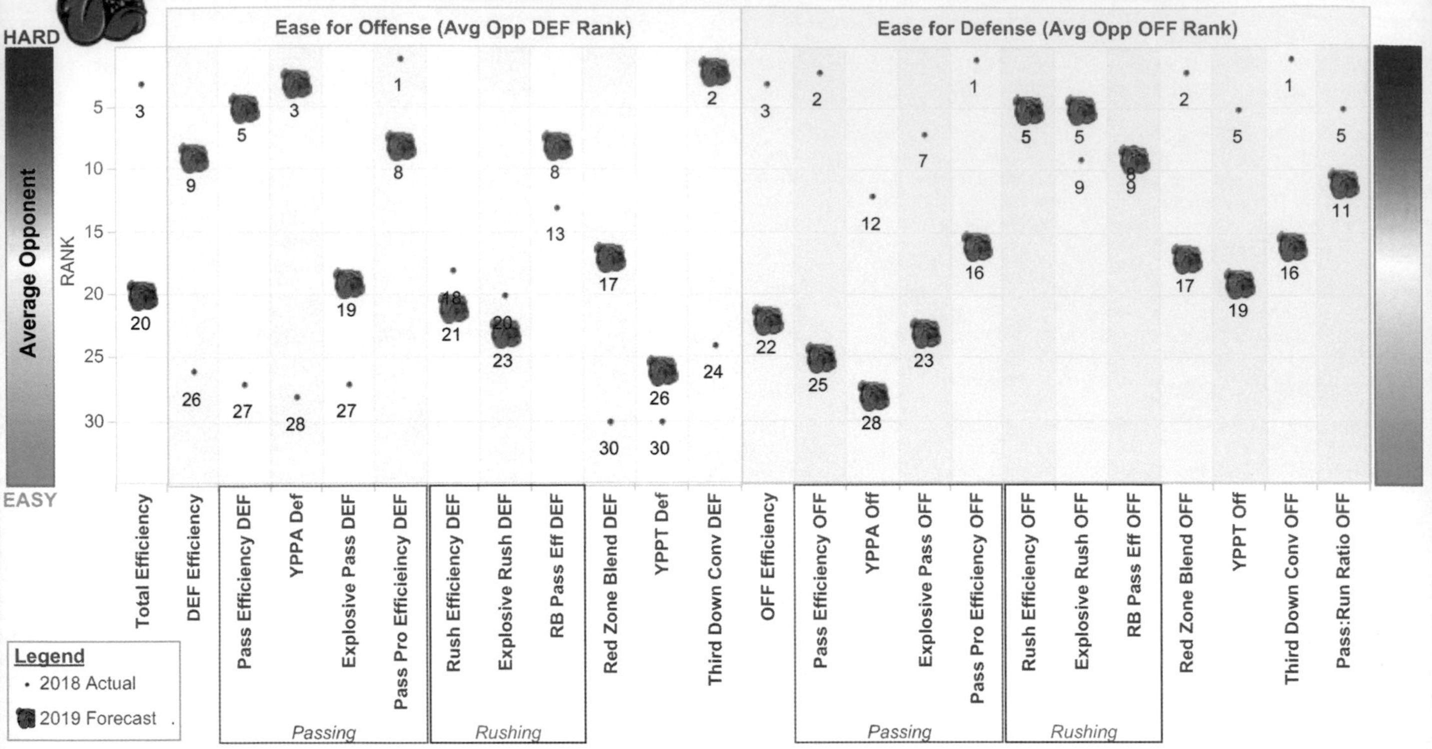

HARD

Average Opponent RANK

EASY

Ease for Offense (Avg Opp DEF Rank)

Metric	2018 Actual	2019 Forecast
Total Efficiency	3	20
DEF Efficiency	26	9
Pass Efficiency DEF	27	5
YPPA Def	28	3
Explosive Pass DEF	27	8
Pass Pro Efficiency DEF	—	19
Rush Efficiency DEF	18	21
Explosive Rush DEF	20	23
RB Pass Eff DEF	13	8
Red Zone Blend DEF	—	17
YPPT Def	30	26
Third Down Conv DEF	30	2, 24

Passing / Rushing

Ease for Defense (Avg Opp OFF Rank)

Metric	2018 Actual	2019 Forecast
OFF Efficiency	3	22
Pass Efficiency OFF	2	25
YPPA Off	7	28
Explosive Pass OFF	12	23
Pass Pro Efficiency OFF	1	16
Rush Efficiency OFF	5	—
Explosive Rush OFF	5	9
RB Pass Eff OFF	9	8
Red Zone Blend OFF	2	17
YPPT Off	5	19
Third Down Conv OFF	16	—
Pass:Run Ratio OFF	1	5, 11

Passing / Rushing

Legend
- 2018 Actual
- 2019 Forecast

2019 v 2018 Schedule Variances* (OFF=Rank of DEF faced, 2019 vs 2018)

Pass OFF Rank	Pass OFF Blend Rk	Rush OFF Rk	Rush OFF Blend Rk	Pass DEF Rk	Pass DEF Blend Rk	Rush DEF Rk	Rush DEF Blend Rk
1	1	19	15	32	32	14	9

* **1**=Hardest Jump in 2019 schedule from 2018 (aka a much harder schedule in 2019), **32**=Easiest Jump in 2019 schedule from 2018 (aka a much easier schedule in 2019);
Pass Blend metric blends 4 metrics: Pass Efficiency, YPPA, Explosive Pass & Pass Rush; **Rush Blend** metric blends 3 metrics: Rush Efficiency, Explosive Rush & RB Targets

Team Records & Trends

	2018	2017	2016
Average line	2.9	6.8	7.1
Average O/U line	46.3	41.3	44.5
Straight Up Record	7-8	0-16	1-15
Against the Spread Record	10-6	4-12	5-11
Over/Under Record	7-8	7-9	8-8
ATS as Favorite	1-1	0-1	0-0
ATS as Underdog	8-5	4-10	5-11
Straight Up Home	5-2	0-7	1-7
ATS Home	5-3	2-5	2-6
Over/Under Home	3-4	1-6	2-6
ATS as Home Favorite	1-1	0-0	0-0
ATS as a Home Dog	4-2	2-4	2-6
Straight Up Away	2-6	0-8	0-8
ATS Away	5-3	2-6	3-5
Over/Under Away	4-4	5-3	6-2
ATS Away Favorite	0-0	0-1	0-0
ATS Away Dog	4-3	2-5	3-5
Six Point Teaser Record	12-4	9-4	13-3
Seven Point Teaser Record	13-3	13-3	9-6
Ten Point Teaser Record	14-1	13-2	13-3

CLE-3

But this wasn't just a 2018 Browns thing. *It was a Hue Jackson thing*. Turnover margins decide games more than any other metric. Teams have won roughly 80% of their games over the last 30 years when winning the takeaway battle. Yet since 2016 when Hue took over as Cleveland's head coach, the Browns' win rate was 37.5% when winning turnover margins. Additionally, no team went to overtime more than Hue's Browns in his 2 ½-year tenure. Cleveland's record should've been around .500 in such affairs, yet Hue went 1-6-1 for a pathetic .143 win rate.

Yet Jackson kept on making excuses. When he went 1-16 in 2016, he claimed the team was in the midst of a long-term rebuild and needed time. When he went 0-16 the next year, he requested a new personnel guy, an offensive coordinator, and a new quarterback. Jackson won his power struggle with EVP **Sashi Brown**, the Browns hired Haley as offensive coordinator, and Mayfield was taken first overall.

(cont'd - see CLE-4)

2019 Rest Analysis

Team More Rest	2
Opp More Rest	4
Net Rest Edge	-2
Week 2 Edge	0
Week 3 Edge	-1
Week 4 Edge	0
Week 5 Edge	
Week 6 Edge	-4
Week 8 Edge	8
Week 9 Edge	0
Week 10 Edge	0
Week 11 Edge	0
Week 12 Edge	3
Week 13 Edge	0
Week 14 Edge	0
Week 15 Edge	0
Week 16 Edge	-3
Week 17 Edge	0

Health by Unit*

2018 Rk	7
2017 Rk	12
2018 v 2017 Rk	12
Off Rk	1
Def Rk	22
QB Rk	1
RB Rk	1
WR Rk	10
TE Rk	7
Oline Rk	4
Dline Rk	13
LB Rk	24
DB Rk	24

Based on the work of Football Outsiders

2018 Weekly Betting Lines (wks 1-16)

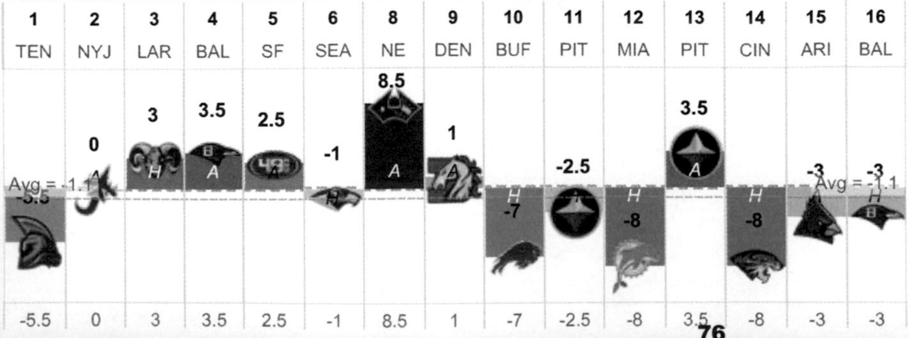

1	2	3	4	5	6	7	8	9	10	11	12	13	14	15	16
TEN	NYJ	LAR	BAL	SF	SEA	NE	DEN	BUF	PIT	MIA	PIT	CIN	ARI	BAL	
-5.5	0	3	3.5	2.5	-1	8.5	1	-7	-2.5	-8	3.5	-8	-3	-3	

Avg = -1.1

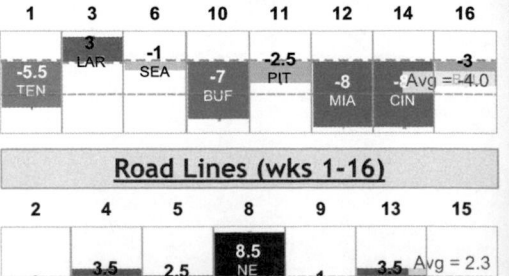

Home Lines (wks 1-16)

1	3	6	10	11	12	14	16
-5.5 TEN	3 LAR	-1 SEA	-7 BUF	-2.5 PIT	-8 MIA	CIN	-3

Avg = -4.0

Road Lines (wks 1-16)

2	4	5	8	9	13	15
0 NYJ	3.5 BAL	2.5 SF	8.5 NE	1 DEN	3.5 PIT	-3 ARI

Avg = 2.3

2018 Play Tendencies

All Pass %	60%
All Pass Rk	15
All Rush %	40%
All Rush Rk	18
1 Score Pass %	56%
1 Score Pass Rk	21
2017 1 Score Pass %	52%
2017 1 Score Pass Rk	28
2018 Pass Increase %	4%
Pass Increase Rk	13
1 Score Rush %	44%
1 Score Rush Rk	12
Up Pass %	46%
Up Pass Rk	23
Up Rush %	54%
Up Rush Rk	10
Down Pass %	66%
Down Pass Rk	16
Down Rush %	34%
Down Rush Rk	17

2018 Down & Distance Tendencies

Down	Distance	Total Plays	Pass Rate	Run Rate	Play Success %
1	Short (1-3)	8	50%	50%	63%
	Med (4-7)	8	50%	50%	38%
	Long (8-10)	309	50%	50%	49%
	XL (11+)	13	62%	38%	31%
2	Short (1-3)	39	38%	62%	74%
	Med (4-7)	75	47%	53%	51%
	Long (8-10)	90	57%	43%	26%
	XL (11+)	46	72%	28%	30%
3	Short (1-3)	34	65%	35%	62%
	Med (4-7)	49	86%	14%	39%
	Long (8-10)	39	90%	10%	21%
	XL (11+)	36	94%	6%	22%
4	Short (1-3)	9	44%	56%	67%
	Med (4-7)	2	50%	50%	50%

Shotgun %:

Under Center	Shotgun
37%	63%

37% AVG 63%

Run Rate:

Under Center	Shotgun
71%	20%

68% AVG 23%

Pass Rate:

Under Center	Shotgun
29%	80%

32% AVG 77%

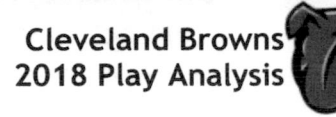

Cleveland Browns 2018 Play Analysis

Short Yardage Intelligence:

2nd and Short Run

Run Freq	Run Rk	NFL Run Freq Avg	Run 1D Rate	Run NFL 1D Avg
54%	29	65%	62%	68%

2nd and Short Pass

Pass Freq	Pass Rk	NFL Pass Freq Avg	Pass 1D Rate	Pass NFL 1D Avg
46%	4	35%	67%	56%

Most Frequent Play

Down	Distance	Play Type	Player	Total Plays	Play Success %
1	Short (1-3)	RUSH	Nick Chubb	3	67%
	Med (4-7)	RUSH	Nick Chubb	3	33%
	Long (8-10)	RUSH	Nick Chubb	81	47%
	XL (11+)	PASS	Nick Chubb	3	67%
		RUSH	Nick Chubb	3	0%
2	Short (1-3)	RUSH	Nick Chubb	12	83%
	Med (4-7)	RUSH	Nick Chubb	24	54%
	Long (8-10)	RUSH	Carlos Hyde	16	0%
	XL (11+)	RUSH	Carlos Hyde	6	17%
3	Short (1-3)	PASS	David Njoku	6	67%
	Med (4-7)	PASS	Duke Johnson	9	33%
			Antonio Callaway	9	56%
	Long (8-10)	PASS	Jarvis Landry	9	22%
	XL (11+)	PASS	Jarvis Landry	8	13%

Most Successful Play*

Down	Distance	Play Type	Player	Total Plays	Play Success %
1	Long (8-10)	PASS	Darren Fells	5	80%
2	Short (1-3)	RUSH	Nick Chubb	12	83%
	Med (4-7)	PASS	Jarvis Landry	6	67%
	Long (8-10)	PASS	Duke Johnson	5	60%
	XL (11+)	PASS	Antonio Callaway	5	40%
3	Short (1-3)	PASS	David Njoku	6	67%
	Med (4-7)	PASS	Antonio Callaway	9	56%
	Long (8-10)	PASS	Jarvis Landry	9	22%
	XL (11+)	PASS	Antonio Callaway	6	17%

*Minimum 5 plays to qualify

2018 Weekly Snap Rates

Wk	Opp	Score	Jarvis Landry	David Njoku	Antonio Callaway	Rashard Higgins	Duke Johnson	Darren Fells	Nick Chubb	Carlos Hyde	Breshad Perriman	Seth DeValve
1	PIT	T 21-21	81 (91%)	78 (88%)	15 (17%)	53 (60%)	41 (46%)	39 (44%)	4 (4%)	47 (53%)		6 (7%)
2	NO	L 21-18	59 (95%)	46 (74%)	50 (81%)	46 (74%)	23 (37%)	25 (40%)	3 (5%)	36 (58%)		
3	NYJ	W 21-17	66 (86%)	62 (81%)	69 (90%)	54 (70%)	29 (38%)	30 (39%)	5 (6%)	45 (58%)		
4	OAK	L 45-42	72 (89%)	68 (84%)	57 (70%)	53 (65%)	29 (36%)	39 (48%)	3 (4%)	49 (60%)		
5	BAL	W 12-9	80 (100%)	72 (90%)	55 (69%)	31 (39%)	41 (51%)	19 (24%)	11 (14%)	28 (35%)		9 (11%)
6	LAC	L 38-14	73 (99%)	60 (81%)	72 (97%)		35 (47%)	19 (26%)	7 (9%)	32 (43%)		1 (1%)
7	TB	L 26-23	67 (99%)	57 (84%)	51 (75%)		35 (51%)	24 (35%)	45 (66%)		11 (16%)	
8	PIT	L 33-18	52 (81%)	53 (83%)	59 (92%)		23 (36%)	25 (39%)	31 (48%)		9 (14%)	5 (8%)
9	KC	L 37-21	73 (97%)	55 (73%)	39 (52%)	29 (39%)	35 (47%)	26 (35%)	37 (49%)		26 (35%)	14 (19%)
10	ATL	W 28-16	36 (68%)	35 (66%)	39 (74%)	22 (42%)	17 (32%)	32 (60%)	42 (79%)		13 (25%)	4 (8%)
12	CIN	W 35-20	39 (61%)	43 (67%)	38 (59%)	20 (31%)	18 (28%)	35 (55%)	46 (72%)		35 (55%)	15 (23%)
13	HOU	L 29-13	46 (81%)	46 (81%)	41 (72%)	33 (58%)	20 (35%)	15 (26%)	27 (47%)		26 (46%)	6 (11%)
14	CAR	W 26-20	42 (81%)	43 (83%)	38 (73%)	26 (50%)	18 (35%)	23 (44%)	33 (63%)		19 (37%)	7 (13%)
15	DEN	W 17-16	57 (85%)	56 (84%)	49 (73%)	30 (45%)	26 (39%)	30 (45%)	40 (60%)		28 (42%)	15 (22%)
16	CIN	W 26-18	58 (84%)	40 (58%)	47 (68%)	43 (62%)	32 (46%)	28 (41%)	39 (57%)		32 (46%)	14 (20%)
17	BAL	L 26-24	56 (95%)	57 (97%)	47 (80%)	43 (73%)	37 (63%)	11 (19%)	22 (37%)		19 (32%)	2 (3%)
	Grand Total		957 (87%)	871 (80%)	766 (71%)	483 (54%)	459 (42%)	420 (39%)	395 (39%)	237 (51%)	218 (35%)	98 (12%)

Personnel Groupings

Personnel	Team %	NFL Avg	Succ. %
1-1 [3WR]	62%	65%	44%
1-2 [2WR]	17%	17%	46%
1-3 [1WR]	14%	3%	42%
1-0 [4WR]	3%	2%	52%
2-1 [2WR]	2%	8%	53%

Grouping Tendencies

Personnel	Pass Rate	Pass Succ. %	Run Succ. %
1-1 [3WR]	71%	42%	49%
1-2 [2WR]	48%	49%	43%
1-3 [1WR]	25%	53%	38%
1-0 [4WR]	69%	45%	67%
2-1 [2WR]	63%	42%	71%

Red Zone Targets (min 3)

Receiver	All	Inside 5	6-10	11-20
Jarvis Landry	18	3	3	12
Antonio Callaway	8	4	1	3
David Njoku	8	3	2	3
Duke Johnson	8	2	1	5
Nick Chubb	5		1	4
Rashard Higgins	3			3
Darren Fells	2	1	1	

Red Zone Rushes (min 3)

Rusher	All	Inside 5	6-10	11-20
Nick Chubb	26	9	9	8
Carlos Hyde	17	10	4	3
Baker Mayfield	7	4		3
Duke Johnson	5			5
Tyrod Taylor	1			1

Early Down Target Rate

RB	TE	WR
21%	21%	58%
23%	21%	56%
	NFL AVG	

Overall Target Success %

RB	TE	WR
45%	50%	47%
#21	#26	#28

Cleveland Browns 2018 Passing Recap & 2019 Outlook

Kitchens and Mayfield set a high bar in last year's second half. In Kitchens-called games, Baker's 8.6 yards per attempt were third highest in the league, and his passer rating (106) and Success Rate (51%) were both top five.

Now, Kitchens and Mayfield have a full offseason together. They're incorporating a Hall of Fame receiver talent in **Odell Beckham**. Kitchens is meshing with ultra-aggressive OC **Todd Monken**.

My two questions: Will a revised offensive line provide proper protection? And how many touchdowns will **Nick Chubb** – and perhaps eventually **Kareem Hunt** – steal from Baker's aerial tally?

2018 Standard Passing Table

QB	Comp	Att	Comp %	Yds	YPA	TDs	INT	Sacks	Rating	Rk
Baker Mayfield	310	486	64%	3,725	7.7	27	14	25	94	21
Tyrod Taylor	42	85	49%	473	5.6	2	2	13	65	49
NFL Avg			62%		7.0				87.5	

2018 Advanced Passing Table

QB	Success %	EDSR Passing Success %	20+ Yd Pass Gains	20+ Yd Pass %	30+ Yd Pass Gains	30+ Yd Pass %	Avg. Air Yds per Comp	Avg. YAC per Comp	20+ Air Yd Comp	20+ Air Yd %
Baker Mayfield	46%	50%	52	11.0%	15	3.0%	6.5	5.5	29	6%
Tyrod Taylor	29%	34%	7	8.0%	4	5.0%	6.5	4.8	5	6%
NFL Avg	44%	48%	29.5	8.4%	12.5	3.7%	5.8	5.1	14.5	6%

Interception Rates by Down

Yards to Go	1st Dwn	2nd Dwn	3rd Dwn	4th Dwn	Total
1 & 2	0.0%	0.0%	0.0%	0.0%	0.0%
3, 4, 5	0.0%	4.8%	2.9%	0.0%	3.3%
6 - 9	0.0%	2.1%	2.2%	0.0%	2.0%
10 - 14	3.3%	0.0%	6.5%	100.0%	3.2%
15+	9.1%	0.0%	0.0%		2.7%
Total	3.4%	1.3%	2.9%	9.1%	2.7%

3rd Down Passing - Short of Sticks Analysis

QB	Avg. Yds to Go	Avg. YIA (of Comp)	Avg Yds Short	Short of Sticks Rate	Short Rk
Baker Mayfield	7.8	7.7	-0.1	65%	9
NFL Avg	7.8	6.4	-1.4	60%	

Air Yds vs YAC

Air Yds %	YAC %	Rk
54%	46%	22
53%	48%	

Baker Mayfield Rating All Downs

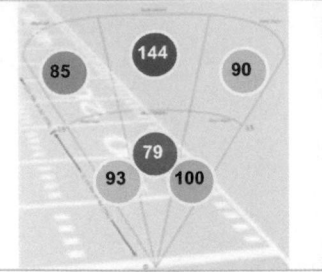

Baker Mayfield Rating Early Downs

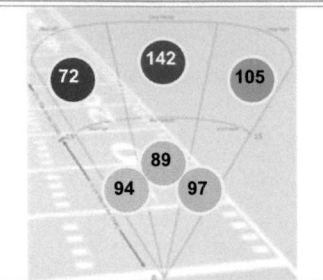

2018 Receiving Recap & 2019 Outlook

On pass plays under Hue and Haley, the 2018 Browns used three-receiver 11 personnel on 79% of plays, resulting in 65 targets for **Jarvis Landry**, 32 for **David Njoku**, 29 for **Antonio Calloway**, and 26 for **Duke Johnson**. Kitchens reduced Cleveland's use of 11 personnel, and Landry's targets fell from 65 in the season's first half to 38 over the Browns' final eight games. Targets were much more evenly distributed with 25 apiece going to **Rashard Higgins** and Johnson, 24 to Calloway, and 19 to Njoku.

Player *Min 50 Targets	Targ	Comp %	YPA	Rating	Success %	Success Rk	Missed YPA Rk	YAS % Rk	YTS % Rk	TDs
Jarvis Landry	148	55%	6.6	78.5	41%	117	164	56	77	3
David Njoku	89	63%	7.2	85.4	45%	102	119	43	113	4
Antonio Calloway	81	53%	7.2	71.3	42%	114	114	56	126	5
Duke Johnson	62	76%	6.9	103.5	47%	95	83	84	113	3
Rashard Higgins	54	72%	10.6	115.7	63%	3	35	11	97	3

Directional Passer Rating Delivered

Receiver	Short Left	Short Middle	Short Right	Deep Left	Deep Middle	Deep Right	Player Total
Jarvis Landry	55	105	75	75	141	78	79
David Njoku	140	69	88	50	110	40	85
Antonio Calloway	95	51	37	5	129	77	71
Duke Johnson	94	89	111	119		40	103
Rashard Higgins	41	36	113	119	119	147	116
Nick Chubb	119	60	111	40	40		104
Breshad Perriman	115	117	81	135	83	141	134
Darren Fells	96	81	131		158		147
Carlos Hyde	77	88	58	40			65
Seth DeValve	17	40	108	119	158		106
Josh Gordon		158		40	0		53
Team Total	88	79	92	78	140	95	92

2018 Rushing Recap & 2019 Outlook

Fully locked in as Cleveland's bellcow back – at least until **Kareem Hunt** is eligible to return from suspension – **Nick Chubb** can no longer worry about **Hue Jackson**'s suboptimal allocation of playing time. This year, Chubb is fortunate to face an easier schedule than he did as a rookie and can benefit from the increasingly aggressive nature of Cleveland's passing game with lighter boxes to run against.

Player *Min 50 Rushes	Rushes	YPC	Success %	Success Rk	Missed YPA Rk	YTS % Rk	YAS % Rk	Early Down Success %	Early Down Success Rk	TDs
Nick Chubb	191	5.2	50%	25	34	67	2	51%	22	8
Carlos Hyde	172	3.4	38%	68	53	49	67	37%	67	5

Yards per Carry by Direction

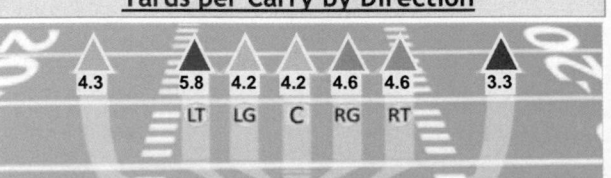

Directional Run Frequency

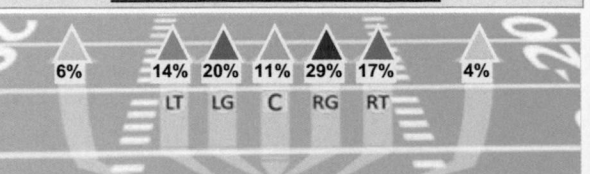

Hue got *everything* he wanted and still couldn't get results.

Last year's Browns won the turnover battle in five of their first eight games but won two. After an overtime loss to the Bucs in Week 7, Jackson threatened to take back play-calling duties from Haley. The same Hue who won 1-of-32 games over the previous two years. After Week 8, Browns ownership finally sent **The Hue Circus** packing. Haley was canned, too.

And that's when the tide turned for Mayfield. Although the rookie shined against the Jets in his NFL debut, Baker's cumulative body of work under Haley and Hue wasn't inspiring. He recorded a 38% Success Rate, 6.4 yards per attempt, and a 76.5 passer rating as Cleveland's starter in Weeks 4-8. Under Kitchens, Mayfield exploded for 50% success, 8.1 YPA, and a 103 rating.

First, Kitchens increased Mayfield's snaps from under center from 34% to 42% in first halves of games. Mayfield's under-center Success Rate spiked from 41% under Hue and Haley to 57% under Kitchens, and his yards per attempt jumped from 7.8 to 9.4.

Kitchens also tweaked personnel packaging, dropping Cleveland's three-receiver 11-personnel usage from 79% to 68% and increasing the use of 12, 13, and 10 personnel. Haley ran two-tight end 12 personnel primarily to take deep shots, yet those plays gained just 4.3 yards per attempt with a putrid 30% Success Rate. Kitchens decreased Mayfield's average depth of target from 13.6 to 8.2 yards in 12 personnel, and Mayfield took zero sacks with a 65% Success Rate on such plays following Hue and Haley's firings. Mayfield deserves credit, but good coaching can unlock

(cont'd - see CLE-5)

Cleveland Browns Fantasy Corner

Odell Beckham arrives in Cleveland for the best quarterback play of his career. **Baker Mayfield's** 7.7 yards-per-attempt average as a rookie is a number **Eli Manning** hasn't touched since 2011 and has reached twice in his 15-year career. PFF charted a league-low 50% of Beckham's 2018 targets as "accurate" – on-frame or in-stride — while Mayfield posted the NFL's fourth-best accuracy from Week 9 on. Despite playing with washed-up Eli, Beckham's receiving line is 102/1,354/9 (13.3 YPR) over his last 16 games with 85-plus yards and/or a touchdown in 12 of them (75%). Although Beckham's target ceiling isn't as lofty as fellow tier-one receivers **Davante Adams** and **DeAndre Hopkins** due to the depth of Cleveland's pass-catcher corps, OBJ's ceiling remains sky high in an efficiency-friendly environment. - Evan Silva

2018 Situational Usage by Player & Position

Usage Rate by Score

		Being Blown Out (14+)	Down Big (9-13)	One Score	Large Lead (9-13)	Blowout Lead (14+)
RUSH	Nick Chubb	11%	11%	56%	4%	18%
	Jarvis Landry			100%		
	Carlos Hyde	7%	4%	88%	1%	
	Duke Johnson	10%	12%	68%	5%	5%
	Antonio Callaway			100%		
	Breshad Perriman			75%		25%
	Total	9%	9%	68%	3%	11%
PASS	Nick Chubb	23%	18%	41%		18%
	Jarvis Landry	22%	12%	59%	1%	6%
	Carlos Hyde	29%	14%	57%		
	Duke Johnson	23%	15%	52%	3%	7%
	Antonio Callaway	16%	17%	60%		7%
	David Njoku	31%	12%	50%	1%	5%
	Rashard Higgins	13%	21%	45%	11%	11%
	Breshad Perriman	26%	4%	57%	4%	9%
	Darren Fells		9%	64%		18%
	Seth DeValve	83%				17%
	Josh Gordon	33%		67%		
	Total	22%	14%	54%	2%	8%

Share of Offensive Plays by Type

	Nick Chubb	Jarvis Landry	Carlos Hyde	Duke Johnson	Antonio Callaway	David Njoku	Rashard Higgins	Breshad Perriman	Darren Fells	Seth DeValve	Josh Gordon
RUSH	54%	1%	32%	12%	1%			1%			
PASS	5%	29%	2%	13%	16%	16%	10%	5%	2%	1%	1%
ALL	26%	17%	15%	12%	9%	9%	6%	3%	1%	1%	0%

Positional Target Distribution vs NFL Average

		NFL Wide				Team Only			
		Left	Middle	Right	Total	Left	Middle	Right	Total
Deep	WR	33%	17%	30%	**81%**	28%	14%	37%	**79%**
	TE	5%	4%	7%	**16%**	4%	4%	7%	**15%**
	RB	1%	0%	2%	**3%**	3%	1%	2%	**6%**
	All	**39%**	**22%**	**39%**	**100%**	**35%**	**18%**	**47%**	**100%**
Short	WR	20%	14%	21%	**55%**	19%	10%	24%	**53%**
	TE	6%	6%	8%	**20%**	5%	8%	10%	**23%**
	RB	10%	5%	10%	**25%**	10%	4%	10%	**24%**
	All	**36%**	**25%**	**39%**	**100%**	**34%**	**22%**	**44%**	**100%**
Total		**37%**	**24%**	**39%**	**100%**	**34%**	**21%**	**45%**	**100%**

Positional Success Rates vs NFL Average

		NFL Wide				Team Only			
		Left	Middle	Right	Total	Left	Middle	Right	Total
Deep	WR	40%	49%	39%	**42%**	33%	47%	54%	**45%**
	TE	44%	52%	42%	**45%**	33%	80%	40%	**48%**
	RB	36%	40%	44%	**42%**	50%	0%	0%	**25%**
	All	**41%**	**50%**	**40%**	**42%**	**35%**	**52%**	**49%**	**45%**
Short	WR	55%	61%	53%	**56%**	47%	49%	46%	**47%**
	TE	55%	63%	55%	**57%**	58%	50%	45%	**49%**
	RB	47%	54%	45%	**48%**	41%	50%	48%	**45%**
	All	**53%**	**60%**	**51%**	**54%**	**47%**	**49%**	**46%**	**47%**
Total		**51%**	**58%**	**49%**	**52%**	**44%**	**50%**	**47%**	**46%**

Division History: Season Wins & 2019 Projection

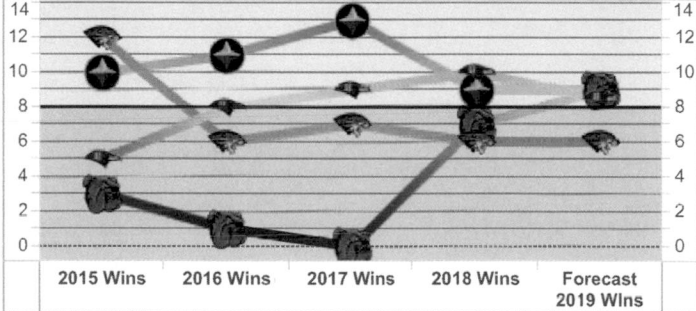

2015 Wins | 2016 Wins | 2017 Wins | 2018 Wins | Forecast 2019 Wins

Rank of 2019 Defensive Pass Efficiency Faced by Week

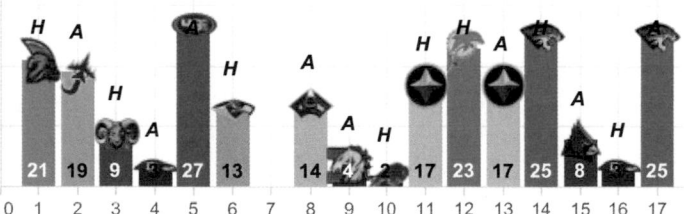

21 19 9 27 13 14 4 2 17 23 17 25 8 25

Rank of 2019 Defensive Rush Efficiency Faced by Week

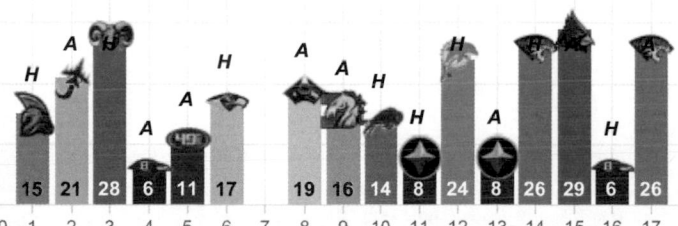

15 21 28 6 11 17 19 16 14 8 24 8 26 29 6 26

79

2018 Detailed Analytics Summary
Success by Play Type & Primary Personnel Groupings

Successful Play Rate 0% — 100%

Type	1-1 [3WR]	1-2 [2WR]	1-3 [1WR]	1-0 [4WR]	2-1 [2WR]	2-2 [1WR]	2-0 [3WR]	2-3 [0WR]	ALL
PASS	42% (414)	49% (76)	53% (32)	45% (20)	42% (12)		50% (2)		43% (556)
RUSH	49% (171)	43% (82)	38% (98)	67% (9)	71% (7)	33% (6)	0% (1)	0% (1)	45% (375)
All	44% (585)	46% (158)	42% (130)	52% (29)	53% (19)	33% (6)	33% (3)	0% (1)	44% (931)

Format   Success Rate (Total # of Plays)

Receiving Success by Top-4 Personnel Groupings
(Min 50 targets)

POS	Player	1-1 [3WR]	1-2 [2WR]	1-0 [4WR]	2-1 [2WR]	4 Grp Total
RB	Duke Johnson	49% (51) 6.9, 104.5	0% (2) 0.0, 39.6	25% (4) 6.5, 93.8	50% (2) 6.0, 91.7	46% (59) 6.6, 101.8
TE	David Njoku	41% (51) 5.8, 75.2	67% (15) 12.9, 158.3	0% (1) 0.0, 39.6	0% (1) 0.0, 39.6	46% (68) 7.2, 94.5
WR	Jarvis Landry	39% (103) 6.6, 74.9	50% (20) 7.9, 84.8	75% (4) 7.0, 93.8	33% (6) 2.3, 70.1	41% (133) 6.6, 76.6
	Antonio Callaway	42% (53) 8.6, 91.2	47% (15) 4.1, 30.1	50% (4) 8.0, 77.1	50% (2) 8.5, 102.1	43% (74) 7.6, 77.8
	Rashard Higgins	62% (45) 10.3, 117.2		50% (6) 7.2, 87.5		61% (51) 9.9, 113.7
	Josh Gordon	33% (3) 5.7, 53.5				33% (3) 5.7, 53.5

Format   Line 1: Success Rate (Total # of Plays)   Line 2: YPA, Passer Rating

Rushing Success by Top-4 Personnel Groupings
(Min 25 carries)

Rusher (Last, First)	1-1 [3WR]	1-2 [2WR]	2-1 [2WR]	2-2 [1WR]	4 Grp Total
Chubb Nick	49% (67) 5.6	50% (46) 6.6	80% (5) 5.0	25% (4) 1.3	50% (122) 5.8
Hyde Carlos	40% (45) 3.8	32% (22) 3.1	0% (1) -1.0	100% (1) 1.0	38% (69) 3.5
Johnson Duke	50% (30) 5.3	0% (4) -0.5	100% (1) 9.0		46% (35) 4.7
Mayfield Baker	50% (14) 6.1	50% (4) 3.8		0% (1) -1.0	47% (19) 5.2

Format   Line 1: Success Rate (Total # of Plays)   Line 2: YPC

Passing by Coverage Scheme

Zone	52% (225) 8.5, 92.8
M2M	41% (176) 6.3, 78.4
Screen	42% (65) 5.3, 92.6
Combo	71% (7) 14.1, 153.3

Passing by Route

Screen	41% (68) 4.9, 97.1
Out	48% (54) 5.7, 72.1
Curl	56% (52) 7.0, 55.6
Slant	53% (36) 6.3, 104.6
Dig	86% (21) 15.5, 134.6
Flat	59% (17) 4.2, 84.1

Throw Types

Level 1	51% (305) 6.3, 86.9
Level 2	46% (130) 9.1, 103.9
Level 3	33% (60) 11.2, 88.2
Shovel	29% (7) 3.4, 81.0
Sidearm	100% (1) 21.0, 118.8

QB Drop Types

3 Step	48% (230) 7.6, 89.3
0/1 Step	50% (105) 5.9, 103.6
5 Step	47% (70) 8.8, 63.8
Basic Screen	42% (38) 6.1, 109.4
7 Step	43% (35) 11.4, 113.9
Designed Rollout Right	50% (10) 5.0, 106.3

QB State at Pass

Planted	48% (328) 7.3, 83.2
Shuffling	45% (74) 6.3, 112.8
Moving	39% (64) 7.7, 84.9

Play Action

	Play Action	No P/A
Under Center	49% (75) 9.1, 95.5	72% (18) 10.4, 147.2
Shotgun	44% (41) 6.8, 103.0	46% (374) 7.1, 86.6
ALL	47% (116) 8.3, 99.1	47% (392) 7.3, 89.4

Run Types

Inside Zone	55% (82) 4.9
Lead	37% (67) 3.4
Outside Zone	47% (53) 6.1
Power	36% (53) 3.5
Pitch	45% (11) 2.6
Stretch	18% (11) 2.4

CLE-5

players, and we saw that happen with Cleveland's franchise quarterback under Kitchens. Neither Kitchens nor Mayfield operated in their current roles entering last season. Kitchens coached the Browns' running backs, and Mayfield was sequestered to the second-team offense. A full offseason together should immensely help both.

And then there is the second-year quarterback bump. Since 2012, quarterbacks drafted within the top-15 picks have gone a combined 45-70 (39%) as rookies, then soared to 97-56 (63%) with huge individual improvements in passing efficiency as sophomores.

Last year's Browns faced the NFL's third-toughest schedule based on total opponent efficiency. By current win totals, I project this year's Browns to face the league's fourth-softest slate. That's the biggest increase is schedule softness of any team in the league.

Cleveland is scheduled to face only two top-ten opponents, fewest in the NFL. But offensively, the Browns project to play the league's ninth-toughest pass-defense schedule, way up from seventh softest last year. In Mayfield's five starts with Kitchens against bottom-half pass defenses (Bengals twice, Falcons, Panthers, Texans), Baker averaged 9.4 yards per attempt with a 57% Success Rate and 122 rating. In three starts against top-half pass defenses (Ravens, Broncos, Chiefs), Mayfield averaged 7.5 yards per attempt with a 45% Success Rate and 86 rating. Anyone should expect a quarterback to struggle against superior pass defenses, particularly as a rookie. But note that Cleveland's pass-defense schedule projects as much tougher in 2019 than last year - the toughest jump in the league.

The Browns now have **Odell Beckham** to make Mayfield and Kitchens look even better. Dorsey *robbed* the hapless Giants in that trade. Losing pass-protection extraordinaire RG **Kevin Zeitler** is a concern, but the Browns are still in great position given Kitchens' scheme. I'm also intrigued by the incorporation of new OC **Todd Monken**, who helped turn the Bucs into a top-three offense last season. Both **Jameis Winston** and **Ryan Fitzpatrick** ranked top three in the NFL in average depth of target with Monken calling plays. An Air Raid proponent, Monken's approach to offense is extraordinarily aggressive.

While the Browns' schedule gets tougher for Kitchens and Monken's offense, defensively the opposite is true. Last year's team faced the league's third-toughest schedule of offenses, and this year's club draws the 22nd-ranked group. Aside from **Tom Brady**, **Russell Wilson**, **Ben Roethlisberger**, and **Jared Goff**, Cleveland's schedule is chock full of average-or-worse starters.

Changes to the Browns' roster have been especially massive on defense. Last year's Browns devoted the NFL's 25th-most cap space to defense. In 2019, that ranking has increased to 2nd. All that while the team shed cap at linebacker. Cleveland's defensive line is the NFL's second-most expensive – up from $16.5 million to $47.9 million – and their secondary hits the cap at $40 million after costing just $25 million in 2018. The Browns went from just two defensive players hitting last year's cap for over $5.3 million (**Myles Garrett**, **Jamie Collins**) to six this year (Garrett, **Olivier Vernon**, **Sheldon Richardson**, **Travis Carrie**, **Christian Kirksey**, **Denzel Ward**).

Dallas Cowboys

Coaches (Prior Yrs)

Head Coach:
Jason Garrett (8 yrs)
Offensive Coordinator:
Kellen Moore (DAL QB) (new)
Defensive Coordinator:
Rod Marinelli (5 yrs)

2019 Forecast

Wins	Div Rank
9	#2

Past Records

2018: 10-6
2017: 9-7
2016: 13-3

EASY   HARD

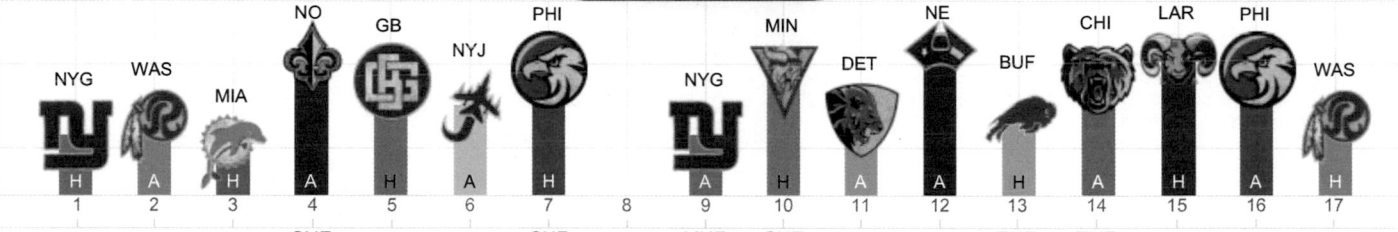

NYG	WAS	MIA	NO	GB	NYJ	PHI		NYG	MIN	DET	NE	BUF	CHI	LAR	PHI	WAS
H	A	H	A	H	A	H		A	H	A	A	H	A	H	A	H
1	2	3	4	5	6	7	8	9	10	11	12	13	14	15	16	17

SNF   SNF   MNF SNF   TNF TNF

Key Players Lost

Player	New
Caraun Reid (DT)	IND
Cole Beasley (WR)	BUF
Damien Wilson (OLB)	KC
Datone Jones (DT)	JAC
David Irving (DT)	Retired
Geoff Swaim (TE)	JAC
Marcus Martin (G)	SEA
Rod Smith (RB)	NYG

Average Line	# Games Favored	# Games Underdog
-1.3	9	4

Regular Season Wins: Past & Current Proj

Forecast 2019 Wins	9
2018 Wins	10
Forecast 2018 Wins	8.5
2017 Wins	9
2016 Wins	13
2015 Wins	4

1 3 5 7 9 11 13 15

2019 Dallas Cowboys Overview

Only one team in NFL history has won double-digit games by one score in a single season.

The 2018 Cowboys joined nine teams in league history to win *nine games* by one score.

In those games, the Cowboys led at halftime by an average score of 11-5 but were outscored in the second half in 6-of-9 games. From Weeks 10-17, the Cowboys won four games by one score. They led by a combined halftime score of 46-10 but were outscored 37-10 in the third quarter yet still more often than not held on for the win.

In first halves, the Cowboys ranked No. 12 in offensive efficiency with a 48% Success Rate. Defensively, they were No. 9 in first-half Success Rate. But in the third quarter, the Cowboys' offense dropped to 25th in efficiency with a 43% Success Rate. And the defense fell to 15th.

In first halves of games, last year's Cowboys faced an average of 6.8 yards to go on third downs, which was better than league average (7.0). And as you might expect due to average yards to go, the Cowboys ranked 15th in in first-down conversation rate (42%).

But third quarters were a different story. The Cowboys ranked third worst in average yards to go on third-down plays (8.4), and far worse than the 6.8 yards they required on third downs in first halves. Resultingly, the Cowboys converted third downs 24% of the time in third quarters, the NFL's third-worst rate. But why? What happened in the third quarter?

Dallas went conservative on first down, resulting in more yards to go on third downs, more punts, less time of possession, worse field position, fewer points, and more

(cont'd - see DAL 2)

Key Free Agents/ Trades Added

Player	AAV (MM)
Christian Covington (DT)	$2.5
George Iloka (FS)	$1
Kerry Hyder (DT)	$1
Randall Cobb (WR)	$5
Robert Quinn (DE)	Trade

Drafted Players

Rd	Pk	Player (College)
2	58	DT - Trysten Hill (UCF)
3	90	G - Connor McGovern (Penn State)
4	128	RB - Tony Pollard (Memphis)
5	158	CB - Michael Jackson (Miami)
5	165	DE - Joe Jackson (Miami)
6*	213	S - Donovan Wilson (Texas A&M)
7	218	RB - Mike Weber (Ohio State)
7	241	DE - Jalen Jelks (Oregon)

Lineup & Cap Hits

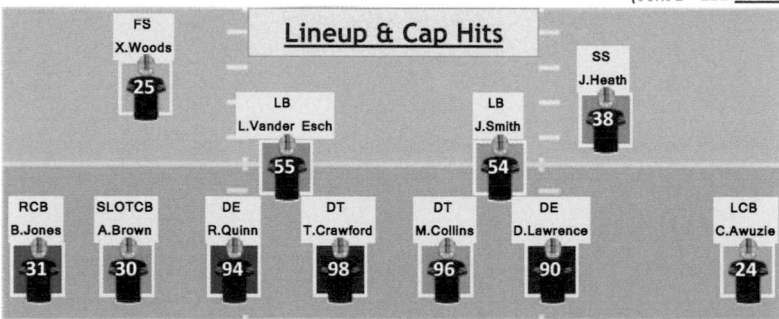

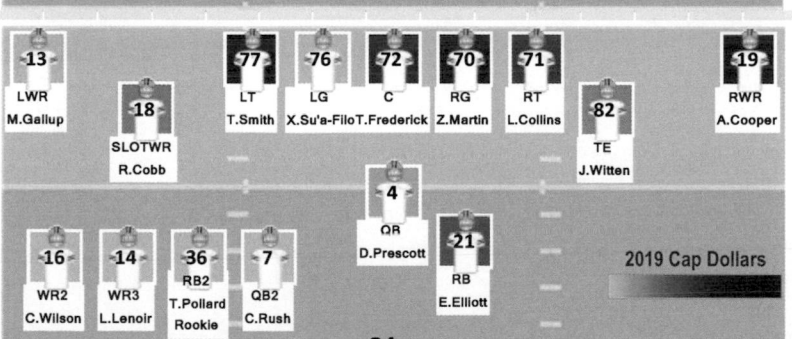

2019 Cap Dollars

2019 Unit Spending

All DEF   All OFF

Positional Spending

	Rank	Total	2017 Rk
All OFF	7	$111.79M	23
QB	32	$3.39M	32
OL	1	$60.66M	1
RB	9	$10.27M	11
WR	6	$30.23M	15
TE	22	$7.24M	32
All DEF	22	$79.19M	22
DL	7	$41.80M	10
LB	21	$17.33M	16
CB	24	$13.21M	28
S	29	$6.86M	31

points for opponents. First-down play calling controls so much of a game with a domino effect creating second- and third-down fallouts. I've been preaching about this for years, most notably through my work with Early Down Success Rate.

On first downs in first halves, last year's Cowboys passed at a 48% clip and recorded a 56% Success Rate with 8.0 yards per attempt. Yet in the third quarter, **Jason Garrett**'s club passed on just 41% of first-down plays, averaging 6.2 YPA. As the Cowboys shifted to nearly 60% first-down runs out of halftime, their first-down rushing Success Rate plummeted from 47% in the first half to 39% in the third quarter.

T*he Cowboys caused this*. Dallas chose to simply ignore what made the offense successful in first halves of games, instead playing conservatively and tentatively on first downs in the third quarter. Ignoring one broken play, the Cowboys' average depth of target on first downs was two full yards shorter in the third quarter than in the first half. On first-half first downs, **Dak Prescott** threw 19 attempts at 12-plus Air Yards. On second-half first downs, Dak threw just one pass of 12-plus Air Yards all year.

I found this shocking. The Cowboys should have understood the impact of their play calling on their third-quarter performances. Someone on their analytics staff should have noticed these -EV tendencies and alerted Garrett. If the Cowboys don't have someone like that on staff, they need to find one.

The Cowboys' conservativism nearly came back to bite them in the playoffs against Seattle. Dallas led 10-6 at halftime but scored zero third-quarter points while allowing eight and had to rally from behind for the win. In the third quarter, each of the Cowboys' first two drives featured **Ezekiel Elliott** runs on first down. Neither run was successful, and Dallas went three and out each time.

One of the biggest fears of going three and out is the lack of positive yardage which can result in great opponent field position. Wouldn't you know; after the second three and out, the Cowboys' punt gave the Seahawks the ball to start their drive on Dallas' 44-yard line. Thanks to great field position, Seattle scored a touchdown to take a 14-10 lead.

Now down by four points, the Cowboys called a Prescott pass play on first down on their final drive of the third quarter. A curl route to **Michael Gallup** traveling eight Air Yards was complete and set up second and short. After converting, the Cowboys drove the length of the field and scored a touchdown to take a lead they would never relinquish.

2018 Passing Performance

QB	1st Dwn	2nd Dwn	3rd Dwn	
Dak Prescott	55%	46%	34%	Success Rate
	7.7	7.4	6.9	YPA
	91.5	99.9	98.3	Rating
Pass Rate	50%	61%	82%	
NFL AVG	53%	47%	36%	Success Rate
	7.7	7.3	6.9	YPA
	95.1	93.7	87.1	Rating
Pass Rate	53%	62%	80%	

2018 Rushing Performance

Offense	1st Dwn	2nd Dwn	3rd Dwn	
DAL	46%	46%	63%	Success Rate
	4.4	4.5	5.0	YPC
Run Rate	50%	39%	18%	
NFL AVG	48%	46%	51%	Success Rate
	4.5	4.4	4.3	YPC
Run Rate	47%	38%	20%	

But the Cowboys never learned how their third-quarter play calling nearly cost them their season. They certainly didn't understand it during the season, and they didn't discover it before the playoffs. My guess is that if Garrett were to pick up this season preview and thumb to the Cowboys' chapter, he would be reading for the first time about his team's abnormally high run-play propensity in third quarters, which forced the Cowboys to need to gain far more yardage on third-down plays. Garrett may have no clue this cost many of Dallas' 2018 leads to evaporate and forced them to scratch and claw their way to *nine* wins by one score, second most in league history.

Had the Cowboys dropped even one of those one-score victories, they might have missed the playoffs, and Garrett might have been fired.

(cont'd - see DAL-3)

2018 Offensive Advanced Metrics

2018 Defensive Advanced Metrics

2018 Weekly EDSR & Season Trending Performance

	1	2	3	4	5	6	7		9	10	11	12	13	14	15	16	17	WEEK
	L	W	L	W	L	W	L		L	W	W	W	W	W	L	W	W	RESULT
	CAR	NYG	SEA	DET	HOU	JAC	WAS		TEN	PHI	ATL	WAS	NO	PHI	IND	TB	NYG	OPP
	A	H	A	H	A	H	A		H	A	H	H	H	A	H	A	H	SITE
	-8	7	-11	2	-3	33	-3		-14	7	3	8	3	6	-23	7	1	MARGIN
	8	20	13	26	16	40	17		14	27	22	31	13	29	0	27	36	PTS
	16	13	24	24	19	7	20		28	20	19	23	10	23	23	20	35	OPP PTS

EDSR by Wk
W=Green
L=Red

OFF/DEF
EDSR
Blue=OFF
(high=good)
Red=DEF
(low=good)

2018 Close Game Records

All 2018 Wins: **10**
FG Games (<=3 pts) W-L: **4-2**
FG Games Win %: **67% (#8)**
FG Games Wins (% of Total Wins): **40% (#6)**
1 Score Games (<=8 pts) W-L: **9-3**
1 Score Games Win %: **75% (#4)**
1 Score Games Wins (% of Total Wins): **90% (#2)**

2018 Critical & Game-Deciding Stats

TO Margin	+2
TO Given	18
INT Given	8
FUM Given	10
TO Taken	20
INT Taken	9
FUM Taken	11
Sack Margin	-17
Sacks	39
Sacks Allow	56
Return TD Margin	+0
Ret TDs	1
Ret TDs Allow	1
Penalty Margin	-15
Penalties	104
Opponent Penalties	89

Dallas Cowboys 2019 Strength of Schedule In Detail (compared to 2018)

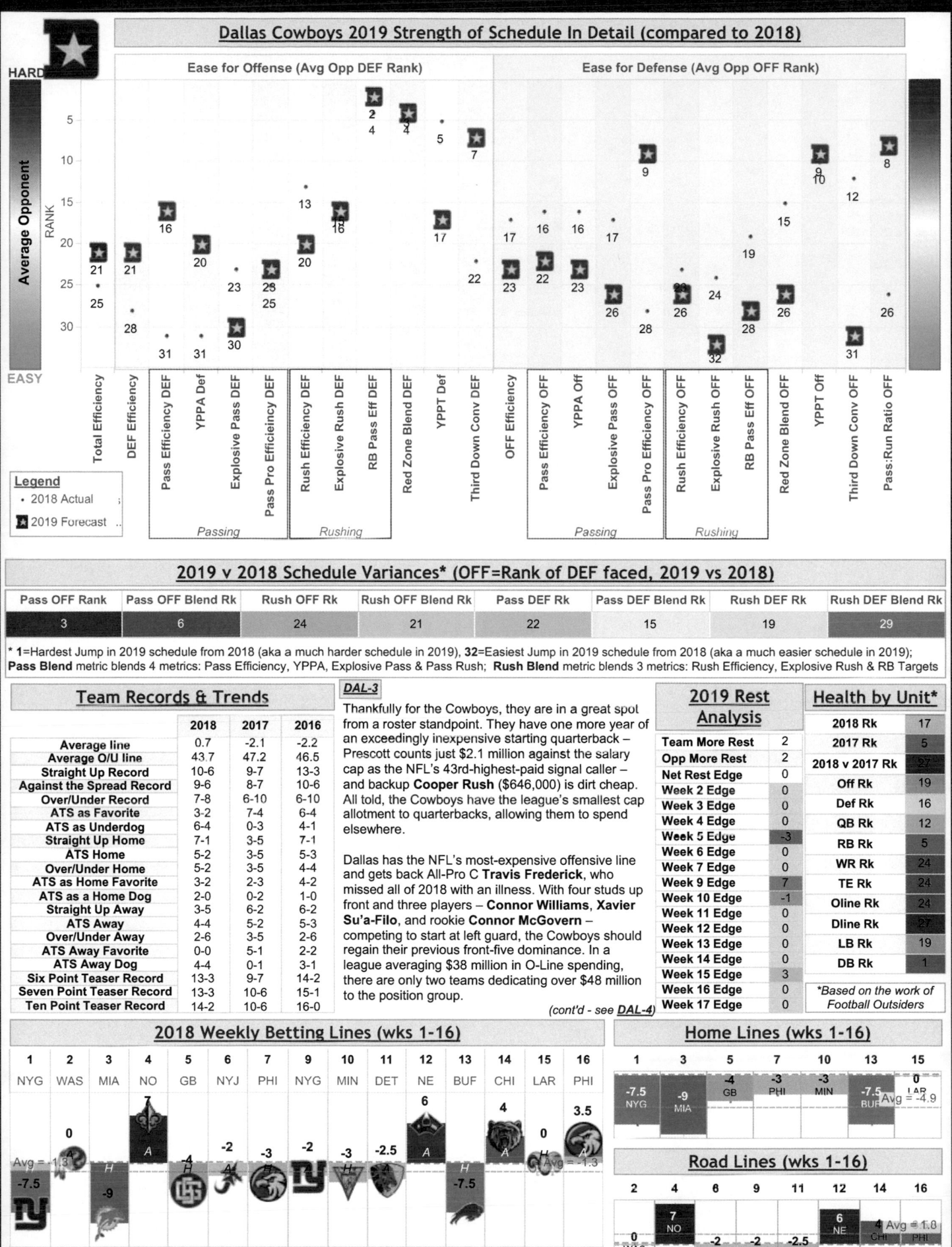

Ease for Offense (Avg Opp DEF Rank) | **Ease for Defense (Avg Opp OFF Rank)**

Legend
- 2018 Actual
- ⭐ 2019 Forecast

2019 v 2018 Schedule Variances* (OFF=Rank of DEF faced, 2019 vs 2018)

Pass OFF Rank	Pass OFF Blend Rk	Rush OFF Rk	Rush OFF Blend Rk	Pass DEF Rk	Pass DEF Blend Rk	Rush DEF Rk	Rush DEF Blend Rk
3	6	24	21	22	15	19	29

* **1**=Hardest Jump in 2019 schedule from 2018 (aka a much harder schedule in 2019), **32**=Easiest Jump in 2019 schedule from 2018 (aka a much easier schedule in 2019);
Pass Blend metric blends 4 metrics: Pass Efficiency, YPPA, Explosive Pass & Pass Rush; **Rush Blend** metric blends 3 metrics: Rush Efficiency, Explosive Rush & RB Targets

Team Records & Trends

	2018	2017	2016
Average line	0.7	-2.1	-2.2
Average O/U line	43.7	47.2	46.5
Straight Up Record	10-6	9-7	13-3
Against the Spread Record	9-6	8-7	10-6
Over/Under Record	7-8	6-10	6-10
ATS as Favorite	3-2	7-4	6-4
ATS as Underdog	6-4	0-3	4-1
Straight Up Home	7-1	3-5	7-1
ATS Home	5-2	3-5	5-3
Over/Under Home	5-2	3-5	4-4
ATS as Home Favorite	3-2	2-3	4-2
ATS as a Home Dog	2-0	0-2	1-0
Straight Up Away	3-5	6-2	6-2
ATS Away	4-4	5-2	5-3
Over/Under Away	2-6	3-5	2-6
ATS Away Favorite	0-0	5-1	2-2
ATS Away Dog	4-4	0-1	3-1
Six Point Teaser Record	13-3	9-7	14-2
Seven Point Teaser Record	13-3	10-6	15-1
Ten Point Teaser Record	14-2	10-6	16-0

DAL-3

Thankfully for the Cowboys, they are in a great spot from a roster standpoint. They have one more year of an exceedingly inexpensive starting quarterback – Prescott counts just $2.1 million against the salary cap as the NFL's 43rd-highest-paid signal caller – and backup **Cooper Rush** ($646,000) is dirt cheap. All told, the Cowboys have the league's smallest cap allotment to quarterbacks, allowing them to spend elsewhere.

Dallas has the NFL's most-expensive offensive line and gets back All-Pro C **Travis Frederick**, who missed all of 2018 with an illness. With four studs up front and three players – **Connor Williams**, **Xavier Su'a-Filo**, and rookie **Connor McGovern** – competing to start at left guard, the Cowboys should regain their previous front-five dominance. In a league averaging $38 million in O-Line spending, there are only two teams dedicating over $48 million to the position group.

(cont'd - see **DAL-4**)

2019 Rest Analysis

Team More Rest	2
Opp More Rest	2
Net Rest Edge	0
Week 2 Edge	0
Week 3 Edge	0
Week 4 Edge	0
Week 5 Edge	-3
Week 6 Edge	0
Week 7 Edge	0
Week 9 Edge	7
Week 10 Edge	-1
Week 11 Edge	0
Week 12 Edge	0
Week 13 Edge	0
Week 14 Edge	0
Week 15 Edge	3
Week 16 Edge	0
Week 17 Edge	0

Health by Unit*

2018 Rk	17
2017 Rk	5
2018 v 2017 Rk	27
Off Rk	19
Def Rk	16
QB Rk	12
RB Rk	5
WR Rk	24
TE Rk	24
Oline Rk	24
Dline Rk	27
LB Rk	19
DB Rk	1

Based on the work of Football Outsiders

2018 Weekly Betting Lines (wks 1-16)

1	2	3	4	5	6	7	9	10	11	12	13	14	15	16
NYG	WAS	MIA	NO	GB	NYJ	PHI	NYG	MIN	DET	NE	BUF	CHI	LAR	PHI
-7.5	0	-9	7	-4	-2	-3	-2	-3	-2.5	6	-7.5	4	0	3.5

Avg = -1.3

Home Lines (wks 1-16)

1	3	5	7	10	13	15
-7.5 NYG	-9 MIA	-4 GB	-3 PHI	-3 MIN	-7.5 BUF	0 LAR

Avg = -4.9

Road Lines (wks 1-16)

2	4	6	9	11	12	14	16
0 WAS	7 NO	-2 NYJ	-2 NYG	-2.5 DET	6 NE	4 CHI	PHI

Avg = 1.8

2018 Play Tendencies

All Pass %	57%
All Pass Rk	23
All Rush %	43%
All Rush Rk	10
1 Score Pass %	58%
1 Score Pass Rk	16
2017 1 Score Pass %	51%
2017 1 Score Pass Rk	30
2018 Pass Increase %	7%
Pass Increase Rk	6
1 Score Rush %	42%
1 Score Rush Rk	17
Up Pass %	50%
Up Pass Rk	16
Up Rush %	50%
Up Rush Rk	17
Down Pass %	66%
Down Pass Rk	19
Down Rush %	34%
Down Rush Rk	14

2018 Down & Distance Tendencies

Down	Distance	Total Plays	Pass Rate	Run Rate	Play Success %
1	Short (1-3)	6	17%	83%	50%
	Med (4-7)	10	50%	50%	30%
	Long (8-10)	332	45%	55%	50%
	XL (11+)	12	58%	42%	42%
2	Short (1-3)	39	26%	74%	72%
	Med (4-7)	93	60%	40%	52%
	Long (8-10)	93	66%	34%	46%
	XL (11+)	50	66%	34%	30%
3	Short (1-3)	54	50%	50%	59%
	Med (4-7)	53	98%	2%	45%
	Long (8-10)	27	100%	0%	26%
	XL (11+)	43	95%	5%	12%
4	Short (1-3)	11	9%	91%	82%

Shotgun %:

Under Center	Shotgun
42%	58%

37% AVG 63%

Run Rate:

Under Center	Shotgun
74%	18%

68% AVG 23%

Pass Rate:

Under Center	Shotgun
26%	82%

32% AVG 77%

Short Yardage Intelligence:

2nd and Short Run

Run Freq	Run Rk	NFL Run Freq Avg	Run 1D Rate	Run NFL 1D Avg
77%	4	65%	71%	68%

2nd and Short Pass

Pass Freq	Pass Rk	NFL Pass Freq Avg	Pass 1D Rate	Pass NFL 1D Avg
23%	29	35%	57%	56%

Most Frequent Play

Down	Distance	Play Type	Player	Total Plays	Play Success %
1	Short (1-3)	RUSH	Ezekiel Elliott	4	25%
	Med (4-7)	RUSH	Ezekiel Elliott	3	33%
	Long (8-10)	RUSH	Ezekiel Elliott	141	48%
	XL (11+)	RUSH	Ezekiel Elliott	3	33%
2	Short (1-3)	RUSH	Ezekiel Elliott	19	79%
	Med (4-7)	RUSH	Ezekiel Elliott	29	41%
	Long (8-10)	RUSH	Ezekiel Elliott	23	52%
	XL (11+)	RUSH	Ezekiel Elliott	13	15%
3	Short (1-3)	RUSH	Ezekiel Elliott	21	67%
	Med (4-7)	PASS	Amari Cooper	9	56%
	Long (8-10)	PASS	Michael Gallup	7	29%
	XL (11+)	PASS	Ezekiel Elliott	10	0%

Most Successful Play*

Down	Distance	Play Type	Player	Total Plays	Play Success %
1	Long (8-10)	PASS	Blake Jarwin	6	83%
2	Short (1-3)	RUSH	Ezekiel Elliott	19	79%
	Med (4-7)	RUSH	Dak Prescott	5	80%
	Long (8-10)	PASS	Amari Cooper	8	75%
	XL (11+)	PASS	Michael Gallup	5	100%
3	Short (1-3)	RUSH	Ezekiel Elliott	21	67%
	Med (4-7)	PASS	Cole Beasley	6	83%
	Long (8-10)	PASS	Michael Gallup	7	29%
	XL (11+)	PASS	Michael Gallup	6	33%
4	Short (1-3)	RUSH	Ezekiel Elliott	7	86%

*Minimum 5 plays to qualify

2018 Weekly Snap Rates

Wk	Opp	Score	Ezekiel Elliott	Cole Beasley	Amari Cooper	Geoff Swaim	Allen Hurns	Blake Jarwin	Dalton Schultz	Rod Smith	Tavon Austin	Terrance Williams
1	CAR	L 16-8	59 (92%)	43 (67%)		58 (91%)	38 (59%)	22 (34%)	2 (3%)	4 (6%)	10 (16%)	19 (30%)
2	NYG	W 20-13	50 (94%)	30 (57%)		50 (94%)	27 (51%)	14 (26%)		3 (6%)	18 (34%)	10 (19%)
3	SEA	L 24-13	56 (95%)	42 (71%)		55 (93%)	39 (66%)	12 (20%)		3 (5%)	19 (32%)	9 (15%)
4	DET	W 26-24	53 (77%)	38 (55%)		64 (93%)	47 (68%)	27 (39%)		13 (19%)	17 (25%)	
5	HOU	L 19-16	50 (81%)	37 (60%)		59 (95%)	38 (61%)	18 (29%)		11 (18%)	23 (37%)	
6	JAC	W 40-7	63 (86%)	42 (58%)		66 (90%)	57 (78%)	22 (30%)		8 (11%)	18 (25%)	
7	WAS	L 20-17	66 (100%)	53 (80%)		47 (71%)	54 (82%)	9 (14%)	19 (29%)			
9	TEN	L 28-14	52 (88%)	44 (75%)	50 (85%)		18 (31%)	27 (46%)	24 (41%)	7 (12%)		
10	PHI	W 27-20	61 (88%)	48 (70%)	54 (78%)	56 (81%)	15 (22%)	3 (4%)	8 (12%)	10 (14%)		
11	ATL	W 22-19	56 (88%)	42 (66%)	51 (80%)	57 (89%)	8 (13%)	3 (5%)	11 (17%)	8 (13%)		
12	WAS	W 31-23	65 (93%)	43 (61%)	47 (67%)		32 (46%)	35 (50%)	42 (60%)	5 (7%)		
13	NO	W 13-10	63 (89%)	47 (66%)	56 (79%)		16 (23%)	28 (39%)	40 (56%)	8 (11%)		
14	PHI	W 29-23	86 (87%)	65 (66%)	90 (91%)		27 (27%)	57 (58%)	46 (46%)	13 (13%)		
15	IND	L 23-0	61 (88%)	44 (64%)	54 (78%)		22 (32%)	43 (62%)	31 (45%)	6 (9%)		
16	TB	W 27-20	49 (94%)	35 (67%)	44 (85%)		4 (8%)	27 (52%)	33 (63%)	3 (6%)		
17	NYG	W 36-35		60 (77%)	66 (85%)		10 (13%)	40 (51%)	44 (56%)	49 (63%)	10 (13%)	
	Grand Total		890 (89%)	713 (66%)	512 (81%)	512 (89%)	452 (42%)	387 (35%)	300 (39%)	151 (14%)	115 (26%)	38 (21%)

Personnel Groupings

Personnel	Team %	NFL Avg	Succ. %
1-1 [3WR]	66%	65%	46%
1-2 [2WR]	14%	17%	52%
2-1 [2WR]	7%	8%	52%
1-3 [1WR]	4%	3%	54%
2-2 [1WR]	3%	3%	32%
1-0 [4WR]	3%	2%	20%

Grouping Tendencies

Personnel	Pass Rate	Pass Succ. %	Run Succ. %
1-1 [3WR]	66%	45%	48%
1-2 [2WR]	35%	55%	50%
2-1 [2WR]	38%	54%	51%
1-3 [1WR]	28%	55%	54%
2-2 [1WR]	19%	67%	24%
1-0 [4WR]	57%	12%	31%

Red Zone Targets (min 3)

Receiver	All	Inside 5	6-10	11-20
Ezekiel Elliott	14		4	10
Cole Beasley	9	1	3	5
Michael Gallup	9	1	2	6
Amari Cooper	8	3	2	3
Allen Hurns	4		1	3
Blake Jarwin	4			4
Geoff Swaim	4	2		2

Red Zone Rushes (min 3)

Rusher	All	Inside 5	6-10	11-20
Ezekiel Elliott	46	16	11	19
Dak Prescott	23	11	5	7
Rod Smith	6	1		5

Early Down Target Rate

RB	TE	WR
20%	18%	62%
23%	21%	56%
	NFL AVG	

Overall Target Success %

RB	TE	WR
40%	56%	53%
#29	#14	#12

Dallas Cowboys 2018 Passing Recap & 2019 Outlook

Amari Cooper's impact was evident in **Dak Prescott**'s passing performance. Pre-Cooper, Dak managed a 22% Success Rate and 5.3 yards per attempt on third-down passes. With Amari, Prescott's third-down passing Success Rate nearly doubled to 40% with 7.7 YPA. Will rookie OC **Kellen Moore** encourage Prescott to stay aggressive with his first-down pass rate, and can the offensive line better protect him? Dak's upward-trending red-zone rushing enhances his fantasy outlook.

Dak Prescott Rating All Downs

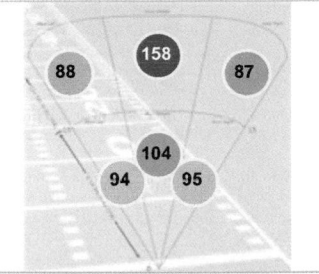

2018 Standard Passing Table

QB	Comp	Att	Comp %	Yds	YPA	TDs	INT	Sacks	Rating	Rk
Dak Prescott	398	590	67%	4,376	7.4	24	9	58	96	15
NFL Avg			62%		7.0				87.5	

2018 Advanced Passing Table

QB	Success %	EDSR Passing Success %	20+ Yd Pass Gains	20+ Yd Pass %	30+ Yd Pass Gains	30+ Yd Pass %	Avg. Air Yds per Comp	Avg. YAC per Comp	20+ Air Yd Comp	20+ Air Yd %
Dak Prescott	46%	51%	46	8.0%	23	4.0%	5.6	5.4	21	4%
NFL Avg	44%	48%	29.5	8.4%	12.5	3.7%	5.8	5.1	14.5	6%

Dak Prescott Rating Early Downs

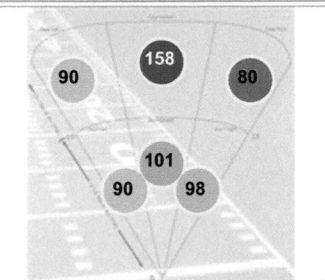

Interception Rates by Down

Yards to Go	1st Dwn	2nd Dwn	3rd Dwn	4th Dwn	Total
1 & 2	0.0%	0.0%	0.0%	0.0%	0.0%
3, 4, 5	0.0%	0.0%	0.0%	0.0%	0.0%
6 - 9	0.0%	1.2%	1.9%		1.4%
10 - 14	1.9%	0.0%	0.0%	20.0%	1.5%
15+	11.1%	5.9%	0.0%	0.0%	4.0%
Total	2.2%	0.9%	0.5%	10.0%	1.4%

3rd Down Passing - Short of Sticks Analysis

QB	Avg. Yds to Go	Avg. YIA (of Comp)	Avg Yds Short	Short of Sticks Rate	Short Rk
Dak Prescott	8.4	4.6	-3.8	69%	37
NFL Avg	7.8	6.4	-1.4	60%	

Air Yds vs YAC

Air Yds %	YAC %	Rk
51%	49%	27
53%	48%	

2018 Receiving Recap & 2019 Outlook

Amari Cooper is the prized jewel, especially with security-blanket slot WR **Cole Beasley** gone to Buffalo. I think the return of **Jason Witten** could be more beneficial than expected for Prescott, albeit not as his primary read. Witten has a solid on-field rapport with Dak and knows where to be as a chain mover in the middle of the field. I'm not as high on the addition of **Randall Cobb**, but the Cowboys needed slot help. I am higher on No. 2 WR **Michael Gallup**, who produced 15.2 yards per target and an 80% Success Rate in the slot after Cooper's arrival.

Player *Min 50 Targets	Targ	Comp %	YPA	Rating	Success %	Success Rk	Missed YPA Rk	YAS % Rk	YTS % Rk	TDs
Ezekiel Elliott	105	79%	5.9	100.7	41%	117	180	119	110	3
Amari Cooper	94	70%	9.5	116.2	59%	21	50	43	97	5
Cole Beasley	91	76%	7.9	109.0	62%	7	11	113	9	3
Michael Gallup	83	49%	7.8	77.6	41%	117	166	18	97	3

Directional Passer Rating Delivered

Receiver	Short Left	Short Middle	Short Right	Deep Left	Deep Middle	Deep Right	Player Total
Ezekiel Elliott	83	84	123			119	101
Amari Cooper	129	128	89	6	135	135	116
Cole Beasley	109	111	78	135	119	119	109
Michael Gallup	76	0	97	86	119	40	78
Blake Jarwin	97	101	90	0	158	149	105
Allen Hurns	88	114	64	149		96	102
Geoff Swaim	98	89	128			40	109
Deonte Thompson	56	107	66			40	65
Tavon Austin	77	119	89	149		0	110
Rod Smith	79	99	70				85
Jamize Olawale	65		56				57
Team Total	96	104	96	89	158	99	101

2018 Rushing Recap & 2019 Outlook

Ezekiel Elliott should benefit from the return of C **Travis Frederick**. After ranking No. 2 in rushing efficiency in 2017, the 2018 Cowboys fell to 19th. Elliott's explosive-run rate grew, but his rushing Success Rate dipped from No. 2 among qualified backs (57%) in 2017 to 29th (49%) last year. Zeke was much more dominant in the receiving game, where he led the Cowboys in targets. I suspect Cooper claims that crown this year, but Elliott still projects as a dominant fantasy producer.

Player *Min 50 Rushes	Rushes	YPC	Success %	Success Rk	Missed YPA Rk	YTS % Rk	YAS % Rk	Early Down Success %	Early Down Success Rk	TDs
Ezekiel Elliott	350	4.6	49%	29	18	56	33	47%	34	8

Yards per Carry by Direction

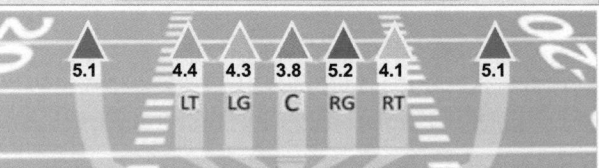

5.1   4.4   4.3   3.8   5.2   4.1   5.1
　　　LT   LG   C   RG   RT

Directional Run Frequency

9%   16%   11%   29%   11%   13%   11%
　　　LT   LG   C   RG   RT

They are the Cowboys ($61 million) and Falcons ($55 million).

Without Frederick, Dallas' offensive line didn't live up to its cost last year. It fell from 15th to 28th in pass-protection efficiency, and Prescott was sacked 49 times on 349 dropbacks (14%) when holding the ball longer than 2.5 seconds. His sack rate was 2.7% when releasing within 2.5 seconds.

These numbers also suggest the Cowboys should emphasize more quicker, higher-efficiency passes. Not only does Dak avoid sacks when getting the ball out fast, he has a 73% completion rate and 7:1 TD-to-INT ratio inside 2.5 seconds versus a 63% completion rate and 15:7 TD-to-INT ratio when holding onto the ball longer.

Following a sack, last year's Cowboys gained a first down only 13% of the time. The other 87% were punts, field goal attempts, or turnovers. When Dak was sacked on early downs, Dallas faced an average of 13.9 yards to go on third downs. The Cowboys scored touchdowns on just 3.7% of drives where Prescott took a sack.

This year's Cowboys need better protection and a commitment from first-year OC **Kellen Moore** to hastening Dak's release time.

There are signs the Cowboys are trusting Dak more, however. As a rookie, Prescott passed the ball on a league-low 45% of early-down plays. That number stayed at 45% in 2017. Last year, Dak's early-down passing rate was 51%, a significant hike but still eighth lowest in the league. Over the first seven weeks, Prescott managed a 38% Success Rate, 6.9 yards per attempt, and an 87.4 passer rating despite facing the NFL's tenth-softest pass-defense schedule.

(cont'd - see **DAL-5**)

Dallas Cowboys Fantasy Corner

Acquired from Oakland for what became the 27th overall pick (SS **Johnathan Abram**), **Amari Cooper** injected immediate dynamism into a 2018 Cowboys offense that had gone boringly stale. Long criticized for his unsure hands, Cooper dropped just 4-of-94 targets and posted a mouth-watering 96/1,303/10 (13.6 YPR) full-season receiving pace across 11 games, including the playoffs. This is **Dak Prescott** and Cooper's first offseason together, and both are in contract years. Still only 25 – Cooper just turned in June -- all signs point to a breakout season as the Cowboys' clear-cut passing-game focal point. Since the 1970 AFL-NFL merger, only six players have had more receiving yards before age 25 than Amari's 3,908. Dak-Cooper stacks in best ball and DFS deserve to be popular against Dallas' soft Weeks 1-6 pass-defense slate.

- Evan Silva

2018 Situational Usage by Player & Position

Usage Rate by Score

		Being Blown Out (14+)	Down Big (9-13)	One Score	Large Lead (9-13)	Blowout Lead (14+)
RUSH	Ezekiel Elliott	7%	2%	74%	11%	7%
	Amari Cooper			100%		
	Rod Smith			80%	7%	13%
	Tavon Austin			86%		14%
	Total	6%	2%	75%	10%	7%
PASS	Ezekiel Elliott	12%	15%	66%	7%	
	Cole Beasley	14%	7%	61%	8%	10%
	Amari Cooper	11%	2%	79%	6%	1%
	Michael Gallup	15%	3%	77%	4%	
	Rod Smith			100%		
	Allen Hurns	6%	9%	70%	6%	9%
	Blake Jarwin	19%	9%	66%	3%	3%
	Geoff Swaim	7%	17%	72%		3%
	Tavon Austin	17%		67%	8%	8%
	Deonte Thompson	19%		56%	25%	
	Jamize Olawale			75%		25%
	Terrance Williams		33%	33%	33%	
	Brice Butler			100%		
	Total	12%	8%	70%	7%	3%

Share of Offensive Plays by Type

	Ezekiel Elliott	Cole Beasley	Amari Cooper	Michael Gallup	Rod Smith	Allen Hurns	Blake Jarwin	Geoff Swaim	Tavon Austin	Deonte Thompson	Jamize Olawale	Terrance Williams	Brice Butler
RUSH	87%		0%		11%				2%				
PASS	18%	18%	18%	15%	2%	7%	7%	6%	3%	3%	1%	1%	0%
ALL	50%	10%	9%	8%	6%	4%	4%	3%	2%	2%	0%	0%	0%

Positional Target Distribution vs NFL Average

		NFL Wide				Team Only			
		Left	Middle	Right	Total	Left	Middle	Right	Total
Deep	WR	33%	17%	30%	**81%**	39%	10%	38%	**87%**
	TE	5%	4%	7%	**16%**	3%	3%	6%	**12%**
	RB	1%	0%	2%	**4%**			1%	**1%**
	All	**39%**	**22%**	**39%**	**100%**	**42%**	**13%**	**45%**	**100%**
Short	WR	20%	14%	21%	**55%**	23%	13%	24%	**60%**
	TE	6%	6%	8%	**20%**	6%	2%	6%	**14%**
	RB	10%	5%	10%	**25%**	9%	6%	11%	**26%**
	All	**36%**	**25%**	**39%**	**100%**	**38%**	**21%**	**41%**	**100%**
Total		**37%**	**24%**	**39%**	**100%**	**38%**	**20%**	**42%**	**100%**

Positional Success Rates vs NFL Average

		NFL Wide				Team Only			
		Left	Middle	Right	Total	Left	Middle	Right	Total
Deep	WR	40%	49%	40%	**42%**	43%	75%	34%	**43%**
	TE	44%	53%	41%	**45%**	0%	100%	40%	**44%**
	RB	38%	33%	42%	**40%**			100%	**100%**
	All	**40%**	**49%**	**40%**	**42%**	**41%**	**80%**	**37%**	**44%**
Short	WR	55%	61%	52%	**55%**	58%	61%	52%	**56%**
	TE	55%	62%	54%	**57%**	65%	44%	59%	**59%**
	RB	47%	54%	45%	**48%**	35%	38%	45%	**40%**
	All	**53%**	**60%**	**51%**	**54%**	**54%**	**53%**	**51%**	**52%**
Total		**50%**	**58%**	**49%**	**52%**	**52%**	**55%**	**49%**	**51%**

Division History: Season Wins & 2019 Projection

2015 Wins | 2016 Wins | 2017 Wins | 2018 Wins | Forecast 2019 Wins

Rank of 2019 Defensive Pass Efficiency Faced by Week

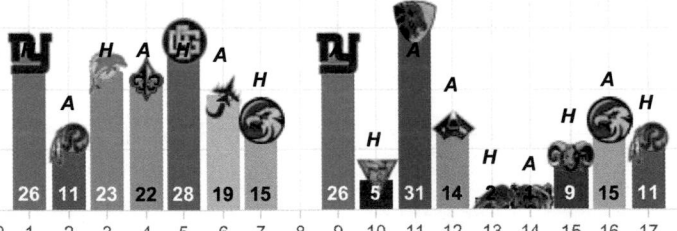

| 26 | 11 | 23 | 22 | 28 | 19 | 15 | | 26 | 5 | 31 | 14 | | | 9 | 15 | 11 |

Rank of 2019 Defensive Rush Efficiency Faced by Week

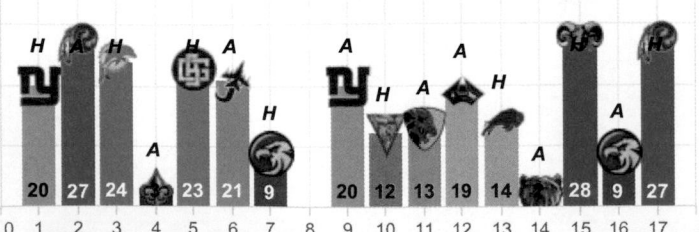

| 20 | 27 | 24 | | 23 | 21 | 9 | | 20 | 12 | 13 | 19 | 14 | | 28 | 9 | 27 |

2018 Detailed Analytics Summary
Success by Play Type & Primary Personnel Groupings

Successful Play Rate 0% ▮▮▮▮▮ 100%

Type	1-1 [3WR]	1-2 [2WR]	2-1 [2WR]	1-3 [1WR]	2-2 [1WR]	1-0 [4WR]	0-1 [4WR]	0-0 [5WR]	2-0 [3WR]	2-3 [0WR]	ALL
PASS	45% (496)	54% (59)	52% (27)	57% (14)	63% (8)	12% (17)	43% (14)	25% (4)	0% (2)	0% (1)	45% (642)
RUSH	49% (255)	49% (110)	49% (49)	55% (29)	28% (32)	31% (13)		100% (2)	0% (1)	100% (1)	48% (492)
All	46% (751)	51% (169)	50% (76)	56% (43)	35% (40)	20% (30)	43% (14)	50% (6)	0% (3)	50% (2)	46% (1,134)

Format Success Rate (Total # of Plays)

Receiving Success by Top-4 Personnel Groupings
(Min 50 targets)

POS	Player	1-1 [3WR]	1-2 [2WR]	2-1 [2WR]	1-0 [4WR]	4 Grp Total
RB	Ezekiel Elliott	36% (83) 5.5, 100.2	83% (12) 9.9, 108.0	33% (3) 2.0, 79.2	0% (4) 4.8, 84.4	40% (102) 5.9, 100.9
WR	Amari Cooper	62% (77) 10.3, 138.0	20% (5) 3.8, 11.7	50% (6) 7.7, 36.1	0% (1) 0.0, 39.6	58% (89) 9.6, 118.0
	Cole Beasley	62% (81) 7.6, 106.5	100% (1) 9.0, 104.2		50% (2) 8.0, 77.1	62% (84) 7.6, 106.3
	Michael Gallup	41% (63) 7.6, 82.5	67% (6) 20.5, 118.8	40% (5) 4.8, 55.4		43% (74) 8.4, 86.7

Format Line 1: Success Rate (Total # of Plays) Line 2: YPA, Passer Rating

Rushing Success by Top-4 Personnel Groupings
(Min 25 carries)

Rusher (Last, First)	1-1 [3WR]	1-2 [2WR]	2-1 [2WR]	2-2 [1WR]	4 Grp Total
Elliott Ezekiel	46% (176) 5.0	54% (83) 4.6	47% (43) 3.8	50% (14) 1.4	48% (316) 4.6
Prescott Dak	62% (47) 6.0	44% (9) 4.1	100% (1) 6.0	11% (18) -0.7	48% (75) 4.1
Smith Rod	35% (23) 3.5	27% (11) 1.8	60% (5) 3.4		36% (39) 3.0

Format Line 1: Success Rate (Total # of Plays) Line 2: YPC

Passing by Coverage Scheme

Zone	56% (239) 8.0, 102.5
M2M	50% (223) 7.3, 95.7
Screen	32% (57) 6.8, 106.6
Combo	71% (7) 9.1, 99.7

Passing by Route

Curl	64% (78) 6.5, 83.6
Out	71% (59) 7.5, 91.0
Screen	34% (50) 7.7, 118.6
Slant	64% (42) 8.3, 106.0
Dig	50% (32) 5.9, 73.7
Flat	59% (29) 6.4, 104.9

Throw Types

Level 1	53% (376) 6.8, 93.0
Level 2	54% (141) 9.1, 112.1
Level 3	27% (45) 10.6, 101.1
Shovel	29% (7) 0.1, 118.8
Touch	50% (2) 5.5, 66.7
Sidearm	50% (2) 5.0, 87.5

QB Drop Types

3 Step	50% (284) 7.3, 98.0
0/1 Step	55% (105) 6.3, 98.1
5 Step	48% (81) 8.8, 78.9
Basic Screen	36% (39) 7.9, 125.2
Designed Rollout Right	54% (26) 8.7, 105.6
7 Step	68% (22) 9.0, 81.3

QB State at Pass

Planted	55% (332) 7.9, 101.4
Shuffling	43% (103) 6.7, 93.9
Moving	46% (84) 7.5, 109.8

Play Action

	Play Action	No P/A
Under Center	65% (65) 10.5, 109.8	62% (42) 7.0, 80.9
Shotgun	44% (70) 6.5, 92.1	49% (399) 7.3, 99.3
ALL	54% (135) 8.4, 100.6	50% (441) 7.3, 97.5

Run Types

Inside Zone	53% (149) 4.4
Outside Zone	47% (95) 4.6
Power	37% (38) 2.7
Lead	37% (30) 4.1
Stretch	36% (14) 3.8
Pitch	20% (10) 1.1

DAL-5

Then, the Cowboys traded for **Amari Cooper**.

Over the final nine games, Prescott's Success Rate launched to 50% -- No. 8 in the NFL over the back half of the season – his YPA moved to 7.7, and his 103 rating was also top eight among 43 qualified passers. Dak's performance with Cooper did come against the NFL's sixth-easiest schedule of pass defenses, but his efficiency enhancement was notable nonetheless.

Despite their general conservatism, the Cowboys took a number of steps forward I hoped they would last year. First was increasing Dak's red-zone usage. Dallas finished 2018 with a bottom-five red-zone offense and was successful on just 38% of its red-zone plays, the NFL's fourth-worst mark. The Cowboys scored touchdowns on just 48% of red-zone trips. And Cooper did not save them in scoring position; the Cowboys' red-zone Success Rate in Amari's nine games was second lowest in the league (35%). Dallas' red-zone struggles came from the passing attack, which produced a league-worst 28% Success Rate inside the opposing 20-yard line.

Red-zone runs featuring Prescott were by far the Cowboys' most-successful scoring-position plays. Dak's 68% Success Rate among quarterbacks with at least ten red-zone carries was highest in the league with six touchdowns on 19 attempts. **Ezekiel Elliott** ranked 25th among running backs with a 44% rushing Success Rate and only five TDs on 39 red-zone runs. Dak's 19 red-zone carries still nearly equaled his 23 red-zone runs from the 2016 and 2017 seasons combined, so at least his usage there took a step forward.

Over the last three seasons among 150 qualified rushers with at least ten red-zone carries, only **Derrick Henry**'s 72% Success Rate is higher than Prescott's 71%. The Cowboys *need* to keep using Dak more and more near the goal line.

The Cowboys also smartly got Elliott more involved in the passing game. The 2016 Cowboys threw only 17% of first-and-ten passes to running backs, and that number decreased to 16% in 2017. Last year's Cowboys threw to backs on 22% of first-down plays with phenomenal play design, producing a 73% Success Rate and 8.0 yards per attempt, which both ranked top four in the league. The only backs with more first-and-ten targets than Zeke's 33 were **Christian McCaffrey** and **Todd Gurley**; Elliott drew just 27 combined first-and-ten targets in his first two NFL seasons.

Dallas also has a rock-solid defense that improved its Early-Down Success Rate from 25th in 2017 to 11th last year and ranked No. 9 in defensive efficiency. Last year's Cowboys finished sixth worst in pass rush but endured the sixth-most injured defensive line and should be healthier this season. Every member of Dallas' starting secondary is on his rookie deal. At this time last year, the 2018 Cowboys were projected underdogs in six of their first ten games.

Denver Broncos

Coaches (Prior Yrs)

Head Coach:
Vic Fangio (CHI DC) (new)
Offensive Coordinator:
Rich Scangarello (SF QB) (new)
Defensive Coordinator:
Ed Donatell (CHI DB) (new)

EASY   HARD

2019 Forecast

Wins	Div Rank
7	#3

Past Records
2018: 6-10
2017: 5-11
2016: 9-7

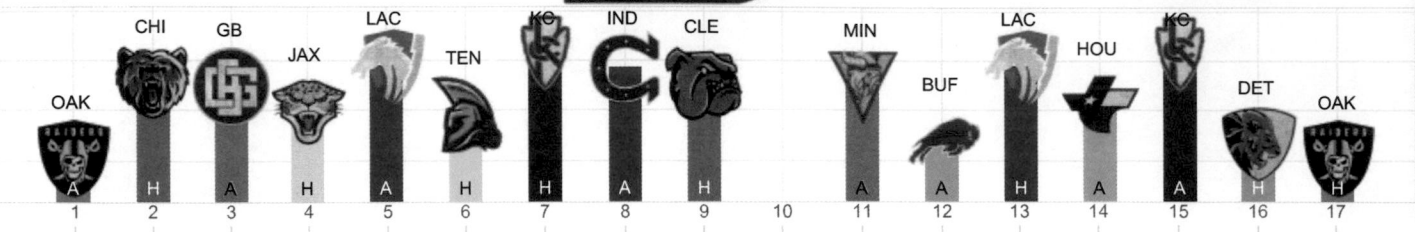

OAK	CHI	GB	JAX	LAC	TEN	KC	IND	CLE		MIN	BUF	LAC	HOU	KC	DET	OAK
A	H	A	H	A	H	H	A	H		A	A	H	A	A	H	H
1	2	3	4	5	6	7	8	9	10	11	12	13	14	15	16	17

MNF   TNF

Key Players Lost

Player	New
Adam-Pacman Jones (CB)	Retired
Billy Turner (G)	GB
Bradley Roby (CB)	HOU
Brandon Marshall (ILB)	OAK
Case Keenum (QB)	WAS
Jamar Taylor (CB)	SEA
Jared Veldheer (RT)	NE
Jordan Taylor (WR)	MIN
Matt LaCosse (TE)	NE
Matt Paradis (C)	CAR
Max Garcia (G)	ARI
Shane Ray (OLB)	BAL
Shaquil Barrett (OLB)	TB
Tramaine Brock (CB)	ARI

Average Line	# Games Favored	# Games Underdog
2.6	5	10

Regular Season Wins: Past & Current Proj

Forecast 2019 Wins — 7
2018 Wins — 6
Forecast 2018 Wins — 7
2017 Wins — 5
2016 Wins — 9
2015 Wins — 12

1 3 5 7 9 11 13 15

2019 Denver Broncos Overview

Last year I called the Bears' re-signing of **Vic Fangio** one of the NFL's most-underrated coaching moves. Fangio's contract expired after 2017. Invited to interview for the Bears' head-coaching vacancy, Fangio lost out to **Matt Nagy** but stayed on for another year. The Bears fielded the league's best defense on Fangio's watch. He is now the Broncos' head coach.

Fangio inherits a strong Denver defense that last year ranked No. 6 in Early Down Success Rate and No. 5 in defensive efficiency despite facing one of the NFL's ten-toughest schedules of opposing offenses. **Von Miller**, **Bradley Chubb**, **Chris Harris**, **Derek Wolfe**, **Adam Gotsis**, and **Todd Davis** make up the corps of a talented group, and the Broncos signed physical S/CB **Kareem Jackson** away from the Texans in free agency. Fangio lured trusty slot CB **Bryce Callahan** with him to Chicago.

But the Broncos' offense is a different story.

Last year's Denver offense was, at best, an enigma. And it's important to understand how they got there. The 2017 Broncos were even more miserable, going 5-11 with horrendous quarterback play from **Brock Osweiler** and **Trevor Siemian** and ranking 31st in passing offense with poor run-game production. They finished -17 in turnover margin and -20 in sack margin, becoming the first team since **Mike Nolan**'s 2008 49ers to finish with at least a -15 takeaway margin and -20 sack margin. The 2017 Broncos were downright atrocious in the most-critical game-deciding metrics.

The 2018 Broncos hitched their wagon to **Case Keenum**. Albeit better than Siemian and Osweiler, Keenum's passing efficiency was subpar across the board when compared to league average. Denver's offensive efficiency did improve from 31st to 14th, primarily

(cont'd - see DEN2)

Key Free Agents/ Trades Added

Player	AAV (MM)
Bryce Callahan (CB)	$7
Dekoda Watson (LB)	Trade
Ja'Wuan James (RT)	$12.
Joe Flacco (QB)	Trade
Kareem Jackson (CB)	$11

Drafted Players

Rd	Pk	Player (College)
1	20	TE - Noah Fant (Iowa)
2	41	OT - Dalton Risner (Kansas State)
	42	QB - Drew Lock (Missouri)
3	71	DT - Dre'mont Jones (Ohio State)
5	156	LB - Justin Hollins (Oregon)
6	187	WR - Juwann Winfree (Colorado)

Lineup & Cap Hits

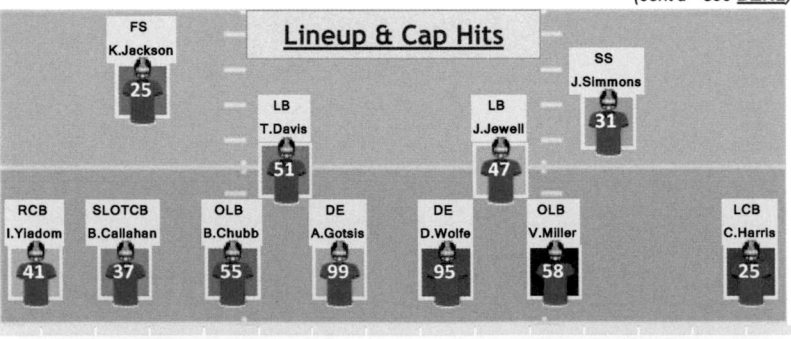

2019 Cap Dollars

2019 Unit Spending

All OFF / All DEF

Positional Spending

	Rank	Total	2017 Rk
All OFF	29	$77.32M	28
QB	17	$20.78M	21
OL	29	$28.32M	18
RB	31	$3.29M	30
WR	20	$19.47M	20
TE	25	$5.46M	29
All DEF	6	$95.44M	8
DL	25	$20.65M	18
LB	1	$44.16M	3
CB	14	$23.09M	6
S	25	$7.54M	17

88

because it jumped from 10th worst to fifth best in rushing efficiency. But the Broncos' pass protection improved dramatically as well, leaping from 29th to 11th as one of Keenum's strengths was avoiding sacks. Keenum was pressured on 36% of dropbacks – ninth most in the league – but ranked No. 8 in sack rate when pressured.

The Broncos also improved critical statistics that correlate to winning with a massive swing from -17 to +7 In turnover margin and -20 to +10 in sack ratio. Over the last 30 years, only nine teams won six games or fewer and improved their turnover and sack margins by 20 the following year. Those nine teams increased their next-year win total by an average of 5.6 games. The Broncos fell into this bucket, yet only improved their record from 5-11 to 6-10. Denver got closer to becoming a competitive team but still couldn't save Vance Joseph's job.

Despite its solid 2018 performance, Denver's biggest offensive concern is the line. C **Matt Paradis** left for Carolina in free agency. RG **Ronald Leary** is returning from a torn Achilles', and LG **Dalton Risner** is a rookie. Projected Paradis replacement **Connor McGovern** ranked 87th in pass blocking among 88 qualified guards last year.

Denver's interior line is particularly important because **Joe Flacco** has been astonishingly terrible when under pressure. Among qualified quarterbacks, Flacco's rankings in under-pressure passer rating were 29th, 26th, 22nd, and 35th over the last four years, and he posted ridiculously high throwaway rates.

But Flacco wasn't pressured often behind Baltimore's sturdy offensive line. He was pressured at the fourth-lowest rate among 33 qualified quarterbacks in 2018, and second lowest in 2017. A statue in the pocket who's battled back and hip injuries down the stretch of his career, Flacco's ineffectiveness handling pass rush will be exacerbated if the Broncos' offensive line takes a step back.

The interior line is also important because of *where* the Broncos run the ball; they ran behind center at the NFL's third-highest rate (42%) last season.

Here is the problem for the Broncos: Against a favorable schedule of opposing offenses, last year's defense already ranked top five in efficiency. Even if this year's defense gets better under Fangio, the defense won't propel them to new heights. The Broncos' missing component is a productive passing attack, and there's little reason to believe they'll field one this year.
 I worry about Flacco in Denver. New OC **Rich Scangarello** called Flacco a "perfect fit" for his offense, praising the veteran's willingness to stand in the

pocket and make throws. In other words, Flacco is big and has a strong arm, and Scangarello evaluates quarterbacks a lot like his boss, GM **John Elway**. Yet Flacco has been one of the worst quarterbacks in the league when pressured. Flacco may be "tough" and can "stand in the pocket" as a matter of fact, but when he does stand in under pressure, the results have been disastrous.

As to Scangarello's notion that Flacco can make all the throws, note that Flacco ranked 32nd among 33 qualified quarterbacks in deep-ball efficiency last season. His 34% completion rate was also 32nd. Over the last three years combined, Flacco's deep accuracy ranks dead last among 27 qualified quarterbacks.

(cont'd - see DEN-3)

2018 Passing Performance

QB	1st Dwn	2nd Dwn	3rd Dwn	
Case Keenum	56%	43%	28%	Success Rate
	7.3	6.9	5.4	YPA
	85.9	86.3	67.8	Rating
Pass Rate	61%	61%	81%	
NFL AVG	53%	47%	36%	Success Rate
	7.7	7.3	6.9	YPA
	95.1	93.7	87.1	Rating
Pass Rate	53%	62%	80%	

2018 Rushing Performance

Offense	1st Dwn	2nd Dwn	3rd Dwn	
DEN	49%	45%	53%	Success Rate
	5.3	4.5	4.5	YPC
Run Rate	39%	39%	19%	
NFL AVG	48%	46%	51%	Success Rate
	4.5	4.4	4.3	YPC
Run Rate	47%	38%	20%	

2018 Offensive Advanced Metrics

Metric	Rank
EDSR Off	22
30 & In Off	25
Red Zone Off	22
3rd Down Off	28
YPPA Off	26
YPPT Off	25
Offensive Efficiency	24
Pass Efficiency Off	14
Pass Pro Efficiency Off	11
RB Pass Eff Off	9
Rush Efficiency Off	5
Explosive Pass Off	19
Explosive Run Off	23

2018 Defensive Advanced Metrics

Metric	Rank
EDSR Def	6
30 & In Def	17
Red Zone Def	5
3rd Down Def	17
YPPA Def	13
YPPT Def	23
Defensive Efficiency	5
Pass Efficiency Def	4
Pass Pro Efficiency Def	9
RB Pass Eff Def	21
Rush Efficiency Def	16
Explosive Pass Def	7
Explosive Run Def	10

2018 Weekly EDSR & Season Trending Performance

	1	2	3	4	5	6	7	8	9	11	12	13	14	15	16	17	WEEK
	W	W	L	L	L	L	W	L	L	W	W	W	L	L	L	L	RESULT
	SEA	OAK	BAL	KC	NYJ	LA	ARI	KC	HOU	LAC	PIT	CIN	SF	CLE	OAK	LAC	OPP
	H	H	A	H	A	H	A	A	A	A	H	A	A	H	A	H	SITE
	3	1	-13	-4	-18	-3	35	-7	-2	1	7	14	-6	-1	-13	-14	MARGIN
	27	20	14	23	16	20	45	23	17	23	24	24	14	16	14	9	PTS
	24	19	27	27	34	23	10	30	19	22	17	10	20	17	27	23	OPP PTS

EDSR by Wk
W=Green
L=Red

OFF/DEF
EDSR
Blue=OFF
(high=good)
Red=DEF
(low=good)

2018 Close Game Records

All 2018 Wins: **6**

FG Games (<=3 pts) W-L: **3-3**
FG Games Win %: **50% (#13)**
FG Games Wins (% of Total Wins):
50% (#3)
1 Score Games (<=8 pts) W-L: **4-6**
1 Score Games Win %: **40% (#22)**
1 Score Games Wins (% of Total Wins): **67% (#8)**

2018 Critical & Game-Deciding Stats

TO Margin	+7
TO Given	21
INT Given	15
FUM Given	6
TO Taken	28
INT Taken	17
FUM Taken	11
Sack Margin	+10
Sacks	44
Sacks Allow	34
Return TD Margin	+0
Ret TDs	2
Ret TDs Allow	2
Penalty Margin	-2
Penalties	125
Opponent Penalties	123

Denver Broncos 2019 Strength of Schedule In Detail (compared to 2018)

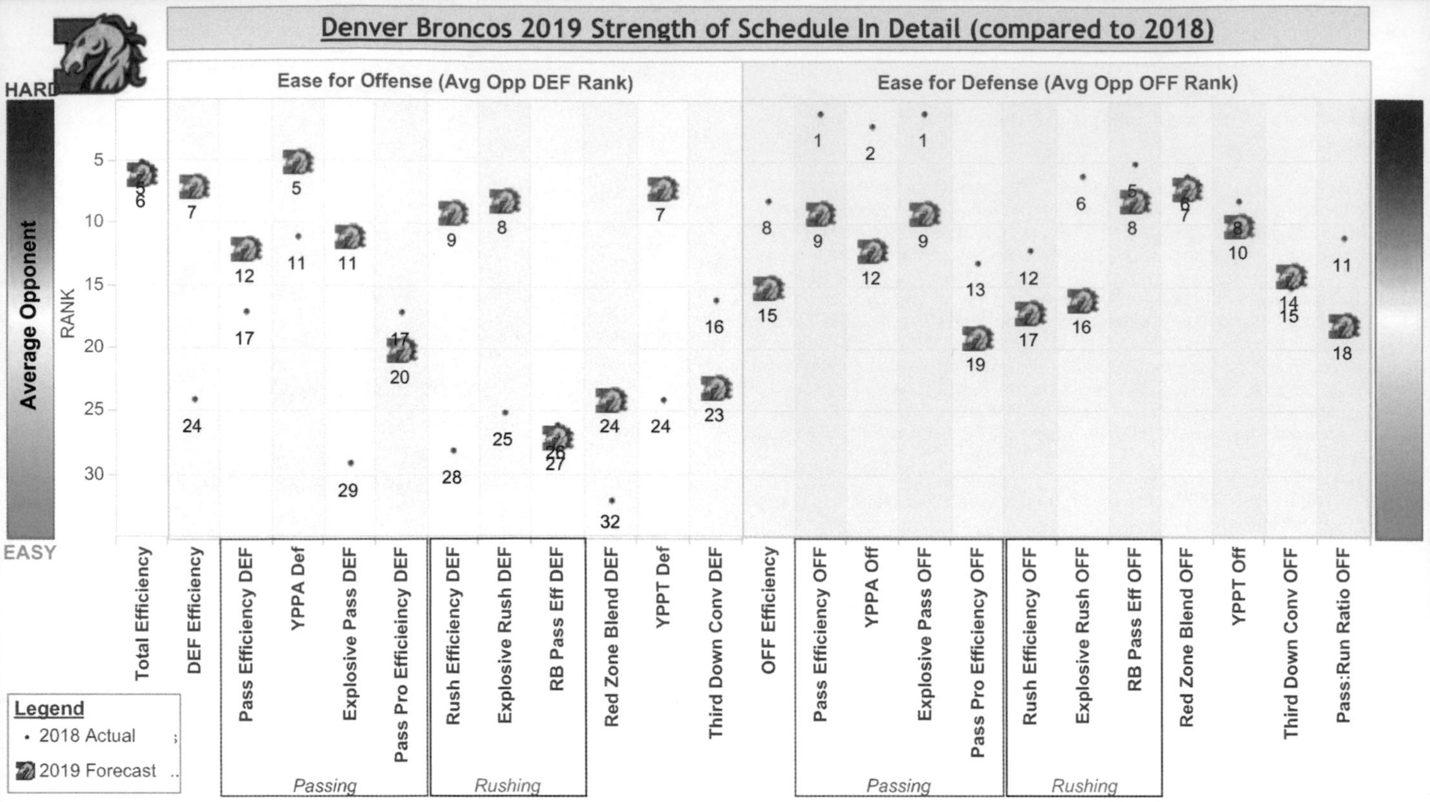

HARD

Ease for Offense (Avg Opp DEF Rank)

Average Opponent RANK

Metric	2019 Forecast	2018 Actual
Total Efficiency	6	—
DEF Efficiency	7	24
Pass Efficiency DEF	12	17
YPPA Def	5	11
Explosive Pass DEF	11	29
Pass Pro Efficiency DEF	20	17
Rush Efficiency DEF	9	28
Explosive Rush DEF	8	25
RB Pass Eff DEF	27	26
Red Zone Blend DEF	24	32
YPPT Def	7	24
Third Down Conv DEF	23	16

Passing / *Rushing*

Ease for Defense (Avg Opp OFF Rank)

Metric	2019 Forecast	2018 Actual
OFF Efficiency	15	8
Pass Efficiency OFF	9	1
YPPA Off	12	2
Explosive Pass OFF	9	1
Pass Pro Efficiency OFF	19	13
Rush Efficiency OFF	17	12
Explosive Rush OFF	16	6
RB Pass Eff OFF	8	5
Red Zone Blend OFF	7	—
YPPT Off	10	8
Third Down Conv OFF	15	14
Pass:Run Ratio OFF	18	11

Passing / *Rushing*

EASY

Legend
- 2018 Actual
- 2019 Forecast

2019 v 2018 Schedule Variances* (OFF=Rank of DEF faced, 2019 vs 2018)

Pass OFF Rank	Pass OFF Blend Rk	Rush OFF Rk	Rush OFF Blend Rk	Pass DEF Rk	Pass DEF Blend Rk	Rush DEF Rk	Rush DEF Blend Rk
9	5	1	4	25	27	21	26

*1=Hardest Jump in 2019 schedule from 2018 (aka a much harder schedule in 2019), 32=Easiest Jump in 2019 schedule from 2018 (aka a much easier schedule in 2019); **Pass Blend** metric blends 4 metrics: Pass Efficiency, YPPA, Explosive Pass & Pass Rush; **Rush Blend** metric blends 3 metrics: Rush Efficiency, Explosive Rush & RB Targets

---

Team Records & Trends

	2018	2017	2016
Average line	1.3	0.3	-1.2
Average O/U line	45.7	41.5	42.7
Straight Up Record	6-10	5-11	9-7
Against the Spread Record	6-8	4-11	9-7
Over/Under Record	3-13	8-8	6-9
ATS as Favorite	2-5	2-5	6-3
ATS as Underdog	4-3	2-5	3-4
Straight Up Home	3-5	4-4	5-3
ATS Home	2-4	3-4	5-3
Over/Under Home	1-7	4-4	3-4
ATS as Home Favorite	0-3	1-3	4-2
ATS as a Home Dog	2-1	2-1	1-1
Straight Up Away	3-5	1-7	4-4
ATS Away	4-4	1-7	4-4
Over/Under Away	2-6	4-4	3-5
ATS Away Favorite	2-2	1-2	2-1
ATS Away Dog	2-2	0-4	2-3
Six Point Teaser Record	11-5	8-7	10-6
Seven Point Teaser Record	11-3	9-7	11-5
Ten Point Teaser Record	14-2	9-7	12-3

DEN-3

Flacco may have a big arm, but it hasn't helped his ability to execute deep passes. And his raw arm strength hasn't translated to downfield passing production in a long time.

After trading for Flacco, Elway rattled off his top attributes. "He's played under the center, his arm strength is still great, he can still throw the ball downfield, and he's a guy who has won." We've already debunked the myth of Flacco's downfield-passing capability. Elway's reference to Flacco's ability to "play under the center" is merely a critique of college quarterbacks whom Elway has struggled to evaluate because they spend so much time in the shotgun.

Baker Mayfield played a ton of shotgun in **Lincoln Riley**'s Air Raid offense at Oklahoma. That a quarterback ran a shotgun-based offense in college should not be viewed as a negative NFL attribute.

(cont'd - see DEN-4)

2019 Rest Analysis

Team More Rest	2
Opp More Rest	3
Net Rest Edge	-1
Week 2 Edge	-4
Week 3 Edge	0
Week 4 Edge	-3
Week 5 Edge	0
Week 6 Edge	0
Week 7 Edge	0
Week 8 Edge	3
Week 9 Edge	0
Week 11 Edge	7
Week 12 Edge	0
Week 13 Edge	-6
Week 14 Edge	0
Week 15 Edge	0
Week 16 Edge	0
Week 17 Edge	0

Health by Unit*

2018 Rk	14
2017 Rk	15
2018 v 2017 Rk	16
Off Rk	23
Def Rk	11
QB Rk	15
RB Rk	15
WR Rk	12
TE Rk	
Oline Rk	22
Dline Rk	4
LB Rk	18
DB Rk	20

Based on the work of Football Outsiders

2018 Weekly Betting Lines (wks 1-16)

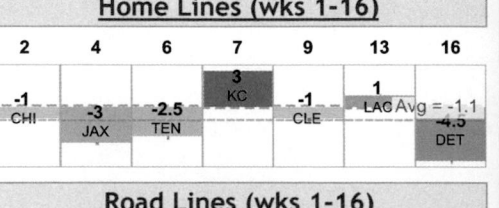

1	2	3	4	5	6	7	8	9	11	12	13	14	15	16
OAK	CHI	GB	JAX	LAC	TEN	KC	IND	CLE	MIN	BUF	LAC	HOU	KC	DET
2.5	-1	6.5	-3	7.5	-2.5	3	7	-1	6	3	1	5.5	9.5	-4.5

Avg = 2.6

Home Lines (wks 1-16)

2	4	6	7	9	13	16
-1	-3	-2.5	3	-1	1	-4.5
CHI	JAX	TEN	KC	CLE	LAC	DET

Avg = -1.1

Road Lines (wks 1-16)

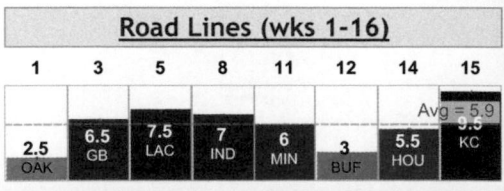

1	3	5	8	11	12	14	15
2.5	6.5	7.5	7	6	3	5.5	9.5
OAK	GB	LAC	IND	MIN	BUF	HOU	KC

Avg = 5.9

2018 Play Tendencies

All Pass %	61%
All Pass Rk	10
All Rush %	39%
All Rush Rk	23
1 Score Pass %	61%
1 Score Pass Rk	9
2017 1 Score Pass %	53%
2017 1 Score Pass Rk	26
2018 Pass Increase %	8%
Pass Increase Rk	4
1 Score Rush %	39%
1 Score Rush Rk	24
Up Pass %	42%
Up Pass Rk	29
Up Rush %	58%
Up Rush Rk	4
Down Pass %	68%
Down Pass Rk	12
Down Rush %	32%
Down Rush Rk	21

2018 Down & Distance Tendencies

Down	Distance	Total Plays	Pass Rate	Run Rate	Play Success %
1	Short (1-3)	4	0%	100%	75%
	Med (4-7)	11	64%	36%	64%
	Long (8-10)	296	54%	46%	52%
	XL (11+)	17	65%	35%	41%
2	Short (1-3)	47	34%	66%	68%
	Med (4-7)	61	62%	38%	43%
	Long (8-10)	90	59%	41%	30%
	XL (11+)	34	62%	38%	32%
3	Short (1-3)	35	57%	43%	54%
	Med (4-7)	50	86%	14%	26%
	Long (8-10)	38	92%	8%	32%
	XL (11+)	26	92%	8%	15%
4	Short (1-3)	6	50%	50%	50%
	Med (4-7)	1	100%	0%	100%

Shotgun %:

Under Center	Shotgun
46%	54%

37% *AVG* 63%

Run Rate:

Under Center	Shotgun
68%	15%

68% *AVG* 23%

Pass Rate:

Under Center	Shotgun
32%	85%

32% *AVG* 77%

Denver Broncos
2018 Play Analysis

Short Yardage Intelligence:

2nd and Short Run

Run Freq	Run Rk	NFL Run Freq Avg	Run 1D Rate	Run NFL 1D Avg
61%	23	65%	87%	68%

2nd and Short Pass

Pass Freq	Pass Rk	NFL Pass Freq Avg	Pass 1D Rate	Pass NFL 1D Avg
39%	10	35%	53%	56%

Most Frequent Play

Down	Distance	Play Type	Player	Total Plays	Play Success %
1	Short (1-3)	RUSH	Royce Freeman	3	67%
	Med (4-7)	RUSH	Phillip Lindsay	3	100%
	Long (8-10)	RUSH	Phillip Lindsay	65	51%
	XL (11+)	PASS	Emmanuel Sanders	4	50%
2	Short (1-3)	RUSH	Phillip Lindsay	14	71%
	Med (4-7)	RUSH	Phillip Lindsay	13	38%
	Long (8-10)	RUSH	Phillip Lindsay	22	27%
	XL (11+)	RUSH	Phillip Lindsay	9	44%
3	Short (1-3)	RUSH	Phillip Lindsay	6	83%
	Med (4-7)	PASS	Courtland Sutton	9	11%
	Long (8-10)	PASS	Courtland Sutton	9	44%
	XL (11+)	PASS	Devontae Booker	5	0%

Most Successful Play*

Down	Distance	Play Type	Player	Total Plays	Play Success %
1	Long (8-10)	PASS	Jeff Heuerman	5	80%
2	Short (1-3)	RUSH	Devontae Booker	5	80%
	Med (4-7)	PASS	Emmanuel Sanders	7	43%
	Long (8-10)	RUSH	Phillip Lindsay	22	27%
	XL (11+)	RUSH	Phillip Lindsay	9	44%
3	Short (1-3)	RUSH	Phillip Lindsay	6	83%
	Med (4-7)	PASS	Courtland Sutton	9	11%
	Long (8-10)	PASS	Courtland Sutton	9	44%
	XL (11+)	PASS	Devontae Booker	5	0%

*Minimum 5 plays to qualify

2018 Weekly Snap Rates

Wk	Opp	Score	Courtland Sutton	Emmanuel Sanders	Jeff Heuerman	DaeSean Hamilton	Phillip Lindsay	Matt LaCosse	Demaryius Thomas	Devontae Booker	Royce Freeman
1	SEA	W 27-24	44 (59%)	64 (86%)	60 (81%)	14 (19%)	26 (35%)	1 (1%)	53 (72%)	19 (26%)	29 (39%)
2	OAK	W 20-19	54 (82%)	54 (82%)	41 (62%)	12 (18%)	28 (42%)	2 (3%)	59 (89%)	22 (33%)	16 (24%)
3	BAL	L 27-14	53 (78%)	60 (88%)	41 (60%)	15 (22%)	11 (16%)	1 (1%)	54 (79%)	26 (38%)	29 (43%)
4	KC	L 27-23	42 (70%)	54 (90%)	53 (88%)	6 (10%)	24 (40%)	15 (25%)	51 (85%)	20 (33%)	16 (27%)
5	NYJ	L 34-16	59 (77%)	73 (95%)	53 (69%)	32 (42%)	29 (38%)	19 (25%)	47 (61%)	22 (29%)	30 (30%)
6	LA	L 23-20	35 (53%)	56 (85%)	58 (88%)	18 (27%)	20 (30%)	27 (41%)	48 (73%)	22 (33%)	25 (38%)
7	ARI	W 45-10	40 (68%)	43 (73%)	48 (81%)	4 (7%)	35 (59%)	18 (31%)	41 (69%)	6 (10%)	18 (31%)
8	KC	L 30-23	49 (67%)	59 (81%)	63 (86%)		41 (56%)	27 (37%)	52 (71%)	32 (44%)	
9	HOU	L 19-17	56 (85%)	61 (92%)	47 (71%)		38 (58%)	25 (38%)		26 (39%)	
11	LAC	W 23-22	50 (89%)	50 (89%)	48 (86%)	14 (25%)	32 (57%)	19 (34%)		11 (20%)	13 (23%)
12	PIT	W 24-17	42 (74%)	44 (77%)	43 (75%)	29 (51%)	36 (63%)	27 (47%)		6 (11%)	15 (26%)
13	CIN	W 24-10	41 (69%)	40 (68%)		47 (80%)	25 (42%)	47 (80%)		13 (22%)	21 (36%)
14	SF	L 20-14	51 (69%)			72 (97%)	48 (65%)	60 (81%)		17 (23%)	9 (12%)
15	CLE	L 17-16	63 (86%)			72 (99%)	39 (53%)	68 (93%)		15 (21%)	18 (25%)
16	OAK	L 27-14	66 (99%)		63 (94%)	21 (31%)				24 (36%)	25 (37%)
17	LAC	L 23-9	74 (94%)		73 (92%)		62 (78%)			35 (44%)	44 (56%)
	Grand Total		819 (76%)	658 (84%)	555 (77%)	471 (49%)	453 (46%)	418 (41%)	405 (75%)	316 (29%)	308 (33%)

Personnel Groupings

Personnel	Team %	NFL Avg	Succ. %
1-1 [3WR]	63%	65%	45%
2-1 [2WR]	12%	8%	47%
1-2 [2WR]	12%	17%	49%
2-2 [1WR]	5%	3%	50%
2-0 [3WR]	4%	1%	48%
1-0 [4WR]	2%	2%	59%

Grouping Tendencies

Personnel	Pass Rate	Pass Succ. %	Run Succ. %
1-1 [3WR]	72%	42%	54%
2-1 [2WR]	31%	56%	42%
1-2 [2WR]	52%	49%	48%
2-2 [1WR]	24%	67%	45%
2-0 [3WR]	57%	54%	39%
1-0 [4WR]	77%	59%	60%

Red Zone Targets (min 3)

Receiver	All	Inside 5	6-10	11-20
Jeff Heuerman	11	3	4	4
Demaryius Thomas	8	3		5
Devontae Booker	7	1	2	4
Emmanuel Sanders	7	3		4
Matt LaCosse	6		4	2
Phillip Lindsay	3		1	2

Red Zone Rushes (min 3)

Rusher	All	Inside 5	6-10	11-20
Phillip Lindsay	29	8	7	14
Royce Freeman	18	5	4	9
Devontae Booker	4		1	3
Case Keenum	2	2		

Early Down Target Rate

	RB	TE	WR
	24%	20%	56%
	23%	*21%*	*56%*
		NFL AVG	

Overall Target Success %

RB	TE	WR
50%	49%	50%
#8	#29	#22

Denver Broncos 2018 Passing Recap & 2019 Outlook

Amari Cooper's impact was evident in **Dak Prescott's** passing performance. Pre-Cooper, Dak managed a 22% Success Rate and 5.3 yards per attempt on third-down passes. With Amari, Prescott's third-down passing Success Rate nearly doubled to 40% with 7.7 YPA. Will rookie OC **Kellen Moore** encourage Prescott to stay aggressive with his first-down pass rate, and can the offensive line better protect him? Dak's upward-trending red-zone rushing enhances his fantasy outlook.

Case Keenum Rating All Downs

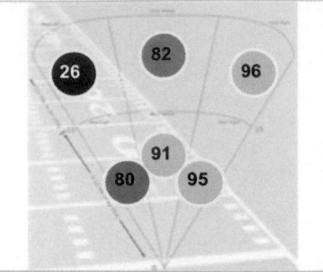

2018 Standard Passing Table

QB	Comp	Att	Comp %	Yds	YPA	TDs	INT	Sacks	Rating	Rk
Case Keenum	366	587	62%	3,916	6.7	19	15	34	82	38
NFL Avg			62%		7.0				87.5	

2018 Advanced Passing Table

QB	Success %	EDSR Passing Success %	20+ Yd Pass Gains	20+ Yd Pass %	30+ Yd Pass Gains	30+ Yd Pass %	Avg. Air Yds per Comp	Avg. YAC per Comp	20+ Air Yd Comp	20+ Air Yd %
Case Keenum	45%	51%	52	9.0%	21	4.0%	5.7	5.0	24	4%
NFL Avg	44%	48%	29.5	8.4%	12.5	3.7%	5.8	5.1	14.5	6%

Case Keenum Rating Early Downs

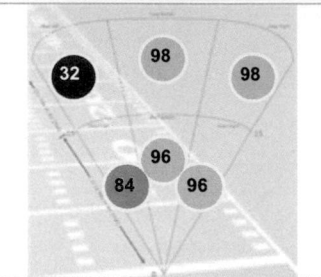

Interception Rates by Down

Yards to Go	1st Dwn	2nd Dwn	3rd Dwn	4th Dwn	Total
1 & 2	0.0%	0.0%	0.0%	0.0%	0.0%
3, 4, 5	0.0%	6.1%	0.0%	0.0%	2.4%
6 - 9	0.0%	1.7%	3.6%	0.0%	2.4%
10 - 14	2.7%	1.6%	2.5%	0.0%	2.4%
15+	0.0%	6.3%	0.0%	100.0%	4.3%
Total	2.3%	2.7%	1.9%	5.6%	2.4%

3rd Down Passing - Short of Sticks Analysis

QB	Avg. Yds to Go	Avg. YIA (of Comp)	Avg Yds Short	Short of Sticks Rate	Short Rk
Case Keenum	7.8	5.7	-2.0	69%	29
NFL Avg	7.8	6.4	-1.4	60%	

Air Yds vs YAC

Air Yds %	YAC %	Rk
53%	47%	25
53%	48%	

2018 Receiving Recap & 2019 Outlook

Amari Cooper is the prized jewel, especially with security-blanket slot WR **Cole Beasley** gone to Buffalo. I think the return of **Jason Witten** could be more beneficial than expected for Prescott, albeit not as his primary read. Witten has a solid on-field rapport with Dak and knows where to be as a chain mover in the middle of the field. I'm not as high on the addition of **Randall Cobb**, but the Cowboys needed slot help. I am higher on No. 2 WR **Michael Gallup**, who produced 15.2 yards per target and an 80% Success Rate in the slot after Cooper's arrival.

Player *Min 50 Targets	Targ	Comp %	YPA	Rating	Success %	Success Rk	Missed YPA Rk	YAS % Rk	YTS % Rk	TDs
Emmanuel Sanders	98	72%	8.8	104.4	56%	37	23	18	87	4
Courtland Sutton	84	50%	8.4	79.7	45%	102	151	11	97	3
Demaryius Thomas	56	64%	7.2	88.5	50%	78	30	106	2	4
Devontae Booker	51	75%	5.4	86.6	53%	52	168	128	1	0

Directional Passer Rating Delivered

Receiver	Short Left	Short Middle	Short Right	Deep Left	Deep Middle	Deep Right	Player Total
Emmanuel Sanders	89	124	99	56	158	93	104
Courtland Sutton	28	119	111	45	53	146	80
Demaryius Thomas	79	122	88	74	40	83	89
Devontae Booker	84	79	93				87
Jeff Heuerman	73	90	88		119	31	75
Phillip Lindsay	111	73	82				93
DaeSean Hamilton	107	107	102	0	119	40	86
Tim Patrick	108	56	81	40	0	158	79
Matt LaCosse	122	35	105	40		40	82
Andy Janovich	106	113	116			119	147
Team Total	83	94	96	26	85	106	89

2018 Rushing Recap & 2019 Outlook

Ezekiel Elliott should benefit from the return of C **Travis Frederick**. After ranking No. 2 in rushing efficiency in 2017, the 2018 Cowboys fell to 19th. Elliott's explosive-run rate grew, but his rushing Success Rate dipped from No. 2 among qualified backs (57%) in 2017 to 29th (49%) last year. Zeke was much more dominant in the receiving game, where he led the Cowboys in targets. I suspect Cooper claims that crown this year, but Elliott still projects as a dominant fantasy producer.

Player *Min 50 Rushes	Rushes	YPC	Success %	Success Rk	Missed YPA Rk	YTS % Rk	YAS % Rk	Early Down Success %	Early Down Success Rk	TDs
Phillip Lindsay	192	5.4	49%	30	32	59	15	49%	26	9
Royce Freeman	130	4.0	45%	46	39	55	45	46%	41	5

Yards per Carry by Direction

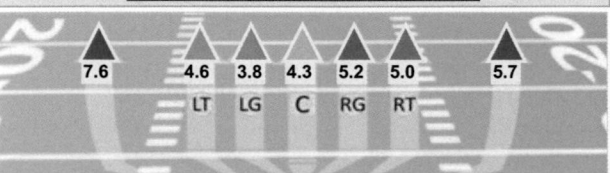

7.6   4.6   3.8   4.3   5.2   5.0   5.7

LT   LG   C   RG   RT

Directional Run Frequency

10%   6%   12%   42%   11%   13%   7%

LT   LG   C   RG   RT

Flacco played in the shotgun 73% of the time himself over the last three years, including 80% last season. Scangarello and **Kyle Shanahan**'s 49ers offense passed from shotgun on 82% of attempts, 11th most in the in the league. They passed from shotgun on 85% of attempts in 2017. Even when adjusting for one-score games only each of the last two years, the 49ers passed from shotgun on over 80% of attempts.

With all due respect, what the hell are these guys talking about? Thinking Flacco will be a great fit with Scangarello because his system calls for frequent under-center passes is mind boggling.

My concerns with Denver's passing game don't end at Flacco or his transitioning offensive line. The team's most-productive 2018 receiver by a long distance was **Emmanuel Sanders**, who averaged 8.8 yards per target with a 56% Success Rate and an explosiveness quotient that ranked 18th among 130 pass catchers. No other Bronco delivered a passer rating when targeted above league average, or a Success Rate north of 50%.

Sanders tore his Achilles' last December 5. Although reports have been positive on his rehab, Sanders is more likely to begin the season on the reserve/PUP list, which would cost him the first six games. He's a 32-year-old player coming off a career-threatening injury that occurred late in the season.

(cont'd - see DEN-5)

Denver Broncos Fantasy Corner

DaeSean Hamilton became **Case Keenum**'s go-to possession target down last year's stretch, parlaying **Demaryius Thomas**' trade to Houston and **Emmanuel Sanders**' Achilles' tear into 25 catches over Denver's final four games. Sanders appears unlikely to factor in before midseason, while Hamilton's skill set reminds of **Derrick Mason**, Flacco's first-ever No. 1 receiver when he broke into the league. Hamilton ran 63% of his routes in the slot last season and figures to stay there between Sutton and **Tim Patrick**, at least until Sanders' return. Hamilton is a route technician capable of becoming a PPR slot machine.

- Evan Silva

Division History: Season Wins & 2019 Projection

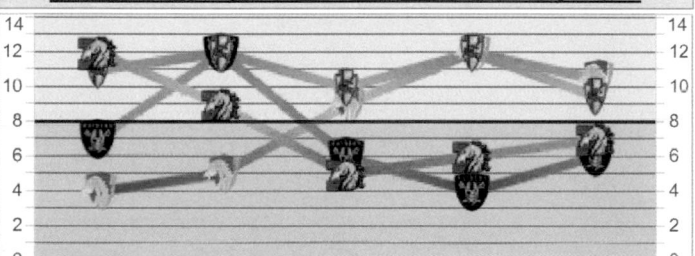

2015 Wins · 2016 Wins · 2017 Wins · 2018 Wins · Forecast 2019 Wins

Rank of 2019 Defensive Pass Efficiency Faced by Week

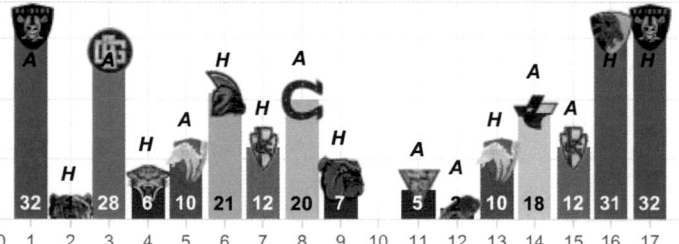

| 32 | | 28 | 6 | 10 | 21 | 12 | 20 | 7 | 5 | | 10 | 18 | 12 | 31 | 32 |

Rank of 2019 Defensive Rush Efficiency Faced by Week

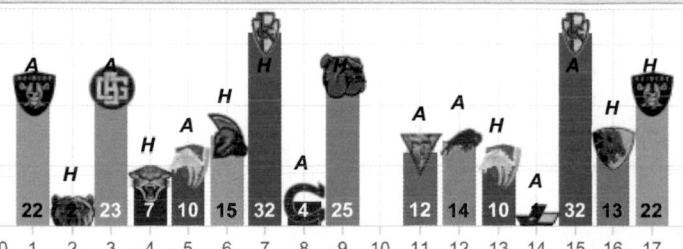

| 22 | | 23 | 7 | 10 | 15 | 32 | 4 | 25 | 12 | 14 | 10 | | 32 | 13 | 22 |

2018 Situational Usage by Player & Position

Usage Rate by Score

		Being Blown Out (14+)	Down Big (9-13)	One Score	Large Lead (9-13)	Blowout Lead (14+)
RUSH	Phillip Lindsay	7%	15%	67%	4%	7%
	Royce Freeman	5%	19%	59%	8%	8%
	Emmanuel Sanders			100%		
	Devontae Booker	15%	35%	50%		
	Courtland Sutton	100%				
	Tim Patrick			100%		
	Andy Janovich	50%	50%			
	Total	8%	18%	63%	5%	6%
PASS	Phillip Lindsay	6%	18%	74%		3%
	Royce Freeman		20%	80%		
	Emmanuel Sanders	4%	17%	69%	3%	8%
	Devontae Booker	7%	32%	59%		2%
	Courtland Sutton	11%	18%	65%	3%	3%
	Demaryius Thomas	2%	35%	53%	2%	7%
	Jeff Heuerman	5%	37%	58%		
	DaeSean Hamilton	18%	9%	73%		
	Matt LaCosse	6%	21%	70%		3%
	Tim Patrick	10%	13%	77%		
	Andy Janovich		22%	78%		
	Total	7%	22%	67%	1%	3%

Share of Offensive Plays by Type

	Phillip Lindsay	Royce Freeman	Emmanuel Sanders	Devontae Booker	Courtland Sutton	Demaryius Thomas	Jeff Heuerman	DaeSean Hamilton	Matt LaCosse	Tim Patrick	Andy Janovich	Andre Holmes
RUSH	52%	36%	1%	9%	0%					1%	1%	
PASS	8%	4%	18%	10%	16%	10%	9%	8%	8%	7%	2%	0%
ALL	29%	18%	10%	10%	9%	5%	5%	4%	4%	4%	1%	0%

Positional Target Distribution vs NFL Average

		NFL Wide				Team Only			
		Left	Middle	Right	Total	Left	Middle	Right	Total
Deep	WR	33%	17%	30%	**81%**	38%	14%	40%	**91%**
	TE	5%	4%	7%	**16%**	1%	1%	6%	**8%**
	RB	1%	0%	2%	**4%**			1%	**1%**
	All	39%	22%	39%	**100%**	39%	15%	47%	**100%**
Short	WR	20%	14%	21%	**55%**	23%	9%	25%	**57%**
	TE	6%	6%	8%	**20%**	6%	4%	9%	**18%**
	RB	10%	5%	10%	**25%**	9%	7%	9%	**25%**
	All	36%	25%	39%	**100%**	37%	20%	42%	**100%**
Total		37%	24%	39%	**100%**	37%	19%	43%	**100%**

Positional Success Rates vs NFL Average

		NFL Wide				Team Only			
		Left	Middle	Right	Total	Left	Middle	Right	Total
Deep	WR	40%	49%	39%	**42%**	27%	50%	54%	**43%**
	TE	44%	53%	42%	**46%**	0%	100%	20%	**29%**
	RB	38%	33%	42%	**40%**			100%	**100%**
	All	41%	50%	40%	**42%**	26%	54%	51%	**42%**
Short	WR	55%	61%	52%	**56%**	45%	65%	53%	**52%**
	TE	55%	62%	54%	**57%**	52%	53%	57%	**54%**
	RB	46%	54%	45%	**47%**	50%	45%	55%	**50%**
	All	53%	60%	51%	**54%**	48%	56%	54%	**52%**
Total		51%	58%	49%	**52%**	44%	55%	54%	**50%**

2018 Detailed Analytics Summary
Success by Play Type & Primary Personnel Groupings

Type	1-1 [3WR]	2-1 [2WR]	1-2 [2WR]	2-2 [1WR]	2-0 [3WR]	1-0 [4WR]	1-3 [1WR]	2-3 [0WR]	0-0 [5WR]	ALL
PASS	42% (459)	56% (39)	49% (61)	67% (12)	54% (24)	59% (17)	33% (3)		100% (1)	45% (616)
RUSH	54% (181)	42% (85)	48% (56)	45% (38)	39% (18)	60% (5)	50% (8)	50% (2)		49% (393)
All	45% (640)	47% (124)	49% (117)	50% (50)	48% (42)	59% (22)	45% (11)	50% (2)	100% (1)	46% (1,009)

Format   Success Rate (Total # of Plays)

Receiving Success by Top-4 Personnel Groupings
(Min 50 targets)

POS	Player	1-1 [3WR]	1-2 [2WR]	2-1 [2WR]	1-0 [4WR]	4 Grp Total
RB	Devontae Booker	52% (44) 5.3, 86.6	50% (2) 4.0, 60.4	100% (1) 2.0, 79.2	25% (4) 4.8, 84.4	51% (51) 5.1, 85.5
	Phillip Lindsay	44% (32) 5.4, 95.1	67% (6) 5.5, 89.6	25% (4) 2.5, 77.1	100% (1) 12.0, 116.7	47% (43) 5.3, 94.0
TE	Jeff Heuerman	46% (35) 5.2, 66.5	60% (5) 7.2, 136.3	100% (2) 13.0, 118.8	67% (3) 5.0, 78.5	51% (45) 5.7, 81.5
WR	Emmanuel Sanders	53% (68) 8.2, 92.6	54% (13) 10.5, 129.3	78% (9) 9.0, 141.2	67% (3) 4.3, 84.7	56% (93) 8.5, 102.8
	Courtland Sutton	46% (65) 8.2, 71.1	50% (4) 12.8, 95.8	40% (5) 6.6, 62.9	50% (2) 10.5, 87.5	46% (76) 8.4, 72.3
	Demaryius Thomas	46% (46) 6.3, 102.4	40% (5) 4.2, 13.3	100% (4) 20.5, 118.8		49% (55) 7.1, 87.8

Format   Line 1: Success Rate (Total # of Plays)   Line 2: YPA, Passer Rating

Rushing Success by Top-4 Personnel Groupings
(Min 25 carries)

Rusher (Last, First)	1-1 [3WR]	2-1 [2WR]	1-2 [2WR]	2-2 [1WR]	4 Grp Total
Lindsay Phillip	59% (99) 6.3	41% (39) 4.5	42% (24) 3.3	40% (10) 3.5	51% (172) 5.3
Freeman Royce	40% (42) 3.7	41% (39) 3.0	56% (27) 6.0	60% (15) 3.9	46% (123) 4.0
Booker Devontae	48% (25) 4.8	50% (2) 14.0	33% (3) 3.3	100% (2) 9.0	50% (32) 5.5
Keenum Case	69% (13) 6.1	50% (2) 4.5	100% (1) 8.0	0% (8) -0.9	46% (24) 3.7

Format   Line 1: Success Rate (Total # of Plays)   Line 2: YPC

Passing by Coverage Scheme

M2M	42% (241) 6.2, 70.0
Zone	57% (237) 7.9, 100.5
Screen	51% (45) 5.6, 90.0
Combo	43% (7) 6.3, 75.9

Passing by Route

Curl	61% (76) 6.8, 95.0
Out	50% (56) 6.1, 85.6
Flat	53% (51) 5.2, 101.5
Screen	45% (44) 5.0, 87.5
Slant	51% (35) 6.2, 66.0
Dig	54% (26) 7.5, 71.4

Throw Types

Level 1	51% (328) 6.1, 90.9
Level 2	51% (147) 7.4, 72.1
Level 3	40% (47) 13.7, 100.8
Sidearm	44% (18) 4.1, 97.7
Shovel	55% (11) 6.6, 94.3

QB Drop Types

3 Step	47% (207) 6.8, 79.9
0/1 Step	51% (185) 6.1, 87.7
5 Step	48% (83) 10.4, 103.7
Designed Rollout Right	68% (34) 6.9, 106.7
7 Step	33% (18) 4.8, 14.8
Basic Screen	29% (14) 3.4, 75.6

QB State at Pass

Planted	49% (371) 7.3, 85.8
Moving	58% (96) 6.6, 95.6
Shuffling	41% (56) 5.1, 78.3

Play Action

	Play Action	No P/A
Under Center	61% (83) 9.5, 110.1	57% (47) 7.7, 89.0
Shotgun	48% (46) 7.2, 97.4	46% (380) 6.3, 79.6
ALL	57% (129) 8.7, 105.5	48% (427) 6.4, 80.6

Run Types

Inside Zone	51% (112) 4.7
Outside Zone	47% (68) 5.4
Lead	35% (37) 2.7
Stretch	54% (28) 4.1
Power	52% (27) 4.3
Pitch	46% (24) 7.3

DEN-5

Opposite Sanders are second-year WRs **Courtland Sutton** and **DaeSean Hamilton**. Primarily an interior receiver, Hamilton struggled to 5.9 yards per target with a 48% Success Rate on 11-personnel targets in the slot. Hamilton could see generous volume, however; last year Flacco targeted slot receivers on 49% of his 11-personnel throws.

My other concern is this offense's 2019 schedule. In my 2018 Football Preview, I predicted the Broncos would face the league's eighth-softest slate of defenses. Their schedule indeed ranked eighth easiest.

This year, I project Denver to face the NFL's seventh-toughest slate of defenses with a particularly significant jump in schedule difficulty for the Broncos' running game. Last year, Denver's rushing attack was fifth-most efficient in the league, albeit against the fifth-easiest schedule. I have them facing the NFL's ninth-toughest run-defense schedule in 2019.

Another concerning scheduling quirk is that the Broncos' lone home game in the first three weeks comes in Week 2, and it's against the Bears. Historically, the Broncos have massively benefited from playing early-season games in Denver's thin air. And the Bears play on Thursday Night Football in Week 1, giving them extra time to prepare and rest before visiting Mile High.

Detroit Lions

Coaches (Prior Yrs)

Head Coach:
  Matt Patricia (1 yr)
Offensive Coordinator:
  Darrell Bevell (SEA OC 2017) (new)
Defensive Coordinator:
  Paul Pasqualoni (1 yr)

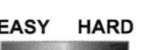

EASY   HARD

2019 Forecast

Wins	Div Rank
6.5	#4

Past Records
2018: 6-10
2017: 9-7
2016: 9-7

ARI	LAC	PHI	KC		GB	MIN	NYG	OAK	CHI	DAL	WAS	CHI	MIN	TB	DEN	GB
A	H	A	H		A	H	H	A	A	H	A	H	A	H	A	H
1	2	3	4	5	6	7	8	9	10	11	12	13	14	15	16	17

MNF   TNF

Key Players Lost

Player	New
Alex Barrett (DE)	OAK
Bruce Ellington (WR)	NE
Eli Harold (OLB)	BUF
Ezekiel Ansah (DE)	SEA
Kerry Hyder (DT)	DAL
Luke Willson (TE)	OAK
Nevin Lawson (CB)	OAK
Nick Bellore (FB)	SEA
T.J. Lang (G)	Retired

Average Line	# Games Favored	# Games Underdog
3.5	3	12

2019 Detroit Lions Overview

In my 2017 Football Preview, I suggested the Lions needed to throw more deep passes on first down. Following their Week 6 bye that year, Detroit began doing so.

Matthew Stafford attempted deep passes on 25% of his first-down throws in Weeks 7-12 that season and had tremendous success despite facing the NFL's sixth-toughest schedule of pass defenses.

While I absolutely recommend teams passing deep more on first down compared to league tendencies, doing so worked for the Lions because they had the requisite personnel for it. Stafford is a big-armed thrower, and **Marvin Jones** and **Kenny Golladay** could win outside. I was hopeful then-OC **Jim Bob Cooter** would expand on this strategy in 2018.

But even though Cooter remained on staff, new coach **Matt Patricia** wanted his imprint on the offense. Two-down power back **LeGarrette Blount** followed Patricia from New England. The Lions drafted OL **Frank Ragnow** in the first round and RB **Kerryon Johnson** in the second. The theory was that if the Lions could maintain passing-game success and manufacture a running game, the offense could make a big jump.

For years, the Lions produced big passing numbers but awful rushing results. The 2016 team ranked 13th in passing efficiency but 25th in rushing. The 2017 Lions ranked 11th in passing efficiency but 30th in rushing.

The 2016 and 2017 Lions both ranked top three in pass attempts and won nine games apiece. They were passing-based teams.

So, were the 2018 Lions aware that analytics show passing is significantly more

(cont'd - see DET2)

Key Free Agents/ Trades Added

Player	AAV (MM)
C.J. Anderson (RB)	$1.5
Danny Amendola (WR)	$4.5
Jermaine Kearse (WR)	$1.3
Jesse James (TE)	$5.7
Justin Coleman (CB)	$9
Tommylee Lewis (WR)	$0.9
Trey Flowers (DE)	$18

Drafted Players

Rd	Pk	Player (College)
1	8	TE - T. J. Hockenson (Iowa)
2	43	LB - Jahlani Tavai (Hawaii)
3	81	S - Will Harris (Boston College)
4	117	DE - Austin Bryant (Clemson)
5	146	CB - Amani Oruwariye (Penn State)
6	184	WR - Travis Fulgham (Old Dominion)
6	186	RB - Ty Johnson (Maryland)
7	224	TE - Isaac Nauta (Georgia)
7	229	DE - P. J. Johnson (Arizona)

Regular Season Wins: Past & Current Proj

Forecast 2019 Wins — 6.5
2018 Wins — 6
Forecast 2018 Wins — 8
2017 Wins — 9
2016 Wins — 9
2015 Wins — 7

1 3 5 7 9 11 13 15

Lineup & Cap Hits

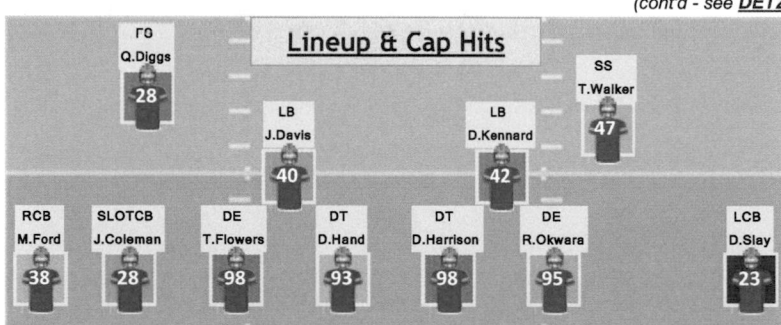

FS Q.Diggs 28
SS T.Walker 47
LB J.Davis 40
LB D.Kennard 42
RCB M.Ford 38
SLOTCB J.Coleman 28
DE T.Flowers 98
DT D.Hand 93
DT D.Harrison 98
DE R.Okwara 95
LCB D.Slay 23

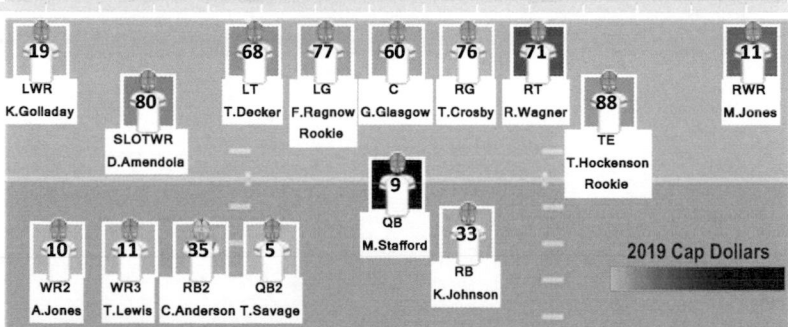

LWR K.Golladay 19
SLOTWR D.Amendola 80
LT T.Decker 68
LG F.Ragnow Rookie 77
C G.Glasgow 60
RG T.Crosby 76
RT R.Wagner 71
TE T.Hockenson Rookie 88
RWR M.Jones 11
QB M.Stafford 9
RB K.Johnson 33
WR2 A.Jones 10
WR3 T.Lewis 11
RB2 C.Anderson 35
QB2 T.Savage 5

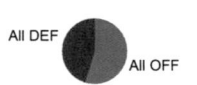
2019 Cap Dollars

2019 Unit Spending

All DEF / All OFF

Positional Spending

	Rank	Total	2017 Rk
All OFF	19	$96.01M	19
QB	2	$30.92M	3
OL	27	$29.29M	23
RB	14	$8.57M	10
WR	22	$18.65M	30
TE	14	$8.58M	22
All DEF	23	$78.98M	21
DL	24	$20.94M	15
LB	19	$19.51M	24
CB	8	$25.92M	21
S	12	$12.61M	7

correlated to winning games than running? Have the Lions chosen good-process ways to build an offense, or were they passing only because their running game was so inefficient?

Unfortunately, the answer was not the former.

While Cooter's prior offenses were high on passing volume, the 2018 Lions were no such thing. Likely from Patricia's influence, last year's Lions went far more run heavy.

When studying play-calling tendencies, it's best to look at early downs in first halves of games, when game script tends to be closer to neutral. The 2016 Lions were the NFL's third pass-heaviest team after this adjustment. The 2017 Lions were the league's No. 1 pass-dedicated club. Last year's Lions dropped all the way to 20th. The offense clearly changed its objectives.

Digging deeper, we can examine first-down play calling. The 2016 Lions passed on 53% of first downs in the first half – tenth highest in the league – and gained 7.0 yards per attempt with a 58% Success Rate. (Their first-down running game averaged a putrid 3.9 yards per carry with 42% success.) The 2017 Lions passed on first-half first downs at the NFL's ninth-highest rate and gained 7.1 YPA with a 51% Success Rate. In 2018, the Lions became the league's ninth run-heaviest team on first downs in first halves.

The 2018 Lions became a test-case team. What happens when a pass-oriented offense coming off consecutive nine-win years overhauls its philosophy to feature the run? Was the shift beneficial? Did better running backs and offensive linemen produce a more efficient overall offense? Did the passing game benefit? Did play action work better? Did opponents blitz less because the Lions were running more? Was it easier to pass on third down or in the red zone?

The answer to all of these questions was no.

The Lions' experiment backfired.

Patricia's team went 6-10, the organization's worst record since 2012. Self-proclaimed football guys say you are what your record says you are, so football guys can see that the shift to a run-first strategy was a failure. But football guys will ignore the poor record and blame execution. They'll blame injuries. And they'll give us coachspeak. "We can't turn the ball over." "We need to eliminate penalties." "We all have to improve." "It's hard to win games in the NFL." These were verbatim quotes from Patricia's post-season press conference.

We can't live in a world of coachspeak, where all that matters is what our record says we are. We're going to show why every single question above was answered in the negative and truly understand the causes behind Detroit's dismal 2018 season.

2018 Passing Performance

QB	1st Dwn	2nd Dwn	3rd Dwn	
Matthew Stafford	53%	46%	36%	Success Rate
	6.8	7.2	6.2	YPA
	95.7	95.8	76.8	Rating
Pass Rate	53%	66%	84%	
NFL AVG	53%	47%	36%	Success Rate
	7.7	7.3	6.9	YPA
	95.1	93.7	87.1	Rating
Pass Rate	53%	62%	80%	

2018 Rushing Performance

Offense	1st Dwn	2nd Dwn	3rd Dwn	
DET	45%	45%	41%	Success Rate
	4.0	4.1	4.1	YPC
Run Rate	47%	34%	16%	
NFL AVG	48%	46%	51%	Success Rate
	4.5	4.4	4.3	YPC
Run Rate	47%	38%	20%	

Did better running backs and offensive linemen produce a more efficient offense? Both the 2017 and 2018 Lions faced the NFL's fourth-toughest schedules of defenses. The 2017 Lions ranked 12th in total offensive efficiency. Last year, Detroit ranked 23rd. The 2017 Lions offense ranked fifth in yards per play. Last year's Lions ranked 20th. The 2017 Lions ranked 17th in third-down conversion rate. Last year's Lions were 25th. The Lions fell from No. 10 to No. 24 in red-zone efficiency.

The Lions' run-game improvement and shift to a run-centric team *made the offense worse*.

Did a run-heavier philosophy assist the passing game? Did it become easier to pass because defenses were playing the run? **Matthew Stafford** produced a substantially worse 2018 season than he did in 2017. Let's start with early downs in the first half. The Lions moved from the NFL's pass-heaviest team in such scenarios in 2017 to 20th most pass-heavy in 2018.

(cont'd - see DET-3)

2018 Offensive Advanced Metrics

Rank values by category: EDSR Off 17, 30 In Off 17, Red Zone Off 23, 3rd Down Off 25, YPPA Off 25, YPPT Off 20, Offensive Efficiency 23, Pass Efficiency Off 22, Pass Pro Efficiency Off 12, RB Pass Eff Off 21, Rush Efficiency Off 25, Explosive Pass Off 28, Explosive Run Off 22

2018 Defensive Advanced Metrics

Rank values by category: EDSR Def 26, 30 & In Def 29, Red Zone Def 11, 3rd Down Def 14, YPPA Def 6, YPPT Def 27, Defensive Efficiency 28, Pass Efficiency Def 31, Pass Pro Efficiency Def 5, RB Pass Eff Def 23, Rush Efficiency Def 13, Explosive Pass Def 30, Explosive Run Def 4

2018 Weekly EDSR & Season Trending Performance

	1	2	3	4	5	7	8	9	10	11	12	13	14	15	16	17	WEEK
	L	L	W	L	W	W	L	L	L	W	L	L	W	L	L	W	RESULT
	NYJ	SF	NE	DAL	GB	MIA	SEA	MIN	CHI	CAR	CHI	LA	ARI	BUF	MIN	GB	OPP
	H	A	H	A	H	A	H	A	H	H	A	H	A	A	H	A	SITE
	-31	-3	16	-2	8	11	-14	-15	-12	1	-7	-14	14	-14	-18	31	MARGIN
	17	27	26	24	31	32	14	9	22	20	16	16	17	13	9	31	PTS
	48	30	10	26	23	21	28	24	34	19	23	30	3	14	27	0	OPP PTS

EDSR by Wk
W=Green
L=Red

OFF/DEF
EDSR
Blue=OFF
(high=good)
Red=DEF
(low=good)

2018 Close Game Records

All 2018 Wins: **6**
FG Games (<=3 pts) W-L: **1-3**
FG Games Win %: **25% (#25)**
FG Games Wins (% of Total Wins): **17% (#25)**
1 Score Games (<=8 pts) W-L: **2-4**
1 Score Games Win %: **33% (#24)**
1 Score Games Wins (% of Total Wins): **33% (#29)**

2018 Critical & Game-Deciding Stats

TO Margin	-5
TO Given	19
INT Given	12
FUM Given	7
TO Taken	14
INT Taken	7
FUM Taken	7
Sack Margin	+2
Sacks	43
Sacks Allow	41
Return TD Margin	-2
Ret TDs	2
Ret TDs Allow	4
Penalty Margin	+0
Penalties	94
Opponent Penalties	94

Detroit Lions 2019 Strength of Schedule In Detail (compared to 2018)

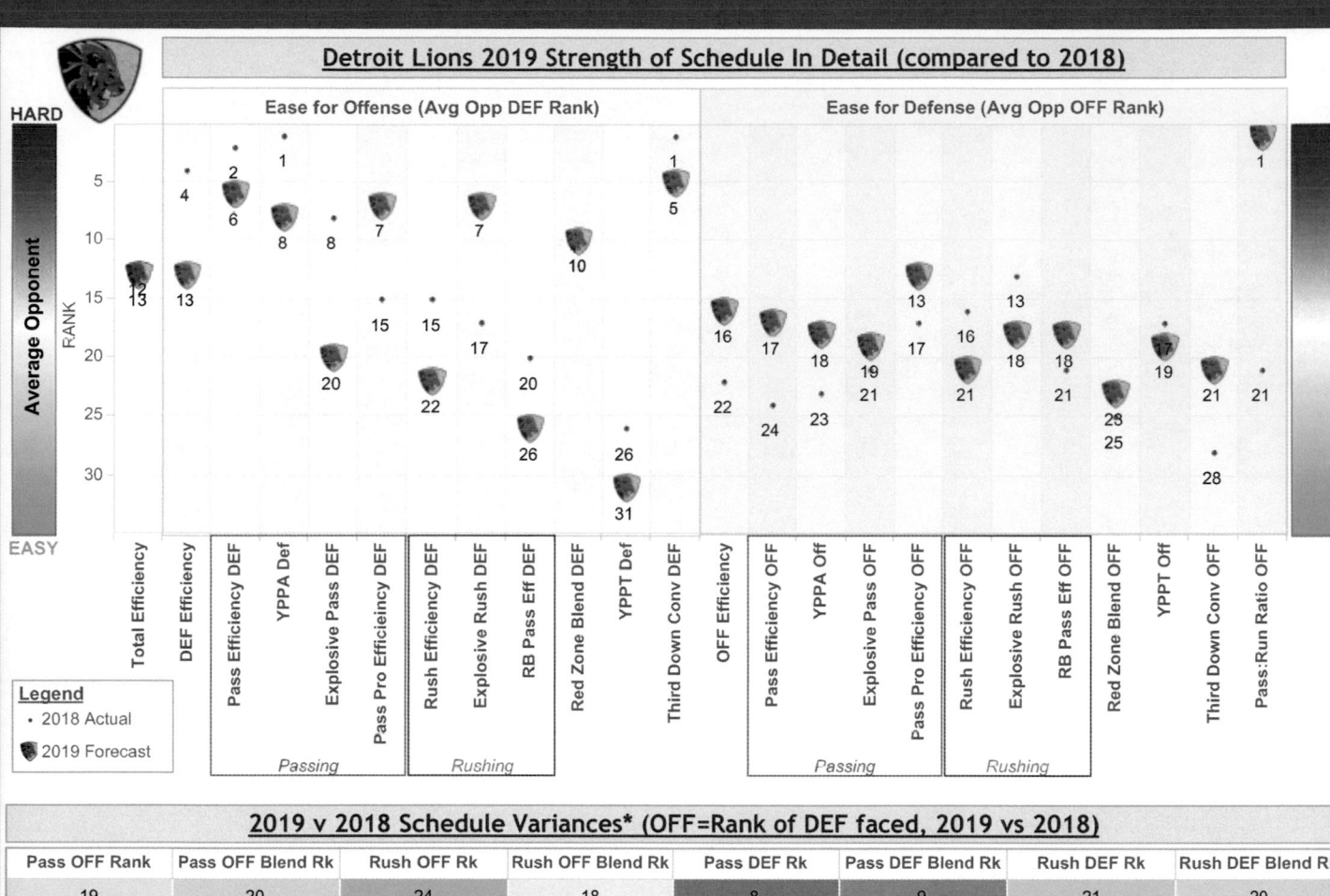

HARD / **EASY** — Average Opponent RANK

Ease for Offense (Avg Opp DEF Rank) | **Ease for Defense (Avg Opp OFF Rank)**

Legend
- 2018 Actual
- 2019 Forecast

2019 v 2018 Schedule Variances* (OFF=Rank of DEF faced, 2019 vs 2018)

Pass OFF Rank	Pass OFF Blend Rk	Rush OFF Rk	Rush OFF Blend Rk	Pass DEF Rk	Pass DEF Blend Rk	Rush DEF Rk	Rush DEF Blend Rk
19	20	24	18	8	9	21	20

* **1**=Hardest Jump in 2019 schedule from 2018 (aka a much harder schedule in 2019), **32**=Easiest Jump in 2019 schedule from 2018 (aka a much easier schedule in 2019);
Pass Blend metric blends 4 metrics: Pass Efficiency, YPPA, Explosive Pass & Pass Rush; **Rush Blend** metric blends 3 metrics: Rush Efficiency, Explosive Rush & RB Targets

---

Team Records & Trends

	2018	2017	2016
Average line	2.8	-0.9	0.8
Average O/U line	46.3	44.8	46.4
Straight Up Record	6-10	9-7	9-7
Against the Spread Record	9-7	8-7	7-8
Over/Under Record	6-10	10-6	6-10
ATS as Favorite	3-2	5-2	2-3
ATS as Underdog	6-5	3-5	4-5
Straight Up Home	3-5	4-4	6-2
ATS Home	3-5	4-4	4-3
Over/Under Home	2-6	6-2	3-5
ATS as Home Favorite	1-2	3-1	2-2
ATS as a Home Dog	2-3	1-3	1-1
Straight Up Away	3-5	5-3	3-5
ATS Away	6-2	4-3	3-5
Over/Under Away	4-4	4-4	3-5
ATS Away Favorite	2-0	2-1	0-1
ATS Away Dog	4-2	2-2	3-4
Six Point Teaser Record	12-4	13-3	12-3
Seven Point Teaser Record	12-4	13-3	15-1
Ten Point Teaser Record	13-3	14-2	15-1

DET-3

In 2017, Stafford averaged 7.3 yards per attempt with a 48% Success Rate and 94 passer rating on these downs. In 2018, he dropped to 6.7 YPA with a 91.3 rating. No, running more did not help Stafford.

Did play action work better? Defenses became programmed to sell out to stop the Lions' running game, opening up the play-action game. Right? Nope. Stafford averaged 10.2 yards per attempt with play action versus 7.3 without it in 2017. In 2018, Stafford averaged 8.1 YPA with play action and 6.5 YPA without it. For the Lions, play action has worked better *when they have rarely run the ball*.

Did teams blitz the Lions less? Not really. Stafford's overall blitz rate dropped mildly from 30% to 28%, but he was still blitzed at a rate above league average (27%). More remarkable was Stafford's production against the blitz; his passer rating when blitzed fell from 93.2 to 79.8 in 2018, and his yards per attempt against the blitz plummeted from 8.1 to 6.7.

(cont'd - see DET-4)

2019 Rest Analysis

Team More Rest	3
Opp More Rest	1
Net Rest Edge	2
Week 2 Edge	0
Week 3 Edge	0
Week 4 Edge	0
Week 6 Edge	7
Week 7 Edge	-1
Week 8 Edge	0
Week 9 Edge	0
Week 10 Edge	0
Week 11 Edge	0
Week 12 Edge	0
Week 13 Edge	0
Week 14 Edge	4
Week 15 Edge	0
Week 16 Edge	0
Week 17 Edge	1

Health by Unit*

2018 Rk	15
2017 Rk	17
2018 v 2017 Rk	13
Off Rk	17
Def Rk	17
QB Rk	20
RB Rk	25
WR Rk	21
TE Rk	22
Oline Rk	15
Dline Rk	22
LB Rk	11
DB Rk	17

*Based on the work of Football Outsiders

2018 Weekly Betting Lines (wks 1-16)

1	2	3	4	5	6	7	8	9	10	11	12	13	14	15	16
ARI	LAC	PHI	KC	GB	MIN	NYG	OAK	CHI	DAL	WAS	CHI	MIN	TB	DEN
-1	4	8	7	7.5	1.5	-3	3	8	2.5	2	3.5	8	-2.5	4.5

Avg = 3.5

Home Lines (wks 1-16)

2	4	7	8	11	13	15
4 LAC	7 KC	1.5 MIN	-3 NYG	2.5 DAL	3.5 CHI	-2.5 TB

Avg = 1.9

Road Lines (wks 1-16)

1	3	6	9	10	12	14	16
-1 ARI	8 PHI	7.5 GB	3 OAK	8 CHI	2 WAS	8 MIN	4.5 DEN

Avg = 5.0

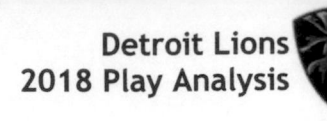

Detroit Lions 2018 Play Analysis

2018 Play Tendencies

All Pass %	60%
All Pass Rk	13
All Rush %	40%
All Rush Rk	20
1 Score Pass %	57%
1 Score Pass Rk	19
2017 1 Score Pass %	64%
2017 1 Score Pass Rk	1
2018 Pass Increase %	-6%
Pass Increase Rk	30
1 Score Rush %	43%
1 Score Rush Rk	14
Up Pass %	49%
Up Pass Rk	18
Up Rush %	51%
Up Rush Rk	15
Down Pass %	71%
Down Pass Rk	7
Down Rush %	29%
Down Rush Rk	26

2018 Down & Distance Tendencies

Down	Distance	Total Plays	Pass Rate	Run Rate	Play Success %
1	Short (1-3)	4	0%	100%	25%
	Med (4-7)	10	40%	60%	50%
	Long (8-10)	296	47%	53%	49%
	XL (11+)	12	58%	42%	33%
2	Short (1-3)	34	24%	76%	62%
	Med (4-7)	81	54%	46%	53%
	Long (8-10)	92	66%	34%	42%
	XL (11+)	41	95%	5%	37%
3	Short (1-3)	45	56%	44%	53%
	Med (4-7)	49	94%	6%	37%
	Long (8-10)	28	100%	0%	32%
	XL (11+)	27	74%	26%	7%
4	Short (1-3)	7	43%	57%	86%

Shotgun %:

Under Center	Shotgun
35%	65%

37% AVG 63%

Run Rate:

Under Center	Shotgun
76%	21%

68% AVG 23%

Pass Rate:

Under Center	Shotgun
24%	79%

32% AVG 77%

Short Yardage Intelligence:

2nd and Short Run

Run Freq	Run Rk	NFL Run Freq Avg	Run 1D Rate	Run NFL 1D Avg
73%	8	65%	68%	68%

2nd and Short Pass

Pass Freq	Pass Rk	NFL Pass Freq Avg	Pass 1D Rate	Pass NFL 1D Avg
27%	25	35%	38%	56%

Most Frequent Play

Down	Distance	Play Type	Player	Total Plays	Play Success %
1	Short (1-3)	RUSH	LeGarrette Blount	3	33%
	Med (4-7)	RUSH	LeGarrette Blount	3	67%
	Long (8-10)	RUSH	LeGarrette Blount	70	36%
	XL (11+)	PASS	Michael Roberts	2	0%
		RUSH	Kerryon Johnson	2	0%
			Zach Zenner	2	50%
2	Short (1-3)	RUSH	LeGarrette Blount	13	46%
	Med (4-7)	RUSH	Kerryon Johnson	15	67%
	Long (8-10)	PASS	Theo Riddick	13	46%
	XL (11+)	PASS	Theo Riddick	9	11%
3	Short (1-3)	PASS	Golden Tate	6	50%
		RUSH	Kerryon Johnson	6	50%
	Med (4-7)	PASS	Kenny Golladay	8	38%
	Long (8-10)	PASS	Kenny Golladay	4	75%
			Marvin Jones	4	75%
	XL (11+)	RUSH	Theo Riddick	4	0%

Most Successful Play*

Down	Distance	Play Type	Player	Total Plays	Play Success %
1	Long (8-10)	PASS	Levine Toilolo	7	100%
2	Short (1-3)	RUSH	Kerryon Johnson	7	100%
	Med (4-7)	RUSH	Kerryon Johnson	15	67%
	Long (8-10)	PASS	Kenny Golladay	6	67%
	XL (11+)	PASS	Kenny Golladay	5	40%
			Marvin Jones	5	40%
3	Short (1-3)	RUSH	LeGarrette Blount	5	60%
	Med (4-7)	PASS	Theo Riddick	5	40%

*Minimum 5 plays to qualify

2018 Weekly Snap Rates

Wk	Opp	Score	Kenny Golladay	Marvin Jones	Levine Toilolo	T.J. Jones	Luke Willson	Theo Riddick	Golden Tate	Kerryon Johnson	LeGarrette Blount
1	NYJ	L 48-17	65 (93%)	62 (89%)	20 (29%)	17 (24%)	14 (20%)	41 (59%)	57 (81%)	16 (23%)	13 (19%)
2	SF	L 30-27	71 (92%)	77 (100%)	22 (29%)	16 (21%)	40 (52%)	28 (36%)	65 (84%)	36 (47%)	17 (22%)
3	NE	W 26-10	64 (88%)	67 (92%)	37 (51%)	12 (16%)	39 (53%)	21 (29%)	54 (74%)	32 (44%)	26 (36%)
4	DAL	L 26-24	53 (98%)	50 (93%)	19 (35%)	11 (20%)	25 (46%)	25 (46%)	42 (78%)	20 (37%)	14 (26%)
5	GB	W 31-23	49 (79%)	58 (94%)	32 (52%)	9 (15%)	34 (55%)	19 (31%)	48 (77%)	29 (47%)	18 (29%)
7	MIA	W 32-21	49 (77%)	56 (88%)	21 (33%)	8 (13%)	41 (64%)		46 (72%)	38 (59%)	21 (33%)
8	SEA	L 28-14	54 (92%)	57 (97%)	14 (24%)		36 (61%)		54 (92%)	48 (81%)	7 (12%)
9	MIN	L 24-9	68 (97%)	63 (90%)	16 (23%)	36 (51%)	34 (49%)	39 (56%)		39 (56%)	11 (16%)
10	CHI	L 34-22	75 (96%)	48 (62%)	38 (49%)	50 (64%)		46 (59%)		55 (71%)	9 (12%)
11	CAR	W 20-19	61 (94%)		42 (65%)	45 (69%)	33 (51%)	27 (42%)		33 (51%)	12 (18%)
12	CHI	L 23-16	65 (98%)		28 (42%)	45 (68%)	20 (30%)	29 (44%)			33 (50%)
13	LA	L 30-16	70 (97%)		54 (75%)	50 (69%)	50 (69%)	38 (53%)			30 (42%)
14	ARI	W 17-3	50 (83%)		48 (80%)	32 (53%)	21 (35%)	25 (42%)			19 (32%)
15	BUF	L 14-13	52 (91%)		40 (70%)	36 (63%)	24 (42%)	25 (44%)			11 (19%)
16	MIN	L 27-9	58 (77%)		46 (61%)	52 (69%)	13 (17%)	33 (44%)			22 (29%)
17	GB	W 31-0			50 (68%)	42 (58%)		19 (26%)			18 (25%)
	Grand Total		904 (90%)	538 (89%)	527 (49%)	461 (45%)	424 (46%)	415 (44%)	366 (80%)	346 (51%)	281 (26%)

Personnel Groupings

Personnel	Team %	NFL Avg	Succ. %
1-1 [3WR]	61%	65%	47%
1-2 [2WR]	15%	17%	42%
2-1 [2WR]	9%	8%	47%
1-0 [4WR]	5%	2%	48%
2-0 [3WR]	5%	1%	36%
2-2 [1WR]	3%	3%	18%

Grouping Tendencies

Personnel	Pass Rate	Pass Succ. %	Run Succ. %
1-1 [3WR]	67%	46%	50%
1-2 [2WR]	38%	47%	39%
2-1 [2WR]	43%	49%	46%
2-0 [3WR]	83%	33%	50%
2-2 [1WR]	7%	50%	15%

Red Zone Targets (min 3)

Receiver	All	Inside 5	6-10	11-20
Kenny Golladay	13	2	2	9
Marvin Jones	10	1	4	5
Theo Riddick	10		1	9
Golden Tate	7	2	3	2
Michael Roberts	7	2	2	3
Kerryon Johnson	6		2	4
T.J. Jones	3	1		2

Red Zone Rushes (min 3)

Rusher	All	Inside 5	6-10	11-20
LeGarrette Blount	26	12	5	9
Kerryon Johnson	17	2	6	9
Zach Zenner	11	3	3	5
Theo Riddick	9		3	6
Matthew Stafford	3		1	2

Early Down Target Rate

	RB	TE	WR
	29%	12%	59%
NFL AVG	23%	21%	56%

Overall Target Success %

	RB	TE	WR
	45%	55%	51%
	#22	#17	#19

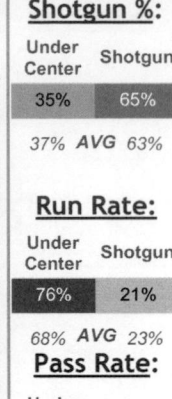

Detroit Lions 2018 Passing Recap & 2019 Outlook

So many areas of **Matthew Stafford**'s game fell off in 2018, but I can't fault him for a portion of those. **Jim Bob Cooter** was Stafford's play caller since 2015, and his quarterbacks coach before that. Cooter knew what Stafford liked and didn't like. I highly doubt Cooter was calling plays that hurt the offense without being forced to some extent by his boss.

Stafford began passing the ball significantly shorter in 2018. His third-down average depth of target was just 5.7 yards, such that his completions fell an average of 1.6 yards short of the sticks. His deep passing was also substantially worse despite the Lions' revamped offensive line. The run-heavy approach certainly didn't mesh with Stafford's style. As new OC **Darrell Bevell** also sports a run-first background, Stafford could be in for another long year.

Matthew Stafford Rating All Downs

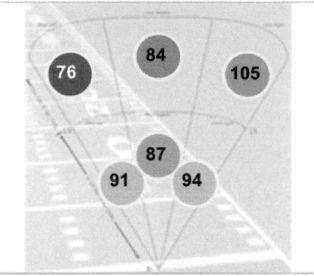

2018 Standard Passing Table

QB	Comp	Att	Comp %	Yds	YPA	TDs	INT	Sacks	Rating	Rk
Matthew Stafford	362	551	66%	3,751	6.8	20	11	39	89	32
NFL Avg			62%		7.0				87.5	

2018 Advanced Passing Table

QB	Success %	EDSR Passing Success %	20+ Yd Pass Gains	20+ Yd Pass %	30+ Yd Pass Gains	30+ Yd Pass %	Avg. Air Yds per Comp	Avg. YAC per Comp	20+ Air Yd Comp	20+ Air Yd %
Matthew Stafford	45%	49%	44	8.0%	17	3.0%	4.8	5.6	20	4%
NFL Avg	44%	48%	29.5	8.4%	12.5	3.7%	5.8	5.1	14.5	6%

Matthew Stafford Rating Early Downs

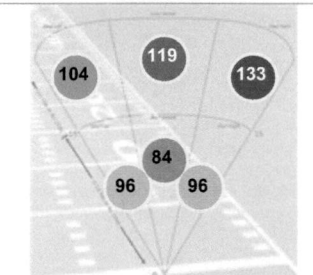

Interception Rates by Down

Yards to Go	1st Dwn	2nd Dwn	3rd Dwn	4th Dwn	Total
1 & 2		0.0%	4.8%	0.0%	3.2%
3, 4, 5	20.0%	0.0%	2.7%	0.0%	2.5%
6 - 9	0.0%	0.0%	3.4%	0.0%	1.4%
10 - 14	1.0%	1.4%	6.3%	0.0%	1.7%
15+	0.0%	0.0%	0.0%	100.0%	2.2%
Total	**1.4%**	**0.5%**	**3.7%**	**11.1%**	**1.8%**

3rd Down Passing - Short of Sticks Analysis

QB	Avg. Yds to Go	Avg. YIA (of Comp)	Avg Yds Short	Short of Sticks Rate	Short Rk
Matthew Stafford	7.4	5.7	-1.6	62%	23
NFL Avg	7.8	6.4	-1.4	60%	

Air Yds vs YAC

Air Yds %	YAC %	Rk
45%	55%	44
53%	48%	

2018 Receiving Recap & 2019 Outlook

Lions passing targets are focused on **Kenny Golladay** and **Marvin Jones**, who both posted 2018 Success Rates of 52% or better and over 8.0 yards per target with top-40 explosiveness quotients. Jones' injury-shortened 2018 season still disappointed after his 107-target breakout campaign in 2017, which featured nine touchdowns. Stafford has been mediocre passing short over the middle of the field over the last two years. If first-round pick **T.J. Hockenson** can fill that void, this passing game's efficiency should rebound somewhat. Hockenson will be joined by new slot receiver **Danny Amendola** inside.

Player *Min 50 Targets*	Targ	Comp %	YPA	Rating	Success %	Success Rk	Missed YPA Rk	YAS % Rk	YTS % Rk	TDs
Kenny Golladay	118	59%	9.0	96.1	54%	47	59	28	59	4
Theo Riddick	75	81%	5.1	82.4	39%	122	176	129	9	0
Golden Tate	69	64%	7.5	94.9	48%	93	51	43	77	5
Marvin Jones	62	56%	8.2	96.7	52%	59	145	36	59	4

Directional Passer Rating Delivered

Receiver	Short Left	Short Middle	Short Right	Deep Left	Deep Middle	Deep Right	Player Total
Kenny Golladay	110	100	89	88	104	79	96
Theo Riddick	70	97	82			40	82
Golden Tate	53	98	80	110	119	158	95
Marvin Jones	111	108	70	57	83	124	97
Kerryon Johnson	104	93	89				98
Bruce Ellington	88	62	87				84
T.J. Jones	90	131	45	62		110	87
Levine Toilolo	144	86	97		119		126
Luke Willson	98	28	80		0		39
LeGarrette Blount	65	80	85				76
Zach Zenner	68	113	83				84
Ameer Abdullah	92		117				104
Team Total	96	94	84	80	84	118	92

2018 Rushing Recap & 2019 Outlook

While rebuking the Lions for their run-first failures was entirely necessary, **Kerryon Johnson** was a fun player to watch with the ball. And it was obvious Detroit's run game regressed when Johnson was lost for the season in Week 11. But through Week 11, Detroit's rushing offense was only 22nd in efficiency. While **LeGarrette Blount**'s departure should prove addition by subtraction, Kerryon's fantasy owners must hope **C.J. Anderson** isn't used as a goal-line back.

Player *Min 50 Rushes*	Rushes	YPC	Success %	Success Rk	Missed YPA Rk	YTS % Rk	YAS % Rk	Early Down Success %	Early Down Success Rk	TDs
LeGarrette Blount	154	2.7	37%	69	57	6	54	36%	71	5
Kerryon Johnson	118	5.4	52%	18	43	64	10	54%	8	3
Zach Zenner	55	4.8	56%	5	12	51	32	54%	8	3

Yards per Carry by Direction

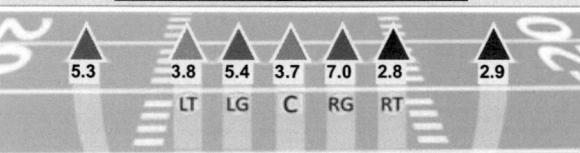

	LT	LG	C	RG	RT	
5.3	3.8	5.4	3.7	7.0	2.8	2.9

Directional Run Frequency

	LT	LG	C	RG	RT	
11%	18%	8%	35%	6%	15%	6%

Did running more make it easier to pass on third down? Nope. Stafford's yards per attempt on third-down passes fell from 8.0 to 6.2, and his third-down passer rating sank from 110.7 to 76.8.

Was Stafford more efficient with defenses loaded up to stop the run? Nope. In 2017 on early-down red-zone plays, Stafford produced a 97 passer rating, 50% completion rate, and 35% Success Rate. In 2018, Stafford's passer rating was 87 with a 49% completion rate on early-down red-zone throws.

The 2017 Lions – with a talent-poor rushing attack featuring **Ameer Abdullah** and **Theo Riddick** – were successful on 50% of their red-zone runs, five percent above league average. The 2018 Lions – with second-round pick **Kerryon Johnson** and free agent signee Blount – were successful on just 46% of run plays, 4% below average. I've said for years the red zone is the optimal area of the field to run the ball, and that is best accomplished from passing looks. And it doesn't take the NFL's highest-paid or highest-drafted running backs to succeed in the red zone when defenses are playing pass. Even passing-down backs have been highly successful on such run plays.

The answer to the question at the beginning of this chapter concerning whether Cooter would expand on his deep-pass intentions from 2017 was no. Under Patricia, the Lions became the NFL's *least likely* team to throw deep on first downs in 2018, shifting almost entirely to shorter passing on such plays. On first downs in the first half, the Lions passed short on *94 percent* of their throws.

In his year-ending press conference, Patricia was asked to address Stafford's regression. "One part of the offense I thought was really improved

(cont'd - see DET-5)

Detroit Lions Fantasy Corner

Kerryon Johnson looked headed for a second-half explosion before a knee sprain that did not require surgery cut his rookie season six games short. Johnson averaged 16.1 touches for 93.9 yards with four touchdowns over his final eight games, shining as a receiver and severely outplaying black-hole RBBC partner **LeGarrette Blount**. Well built (6'0/213) with adequate speed (4.52), Johnson resembles **DeMarco Murray** as a tall but crafty inside runner with plus versatility. His biggest 2019 concern is volume; the Lions have repeatedly gone out of their way to promise Johnson won't be overworked. Still, Johnson is capable of flirting with RB1 value if he stays healthy in an offense committed to the run. The Lions are missing 40% of their rushing attempts from last year's team, clearing a healthy dose of wide-open opportunity.

- Evan Silva

2018 Situational Usage by Player & Position

Usage Rate by Score

		Being Blown Out (14+)	Down Big (9-13)	One Score	Large Lead (9-13)	Blowout Lead (14+)
RUSH	LeGarrette Blount	7%	6%	69%	14%	4%
	Kerryon Johnson	10%	8%	61%	15%	5%
	Theo Riddick	5%	15%	68%	8%	5%
	Kenny Golladay			100%		
	Golden Tate			67%	33%	
	Zach Zenner	2%	2%	62%		35%
	Bruce Ellington			100%		
	Ameer Abdullah				100%	
	Total	7%	7%	65%	12%	9%
PASS	LeGarrette Blount	17%		83%		
	Kerryon Johnson	35%	19%	38%	8%	
	Theo Riddick	21%	13%	63%	3%	
	Kenny Golladay	23%	15%	57%	5%	
	Golden Tate	29%	10%	53%	8%	
	Zach Zenner	30%		50%		20%
	Marvin Jones	36%	9%	48%	7%	
	Bruce Ellington		19%	81%		
	T.J. Jones	32%		56%	8%	4%
	Levine Toilolo	14%	14%	62%		10%
	Luke Willson	42%		47%	11%	
	Ameer Abdullah	50%			50%	
	Total	26%	12%	56%	5%	1%

Share of Offensive Plays by Type

	LeGarrette Blount	Kerryon Johnson	Theo Riddick	Kenny Golladay	Golden Tate	Zach Zenner	Marvin Jones	Bruce Ellington	T.J. Jones	Levine Toilolo	Luke Willson	Ameer Abdullah
RUSH	41%	32%	11%	0%	1%	15%		0%				0%
PASS	3%	8%	15%	24%	14%	2%	13%	6%	6%	5%	4%	0%
ALL	20%	19%	13%	13%	8%	8%	7%	3%	3%	3%	2%	0%

Positional Target Distribution vs NFL Average

		NFL Wide				Team Only			
		Left	Middle	Right	Total	Left	Middle	Right	Total
Deep	WR	33%	17%	30%	81%	41%	11%	38%	90%
	TE	5%	4%	7%	16%		8%		8%
	RB	1%	0%	2%	4%			1%	1%
	All	39%	22%	39%	100%	41%	20%	39%	100%
Short	WR	20%	14%	21%	55%	18%	15%	24%	58%
	TE	6%	6%	8%	21%	3%	3%	3%	9%
	RB	10%	5%	10%	25%	14%	8%	12%	33%
	All	36%	25%	39%	100%	35%	26%	40%	100%
Total		37%	24%	39%	100%	36%	25%	40%	100%

Positional Success Rates vs NFL Average

		NFL Wide				Team Only			
		Left	Middle	Right	Total	Left	Middle	Right	Total
Deep	WR	40%	49%	40%	42%	38%	63%	48%	45%
	TE	44%	52%	41%	45%		83%		83%
	RB	38%	33%	43%	41%			0%	0%
	All	40%	49%	40%	42%	38%	71%	46%	48%
Short	WR	55%	61%	53%	56%	57%	61%	44%	53%
	TE	55%	62%	54%	57%	83%	64%	50%	65%
	RB	46%	53%	46%	48%	47%	56%	36%	45%
	All	53%	59%	51%	54%	55%	60%	42%	51%
Total		50%	58%	49%	52%	52%	61%	43%	51%

Division History: Season Wins & 2019 Projection

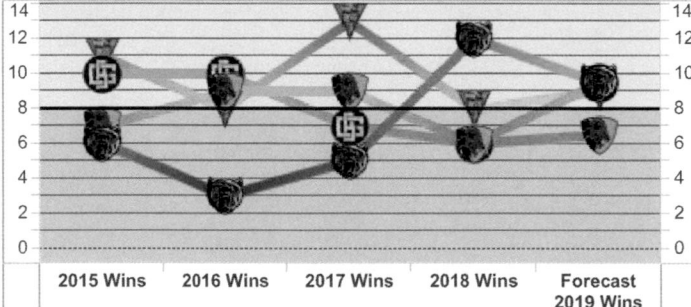

2015 Wins · 2016 Wins · 2017 Wins · 2018 Wins · Forecast 2019 Wins

Rank of 2019 Defensive Pass Efficiency Faced by Week

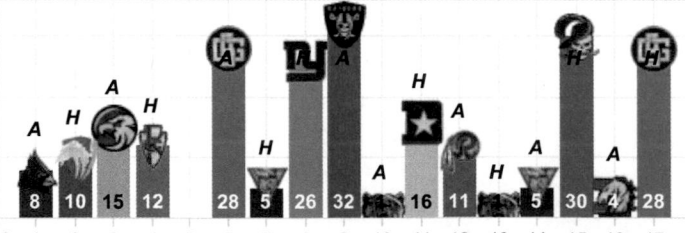

8 · 10 · 15 · 12 · 28 · 5 · 26 · 32 · 16 · 11 · 5 · 30 · 4 · 28

Rank of 2019 Defensive Rush Efficiency Faced by Week

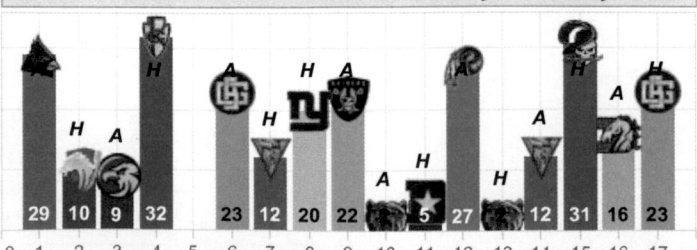

29 · 10 · 9 · 32 · 23 · 12 · 20 · 22 · 5 · 27 · 12 · 31 · 16 · 23

2018 Detailed Analytics Summary
Success by Play Type & Primary Personnel Groupings

Type	1-1 [3WR]	1-2 [2WR]	2-1 [2WR]	1-0 [4WR]	2-0 [3WR]	2-2 [1WR]	1-3 [1WR]	0-0 [5WR]	ALL
PASS	46% (416)	47% (57)	49% (41)	48% (52)	33% (39)	50% (2)	100% (1)	100% (1)	46% (609)
RUSH	50% (201)	39% (93)	46% (54)		50% (8)	15% (26)	56% (16)	100% (1)	45% (399)
All	47% (617)	42% (150)	47% (95)	48% (52)	36% (47)	18% (28)	59% (17)	100% (2)	46% (1,008)

Format   Success Rate (Total # of Plays)

Receiving Success by Top-4 Personnel Groupings
(Min 50 targets)

POS	Player	1-1 [3WR]	1-0 [4WR]	2-1 [2WR]	1-2 [2WR]	4 Grp Total
RB	Theo Riddick	41% (37) 4.9, 84.7	43% (7) 6.1, 87.2	50% (12) 5.0, 85.4	40% (5) 3.4, 66.3	43% (61) 4.9, 85.8
WR	Kenny Golladay	54% (78) 9.4, 98.0	58% (12) 9.3, 89.2	64% (11) 7.6, 117.2	60% (10) 10.6, 110.8	56% (111) 9.3, 100.3
	Golden Tate	50% (46) 6.5, 87.0	60% (15) 9.7, 125.7	0% (1) 0.0, 39.6	50% (2) 2.5, 79.2	52% (64) 7.0, 95.1
	Marvin Jones	51% (45) 8.1, 93.1	33% (3) 5.3, 52.1	50% (2) 6.5, 93.8	83% (6) 13.2, 158.3	54% (56) 8.4, 101.1

Format   Line 1: Success Rate (Total # of Plays)   Line 2: YPA, Passer Rating

Rushing Success by Top-4 Personnel Groupings
(Min 25 carries)

Rusher (Last, First)	1-1 [3WR]	1-2 [2WR]	2-1 [2WR]	2-2 [1WR]	4 Grp Total
Blount LeGarrette	42% (60) 3.2	31% (49) 2.9	43% (21) 2.5	14% (14) 0.9	35% (144) 2.8
Johnson Kerryon	55% (65) 5.9	47% (19) 4.8	52% (23) 5.4	0% (2) -0.5	52% (109) 5.5
Zenner Zach	50% (26) 5.1	56% (16) 5.8	50% (8) 3.1	50% (2) 3.5	52% (52) 5.0
Riddick Theo	44% (34) 4.4	50% (4) 4.3	0% (1) 3.0		44% (39) 4.3

Format   Line 1: Success Rate (Total # of Plays)   Line 2: YPC

Passing by Coverage Scheme

Zone	51% (258) 6.6, 80.3
M2M	51% (194) 7.8, 97.4
Screen	43% (68) 5.4, 93.9
Combo	54% (13) 11.4, 139.3

Passing by Route

Out	59% (64) 6.5, 76.2
Screen	44% (62) 5.7, 101.1
Curl	59% (58) 6.3, 92.7
Dig	60% (53) 5.9, 99.1
Flat	50% (46) 4.9, 92.5
Slant	43% (28) 4.3, 64.4

Throw Types

Level 1	56% (335) 6.5, 95.6
Level 2	48% (144) 7.9, 92.7
Level 3	29% (42) 9.5, 58.6
Sidearm	30% (23) 3.4, 77.4
Shovel	25% (4) 6.5, 93.8

QB Drop Types

3 Step	49% (306) 6.6, 87.4
5 Step	49% (95) 9.2, 89.6
0/1 Step	53% (73) 5.2, 96.5
Basic Screen	52% (29) 7.7, 110.2
Designed Rollout Right	58% (26) 6.9, 105.0
7 Step	57% (14) 8.9, 92.9

QB State at Pass

Planted	55% (380) 7.6, 95.7
Shuffling	35% (97) 5.1, 72.1
Moving	36% (42) 4.3, 71.6

Play Action

	Play Action	No P/A
Under Center	60% (58) 8.9, 116.9	46% (13) 5.5, 76.1
Shotgun	55% (44) 7.0, 99.3	49% (434) 6.7, 87.5
ALL	58% (102) 8.1, 109.3	49% (447) 6.7, 87.2

Run Types

Inside Zone	40% (108) 3.8
Outside Zone	48% (64) 4.1
Lead	50% (58) 4.0
Power	38% (45) 4.2
Stretch	35% (20) 2.9
Pitch	67% (12) 4.8

DET-5

was the run game, which was obviously a big part of the questioning that I got when I first got here," Patricia stated. "And that's half of the game, you know, so I'll take that as a positive and we'll build from there."

It was a perfect politician's answer: Ignore the negative, even if it is the entirety of the question, and speak only about topics that reflect positively on you. And Patricia's claim that running the ball is "half of the game" is a major red flag. Not only do teams pass far more than they run, but (depending on your metrics of choice) passing efficiency is roughly *four times more correlated* to win-loss outcomes. The run game is nowhere near equally important as the pass game.

Patricia was also asked about the NFL being a passing league and whether he thought the Lions were falling behind due to his run-first mentality. "You know what's interesting," Patricia replied. "Most of the teams that win in the playoffs are running the ball and winning the big games in the end. Teams that can run the ball, stop the run, and control the game towards the end of the season are really the teams that will have the most chance to win. There is a fundamental philosophy that I do believe with the run game and stopping the run and covering kicks, and that is true. And that's held true so far through the course of seasons."

I know what *I saw* on the field in 2018. Football guy knows the 6-10 Lions regressed from their back-to-back nine-win seasons. Analytics show they regressed substantially based on the design of the team.

Now, Patricia has a choice. And a new offensive coordinator in **Darrell Bevell**. Will Patricia allow the offense to pass more because it is more efficient after seeing how the run-centric shift sunk his 2018 Lions? Or will he stick to outdated football-guy clichés that were true decades ago but are plainly wrong in today's NFL?

If Patricia truly wants what's best for his team, we'll see the 2019 Lions revert to a passing-focused offense. If he sticks with a run-based mentality, he will be putting his dinosaur beliefs ahead of giving his team the best chance to win.

I can't wait to watch.

Coaches (Prior Yrs)

Head Coach:
Matt LaFleur (TEN OC, Calls Plays) (new)

Offensive Coordinator:
Nathaniel Hackett (JAC OC) (new)

Defensive Coordinator:
Mike Pettine (1 yr)

EASY HARD

2019 Forecast

Wins	Div Rank
9.5	#2

Past Records

2018: 6-10
2017: 7-9
2016: 10-6

	CHI	MIN	DEN	PHI	DAL	DET	OAK	KC	LAC	CAR		SF	NYG	WAS	CHI	MIN	DET
	A	H	H	H	A	H	H	A	H	H		A	A	H	H	A	A
	1	2	3	4	5	6	7	8	9	10	11	12	13	14	15	16	17
	TNF			TNF		MNF		SNF								MNF	

Key Players Lost

Player	New
Bashaud Breeland (CB)	KC
Clay Matthews (OLB)	LAR
Jake Ryan (ILB)	JAC
Kentrell Brice (S)	TB
Nico Siragusa (G)	IND
Quinton Dial (DT)	Retired
Randall Cobb (WR)	DAL

Average Line	# Games Favored	# Games Underdog
-1.8	9	5

2019 Green Bay Packers Overview

Aaron Rodgers played all 16 games last year with a tibial plateau fracture and MCL sprain. A quarterback playing hurt should get as much help as possible from his coaches to more easily work within offensive structure. Rodgers didn't get that from **Mike McCarthy**.

How much of Rodgers' downturn over the past few seasons can be blamed on McCarthy's archaic offensive design? It's a question we may never answer. But we do know last year's Packers offense was inefficient, and things need to change under rookie coach **Matt LaFleur**.

For years under McCarthy, the Packers threw to running backs on early downs at a below-average rate. They targeted backs on early downs 5% below league average in 2018, despite a better Success Rate (59%) when passing to running backs on early downs in the first half than wide receivers (57%) and tight ends (45%). Green Bay's running back passes averaged 7.3 yards per target, well above league average (6.2 YPT). They finished 25th in yards per target to wide receivers and 29th in yards per target to tight ends, but targeted running backs at an 18% rate, fourth lowest in the league.

Early-down running back passes make a quarterback's life easier because they are so efficient. And that's why teams with great quarterbacks like the Patriots and Saints throw so often to running backs on early downs. New England threw to backs on a whopping 35% of early-down passes in first halves last year, and 34% in 2017. The Saints did so at 30% in 2018 and 41% the year before. The Patriots and Saints are overseen by two of the NFL's most-creative minds, and both **Bill Belichick** and **Sean Payton** are keenly aware of the benefits of early-down running back targets.

Another play call that eases a quarterback's job is running on second and short.

(cont'd - see GB2)

Key Free Agents/ Trades Added

Player	AAV (MM)
Adrian Amos (FS)	$9
Billy Turner (G)	$7
Preston Smith (OLB)	$13
Za'Darius Smith (OLB)	$16.

Drafted Players

Rd	Pk	Player (College)
1	12	LB - Rashan Gary (Michigan)
	21	S - Darnell Savage Jr. (Maryland)
2	44	C - Elgton Jenkins (Mississippi State)
3	75	TE - Jace Sternberger (Texas A&M)
5	150	DT - Kingsley Keke (Texas A&M)
6	185	CB - Ka'dar Hollman (Toledo)
	194	RB - Dexter Williams (Notre Dame)
7	226	LB - Ty Summers (TCU)

Regular Season Wins: Past & Current Proj

	Wins
Forecast 2019 Wins	9.5
2018 Wins	6
Forecast 2018 Wins	10
2017 Wins	7
2016 Wins	10
2015 Wins	10

1 3 5 7 9 11 13 15

Lineup & Cap Hits

FS D.Savage Rookie -26-
SS A.Amos -38-
LB O.Burks -42-
LB B.Martinez -50-
OLB R.Gary Rookie -52-
RCB K.King -20-
SLOTCB J.Jackson -37-
DE M.Daniels -76-
DE K.Clark -97-
OLB D.Lowry -94-
LCB J.Alexander -23-

LWR D.Adams -17-
SLOTWR M.Valdes-Scantling -83-
LT D.Bakhtiari -69-
LG L.Taylor -65-
C C.Linsley -63-
RG B.Turner -77-
RT B.Bulaga -75-
TE J.Graham -80-
RWR G.Allison -81-

QB A.Rodgers -12-
RB A.Jones -33-

WR2 J.Moore -82-
WR3 E.St. Brown -19-
RB2 J.Williams -30-
QB2 D.Kizer -9-

2019 Cap Dollars

2019 Unit Spending

All DEF / All OFF

Positional Spending

	Rank	Total	2017 Rk
All OFF	5	$116.03M	4
QB	6	$28.48M	17
OL	3	$47.58M	13
RB	30	$3.39M	31
WR	21	$19.11M	2
TE	2	$17.47M	8
All DEF	28	$72.93M	27
DL	27	$20.11M	19
LB	8	$25.51M	7
CB	29	$9.33M	26
S	7	$17.99M	-

The NFL averages 66% run plays on second and short with a 68% Success Rate. Second-and-short passes average a far-worse 56% Success Rate. Studying the best offenses in the league can clue us into the best strategies. And there are reasons the Patriots and Saints are among the league leaders in run rate on second and short. Last year, New Orleans rushed on 87% of second-and-short plays with a 71% conversion rate. New England ran on 73% of second-and-short plays with 67% success. The Packers' second-and-short conversion rate was 76% on run plays, but Green Bay ran on second and short at the league's fourth-lowest frequency.

When your quarterback is injured, you have to take slam-dunk plays where you can.

So with Rodgers back at full health, how will LaFleur deal with making these simple but necessary adjustments?

LaFleur spent 2017 on the Rams' offensive staff and took over as the Titans' play caller last year. The 2017 Rams targeted running backs on 25% of early-down passes in the first half, 2% above league average. The 2018 Titans targeted backs on 24% of early-down first-half throws, also slightly above average. But both percentages were significantly higher than the Packers' early-down running back target rates in McCarthy's final two years.

The 2017 Rams ran the ball on 73% of second-and-short situations, the eighth-highest rate in the league. LaFleur's 2018 Titans ran on second and short at the exact same clip (73%).

While this seems to bode well for the 2019 Packers, the jury remains out on LaFleur. He learned under **Kyle Shanahan** in Atlanta and **Sean McVay** in Los Angeles, but what we saw from LaFleur's 2018 Titans play-calling debut was anything but encouraging.

Mike Mularkey coached the Titans' tight ends for two years before becoming their head coach in 2016. His "exotic smashmouth" offense was a disaster, and Mularkey was fired after two years. **Mike Vrabel** tabbed LaFleur to run the Titans' offense. LaFleur proceeded to call runs on early downs *even more* than Mularkey, specifically spiking the Titans' run rate on early downs from 54% and 51% under Mularkey to 56% last season. And that was despite less success; LaFleur's early-down run-play Success Rate was just 44% compared to 52% and 45% under Mularkey.

My hope was that LaFleur leaned so run heavy because he believed the Titans lacked passing-game weaponry, or because **Marcus Mariota** has limitations to his game. Or because defensive-minded Vrabel desired a run-oriented approach.

Then, I heard LaFleur speak at February's Scouting Combine, and my fears returned. LaFleur said he wants the Packers to be "as balanced as possible on first and second down because it makes the quarterback's job easier and extends a quarterback's career." LaFleur added that he "builds his offense through the run game."

2018 Passing Performance

QB	1st Dwn	2nd Dwn	3rd Dwn	
Aaron Rodgers	52%	47%	34%	Success Rate
	6.8	6.9	9.6	YPA
	94.6	98.9	101.5	Rating
Pass Rate	65%	69%	87%	
NFL AVG	53%	47%	36%	Success Rate
	7.7	7.3	6.9	YPA
	95.1	93.7	87.1	Rating
Pass Rate	53%	62%	80%	

2018 Rushing Performance

Offense	1st Dwn	2nd Dwn	3rd Dwn	
GB	56%	47%	53%	Success Rate
	5.1	4.6	4.9	YPC
Run Rate	35%	31%	14%	
NFL AVG	48%	46%	51%	Success Rate
	4.5	4.4	4.3	YPC
Run Rate	47%	38%	20%	

These are legitimate concerns. I'm wholly in favor of making the quarterback's job easier, but my suggestions never involve building the offense through the run or having run-pass balance on early downs. Because those methods are inherently inefficient, and inefficiency does not make a quarterback's job easier.

But evidence from LaFleur's lone play-calling season indicates he is telling the truth. On early downs in first halves of games – when teams are executing their original game plans – last year's Titans were the NFL's third run-heaviest team, running on 55% of all play calls.

LaFleur must have missed how his mentor McVay "protected" **Jared Goff** after taking over as the Rams' play caller in 2017. After **Jeff Fisher**'s 2016 Rams ran the ball on nearly 50% of early downs in first halves, McVay ratcheted up the 2017 Rams' early-down pass rate to fifth highest in the league.

(cont'd - see GB-3)

2018 Offensive Advanced Metrics

Rank (by category):
EDSR Off: 13; 30 & In Off: 10; Red Zone Off: 21; 3rd Down Off: 22; YPPA Off: 21; YPPT Off: 11; Offensive Efficiency: 7; Pass Efficiency Off: 12; Pass Pro Efficiency Off: 21; RB Pass Eff Off: 12; Rush Efficiency Off: 3; Explosive Pass Off: 17; Explosive Run Off: 24

2018 Defensive Advanced Metrics

Rank (by category):
EDSR Def: 17; 30 & In Def: 27; Red Zone Def: 24; 3rd Down Def: 8; YPPA Def: 25; YPPT Def: 31; Defensive Efficiency: 29; Pass Efficiency Def: 28; Pass Pro Efficiency Def: 10; RB Pass Eff Def: 27; Rush Efficiency Def: 23; Explosive Pass Def: 3; Explosive Run Def: 8

2018 Weekly EDSR & Season Trending Performance

	1	2	3	4	5	6	8	9	10	11	12	13	14	15	16	17	
	W	T	L	W	L	W	L	L	W	L	L	L	W	L	W	L	WEEK / RESULT
OPP	CHI	MIN	WAS	BUF	DET	SF	LA	NE	MIA	SEA	MIN	ARI	ATL	CHI	NYJ	DET	
SITE	H	A	H	A	H	A	A	A	H	A	A	H	A	H	A	A	
MARGIN	1	0	-14	22	-8	3	-2	-14	19	-3	-7	-3	14	-7	6	-31	
PTS	24	29	17	22	23	33	27	17	31	24	17	17	34	17	44	0	
OPP PTS	23	29	31	0	31	30	29	31	12	27	24	20	20	24	38	31	

EDSR by Wk
W=Green
L=Red

OFF / DEF
EDSR
Blue=OFF
(high=good)
Red=DEF
(low=good)

2018 Close Game Records

All 2018 Wins: **6**
FG Games (<=3 pts) W-L: **2-3**
FG Games Win %: **40% (#18)**
FG Games Wins (% of Total Wins): **33% (#11)**
1 Score Games (<=8 pts) W-L: **3-6**
1 Score Games Win %: **33% (#24)**
1 Score Games Wins (% of Total Wins): **50% (#15)**

2018 Critical & Game-Deciding Stats

TO Margin	+0
TO Given	15
INT Given	4
FUM Given	11
TO Taken	15
INT Taken	7
FUM Taken	8
Sack Margin	-9
Sacks	44
Sacks Allow	53
Return TD Margin	+0
Ret TDs	2
Ret TDs Allow	2
Penalty Margin	-11
Penalties	108
Opponent Penalties	97

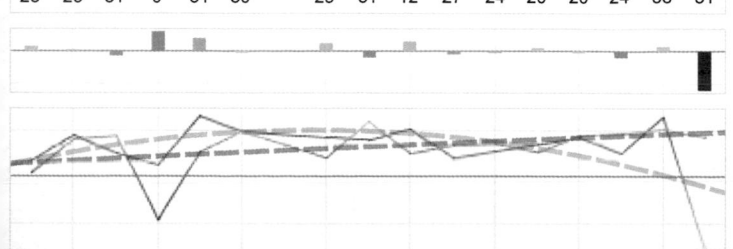

Green Bay Packers 2019 Strength of Schedule In Detail (compared to 2018)

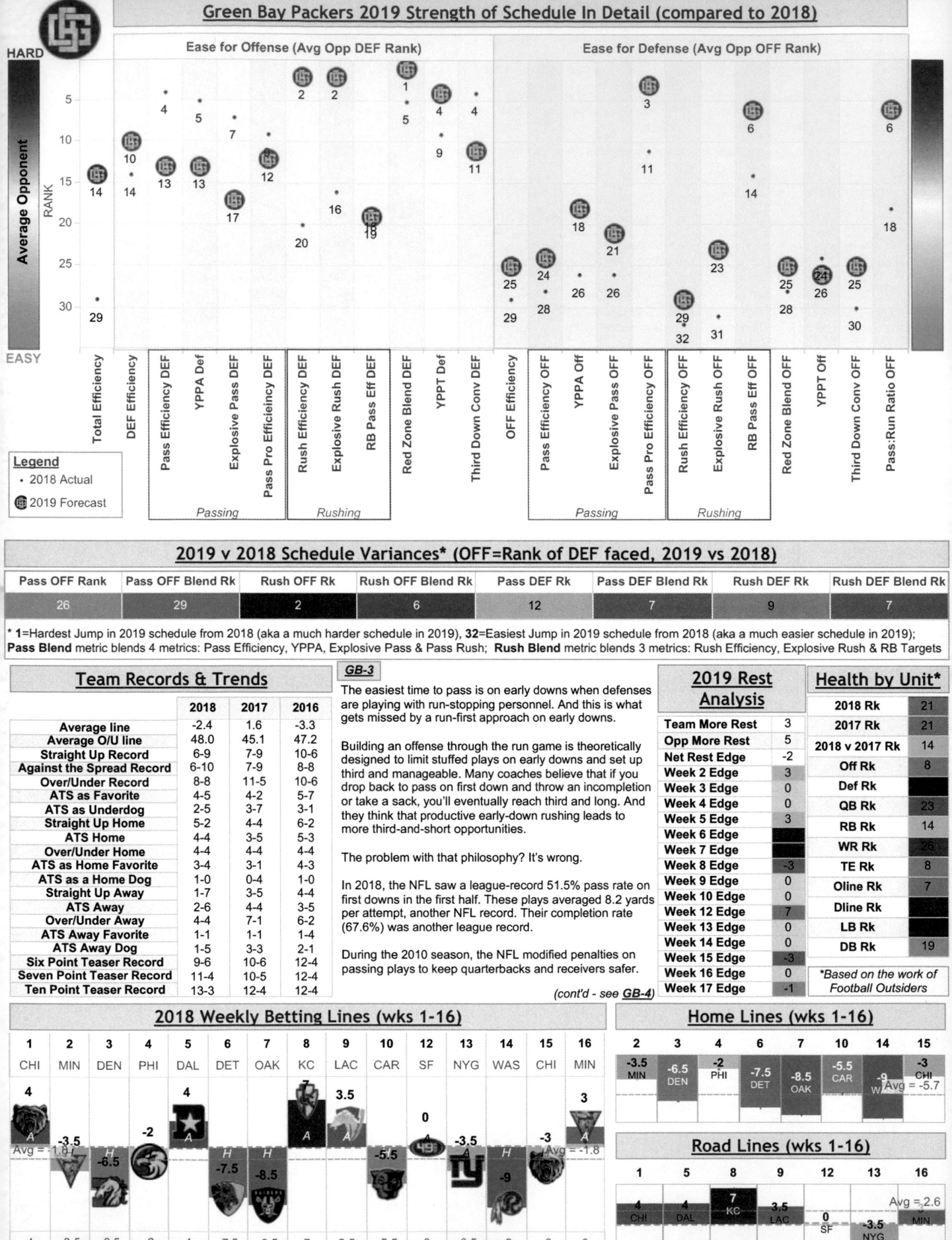

2019 v 2018 Schedule Variances* (OFF=Rank of DEF faced, 2019 vs 2018)

Pass OFF Rank	Pass OFF Blend Rk	Rush OFF Rk	Rush OFF Blend Rk	Pass DEF Rk	Pass DEF Blend Rk	Rush DEF Rk	Rush DEF Blend Rk
26	29	2	6	12	7	9	7

* **1**=Hardest Jump in 2019 schedule from 2018 (aka a much harder schedule in 2019), **32**=Easiest Jump in 2019 schedule from 2018 (aka a much easier schedule in 2019);
Pass Blend metric blends 4 metrics: Pass Efficiency, YPPA, Explosive Pass & Pass Rush; **Rush Blend** metric blends 3 metrics: Rush Efficiency, Explosive Rush & RB Targets

Team Records & Trends

	2018	2017	2016
Average line	-2.4	1.6	-3.3
Average O/U line	48.0	45.1	47.2
Straight Up Record	6-9	7-9	10-6
Against the Spread Record	6-10	7-9	8-8
Over/Under Record	8-8	11-5	10-6
ATS as Favorite	4-5	4-2	5-7
ATS as Underdog	2-5	3-7	3-1
Straight Up Home	5-2	4-4	6-2
ATS Home	4-4	3-5	5-3
Over/Under Home	4-4	4-4	4-4
ATS as Home Favorite	3-4	3-1	4-3
ATS as a Home Dog	1-0	0-4	1-0
Straight Up Away	1-7	3-5	4-4
ATS Away	2-6	4-4	3-5
Over/Under Away	4-4	7-1	6-2
ATS Away Favorite	1-1	1-1	1-4
ATS Away Dog	1-5	3-3	2-1
Six Point Teaser Record	9-6	10-6	12-4
Seven Point Teaser Record	11-4	10-5	12-4
Ten Point Teaser Record	13-3	12-4	12-4

GB-3

The easiest time to pass is on early downs when defenses are playing with run-stopping personnel. And this is what gets missed by a run-first approach on early downs.

Building an offense through the run game is theoretically designed to limit stuffed plays on early downs and set up third and manageable. Many coaches believe that if you drop back to pass on first down and throw an incompletion or take a sack, you'll eventually reach third and long. And they think that productive early-down rushing leads to more third-and-short opportunities.

The problem with that philosophy? It's wrong.

In 2018, the NFL saw a league-record 51.5% pass rate on first downs in the first half. These plays averaged 8.2 yards per attempt, another NFL record. Their completion rate (67.6%) was another league record.

During the 2010 season, the NFL modified penalties on passing plays to keep quarterbacks and receivers safer.

(cont'd - see **GB-4**)

2019 Rest Analysis

Team More Rest	3
Opp More Rest	5
Net Rest Edge	-2
Week 2 Edge	3
Week 3 Edge	0
Week 4 Edge	0
Week 5 Edge	3
Week 6 Edge	
Week 7 Edge	
Week 8 Edge	-3
Week 9 Edge	0
Week 10 Edge	0
Week 12 Edge	7
Week 13 Edge	0
Week 14 Edge	0
Week 15 Edge	-3
Week 16 Edge	0
Week 17 Edge	-1

Health by Unit*

2018 Rk	21
2017 Rk	21
2018 v 2017 Rk	14
Off Rk	8
Def Rk	
QB Rk	23
RB Rk	14
WR Rk	26
TE Rk	8
Oline Rk	7
Dline Rk	
LB Rk	
DB Rk	19

*Based on the work of Football Outsiders

2018 Weekly Betting Lines (wks 1-16)

1	2	3	4	5	6	7	8	9	10	12	13	14	15	16
CHI	MIN	DEN	PHI	DAL	DET	OAK	KC	LAC	CAR	SF	NYG	WAS	CHI	MIN
4	-3.5	-6.5	-2	4	-7.5	-8.5	7	3.5	-5.5	0	-3.5	-9	-3	3

Avg = -1.8

Home Lines (wks 1-16)

2	3	4	6	7	10	14	15
-3.5 MIN	-6.5 DEN	-2 PHI	-7.5 DET	-8.5 OAK	-5.5 CAR	-9 WAS	-3 CHI

Avg = -5.7

Road Lines (wks 1-16)

1	5	8	9	12	13	16
4 CHI	4 DAL	7 KC	3.5 LAC	0 SF	-3.5 NYG	3 MIN

Avg = 2.6

2018 Play Tendencies

All Pass %	67%
All Pass Rk	1
All Rush %	33%
All Rush Rk	32
1 Score Pass %	65%
1 Score Pass Rk	3
2017 1 Score Pass %	55%
2017 1 Score Pass Rk	22
2018 Pass Increase %	9%
Pass Increase Rk	2
1 Score Rush %	35%
1 Score Rush Rk	30
Up Pass %	61%
Up Pass Rk	1
Up Rush %	39%
Up Rush Rk	32
Down Pass %	74%
Down Pass Rk	4
Down Rush %	26%
Down Rush Rk	29

2018 Down & Distance Tendencies

Down	Distance	Total Plays	Pass Rate	Run Rate	Play Success %
1	Short (1-3)	6	67%	33%	50%
	Med (4-7)	7	29%	71%	86%
	Long (8-10)	320	58%	42%	54%
	XL (11+)	9	78%	22%	33%
2	Short (1-3)	53	53%	47%	68%
	Med (4-7)	70	60%	40%	43%
	Long (8-10)	95	72%	28%	41%
	XL (11+)	31	87%	13%	39%
3	Short (1-3)	43	63%	37%	60%
	Med (4-7)	43	91%	9%	44%
	Long (8-10)	34	91%	9%	32%
	XL (11+)	30	93%	7%	10%
4	Short (1-3)	4	75%	25%	0%
	Med (4-7)	4	50%	50%	75%
	XL (11+)	1	100%	0%	100%

Shotgun %:

	Under Center	Shotgun
	29%	71%

37% *AVG* 63%

Run Rate:

	Under Center	Shotgun
	56%	21%

68% *AVG* 23%

Pass Rate:

	Under Center	Shotgun
	44%	79%

32% *AVG* 77%

Short Yardage Intelligence:

2nd and Short Run

Run Freq	Run Rk	NFL Run Freq Avg	Run 1D Rate	Run NFL 1D Avg
54%	26	65%	76%	68%

2nd and Short Pass

Pass Freq	Pass Rk	NFL Pass Freq Avg	Pass 1D Rate	Pass NFL 1D Avg
46%	7	35%	57%	56%

Most Frequent Play

Down	Distance	Play Type	Player	Total Plays	Play Success %
1	Short (1-3)	PASS	Jimmy Graham	2	0%
		RUSH	Aaron Jones	2	50%
	Med (4-7)	RUSH	Jamaal Williams	2	50%
	Long (8-10)	RUSH	Aaron Jones	62	56%
	XL (11+)	PASS	Aaron Jones	3	33%
2	Short (1-3)	RUSH	Aaron Jones	10	80%
			Jamaal Williams	10	80%
	Med (4-7)	RUSH	Aaron Jones	14	50%
	Long (8-10)	RUSH	Jamaal Williams	13	31%
	XL (11+)	PASS	Davante Adams	7	43%
3	Short (1-3)	RUSH	Aaron Jones	6	83%
			Aaron Rodgers	6	83%
	Med (4-7)	PASS	Davante Adams	7	57%
			Randall Cobb	7	43%
	Long (8-10)	PASS	Davante Adams	8	50%
	XL (11+)	PASS	Jamaal Williams	2	0%
			Geronimo Allison	2	50%

Most Successful Play*

Down	Distance	Play Type	Player	Total Plays	Play Success %
1	Long (8-10)	RUSH	Aaron Rodgers	10	80%
2	Short (1-3)	RUSH	Aaron Jones	10	80%
			Jamaal Williams	10	80%
	Med (4-7)	RUSH	Aaron Jones	14	50%
	Long (8-10)	PASS	Jamaal Williams	6	83%
	XL (11+)	PASS	Davante Adams	7	43%
3	Short (1-3)	RUSH	Aaron Jones	6	83%
			Aaron Rodgers	6	83%
	Med (4-7)	PASS	Davante Adams	7	57%
	Long (8-10)	PASS	Davante Adams	8	50%
	XL (11+)	PASS	Davante Adams	8	13%

Minimum 5 plays to qualify

2018 Weekly Snap Rates

Wk	Opp	Score	Davante Adams	Jimmy Graham	Marquez Valdes-Scan..	Jamaal Williams	Randall Cobb	Aaron Jones	Equanimeous St. Brown
1	CHI	W 24-23	59 (98%)	59 (98%)	2 (3%)	37 (62%)	52 (87%)		
2	MIN	T 29-29	75 (97%)	58 (75%)	6 (8%)	47 (61%)	71 (92%)		
3	WAS	L 31-17	68 (99%)	64 (93%)	12 (17%)	30 (43%)	65 (94%)	17 (25%)	
4	BUF	W 22-0	76 (100%)	54 (71%)	54 (71%)	28 (37%)		29 (38%)	
5	DET	L 31-23	71 (88%)	66 (81%)	77 (95%)	33 (41%)		22 (27%)	60 (74%)
6	SF	W 33-30	63 (89%)	56 (79%)	66 (93%)	27 (38%)		19 (27%)	35 (49%)
8	LA	L 29-27	40 (77%)	46 (88%)	31 (60%)	13 (25%)	24 (46%)	32 (62%)	6 (12%)
9	NE	L 31-17	71 (96%)	59 (80%)	60 (81%)	31 (42%)	56 (76%)	43 (58%)	15 (20%)
10	MIA	W 31-12	53 (93%)	39 (68%)	54 (95%)	14 (25%)		42 (74%)	33 (58%)
11	SEA	L 27-24	46 (94%)	21 (43%)	48 (98%)	4 (8%)		44 (90%)	43 (88%)
12	MIN	L 24-17	53 (100%)	22 (42%)	44 (83%)	13 (25%)		40 (75%)	36 (68%)
13	ARI	L 20-17	72 (95%)	54 (71%)	64 (84%)	38 (50%)	61 (80%)	39 (51%)	15 (20%)
14	ATL	W 34-20	56 (86%)	47 (72%)	30 (46%)	24 (37%)	44 (68%)	42 (65%)	34 (52%)
15	CHI	L 24-17	64 (94%)	47 (69%)	21 (31%)	59 (87%)	47 (69%)	7 (10%)	42 (62%)
16	NYJ	W 44-38	87 (96%)	64 (70%)	72 (79%)	86 (95%)			39 (43%)
17	DET	L 31-0		39 (70%)	51 (91%)	39 (70%)	46 (82%)		
	Grand Total		954 (93%)	795 (73%)	692 (65%)	523 (46%)	466 (77%)	376 (50%)	358 (50%)

Personnel Groupings

Personnel	Team %	NFL Avg	Succ. %
1-1 [3WR]	77%	65%	48%
1-2 [2WR]	16%	17%	49%
1-3 [1WR]	4%	3%	44%

Grouping Tendencies

Personnel	Pass Rate	Pass Succ. %	Run Succ. %
1-1 [3WR]	72%	44%	59%
1-2 [2WR]	58%	52%	45%
1-3 [1WR]	25%	44%	44%

Red Zone Targets (min 3)

Receiver	All	Inside 5	6-10	11-20
Davante Adams	28	2	5	21
Jimmy Graham	9	3	2	4
Marquez Valdes-Scan..	6	2		4
Randall Cobb	4			4
Aaron Jones	3			3
Geronimo Allison	3		1	2
Jamaal Williams	2			2

Red Zone Rushes (min 3)

Rusher	All	Inside 5	6-10	11-20
Aaron Jones	18	4	4	10
Jamaal Williams	14	2	4	8
Aaron Rodgers	8	2		6
Ty Montgomery	3	1	1	1

Early Down Target Rate

RB	TE	WR
19%	21%	60%
23%	21%	56%
	NFL AVG	

Overall Target Success %

RB	TE	WR
49%	50%	51%
#12	#24	#18

Green Bay Packers 2018 Passing Recap & 2019 Outlook

After **Mike McCarthy** was fired midseason, reports emerged about his behind-the-scenes conflict with **Aaron Rodgers** as Rodgers' play has deteriorated mildly but steadily in recent years. One of the main differences in Rodgers' play has come in the red zone. When Rodgers threw 40 touchdown passes in 2016, outside the red zone he completed 66% of throws at 8.0 yards per attempt with a 50% Success Rate. Last year, Rodgers completed 65% of his passes at 8.0 YPA with a 47% Success Rate on non-red-zone plays. But in the red zone in 2016, he threw 33 touchdowns on 115 attempts (29% TD rate) with a 48% Success Rate and 111 rating. Last year, Rodgers threw 16 touchdowns on 73 red-zone attempts (22% TD rate) with 37% success and an 85 rating. LaFleur *must* improve the Packers' red-zone offense. An additional nugget: Rodgers was incredible when planted in the pocket last season but awful when throwing on the move or throwing when shuffling. Rodgers' 2018 struggles on the move may be attributable to the tibial plateau fracture and MCL sprain he suffered in Week 1.

2018 Standard Passing Table

QB	Comp	Att	Comp %	Yds	YPA	TDs	INT	Sacks	Rating	Rk
Aaron Rodgers	372	597	62%	4,442	7.4	25	2	49	98	13
DeShone Kizer	20	42	48%	187	4.5	0	2	4	41	54
NFL Avg			62%		7.0				87.5	

2018 Advanced Passing Table

QB	Success %	EDSR Passing Success %	20+ Yd Pass Gains	20+ Yd Pass %	30+ Yd Pass Gains	30+ Yd Pass %	Avg. Air Yds per Comp	Avg. YAC per Comp	20+ Air Yd Comp	20+ Air Yd %
Aaron Rodgers	46%	50%	55	9.0%	25	4.0%	6.1	5.9	29	5%
DeShone Kizer	30%	29%	2	5.0%			6.1	3.3	1	2%
NFL Avg	44%	48%	29.5	8.4%	12.5	3.7%	5.8	5.1	14.5	6%

Aaron Rodgers Rating All Downs

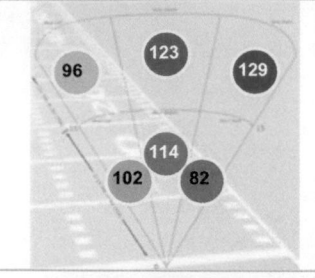

Aaron Rodgers Rating Early Downs

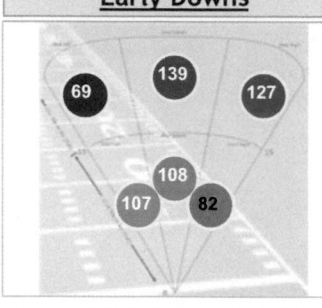

Interception Rates by Down

Yards to Go	1st Dwn	2nd Dwn	3rd Dwn	4th Dwn	Total
1 & 2	0.0%	0.0%	0.0%	0.0%	0.0%
3, 4, 5		2.4%	0.0%	0.0%	1.2%
6 - 9	0.0%	0.0%	2.3%	0.0%	0.9%
10 - 14	0.0%	0.0%	0.0%	0.0%	0.0%
15+	0.0%	0.0%	0.0%	0.0%	0.0%
Total	0.0%	0.5%	0.6%	0.0%	0.3%

3rd Down Passing - Short of Sticks Analysis

QB	Avg. Yds to Go	Avg. YIA (of Comp)	Avg Yds Short	Short of Sticks Rate	Short Rk
Aaron Rodgers	8.0	10.3	0.0	52%	1
NFL Avg	7.8	6.4	-1.4	60%	

Air Yds vs YAC

Air Yds %	YAC %	Rk
51%	49%	29
53%	48%	

2018 Receiving Recap & 2019 Outlook

For how many years will the Packers continue to lean on **Davante Adams** and miscellaneous pieces? Since 2012 – apart from retired **James Jones** – the Packers have had zero receivers post 50-plus catches in a season beyond Adams, **Jordy Nelson**, and **Randall Cobb**.

Adams drew a ridiculous 28 red-zone targets in 2018 – the next-closest Packer had nine – and 23 red-zone targets in 2017. Although Adams is an obvious fantasy stud, Rodgers is desperate for another weapon in real life. Young players **Geronimo Allison**, **Marquez Valdes-Scantling**, **Equanimeous St. Brown**, and **Jake Kumerow** have flashed promise but lack consistency.

Player *Min 50 Targets	Targ	Comp %	YPA	Rating	Success %	Success Rk	Missed YPA Rk	YAS % Rk	YTS % Rk	TDs
Davante Adams	169	66%	8.2	116.6	53%	52	105	59	67	11
Jimmy Graham	91	60%	7.0	79.7	46%	99	143	75	97	2
Marquez Valdes-Sca..	72	53%	8.1	88.9	44%	110	136	3	126	1
Randall Cobb	61	62%	6.3	91.2	46%	99	160	67	67	1

Directional Passer Rating Delivered

Receiver	Short Left	Short Middle	Short Right	Deep Left	Deep Middle	Deep Right	Player Total
Davante Adams	124	152	78	92	130	128	117
Jimmy Graham	111	49	74	102	62	50	80
Marquez Valdes-Scan..	81	115	61	82	110	122	89
Randall Cobb	77	140	85	88	40	50	91
Jamaal Williams	84	109	69	40			78
Equanimeous St. Bro..	87	119	91	67	80	102	89
Aaron Jones	67	85	98			158	98
Geronimo Allison	86	119	100		158	94	122
Lance Kendricks	78	119	128	55		40	103
Ty Montgomery	86	34	73	119			69
Kapri Bibbs	56	85	0				25
Marcedes Lewis	106		83				105
Team Total	101	104	81	92	124	111	96

2018 Rushing Recap & 2019 Outlook

I loved what **Aaron Jones** did for the Packers' 2018 offense. Out of 59 backs with 75-plus carries, Jones was the NFL's only running back to rank top ten in Success Rate, YAS (explosiveness), and missed yards per attempt (production on unsuccessful plays). LaFleur's idea to go more run heavy should enhance Jones' volume. Targeted by early fantasy drafters as the RB18, Jones could easily beat that Average Draft Position if LaFleur commits to him over **Jamaal Williams** and rookie **Dexter Williams**.

Player *Min 50 Rushes	Rushes	YPC	Success %	Success Rk	Missed YPA Rk	YTS % Rk	YAS % Rk	Early Down Success %	Early Down Success Rk	TDs
Aaron Jones	133	5.5	54%	11	9	58	5	54%	8	8
Jamaal Williams	121	3.8	45%	44	37	25	59	47%	34	3

Yards per Carry by Direction

	LT	LG	C	RG	RT		
	5.2	3.4	3.5	5.2	5.1	4.4	4.0

Directional Run Frequency

	LT	LG	C	RG	RT		
	20%	13%	7%	28%	9%	10%	13%

This helped increase passing efficiency; league-wide completion rates on first-down passes moved from 62.1% in 2011 to 63% in 2013, 65% in 2014, and nearly 68% in 2018. *Passing is easier*. We've reached a point where nearly 7-of-10 first-down passes are complete.

Knowing that, offenses *must* become more aggressive passing on first and ten. And they are shifting in the right direction. Aggressive early-down passing also helps to open up the running game.

Teams that bucked that trend the most and opted for heavy early-down rushing in first halves of games were Seattle, Buffalo, Tennessee, and Jacksonville last year. It's understandable to some extent why coaches of these teams wanted to run often; they didn't believe in their quarterbacks. But the goal of any series is to, first, avoid third down, and second, try to set up the fewest yards to go possible should you encounter third down.

The Jaguars were the only team of the four above to average significantly fewer yards to go on third down (6.1) than league average (7.0 in the first half). But the Jaguars ranked 31st in Early Down Success Rate, which effectively measures third-down avoidance. So, Jacksonville still punted on the NFL's third-highest rate of drives.

LaFleur's Titans were just below average in yards to go on third down (7.1) and 26th in EDSR, showing that all that running hurt *(cont'd - see GB-5)*

Green Bay Packers Fantasy Corner

Geronimo Allison got off to a scorching-hot 2018 start, playing 75% of Green Bay's offensive snaps in Weeks 1-4 and putting together a 76/1,156/8 full-season pace only to suffer a Week 4 concussion, a Week 5 hamstring strain, and a Week 8 groin strain that required year-ending surgery. The Packers re-signed Allison to a one-year, $2.8 million deal and inserted him at slot receiver during OTAs. Although Allison doesn't stand out from a speed (4.67) or athleticism standpoint, he looks like the best bet to finish second on the Packers in targets. He's one of my favorite late-round wideout picks.

- Evan Silva

2018 Situational Usage by Player & Position

Usage Rate by Score

		Being Blown Out (14+)	Down Big (9-13)	One Score	Large Lead (9-13)	Blowout Lead (14+)
RUSH	Aaron Jones	7%	5%	69%	4%	16%
	Jamaal Williams	17%	11%	61%	7%	5%
	Marquez Valdes-Sca..			100%		
	Ty Montgomery	19%	12%	54%	4%	12%
	Kapri Bibbs	100%				
	Total	12%	8%	64%	5%	11%
PASS	Aaron Jones	10%		83%	3%	3%
	Jamaal Williams	19%	11%	69%		
	Davante Adams	8%	14%	66%	3%	8%
	Jimmy Graham	16%	16%	57%	5%	5%
	Marquez Valdes-Sca..	23%	3%	62%	7%	5%
	Randall Cobb	24%	20%	49%	7%	
	Ty Montgomery	20%	30%	40%	10%	
	Geronimo Allison	23%	13%	23%	20%	20%
	Lance Kendricks	13%	17%	58%	4%	8%
	Kapri Bibbs	100%				
	Marcedes Lewis			75%	25%	
	Total	17%	13%	59%	6%	6%

Share of Offensive Plays by Type

	Aaron Jones	Jamaal Williams	Davante Adams	Jimmy Graham	Marquez Valdes-Scantling	Randall Cobb	Ty Montgomery	Geronimo Allison	Lance Kendricks	Kapri Bibbs	Marcedes Lewis
RUSH	47%	43%			1%		9%			0%	
PASS	6%	7%	30%	15%	12%	11%	4%	6%	5%	1%	1%
ALL	21%	20%	19%	10%	8%	7%	6%	4%	3%	1%	1%

Positional Target Distribution vs NFL Average

		NFL Wide				Team Only			
		Left	Middle	Right	Total	Left	Middle	Right	Total
Deep	WR	33%	17%	31%	**81%**	39%	14%	29%	**81%**
	TE	5%	4%	7%	**16%**	8%	5%	5%	**17%**
	RB	1%	0%	2%	**4%**	2%		1%	**2%**
	All	**39%**	**22%**	**40%**	**100%**	**48%**	**18%**	**34%**	**100%**
Short	WR	20%	14%	21%	**55%**	25%	10%	22%	**57%**
	TE	6%	6%	8%	**20%**	9%	6%	7%	**21%**
	RB	10%	5%	10%	**25%**	8%	4%	10%	**22%**
	All	**36%**	**25%**	**39%**	**100%**	**41%**	**20%**	**38%**	**100%**
Total		**37%**	**24%**	**39%**	**100%**	**43%**	**20%**	**37%**	**100%**

Positional Success Rates vs NFL Average

		NFL Wide				Team Only			
		Left	Middle	Right	Total	Left	Middle	Right	Total
Deep	WR	40%	49%	40%	**42%**	31%	56%	39%	**38%**
	TE	43%	54%	42%	**46%**	50%	33%	17%	**36%**
	RB	37%	33%	42%	**40%**	50%		100%	**67%**
	All	**41%**	**50%**	**40%**	**43%**	**35%**	**50%**	**38%**	**39%**
Short	WR	55%	60%	52%	**55%**	51%	72%	50%	**55%**
	TE	55%	63%	54%	**57%**	58%	48%	53%	**54%**
	RB	47%	53%	45%	**47%**	43%	65%	45%	**49%**
	All	**53%**	**59%**	**51%**	**54%**	**51%**	**64%**	**50%**	**53%**
Total		**50%**	**58%**	**49%**	**52%**	**47%**	**61%**	**47%**	**50%**

Division History: Season Wins & 2019 Projection

2015 Wins | 2016 Wins | 2017 Wins | 2018 Wins | Forecast 2019 Wins

Rank of 2019 Defensive Pass Efficiency Faced by Week

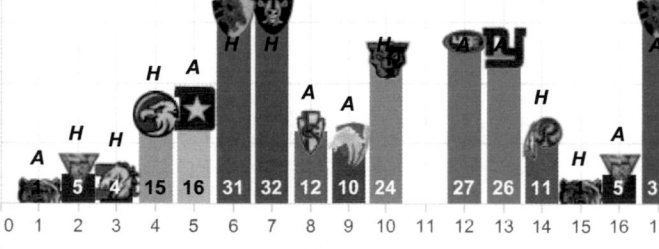

Rank of 2019 Defensive Rush Efficiency Faced by Week

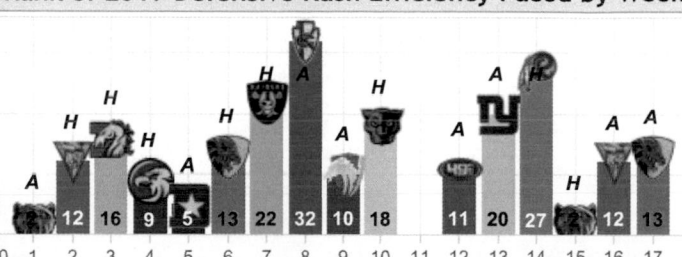

2018 Detailed Analytics Summary
Success by Play Type & Primary Personnel Groupings

Type	1-1 [3WR]	1-2 [2WR]	1-3 [1WR]	2-1 [2WR]	2-0 [3WR]	1-0 [4WR]	2-2 [1WR]	0-0 [5WR]	0-1 [4WR]	2-3 [0WR]	ALL
PASS	44% (567)	52% (94)	44% (9)	0% (3)	100% (2)	0% (2)		0% (1)	0% (2)	0% (1)	45% (681)
RUSH	59% (216)	45% (69)	44% (27)	14% (7)	100% (3)	50% (2)	50% (4)	100% (1)			54% (329)
All	48% (783)	49% (163)	44% (36)	10% (10)	100% (5)	25% (4)	50% (4)	50% (2)	0% (2)	0% (1)	48% (1,010)

Format Success Rate (Total # of Plays)

Receiving Success by Top-4 Personnel Groupings
(Min 50 targets)

POS	Player	1-1 [3WR]	1-2 [2WR]	4 Grp Total
TE	Jimmy Graham	49% (69) 6.5, 82.2	43% (14) 11.6, 92.0	48% (83) 7.3, 83.9
WR	Davante Adams	52% (147) 8.6, 117.1	59% (22) 5.9, 113.6	53% (169) 8.2, 116.6
	Marquez Valdes-Scantling	46% (56) 8.9, 97.1	33% (12) 4.8, 56.6	44% (68) 8.1, 90.0
	Randall Cobb	45% (55) 6.4, 93.9	75% (4) 8.3, 99.0	47% (59) 6.5, 94.2

Format Line 1: Success Rate (Total # of Plays) Line 2: YPA, Passer Rating

Rushing Success by Top-4 Personnel Groupings
(Min 25 carries)

Rusher (Last, First)	1-1 [3WR]	1-2 [2WR]	2-1 [2WR]	2-2 [1WR]	4 Grp Total
Jones Aaron	56% (84) 6.0	52% (31) 4.6	33% (3) 2.3	100% (2) 9.5	55% (120) 5.6
Williams Jamaal	52% (77) 4.2	43% (23) 3.6	0% (3) 0.0		49% (103) 3.9
Rodgers Aaron	77% (35) 7.5	43% (7) 1.3		0% (1) -1.0	70% (43) 6.3
Montgomery Ty	58% (12) 4.8	25% (8) 3.3	0% (1) -6.0		43% (21) 3.7

Format Line 1: Success Rate (Total # of Plays) Line 2: YPC

Passing by Coverage Scheme

M2M	49% (299) 7.8, 92.5
Zone	56% (209) 7.9, 106.7
Screen	49% (67) 6.1, 90.9
Combo	50% (14) 7.4, 126.2

Passing by Route

Out	49% (79) 5.7, 83.9
Screen	50% (66) 6.2, 91.3
Flat	60% (63) 4.8, 97.1
Curl	64% (61) 6.5, 97.6
Slant	70% (40) 8.4, 116.0
Dig	48% (23) 9.9, 83.2

Throw Types

Level 1	54% (387) 6.5, 95.9
Level 2	54% (134) 10.8, 119.8
Level 3	18% (60) 7.2, 77.9
Sidearm	82% (17) 10.5, 130.1
Shovel	100% (1) 22.0, 118.8

QB Drop Types

3 Step	54% (270) 8.9, 108.8
0/1 Step	46% (138) 5.1, 87.4
5 Step	41% (103) 6.5, 80.2
Basic Screen	64% (33) 9.5, 103.5
Designed Rollout Right	38% (24) 6.5, 67.2
7 Step	63% (16) 14.4, 106.3

QB State at Pass

Planted	57% (360) 8.4, 107.1
Shuffling	45% (123) 5.8, 87.3
Moving	38% (92) 6.9, 77.9

Play Action

	Play Action	No P/A
Under Center	48% (65) 8.6, 89.0	66% (44) 8.4, 124.4
Shotgun	50% (54) 4.8, 102.5	50% (443) 7.7, 96.9
ALL	49% (119) 6.9, 95.1	51% (487) 7.7, 99.6

Run Types

Inside Zone	50% (96) 4.6
Outside Zone	48% (86) 4.3
Pitch	61% (23) 5.4
Lead	62% (21) 5.4
Power	46% (13) 3.8
Stretch	40% (10) 1.1

GB-5

the team and led to a below-average scoring rate. The Bills were terrible in both metrics, averaging 8.3 yards to go on third downs and finishing fourth worst in EDSR. Seattle was nearly average in third-down distance (6.9 vs. 7.0) but just below average in EDSR (19th).

Ideally, LaFleur will take a page from McVay and instill a higher early-down passing rate than he's hinted at publicly. Rodgers is much better than Mariota, and there is no need to "protect" him now that Rodgers is healthy. "Protecting" quarterbacks typically hurts an offense. LaFleur can still make Rodgers' job easier with minor tweaks that will make a big difference.

Fortunately, LaFleur inherits a strong offensive line to which the Packers have devoted the NFL's third-most monetary resources. Their run game ranked third best in the league last year. But this year I'm projecting the Packers to face the NFL's second-toughest run-defense slate.

Another schedule specific I don't love for the Packers is their rest disadvantage down the stretch. Over its final 11 games, Green Bay faces a one-on-one rest disadvantage in five and has a rest advantage in only one. The Packers must play the Lions and Raiders immediately after those teams' byes. They face a Chiefs team coming off a mini-bye Thursday night game. They face the Bears in Week 15 off a mini bye and the Lions in Week 17 on a short week.

Last year's Packers schedule wound up being especially soft – fourth easiest in the NFL – fueled by facing every rookie quarterback besides **Baker Mayfield**, plus **Brock Osweiler**. But their defense still ranked bottom four in efficiency.

DC **Mike Pettine** must fix his defense for Green Bay to return to the playoffs after a two-year absence.

The Packers haven't gone three straight years without a postseason berth since the pre-Favre era.

Houston Texans

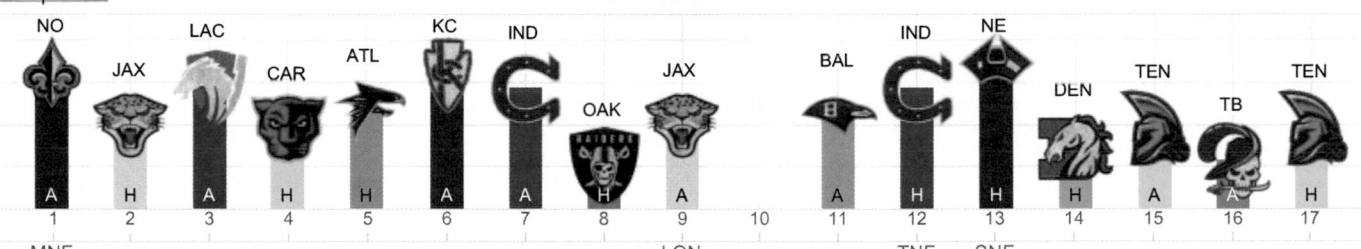

Coaches (Prior Yrs)

Head Coach:
 Bill O'Brien (Calls Plays) (5 yrs)
Offensive Coordinator:
 Tim Kelly (HOU TE) (new)
Defensive Coordinator:
 Romeo Crennel (5 yrs)

EASY   HARD

2019 Forecast

Wins	Div Rank
8.5	#2

Past Records
2018: 11-5
2017: 4-12
2016: 9-7

Schedule:
NO(A) 1 MNF / JAX(H) 2 / LAC(A) 3 / CAR(H) 4 / ATL(H) 5 / KC(A) 6 / IND(A) 7 / OAK(H) 8 / JAX(A) 9 / 10 / BAL(A) 11 / IND(H) 12 TNF / NE(H) 13 SNF / DEN(H) 14 / TEN(A) 15 / TB(A) 16 / TEN(H) 17
LON (at week 7 area)

Key Players Lost

Player	New
Alfred Blue (RB)	JAC
Andre Hal (FS)	Retired
Christian Covington (DT)	DAL
Demaryius Thomas (WR)	NE
Kareem Jackson (CB)	DEN
Kendall Lamm (RT)	CLE
Kevin Johnson (CB)	BUF
Shane Lechler (P)	Retired
Tyrann Mathieu (FS)	KC

Average Line	# Games Favored	# Games Underdog
0.1	7	7

2019 Houston Texans Overview

Strength of schedule matters.

And that's why I track SOS at Sharp Football Stats using roughly 30 different metrics to slice and dice team schedules. In 2018, five of the teams with the ten-softest schedules based on opponent efficiency made the playoffs (Colts, Bears, Texans, Patriots, Cowboys). The only team among them that made the playoffs the previous year was New England. The Chiefs were the only team to make the playoffs with one of last year's ten-toughest slates.

The 2017 Texans finished 4-12 against the league's 12th-toughest schedule. In last year's preview, I projected Houston to face the NFL's softest slate based on both opponent efficiency and a Vegas-based schedule comparison I first introduced several years ago. I believed the Texans would bounce back thanks in large part to their easier road.

The 2018 Texans finished 11-5, winning the AFC South. They weren't the betting favorite to win the division, but they did. And as it turned out, the Texans were one of the easiest fades in the playoffs I've seen in some time. All of this revolved around schedule strength.

I also forecast the 2018 Texans to face the easiest schedule of opponent passing offenses. Sure enough, they drew the league's easiest pass-offense slate. In fact, it was the easiest pass-offense schedule *in the last four years*. Their list of quarterbacks faced included **Brock Osweiler, Blaine Gabbert, Blake Bortles, Cody Kessler, Colt McCoy, Case Keenum, Nathan Peterman, Marcus Mariota, Dak Prescott, Eli Manning, Nick Foles,** and three rookies (**Josh Allen, Sam Darnold, Baker Mayfield**).

We may be hard pressed to *ever again* see a defense face a combination of as many

(cont'd - see HOU2)

Key Free Agents/ Trades Added

Player	AAV (MM)
A.J. McCarron (QB)	$3
Bradley Roby (CB)	$10
Briean Boddy-Calhoun (S)	$0.9
Darren Fells (TE)	$1.5
Jahleel Addae (SS)	$1.1
Matt Kalil (LT)	$7.5
Taiwan Jones (RB)	$1
Tashaun Gipson (FS)	$7.5

Drafted Players

Rd	Pk	Player (College)
1	23	OT - Tytus Howard (Alabama State)
2	54	CB - Lonnie Johnson Jr. (Kentucky)
2	55	OT - Max Scharping (Northern Illinois)
3	86	TE - Kahale Warring (San Diego State)
5	161	DE - Charles Omenihu (Texas)
6	195	CB - Xavier Crawford (Central Michigan)
7	220	RB - Cullen Gillaspia (Texas A&M)

Regular Season Wins: Past & Current Proj

Forecast 2019 Wins — 8.5
2018 Wins — 11
Forecast 2018 Wins — 8.5
2017 Wins — 4
2016 Wins — 9
2015 Wins — 9

1 3 5 7 9 11 13 15

Lineup & Cap Hits

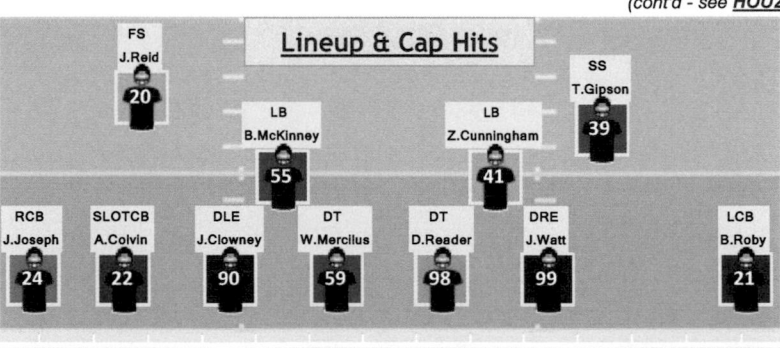

FS J.Reid 20
SS T.Gipson 39
LB B.McKinney 55
LB Z.Cunningham 41
RCB J.Joseph 24
SLOTCB A.Colvin 22
DLE J.Clowney 90
DT W.Mercilus 59
DT D.Reader 98
DRE J.Watt 99
LCB B.Roby 21

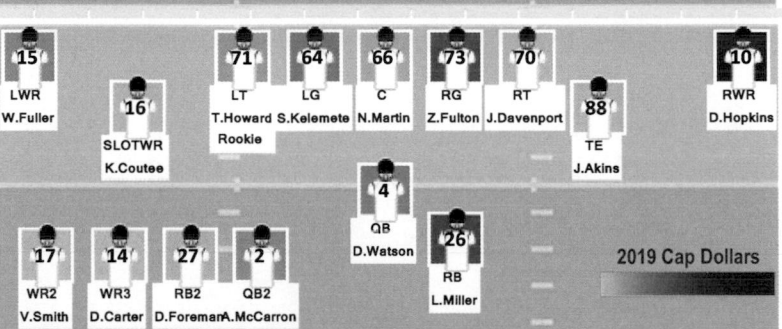

LWR W.Fuller 15
SLOTWR K.Coutee 16
LT T.Howard Rookie 71
LG S.Kelemete 64
C N.Martin 66
RG Z.Fulton 73
RT J.Davenport 70
TE J.Akins 88
RWR D.Hopkins 10
QB D.Watson 4
RB L.Miller 26
WR2 V.Smith 17
WR3 D.Carter 14
RB2 D.Foreman 27
QB2 A.McCarron 2

2019 Cap Dollars

2019 Unit Spending

All OFF
All DEF

Positional Spending

	Rank	Total	2017 Rk
All OFF	30	$74.31M	30
QB	28	$7.51M	31
OL	26	$29.57M	27
RB	7	$11.02M	5
WR	16	$22.18M	7
TE	32	$4.03M	25
All DEF	1	$108.61M	2
DL	18	$29.33M	20
LB	2	$37.54M	5
CB	4	$30.72M	1
S	15	$11.02M	10

below-average to downright backup-level quarterbacks as last year's Texans did.

The only other two quarterbacks the Texans faced were **Tom Brady** and **Andrew Luck**. They went 1-3 against those quarterbacks, the lone win coming on an overtime play call where **Frank Reich**'s Colts risked going for it on fourth down in their own territory rather than playing for the tie.

Your pass defense *might be bad* when you face a league-worst quarterback slate yet rank No. 18 in pass-defense efficiency. It might also be bad if it allows **Nick Foles** to set a franchise record in passing yards (497) and average 9.8 yards per attempt with four touchdowns. Your pass defense *might be bad* if it allows **Marcus Mariota** to go 22-of-23 for 303 yards (13.2 YPA) and a 148 passer rating. It might be an abject failure if the petrified remains of **Eli Manning** lights it up for 25-of-29 passing, 297 yards (10.2 YPA), and a season-best 69% Success Rate.

On account of accurately forecasting the strength of their 2018 schedule, I wasn't surprised the Texans made the playoffs. And I was even less surprised they went one and done in a two-touchdown loss to the Colts. Hosting their Wild Card game, the Texans trailed Indianapolis 21-0 at halftime. It was just the second time in the last ten years that a home playoff favorite was held scoreless in the first half. The last time a Wild Card team trailed at home by 21 points? **Bill O'Brien**'s 2015 Texans, who were shellacked 30-0 by the Chiefs.

Unfortunately for this year's Texans, I project them to face the NFL's fifth-toughest slate of opposing passing offenses and the third-toughest overall schedule of offenses. Inside the division, the Jaguars upgraded from Bortles to Foles, and Tennessee has a new offensive coordinator. In addition to running it back against Luck (twice) and Brady, the 2019 Texans draw **Patrick Mahomes**, **Philip Rivers**, and **Drew Brees**, who quarterbacked last year's Nos. 1, 2, and 3 pass-efficiency offenses. Houston also draws **Matt Ryan**, **Bruce Arians**' Bucs, **Cam Newton**, and **Derek Carr** at the helm of a remade Raiders passing attack.

The 2018 Texans had an easy schedule and won. But their schedule-strength swing is the biggest in football heading into 2019. Based on Opponent Win Totals, the Texans move from the NFL's softest 2018 slate to this year's toughest draw. And that will impact their outcomes.

To increase their odds of success, the Texans must improve their efficiency wherever possible. How does a team with a great dual-threat quarterback that finishes No. 13 in passing efficiency end up with an overall efficiency ranking of No. 21? Only if their non-quarterback rushing stats are terrible, and the team runs in inefficient circumstances. Because strong passing teams with bad running backs can just become pass heavier and avoid pounding their heads into walls.

The 2018 Texans indeed ran inefficiently and called run plays in inefficient circumstances.

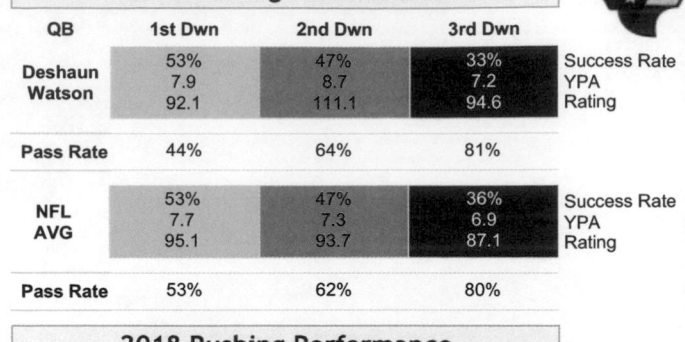

2018 Passing Performance

QB	1st Dwn	2nd Dwn	3rd Dwn	
Deshaun Watson	53%	47%	33%	Success Rate
	7.9	8.7	7.2	YPA
	92.1	111.1	94.6	Rating
Pass Rate	44%	64%	81%	
NFL AVG	53%	47%	36%	Success Rate
	7.7	7.3	6.9	YPA
	95.1	93.7	87.1	Rating
Pass Rate	53%	62%	80%	

2018 Rushing Performance

Offense	1st Dwn	2nd Dwn	3rd Dwn	
HOU	45%	46%	47%	Success Rate
	4.0	4.5	5.5	YPC
Run Rate	56%	36%	19%	
NFL AVG	48%	46%	51%	Success Rate
	4.5	4.4	4.3	YPC
Run Rate	47%	38%	20%	

Houston was the NFL's eighth run-heavy team in 2018 raw totals, but a deeper look reveals they were even run heavier than that. O'Brien's team went just 38% pass on first downs in first halves of games. They were the NFL's single-most run-heavy team on such plays.

Lamar Miller's first-half first-down rushing stats are skewed because one of his 72 attempts in such scenarios went for a 95-yard touchdown. He ranked 30th among 40 qualified backs in Success Rate (44%) on first-down runs in the first half. He averaged 5.4 yards per carry but only 4.1 YPC if you eliminate that 95-yard score. Miller was a boom-bust runner, gaining six-plus yards at the third-highest rate in the league on first-half first downs but gaining zero or losing yardage at the league's third-highest clip (25%). In one-score games, Miller posted an anemic 38% Success Rate on first-down runs, which ranked 41st among 43 qualified backs.

The Texans' running game also sputtered in the red zone. *(cont'd - see **HOU-3**)*

2018 Offensive Advanced Metrics

Rank (y-axis): 1, 5, 10, 15, 20, 25, 30

Metric	Rank
EDSR Off	11
30 & In Off	11
Red Zone Off	17
3rd Down Off	20
YPPA Off	7
YPPT Off	8
Offensive Efficiency	21
Pass Efficiency Off	13
Pass Pro Efficiency Off	29
RB Pass Eff Off	26
Rush Efficiency Off	10
Explosive Pass Off	13
Explosive Run Off	

2018 Defensive Advanced Metrics

Metric	Rank
EDSR Def	4
30 & In Def	20
Red Zone Def	23
3rd Down Def	20
YPPA Def	19
YPPT Def	7
Defensive Efficiency	7
Pass Efficiency Def	18
Pass Pro Efficiency Def	8
RB Pass Eff Def	13
Rush Efficiency Def	1
Explosive Pass Def	19
Explosive Run Def	1

2018 Weekly EDSR & Season Trending Performance

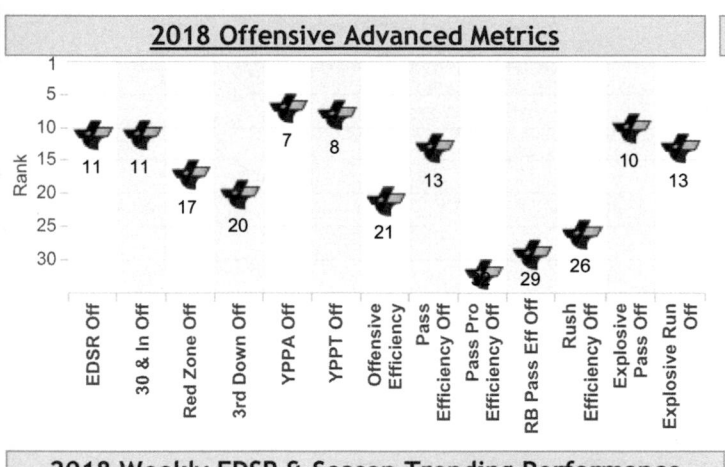

	1	2	3	4	5	6	7	8	9		11	12	13	14	15	16	17	
RESULT	L	L	L	W	W	W	W	W	W		W	W	W	L	W	L	W	**WEEK**
OPP	NE	TEN	NYG	IND	DAL	BUF	JAC	MIA	DEN		WAS	TEN	CLE	IND	NYJ	PHI	JAC	
SITE	A	A	H	H	A	A	H	A	H		A	H	H	H	A	A	H	
MARGIN	-7	-3	-5	3	3	7	13	19	2		2	17	16	-3	7	-2	17	
PTS	20	17	22	37	19	20	20	42	19		23	34	29	21	29	30	20	
OPP PTS	27	20	27	34	16	13	7	23	17		21	17	13	24	22	32	3	

EDSR by Wk
W=Green
L=Red

OFF/DEF
EDSR
Blue=OFF
(high=good)
Red=DEF
(low=good)

2018 Close Game Records

All 2018 Wins: **11**
FG Games (<=3 pts) W-L: **4-3**
FG Games Win %: **0% (#30)**
FG Games Wins (% of Total Wins): **36% (#10)**
1 Score Games (<=8 pts) W-L: **6-5**
1 Score Games Win %: **55% (#13)**
1 Score Games Wins (% of Total Wins): **55% (#14)**

2018 Critical & Game-Deciding Stats

TO Margin	+13
TO Given	16
INT Given	9
FUM Given	7
TO Taken	29
INT Taken	15
FUM Taken	14
Sack Margin	-19
Sacks	43
Sacks Allow	62
Return TD Margin	+4
Ret TDs	4
Ret TDs Allow	0
Penalty Margin	+12
Penalties	105
Opponent Penalties	117

Houston Texans 2019 Strength of Schedule In Detail (compared to 2018)

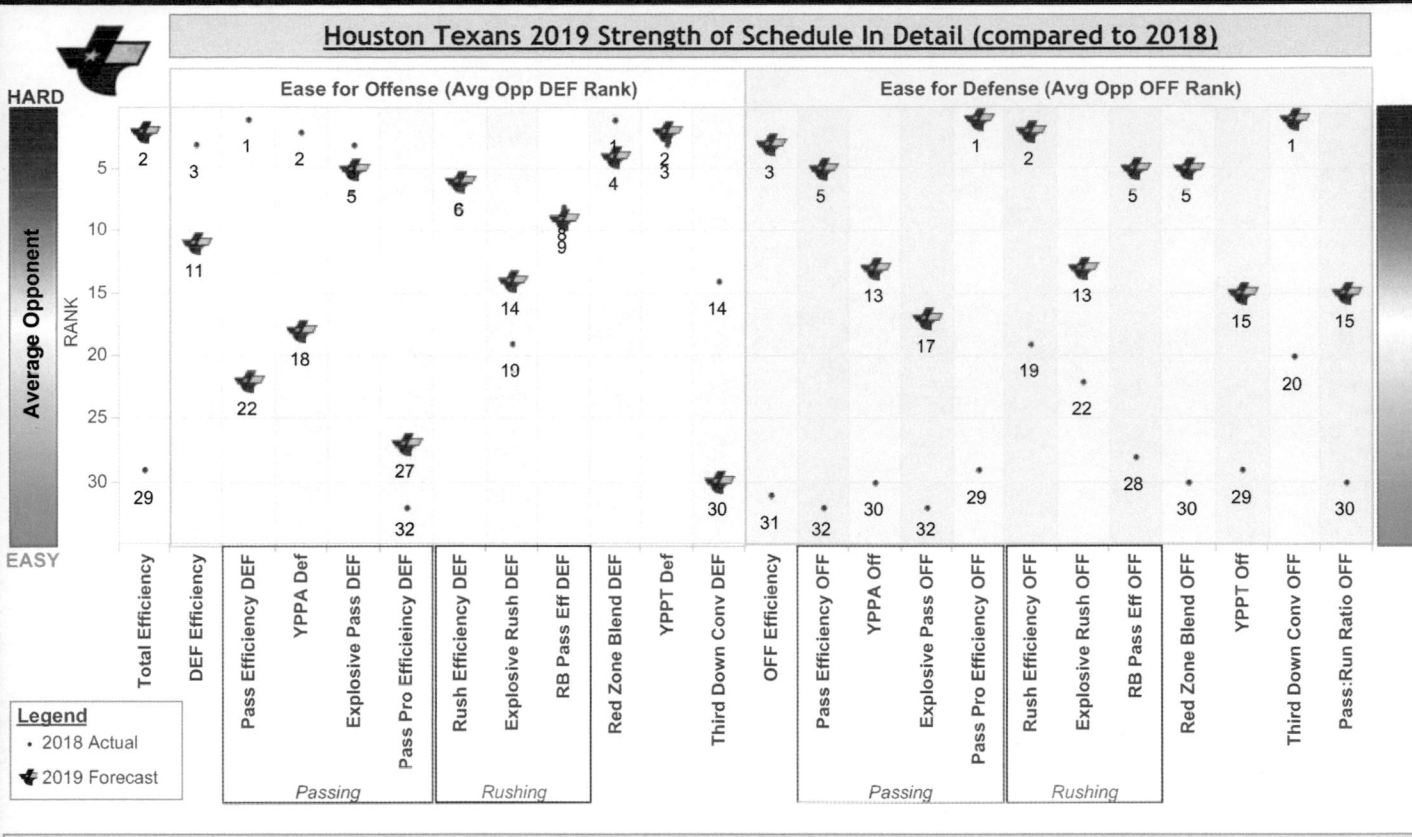

2019 v 2018 Schedule Variances* (OFF=Rank of DEF faced, 2019 vs 2018)

Pass OFF Rank	Pass OFF Blend Rk	Rush OFF Rk	Rush OFF Blend Rk	Pass DEF Rk	Pass DEF Blend Rk	Rush DEF Rk	Rush DEF Blend Rk
32	31	14	12	1	1	2	2

* **1**=Hardest Jump in 2019 schedule from 2018 (aka a much harder schedule in 2019), **32**=Easiest Jump in 2019 schedule from 2018 (aka a much easier schedule in 2019);
Pass Blend metric blends 4 metrics: Pass Efficiency, YPPA, Explosive Pass & Pass Rush; **Rush Blend** metric blends 3 metrics: Rush Efficiency, Explosive Rush & RB Targets

Team Records & Trends

	2018	2017	2016
Average line	-3.0	3.6	1.1
Average O/U line	44.4	42.5	42.9
Straight Up Record	11-5	4-12	9-7
Against the Spread Record	8-7	7-9	6-8
Over/Under Record	7-9	8-8	7-9
ATS as Favorite	5-6	2-3	4-1
ATS as Underdog	3-1	5-6	1-6
Straight Up Home	6-2	3-5	7-1
ATS Home	4-4	4-4	4-2
Over/Under Home	3-5	4-4	3-5
ATS as Home Favorite	4-4	2-3	4-1
ATS as a Home Dog	0-0	1-2	0-1
Straight Up Away	5-3	1-7	2-5
ATS Away	4-3	4-4	2-5
Over/Under Away	4-4	4-4	3-4
ATS Away Favorite	1-2	0-0	0-0
ATS Away Dog	3-1	4-4	1-4
Six Point Teaser Record	14-2	9-6	13-3
Seven Point Teaser Record	14-1	10-6	13-3
Ten Point Teaser Record	15-1	10-6	14-2

HOU-3

Whereas Watson's red-zone rushing produced a 62% Success Rate and 4.8 yards per carry, Miller's Success Rate (32%) and yards per carry (1.8) were pathetic. No. 2 back **Alfred Blue** (21% success, 1.1 YPC) was even worse.

It's hard to build a rushing offense around a boom-bust, inefficient back. And it's especially important for the Texans to succeed on first downs in the first half because they've historically struggled to play from behind. Last year's Texans went 11-0 when leading by more than three points at halftime. They went 0-6 when trailing or leading by two or fewer points. The 2017 Texans went 1-11 when trailing or tied at halftime and were 3-1 when up by more than three points at the break. Over the last two seasons, Houston is 1-16 when tied or behind at the half. It's the worst win rate in the NFL.

The Texans will take more halftime leads if they improve early-down efficiency by scrapping the NFL's run-heaviest offense on first downs in the first half. O'Brien must

(cont'd - see HOU-4)

2019 Rest Analysis

Team More Rest	2
Opp More Rest	2
Net Rest Edge	0
Week 2 Edge	-1
Week 3 Edge	0
Week 4 Edge	0
Week 5 Edge	0
Week 6 Edge	0
Week 7 Edge	
Week 8 Edge	0
Week 9 Edge	0
Week 11 Edge	7
Week 12 Edge	0
Week 13 Edge	3
Week 14 Edge	0
Week 15 Edge	0
Week 16 Edge	0
Week 17 Edge	0

Health by Unit*

2018 Rk	20
2017 Rk	
2018 v 2017 Rk	9
Off Rk	20
Def Rk	26
QB Rk	19
RB Rk	10
WR Rk	
TE Rk	13
Oline Rk	20
Dline Rk	9
LB Rk	21
DB Rk	

*Based on the work of Football Outsiders

2018 Weekly Betting Lines (wks 1-16)

1	2	3	4	5	6	7	8	9	11	12	13	14	15	16
NO	JAX	LAC	CAR	ATL	KC	IND	OAK	JAX	BAL	IND	NE	DEN	TEN	TB
7	-3.5	5.5	-4.5	-3.5	7	4	-7	0	2.5	-2	3	-5.5	1	-2

Avg = 0.1   Avg = 0.1

Home Lines (wks 1-16)

2	4	5	8	12	13	14
-3.5 JAX	-4.5 CAR	-3.5 ATL	-7 OAK	-2 IND	3 NE	Avg = -3.3 DEN

Road Lines (wks 1-16)

1	3	6	7	9	11	15	16
7 NO	5.5 LAC	7 KC	4 IND	0 JAX	2.5 BAL	1 TEN	-2 TB

Avg = 3.1

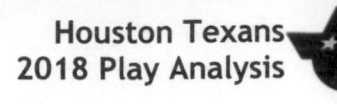

2018 Play Tendencies

All Pass %	55%
All Pass Rk	26
All Rush %	45%
All Rush Rk	7
1 Score Pass %	55%
1 Score Pass Rk	27
2017 1 Score Pass %	57%
2017 1 Score Pass Rk	19
2018 Pass Increase %	-2%
Pass Increase Rk	22
1 Score Rush %	45%
1 Score Rush Rk	6
Up Pass %	48%
Up Pass Rk	21
Up Rush %	52%
Up Rush Rk	12
Down Pass %	61%
Down Pass Rk	29
Down Rush %	39%
Down Rush Rk	4

2018 Down & Distance Tendencies

Down	Distance	Total Plays	Pass Rate	Run Rate	Play Success %
1	Short (1-3)	2	0%	100%	50%
	Med (4-7)	12	33%	67%	50%
	Long (8-10)	339	35%	65%	50%
	XL (11+)	16	69%	31%	19%
2	Short (1-3)	43	35%	65%	51%
	Med (4-7)	83	58%	42%	55%
	Long (8-10)	90	71%	29%	48%
	XL (11+)	59	85%	15%	34%
3	Short (1-3)	44	59%	41%	61%
	Med (4-7)	41	93%	7%	39%
	Long (8-10)	35	83%	17%	26%
	XL (11+)	42	79%	21%	12%
4	Short (1-3)	8	75%	25%	63%
	Med (4-7)	3	100%	0%	33%

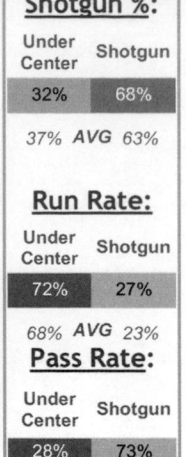

Shotgun %:

Under Center	Shotgun
32%	68%

37% *AVG* 63%

Run Rate:

Under Center	Shotgun
72%	27%

68% *AVG* 23%

Pass Rate:

Under Center	Shotgun
28%	73%

32% *AVG* 77%

Short Yardage Intelligence:

2nd and Short Run

Run Freq	Run Rk	NFL Run Freq Avg	Run 1D Rate	Run NFL 1D Avg
71%	10	65%	56%	68%

2nd and Short Pass

Pass Freq	Pass Rk	NFL Pass Freq Avg	Pass 1D Rate	Pass NFL 1D Avg
29%	23	35%	50%	56%

Most Frequent Play

Down	Distance	Play Type	Player	Total Plays	Play Success %
1	Med (4-7)	RUSH	Alfred Blue	3	33%
			Deshaun Watson	3	100%
	Long (8-10)	RUSH	Lamar Miller	110	41%
	XL (11+)	PASS	DeAndre Hopkins	3	0%
		RUSH	Deshaun Watson	3	33%
2	Short (1-3)	RUSH	Lamar Miller	15	60%
	Med (4-7)	RUSH	Lamar Miller	19	63%
	Long (8-10)	PASS	DeAndre Hopkins	16	63%
		RUSH	Lamar Miller	16	25%
	XL (11+)	PASS	DeAndre Hopkins	10	60%
3	Short (1-3)	RUSH	Alfred Blue	9	78%
	Med (4-7)	PASS	DeAndre Hopkins	14	71%
	Long (8-10)	PASS	DeAndre Hopkins	6	50%
		RUSH	Deshaun Watson	6	17%
	XL (11+)	PASS	Keke Coutee	7	14%
		RUSH	Deshaun Watson	7	14%

Most Successful Play*

Down	Distance	Play Type	Player	Total Plays	Play Success %
1	Long (8-10)	PASS	Demaryius Thomas	7	86%
2	Short (1-3)	RUSH	Lamar Miller	15	60%
	Med (4-7)	PASS	Will Fuller	6	67%
		RUSH	Deshaun Watson	9	67%
	Long (8-10)	PASS	DeAndre Carter	5	80%
	XL (11+)	PASS	DeAndre Hopkins	10	60%
3	Short (1-3)	RUSH	Deshaun Watson	7	86%
	Med (4-7)	PASS	Will Fuller	5	80%
	Long (8-10)	PASS	DeAndre Hopkins	6	50%
	XL (11+)	PASS	Lamar Miller	5	20%
		PASS	DeAndre Hopkins	5	20%

Minimum 5 plays to qualify

2018 Weekly Snap Rates

Wk	Opp	Score	DeAndre Hopkins	Ryan Griffin	Lamar Miller	Jordan Thomas	Jordan Akins	Will Fuller	Demaryius Thomas	Keke Coutee
1	NE	L 27-20	73 (99%)	63 (85%)	57 (77%)	14 (19%)	37 (50%)			
2	TEN	L 20-17	67 (100%)	52 (78%)	51 (76%)	24 (36%)	15 (22%)	55 (82%)		
3	NYG	L 27-22	68 (100%)	52 (76%)	52 (76%)	15 (22%)	25 (37%)	68 (100%)		
4	IND	W 37-34	86 (100%)	59 (69%)	46 (53%)	27 (31%)	37 (43%)	27 (31%)		80 (93%)
5	DAL	W 19-16	80 (100%)	57 (71%)		29 (36%)	18 (23%)	77 (96%)		57 (71%)
6	BUF	W 20-13	61 (100%)	51 (84%)	41 (67%)	21 (34%)	8 (13%)	52 (85%)		45 (74%)
7	JAC	W 20-7	64 (100%)		45 (70%)	55 (86%)	30 (47%)	52 (81%)		16 (25%)
8	MIA	W 42-23	59 (97%)		34 (56%)	54 (89%)	34 (56%)	44 (72%)		
9	DEN	W 19-17	61 (98%)	47 (76%)	40 (65%)	39 (63%)	36 (58%)		49 (79%)	
11	WAS	W 23-21	63 (100%)	47 (75%)	46 (73%)	34 (54%)	18 (29%)		46 (73%)	42 (67%)
12	TEN	W 34-17	64 (98%)	43 (66%)	40 (62%)	33 (51%)	25 (38%)		54 (83%)	27 (42%)
13	CLE	W 29-13	75 (99%)	61 (80%)	41 (54%)	40 (53%)	21 (28%)		60 (79%)	
14	IND	L 24-21	72 (100%)	59 (82%)	51 (71%)	33 (46%)	15 (21%)		68 (94%)	
15	NYJ	W 29-22	51 (96%)	44 (83%)	11 (21%)	24 (45%)	14 (26%)		47 (89%)	
16	PHI	L 32-30	65 (100%)	47 (72%)		15 (23%)	24 (37%)		35 (54%)	
17	JAC	W 20-3	75 (97%)	61 (79%)	64 (83%)	13 (17%)	31 (40%)			
	Grand Total		1,084 (99%)	743 (77%)	619 (65%)	470 (44%)	388 (35%)	375 (78%)	359 (79%)	267 (62%)

Personnel Groupings

Personnel	Team %	NFL Avg	Succ. %
1-1 [3WR]	55%	65%	43%
1-2 [2WR]	37%	17%	48%
1-3 [1WR]	4%	3%	39%

Grouping Tendencies

Personnel	Pass Rate	Pass Succ. %	Run Succ. %
1-1 [3WR]	62%	43%	42%
1-2 [2WR]	49%	54%	43%
1-3 [1WR]	13%	20%	42%

Red Zone Targets (min 3)

Receiver	All	Inside 5	6-10	11-20
DeAndre Hopkins	19	7	4	8
Jordan Thomas	8	1	3	4
Alfred Blue	7	1	1	5
Keke Coutee	6	1	2	3
Ryan Griffin	5		1	4
Will Fuller	5	2	1	2
Demaryius Thomas	4		1	3

Red Zone Rushes (min 3)

Rusher	All	Inside 5	6-10	11-20
Lamar Miller	31	7	6	18
Deshaun Watson	21	9	4	8
Alfred Blue	14	4	4	6

Early Down Target Rate

	RB	TE	WR
	14%	18%	68%
NFL AVG	23%	21%	56%

Overall Target Success %

	RB	TE	WR
	42%	49%	55%
	#25	#30	#10

Houston Texans 2018 Passing Recap & 2019 Outlook

Although I'm not high on the 2019 Texans from a win-loss perspective, I am extremely high on **Deshaun Watson** as a fantasy pick. Watson finished as last year's QB4 despite myriad obstacles, including playing without **Will Fuller** (ACL) for most of the season and having slot receiver **Keke Coutee** (hamstring) for only five weeks. Watson also faced the NFL's toughest pass-defense schedule. That schedule will be softer this year. Watson also finished second among quarterbacks in red-zone carries behind **Lamar Jackson** last season. Even if O'Brien continues to work against him, Watson should dominate box scores in 2019.

2018 Standard Passing Table

QB	Comp	Att	Comp %	Yds	YPA	TDs	INT	Sacks	Rating	Rk
Deshaun Watson	374	554	68%	4,400	7.9	27	10	65	100	11
NFL Avg			62%		7.0				87.5	

2018 Advanced Passing Table

QB	Success %	EDSR Passing Success %	20+ Yd Pass Gains	20+ Yd Pass %	30+ Yd Pass Gains	30+ Yd Pass %	Avg. Air Yds per Comp	Avg. YAC per Comp	20+ Air Yd Comp	20+ Air Yd %
Deshaun Watson	45%	50%	52	9.0%	20	4.0%	6.7	5.1	24	4%
NFL Avg	44%	48%	29.5	8.4%	12.5	3.7%	5.8	5.1	14.5	6%

Deshaun Watson Rating All Downs

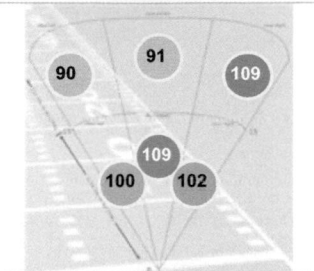

Deshaun Watson Rating Early Downs

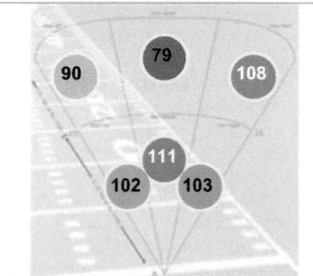

Interception Rates by Down

Yards to Go	1st Dwn	2nd Dwn	3rd Dwn	4th Dwn	Total
1 & 2		0.0%	0.0%	0.0%	0.0%
3, 4, 5	0.0%	2.6%	2.1%	25.0%	3.1%
6 - 9	0.0%	2.4%	0.0%	0.0%	1.4%
10 - 14	1.1%	0.0%	5.1%	0.0%	1.4%
15+	0.0%	5.3%	0.0%		2.0%
Total	1.0%	1.7%	1.7%	7.1%	1.6%

3rd Down Passing - Short of Sticks Analysis

QB	Avg. Yds to Go	Avg. YIA (of Comp)	Avg Yds Short	Short of Sticks Rate	Short Rk
Deshaun Watson	7.7	5.7	-2.0	57%	28
NFL Avg	7.8	6.4	-1.4	60%	

Air Yds vs YAC

Air Yds %	YAC %	Rk
56%	44%	12
53%	48%	

2018 Receiving Recap & 2019 Outlook

The Texans' three-receiver package is among the NFL's most talented. They just need to stay healthy. **DeAndre Hopkins** has stayed reliable amid shaky quarterback play. **Will Fuller** is a difference-making field stretcher; in his career, Watson averages 8.8 yards per attempt with Fuller in the lineup but only 7.4 without him. And Coutee was tremendous in a small sample size working in the slot last season. The most disappointing elements of Houston's passing attack were the backs and tight ends, who finished 25th and 30th in Success Rate.

Player *Min 50 Targets	Targ	Comp %	YPA	Rating	Success %	Success Rk	Missed YPA Rk	YAS % Rk	YTS % Rk	TDs
DeAndre Hopkins	173	69%	9.3	112.6	60%	14	34	28	67	10
Keke Coutee	55	71%	7.2	88.2	49%	85	158	121	26	1

Directional Passer Rating Delivered

Receiver	Short Left	Short Middle	Short Right	Deep Left	Deep Middle	Deep Right	Player Total
DeAndre Hopkins	103	123	103	68	113	115	113
Keke Coutee	132	79	77	50	58		88
Ryan Griffin	75	50	66	40	56	40	55
Lamar Miller	58	122	77			0	73
Will Fuller	95	158	115	110	119	149	138
Demaryius Thomas	103	64	147	40	119	58	115
Alfred Blue	89	93	79				89
Jordan Akins	101	65	94	119		67	93
Jordan Thomas	111	110	154	119		40	137
DeAndre Carter	115	102	84	119			102
Bruce Ellington	59	152	88		40	119	117
Team Total	101	110	103	68	98	101	103

2018 Rushing Recap & 2019 Outlook

Calling the Texans' running back group disappointing would be an understatement. **Lamar Miller**'s 2018 yards-per-carry average looks reasonable on paper at 4.6, but he ranked 52nd in Early Down Success Rate and 50th in overall success.

Texans backs also ranked dead last in the league in both rushing Success Rate in the red zone (28%) and yards per carry (1.5) inside opponents' 20-yard line. The red zone should be the easiest area on the field to run the ball, yet the Texans weren't even close to league average (50%) in red-zone rushing success.

Yards per Carry by Direction

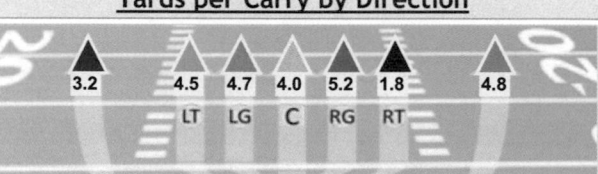

	LT	LG	C	RG	RT	
	3.2	4.5	4.7	4.0	5.2	1.8	4.8

Directional Run Frequency

	LT	LG	C	RG	RT	
	9%	11%	11%	30%	17%	15%	7%

Player *Min 50 Rushes	Rushes	YPC	Success %	Success Rk	Missed YPA Rk	YTS % Rk	YAS % Rk	Early Down Success %	Early Down Success Rk	TDs
Lamar Miller	216	4.6	44%	50	50	63	11	44%	52	5
Alfred Blue	151	3.4	42%	56	28	15	61	41%	58	2

develop a more aggressive first-down passing strategy.

Several other play-calling tweaks could help Houston. After a first-and-ten incompletion, the NFL average in 2018 was 61% pass on second and ten. Yet the Texans were 47% run, the seventh-highest rate in the league. Those second-and-ten runs produced an abysmal 14% Success Rate and 3.8 yards per carry. Second-and-ten passes by the Texans produced a 50% Success Rate and 10.2 yards per attempt.

O'Brien has been doing this for years. The three-year league average is 59% pass on second-and-ten plays; O'Brien went a league-high 53% run on second-and-ten plays during that time. If you eliminate fourth-quarter plays, O'Brien jumps to 62% run on second and ten. The 2018 Cowboys led the league at 63% last year but averaged 6.3 yards per carry with a 47% Success Rate. The Texans averaged 3.9 YPC with just 20% success.

Another frustration with the Texans is their usage of the same running back immediately after an explosive run. League wide over the last three years, when teams hand off to a different running back following a rush of ten or more yards, the next play averages 4.8 YPC with a 49% Success Rate. When teams hand off to the same running back who executed the original explosive play, their yards per carry fall to 4.1 and Success Rate to 43%.

(cont'd - see HOU-5)

Houston Texans Fantasy Corner

Keke Coutee was limited to six regular season games by a recurring hamstring injury as a rookie, but he was a major factor whenever on the field. Coutee played 30-plus snaps in five games including the playoffs, registering stat lines of 11/109/0, 6/51/1, 3/33/0, 5/77/0, and 11/110/1 on robust target counts of 15, 7, 5, 9, and 14. **Will Fuller** did miss the latter two games – freeing up opportunity for Coutee – but Coutee added a new dimension to Houston's offense on high-percentage quick hitters in the middle of the field, critical for **Deshaun Watson** as his pass protection struggled. As the Texans' offensive line still projects as one of the worst in the league, Coutee is one of my favorite late-round wide receiver picks in PPR leagues.

- Evan Silva

2018 Situational Usage by Player & Position

Usage Rate by Score

		Being Blown Out (14+)	Down Big (9-13)	One Score	Large Lead (9-13)	Blowout Lead (14+)
PASS	Lamar Miller	31%	10%	41%	15%	3%
	Alfred Blue	10%	20%	50%	5%	15%
	DeAndre Hopkins	15%	9%	52%	10%	15%
	Keke Coutee	27%		56%	15%	2%
	Will Fuller	7%	14%	64%	5%	10%
	Ryan Griffin	29%	12%	41%	12%	6%
	Demaryius Thomas		4%	70%	11%	15%
	Bruce Ellington	58%		42%		
	D'Onta Foreman	33%	33%	33%		
	Sammie Coates			100%		
	Total	19%	9%	53%	10%	10%
RUSH	Lamar Miller	6%	8%	57%	15%	13%
	Alfred Blue	9%	4%	58%	11%	19%
	DeAndre Hopkins	100%				
	Keke Coutee			100%		
	D'Onta Foreman	13%		88%		
	Total	8%	6%	58%	13%	15%

Share of Offensive Plays by Type

	Lamar Miller	Alfred Blue	DeAndre Hopkins	Keke Coutee	Will Fuller	Ryan Griffin	Demaryius Thomas	Bruce Ellington	D'Onta Foreman	Sammie Coates
PASS	10%	5%	40%	13%	11%	9%	7%	3%	1%	1%
RUSH	57%	40%	0%	1%					2%	
ALL	34%	23%	20%	7%	6%	4%	4%	2%	1%	0%

Positional Target Distribution vs NFL Average

		NFL Wide				Team Only			
		Left	Middle	Right	Total	Left	Middle	Right	Total
Deep	WR	33%	17%	31%	81%	32%	21%	27%	80%
	TE	5%	4%	7%	16%	5%	5%	7%	17%
	RB	1%	0%	2%	3%			2%	2%
	All	39%	22%	39%	100%	37%	26%	37%	100%
Short	WR	20%	14%	21%	55%	23%	16%	24%	63%
	TE	6%	6%	8%	20%	7%	4%	9%	20%
	RB	10%	5%	10%	25%	7%	5%	5%	16%
	All	36%	25%	39%	100%	37%	25%	38%	100%
Total		37%	24%	39%	100%	37%	25%	38%	100%

Positional Success Rates vs NFL Average

		NFL Wide				Team Only			
		Left	Middle	Right	Total	Left	Middle	Right	Total
Deep	WR	40%	49%	39%	42%	35%	65%	64%	52%
	TE	43%	54%	42%	46%	50%	50%	17%	36%
	RB	38%	33%	44%	41%			0%	0%
	All	40%	50%	40%	42%	37%	62%	50%	48%
Short	WR	55%	60%	52%	55%	54%	64%	55%	57%
	TE	55%	62%	54%	57%	47%	47%	55%	51%
	RB	47%	54%	45%	48%	43%	50%	36%	43%
	All	53%	59%	51%	54%	51%	59%	52%	53%
Total		50%	58%	49%	52%	48%	59%	52%	53%

Division History: Season Wins & 2019 Projection

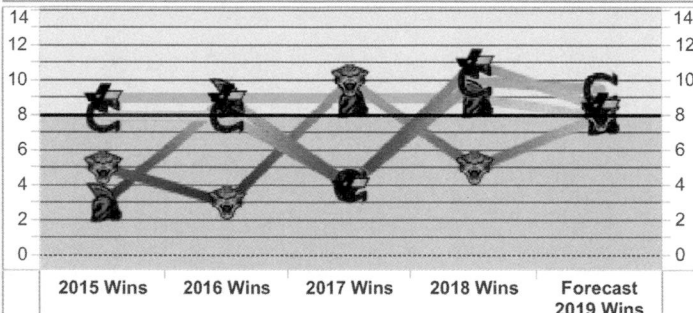

Rank of 2019 Defensive Pass Efficiency Faced by Week

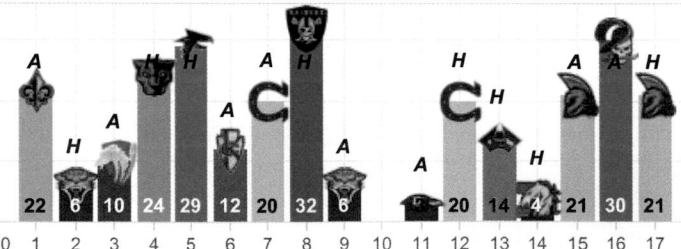

Rank of 2019 Defensive Rush Efficiency Faced by Week

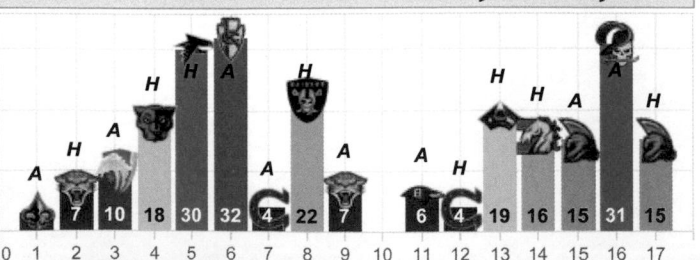

Successful Play Rate 0% ▬▬▬ 100%

Type	1-1 [3WR]	1-2 [2WR]	1-3 [1WR]	2-1 [2WR]	2-0 [3WR]	2-2 [1WR]	1-0 [4WR]	2-3 [0WR]	ALL
PASS	43% (403)	53% (192)	20% (5)	29% (7)	43% (7)	100% (1)	100% (1)		46% (616)
RUSH	44% (229)	43% (197)	44% (34)	44% (9)	50% (8)	33% (3)		0% (1)	43% (481)
All	43% (632)	48% (389)	41% (39)	38% (16)	47% (15)	50% (4)	100% (1)	0% (1)	45% (1,097)

Format Success Rate (Total # of Plays)

Receiving Success by Top-4 Personnel Groupings
(Min 50 targets)

POS	Player	1-1 [3WR]	1-2 [2WR]	1-0 [4WR]	2-1 [2WR]	4 Grp Total
TE	Ryan Griffin	36% (33) 6.8, 58.1	64% (14) 6.2, 51.8			45% (47) 6.6, 56.3
WR	DeAndre Hopkins	58% (111) 9.3, 118.3	66% (56) 9.2, 104.2		100% (1) 9.0, 104.2	61% (168) 9.3, 113.7
	Keke Coutee	45% (44) 7.1, 94.0	67% (9) 9.0, 64.6	100% (1) 5.0, 87.5		50% (54) 7.4, 89.8
	Demaryius Thomas	50% (14) 8.4, 114.3	50% (18) 8.8, 121.8			50% (32) 8.6, 118.6

Format Line 1: Success Rate (Total # of Plays) Line 2: YPA, Passer Rating

Rushing Success by Top-4 Personnel Groupings
(Min 25 carries)

Rusher (Last, First)	1-1 [3WR]	1-2 [2WR]	2-1 [2WR]	2-2 [1WR]	4 Grp Total
Miller Lamar	43% (87) 3.8	41% (106) 5.3	60% (5) 4.8	100% (1) 4.0	42% (199) 4.6
Blue Alfred	35% (66) 3.1	40% (62) 3.6	0% (2) 2.5	0% (1) 1.0	37% (131) 3.3
Watson Deshaun	58% (69) 6.9	65% (23) 5.5	50% (3) 3.5	0% (1) -1.0	59% (95) 6.4

Format Line 1: Success Rate (Total # of Plays) Line 2: YPC

Passing by Coverage Scheme

Zone	56% (258) 8.9, 103.1
M2M	52% (211) 7.8, 101.3
Screen	34% (44) 5.6, 88.2
Combo	33% (6) 3.3, 120.1

Passing by Route

Out	70% (66) 8.4, 104.2
Curl	63% (64) 7.9, 97.3
Slant	64% (47) 8.0, 106.3
Screen	29% (38) 5.9, 80.3
Dig	67% (33) 10.8, 102.8
Flat	50% (16) 4.1, 76.6

Throw Types

Level 1	53% (419) 7.4, 101.1
Level 2	64% (66) 14.1, 123.6
Level 3	17% (41) 5.8, 51.3
Shovel	67% (9) 6.1, 129.2
Sidearm	75% (4) 5.0, 127.1

QB Drop Types

3 Step	54% (267) 7.9, 104.8
0/1 Step	55% (106) 6.9, 100.1
5 Step	48% (93) 9.9, 90.1
Designed Rollout Right	61% (28) 6.2, 127.1
Basic Screen	32% (19) 5.8, 69.1
7 Step	44% (16) 12.8, 90.6

QB State at Pass

Planted	56% (385) 8.6, 105.7
Moving	54% (68) 7.9, 108.6
Shuffling	29% (59) 5.7, 72.4

Play Action

	Play Action	No P/A
Under Center	55% (62) 9.6, 106.5	54% (13) 6.8, 113.9
Shotgun	61% (57) 9.6, 112.5	50% (411) 7.7, 99.9
ALL	58% (119) 9.6, 109.3	50% (424) 7.7, 100.4

Run Types

Outside Zone	33% (126) 3.5
Inside Zone	40% (97) 2.9
Power	54% (69) 6.9
Stretch	30% (23) 3.8
Lead	33% (18) 3.3
Pitch	60% (5) 5.4

HOU-5

When the same back gets the ball for the Texans following an explosive run, they average 2.6 YPC with a 24% Success Rate. But when they hand off to a new back, that back has averaged 6.2 YPC with a 50% Success Rate. Yet 59% of the time, O'Brien has left in the original back.

Frankly, **Bill O'Brien**'s Texans are on the unintelligent end of the play-calling spectrum.

And time is running out for the Texans to compete for a championship in **Deshaun Watson**'s rookie-contract window. 7-of-12 playoff teams last season had quarterbacks on rookie deals. It gives clubs a huge roster-building edge. Watson's cheap $3-4 million cap hit will expire after the 2020 season, and the Texans have done a terrible job of protecting their young passer. After being pressured on nearly 48% of dropbacks as a 2017 rookie – most in the NFL among 42 qualified passers – Watson was again pressured on a league-high 45% of dropbacks last year.

O'Brien seems to think he knows how to "protect" Watson, which is by calling first-down runs and getting to third and manageable. O'Brien is wrong. First downs provide offenses with their easiest opportunities to pass the ball. So O'Brien is *hurting* Watson's ability to produce by running when defenses are geared up to stop the run.

O'Brien is also too predictable. Due to his league-high first-down run rate, O'Brien follows runs that gain 0-1 yards with passes on second and long at an extraordinary 80% clip. No team threw more second-and-long passes after run stuffs last season, and those predictable throws managed a 42% Success Rate. Unsuccessful second-and-long passes put Watson into too many third-and-long situations. On average, last year's Texans needed 7.8 yards to go on third downs in the first half, ranking 26th in the NFL.

For years prior to Watson, O'Brien's quarterback room was an ever-changing mess he pretended he could coach up. He collected bad quarterbacks, shipped them off, then welcomed them back in a circus-like atmosphere.

And now that he has an actual franchise quarterback, O'Brien doesn't know how to optimize his play calling to get the most out of Houston's offense. In desperate need of improving Watson's protection, the Texans were leapfrogged by the forward-thinking Eagles for prized OT **Andre Dillard** in the draft. The Texans settled for Alabama State OT **Tytus Howard** instead, then doubled down with Northern Illinois G/T **Max Scharping** in the second round. But O'Brien needs to do his share from a play-calling standpoint, especially against a brutal schedule.

Indianapolis Colts

Coaches (Prior Yrs)

Head Coach:
Frank Reich (Calls Plays) (1 yr)
Offensive Coordinator:
Nick Sirianni (1 yr)
Defensive Coordinator:
Matt Eberflus (1 yr)

EASY   HARD

2019 Forecast

Wins	Div Rank
9.5	#1

Past Records

2018: 10-6
2017: 4-12
2016: 8-8

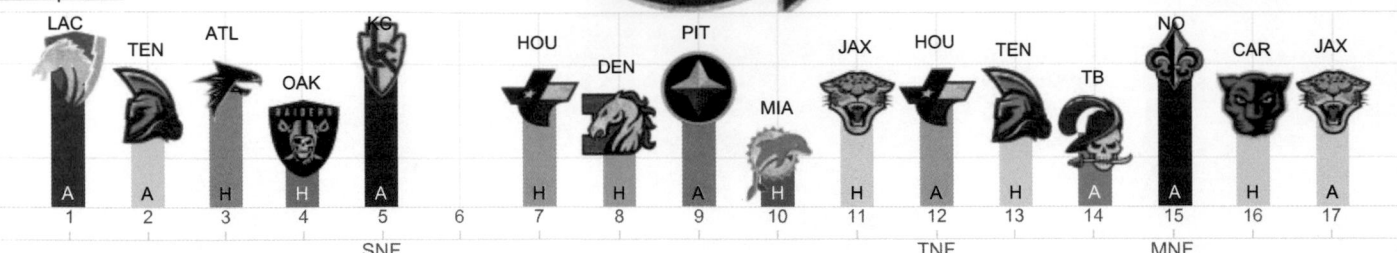

LAC	TEN	ATL	OAK	KC		HOU	DEN	PIT	MIA	JAX	HOU	TEN	TB	NO	CAR	JAX
A	A	H	H	A		H	H	A	H	H	A	H	A	A	H	A
1	2	3	4	5	6	7	8	9	10	11	12	13	14	15	16	17

SNF   TNF   MNF

Key Players Lost

Player	New
Al Woods (DT)	SEA
DeShawn Williams (DT)	DEN
Dontrelle Inman (WR)	NE
Erik Swoope (TE)	OAK
Hassan Ridgeway (DE)	PHI
J.J. Wilcox (FS)	ATL
Matt Slauson (G)	Retired
Najee Goode (OLB)	JAC
Ryan Grant (WR)	OAK

Average Line	# Games Favored	# Games Underdog
-2.5	9	5

Regular Season Wins: Past & Current Proj

Forecast 2019 Wins — 9.5
2018 Wins — 10
Forecast 2018 Wins — 6.5
2017 Wins — 4
2016 Wins — 8
2015 Wins — 8

1 3 5 7 9 11 13 15

2019 Indianapolis Colts Overview

"I wholly disapprove of what you say – and will defend to the death your right to say it."

I think back to this Voltairean principle when reflecting on a 2018 offseason brimming with **Andrew Luck** skepticism. Twitter was aflame with both real individuals and nameless eggs marching on internet Main Street, torches in hand, doubting Luck's ability to return to health following his lost 2017. Twitter didn't approve of Luck's absence from offseason workouts. It's fun to join the angry mob and find something to get really mad about online.

But it's best to form your own opinion rather than rush in with rage. I took a good, long look at Luck. I researched the 2017 Colts for their chapter in my 2018 Football Preview. They went 4-12. Public sentiment held in May through June that the Colts were trash and Luck was done.

After the Colts fired **Chuck Pagano**, they had **Josh McDaniels** in the bag. But he backed out at the last minute, on February 6. Rumors began that McDaniels knew something about Luck's recovery that the public did not. Whispers surfaced that Luck might need another surgery.

On February 7, GM **Chris Ballard** squashed the rumor mill. He stated Luck didn't need more surgery and was working on building arm speed before picking up a regulation-sized ball.

By March, questions revolved around Luck's throwing distance. In April, reports emerged that Luck had indeed begun throwing, but he did not throw at the Colts' veteran minicamp in late April. By late May, the countdown was in full force.

When Reich stated publicly on May 23 that Luck was still not throwing actual footballs, Twitter determined it'd been 507 days since Luck had done so. "He'll never come back from such a layoff," they said. Luck finally resumed throwing regulation balls on June 12, 527 days since he had last done so. But reporters noted Luck wasn't throwing difficult or high-velocity passes.

In the middle of July, Ballard confirmed publicly Luck would be all systems go for the start

*(cont'd - see **IND2**)*

Key Free Agents/ Trades Added

Player	AAV (MM)
Caraun Reid (DT)	$0.8
Devin Funchess (WR)	$10
Justin Houston (DE)	$12
Nico Siragusa (G)	$0.5
Spencer Ware (RB)	$1.3

Drafted Players

Rd	Pk	Player (College)
	34	CB - Rock Ya-Sin (Temple)
2	49	LB - Ben Banogu (TCU)
	59	WR - Parris Campbell (Ohio State)
3	89	LB - Bobby Okereke (Stanford)
4	109	S - Khari Willis (Michigan State)
5	144	S - Marvell Tell III (USC)
	164	LB - E. J. Speed (Tarleton State)
6	199	DE - Gerri Green (Mississippi State)
7	240	OT - Jackson Barton (Utah)
	246	C - Javon Patterson (Ole Miss)

Lineup & Cap Hits

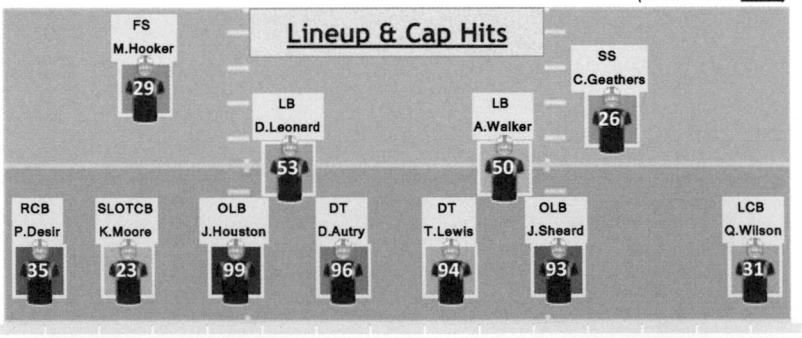

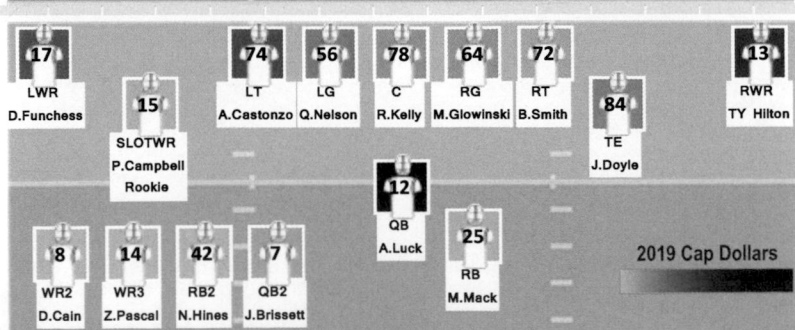

2019 Cap Dollars

2019 Unit Spending

All DEF   All OFF

Positional Spending

	Rank	Total	2017 Rk
All OFF	4	$116.70M	9
QB	5	$30.05M	7
OL	21	$33.90M	24
RB	29	$4.09M	29
WR	2	$33.40M	10
TE	3	$15.27M	4
All DEF	26	$75.11M	32
DL	19	$26.49M	17
LB	18	$19.67M	32
CB	23	$15.56M	30
S	11	$13.39M	24

116

of training camp, and his surgically repaired shoulder was pain free.

On July 29, Luck participated in the Colts' first full-padded practice of training camp. Reporters hawked him like a buzzard on fresh roadkill. He went 19-of-22, including 12-of-14 in 11-on-11 situations. Beat writers live tweeted the "event."

But through two preseason games, Luck was just 12-of-22 for 114 yards (5.2 YPA), zero touchdowns, and a pick. Twitter chimed back in. "See, we told you in April he was done!"

The world got mad online about an elite athlete trying to recover from years of shoulder problems and return to greatness. And it really was "years." Luck first injured his throwing shoulder on September 27 of 2015. He missed the first game of his career, then later suffered a kidney laceration and partially torn abdominal muscle, shutting him down for the year. Luck played all of 2016 with a torn labrum in his throwing shoulder. Post-season surgery didn't go well, and cost him all of 2017.

Warren Buffet has a legendary saying on investing: "Be fearful when others are greedy and greedy when others are fearful." Twitter was on an anti-Luck witch hunt all last offseason, and everyone wanted to be "first" with a Luck-is-done scoop to reap the retweet rewards.

I stayed quiet. I was researching. I was in X-files, "I want to believe" mode.

My first step was researching the 2017 Colts. I wanted to know why they finished 4-12 and if they were as bad as their record showed. I discovered that the 2017 Colts led nine games entering the fourth quarter but went 4-5 in them due to terribly predictable play calling. Over their first 11 games, they led entering the fourth quarter eight times, the third-highest total in the league. But they won just three of eight.

I then researched new coach **Frank Reich**'s background. And I came away confident in his coaching ability. He wouldn't blow fourth-quarter leads with bad play calls. Coming from the forward-thinking Eagles organization, Reich was too smart repeat the mistakes that got Pagano fired.

Now, I needed the best information on Luck. I researched everything I could find. The seminal moment came in late May when I discovered a picture of Luck riding his bike to the Indy 500. In a tank top, Luck looked jacked. Shoulders, biceps, traps. And keep in mind, this was in late May, when Luck still wasn't throwing a regulation football. Yet Twitter remained confident Luck would never be the same.

I wanted to compare to see how Luck looked in early summer of 2017, before missing the entire season. There weren't many photos available from that time, but thank goodness Luck is a total nerd. I stumbled onto his book club, where Luck snaps pictures of the latest books he's having the club read.

I searched back to 2017, and *jackpot.* Luck looked as thin as a rail in his April, May,

and June pictures from 2017. I could barely believe one picture from June 6 of 2017 was even actually him. He was holding an old copy of the book "Dune" and had a pencil-thin neck without any shoulder muscle. It was night and day from how rocked up Luck looked only 12 months later.

While this obviously wasn't definite proof Luck would play again let alone regain his early-career form, it did provide some evidence Luck was in a better state of rehab. *He was looking like a football player again.*

I tweeted out the pictures, and Twitter remained skeptical. "But he hasn't thrown a football." "Bicep size doesn't correlate to passing efficiency." "Luck is done."

I am thankful for the hate. Because it gave me more time to get down my bets on Colts futures. We max bet the Colts on over six wins. Then, a sportsbook operator in Las Vegas posted lines on all games from Weeks 2-16.

(cont'd - see IND-3)

2018 Passing Performance

QB	1st Dwn	2nd Dwn	3rd Dwn	
Andrew Luck	54%	54%	46%	Success Rate
	6.9	7.5	7.2	YPA
	97.8	101.1	92.8	Rating
Pass Rate	61%	58%	80%	
NFL AVG	53%	47%	36%	Success Rate
	7.7	7.3	6.9	YPA
	95.1	93.7	87.1	Rating
Pass Rate	53%	62%	80%	

2018 Rushing Performance

Offense	1st Dwn	2nd Dwn	3rd Dwn	
IND	55%	44%	54%	Success Rate
	5.0	3.8	3.8	YPC
Run Rate	39%	42%	20%	
NFL AVG	48%	46%	51%	Success Rate
	4.5	4.4	4.3	YPC
Run Rate	47%	38%	20%	

2018 Offensive Advanced Metrics

2018 Defensive Advanced Metrics

2018 Weekly EDSR & Season Trending Performance

	1	2	3	4	5	6	7	8	10	11	12	13	14	15	16	17	
RESULT	L	L	L	L	L	W	W	W	W	W	W	L	W	W	W	W	WEEK
OPP	CIN	WAS	PHI	HOU	NE	NYJ	BUF	OAK	JAC	TEN	MIA	JAC	HOU	DAL	NYG	TEN	
SITE	H	A	A	H	A	H	A	A	H	H	H	A	A	H	H	A	
MARGIN	-11	12	-4	-3	-14	-8	32	14	3	28	3	-6	3	23	1	16	
PTS	23	21	16	34	24	34	37	42	29	38	27	0	24	23	28	33	
OPP PTS	34	9	20	37	38	42	5	28	26	10	24	6	21	0	27	17	

EDSR by Wk
W=Green
L=Red

OFF/DEF EDSR
Blue=OFF (high=good)
Red=DEF (low=good)

2018 Close Game Records

All 2018 Wins: **10**

FG Games (<=3 pts) W-L: **4-1**
FG Games Win %: **80% (#4)**
FG Games Wins (% of Total Wins): **40% (#6)**

1 Score Games (<=8 pts) W-L: **4-4**
1 Score Games Win %: **50% (#15)**
1 Score Games Wins (% of Total Wins): 40% (#25)

2018 Critical & Game-Deciding Stats

TO Margin	+3
TO Given	24
INT Given	15
FUM Given	9
TO Taken	27
INT Taken	15
FUM Taken	12
Sack Margin	+20
Sacks	38
Sacks Allow	18
Return TD Margin	-4
Ret TDs	0
Ret TDs Allow	4
Penalty Margin	+11
Penalties	120
Opponent Penalties	131

Indianapolis Colts 2019 Strength of Schedule In Detail (compared to 2018)

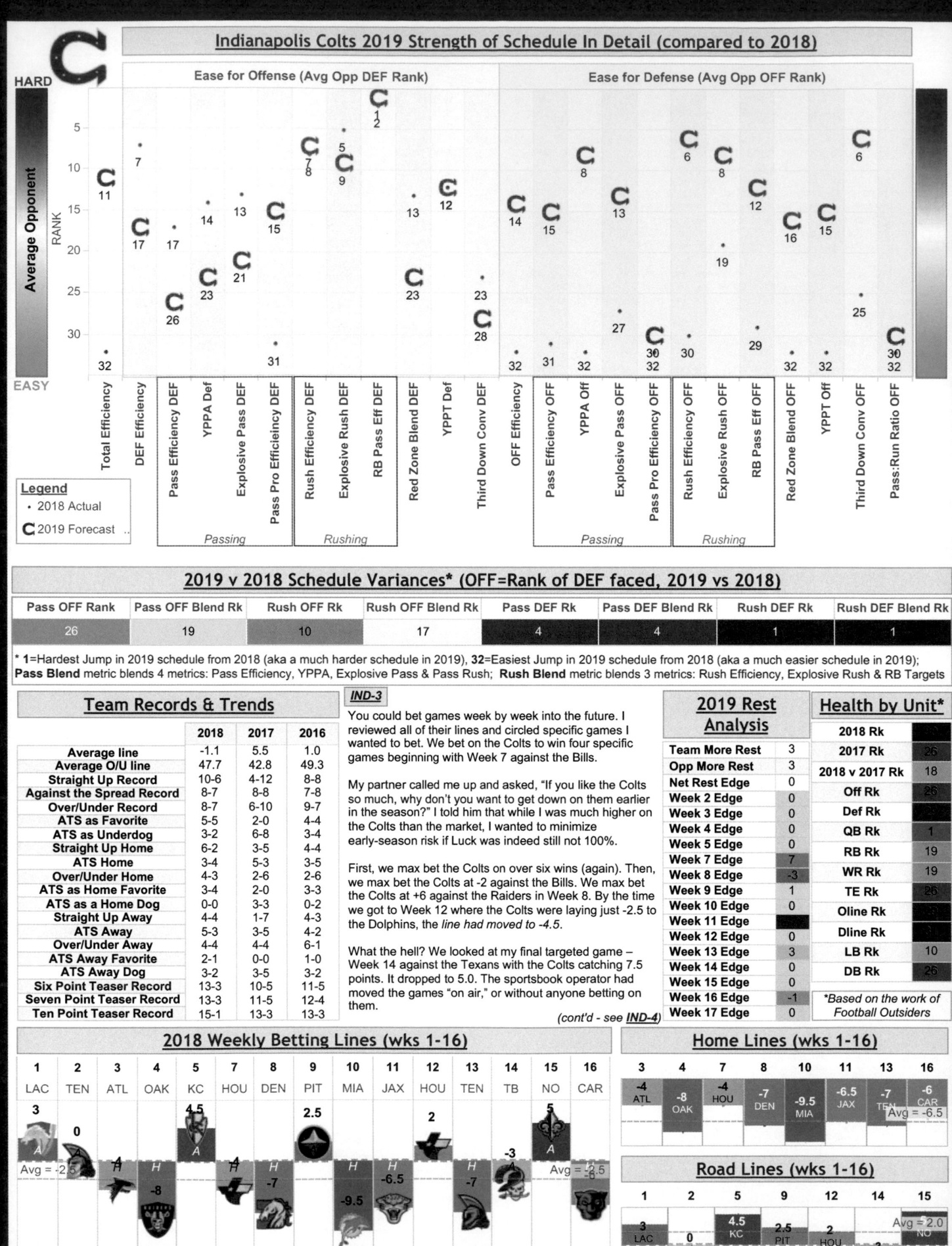

HARD / EASY — Average Opponent RANK

Legend
- 2018 Actual
- C 2019 Forecast

2019 v 2018 Schedule Variances* (OFF=Rank of DEF faced, 2019 vs 2018)

Pass OFF Rank	Pass OFF Blend Rk	Rush OFF Rk	Rush OFF Blend Rk	Pass DEF Rk	Pass DEF Blend Rk	Rush DEF Rk	Rush DEF Blend Rk
26	19	10	17	4	4	1	1

* **1**=Hardest Jump in 2019 schedule from 2018 (aka a much harder schedule in 2019), **32**=Easiest Jump in 2019 schedule from 2018 (aka a much easier schedule in 2019);
Pass Blend metric blends 4 metrics: Pass Efficiency, YPPA, Explosive Pass & Pass Rush; **Rush Blend** metric blends 3 metrics: Rush Efficiency, Explosive Rush & RB Targets

---

Team Records & Trends

	2018	2017	2016
Average line	-1.1	5.5	1.0
Average O/U line	47.7	42.8	49.3
Straight Up Record	10-6	4-12	8-8
Against the Spread Record	8-7	8-8	7-8
Over/Under Record	8-7	6-10	9-7
ATS as Favorite	5-5	2-0	4-4
ATS as Underdog	3-2	6-8	3-4
Straight Up Home	6-2	3-5	4-4
ATS Home	3-4	5-3	3-5
Over/Under Home	4-3	2-6	2-6
ATS as Home Favorite	3-4	2-0	3-3
ATS as a Home Dog	0-0	3-3	0-2
Straight Up Away	4-4	1-7	4-3
ATS Away	5-3	3-5	4-2
Over/Under Away	4-4	4-4	6-1
ATS Away Favorite	2-1	0-0	1-0
ATS Away Dog	3-2	3-5	3-2
Six Point Teaser Record	13-3	10-5	11-5
Seven Point Teaser Record	13-3	11-5	12-4
Ten Point Teaser Record	15-1	13-3	13-3

IND-3

You could bet games week by week into the future. I reviewed all of their lines and circled specific games I wanted to bet. We bet on the Colts to win four specific games beginning with Week 7 against the Bills.

My partner called me up and asked, "If you like the Colts so much, why don't you want to get down on them earlier in the season?" I told him that while I was much higher on the Colts than the market, I wanted to minimize early-season risk if Luck was indeed still not 100%.

First, we max bet the Colts on over six wins (again). Then, we max bet the Colts at -2 against the Bills. We max bet the Colts at +6 against the Raiders in Week 8. By the time we got to Week 12 where the Colts were laying just -2.5 to the Dolphins, the *line had moved to -4.5.*

What the hell? We looked at my final targeted game – Week 14 against the Texans with the Colts catching 7.5 points. It dropped to 5.0. The sportsbook operator had moved the games "on air," or without anyone betting on them.

(cont'd - see IND-4)

2019 Rest Analysis

Team More Rest	3
Opp More Rest	3
Net Rest Edge	0
Week 2 Edge	0
Week 3 Edge	0
Week 4 Edge	0
Week 5 Edge	0
Week 7 Edge	7
Week 8 Edge	-3
Week 9 Edge	1
Week 10 Edge	0
Week 11 Edge	
Week 12 Edge	0
Week 13 Edge	3
Week 14 Edge	0
Week 15 Edge	0
Week 16 Edge	-1
Week 17 Edge	0

Health by Unit*

2018 Rk	
2017 Rk	26
2018 v 2017 Rk	18
Off Rk	26
Def Rk	
QB Rk	1
RB Rk	19
WR Rk	19
TE Rk	26
Oline Rk	
Dline Rk	
LB Rk	10
DB Rk	26

*Based on the work of Football Outsiders

2018 Weekly Betting Lines (wks 1-16)

1	2	3	4	5	7	8	9	10	11	12	13	14	15	16
LAC	TEN	ATL	OAK	KC	HOU	DEN	PIT	MIA	JAX	HOU	TEN	TB	NO	CAR
3	0	-4	-8	4.5	-4	-7	2.5	-9.5	-6.5	2	-7	-3	5	-6

Avg = -2.5 ... Avg = -6

Home Lines (wks 1-16)

3	4	7	8	10	11	13	16
-4 ATL	-8 OAK	-4 HOU	-7 DEN	-9.5 MIA	-6.5 JAX	-7 TEN	-6 CAR

Avg = -6.5

Road Lines (wks 1-16)

1	2	5	9	12	14	15
3 LAC	0 TEN	4.5 KC	2.5 PIT	2 HOU	-3 TB	NO

Avg = 2.0

Indianapolis Colts 2018 Play Analysis

2018 Play Tendencies

All Pass %	62%
All Pass Rk	7
All Rush %	38%
All Rush Rk	26
1 Score Pass %	65%
1 Score Pass Rk	2
2017 1 Score Pass %	52%
2017 1 Score Pass Rk	29
2018 Pass Increase %	13%
Pass Increase Rk	1
1 Score Rush %	35%
1 Score Rush Rk	31
Up Pass %	51%
Up Pass Rk	12
Up Rush %	49%
Up Rush Rk	21
Down Pass %	73%
Down Pass Rk	5
Down Rush %	27%
Down Rush Rk	28

2018 Down & Distance Tendencies

Down	Distance	Total Plays	Pass Rate	Run Rate	Play Success %
1	Short (1-3)	6	33%	67%	67%
	Med (4-7)	14	57%	43%	79%
	Long (8-10)	349	60%	40%	52%
	XL (11+)	19	68%	32%	42%
2	Short (1-3)	47	40%	60%	60%
	Med (4-7)	91	51%	49%	53%
	Long (8-10)	108	60%	40%	43%
	XL (11+)	40	70%	30%	38%
3	Short (1-3)	58	59%	41%	64%
	Med (4-7)	55	91%	9%	49%
	Long (8-10)	31	97%	3%	48%
	XL (11+)	26	96%	4%	19%
4	Short (1-3)	6	50%	50%	67%
	Med (4-7)	1	100%	0%	0%

Shotgun %:

Under Center	Shotgun
25%	75%

37% AVG 63%

Run Rate:

Under Center	Shotgun
70%	25%

68% AVG 23%

Pass Rate:

Under Center	Shotgun
30%	75%

32% AVG 77%

Short Yardage Intelligence:

2nd and Short Run

Run Freq	Run Rk	NFL Run Freq Avg	Run 1D Rate	Run NFL 1D Avg
67%	13	65%	58%	68%

2nd and Short Pass

Pass Freq	Pass Rk	NFL Pass Freq Avg	Pass 1D Rate	Pass NFL 1D Avg
33%	19	35%	62%	56%

Most Frequent Play

Down	Distance	Play Type	Player	Total Plays	Play Success %
1	Short (1-3)	RUSH	Marlon Mack	3	33%
	Med (4-7)	RUSH	Marlon Mack	4	100%
	Long (8-10)	RUSH	Marlon Mack	79	51%
	XL (11+)	RUSH	Nyheim Hines	4	50%
2	Short (1-3)	RUSH	Marlon Mack	14	64%
	Med (4-7)	RUSH	Marlon Mack	29	48%
	Long (8-10)	RUSH	Marlon Mack	22	36%
	XL (11+)	PASS	Dontrelle Inman	5	40%
		RUSH	Andrew Luck	5	20%
3	Short (1-3)	RUSH	Marlon Mack	12	67%
	Med (4-7)	PASS	Ty Hilton	18	50%
	Long (8-10)	PASS	Eric Ebron	6	50%
	XL (11+)	PASS	Nyheim Hines	6	0%
			Ty Hilton	6	50%

Most Successful Play*

Down	Distance	Play Type	Player	Total Plays	Play Success %
1	Long (8-10)	PASS	Dontrelle Inman	15	87%
2	Short (1-3)	RUSH	Nyheim Hines	10	70%
	Med (4-7)	PASS	Ty Hilton	12	83%
	Long (8-10)	PASS	Jordan Wilkins	6	83%
	XL (11+)	PASS	Dontrelle Inman	5	40%
3	Short (1-3)	PASS	Ty Hilton	7	71%
	Med (4-7)	PASS	Ty Hilton	18	50%
	Long (8-10)	PASS	Ty Hilton	5	60%
	XL (11+)	PASS	Ty Hilton	6	50%

*Minimum 5 plays to qualify

2018 Weekly Snap Rates

Wk	Opp	Score	Ty Hilton	Eric Ebron	Chester Rogers	Ryan Grant	Zach Pascal	Nyheim Hines	Marlon Mack	Dontrelle Inman	Jack Doyle	Ryan Hewitt
1	CIN	L 34-23	80 (98%)	37 (45%)	47 (57%)	65 (79%)	10 (12%)	37 (45%)			77 (94%)	
2	WAS	W 21-9	55 (90%)	16 (26%)	26 (43%)	43 (70%)	18 (30%)	25 (41%)	18 (30%)		59 (97%)	17 (28%)
3	PHI	L 20-16	59 (100%)	52 (88%)	40 (68%)	50 (85%)	6 (10%)	43 (73%)				16 (27%)
4	HOU	L 37-34	43 (47%)	76 (84%)	73 (80%)	72 (79%)	45 (49%)	62 (68%)				14 (15%)
5	NE	L 38-24		59 (71%)	64 (77%)	68 (82%)	64 (77%)	56 (67%)				16 (19%)
6	NYJ	L 42-34		49 (71%)	46 (67%)	40 (58%)	61 (88%)	30 (43%)	24 (35%)			12 (17%)
7	BUF	W 37-5	35 (53%)	33 (50%)	36 (55%)		41 (62%)	17 (26%)	37 (56%)	42 (64%)		26 (39%)
8	OAK	W 42-28	64 (82%)	17 (22%)	39 (50%)		28 (36%)	28 (36%)	49 (63%)	58 (74%)	57 (73%)	21 (27%)
10	JAC	W 29-26	43 (77%)	21 (38%)	16 (29%)	29 (52%)	15 (27%)	20 (36%)	34 (61%)	19 (34%)	49 (88%)	
11	TEN	W 38-10	42 (68%)	25 (40%)	21 (34%)	24 (39%)	24 (39%)	16 (26%)	38 (61%)	29 (47%)	51 (82%)	
12	MIA	W 27-24	60 (87%)	49 (71%)	32 (46%)	27 (39%)	11 (16%)	26 (38%)	36 (52%)	46 (67%)	39 (57%)	
13	JAC	L 6-0	66 (87%)	58 (76%)	1 (1%)	42 (55%)	42 (55%)	45 (59%)	29 (38%)	54 (71%)		13 (17%)
14	HOU	W 24-21	54 (81%)	45 (67%)	25 (37%)	49 (73%)	35 (52%)	28 (42%)	40 (60%)			26 (39%)
15	DAL	W 23-0	41 (57%)	38 (53%)	37 (51%)	17 (24%)	49 (68%)	29 (40%)	44 (61%)	36 (50%)		9 (13%)
16	NYG	W 28-27	58 (87%)	20 (30%)	46 (69%)	28 (42%)	35 (52%)	23 (34%)	43 (64%)	39 (58%)		4 (6%)
17	TEN	W 33-17	63 (80%)	39 (49%)	46 (58%)	7 (9%)	43 (54%)	14 (18%)	53 (67%)	49 (62%)		8 (10%)
	Grand Total		763 (78%)	634 (55%)	595 (51%)	561 (56%)	527 (46%)	499 (43%)	445 (54%)	372 (59%)	332 (82%)	182 (21%)

Personnel Groupings

Personnel	Team %	NFL Avg	Succ. %
1-1 [3WR]	70%	65%	52%
1-2 [2WR]	19%	17%	52%
1-3 [1WR]	5%	3%	35%
2-1 [2WR]	3%	8%	55%
1-0 [4WR]	2%	2%	52%

Grouping Tendencies

Personnel	Pass Rate	Pass Succ. %	Run Succ. %
1-1 [3WR]	65%	52%	54%
1-2 [2WR]	56%	59%	42%
1-3 [1WR]	37%	47%	27%
2-1 [2WR]	45%	38%	69%
1-0 [4WR]	91%	48%	100%

Red Zone Targets (min 3)

Receiver	All	Inside 5	6-10	11-20
Eric Ebron	19	2	4	13
Ty Hilton	18	8	2	8
Nyheim Hines	10	2	2	6
Dontrelle Inman	7	2	2	3
Jack Doyle	7	2	2	3
Zach Pascal	7	1	1	5
Chester Rogers	6	1		5
Marlon Mack	5		3	2

Red Zone Rushes (min 3)

Rusher	All	Inside 5	6-10	11-20
Marlon Mack	37	14	9	14
Nyheim Hines	22	3	3	16
Andrew Luck	8	1	5	2
Jordan Wilkins	5	1	1	3

Early Down Target Rate

RB	TE	WR
21%	27%	53%
23%	21%	56%
	NFL AVG	

Overall Target Success %

RB	TE	WR
47%	53%	58%
#15	#20	#2

119

Indianapolis Colts 2018 Passing Recap & 2019 Outlook

Andrew Luck should experience an efficiency explosion if 2019 breaks right. The Colts draw the NFL's seventh-softest pass-defense schedule and the league's tenth-toughest schedule of defenses against the run.

Luck enjoyed an injury-free offseason for the first time in four years. He's in year two with Reich. We all know about the sophomore-quarterback breakout trend, and a similar effect could be felt by Luck. And we know about Indianapolis' receiving additions. The Colts return all five starters from last year's offensive line and also return their top-two offensive line reserves.

Andrew Luck Rating All Downs

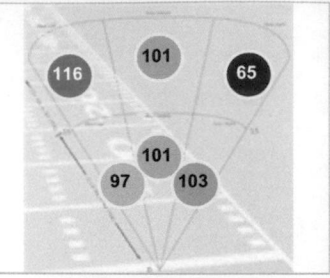

Andrew Luck Rating Early Downs

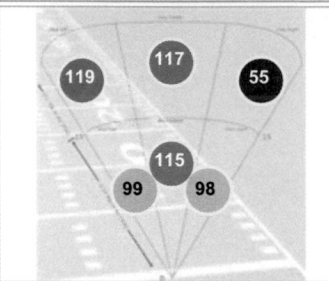

2018 Standard Passing Table

QB	Comp	Att	Comp %	Yds	YPA	TDs	INT	Sacks	Rating	Rk
Andrew Luck	467	706	66%	5,022	7.1	42	16	21	97	14
NFL Avg			62%		7.0				87.5	

2018 Advanced Passing Table

QB	Success %	EDSR Passing Success %	20+ Yd Pass Gains	20+ Yd Pass %	30+ Yd Pass Gains	30+ Yd Pass %	Avg. Air Yds per Comp	Avg. YAC per Comp	20+ Air Yd Comp	20+ Air Yd %
Andrew Luck	52%	54%	59	8.0%	17	2.0%	6.4	4.4	31	4%
NFL Avg	44%	48%	29.5	8.4%	12.5	3.7%	5.8	5.1	14.5	6%

Interception Rates by Down

Yards to Go	1st Dwn	2nd Dwn	3rd Dwn	4th Dwn	Total
1 & 2	0.0%	0.0%	0.0%	0.0%	0.0%
3, 4, 5	0.0%	2.6%	3.3%	0.0%	2.7%
6 - 9	0.0%	0.0%	2.2%	0.0%	0.8%
10 - 14	2.8%	2.5%	5.3%		3.0%
15+	0.0%	0.0%	0.0%		0.0%
Total	2.5%	1.4%	2.7%	0.0%	2.2%

3rd Down Passing - Short of Sticks Analysis

QB	Avg. Yds to Go	Avg. YIA (of Comp)	Avg Yds Short	Short of Sticks Rate	Short Rk
Andrew Luck	7.1	6.8	-0.3	55%	10
NFL Avg	7.8	6.4	-1.4	60%	

Air Yds vs YAC

Air Yds %	YAC %	Rk
59%	41%	7
53%	48%	

2018 Receiving Recap & 2019 Outlook

My biggest question mark relates to how Reich deploys personnel groupings and snaps behind **T.Y. Hilton**. Despite not seeing full run due to **Jack Doyle**'s presence in Weeks 1-2 and 8-12, **Eric Ebron** led last year's Colts in red-zone targets with Hilton one off the pace, followed by a large cluster of receivers much further down the list. Will Reich have a better handle on the Colts' most-effective offensive sets, or will he still rotate guys through on a weekly basis? I love Luck's fantasy ceiling in 2019, but it's difficult to isolate which of his pass catchers will emerge as values. Which is why Hilton is the Colts' lone wide receiver with an ADP before the 11th round. I'm intrigued by rookie **Parris Campbell** as a late-round fantasy option.

Player *Min 50 Targets	Targ	Comp %	YPA	Rating	Success %	Success Rk	Missed YPA Rk	YAS % Rk	YTS % Rk	TDs
Ty Hilton	140	61%	10.1	102.5	58%	27	86	11	97	7
Eric Ebron	125	59%	6.6	109.7	51%	64	41	88	18	11
Chester Rogers	83	75%	6.8	95.5	55%	43	76	94	13	2
Nyheim Hines	81	78%	5.2	86.5	47%	95	175	84	18	2
Ryan Grant	51	69%	6.5	84.9	59%	21	8	97	4	1
Zach Pascal	51	57%	5.5	69.2	45%	102	138	119	7	1

Directional Passer Rating Delivered

Receiver	Short Left	Short Middle	Short Right	Deep Left	Deep Middle	Deep Right	Player Total
Ty Hilton	81	60	114	131	158	65	103
Eric Ebron	130	95	120	81	69	66	110
Chester Rogers	101	100	86	110	96	40	96
Nyheim Hines	89	111	82	0		96	86
Ryan Grant	109	97	87	110	0	58	85
Zach Pascal	88	92	80	76	17	40	69
Dontrelle Inman	116	89	140	127	85	119	131
Jack Doyle	96	123	85			40	105
Marlon Mack	32	67	96				53
Jordan Wilkins	88	100	79				86
Erik Swoope	121	148	81		119	119	143
Team Total	98	99	103	105	88	72	98

2018 Rushing Recap & 2019 Outlook

Marlon Mack recorded 37 red-zone carries last year – tenth most in the NFL – and Mack barely played until Week 6. His ten rushing touchdowns on 37 red-zone runs gave Mack the NFL's third-highest rate for backs with at least 35 red-zone carries, and Mack's 62% Success Rate on red-zone rushes was second best.

Mack was shut down by the Jaguars and Texans but fared exceedingly well versus the Titans and outside the AFC South. Mack may go undervalued in fantasy drafts this year.

Player *Min 50 Rushes	Rushes	YPC	Success %	Success Rk	Missed YPA Rk	YTS % Rk	YAS % Rk	Early Down Success %	Early Down Success Rk	TDs
Marlon Mack	228	4.8	54%	12	6	31	23	52%	17	10
Nyheim Hines	88	3.8	48%	36	20	21	53	48%	29	2
Jordan Wilkins	62	5.6	58%	4	5	52	12	57%	4	1

Yards per Carry by Direction

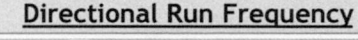

Directional Run Frequency

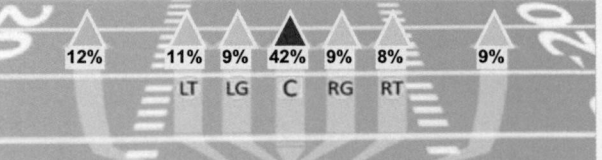

The sportsbook saw we were going hard on the Colts, and they flagged our account as "super sharp," or the highest level of risk. The book operator was alerted that Colts futures were repeatedly being smacked by a "super sharp" account on a random weekday in May. So, he moved the rest of the lines to effectively block our action. After a few phone calls and thanks to some in-place relationships, we were able to get the original lines on our two final bets.

Buffett was right about being greedy when others are fearful.

Final tally? 4-0 on the four Colts specific-game bets, and we got tremendous value on all four. Colts -2 against the Bills closed at Colts -7.5, and Indianapolis won the game 37-5. Colts +6 against the Raiders closed with Indy favored by -3.5, and they won 42-28. Colts -2.5 against the Dolphins closed at -7.5, and Indy won 24-21. And I was right about avoiding Colts early-season bets, too. Indianapolis went 1-5 straight up and 2-4 against the spread in Weeks 1-6.

But Luck definitely needed some live-game action to shake off the rust and pick up the nuances of Reich's offense. The Colts lost the Early Down Success Rate battle in each of their first five games, finishing 1-4. But from that point onward, the Colts won EDSR in every single game, propelling a 9-1 finish and first-round playoff win.

Reich is smart. The Colts were dealing with a quarterback coming off a multi-year injury, and yet on first downs in the first half, Reich passed at the third-highest rate in the NFL (60%). Coaches like **Bill O'Brien** rely on their run game on first-half first downs to "protect" their quarterback. Not Reich, whose Colts were the NFL's fourth pass-heaviest

(cont'd - see IND-5)

Indianapolis Colts Fantasy Corner

Last year's Colts offensive line dominated on the ground, where it ranked top four in Football Outsiders' Adjusted Line Yards and tackle for loss rate allowed. **Marlon Mack** capitalized, shaking off early-season hamstring woes to average 18.8 touches for 88.2 yards with ten TDs over Indy's final ten regular season games. Mack also starred in the Colts' playoff win, pouring 154 yards and a touchdown on the Texans in a 26-touch effort. He lost passing-down work to **Nyheim Hines** for most of last year, although Mack's average number of routes run spiked from 13.5 to 23.3 in Indianapolis' final four games, and he's been a capable pass catcher since college. The Colts gave Mack a vote of confidence by making journeyman **Spencer Ware** their lone significant backfield addition. Even if his receiving role remains limited, the trustworthiness of Indy's offense and Mack's scoring upside render him a fourth-round value pick.

- Evan Silva

2018 Situational Usage by Player & Position

Usage Rate by Score

		Being Blown Out (14+)	Down Big (9-13)	One Score	Large Lead (9-13)	Blowout Lead (14+)
RUSH	Marlon Mack	6%	6%	56%	5%	27%
	Nyheim Hines	19%	1%	65%	2%	13%
	Eric Ebron			100%		
	Jordan Wilkins	8%	8%	61%	5%	18%
	Chester Rogers			100%		
	Zach Pascal	33%		67%		
	Robert Turbin			100%		
	Christine Michael			100%		
	Total	9%	5%	60%	4%	21%
PASS	Marlon Mack	7%	3%	79%	3%	7%
	Nyheim Hines	10%	6%	72%	4%	7%
	Ty Hilton	10%	2%	71%	3%	14%
	Eric Ebron	14%	7%	69%		11%
	Jordan Wilkins	13%		88%		
	Chester Rogers	20%	14%	55%	2%	11%
	Dontrelle Inman	11%	6%	64%	2%	17%
	Ryan Grant	2%	10%	83%		5%
	Zach Pascal	8%	26%	55%		11%
	Jack Doyle		9%	85%	6%	
	Robert Turbin			100%		
	Total	11%	8%	70%	2%	10%

Share of Offensive Plays by Type

	Marlon Mack	Nyheim Hines	Ty Hilton	Eric Ebron	Jordan Wilkins	Chester Rogers	Dontrelle Inman	Ryan Grant	Zach Pascal	Jack Doyle	Robert Turbin	Christine Michael
RUSH	58%	23%		1%	16%	0%			1%		1%	1%
PASS	5%	12%	23%	18%	3%	12%	8%	7%	7%	6%	0%	
ALL	27%	16%	13%	11%	8%	7%	5%	4%	4%	3%	1%	0%

Positional Target Distribution vs NFL Average

		NFL Wide				Team Only			
		Left	Middle	Right	Total	Left	Middle	Right	Total
Deep	WR	33%	17%	31%	81%	28%	15%	27%	71%
	TE	6%	4%	6%	15%	2%	9%	14%	25%
	RB	1%	0%	2%	3%	3%		2%	5%
	All	39%	22%	39%	100%	33%	25%	43%	100%
Short	WR	20%	14%	21%	55%	20%	11%	22%	52%
	TE	6%	6%	8%	20%	9%	8%	8%	25%
	RB	10%	5%	10%	25%	10%	4%	8%	22%
	All	36%	25%	39%	100%	39%	23%	38%	100%
Total		37%	24%	39%	100%	38%	23%	39%	100%

Positional Success Rates vs NFL Average

		NFL Wide				Team Only			
		Left	Middle	Right	Total	Left	Middle	Right	Total
Deep	WR	39%	49%	40%	42%	58%	53%	37%	49%
	TE	44%	55%	42%	46%	50%	40%	33%	37%
	RB	41%	33%	42%	41%	0%		50%	20%
	All	40%	50%	40%	42%	53%	48%	36%	45%
Short	WR	55%	61%	52%	55%	59%	63%	58%	60%
	TE	55%	62%	54%	57%	61%	58%	55%	58%
	RB	46%	53%	46%	48%	51%	70%	33%	48%
	All	53%	59%	51%	54%	58%	63%	52%	57%
Total		50%	58%	49%	51%	57%	60%	49%	55%

Division History: Season Wins & 2019 Projection

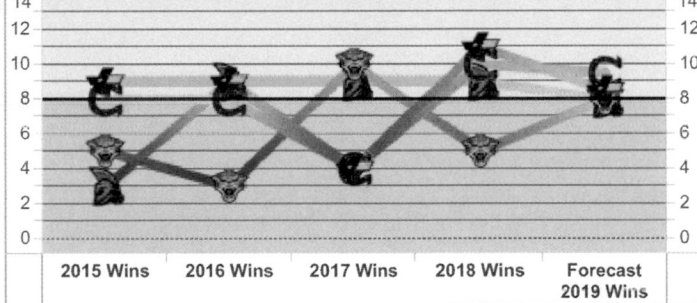

2015 Wins | 2016 Wins | 2017 Wins | 2018 Wins | Forecast 2019 Wins

Rank of 2019 Defensive Pass Efficiency Faced by Week

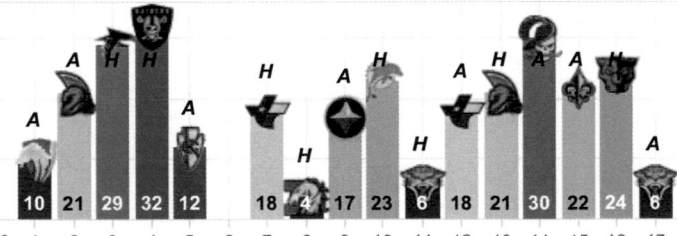

10 | 21 | 29 | 32 | 12 | | 18 | 4 | 17 | 23 | 6 | 18 | 21 | 30 | 22 | 24 | 6

0 1 2 3 4 5 6 7 8 9 10 11 12 13 14 15 16 17

Rank of 2019 Defensive Rush Efficiency Faced by Week

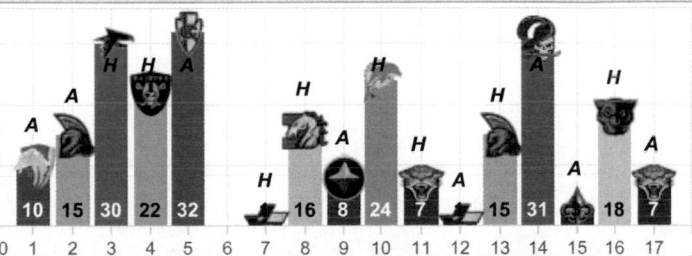

10 | 15 | 30 | 22 | 32 | | 16 | 8 | 24 | 7 | | 15 | 31 | | 18 | 7

0 1 2 3 4 5 6 7 8 9 10 11 12 13 14 15 16 17

Success by Play Type & Primary Personnel Groupings

Successful Play Rate 0% ▬▬▬ 100%

Type	1-1 [3WR]	1-2 [2WR]	1-3 [1WR]	2-1 [2WR]	1-0 [4WR]	2-2 [1WR]	0-0 [5WR]	0-1 [4WR]	ALL
PASS	51% (550)	58% (113)	48% (23)	36% (14)	50% (22)	100% (4)	0% (1)	100% (1)	52% (728)
RUSH	53% (301)	42% (95)	27% (33)	71% (17)	100% (2)	0% (4)	0% (3)	0% (1)	49% (456)
All	52% (851)	51% (208)	36% (56)	55% (31)	54% (24)	50% (8)	0% (4)	50% (2)	51% (1,184)

Format Success Rate (Total # of Plays)

Receiving Success by Top-4 Personnel Groupings
(Min 50 targets)

POS	Player	1-1 [3WR]	1-2 [2WR]	1-0 [4WR]	2-1 [2WR]	4 Grp Total
RB	Nyheim Hines	50% (64) 5.4, 91.7	40% (5) 6.4, 78.8	50% (4) 7.5, 95.8	29% (7) 2.9, 62.2	48% (80) 5.3, 90.9
TE	Eric Ebron	51% (93) 6.7, 102.4	57% (23) 7.6, 127.5		33% (3) 3.3, 43.8	51% (119) 6.7, 106.5
WR	T.Y. Hilton	57% (102) 9.5, 92.4	62% (29) 11.0, 125.6	100% (2) 16.0, 118.8		59% (133) 9.9, 100.5
	Chester Rogers	56% (78) 6.7, 90.8	50% (2) 8.5, 118.8	33% (3) 8.0, 100.0		55% (83) 6.8, 95.5
	Ryan Grant	55% (42) 6.1, 79.2	71% (7) 8.4, 101.8		100% (1) 13.0, 118.8	58% (50) 6.6, 84.5
	Zach Pascal	40% (43) 4.4, 53.4	100% (1) 15.0, 118.8	50% (4) 8.3, 78.1		42% (48) 5.0, 57.5
	Dontrelle Inman	73% (37) 8.6, 129.6	67% (3) 13.7, 118.8	50% (6) 6.7, 111.1	100% (1) 12.0, 116.7	70% (47) 8.8, 130.8

Format Line 1: Success Rate (Total # of Plays)   Line 2: YPA, Passer Rating

Rushing Success by Top-4 Personnel Groupings
(Min 25 carries)

Rusher (Last, First)	1-1 [3WR]	1-2 [2WR]	2-1 [2WR]	4 Grp Total
Mack Marlon	54% (157) 5.4	49% (51) 3.9	60% (5) 5.2	53% (213) 5.1
Hines Nyheim	49% (65) 4.0	23% (13) 1.6	60% (5) 6.4	46% (83) 3.8
Wilkins Jordan	61% (31) 5.4	45% (20) 3.6	83% (6) 15.2	58% (57) 5.8
Luck Andrew	53% (38) 5.0	13% (8) -0.3	100% (1) 4.0	47% (47) 4.1

Format Line 1: Success Rate (Total # of Plays)   Line 2: YPC

Passing by Coverage Scheme

M2M	51% (316) 6.4, 100.9
Zone	61% (248) 8.2, 100.2
Screen	50% (60) 5.8, 89.4
Combo	47% (19) 7.3, 106.9

Passing by Route

Curl	68% (106) 7.6, 94.2
Screen	45% (60) 5.6, 88.4
Out	60% (57) 7.0, 116.0
Dig	50% (50) 7.2, 55.4
Slant	45% (42) 4.7, 73.3
Flat	70% (27) 4.6, 110.5

Throw Types

Level 1	58% (479) 6.3, 98.2
Level 2	53% (158) 8.7, 107.1
Level 3	41% (37) 13.6, 101.5
Sidearm	36% (14) 4.7, 86.3
Shovel	0% (3) -1.3, 79.2

QB Drop Types

3 Step	54% (219) 7.0, 106.5
5 Step	53% (191) 7.7, 83.6
0/1 Step	57% (185) 5.9, 103.1
7 Step	65% (40) 14.3, 125.0
Basic Screen	28% (25) 5.2, 84.8
Designed Rollout Right	69% (13) 6.7, 81.3

QB State at Pass

Planted	56% (508) 7.6, 100.4
Shuffling	43% (61) 3.9, 92.0
Moving	56% (55) 6.3, 97.8

Play Action

	Play Action	No P/A
Under Center	63% (59) 12.7, 116.3	63% (19) 6.7, 122.0
Shotgun	59% (87) 7.0, 110.6	53% (530) 6.6, 95.7
ALL	60% (146) 9.3, 113.2	53% (549) 6.6, 96.6

Run Types

Inside Zone	55% (113) 3.9
Power	49% (76) 4.6
Outside Zone	39% (64) 4.8
Stretch	81% (16) 6.8
Pitch	60% (15) 8.3
Lead	71% (7) 3.4

IND-5

team on early downs combined. Reich's aggressiveness allowed for Indianapolis to face the league's second-fewest average yards to go on third-down plays (6.3). And because they were No. 6 in EDSR on the season, the Colts were great at bypassing third downs altogether.

So, the 2018 Colts were the NFL's best team at converting third downs, thanks to shorter distances needed and outstanding play calling. It's amazing, isn't it? Offense becomes *a lot* easier when you're smart on first down, bypass third down, or at very least reduce average third-down yardage to go.

Chris Ballard hiring a smart coach is no surprise. Having famously stated "the rivalry is back on" when **Josh McDaniels** walked out on him and returned to the Patriots, Ballard is as competitive as it gets, and has continued to make smart to decisions from top to bottom since signing on to reset the Colts' post-**Ryan Grigson** era.

It's tough to build a complete roster around a quarterback hitting the salary cap for as much as Luck is. He had a top-five cap cost in 2018, and it will be top three this year. The four teams with more cap space devoted to one player than Indianapolis last season went a combined 24-40. When the Colts had success on Grigson's watch (2012-2014), Luck was hitting the salary cap for only $4-6 million. Ballard built a playoff team with Luck costing $27.5 million, and *still* entered 2019 with the most available cap room in the NFL. That's not just impressive. It's voodoo.

And Ballard made significant improvements at wide receiver this offseason, signing plus-sized **Devin Funchess** away from Carolina and drafting Ohio State speedster **Parris Campbell** in the second round. Just as he was regarding touchdown-machine **Eric Ebron** at this time last year, Reich was ebullient watching Funchess' film and called him a "physical monster" with underrated route-running skills. Reich banged the table for Campbell in the draft.

Last year, the Colts went into Kansas City for their Divisional Round playoff game with Ebron, **Chester Rogers**, **Dontrelle Inman**, and **Zach Pascal** behind a banged-up **T.Y. Hilton**. Add Funchess, Campbell, and a healthy **Jack Doyle**, and this is one of the deepest pass-catcher corps in the league.

Due to the depth, Reich's 2019 personnel packaging will be fascinating to watch. During the six weeks where Doyle was healthy, Indianapolis used the NFL's third-highest rate of two-tight end 12 personnel (34%) and the third-lowest rate of three-receiver 11 on early downs. After Doyle went down, Indy's 11-personnel usage skyrocketed from third-least utilized (57%) to second most (79%) on early-down passes. Clearly, Reich adapts to the strengths and weaknesses of his personnel. Entering this year, the Colts' receiver and tight end groups are *both* strengths.

Considering Luck's shoulder issue, it's notable that his accuracy on passes to his deep right was much worse than his historical rate. In 2016, Luck averaged 16.6 yards per attempt with a 59% Success Rate on deep-right throws playing through a torn shoulder labrum. *(cont'd - see Page 246)*

Jacksonville Jaguars

Coaches (Prior Yrs)

Head Coach:
Doug Marrone (2 yrs)
Offensive Coordinator:
John DeFilippo (MIN OC) (new)
Defensive Coordinator:
Todd Wash (3 yrs)

2019 Forecast

Wins	Div Rank
8	#4

Past Records

2018: 5-11
2017: 10-6
2016: 3-13

EASY   HARD

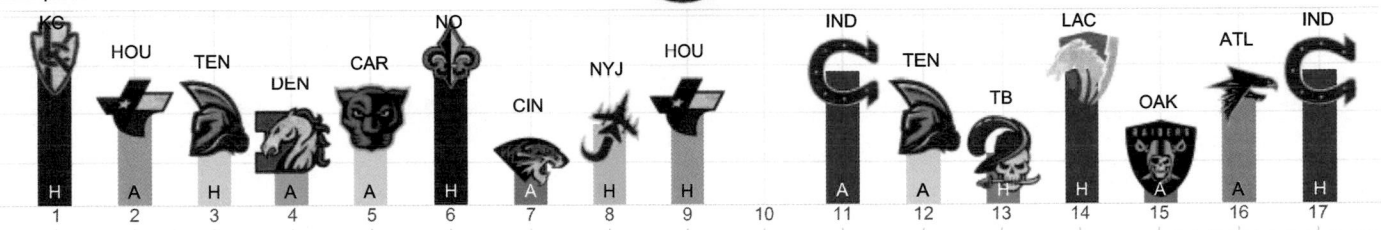

	KC	HOU	TEN	DEN	CAR	NO	CIN	NYJ	HOU		IND	TEN	TB	LAC	OAK	ATL	IND
	H	A	H	A	A	H	A	H	H		A	A	H	H	A	A	H
	1	2	3	4	5	6	7	8	9	10	11	12	13	14	15	16	17

TNF   LON

2019 Jacksonville Jaguars Overview

The 2017 Jaguars finished the regular season 10-6, grabbed a ten-point lead in the fourth quarter of the AFC Championship Game in Foxboro, and lost the game.

They regrouped, refocused, and came into 2018 to exact revenge on the Patriots in Week 2 as part of a 3-1 start. It was all downhill from there. The Jaguars lost their next three in a row by double digits as part of a seven-game losing streak, and dropped ten of their final 12 games.

The defense pointed fingers at **Blake Bortles**, and neither Bortles nor OC **Nathaniel Hackett** survived the 5-11 season. Replacing them is Philly South; ex-Eagles QBs coach **John DeFilippo** was reunited with Super Bowl 52 MVP **Nick Foles** in Jacksonville.

But Jacksonville's 2018 defense had every right to be upset. Even if the Jags couldn't repeat 2017's twin No. 1 finishes in Early Down Success Rate and defensive efficiency, they remained a top-six unit in both metrics while facing a schedule of opposing offenses that went from 2017's third softest to 2018's 11th toughest.

The Jaguars' biggest drop off came in pass rush. After a 55-sack campaign and No. 2 ranking in pass-rush efficiency, the 2018 Jags fell to 37 sacks with a 15th-place finish in pass-rush efficiency. By causing disruption, pass rush can have a trickle-down effect on turnovers. The 2017 Jaguars recorded 33 takeaways, and last year's defense just barely recorded half (17). Last year's defense remained rock solid, but losing so many sacks and turnovers really hurt.

Jacksonville's downturn in defensive dominance put more on the offense's plate, and it didn't go well. Hackett's unit plummeted from 11th in Early Down Success Rate to 31st, and 16th to 30th in offensive efficiency. Numerous offensive line injuries caused Jacksonville to drop from fifth in pass protection to 27th.

The Jaguars' 2017 offense faced the NFL's second-toughest schedule of run defenses and fourth-softest pass-defense slate. Last year's team faced the league's third-toughest

(cont'd - see JAC2)

Key Players Lost

Player	New
Austin Seferian-Jenkins (TE)	NE
Blake Bell (TE)	KC
Blake Bortles (QB)	LAR
Carlos Hyde (RB)	KC
Chris Reed (G)	MIA
Donte Moncrief (WR)	PIT
Ereck Flowers (RT)	WAS
Landry Jones (QB)	OAK
Malik Jackson (DT)	PHI
T.J. Yeldon (RB)	BUF
Tashaun Gipson (FS)	HOU

Average Line	# Games Favored	# Games Underdog
1.5	3	9

Key Free Agents/ Trades Added

Player	AAV (MM)
Alfred Blue (RB)	$0.9
Cedric Ogbuehi (LT)	$0.9
Chris Conley (WR)	$2.2
Datone Jones (DT)	$0.8
Geoff Swaim (TE)	$3.2
Jake Ryan (ILB)	$3.7
Nick Foles (QB)	$22

Drafted Players

Rd	Pk	Player (College)
1	7	DE - Josh Allen (Kentucky)
2	35	OT - Jawaan Taylor (Florida)
3	69	TE - Josh Oliver (San Jose State)
3*	98	LB - Quincy Williams (Murray State)
5	140	RB - Ryquell Armstead (Temple)
6	178	QB - Gardner Minshew (Washington State)
7	235	DT - Dontavius Russell (Auburn)

Regular Season Wins: Past & Current Proj

Forecast 2019 Wins	8
2018 Wins	5
Forecast 2018 Wins	9
2017 Wins	10
2016 Wins	3
2015 Wins	5

1 3 5 7 9 11 13 15

Lineup & Cap Hits

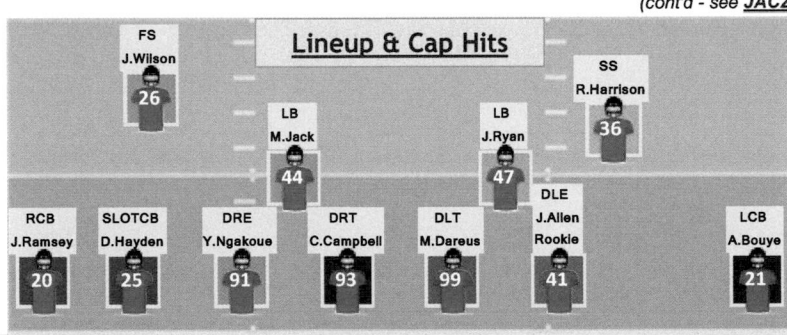

2019 Cap Dollars

2019 Unit Spending

All OFF
All DEF

Positional Spending

	Rank	Total	2017 Rk
All OFF	28	$78.46M	22
QB	21	$13.65M	23
OL	22	$33.53M	16
RB	10	$10.12M	2
WR	27	$16.01M	16
TE	26	$5.15M	21
All DEF	4	$100.10M	1
DL	13	$34.27M	2
LB	10	$24.42M	25
CB	2	$33.75M	4
S	24	$7.66M	13

run-defense schedule and 12th-friendliest pass-defense slate. Scheduling alone doesn't explain the offense's dramatic drop in performance, but it was a factor.

A larger factor was Jacksonville's offensive health. They were the league's sixth-healthiest team in 2017, then fell to sixth-most injured last year. It was the biggest shift for any NFL team. The Jaguars' offensive line lost four starters to injured reserve. Their tight ends were second most-injured in the league, and their wide receivers suffered injuries at the third-highest rate. Thus, the bulk of Jacksonville's non-quarterback passing offense was severely impacted by injuries.

Leonard Fournette only played in eight games and finished only six. As a unit, 2017 Jaguars running backs produced a 43% Success Rate and 3.8 yards per carry on early downs. Last year's Jaguars backs produced a 43% Success Rate and 3.5 YPC on early downs. On all downs, both offenses produced a 44% Success Rate. Last year's Jags were slightly worse in yards per carry, but Fournette's absence wasn't a major factor in their offensive woes.

Beyond injuries, what was the 2018 Jaguars' greatest problem? The team did go 2-6 in games decided by one score, an unfortunate record that should regress back toward the mean. Bortles deserves blame for being terrible in close games in the fourth quarter, although he was slightly *better* in such game circumstances than he was in 2017. Bortles' 2017 Success Rate was 33% and his passer rating 21.8 in fourth quarters of games within one score. His 2018 Success Rate was 33% with a 47.2 passer rating in such scenarios.

The Jaguars benched Bortles for **Cody Kessler** late in the season, but it solved nothing. And Jacksonville's pass protection only got worse; Bortles faced pressure on 36% of dropbacks, taking sacks on 18%. Kessler was pressured at a 43% rate and took sacks on 29% of his drops.

The Jaguars' sack margin plummeted from +31 to -16, a 47-sack swing that was the largest year to year over the past 30 NFL seasons. Their turnover margin sank from +10 to -12.

Early Down Success Rate is highly correlated to wins. In 2018, the 5-11 Jaguars won EDSR in just five games. The 10-6 Jags the year before won EDSR in exactly ten games. In order to win EDSR, it should be no shock the Jaguars must make better early-down play calls.

If forcing Hackett to call first-down running plays at a high frequency was forced on him by coach **Doug Marrone**, Marrone might be surprised by DeFilippo's background. As the Vikings' offensive coordinator last year, DeFilippo called the NFL's third-highest rate of passes on first down (60%) and the fifth-highest pass rate on first downs in the first half (59%). Even if Fournette comes back healthy, a higher first-down pass rate is exactly what Jacksonville needs to boost their EDSR.

2018 Passing Performance

QB	1st Dwn	2nd Dwn	3rd Dwn	
Blake Bortles	53%	42%	34%	Success Rate
	7.0	6.8	6.4	YPA
	84.5	75.7	79.9	Rating
Pass Rate	53%	60%	76%	
NFL AVG	53%	47%	36%	Success Rate
	7.7	7.3	6.9	YPA
	95.1	93.7	87.1	Rating
Pass Rate	53%	62%	80%	

2018 Rushing Performance

Offense	1st Dwn	2nd Dwn	3rd Dwn	
JAC	47%	41%	60%	Success Rate
	4.1	3.7	5.3	YPC
Run Rate	47%	40%	24%	
NFL AVG	48%	46%	51%	Success Rate
	4.5	4.4	4.3	YPC
Run Rate	47%	38%	20%	

With Fournette on the field, the 2018 Jaguars made 103 first-down play calls in first halves of games. They ran on an astonishing 67%; league average was 49%. Most run-heavy teams across the league averaged 60-62% run on first-down play calls in the first half.

The lone game in which the Jaguars consistently called first-down pass plays in the first half was in that Week 2 upset of the Patriots, although they shifted pass heavier after Fournette left early in Weeks 1 and 4. All told, Jacksonville went 3-0 in those games.

In Week 1, the Jaguars ran the ball on 8-of-12 first downs (67%) before Fournette went down, producing a 25% Success Rate and 3.0 yards per carry. Fournette left in the second quarter. In the first series without Fournette, the Jaguars passed on 3-of-4 first-down plays producing a 100% Success Rate and 12.7 yards per attempt.

*(cont'd - see **JAC-3**)*

2018 Offensive Advanced Metrics

Rank (y-axis: 1, 5, 10, 15, 20, 25, 30)

Metric	Rank
EDSR Off	31
30 & In Off	18
Red Zone Off	32
3rd Down Off	10
YPPA Off	31
YPPT Off	29
Offensive Efficiency	30
Pass Efficiency Off	30
Pass Pro Efficiency Off	27
RB Pass Eff Off	17
Rush Efficiency Off	22
Explosive Pass Off	29
Explosive Run Off	4

2018 Defensive Advanced Metrics

Rank (y-axis: 1, 5, 10, 15, 20, 25, 30)

Metric	Rank
EDSR Def	3
30 & In Def	3
Red Zone Def	7
3rd Down Def	5
YPPA Def	6
YPPT Def	22
Defensive Efficiency	6
Pass Efficiency Def	15
Pass Pro Efficiency Def	14
RB Pass Eff Def	7
Rush Efficiency Def	18
Explosive Pass Def	12
Explosive Run Def	15

2018 Weekly EDSR & Season Trending Performance

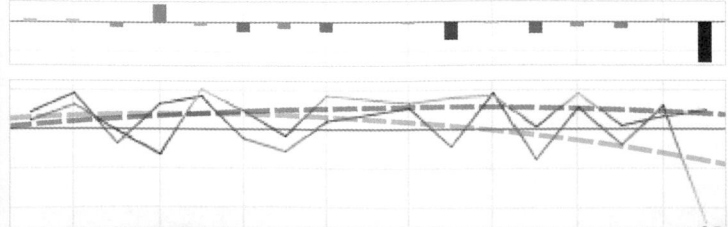

WEEK	1	2	3	4	5	6	7	8	10	11	12	13	14	15	16	17
RESULT	W	W	L	W	L	L	L	L	L	L	L	W	L	L	W	L
OPP	NYG	NE	TEN	NYJ	KC	DAL	HOU	PHI	IND	PIT	BUF	IND	TEN	WAS	MIA	HOU
SITE	A	H	H	H	A	A	H	N	A	H	A	H	A	H	A	A
MARGIN	5	11	-3	19	-16	-33	-13	-6	-3	-4	-3	6	-21	-3	10	-17
PTS	20	31	6	31	14	7	7	18	26	16	21	6	9	13	17	3
OPP PTS	15	20	9	12	30	40	20	24	29	20	24	0	30	16	7	20

EDSR by Wk
W=Green
L=Red

OFF/DEF
EDSR
Blue=OFF
(high=good)
Red=DEF
(low=good)

2018 Close Game Records

All 2018 Wins: **5**
FG Games (<=3 pts) W-L: **0-4**
FG Games Win %: **0% (#30)**
FG Games Wins (% of Total Wins): **0% (#31)**
1 Score Games (<=8 pts) W-L: **2-6**
1 Score Games Win %: **25% (#31)**
1 Score Games Wins (% of Total Wins): **40% (#25)**

2018 Critical & Game-Deciding Stats

TO Margin	-12
TO Given	29
INT Given	13
FUM Given	16
TO Taken	17
INT Taken	11
FUM Taken	6
Sack Margin	-16
Sacks	37
Sacks Allow	53
Return TD Margin	+2
Ret TDs	3
Ret TDs Allow	1
Penalty Margin	-29
Penalties	121
Opponent Penalties	92

Jacksonville Jaguars 2019 Strength of Schedule In Detail (compared to 2018)

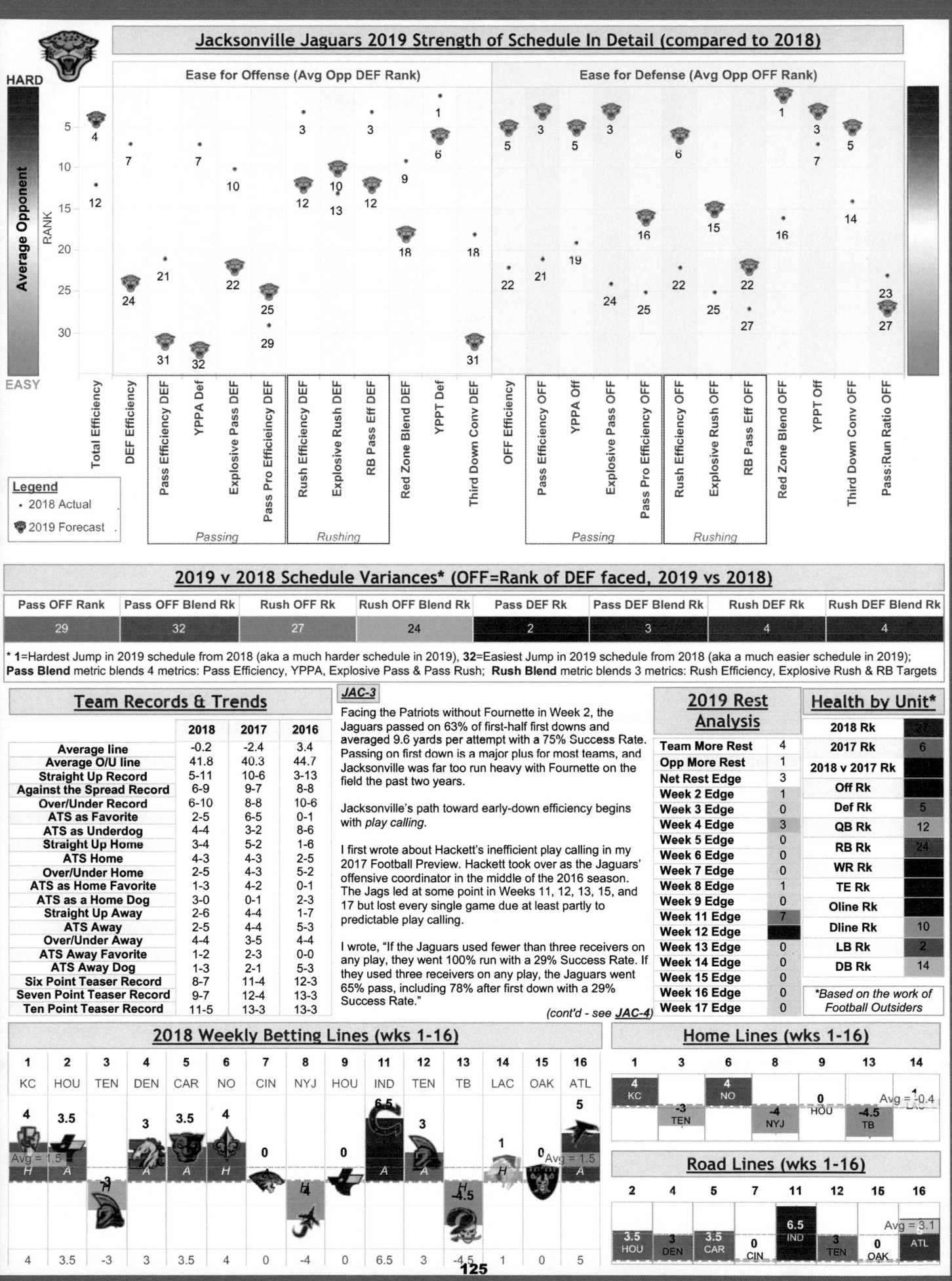

2019 v 2018 Schedule Variances* (OFF=Rank of DEF faced, 2019 vs 2018)

Pass OFF Rank	Pass OFF Blend Rk	Rush OFF Rk	Rush OFF Blend Rk	Pass DEF Rk	Pass DEF Blend Rk	Rush DEF Rk	Rush DEF Blend Rk
29	32	27	24	2	3	4	4

* **1**=Hardest Jump in 2019 schedule from 2018 (aka a much harder schedule in 2019), **32**=Easiest Jump in 2019 schedule from 2018 (aka a much easier schedule in 2019);
Pass Blend metric blends 4 metrics: Pass Efficiency, YPPA, Explosive Pass & Pass Rush; **Rush Blend** metric blends 3 metrics: Rush Efficiency, Explosive Rush & RB Targets

Team Records & Trends

	2018	2017	2016
Average line	-0.2	-2.4	3.4
Average O/U line	41.8	40.3	44.7
Straight Up Record	5-11	10-6	3-13
Against the Spread Record	6-9	9-7	8-8
Over/Under Record	6-10	8-8	10-6
ATS as Favorite	2-5	6-5	0-1
ATS as Underdog	4-4	3-2	8-6
Straight Up Home	3-4	5-2	1-6
ATS Home	4-3	4-3	2-5
Over/Under Home	2-5	4-3	5-2
ATS as Home Favorite	1-3	4-2	0-1
ATS as a Home Dog	3-0	0-1	2-3
Straight Up Away	2-6	4-4	1-7
ATS Away	2-5	4-4	5-3
Over/Under Away	4-4	3-5	4-4
ATS Away Favorite	1-2	2-3	0-0
ATS Away Dog	1-3	2-1	5-3
Six Point Teaser Record	8-7	11-4	12-3
Seven Point Teaser Record	9-7	12-4	13-3
Ten Point Teaser Record	11-5	13-3	13-3

JAC-3

Facing the Patriots without Fournette in Week 2, the Jaguars passed on 63% of first-half first downs and averaged 9.6 yards per attempt with a 75% Success Rate. Passing on first down is a major plus for most teams, and Jacksonville was far too run heavy with Fournette on the field the past two years.

Jacksonville's path toward early-down efficiency begins with *play calling*.

I first wrote about Hackett's inefficient play calling in my 2017 Football Preview. Hackett took over as the Jaguars' offensive coordinator in the middle of the 2016 season. The Jags led at some point in Weeks 11, 12, 13, 15, and 17 but lost every single game due at least partly to predictable play calling.

I wrote, "If the Jaguars used fewer than three receivers on any play, they went 100% run with a 29% Success Rate. If they used three receivers on any play, the Jaguars went 65% pass, including 78% after first down with a 29% Success Rate."

(cont'd - see JAC-4)

2019 Rest Analysis

Team More Rest	4
Opp More Rest	1
Net Rest Edge	3
Week 2 Edge	1
Week 3 Edge	0
Week 4 Edge	3
Week 5 Edge	0
Week 6 Edge	0
Week 7 Edge	0
Week 8 Edge	1
Week 9 Edge	0
Week 11 Edge	7
Week 12 Edge	
Week 13 Edge	0
Week 14 Edge	0
Week 15 Edge	0
Week 16 Edge	0
Week 17 Edge	0

Health by Unit*

2018 Rk	27
2017 Rk	6
2018 v 2017 Rk	
Off Rk	
Def Rk	5
QB Rk	12
RB Rk	24
WR Rk	
TE Rk	
Oline Rk	
Dline Rk	10
LB Rk	2
DB Rk	14

Based on the work of Football Outsiders

2018 Weekly Betting Lines (wks 1-16)

1	2	3	4	5	6	7	8	9	11	12	13	14	15	16
KC	HOU	TEN	DEN	CAR	NO	CIN	NYJ	HOU	IND	TEN	TB	LAC	OAK	ATL
4	3.5	-3	3	3.5	4	0	-4	0	6.5	3	-4.5	1	0	5

Avg = 1.5 (Home) / Avg = 1.5 (Away)

Home Lines (wks 1-16)

1	3	6	8	9	13	14
4 KC	-3 TEN	4 NO	-4 NYJ	0 HOU	-4.5 TB	

Avg = -0.4

Road Lines (wks 1-16)

2	4	5	7	11	12	15	16
3.5 HOU	3 DEN	3.5 CAR	0 CIN	6.5 IND	3 TEN	0 OAK	ATL

Avg = 3.1

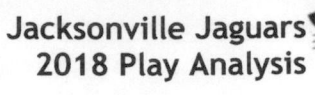

2018 Play Tendencies

All Pass %	59%
All Pass Rk	17
All Rush %	41%
All Rush Rk	16
1 Score Pass %	52%
1 Score Pass Rk	28
2017 1 Score Pass %	54%
2017 1 Score Pass Rk	24
2018 Pass Increase %	-2%
Pass Increase Rk	21
1 Score Rush %	48%
1 Score Rush Rk	5
Up Pass %	55%
Up Pass Rk	8
Up Rush %	45%
Up Rush Rk	25
Down Pass %	66%
Down Pass Rk	15
Down Rush %	34%
Down Rush Rk	18

2018 Down & Distance Tendencies

Down	Distance	Total Plays	Pass Rate	Run Rate	Play Success %
1	Short (1-3)	5	40%	60%	80%
	Med (4-7)	5	40%	60%	80%
	Long (8-10)	287	47%	53%	51%
	XL (11+)	12	58%	42%	42%
2	Short (1-3)	42	36%	64%	62%
	Med (4-7)	83	47%	53%	39%
	Long (8-10)	88	60%	40%	36%
	XL (11+)	29	79%	21%	21%
3	Short (1-3)	49	57%	43%	73%
	Med (4-7)	56	82%	18%	43%
	Long (8-10)	36	83%	17%	17%
	XL (11+)	23	87%	13%	17%
	38	1	100%	0%	0%
4	Short (1-3)	3	33%	67%	33%
	Med (4-7)	3	67%	33%	67%

Shotgun %:

Under Center	Shotgun
34%	66%

37% AVG 63%

Run Rate:

Under Center	Shotgun
70%	24%

68% AVG 23%

Pass Rate:

Under Center	Shotgun
30%	76%

32% AVG 77%

Short Yardage Intelligence:

2nd and Short Run

Run Freq	Run Rk	NFL Run Freq Avg	Run 1D Rate	Run NFL 1D Avg
65%	17	65%	64%	68%

2nd and Short Pass

Pass Freq	Pass Rk	NFL Pass Freq Avg	Pass 1D Rate	Pass NFL 1D Avg
35%	16	35%	33%	56%

Most Frequent Play

Down	Distance	Play Type	Player	Total Plays	Play Success %
1	Short (1-3)	RUSH	Leonard Fournette	2	100%
	Med (4-7)	RUSH	Leonard Fournette	3	100%
	Long (8-10)	RUSH	Leonard Fournette	59	49%
	XL (11+)	PASS	Keelan Cole	2	100%
		RUSH	Leonard Fournette	2	50%
			T.J. Yeldon	2	0%
2	Short (1-3)	RUSH	Leonard Fournette	11	73%
	Med (4-7)	RUSH	Leonard Fournette	18	33%
	Long (8-10)	RUSH	Leonard Fournette	11	9%
			T.J. Yeldon	11	18%
	XL (11+)	PASS	Dede Westbrook	4	25%
			Donte Moncrief	4	50%
			Keelan Cole	4	50%
3	Short (1-3)	RUSH	Leonard Fournette	8	88%
	Med (4-7)	PASS	Dede Westbrook	9	56%
	Long (8-10)	PASS	Dede Westbrook	6	50%
	XL (11+)	PASS	T.J. Yeldon	5	0%

Most Successful Play*

Down	Distance	Play Type	Player	Total Plays	Play Success %
1	Long (8-10)	PASS	Leonard Fournette	9	78%
2	Short (1-3)	RUSH	Leonard Fournette	11	73%
	Med (4-7)	PASS	Donte Moncrief	7	57%
	Long (8-10)	PASS	Donte Moncrief	5	60%
3	Short (1-3)	RUSH	Leonard Fournette	8	88%
	Med (4-7)	PASS	Austin Seferian-Jenkins	5	80%
	Long (8-10)	PASS	Dede Westbrook	6	50%
	XL (11+)	PASS	T.J. Yeldon	5	0%

*Minimum 5 plays to qualify

2018 Weekly Snap Rates

Wk	Opp	Score	Donte Moncrief	Dede Westbrook	Keelan Cole	T.J. Yeldon	Leonard Fournette	Austin Seferian-J..	Blake Bell	Carlos Hyde
1	NYG	W 20-15	43 (68%)	31 (49%)	47 (75%)	39 (62%)	21 (33%)	55 (87%)		
2	NE	W 31-20	51 (72%)	51 (72%)	59 (83%)	41 (58%)		60 (85%)		
3	TEN	L 9-6	48 (84%)	39 (68%)	53 (93%)	38 (67%)		47 (82%)		
4	NYJ	W 31-12	60 (78%)	57 (74%)	60 (78%)	48 (62%)	24 (31%)	36 (47%)		
5	KC	L 30-14	68 (82%)	61 (73%)	74 (89%)	77 (93%)		23 (28%)		
6	DAL	L 40-7	38 (79%)	44 (92%)	45 (94%)	31 (65%)				
7	HOU	L 20-7	55 (81%)	50 (74%)	52 (76%)	56 (82%)			22 (32%)	
8	PHI	L 24-18	56 (88%)	58 (91%)	15 (23%)	37 (58%)			32 (50%)	28 (44%)
10	IND	L 29-26	61 (81%)	60 (80%)	22 (29%)	27 (36%)	39 (52%)		27 (36%)	9 (12%)
11	PIT	L 20-16	51 (74%)	49 (71%)	16 (23%)	23 (33%)	35 (51%)		25 (36%)	11 (16%)
12	BUF	L 24-21	53 (76%)	50 (71%)	50 (71%)	24 (34%)	31 (44%)		16 (23%)	15 (21%)
13	IND	W 6-0	45 (78%)	51 (88%)	36 (62%)	35 (60%)			18 (31%)	23 (40%)
14	TEN	L 30-9	53 (75%)	65 (92%)	51 (72%)	12 (17%)	55 (77%)		23 (32%)	3 (4%)
15	WAS	L 16-13	40 (77%)	43 (83%)	39 (75%)	19 (37%)	26 (50%)		19 (37%)	
16	MIA	W 17-7	53 (79%)	52 (78%)	35 (52%)		49 (73%)		25 (37%)	16 (24%)
17	HOU	L 20-3	40 (85%)	44 (94%)	33 (70%)				14 (30%)	43 (91%)
	Grand Total		815 (79%)	805 (78%)	687 (67%)	507 (55%)	280 (52%)	221 (66%)	221 (34%)	148 (32%)

Personnel Groupings

Personnel	Team %	NFL Avg	Succ. %
1-1 [3WR]	64%	65%	42%
1-2 [2WR]	12%	17%	49%
2-1 [2WR]	9%	8%	51%
2-2 [1WR]	6%	3%	47%
1-3 [1WR]	4%	3%	45%
1-0 [4WR]	3%	2%	50%

Grouping Tendencies

Personnel	Pass Rate	Pass Succ. %	Run Succ. %
1-1 [3WR]	71%	40%	47%
1-2 [2WR]	43%	47%	51%
2-1 [2WR]	31%	74%	41%
2-2 [1WR]	11%	67%	45%
1-3 [1WR]	34%	46%	44%
1-0 [4WR]	83%	48%	60%

Red Zone Targets (min 3)

Receiver	All	Inside 5	6-10	11-20
Dede Westbrook	11		5	6
Keelan Cole	4			4
Donte Moncrief	3	1	1	1
Leonard Fournette	3	1		2
T.J. Yeldon	3	1	1	1

Red Zone Rushes (min 3)

Rusher	All	Inside 5	6-10	11-20
Leonard Fournette	22	11	3	8
T.J. Yeldon	12	2	3	7
Carlos Hyde	6	1	1	4
Blake Bortles	5		3	2
Cody Kessler	4	2		2

Early Down Target Rate

	RB	TE	WR
	28%	17%	55%
NFL AVG	23%	21%	56%

Overall Target Success %

	RB	TE	WR
	46%	49%	49%
	#16	#28	#26

Jacksonville Jaguars 2018 Passing Recap & 2019 Outlook

No offensive coordinator wants to be chained to a turnover-prone quarterback like **Blake Bortles**. But the Jags took leads in many games with Bortles at the helm, then blew them for reasons other than him.

Fortunately for new OC **John DeFilippo**, the Jaguars have belief in their new quarterback. Said DE **Calais Campbell** of Nick Foles, "He won a Super Bowl MVP, but really what he brings is that confidence. He's a natural leader. What he can do throwing the ball is great, but it's what he does for the actual overall team, giving us more confidence and belief."

Especially after the Jaguars' defense was so often at odds with last year's offense, hearing a team leader like Campbell offer up such effusive praise for Foles is certainly noteworthy.

2018 Standard Passing Table

QB	Comp	Att	Comp %	Yds	YPA	TDs	INT	Sacks	Rating	Rk
Blake Bortles	243	403	60%	2,711	6.7	13	11	31	80	40
NFL Avg			62%		7.0				87.5	

2018 Advanced Passing Table

QB	Success %	EDSR Passing Success %	20+ Yd Pass Gains	20+ Yd Pass %	30+ Yd Pass Gains	30+ Yd Pass %	Avg. Air Yds per Comp	Avg. YAC per Comp	20+ Air Yd Comp	20+ Air Yd %
Blake Bortles	44%	48%	36	9.0%	12	3.0%	5.1	6.1	13	3%
NFL Avg	44%	48%	29.5	8.4%	12.5	3.7%	5.8	5.1	14.5	6%

Interception Rates by Down

Yards to Go	1st Dwn	2nd Dwn	3rd Dwn	4th Dwn	Total
1 & 2	0.0%	0.0%	0.0%	0.0%	0.0%
3, 4, 5	0.0%	3.4%	0.0%	0.0%	1.4%
6 - 9	0.0%	2.4%	0.0%		1.4%
10 - 14	3.4%	3.7%	3.0%	0.0%	3.4%
15+	0.0%	8.3%	0.0%		3.7%
Total	**3.2%**	**3.4%**	**0.8%**	**0.0%**	**2.5%**

3rd Down Passing - Short of Sticks Analysis

QB	Avg. Yds to Go	Avg. YIA (of Comp)	Avg Yds Short	Short of Sticks Rate	Short Rk
Blake Bortles	7.2	5.0	-2.3	63%	31
NFL Avg	7.8	6.4	-1.4	60%	

Air Yds vs YAC

Air Yds %	YAC %	Rk
45%	55%	45
53%	48%	

Blake Bortles Rating All Downs

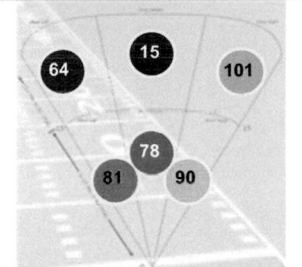

Blake Bortles Rating Early Downs

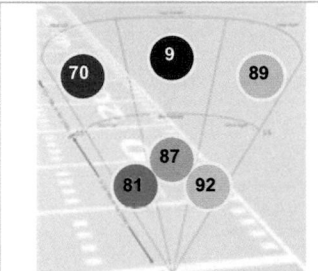

2018 Receiving Recap & 2019 Outlook

The Jaguars have a diverse receiving room that isn't well known on account of the team's run-first philosophy and poor quarterback play.

Nick Foles' solid deep ball should give this position group some life. In 2017, **Keelan Cole** ranked No. 2 in yards per target in early downs (12.2) ahead of more recognizable studs **JuJu Smith-Schuster**, **Tyreek Hill**, and **Chris Godwin**. Cole's productivity and playing time fell due to ball-security issues in 2018, but he still led all Jaguars receivers in yards per target (7.8). One overlooked offseason addition could be **Terrelle Pryor**.

Player *Min 50 Targets	Targ	Comp %	YPA	Rating	Success %	Success Rk	Missed YPA Rk	YAS % Rk	YTS % Rk	TDs
Dede Westbrook	101	65%	7.1	90.2	50%	78	98	75	51	4
Donte Moncrief	90	53%	7.5	79.5	50%	78	120	26	77	3
T.J. Yeldon	77	70%	6.1	88.2	45%	102	111	125	38	2
Keelan Cole	70	54%	7.0	69.4	50%	78	57	97	7	1

Directional Passer Rating Delivered

Receiver	Short Left	Short Middle	Short Right	Deep Left	Deep Middle	Deep Right	Player Total
Dede Westbrook	105	95	97	11	104	83	90
Donte Moncrief	85	54	93	18	50	126	79
T.J. Yeldon	58	90	101				88
Keelan Cole	47	93	60	98		80	69
James O'Shaughnessy	97	75	90		0	40	56
Leonard Fournette	90	92	119				109
Austin Seferian-Jenki..	98	24	83				63
Niles Paul	119	86	95	40		119	98
Corey Grant	103	81	60	40			88
Blake Bell		65	99			40	88
Carlos Hyde		40	79				62
Jamaal Charles		56	79				70
Team Total	84	76	95	33	26	103	82

2018 Rushing Recap & 2019 Outlook

T.J. Yeldon's departure increases **Leonard Fournette**'s importance, meaning the Jaguars need to begin running Fournette in more +EV situations and avoid banging his injury-riddled body into the middle of the line on predictable run plays. After taking the Jaguars' offensive coordinator job, DeFilippo insisted Fournette will remain "a big part of the offense" and a "major reason for where our offense goes."

Incorporating Fournette on more early-down targets would help do the trick. A plenty capable receiver, Fournette averaged 8.4 yards per reception with a nearly 80% catch rate in his first two NFL seasons.

Player *Min 50 Rushes	Rushes	YPC	Success %	Success Rk	Missed YPA Rk	YTS % Rk	YAS % Rk	Early Down Success %	Early Down Success Rk	TDs
Leonard Fournette	133	3.3	47%	37	44	3	57	45%	46	5
T.J. Yeldon	104	4.0	47%	39	29	17	68	47%	34	1
Carlos Hyde	172	3.3	40%	65	35	5	64	37%	67	5

Yards per Carry by Direction

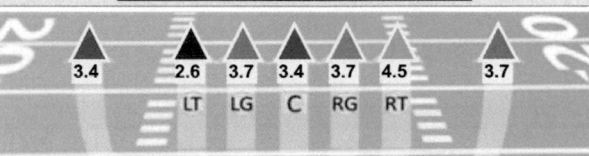

Directional Run Frequency

I urged the Jaguars to stay aggressive with a lead. That was prescient; in 2017's AFC title game, Hackett once again resorted to horribly predictable and conservative play calling with a ten-point fourth-quarter lead that cost the Jaguars a Super Bowl trip. I documented their repetitive play calling down by down in a Twitter thread. Nevertheless, Hackett stayed on as the Jaguars' offensive coordinator for 2018. He held that position until more predictable play calling cost the Jaguars a win over the Steelers.

Last Week 11, Jacksonville took a 16-0 lead over Pittsburgh. After the Steelers scored on their next drive, the Jaguars had possession leading 16-6 with 1:17 left in the third quarter. All four of Jacksonville's ensuing four drives went three and out.

On each of their four drives with a lead, every single first-down play call was a run in heavy personnel (one wide receiver) from under center into loaded boxes with the run direction going directly behind backup C **Tyler Shatley**. (Starting C **Brandon Linder** had just gone on injured reserve.) These runs averaged 1.25 yards per carry.

Hackett's four second-down play calls on these drives featured three runs, each from under center with the ball carrier running directly behind Shatley into loaded boxes. These predictable, repetitive, and unimaginative second-down rushing attempts averaged 0.0 YPC. In sum, the Jaguars unsuccessfully ran the ball on 7-of-8 early-down plays into loaded boxes behind a backup center. On their four third-down plays – all from third and long – the Jaguars went 100-percent pass from 11 personnel in shotgun and not once gained a first down.

(cont'd - see JAC-5)

Jacksonville Jaguars Fantasy Corner

Dede Westbrook emerged as Jacksonville's No. 1 receiver in his sophomore campaign, leading the team in targets (101), catches (66), yards (717), and receiving scores (5) amid horrific quarterback play. A **T.Y. Hilton** clone with 4.44 speed and vertical ability out of the slot, Westbrook gained 90% of his 2018 yards on interior routes and shined with the ball in his hands by averaging 14.0 yards per punt return with a Week 15 74-yard score. No stranger to force feeding slot receivers, **Nick Foles** targeted **Nelson Agholor** second most behind only **Zach Ertz** the past two years in Philadelphia, and **Tavon Austin** was Foles' most-targeted receiver in 11 starts for the 2015 Rams. With the Jaguars missing the NFL's third-most targets from last year's team, Westbrook has a great chance to further ascend as a third-year breakout.

- Evan Silva

2018 Situational Usage by Player & Position

Usage Rate by Score

		Being Blown Out (14+)	Down Big (9-13)	One Score	Large Lead (9-13)	Blowout Lead (14+)
RUSH	T.J. Yeldon	8%	10%	59%	13%	12%
	Leonard Fournette	9%	6%	76%	9%	
	Dede Westbrook	11%		67%	11%	11%
	Carlos Hyde	17%		71%	12%	
	Corey Grant		8%	54%	15%	23%
	Jamaal Charles	67%	17%	17%		
	Total	11%	6%	67%	11%	5%
PASS	T.J. Yeldon	15%	12%	64%	6%	3%
	Leonard Fournette	4%	13%	74%	9%	
	Dede Westbrook	17%	9%	56%	13%	5%
	Donte Moncrief	17%	9%	60%	3%	11%
	Carlos Hyde	50%	17%	33%		
	Keelan Cole	26%	4%	57%	6%	8%
	James O'Shaughnes..	21%	11%	64%	4%	
	Corey Grant			50%	25%	25%
	Austin Seferian-Jenki..			63%	32%	5%
	Jamaal Charles	67%	33%			
	Total	17%	9%	59%	9%	6%

Share of Offensive Plays by Type

	T.J. Yeldon	Leonard Fournette	Dede Westbrook	Donte Moncrief	Carlos Hyde	Keelan Cole	James O'Shaughnessy	Corey Grant	Austin Seferian-Jenkins	Jamaal Charles
RUSH	32%	41%	3%		18%			4%		2%
PASS	18%	6%	24%	18%	2%	15%	8%	3%	5%	1%
ALL	25%	23%	14%	10%	9%	8%	4%	4%	3%	1%

Positional Target Distribution vs NFL Average

		NFL Wide				Team Only			
		Left	Middle	Right	Total	Left	Middle	Right	Total
Deep	WR	33%	17%	31%	**81%**	41%	13%	33%	**87%**
	TE	5%	4%	7%	**16%**	1%	3%	7%	**11%**
	RB	1%	0%	2%	**4%**	1%			**1%**
	All	39%	22%	39%	**100%**	44%	16%	40%	**100%**
Short	WR	20%	14%	21%	**55%**	16%	12%	22%	**50%**
	TE	6%	6%	8%	**20%**	5%	7%	7%	**19%**
	RB	10%	5%	10%	**25%**	8%	9%	15%	**31%**
	All	36%	25%	39%	**100%**	29%	28%	43%	**100%**
Total		37%	24%	39%	**100%**	31%	26%	43%	**100%**

Positional Success Rates vs NFL Average

		NFL Wide				Team Only			
		Left	Middle	Right	Total	Left	Middle	Right	Total
Deep	WR	40%	49%	40%	**42%**	34%	44%	39%	**38%**
	TE	44%	54%	42%	**46%**	0%	0%	20%	**13%**
	RB	39%	33%	42%	**41%**	0%			**0%**
	All	40%	50%	40%	**43%**	32%	36%	36%	**34%**
Short	WR	55%	61%	52%	**55%**	55%	57%	51%	**54%**
	TE	55%	63%	55%	**57%**	63%	46%	48%	**51%**
	RB	47%	53%	45%	**48%**	42%	56%	41%	**45%**
	All	53%	60%	51%	**54%**	53%	54%	47%	**51%**
Total		50%	58%	49%	**52%**	48%	52%	45%	**48%**

Division History: Season Wins & 2019 Projection

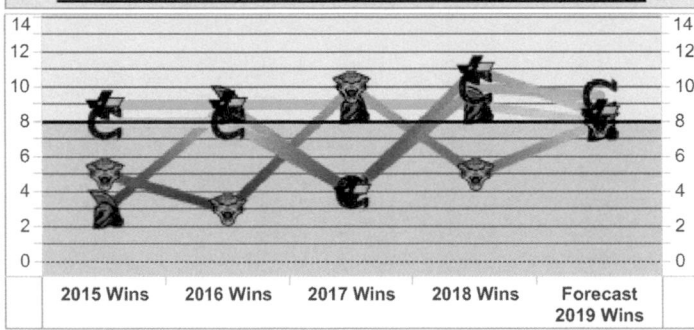

2015 Wins | 2016 Wins | 2017 Wins | 2018 Wins | Forecast 2019 Wins

Rank of 2019 Defensive Pass Efficiency Faced by Week

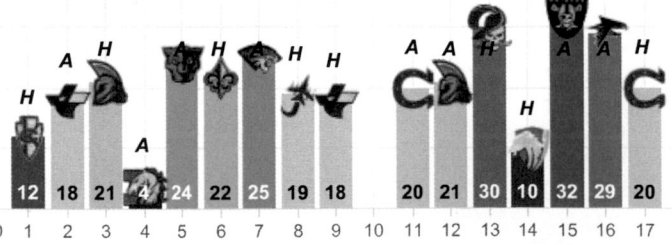

| 12 | 18 | 21 | 4 | 24 | 22 | 25 | 19 | 18 | | 20 | 21 | 30 | 10 | 32 | 29 | 20 |

0 1 2 3 4 5 6 7 8 9 10 11 12 13 14 15 16 17

Rank of 2019 Defensive Rush Efficiency Faced by Week

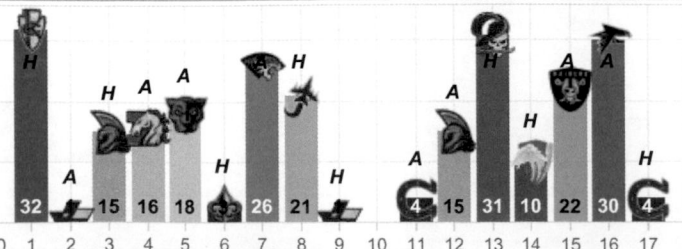

| 32 | | 15 | 16 | 18 | | 26 | 21 | | | 4 | 15 | 31 | 10 | 22 | 30 | 4 |

0 1 2 3 4 5 6 7 8 9 10 11 12 13 14 15 16 17

2018 Detailed Analytics Summary
Success by Play Type & Primary Personnel Groupings

Type	1-1 [3WR]	1-2 [2WR]	2-1 [2WR]	2-2 [1WR]	1-3 [1WR]	1-0 [4WR]	2-0 [3WR]	2-3 [0WR]	0-0 [5WR]	ALL
PASS	40% (455)	47% (51)	74% (27)	67% (6)	46% (13)	48% (25)	60% (10)		100% (1)	44% (588)
RUSH	47% (190)	51% (69)	41% (61)	45% (51)	44% (25)	60% (5)	43% (7)	20% (5)	0% (1)	46% (414)
All	42% (645)	49% (120)	51% (88)	47% (57)	45% (38)	50% (30)	53% (17)	20% (5)	50% (2)	45% (1,002)

Format Success Rate (Total # of Plays)

Receiving Success by Top-4 Personnel Groupings
(Min 50 targets)

POS	Player	1-1 [3WR]	1-2 [2WR]	2-1 [2WR]	1-0 [4WR]	4 Grp Total
RB	T.J. Yeldon	48% (60) 6.6, 100.5	29% (7) 4.6, 80.7		75% (4) 6.0, 50.0	48% (71) 6.4, 92.0
WR	Dede Westbrook	51% (87) 7.3, 92.8	33% (3) 3.0, 70.1	25% (4) 5.5, 50.0	67% (3) 3.3, 71.5	49% (97) 7.0, 89.5
	Donte Moncrief	45% (69) 8.1, 79.3	73% (11) 5.7, 86.6	60% (5) 6.6, 79.6	100% (3) 9.7, 106.9	51% (88) 7.8, 81.8
	Keelan Cole	43% (56) 6.1, 49.9	100% (5) 9.0, 104.2	100% (4) 15.5, 158.3	67% (3) 8.7, 93.8	51% (68) 7.0, 68.0

Format Line 1: Success Rate (Total # of Plays) Line 2: YPA, Passer Rating

Rushing Success by Top-4 Personnel Groupings
(Min 25 carries)

Rusher (Last, First)	1-1 [3WR]	1-2 [2WR]	2-1 [2WR]	2-2 [1WR]	4 Grp Total
Fournette Leonard	43% (40) 3.5	52% (29) 3.9	43% (28) 3.1	52% (21) 2.2	47% (118) 3.3
Yeldon T.J.	46% (54) 3.9	44% (16) 3.8	50% (12) 3.8	36% (11) 4.3	45% (93) 3.9
Bortles Blake	64% (42) 7.3	100% (4) 8.8	33% (3) 3.7	25% (4) -0.3	62% (53) 6.6
Hyde Carlos	39% (18) 3.4	45% (11) 3.0	38% (13) 2.8	45% (11) 3.8	42% (53) 3.2

Format Line 1: Success Rate (Total # of Plays) Line 2: YPC

Passing by Coverage Scheme

Zone	54% (253) 6.6, 83.7
M2M	43% (176) 7.1, 70.2
Screen	39% (41) 4.7, 76.0
Combo	63% (16) 4.1, 116.1

Passing by Route

Curl	53% (70) 6.2, 61.1
Screen	42% (43) 5.3, 78.9
Flat	49% (37) 5.0, 105.4
Out	57% (30) 5.8, 93.1
Dig	45% (29) 6.7, 41.3
Slant	50% (16) 6.8, 51.0

Throw Types

Level 1	53% (322) 6.1, 81.8
Level 2	46% (138) 6.8, 83.5
Level 3	29% (34) 10.9, 67.6
Sidearm	50% (20) 6.5, 93.5
Shovel	25% (4) 2.3, 56.3

QB Drop Types

3 Step	48% (282) 6.8, 75.5
5 Step	56% (106) 7.7, 90.9
0/1 Step	42% (65) 4.4, 65.2
7 Step	73% (22) 8.3, 101.3
Designed Rollout Right	53% (19) 4.5, 112.8
Basic Screen	42% (19) 6.4, 93.2

QB State at Pass

Planted	49% (354) 6.6, 78.0
Moving	47% (62) 6.4, 77.0
Shuffling	46% (54) 7.4, 82.1

Play Action

	Play Action	No P/A
Under Center	59% (39) 6.9, 88.4	75% (44) 7.9, 122.2
Shotgun	40% (50) 5.9, 68.5	47% (387) 6.5, 77.4
ALL	48% (89) 6.3, 77.2	50% (431) 6.6, 82.1

Run Types

Inside Zone	41% (95) 3.0
Outside Zone	49% (73) 4.5
Lead	48% (69) 3.3
Power	36% (36) 2.9
Stretch	48% (29) 4.3
Pitch	25% (4) 1.3

JAC-5

Entering that Week 11 game, the Jaguars had attempted 17 runs behind center in the second half when leading. Those runs averaged 1.7 yards per carry. In Week 11 with Linder on injured reserve, the Jaguars ran the ball *16 times* in the second half against the Steelers, with 15 of them going directly behind their backup center.

As the Jaguars failed to maintain possession and squandered their two-score lead, the Steelers came back and won. This loss occurred on Sunday, November 18. I wrote a Twitter thread on Wednesday, November 21 detailing Hackett's backbreaking play calling spliced with film cutups and statistics. I also noted how these tendencies were typical of Hackett in both 2016 and 2017.

On Monday, November 26, the Jaguars fired **Nathaniel Hackett.**

When playing with a second-half lead, the 2018 Jaguars ran the ball 59% of the time directly behind center. League average is just over 30%. And the Jags *weren't even good at running behind center*, averaging 1.7 yards per carry on 54 behind-center runs when trying to protect second-half leads. With offenses around the league becoming more creative and dynamic, the Bortles-Hackett offense stood out like a sore thumb.

I realize that when you draft a running back fourth overall, you want him to return value on your investment. And he should be able to run the ball in the fourth quarter with a lead. But last year, Fournette's 1.9 yards-per-carry average with a second-half lead ranked 68th among 69 qualified running backs. Out of 66 qualified running backs over the past three years, Fournette ranks 60th with a 35% Success Rate on fourth-quarter rushing attempts with a second-half lead.

Jaguars WLB **Telvin Smith** is taking the year off for personal reasons, and his loss is notable. Smith's absence wasn't announced until May 9, preventing the Jaguars from using free agency or the draft to replace him. Smith is one of only 13 players in NFL history to record 100-plus tackles in each of his first five seasons. He is also a critical pass-coverage linebacker.

But thanks to the Raiders' wild overdraft of **Clelin Ferrill** at No. 4 overall, Kentucky EDGE rusher **Josh Allen** fell into Jacksonville's lap at No. 7. Up front on offense, the Jaguars added Florida OT **Jawaan Taylor** at No. 35 overall.

I'm cautiously optimistic that with **Nick Foles**, a new offensive coordinator, and smarter play calling, the Jaguars will be much improved facing the NFL's second-softest schedule of pass defenses. How much that can do for the psyche and spirit of a still-elite defense may be immeasurable, but more pressure and takeaways could get this team back into the competitive ranks quickly.

Kansas City Chiefs

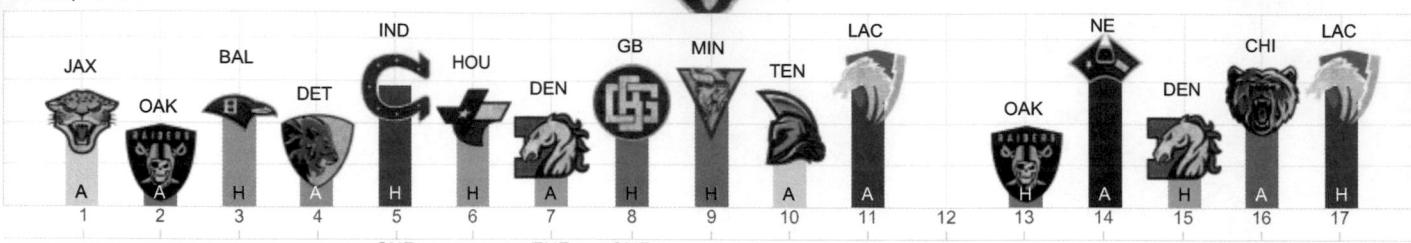

Coaches (Prior Yrs)

Head Coach:
Andy Reid (6 yrs)
Offensive Coordinator:
Eric Bieniemy (1 yr)
Defensive Coordinator:
Steve Spagnuolo (NYG DC) (new)

EASY   HARD

2019 Forecast

Wins	Div Rank
10.5	#1

Past Records

2018: 12-4
2017: 10-6
2016: 12-4

	JAX	OAK	BAL	DET	IND	HOU	DEN	GB	MIN	TEN	LAC		OAK	NE	DEN	CHI	LAC
	A	A	H	A	H	H	A	H	H	A	A		A	H	H	A	H
	1	2	3	4	5	6	7	8	9	10	11	12	13	14	15	16	17

SNF   TNF   SNF   MEX

Key Players Lost

Player	New
Chris Conley (WR)	JAC
Dee Ford (OLB)	SF
Demetrius Harris (TE)	CLE
Derrick Johnson (ILB)	Retired
E.J. Manuel (QB)	Retired
Eric Murray (CB)	CLE
Jamaal Charles (RB)	Retired
Jordan Devey (G)	OAK
Justin Houston (DE)	IND
Kareem Hunt (RB)	CLE
Martrell Spaight (ILB)	Retired
Mitch Morse (C)	BUF
Spencer Ware (RB)	IND
Steven Nelson (CB)	PIT

Average Line	# Games Favored	# Games Underdog
-5.1	13	1

2019 Kansas City Chiefs Overview

Over the last three seasons, first-and-ten passes to running backs delivered a 57% Success Rate and 76% completion rate. First-and-ten passes to wide receivers succeeded 56% of the time and were completed at a 65% rate.

On first and second downs combined, passes to running backs have a 54% Success Rate and 76% completion rate. Passes to wide receivers have a 55% Success Rate and 63% completion rate. With both types of passes producing similar Success Rates, but those to backs completed at a 13% higher rate, many smart coaches have begun to notice. Early adapters of the running back pass were **Bill Belichick** and **Sean Payton**, but it's fair to say one of the godfathers of the early-down running back pass is **Andy Reid**.

From **Brian Westbrook** to **Duce Staley** to **LeSean McCoy** with the Eagles and **Jamaal Charles** to **Spencer Ware** to **Kareem Hunt**, and now, **Damien Williams** with the Chiefs, Reid has been doing this for years.

Reid has his own unique style with regard to passes to running backs, rarely calling plays that end up in a catch by a back on second down. Kansas City is averaging an NFL-low 14% target rate to running backs on second down over the past three seasons. But on first down, Reid loves drawing them up, and he does a masterful job. Over the last three years, the Chiefs' first-down passes to backs have produced a league-leading 9.3 YPA and a fourth-ranked 64% Success Rate.

Patrick Mahomes is known most for his downfield missiles regardless of down and distance, but he also led the league in first-down passing to running backs, posting a 69% Success Rate, 10.1 YPA, and a 148.4 passer rating on such throws.

(cont'd - see KC2)

Key Free Agents/ Trades Added

Player	AAV (MM)
Alex Okafor (DE)	$6
Bashaud Breeland (CB)	$2
Carlos Hyde (RB)	$2.7
Damien Wilson (OLB)	$2.8
Darron Lee (LB)	Trade
Emmanuel Ogbah (DE)	Trade
Frank Clark (DE)	Trade
Tyrann Mathieu (FS)	$14

Drafted Players

Rd	Pk	Player (College)
2	56	WR - Mecole Hardman (Georgia)
	63	S - Juan Thornhill (Virginia)
3	84	DT - Khalen Saunders (Western Illinois)
6	201	CB - Rashad Fenton (South Carolina)
6*	214	RB - Darwin Thompson (Utah State)
7	216	G - Nick Allegretti (Illinois)

Regular Season Wins: Past & Current Proj

Forecast 2019 Wins	10.5
2018 Wins	12
Forecast 2018 Wins	8.5
2017 Wins	10
2016 Wins	12
2015 Wins	11

1 3 5 7 9 11 13 15

Lineup & Cap Hits

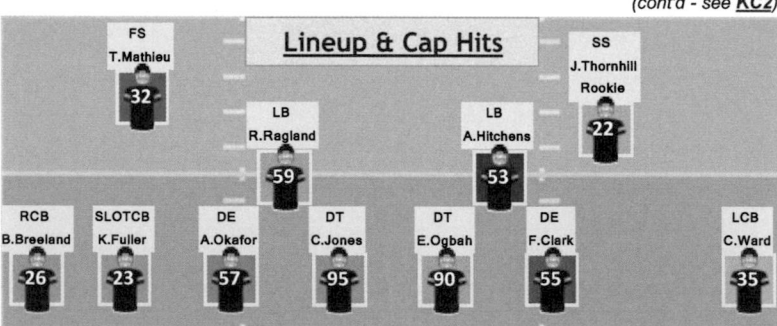

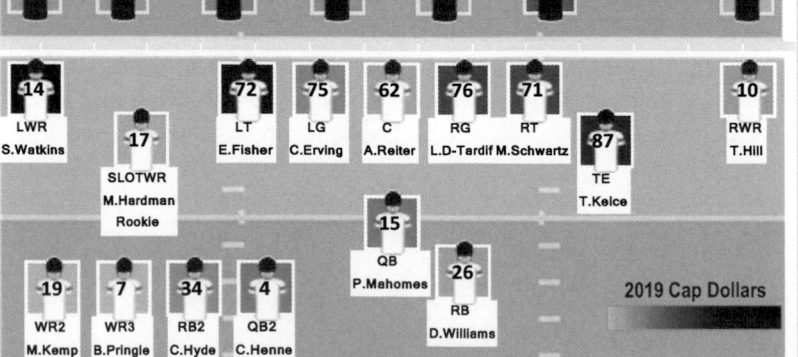

2019 Cap Dollars

2019 Unit Spending

All DEF   All OFF

Positional Spending

	Rank	Total	2017 Rk
All OFF	17	$97.21M	24
QB	25	$10.56M	28
OL	12	$39.40M	10
RB	18	$6.80M	26
WR	11	$27.93M	22
TE	5	$12.52M	5
All DEF	20	$81.94M	10
DL	21	$23.67M	28
LB	20	$18.20M	2
CB	31	$8.70M	29
S	1	$31.37M	3

In fact, despite leading the league in deep passing yards (1,804), Mahomes ranked 28th in percentage of his total passing yards through the air. That's simply amazing, and it is a credit to Reid.

Reid is going to have to work more of his magic if the Chiefs lose **Tyreek Hill**, who could be facing a suspension stemming from a legal case involving his child. Hill's impact goes beyond the catches he makes; just the threat of him opens things up for all of his teammates. Without Hill on the field, Mahomes was just two percent above league average in YPA, and Hill was on the field for all but one of the Chiefs' rushing touchdowns. That's not to say he's not also one of the most impactful players in the league when the ball comes his way. The 4.27 speedster delivered a 10.4 YPA and visited the end zone 12 times through the air.

The Chiefs began preparation for life without Hill by using their first draft pick (No. 56 overall) to take 4.33 burner **Mecole Hardman**. The former Georgia Bulldog caught only 59 passes in three years, but he operated primarily out of the slot, which is exactly where the Chiefs would likely use him while **Sammy Watkins** takes over as the No. 1 receiver and tight end **Travis Kelce** continues to wreak havoc all over the field.

The good news for the Chiefs is that Mahomes was stellar to slot receivers last year. His 57% Success Rate, 10.1 YPA, and 15 touchdowns to wide receivers in the slot were far more efficient than his numbers to receivers aligned out wide. No quarterback averaged more air yardage per attempt to slot receivers than Mahomes' mark of 12.9 last season, 3.0 yards above average.

The Chiefs made major strides offensively last year thanks to the Mahomes-Reid marriage. They improved their Early Down Success Rate from sixth to first, their offensive efficiency from fourth to first, their pass protection from 17th to fifth, and their red-zone offense from 19th to first.

Reid has always led the NFL's pass-first movement. On first downs in the first half, his Chiefs passed the ball 4% above the league average in 2016, 7% above average in 2017, and 8% above average last season. As much as it would help any offense to have Mahomes, don't doubt for even a millisecond that Reid's offense helps Mahomes as well. It also helps young players such as Hill and Kelce come into their own quickly, so it's likely to do the same for Hardman.

And of course, the main beneficiary is often the running back. Locked in as the starter, **Damien Williams** should not be overlooked early in fantasy drafts despite his lack of a substantial track record.

He has upside to surpass his RB12 average draft position.

But unless you've been residing under a rock, I don't even need to give you advanced metrics to tell you the Chiefs' offense is good. The question marks come on defense. That the defense ranked 32nd in EDSR and 26th in efficiency and yet the Chiefs still made -- and nearly won -- the AFC Championship Game is a testament to just how elite the offense truly was and is.

The 2018 defense was quite similar to the 2017 version with one major exception: a superior pass rush. The Chiefs improved from 26th in pass-rush efficiency in 2017 to seventh in 2018, and that increased pressure helped vault their pass defense from 23rd in 2017 to 12th in 2018. It also improved

(cont'd - see KC-3)

2018 Passing Performance

QB	1st Dwn	2nd Dwn	3rd Dwn	
Patrick Mahomes	53%	55%	47%	Success Rate
	8.4	8.2	9.5	YPA
	106.0	116.4	109.9	Rating
Pass Rate	61%	68%	80%	
NFL AVG	53%	47%	36%	Success Rate
	7.7	7.3	6.9	YPA
	95.1	93.7	87.1	Rating
Pass Rate	53%	62%	80%	

2018 Rushing Performance

Offense	1st Dwn	2nd Dwn	3rd Dwn	
KC	55%	61%	42%	Success Rate
	4.6	5.5	4.1	YPC
Run Rate	39%	32%	20%	
NFL AVG	48%	46%	51%	Success Rate
	4.5	4.4	4.3	YPC
Run Rate	47%	38%	20%	

2018 Offensive Advanced Metrics

Rank

Metric	Rank
EDSR Off	1
30 & In Off	5
Red Zone Off	1
3rd Down Off	4
YPPA Off	1
YPPT Off	1
Offensive Efficiency	1
Pass Efficiency Off	1
Pass Pro Efficiency Off	5
RB Pass Eff Off	1
Rush Efficiency Off	1
Explosive Pass Off	4
Explosive Run Off	26

2018 Defensive Advanced Metrics

Rank

Metric	Rank
EDSR Def	32
30 & In Def	22
Red Zone Def	32
3rd Down Def	25
YPPA Def	3
YPPT Def	26
Defensive Efficiency	12
Pass Efficiency Def	7
Pass Pro Efficiency Def	26
RB Pass Eff Def	12
Rush Efficiency Def	32
Explosive Pass Def	9
Explosive Run Def	27

2018 Weekly EDSR & Season Trending Performance

	1	2	3	4	5	6	7	8	9	10	11		13	14	15	16	17	WEEK
RESULT	W	W	W	W	W	L	W	W	W	W	L		W	W	L	L	W	
OPP	LAC	PIT	SF	DEN	JAC	NE	CIN	DEN	CLE	ARI	LA		OAK	BAL	LAC	SEA	OAK	
SITE	A	A	H	A	H	A	H	H	H	A	A		A	H	H	A	H	
MARGIN	10	5	11	4	16	-3	35	7	16	12	-3		7	3	-1	-7	32	
PTS	38	42	38	27	30	40	45	30	37	26	51		40	27	28	31	35	
OPP PTS	28	37	27	23	14	43	10	23	21	14	54		33	24	29	38	3	

EDSR by Wk
W=Green
L=Red

OFF/DEF
EDSR
Blue=OFF
(high=good)
Red=DEF
(low=good)

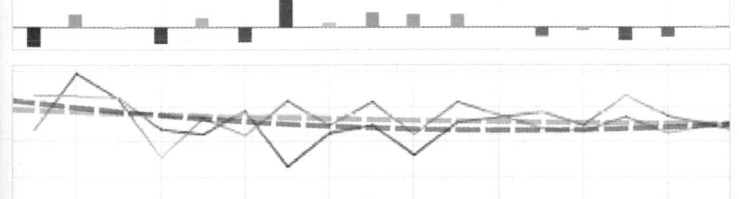

2018 Close Game Records

All 2018 Wins: **12**

FG Games (<=3 pts) W-L: **1-3**
FG Games Win %: **25% (#25)**
FG Games Wins (% of Total Wins): **8% (#29)**
1 Score Games (<=8 pts) W-L: **5-4**
1 Score Games Win %: **56% (#11)**
1 Score Games Wins (% of Total Wins): **42% (#24)**

2018 Critical & Game-Deciding Stats

TO Margin	+9
TO Given	18
INT Given	12
FUM Given	6
TO Taken	27
INT Taken	15
FUM Taken	12
Sack Margin	+27
Sacks	53
Sacks Allow	26
Return TD Margin	+3
Ret TDs	5
Ret TDs Allow	2
Penalty Margin	-30
Penalties	137
Opponent Penalties	107

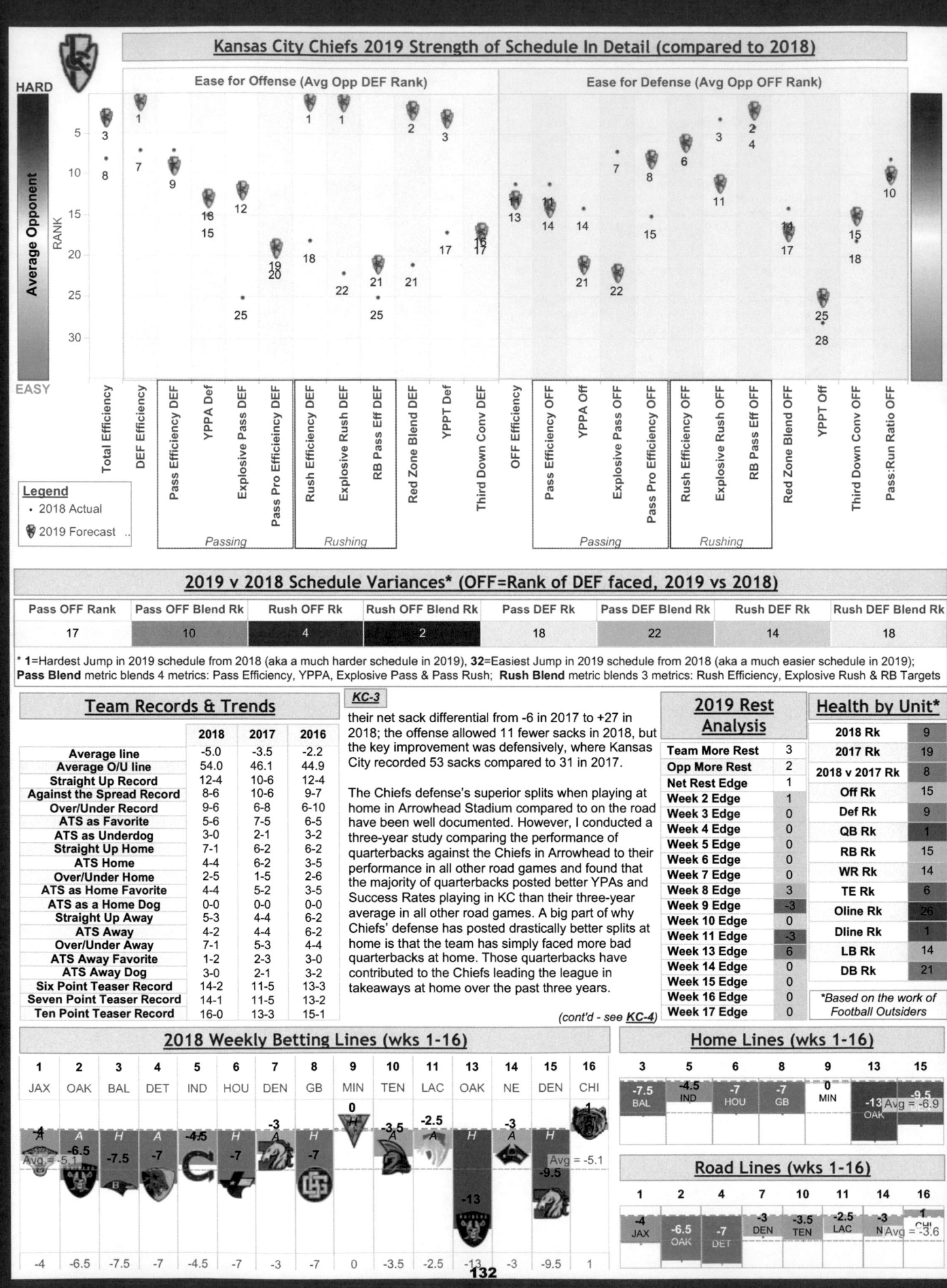

Kansas City Chiefs 2019 Strength of Schedule In Detail (compared to 2018)

HARD / **EASY** — Average Opponent — RANK

Ease for Offense (Avg Opp DEF Rank) | **Ease for Defense (Avg Opp OFF Rank)**

Categories (left to right): Total Efficiency, DEF Efficiency, Pass Efficiency DEF, YPPA Def, Explosive Pass DEF, Pass Pro Efficiency DEF *(Passing)*, Rush Efficiency DEF, Explosive Rush DEF, RB Pass Eff DEF *(Rushing)*, Red Zone Blend DEF, YPPT Def, Third Down Conv DEF, OFF Efficiency, Pass Efficiency OFF, YPPA Off, Explosive Pass OFF, Pass Pro Efficiency OFF *(Passing)*, Rush Efficiency OFF, Explosive Rush OFF, RB Pass Eff OFF *(Rushing)*, Red Zone Blend OFF, YPPT Off, Third Down Conv OFF, Pass:Run Ratio OFF

Legend
- 2018 Actual
- 2019 Forecast

2019 v 2018 Schedule Variances* (OFF=Rank of DEF faced, 2019 vs 2018)

Pass OFF Rank	Pass OFF Blend Rk	Rush OFF Rk	Rush OFF Blend Rk	Pass DEF Rk	Pass DEF Blend Rk	Rush DEF Rk	Rush DEF Blend Rk
17	10	4	2	18	22	14	18

** **1**=Hardest Jump in 2019 schedule from 2018 (aka a much harder schedule in 2019), **32**=Easiest Jump in 2019 schedule from 2018 (aka a much easier schedule in 2019);*
***Pass Blend** metric blends 4 metrics: Pass Efficiency, YPPA, Explosive Pass & Pass Rush; **Rush Blend** metric blends 3 metrics: Rush Efficiency, Explosive Rush & RB Targets*

Team Records & Trends

	2018	2017	2016
Average line	-5.0	-3.5	-2.2
Average O/U line	54.0	46.1	44.9
Straight Up Record	12-4	10-6	12-4
Against the Spread Record	8-6	10-6	9-7
Over/Under Record	9-6	6-8	6-10
ATS as Favorite	5-6	7-5	6-5
ATS as Underdog	3-0	2-1	3-2
Straight Up Home	7-1	6-2	6-2
ATS Home	4-4	6-2	3-5
Over/Under Home	2-5	1-5	2-6
ATS as Home Favorite	4-4	5-2	3-5
ATS as a Home Dog	0-0	0-0	0-0
Straight Up Away	5-3	4-4	6-2
ATS Away	4-2	4-4	6-2
Over/Under Away	7-1	5-3	4-4
ATS Away Favorite	1-2	2-3	3-0
ATS Away Dog	3-0	2-1	3-2
Six Point Teaser Record	14-2	11-5	13-3
Seven Point Teaser Record	14-1	11-5	13-2
Ten Point Teaser Record	16-0	13-3	15-1

KC-3

their net sack differential from -6 in 2017 to +27 in 2018; the offense allowed 11 fewer sacks in 2018, but the key improvement was defensively, where Kansas City recorded 53 sacks compared to 31 in 2017.

The Chiefs defense's superior splits when playing at home in Arrowhead Stadium compared to on the road have been well documented. However, I conducted a three-year study comparing the performance of quarterbacks against the Chiefs in Arrowhead to their performance in all other road games and found that the majority of quarterbacks posted better YPAs and Success Rates playing in KC than their three-year average in all other road games. A big part of why Chiefs' defense has posted drastically better splits at home is that the team has simply faced more bad quarterbacks at home. Those quarterbacks have contributed to the Chiefs leading the league in takeaways at home over the past three years.

*(cont'd - see **KC-4**)*

2019 Rest Analysis

Team More Rest	3
Opp More Rest	2
Net Rest Edge	1
Week 2 Edge	1
Week 3 Edge	0
Week 4 Edge	0
Week 5 Edge	0
Week 6 Edge	0
Week 7 Edge	0
Week 8 Edge	3
Week 9 Edge	-3
Week 10 Edge	0
Week 11 Edge	-3
Week 13 Edge	6
Week 14 Edge	0
Week 15 Edge	0
Week 16 Edge	0
Week 17 Edge	0

Health by Unit*

2018 Rk	9
2017 Rk	19
2018 v 2017 Rk	8
Off Rk	15
Def Rk	9
QB Rk	1
RB Rk	15
WR Rk	14
TE Rk	6
Oline Rk	26
Dline Rk	1
LB Rk	14
DB Rk	21

*Based on the work of Football Outsiders

2018 Weekly Betting Lines (wks 1-16)

1	2	3	4	5	6	7	8	9	10	11	13	14	15	16
JAX	OAK	BAL	DET	IND	HOU	DEN	GB	MIN	TEN	LAC	OAK	NE	DEN	CHI
-4	-6.5	-7.5	-7	-4.5	-7	-3	-7	0	-3.5	-2.5	-13	-3	-9.5	1

Avg = -5.1 (weeks 1-8) ; Avg = -5.1 (weeks 9-16)

Home Lines (wks 1-16)

3	5	6	8	9	13	15
BAL	IND	HOU	GB	MIN	OAK	DEN
-7.5	-4.5	-7	-7	0	-13	-9.5

Avg = -6.9

Road Lines (wks 1-16)

1	2	4	7	10	11	14	16
JAX	OAK	DET	DEN	TEN	LAC	NE	CHI
-4	-6.5	-7	-3	-3.5	-2.5	-3	1

Avg = -3.6

Kansas City Chiefs 2018 Play Analysis

2018 Play Tendencies

All Pass %	61%
All Pass Rk	11
All Rush %	39%
All Rush Rk	22
1 Score Pass %	64%
1 Score Pass Rk	4
2017 1 Score Pass %	60%
2017 1 Score Pass Rk	6
2018 Pass Increase %	4%
Pass Increase Rk	10
1 Score Rush %	36%
1 Score Rush Rk	29
Up Pass %	57%
Up Pass Rk	4
Up Rush %	43%
Up Rush Rk	29
Down Pass %	70%
Down Pass Rk	8
Down Rush %	30%
Down Rush Rk	25

2018 Down & Distance Tendencies

Down	Distance	Total Plays	Pass Rate	Run Rate	Play Success %
1	Short (1-3)	11	27%	73%	82%
	Med (4-7)	17	47%	53%	65%
	Long (8-10)	363	60%	40%	54%
	XL (11+)	15	73%	27%	20%
2	Short (1-3)	39	41%	59%	77%
	Med (4-7)	84	62%	38%	70%
	Long (8-10)	112	77%	23%	58%
	XL (11+)	36	89%	11%	33%
3	Short (1-3)	40	53%	48%	60%
	Med (4-7)	36	89%	11%	58%
	Long (8-10)	37	95%	5%	43%
	XL (11+)	26	92%	8%	35%
4	Short (1-3)	9	11%	89%	89%
	Med (4-7)	1	100%	0%	0%

Shotgun %:

Under Center	Shotgun
20%	80%

37% *AVG* 63%

Run Rate:

Under Center	Shotgun
68%	29%

68% *AVG* 23%

Pass Rate:

Under Center	Shotgun
32%	71%

32% *AVG* 77%

Short Yardage Intelligence:

2nd and Short Run

Run Freq	Run Rk	NFL Run Freq Avg	Run 1D Rate	Run NFL 1D Avg
58%	25	65%	81%	68%

2nd and Short Pass

Pass Freq	Pass Rk	NFL Pass Freq Avg	Pass 1D Rate	Pass NFL 1D Avg
42%	8	35%	53%	56%

Most Frequent Play

Down	Distance	Play Type	Player	Total Plays	Play Success %
1	Short (1-3)	RUSH	Kareem Hunt	5	100%
	Med (4-7)	RUSH	Patrick Mahomes	4	50%
	Long (8-10)	RUSH	Kareem Hunt	72	51%
	XL (11+)	PASS	Tyreek Hill	3	33%
2	Short (1-3)	RUSH	Kareem Hunt	13	85%
	Med (4-7)	PASS	Travis Kelce	15	67%
	Long (8-10)	PASS	Travis Kelce	17	71%
	XL (11+)	PASS	Travis Kelce	4	50%
			Tyreek Hill	4	25%
			Sammy Watkins	4	75%
			Chris Conley	4	75%
3	Short (1-3)	RUSH	Patrick Mahomes	7	100%
	Med (4-7)	PASS	Travis Kelce	11	64%
	Long (8-10)	PASS	Tyreek Hill	10	30%
	XL (11+)	PASS	Tyreek Hill	5	60%

Most Successful Play*

Down	Distance	Play Type	Player	Total Plays	Play Success %
1	Short (1-3)	RUSH	Kareem Hunt	5	100%
	Long (8-10)	PASS	Kareem Hunt	10	80%
2	Short (1-3)	RUSH	Kareem Hunt	13	85%
	Med (4-7)	RUSH	Tyreek Hill	5	80%
			Patrick Mahomes	5	80%
	Long (8-10)	RUSH	Damien Williams	8	88%
3	Short (1-3)	RUSH	Patrick Mahomes	7	100%
	Med (4-7)	PASS	Travis Kelce	11	64%
	Long (8-10)	PASS	Travis Kelce	6	83%
	XL (11+)	PASS	Tyreek Hill	5	60%

Minimum 5 plays to qualify

2018 Weekly Snap Rates

Wk	Opp	Score	Travis Kelce	Tyreek Hill	Chris Conley	Kareem Hunt	Sammy Watkins	Demarcus Robinson	Demetrius Harris	Spencer Ware	Damien Williams
1	LAC	W 38-28	56 (100%)	40 (71%)	35 (63%)	40 (71%)	51 (91%)	5 (9%)		9 (16%)	7 (13%)
2	PIT	W 42-37	57 (98%)	51 (88%)	36 (62%)	40 (69%)	47 (81%)	7 (12%)	18 (31%)	6 (10%)	9 (16%)
3	SF	W 38-27	71 (95%)	68 (91%)	49 (65%)	46 (61%)	67 (89%)	11 (15%)	25 (33%)	18 (24%)	7 (9%)
4	DEN	W 27-23	73 (94%)	70 (90%)	73 (94%)	45 (58%)	12 (15%)	45 (58%)	31 (40%)	24 (31%)	3 (4%)
5	JAC	W 30-14	66 (94%)	64 (91%)	43 (61%)	52 (74%)	60 (86%)	9 (13%)	29 (41%)	8 (11%)	2 (3%)
6	NE	L 43-40	51 (94%)	53 (98%)	38 (70%)	31 (57%)	54 (100%)	6 (11%)	16 (30%)	16 (30%)	3 (6%)
7	CIN	W 45-10	60 (86%)	52 (74%)	46 (66%)	46 (66%)	60 (86%)	11 (16%)	35 (50%)	22 (31%)	2 (3%)
8	DEN	W 30-23	55 (95%)	48 (83%)	30 (52%)	49 (84%)	55 (95%)	20 (34%)	20 (34%)	9 (16%)	
9	CLE	W 37-21	60 (95%)	61 (97%)	34 (54%)	49 (78%)	48 (76%)	18 (29%)	22 (35%)	14 (22%)	
10	ARI	W 26-14	58 (98%)	54 (92%)	54 (92%)	43 (73%)		43 (73%)	14 (24%)	20 (34%)	1 (2%)
11	LA	L 54-51	72 (100%)	69 (96%)	64 (89%)	62 (86%)	5 (7%)	35 (49%)	39 (54%)	11 (15%)	
13	OAK	W 40-33	69 (97%)	63 (89%)	65 (92%)			42 (59%)	31 (44%)	49 (69%)	19 (27%)
14	BAL	W 27-24	85 (99%)	65 (76%)	85 (99%)			56 (65%)	28 (33%)	41 (48%)	43 (50%)
15	LAC	L 29-28	60 (100%)	53 (88%)	57 (95%)			36 (60%)	18 (30%)		44 (73%)
16	SEA	L 38-31	60 (98%)	58 (95%)	57 (93%)			40 (66%)	16 (26%)		39 (64%)
17	OAK	W 35-3	40 (74%)	36 (67%)	36 (67%)			35 (65%)	29 (54%)		28 (52%)
	Grand Total		993 (95%)	905 (87%)	802 (76%)	503 (71%)	459 (73%)	419 (40%)	371 (37%)	247 (27%)	207 (25%)

Personnel Groupings

Personnel	Team %	NFL Avg	Succ. %
1-1 [3WR]	61%	65%	56%
1-2 [2WR]	26%	17%	52%
2-1 [2WR]	7%	8%	49%
2-2 [1WR]	4%	3%	38%
0-1 [4WR]	2%	1%	60%

Grouping Tendencies

Personnel	Pass Rate	Pass Succ. %	Run Succ. %
1-1 [3WR]	65%	55%	57%
1-2 [2WR]	61%	50%	55%
2-1 [2WR]	44%	53%	45%
2-2 [1WR]	24%	67%	29%
0-1 [4WR]	80%	63%	50%

Red Zone Targets (min 3)

Receiver	All	Inside 5	6-10	11-20
Travis Kelce	22	5	5	12
Tyreek Hill	10	4	2	4
Damien Williams	8	3		5
Kareem Hunt	8	2	2	4
Sammy Watkins	8		4	4
Chris Conley	7	4	2	1
Demetrius Harris	4			4
Demarcus Robinson	3	2		1

Red Zone Rushes (min 3)

Rusher	All	Inside 5	6-10	11-20
Kareem Hunt	27	11	11	5
Patrick Mahomes	16	7	3	6
Spencer Ware	12	5	3	4

Early Down Target Rate

RB	TE	WR
18%	30%	53%
23%	21%	56%
	NFL AVG	

Overall Target Success %

RB	TE	WR
61%	58%	56%
#1	#7	#7

133

Kansas City Chiefs 2018 Passing Recap & 2019 Outlook

What made Mahomes toughest to stop last year was how difficult it was to disrupt him. Of the 30 quarterbacks that were pressured on at least 30% of throws, Mahomes was sacked the least often, at 11.6%. His stats when blitzed were pristine: 82% completion rate, 9.3 YPA, 125 passer rating.

When Mahomes found himself in third down, he posted a 49% first-down rate and 9.7 YPA, both league bests.

Overall, Mahomes displayed an uncanny accuracy level despite a depth of target near the top of the league. There is no telling just how high his ceiling truly is. He is technically a third-year quarterback but played only one game as a rookie, and most quarterbacks tend to take a jump after their first full season.

2018 Standard Passing Table

QB	Comp	Att	Comp %	Yds	YPA	TDs	INT	Sacks	Rating	Rk
Patrick Mahomes	426	653	65%	5,657	8.7	53	12	33	112	5
NFL Avg			62%		7.0				87.5	

2018 Advanced Passing Table

QB	Success %	EDSR Passing Success %	20+ Yd Pass Gains	20+ Yd Pass %	30+ Yd Pass Gains	30+ Yd Pass %	Avg. Air Yds per Comp	Avg. YAC per Comp	20+ Air Yd Comp	20+ Air Yd %
Patrick Mahomes	53%	54%	85	13.0%	39	6.0%	6.4	6.9	41	6%
NFL Avg	44%	48%	29.5	8.4%	12.5	3.7%	5.8	5.1	14.5	6%

Patrick Mahomes Rating All Downs

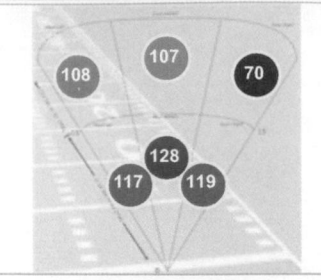

Patrick Mahomes Rating Early Downs

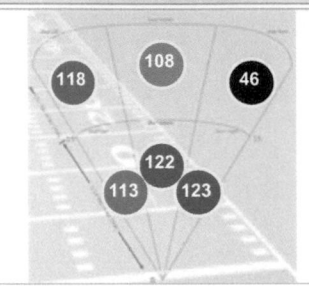

Interception Rates by Down

Yards to Go	1st Dwn	2nd Dwn	3rd Dwn	4th Dwn	Total
1 & 2	0.0%	0.0%	4.8%	0.0%	2.2%
3, 4, 5	0.0%	0.0%	0.0%	0.0%	0.0%
6 - 9	0.0%	1.6%	2.3%	0.0%	1.7%
10 - 14	2.6%	0.0%	5.6%		2.3%
15+	0.0%	0.0%	0.0%		0.0%
Total	2.3%	0.4%	2.6%	0.0%	1.7%

3rd Down Passing - Short of Sticks Analysis

QB	Avg. Yds to Go	Avg. YIA (of Comp)	Avg Yds Short	Short of Sticks Rate	Short Rk
Patrick Mahomes	7.6	9.4	0.0	49%	3
NFL Avg	7.8	6.4	-1.4	60%	

Air Yds vs YAC

Air Yds %	YAC %	Rk
48%	52%	37
53%	48%	

2018 Receiving Recap & 2019 Outlook

The biggest question mark in regard to the Chiefs' pass catchers is obviously the availability of Hill, whose speed and playmaking presence on the field causes defenses to overplay and/or tip their hand pre-snap. If Hill is not available, Hardman will be counted on to play a major role in Year 1. A key for him will be successfully running Reid's staple fly sweep plays and become a good enough route runner to create enough deception for the offense to continue to operate at peak levels. As a receiver, it's all about deception. If things go as planned, Hardman will have ample opportunity to rack up easy fantasy points.

Player *Min 50 Targets	Targ	Comp %	YPA	Rating	Success %	Success Rk	Missed YPA Rk	YAS % Rk	YTS % Rk	TDs
Travis Kelce	165	68%	8.9	110.8	62%	7	10	43	51	9
Tyreek Hill	153	63%	10.4	107.6	54%	47	94	2	126	12
Sammy Watkins	71	70%	9.8	115.6	63%	3	29	11	97	3
Chris Conley	55	58%	6.1	98.6	51%	64	39	106	12	5

Directional Passer Rating Delivered

Receiver	Short Left	Short Middle	Short Right	Deep Left	Deep Middle	Deep Right	Player Total
Travis Kelce	101	126	122	10	147	63	111
Tyreek Hill	127	134	99	119	79	42	108
Sammy Watkins	113	127	98	62	119	88	116
Chris Conley	79	112	114	40	117	7	99
Damien Williams	118	83	136			40	129
Kareem Hunt	148	126	144			149	149
Demarcus Robinson	94	0	125	96	149	86	124
Demetrius Harris	48	110	61	40		144	89
Spencer Ware	109	40	108		119	88	109
Anthony Sherman	117	88	99	158			148
De'Anthony Thomas	119	119	119		40	40	116
Kelvin Benjamin	63	40				119	57
Charcandrick West	158		69				149
Team Total	115	128	120	108	107	71	116

2018 Rushing Recap & 2019 Outlook

I'm on the record as a huge believer in the fantasy upside of **Damien Williams**. Among running backs with more than 50 combined rushes and targets in 2018, Williams was the only one to rank top 20 in Success Rate (second), Missed YPA (ninth) and explosiveness (11th).

It's hard for a back not to be productive playing in a Reid offense with Mahomes at quarterback. Last season, Chiefs running backs collectively received 74 red-zone opportunities, and while Williams could share duties with **Carlos Hyde**, he is still expected to get the bulk of the load.

Player *Min 50 Rushes	Rushes	YPC	Success %	Success Rk	Missed YPA Rk	YTS % Rk	YAS % Rk	Early Down Success %	Early Down Success Rk	TDs
Kareem Hunt	181	4.6	54%	10	41	24	21	55%	7	7
Damien Williams	85	4.9	64%	2	11	9	14	64%	1	6
Spencer Ware	51	4.8	45%	47	40	66	28	48%	29	2

Yards per Carry by Direction

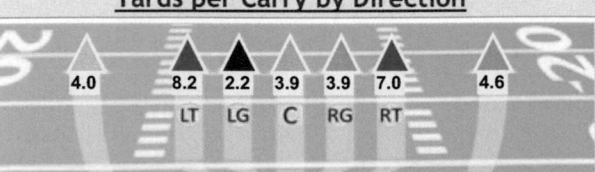

4.0	8.2	2.2	3.9	3.9	7.0	4.6
	LT	LG	C	RG	RT	

Directional Run Frequency

10%	8%	4%	48%	8%	10%	12%
	LT	LG	C	RG	RT	

Last year at home, the Chiefs allowed a 44% Success Rate, 5.4 YPA, and 76.8 rating (third best) – all of which ranked top six league wide. On the road, though, they allowed a 48% Success Rate, 7.3 YPA and 106.6 rating. Over the past three years, the Chiefs have the NFL's best pass defense at home but the 25th-rated unit on the road. Those are obviously measurable drops, but they only tell part of the story; the rest is told by pressure stats.

At home last season, the Chiefs posted a hurry rate of 37%, hit rate of 20%, and sack rate of 9.8%. On the road, their hurry rate was 24%; hit rate 15%; and sack rate 5.6%.

Pressures generate hits, which generate sacks, which can, in turn, lead to turnovers. Pressures also generate disruptions, which can end up generating turnovers. Over the past three seasons, the Chiefs recorded 32 interceptions on 894 attempts at home, but came away with just 17 interceptions on 906 attempts on the road.

To dig deeper, I studied all quarterbacks that faced the Chiefs in Kansas City over the last three years as compared to those same quarterbacks when playing elsewhere on the road. Of those 20 quarterbacks, 13 posted a better Success Rate in Arrowhead than elsewhere on the road, while 12 posted a better YPA in KC

(cont'd - see KC-5)

Kansas City Chiefs Fantasy Corner

Mecole Hardman's fantasy stock skyrocketed landing in an optimal destination in April's draft. A projected third-day pick, the Chiefs *traded up* for Hardman at No. 56 overall to become **Tyreek Hill**'s potential replacement. On tape, Hardman reminded me of Marquise Goodwin as a vertical burner capable of playing outside and in the slot. Hardman lacks the physicality and contested-catch prowess of Hill as a finesse deep threat with 4.33 jets at 5-foot-10, 183. Hardman may have more growth potential than his 59-catch college career suggests, however; he didn't even play wide receiver in high school and showed elite ability with the ball in his hands by averaging 15.2 yards per punt return with a touchdown over his final two seasons at Georgia. Many "small" WR hits dominated in the return game in college, such as **Odell Beckham**, **Antonio Brown**, **DeSean Jackson**, **T.Y. Hilton**, and **Steve Smith**.

- Evan Silva

2018 Situational Usage by Player & Position

Usage Rate by Score

		Being Blown Out (14+)	Down Big (9-13)	One Score	Large Lead (9-13)	Blowout Lead (14+)
RUSH	Kareem Hunt	1%	6%	51%	22%	20%
	Tyreek Hill		4%	70%	9%	17%
	Damien Williams	1%	2%	54%	16%	26%
	Spencer Ware		6%	53%	22%	20%
	Sammy Watkins			50%	17%	33%
	Anthony Sherman			100%		
	Charcandrick West			50%		50%
	De'Anthony Thomas			100%		
	Total	1%	5%	54%	19%	22%
PASS	Kareem Hunt	3%	14%	59%	10%	14%
	Tyreek Hill	3%	8%	60%	12%	18%
	Travis Kelce	3%	6%	60%	11%	20%
	Damien Williams	3%	18%	55%	3%	21%
	Spencer Ware	11%	6%	44%	28%	11%
	Sammy Watkins	2%	5%	53%	21%	19%
	Chris Conley		5%	71%	15%	10%
	Demarcus Robinson		4%	65%	17%	13%
	Demetrius Harris			58%	26%	16%
	Anthony Sherman		14%	43%	29%	14%
	Charcandrick West		67%	33%		
	Kelvin Benjamin			80%		20%
	De'Anthony Thomas			100%		
	Total	2%	8%	59%	14%	17%

Share of Offensive Plays by Type

	Kareem Hunt	Tyreek Hill	Travis Kelce	Damien Williams	Spencer Ware	Sammy Watkins	Chris Conley	Demarcus Robinson	Demetrius Harris	Anthony Sherman	Charcandrick West	Kelvin Benjamin	De'Anthony Thomas
RUSH	52%	7%		24%	15%	2%					0%	1%	0%
PASS	6%	24%	27%	7%	4%	12%	8%	5%	4%	1%	1%	1%	0%
ALL	25%	17%	16%	14%	8%	8%	5%	3%	2%	1%	1%	1%	0%

Positional Target Distribution vs NFL Average

		NFL Wide				Team Only			
		Left	Middle	Right	Total	Left	Middle	Right	Total
Deep	WR	34%	17%	31%	82%	22%	18%	26%	66%
	TE	5%	4%	6%	15%	6%	8%	14%	28%
	RB	1%	0%	2%	3%	1%	1%	5%	6%
	All	39%	21%	39%	100%	29%	27%	45%	100%
Short	WR	20%	14%	21%	55%	17%	12%	18%	48%
	TE	6%	6%	8%	20%	9%	9%	13%	32%
	RB	10%	5%	10%	25%	8%	2%	11%	21%
	All	36%	25%	39%	100%	35%	23%	42%	100%
Total		37%	24%	39%	100%	33%	24%	43%	100%

Positional Success Rates vs NFL Average

		NFL Wide				Team Only			
		Left	Middle	Right	Total	Left	Middle	Right	Total
Deep	WR	40%	49%	40%	42%	45%	46%	38%	43%
	TE	45%	53%	41%	45%	22%	64%	50%	48%
	RB	36%	20%	42%	39%	100%	100%	43%	56%
	All	40%	50%	40%	42%	41%	53%	42%	45%
Short	WR	55%	61%	52%	55%	64%	59%	60%	61%
	TE	55%	62%	54%	57%	60%	67%	58%	61%
	RB	46%	54%	45%	47%	64%	50%	61%	61%
	All	52%	59%	51%	53%	63%	61%	59%	61%
Total		50%	58%	49%	51%	59%	59%	55%	57%

Division History: Season Wins & 2019 Projection

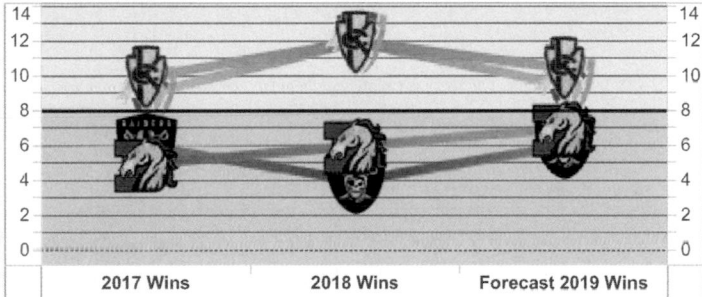

| 2017 Wins | 2018 Wins | Forecast 2019 Wins |

Rank of 2019 Defensive Pass Efficiency Faced by Week

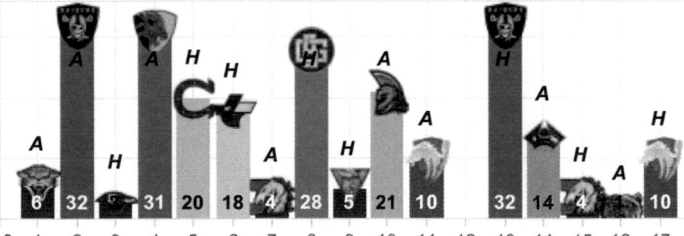

| 6 | 32 | | 31 | 20 | 18 | 4 | 28 | 5 | 21 | 10 | | 32 | 14 | 4 | | 10 |

0 1 2 3 4 5 6 7 8 9 10 11 12 13 14 15 16 17

Rank of 2019 Defensive Rush Efficiency Faced by Week

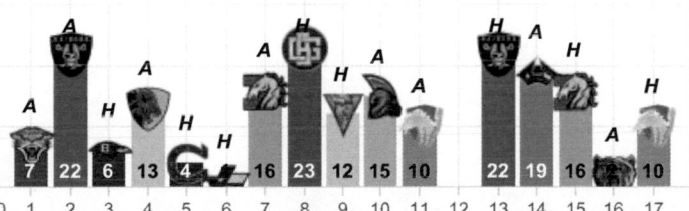

| 7 | 22 | 6 | 13 | 4 | | 16 | 23 | 12 | 15 | 10 | | 22 | 19 | 16 | | 10 |

0 1 2 3 4 5 6 7 8 9 10 11 12 13 14 15 16 17

Successful Play Rate 0% ▮▮▮ 100%

Type	1-1 [3WR]	1-2 [2WR]	2-1 [2WR]	2-2 [1WR]	0-1 [4WR]	2-0 [3WR]	0-0 [5WR]	1-3 [1WR]	ALL
PASS	53% (434)	50% (191)	53% (30)	67% (12)	63% (16)	100% (2)			53% (685)
RUSH	57% (238)	55% (118)	46% (39)	33% (30)	50% (4)		0% (1)	100% (1)	54% (431)
All	55% (672)	52% (309)	49% (69)	43% (42)	60% (20)	100% (2)	0% (1)	100% (1)	53% (1,116)

Format Success Rate (Total # of Plays)

Receiving Success by Top-4 Personnel Groupings
(Min 50 targets)

POS	Player	1-1 [3WR]	1-2 [2WR]	2-1 [2WR]	2-2 [1WR]	4 Grp Total
TE	Travis Kelce	62% (106) 8.9, 107.5	59% (46) 8.0, 102.4	80% (5) 11.6, 115.0	67% (3) 6.0, 122.2	62% (160) 8.7, 110.1
WR	Tyreek Hill	54% (100) 9.2, 96.1	61% (41) 13.5, 131.4	33% (6) 14.0, 135.4		55% (147) 10.6, 109.6
	Sammy Watkins	62% (42) 9.3, 122.0	70% (23) 11.7, 115.6	67% (3) 8.7, 93.8		65% (68) 10.1, 118.8
	Chris Conley	53% (40) 5.5, 95.8	58% (12) 8.3, 119.8	100% (1) 15.0, 118.8		55% (53) 6.3, 102.2
	Kelvin Benjamin	40% (5) 5.2, 57.1				40% (5) 5.2, 57.1

Format Line 1: Success Rate (Total # of Plays) Line 2: YPA, Passer Rating

Rushing Success by Top-4 Personnel Groupings
(Min 25 carries)

Rusher (Last, First)	1-1 [3WR]	1-2 [2WR]	2-1 [2WR]	2-2 [1WR]	4 Grp Total
Hunt Kareem	53% (92) 4.5	52% (58) 5.5	42% (19) 2.4	55% (11) 3.5	52% (180) 4.5
Williams Damien	65% (55) 4.9	50% (24) 4.8	75% (4) 7.0	50% (2) 1.0	61% (85) 4.9
Mahomes Patrick	69% (26) 7.1	69% (13) 5.4	63% (8) 2.0	14% (14) 0.3	56% (61) 4.5
Ware Spencer	45% (33) 5.8	42% (12) 3.8	40% (5) 2.2	0% (1) 0.0	43% (51) 4.8

Format Line 1: Success Rate (Total # of Plays) Line 2: YPC

Passing by Coverage Scheme

Zone	57% (240) 9.1, 114.8
M2M	58% (228) 9.3, 114.0
Screen	61% (96) 7.6, 125.9
Combo	55% (11) 7.2, 69.9

Passing by Route

Curl	64% (78) 7.4, 96.1
Screen	64% (73) 7.7, 116.8
Out	71% (45) 9.6, 116.3
Slant	57% (44) 9.1, 97.0
Dig	55% (31) 7.4, 111.0
Flat	61% (31) 7.9, 132.0

Throw Types

Level 1	63% (374) 7.6, 121.2
Level 2	59% (160) 11.4, 120.9
Level 3	33% (58) 14.8, 81.5
Shovel	60% (15) 6.1, 131.8
Sidearm	29% (14) 4.6, 57.1

QB Drop Types

3 Step	58% (216) 8.9, 104.2
0/1 Step	62% (203) 8.4, 128.2
5 Step	46% (72) 11.2, 103.2
Designed Rollout Right	62% (42) 9.0, 138.7
Basic Screen	61% (38) 9.2, 131.3
7 Step	58% (19) 12.6, 102.4

QB State at Pass

Planted	61% (353) 9.0, 118.1
Moving	52% (121) 9.1, 116.4
Shuffling	56% (90) 8.3, 120.0

Play Action

	Play Action	No P/A
Under Center	61% (44) 13.2, 131.8	68% (22) 7.3, 113.8
Shotgun	53% (136) 8.2, 98.8	59% (423) 9.1, 118.9
ALL	55% (180) 9.4, 107.5	60% (445) 9.0, 121.2

Run Types

Inside Zone	55% (97) 4.1
Outside Zone	53% (77) 4.7
Stretch	43% (56) 4.1
Power	69% (42) 4.1
Pitch	56% (9) 8.0
Lead	33% (9) 2.4

KC-5

than on the road.

The bottom line is, the Arrowhead crowd is a bigger factor than most other home crowds around the NFL. Arrowhead broke the record for loudest crowd noise in a stadium, hitting levels exceeding 140 dbA -- louder than the sound on the deck of an aircraft carrier. This impacts opponents' snap counts, forcing them into simpler, more predictable calls which in turn allow the Chiefs' pass rush to be even more dangerous.

The Chiefs' run defense has been the league's worst for two straight years, but opponents aren't in position to run the ball as much if they're trailing. Thus, the goal is for the high-powered Chiefs offense to get a halftime lead to compensate for its porous run defense, forcing their opponent to abandon the run and instead have to contend with a pass rush that improved from 26th in 2017 to seventh in 2018.

Offseason additions could help. Along the line, the Chiefs added **Frank Clark** from the Seahawks, **Emmanuel Ogbah** from the Browns, and **Alex Okafor** from the Saints – all of whom are in their prime at age 26-28. On the back end, safety **Tyrann Mathieu** was added from the Texans.

Issues remain, though. Leading pass rusher **Dee Ford** was not brought back because the Chiefs are switching to a new scheme under new defensive coordinator **Steve Spagnuolo** after firing **Bob Sutton**. The aforementioned additions are further offset by the loss of edge rusher **Justin Houston** and cornerback **Steven Nelson**. And while **Eric Berry** is past his prime, his loss in the locker room is sure to sting as well.

From a schedule perspective, the Chiefs are projected to face the ninth-toughest slate of pass defenses and the NFL's toughest schedule of run defenses. Their Week 11 game in Mexico against the Chargers comes with a three-day rest disadvantage. It's hard to envision the Chiefs dropping off substantially -- they are too great at what matters most in quarterback play and offensive play calling -- but their schedule will be challenging.

Coaches (Prior Yrs)

Head Coach:
Anthony Lynn (2 yrs)
Offensive Coordinator:
Ken Whisenhunt (3 yrs)
Defensive Coordinator:
Gus Bradley (1 yr)

EASY   HARD

2019 Forecast

Wins	Div Rank
9.5	#2

Past Records
2018: 12-4
2017: 9-7
2016: 5-11

IND	DET	HOU	MIA	DEN	PIT	TEN	CHI	GB	OAK	KC		DEN	JAX	MIN	OAK	KC
H	A	H	A	H	H	A	A	H	A	H		A	A	H	H	A
1	2	3	4	5	6	7	8	9	10	11	12	13	14	15	16	17

SNF   TNF   LON

Key Players Lost

Player	New
Darius Philon (DT)	ARI
Jahleel Addae (SS)	HOU
Jason Verrett (CB)	SF
Kyle Emanuel (OLB)	Retired
Tyrell Williams (WR)	OAK

Average Line	# Games Favored	# Games Underdog
-3.1	12	2

2019 Los Angeles Chargers Overview

I was *furious* with the 2017 Chargers.

As I wrote in my 2018 Football Preview, the previous year's Bolts "should have been an 11- to 12-win team that could have hosted a playoff game in their first year in Los Angeles."

But the Rams captured the city in last year's two-team move purely through better on-field decision making.

The 2017 Chargers made fundamental errors. They ran way too much on first and ten and began the season 0-4. Finally smartening up with more early-down throws to **Melvin Gordon**, the 2017 Chargers closed out the year 6-1. But they waited far too long to get smart. And they waited far too long to transition from **Antonio Gates** to **Hunter Henry**.

But I was not surprised last year's club beat its 9.5-win expectation. The Chargers were a very good team in both 2017 and 2018. And they look even better this year. It starts with the players, specifically players that weren't on the 2018 team but were there in spirit.

*It starts with **Hunter Henry**.*

Over 2016 and 2017, Henry was the NFL's most-successful tight end target. He ranked No. 2 in Success Rate among all positions, and he ranked as the NFL's best player in missed yards per attempt, a metric measuring efficiency on plays graded as unsuccessful. Henry was a major difference maker in the passing game.

But on May 22 of 2018, Henry tore his ACL. The Chargers were forced to bring back Gates, who averaged a sloth-like 7.1 yards per target with a 50% Success Rate that

(cont'd - see LAC2)

Key Free Agents/ Trades Added

Player	AAV (MM)
Thomas Davis (OLB)	$5.2
Tyrod Taylor (QB)	$5.5

Drafted Players

Rd	Pk	Player (College)
1	28	DT - Jerry Tillery (Notre Dame)
2	60	S - Nasir Adderley (Delaware)
3	91	OT - Trey Pipkins (Sioux Falls)
4	130	LB - Drue Tranquill (Notre Dame)
5	166	QB - Easton Stick (North Dakota State)
6	200	LB - Emeke Egbule (Houston)
7	242	DT - Cortez Broughton (Cincinnati)

Regular Season Wins: Past & Current Proj

Forecast 2019 Wins	9.5
2018 Wins	12
Forecast 2018 Wins	9.5
2017 Wins	9
2016 Wins	5
2015 Wins	4

1 3 5 7 9 11 13 15

Lineup & Cap Hits

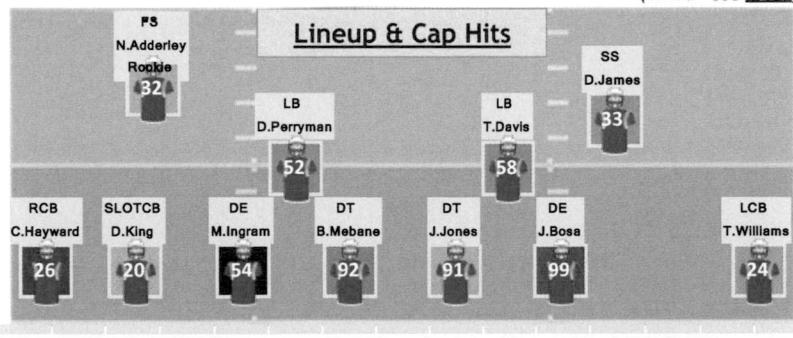

FS N.Adderley Rookie 32

SS D.James 33

LB D.Perryman 52

LB T.Davis 58

RCB C.Hayward 26

SLOTCB D.King 20

DE M.Ingram 54

DT B.Mebane 92

DT J.Jones 91

DE J.Bosa 99

LCB T.Williams 24

LWR 12 T.Benjamin

LT 76 R.Okung

LG 66 D.Feeney

C 53 M.Pouncey

RG 75 M.Schofield

RT 69 S.Tevi

TE 86 H.Henry

RWR 16 M.Williams

SLOTWR 13 K.Allen

QB 17 P.Rivers

RB 28 M.Gordon

WR2 84 D.Cantrell

WR3 11 G.Davis

RB2 30 A.Ekeler

QB2 5 T.Taylor

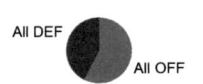
2019 Cap Dollars

2019 Unit Spending

All DEF / All OFF

Positional Spending

	Rank	Total	2017 Rk
All OFF	8	$106.64M	8
QB	8	$27.71M	12
OL	16	$37.72M	19
RB	16	$8.53M	22
WR	14	$25.06M	5
TE	19	$7.61M	19
All DEF	25	$78.07M	15
DL	10	$38.16M	9
LB	23	$16.09M	31
CB	22	$16.51M	16
S	27	$7.32M	16

ranked 78th in the league. Gates' explosiveness quotient ranked 111th.

Chargers DE **Joey Bosa** missed Weeks 1-10 with a foot injury. MLB **Denzel Perryman** suffered a year-ending LCL tear in Week 10 and didn't return. Way back in training camp, CB **Jason Verrett** tore his Achilles. Verrett's replacement, Trevor Williams, missed seven games.

The Chargers re-signed Perryman, added longtime Panthers stud WLB **Thomas Davis**, drafted DT **Jerry Tillery** in the first round, and get back a healthy Bosa. They drafted FS **Nasir Adderley** out of Delaware in the second round.

This defense is *stacked*.

DC **Gus Bradley**'s unit is flush with dominant talent from Bosa and **Melvin Ingram** on the edges to Perryman and Davis at linebacker, and **Derwin James**, **Casey Hayward**, and **Desmond King** in the secondary. And they have an extraordinary mix of youth and veteran stalwarts.

Bradley helped architect Seattle's Legion of Boom but unfortunately left for Jacksonville's head-coaching opportunity before the Seahawks' Super Bowl win. Bradley improved Seattle's defense from No. 29 in efficiency in 2009 and 2010 to No. 10 in 2011 and No. 2 in 2012. They rose to No. 1 in 2013. Bradley improved the Chargers' defense from No. 12 in 2017 to No. 8 last year, despite the Chargers fielding NFL's fifth most-injured defense.

Bradley was a flawed head coach, but he knows how to coach defense. The Chargers gave him a much better defense to mold than Seattle or Jacksonville did. I'm forecasting Bradley's unit to face a slightly softer schedule of offenses than last year's Chargers defense did. And in 2018, they were seventh in Early Down Success Rate and eighth in defensive efficiency despite Bosa, Perryman, Verrett, and Williams getting hurt.

With top-three talent, an intelligent coordinator, an easier-than-average schedule of opposing offenses, and presumably improved health, this year's Chargers should field a top-five defense.

The 2017 Chargers had a kicking crisis. **YoungHoe Koo** couldn't made field goals and was replaced by **Nick Novak**. In the end, the Bolts lost multiple games due to their inability to make kicks. They went 1-4 in games decided by field goals and 3-5 in games decided by one score.

Last year's Chargers still juggled their kickers some, switching to rookie

Michael Badgley later in the season. But they were much better in field-goal rate. In games with ten minutes left and the score between -11 and +6, the Chargers went 5-of-6 on field-goal attempts.

That partly resulted in the Chargers' 6-1 record in one-score games, after going 3-5 in 2017. The Chargers won 4-of-5 games decided by three points or fewer in 2018 after losing 4-of-5 such games the year before.

Those improvements helped vault the Bolts from 9-7 to 12-4. But there is room for further optimization.

The 2018 Chargers offense ranked 26th in efficiency in first quarters of games, then fifth in the remainder of games. They ranked 31st in

(cont'd - see LAC-3)

2018 Passing Performance

QB	1st Dwn	2nd Dwn	3rd Dwn	
Philip Rivers	58% / 8.9 / 117.2	50% / 8.0 / 107.0	38% / 6.9 / 71.8	Success Rate / YPA / Rating
Pass Rate	49%	65%	89%	
NFL AVG	53% / 7.7 / 95.1	47% / 7.3 / 93.7	36% / 6.9 / 87.1	Success Rate / YPA / Rating
Pass Rate	53%	62%	80%	

2018 Rushing Performance

Offense	1st Dwn	2nd Dwn	3rd Dwn	
LAC	49% / 4.7	43% / 4.6	48% / 2.0	Success Rate / YPC
Run Rate	51%	35%	11%	
NFL AVG	48% / 4.5	46% / 4.4	51% / 4.3	Success Rate / YPC
Run Rate	47%	38%	20%	

2018 Offensive Advanced Metrics

2018 Defensive Advanced Metrics

2018 Weekly EDSR & Season Trending Performance

	1	2	3	4	5	6	7		9	10	11	12	13	14	15	16	17	WEEK
	L	W	L	W	W	W	W		W	W	W	W	L	W	W	L	W	RESULT
	KC	BUF	LA	SF	OAK	CLE	TEN		SEA	OAK	DEN	ARI	PIT	CIN	KC	BAL	DEN	OPP
	H	A	A	H	H	A	N		A	A	H	H	A	H	A	H	A	SITE
	-10	11	-12	2	16	24	1		8	14	-1	35	3	5	1	-12	14	MARGIN
	28	31	23	29	26	38	20		25	20	22	45	33	26	29	10	23	PTS
	38	20	35	27	10	14	19		17	6	23	10	30	21	28	22	9	OPP PTS

EDSR by Wk
W=Green
L=Red

OFF/DEF
EDSR
Blue=OFF
(high=good)
Red=DEF
(low=good)

2018 Close Game Records

All 2018 Wins: **12**
FG Games (<=3 pts) W-L: **4-1**
FG Games Win %: **80% (#4)**
FG Games Wins (% of Total Wins): **33% (#11)**
1 Score Games (<=8 pts) W-L: **6-1**
1 Score Games Win %: **86% (#2)**
1 Score Games Wins (% of Total Wins): **50% (#15)**

2018 Critical & Game-Deciding Stats

TO Margin	+1
TO Given	19
INT Given	12
FUM Given	7
TO Taken	20
INT Taken	13
FUM Taken	7
Sack Margin	+4
Sacks	38
Sacks Allow	34
Return TD Margin	-1
Ret TDs	3
Ret TDs Allow	4
Penalty Margin	-10
Penalties	113
Opponent Penalties	103

Los Angeles Chargers 2019 Strength of Schedule In Detail (compared to 2018)

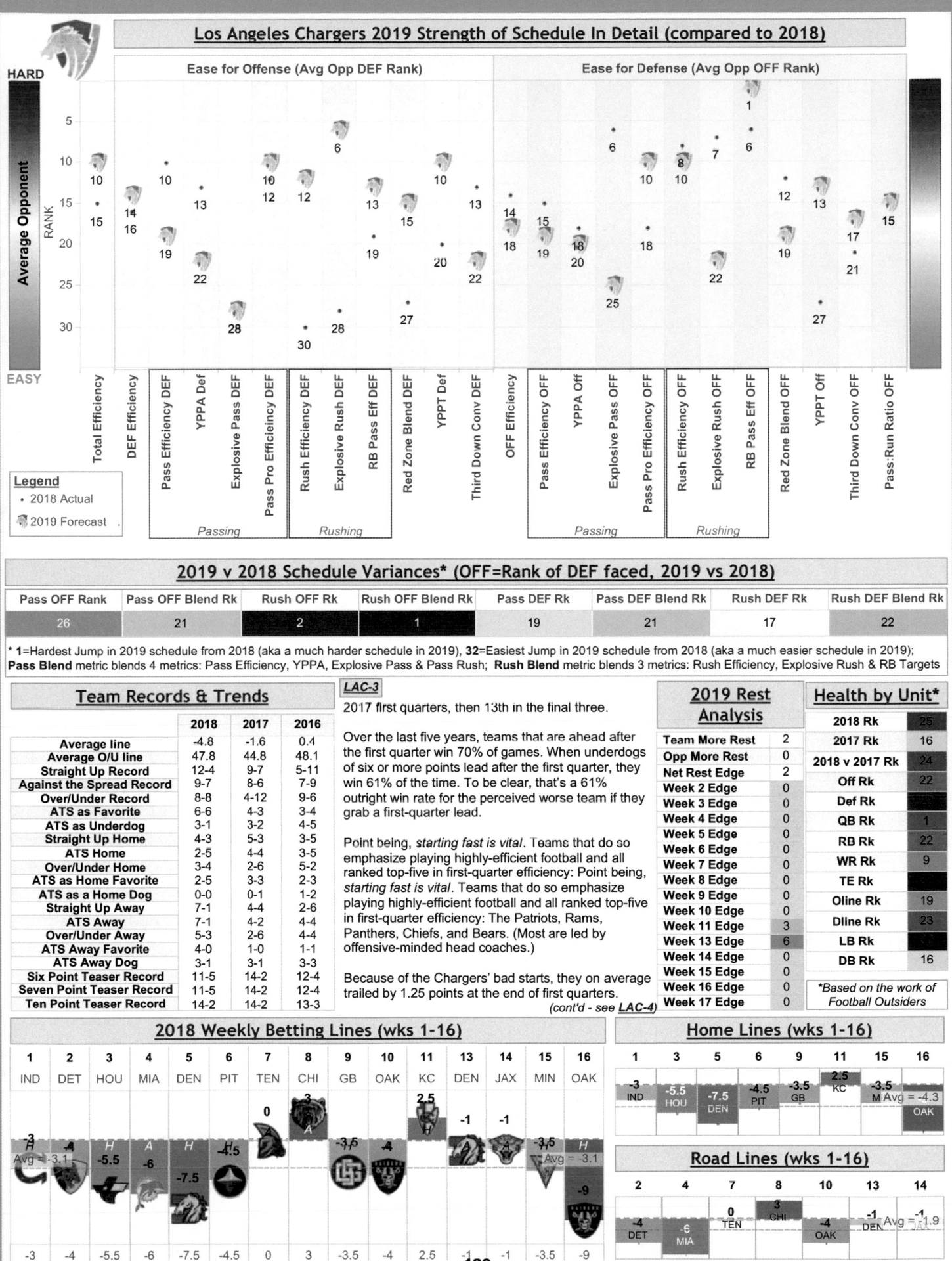

HARD

EASY

Average Opponent | RANK

Ease for Offense (Avg Opp DEF Rank)

Ease for Defense (Avg Opp OFF Rank)

Legend
- 2018 Actual
- 2019 Forecast

Offense axis labels: Total Efficiency | DEF Efficiency | Pass Efficiency DEF | YPPA Def | Explosive Pass DEF | Pass Pro Efficiency DEF | Rush Efficiency DEF | Explosive Rush DEF | RB Pass Eff DEF | Red Zone Blend DEF | YPPT Def | Third Down Conv DEF — *Passing* / *Rushing*

Defense axis labels: OFF Efficiency | Pass Efficiency OFF | YPPA Off | Explosive Pass OFF | Pass Pro Efficiency OFF | Rush Efficiency OFF | Explosive Rush OFF | RB Pass Eff OFF | Red Zone Blend OFF | YPPT Off | Third Down Conv OFF | Pass:Run Ratio OFF — *Passing* / *Rushing*

2019 v 2018 Schedule Variances* (OFF=Rank of DEF faced, 2019 vs 2018)

Pass OFF Rank	Pass OFF Blend Rk	Rush OFF Rk	Rush OFF Blend Rk	Pass DEF Rk	Pass DEF Blend Rk	Rush DEF Rk	Rush DEF Blend Rk
26	21	2	1	19	21	17	22

* **1**=Hardest Jump in 2019 schedule from 2018 (aka a much harder schedule in 2019), **32**=Easiest Jump in 2019 schedule from 2018 (aka a much easier schedule in 2019);
Pass Blend metric blends 4 metrics: Pass Efficiency, YPPA, Explosive Pass & Pass Rush; **Rush Blend** metric blends 3 metrics: Rush Efficiency, Explosive Rush & RB Targets

Team Records & Trends

	2018	2017	2016
Average line	-4.8	-1.6	0.4
Average O/U line	47.8	44.8	48.1
Straight Up Record	12-4	9-7	5-11
Against the Spread Record	9-7	8-6	7-9
Over/Under Record	8-8	4-12	9-6
ATS as Favorite	6-6	4-3	3-4
ATS as Underdog	3-1	3-2	4-5
Straight Up Home	4-3	5-3	3-5
ATS Home	2-5	4-4	3-5
Over/Under Home	3-4	2-6	5-2
ATS as Home Favorite	2-5	3-3	2-3
ATS as a Home Dog	0-0	0-1	1-2
Straight Up Away	7-1	4-4	2-6
ATS Away	7-1	4-2	4-4
Over/Under Away	5-3	2-6	4-4
ATS Away Favorite	4-0	1-0	1-1
ATS Away Dog	3-1	3-1	3-3
Six Point Teaser Record	11-5	14-2	12-4
Seven Point Teaser Record	11-5	14-2	12-4
Ten Point Teaser Record	14-2	14-2	13-3

LAC-3

2017 first quarters, then 13th in the final three.

Over the last five years, teams that are ahead after the first quarter win 70% of games. When underdogs of six or more points lead after the first quarter, they win 61% of the time. To be clear, that's a 61% outright win rate for the perceived worse team if they grab a first-quarter lead.

Point being, *starting fast is vital*. Teams that do so emphasize playing highly-efficient football and all ranked top-five in first-quarter efficiency: Point being, *starting fast is vital*. Teams that do so emphasize playing highly-efficient football and all ranked top-five in first-quarter efficiency: The Patriots, Rams, Panthers, Chiefs, and Bears. (Most are led by offensive-minded head coaches.)

Because of the Chargers' bad starts, they on average trailed by 1.25 points at the end of first quarters.

(cont'd - see LAC-4)

2019 Rest Analysis

Team More Rest	2
Opp More Rest	0
Net Rest Edge	2
Week 2 Edge	0
Week 3 Edge	0
Week 4 Edge	0
Week 5 Edge	0
Week 6 Edge	0
Week 7 Edge	0
Week 8 Edge	0
Week 9 Edge	0
Week 10 Edge	0
Week 11 Edge	3
Week 13 Edge	6
Week 14 Edge	0
Week 15 Edge	0
Week 16 Edge	0
Week 17 Edge	0

Health by Unit*

2018 Rk	25
2017 Rk	16
2018 v 2017 Rk	24
Off Rk	22
Def Rk	
QB Rk	1
RB Rk	22
WR Rk	9
TE Rk	
Oline Rk	19
Dline Rk	23
LB Rk	
DB Rk	16

Based on the work of Football Outsiders

2018 Weekly Betting Lines (wks 1-16)

1	2	3	4	5	6	7	8	9	10	11	12	13	14	15	16
IND	DET	HOU	MIA	DEN	PIT	TEN	CHI	GB	OAK	KC		DEN	JAX	MIN	OAK
-3	-4	-5.5	-6	-7.5	-4.5	0	3	-3.5	-4	2.5		-1	-1	-3.5	-9

Avg = -3.1

Home Lines (wks 1-16)

1	3	5	6	9	11	15	16
-3 IND	-5.5 HOU	-7.5 DEN	-4.5 PIT	-3.5 GB	2.5 KC	-3.5	
							OAK

Avg = -4.3

Road Lines (wks 1-16)

2	4	7	8	10	13	14
-4 DET	-6 MIA	0 TEN	3 CHI	-4 OAK	-1 DEN	

Avg = -1.9

Los Angeles Chargers 2018 Play Analysis

2018 Play Tendencies

All Pass %	58%
All Pass Rk	19
All Rush %	42%
All Rush Rk	14
1 Score Pass %	59%
1 Score Pass Rk	12
2017 1 Score Pass %	61%
2017 1 Score Pass Rk	2
2018 Pass Increase %	-2%
Pass Increase Rk	25
1 Score Rush %	41%
1 Score Rush Rk	21
Up Pass %	50%
Up Pass Rk	13
Up Rush %	50%
Up Rush Rk	20
Down Pass %	67%
Down Pass Rk	14
Down Rush %	33%
Down Rush Rk	19

2018 Down & Distance Tendencies

Down	Distance	Total Plays	Pass Rate	Run Rate	Play Success %
1	Short (1-3)	6	33%	67%	50%
	Med (4-7)	13	54%	46%	69%
	Long (8-10)	342	47%	53%	53%
	XL (11+)	9	78%	22%	44%
2	Short (1-3)	36	39%	61%	58%
	Med (4-7)	73	64%	36%	63%
	Long (8-10)	107	66%	34%	38%
	XL (11+)	34	82%	18%	38%
3	Short (1-3)	40	55%	45%	58%
	Med (4-7)	45	98%	2%	47%
	Long (8-10)	34	100%	0%	21%
	XL (11+)	27	96%	4%	30%
4	Short (1-3)	5	20%	80%	100%

Shotgun %:

	Under Center	Shotgun
	43%	57%
AVG	37%	63%

Run Rate:

	Under Center	Shotgun
	71%	20%
AVG	68%	23%

Pass Rate:

	Under Center	Shotgun
	29%	80%
AVG	32%	77%

Short Yardage Intelligence:

2nd and Short Run

Run Freq	Run Rk	NFL Run Freq Avg	Run 1D Rate	Run NFL 1D Avg
69%	11	65%	39%	68%

2nd and Short Pass

Pass Freq	Pass Rk	NFL Pass Freq Avg	Pass 1D Rate	Pass NFL 1D Avg
31%	21	35%	75%	56%

Most Frequent Play

Down	Distance	Play Type	Player	Total Plays	Play Success %
1	Short (1-3)	PASS	Mike Williams	2	100%
		RUSH	Melvin Gordon	2	0%
	Med (4-7)	RUSH	Melvin Gordon	5	100%
	Long (8-10)	RUSH	Melvin Gordon	98	43%
	XL (11+)	PASS	Keenan Allen	2	50%
2	Short (1-3)	RUSH	Melvin Gordon	15	60%
	Med (4-7)	RUSH	Melvin Gordon	11	55%
			Austin Ekeler	11	64%
	Long (8-10)	RUSH	Melvin Gordon	21	33%
	XL (11+)	PASS	Keenan Allen	6	17%
3	Short (1-3)	PASS	Keenan Allen	6	50%
			Tyrell Williams	6	67%
		RUSH	Melvin Gordon	6	83%
	Med (4-7)	PASS	Antonio Gates	10	60%
	Long (8-10)	PASS	Antonio Gates	6	50%
	XL (11+)	PASS	Keenan Allen	7	29%

Most Successful Play*

Down	Distance	Play Type	Player	Total Plays	Play Success %
1	Med (4-7)	RUSH	Melvin Gordon	5	100%
	Long (8-10)	PASS	Keenan Allen	35	71%
2	Short (1-3)	RUSH	Melvin Gordon	15	60%
	Med (4-7)	PASS	Tyrell Williams	6	83%
	Long (8-10)	PASS	Keenan Allen	10	70%
	XL (11+)	PASS	Keenan Allen	6	17%
3	Short (1-3)	RUSH	Justin Jackson	5	100%
	Med (4-7)	PASS	Keenan Allen	8	63%
	Long (8-10)	PASS	Antonio Gates	6	50%
	XL (11+)	PASS	Mike Williams	5	100%

*Minimum 5 plays to qualify

2018 Weekly Snap Rates

Wk	Opp	Score	Keenan Allen	Tyrell Williams	Virgil Green	Mike Williams	Melvin Gordon	Antonio Gates	Austin Ekeler	Travis Benjamin	Derek Watt
1	KC	L 38-28	72 (88%)	62 (76%)	44 (54%)	44 (54%)	62 (76%)	33 (40%)	22 (27%)	47 (57%)	7 (9%)
2	BUF	W 31-20	50 (89%)	45 (80%)	41 (73%)	39 (70%)	36 (64%)	11 (20%)	23 (41%)		7 (13%)
3	LA	L 35-23	40 (77%)	38 (73%)	33 (63%)	35 (67%)	40 (77%)	22 (42%)	18 (35%)		8 (15%)
4	SF	W 29-27	57 (84%)	55 (81%)	50 (74%)	46 (68%)	49 (72%)	23 (34%)	23 (34%)	5 (7%)	11 (16%)
5	OAK	W 26-10	49 (77%)	46 (72%)	46 (72%)	45 (70%)	45 (70%)	23 (36%)	23 (36%)		14 (22%)
6	CLE	W 38-14	39 (65%)	49 (82%)	48 (80%)	38 (63%)	38 (63%)	16 (27%)	21 (35%)		10 (17%)
7	TEN	W 20-19	40 (91%)	36 (82%)	32 (73%)	30 (68%)		13 (30%)	42 (95%)	5 (11%)	3 (7%)
9	SEA	W 25-17	43 (84%)	47 (92%)	34 (67%)	15 (29%)	45 (88%)	16 (31%)	9 (18%)	18 (35%)	11 (22%)
10	OAK	W 20-6	50 (89%)	45 (80%)	47 (84%)	26 (46%)	45 (80%)	11 (20%)	20 (36%)	13 (23%)	11 (20%)
11	DEN	L 23-22	69 (90%)	67 (87%)	54 (70%)	45 (58%)	64 (83%)	25 (32%)	18 (23%)	19 (25%)	10 (13%)
12	ARI	W 45-10	52 (75%)	9 (13%)	45 (65%)	63 (91%)	26 (38%)	26 (38%)	26 (38%)	44 (64%)	12 (17%)
13	PIT	W 33-30	58 (92%)	50 (79%)	41 (65%)	34 (54%)		24 (38%)	49 (78%)	28 (44%)	2 (3%)
14	CIN	W 26-21	54 (95%)	48 (84%)	40 (70%)	29 (51%)		23 (40%)	39 (68%)	20 (35%)	10 (18%)
15	KC	W 29-28	17 (23%)	65 (88%)	43 (58%)	66 (89%)		42 (57%)		44 (59%)	6 (8%)
16	BAL	L 22-10	59 (94%)	58 (92%)	29 (46%)	40 (63%)	42 (67%)	42 (67%)		21 (33%)	3 (5%)
17	DEN	W 23-9	45 (76%)	41 (69%)	47 (80%)	27 (46%)	32 (54%)	14 (24%)	15 (25%)	14 (24%)	21 (36%)
	Grand Total		794 (81%)	761 (77%)	674 (68%)	622 (62%)	524 (69%)	364 (36%)	348 (42%)	278 (35%)	146 (15%)

Personnel Groupings

Personnel	Team %	NFL Avg	Succ. %
1-1 [3WR]	64%	65%	52%
1-2 [2WR]	13%	17%	46%
2-1 [2WR]	10%	8%	46%
2-2 [1WR]	9%	3%	46%

Grouping Tendencies

Personnel	Pass Rate	Pass Succ. %	Run Succ. %
1-1 [3WR]	69%	52%	52%
1-2 [2WR]	50%	48%	45%
2-1 [2WR]	33%	50%	45%
2-2 [1WR]	14%	58%	44%

Red Zone Targets (min 3)

Receiver	All	Inside 5	6-10	11-20
Melvin Gordon	13	1	7	5
Keenan Allen	12	3	3	6
Mike Williams	12	4	5	3
Antonio Gates	11	4	4	3
Tyrell Williams	7	1	2	4
Austin Ekeler	5			5
Virgil Green	5	2	1	2

Red Zone Rushes (min 3)

Rusher	All	Inside 5	6-10	11-20
Melvin Gordon	35	11	6	18
Austin Ekeler	17	6	1	10
Philip Rivers	9	4	4	1
Justin Jackson	5	2		3

Early Down Target Rate

	RB	TE	WR
	32%	14%	54%
NFL AVG	23%	21%	56%

Overall Target Success %

	RB	TE	WR
	49%	53%	55%
	#11	#23	#8

Los Angeles Chargers 2018 Passing Recap & 2019 Outlook

Philip Rivers' 2018 season was very underrated, completing his highest rate of passes (68.3%) since 2013 and averaging his most yards per attempt (8.7) since 2010. Rivers' passer rating was the best of his entire career, and this came against the NFL's tenth-toughest schedule of pass defenses without **Hunter Henry**.

With Henry back and the Bolts facing a much softer pass-defense schedule, Rivers looks set up for another big year. In fantasy, Rivers was last year's QB11. This year, his ADP is QB14.

Philip Rivers Rating All Downs

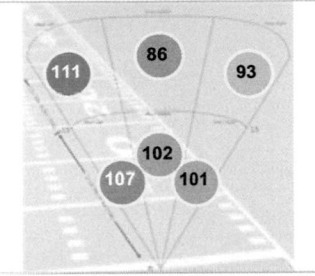

2018 Standard Passing Table

QB	Comp	Att	Comp %	Yds	YPA	TDs	INT	Sacks	Rating	Rk
Philip Rivers	394	591	67%	4,799	8.1	35	13	35	102	8
NFL Avg			62%		7.0				87.5	

2018 Advanced Passing Table

QB	Success %	EDSR Passing Success %	20+ Yd Pass Gains	20+ Yd Pass %	30+ Yd Pass Gains	30+ Yd Pass %	Avg. Air Yds per Comp	Avg. YAC per Comp	20+ Air Yd Comp	20+ Air Yd %
Philip Rivers	50%	54%	67	11.0%	20	3.0%	6.3	5.9	28	5%
NFL Avg	44%	48%	29.5	8.4%	12.5	3.7%	5.8	5.1	14.5	6%

Philip Rivers Rating Early Downs

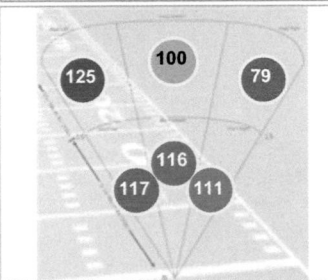

Interception Rates by Down

Yards to Go	1st Dwn	2nd Dwn	3rd Dwn	4th Dwn	Total
1 & 2	0.0%	0.0%	0.0%	0.0%	0.0%
3, 4, 5	0.0%	0.0%	4.9%		2.5%
6 - 9	0.0%	1.4%	8.3%	0.0%	4.0%
10 - 14	0.5%	1.3%	6.5%	0.0%	1.5%
15+	0.0%	5.6%	0.0%		2.1%
Total	**0.4%**	**1.4%**	**5.2%**	**0.0%**	**2.1%**

3rd Down Passing - Short of Sticks Analysis

QB	Avg. Yds to Go	Avg. YIA (of Comp)	Avg Yds Short	Short of Sticks Rate	Short Rk
Philip Rivers	8.0	7.6	-0.4	56%	11
NFL Avg	7.8	6.4	-1.4	60%	

Air Yds vs YAC

Air Yds %	YAC %	Rk
51%	49%	28
53%	48%	

2018 Receiving Recap & 2019 Outlook

The Chargers get the Steelers in Week 6, so **Keenan Allen** can only hope Pittsburgh continues to cover him with linebackers. The Steelers aligned a linebacker on Allen even in two-receiver sets last season, and he drew nine targets with a linebacker in coverage in that game alone. He finished with 148 yards and a touchdown.

After a rough rookie year, **Mike Williams** was particularly spectacular as a sophomore. Coming off a ten-touchdown campaign, I'd lean toward Williams' value at his WR25 ADP over Allen at his WR11 cost.

Player *Min 50 Targets	Targ	Comp %	YPA	Rating	Success %	Success Rk	Missed YPA Rk	YAS % Rk	YTS % Rk	TDs
Keenan Allen	149	69%	8.8	103.5	60%	14	79	59	51	6
Mike Williams	82	61%	9.4	126.7	56%	37	68	43	38	10
Tyrell Williams	75	64%	10.1	91.9	53%	52	140	5	122	5
Melvin Gordon	69	75%	7.3	108.6	49%	85	95	88	87	4
Austin Ekeler	62	74%	7.0	109.4	52%	59	40	102	26	2
Antonio Gates	58	64%	7.1	94.7	50%	78	137	111	18	3

Directional Passer Rating Delivered

Receiver	Short Left	Short Middle	Short Right	Deep Left	Deep Middle	Deep Right	Player Total
Keenan Allen	101	114	91	65	119	87	104
Mike Williams	126	118	121	104	145	89	127
Tyrell Williams	40	104	110	149	41	89	92
Melvin Gordon	139	42	114			40	109
Austin Ekeler	126	95	89	119		100	109
Antonio Gates	79	90	121	96	40	40	95
Travis Benjamin	84	74	49	40	9	135	56
Virgil Green	118	94	88		119		117
Justin Jackson	85	100	96				95
Hunter Henry				40			40
Team Total	107	101	101	110	86	93	104

2018 Rushing Recap & 2019 Outlook

Melvin Gordon missed four games last year yet still recorded 35 red-zone carries and led the Chargers in red-zone targets. He's a scoring-position usage machine, and the fact that the Chargers have begun throwing so many early-down running back passes provides a massive boost to his floor. Gordon's 2019 schedule toughens, however; the Chargers are projected to face the league's 12th-hardest run-defense schedule after drawing last year's third-softest slate.

Player *Min 50 Rushes	Rushes	YPC	Success %	Success Rk	Missed YPA Rk	YTS % Rk	YAS % Rk	Early Down Success %	Early Down Success Rk	TDs
Melvin Gordon	201	4.7	51%	22	26	43	16	49%	26	12
Austin Ekeler	117	5.0	50%	23	31	33	18	52%	17	2
Justin Jackson	53	4.1	53%	15	24	22	35	47%	34	2

Yards per Carry by Direction

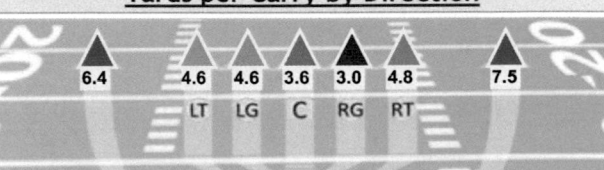

	6.4	4.6	4.6	3.6	3.0	4.8		7.5
		LT	LG	C	RG	RT		

Directional Run Frequency

	15%		13%	11%	31%	11%	10%		9%
			LT	LG	C	RG	RT		

Only four other teams in the last 30 years trailed by an average of at least 1.2 points at the end of the first quarter and won over 11 games.

They were the 1990 Montana 49ers, the 2001 Garcia-T.O. Niners, the 2007 Romo Cowboys, and the 2009 Brees Saints.

Incredibly, the Chargers trailed after the first quarter in half of their 12 wins. Only 11 teams in the last 30 years trailed after the first quarter and won six or more of those games. It was last done by the 2015 Super Bowl Panthers.

Chargers OC **Ken Whisenhunt** must figure out how to better script offensive plays at the beginning of games. This, of course, reeks of a team that lacks an analytics department to grow its awareness of its own early-game ineptitude, let alone one that knows how to fix it.

And it all starts with better early-down efficiency. The Chargers averaged the NFL's fourth-most yards to go on third downs in the first quarter (7.9) last year and were highly unsuccessful on those third downs, converting just 25% (second worst). Throughout the rest of the game, they averaged 7.2 yards to go on third down – still below average – but converted at the league's ninth-highest rate.

Philip Rivers wasn't great on third down, though. He threw a league-high six third-down interceptions, and his third-down yards per attempt were 7.2 with a 57% completion rate.

*(cont'd – see **LAC-5**)*

Los Angeles Chargers Fantasy Corner

Hunter Henry returns as a top-five fantasy tight end after tearing his ACL last May, then cameoing for 14 snaps in the Chargers' playoff loss to the Patriots. Henry didn't do much, but the fact that he was medically cleared so soon after the tear bodes well for his full-health return in 2019. Henry scored eight TDs on just 53 targets as a 2016 rookie, then ranked No. 2 among 43 qualified tight ends as a 2017 sophomore. I have Henry ranked along with **Evan Engram** in my second tight end tier behind **Travis Kelce**, **George Kittle**, **Zach Ertz**, and **O.J. Howard**.

- Evan Silva

2018 Situational Usage by Player & Position

Usage Rate by Score

		Being Blown Out (14+)	Down Big (9-13)	One Score	Large Lead (9-13)	Blowout Lead (14+)
RUSH	Melvin Gordon	7%	5%	59%	13%	16%
	Austin Ekeler	8%	5%	53%	11%	23%
	Keenan Allen			67%	11%	22%
	Mike Williams	14%		71%		14%
	Justin Jackson	28%		47%	2%	23%
	Tyrell Williams	50%				50%
	Travis Benjamin			86%	14%	
	Total	10%	4%	56%	11%	19%
PASS	Melvin Gordon	12%	14%	57%	6%	11%
	Austin Ekeler	9%	17%	44%	15%	15%
	Keenan Allen	16%	11%	50%	11%	11%
	Mike Williams	29%	10%	47%	14%	
	Justin Jackson	29%		67%		5%
	Tyrell Williams	25%	4%	54%	9%	9%
	Antonio Gates	33%	4%	54%	7%	2%
	Travis Benjamin	7%	21%	57%	7%	7%
	Virgil Green	21%		43%	25%	11%
	Hunter Henry	100%				
	Total	20%	10%	51%	11%	8%

Share of Offensive Plays by Type

	Melvin Gordon	Austin Ekeler	Keenan Allen	Mike Williams	Justin Jackson	Tyrell Williams	Antonio Gates	Travis Benjamin	Virgil Green	Hunter Henry
RUSH	51%	30%	2%	2%	13%	1%		2%		
PASS	12%	10%	25%	14%	4%	13%	10%	5%	5%	0%
ALL	29%	19%	15%	9%	8%	8%	6%	4%	3%	0%

Positional Target Distribution vs NFL Average

		NFL Wide				Team Only			
		Left	Middle	Right	Total	Left	Middle	Right	Total
Deep	WR	33%	17%	31%	**81%**	32%	27%	30%	**88%**
	TE	5%	4%	7%	**16%**	3%	4%	1%	**7%**
	RB	1%	0%	2%	**3%**	1%		4%	**4%**
	All	39%	21%	40%	**100%**	35%	30%	35%	**100%**
Short	WR	20%	14%	21%	**55%**	18%	16%	17%	**51%**
	TE	6%	6%	8%	**20%**	5%	5%	7%	**17%**
	RB	10%	5%	10%	**25%**	11%	7%	14%	**32%**
	All	36%	25%	39%	**100%**	34%	28%	38%	**100%**
Total		37%	24%	39%	**100%**	34%	29%	37%	**100%**

Positional Success Rates vs NFL Average

		NFL Wide				Team Only			
		Left	Middle	Right	Total	Left	Middle	Right	Total
Deep	WR	40%	49%	40%	**42%**	50%	57%	44%	**50%**
	TE	44%	54%	42%	**45%**	33%	50%	0%	**38%**
	RB	36%	33%	44%	**40%**	100%		25%	**40%**
	All	40%	50%	40%	**42%**	50%	56%	41%	**49%**
Short	WR	55%	60%	52%	**55%**	54%	71%	51%	**58%**
	TE	55%	62%	54%	**57%**	52%	48%	59%	**54%**
	RB	46%	54%	45%	**47%**	53%	48%	48%	**50%**
	All	53%	59%	51%	**54%**	53%	61%	51%	**55%**
Total		50%	58%	49%	**52%**	53%	60%	49%	**54%**

Division History: Season Wins & 2019 Projection

2015 Wins	2016 Wins	2017 Wins	2018 Wins	Forecast 2019 Wins

Rank of 2019 Defensive Pass Efficiency Faced by Week

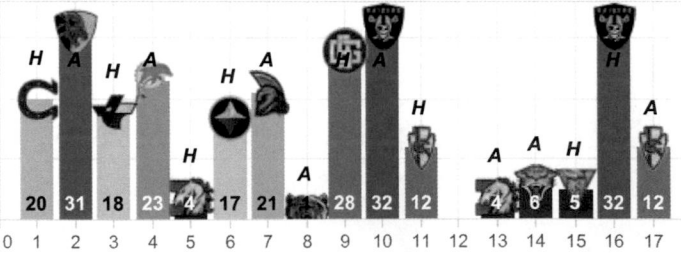

20	31	18	23	4	17	21	1	28	32	12	4	8	5	32	12

0 1 2 3 4 5 6 7 8 9 10 11 12 13 14 15 16 17

Rank of 2019 Defensive Rush Efficiency Faced by Week

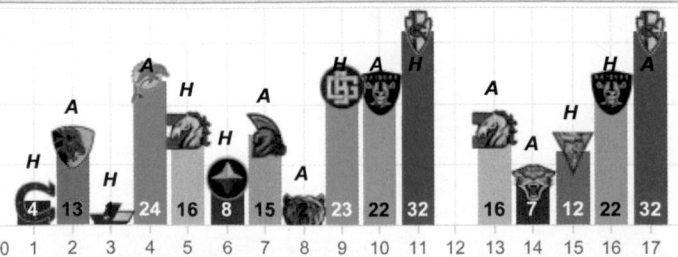

4	13	24	16	8	15	23	22	32	16	7	12	22	32

0 1 2 3 4 5 6 7 8 9 10 11 12 13 14 15 16 17

Successful Play Rate
0% ▓▓▓▓ 100%

2018 Detailed Analytics Summary
Success by Play Type & Primary Personnel Groupings

Type	1-1 [3WR]	1-2 [2WR]	2-1 [2WR]	2-2 [1WR]	1-0 [4WR]	1-3 [1WR]	0-0 [5WR]	2-0 [3WR]	2-3 [0WR]	0-1 [4WR]	ALL
PASS	50% (492)	48% (62)	44% (36)	62% (13)	36% (14)	71% (7)		50% (2)	0% (1)	0% (1)	49% (628)
RUSH	51% (211)	43% (69)	43% (70)	44% (78)	100% (1)	0% (7)	0% (3)	100% (1)	50% (2)		46% (442)
All	50% (703)	46% (131)	43% (106)	46% (91)	40% (15)	36% (14)	0% (3)	67% (3)	33% (3)	0% (1)	48% (1,070)

Format   Success Rate (Total # of Plays)

Receiving Success by Top-4 Personnel Groupings
(Min 50 targets)

POS	Player	1-1 [3WR]	1-2 [2WR]	2-1 [2WR]	1-0 [4WR]	4 Grp Total
RB	Austin Ekeler	56% (48) 7.1, 110.2	40% (5) 10.4, 118.3	33% (6) 4.0, 74.3	0% (2) 3.0, 56.3	51% (61) 7.0, 108.9
	Melvin Gordon	50% (40) 9.3, 128.2	50% (12) 5.3, 79.5	50% (6) 4.2, 84.0	0% (2) -1.0, 56.3	48% (60) 7.6, 113.0
TE	Antonio Gates	52% (50) 6.7, 103.5	75% (4) 12.5, 116.7			54% (54) 7.2, 104.5
WR	Keenan Allen	59% (121) 8.8, 102.2	63% (16) 5.9, 99.7	100% (5) 13.6, 158.3	33% (3) 6.7, 85.4	60% (145) 8.6, 105.3
	Mike Williams	56% (71) 8.3, 124.7	50% (4) 14.8, 156.3	50% (2) 9.0, 81.3	50% (4) 13.0, 95.8	56% (81) 8.9, 126.5
	Tyrell Williams	52% (60) 7.7, 77.1	50% (8) 23.6, 135.4	60% (5) 10.2, 55.0		52% (73) 9.6, 84.3

Format   Line 1: Success Rate (Total # of Plays)   Line 2: YPA, Passer Rating

Rushing Success by Top-4 Personnel Groupings
(Min 25 carries)

Rusher (Last, First)	1-1 [3WR]	2-1 [2WR]	2-2 [1WR]	1-2 [2WR]	4 Grp Total
Gordon Melvin	53% (93) 4.6	44% (36) 4.8	50% (30) 5.3	49% (37) 5.0	50% (196) 4.8
Ekeler Austin	50% (54) 5.1	55% (22) 6.2	42% (19) 4.9	41% (17) 3.4	48% (112) 5.0
Jackson Justin	52% (31) 4.5	14% (7) 2.1	64% (11) 3.7	50% (4) 5.0	49% (53) 4.1

Format   Line 1: Success Rate (Total # of Plays)   Line 2: YPC

Passing by Coverage Scheme

M2M	50% (268) 7.6, 96.5
Zone	60% (225) 9.2, 115.1
Screen	40% (43) 6.5, 92.0
Combo	69% (13) 7.8, 138.6

Passing by Route

Curl	48% (60) 5.9, 78.0
Out	62% (42) 6.9, 100.2
Screen	35% (37) 7.0, 91.9
Dig	74% (35) 11.6, 115.0
Slant	65% (34) 7.1, 97.9
Flat	61% (23) 8.3, 115.8

Throw Types

Level 1	57% (322) 7.2, 98.7
Level 2	52% (175) 8.6, 106.9
Level 3	43% (54) 14.8, 107.6
Sidearm	44% (18) 4.7, 81.9
Shovel	80% (5) 7.6, 98.3

QB Drop Types

3 Step	54% (263) 7.8, 106.3
5 Step	50% (168) 8.8, 90.5
0/1 Step	55% (67) 5.5, 99.6
7 Step	67% (46) 12.7, 139.3
Basic Screen	42% (24) 9.3, 127.8
Designed Rollout Right	50% (6) 4.3, 84.7

QB State at Pass

Planted	56% (406) 8.4, 102.0
Shuffling	48% (92) 7.7, 116.8
Moving	42% (38) 6.4, 94.7

Play Action

	Play Action	No P/A
Under Center	64% (89) 10.3, 125.7	71% (35) 14.2, 147.3
Shotgun	56% (27) 7.0, 123.8	50% (426) 7.4, 95.1
ALL	62% (116) 9.6, 125.3	52% (461) 7.9, 100.1

Run Types

Inside Zone	39% (84) 3.3
Outside Zone	45% (66) 3.7
Lead	46% (50) 3.9
Power	44% (50) 5.0
Pitch	53% (38) 5.8
Stretch	80% (5) 6.0

LAC-5

Rivers' high third-down conversion rate despite unimpressive third-down passing metrics suggests he caught the positive side of variance last year. So the coaching staff must concoct higher-efficiency early-down plays, which boils down to Whisenhunt's play calling.

The Chargers have also struggled to expose and exploit opponent weaknesses, typically done through analytics. But they don't invest much in analytics. Look no further than January's Divisional Round loss to the Patriots.

New England's run defense was a disaster against 11 personnel. The Pats allowed league highs in yards per carry (6.8) and Success Rate (61%) on 11-personnel runs from Week 11 onward. The Chargers *didn't run once* from 11 personnel in the first quarter. Over the course of the game, **Melvin Gordon** rushed just four times from an 11-personnel grouping.

Henry's return can make the Chargers' offense more multiple. With Henry healthy in 2017, the Chargers used two-tight end 12 personnel on 22% of snaps. That number dropped to 13% last year. The Chargers lost **Tyrell Williams**, freeing up 75 passing-game targets. This opens up more opportunity for **Mike Williams**, Henry, and **Travis Benjamin**. Whisenhunt's 11-personnel offense still looks downright nasty with Williams and Benjamin outside, **Keenen Allen** in the slot, and Henry at tight end.

Once concern with the Chargers' 11-personnel package was how many sacks Rivers took when running it. From 2017 to 2018, Rivers' pressure rate dropped from 37.2% to 35.5%, but his sack rate more than doubled from 8.1% to 16.7%. The Chargers may resort to more two-tight end 12 personnel with **Virgil Green** blocking across from Henry and Allen and Williams aligning out wide. Green was a top-ten pass-blocking tight end out of 81 qualifiers last year, allowing zero sacks, zero hits, and only two QB pressures all season.

The Chargers should be commended for stepping up their early-down target rate to running backs in a major way. The 2016 Chargers targeted backs on early downs on just 21% of attempts. It increased to 25% in 2017, then 32% last season, 9% above league average. And they were incredible on such plays. The Chargers' 58% Success Rate on early-down passes to running backs ranked second highest in the league, and their 7.7 yards per attempt ranked third.

If the Chargers' offensive line can stay intact, I have strong confidence they'll resume playoff competitiveness in 2019. Their projected Win Total sits between 9.5 and 10. They must play a home game in Mexico, but they get that game after nine days rest, while their opponent Chiefs play at altitude on only six days rest. The Chargers face two Florida teams in Florida, but neither takes place in the hottest early-season weeks. The Bolts also don't have to play in Denver early in the year. They host the Steelers in a night game, adding to their minimal homefield edge. And there is a chance the Chargers will play their second Chiefs game against a resting Kansas City squad in Week 17. **Andy Reid** loves resting his starters with a playoff berth clinched.

Los Angeles Rams

Coaches (Prior Yrs)

Head Coach:
Sean McVay (Calls Plays) (2 yrs)
Offensive Coordinator:
n/a ()
Defensive Coordinator:
Wade Phillips (1 yr)

2019 Forecast

Wins	Div Rank
10.5	#1

Past Records
2018: 13-3
2017: 11-5
2016: 4-12

EASY   HARD

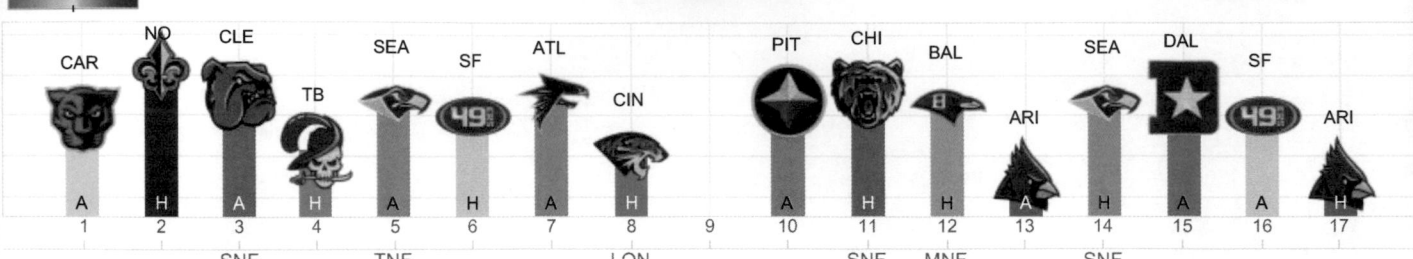

CAR	NO	CLE	TB	SEA	SF	ATL	CIN		PIT	CHI	BAL	ARI	SEA	DAL	SF	ARI
A	H	A	H	A	H	A	H		A	H	H	A	H	A	A	H
1	2	3	4	5	6	7	8	9	10	11	12	13	14	15	16	17
	SNF		TNF			LON				SNF	MNF		SNF			

Key Players Lost

Player	New
C.J. Anderson (RB)	DET
LaMarcus Joyner (FS)	OAK
Mark Barron (ILB)	PIT
Ndamukong Suh (DT)	TB
Ramik Wilson (ILB)	JAC
Rodger Saffold (G)	TEN
Sean Mannion (QB)	MIN

Average Line	# Games Favored	# Games Underdog
-5.0	13	

2019 Los Angeles Rams Overview

An inch. A second. That's why we love sports.

A single inch or second can change the outcome of any competitive affair. Close races. Shots. Pitches. Goals. Touchdowns.

In the case of the Rams, that's not being theatrical. On the Patriots' 29-yard line in Super Bowl 53, **Jared Goff** hits wide-open **Brandin Cooks** for a touchdown if he throws the ball a split second earlier to give the Rams a 7-3 second-half lead. That single inch or half second might have given us a different world champion.

And in the previous breath, the Rams wouldn't have been in Super Bowl position had officials correctly thrown a blatant pass-interference flag on **Nickell Robey-Coleman** for running into Saints WR **Tommylee Lewis** in the NFC Championship Game.

I can't imagine being that close to a conference or world championship and the psychological toll of coming up shy. But it's just an excuse.

Looking forward, the "real" element is tax spent on players' bodies when their seasons continue into early February. Super Bowl winners experience the same physical tax. It gets back to sports psychology, and that tax can be handled positively or negatively by teams and players.

Sean McVay has already analyzed it. He admitted to being "overprepared" for the Super Bowl, watching too much film in the leadup to the game. McVay suggested so much preparation "watered down" his thought process.

My perspective is different. As an outsider analyst, I can avoid pre-Super Bowl distractions. I can lock myself in my office and crank away on analysis and predictions. And that's what I did. I analyzed the Rams-Patriots Super Bowl in a style that is my own. And I approach the game differently than most NFL teams.

(cont'd - see LA2)

Key Free Agents/Trades Added

Player	AAV (MM)
Blake Bortles (QB)	$1
Clay Matthews (OLB)	$4.5
Eric Weddle (FS)	$5.2

Drafted Players

Rd	Pk	Player (College)
2	61	S - Taylor Rapp (Washington)
3	70	RB - Darrell Henderson (Memphis)
	79	CB - David Long (Michigan)
3*	97	OT - Bobby Evans (Oklahoma)
4	134	DT - Greg Gaines (Washington)
5	169	OT - David Edwards (Wisconsin)
7	243	S - Nick Scott (Penn State)
7*	251	LB - Dakota Allen (Texas Tech)

Regular Season Wins: Past & Current Proj

Forecast 2019 Wins	10.5
2018 Wins	13
Forecast 2018 Wins	9.5
2017 Wins	11
2016 Wins	4
2015 Wins	7

1 3 5 7 9 11 13 15

Lineup & Cap Hits

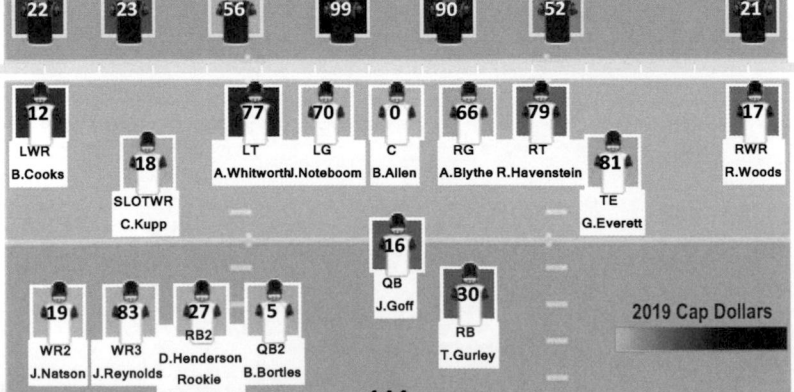

FS E.Weddle 32
SS J.Johnson 43
LB C.Littleton 58
LB S.Ebukam 50
RCB M.Peters 22
SLOTCB N.Robey-Coleman 23
OLB D.Fowler 56
DT A.Donald 99
DT M.Brockers 90
OLB C.Matthews 52
LCB A.Talib 21

LWR B.Cooks 12
SLOTWR C.Kupp 18
LT A.Whitworth 77
LG J.Noteboom 70
C B.Allen 0
RG A.Blythe 66
RT R.Havenstein 79
TE G.Everett 81
RWR R.Woods 17

QB J.Goff 16
RB T.Gurley 30
WR2 J.Natson 19
WR3 J.Reynolds 83
RB2 D.Henderson Rookie 27
QB2 B.Bortles 5

2019 Cap Dollars

2019 Unit Spending

All OFF
All DEF

Positional Spending

	Rank	Total	2017 Rk
All OFF	20	$92.38M	29
QB	24	$11.03M	27
OL	23	$33.16M	17
RB	3	$13.58M	4
WR	9	$28.23M	21
TE	24	$6.37M	30
All DEF	8	$95.37M	5
DL	5	$44.46M	7
LB	27	$13.52M	18
CB	6	$28.79M	9
S	19	$8.60M	9

Every team has access to similar information. Why would they need help from someone like me? I'm a consultant for multiple NFL teams and have met with a significant percentage of teams around the league.

The answer is within the NFL. It's the same reason why **Bill Belichick**'s game plan to slow down the Rams' offense was different than **Sean Payton**'s, and whose approach was different than **Jason Garrett**'s.

Think back to tenth-grade math class. Everyone studies the same textbooks. But not everyone walks away with the same level of subject understanding, and nor will everyone score the same on the final exam. People have different IQs, of course, but this is also true in the NFL.

Everyone attacks problems differently. Many rely on their own experiences when devising a strategy. And in the NFL, we're not taking true-or-false tests with definitively right or wrong answers. Teams play games on Sunday afternoons, and within 48 hours must establish a game plan for the ensuing week. Injuries, performance, and opponent scouting factor into that plan.

I have the benefit of watching all 256 games, and I've done so for over a decade. Each week, there are plays and series I go back to re-watch. Sometimes, it's film study. Other times, it's a few possessions on Game Rewind. For others, it's a particular sequence I need to study and even listen to the broadcasters, who provide special insights. I try to spot injuries, player reactions, and sideline interactions. I try to study the game as a play caller, then pore over my robust charting data. I run it through models of *my own* creation.

My suggestions are delivered to teams as quickly as 24 hours after games conclude. In most cases, my takeaways and recommendations are quite different from other analysts. Even though the Patriots, Saints, and Cowboys have competent advisers and can strategize based on similar data, we all come up with different plans to stop opponents.

McVay thought his problem was overpreparation, but he was unfortunate to miss some of the edges I unearthed in my pre-Super Bowl analysis. I didn't work for the Rams, but I published my analysis early that week.

My first recommendation was for the Rams to pass more from two-tight end 12 personnel. The Patriots fielded the NFL's third-most efficient defense against three-receiver 11-personnel passes, holding opponents to a 35% Success Rate and 6.2 yards per attempt. The Patriots' defense was especially effective on third downs, yielding just 3.0 yards per attempt and a 23% Success Rate to wide receivers on third-down targets over their previous six games.

Missing **Cooper Kupp**, the Rams managed a 47% Success Rate and 6.1 yards per attempt on 11-personnel passes to close out the season. On 12-personnel passes, however, the Rams logged a 67% Success Rate and 8.2 yards per attempt.

2018 Passing Performance

QB	1st Dwn	2nd Dwn	3rd Dwn	
Jared Goff	55%	51%	40%	Success Rate
	8.9	7.8	7.1	YPA
	101.7	97.6	85.4	Rating
Pass Rate	49%	61%	77%	
NFL AVG	53%	47%	36%	Success Rate
	7.7	7.3	6.9	YPA
	95.1	93.7	87.1	Rating
Pass Rate	53%	62%	80%	

2018 Rushing Performance

Offense	1st Dwn	2nd Dwn	3rd Dwn	
LA	58%	57%	54%	Success Rate
	5.1	4.4	4.8	YPC
Run Rate	51%	39%	23%	
NFL AVG	48%	46%	51%	Success Rate
	4.5	4.4	4.3	YPC
Run Rate	47%	38%	20%	

And New England's defense was 26th in Success Rate allowed on 12-personnel throws.

I assume the Rams knew about this competitive edge and simply decided not to exploit it.

The Rams' first 12-personnel pass didn't come until *3:42 left in the third quarter*. On first and ten at the Patriots' 29-yard line, Goff missed Cooks for the aforementioned would-be TD. Because both tight ends were blocking, Goff's line double teamed both Patriots defensive tackles and gave its quarterback time to step up in the pocket without any pressure in his face. Goff actually wound up with *too much time*, because he was late on the throw.

All told, the Rams had 36 dropbacks from 11 personnel but only six dropbacks in 12 during Super Bowl 53.

(cont'd - see LA-3)

2018 Offensive Advanced Metrics

2018 Defensive Advanced Metrics

2018 Weekly EDSR & Season Trending Performance

	1	2	3	4	5	6	7	8	9	10	11		13	14	15	16	17	WEEK
	W	W	W	W	W	W	W	W	L	W	W		W	L	L	W	W	RESULT
	OAK	ARI	LAC	MIN	SEA	DEN	SF	GB	NO	SEA	KC		DET	CHI	PHI	ARI	SF	OPP
	A	H	H	H	A	A	A	H	A	H	H		A	A	H	A	H	SITE
	20	34	12	7	2	3	29	2	-10	5	3		14	-9	-7	22	16	MARGIN
	33	34	35	38	33	23	39	29	35	36	54		30	6	23	31	48	PTS
	13	0	23	31	31	20	10	27	45	31	51		16	15	30	9	32	OPP PTS

EDSR by Wk
W=Green
L=Red

OFF / DEF
EDSR
Blue=OFF
(high=good)
Red=DEF
(low=good)

2018 Close Game Records

All 2018 Wins: **13**

FG Games (<=3 pts) W-L: **4-0**

FG Games Win %: **100% (#1)**

FG Games Wins (% of Total Wins): **31% (#15)**

1 Score Games (<=8 pts) W-L: **6-1**

1 Score Games Win %: **86% (#2)**

1 Score Games Wins (% of Total Wins): **46% (#21)**

2018 Critical & Game-Deciding Stats

TO Margin	+11
TO Given	19
INT Given	13
FUM Given	6
TO Taken	30
INT Taken	18
FUM Taken	12
Sack Margin	+8
Sacks	41
Sacks Allow	33
Return TD Margin	+4
Ret TDs	5
Ret TDs Allow	1
Penalty Margin	+3
Penalties	96
Opponent Penalties	99

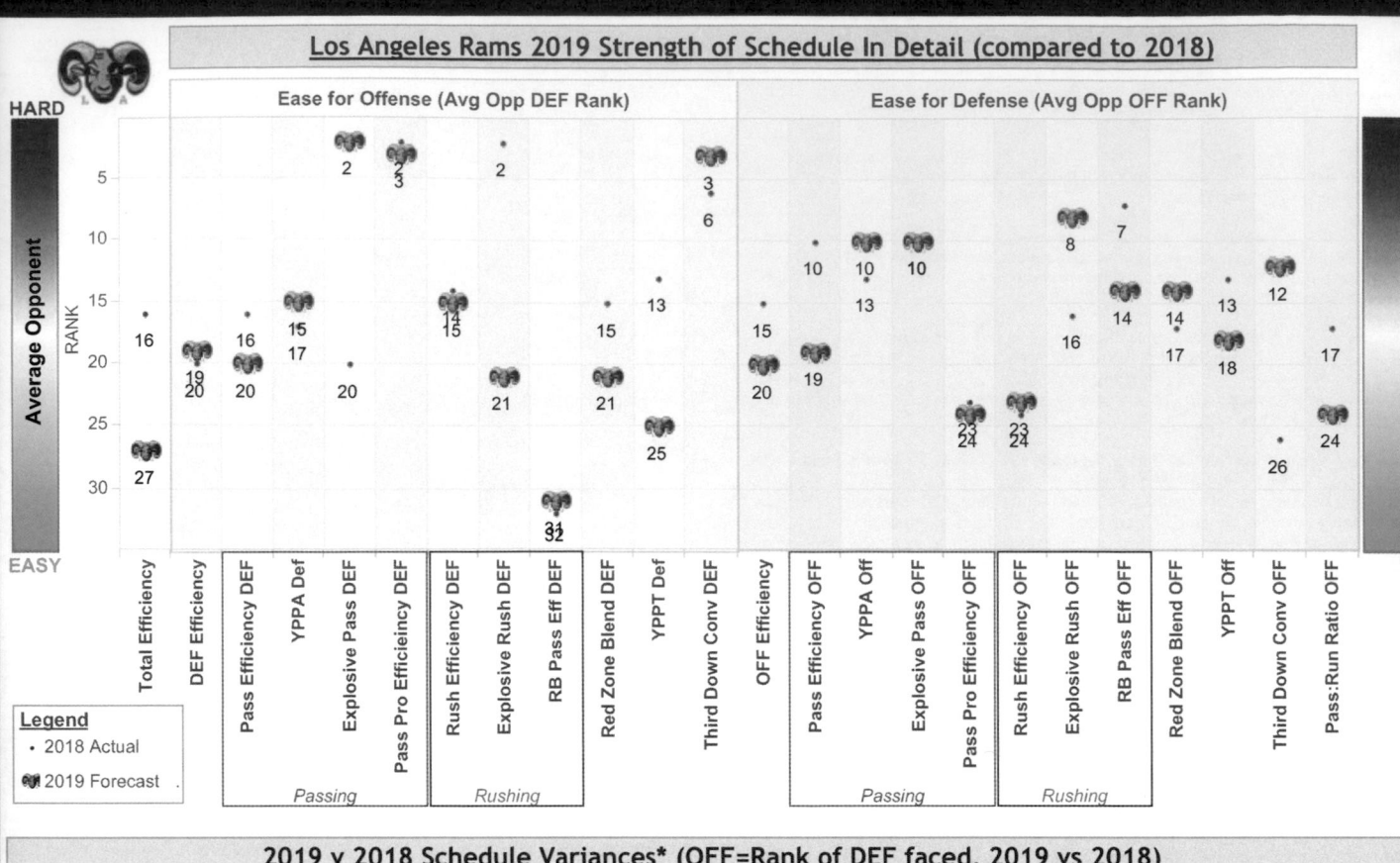

2019 v 2018 Schedule Variances* (OFF=Rank of DEF faced, 2019 vs 2018)

Pass OFF Rank	Pass OFF Blend Rk	Rush OFF Rk	Rush OFF Blend Rk	Pass DEF Rk	Pass DEF Blend Rk	Rush DEF Rk	Rush DEF Blend Rk
19	9	16	26	27	17	12	11

* **1**=Hardest Jump in 2019 schedule from 2018 (aka a much harder schedule in 2019), **32**=Easiest Jump in 2019 schedule from 2018 (aka a much easier schedule in 2019);
Pass Blend metric blends 4 metrics: Pass Efficiency, YPPA, Explosive Pass & Pass Rush; **Rush Blend** metric blends 3 metrics: Rush Efficiency, Explosive Rush & RB Targets

Team Records & Trends

	2018	2017	2016
Average line	-7.7	-2.0	4.3
Average O/U line	51.6	46.3	42.1
Straight Up Record	13-3	11-5	4-12
Against the Spread Record	7-7	9-7	4-10
Over/Under Record	7-8	11-5	7-9
ATS as Favorite	7-7	6-4	0-2
ATS as Underdog	0-0	3-2	3-6
Straight Up Home	7-1	3-4	1-6
ATS Home	3-3	3-4	1-5
Over/Under Home	5-2	4-3	4-3
ATS as Home Favorite	3-3	3-2	0-1
ATS as a Home Dog	0-0	0-1	1-2
Straight Up Away	6-2	7-1	3-5
ATS Away	4-4	5-3	3-4
Over/Under Away	2-6	7-1	3-5
ATS Away Favorite	4-4	2-2	0-1
ATS Away Dog	0-0	3-1	2-3
Six Point Teaser Record	13-3	11-5	10-5
Seven Point Teaser Record	13-3	11-4	11-5
Ten Point Teaser Record	13-3	14-2	11-5

LA-3

11-personnel passes delivered 5.6 yards per attempt and a 29% Success Rate, while 12-personnel throws averaged 8.8 yards with a 60% Success Rate. The Rams had only two other passes from 12 personnel where both tight ends stayed in to block: a 16-yard completion on first and ten and a nine-yard completion on first and ten.

But I *really* wanted the Rams to use play action *often* to mute the Patriots' pass rush. New England's defense was especially effective against non-play-action throws, recording 16-of-17 sacks on such plays in their games preceding Super Bowl 53. On play-action passes, the Patriots allowed a 53% Success Rate and 10.2 yards per attempt. Without play action, New England held its most-recent opponents to a 40% Success Rate and 6.1 yards per attempt.

On the season, the Rams used play action on 35% of dropbacks. But that rate dipped to 24% in the Super Bowl. Early-down splits showed the Rams gained 6.5 YPA with a 38% Success Rate on non-play-action throws, but 7.6 YPA with 56% success on play-action passes.

(cont'd - see **LA-4**)

2019 Rest Analysis

Team More Rest	5
Opp More Rest	2
Net Rest Edge	3
Week 2 Edge	1
Week 3 Edge	1
Week 4 Edge	0
Week 5 Edge	0
Week 6 Edge	4
Week 7 Edge	0
Week 8 Edge	0
Week 10 Edge	7
Week 11 Edge	0
Week 12 Edge	0
Week 13 Edge	
Week 14 Edge	1
Week 15 Edge	-3
Week 16 Edge	0
Week 17 Edge	0

Health by Unit*

2018 Rk	4
2017 Rk	1
2018 v 2017 Rk	20
Off Rk	2
Def Rk	13
QB Rk	1
RB Rk	13
WR Rk	16
TE Rk	4
Oline Rk	1
Dline Rk	1
LB Rk	
DB Rk	13

*Based on the work of Football Outsiders

2018 Weekly Betting Lines (wks 1-16)

1	2	3	4	5	6	7	8	10	11	12	13	14	15	16
CAR	NO	CLE	TB	SEA	SF	ATL	CIN	PIT	CHI	BAL	ARI	SEA	DAL	SF
-3	-3	-3	-11	-1	-8.5	-2	-13	0	-5.5	-7.5	-8	-7.5	0	-2

Avg = -5.0 (home) · Avg = -5.0 (away)

Home Lines (wks 1-16)

2	4	6	8	11	12	14
-3 NO	-11 TB	-8.5 SF	-13 CIN	-5.5 CHI	-7.5 BAL	-7.5 SEA

Avg = -8.0

Road Lines (wks 1-16)

1	3	5	7	10	13	15	16
-3 CAR	-3 CLE	-1 SEA	-2 ATL	0 PIT	-8 ARI	0 DAL	SF

Avg = -2.4

2018 Play Tendencies

All Pass %	57%
All Pass Rk	24
All Rush %	43%
All Rush Rk	9
1 Score Pass %	59%
1 Score Pass Rk	13
2017 1 Score Pass %	60%
2017 1 Score Pass Rk	8
2018 Pass Increase %	-1%
Pass Increase Rk	18
1 Score Rush %	41%
1 Score Rush Rk	20
Up Pass %	48%
Up Pass Rk	22
Up Rush %	52%
Up Rush Rk	11
Down Pass %	68%
Down Pass Rk	11
Down Rush %	32%
Down Rush Rk	22

2018 Down & Distance Tendencies

Down	Distance	Total Plays	Pass Rate	Run Rate	Play Success %
1	Short (1-3)	12	8%	92%	75%
	Med (4-7)	14	21%	79%	64%
	Long (8-10)	423	51%	49%	60%
	XL (11+)	6	50%	50%	50%
2	Short (1-3)	62	39%	61%	68%
	Med (4-7)	102	57%	43%	61%
	Long (8-10)	97	73%	27%	43%
	XL (11+)	32	94%	6%	41%
3	Short (1-3)	56	57%	43%	54%
	Med (4-7)	51	96%	4%	45%
	Long (8-10)	35	91%	9%	34%
	XL (11+)	18	94%	6%	22%
4	Short (1-3)	5	40%	60%	100%
	Med (4-7)	4	75%	25%	50%
	Long (8-10)	1	100%	0%	0%

Shotgun %:

Under Center	Shotgun
63%	38%

37% *AVG* 63%

Run Rate:

Under Center	Shotgun
66%	4%

68% *AVG* 23%

Pass Rate:

Under Center	Shotgun
34%	96%

32% *AVG* 77%

Los Angeles Rams
2018 Play Analysis

Short Yardage Intelligence:

2nd and Short Run

Run Freq	Run Rk	NFL Run Freq Avg	Run 1D Rate	Run NFL 1D Avg
63%	19	65%	69%	68%

2nd and Short Pass

Pass Freq	Pass Rk	NFL Pass Freq Avg	Pass 1D Rate	Pass NFL 1D Avg
37%	14	35%	71%	56%

Most Frequent Play

Down	Distance	Play Type	Player	Total Plays	Play Success %
1	Short (1-3)	RUSH	Todd Gurley	7	71%
	Med (4-7)	RUSH	Todd Gurley	6	67%
	Long (8-10)	RUSH	Todd Gurley	126	60%
	XL (11+)	RUSH	Todd Gurley	2	0%
2	Short (1-3)	RUSH	Todd Gurley	21	71%
	Med (4-7)	RUSH	Todd Gurley	20	55%
	Long (8-10)	RUSH	Todd Gurley	14	29%
	XL (11+)	PASS	Robert Woods	10	40%
3	Short (1-3)	RUSH	Todd Gurley	15	53%
	Med (4-7)	PASS	Robert Woods	14	64%
	Long (8-10)	PASS	Brandin Cooks	9	56%
	XL (11+)	PASS	Robert Woods	4	50%
			Brandin Cooks	4	50%

Most Successful Play*

Down	Distance	Play Type	Player	Total Plays	Play Success %
1	Short (1-3)	RUSH	Todd Gurley	7	71%
	Med (4-7)	RUSH	Todd Gurley	6	67%
	Long (8-10)	RUSH	Malcolm Brown	9	78%
2	Short (1-3)	RUSH	C.J. Anderson	11	82%
	Med (4-7)	RUSH	Malcolm Brown	5	80%
	Long (8-10)	PASS	Robert Woods	12	75%
	XL (11+)	PASS	Robert Woods	10	40%
3	Short (1-3)	PASS	Brandin Cooks	5	60%
	Med (4-7)	PASS	Robert Woods	14	64%
	Long (8-10)	PASS	Brandin Cooks	9	56%

Minimum 5 plays to qualify

2018 Weekly Snap Rates

Wk	Opp	Score	Robert Woods	Brandin Cooks	Todd Gurley	Tyler Higbee	Josh Reynolds	Cooper Kupp	Gerald Everett	Malcolm Brown
1	OAK	W 33-13	61 (97%)	61 (97%)	59 (94%)	60 (95%)	2 (3%)	61 (97%)	5 (8%)	4 (6%)
2	ARI	W 34-0	70 (97%)	72 (100%)	49 (68%)	64 (89%)	2 (3%)	72 (100%)	8 (11%)	23 (32%)
3	LAC	W 35-23	74 (96%)	74 (96%)	64 (83%)	58 (75%)	4 (5%)	75 (97%)	21 (27%)	13 (17%)
4	MIN	W 38-31	55 (100%)	52 (95%)	53 (96%)	34 (62%)	1 (2%)	53 (96%)	23 (42%)	2 (4%)
5	SEA	W 33-31	66 (100%)	28 (42%)	66 (100%)	53 (80%)	36 (55%)	36 (55%)	16 (24%)	
6	DEN	W 23-20	72 (97%)	68 (92%)	58 (78%)	55 (74%)	46 (62%)	28 (38%)	21 (28%)	16 (22%)
7	SF	W 39-10	50 (82%)	50 (82%)	36 (59%)	42 (69%)	51 (84%)		22 (36%)	25 (41%)
8	GB	W 29-27	76 (97%)	75 (96%)	70 (90%)	62 (79%)	69 (88%)		17 (22%)	9 (12%)
9	NO	L 45-35	58 (97%)	59 (98%)	54 (90%)	42 (70%)	2 (3%)	60 (100%)	18 (30%)	6 (10%)
10	SEA	W 36-31	64 (98%)	63 (97%)	58 (89%)	50 (77%)	10 (15%)	54 (83%)	16 (25%)	8 (12%)
11	KC	W 54-51	79 (99%)	70 (88%)	68 (85%)	59 (74%)	78 (98%)		23 (29%)	14 (18%)
13	DET	W 30-16	66 (96%)	66 (96%)	65 (94%)	47 (68%)	67 (97%)		24 (35%)	3 (4%)
14	CHI	L 15-6	63 (100%)	62 (98%)	62 (98%)	27 (43%)	63 (100%)		36 (57%)	
15	PHI	L 30-23	76 (100%)	76 (100%)	63 (83%)	42 (55%)	75 (99%)		34 (45%)	
16	ARI	W 31-9	60 (88%)	59 (87%)		50 (74%)	35 (51%)		51 (75%)	
17	SF	W 48-32	51 (70%)	54 (74%)		43 (59%)	70 (96%)		45 (62%)	
	Grand Total		1,041 (95%)	989 (90%)	825 (86%)	788 (71%)	611 (54%)	439 (83%)	380 (35%)	123 (16%)

Personnel Groupings

Personnel	Team %	NFL Avg	Succ. %
1-1 [3WR]	90%	65%	54%
1-2 [2WR]	7%	17%	58%

Grouping Tendencies

Personnel	Pass Rate	Pass Succ. %	Run Succ. %
1-1 [3WR]	60%	50%	59%
1-2 [2WR]	21%	60%	57%

Red Zone Targets (min 3)

Receiver	All	Inside 5	6-10	11-20
Brandin Cooks	18	4	6	8
Todd Gurley	18	1	5	12
Josh Reynolds	14	4	1	9
Robert Woods	13	3	5	5
Cooper Kupp	11		6	5
Gerald Everett	9	1	5	3
Tyler Higbee	7	2	1	4
C.J. Anderson	2		1	1

Red Zone Rushes (min 3)

Rusher	All	Inside 5	6-10	11-20
Todd Gurley	66	22	15	29
C.J. Anderson	25	8	6	11
Jared Goff	10	5	1	4
Malcolm Brown	8	1	2	5
Brandin Cooks	3		1	2

Early Down Target Rate

	RB	TE	WR
	18%	15%	67%
NFL AVG	*23%*	*21%*	*56%*

Overall Target Success %

	RB	TE	WR
	48%	54%	56%
	#14	#18	#5

147

Los Angeles Rams 2018 Passing Recap & 2019 Outlook

Entering 2018, I wrote that I was more impressed than the public during **Jared Goff**'s 2016 campaign and less impressed than the public with Goff's 2017, attributing much of his improvement to **Sean McVay**. So I wasn't surprised when the Rams had a great 2018 season but Goff's performance was similar to his 2017.

From third downs to early downs to red zone and under center versus shotgun, Goff's play held steady. He did look downfield more often with a deeper average depth of target, and Goff's adjusted completion percent rose from 72% to 75%. With **Brandin Cooks**, **Robert Woods**, and the return of **Cooper Kupp**, everything is in place for Goff to take another step.

One interesting note: Goff was terrible on the road with an 11:10 TD-to-INT ratio and 1.1-yard drop in yards per attempt. His home-game TD-to-INT ratio was 22:4.

Jared Goff Rating All Downs

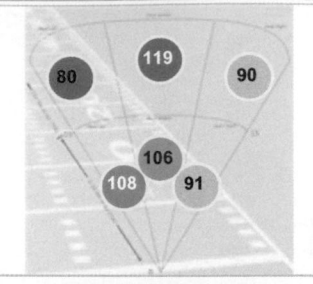

2018 Standard Passing Table

QB	Comp	Att	Comp %	Yds	YPA	TDs	INT	Sacks	Rating	Rk
Jared Goff	423	669	63%	5,392	8.1	33	15	37	96	18
NFL Avg			62%		7.0				87.5	

2018 Advanced Passing Table

QB	Success %	EDSR Passing Success %	20+ Yd Pass Gains	20+ Yd Pass %	30+ Yd Pass Gains	30+ Yd Pass %	Avg. Air Yds per Comp	Avg. YAC per Comp	20+ Air Yd Comp	20+ Air Yd %
Jared Goff	50%	53%	77	12.0%	27	4.0%	7.1	5.7	30	4%
NFL Avg	44%	48%	29.5	8.4%	12.5	3.7%	5.8	5.1	14.5	6%

Jared Goff Rating Early Downs

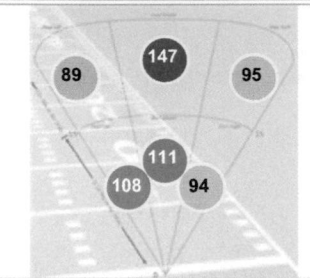

Interception Rates by Down

Yards to Go	1st Dwn	2nd Dwn	3rd Dwn	4th Dwn	Total
1 & 2	0.0%	5.0%	4.0%	0.0%	4.2%
3, 4, 5	0.0%	0.0%	2.2%	0.0%	1.0%
6 - 9	0.0%	1.4%	6.1%	0.0%	3.1%
10 - 14	1.5%	1.2%	0.0%	100.0%	1.5%
15+	11.1%	0.0%	11.1%		5.6%
Total	1.8%	1.2%	3.5%	20.0%	2.1%

3rd Down Passing - Short of Sticks Analysis

QB	Avg. Yds to Go	Avg. YIA (of Comp)	Avg Yds Short	Short of Sticks Rate	Short Rk
Jared Goff	7.1	5.7	-1.4	57%	17
NFL Avg	7.8	6.4	-1.4	60%	

Air Yds vs YAC

Air Yds %	YAC %	Rk
55%	45%	16
53%	48%	

2018 Receiving Recap & 2019 Outlook

The Rams' loss of **Cooper Kupp** to an ACL tear at midseason hurt but wasn't crippling. I would like to have seen **Sean McVay** implement more two-tight end 12 personnel as a result, but he did not.

In fact, McVay's 11-personnel usage (90%) was even higher in 2018 than 2017 (81%). When the Rams passed, they were in 11 personnel at an unheard-of 96% rate. Even when all three of the Rams' top-three receivers were healthy, **Robert Woods** led the team in targets and Success Rate.

Player *Min 50 Targets	Targ	Comp %	YPA	Rating	Success %	Success Rk	Missed YPA Rk	YAS % Rk	YTS % Rk	TDs
Robert Woods	159	65%	8.7	97.2	58%	27	73	36	67	6
Brandin Cooks	143	69%	10.5	106.3	59%	21	27	18	113	5
Todd Gurley	88	72%	6.6	95.1	49%	85	84	36	87	4
Josh Reynolds	71	52%	7.4	76.2	46%	99	127	11	97	5
Gerald Everett	58	60%	6.4	89.0	47%	95	113	94	38	3
Cooper Kupp	56	71%	10.1	132.0	59%	21	46	5	113	5

Directional Passer Rating Delivered

Receiver	Short Left	Short Middle	Short Right	Deep Left	Deep Middle	Deep Right	Player Total
Robert Woods	98	93	101	53	156	109	97
Brandin Cooks	114	107	111	124	138	30	106
Todd Gurley	110	57	107	119	40	40	95
Josh Reynolds	124	136	37	25	119	67	76
Gerald Everett	59	143	52			127	89
Cooper Kupp	115	113	124	96	0	141	132
Tyler Higbee	117	119	135	78		119	123
C.J. Anderson	77	97	40				68
Malcolm Brown	158		73				132
Pharoh Cooper			40				40
Team Total	108	106	91	80	119	89	100

2018 Rushing Recap & 2019 Outlook

Third-round pick **Darrell Henderson** could take the football world by storm. **Todd Gurley**'s fantasy football Average Draft Position has dropped into the second round, whereas Henderson's ADP is creeping into the sixth.

Running backs are bound to produce in **Sean McVay**'s offense, and with Gurley's usage near certain to be scaled back, Henderson can at very least lighten Gurley's load. When the Rams are in shotgun, they run the ball on only 4% of snaps. Yet they occasionally use play action from the gun and delivered 7.4 yards per attempt with a 125 passer rating on such plays last year.

Player *Min 50 Rushes	Rushes	YPC	Success %	Success Rk	Missed YPA Rk	YTS % Rk	YAS % Rk	Early Down Success %	Early Down Success Rk	TDs
Todd Gurley	286	4.9	56%	6	22	37	19	57%	4	19
C.J. Anderson	113	5.5	70%	1	1	23	22	52%	17	4

Yards per Carry by Direction

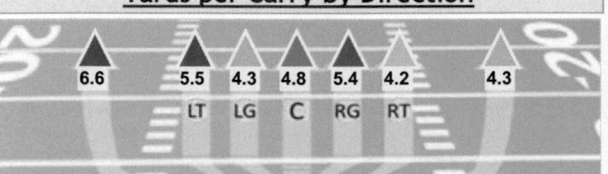

6.6 | 5.5 | 4.3 | 4.8 | 5.4 | 4.2 | 4.3
LT | LG | C | RG | RT

Directional Run Frequency

7% | 21% | 12% | 27% | 8% | 18% | 7%
LT | LG | C | RG | RT

I was also surprised by the Rams' use of tempo. It was nearly impossible to use in the hostile Superdome in the NFC Championship Game, but far too often the Rams snapped the ball with five or fewer seconds left on the play clock for disastrous Super Bowl results. These 18 plays generated a paltry average gain of 1.4 yards with an interception. Plays snapped with just one second on the clock averaged 0.2 yards.

McVay also made minimal halftime adjustments. Each of the Rams' first five plays after the break saw them snap the ball with fewer than ten seconds left on the play clock, including three snaps with three seconds or fewer. And of their final nine snaps before their desperation final drive, seven saw the Rams snap the ball with fewer than ten seconds on the clock, including six with five seconds remaining or fewer.

Somewhere along the way, the Rams presumably received information that continuing to field heavy 11 personnel was their best strategy. That play action wasn't particularly necessary, and that running down the play clock was optimal. My recommendations were the opposite of all of those. We had access to the same data but came away with completely different notions of an optimal approach.

And that's why consulting with different perspectives and incorporating divergent ideas – even from those "outside the building" – can be valuable. Ultimately, what a team does with its data-backed recommendations is up to the coach. But at least they should have access to the ideas.

Despite the Super Bowl loss, the Rams are in good shape entering the 2019 season. And Super Bowl hangovers aren't really a thing. Nine of the last ten

(cont'd - see LA-5)

Los Angeles Rams Fantasy Corner

After trading up for **Darrell Henderson** at the 70th pick, GM **Les Snead** likened his projected role to **Alvin Kamara** as a versatile space player with immense big-play upside. A 4.49 speedster at 5-foot-8, 208, Henderson averaged an otherworldly 8.2 career yards per carry at Memphis and led the nation in yards after contact per rushing attempt (6.2) in his final year. He caught 63 passes across three seasons, averaging 12.0 yards per catch. Behind arthritic-kneed **Todd Gurley**, Henderson's floor looks to be a 9-12 touches-per-game back with league-winning upside if Gurley breaks down. After he landed in an elite offense, no one should be surprised if Henderson emerges as the most-valuable running back in this rookie class.

- Evan Silva

2018 Situational Usage by Player & Position

Usage Rate by Score

		Being Blown Out (14+)	Down Big (9-13)	One Score	Large Lead (9-13)	Blowout Lead (14+)
RUSH	Todd Gurley	1%	5%	77%	14%	3%
	Robert Woods	4%		87%	4%	4%
	Brandin Cooks			91%	9%	
	C.J. Anderson		11%	57%	9%	22%
	Josh Reynolds		25%	75%		
	Cooper Kupp			75%	25%	
	Gerald Everett				50%	50%
	Malcolm Brown			28%	12%	60%
	John Kelly	4%		15%		81%
	Total	1%	5%	66%	12%	16%
PASS	Todd Gurley	11%	8%	70%	8%	4%
	Robert Woods	6%	6%	73%	8%	7%
	Brandin Cooks	2%	10%	67%	10%	11%
	C.J. Anderson		9%	45%	18%	27%
	Josh Reynolds	5%	11%	62%	8%	13%
	Cooper Kupp	2%		83%	9%	6%
	Gerald Everett	17%	6%	58%	10%	8%
	Malcolm Brown	14%		43%	14%	29%
	Tyler Higbee	6%	8%	75%		11%
	John Kelly				33%	67%
	Pharoh Cooper			100%		
	Total	6%	7%	68%	9%	10%

Share of Offensive Plays by Type

	Todd Gurley	Robert Woods	Brandin Cooks	C.J. Anderson	Josh Reynolds	Cooper Kupp	Gerald Everett	Malcolm Brown	Tyler Higbee	John Kelly	Pharoh Cooper
RUSH	58%	5%	2%	18%	1%	1%	0%	9%		6%	
PASS	13%	25%	24%	2%	11%	8%	8%	1%	6%	1%	0%
ALL	34%	15%	14%	9%	6%	5%	5%	5%	3%	3%	0%

Positional Target Distribution vs NFL Average

		NFL Wide				Team Only			
		Left	Middle	Right	Total	Left	Middle	Right	Total
Deep	WR	33%	17%	30%	81%	35%	16%	38%	88%
	TE	5%	4%	7%	16%	5%		5%	9%
	RB	1%	0%	2%	4%	1%	1%	1%	2%
	All	39%	22%	39%	100%	40%	17%	43%	100%
Short	WR	20%	13%	21%	55%	24%	19%	19%	62%
	TE	6%	6%	8%	20%	7%	3%	8%	17%
	RB	10%	5%	10%	25%	9%	5%	7%	20%
	All	36%	25%	39%	100%	40%	27%	34%	100%
Total		37%	24%	39%	100%	40%	25%	36%	100%

Positional Success Rates vs NFL Average

		NFL Wide				Team Only			
		Left	Middle	Right	Total	Left	Middle	Right	Total
Deep	WR	39%	49%	40%	42%	53%	67%	35%	48%
	TE	44%	53%	41%	45%	33%		50%	42%
	RB	36%	40%	43%	41%	100%	0%	0%	33%
	All	40%	49%	40%	42%	52%	64%	36%	47%
Short	WR	55%	60%	53%	55%	61%	68%	49%	59%
	TE	55%	62%	54%	57%	46%	86%	55%	56%
	RB	46%	54%	45%	48%	51%	50%	42%	48%
	All	53%	59%	51%	54%	56%	66%	49%	56%
Total		50%	58%	49%	51%	55%	66%	46%	54%

Division History: Season Wins & 2019 Projection

2015 Wins | 2016 Wins | 2017 Wins | 2018 Wins | Forecast 2019 Wins

Rank of 2019 Defensive Pass Efficiency Faced by Week

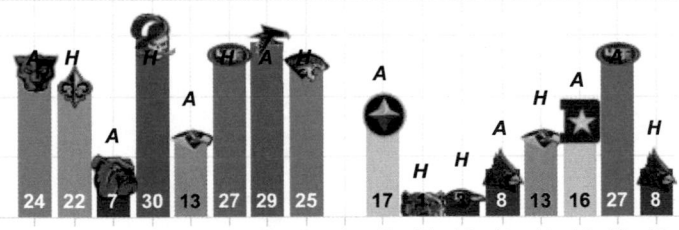

| 24 | 22 | 7 | 30 | 13 | 27 | 29 | 25 | | 17 | | | 8 | 13 | 16 | 27 | 8 |
| 0 | 1 | 2 | 3 | 4 | 5 | 6 | 7 | 8 | 9 | 10 | 11 | 12 | 13 | 14 | 15 | 16 | 17 |

Rank of 2019 Defensive Rush Efficiency Faced by Week

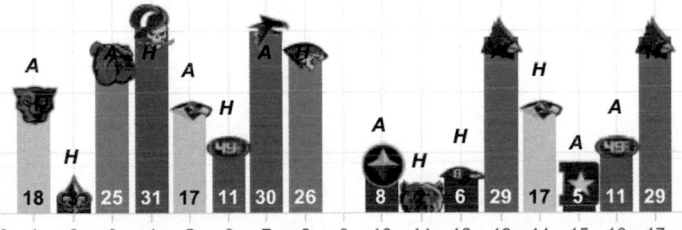

| 18 | | 25 | 31 | 17 | 11 | 30 | 26 | | 8 | 6 | 29 | 17 | 5 | 11 | 29 |
| 0 | 1 | 2 | 3 | 4 | 5 | 6 | 7 | 8 | 9 | 10 | 11 | 12 | 13 | 14 | 15 | 16 | 17 |

2018 Detailed Analytics Summary
Success by Play Type & Primary Personnel Groupings

Successful Play Rate 0% ▮▮▮▮ 100%

Type	1-1 [3WR]	1-2 [2WR]	1-3 [1WR]	2-2 [1WR]	0-0 [5WR]	1-0 [4WR]	0-1 [4WR]	2-3 [0WR]	ALL
PASS	50% (630)	68% (22)	50% (2)		75% (4)	67% (3)	0% (3)		50% (664)
RUSH	59% (436)	60% (70)	20% (15)	0% (7)		0% (1)		0% (2)	57% (531)
All	53% (1,066)	62% (92)	24% (17)	0% (7)	75% (4)	50% (4)	0% (3)	0% (2)	53% (1,195)

Format Success Rate (Total # of Plays)

Receiving Success by Top-4 Personnel Groupings
(Min 50 targets)

POS	Player	1-1 [3WR]	1-2 [2WR]	1-0 [4WR]	1-3 [1WR]	4 Grp Total
RB	Todd Gurley	51% (82) 6.7, 96.9				51% (82) 6.7, 96.9
TE	Gerald Everett	47% (53) 6.8, 93.3	50% (2) 1.5, 56.3			47% (55) 6.6, 91.7
WR	Robert Woods	57% (140) 8.6, 92.7	86% (7) 15.3, 158.3	0% (1) 0.0, 39.6	100% (1) 9.0, 104.2	58% (149) 8.9, 98.9
	Brandin Cooks	57% (125) 10.2, 107.9	100% (2) 14.5, 118.8	100% (2) 16.5, 118.8		58% (129) 10.3, 109.2
	Josh Reynolds	47% (59) 7.8, 74.1	100% (1) 2.0, 118.8			48% (60) 7.7, 80.0
	Cooper Kupp	61% (54) 10.5, 136.8				61% (54) 10.5, 136.8

Format Line 1: Success Rate (Total # of Plays)   Line 2: YPA, Passer Rating

Rushing Success by Top-4 Personnel Groupings
(Min 25 carries)

Rusher (Last, First)	1-1 [3WR]	1-2 [2WR]	2-2 [1WR]	4 Grp Total
Gurley Todd	57% (267) 5.0	29% (7) 1.7		56% (274) 5.0
Anderson C.J.	65% (57) 5.9	83% (23) 5.6		70% (80) 5.8
Brown Malcolm	64% (36) 5.1	83% (6) 4.0		67% (42) 4.9
Goff Jared	48% (31) 4.1	50% (6) 2.7	0% (3) -1.0	45% (40) 3.5
Kelly John	67% (6) 4.3	33% (21) 2.3		41% (27) 2.7

Format Line 1: Success Rate (Total # of Plays)   Line 2: YPC

Passing by Coverage Scheme

Zone	59% (253) 8.7, 97.2
M2M	54% (201) 9.2, 112.1
Screen	47% (66) 7.6, 113.5
Combo	54% (13) 7.2, 115.2

Passing by Route

Out	62% (77) 7.1, 84.6
Screen	45% (53) 8.4, 114.3
Curl	59% (49) 7.2, 98.5
Dig	70% (44) 11.3, 121.1
Flat	30% (20) 3.7, 84.2
Slant	93% (15) 17.1, 118.8

Throw Types

Level 1	58% (412) 7.7, 100.6
Level 2	58% (132) 10.9, 120.3
Level 3	26% (34) 10.8, 76.8
Shovel	46% (13) 4.7, 111.4
Sidearm	50% (4) 9.3, 103.1

QB Drop Types

3 Step	59% (264) 8.5, 96.2
5 Step	46% (106) 7.6, 87.1
7 Step	56% (72) 11.6, 110.5
0/1 Step	52% (58) 6.2, 107.0
Basic Screen	43% (44) 7.3, 111.9
Designed Rollout Right	55% (33) 8.6, 130.4

QB State at Pass

Planted	56% (376) 9.2, 104.6
Shuffling	52% (85) 6.6, 99.4
Moving	56% (59) 8.6, 122.8

Play Action

	Play Action	No P/A
Under Center	61% (186) 10.5, 119.8	62% (37) 8.9, 120.3
Shotgun	50% (20) 7.4, 124.6	52% (354) 7.5, 90.6
ALL	60% (206) 10.2, 120.2	53% (391) 7.6, 93.4

Run Types

Outside Zone	61% (246) 5.5
Inside Zone	55% (101) 4.0
Stretch	51% (35) 3.7
Pitch	48% (23) 5.4
Power	63% (8) 4.1
Lead	100% (1) 5.0

LA-5

Super Bowl losers have won double-digit games the following year. Multiple teams made it back to the conference title game, and last year's Patriots went from Super Bowl losers to world champs.

Unfortunately, the Rams are also saddled with an albatross contract for a running back who may not deliver the production the team initially envisioned. Last season was **Todd Gurley**'s first of his four-year, $57.5 million deal. His $9.2 million cap hit is second highest among running backs this year, and his projected 2020 hit of $17.25 million is highest in the league. If the Rams want to cut Gurley in 2021, they would have to accept $8.4 million in dead cap space.

Many in the analytics community didn't love Gurley's second contract. I'm wondering how many in the non-analytics world – as well as the Rams – are having second thoughts entering the deal's second season. Gurley was unbelievable when healthy in 2018, but he was hurt late with what appears to be a chronic injury.

Gurley tore his left ACL in November of 2014. He suffered an unspecified left knee injury in Week 1 last year, then played through it until the final two games of the regular season. His playoff debut came nearly a month later, and Gurley's efficiency in that game (16 carries, 56% success, 7.2 yards per carry) was inferior to teammate **C.J. Anderson**'s (23 carries, 70% success, 5.3 YPC). On seven days rest, Gurley was given only four carries the following week and totaled ten yards. On two weeks rest in the Super Bowl, Gurley managed a 40% Success Rate and 3.5 YPC.

There are three reasons to be concerned if you're the Rams, or someone invested heavily in their and **Todd Gurley**'s success.

First, it's become clear the Rams can no longer and will no longer use Gurley in the every-down workhorse hole they paid him for, and his contract has no outs for at least two more seasons. The organization outwardly expressed its Gurley concern by trading up for **Darrell Henderson** in the top-75 picks of the draft. So not only are the Rams allocating $26.5 million in combined cap space to a running back, but they've also spent significant draft capital on another player at the same replaceable position.

Second, Gurley was flatly outplayed by street free agent **C.J. Anderson** last year. Key reasons for Gurley's greatness were McVay's scheme and the performance of his teammates, especially on the offensive line. In Anderson's two spot starts, he averaged 7.0 yards per carry with a 77% Success Rate. Anderson's playoff carries scored rock-solid results in Success Rate (63%) and YPC (4.2). Anderson isn't even remotely close to as talented as Gurley yet produced on par or better when given the opportunity to play within Gurley's elite supporting-cast confines.

Third, running back suffers the highest injury rate of any position in the NFL. Paying a player as much as the Rams did Gurley at the league's most-injured position is definitively poor process.

(cont'd – see Page 246)

Miami Dolphins

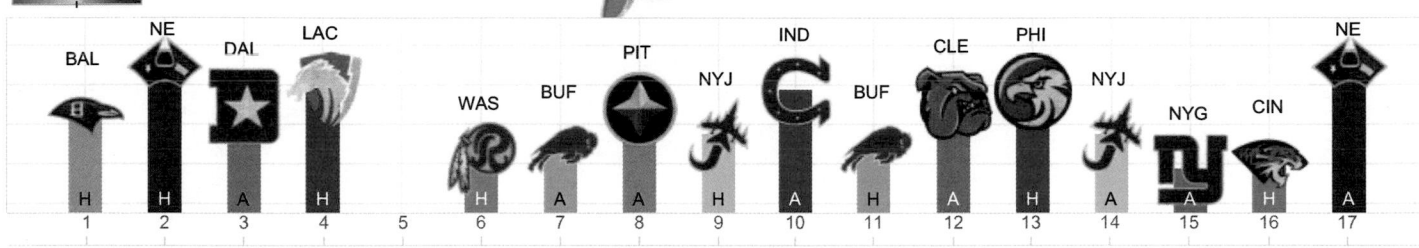

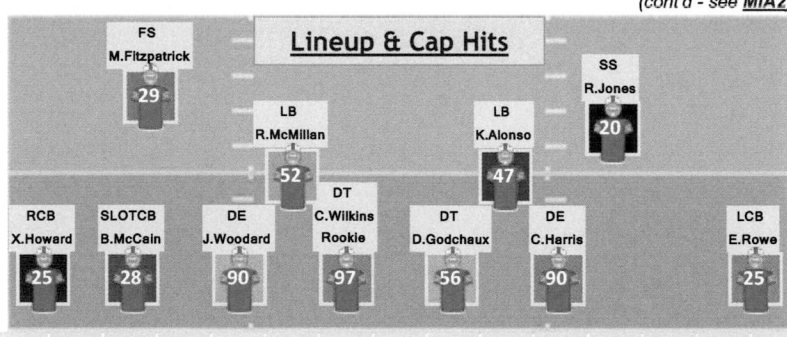

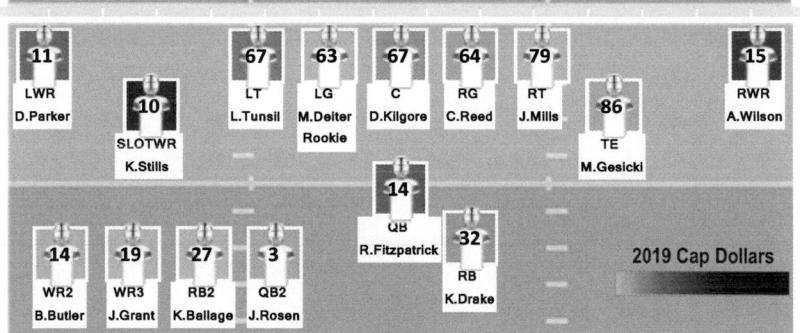

Coaches (Prior Yrs)

Head Coach:
Brian Flores (NE DC) (new)
Offensive Coordinator:
Chad O'Shea (NE WR) (new)
Defensive Coordinator:
Patrick Graham (GB LB) (new)

EASY   HARD

BAL	NE	DAL	LAC		WAS	BUF	PIT	NYJ	IND	BUF	CLE	PHI	NYJ	NYG	CIN	NE
H	H	A	H		H	A	A	H	A	H	A	H	A	A	H	A
1	2	3	4	5	6	7	8	9	10	11	12	13	14	15	16	17

MNF

2019 Forecast

Wins	Div Rank
5	#4

Past Records

2018: 7-9
2017: 6-10
2016: 10-6

Key Players Lost

Player	New
Alterraun Verner (CB)	Retired
Brandon Bolden (RB)	NE
Cameron Wake (DE)	TEN
Danny Amendola (WR)	DET
Frank Gore (RB)	BUF
Ja'Wuan James (RT)	DEN
Jake Brendel (C)	DEN
Josh Sitton (G)	Retired
Robert Quinn (DE)	DAL
Ryan Tannehill (QB)	TEN
Senorise Perry (RB)	BUF
Ted Larsen (G)	CHI
Travis Swanson (C)	Retired

Average Line	# Games Favored	# Games Underdog
4.3	3	11

Regular Season Wins: Past & Current Proj

Forecast 2019 Wins — 5
2018 Wins — 7
Forecast 2018 Wins — 6
2017 Wins — 6
2016 Wins — 10
2015 Wins — 6

1 3 5 7 9 11 13 15

2019 Miami Dolphins Overview

"You are what you record says you are." – **Bill Parcells**.

Wrong. The 2018 Dolphins were much worse than their 7-9 record, and they knew it.

Last year's Fins played the NFL's fifth-softest schedule based on Early Down Success Rate, yet Miami ranked No. 25 in defensive efficiency and No. 29 in offensive efficiency. The Dolphins were No. 31 in both third-down and red-zone efficiency.

Zooming in to a game-by-game basis, Miami posted a superior EDSR to its opponent in just two games all year: Week 1 against the Titans and Week 14 against the Patriots. Tennessee lost **Marcus Mariota** amid a rainstorm, before Week 14 was dubbed the "Miami Miracle" as the Dolphins won on one of the most improbable final play hook-and-ladder sequences in NFL history. Miami also won five games where it trailed by EDSR, accounting for the team's seven wins.

The Dolphins made 90% of their field goal attempts (No. 7 in the NFL), while opponents made only 75% of their field goal attempts, third worst. The team's field goal edge contributed to +15% of Miami's 2018 point differential.

Beyond a soft schedule and serendipitous special teams outcomes, Miami's +5 turnover margin was unsustainable, and Week 9 vs. the Jets provided a perfect microcosm. The Jets had *six* explosive plays to only one by the **Brock Osweiler**-led Dolphins. New York more than doubled the amount of first downs recorded by the Dolphins, gained over 67% more yards, and held the Miami offense to just 168 total yards. However, Miami's +4 turnover margin with a pick-six sealed the 13-6 victory. It was the least-impressive win in the NFL last season given that teams enjoying a +4 in turnover margin and scoring a non-offensive touchdown are 73-0 over the last eight seasons, winning by an average

(cont'd - see MIA2)

Key Free Agents/ Trades Added

Player	AAV (MM)
Adolphus Washington (DT)	$0.6
Chris Reed (G)	$1.5
Clive Walford (TE)	$0.6
Dwayne Allen (TE)	$3.2
Eric Rowe (CB)	$3.5
Josh Rosen (QB)	Trade
Ricardo Louis (WR)	$0.5
Ryan Fitzpatrick (QB)	$5.5

Drafted Players

Rd	Pk	Player (College)
1	13	DT - Christian Wilkins (Clemson)
3	78	G - Michael Deiter (Wisconsin)
5	151	LB - Andrew Van Ginkel (Wisconsin)
6	202	OT - Isaiah Prince (Ohio State)
7	233	RB - Chandler Cox (Auburn)
7	234	RB - Myles Gaskin (Washington)

Lineup & Cap Hits

FS M.Fitzpatrick 29
SS R.Jones 20
LB R.McMillan 52
LB K.Alonso 47
RCB X.Howard 25
SLOTCB B.McCain 28
DE J.Woodard 90
DT C.Wilkins Rookie 97
DT D.Godchaux 56
DE C.Harris 90
LCB E.Rowe 25

LWR D.Parker 11
SLOTWR K.Stills 10
LT L.Tunsil 67
LG M.Deiter Rookie 63
C D.Kilgore 67
RG C.Reed 64
RT J.Mills 79
TE M.Gesicki 86
RWR A.Wilson 15

QB R.Fitzpatrick 14
RB K.Drake 32

WR2 B.Butler 14
WR3 J.Grant 19
RB2 K.Ballage 27
QB2 J.Rosen 3

2019 Cap Dollars

2019 Unit Spending

All OFF / All DEF

Positional Spending

	Rank	Total	2017 Rk
All OFF	32	$60.58M	21
QB	29	$7.42M	25
OL	32	$13.88M	15
RB	27	$4.53M	24
WR	13	$26.95M	4
TE	17	$7.80M	24
All DEF	17	$85.34M	13
DL	29	$15.61M	3
LB	24	$15.80M	23
CB	10	$24.61M	32
S	3	$29.32M	11

151

of 22 points.

Through their Week 11 bye, Miami posted an abysmal 45% Success Rate and 6.7 yards per attempt when passing from 11 personnel. From 12 personnel, the offense posted a 61% Success Rate and 13.6 YPA. Yet OC **Dowell Loggains** utilized 11 personnel on 86% of plays, second only to the Rams. These suboptimal personnel tendencies contributed to the Dolphins' anemic offensive efficiency.

After the bye, Miami upped its usage of 12 personnel to 21%, and the team was much more competitive, winning its next three games as well as going up 24-14 against the Colts prior to an epic fourth-quarter meltdown. During this stretch, Miami averaged a 63% Success Rate in 12 personnel. The team's sack rate dropped by more than 50% in 12 personnel vs. 11 personnel.

Beyond any midseason strategy improvements, Miami was the luckiest team in the NFL last season, going 7-1 (87.5% win rate) in one-score games. To put in context, 21 teams since 1995 posted an 87.5% or better win rate in one-score games, and each of those teams finished 10-6 or better.

Except the 2018 Dolphins. Let that sink in.

These lucky teams posted a .519 average winning percentage in one-score games the following season. Translation: Winning close games is more random than skillful, and when bad teams get extraordinarily lucky, a catastrophic season often follows.

Fortunately for fans, no one understands this predicament better than Dolphins management. With no room for meaningful short-term improvement, new GM **Chris Grier** arrived knowing a full rebuild would be required for the Dolphins to compete with Grier's former club, the Patriots.

Grier kicked off his tenure by signaling a radically different organizational philosophy. He started with several intelligent moves made on draft day. The Dolphins acquired the Saints' 2020 second-round pick, so now Miami has a first and a pair of seconds. They also acquired an extra fourth when they traded away **Ryan Tannehill**. In a very shrewd move, Miami flipped its late second-round pick and a future fifth to pick up **Josh Rosen**. From there, Miami added a sixth when they traded away **Robert Quinn** and gained an extra seventh when they traded away **Jordan Lucas**.

The Dolphins then began to work the compensatory pick market. You're

familiar with that market, where the NFL literally gives away 32 free draft picks to teams that "lost" the highest-priced free agents. (As if losing players who are getting massively overpaid and saving that cap space is a bad thing.)

Amazingly, in the five years from 2015-2019, the Dolphins received only three comp picks. The only way such a thing happens is heavy investment in free agency. But the Dolphins have turned the page on that. In the 2020 draft, it appears they will receive an extra third and an extra fifth-round pick thanks to the compensatory distribution.

In sum, the Dolphins have two 2020 picks in every round except the first and fifth rounds – an impressive war chest. With that stockpile, the Dolphins

(cont'd - see MIA-3)

2018 Passing Performance

QB	1st Dwn	2nd Dwn	3rd Dwn	
Ryan Tannehill	52%	48%	22%	Success Rate
	7.6	7.4	5.8	YPA
	101.6	102.0	65.4	Rating
Pass Rate	51%	60%	82%	
NFL AVG	53%	47%	36%	Success Rate
	7.7	7.3	6.9	YPA
	95.1	93.7	87.1	Rating
Pass Rate	53%	62%	80%	

2018 Rushing Performance

Offense	1st Dwn	2nd Dwn	3rd Dwn	
MIA	49%	42%	36%	Success Rate
	4.7	4.7	3.9	YPC
Run Rate	49%	40%	18%	
NFL AVG	48%	46%	51%	Success Rate
	4.5	4.4	4.3	YPC
Run Rate	47%	38%	20%	

2018 Offensive Advanced Metrics

Rank (by category):
- EDSR Off: 29
- 30 & In Off: 22
- Red Zone Off: 31
- 3rd Down Off: 31
- YPPA Off: 24
- YPPT Off: 10
- Offensive Efficiency: 26
- Pass Efficiency Off: 27
- Pass Pro Efficiency Off: 31
- RB Pass Eff Off: 11
- Rush Efficiency Off: 15
- Explosive Pass Off: 31
- Explosive Run Off: 31

2018 Defensive Advanced Metrics

Rank (by category):
- EDSR Def: 27
- 30 & In Def: 24
- Red Zone Def: 29
- 3rd Down Def: 27
- YPPA Def: 31
- YPPT Def: 17
- Defensive Efficiency: 25
- Pass Efficiency Def: 23
- Pass Pro Efficiency Def: 28
- RB Pass Eff Def: 11
- Rush Efficiency Def: 24
- Explosive Pass Def: 24
- Explosive Run Def: 22

2018 Weekly EDSR & Season Trending Performance

	1	2	3	4	5	6	7	8	9	10	12	13	14	15	16	17	WEEK
RESULT	W	W	W	L	L	W	L	L	W	L	L	W	W	L	L	L	
OPP	TEN	NYJ	OAK	NE	CIN	CHI	DET	HOU	NYJ	GB	IND	BUF	NE	MIN	JAC	BUF	
SITE	H	A	H	A	A	H	H	A	H	A	A	H	H	A	H	A	
MARGIN	7	8	8	-31	-10	3	-11	-19	7	-19	-3	4	1	-24	-10	-25	
PTS	27	20	28	7	17	31	21	23	13	12	24	21	34	17	7	17	
OPP PTS	20	12	20	38	27	28	32	42	6	31	27	17	33	41	17	42	

EDSR by Wk
W=Green
L=Red

OFF/DEF
EDSR
Blue=OFF
(high=good)
Red=DEF
(low=good)

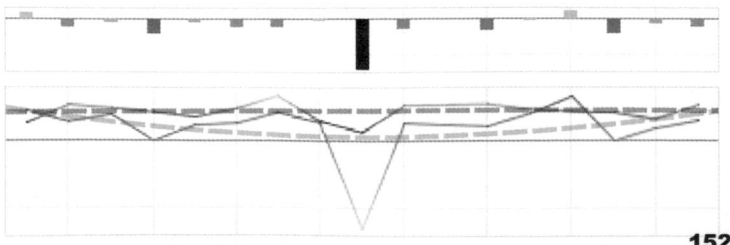

2018 Close Game Records

All 2018 Wins: **7**
FG Games (<=3 pts) W-L: **2-1**
FG Games Win %: **67% (#8)**
FG Games Wins (% of Total Wins): **29% (#17)**
1 Score Games (<=8 pts) W-L: **7-1**
1 Score Games Win %: **88% (#1)**
1 Score Games Wins (% of Total Wins): **100% (#1)**

2018 Critical & Game-Deciding Stats

TO Margin	+5
TO Given	23
INT Given	13
FUM Given	10
TO Taken	28
INT Taken	21
FUM Taken	7
Sack Margin	-21
Sacks	31
Sacks Allow	52
Return TD Margin	+1
Ret TDs	5
Ret TDs Allow	4
Penalty Margin	-1
Penalties	108
Opponent Penalties	107

Miami Dolphins 2019 Strength of Schedule In Detail (compared to 2018)

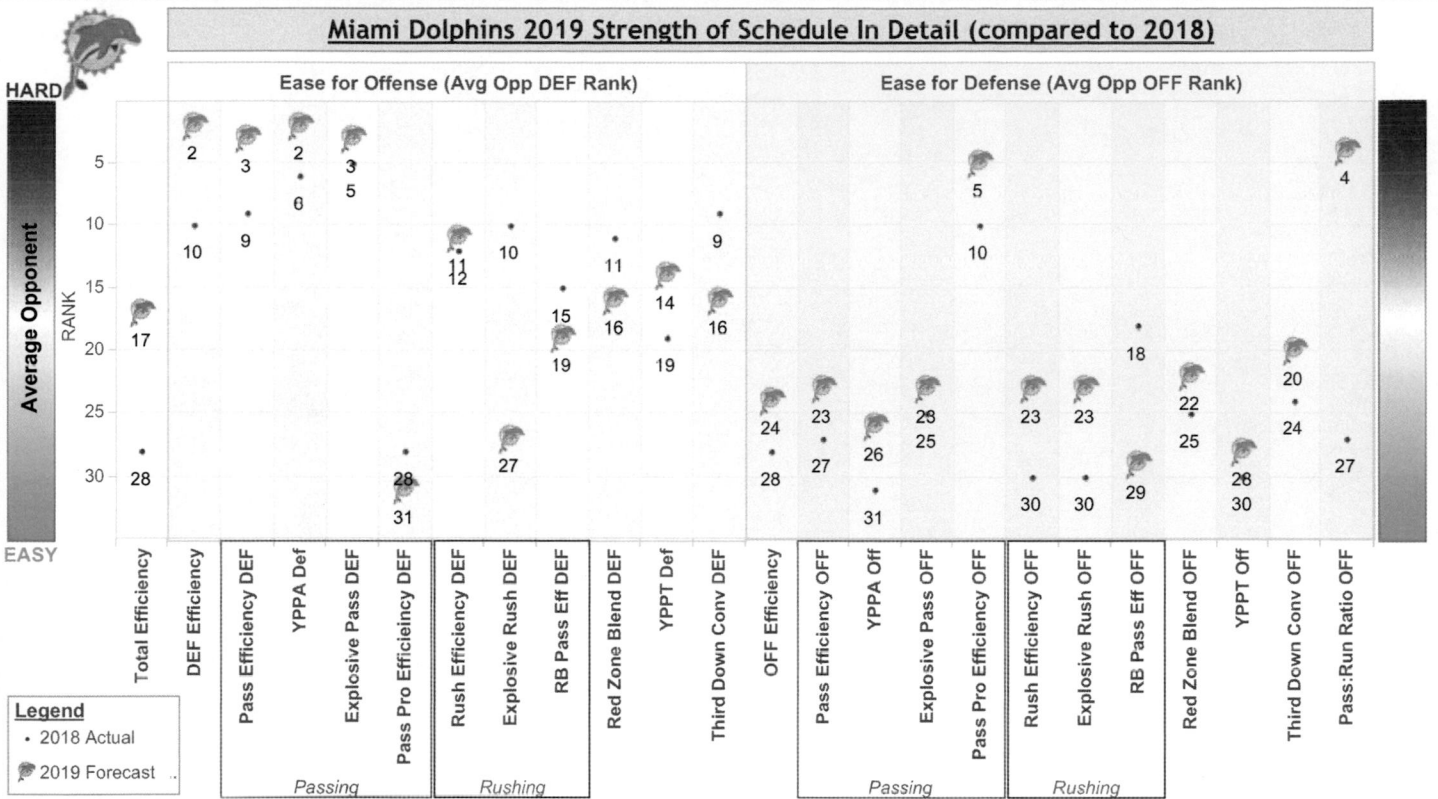

Legend
- 2018 Actual
- 2019 Forecast

2019 v 2018 Schedule Variances* (OFF=Rank of DEF faced, 2019 vs 2018)

Pass OFF Rank	Pass OFF Blend Rk	Rush OFF Rk	Rush OFF Blend Rk	Pass DEF Rk	Pass DEF Blend Rk	Rush DEF Rk	Rush DEF Blend Rk
7	13	10	27	12	10	8	9

* **1**=Hardest Jump in 2019 schedule from 2018 (aka a much harder schedule in 2019), **32**=Easiest Jump in 2019 schedule from 2018 (aka a much easier schedule in 2019);
Pass Blend metric blends 4 metrics: Pass Efficiency, YPPA, Explosive Pass & Pass Rush; **Rush Blend** metric blends 3 metrics: Rush Efficiency, Explosive Rush & RB Targets

Team Records & Trends

MIA-3

	2018	2017	2016
Average line	3.5	4.6	1.8
Average O/U line	44.9	43.3	44.2
Straight Up Record	7-9	6-10	10-6
Against the Spread Record	7-9	5-9	9-7
Over/Under Record	8-7	8-8	12-4
ATS as Favorite	2-2	0-1	2-3
ATS as Underdog	4-7	4-8	6-4
Straight Up Home	6-2	4-3	6-2
ATS Home	5-3	3-2	4-4
Over/Under Home	5-3	4-3	7-1
ATS as Home Favorite	2-2	0-0	1-3
ATS as a Home Dog	2-1	2-2	3-1
Straight Up Away	1-7	2-6	4-4
ATS Away	2-6	2-6	5-3
Over/Under Away	3-4	4-4	5-3
ATS Away Favorite	0-0	0-1	1-0
ATS Away Dog	2-6	2-5	3-3
Six Point Teaser Record	9-7	11-5	12-4
Seven Point Teaser Record	9-7	11-5	12-4
Ten Point Teaser Record	11-5	12-4	13-3

can dig hardcore into their rebuild and either select players they believe to be worth the pick, or package picks in other trades to target a truly coveted player.

In either case, step one is complete: Acquire draft capital. The harder part is properly analyzing the right way to build a team and execute by selecting good players that fill needs.

Many teams have tried to build through the draft, but they end up spending draft capital on positions that aren't worthy of such investment, or players whose college performance doesn't translate to the NFL as envisioned. Before making any picks, it's vital the Dolphins do their research to understand positional value and optimal roster design to take advantage of the most current rules as well as projecting the future direction of the league. Foresight will be valuable.

*(cont'd - see **MIA-4**)*

2019 Rest Analysis

Team More Rest	2
Opp More Rest	4
Net Rest Edge	-2
Week 2 Edge	0
Week 3 Edge	0
Week 4 Edge	0
Week 6 Edge	7
Week 7 Edge	
Week 8 Edge	
Week 9 Edge	-1
Week 10 Edge	0
Week 11 Edge	0
Week 12 Edge	-3
Week 13 Edge	0
Week 14 Edge	0
Week 15 Edge	1
Week 16 Edge	0
Week 17 Edge	0

Health by Unit*

2018 Rk	22
2017 Rk	
2018 v 2017 Rk	7
Off Rk	
Def Rk	12
QB Rk	27
RB Rk	17
WR Rk	
TE Rk	22
Oline Rk	27
Dline Rk	25
LB Rk	3
DB Rk	11

*Based on the work of Football Outsiders

2018 Weekly Betting Lines (wks 1-16)

1	2	3	4	6	7	8	9	10	11	12	13	14	15	16
BAL	NE	DAL	LAC	WAS	BUF	PIT	NYJ	IND	BUF	CLE	PHI	NYJ	NYG	CIN
4	8.5	9	6	-1	4.5	10	0	9.5	-2.5	8	4	3	3	-1.5

Avg = 4.3

Home Lines (wks 1-16)

1	2	4	6	9	11	13	16
4	8.5	6	-1	0	-2.5	4	-1.5
BAL	NE	LAC	WAS	NYJ	BUF	PHI	CIN

Avg = 2.2

Road Lines (wks 1-16)

3	7	8	10	12	14	15
9	4.5	10	9.5	8	3	3
DAL	BUF	PIT	IND	CLE	NYJ	NYG

Avg = 6.7

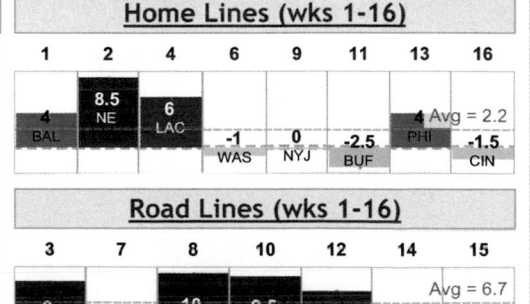

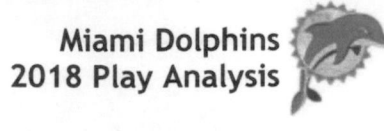
2018 Play Tendencies

All Pass %	58%
All Pass Rk	20
All Rush %	42%
All Rush Rk	13
1 Score Pass %	56%
1 Score Pass Rk	22
2017 1 Score Pass %	58%
2017 1 Score Pass Rk	14
2018 Pass Increase %	-2%
Pass Increase Rk	23
1 Score Rush %	44%
1 Score Rush Rk	11
Up Pass %	51%
Up Pass Rk	10
Up Rush %	49%
Up Rush Rk	23
Down Pass %	64%
Down Pass Rk	26
Down Rush %	36%
Down Rush Rk	7

2018 Down & Distance Tendencies

Down	Distance	Total Plays	Pass Rate	Run Rate	Play Success %
1	Short (1-3)	1	100%	0%	100%
	Med (4-7)	8	38%	63%	63%
	Long (8-10)	275	45%	55%	54%
	XL (11+)	13	46%	54%	31%
2	Short (1-3)	35	49%	51%	71%
	Med (4-7)	78	64%	36%	62%
	Long (8-10)	72	47%	53%	28%
	XL (11+)	37	57%	43%	19%
3	Short (1-3)	33	64%	36%	52%
	Med (4-7)	47	91%	9%	36%
	Long (8-10)	33	88%	12%	18%
	XL (11+)	29	86%	14%	17%
4	Short (1-3)	7	57%	43%	71%

Shotgun %:

Under Center	Shotgun
35%	65%

37% AVG 63%

Run Rate:

Under Center	Shotgun
67%	30%

68% AVG 23%

Pass Rate:

Under Center	Shotgun
33%	70%

32% AVG 77%

Short Yardage Intelligence:

2nd and Short Run

Run Freq	Run Rk	NFL Run Freq Avg	Run 1D Rate	Run NFL 1D Avg
53%	30	65%	69%	68%

2nd and Short Pass

Pass Freq	Pass Rk	NFL Pass Freq Avg	Pass 1D Rate	Pass NFL 1D Avg
47%	2	35%	57%	56%

Most Frequent Play

Down	Distance	Play Type	Player	Total Plays	Play Success %
1	Med (4-7)	RUSH	Kenyan Drake	2	100%
			Frank Gore	2	50%
	Long (8-10)	RUSH	Frank Gore	76	54%
	XL (11+)	RUSH	Frank Gore	5	40%
2	Short (1-3)	RUSH	Frank Gore	9	67%
	Med (4-7)	RUSH	Frank Gore	14	57%
	Long (8-10)	RUSH	Kenyan Drake	17	29%
			Frank Gore	17	35%
	XL (11+)	RUSH	Kenyan Drake	7	0%
3	Short (1-3)	PASS	Danny Amendola	4	75%
		RUSH	Kenyan Drake	4	50%
	Med (4-7)	PASS	Kenyan Drake	10	60%
	Long (8-10)	PASS	DeVante Parker	6	17%
	XL (11+)	PASS	Kenyan Drake	4	0%
			Danny Amendola	4	0%

Most Successful Play*

Down	Distance	Play Type	Player	Total Plays	Play Success %
1	Long (8-10)	PASS	Danny Amendola	19	79%
	XL (11+)	RUSH	Frank Gore	5	40%
2	Short (1-3)	RUSH	Frank Gore	9	67%
	Med (4-7)	RUSH	Kenyan Drake	8	75%
	Long (8-10)	RUSH	Frank Gore	17	35%
	XL (11+)	PASS	Danny Amendola	5	0%
		RUSH	Kenyan Drake	7	0%
3	Med (4-7)	PASS	Kenyan Drake	10	60%
	Long (8-10)	PASS	DeVante Parker	6	17%

*Minimum 5 plays to qualify

2018 Weekly Snap Rates

Wk	Opp	Score	Kenny Stills	Danny Amendola	Kenyan Drake	DeVante Parker	Mike Gesicki	Nick O'Leary	Frank Gore	Jakeem Grant	Albert Wilson
1	TEN	W 27-20	59 (95%)	45 (73%)	46 (74%)		21 (34%)		18 (29%)	25 (40%)	34 (55%)
2	NYJ	W 20-12	56 (93%)	44 (73%)	36 (60%)		33 (55%)		24 (40%)	32 (53%)	29 (48%)
3	OAK	W 28-20	40 (91%)	31 (70%)	29 (66%)	33 (75%)	28 (64%)		16 (36%)	9 (20%)	10 (23%)
4	NE	L 38-7	38 (78%)	42 (86%)	22 (45%)		41 (84%)		25 (51%)	31 (63%)	37 (76%)
5	CIN	L 27-17	60 (94%)	53 (83%)	41 (64%)		30 (47%)	28 (44%)	26 (41%)	15 (23%)	58 (91%)
6	CHI	W 31-28	67 (86%)	75 (96%)	49 (63%)	4 (5%)	27 (35%)	52 (67%)	30 (38%)	31 (40%)	50 (64%)
7	DET	L 32-21	49 (88%)	55 (98%)	36 (64%)		16 (29%)	39 (70%)	25 (45%)	39 (70%)	14 (25%)
8	HOU	L 42-23		65 (98%)	37 (56%)	66 (100%)	16 (24%)	49 (74%)	29 (44%)	63 (95%)	
9	NYJ	W 13-6	28 (49%)	47 (82%)	28 (49%)	51 (89%)	27 (47%)	33 (58%)	29 (51%)	29 (51%)	
10	GB	L 31-12	65 (96%)	66 (97%)	34 (50%)	45 (66%)	20 (29%)	21 (31%)	29 (43%)	8 (12%)	
12	IND	L 27-24	51 (96%)	14 (26%)	24 (45%)	24 (45%)	37 (70%)	30 (57%)	29 (55%)		
13	BUF	W 21-17	48 (87%)		30 (55%)	46 (84%)	22 (40%)	32 (58%)	20 (36%)		
14	NE	W 34-33	40 (83%)	25 (52%)	24 (50%)	42 (88%)	24 (50%)	24 (50%)	23 (48%)		
15	MIN	L 41-17	51 (96%)	39 (74%)	28 (53%)	19 (36%)	25 (47%)	25 (47%)	7 (13%)		
16	JAC	L 17-7	37 (80%)	31 (67%)	39 (85%)	32 (70%)	16 (35%)	16 (35%)			
17	BUF	L 42-17	56 (92%)	50 (82%)	42 (69%)	49 (80%)	21 (34%)	23 (38%)			
	Grand Total		745 (87%)	682 (77%)	545 (59%)	411 (67%)	400 (45%)	372 (52%)	330 (41%)	282 (47%)	232 (54%)

Personnel Groupings

Personnel	Team %	NFL Avg	Succ. %
1-1 [3WR]	74%	65%	46%
1-2 [2WR]	12%	17%	50%
2-1 [2WR]	4%	8%	58%
1-3 [1WR]	3%	3%	23%

Grouping Tendencies

Personnel	Pass Rate	Pass Succ. %	Run Succ. %
1-1 [3WR]	62%	43%	51%
1-2 [2WR]	51%	56%	43%
2-1 [2WR]	39%	33%	74%
1-3 [1WR]	30%	33%	19%

Red Zone Targets (min 3)

Receiver	All	Inside 5	6-10	11-20
Kenyan Drake	7	2	1	4
DeVante Parker	5		2	3
Mike Gesicki	5	2		3
Frank Gore	3		1	2
Kenny Stills	3	1	1	1
A.J. Derby	2		1	1
Danny Amendola	2		2	

Red Zone Rushes (min 3)

Rusher	All	Inside 5	6-10	11-20
Frank Gore	13	1	4	8
Kenyan Drake	12	1	3	8
Ryan Tannehill	4			4
Brandon Bolden	2		1	1

Early Down Target Rate

	RB	TE	WR
	23%	14%	63%
	23%	21%	56%
		NFL AVG	

Overall Target Success %

	RB	TE	WR
	50%	53%	49%
	#10	#19	#23

Miami Dolphins 2018 Passing Recap & 2019 Outlook

Ryan Fitzpatrick is one "hellafun" NFL quarterback. If your priority is evaluating your roster and trying to be something more than bland and putrid, Fitzpatrick is a decent option. Which direction the Dolphins go at starting quarterback will be interesting. There is no need to sit Rosen to let him get experience. He got plenty in Arizona. If the priority is seeing what guys have, then let Rosen start Week 1, so long as he's free of any major red flags through the preseason.

I want to see how he performs and adapts. I'd want to see if he *could* be a franchise quarterback for my roster. That said, regardless of who starts, it's likely going to look ugly for a while. The first six games of the season come against nothing but above-average pass defenses from 2018, including three that ranked top ten. It's not until the second half of the season where the passing schedule lightens up a bit and where Rosen should definitely see playing time.

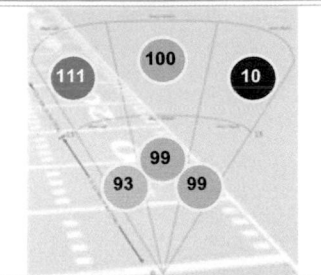

Ryan Tannehill Rating All Downs

2018 Standard Passing Table

QB	Comp	Att	Comp %	Yds	YPA	TDs	INT	Sacks	Rating	Rk
Ryan Tannehill	176	274	64%	1,924	7.0	17	9	35	92	25
Brock Osweiler	113	178	63%	1,247	7.0	6	4	17	86	33
NFL Avg			62%		7.0				87.5	

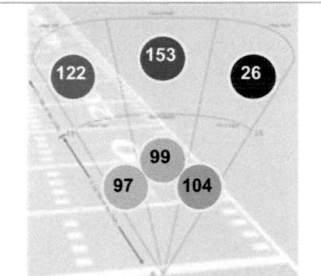

Ryan Tannehill Rating Early Downs

2018 Advanced Passing Table

QB	Success %	EDSR Passing Success %	20+ Yd Pass Gains	20+ Yd Pass %	30+ Yd Pass Gains	30+ Yd Pass %	Avg. Air Yds per Comp	Avg. YAC per Comp	20+ Air Yd Comp	20+ Air Yd %
Ryan Tannehill	42%	50%	18	7.0%	8	3.0%	5.0	5.9	9	3%
Brock Osweiler	44%	46%	13	7.0%	6	3.0%	5.0	6.1	4	2%
NFL Avg	44%	48%	29.5	8.4%	12.5	3.7%	5.8	5.1	14.5	6%

Interception Rates by Down

Yards to Go	1st Dwn	2nd Dwn	3rd Dwn	4th Dwn	Total
1 & 2		0.0%	0.0%	0.0%	0.0%
3, 4, 5		6.3%	0.0%		2.9%
6 - 9	0.0%	2.9%	3.3%		2.9%
10 - 14	1.8%	3.4%	0.0%	0.0%	1.9%
15+	16.7%	0.0%	11.8%		8.8%
Total	2.5%	3.1%	3.3%	0.0%	2.9%

3rd Down Passing - Short of Sticks Analysis

QB	Avg. Yds to Go	Avg. YIA (of Comp)	Avg Yds Short	Short of Sticks Rate	Short Rk
Ryan Tannehill	9.3	3.7	-5.6	81%	40
NFL Avg	7.8	6.4	-1.4	60%	

Air Yds vs YAC

Air Yds %	YAC %	Rk
45%	55%	43
53%	48%	

2018 Receiving Recap & 2019 Outlook

Embarrassingly, the 2018 Dolphins' leading receiver was 33-year-old **Danny Amendola** despite a Success Rate that ranked No. 47 in the league and a No. 97-ranked explosiveness quotient. Another problem for Miami was its receiver corps was the second-most injured group in the league. Unfortunately, the Dolphins don't have anyone new beating down the door to target. **DaVante Parker**, **Albert Wilson**, and **Kenny Stills** will still be the team's primary three receivers. If the offensive line provides better protection, whomever the quarterback is may have time to work the ball downfield to these guys, because last year's group rarely had that opportunity.

Player *Min 50 Targets*	Targ	Comp %	YPA	Rating	Success %	Success Rk	Missed YPA Rk	YAS % Rk	YTS % Rk	TDs
Danny Amendola	79	75%	7.3	83.0	54%	47	97	97	67	1
Kenyan Drake	73	73%	5.8	105.1	45%	102	93	121	26	3
Kenny Stills	64	58%	8.6	103.2	53%	52	139	28	97	5

Directional Passer Rating Delivered

Receiver	Short Left	Short Middle	Short Right	Deep Left	Deep Middle	Deep Right	Player Total
Danny Amendola	76	79	93	67	0	149	83
Kenyan Drake	95	95	102	100		135	105
Kenny Stills	131	78	104	87	88	27	103
DeVante Parker	84	75	84	40	133	18	70
Albert Wilson	79	158	85	40	119	0	125
Jakeem Grant	87	57	113		0	156	94
Mike Gesicki	48	95	89	40	40	67	73
Frank Gore	115	55	129				118
Nick O'Leary	106	40	155				136
A.J. Derby	40		119		158		132
Team Total	91	108	109	73	87	70	97

2018 Rushing Recap & 2019 Outlook

Frank Gore surprised skeptics by producing a 50% Success Rate in all game situations. However, Gore is gone and now the clear-cut leader of the running back room is **Kenyan Drake** playing in a contract year. Drake was the Dolphins' second-leading receiver in 2018 by targets and led the team with 19 total red-zone touches. The enigmatic oversized satellite back **Kalen Ballage** is the wildcard in this backfield. No team targeted running backs on early downs more over the last three years than the Patriots, where new OC **Chad O'Shea** coached the past ten years.

Yards per Carry by Direction

	5.9	6.0	4.4	4.0	4.3	7.5	4.2
		LT	LG	C	RG	RT	

Directional Run Frequency

	7%	13%	16%	36%	10%	10%	8%
		LT	LG	C	RG	RT	

Player *Min 50 Rushes*	Rushes	YPC	Success %	Success Rk	Missed YPA Rk	YTS % Rk	YAS % Rk	Early Down Success %	Early Down Success Rk	TDs
Frank Gore	156	4.6	50%	26	13	18	56	50%	24	0
Kenyan Drake	120	4.5	45%	48	72	39	37	47%	34	4

The lone 2020 pick the Dolphins gave away was a fifth-rounder to Arizona in the **Josh Rosen** trade. The amazing part of the move is that the Cardinals already paid all the big money to Rosen from his rookie deal. He will *only* cost the Dolphins $6.3 million over the next three years.

Even though most people are now down on Rosen, I was a huge fan of the move. Those same people also didn't like **Jared Goff** after his rookie year. After all, Goff averaged 5.3 YPA, recorded a dreadful 63.6 passer rating, and only completed 54.6 percent of his passes. Rosen was superior in all of those stats, although not by much. Both players were coached their rookie year in a terrible offense with head coaches that were fired with minimal talent at receiver.

Rosen is not dead yet.

Last year, Rosen faced the NFL's worst pass-blocking offensive line under an uncreative offensive coordinator who was fired midseason with a group of extremely young wide receivers paired with the game's oldest wide receiver, and the toughest schedule of opposing pass defenses for any rookie quarterback.

Rosen was set up to fail in Arizona, and his best years are undoubtedly ahead of him.

(cont'd - see MIA-5)

Miami Dolphins Fantasy Corner

Kenyan Drake looked like a massive reach in the early third round after posting less than 1500 rushing yards and less than 50 receptions in four years at Alabama. Then, something changed. After receiving just 42 touches in 2016, Drake's efficiency climbed as he added weight while keeping his explosiveness, evidenced by a 107.1 (85th-percentile) Speed Score on Player Profiler. In 2018, Drake's 5.8 yards per touch ranked No. 10 and his 34.7% Juke Rate (evaded tackles per touch) ranked No. 7 among qualified backs. With Gore in Buffalo, Drake is poised to finally come full circle in his NFL career and assume a bellcow role in Miami. **Ryan Fitzpatrick**'s possible presence under center should lead to more red-zone opportunities after Drake secured just 15 red-zone touches in 2018. Drake's athletic profile raises his ceiling while his projected workload bolsters his floor, making Drake an excellent value in the fifth round of fantasy drafts. - Matt Kelley

2018 Situational Usage by Player & Position

Usage Rate by Score

		Being Blown Out (14+)	Down Big (9-13)	One Score	Large Lead (9-13)	Blowout Lead (14+)
RUSH	Kenyan Drake	15%	11%	68%	3%	4%
	Frank Gore	10%	10%	75%	1%	4%
	Danny Amendola		100%			
	Kalen Ballage	57%	3%	40%		
	Albert Wilson	13%		75%		13%
	Jakeem Grant			100%		
	Brandon Bolden	13%		88%		
	Total	17%	9%	69%	1%	4%
PASS	Kenyan Drake	20%	16%	59%		5%
	Frank Gore	20%	13%	67%		
	Danny Amendola	23%	16%	59%		1%
	Kenny Stills	24%	6%	66%		4%
	Kalen Ballage	18%		82%		
	DeVante Parker	19%	16%	65%		
	Albert Wilson	10%	3%	76%	3%	7%
	Jakeem Grant	15%	6%	70%	3%	6%
	Brandon Bolden	50%		50%		
	Nick O'Leary	30%	20%	50%		
	Brice Butler	38%		63%		
	A.J. Derby	20%	20%	40%		20%
	Total	21%	12%	64%	1%	3%

Share of Offensive Plays by Type

	Kenyan Drake	Frank Gore	Danny Amendola	Kenny Stills	Kalen Ballage	DeVante Parker	Albert Wilson	Jakeem Grant	Brandon Bolden	Nick O'Leary	Brice Butler	A.J. Derby
RUSH	36%	47%	0%		11%		2%	0%	2%			
PASS	18%	4%	22%	15%	3%	13%	9%	10%	1%	3%	2%	1%
ALL	27%	26%	11%	7%	7%	6%	6%	5%	1%	1%	1%	1%

Positional Target Distribution vs NFL Average

		NFL Wide				Team Only			
		Left	Middle	Right	Total	Left	Middle	Right	Total
Deep	WR	33%	17%	30%	**81%**	25%	21%	37%	**83%**
	TE	5%	4%	7%	**16%**	3%	3%	4%	**10%**
	RB	1%	0%	2%	**3%**	4%		3%	**7%**
	All	**39%**	**22%**	**39%**	**100%**	**32%**	**24%**	**44%**	**100%**
Short	WR	20%	14%	21%	**55%**	23%	15%	25%	**63%**
	TE	6%	6%	8%	**20%**	4%	4%	5%	**12%**
	RB	10%	5%	10%	**25%**	11%	5%	10%	**25%**
	All	**36%**	**25%**	**39%**	**100%**	**38%**	**23%**	**39%**	**100%**
Total		**37%**	**24%**	**39%**	**100%**	**37%**	**24%**	**40%**	**100%**

Positional Success Rates vs NFL Average

		NFL Wide				Team Only			
		Left	Middle	Right	Total	Left	Middle	Right	Total
Deep	WR	40%	50%	40%	**42%**	17%	40%	35%	**31%**
	TE	44%	53%	42%	**46%**	0%	50%	33%	**29%**
	RB	38%	33%	42%	**40%**	33%		50%	**40%**
	All	**41%**	**50%**	**40%**	**43%**	**17%**	**41%**	**35%**	**31%**
Short	WR	55%	61%	52%	**55%**	51%	60%	54%	**55%**
	TE	55%	62%	54%	**57%**	54%	50%	67%	**58%**
	RB	46%	54%	45%	**47%**	53%	44%	50%	**50%**
	All	**53%**	**60%**	**51%**	**54%**	**52%**	**55%**	**55%**	**54%**
Total		**50%**	**58%**	**49%**	**52%**	**47%**	**53%**	**51%**	**50%**

Division History: Season Wins & 2019 Projection

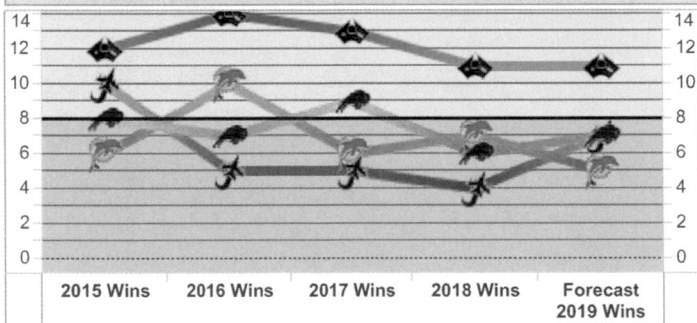

2015 Wins | 2016 Wins | 2017 Wins | 2018 Wins | Forecast 2019 Wins

Rank of 2019 Defensive Pass Efficiency Faced by Week

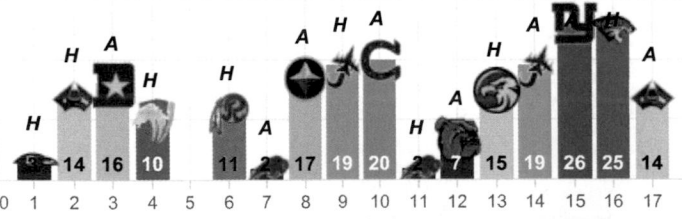

Rank of 2019 Defensive Rush Efficiency Faced by Week

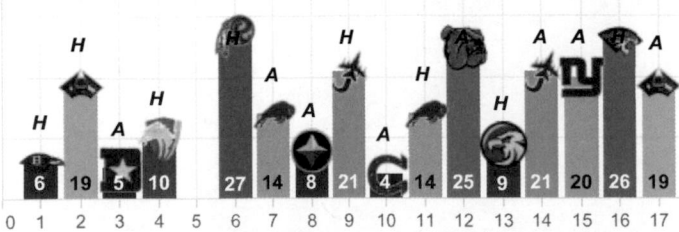

2018 Detailed Analytics Summary
Success by Play Type & Primary Personnel Groupings

Successful Play Rate 0% ▬▬▬ 100%

Type	1-1 [3WR]	1-2 [2WR]	2-1 [2WR]	1-3 [1WR]	0-1 [4WR]	1-0 [4WR]	2-0 [3WR]	2-3 [0WR]	0-0 [5WR]	ALL
PASS	43% (401)	56% (52)	33% (12)	33% (9)	11% (9)	44% (9)	33% (6)			43% (498)
RUSH	51% (245)	43% (49)	74% (19)	19% (21)	80% (5)	40% (5)	25% (8)	0% (10)	100% (1)	48% (363)
All	46% (646)	50% (101)	58% (31)	23% (30)	36% (14)	43% (14)	29% (14)	0% (10)	100% (1)	45% (861)

Format   Success Rate (Total # of Plays)

Receiving Success by Top-4 Personnel Groupings
(Min 50 targets)

POS	Player	1-1 [3WR]	1-2 [2WR]	1-0 [4WR]	2-1 [2WR]	4 Grp Total
RB	Kenyan Drake	48% (56) 5.8, 100.6	60% (5) 8.4, 141.3	67% (3) 13.3, 149.3	0% (2) 2.0, 56.3	48% (66) 6.2, 110.0
WR	Danny Amendola	57% (70) 7.5, 83.2	100% (2) 12.5, 118.8	0% (1) 0.0, 39.6	50% (2) 5.0, 64.6	57% (75) 7.4, 83.1
	Kenny Stills	54% (48) 8.3, 95.8	67% (9) 18.3, 149.3	0% (2) 0.0, 39.6	50% (2) 10.5, 87.5	54% (61) 9.6, 109.1

Format   Line 1: Success Rate (Total # of Plays)   Line 2: YPA, Passer Rating

Rushing Success by Top-4 Personnel Groupings
(Min 25 carries)

Rusher (Last, First)	1-1 [3WR]	1-2 [2WR]	2-1 [2WR]	4 Grp Total
Gore Frank	56% (114) 5.3	38% (26) 2.9	67% (3) 4.3	53% (143) 4.9
Drake Kenyan	49% (91) 5.1	43% (14) 1.9	75% (4) 8.0	50% (109) 4.8
Ballage Kalen	38% (16) 3.6	100% (3) 8.7	67% (6) 15.5	52% (25) 7.0
Tannehill Ryan	46% (13) 5.2	40% (5) 5.0	100% (1) 5.0	47% (19) 5.2

Format   Line 1: Success Rate (Total # of Plays)   Line 2: YPC

Passing by Coverage Scheme

M2M	51% (179) 7.4, 91.3
Zone	55% (163) 7.6, 94.1
Screen	47% (62) 8.1, 132.9
Combo	30% (10) 3.8, 45.0

Passing by Route

Flat	59% (54) 4.7, 115.5
Curl	71% (48) 8.8, 109.7
Out	46% (46) 4.9, 53.4
Screen	48% (44) 7.2, 111.9
Dig	59% (27) 12.1, 123.4
Slant	73% (15) 10.2, 105.7

Throw Types

Level 1	55% (272) 7.0, 98.1
Level 2	53% (96) 9.5, 118.9
Level 3	19% (47) 7.5, 58.3
Shovel	83% (6) 19.8, 158.3
Sidearm	50% (4) 5.3, 88.5

QB Drop Types

3 Step	51% (196) 7.9, 94.7
0/1 Step	52% (134) 6.7, 107.9
5 Step	52% (48) 9.4, 100.3
7 Step	45% (22) 5.5, 46.0
Basic Screen	45% (11) 11.0, 152.1
Designed Rollout Right	30% (10) 3.1, 40.0

QB State at Pass

Planted	53% (340) 7.9, 100.7
Moving	47% (36) 6.7, 101.9
Shuffling	39% (28) 5.4, 99.0

Play Action

	Play Action	No P/A
Under Center	60% (57) 8.8, 85.7	64% (22) 9.3, 105.3
Shotgun	56% (36) 6.6, 103.2	47% (316) 7.5, 101.3
ALL	58% (93) 8.0, 93.5	49% (338) 7.6, 101.6

Run Types

Inside Zone	48% (113) 4.4
Outside Zone	51% (91) 5.2
Stretch	47% (32) 3.9
Power	48% (29) 5.9
Lead	42% (12) 3.4
Pitch	67% (9) 2.6

MIA-5

Unfortunately, Rosen's supporting cast will be no better in Miami. For starters, Rosen will be working with his sixth offensive coordinator in the last five years. He's he's also going to be playing behind what could be 2019's worst pass-blocking offensive line. Last year the Dolphins offensive line ranked sixth worst in pass blocking, and this past offseason, Miami cut its offensive line spending in half. They were spending a league-average $30.6 million on the line in 2018, but in 2019, Miami will spend a league-low $15 million on offensive linemen. The Dolphins will feature the NFL's least expensive offense in 2019, setting up Rosen for another demoralizing year.

Miami also draws a brutal schedule.

The Dolphins face the league's tenth-toughest schedule of defenses in 2019, as well as the league's second-hardest schedule of defenses, including the NFL's most-difficult slate against the pass.

Facing stout defenses behind a porous offensive line feels like Groundhog Day for Rosen. Beyond that, there are other elements of the schedule not in Miami's favor. For three consecutive weeks (Weeks 7-9), they will be playing teams benefiting from extra rest. They face the Bills and Steelers in consecutive weeks, and coming off of their byes, and both games are on the road. Miami returns home in Week 9, but since that Steelers game is on Monday night, they'll face the Jets on a short week.

Three weeks later, the Dolphins travel to Cleveland where the Browns will have gotten their "mini-bye," having played the Thursday prior. Miami will then travel to the Northeast throughout December, playing the Jets and Giants in Weeks 14-15 and closing the season at New England for Week 17.

Questions across the skill position group abound. Will the young secondary led by the newly-extended **Xavien Howard** and playmakers **Minkah Fitzpatrick** and **Reshad Jones** make a leap? Can **Christian Wilkins** and **Laremy Tunsil** adequately anchor the defensive and offensive lines? What skill players will emerge? **Kenyan Drake** is in his contract year. What about the young **Kalen Ballage**? Which receivers will mesh with new offensive coordinator **Chad O'Shea**? And who is the real **Josh Rosen**?

Minnesota Vikings

Coaches (Prior Yrs)

Head Coach:
Mike Zimmer (5 yrs)
Offensive Coordinator:
Kevin Stefanski (MIN QB) (new)
Defensive Coordinator:
George Edwards (5 yrs)

EASY   HARD

2019 Forecast

Wins	Div Rank
9	#3

Past Records

2018: 8-8
2017: 13-3
2016: 8-8

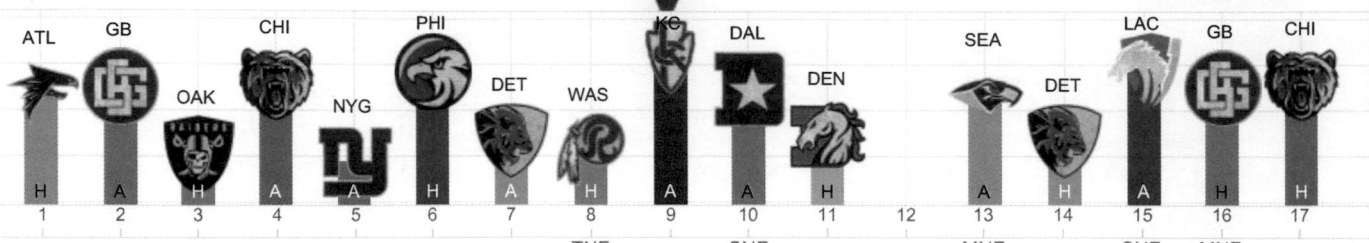

	ATL	GB	OAK	CHI	NYG	PHI	DET	WAS	KC	DAL	DEN		SEA	DET	LAC	GB	CHI
	H	A	H	A	A	H	A	H	A	A	H		A	H	A	H	H
	1	2	3	4	5	6	7	8	9	10	11	12	13	14	15	16	17

TNF   SNF   MNF   SNF   MNF

Key Players Lost

Player	New
Aldrick Robinson (WR)	CAR
Andrew Sendejo (SS)	PHI
Brian Robison (DE)	Retired
Cedrick Lang (T)	NE
George Iloka (FS)	DAL
Latavius Murray (RB)	NO
Marcus Sherels (CB)	NO
Mike Remmers (RT)	NYG
Nick Easton (C)	NO
Sheldon Richardson (DT)	CLE
Tom Compton (G)	NYJ
Trevor Siemian (QB)	NYJ

Average Line	# Games Favored	# Games Underdog
-1.7	9	5

2019 Minnesota Vikings Overview

In the 2017 NFC Championship, the 13-3 Vikings lost the Eagles 38-7, and the game wasn't even that close.

Flash forward to 2018. That fateful championship game was clearly a topic of conversation when former Eagles quarterbacks coach **John DeFilippo** interviewed for Minnesota's offensive coordinator position.

Doug Pederson and **Frank Reich** get the credit for architecting the Eagles' Super Bowl run, but DeFilippo was part of the effort that put **Mike Zimmer**'s proud, No. 2-ranked defense on skates. An effort that included a 17-point second quarter and three total punts.

From 2016 to 2017, the Eagles were among the NFL's most pass-heavy teams with DeFilippo on board. The Vikings skewed more toward the run. The philosophies of these coaches couldn't have been more different. A phenomenon that played itself out across 2018.

To better understand a team's general philosophy, it's vital to study first-down usage. Minnesota ranked near the bottom of the league in first-down Success Rate and yards per carry in both 2016 and 2017. You can blame that on a weak interior offensive line that struggled to get push and movement. Averaging 3.1 YPC when running behind the center or guards is not good.

From his time in Philadelphia, DeFilippo had to believe that continuing in this manner would be unideal. That first-down efficiency is an important marker for success. With **Adam Thielen**, **Stefon Diggs** and **Dalvin Cook** available to operate in space, why play to your weaknesses?

(cont'd - see MIN2)

Key Free Agents/ Trades Added

Player	AAV (MM)
Dakota Dozier (G)	$0.9
Jordan Taylor (WR)	$0.6
Josh Kline (G)	$5.2
Sean Mannion (QB)	$0.9
Shamar Stephen (DT)	$4.2

Drafted Players

Rd	Pk	Player (College)
1	18	C - Garrett Bradbury (NC Sta..
2	50	TE - Irv Smith Jr. (Alabama)
3*	102	RB - Alexander Mattison (Boi..
4	114	G - Dru Samia (Oklahoma)
5	162	LB - Cameron Smith (USC)
	190	DT - Armon Watts (Arkansas)
6	191	S - Marcus Epps (Wyoming)
	193	OT - Oli Udoh (Elon)
7	217	CB - Kris Boyd (Texas)
	239	WR - Dillon Mitchell (Oregon)
7*	247	WR - Olabisi Johnson (Color..
	250	LS - Austin Cutting (Air Force)

Regular Season Wins: Past & Current Proj

Forecast 2019 Wins — 9
2018 Wins — 8
Forecast 2018 Wins — 10
2017 Wins — 13
2016 Wins — 8
2015 Wins — 11

1 3 5 7 9 11 13 15

Lineup & Cap Hits

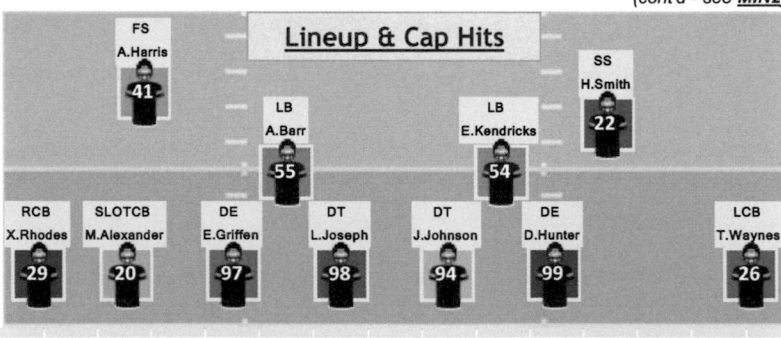
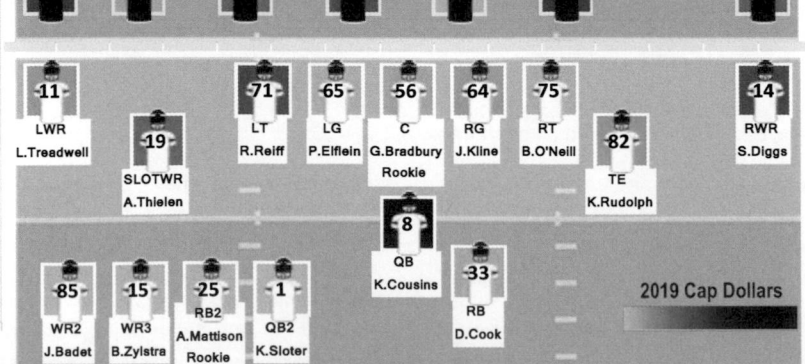

2019 Cap Dollars

2019 Unit Spending

All DEF / All OFF

Positional Spending

	Rank	Total	2017 Rk
All OFF	12	$101.95M	10
QB	3	$30.88M	5
OL	31	$26.86M	22
RB	26	$4.96M	6
WR	10	$28.11M	19
TE	9	$11.14M	11
All DEF	3	$101.50M	3
DL	8	$41.64M	8
LB	26	$14.83M	14
CB	7	$28.69M	8
S	8	$16.34M	6

Philosophically and schematically, DeFilippo wanting to pass more made sense. It's the way the league is trending because it's the most efficient way to play. Especially since 2011, when new league rules that have made passing more efficient were put into effect. First-down passes were completed at a 67.6% clip and averaged 8.2 YPA in 2018, both NFL records. A 51.5% league-wide pass rate on first down also set a new benchmark. The league was still passing on only 47.9% of first-half first downs as recently as five years ago.

This is progress.

Minnesota's run-first approach led to two years of league-worst first-down YPC numbers in the first half. A pass-first approach is far more efficient due to the rules, particularly throwing on first down in the first half -- a key to the Eagles' 2017 Super Bowl run. With an elite wide receiver duo, a dynamic all-purpose running back, and newly-minted quarterback **Kirk Cousins** under center, the rational play-calling tendency was clear.

Throw. The. Ball.

But none of that matters when your head coach isn't just a coach, but also the architect of his defense. As a former defensive coordinator, **Mike Zimmer** seems to care about preventing points more than scoring them. Zimmer's offenses chew up clock by running the ball, even with below-average gains. If forced to punt and give the opponent poor field position, all the better for the defense.

It would be interesting to get inside Zimmer's head to see which style he thinks presents more problems. To see whether he prefers facing an inefficient run-heavy offense or an aggressive offense that skews toward early-down passing. Theoretically, he should want his offense playing the style he feels is tougher to defend. That answer seems obvious if you're looking at it from the offensive perspective. It seems less obvious if you're the coach of the defense, despite evidence to the contrary.

From 2016 to 2018, the Vikings went 9-12 against teams ranked top 15 in both pass rate and pass efficiency. Their record was 21-7 in all other games. The 2018 Vikings went 0-4 against top-10 passing offenses. All four of their losses in 2017, playoffs included, were against above-average pass offenses. And they went 2-6 against above-average pass offenses in 2016.

John DeFilippo changed the structure of the Vikings' offense from his first game on the job. The Vikings called pass plays on 63% of their first-half first downs in Week 1.

2018 Passing Performance

QB	1st Dwn	2nd Dwn	3rd Dwn	
Kirk Cousins	57%	52%	35%	Success Rate
	7.5	7.1	6.6	YPA
	100.5	102.4	92.6	Rating
Pass Rate	68%	64%	85%	
NFL AVG	53%	47%	36%	Success Rate
	7.7	7.3	6.9	YPA
	95.1	93.7	87.1	Rating
Pass Rate	53%	62%	80%	

2018 Rushing Performance

Offense	1st Dwn	2nd Dwn	3rd Dwn	
MIN	45%	38%	39%	Success Rate
	4.5	3.9	3.7	YPC
Run Rate	42%	36%	15%	
NFL AVG	48%	46%	51%	Success Rate
	4.5	4.4	4.3	YPC
Run Rate	47%	38%	20%	

Those numbers jumped to 73% in Week 2 and 75% in Week 3. Their total through seven weeks stood at 66%, tied with the Eagles as the most pass-first offense in the NFL. More importantly, the Vikings' record was 4-2-1 and Minnesota's 64% offensive Success Rate ranked No. 2 in the NFL.

Despite this success, Zimmer seemed more fixated on controlling the tempo of the game than scoring points. A Week 8 tilt against the Saints was the first indication that all was not right in the North. The Vikings went 56% run on first-half first downs, the first time they were above 50% all year.

The difference was immediately noticeable, and it made no sense. Zimmer picked a bad time to force his hand, as he was facing the NFL's best run defense.

(cont'd - see MIN-3)

2018 Offensive Advanced Metrics

EDSR Off: 15; 30 & In Off: 2; Red Zone Off: 20; 3rd Down Off: 19; YPPA Off: 18; YPPT Off: 24; Offensive Efficiency: 18; Pass Efficiency Off: 16; Pass Pro Efficiency Off: 9; RB Pass Eff Off: 19; Rush Efficiency Off: 28; Explosive Pass Off: 26; Explosive Run Off: 10

2018 Defensive Advanced Metrics

EDSR Def: 25; 30 & In Def: 2; Red Zone Def: 3; 3rd Down Def: 1; YPPA Def: 4; YPPT Def: 25; Defensive Efficiency: 4; Pass Efficiency Def: 5; Pass Pro Efficiency Def: 2; RB Pass Eff Def: 13; Rush Efficiency Def: 12; Explosive Pass Def: 22; Explosive Run Def: 6

2018 Weekly EDSR & Season Trending Performance

	1	2	3	4	5	6	7	8	9		11	12	13	14	15	16	17	WEEK
	W	W	L	L	W	W	W	W	W		L	W	L	L	W	W	L	RESULT
	SF	GB	BUF	LA	PHI	ARI	NYJ	NO	DET		CHI	GB	NE	SEA	MIA	DET	CHI	OPP
	H	A	H	A	A	H	A	H	H		A	H	A	A	H	A	H	SITE
	8	0	-21	-7	2	10	20	-10	15		-5	7	-14	-14	24	18	-14	MARGIN
	24	29	6	31	23	27	37	20	24		20	24	10	7	41	27	10	PTS
	16	29	27	38	21	17	17	30	9		25	17	24	21	17	9	24	OPP PTS

EDSR by Wk
W=Green
L=Red

OFF/DEF
EDSR
Blue=OFF
(high=good)
Red=DEF
(low=good)

2018 Close Game Records

All 2018 Wins: **8**

FG Games (<=3 pts) W-L: **1-0**
FG Games Win %: **100% (#1)**
FG Games Wins (% of Total Wins): **13% (#27)**

1 Score Games (<=8 pts) W-L: **3-2**
1 Score Games Win %: **60% (#7)**
1 Score Games Wins (% of Total Wins): **38% (#28)**

2018 Critical & Game-Deciding Stats

TO Margin	+0
TO Given	20
INT Given	10
FUM Given	10
TO Taken	20
INT Taken	12
FUM Taken	8
Sack Margin	+10
Sacks	50
Sacks Allow	40
Return TD Margin	-3
Ret TDs	3
Ret TDs Allow	6
Penalty Margin	+14
Penalties	92
Opponent Penalties	106

Minnesota Vikings 2019 Strength of Schedule In Detail (compared to 2018)

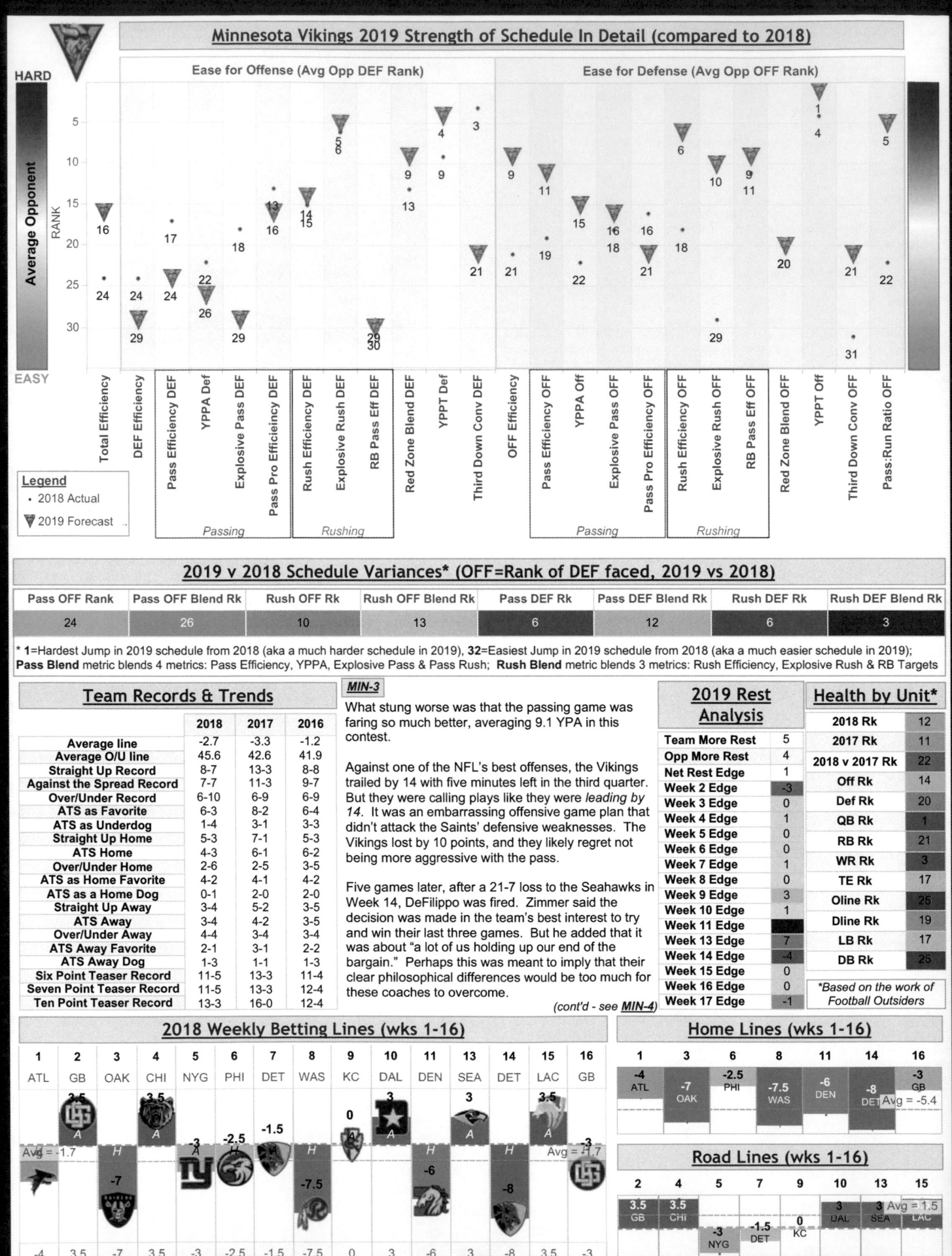

2019 v 2018 Schedule Variances* (OFF=Rank of DEF faced, 2019 vs 2018)

Pass OFF Rank	Pass OFF Blend Rk	Rush OFF Rk	Rush OFF Blend Rk	Pass DEF Rk	Pass DEF Blend Rk	Rush DEF Rk	Rush DEF Blend Rk
24	26	10	13	6	12	6	3

* **1**=Hardest Jump in 2019 schedule from 2018 (aka a much harder schedule in 2019), **32**=Easiest Jump in 2019 schedule from 2018 (aka a much easier schedule in 2019);
Pass Blend metric blends 4 metrics: Pass Efficiency, YPPA, Explosive Pass & Pass Rush; **Rush Blend** metric blends 3 metrics: Rush Efficiency, Explosive Rush & RB Targets

Team Records & Trends

	2018	2017	2016
Average line	-2.7	-3.3	-1.2
Average O/U line	45.6	42.6	41.9
Straight Up Record	8-7	13-3	8-8
Against the Spread Record	7-7	11-3	9-7
Over/Under Record	6-10	6-9	6-9
ATS as Favorite	6-3	8-2	6-4
ATS as Underdog	1-4	3-1	3-3
Straight Up Home	5-3	7-1	5-3
ATS Home	4-3	6-1	6-2
Over/Under Home	2-6	2-5	3-5
ATS as Home Favorite	4-2	4-1	4-2
ATS as a Home Dog	0-1	2-0	2-0
Straight Up Away	3-4	5-2	3-5
ATS Away	3-4	4-2	3-5
Over/Under Away	4-4	3-4	3-4
ATS Away Favorite	2-1	3-1	2-2
ATS Away Dog	1-3	1-1	1-3
Six Point Teaser Record	11-5	13-3	11-4
Seven Point Teaser Record	11-5	13-3	12-4
Ten Point Teaser Record	13-3	16-0	12-4

MIN-3

What stung worse was that the passing game was faring so much better, averaging 9.1 YPA in this contest.

Against one of the NFL's best offenses, the Vikings trailed by 14 with five minutes left in the third quarter. But they were calling plays like they were *leading by 14*. It was an embarrassing offensive game plan that didn't attack the Saints' defensive weaknesses. The Vikings lost by 10 points, and they likely regret not being more aggressive with the pass.

Five games later, after a 21-7 loss to the Seahawks in Week 14, DeFilippo was fired. Zimmer said the decision was made in the team's best interest to try and win their last three games. But he added that it was about "a lot of us holding up our end of the bargain." Perhaps this was meant to imply that their clear philosophical differences would be too much for these coaches to overcome.

(cont'd - see MIN-4)

2019 Rest Analysis

Team More Rest	5
Opp More Rest	4
Net Rest Edge	1
Week 2 Edge	-3
Week 3 Edge	0
Week 4 Edge	1
Week 5 Edge	0
Week 6 Edge	0
Week 7 Edge	1
Week 8 Edge	0
Week 9 Edge	3
Week 10 Edge	1
Week 11 Edge	
Week 13 Edge	7
Week 14 Edge	-4
Week 15 Edge	0
Week 16 Edge	0
Week 17 Edge	-1

Health by Unit*

2018 Rk	12
2017 Rk	11
2018 v 2017 Rk	22
Off Rk	14
Def Rk	20
QB Rk	1
RB Rk	21
WR Rk	3
TE Rk	17
Oline Rk	25
Dline Rk	19
LB Rk	17
DB Rk	25

Based on the work of Football Outsiders

2018 Weekly Betting Lines (wks 1-16)

1	2	3	4	5	6	7	8	9	10	11	13	14	15	16
ATL	GB	OAK	CHI	NYG	PHI	DET	WAS	KC	DAL	DEN	SEA	DET	LAC	GB
-4	3.5	-7	3.5	-3	-2.5	-1.5	-7.5	0	3	-6	3	-8	3.5	-3

Avg = -1.7 ... Avg = -1.7

Home Lines (wks 1-16)

1	3	6	8	11	14	16
-4 ATL	-7 OAK	-2.5 PHI	-7.5 WAS	-6 DEN	-8 DET	-3 GB

Avg = -5.4

Road Lines (wks 1-16)

2	4	5	7	9	10	13	15
3.5 GB	3.5 CHI	-3 NYG	-1.5 DET	0 KC	3 DAL	3 SEA	LAC

Avg = 1.5

Minnesota Vikings
2018 Play Analysis

2018 Play Tendencies

All Pass %	64%
All Pass Rk	4
All Rush %	36%
All Rush Rk	29
1 Score Pass %	62%
1 Score Pass Rk	7
2017 1 Score Pass %	55%
2017 1 Score Pass Rk	23
2018 Pass Increase %	7%
Pass Increase Rk	5
1 Score Rush %	38%
1 Score Rush Rk	26
Up Pass %	50%
Up Pass Rk	14
Up Rush %	50%
Up Rush Rk	19
Down Pass %	76%
Down Pass Rk	2
Down Rush %	24%
Down Rush Rk	31

2018 Down & Distance Tendencies

Down	Distance	Total Plays	Pass Rate	Run Rate	Play Success %
1	Short (1-3)	6	33%	67%	50%
	Med (4-7)	3	33%	67%	67%
	Long (8-10)	304	55%	45%	53%
	XL (11+)	15	67%	33%	33%
2	Short (1-3)	36	50%	50%	67%
	Med (4-7)	78	69%	31%	54%
	Long (8-10)	83	55%	45%	37%
	XL (11+)	40	73%	28%	25%
3	Short (1-3)	44	77%	23%	55%
	Med (4-7)	50	94%	6%	32%
	Long (8-10)	29	97%	3%	34%
	XL (11+)	27	96%	4%	7%
4	Short (1-3)	9	56%	44%	67%

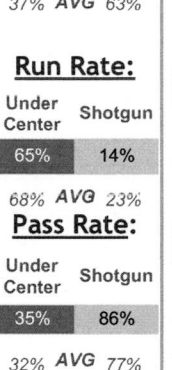

Shotgun %:

Under Center	Shotgun
40%	60%

37% AVG 63%

Run Rate:

Under Center	Shotgun
65%	14%

68% AVG 23%

Pass Rate:

Under Center	Shotgun
35%	86%

32% AVG 77%

Short Yardage Intelligence:

2nd and Short Run

Run Freq	Run Rk	NFL Run Freq Avg	Run 1D Rate	Run NFL 1D Avg
66%	15	65%	58%	68%

2nd and Short Pass

Pass Freq	Pass Rk	NFL Pass Freq Avg	Pass 1D Rate	Pass NFL 1D Avg
34%	18	35%	50%	56%

Most Frequent Play

Down	Distance	Play Type	Player	Total Plays	Play Success %
1	Short (1-3)	PASS	Stefon Diggs	2	50%
		RUSH	Latavius Murray	2	100%
	Long (8-10)	RUSH	Dalvin Cook	64	48%
	XL (11+)	PASS	Stefon Diggs	3	0%
2	Short (1-3)	RUSH	Dalvin Cook	9	56%
	Med (4-7)	PASS	Stefon Diggs	12	58%
	Long (8-10)	PASS	Stefon Diggs	12	58%
		RUSH	Dalvin Cook	12	25%
			Latavius Murray	12	42%
	XL (11+)	PASS	Stefon Diggs	6	33%
			Adam Thielen	6	33%
		RUSH	Dalvin Cook	6	17%
3	Short (1-3)	PASS	Stefon Diggs	6	33%
	Med (4-7)	PASS	Adam Thielen	16	50%
	Long (8-10)	PASS	Stefon Diggs	6	17%
	XL (11+)	PASS	Adam Thielen	6	33%

Most Successful Play*

Down	Distance	Play Type	Player	Total Plays	Play Success %
1	Long (8-10)	PASS	Adam Thielen	38	76%
2	Short (1-3)	RUSH	Kirk Cousins	6	67%
	Med (4-7)	PASS	Adam Thielen	11	82%
	Long (8-10)	RUSH	Stefon Diggs	6	67%
	XL (11+)	PASS	Kyle Rudolph	5	60%
3	Short (1-3)	PASS	Kyle Rudolph	5	80%
	Med (4-7)	PASS	Adam Thielen	16	50%
	Long (8-10)	PASS	Adam Thielen	5	60%
	XL (11+)	PASS	Adam Thielen	6	33%

*Minimum 5 plays to qualify

2018 Weekly Snap Rates

Wk	Opp	Score	Adam Thielen	Kyle Rudolph	Stefon Diggs	Laquon Treadwell	Dalvin Cook	Latavius Murray	David Morgan	C.J. Ham
1	SF	W 24-16	68 (96%)	59 (83%)	61 (86%)	38 (54%)	57 (80%)	14 (20%)	30 (42%)	13 (18%)
2	GB	T 29-29	70 (96%)	63 (86%)	62 (85%)	45 (62%)	50 (68%)	23 (32%)	22 (30%)	7 (10%)
3	BUF	L 27-6	66 (100%)	64 (97%)	57 (86%)	58 (88%)		38 (58%)		17 (26%)
4	LA	L 38-31	73 (99%)	60 (81%)	63 (85%)	46 (62%)	18 (24%)	41 (55%)	23 (31%)	20 (27%)
5	PHI	W 23-21	60 (97%)	54 (87%)	53 (85%)	30 (48%)		46 (74%)	20 (32%)	8 (13%)
6	ARI	W 27-17	69 (97%)	60 (85%)	63 (89%)	38 (54%)		58 (82%)	30 (42%)	14 (20%)
7	NYJ	W 37-17	66 (96%)	56 (81%)	63 (91%)	51 (74%)		58 (84%)	24 (35%)	2 (3%)
8	NO	L 30-20	69 (95%)	63 (86%)	64 (88%)	46 (63%)		61 (84%)	17 (23%)	10 (14%)
9	DET	W 24-9	45 (92%)	46 (94%)		41 (84%)	28 (57%)	22 (45%)	8 (16%)	2 (4%)
11	CHI	L 25-20	67 (100%)	61 (91%)	62 (93%)	29 (43%)	59 (88%)	6 (9%)		3 (4%)
12	GB	W 24-17	68 (97%)	64 (91%)	66 (94%)	33 (47%)	41 (59%)	28 (40%)		8 (11%)
13	NE	L 24-10	61 (100%)	60 (98%)	47 (77%)	22 (36%)	47 (77%)	12 (20%)		5 (8%)
14	SEA	L 21-7	56 (97%)	57 (98%)	50 (86%)	30 (52%)	49 (84%)	8 (14%)		10 (17%)
15	MIA	W 41-17	63 (91%)	51 (74%)	55 (80%)	22 (32%)	42 (61%)	27 (39%)	23 (33%)	18 (26%)
16	DET	W 27-9	57 (93%)	58 (95%)	52 (85%)		46 (75%)	15 (25%)	23 (38%)	3 (5%)
17	CHI	L 24-10	53 (93%)	49 (86%)	56 (98%)	14 (25%)	53 (93%)	4 (7%)	11 (19%)	
	Grand Total		1,011 (96%)	925 (88%)	874 (87%)	543 (55%)	490 (70%)	461 (43%)	231 (31%)	140 (14%)

Personnel Groupings

Personnel	Team %	NFL Avg	Succ. %
1-1 [3WR]	68%	65%	47%
1-2 [2WR]	19%	17%	52%
2-1 [2WR]	7%	8%	46%
2-2 [1WR]	2%	3%	35%

Grouping Tendencies

Personnel	Pass Rate	Pass Succ. %	Run Succ. %
1-1 [3WR]	74%	48%	44%
1-2 [2WR]	46%	60%	45%
2-1 [2WR]	41%	52%	43%
2-2 [1WR]	22%	80%	22%

Red Zone Targets (min 3)

Receiver	All	Inside 5	6-10	11-20
Adam Thielen	18	4	2	12
Stefon Diggs	16	5	3	8
Kyle Rudolph	14	5	3	6
Aldrick Robinson	3			3
Dalvin Cook	3		2	1
Laquon Treadwell	3		1	2

Red Zone Rushes (min 3)

Rusher	All	Inside 5	6-10	11-20
Latavius Murray	22	4	4	14
Dalvin Cook	16	3	4	9
Kirk Cousins	6	1	2	3

Early Down Target Rate

	RB	TE	WR
	20%	16%	64%
	23%	21%	56%
		NFL AVG	

Overall Target Success %

	RB	TE	WR
	45%	63%	54%
	#19	#1	#11

Minnesota Vikings 2018 Passing Recap & 2019 Outlook

Minnesota's passing offense will face an easier schedule than will the rushing game. Hopefully that reflects positively on the fantasy values of the team's top two receivers. **Adam Thielen**'s Success Rate exploded with **Kirk Cousins** at quarterback in 2018, increasing from 51% to 63%. His passer rating delivered increased from 90 to 111.

The problem for the Vikings is that when they put three WRs on the field, the third was most often **Laquon Treadwell**. He was an abject failure, delivering just 5.7 YPA, a 45% success rate and a 71.4 passer rating. Minnesota should increase its passing from 12 personnel rather than continue to trot Treadwell out there. Every key receiver was better from 12 personnel than from 11. Even targets to Cook were more efficient from this grouping.

2018 Standard Passing Table

QB	Comp	Att	Comp %	Yds	YPA	TDs	INT	Sacks	Rating	Rk
Kirk Cousins	425	606	70%	4,298	7.1	30	10	40	100	12
NFL Avg			62%		7.0				87.5	

2018 Advanced Passing Table

QB	Success %	EDSR Passing Success %	20+ Yd Pass Gains	20+ Yd Pass %	30+ Yd Pass Gains	30+ Yd Pass %	Avg. Air Yds per Comp	Avg. YAC per Comp	20+ Air Yd Comp	20+ Air Yd %
Kirk Cousins	49%	55%	47	8.0%	16	3.0%	5.5	4.7	21	3%
NFL Avg	44%	48%	29.5	8.4%	12.5	3.7%	5.8	5.1	14.5	6%

Interception Rates by Down

Yards to Go	1st Dwn	2nd Dwn	3rd Dwn	4th Dwn	Total
1 & 2	0.0%	10.0%	4.0%	0.0%	4.4%
3, 4, 5	0.0%	0.0%	0.0%	0.0%	0.0%
6 - 9	0.0%	1.4%	0.0%	0.0%	0.7%
10 - 14	2.1%	1.5%	0.0%	0.0%	1.8%
15+	0.0%	0.0%	6.7%		2.4%
Total	2.0%	1.5%	1.2%	0.0%	1.5%

3rd Down Passing - Short of Sticks Analysis

QB	Avg. Yds to Go	Avg. YIA (of Comp)	Avg Yds Short	Short of Sticks Rate	Short Rk
Kirk Cousins	7.2	6.7	-0.5	63%	12
NFL Avg	7.8	6.4	-1.4	60%	

Air Yds vs YAC

Air Yds %	YAC %	Rk
54%	46%	21
53%	48%	

2018 Receiving Recap & 2019 Outlook

Hiring **Kevan Stefanski** and investing significantly at the offensive point of attack tipped the Vikings' hand -- expect more 12 personnel and a higher run-to-pass ratio. Thielen, and Diggs should leverage stronger pass protection to create more separation downfield. **Irv Smith** and **Kyle Rudolph** should be on the field together, especially to sell play-action passes. Great players elevate systems more than systems elevate players. While Zimmer's refusal to optimize play-calling based on game situation will throttle the Vikings' point-scoring potential, **Rick Spielman**'s significant investments in difference-making offensive talents should propel the Vikings forward and into the playoffs in spite of the backwards-looking fossils at the controls.

Player *Min 50 Targets	Targ	Comp %	YPA	Rating	Success %	Success Rk	Missed YPA Rk	YAS % Rk	YTS % Rk	TDs
Adam Thielen	155	73%	8.9	111.0	63%	3	38	67	38	8
Stefon Diggs	148	69%	6.9	102.9	49%	85	112	43	77	9
Kyle Rudolph	81	79%	7.8	110.6	62%	7	7	88	26	4
Laquon Treadwell	53	66%	5.7	71.4	45%	102	154	117	77	1

Directional Passer Rating Delivered

Receiver	Short Left	Short Middle	Short Right	Deep Left	Deep Middle	Deep Right	Player Total
Adam Thielen	107	124	103	58	104	115	111
Stefon Diggs	119	63	96	119	118	49	103
Kyle Rudolph	111	85	115	79	119	117	111
Laquon Treadwell	99	60	76	40		0	71
Dalvin Cook	87	124	105				106
Aldrick Robinson	81	110	61	55	108	135	98
Latavius Murray	85	38	94				73
C.J. Ham	79		93				87
David Morgan		100	74				92
Ameer Abdullah		108				40	65
Team Total	106	94	99	85	110	98	103

2018 Rushing Recap & 2019 Outlook

Minnesota needs **Dalvin Cook** to be healthy. Their recent rushing attack has been terrible, ranking Nos. 28, 18 and 21 over the last three years. Despite its growing inefficiency across the league, **Mike Zimmer** and his like-minded lieutenants remain committed to running on first down. The team has no choice but to improve its first-down efficiency. The Vikings averaged 5.2 YPC from outside zone in 2018 and will look to continue to use it significantly. First-round **Garrett Bradbury** and rookie OG **Dru Samia** should bolster the offensive line, especially the team's anemic run-blocking efficiency. With only rookie **Alexander Mattison** seriously competing for touches, Cook is teed up for a hugely productive season.

Player *Min 50 Rushes	Rushes	YPC	Success %	Success Rk	Missed YPA Rk	YTS % Rk	YAS % Rk	Early Down Success %	Early Down Success Rk	TDs
Latavius Murray	140	4.1	46%	42	38	28	51	46%	41	6
Dalvin Cook	133	4.6	40%	64	46	69	41	40%	62	2

Kirk Cousins Rating All Downs

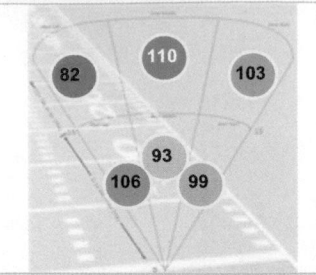

Kirk Cousins Rating Early Downs

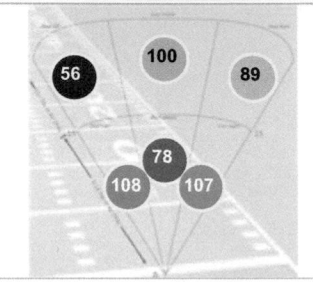

Yards per Carry by Direction

Directional Run Frequency

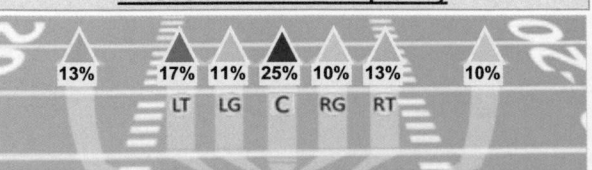

A defensive-minded head coach and creative offensive coordinator is a great marriage, if the coach allows the OC freedom to be creative. **Kyle Shanahan** with **Dan Quinn** and **Josh McDaniels** with **Bill Belichick** are great examples. But a defensive coach who meddles with the offense, forcing them to run heavy with a bad rushing offense, sadly, delivers negative expected value.

In firing DeFilippo, Zimmer was reaching for the ghost of the 2017 season. That year's team was run heavy, inefficient on the ground and still won 13 games. Zimmer didn't care that their offense wasn't optimized, as long as they controlled the pace and tone of the game. *The answer for last year's Vikings team was not more running.* When trying to establish the run with a first quarter run rate of 45% or higher on early downs, the team went 1-5.

In steps new offensive coordinator **Kevan Stefanski**, who implemented his player personnel preferences right away. The Vikings went from passing out of 12 personnel (2-tight end sets) 16% of the time to 32% after he took over in Week 15. Minnesota enjoyed a 58% Success Rate and 9.4 YPA from 12 personnel, compared to a 49% Success Rate and 5.9 YPA from 11 personnel. For that reason, **Irv Smith** could play a key role in 2019.

(cont'd - see MIN-5)

Minnesota Vikings Fantasy Corner

Dalvin Cook will be a first-round fantasy pick in 2020. Turning 24 this summer, Cook enters the prime of his career checking all elite fantasy-back boxes: Bellcow size, sub-4.5 speed, dominant college production profile, and excellent receiving skills. Cook demands touches and delivers efficient outcomes in all phases. After a lost offseason rehabilitating a torn ACL, Cook commanded a 65% Opportunity Share, 4.5 targets per game, 1.7 red-zone touches per game, and a 38% Juke Rate (evaded tackles per touch), which ranked No. 2 among qualified NFL running backs on PlayerProfiler.com. Opportunity + Efficiency = Fantasy Points, particularly in the context of an efficient Vikings offense that has re-committed to the run even after losing **Latavius Murray** to the Saints. These converging forces will propel Cook's 2019 production, making him a slam-dunk selection in the second round of fantasy drafts.

- Matt Kelley

Division History: Season Wins & 2019 Projection

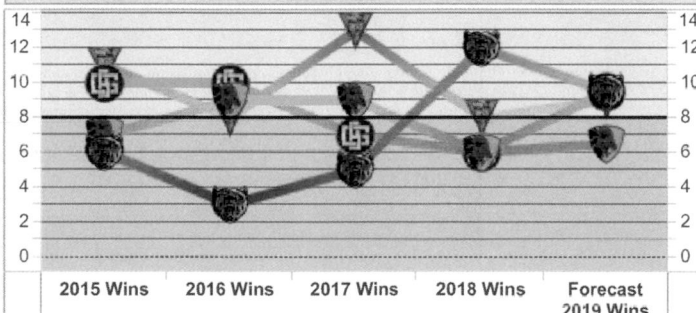

Rank of 2019 Defensive Pass Efficiency Faced by Week

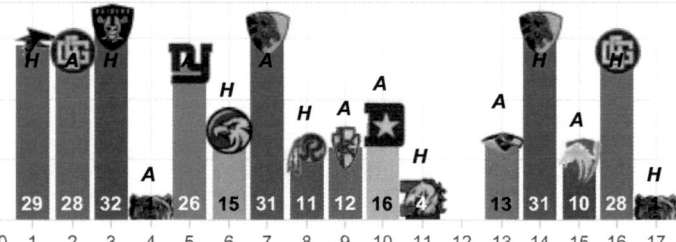

Rank of 2019 Defensive Rush Efficiency Faced by Week

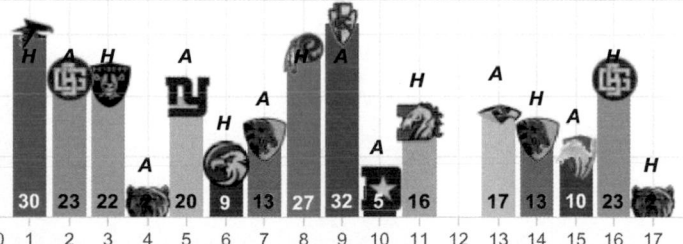

2018 Situational Usage by Player & Position

Usage Rate by Score

		Being Blown Out (14+)	Down Big (9-13)	One Score	Large Lead (9-13)	Blowout Lead (14+)
RUSH	Dalvin Cook	3%	11%	69%	11%	5%
	Latavius Murray	4%	4%	60%	15%	17%
	Adam Thielen		20%	80%		
	Stefon Diggs		10%	90%		
	C.J. Ham		17%	83%		
	Total	3%	8%	66%	12%	11%
PASS	Dalvin Cook	12%	18%	63%	6%	
	Latavius Murray	33%	17%	46%	4%	
	Adam Thielen	26%	10%	55%	6%	3%
	Stefon Diggs	19%	20%	51%	6%	4%
	Kyle Rudolph	14%	16%	63%	4%	3%
	Laquon Treadwell	24%	10%	59%	4%	2%
	Aldrick Robinson	21%	12%	47%	18%	3%
	C.J. Ham	43%		36%	21%	
	Ameer Abdullah		50%	50%		
	Total	21%	15%	55%	7%	3%

Share of Offensive Plays by Type

	Dalvin Cook	Latavius Murray	Adam Thielen	Stefon Diggs	Kyle Rudolph	Laquon Treadwell	Aldrick Robinson	C.J. Ham	Ameer Abdullah
RUSH	45%	48%	2%	3%				2%	
PASS	9%	5%	27%	26%	14%	9%	6%	3%	0%
ALL	22%	20%	18%	18%	9%	6%	4%	2%	0%

Positional Target Distribution vs NFL Average

		NFL Wide				Team Only			
		Left	Middle	Right	Total	Left	Middle	Right	Total
Deep	WR	33%	17%	30%	81%	31%	20%	37%	88%
	TE	5%	4%	7%	16%	2%	4%	5%	11%
	RB	1%	0%	2%	4%			1%	1%
	All	39%	22%	39%	100%	33%	24%	43%	100%
Short	WR	20%	14%	21%	55%	25%	12%	28%	65%
	TE	6%	6%	8%	20%	5%	5%	6%	16%
	RB	10%	5%	10%	25%	6%	3%	10%	19%
	All	36%	25%	39%	100%	36%	20%	44%	100%
Total		37%	24%	39%	100%	36%	21%	44%	100%

Positional Success Rates vs NFL Average

		NFL Wide				Team Only			
		Left	Middle	Right	Total	Left	Middle	Right	Total
Deep	WR	40%	50%	40%	42%	31%	35%	45%	38%
	TE	44%	52%	41%	45%	50%	100%	75%	78%
	RB	38%	33%	43%	41%			0%	0%
	All	40%	50%	40%	42%	32%	45%	47%	42%
Short	WR	55%	61%	52%	55%	61%	56%	55%	57%
	TE	55%	62%	54%	57%	61%	63%	58%	60%
	RB	47%	54%	45%	47%	40%	50%	55%	49%
	All	53%	60%	51%	54%	57%	57%	55%	56%
Total		50%	58%	49%	52%	54%	55%	54%	54%

163

2018 Detailed Analytics Summary
Success by Play Type & Primary Personnel Groupings

Successful Play Rate 0% ▭ 100%

Type	1-1 [3WR]	1-2 [2WR]	2-1 [2WR]	2-2 [1WR]	1-3 [1WR]	1-0 [4WR]	2-0 [3WR]	2-3 [0WR]	0-0 [5WR]	ALL
PASS	48% (507)	60% (89)	52% (29)	80% (5)	40% (5)	0% (4)	50% (2)	0% (1)	0% (1)	49% (643)
RUSH	44% (174)	45% (103)	43% (42)	22% (18)	40% (10)	0% (2)	0% (3)	50% (2)		42% (354)
All	47% (681)	52% (192)	46% (71)	35% (23)	40% (15)	0% (6)	20% (5)	33% (3)	0% (1)	47% (997)

Format Success Rate (Total # of Plays)

Receiving Success by Top-4 Personnel Groupings
(Min 50 targets)

POS	Player	1-1 [3WR]	1-2 [2WR]	2-1 [2WR]	1-0 [4WR]	4 Grp Total
RB	Dalvin Cook	46% (39) 5.0, 104.1	71% (7) 12.7, 118.8	100% (2) 8.5, 102.1		52% (48) 6.3, 106.7
TE	Kyle Rudolph	58% (59) 7.7, 104.9	79% (19) 8.4, 119.3			63% (78) 7.9, 111.3
WR	Adam Thielen	61% (120) 8.9, 108.5	77% (22) 9.0, 134.3	75% (8) 11.6, 113.0	0% (1) 0.0, 39.6	64% (151) 9.0, 112.8
WR	Stefon Diggs	48% (122) 6.4, 102.7	53% (17) 8.6, 116.3	44% (9) 9.8, 98.4		49% (148) 6.9, 104.0
WR	Laquon Treadwell	47% (49) 5.8, 77.3	0% (2) 1.5, 56.3		0% (1) 6.0, 91.7	44% (52) 5.7, 76.9

Format Line 1: Success Rate (Total # of Plays) Line 2: YPA, Passer Rating

Rushing Success by Top-4 Personnel Groupings
(Min 25 carries)

Rusher (Last, First)	1-1 [3WR]	1-2 [2WR]	2-1 [2WR]	2-2 [1WR]	4 Grp Total
Murray Latavius	40% (52) 4.1	44% (54) 4.9	39% (23) 3.1	33% (3) 1.3	42% (132) 4.2
Cook Dalvin	43% (79) 5.4	39% (31) 3.2	54% (13) 4.5	20% (5) 2.4	42% (128) 4.7
Cousins Kirk	45% (22) 4.5	57% (7) 2.1	33% (3) 3.3	0% (7) -0.7	38% (39) 3.1

Format Line 1: Success Rate (Total # of Plays) Line 2: YPC

Passing by Coverage Scheme

M2M	51% (251) 7.2, 105.6
Zone	56% (239) 7.1, 98.2
Screen	51% (39) 6.8, 101.5
Combo	67% (15) 9.9, 147.6

Passing by Route

Curl	59% (74) 6.3, 99.4
Out	52% (64) 6.5, 102.0
Slant	48% (46) 6.0, 79.4
Flat	58% (38) 5.8, 96.6
Screen	50% (38) 6.1, 89.9
Dig	59% (29) 7.9, 95.2

Throw Types

Level 1	55% (423) 6.3, 96.9
Level 2	57% (121) 8.9, 118.2
Level 3	29% (38) 10.6, 90.0
Sidearm	100% (1) 4.0, 83.3

QB Drop Types

3 Step	53% (214) 7.6, 106.4
0/1 Step	54% (155) 6.1, 98.4
5 Step	49% (113) 7.7, 96.8
Designed Rollout Right	53% (36) 5.3, 91.3
7 Step	65% (26) 10.5, 123.1
Basic Screen	46% (24) 5.8, 101.4

QB State at Pass

Planted	53% (381) 7.4, 105.2
Moving	55% (76) 5.9, 111.1
Shuffling	51% (72) 6.9, 79.5

Play Action

	Play Action	No P/A
Under Center	62% (92) 8.0, 117.4	71% (34) 10.3, 128.2
Shotgun	71% (28) 10.6, 107.9	49% (435) 6.6, 96.9
ALL	64% (120) 8.6, 115.2	51% (469) 6.9, 99.2

Run Types

Outside Zone	45% (101) 5.2
Inside Zone	40% (92) 3.6
Stretch	41% (27) 4.9
Lead	39% (18) 3.7
Power	38% (16) 5.0
Pitch	22% (9) -0.1

MIN-5

The target depth under Stefanski is also notable. Cousins aimed passes 10.1 yards downfield from 11 personnel, compared to 5.3 yards downfield from 12 personnel.

The Vikings struggled in all phases in 2018. On one particular onside kick attempt, the positions of their "hands" team members were: SS, LB, DE, RB and S. Needless to say, they didn't have the speed or hands to recover the kick.

Most importantly, Zimmer's defense underachieved.

Minnesota's Early Down Success Rate (EDSR) ranking dropped from No. 13 in 2017 to No. 25 last year. The Vikings won the EDSR battle in 11 straight games in 2017, closing the season 10-1 over that timeframe. They never strung more than two EDSR wins together at any point last year. And it only gets harder for the defense in 2019. Minnesota's offense will face the No. 9 most-difficult projected schedule, a substantial jump in difficulty from last year's No. 17 slate.

Additionally, the Vikings have won only one outdoor road game against a team with a winning record since Zimmer became head coach in 2014. That came all the way back in 2015.

They went 0-4-1 in such games last year and are 0-10-1 both straight up and against the spread since 2016. This year they play in Green Bay, Chicago, Kansas City, Seattle, and Los Angeles (Chargers). All of those games will be outdoors against teams projected to finish with winning records.

New England Patriots

Head Coach:
Bill Belichick (19 yrs)
Offensive Coordinator:
Josh McDaniels (7 yrs)
Defensive Coordinator:
TBD (new)

2019 Forecast

Wins	Div Rank
11	#1

Past Records

2018: 11-5
2017: 13-3
2016: 14-2

EASY HARD

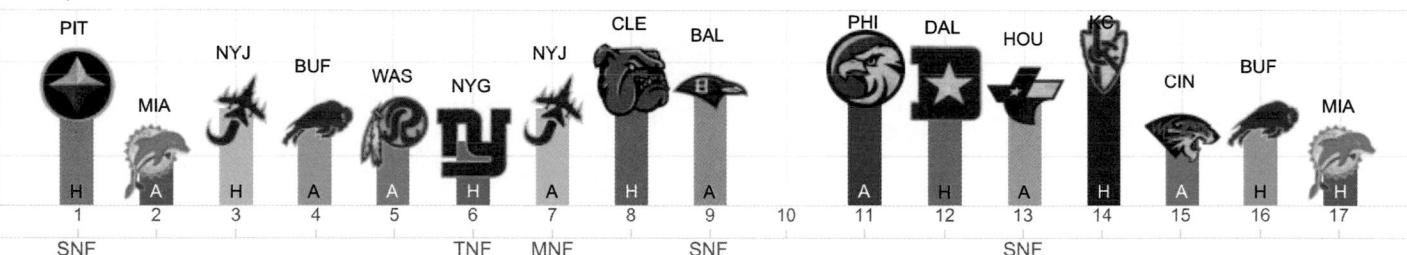

PIT	MIA	NYJ	BUF	WAS	NYG	NYJ	CLE	BAL		PHI	DAL	HOU	KC	CIN	BUF	MIA
H	A	H	A	H	H	A	H	A		A	H	A	H	A	H	H
1	2	3	4	5	6	7	8	9	10	11	12	13	14	15	16	17

SNF — TNF MNF — SNF — SNF

Key Players Lost

Player	New
Adrian Clayborn (DE)	ATL
Chris Hogan (WR)	CAR
Cody Hollister (WR)	TEN
Cordarrelle Patterson (WR)	CHI
Dwayne Allen (TE)	MIA
Eric Rowe (CB)	MIA
Jacob Hollister (TE)	SEA
Jared Veldheer (RT)	Retired
LaAdrian Waddle (RT)	BUF
Malcolm Mitchell (WR)	Retired
Malcom Brown (DT)	NO
Rob Gronkowski (TE)	Retired
Trenton Brown (RT)	OAK
Trey Flowers (DE)	DET

Average Line	# Games Favored	# Games Underdog
-5.9	13	2

Regular Season Wins: Past & Current Proj

Forecast 2019 Wins	11
2018 Wins	11
Forecast 2018 Wins	11
2017 Wins	13
2016 Wins	14
2015 Wins	12

1 3 5 7 9 11 13 15

2019 New England Patriots Overview

Building a team from the inside out is a proven successful philosophy for winning in the NFL. Many top-10 teams in both offensive and defensive line expenditure opt to use substantial cap space on veteran linemen. The Cowboys, Steelers, Rams, Chargers and Browns are examples. The projected offensive line starters for the New England Patriots, meanwhile, were all either draft picks or undrafted free agent signings. This strategy allows them to avoid contractual land mines.

The starting left tackle for the Super Bowl Champions, **Trent Brown** was a candidate to be overpaid as a free agent. This despite his contributions to a No. 1-ranked pass protecting line. On cue, the Raiders signed him to a four-year, $66 million contract. One with cap hits of $15.25 and $21.5 million the next two years. His 2018 cap hit with the Pats was only $1.9 million.

Brown was a seventh-round draft pick of the 49ers in 2015, starting at right tackle in his second year. An injury derailed his 2017 season. **Kyle Shanahan** and company subsequently drafted his replacement, **Mike McGlinchy**, number nine overall in 2018. Entering the final year of his rookie deal, Brown was recovering from shoulder surgery and was a limited offseason program participant. With San Francisco undervaluing him, the Patriots traded a third-round pick in exchange for Brown and a fifth-round pick.

The move saved New England's season, with 2018 first round pick **Isiah Wynn** suffering a torn Achilles in the preseason. Despite filling the void and helping the Pats win the Super Bowl, the team opted not to re-sign Brown. They received a third-round comp pick for Brown leaving, and can roll with a now-healthy Wynn because they planned ahead.

To recap, they traded a 2018 third-round pick for a one-year rental, won a Super Bowl and now get a 2020 third-round compensatory pick. An amazing example of shrewd

(cont'd - see NE2)

Key Free Agents/ Trades Added

Player	AAV (MM)
Benjamin Watson (TE)	$3
Brandon Bolden (RB)	$1.8
Demaryius Thomas (WR)	$2.8
Jamie Collins (OLB)	$2
Jared Veldheer (RT)	$3.5
Michael Bennett (DE)	Trade
Mike Pennel (DE)	$2.5

Drafted Players

Rd	Pk	Player (College)
1	32	WR - N'Keal Harry (Arizona State)
2	45	CB - Joejuan Williams (Vanderbilt)
3	77	DE - Chase Winovich (Michigan)
	87	RB - Damien Harris (Alabama)
3*	101	OT - Yodny Cajuste (West Virginia)
4	118	G - Hjalte Froholdt (Arkansas)
	133	QB - Jarrett Stidham (Auburn)
5	159	DT - Byron Cowart (Maryland)
	163	P - Jake Bailey (Stanford)
7*	252	CB - Ken Webster (Ole Miss)

Lineup & Cap Hits

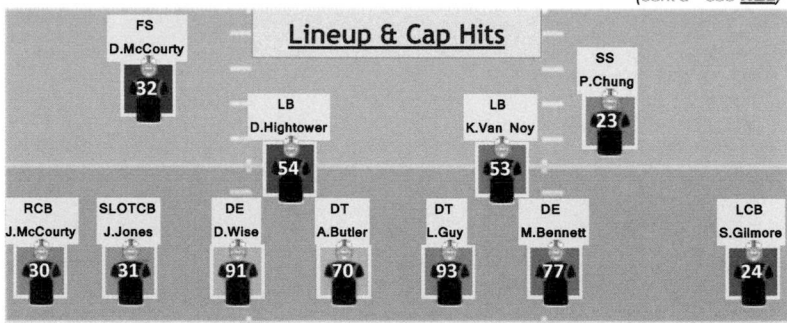

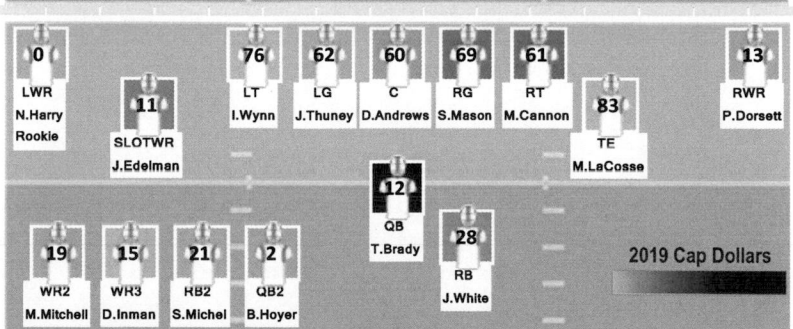

2019 Cap Dollars

2019 Unit Spending

All DEF — All OFF

Positional Spending

	Rank	Total	2017 Rk
All OFF	14	$100.81M	13
QB	1	$31.15M	13
OL	24	$32.38M	29
RB	5	$12.51M	9
WR	17	$20.68M	18
TE	31	$4.09M	1
All DEF	12	$92.16M	16
DL	26	$20.37M	22
LB	14	$22.22M	20
CB	18	$19.89M	19
S	2	$29.68M	2

maneuvering coming full circle.

The Patriots have the fourth-cheapest line in the NFL, but don't mistake cheap with poor. **David Andrews**, **Marcus Cannon** and Wynn have two, three and three more years on their current deals. And Shaq Mason was recently signed to a five-year contract. By building through the draft, they're set along the offensive line with home-grown talent on reasonable deals. Additionally, these players receive ample coaching from arguably the best offensive line coach in the industry in Dante Scarnecchia.

The Patriots shifted too pass-heavy near the goal line in 2017. In 2016, when inside the five-yard line, the Patriots were 67-percent run with a 59-percent success rate. In those same situations in 2017, they were 60-percent pass with a 51-percent success rate. They returned to their 2016 ways last year by replicating their 67-percent run rate. This plan averaged a 65-percent success rate compared to a mere 30-percent success rate on passes. Another wise decision evidenced by **Sony Michel**'s 67-percent success rate and seven rushing touchdowns. They ranked top-3 in the league with a 76-percent run rate on plays after a ten-yard gain that put them in the red zone. This was nearly 20-percent above league average.

The Patriots were also efficient on second downs. After first and ten incompletions, the league is shockingly only 53-percent pass on second and ten. Not the Patriots, who went 69-percent pass in 2018. This ranked No. 4 in the league behind only the Steelers, Chiefs and Rams. Unsurprisingly, all of these teams have great offenses. Teams with veteran quarterbacks like the Falcons and Titans still ran on roughly 60-percent of their second-and-ten plays following an incompletion. This resulted in an underwhelming sub 30-percent success rate. Compare that with the pass-heavy teams producing gains of over 7 YPA through the air and over 50-percent success rates. The Patriots also went run-heavy on second and shorts, converting first downs with regularity. Per the proprietary Early Down Success Rate (EDSR) metric, the Patriots are 20-0 during the last two regular seasons when winning the EDSR battle. They're 4-8 when losing it.

Rob Gronkowski is fully retired, for now. Whether or not that changes, the Patriots have to learn to succeed without the league's biggest mismatch for opposing defenses. With one command from **Tom Brady**, Gronk could be motioned to uncoverable receiver or incredible blocker due to his flexibility. No other offense had that luxury.

There's no replacing Gronkowski with a single player. Last year in 21 personnel formations, he saw the most targets and was No. 2 on the Patriots with 9.0 YPA.

He was the third-most targeted player from 11 personnel, but his presence benefitted the offense by dictating defenses. Brady averaged 0.8 more career YPA, a 60-percent better TD:INT rate and a nearly 15-point higher passer rating with Gronkowski on the field. An unspecified back injury limited him as a receiver in 2018. But his utility as a blocker helped New England's top-ten rushing attack dominate, despite playing a top-ten run defense schedule.

Brady still wants the tight end position to be a strength, even if it's via multiple players. That approach is pragmatic, but hurts New England's ability to be as multiple because opponents can track tendencies. Belichick is great at tossing in "junk" plays late in games to obfuscate tendencies, but that only goes so far.

*(cont'd - see **NE-3**)*

2018 Passing Performance

QB	1st Dwn	2nd Dwn	3rd Dwn	
Tom Brady	61% / 8.6 / 105.4	53% / 7.2 / 85.8	40% / 6.8 / 95.0	Success Rate / YPA / Rating
Pass Rate	47%	64%	70%	
NFL AVG	53% / 7.7 / 95.1	47% / 7.3 / 93.7	36% / 6.9 / 87.1	Success Rate / YPA / Rating
Pass Rate	53%	62%	80%	

2018 Rushing Performance

Offense	1st Dwn	2nd Dwn	3rd Dwn	
NE	48% / 4.3	56% / 4.8	51% / 2.7	Success Rate / YPC
Run Rate	53%	36%	30%	
NFL AVG	48% / 4.5	46% / 4.4	51% / 4.3	Success Rate / YPC
Run Rate	47%	38%	20%	

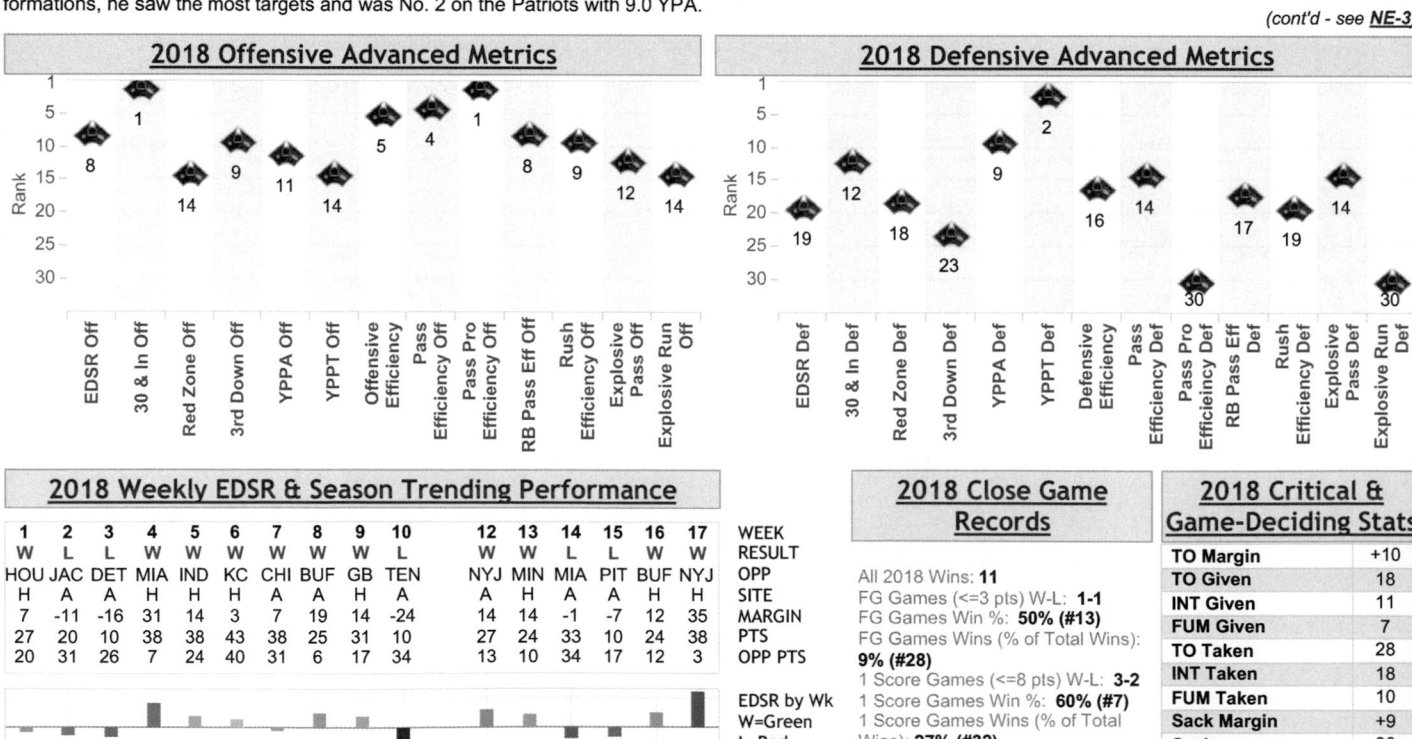

2018 Offensive Advanced Metrics

Rank (lower=better): EDSR Off 8, 30 & In Off 1, Red Zone Off 14, 3rd Down Off 9, YPPA Off 11, YPPT Off 14, Offensive Efficiency 5, Pass Efficiency Off 4, Pass Pro Efficiency Off 1, RB Pass Eff Off 8, Rush Efficiency Off 9, Explosive Pass Off 12, Explosive Run Off 14

2018 Defensive Advanced Metrics

Rank: EDSR Def 19, 30 & In Def 12, Red Zone Def 18, 3rd Down Def 23, YPPA Def 9, YPPT Def 2, Defensive Efficiency 16, Pass Efficiency Def 14, Pass Pro Efficiency Def 30, RB Pass Eff Def 17, Rush Efficiency Def 19, Explosive Pass Def 14, Explosive Run Def 30

2018 Weekly EDSR & Season Trending Performance

	1	2	3	4	5	6	7	8	9	10		12	13	14	15	16	17
RESULT	W	L	L	W	W	W	W	W	W	L		W	W	L	W	W	W
OPP	HOU	JAC	DET	MIA	IND	KC	CHI	BUF	GB	TEN		NYJ	MIN	MIA	PIT	BUF	NYJ
SITE	H	A	A	H	H	H	A	A	H	A		A	H	A	A	H	H
MARGIN	7	-11	-16	31	14	3	7	19	14	-24		14	14	-1	-7	12	35
PTS	27	20	10	38	38	43	38	25	31	10		27	24	33	10	24	38
OPP PTS	20	31	26	7	24	40	31	6	17	34		13	10	34	17	12	3

WEEK / RESULT / OPP / SITE / MARGIN / PTS / OPP PTS

EDSR by Wk W=Green L=Red

OFF/DEF EDSR Blue=OFF (high=good) Red=DEF (low=good)

2018 Close Game Records

All 2018 Wins: **11**
FG Games (<=3 pts) W-L: **1-1**
FG Games Win %: **50% (#13)**
FG Games Wins (% of Total Wins): **9% (#28)**
1 Score Games (<=8 pts) W-L: **3-2**
1 Score Games Win %: **60% (#7)**
1 Score Games Wins (% of Total Wins): **27% (#32)**

2018 Critical & Game-Deciding Stats

TO Margin	+10
TO Given	18
INT Given	11
FUM Given	7
TO Taken	28
INT Taken	18
FUM Taken	10
Sack Margin	+9
Sacks	30
Sacks Allow	21
Return TD Margin	+4
Ret TDs	4
Ret TDs Allow	0
Penalty Margin	-2
Penalties	93
Opponent Penalties	91

New England Patriots 2019 Strength of Schedule In Detail (compared to 2018)

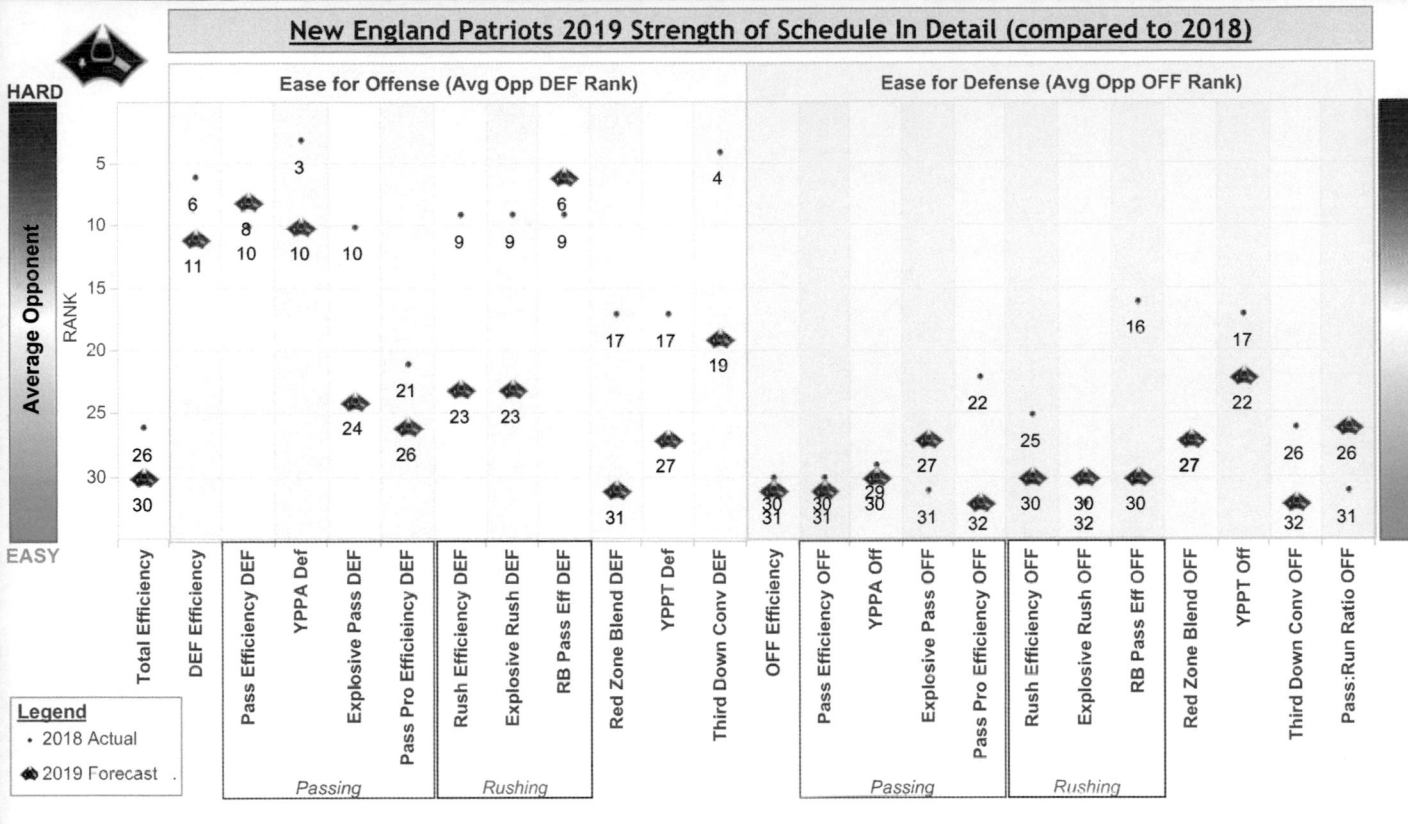

2019 v 2018 Schedule Variances* (OFF=Rank of DEF faced, 2019 vs 2018)

Pass OFF Rank	Pass OFF Blend Rk	Rush OFF Rk	Rush OFF Blend Rk	Pass DEF Rk	Pass DEF Blend Rk	Rush DEF Rk	Rush DEF Blend Rk
10	25	29	28	17	18	21	24

* **1**=Hardest Jump in 2019 schedule from 2018 (aka a much harder schedule in 2019), **32**=Easiest Jump in 2019 schedule from 2018 (aka a much easier schedule in 2019);
Pass Blend metric blends 4 metrics: Pass Efficiency, YPPA, Explosive Pass & Pass Rush; **Rush Blend** metric blends 3 metrics: Rush Efficiency, Explosive Rush & RB Targets

Team Records & Trends

	2018	2017	2016
Average line	-7.4	-8.9	-6.9
Average O/U line	49.5	49.7	45.8
Straight Up Record	11-5	13-3	14-2
Against the Spread Record	9-7	10-5	12-3
Over/Under Record	5-11	6-9	6-10
ATS as Favorite	9-7	10-5	10-3
ATS as Underdog	0-0	0-0	1-0
Straight Up Home	8-0	6-2	6-2
ATS Home	6-2	5-3	6-2
Over/Under Home	2-6	5-3	4-4
ATS as Home Favorite	6-2	5-3	5-2
ATS as a Home Dog	0-0	0-0	0-0
Straight Up Away	3-5	6-1	8-0
ATS Away	3-5	4-2	6-1
Over/Under Away	3-5	1-5	2-6
ATS Away Favorite	3-5	4-2	5-1
ATS Away Dog	0-0	0-0	1-0
Six Point Teaser Record	11-5	12-4	14-2
Seven Point Teaser Record	11-5	12-4	14-2
Ten Point Teaser Record	13-3	12-4	14-2

NE-3

Personnel usage will be a challenge without Gronk, as only the 49ers used more 21 personnel. The Patriots already used the least amount of 12 personnel in the league. And they had the second-fewest pass snaps from 2-TE sets even with Gronkowski.

It'd be shocking if the 2019 Patriots don't have ample snaps from 21 and 11 personnel.

Bellichick may use multi-TE sets more often, which is the exact opposite of their recent tendencies with Gronkowski. This high-risk, high-reward strategy reduces substitutions. Which allows the Patriots to confuse defenses by using the same personnel and quickly audibling at the line between pass and run formations.

The obvious drawback is potentially not having your best 11 on the field.

(cont'd - see NE-4)

2019 Rest Analysis

Team More Rest	2
Opp More Rest	3
Net Rest Edge	-1
Week 2 Edge	0
Week 3 Edge	1
Week 4 Edge	0
Week 5 Edge	0
Week 6 Edge	0
Week 7 Edge	3
Week 8 Edge	
Week 9 Edge	
Week 11 Edge	0
Week 12 Edge	0
Week 13 Edge	-3
Week 14 Edge	0
Week 15 Edge	0
Week 16 Edge	0
Week 17 Edge	0

Health by Unit*

2018 Rk	18
2017 Rk	14
2018 v 2017 Rk	19
Off Rk	18
Def Rk	18
QB Rk	17
RB Rk	27
WR Rk	5
TE Rk	19
Oline Rk	23
Dline Rk	14
LB Rk	26
DB Rk	18

Based on the work of Football Outsiders

2018 Weekly Betting Lines (wks 1-16)

1	2	3	4	5	6	7	8	9	11	12	13	14	15	16
PIT	MIA	NYJ	BUF	WAS	NYG	NYJ	CLE	BAL	PHI	DAL	HOU	KC	CIN	BUF
-6	-8.5	-10	-6.5	-6.5	-11	-4.5	-8.5	-2.5	1	-6	-3	3	-7	-13

Avg = -5.9

Home Lines (wks 1-16)

1	3	6	8	12	14	16
-6 PIT	-10 NYJ	-11 NYG	-8.5 CLE	-6 DAL	3 KC	BUF

Avg = -7.4

Road Lines (wks 1-16)

2	4	5	7	9	11	13	15
-8.5 MIA	-6.5 BUF	-6.5 WAS	-4.5 NYJ	-2.5 BAL	PHI	-3 HOU	CIN

Avg = -4.7

New England Patriots
2018 Play Analysis

2018 Play Tendencies

All Pass %	55%
All Pass Rk	25
All Rush %	45%
All Rush Rk	8
1 Score Pass %	58%
1 Score Pass Rk	15
2017 1 Score Pass %	61%
2017 1 Score Pass Rk	4
2018 Pass Increase %	-2%
Pass Increase Rk	26
1 Score Rush %	42%
1 Score Rush Rk	18
Up Pass %	51%
Up Pass Rk	11
Up Rush %	49%
Up Rush Rk	22
Down Pass %	65%
Down Pass Rk	22
Down Rush %	35%
Down Rush Rk	11

2018 Down & Distance Tendencies

Down	Distance	Total Plays	Pass Rate	Run Rate	Play Success %
1	Short (1-3)	8	25%	75%	38%
	Med (4-7)	16	13%	88%	63%
	Long (8-10)	412	48%	52%	54%
	XL (11+)	17	88%	12%	53%
2	Short (1-3)	62	26%	74%	68%
	Med (4-7)	109	63%	37%	58%
	Long (8-10)	126	77%	23%	48%
	XL (11+)	31	90%	10%	39%
3	Short (1-3)	66	47%	53%	58%
	Med (4-7)	67	87%	13%	45%
	Long (8-10)	39	97%	3%	28%
	XL (11+)	14	86%	14%	29%
4	Short (1-3)	10	60%	40%	60%
	Med (4-7)	1	100%	0%	100%

Shotgun %:

Under Center	Shotgun
55%	45%

37% *AVG* 63%

Run Rate:

Under Center	Shotgun
70%	14%

68% *AVG* 23%

Pass Rate:

Under Center	Shotgun
30%	86%

32% *AVG* 77%

Short Yardage Intelligence:

2nd and Short Run

Run Freq	Run Rk	NFL Run Freq Avg	Run 1D Rate	Run NFL 1D Avg
73%	7	65%	67%	68%

2nd and Short Pass

Pass Freq	Pass Rk	NFL Pass Freq Avg	Pass 1D Rate	Pass NFL 1D Avg
27%	26	35%	46%	56%

Most Frequent Play

Down	Distance	Play Type	Player	Total Plays	Play Success %
1	Short (1-3)	RUSH	Sony Michel	5	60%
	Med (4-7)	RUSH	Sony Michel	9	78%
	Long (8-10)	RUSH	Sony Michel	122	48%
	XL (11+)	PASS	Julian Edelman	2	50%
			Rob Gronkowski	2	100%
			Cordarrelle Patterson	2	50%
			Josh Gordon	2	100%
2	Short (1-3)	RUSH	Sony Michel	26	62%
	Med (4-7)	RUSH	Sony Michel	24	58%
	Long (8-10)	PASS	Julian Edelman	21	62%
	XL (11+)	PASS	James White	6	33%
			Julian Edelman	6	67%
3	Short (1-3)	RUSH	Sony Michel	14	57%
	Med (4-7)	PASS	James White	18	56%
	Long (8-10)	PASS	Julian Edelman	6	83%
	XL (11+)	PASS	Rob Gronkowski	3	67%

Most Successful Play*

Down	Distance	Play Type	Player	Total Plays	Play Success %
1	Short (1-3)	RUSH	Sony Michel	5	60%
	Med (4-7)	RUSH	Sony Michel	9	78%
	Long (8-10)	RUSH	Cordarrelle Patterson	13	77%
2	Short (1-3)	RUSH	Rex Burkhead	6	67%
	Med (4-7)	PASS	Julian Edelman	12	67%
	Long (8-10)	PASS	Rob Gronkowski	7	71%
			Phillip Dorsett	7	71%
	XL (11+)	PASS	Julian Edelman	6	67%
3	Short (1-3)	RUSH	Tom Brady	5	80%
	Med (4-7)	RUSH	James White	5	60%
	Long (8-10)	PASS	Julian Edelman	6	83%

*Minimum 5 plays to qualify

2018 Weekly Snap Rates

Wk	Opp	Score	Rob Gronkowski	Chris Hogan	Julian Edelman	James White	Dwayne Allen	Sony Michel	Cordarrelle Patterson	Rex Burkhead
1	HOU	W 27-20	75 (100%)	68 (91%)		36 (48%)	23 (31%)		16 (21%)	38 (51%)
2	JAC	L 31-20	58 (95%)	55 (90%)		34 (56%)	14 (23%)	13 (21%)	28 (46%)	14 (23%)
3	DET	L 26-10	48 (100%)	48 (100%)		25 (52%)	17 (35%)	23 (48%)	19 (40%)	7 (15%)
4	MIA	W 38-7	54 (67%)	70 (86%)		40 (49%)	45 (56%)	33 (41%)	41 (51%)	
5	IND	W 38-24	63 (91%)	63 (91%)	48 (70%)	43 (62%)	12 (17%)	27 (39%)	8 (12%)	
6	KC	W 43-40	77 (99%)	47 (60%)	71 (91%)	33 (42%)	11 (14%)	37 (47%)	6 (8%)	
7	CHI	W 38-31		42 (66%)	63 (98%)	45 (70%)	55 (86%)	6 (9%)	6 (9%)	
8	BUF	W 25-6	68 (89%)	45 (59%)	73 (96%)	61 (80%)	12 (16%)		13 (17%)	
9	GB	W 31-17		53 (75%)	64 (90%)	56 (79%)	66 (93%)		13 (18%)	
10	TEN	L 34-10		54 (82%)	54 (82%)	42 (64%)	44 (67%)	18 (27%)	10 (15%)	
12	NYJ	W 27-13	69 (99%)	28 (40%)	60 (86%)	37 (53%)		30 (43%)	22 (31%)	
13	MIN	W 24-10	73 (99%)	32 (43%)	66 (89%)	33 (45%)		30 (41%)	8 (11%)	17 (23%)
14	MIA	L 34-33	77 (95%)	33 (41%)	74 (91%)	33 (41%)		33 (41%)	18 (22%)	17 (21%)
15	PIT	L 17-10	62 (100%)	39 (63%)	58 (94%)	26 (42%)	3 (5%)	22 (35%)	5 (8%)	16 (26%)
16	BUF	W 24-12	59 (79%)	62 (83%)	58 (77%)	29 (39%)	37 (49%)	23 (31%)	17 (23%)	25 (33%)
17	NYJ	W 38-3	55 (81%)	64 (94%)	58 (85%)	27 (40%)	26 (38%)	25 (37%)		17 (25%)
	Grand Total		838 (92%)	803 (73%)	747 (87%)	600 (54%)	365 (41%)	320 (35%)	230 (22%)	151 (27%)

Personnel Groupings

Personnel	Team %	NFL Avg	Succ. %
1-1 [3WR]	56%	65%	52%
2-1 [2WR]	29%	8%	50%
2-2 [1WR]	7%	3%	45%
1-2 [2WR]	5%	17%	58%

Grouping Tendencies

Personnel	Pass Rate	Pass Succ. %	Run Succ. %
1-1 [3WR]	68%	52%	50%
2-1 [2WR]	41%	52%	48%
2-2 [1WR]	14%	30%	48%
1-2 [2WR]	58%	55%	64%

Red Zone Targets (min 3)

Receiver	All	Inside 5	6-10	11-20
James White	22	2	7	13
Julian Edelman	19	4	5	10
Chris Hogan	9	1	3	5
Rob Gronkowski	7	1	2	4
Rex Burkhead	6			6
Cordarrelle Patterson	3	1		2

Red Zone Rushes (min 3)

Rusher	All	Inside 5	6-10	11-20
Sony Michel	59	20	16	23
James White	21	9	6	6
Rex Burkhead	10	3	3	4
Cordarrelle Patters..	9	4		5
Tom Brady	6	2	2	2
James Develin	4	4		

Early Down Target Rate

	RB	TE	WR
	33%	14%	54%
NFL AVG	23%	21%	56%

Overall Target Success %

	RB	TE	WR
	51%	62%	56%
	#5	#2	#6

New England Patriots 2018 Passing Recap & 2019 Outlook

The Patriots are unlikely to notice the loss of LT **Trent Brown**. With **Isiah Wynn** set to step into his shoes, and no other changes, it's a near perfect offensive line. Tom Brady was pressured on 26-percent of his drop backs last year, third-fewest in the NFL. Much of that is a credit to the offensive scheme and Brady's ability to make the proper pre-snap reads and adjustments. But the line was exceedingly strong, and that isn't changing in 2019. The Patriots shifted run-heavy in the red zone from 2017 to 2018. As a result, **Tom Brady**'s red zone drop backs regressed from 31 to 19. His passing TDs dropped from 15 to 6.

Tom Brady Rating All Downs

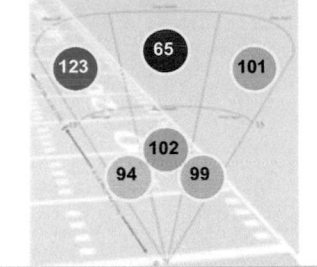

Tom Brady Rating Early Downs

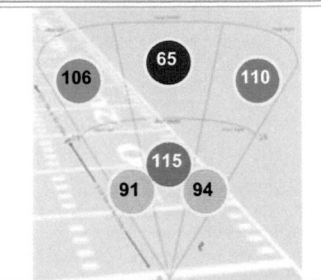

2018 Standard Passing Table

QB	Comp	Att	Comp %	Yds	YPA	TDs	INT	Sacks	Rating	Rk
Tom Brady	460	695	66%	5,308	7.6	31	14	22	96	17
NFL Avg			62%		7.0				87.5	

2018 Advanced Passing Table

QB	Success %	EDSR Passing Success %	20+ Yd Pass Gains	20+ Yd Pass %	30+ Yd Pass Gains	30+ Yd Pass %	Avg. Air Yds per Comp	Avg. YAC per Comp	20+ Air Yd Comp	20+ Air Yd %
Tom Brady	52%	56%	67	10.0%	20	3.0%	5.7	5.8	21	3%
NFL Avg	44%	48%	29.5	8.4%	12.5	3.7%	5.8	5.1	14.5	6%

Interception Rates by Down

Yards to Go	1st Dwn	2nd Dwn	3rd Dwn	4th Dwn	Total
1 & 2	0.0%	0.0%	9.5%	0.0%	4.8%
3, 4, 5	0.0%	0.0%	0.0%	0.0%	0.0%
6 - 9	0.0%	5.3%	3.3%	0.0%	4.5%
10 - 14	0.4%	1.2%	0.0%	0.0%	0.6%
15+	0.0%	10.0%	0.0%	0.0%	4.4%
Total	0.4%	3.3%	2.4%	0.0%	2.0%

3rd Down Passing - Short of Sticks Analysis

QB	Avg. Yds to Go	Avg. YIA (of Comp)	Avg Yds Short	Short of Sticks Rate	Short Rk
Tom Brady	6.6	7.4	0.0	58%	5
NFL Avg	7.8	6.4	-1.4	60%	

Air Yds vs YAC

Air Yds %	YAC %	Rk
49%	51%	31
53%	48%	

2018 Receiving Recap & 2019 Outlook

The 2019 passing offense will look drastically different. In 12-team leagues, the only receivers currently being drafted are Edelman and Harry. **Julian Edelman** earned Super Bowl MVP honors with 141 receiving yards, second-most in history, and will see massive volume in 2019. Unfortunately, his efficiency may drop without Gronkowski and Hogan demanding defensive attention.

Player *Min 50 Targets	Targ	Comp %	YPA	Rating	Success %	Success Rk	Missed YPA Rk	YAS % Rk	YTS % Rk	TDs
James White	150	71%	6.0	99.4	51%	64	62	102	13	6
Julian Edelman	143	70%	8.7	101.7	62%	7	33	43	51	5
Rob Gronkowski	91	66%	9.6	94.3	62%	7	47	43	59	2
Chris Hogan	71	61%	8.3	89.5	51%	64	126	9	122	3
Josh Gordon	68	59%	10.6	109.9	53%	52	82	5	113	3
Phillip Dorsett	50	74%	7.2	102.1	60%	14	90	106	13	5

Directional Passer Rating Delivered

Receiver	Short Left	Short Middle	Short Right	Deep Left	Deep Middle	Deep Right	Player Total
James White	93	99	115	40		96	99
Julian Edelman	105	99	93	96	119	96	102
Rob Gronkowski	91	76	124	149	90	53	94
Chris Hogan	69	145	43	85	82	127	90
Josh Gordon	73	149	88	127	110	109	110
Phillip Dorsett	143	99	116	149	0	41	102
Cordarrelle Patterson	105	91	89	149	40	135	123
Rex Burkhead	81	64	95			121	91
James Develin	76		39				53
Dwayne Allen		108	102			40	93
Jeremy Hill	92						92
Team Total	96	102	99	123	65	103	99

2018 Rushing Recap & 2019 Outlook

The Patriots could improve their run game with better play sequencing. Last year, after an explosive gain by a running back, they handed off to that same back 19 times. This produced a 32-percent success rate and only 3.7 YPC. When they handed to a different running back, those runs produced a 71-percent success rate and 7.0 YPC. If Brady passed on the following play, they averaged an identical 71-percent success rate and gained 11.6 YPA. With **Sony Michel** absent in OTAs, rookie third-round pick **Damien Harris** has earned more attention. Michel has dealt with knee issues since his time at Georgia, so he's being managed during the offseason. If the Patriots continue their run-heavy approach in the red zone, a running back getting those carries will be valuable in fantasy. Michel had an unreal 59 red zone carries as a rookie.

Player *Min 50 Rushes	Rushes	YPC	Success %	Success Rk	Missed YPA Rk	YTS % Rk	YAS % Rk	Early Down Success %	Early Down Success Rk	TDs
Sony Michel	280	4.5	53%	14	3	45	30	53%	12	12
James White	102	4.4	47%	40	27	48	50	48%	29	5
Rex Burkhead	80	3.5	40%	63	45	53	66	41%	58	3

Yards per Carry by Direction

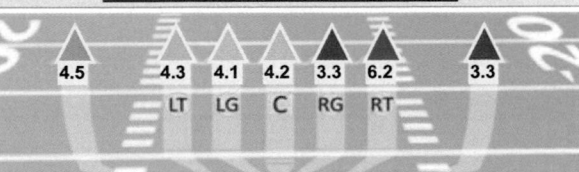

4.5		4.3	4.1	4.2	3.3	6.2		3.3
		LT	LG	C	RG	RT		

Directional Run Frequency

10%		13%	12%	33%	13%	12%		7%
		LT	LG	C	RG	RT		

With **Chris Hogan** gone, New England's WR-depth is a question mark. **Josh Gordon** signed his RFA tender to stay with the team. But he's serving an indefinite NFL suspension for violating his reinstatement terms under the league's substance abuse policy. In his absence, the Patriots will trot out **Julian Edelman** with 2019 first round pick **N'Keal Harry**.

The highest drafted Patriots wide receiver in the Brady-era was **Chad Jackson**, drafted 36th overall. They haven't drafted a wide receiver in the first round since 1996. This isn't to suggest Harry can't make a splash in his rookie season. He's a big, physical receiver similar to **Anquan Boldin**, and needs to make waves for the team to achieve their 2019 goals. Beating **Deion Branch**'s rookie season mark of 43 catches, and/or **Aaron Dobson**'s rookie year mark of 519 yards, would be a great starting point.

Despite question marks in the receiving game, the Patriots can look back to last season for optimism. 2018 was the first season since 2010 where they failed to have multiple wide receivers or tight ends catch at least 50 passes. Only Edelman exceeded that number. Yet they still won it all.

Fortunately, the Patriots still have RB **James White**. He led last year's team with 123 targets and 108 receptions, also earning the most red zone targets. With no **Dwayne Allen** and Gronkowski not at 100-percent, the team targeted RBs a league-high 31-percent of the time. The position was targeted 33-percent of the time on early downs. These RB targets resulted in a No. 10 ranked success rate. If **Josh McDaniels** further increases passes to RBs, it will accentuate a positive given how adept their offensive line is at blocking those plays.

(cont'd - see **NE-5**)

New England Patriots Fantasy Corner

Sony Michel is a late-third rd selection, and **James White** is an early-sixth rd pick in fantasy drafts. Michel missed mini-camp recuperating from his third knee procedure in the last 12-months. He is the signature high-risk early-round back to avoid. While Michel's downside is terrifying, James White's weekly volatility diminishes his value. Game script-depended satellite backs like White may be attractive in best ball, but lack predictable usable weeks for traditional leagues. With both overvalued, the third back off the board, **Damien Harris**, is the Patriot back to own in fantasy football. Harris offers feature back size, a 60th-percentile Speed Score, and a productive collegiate résumé. After back-to-back 1000-yard seasons at Alabama, Harris out-touched first rounder Josh Jacobs. A better receiver than Michel and a better runner than White, few running backs offer more fantasy upside in the double-digit rds than New England's bell cow-in-waiting.

- Matt Kelley

2018 Situational Usage by Player & Position

Usage Rate by Score

		Being Blown Out (14+)	Down Big (9-13)	One Score	Large Lead (9-13)	Blowout Lead (14+)
RUSH	Sony Michel	5%	5%	65%	4%	20%
	James White	7%	2%	74%	4%	14%
	Julian Edelman			55%		45%
	Rex Burkhead	4%		66%	4%	26%
	Cordarrelle Patterson	11%		67%	2%	20%
	Phillip Dorsett					100%
	James Develin	13%		38%		50%
	Kenjon Barner			79%		21%
	Jeremy Hill			75%		25%
	Total	6%	3%	67%	3%	22%
PASS	Sony Michel	8%	15%	77%		
	James White	8%	5%	69%	2%	16%
	Julian Edelman	8%		81%		11%
	Rex Burkhead		12%	76%		12%
	Rob Gronkowski	3%	7%	74%	4%	13%
	Cordarrelle Patterson	17%	3%	60%	3%	17%
	Chris Hogan	9%	3%	65%	5%	18%
	Josh Gordon	9%		86%		5%
	Phillip Dorsett	19%	6%	45%	6%	23%
	James Develin	5%	5%	79%	5%	5%
	Jeremy Hill			100%		
	Dwayne Allen	25%		25%		50%
	Total	9%	4%	71%	2%	14%

Share of Offensive Plays by Type

	Sony Michel	James White	Julian Edelman	Rex Burkhead	Rob Gronkowski	Cordarrelle Patterson	Chris Hogan	Josh Gordon	Phillip Dorsett	James Develin	Kenjon Barner	Jeremy Hill	Dwayne Allen
RUSH	51%	18%	2%	14%		8%			1%	1%	3%	1%	
PASS	2%	22%	21%	4%	13%	5%	11%	9%	8%	3%		0%	1%
ALL	26%	20%	12%	9%	7%	7%	6%	5%	4%	2%	2%	0%	0%

Positional Target Distribution vs NFL Average

		NFL Wide				Team Only			
		Left	Middle	Right	Total	Left	Middle	Right	Total
Deep	WR	33%	17%	31%	81%	22%	30%	21%	72%
	TE	5%	4%	7%	15%	5%	6%	10%	22%
	RB	1%	0%	2%	3%	3%		3%	6%
	All	39%	21%	40%	100%	30%	36%	35%	100%
Short	WR	20%	14%	21%	55%	22%	13%	18%	52%
	TE	6%	6%	8%	21%	4%	5%	4%	13%
	RB	9%	5%	10%	24%	16%	6%	12%	35%
	All	36%	25%	39%	100%	42%	24%	34%	100%
Total		37%	24%	39%	100%	40%	26%	34%	100%

Positional Success Rates vs NFL Average

		NFL Wide				Team Only			
		Left	Middle	Right	Total	Left	Middle	Right	Total
Deep	WR	40%	49%	40%	42%	52%	53%	38%	48%
	TE	43%	55%	43%	46%	67%	29%	17%	32%
	RB	41%	33%	42%	41%	0%		50%	29%
	All	40%	50%	41%	42%	50%	49%	33%	43%
Short	WR	55%	61%	52%	55%	52%	64%	63%	58%
	TE	55%	62%	54%	56%	61%	78%	75%	71%
	RB	46%	54%	45%	47%	51%	54%	55%	53%
	All	53%	59%	51%	54%	52%	64%	61%	58%
Total		50%	58%	49%	51%	52%	60%	56%	56%

Division History: Season Wins & 2019 Projection

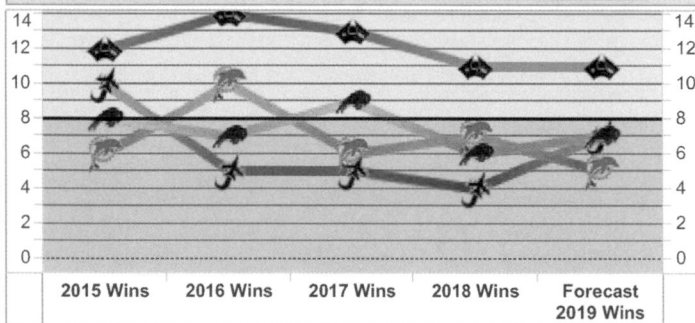

2015 Wins | 2016 Wins | 2017 Wins | 2018 Wins | Forecast 2019 Wins

Rank of 2019 Defensive Pass Efficiency Faced by Week

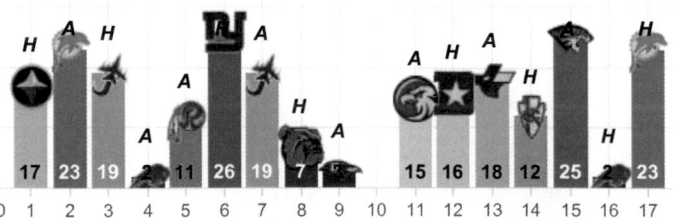

17 | 23 | 19 | 2 | 11 | 26 | 19 | 7 | | 15 | 16 | 18 | 12 | 25 | 2 | 23

Rank of 2019 Defensive Rush Efficiency Faced by Week

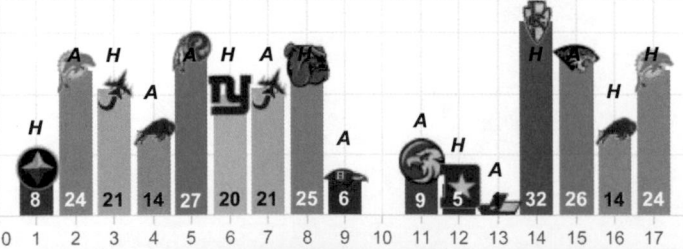

8 | 24 | 21 | 14 | 27 | 20 | 21 | 25 | 6 | 9 | 5 | | 32 | 26 | 14 | 24

2018 Detailed Analytics Summary
Success by Play Type & Primary Personnel Groupings

Type	1-1 [3WR]	2-1 [2WR]	2-2 [1WR]	1-2 [2WR]	1-0 [4WR]	0-1 [4WR]	2-0 [3WR]	2-3 [0WR]	0-0 [5WR]	1-3 [1WR]	ALL
PASS	52% (465)	54% (138)	53% (19)	53% (32)	47% (15)	50% (4)	40% (5)	0% (1)	0% (1)	100% (1)	53% (681)
RUSH	60% (223)	50% (210)	43% (81)	62% (26)	50% (2)	20% (5)	33% (3)	80% (5)			49% (555)
All	52% (688)	51% (348)	45% (100)	57% (58)	47% (17)	33% (9)	38% (8)	50% (6)	0% (1)	100% (1)	51% (1,236)

Format Success Rate (Total # of Plays)

Receiving Success by Top-4 Personnel Groupings
(Min 50 targets)

POS	Player	1-1 [3WR]	2-1 [2WR]	1-2 [2WR]	1-0 [4WR]	4 Grp Total
RB	James White	50% (113) 5.7, 95.3	59% (22) 7.5, 101.5	33% (3) 7.0, 126.4	67% (3) 7.0, 126.4	51% (141) 6.1, 100.7
TE	Rob Gronkowski	62% (53) 9.2, 90.8	50% (20) 9.0, 102.1	100% (5) 12.8, 118.8		62% (78) 9.4, 96.7
WR	Julian Edelman	62% (104) 8.8, 102.8	65% (17) 9.4, 114.6	25% (4) 2.8, 39.6	100% (1) 8.0, 100.0	61% (126) 8.7, 102.3
WR	Josh Gordon	57% (44) 12.1, 130.2	57% (14) 8.6, 85.4	50% (2) 9.5, 83.3	33% (6) 8.0, 63.2	55% (66) 10.9, 113.2
WR	Chris Hogan	57% (42) 10.8, 112.4	53% (15) 6.0, 77.1	60% (5) 8.2, 86.3	0% (1) 0.0, 39.6	56% (63) 9.3, 100.2
WR	Phillip Dorsett	59% (37) 7.2, 110.0	50% (6) 6.2, 29.9	75% (4) 5.8, 88.5	100% (2) 12.5, 118.8	61% (49) 7.2, 100.0

Format Line 1: Success Rate (Total # of Plays) Line 2: YPA, Passer Rating

Rushing Success by Top-4 Personnel Groupings
(Min 25 carries)

Rusher (Last, First)	1-1 [3WR]	2-1 [2WR]	2-2 [1WR]	1-2 [2WR]	4 Grp Total
Michel Sony	48% (73) 4.4	53% (133) 5.2	42% (33) 2.3	56% (18) 4.2	51% (257) 4.6
White James	47% (79) 4.6	44% (18) 4.3	33% (3) 2.0		46% (100) 4.5
Burkhead Rex	25% (20) 3.1	37% (30) 3.3	55% (20) 3.5	100% (2) 4.5	40% (72) 3.3
Patterson Cordarrelle	63% (27) 4.9	0% (1) 3.0	100% (2) 11.5	75% (4) 10.0	65% (34) 5.9
Brady Tom	80% (5) 3.4	29% (7) 0.6	11% (9) -0.4	50% (2) 0.5	35% (23) 0.8

Format Line 1: Success Rate (Total # of Plays) Line 2: YPC

Passing by Coverage Scheme

M2M	54% (256) 7.5, 94.3
Zone	58% (244) 8.0, 99.1
Screen	48% (67) 7.0, 101.0
Combo	71% (7) 12.3, 152.4

Passing by Route

Curl	64% (89) 6.6, 90.2
Screen	46% (56) 6.5, 105.5
Out	55% (55) 5.8, 83.8
Dig	62% (52) 10.5, 103.6
Flat	50% (40) 5.7, 84.3
Slant	69% (32) 9.3, 131.9

Throw Types

Level 1	58% (428) 7.2, 98.8
Level 2	57% (168) 9.6, 105.5
Level 3	21% (33) 7.8, 77.2
Shovel	57% (7) 7.6, 137.8
Sidearm	100% (2) 14.5, 118.8

QB Drop Types

3 Step	54% (299) 7.1, 93.8
0/1 Step	57% (134) 7.2, 103.1
5 Step	60% (126) 10.1, 115.4
7 Step	61% (36) 9.6, 88.4
Basic Screen	50% (30) 7.9, 98.8
Designed Rollout Right	40% (5) 7.4, 97.5

QB State at Pass

Planted	57% (461) 7.9, 98.5
Shuffling	43% (82) 6.3, 89.4
Moving	46% (24) 7.1, 110.1

Play Action

	Play Action	No P/A
Under Center	64% (114) 11.3, 118.0	57% (68) 6.0, 82.1
Shotgun	59% (61) 8.8, 106.9	53% (397) 7.2, 96.8
ALL	62% (175) 10.4, 114.1	54% (465) 7.0, 94.7

Run Types

Lead	51% (162) 4.5
Power	51% (98) 5.1
Inside Zone	41% (61) 2.6
Outside Zone	52% (48) 4.1
Pitch	57% (30) 5.5
Stretch	41% (27) 3.5

NE-5

Writing last year's preview I noticed the Patriots had shifted too pass-heavy near the goal line. Inside the five-yard line in 2017, the Patriots went 60 percent pass (67 percent run in 2016). Their passes were far less successful (51 percent as compared to 59 percent from runs). I urged the Patriots to shift to a more run-heavy approach in 2018. They listened. They replicated their 2016 run rate of 67 percent. And runs were tremendously productive. Run plays averaged a 65 percent success rate compared to passes which produced a mere 30 percent success rate. It was wise for the Patriots to go more run-heavy. Sony Michel's 67 percent success rate and seven rushing touchdowns led the way.

It wasn't the only efficient play calling strategy the Patriots employed in 2018. After first and ten incompletions, the league is shockingly only 53 percent pass on second and ten. Not the Patriots. They went 69 percent pass in 2018, the fourth-highest rate in the league, behind only the Steelers, Chiefs and Rams. Not surprisingly, all four of these teams have great offenses. It still amazes me in this day and age, there are teams with veteran quarterbacks like the Falcons and Titans, who went run on roughly 60 percent of their second-and-ten plays following an incompletion. They deserve the roughly 30 percent success rate on those run plays, while the pass-heavy teams are producing gains of over 7 YPA through the air to go with over 50 percent success rates. The Patriots also went very run-heavy on second and shorts and converted first downs with regularity, another extremely smart decision which too many teams don't take advantage of.

Trent Brown was not the only offseason loss. **Bill Belichick** will be tested once again this offseason as the New England lost key playmakers on defense. **Trey Flowers** is gone after recording two double-digit sack campaigns, with 51 quarterback hurries and 11 sacks coming last season.

Jamie Collins, who thrived in their scheme before an unsuccessful run in Cleveland, is back to replace that production. They also drafted Michigan EDGE **Chase Winovich**, one of the 2019 class's top pass-rushers. Additionally, they signed **Michael Bennett** in free agency to a two-year $16.75 million contract after the Seahawks cut him. Bennett's $2 million dead cap in 2020 allows the Patriots to cut him and save over $6M in salary cap if necessary.

Similar to 2018, New England's 2019 strength of schedule will be soft as they face the NFL's easiest projected slate of opponents. In 2017, the Patriots defense faced the No. 21-ranked offenses and the No. 19-ranked passing offenses. Last year they faced the third-easiest schedule of defenses and the third-easiest of pass defenses, as predicted. This year, they face the second-easiest schedule both overall and of pass defenses. An interesting scheduling quirk is that they won't get a real bye week rest advantage because their opponent has the same bye week. They face the Browns in Week 8, as they come off their own bye week. They face the Ravens off a bye in the following week, and the Texans off a mini bye in Week 13.

Repeating as Super Bowl Champs is never easy. After making only one top-50 pick from 2015 to 2017, the Patriots made four top-50 selections in the last two years. By filling key positions with home-grown talent and continuing to win on early downs, the Patriots are poised for another successful season.

Coaches (Prior Yrs)

Head Coach:
Sean Payton (13 yrs)
Offensive Coordinator:
Pete Carmichael (10 yrs)
Defensive Coordinator:
Dennis Allen (4 yrs)

New Orleans Saints

2019 Forecast

Wins	Div Rank
10.5	#1

Past Records
2018: 13-3
2017: 11-5
2016: 7-9

EASY   HARD

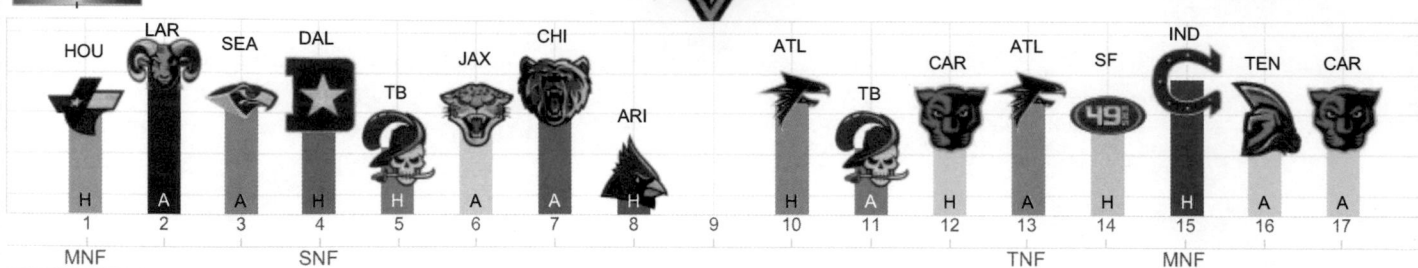

HOU	LAR	SEA	DAL	TB	JAX	CHI	ARI		ATL	TB	CAR	ATL	SF	IND	TEN	CAR
H	A	A	H	H	A	H	H		H	A	H	A	H	H	A	A
1	2	3	4	5	6	7	8	9	10	11	12	13	14	15	16	17

MNF   SNF   TNF   MNF

Key Players Lost

Player	New
Alex Okafor (DE)	KC
Benjamin Watson (TE)	NE
John Kuhn (FB)	Retired
Mark Ingram (RB)	BAL
Max Unger (C)	Retired
Tommylee Lewis (WR)	DET
Tyeler Davison (DT)	ATL

Average Line	# Games Favored	# Games Underdog
-5.2	12	2

2019 New Orleans Saints Overview

Since **Drew Brees** landed in New Orleans, the Saints' offense has melted faces with its high- octane passing game and high-efficiency running game, especially over the last two seasons. The 2016 Saints team was a strange outlier. That year, they ranked No. 1 in third-down conversion rate and finished 7-9. Woof.

With the emergence of **Cameron Jordan** and **Michael Thomas** and the arrival of **Alvin Kamara** and **Marshon Lattimore** in the Bayou, the Saints' offensive and defensive efficiency surged in 2017, but the team's third-down conversion rate collapsed to No. 22 in the NFL. After averaging a conversion-friendly 5.7 yards to go on third down in 2016, New Orleans averaged a not-so-nice 6.9 yards to go in 2017. This steep increase was a direct result of **Sean Payton**'s misguided first down play-calling tendencies. After passing on first-half first downs at a 56% rate in 2016, the Saints inexplicably passed on only 48% of first downs in 2017.

In 2018, everything clicked.

More rational play-calling finally unlocked New Orleans' talent-rich roster as Payton called pass plays on 54% of first-half first downs, up 6% from 2017. Thanks to a more pass-heavy and aggressive attack, the Saints found themselves with less yards to go, and their third-down conversion rate jumped back into the top five.

Better performance on third down could be one reason for the team's substantially better record in one-score games. They went 2-3 in one-score games in 2017, improving to 5-2 last year. The 2018 Saints were 8-1 in all other games, while the 2017 Saints went 9-2. Better third-down performance in close games allowed the Saints to go 13-3 last season.

Not every team needs to be pass heavy on first down to get short third downs.

(cont'd - see **NO2**)

Key Free Agents/ Trades Added

Player	AAV (MM)
Jared Cook (TE)	$7.5
Javorius Allen (RB)	$0.9
Latavius Murray (RB)	$3.6
Malcom Brown (DT)	$5
Marcus Sherels (CB)	$1
Mario Edwards (DT)	$2.3
Nick Easton (C)	$5.5

Drafted Players

Rd	Pk	Player (College)
2	48	C - Erik McCoy (Texas A&M)
4	105	S - Chauncey Gardner-Johnson (Florida)
6	177	S - Saquan Hampton (Rutgers)
7	231	TE - Alizé Mack (Notre Dame)
7	244	LB - Kaden Elliss (Idaho)

Regular Season Wins: Past & Current Proj

Forecast 2019 Wins — 10.5
2018 Wins — 13
Forecast 2018 Wins — 9.5
2017 Wins — 11
2016 Wins — 7
2015 Wins — 7

1 3 5 7 9 11 13 15

Lineup & Cap Hits

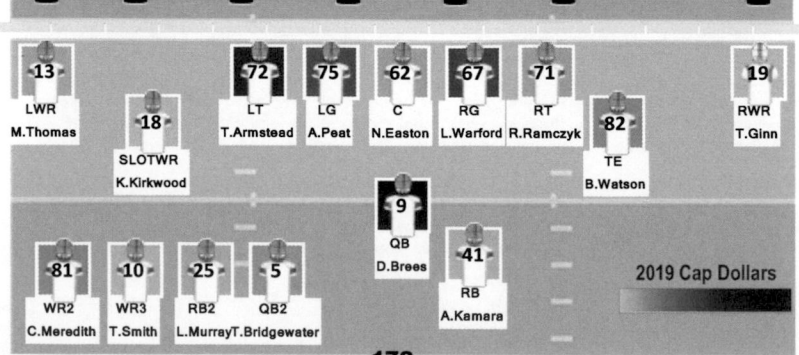

2019 Cap Dollars

2019 Unit Spending

All DEF   All OFF

Positional Spending

	Rank	Total	2017 Rk
All OFF	16	$98.72M	7
QB	9	$27.09M	4
OL	5	$45.47M	6
RB	28	$4.12M	14
WR	29	$14.59M	26
TE	21	$7.46M	15
All DEF	27	$74.40M	29
DL	16	$30.77M	12
LB	17	$19.85M	22
CB	21	$17.56M	24
S	32	$6.22M	21

But Brees is the league's most efficient first-down passer over the last three years. He ranked No. 1 on first down with a 72% completion rate, 62% Success Rate and 111 passer rating last season. Not going pass heavy to take advantage of this skill set would be hard to justify.

Last year's Saints preview was written almost entirely about Brees. Fewer people were talking about him heading into 2018 than at any time in recent memory. This was primarily due to his poor fantasy production in 2017. Which was mainly a product of the team running the ball more.

Brees' efficiency didn't take a backseat to anyone. His 8.1 yards per attempt were his most since 2011 and led the NFL. He also posted the NFL's second-best passer rating to go along with a career-low interception rate. If not for blatantly erroneous officiating, he would've taken the Saints to the Super Bowl.

Brees was ridiculous in the red zone and on third downs. His completion percentage was 3% higher than in 2017, and his league-best adjusted completion rate was off the charts. Brees was dominant. But he could've been even better if not for a hit he took on Thanksgiving.

The quality of pass defenses New Orleans faced in 2018 was largely overestimated in the preseason. The Steelers, Bengals, Giants, Falcons and Panthers were worse against the pass than predicted. The Saints ended up facing the fifth-easiest schedule for passing and project to do the same in 2019.

Two of Brees' toughest 2019 challenges come against defenses with extra time to prepare. He travels to face a Rams team coming off an extra day of rest in Week 2. The Saints travel to Chicago in Week 7, when the Bears will be coming off a bye. They'll be in Jacksonville the week before. This Weeks 6-7 stretch will mark the Saints' second set of three back-to-back road games on the year.

The Saints making a substantial shift toward 11 personnel was anticipated in the 2018 Preview. They used it only 48% of the time in 2017, including on only 58% of pass plays. Both were at least 10% below league average. In 2018, the Saints went 11 personnel 55% of the time, including on 65% of their pass plays. Both were still below-average numbers but were dramatic increases. The Saints' number of total plays from 11 personnel increased from 482 to 626.

The team's primary targets in 11-personnel formations were **Michael Thomas** with 104, **Alvin Kamara** with 86, **Ted Ginn** with 36, and **Tre'Quan Smith** with 29. It's telling that in only five games played, Ginn still saw 11 more targets

than Smith earned all season.

Brees took a hard shot in the first quarter of the Thanksgiving game. This happened after he overthrew a third-down pass which was intercepted. Though the defensive back ran the ball back for an apparent touchdown, he was later ruled down by contact. Brees didn't know he was down, so the play continued. Brees threw his shoulder into the convoy's lead blocker at his own five-yard line, jarring and taking himself to the ground. He finished the game and never showed up on the injury report.

Little things like this are what you seek out when you're hunting for any possible betting edge. Coincidence or not, Breeds' deep ball wasn't the same for the rest of the year. His deep passes averaged 63% completions,

(cont'd - see NO-3)

2018 Passing Performance

QB	1st Dwn	2nd Dwn	3rd Dwn	
Drew Brees	66%	52%	43%	Success Rate
	8.9	7.5	7.0	YPA
	123.3	97.2	109.1	Rating
Pass Rate	49%	57%	74%	
NFL AVG	53%	47%	36%	Success Rate
	7.7	7.3	6.9	YPA
	95.1	93.7	87.1	Rating
Pass Rate	53%	62%	80%	

2018 Rushing Performance

Offense	1st Dwn	2nd Dwn	3rd Dwn	
NO	52%	53%	54%	Success Rate
	4.9	3.5	2.9	YPC
Run Rate	51%	43%	26%	
NFL AVG	48%	46%	51%	Success Rate
	4.5	4.4	4.3	YPC
Run Rate	47%	38%	20%	

2018 Offensive Advanced Metrics

Rank (high on chart = good)

Metric	Rank
EDSR Off	2
30 & In Off	3
Red Zone Off	2
3rd Down Off	7
YPPA Off	5
YPPT Off	2
Offensive Efficiency	4
Pass Efficiency Off	3
Pass Pro Efficiency Off	3
RB Pass Eff Off	13
Rush Efficiency Off	8
Explosive Pass Off	5
Explosive Run Off	20

2018 Defensive Advanced Metrics

Metric	Rank
EDSR Def	31
30 & In Def	23
Red Zone Def	10
3rd Down Def	22
YPPA Def	12
YPPT Def	11
Defensive Efficiency	28
Pass Efficiency Def	22
Pass Pro Efficiency Def	4
RB Pass Eff Def	25
Rush Efficiency Def	31
Explosive Pass Def	3
Explosive Run Def	3

2018 Weekly EDSR & Season Trending Performance

	1	2	3	4	5	7	8	9	10	11	12	13	14	15	16	17	WEEK
	L	W	W	W	W	W	W	W	W	W	W	L	W	W	W	L	RESULT
	TB	CLE	ATL	NYG	WAS	BAL	MIN	LA	CIN	PHI	ATL	DAL	TB	CAR	PIT	CAR	OPP
	H	H	A	A	H	A	A	H	A	H	H	A	A	H	H	H	SITE
	-8	3	6	15	24	1	10	10	37	41	14	-3	14	3	3	-19	MARGIN
	40	21	43	33	43	24	30	45	51	48	31	10	28	12	31	14	PTS
	48	18	37	18	19	23	20	35	14	7	17	13	14	9	28	33	OPP PTS

EDSR by Wk
W=Green
L=Red

OFF/DEF
EDSR
Blue=OFF
(high=good)
Red=DEF
(low=good)

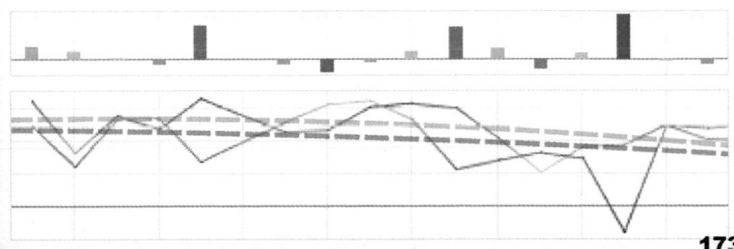

2018 Close Game Records

All 2018 Wins: **13**

FG Games (<=3 pts) W-L: **4-1**
FG Games Win %: **80% (#4)**
FG Games Wins (% of Total Wins): **31% (#15)**

1 Score Games (<=8 pts) W-L: **5-2**
1 Score Games Win %: **71% (#5)**
1 Score Games Wins (% of Total Wins): **38% (#27)**

2018 Critical & Game-Deciding Stats

TO Margin	+8
TO Given	16
INT Given	7
FUM Given	9
TO Taken	24
INT Taken	12
FUM Taken	12
Sack Margin	+29
Sacks	49
Sacks Allow	20
Return TD Margin	+0
Ret TDs	1
Ret TDs Allow	1
Penalty Margin	-9
Penalties	94
Opponent Penalties	85

New Orleans Saints 2019 Strength of Schedule In Detail (compared to 2018)

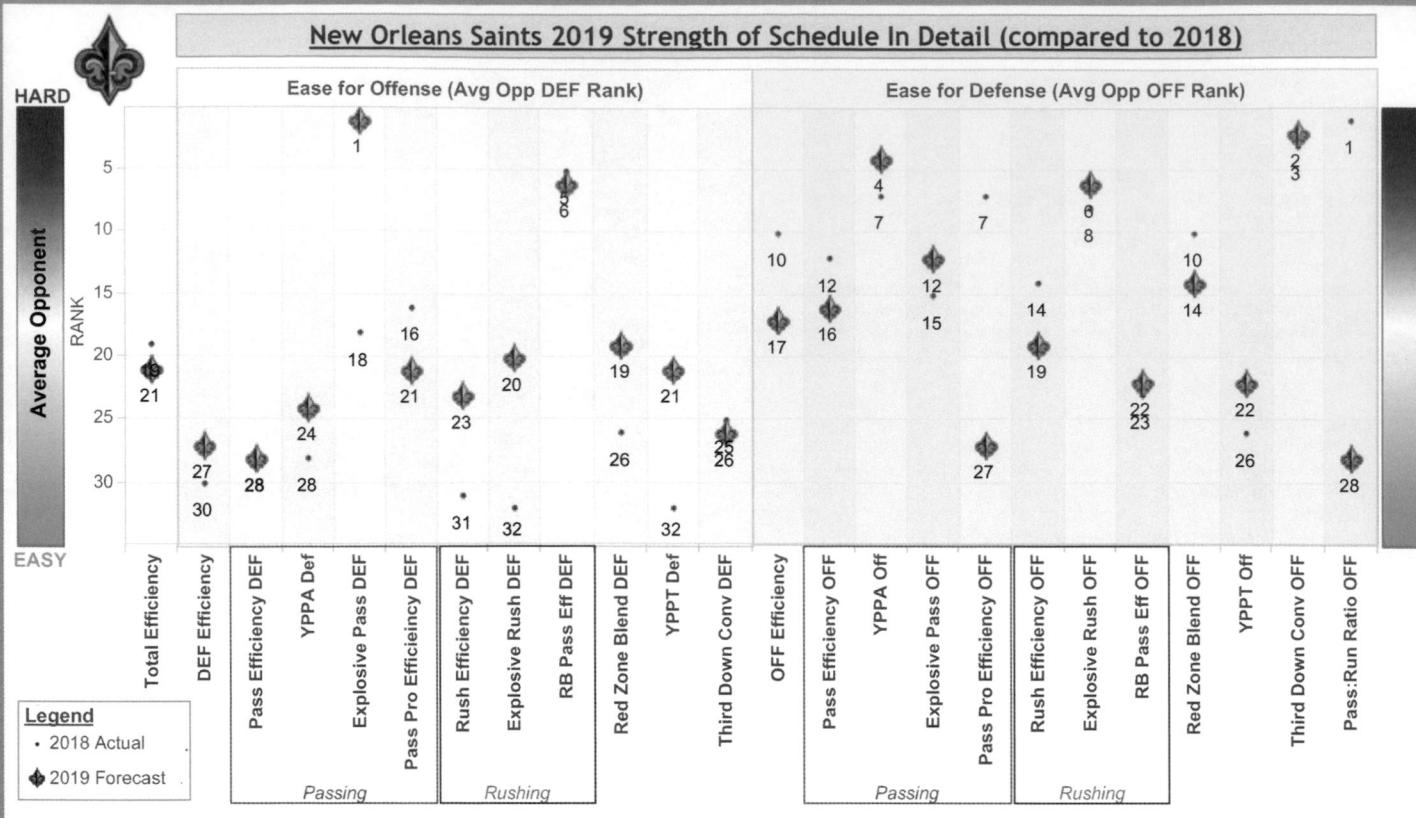

HARD / EASY

Average Opponent RANK

Ease for Offense (Avg Opp DEF Rank) | Ease for Defense (Avg Opp OFF Rank)

Ease for Offense categories: Total Efficiency, DEF Efficiency, Pass Efficiency DEF, YPPA Def, Explosive Pass DEF, Pass Pro Efficiency DEF, Rush Efficiency DEF, Explosive Rush DEF, RB Pass Eff DEF, Red Zone Blend DEF, YPPT Def, Third Down Conv DEF

Ease for Defense categories: OFF Efficiency, Pass Efficiency OFF, YPPA Off, Explosive Pass OFF, Pass Pro Efficiency OFF, Rush Efficiency OFF, Explosive Rush OFF, RB Pass Eff OFF, Red Zone Blend OFF, YPPT Off, Third Down Conv OFF, Pass:Run Ratio OFF

Passing / *Rushing*

Legend
- 2018 Actual
- ◆ 2019 Forecast

2019 v 2018 Schedule Variances* (OFF=Rank of DEF faced, 2019 vs 2018)

Pass OFF Rank	Pass OFF Blend Rk	Rush OFF Rk	Rush OFF Blend Rk	Pass DEF Rk	Pass DEF Blend Rk	Rush DEF Rk	Rush DEF Blend Rk
16	8	8	9	19	22	21	14

* **1**=Hardest Jump in 2019 schedule from 2018 (aka a much harder schedule in 2019), **32**=Easiest Jump in 2019 schedule from 2018 (aka a much easier schedule in 2019);
Pass Blend metric blends 4 metrics: Pass Efficiency, YPPA, Explosive Pass & Pass Rush; **Rush Blend** metric blends 3 metrics: Rush Efficiency, Explosive Rush & RB Targets

Team Records & Trends

	2018	2017	2016
Average line	-5.6	-3.3	0.3
Average O/U line	52.6	49.9	51.8
Straight Up Record	13-3	11-5	7-9
Against the Spread Record	10-6	8-8	11-5
Over/Under Record	7-9	6-7	9-7
ATS as Favorite	7-6	7-4	3-4
ATS as Underdog	3-0	1-4	8-1
Straight Up Home	6-2	7-1	4-4
ATS Home	4-4	4-4	4-4
Over/Under Home	5-3	4-3	5-3
ATS as Home Favorite	3-4	4-3	2-4
ATS as a Home Dog	1-0	0-1	2-0
Straight Up Away	7-1	3-4	3-5
ATS Away	6-2	3-4	7-1
Over/Under Away	2-6	2-3	4-4
ATS Away Favorite	4-2	2-1	1-0
ATS Away Dog	2-0	1-3	6-1
Six Point Teaser Record	12-3	12-3	14-2
Seven Point Teaser Record	13-3	14-2	14-2
Ten Point Teaser Record	13-2	15-1	14-2

NO-3

18.1 YPA, a 6:0 TD:INT ratio and a passer rating of 144 before Thanksgiving. Post-Thanksgiving, they averaged 41% completions, 10.2 YPA, a 1:2 TD:INT rate and a passer rating of 63. Brees threw deep only four times in the NFC Championship against the Rams. He completed just one, for an average of 10.8 YPA and a 71.9 passer rating.

Looking at some of his deeper routes, we can see the change more granularly. Brees was 8 for 11 with a 5:0 touchdown to interception ratio on go and fly routes before the hit. He went 2 for 6 and his passer rating fell by 30 points on fly routes thereafter. Brees' 2:0 ratio and 140.0 passer rating on pre-hit post routes collapsed to a 0:1 TD:INT ratio and a 61 passer rating post-hit.

On one of Brees' favorite routes, the stick-nod, he was 8 for 14 with a 98.8 rating and 11.8 YPA pre-hit, which then dropped to 2 for 8 with a 0:2 TD:INT ratio, *(cont'd - see NO-4)*

2019 Rest Analysis

Team More Rest	1
Opp More Rest	3
Net Rest Edge	-2
Week 2 Edge	-1
Week 3 Edge	0
Week 4 Edge	0
Week 5 Edge	0
Week 6 Edge	0
Week 7 Edge	
Week 8 Edge	0
Week 10 Edge	0
Week 11 Edge	0
Week 12 Edge	0
Week 13 Edge	0
Week 14 Edge	3
Week 15 Edge	0
Week 16 Edge	-1
Week 17 Edge	0

Health by Unit*

2018 Rk	6
2017 Rk	24
2018 v 2017 Rk	3
Off Rk	9
Def Rk	8
QB Rk	1
RB Rk	5
WR Rk	
TE Rk	1
Oline Rk	11
Dline Rk	18
LB Rk	6
DB Rk	15

Based on the work of Football Outsiders

2018 Weekly Betting Lines (wks 1-16)

1	2	3	4	5	6	7	8	10	11	12	13	14	15	16
HOU	LAR	SEA	DAL	TB	JAX	CHI	ARI	ATL	TB	CAR	ATL	SF	IND	TEN
	3	0				1					-2.5			-3
-7			-7	-10.5	-4		-7	-4		-9		-8.5	-5	
							-14.5							
Avg = -5.2														
-7	3	0	-7	-10.5	-4	1	-14.5	-4	-4	-9	-2.5	-8.5	-5	-3

Home Lines (wks 1-16)

1	4	5	8	10	12	14	15
-7 HOU	-7 DAL	-10.5 TB	-14.5 ARI	-7 ATL	-9 CAR	-8.5 SF	-5 IND

Avg = -8.6

Road Lines (wks 1-16)

2	3	6	7	11	13	16
3 LAR	0 SEA	-4 JAX	1 CHI	-4 TB	-2.5 ATL	-3 TEN

Avg = -1.4

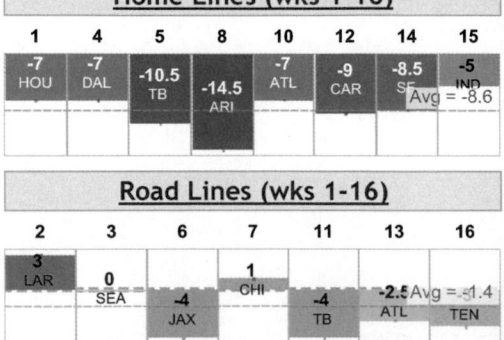

2018 Play Tendencies

All Pass %	53%
All Pass Rk	29
All Rush %	47%
All Rush Rk	4
1 Score Pass %	57%
1 Score Pass Rk	17
2017 1 Score Pass %	59%
2017 1 Score Pass Rk	11
2018 Pass Increase %	-2%
Pass Increase Rk	20
1 Score Rush %	43%
1 Score Rush Rk	16
Up Pass %	45%
Up Pass Rk	26
Up Rush %	55%
Up Rush Rk	7
Down Pass %	59%
Down Pass Rk	30
Down Rush %	41%
Down Rush Rk	3

2018 Down & Distance Tendencies

Down	Distance	Total Plays	Pass Rate	Run Rate	Play Success %
1	Short (1-3)	14	50%	50%	64%
	Med (4-7)	9	56%	44%	67%
	Long (8-10)	368	51%	49%	59%
	XL (11+)	11	82%	18%	55%
2	Short (1-3)	53	17%	83%	66%
	Med (4-7)	88	68%	32%	60%
	Long (8-10)	89	63%	37%	46%
	XL (11+)	34	94%	6%	29%
3	Short (1-3)	58	55%	45%	67%
	Med (4-7)	41	88%	12%	44%
	Long (8-10)	31	97%	3%	29%
	XL (11+)	20	100%	0%	15%
4	Short (1-3)	11	27%	73%	73%

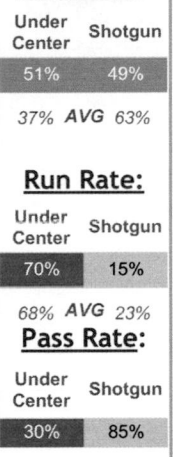

Shotgun %:

Under Center	Shotgun
51%	49%

37% *AVG* 63%

Run Rate:

Under Center	Shotgun
70%	15%

68% *AVG* 23%

Pass Rate:

Under Center	Shotgun
30%	85%

32% *AVG* 77%

New Orleans Saints
2018 Play Analysis

Short Yardage Intelligence:

2nd and Short Run

Run Freq	Run Rk	NFL Run Freq Avg	Run 1D Rate	Run NFL 1D Avg
87%	2	65%	69%	68%

2nd and Short Pass

Pass Freq	Pass Rk	NFL Pass Freq Avg	Pass 1D Rate	Pass NFL 1D Avg
13%	31	35%	86%	56%

Most Frequent Play

Down	Distance	Play Type	Player	Total Plays	Play Success %
1	Short (1-3)	RUSH	Mark Ingram	4	75%
	Med (4-7)	RUSH	Alvin Kamara	3	67%
	Long (8-10)	RUSH	Alvin Kamara	81	54%
	XL (11+)	PASS	Ted Ginn	3	33%
2	Short (1-3)	RUSH	Alvin Kamara	17	71%
	Med (4-7)	RUSH	Alvin Kamara	16	63%
	Long (8-10)	PASS	Michael Thomas	19	63%
	XL (11+)	PASS	Alvin Kamara	9	11%
3	Short (1-3)	RUSH	Mark Ingram	10	30%
	Med (4-7)	PASS	Michael Thomas	7	71%
	Long (8-10)	PASS	Alvin Kamara	9	22%
			Michael Thomas	9	33%
	XL (11+)	PASS	Michael Thomas	5	40%

Most Successful Play*

Down	Distance	Play Type	Player	Total Plays	Play Success %
1	Long (8-10)	PASS	Dan Arnold	5	100%
2	Short (1-3)	RUSH	Zach Line	5	80%
	Med (4-7)	PASS	Tre'Quan Smith	5	100%
	Long (8-10)	PASS	Benjamin Watson	6	67%
	XL (11+)	PASS	Michael Thomas	7	43%
3	Short (1-3)	RUSH	Alvin Kamara	8	100%
	Med (4-7)	PASS	Michael Thomas	7	71%
	Long (8-10)	PASS	Michael Thomas	9	33%
	XL (11+)	PASS	Michael Thomas	5	40%

*Minimum 5 plays to qualify

2018 Weekly Snap Rates

Wk	Opp	Score	Michael Thomas	Alvin Kamara	Josh Hill	Tre'Quan Smith	Benjamin Watson	Mark Ingram	Austin Carr	Ted Ginn	Cameron Meredith
1	TB	L 48-40	61 (95%)	52 (81%)	24 (38%)	11 (17%)	51 (80%)		44 (69%)	50 (78%)	
2	CLE	W 21-18	58 (88%)	51 (77%)	39 (59%)	22 (33%)	54 (82%)		32 (48%)	30 (45%)	
3	ATL	W 43-37	76 (96%)	67 (85%)	49 (62%)	26 (33%)	45 (57%)		13 (16%)	51 (65%)	34 (43%)
4	NYG	W 33-18	66 (94%)	59 (84%)	43 (61%)	26 (37%)	37 (53%)		12 (17%)	38 (54%)	22 (31%)
5	WAS	W 43-19	51 (77%)	31 (47%)	38 (58%)	44 (67%)	36 (55%)	36 (55%)	14 (21%)		30 (45%)
7	BAL	W 24-23	65 (92%)	39 (55%)	44 (62%)	52 (73%)	36 (51%)	35 (49%)	15 (21%)		18 (25%)
8	MIN	W 30-20	51 (96%)	38 (72%)	34 (64%)	41 (77%)	14 (26%)	23 (43%)	19 (36%)		9 (17%)
9	LA	W 45-35	65 (92%)	41 (58%)	55 (77%)	48 (68%)	33 (46%)	34 (48%)	15 (21%)		13 (18%)
10	CIN	W 51-14	46 (61%)	34 (45%)	43 (57%)	50 (67%)	29 (39%)	31 (41%)	22 (29%)		
11	PHI	W 48-7	57 (81%)	44 (63%)	46 (66%)	50 (71%)	21 (30%)	30 (43%)	31 (44%)		
12	ATL	W 31-17	52 (91%)	37 (65%)	31 (54%)		18 (32%)	27 (47%)	18 (32%)		
13	DAL	L 13-10	51 (98%)	35 (67%)	26 (50%)	44 (85%)	20 (38%)	21 (40%)	15 (29%)		
14	TB	W 28-14	58 (91%)	41 (64%)	45 (70%)	41 (64%)	28 (44%)	29 (45%)	14 (22%)		
15	CAR	W 12-9	69 (93%)	47 (64%)	51 (69%)	46 (62%)	32 (43%)	33 (45%)			
16	PIT	W 31-28	61 (92%)	40 (61%)	46 (70%)	26 (39%)	25 (38%)	32 (48%)		27 (41%)	
17	CAR	L 33-14	41 (79%)		38 (73%)	40 (77%)	27 (52%)	19 (37%)	11 (21%)		
	Grand Total		928 (89%)	656 (66%)	652 (62%)	567 (58%)	506 (48%)	350 (45%)	275 (31%)	196 (57%)	126 (30%)

Personnel Groupings

Personnel	Team %	NFL Avg	Succ. %
1-1 [3WR]	55%	65%	57%
1-2 [2WR]	15%	17%	55%
2-1 [2WR]	13%	8%	51%
2-2 [1WR]	8%	3%	46%
1-3 [1WR]	2%	3%	63%
2-0 [3WR]	2%	1%	81%

Grouping Tendencies

Personnel	Pass Rate	Pass Succ. %	Run Succ. %
1-1 [3WR]	63%	57%	59%
1-2 [2WR]	52%	57%	53%
2-1 [2WR]	41%	48%	53%
2-2 [1WR]	21%	53%	45%
1-3 [1WR]	38%	56%	67%
2-0 [3WR]	81%	76%	100%

Red Zone Targets (min 3)

Receiver	All	Inside 5	6-10	11-20
Michael Thomas	31	9	7	15
Alvin Kamara	29	4	5	20
Tre'Quan Smith	11	2	4	5
Benjamin Watson	9	4	2	3
Ted Ginn	6	1		5
Cameron Meredith	2			2

Red Zone Rushes (min 3)

Rusher	All	Inside 5	6-10	11-20
Alvin Kamara	55	16	18	21
Mark Ingram	30	15	5	10
Taysom Hill	16	4	5	7
Drew Brees	6	4	1	1
Teddy Bridgewater	4		1	3

Early Down Target Rate

	RB	TE	WR
	29%	15%	57%
	23%	21%	56%
		NFL AVG	

Overall Target Success %

	RB	TE	WR
	50%	61%	62%
	#7	#3	#1

New Orleans Saints 2018 Passing Recap & 2019 Outlook

Over the last two years, **Drew Brees** hasn't had much to work with at wide receiver outside of **Michael Thomas**. Between **Ben Watson**, **Tre'Quan Smith**, **Brandon Coleman**, **Coby Fleener**, **Josh Hill** and **Keith Kirkwood**, Brees hasn't had a capable tight end or an above-average WR2. Yet, no one other than **Patrick Mahomes** has a higher adjusted YPA over that span. Brees completed a staggering 73.2% of his passes in over 1,000 attempts from 2017-2018. He's the only quarterback in NFL history to hit 72% completions in consecutive seasons and 70% completions in three consecutive seasons. He's also one of only three players to earn a 100-plus passer rating in four straight years, joining **Steve Young** and **Aaron Rodgers**. Projected to face the NFL's fifth-easiest schedule of opposing pass defenses, Brees is set to dominate again. Payton and Brees had found real play-calling and playmaking harmony, and the Saints were a 10-1 juggernaut heading into Thanksgiving. But Brees was not the same player thereafter. With only five selections in the 2019 NFL Draft (one pick in the top 100), there is no time to reload. This is *the year* for the Saints. The NFL's best 2018 team through 12 weeks should enter 2019 as a favorite to represent the NFC in the Super Bowl.

Drew Brees Rating All Downs

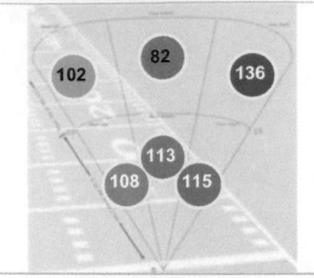

2018 Standard Passing Table

QB	Comp	Att	Comp %	Yds	YPA	TDs	INT	Sacks	Rating	Rk
Drew Brees	418	567	74%	4,542	8.0	36	7	21	113	3
Teddy Bridgewater	14	23	61%	118	5.1	1	1	2	71	45
NFL Avg			62%		7.0				87.5	

2018 Advanced Passing Table

QB	Success %	EDSR Passing Success %	20+ Yd Pass Gains	20+ Yd Pass %	30+ Yd Pass Gains	30+ Yd Pass %	Avg. Air Yds per Comp	Avg. YAC per Comp	20+ Air Yd Comp	20+ Air Yd %
Drew Brees	56%	60%	68	12.0%	21	4.0%	5.9	5.0	31	5%
Teddy Bridgewater	36%	38%	0	0.0%			4.6	3.8		0%
NFL Avg	44%	48%	29.5	8.4%	12.5	3.7%	5.8	5.1	14.5	6%

Drew Brees Rating Early Downs

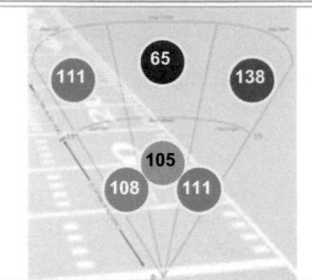

Interception Rates by Down

Yards to Go	1st Dwn	2nd Dwn	3rd Dwn	4th Dwn	Total
1 & 2	0.0%	0.0%	0.0%	0.0%	0.0%
3, 4, 5	0.0%	2.7%	2.5%	0.0%	2.3%
6 - 9	0.0%	2.4%	0.0%	0.0%	1.5%
10 - 14	0.5%	2.1%	0.0%		0.7%
15+	0.0%	4.5%	0.0%		2.2%
Total	**0.4%**	**2.6%**	**0.7%**	**0.0%**	**1.2%**

3rd Down Passing - Short of Sticks Analysis

QB	Avg. Yds to Go	Avg. YIA (of Comp)	Avg Yds Short	Short of Sticks Rate	Short Rk
Drew Brees	7.2	5.6	-1.6	66%	21
NFL Avg	7.8	6.4	-1.4	60%	

Air Yds vs YAC

Air Yds %	YAC %	Rk
54%	46%	20
53%	48%	

2018 Receiving Recap & 2019 Outlook

Michael Thomas is entering the final year of his rookie deal. It would shock me if the Saints didn't sign him to a lucrative extension before the 2019 season begins. He and **Drew Brees** have been in lock step together. Last year, Thomas caught 83% of his targets for 9.5 YPA and a No. 1 Success Rate of 68%. The top three wide receivers off the board in fantasy drafts are **DeAndre Hopkins**, **Davante Adams** and Thomas. Of these players, Thomas faces the easiest projected schedule. And he plays on the team most likely to go more pass heavy in 2019, given the loss of **Mark Ingram**. If the wide receiver corps is healthier in 2019 and **Jared Cook** delivers, it hurts **Alvin Kamara** more than Thomas.

Player *Min 50 Targets	Targ	Comp %	YPA	Rating	Success %	Success Rk	Missed YPA Rk	YAS % Rk	YTS % Rk	TDs
Michael Thomas	170	83%	9.5	123.3	68%	1	1	75	51	10
Alvin Kamara	122	79%	6.9	102.9	54%	47	77	102	51	4

Directional Passer Rating Delivered

Receiver	Short Left	Short Middle	Short Right	Deep Left	Deep Middle	Deep Right	Player Total
Michael Thomas	117	115	114	153	119	68	123
Alvin Kamara	99	110	97	40		135	103
Benjamin Watson	76	98	130	119	40	65	108
Tre'Quan Smith	108	145	97	90	119	146	131
Ted Ginn	59	119	123	51	48	129	73
Mark Ingram	112	85	56				89
Josh Hill	40	102	118	40			106
Keith Kirkwood	140	96	126	19	83	135	117
Cameron Meredith	92	158	79		96		148
Tommylee Lewis	117		40	158			156
Team Total	108	116	109	121	69	124	114

2018 Rushing Recap & 2019 Outlook

Mark Ingram signed with Baltimore, but **Latavius Murray** should fill the void as the new complement to **Alvin Kamara**. If Murray doesn't deliver like Ingram did, the Saints could shift even more pass heavy in 2019. Either way, Kamara should still be in store for a huge season. Players like **Ezekiel Elliott** and **Saquon Barkley** project to see more rushing usage. But Kamara will receive enough carries to validate his top-five fantasy pick status. He ranked No. 1 in total red-zone opportunities last year, with a whopping 55 carries and 29 targets. The only other player to see more than 64 total red-zone plays was **Todd Gurley**. With Gurley banged up and a reduced workload likely, he shouldn't come close to Kamara in that category this year. Especially if Kamara sees more goal-line touches without Ingram around.

Player *Min 50 Rushes	Rushes	YPC	Success %	Success Rk	Missed YPA Rk	YTS % Rk	YAS % Rk	Early Down Success %	Early Down Success Rk	TDs
Alvin Kamara	217	4.4	56%	8	10	19	40	54%	8	14
Mark Ingram	155	4.6	56%	7	4	27	36	58%	3	6

Yards per Carry by Direction

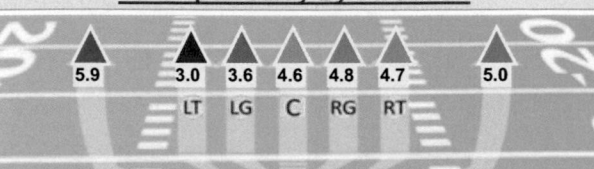

	LT	LG	C	RG	RT	
5.9	3.0	3.6	4.6	4.8	4.7	5.0

Directional Run Frequency

	LT	LG	C	RG	RT	
8%	11%	16%	10%	28%	18%	10%

4.9 YPA and a 7.8 passer rating post-hit. Essentially, Brees struggled tremendously with all throws 10 yards or deeper.

Ouch.

Brees was likely playing hurt, because the pass defenses he faced in December were actually more pass friendly. Brees faced six above-average pass defenses prior to Thanksgiving, including four in the top ten. Afterwards, Brees faced just two above-average pass defenses, both in the playoffs, and only one top-ten pass defense, in the playoff loss to the Rams.

The Saints' entire starting secondary remains on rookie deals. The inexperience showed last year, despite moments of promise. The defense ranked No. 22 in pass efficiency and No. 31 in both explosive pass defense and Early Down Success Rate (EDSR).

Their secondary must improve. With solid pieces in **Marshon Lattimore** outside and **Vonn Bell** at strong safety, the team wisely drafted a dominant college slot corner in Florida's **Chauncey Gardner-Johnson**. If the secondary takes a forward leap, there are very few impediments to **Sean Payton** and **Drew Brees** competing for another Super Bowl in 2019.

(cont'd - see NO-5)

New Orleans Saints Fantasy Corner

Mark Ingram is the quintessential system running back. A sub-athlete compiler propped up by Alabama brand equity and misguided draft capital, Ingram somehow averaged 17.6 PPR fantasy points per game in 2017 prior to his 2018 suspension and subsequent reduced role. Ingram's stunning fantasy output in New Orleans was fueled by parallel forces: 1. The NFL's most efficient run-blocking offensive line the last three seasons and 2. The NFL's best screen- game quarterback. **Drew Brees** is the all-time leader in running back targets and RB yards per reception, and no one is close. Into Running Back Valhalla steps **Latavius Murray**, a big, explosive runner who lacks wiggle. The space the Saints create for skill players in all phases fits perfectly with Murray's skill set. Murray should deliver more explosive plays per touch than Ingram in a similar role. Murray is one of the best-value upside plays in fantasy football.

- Matt Kelley

2018 Situational Usage by Player & Position

Usage Rate by Score

		Being Blown Out (14+)	Down Big (9-13)	One Score	Large Lead (9-13)	Blowout Lead (14+)
RUSH	Alvin Kamara	3%	9%	68%	9%	11%
	Mark Ingram	2%	9%	60%	7%	22%
	Tre'Quan Smith			100%		
	Ted Ginn			67%	33%	
	Dwayne Washington	41%		7%		52%
	Zach Line	30%		40%		30%
	Mike Gillislee		6%	88%	6%	
	Tommylee Lewis		50%	50%		
	Jonathan Williams			100%		
	Total	5%	8%	62%	8%	17%
PASS	Alvin Kamara	7%	8%	75%	5%	5%
	Mark Ingram	4%	11%	75%	4%	7%
	Michael Thomas	12%	11%	66%	4%	6%
	Tre'Quan Smith	4%	11%	50%	20%	15%
	Ted Ginn	9%		88%	2%	
	Benjamin Watson	11%	5%	70%	2%	11%
	Josh Hill	7%	4%	78%	7%	4%
	Zach Line	11%		56%	11%	22%
	Mike Gillislee			100%		
	Cameron Meredith			50%	20%	30%
	Tommylee Lewis	33%		67%		
	Jonathan Williams			100%		
	Total	9%	8%	70%	6%	7%

Share of Offensive Plays by Type

	Alvin Kamara	Mark Ingram	Michael Thomas	Tre'Quan Smith	Ted Ginn	Benjamin Watson	Dwayne Washington	Josh Hill	Zach Line	Mike Gillislee	Cameron Meredith	Tommylee Lewis	Jonathan Williams
RUSH	50%	36%		0%	1%		6%		2%	4%		0%	1%
PASS	24%	6%	32%	9%	9%	9%		6%	2%	0%	2%	1%	0%
ALL	36%	20%	17%	5%	5%	5%	3%	3%	2%	2%	1%	1%	0%

Positional Target Distribution vs NFL Average

		NFL Wide				Team Only			
		Left	Middle	Right	Total	Left	Middle	Right	Total
Deep	WR	33%	17%	31%	81%	25%	18%	34%	78%
	TE	5%	4%	7%	16%	3%	1%	11%	16%
	RB	1%	0%	2%	3%	1%		5%	6%
	All	39%	22%	39%	100%	30%	20%	51%	100%
Short	WR	20%	14%	21%	55%	22%	10%	21%	52%
	TE	6%	6%	8%	20%	1%	4%	9%	14%
	RB	9%	5%	10%	25%	14%	5%	14%	34%
	All	36%	25%	39%	100%	37%	19%	44%	100%
Total		37%	24%	39%	100%	36%	19%	45%	100%

Positional Success Rates vs NFL Average

		NFL Wide				Team Only			
		Left	Middle	Right	Total	Left	Middle	Right	Total
Deep	WR	40%	49%	40%	42%	55%	69%	47%	54%
	TE	43%	54%	41%	45%	67%	0%	60%	57%
	RB	39%	33%	42%	40%	0%		50%	40%
	All	40%	50%	40%	42%	54%	65%	50%	54%
Short	WR	55%	60%	52%	55%	65%	75%	62%	66%
	TE	55%	62%	54%	57%	20%	59%	69%	62%
	RB	46%	54%	45%	47%	48%	48%	56%	51%
	All	53%	59%	51%	54%	57%	64%	61%	61%
Total		50%	58%	49%	51%	57%	64%	59%	59%

Division History: Season Wins & 2019 Projection

| 2015 Wins | 2016 Wins | 2017 Wins | 2018 Wins | Forecast 2019 Wins |

Rank of 2019 Defensive Pass Efficiency Faced by Week

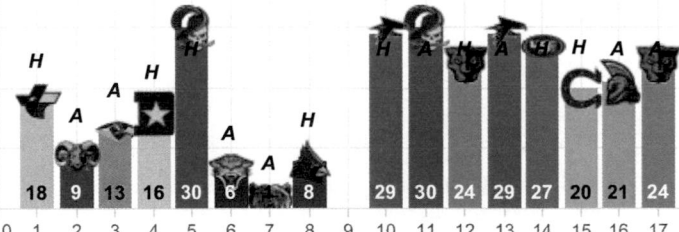

Rank of 2019 Defensive Rush Efficiency Faced by Week

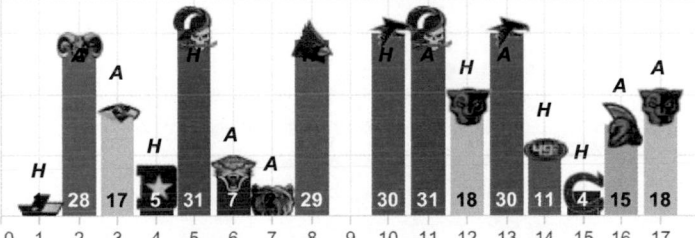

2018 Detailed Analytics Summary
Success by Play Type & Primary Personnel Groupings

Successful Play Rate 0% ▮▮▮ 100%

Type	1-1 [3WR]	1-2 [2WR]	2-1 [2WR]	2-2 [1WR]	1-3 [1WR]	1-0 [4WR]	2-0 [3WR]	2-3 [0WR]	0-0 [5WR]	0-1 [4WR]	ALL
PASS	55% (400)	57% (92)	49% (61)	53% (17)	50% (10)	46% (13)	78% (18)		50% (2)	0% (1)	55% (614)
RUSH	57% (226)	55% (83)	53% (88)	43% (70)	58% (19)	27% (11)	100% (4)	60% (5)	100% (1)		54% (507)
All	55% (626)	56% (175)	52% (149)	45% (87)	55% (29)	38% (24)	82% (22)	60% (5)	67% (3)	0% (1)	54% (1,121)

Format Success Rate (Total # of Plays)

Receiving Success by Top-4 Personnel Groupings
(Min 50 targets)

POS	Player	1-1 [3WR]	1-2 [2WR]	2-1 [2WR]	1-0 [4WR]	4 Grp Total
RB	Alvin Kamara	57% (86) 7.7, 109.3	55% (11) 4.9, 68.0	33% (15) 5.1, 78.8	50% (4) 4.8, 86.5	53% (116) 7.0, 103.6
WR	Michael Thomas	70% (104) 8.7, 121.5	64% (28) 8.9, 115.8	76% (17) 11.4, 114.2	50% (6) 10.0, 108.3	69% (155) 9.1, 119.2

Format Line 1: Success Rate (Total # of Plays) Line 2: YPA, Passer Rating

Rushing Success by Top-4 Personnel Groupings
(Min 25 carries)

Rusher (Last, First)	1-1 [3WR]	2-1 [2WR]	1-2 [2WR]	2-2 [1WR]	4 Grp Total
Kamara Alvin	60% (129) 4.5	55% (20) 7.1	51% (35) 4.0	57% (14) 3.0	58% (198) 4.6
Ingram Mark	38% (39) 3.0	57% (49) 5.7	60% (30) 5.9	50% (26) 3.7	51% (144) 4.6
Hill Taysom	63% (30) 5.4	25% (4) 6.3	50% (2) 2.5	100% (1) 4.0	59% (37) 5.3
Washington Dwayne	55% (11) 4.5	0% (6) 1.0	60% (5) 8.6	50% (4) 13.3	42% (26) 5.8
Brees Drew	83% (6) 5.0	0% (1) 0.0	100% (1) 2.0	12% (17) -0.8	32% (25) 0.8

Format Line 1: Success Rate (Total # of Plays) Line 2: YPC

Passing by Coverage Scheme

Zone	60% (228) 7.8, 104.3
M2M	63% (227) 8.7, 123.6
Screen	36% (59) 5.1, 97.9
Combo	50% (6) 16.2, 79.2

Passing by Route

Out	69% (78) 7.9, 107.1
Curl	67% (69) 7.1, 101.1
Screen	40% (55) 5.8, 95.5
Slant	75% (36) 9.4, 112.8
Flat	63% (32) 4.4, 114.3
Dig	73% (26) 11.6, 140.2

Throw Types

Level 1	60% (349) 6.7, 105.6
Level 2	57% (152) 9.5, 113.7
Level 3	43% (44) 12.9, 110.8
Sidearm	80% (5) 11.6, 115.0
Shovel	100% (1) 3.0, 118.8

QB Drop Types

3 Step	64% (209) 8.7, 115.8
5 Step	52% (148) 8.5, 110.3
0/1 Step	54% (79) 5.3, 107.5
7 Step	66% (50) 9.8, 104.4
Basic Screen	44% (32) 7.2, 106.9
Designed Rollout Right	64% (28) 6.5, 115.5

QB State at Pass

Planted	62% (371) 8.8, 113.6
Shuffling	42% (83) 5.4, 103.9
Moving	60% (60) 6.0, 121.3

Play Action

	Play Action	No P/A
Under Center	67% (93) 8.5, 126.2	55% (65) 7.4, 121.4
Shotgun	38% (13) 7.2, 90.7	58% (382) 8.0, 107.4
ALL	63% (106) 8.3, 124.8	57% (447) 8.0, 109.4

Run Types

Inside Zone	54% (141) 4.0
Outside Zone	50% (120) 4.5
Pitch	64% (44) 6.0
Lead	47% (43) 4.4
Power	55% (33) 5.1
Stretch	44% (9) 1.6

NO-5

Arriving in New Orleans as part of the **Jimmy Graham** trade, **Max Unger** anchored the offensive line from 2015-2018. After his retirement this offseason, the Saints quickly signed **Nick Easton** to a four-year, $24 million contract. They did this even though he missed all of 2018 with a neck injury.

They also spent their only top-100 pick, No. 48 overall, on Texas A&M center **Erik McCoy**.

Center is a massively underrated position. But it's especially important for Brees, who must see passing lanes open up in front of him due to his size. He'll need both McCoy and Easton to maintain a high success rate on pass blocks to provide a safe haven from edge pressure.

Another major change is the insertion of tight end **Jared Cook** into the offense. He can move downfield and provides an exceptional catch radius. Brees already indicated he felt confident throwing Cook 50-50 balls.

No Saints tight end has seen at least 50 targets since **Coby Fleener** in 2016. If Cook becomes the mismatch up the seam that Brees has been missing in recent years, the offense will continue to dominate.

The Saints were the No. 3 passing offense in 2018 with only one pass catcher and one running back drawing at least 50 targets. This speaks to the genius of Payton and the quality of Brees' play at quarterback. It's amazing that such an incredibly efficient passing offense can be designed and executed while funneling targets to only **Michael Thomas** and **Alvin Kamara**.

Part of the reason for the funneling of targets was injuries at the wide receiver position. The Saints were the sixth-healthiest team overall, but fifth-most injured at wide receiver, specifically missing **Ted Ginn** and **Cameron Meredith**.

Coaches (Prior Yrs)

Head Coach:
Pat Shurmur (1 yr)
Offensive Coordinator:
Mike Shula (1 yr)
Defensive Coordinator:
James Bettcher (1 yr)

EASY   HARD

New York Giants

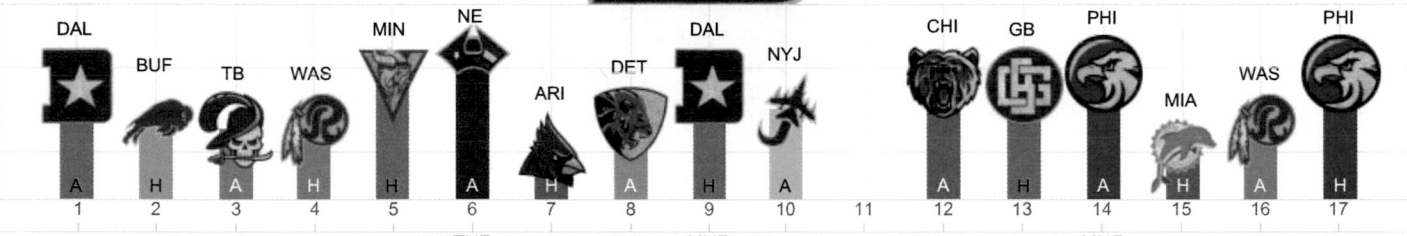

2019 Forecast

Wins	Div Rank
6	#4

Past Records

2018: 5-11
2017: 3-13
2016: 11-5

Schedule:
DAL (A) 1, BUF (H) 2, TB (A) 3, WAS (H) 4, MIN (H) 5, NE (A) 6, ARI (H) 7, DET (A) 8, DAL (H) 9, NYJ (A) 10, 11, CHI (A) 12, GB (H) 13, PHI (A) 14, MIA (H) 15, WAS (A) 16, PHI (H) 17
TNF (5), MNF (9), MNF (14)

Key Players Lost

Player	New
B.W. Webb (CB)	CIN
Curtis Riley (FS)	OAK
Jamon Brown (G)	ATL
Josh Mauro (DT)	OAK
Kerry Wynn (DT)	CIN
Landon Collins (FS)	WAS
Mario Edwards (DT)	NO
Odell Beckham Jr. (WR)	CLE
Oliver Vernon (OLB)	CLE

Average Line	# Games Favored	# Games Underdog
3.0	4	11

2019 New York Giants Overview

Eli Manning was significantly more productive targeting **Odell Beckham** than any other receiver in his career. But Manning was also more productive when simply *sharing the same field* as OBJ. Beckham's presence commanded double teams and created favorable matchups for teammates.

Know a position that doesn't command double teams or free up favorable matchups?

Running back.

It's been proven time and time again that running is devalued. I've discussed it ad nauseum and won't put you through that again. But it's a fact. And understanding the devaluation of the running game is the measure of a quality pro-football analyst. Running is favorable in short-yardage situations and some areas of the red zone, but it is -EV virtually everywhere else.

Imagine for a moment you're GM of an NFL team with full autonomy. You have two drafts and two free agency periods to remake your roster. You understand passing correlates more to wins than rushing. You understand quarterbacks, receivers, left tackles, pass rushers, and corners are more valuable than running backs, fullbacks, blocking tight ends, and nose tackles.

Understanding the basics of the game, which player grouping would you choose?

Option one: **Sam Darnold**, **Odell Beckham**, and Kentucky EDGE rusher **Josh Allen**
Option two: **Daniel Jones**, **Saquon Barkley**, and Clemson NT **Dexter Lawrence**

Giants GM **Dave Gettleman** cast his die in the 2018 draft, selecting the running back over the highest-graded quarterback remaining (Darnold). Most draft analysts gave at least three quarterbacks selected in 2018 higher grades than any current eligible this year. The Giants were badly in quarterback need, yet took a running back instead. Gettleman then openly suggested they may build around Eli for several more years.

(cont'd - see NYG2)

Key Free Agents/ Trades Added

Player	AAV (MM)
Antoine Bethea (FS)	$3.2
Golden Tate (WR)	$9.4
Jabrill Peppers (FS)	Trade
Kevin Zeitler (OG)	Trade
Markus Golden (DE)	$3.7
Mike Remmers (RT)	$2.5
Olsen Pierre (DT)	$1
Rod Smith (RB)	$0.8

Drafted Players

Rd	Pk	Player (College)
1	6	QB - Daniel Jones (Duke)
1	17	DT - Dexter Lawrence (Clemson)
1	30	CB - Deandre Baker (Georgia)
3	95	DE - Oshane Ximines (Old Dominion)
4	108	CB - Julian Love (Notre Dame)
5	143	LB - Ryan Connelly (Wisconsin)
5*	171	WR - Darius Slayton (Auburn)
6	180	CB - Corey Ballentine (Washburn)
7	232	OT - George Asafo-Adjei (Kentucky)
7	245	DT - Chris Slayton (Syracuse)

Regular Season Wins: Past & Current Proj

Forecast 2019 Wins: 6
2018 Wins: 5
Forecast 2018 Wins: 6.5
2017 Wins: 3
2016 Wins: 11
2015 Wins: 6

Lineup & Cap Hits

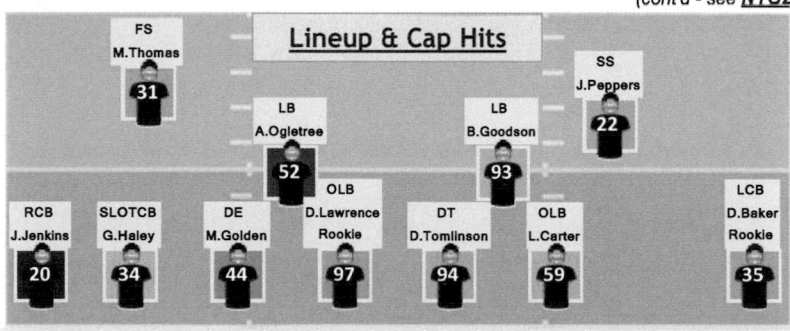

FS M.Thomas 31
SS J.Peppers 22
LB A.Ogletree 52
LB B.Goodson 93
OLB D.Lawrence Rookie 97
RCB J.Jenkins 20
SLOTCB G.Haley 34
DE M.Golden 44
DT D.Tomlinson 94
OLB L.Carter 59
LCB D.Baker Rookie 35

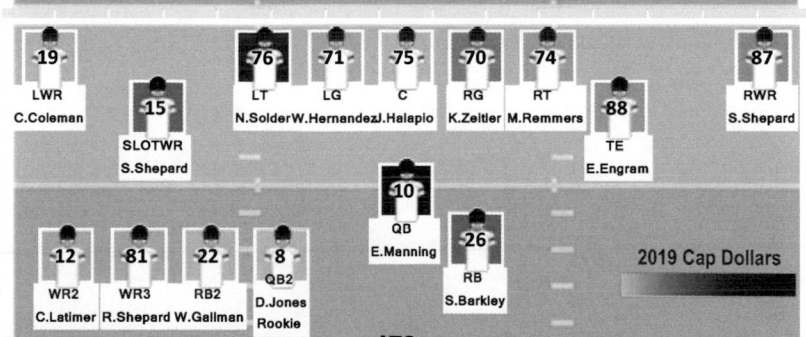

LWR C.Coleman 19
SLOTWR S.Shepard 15
LT N.Solder 76
LG W.Hernandez 71
C J.Halapio 75
RG K.Zeitler 70
RT M.Remmers 74
TE E.Engram 88
RWR S.Shepard 87
QB E.Manning 10
RB S.Barkley 26
WR2 C.Latimer 12
WR3 R.Shepard 81
RB2 W.Gallman 22
QB2 D.Jones Rookie 8

2019 Cap Dollars

2019 Unit Spending

All DEF / All OFF

Positional Spending

	Rank	Total	2017 Rk
All OFF	18	$97.01M	26
QB	11	$26.05M	11
OL	25	$32.03M	31
RB	8	$10.41M	3
WR	23	$18.04M	28
TE	10	$10.48M	18
All DEF	30	$63.00M	30
DL	32	$9.55M	32
LB	11	$23.66M	6
CB	17	$20.18M	20
S	17	$9.62M	30

It was a prime example of the cascading nature of decision making. After the draft, Gettleman claimed his thought process was, "If Baker (Mayfield) is gone, we're taking Saquon and we're going to run the ball."

But the 2018 Giants weren't even as run heavy as 2016 and 2017's teams. The 2016 Giants went 54% run on first-half first downs. They were the NFL's fifth run-heaviest team in 2017 (59%) on first-half first downs. They dipped to 52% run on first-half first downs in 2018, much more balanced that Gettleman planned.

With Barkley on board, the 2018 Giants' first-down run plays produced a 44% Success Rate and 4.5 yards per carry. That Success Rate ranked 27th in the league. The Giants' highly-drafted running back didn't make a difference on first-half first-down runs. The pre-Barkley 2017 Giants recorded the eighth-best Success Rate in the league (48%) with a yards per carry (4.3) that was above league average (4.0).

And that came despite a 2017 Giants offensive line that was less talented and more injured than last year's version. There was no Saquon, and **Ben McAdoo** was coaching in his final season. The 2017 Giants also ran the ball at a 7% higher rate on first-half first downs, making the run game more predictable yet sustaining more success than last year's version.

McAdoo benched **Eli Manning** in 2017, and Eli spent 2018 clinging to a starting job. Manning's traditional statistics – completion rate, yards per attempt, passer rating -- weren't much worse and were in some cases better than his 2017 marks. But 2017 was a year spent almost entirely without **Odell Beckham**, and **Sterling Shepard** also missed time.

Once the 2018 season ended, Gettleman and coach **Pat Shurmur** embraced spin-zone mode with strategic talking points.

"We saw enough in the second half of the season to roll it back one more time." I'm not sure *who* was buying that. In the second half of last year, Eli's passer rating (93.6) and yards per attempt (7.3) were league average. His 45% Success Rate ranked 25th. This was despite Eli facing just two above-average pass defenses over the final eight weeks.

In the first of those two games (vs. Bears), Manning went 19-of-35, averaged 4.9 yards per attempt, and posted a 39% Success Rate. In the second, the Giants beat the **Mark Sanchez**- and **Josh Johnson**-quarterbacked Redskins without Eli needing to do much.

Last year's Giants drew the NFL's seventh-softest schedule and won five games. No teams lost more one-score games (eight). When trailing in the second half and in vital need of production in one-score contests, Manning's 43% Success Rate ranked 31st among 34 qualified quarterbacks. Only rookies **Josh Rosen**, **Josh Allen**, and **Sam Darnold** rated worse.

I'm not confident in Eli for 2019, and that confidence is further reduced by Odell's

departure. Including Odell's trade-induced dead money, it's amazing that the Giants are carrying $39.2 million on this year's salary cap for Manning and Beckham. *That's nearly 21% of their cap.*

Last year's Giants ranked 26th in third-down efficiency, largely because of their reliance on Barkley as a third-down receiver. Saquon drew 32 third-down targets – just three fewer than team leader **Sterling Shepard** – but converted first downs on just 25% of them, by far worst on the Giants. Shepard converted 49% of his third-down targets into chain-moving gains, and OBJ converted 48%. Barkley was barely half as likely to convert.

But that's not a knock on Barkley. NFL running backs have converted exactly 32% of third-down targets into first downs over the last three years. Wide receivers and tight ends are far likelier to convert. And the conversion-rate difference between Giants third-down passes to wide receivers and tight ends (50%) and

(cont'd - see NYG-3)

2018 Passing Performance

QB	1st Dwn	2nd Dwn	3rd Dwn	
Eli Manning	46%	45%	37%	Success Rate
	7.2	7.4	8.0	YPA
	85.7	88.0	106.0	Rating
Pass Rate	56%	67%	90%	
NFL AVG	53%	47%	36%	Success Rate
	7.7	7.3	6.9	YPA
	95.1	93.7	87.1	Rating
Pass Rate	53%	62%	80%	

2018 Rushing Performance

Offense	1st Dwn	2nd Dwn	3rd Dwn	
NYG	42%	40%	43%	Success Rate
	4.4	5.4	3.2	YPC
Run Rate	44%	33%	10%	
NFL AVG	48%	46%	51%	Success Rate
	4.5	4.4	4.3	YPC
Run Rate	47%	38%	20%	

2018 Offensive Advanced Metrics

Rank (y-axis): 1, 5, 10, 15, 20, 25, 30

Metric	Rank
EDSR Off	26
30 & In Off	31
Red Zone Off	24
3rd Down Off	26
YPPA Off	13
YPPT Off	13
Offensive Efficiency	13
Pass Efficiency Off	15
Pass Pro Efficiency Off	20
RB Pass Eff Off	30
Rush Efficiency Off	18
Explosive Pass Off	9
Explosive Run Off	29

2018 Defensive Advanced Metrics

Rank (y-axis): 1, 5, 10, 15, 20, 25, 30

Metric	Rank
EDSR Def	13
30 & In Def	6
Red Zone Def	16
3rd Down Def	16
YPPA Def	22
YPPT Def	28
Defensive Efficiency	24
Pass Efficiency Def	26
Pass Pro Efficiency Def	7
RB Pass Eff Def	20
Rush Efficiency Def	27
Explosive Pass Def	18

2018 Weekly EDSR & Season Trending Performance

	1	2	3	4	5	6	7	8	10	11	12	13	14	15	16	17
WEEK	1	2	3	4	5	6	7	8	10	11	12	13	14	15	16	17
RESULT	L	L	W	L	L	L	L	L	W	W	L	W	W	W	L	L
OPP	JAC	DAL	HOU	NO	CAR	PHI	ATL	WAS	SF	TB	PHI	CHI	WAS	TEN	IND	DAL
SITE	H	A	A	H	A	H	A	H	A	H	A	H	A	H	A	H
MARGIN	-5	-7	5	-15	-2	-21	-3	-7	4	3	-3	3	24	-17	-1	-1
PTS	15	13	27	18	31	13	20	13	27	38	22	30	40	0	27	35
OPP PTS	20	20	22	33	33	34	23	20	23	35	25	27	16	17	28	36

EDSR by Wk
W=Green
L=Red

OFF/DEF
EDSR
Blue=OFF
(high=good)
Red=DEF
(low=good)

2018 Close Game Records

All 2018 Wins: **5**

FG Games (<=3 pts) W-L: **2-5**

FG Games Win %: **29% (#24)**

FG Games Wins (% of Total Wins): **40% (#6)**

1 Score Games (<=8 pts) W-L: **4-8**

1 Score Games Win %: **33% (#24)**

1 Score Games Wins (% of Total Wins): **80% (#3)**

2018 Critical & Game-Deciding Stats

TO Margin	+2
TO Given	19
INT Given	12
FUM Given	7
TO Taken	21
INT Taken	16
FUM Taken	5
Sack Margin	-17
Sacks	30
Sacks Allow	47
Return TD Margin	+0
Ret TDs	3
Ret TDs Allow	3
Penalty Margin	-4
Penalties	114
Opponent Penalties	110

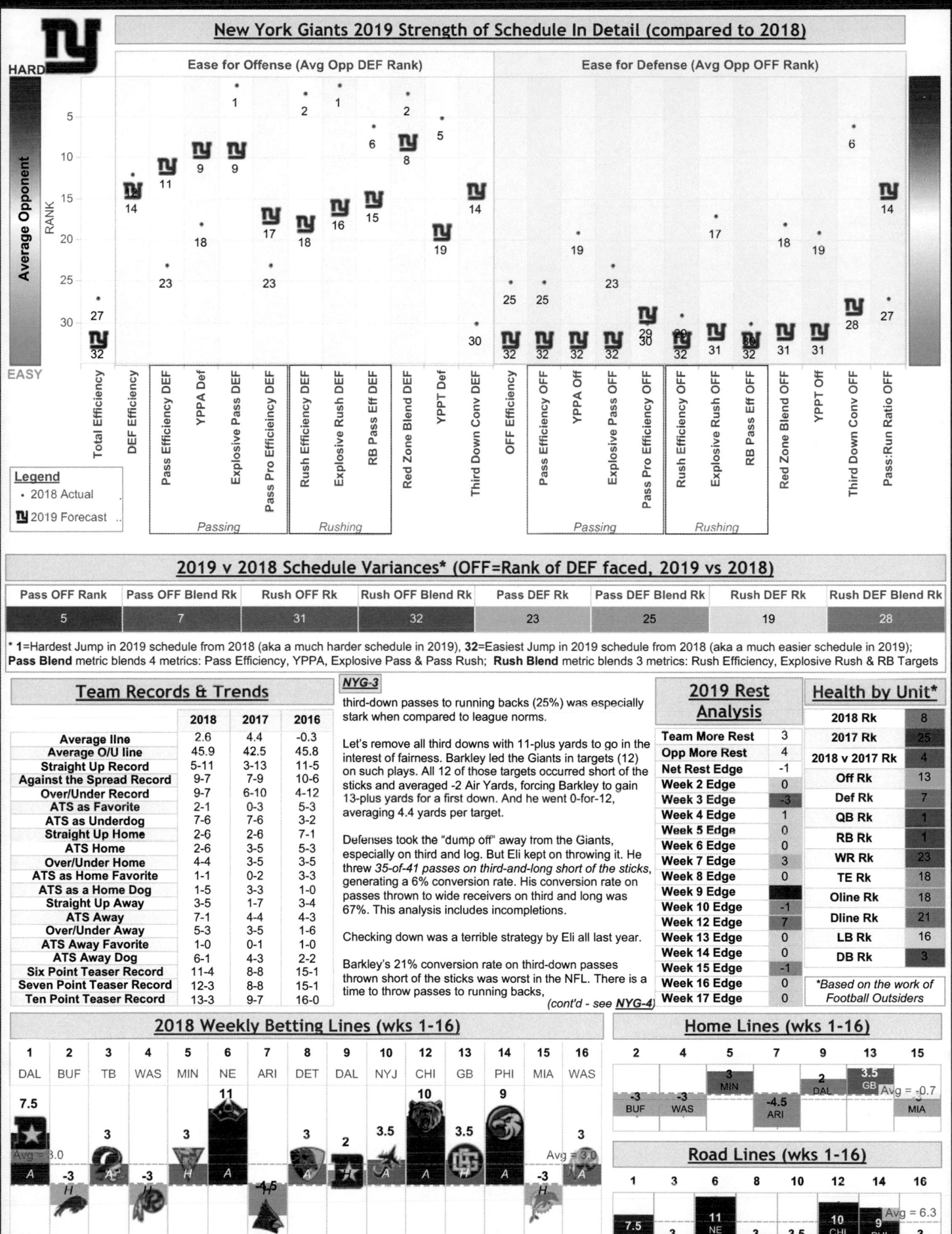

New York Giants 2019 Strength of Schedule In Detail (compared to 2018)

HARD

Ease for Offense (Avg Opp DEF Rank) | **Ease for Defense (Avg Opp OFF Rank)**

Average Opponent RANK

Legend
- 2018 Actual
- 2019 Forecast

Passing — *Rushing* — *Passing* — *Rushing*

EASY

2019 v 2018 Schedule Variances* (OFF=Rank of DEF faced, 2019 vs 2018)

Pass OFF Rank	Pass OFF Blend Rk	Rush OFF Rk	Rush OFF Blend Rk	Pass DEF Rk	Pass DEF Blend Rk	Rush DEF Rk	Rush DEF Blend Rk
5	7	31	32	23	25	19	28

* **1**=Hardest Jump in 2019 schedule from 2018 (aka a much harder schedule in 2019), **32**=Easiest Jump in 2019 schedule from 2018 (aka a much easier schedule in 2019);
Pass Blend metric blends 4 metrics: Pass Efficiency, YPPA, Explosive Pass & Pass Rush; **Rush Blend** metric blends 3 metrics: Rush Efficiency, Explosive Rush & RB Targets

Team Records & Trends

	2018	2017	2016
Average line	2.6	4.4	-0.3
Average O/U line	45.9	42.5	45.8
Straight Up Record	5-11	3-13	11-5
Against the Spread Record	9-7	7-9	10-6
Over/Under Record	9-7	6-10	4-12
ATS as Favorite	2-1	0-3	5-3
ATS as Underdog	7-6	7-6	3-2
Straight Up Home	2-6	2-6	7-1
ATS Home	2-6	3-5	5-3
Over/Under Home	4-4	3-5	3-5
ATS as Home Favorite	1-1	0-2	3-3
ATS as a Home Dog	1-5	3-3	1-0
Straight Up Away	3-5	1-7	3-4
ATS Away	7-1	4-4	4-3
Over/Under Away	5-3	3-5	1-6
ATS Away Favorite	1-0	0-1	1-0
ATS Away Dog	6-1	4-3	2-2
Six Point Teaser Record	11-4	8-8	15-1
Seven Point Teaser Record	12-3	8-8	15-1
Ten Point Teaser Record	13-3	9-7	16-0

NYG-3

third-down passes to running backs (25%) was especially stark when compared to league norms.

Let's remove all third downs with 11-plus yards to go in the interest of fairness. Barkley led the Giants in targets (12) on such plays. All 12 of those targets occurred short of the sticks and averaged -2 Air Yards, forcing Barkley to gain 13-plus yards for a first down. And he went 0-for-12, averaging 4.4 yards per target.

Defenses took the "dump off" away from the Giants, especially on third and log. But Eli kept on throwing it. He threw *35-of-41 passes on third-and-long short of the sticks*, generating a 6% conversion rate. His conversion rate on passes thrown to wide receivers on third and long was 67%. This analysis includes incompletions.

Checking down was a terrible strategy by Eli all last year.

Barkley's 21% conversion rate on third-down passes thrown short of the sticks was worst in the NFL. There is a time to throw passes to running backs, *(cont'd - see NYG-4)*

2019 Rest Analysis

Team More Rest	3
Opp More Rest	4
Net Rest Edge	-1
Week 2 Edge	0
Week 3 Edge	-3
Week 4 Edge	1
Week 5 Edge	0
Week 6 Edge	0
Week 7 Edge	3
Week 8 Edge	0
Week 9 Edge	
Week 10 Edge	-1
Week 12 Edge	7
Week 13 Edge	0
Week 14 Edge	0
Week 15 Edge	-1
Week 16 Edge	0
Week 17 Edge	0

Health by Unit*

2018 Rk	8
2017 Rk	25
2018 v 2017 Rk	4
Off Rk	13
Def Rk	7
QB Rk	1
RB Rk	1
WR Rk	23
TE Rk	18
Oline Rk	18
Dline Rk	21
LB Rk	16
DB Rk	3

*Based on the work of Football Outsiders

2018 Weekly Betting Lines (wks 1-16)

1	2	3	4	5	6	7	8	9	10	12	13	14	15	16
DAL	BUF	TB	WAS	MIN	NE	ARI	DET	DAL	NYJ	CHI	GB	PHI	MIA	WAS
7.5	-3	3	-3	3	11	-4.5	3	2	3.5	10	3.5	9	-3	3
A	H	A	H	H	A	H	H	A	A	A	A	A	H	A

Avg = 3.0 / Avg = 3.0

Home Lines (wks 1-16)

2	4	5	7	9	13	15
-3 BUF	-3 WAS	3 MIN	-4.5 ARI	2 DAL	3.5 GB	MIA

Avg = -0.7

Road Lines (wks 1-16)

1	3	6	8	10	12	14	16
7.5 DAL	3 TB	11 NE	3 DET	3.5 NYJ	10 CHI	9 PHI	3 WAS

Avg = 6.3

New York Giants 2018 Play Analysis

2018 Play Tendencies

All Pass %	64%
All Pass Rk	5
All Rush %	36%
All Rush Rk	28
1 Score Pass %	60%
1 Score Pass Rk	10
2017 1 Score Pass %	58%
2017 1 Score Pass Rk	13
2018 Pass Increase %	3%
Pass Increase Rk	14
1 Score Rush %	40%
1 Score Rush Rk	23
Up Pass %	52%
Up Pass Rk	9
Up Rush %	48%
Up Rush Rk	24
Down Pass %	71%
Down Pass Rk	6
Down Rush %	29%
Down Rush Rk	27

2018 Down & Distance Tendencies

Down	Distance	Total Plays	Pass Rate	Run Rate	Play Success %
1	Short (1-3)	5	20%	80%	40%
	Med (4-7)	7	57%	43%	43%
	Long (8-10)	282	45%	55%	46%
	XL (11+)	18	67%	33%	22%
2	Short (1-3)	28	29%	71%	46%
	Med (4-7)	62	68%	32%	61%
	Long (8-10)	98	65%	35%	35%
	XL (11+)	47	77%	23%	34%
3	Short (1-3)	26	73%	27%	69%
	Med (4-7)	45	100%	0%	40%
	Long (8-10)	33	97%	3%	30%
	XL (11+)	38	87%	13%	11%
4	Short (1-3)	9	56%	44%	67%
	Long (8-10)	1	0%	100%	100%

Shotgun %:

Under Center	Shotgun
43%	57%

37% AVG 63%

Run Rate:

Under Center	Shotgun
65%	16%

68% AVG 23%

Pass Rate:

Under Center	Shotgun
35%	84%

32% AVG 77%

Short Yardage Intelligence:

2nd and Short Run

Run Freq	Run Rk	NFL Run Freq Avg	Run 1D Rate	Run NFL 1D Avg
75%	6	65%	57%	68%

2nd and Short Pass

Pass Freq	Pass Rk	NFL Pass Freq Avg	Pass 1D Rate	Pass NFL 1D Avg
25%	27	35%	57%	56%

Most Frequent Play

Down	Distance	Play Type	Player	Total Plays	Play Success %
1	Short (1-3)	RUSH	Saquon Barkley	3	0%
	Med (4-7)	RUSH	Saquon Barkley	3	33%
	Long (8-10)	RUSH	Saquon Barkley	124	43%
	XL (11+)	RUSH	Saquon Barkley	5	20%
2	Short (1-3)	RUSH	Saquon Barkley	18	56%
	Med (4-7)	RUSH	Saquon Barkley	15	60%
	Long (8-10)	RUSH	Saquon Barkley	25	24%
	XL (11+)	PASS	Sterling Shepard	9	44%
3	Short (1-3)	PASS	Sterling Shepard	6	83%
		RUSH	Saquon Barkley	6	67%
	Med (4-7)	PASS	Sterling Shepard	11	45%
	Long (8-10)	PASS	Odell Beckham Jr.	5	40%
	XL (11+)	PASS	Saquon Barkley	9	0%

Most Successful Play*

Down	Distance	Play Type	Player	Total Plays	Play Success %
1	Long (8-10)	PASS	Evan Engram	8	63%
	XL (11+)	RUSH	Saquon Barkley	5	20%
2	Short (1-3)	RUSH	Saquon Barkley	18	56%
	Med (4-7)	PASS	Sterling Shepard	6	83%
	Long (8-10)	PASS	Sterling Shepard	9	44%
	XL (11+)	PASS	Sterling Shepard	9	44%
3	Short (1-3)	PASS	Sterling Shepard	6	83%
	Med (4-7)	PASS	Odell Beckham Jr.	7	57%
	Long (8-10)	PASS	Odell Beckham Jr.	5	40%
	XL (11+)	PASS	Saquon Barkley	9	0%

*Minimum 5 plays to qualify

2018 Weekly Snap Rates

Wk	Opp	Score	Sterling Shepard	Saquon Barkley	Odell Beckham..	Rhett Ellison	Evan Engram	Bennie Fowler	Cody Latimer	Russell Shepard	Corey Coleman
1	JAC	L 20-15	61 (86%)	55 (77%)	68 (96%)	29 (41%)	64 (90%)		47 (66%)	3 (4%)	
2	DAL	L 20-13	65 (96%)	58 (85%)	66 (97%)	24 (35%)	60 (88%)		44 (65%)	6 (9%)	
3	HOU	W 27-22	59 (95%)	44 (71%)	59 (95%)	54 (87%)	13 (21%)		40 (65%)	1 (2%)	
4	NO	L 33-18	59 (95%)	54 (87%)	59 (95%)	54 (87%)				51 (82%)	
5	CAR	L 33-31	56 (100%)	48 (86%)	52 (93%)	55 (98%)				32 (57%)	
6	PHI	L 34-13	63 (97%)	50 (77%)	63 (97%)				32 (49%)		
7	ATL	L 23-20	59 (92%)	59 (92%)	61 (95%)	32 (50%)	52 (81%)	35 (55%)			
8	WAS	L 20-13	67 (96%)	68 (97%)	67 (96%)	28 (40%)	62 (89%)	48 (69%)		2 (3%)	
10	SF	W 27-23	56 (95%)	54 (92%)	56 (95%)	33 (56%)	36 (61%)	26 (44%)		1 (2%)	8 (14%)
11	TB	W 38-35	46 (87%)	47 (89%)	46 (87%)	40 (75%)	17 (32%)	17 (32%)		7 (13%)	5 (9%)
12	PHI	L 25-22	56 (92%)	47 (77%)	52 (85%)	54 (89%)		26 (43%)		13 (21%)	13 (21%)
13	CHI	W 30-27	57 (79%)	57 (79%)	67 (93%)	68 (94%)		32 (44%)		7 (10%)	11 (15%)
14	WAS	W 40-16	43 (67%)	31 (48%)		33 (52%)	33 (52%)	26 (41%)		26 (41%)	42 (66%)
15	TEN	L 17-0	65 (100%)	65 (100%)		28 (43%)	45 (69%)	46 (71%)		34 (52%)	22 (34%)
16	IND	L 28-27	58 (89%)	57 (88%)		25 (38%)	42 (65%)	54 (83%)	20 (31%)	15 (23%)	
17	DAL	L 36-35	66 (93%)	59 (83%)			51 (72%)	60 (85%)	26 (37%)	16 (23%)	
	Grand Total		936 (91%)	853 (83%)	716 (94%)	557 (63%)	475 (65%)	370 (57%)	209 (52%)	183 (25%)	132 (26%)

Personnel Groupings

Personnel	Team %	NFL Avg	Succ. %
1-1 [3WR]	61%	65%	40%
1-2 [2WR]	24%	17%	44%
2-1 [2WR]	8%	8%	51%
2-2 [1WR]	3%	3%	39%

Grouping Tendencies

Personnel	Pass Rate	Pass Succ. %	Run Succ. %
1-1 [3WR]	74%	41%	38%
1-2 [2WR]	50%	45%	43%
2-1 [2WR]	45%	49%	53%
2-2 [1WR]	33%	64%	27%

Red Zone Targets (min 3)

Receiver	All	Inside 5	6-10	11-20
Odell Beckham Jr.	18	5	3	10
Sterling Shepard	16	4	2	10
Saquon Barkley	14	1	4	9
Evan Engram	7	2	1	4
Scott Simonson	6	4		2
Bennie Fowler	4	2		2

Red Zone Rushes (min 3)

Rusher	All	Inside 5	6-10	11-20
Saquon Barkley	50	18	12	20
Wayne Gallman	14	3	2	9
Eli Manning	6	3	1	2

Early Down Target Rate

	RB	TE	WR
	29%	19%	52%
NFL AVG	23%	21%	56%

Overall Target Success %

	RB	TE	WR
	38%	50%	50%
	#30	#26	#20

New York Giants 2018 Passing Recap & 2019 Outlook

Giants GM **David Gettleman** and coach **Pat Shurmur** defended using 2018's No. 2 overall pick on **Saquon Barkley** by suggesting **Eli Manning** improved in the second half of last season. But Eli wasn't even a league-average quarterback during that span, managing league-average production against below-average competition. Gettleman and Shurmur said they planned to "roll it back" with Eli, laughably comparing their team's situation to Kansas City's **Alex Smith-Patrick Mahomes** transition even before drafting **Daniel Jones** with the No. 6 overall pick. But just as the Giants' offseason program was closing in June, Shurmur stated Jones was "on track to play day one" and promised to "play the very best player," ostensibly opening the Giants' quarterback job to competition. If the rookie from Duke can outplay Eli by such a wide margin in practice sessions, consider how *wrong* the Giants were about Manning turning an imaginary corner in the second half of last year. And consider how *wrong* Gettleman was for selecting a running back with the No. 2 overall pick. And consider how *wrong* the Giants were for trading away the best player on their team, **Odell Beckham**.

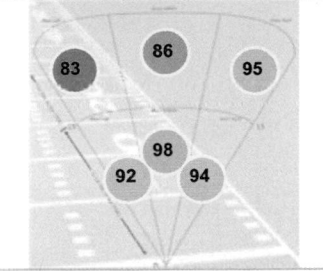

Eli Manning Rating — All Downs

2018 Standard Passing Table

QB	Comp	Att	Comp %	Yds	YPA	TDs	INT	Sacks	Rating	Rk
Eli Manning	379	576	66%	4,292	7.5	21	11	46	92	24
NFL Avg			62%		7.0				87.5	

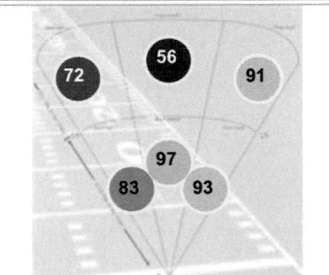

Eli Manning Rating — Early Downs

2018 Advanced Passing Table

QB	Success %	EDSR Passing Success %	20+ Yd Pass Gains	20+ Yd Pass %	30+ Yd Pass Gains	30+ Yd Pass %	Avg. Air Yds per Comp	Avg. YAC per Comp	20+ Air Yd Comp	20+ Air Yd %
Eli Manning	43%	45%	57	10.0%	25	4.0%	5.5	5.9	27	5%
NFL Avg	44%	48%	29.5	8.4%	12.5	3.7%	5.8	5.1	14.5	6%

Interception Rates by Down

Yards to Go	1st Dwn	2nd Dwn	3rd Dwn	4th Dwn	Total
1 & 2	0.0%	14.3%	0.0%	0.0%	3.8%
3, 4, 5	0.0%	0.0%	1.9%	0.0%	1.1%
6 - 9	0.0%	2.9%	0.0%	0.0%	1.6%
10 - 14	1.5%	2.6%	0.0%	0.0%	1.6%
15+	0.0%	0.0%	8.0%		3.1%
Total	1.3%	2.4%	1.7%	0.0%	1.8%

3rd Down Passing - Short of Sticks Analysis

QB	Avg. Yds to Go	Avg. YIA (of Comp)	Avg Yds Short	Short of Sticks Rate	Short Rk
Eli Manning	8.1	5.8	-2.3	65%	32
NFL Avg	7.8	6.4	-1.4	60%	

Air Yds vs YAC

Air Yds %	YAC %	Rk
48%	52%	38
53%	48%	

2018 Receiving Recap & 2019 Outlook

I'm skeptical of **Golden Tate**, who turns 31 before the season and is coming off one of the worst years of his career. Tate's skill set is redundant with **Sterling Shepard**'s, and Tate's presence on the interior will force Shepard outside. Tate also won't command nearly the defensive attention Beckham did. The Giants are now completely devoid of vertical elements in their passing game, and their lone notable rookie receiver is drop-prone **Darius Slayton** of Auburn, who was the 171st pick in the draft. They're counting on retreads **Corey Coleman**, **Bennie Fowler**, and **Cody Latimer** to step up across from Tate and Shepard in three-receiver 11-personnel packages.

Player *Min 50 Targets*	Targ	Comp %	YPA	Rating	Success %	Success Rk	Missed YPA Rk	YAS % Rk	YTS % Rk	TDs
Odell Beckham Jr.	124	62%	8.5	91.9	51%	64	99	28	77	5
Saquon Barkley	121	75%	6.0	97.2	38%	124	165	111	77	2
Sterling Shepard	107	62%	8.1	92.1	51%	64	104	43	59	3
Evan Engram	64	70%	9.0	113.9	44%	110	132	84	120	3

Directional Passer Rating Delivered

Receiver	Short Left	Short Middle	Short Right	Deep Left	Deep Middle	Deep Right	Player Total
Odell Beckham Jr.	106	116	59	88	64	130	92
Saquon Barkley	90	89	93			135	97
Sterling Shepard	90	97	95	62	65	83	92
Evan Engram	96	104	120		158	80	114
Rhett Ellison	93	73	118	119		96	104
Bennie Fowler	75	142	92	49	0		64
Wayne Gallman	79	72	75	40			72
Russell Shepard	88	0	74	50	158	96	83
Cody Latimer	108	84	99	118	119	96	130
Corey Coleman	101		40	119		40	91
Team Total	93	97	91	81	110	108	95

2018 Rushing Recap & 2019 Outlook

I anticipated last year's Giants facing a tough schedule that would translate to fewer rushing opportunities. I hope Shurmur makes better decisions in third-and-long situations as detailed above. Passing to **Saquon Barkley** in such scenarios doesn't work. But Barkley is a true three-down workhorse and the most-valuable short- and long-term asset in fantasy football. Barkley's 2019 run-defense schedule also softens considerably. As last year's Giants won only five games, Barkley was the NFL's lone running back to exceed 40 targets with his team trailing by more than one score and the league's only back to exceed 80 targets when down by any margin.

Player *Min 50 Rushes*	Rushes	YPC	Success %	Success Rk	Missed YPA Rk	YTS % Rk	YAS % Rk	Early Down Success %	Early Down Success Rk	TDs
Saquon Barkley	261	5.0	41%	61	63	72	1	41%	58	11
Wayne Gallman	51	3.5	39%	66	54	13	73	39%	64	1

Yards per Carry by Direction

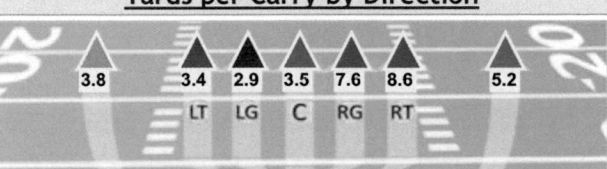

	LT	LG	C	RG	RT	
3.8	3.4	2.9	3.5	7.6	8.6	5.2

Directional Run Frequency

	LT	LG	C	RG	RT	
11%	12%	15%	30%	10%	14%	8%

but third down is not that time. When Eli threw to Barkley short of the sticks on early downs, Saquon's Success Rate was 45%. Even with ten or more yards to go, Barkley's Success Rate was 43%. The Giants need to realize they are wasting plays and ending drives when Eli targets Saquon on third downs.

Rather than spoon feed the Giants answers on when to target Barkley with third-down passes, I'll let their analytics department figure out Barkley's third-down receiving Success Rates and do their own math on play efficiencies. But most of the time, you want your third-down play call to *try to actually convert* to stay on the field.

Barkley drew four third-down targets with ten-plus yards to go where the Giants were in fringe field-goal range and appeared to use the play to get into better range. Saquon gained nine yards on third and 17 from the Panthers' 32, and the Giants made the ensuing 42-yard kick. But after a Barkley catch gained just four yards on third and 11 at the Falcons' 45, the Giants punted from the 41-yard line.

The very next week, Barkley was targeted on third-and-15 at the Redskins' 39-yard line. He gained four yards, and the Giants punted at the Redskins' 39. In Week 12, he drew a third-and-15 target at the Eagles' 39. Barkley's six-yard catch set up a 51-yard field goal at the Eagles' 33.

The Giants lost all of these games by one-score margins. They lost to the Panthers 33-31. To the Falcons 23-20. To the Redskins 20-13, and the Eagles 25-23.

Regarding fourth downs, here is a shocking stat:

New York Giants Fantasy Corner

The Giants are an offense to avoid where possible based on their short-area passing game and potential in-season quarterback controversy, but **Saquon Barkley** showed transcendent scoring ability in a similarly poor 2018 environment. Despite his down-to-down inefficiency as a runner, Barkley led the NFL in yards from scrimmage (2,028) and accounted for 42% of the Giants' touchdowns by drawing the league's sixth-most red-zone targets (15) and third-most red-zone carries (50) among running backs. Coach **Pat Shurmur**'s emphasis on feeding Barkley should be even greater in the post-**Odell Beckham** era.

- Evan Silva

(cont'd - see **NYG-5**)

Division History: Season Wins & 2019 Projection

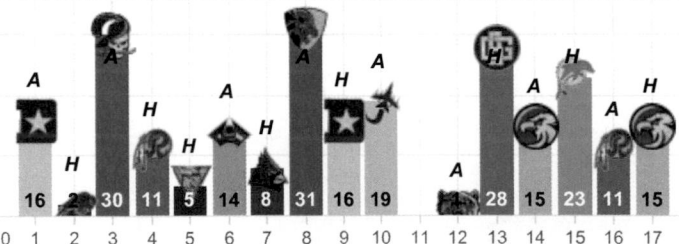

	2015 Wins	2016 Wins	2017 Wins	2018 Wins	Forecast 2019 Wins

Rank of 2019 Defensive Pass Efficiency Faced by Week

16	2	30	11	5	14	8	31	16	19		28	15	23	11	15

0 1 2 3 4 5 6 7 8 9 10 11 12 13 14 15 16 17

Rank of 2019 Defensive Rush Efficiency Faced by Week

5	14	31	27	12	19	29	13	5	21		23	9	24	27	9

0 1 2 3 4 5 6 7 8 9 10 11 12 13 14 15 16 17

2018 Situational Usage by Player & Position

Usage Rate by Score

		Being Blown Out (14+)	Down Big (9-13)	One Score	Large Lead (9-13)	Blowout Lead (14+)
RUSH	Saquon Barkley	7%	9%	73%	6%	5%
	Odell Beckham Jr.			100%		
	Sterling Shepard			100%		
	Wayne Gallman	6%	6%	57%	4%	27%
	Evan Engram			100%		
	Elijhaa Penny			29%		71%
	Corey Coleman			100%		
	Jonathan Stewart		33%	67%		
	Total	6%	9%	71%	5%	9%
PASS	Saquon Barkley	21%	14%	60%	4%	1%
	Odell Beckham Jr.	16%	15%	60%	7%	1%
	Sterling Shepard	14%	19%	64%	3%	
	Wayne Gallman	20%	15%	45%	15%	5%
	Evan Engram	24%	14%	61%		2%
	Rhett Ellison	9%	13%	59%	16%	3%
	Bennie Fowler	19%	4%	77%		
	Cody Latimer	38%	19%	38%		6%
	Elijhaa Penny			63%	38%	
	Russell Shepard	18%	9%	64%	9%	
	Corey Coleman	17%		83%		
	Total	18%	14%	61%	5%	1%

Share of Offensive Plays by Type

	Saquon Barkley	Odell Beckham Jr.	Sterling Shepard	Wayne Gallman	Evan Engram	Rhett Ellison	Bennie Fowler	Cody Latimer	Elijhaa Penny	Russell Shepard	Corey Coleman	Jonathan Stewart
RUSH	77%	1%	1%	15%	1%				2%		0%	2%
PASS	23%	22%	19%	4%	12%	6%	5%	3%	2%	2%	1%	
ALL	45%	14%	12%	9%	7%	4%	3%	2%	2%	1%	1%	1%

Positional Target Distribution vs NFL Average

		NFL Wide				Team Only			
		Left	Middle	Right	Total	Left	Middle	Right	Total
Deep	WR	33%	17%	31%	**81%**	45%	13%	28%	**86%**
	TE	5%	4%	7%	**16%**	1%	2%	7%	**10%**
	RB	1%	0%	2%	**3%**	1%		4%	**5%**
	All	39%	22%	39%	**100%**	47%	14%	38%	**100%**
Short	WR	20%	14%	21%	**55%**	15%	13%	20%	**48%**
	TE	6%	6%	8%	**20%**	6%	5%	9%	**20%**
	RB	10%	5%	10%	**25%**	13%	5%	14%	**31%**
	All	36%	25%	39%	**100%**	34%	23%	43%	**100%**
Total		37%	24%	39%	**100%**	37%	21%	42%	**100%**

Positional Success Rates vs NFL Average

		NFL Wide				Team Only			
		Left	Middle	Right	Total	Left	Middle	Right	Total
Deep	WR	40%	49%	40%	**42%**	47%	46%	45%	**46%**
	TE	43%	53%	41%	**45%**	100%	100%	43%	**60%**
	RB	39%	33%	42%	**40%**	0%		50%	**40%**
	All	40%	50%	40%	**42%**	47%	53%	45%	**47%**
Short	WR	55%	61%	53%	**56%**	49%	61%	49%	**52%**
	TE	56%	62%	55%	**57%**	39%	52%	50%	**47%**
	RB	47%	54%	46%	**48%**	36%	55%	32%	**37%**
	All	53%	60%	51%	**54%**	42%	58%	44%	**46%**
Total		51%	58%	49%	**52%**	44%	57%	44%	**47%**

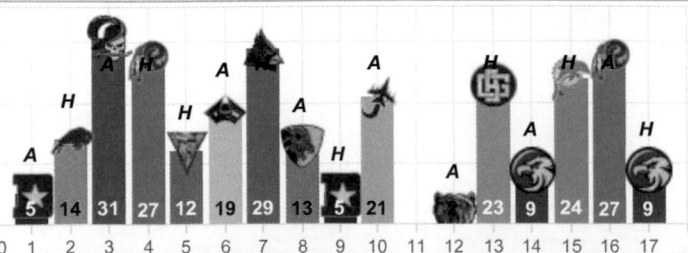

Successful Play Rate 0% — 100%

Type	1-1 [3WR]	1-2 [2WR]	2-1 [2WR]	2-2 [1WR]	1-3 [1WR]	2-0 [3WR]	1-0 [4WR]	0-0 [5WR]	ALL
PASS	41% (441)	45% (117)	49% (35)	64% (11)	44% (9)	67% (9)	0% (6)		43% (628)
RUSH	38% (155)	43% (117)	53% (43)	27% (22)	70% (10)	0% (4)	0% (2)	100% (1)	41% (354)
All	40% (596)	44% (234)	51% (78)	39% (33)	58% (19)	46% (13)	0% (8)	100% (1)	42% (982)

Format Success Rate (Total # of Plays)

Receiving Success by Top-4 Personnel Groupings
(Min 50 targets)

POS	Player	1-1 [3WR]	1-2 [2WR]	2-1 [2WR]	1-0 [4WR]	4 Grp Total
RB	Saquon Barkley	39% (82) 6.2, 91.0	32% (22) 6.5, 109.1	43% (7) 3.9, 65.8	0% (2) 2.0, 79.2	37% (113) 6.1, 93.7
TE	Evan Engram	38% (52) 7.5, 110.1	70% (10) 15.7, 118.8	50% (2) 16.0, 95.8		44% (64) 9.0, 113.9
WR	Odell Beckham	54% (83) 8.0, 95.6	39% (31) 7.8, 83.0	67% (6) 19.5, 118.8	0% (2) 0.0, 0.0	50% (122) 8.4, 90.9
WR	Sterling Shepard	49% (73) 7.4, 95.6	54% (24) 9.5, 76.2	60% (5) 13.6, 104.2	0% (1) 3.0, 79.2	50% (103) 8.1, 91.8

Format Line 1: Success Rate (Total # of Plays)   Line 2: YPA, Passer Rating

Rushing Success by Top-4 Personnel Groupings
(Min 25 carries)

Rusher (Last, First)	1-1 [3WR]	1-2 [2WR]	2-1 [2WR]	2-2 [1WR]	4 Grp Total
Barkley Saquon	37% (116) 5.5	42% (92) 5.4	47% (30) 4.5	33% (15) 0.9	40% (253) 5.1
Gallman Wayne	45% (22) 4.2	40% (20) 3.0	50% (6) 3.8	0% (1) -1.0	43% (49) 3.6

Format Line 1: Success Rate (Total # of Plays)   Line 2: YPC

Passing by Coverage Scheme

Zone	49% (259) 8.5, 90.2
M2M	50% (206) 7.6, 100.7
Screen	33% (42) 6.5, 101.6
Combo	63% (8) 7.6, 96.4

Passing by Route

Curl	59% (58) 6.9, 98.5
Flat	40% (50) 4.2, 111.2
Screen	34% (44) 7.0, 103.6
Out	62% (42) 7.5, 98.6
Slant	67% (39) 8.7, 106.7
Dig	50% (32) 8.6, 45.7

Throw Types

Level 1	50% (336) 6.5, 97.5
Level 2	45% (170) 8.8, 86.8
Level 3	40% (53) 12.6, 111.0
Sidearm	0% (1) -1.0, 79.2

QB Drop Types

3 Step	44% (219) 7.4, 84.9
0/1 Step	55% (116) 7.7, 98.9
5 Step	43% (95) 8.2, 86.1
Designed Rollout Right	59% (49) 7.4, 133.8
7 Step	46% (41) 9.9, 94.0
Basic Screen	34% (32) 6.6, 104.4

QB State at Pass

Planted	48% (339) 8.7, 94.2
Moving	59% (87) 8.0, 123.4
Shuffling	33% (81) 4.7, 75.0

Play Action

	Play Action	No P/A
Under Center	54% (98) 8.5, 117.6	47% (36) 9.3, 130.7
Shotgun	47% (32) 7.6, 41.7	46% (394) 7.5, 91.9
ALL	52% (130) 8.3, 98.9	46% (430) 7.6, 95.1

Run Types

Inside Zone	47% (120) 5.4
Outside Zone	39% (93) 4.1
Pitch	38% (40) 4.3
Power	28% (18) 6.7
Lead	44% (16) 2.0
Stretch	30% (10) 5.4

NYG-5

the 2018 Giants *attempted only one fourth down when tied or leading*. They kicked or punted 48 times and went for it once, resulting in a touchdown against the Bears. Outside of two-minute drills and fourth-quarter deficits, the Giants attempted just eight fourth downs all year long.

There are simple checks anyone can do based on play-by-play data. They are quick evaluations of a team's fourth-down philosophy. When tied or leading, what is a team's fourth-down attempt rate? And when tied or leading, what is a team's fourth-down attempt rate outside an opponent's five-yard line with over one yard to go? Studying both provides a sense as to which teams are making optimal fourth-down decisions.

Last year's ten-most aggressive teams by these metrics included the Saints, Panthers, Patriots, Rams, Eagles, Ravens, and Packers. Bottom-ten teams included the 49ers, Giants, Chargers, Cardinals, Seahawks, Jaguars, Broncos, and Lions.

Put simply, the Giants need to optimize their fourth-down decision making.

Further discouraging is that the Giants' prized No. 2 overall draft pick received just one fourth-down rushing attempt all year.

Smart teams that use analytics are getting more aggressive on fourth downs, including the Patriots, Eagles, Rams, and Saints. Those teams have accounted for the last three Super Bowl wins and many more conference championship appearances. When teams optimize their ability to win, it becomes even harder for teams like the Giants with worse personnel, worse coaches, and an unwillingness to be aggressive on fourth downs to offset their edges.

Shurmur *must* begin to employ a more aggressive fourth-down strategy in 2019. It's just that simple.

One interesting quirk of the Giants' running game is that for two years now, their backs have dominated running to right side of center but are abysmal running from center to the left. Last year's Giants averaged 3.5 yards per carry with a league-low 41% Success Rate on center-to-left runs. Runs to right of the center gained a whopping 7.4 yards per carry with a 47% Success Rate.

But the story was similar in pre-Saquon 2017. Runs to the right of center gained 4.6 YPC with a 48% Success Rate, while runs behind center or to the left gained only 3.7 YPC with 41% success. Despite offensive line and backfield turnover, rushing behind center or to the left side has remained unproductive for New York.

Up front, centers **Spencer Pulley** and **John Greco** split starts in 2018, and projected starter **Jon Halapio** returns from injury. *(cont'd - see Page 246)*

Coaches (Prior Yrs)

Head Coach:
Adam Gase (MIA HC, Calls Plays) (new)
Offensive Coordinator:
Dowell Loggains (MIA OC) (new)
Defensive Coordinator:
Gregg Williams (CLE DC) (new)

EASY HARD

New York Jets

2019 Forecast

Wins	Div Rank
7	#2

Past Records
2018: 4-12
2017: 5-11
2016: 5-11

Game	Opp	H/A	#
	BUF	H	1
	CLE	H	2
	NE	A	3
			4
	PHI	A	5
	DAL	H	6
	NE	H	7
	JAX	A	8
	MIA	A	9
	NYG	H	10
	WAS	H	11
	OAK	H	12
	CIN	H	13
	MIA	H	14
	BAL	A	15
	PIT	H	16
	BUF	A	17

MNF (1-3), MNF (5-7), TNF (15)

Key Players Lost

Player	New
Andre Roberts (WR)	BUF
Buster Skrine (CB)	CHI
Clive Walford (TE)	MIA
Dakota Dozier (G)	MIN
Darron Lee (LB)	KC
Isaiah Crowell (RB)	OAK
James Carpenter (G)	ATL
Jason Myers (K)	SEA
Jeremiah Attaochu (OLB)	KC
Jermaine Kearse (WR)	DET
Mike Pennel (DE)	NE
Spencer Long (C)	BUF
Terrence Brooks (FS)	NE

Average Line	# Games Favored	# Games Underdog
1.8	4	9

2019 New York Jets Overview

In 2002, rookie quarterback **David Carr** took 76 sacks behind the offensive line of the expansion Houston Texans. Having watched that ruin his career, it's hard not to be sensitive to the treatment of young players at the league's most important position.

Franchise quarterbacks require a significant draft capital investment and will eventually command a big salary cap hit. Most think they can step into the league and become **Brett Favre** from day one. Which isn't surprising, as they're praised and adored throughout the draft process after coming out of college with great numbers. As such, it's vital for a play caller to do everything in his power to make their NFL transitions easy more **Patrick Mahomes** than **Deshone Kizer**.

Play-calling drives quarterback development. In **Sam Darnold**'s case, offensive coordinator **Jeremy Bates**' schizophrenic play-calling, especially on second down, did Darnold no favors. Bates was on an island running the ball on second and long, but it limited Darnold's ability to find a rhythm and maintain confidence, especially early in the season.

Bates called runs on 60-percent of Darnold's second-and-ten plays after incompletions on first-and-ten. This was 12-percent above league average, ranking No. 3 in the NFL behind only Houston and Dallas. These runs gained 3.4 yards per carry (YPC) and produced a mere 25 percent-success rate. Meanwhile, Darnold's passes in such situations produced a 49-percent success rate and gained 7.2 YPA. Twenty-six percent of these passes converted a first down.

(cont'd - see NYJ2)

Key Free Agents/ Trades Added

Player	AAV (MM)
Brian Poole (CB)	$3
Chandler Catanzaro (K)	$2.2
Jamison Crowder (WR)	$9.5
Josh Bellamy (WR)	$2.5
Kelechi Osemele (OG)	Trade
Le'Veon Bell (RB)	$13.

Drafted Players

Rd	Pk	Player (College)
1	3	DT - Quinnen Williams (Alabama)
3	68	LB - Jachai Polite (Florida)
	92	OT - Chuma Edoga (USC)
4	121	TE - Trevon Wesco (West Virginia)
5	157	LB - Blake Cashman (Minnesota)
6	196	CB - Blessuan Austin (Rutgers)

Regular Season Wins: Past & Current Proj

Forecast 2019 Wins	7
2018 Wins	4
Forecast 2018 Wins	6
2017 Wins	5
2016 Wins	5
2015 Wins	10

1 3 5 7 9 11 13 15

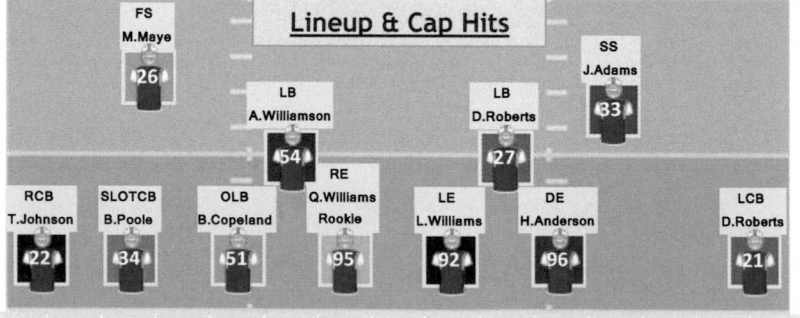

Lineup & Cap Hits

FS M.Maye 26
LB A.Williamson 54
RE Q.Williams Rookie 95
LB D.Roberts 27
SS J.Adams 33
RCB T.Johnson 22
SLOTCB B.Poole 34
OLB B.Copeland 51
LE L.Williams 92
DE H.Anderson 96
LCB D.Roberts 21

LWR J.Crowder 82
SLOTWR Q.Enunwa 81
LT K.Beachum 68
LG K.Osemele 70
C J.Harrison 78
RG B.Winters 67
RT B.Shell 72
TE C.Herndon 89
RWR R.Anderson 11
QB S.Darnold 14
RB L.Bell 26
WR2 J.Bellamy 15
WR3 C.Peake 17
RB2 B.Powell 29
QB2 T.Siemian 3

2019 Cap Dollars

2019 Unit Spending

All OFF / All DEF

Positional Spending

	Rank	Total	2017 Rk
All OFF	26	$85.63M	18
QB	26	$10.09M	20
OL	14	$38.88M	3
RB	6	$12.14M	8
WR	18	$19.93M	24
TE	29	$4.60M	26
All DEF	5	$96.90M	14
DL	15	$32.35M	24
LB	6	$28.60M	17
CB	12	$24.13M	2
S	14	$11.82M	15

Bates was reluctant to have Darnold go pass-pass to start a series. After a first-and-ten pass, regardless of what it gained if it resulted in second down, Bates then called a run play 57-percent of the time. Runs on second-and-ten or longer gained a league-worst 2.9 yards per carry (YPC) with a No. 31-ranked success rate of 15-percent. The percentage was buoyed by Darnold runs on eight such plays, which produced a 50-percent success rate.

On non-Darnold runs, the team was successful on just eight-percent of their second and long rushes, gaining a pathetic 1.9 YPC. Both ranked last in the league, yet they were one of the top-five most run-heavy teams in this situation. Leaving them with a disastrous average of 7.9 yards-to-go on third down. Which tied them for third-worst in games that Darnold started.

The Jets called 50 RB-runs on second-and-ten or longer. The majority of these runs set up third and long, which the Jets converted only nine-percent for first downs. Predictability, especially on third down, is particularly challenging and demoralizing for rookie quarterbacks, evidenced by Darnold's sub-3.5 yards per attempt in these situations.

While running on second-and-ten or more ultimately resulted in a 19-percent first down rate, passing on second-and-ten or more ultimately resulted in a 45-percent first down rate, a massive differential. Yet, Bates and the Jets insisted on running the ball more than passing on these second and long plays, strangling Darnold's ability to extend drives.

Like most rookie quarterbacks, Darnold's passing yards and touchdown to interception ratio underwhelmed in his rookie season. Then the cold weather arrived, and Darnold heated up. Darnold's led all NFL quarterbacks in QBR (ESPN's signature quarterback efficiency metric) in the month of December. That happened.

Remember, Darnold was the youngest quarterback to ever start an NFL game *and* faced a brutal schedule of defenses, surrounded by lackluster weaponry. The Jets played the third-toughest schedule of opposing defenses, which included the third-toughest pass defenses and fifth-toughest run defenses. They did so with the fourth-most injured running back room and the 11th-most injured wide receiver room.

2018 Passing Performance

QB	1st Dwn	2nd Dwn	3rd Dwn	
Sam Darnold	51%	43%	33%	Success Rate
	7.4	6.6	6.7	YPA
	82.1	73.7	83.5	Rating
Pass Rate	55%	58%	80%	
NFL AVG	53%	47%	36%	Success Rate
	7.7	7.3	6.9	YPA
	95.1	93.7	87.1	Rating
Pass Rate	53%	62%	80%	

2018 Rushing Performance

Offense	1st Dwn	2nd Dwn	3rd Dwn	
NYJ	38%	39%	37%	Success Rate
	4.0	4.3	2.7	YPC
Run Rate	45%	42%	20%	
NFL AVG	48%	46%	51%	Success Rate
	4.5	4.4	4.3	YPC
Run Rate	47%	38%	20%	

Players like **Robby Anderson** and **Quincy Enunwa** were in and out of the lineup all season.

Darnold's pre-draft scouting profile showed a lack of ball security when being pressured. His passer rating under pressure during his rookie season was 39.7, ranking No. 38 out of 39 NFL quarterbacks. A more creative offensive structure would've been beneficial, helping provide some relief when being pressured.

The bad news for Darnold is the schedule isn't likely to get much easier in 2019. He's projected to face the seventh-toughest slate of pass defenses. Including five games against top-ten pass defenses from

(cont'd - see **NYJ-3**)

2018 Offensive Advanced Metrics

EDSR Off	30 & In Off	Red Zone Off	3rd Down Off	YPPA Off	YPPT Off	Offensive Efficiency	Pass Efficiency Off	Pass Pro Efficiency Off	RB Pass Eff Off	Rush Efficiency Off	Explosive Pass Off	Explosive Run Off
30	22	26	29	27	27	29	28	18	23	30	22	21

2018 Defensive Advanced Metrics

EDSR Def	30 & In Def	Red Zone Def	3rd Down Def	YPPA Def	YPPT Def	Defensive Efficiency	Pass Efficiency Def	Pass Pro Efficiency Def	RB Pass Eff Def	Rush Efficiency Def	Explosive Pass Def	Explosive Run Def
14	21	14	2	18	30	21	19	21	15	21	26	23

2018 Weekly EDSR & Season Trending Performance

	1	2	3	4	5	6	7	8	9	10		12	13	14	15	16	17	WEEK
RESULT	W	L	L	W	W	L	L	L	L	L		L	L	W	L	L	L	
OPP	DET	MIA	CLE	JAC	DEN	IND	MIN	CHI	MIA	BUF		NE	TEN	BUF	HOU	GB	NE	
SITE	A	H	A	A	H	H	H	A	A	H		H	A	A	H	H	A	
MARGIN	31	-8	-4	-19	18	8	-20	-14	-7	-31		-14	-4	4	-7	-6	-35	
PTS	48	12	17	12	34	42	17	10	6	10		13	22	27	22	38	3	
OPP PTS	17	20	21	31	16	34	37	24	13	41		27	26	23	29	44	38	

EDSR by Wk
W=Green
L=Red

OFF/DEF
EDSR
Blue=OFF
(high=good)
Red=DEF
(low=good)

2018 Close Game Records

All 2018 Wins: **4**
FG Games (<=3 pts) W-L: **0-0**
FG Games Win %: **0% (#30)**
FG Games Wins (% of Total Wins): **0% (#31)**
1 Score Games (<=8 pts) W-L: **2-6**
1 Score Games Win %: **25% (#31)**
1 Score Games Wins (% of Total Wins): **50% (#15)**

2018 Critical & Game-Deciding Stats

TO Margin	-10
TO Given	30
INT Given	19
FUM Given	11
TO Taken	20
INT Taken	13
FUM Taken	7
Sack Margin	+2
Sacks	39
Sacks Allow	37
Return TD Margin	+1
Ret TDs	5
Ret TDs Allow	4
Penalty Margin	-19
Penalties	114
Opponent Penalties	95

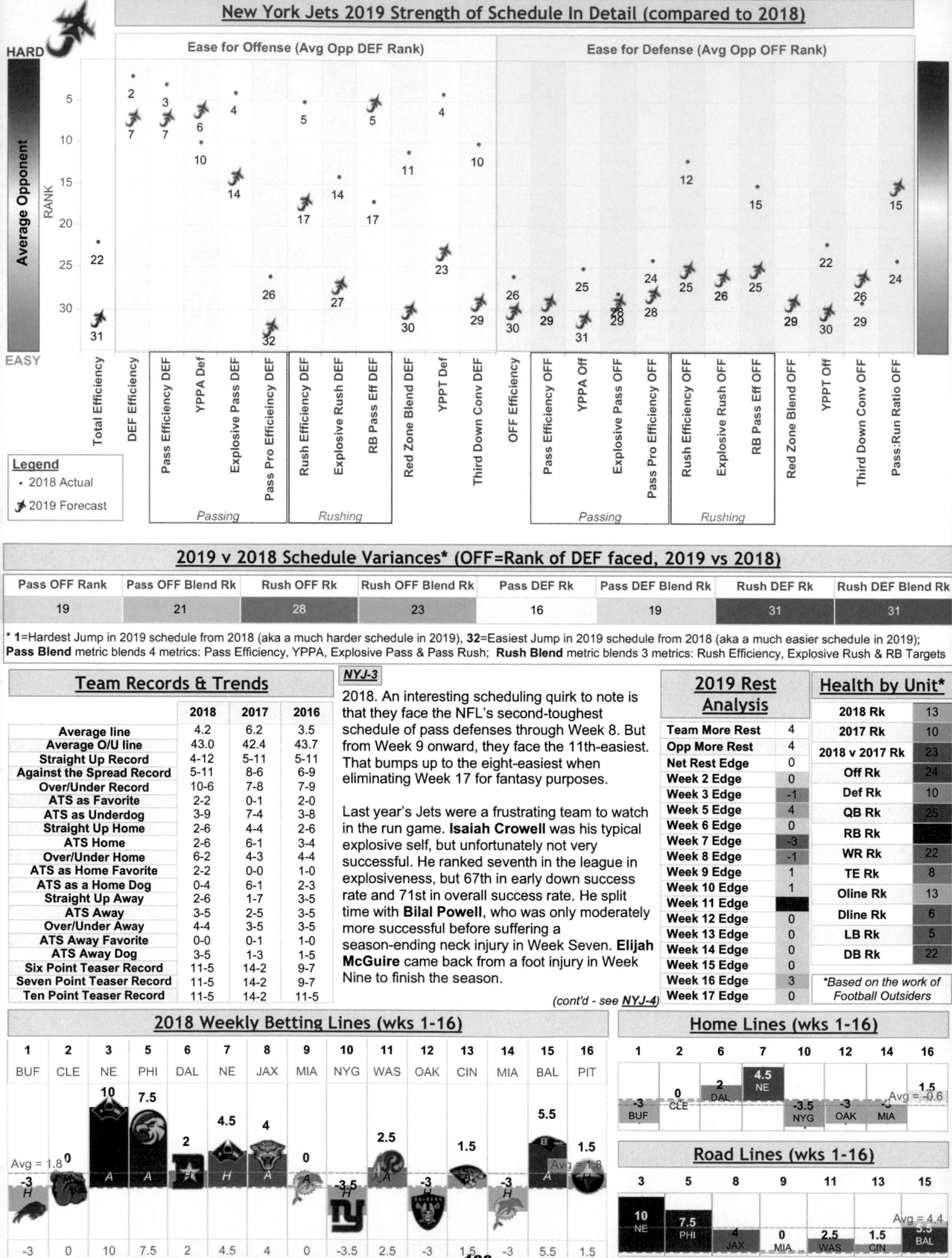

Ease for Offense (Avg Opp DEF Rank)

Category	2018 Actual	2019 Forecast
Total Efficiency	22	31
DEF Efficiency	2	7
Pass Efficiency DEF	3	7
YPPA Def	6	10
Explosive Pass DEF	4	14
Pass Pro Efficieincy DEF	26	32
Rush Efficiency DEF	5	17
Explosive Rush DEF	27	14
RB Pass Eff DEF	5	17
Red Zone Blend DEF	11	30
YPPT Def	4	23
Third Down Conv DEF	10	29

Ease for Defense (Avg Opp OFF Rank)

Category	2018 Actual	2019 Forecast
OFF Efficiency	26	30
Pass Efficiency OFF	25	29
YPPA Off	31	25
Explosive Pass OFF	28	29
Pass Pro Efficiency OFF	24	28
Rush Efficiency OFF	12	25
Explosive Rush OFF	26	25
RB Pass Eff OFF	15	25
Red Zone Blend OFF	29	29
YPPT Off	22	30
Third Down Conv OFF	26	29
Pass:Run Ratio OFF	15	24

Average Opponent RANK — HARD (top) / EASY (bottom)

Passing / **Rushing** (Offense side); **Passing** / **Rushing** (Defense side)

Legend
- • 2018 Actual
- 🦎 2019 Forecast

2019 v 2018 Schedule Variances* (OFF=Rank of DEF faced, 2019 vs 2018)

Pass OFF Rank	Pass OFF Blend Rk	Rush OFF Rk	Rush OFF Blend Rk	Pass DEF Rk	Pass DEF Blend Rk	Rush DEF Rk	Rush DEF Blend Rk
19	21	28	23	16	19	31	31

* **1**=Hardest Jump in 2019 schedule from 2018 (aka a much harder schedule in 2019), 32=Easiest Jump in 2019 schedule from 2018 (aka a much easier schedule in 2019);
Pass Blend metric blends 4 metrics: Pass Efficiency, YPPA, Explosive Pass & Pass Rush; **Rush Blend** metric blends 3 metrics: Rush Efficiency, Explosive Rush & RB Targets

---

Team Records & Trends

	2018	2017	2016
Average line	4.2	6.2	3.5
Average O/U line	43.0	42.4	43.7
Straight Up Record	4-12	5-11	5-11
Against the Spread Record	5-11	8-6	6-9
Over/Under Record	10-6	7-8	7-9
ATS as Favorite	2-2	0-1	2-0
ATS as Underdog	3-9	7-4	3-8
Straight Up Home	2-6	4-4	2-6
ATS Home	2-6	6-1	3-4
Over/Under Home	6-2	4-3	4-4
ATS as Home Favorite	2-2	0-0	1-0
ATS as a Home Dog	0-4	6-1	2-3
Straight Up Away	2-6	1-7	3-5
ATS Away	3-5	2-5	3-5
Over/Under Away	4-4	3-5	3-5
ATS Away Favorite	0-0	0-1	1-0
ATS Away Dog	3-5	1-3	1-5
Six Point Teaser Record	11-5	14-2	9-7
Seven Point Teaser Record	11-5	14-2	9-7
Ten Point Teaser Record	11-5	14-2	11-5

NYJ-3

2018. An interesting scheduling quirk to note is that they face the NFL's second-toughest schedule of pass defenses through Week 8. But from Week 9 onward, they face the 11th-easiest. That bumps up to the eight-easiest when eliminating Week 17 for fantasy purposes.

Last year's Jets were a frustrating team to watch in the run game. **Isaiah Crowell** was his typical explosive self, but unfortunately not very successful. He ranked seventh in the league in explosiveness, but 67th in early down success rate and 71st in overall success rate. He split time with **Bilal Powell**, who was only moderately more successful before suffering a season-ending neck injury in Week Seven. **Elijah McGuire** came back from a foot injury in Week Nine to finish the season.

(cont'd - see **NYJ-4**)

2019 Rest Analysis

Team More Rest	4
Opp More Rest	4
Net Rest Edge	0
Week 2 Edge	0
Week 3 Edge	-1
Week 5 Edge	4
Week 6 Edge	0
Week 7 Edge	-3
Week 8 Edge	-1
Week 9 Edge	1
Week 10 Edge	1
Week 11 Edge	
Week 12 Edge	0
Week 13 Edge	0
Week 14 Edge	0
Week 15 Edge	0
Week 16 Edge	3
Week 17 Edge	0

Health by Unit*

2018 Rk	13
2017 Rk	10
2018 v 2017 Rk	23
Off Rk	24
Def Rk	10
QB Rk	25
RB Rk	
WR Rk	22
TE Rk	8
Oline Rk	13
Dline Rk	6
LB Rk	5
DB Rk	22

*Based on the work of Football Outsiders

2018 Weekly Betting Lines (wks 1-16)

1	2	3	5	6	7	8	9	10	11	12	13	14	15	16
BUF	CLE	NE	PHI	DAL	NE	JAX	MIA	NYG	WAS	OAK	CIN	MIA	BAL	PIT
-3	0	10	7.5	2	4.5	4	0	-3.5	2.5	-3	1.5	-3	5.5	1.5

Avg = 1.8

| -3 | 0 | 10 | 7.5 | 2 | 4.5 | 4 | 0 | -3.5 | 2.5 | -3 | 1.5 | -3 | 5.5 | 1.5 |

Home Lines (wks 1-16)

1	2	6	7	10	12	14	16
-3 BUF	0 CLE	2 DAL	4.5 NE	-3.5 NYG	-3 OAK	-3 MIA	1.5 BAL

Avg = -0.6

Road Lines (wks 1-16)

3	5	8	9	11	13	15
10 NE	7.5 PHI	4 JAX	0 MIA	2.5 WAS	1.5 CIN	5.5 BAL

Avg = 4.4

New York Jets 2018 Play Analysis

2018 Play Tendencies

All Pass %	58%
All Pass Rk	18
All Rush %	42%
All Rush Rk	15
1 Score Pass %	55%
1 Score Pass Rk	23
2017 1 Score Pass %	56%
2017 1 Score Pass Rk	20
2018 Pass Increase %	-1%
Pass Increase Rk	16
1 Score Rush %	45%
1 Score Rush Rk	10
Up Pass %	45%
Up Pass Rk	25
Up Rush %	55%
Up Rush Rk	8
Down Pass %	64%
Down Pass Rk	25
Down Rush %	36%
Down Rush Rk	8

2018 Down & Distance Tendencies

Down	Distance	Total Plays	Pass Rate	Run Rate	Play Success %
1	Med (4-7)	8	50%	50%	75%
	Long (8-10)	280	47%	53%	44%
	XL (11+)	17	47%	53%	41%
2	Short (1-3)	21	29%	71%	71%
	Med (4-7)	72	46%	54%	46%
	Long (8-10)	91	58%	42%	37%
	XL (11+)	38	55%	45%	26%
3	Short (1-3)	39	49%	51%	56%
	Med (4-7)	42	95%	5%	45%
	Long (8-10)	40	93%	8%	30%
	XL (11+)	29	76%	24%	7%
4	Short (1-3)	6	33%	67%	50%
	Med (4-7)	1	100%	0%	100%

Shotgun %:

	Under Center	Shotgun
	42%	58%
	37% AVG 63%	

Run Rate:

	Under Center	Shotgun
	70%	21%
	68% AVG 23%	

Pass Rate:

	Under Center	Shotgun
	30%	79%
	32% AVG 77%	

Short Yardage Intelligence:

2nd and Short Run

Run Freq	Run Rk	NFL Run Freq Avg	Run 1D Rate	Run NFL 1D Avg
76%	5	65%	63%	68%

2nd and Short Pass

Pass Freq	Pass Rk	NFL Pass Freq Avg	Pass 1D Rate	Pass NFL 1D Avg
24%	28	35%	60%	56%

Most Frequent Play

Down	Distance	Play Type	Player	Total Plays	Play Success %
1	Long (8-10)	RUSH	Isaiah Crowell	64	38%
	XL (11+)	RUSH	Elijah McGuire	4	25%
2	Short (1-3)	RUSH	Isaiah Crowell	6	67%
	Med (4-7)	RUSH	Isaiah Crowell	20	45%
	Long (8-10)	RUSH	Isaiah Crowell	10	20%
	XL (11+)	RUSH	Isaiah Crowell	10	10%
3	Short (1-3)	RUSH	Isaiah Crowell	9	44%
	Long (8-10)	PASS	Robby Anderson	5	20%
	XL (11+)	PASS	Quincy Enunwa	4	25%
		RUSH	Isaiah Crowell	4	0%

Most Successful Play*

Down	Distance	Play Type	Player	Total Plays	Play Success %
1	Long (8-10)	PASS	Chris Herndon	20	75%
2	Short (1-3)	RUSH	Isaiah Crowell	6	67%
	Med (4-7)	PASS	Robby Anderson	6	67%
	Long (8-10)	PASS	Quincy Enunwa	7	57%
	XL (11+)	RUSH	Isaiah Crowell	10	10%
3	Short (1-3)	RUSH	Sam Darnold	6	100%
	Med (4-7)	PASS	Jermaine Kearse	8	50%
		PASS	Quincy Enunwa	6	50%
	Long (8-10)	PASS	Jermaine Kearse	5	40%

*Minimum 5 plays to qualify

2018 Weekly Snap Rates

Wk	Opp	Score	Robby Anderson	Jermaine Kearse	Chris Herndon	Quincy Enunwa	Eric Tomlinson	Isaiah Crowell	Jordan Leggett	Elijah McGuire	Bilal Powell
1	DET	W 48-17	35 (58%)		34 (57%)	40 (67%)	29 (48%)	24 (40%)	15 (25%)		24 (40%)
2	MIA	L 20-12	53 (82%)	20 (31%)	44 (68%)	52 (80%)	37 (57%)	31 (48%)			34 (52%)
3	CLE	L 21-17	42 (67%)	34 (54%)	34 (54%)	53 (84%)	24 (38%)	29 (46%)	19 (30%)		34 (54%)
4	JAC	L 31-12	42 (75%)	48 (86%)	36 (64%)	53 (95%)	13 (23%)	20 (36%)	27 (48%)		36 (64%)
5	DEN	W 34-16	32 (52%)	39 (63%)	41 (66%)	48 (77%)	46 (74%)	25 (40%)	29 (47%)		34 (55%)
6	IND	W 42-34	53 (75%)	59 (83%)	28 (39%)	15 (21%)	27 (38%)	29 (41%)	22 (31%)		32 (45%)
7	MIN	L 37-17	62 (87%)	64 (90%)	24 (34%)		26 (37%)	33 (46%)	22 (31%)		14 (20%)
8	CHI	L 24-10		52 (96%)	27 (50%)		6 (11%)	25 (46%)	12 (22%)		
9	MIA	L 13-6	47 (71%)	48 (73%)	42 (64%)	48 (73%)	24 (36%)	23 (35%)	33 (50%)	36 (55%)	
10	BUF	L 41-10		50 (89%)	36 (64%)	54 (96%)	13 (23%)	19 (34%)	17 (30%)	32 (57%)	
12	NE	L 27-13	48 (75%)	40 (63%)	51 (80%)	60 (94%)	23 (36%)	26 (41%)	17 (27%)	35 (55%)	
13	TEN	L 26-22	49 (72%)	48 (71%)	50 (74%)	59 (87%)	21 (31%)	43 (63%)	23 (34%)	25 (37%)	
14	BUF	W 27-23	38 (70%)	28 (52%)	41 (76%)	44 (81%)	21 (39%)	5 (9%)	19 (35%)	40 (74%)	
15	HOU	L 29-22	71 (95%)	62 (83%)	52 (69%)		26 (35%)		26 (35%)	56 (75%)	
16	GB	L 44-38	56 (93%)	34 (57%)	39 (65%)		17 (28%)		16 (27%)	51 (85%)	
17	NE	L 38-3	54 (96%)		46 (82%)				29 (52%)	43 (77%)	
	Grand Total		682 (76%)	626 (71%)	625 (63%)	526 (78%)	353 (37%)	332 (40%)	326 (35%)	318 (64%)	208 (47%)

Personnel Groupings

Personnel	Team %	NFL Avg	Succ. %
1-1 [3WR]	59%	65%	38%
1-2 [2WR]	22%	17%	45%
1-3 [1WR]	10%	3%	39%
2-1 [2WR]	5%	8%	50%
1-0 [4WR]	2%	2%	40%

Grouping Tendencies

Personnel	Pass Rate	Pass Succ. %	Run Succ. %
1-1 [3WR]	66%	39%	36%
1-2 [2WR]	47%	49%	42%
1-3 [1WR]	30%	50%	35%
2-1 [2WR]	42%	60%	43%
1-0 [4WR]	85%	41%	33%

Red Zone Targets (min 3)

Receiver	All	Inside 5	6-10	11-20
Chris Herndon	8	1		7
Jermaine Kearse	8	2	1	5
Quincy Enunwa	7		2	5
Robby Anderson	5	2		3
Andre Roberts	4			4
Elijah McGuire	2			2

Red Zone Rushes (min 3)

Rusher	All	Inside 5	6-10	11-20
Isaiah Crowell	16	3	4	9
Elijah McGuire	15	7	1	7
Sam Darnold	11	3	3	5
Bilal Powell	10	1	2	7
Trenton Cannon	4	1		3

Early Down Target Rate

RB	TE	WR
20%	25%	55%
23%	21%	56%
	NFL AVG	

Overall Target Success %

RB	TE	WR
44%	57%	43%
#24	#10	#31

189

New York Jets 2018 Passing Recap & 2019 Outlook

Sam Darnold's rookie season went as well as it reasonably could've given the context of what he was working with. His performance after returning from an ankle injury gives hope for his sophomore season development. Since 2012, quarterbacks drafted in the top-15 overall went a combined 45-70 as rookies. In year two, they went a combined 97-56. The reason the records improved as they did was because of the underlying play, which dramatically improved statistics that correlate with winning. Sam Darnold went 4-9 as a rookie facing the league's third-most difficult schedule of pass defenses. And he did so with one of the NFL's most injured skill position groups. Not to mention an offensive line that leaked pressure at an incredibly high rate, and play calling that left a lot to be desired. The defense should be stronger in 2019, which will put Darnold and the offense in a better position to be creative. Last year 76-percent of Darnold's pass attempts came when trailing, giving the defense an edge before the ball was even snapped. Darnold delivered 7.8 YPA, a 52-percent success rate and a 113 passer rating in the second half when leading. But he only averaged 5.5 YPA, a 34 percent-success rate and a passer rating of 54 when trailing.

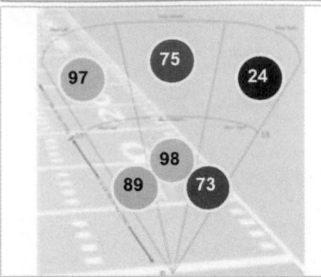

Sam Darnold Rating All Downs

2018 Standard Passing Table

QB	Comp	Att	Comp %	Yds	YPA	TDs	INT	Sacks	Rating	Rk
Sam Darnold	239	414	58%	2,865	6.9	17	15	30	78	42
Josh McCown	60	110	55%	539	4.9	1	4	7	56	53
NFL Avg			62%		7.0				87.5	

2018 Advanced Passing Table

QB	Success %	EDSR Passing Success %	20+ Yd Pass Gains	20+ Yd Pass %	30+ Yd Pass Gains	30+ Yd Pass %	Avg. Air Yds per Comp	Avg. YAC per Comp	20+ Air Yd Comp	20+ Air Yd %
Sam Darnold	43%	47%	40	10.0%	9	2.0%	6.6	5.3	15	4%
Josh McCown	38%	44%	4	4.0%	1	1.0%	3.7	5.3	1	1%
NFL Avg	44%	48%	29.5	8.4%	12.5	3.7%	5.8	5.1	14.5	6%

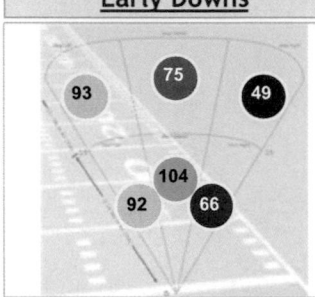

Sam Darnold Rating Early Downs

Interception Rates by Down

Yards to Go	1st Dwn	2nd Dwn	3rd Dwn	4th Dwn	Total
1 & 2		0.0%	0.0%	0.0%	0.0%
3, 4, 5	0.0%	0.0%	4.3%	0.0%	2.2%
6 - 9		3.9%	2.2%		3.1%
10 - 14	3.3%	5.6%	2.4%	25.0%	4.0%
15+	0.0%	0.0%	0.0%	50.0%	3.1%
Total	3.0%	3.6%	2.3%	18.2%	3.4%

3rd Down Passing - Short of Sticks Analysis

QB	Avg. Yds to Go	Avg. YIA (of Comp)	Avg Yds Short	Short of Sticks Rate	Short Rk	Air Yds %	YAC %	Rk
Sam Darnold	8.5	7.6	-0.9	56%	14	55%	45%	14
NFL Avg	7.8	6.4	-1.4	60%		53%	48%	

Air Yds vs YAC

2018 Receiving Recap & 2019 Outlook

Last year the Jets faced pass defenses which ranked the fourth-best at defending explosive passes. This year's schedule projects to be closer to league-average. This should open things up even more for **Robby Anderson**. He'll deliver below average success rates because of how deep he is targeted on many passes. But if the team can get solid slot performance from **Jamison Crowder** and **Sam Darnold**'s protection is improved, better things will happen for Anderson downfield. His primary concern is that his red zone target rate is extremely low. But Darnold confidently fed him 10.3 targets per game after returning from injury last year. He averaged 104 yards and a touchdown per game in Darnold's first three weeks back.

Player *Min 50 Targets	Targ	Comp %	YPA	Rating	Success %	Success Rk	Missed YPA Rk	YAS % Rk	YTS % Rk	TDs
Robby Anderson	93	54%	8.1	84.2	45%	102	141	80	67	3
Jermaine Kearse	76	49%	4.9	50.9	39%	122	170	113	2	1
Quincy Enunwa	69	55%	6.5	67.8	41%	117	146	59	97	1
Chris Herndon	56	70%	9.0	106.4	61%	13	53	11	77	4

Directional Passer Rating Delivered

Receiver	Short Left	Short Middle	Short Right	Deep Left	Deep Middle	Deep Right	Player Total
Robby Anderson	104	138	71	88	9	59	84
Jermaine Kearse	66	55	69	40	90	0	51
Quincy Enunwa	78	62	76	79	40	37	68
Chris Herndon	124	106	112	153	110	39	106
Elijah McGuire	125	87	79			40	90
Isaiah Crowell	86	97	82				87
Trenton Cannon	95	87	84	39		40	66
Terrelle Pryor	50	94	48	158	119	110	111
Andre Roberts	85	44	87	0		40	46
Bilal Powell	17	104	133			40	74
Eric Tomlinson	85	92	28		40		41
Neal Sterling	67	103	88			40	89
Team Total	87	85	76	94	42	16	76

2018 Rushing Recap & 2019 Outlook

The hope is that **Le'Veon Bell** can perform better than last year's stable of Jets running backs. **Isaiah Crowell**'s 37-percent success rate on first down rushes ranked 50th out of 53 qualifiers, and **Bilal Powell**'s 42-percent ranked 45th. Of the 55 backs with at least 125 first down carries over the last three years, Bell boasts a No. 9-ranked success rate of 51-percent. Factors such as defenses needing to respect the passing attack of the Steelers more than they do of the Jets play into that. But it's still an upgrade. There will be concerns with Bell after he took a year off. There will be concerns as to how his patient style will work behind linemen that he's less familiar with. Getting him enough preseason work is vital, even though the Jets will try to limit him.

Yards per Carry by Direction

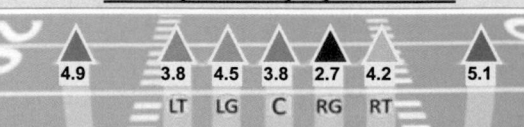

4.9	3.8	4.5	3.8	2.7	4.2	5.1
	LT	LG	C	RG	RT	

Player *Min 50 Rushes	Rushes	YPC	Success %	Success Rk	Missed YPA Rk	YTS % Rk	YAS % Rk	Early Down Success %	Early Down Success Rk	TDs
Isaiah Crowell	143	4.8	36%	71	68	73	7	37%	67	6
Elijah McGuire	92	3.0	36%	72	73	36	48	34%	72	3
Bilal Powell	80	4.3	44%	53	62	40	17	45%	46	0

Directional Run Frequency

14%	10%	8%	31%	14%	10%	12%
	LT	LG	C	RG	RT	

Despite primarily facing below-average rushing defenses, he averaged only 3.0 YPC and trailed Crowell with a No. 72-ranked success rate.

Tying up so much cap in the contract of a running back, even if it's **Le'Veon Bell**, isn't always optimal. But the time to make such a move is when your quarterback is on their rookie deal. The ramifications of moving on from Bell after 2020, if need be, aren't bad. If he's cut before June 1st in 2021, the team would eat $4 million in dead cap. But they'd save $9.5 million overall because they aren't paying his $13.5 million cap hit. They could also spread out the cap hit by cutting Bell post-June 1st, and take $2 million hits in both 2021 and 2022. Though they should've spent their money more wisely, Bell should make an impact and help **Sam Darnold** offer more consistency.

The offensive line's ability to run block should be a concern for whoever is running the ball. The team hasn't made enough upgrades on last year's poor unit. Fans expecting Pittsburgh-level Bell should realize the Steelers had one of the league's most talented offensive lines and best line coaches in **Mike Munchak**. On a positive note, **Adam Gase** helped the NFL's worst run-blocking line ability-wise produce last year's 15th-most efficient rushing attack. One which saw **Frank Gore** produce a

(cont'd - see NYJ-5)

New York Jets Fantasy Corner

After beginning the season as the youngest starting quarterback in NFL history, **Sam Darnold** led all quarterbacks in QBR and several other advanced stats and metrics on PlayerProfiler.com in the month of December. **Robby Anderson** was the prime beneficiary of Darnold's ascendance, posting a league-winning 23.1 PPR fantasy points per game during the fantasy football playoffs (weeks 14-16). Flashing 4.4 speed and a 35-percent College Dominator Rating at Temple, Anderson is one of the most impressive wide receiver prospects to go undrafted in years. Heading into 2019, Anderson is the entrenched No. 1 receiver tethered to an understated version of Baker Mayfield on a Jets team that will need to throw the ball to compete each week. His 20.8-percent Target Share (No. 29) and explosive playmaking make Anderson the ideal upside WR play in the seventh round of fantasy football drafts. - Matt Kelley

2018 Situational Usage by Player & Position

Usage Rate by Score

		Being Blown Out (14+)	Down Big (9-13)	One Score	Large Lead (9-13)	Blowout Lead (14+)
RUSH	Isaiah Crowell	13%	3%	62%	15%	6%
	Elijah McGuire	20%	10%	67%	3%	
	Bilal Powell	9%		59%	18%	15%
	Robby Anderson			100%		
	Trenton Cannon	18%	11%	53%		18%
	Quincy Enunwa			100%		
	Andre Roberts			100%		
	Total	14%	5%	62%	11%	8%
PASS	Isaiah Crowell	15%	8%	54%	23%	
	Elijah McGuire	33%	7%	56%	4%	
	Bilal Powell	39%	17%	44%		
	Robby Anderson	17%	15%	57%	11%	
	Jermaine Kearse	23%	3%	70%	4%	
	Trenton Cannon	50%	8%	29%	4%	8%
	Quincy Enunwa	22%	5%	63%	8%	2%
	Chris Herndon	24%	7%	61%	7%	
	Terrelle Pryor	24%	14%	38%	19%	5%
	Andre Roberts	44%	13%	38%	6%	
	Neal Sterling	13%		88%		
	Charone Peake	100%				
	Rishard Matthews	50%		50%		
	Total	26%	9%	57%	8%	1%

Share of Offensive Plays by Type

	Isaiah Crowell	Elijah McGuire	Bilal Powell	Robby Anderson	Jermaine Kearse	Trenton Cannon	Quincy Enunwa	Chris Herndon	Terrelle Pryor	Andre Roberts	Neal Sterling	Charone Peake	Rishard Matthews
RUSH	40%	26%	22%	1%		11%	0%			1%			
PASS	6%	7%	4%	20%	17%	6%	15%	13%	5%	4%	2%	1%	0%
ALL	22%	15%	13%	11%	9%	8%	8%	7%	3%	2%	1%	0%	0%

Positional Target Distribution vs NFL Average

		NFL Wide				Team Only			
		Left	Middle	Right	Total	Left	Middle	Right	Total
Deep	WR	33%	18%	31%	**81%**	33%	10%	28%	**72%**
	TE	5%	4%	7%	**15%**	7%	4%	8%	**20%**
	RB	1%	0%	2%	**3%**	3%		5%	**8%**
	All	39%	22%	39%	**100%**	44%	15%	42%	**100%**
Short	WR	20%	14%	21%	**55%**	24%	13%	22%	**58%**
	TE	6%	6%	8%	**20%**	5%	4%	7%	**16%**
	RB	10%	5%	10%	**25%**	9%	5%	11%	**26%**
	All	36%	25%	39%	**100%**	38%	22%	40%	**100%**
Total		37%	24%	39%	**100%**	39%	20%	40%	**100%**

Positional Success Rates vs NFL Average

		NFL Wide				Team Only			
		Left	Middle	Right	Total	Left	Middle	Right	Total
Deep	WR	40%	50%	40%	**42%**	44%	30%	26%	**35%**
	TE	42%	54%	42%	**45%**	71%	50%	38%	**53%**
	RB	38%	33%	46%	**43%**	33%		0%	**13%**
	All	40%	50%	41%	**43%**	48%	36%	25%	**36%**
Short	WR	55%	61%	53%	**56%**	48%	46%	43%	**46%**
	TE	55%	62%	54%	**57%**	65%	64%	56%	**61%**
	RB	47%	54%	45%	**48%**	44%	50%	48%	**47%**
	All	53%	60%	51%	**54%**	50%	50%	46%	**48%**
Total		50%	58%	49%	**52%**	49%	48%	42%	**46%**

Division History: Season Wins & 2019 Projection

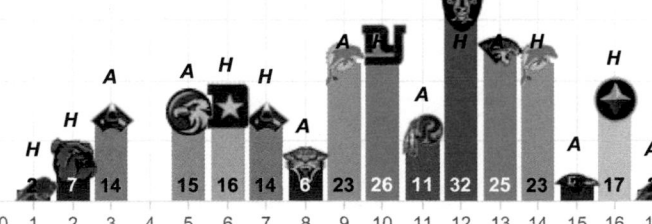

2015 Wins | 2016 Wins | 2017 Wins | 2018 Wins | Forecast 2019 Wins

Rank of 2019 Defensive Pass Efficiency Faced by Week

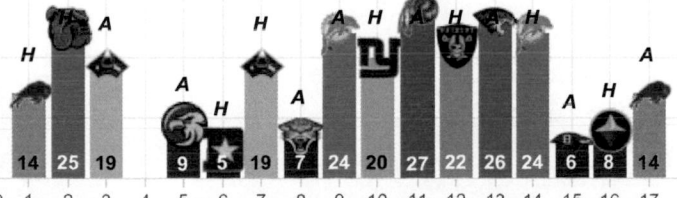

Rank of 2019 Defensive Rush Efficiency Faced by Week

2018 Detailed Analytics Summary
Success by Play Type & Primary Personnel Groupings

Type	1-1 [3WR]	1-2 [2WR]	1-3 [1WR]	2-1 [2WR]	1-0 [4WR]	0-1 [4WR]	2-0 [3WR]	2-2 [1WR]	0-0 [5WR]	ALL
PASS	39% (377)	49% (101)	50% (28)	60% (20)	41% (17)	50% (8)	33% (3)			42% (554)
RUSH	36% (193)	42% (112)	35% (66)	43% (28)	33% (3)		33% (3)	0% (4)	100% (1)	38% (410)
All	38% (570)	45% (213)	39% (94)	50% (48)	40% (20)	50% (8)	33% (6)	0% (4)	100% (1)	40% (964)

Format Success Rate (Total # of Plays)

Receiving Success by Top-4 Personnel Groupings
(Min 50 targets)

POS	Player	1-1 [3WR]	1-2 [2WR]	1-0 [4WR]	2-1 [2WR]	4 Grp Total
TE	Chris Herndon	55% (31) 8.1, 73.5	63% (16) 11.4, 132.8		100% (2) 6.5, 133.3	59% (49) 9.1, 101.2
WR	Robby Anderson	47% (58) 7.5, 85.2	48% (21) 9.9, 87.0	0% (3) 1.7, 2.8	75% (4) 11.8, 153.1	47% (86) 8.1, 84.3
	Jermaine Kearse	37% (60) 4.6, 51.7	50% (6) 7.5, 75.0	25% (4) 5.3, 26.0		37% (70) 4.9, 48.6
	Quincy Enunwa	34% (47) 5.0, 45.8	70% (10) 14.9, 145.8	67% (6) 8.7, 93.8		43% (63) 6.9, 67.8

Format Line 1: Success Rate (Total # of Plays)   Line 2: YPA, Passer Rating

Rushing Success by Top-4 Personnel Groupings
(Min 25 carries)

Rusher (Last, First)	1-1 [3WR]	1-2 [2WR]	2-1 [2WR]	2-2 [1WR]	4 Grp Total
Crowell Isaiah	29% (68) 4.4	39% (44) 4.7	0% (1) -1.0		33% (113) 4.5
McGuire Elijah	30% (44) 3.0	48% (27) 2.0	43% (14) 3.9	0% (1) 0.0	37% (86) 2.8
Powell Bilal	38% (34) 4.1	38% (29) 3.8			38% (63) 3.9
Cannon Trenton	40% (20) 3.5	75% (4) 4.0	30% (10) 2.2		41% (34) 3.2
Darnold Sam	55% (22) 3.9	33% (3) 4.3	100% (2) 17.0	0% (3) -1.0	50% (30) 4.3

Format Line 1: Success Rate (Total # of Plays)   Line 2: YPC

Passing by Coverage Scheme

Zone	49% (233) 6.8, 76.0
M2M	43% (172) 6.5, 78.0
Screen	43% (51) 5.8, 78.5
Combo	83% (6) 6.2, 92.4

Passing by Route

Curl	59% (74) 6.6, 84.6
Out	56% (54) 6.9, 91.1
Screen	49% (47) 7.4, 94.9
Slant	47% (34) 7.2, 39.3
Flat	58% (33) 5.2, 99.3
Dig	58% (24) 11.4, 105.0

Throw Types

Level 1	50% (318) 6.2, 83.6
Level 2	48% (129) 8.0, 82.0
Level 3	13% (39) 5.3, 35.3
Sidearm	50% (2) 11.5, 91.7
Shovel	0% (1) 2.0, 79.2

QB Drop Types

3 Step	41% (237) 6.2, 65.5
0/1 Step	52% (111) 6.6, 100.1
5 Step	45% (53) 6.1, 65.2
7 Step	70% (30) 10.7, 94.0
Designed Rollout Right	45% (22) 5.5, 70.6
Basic Screen	53% (19) 8.7, 99.7

QB State at Pass

Planted	50% (330) 7.1, 84.4
Moving	42% (67) 5.7, 61.9
Shuffling	31% (59) 4.4, 53.1

Play Action

	Play Action	No P/A
Under Center	52% (75) 7.4, 70.5	65% (31) 8.0, 110.7
Shotgun	51% (51) 7.7, 104.5	43% (334) 6.2, 70.9
ALL	52% (126) 7.5, 84.3	44% (365) 6.3, 74.3

Run Types

Inside Zone	44% (104) 4.4
Outside Zone	34% (91) 4.6
Power	36% (44) 3.3
Pitch	46% (41) 3.5
Stretch	36% (28) 4.9
Lead	11% (18) 0.9

NYJ-5

No. 26 success rate of 50-percent and average 4.6 YPC.

It'll be interesting to see how **Gregg Williams** finds a way to minimize the capabilities of an ultra-talented defense. **Leonard Williams** is one of the NFL's best run-blocking interior defenders, while third-overall draft pick **Quinnen Williams** was one of college football's best pass-rushing interior defenders. Combining the two should force opposing offensive lines to overcompensate, which will allow for edge pressure. And when they don't, the pressure will come from right up the gut. Which will quickly put quarterbacks on their heels and in an uncomfortable position.

Spending $85 million on a linebacker like **C.J. Mosley** is steep, but it's the price of amassing one of the league's more talented defenses. With Mosely at the second level and **Jamal Adams** anchoring the secondary, EDGE rusher **Jachai Polite** was added in the third round of this year's draft. He's a player who slid in pre-draft grades, but had tremendous productivity during his final year at Florida.

They've become aggressive with their rookie-deal quarterback, beginning to put pieces around him to in the hopes of building a contender. The addition of **Jamison Crowder** in the slot paired with **Robby Anderson** over the top is something defenses will have to respect. New Jets head coach and signal caller **Adam Gase** needs to help **Sam Darnold** excel in ways that **Jeremy Bates** didn't. His last season as Miami's head coach in 2018 should raise at least some concerns as to whether he can. Through their Week 11 bye, the Dolphins had a mere 45-percent success rate when passing from 11 personnel and averaged only 6.7 YPA. This despite running plays from 11 personnel 86-percent of the time, behind only the Rams. When passing from 12 personnel, they had a 61 percent-success rate and averaged 13.6 YPA. Yet they ran plays from 12 personnel only five-percent of the time, ahead of only the Rams. To their credit, they adjusted after the bye week and passed more out of 12 with better results down the stretch. But it's concerning that it took so long for a change to be made.

The early schedule is brutal, with games against the Browns, Eagles, Cowboys and Patriots twice in the season's first seven weeks. Though the schedule lightens up considerably after that, they need to come out of the gates quickly. The Jets have the NFL's second-easiest schedule based on win totals. They're the only team in the league projected to face as many as five bottom-5 opponents and as many as eight bottom-10 opponents.   They'll need to be playing great football down the stretch to hit their win total. They'll also have to reverse their recent trend of failure in close games, with a 5-12 record over the last two years. If **Sam Darnold** takes a sophomore jump, like many recent young quarterbacks, there could at least be one exciting team in New York in 2019.

The arrival of Adam Gase will surely help propel Sam Darnold's precocious breakout, but the presence of Gregg Williams on the other side is worst case scenario for what could have been an ascending defense. Entering 2019 with a 22-year old quarterback and fresh faces on the field and roaming the sidelines, the Jets are one of the most enigmatic franchises in the NFL. In light of this uncertainty, accurately forecasting the Jets' game outcomes is particularly challenging this season.

Oakland Raiders

Coaches (Prior Yrs)

Head Coach:
Jon Gruden (1 yr)
Offensive Coordinator:
Greg Olson (1 yr)
Defensive Coordinator:
Paul Guenther (1 yr)

EASY   HARD

2019 Forecast

Wins	Div Rank
6	#4

Past Records

2018: 4-12
2017: 6-10
2016: 12-4

Schedule: DEN (H), KC (H), MIN (A), IND (A), CHI (H), bye, GB (A), HOU (A), DET (H), LAC (H), CIN (H), NYJ (A), KC (A), TEN (H), JAX (H), LAC (A), DEN (A)
Weeks 1-17. MNF, LON, TNF.

Key Players Lost

Player	New
A.J. McCarron (QB)	HOU
Jared Cook (TE)	NO
Jon Feliciano (G)	BUF
Jordy Nelson (WR)	Retired
Kelechi Osemele (OG)	NYJ
Lee Smith (TE)	BUF
Navorro Bowman (ILB)	Retired
Shilique Calhoun (OLB)	NE
T.J. Clemmings (RT)	CHI

Average Line	# Games Favored	# Games Underdog
4.2	3	10

Regular Season Wins: Past & Current Proj

Forecast 2019 Wins — 6
2018 Wins — 4
Forecast 2018 Wins — 8
2017 Wins — 6
2016 Wins — 12
2015 Wins — 7

1 3 5 7 9 11 13 15

2019 Oakland Raiders Overview

One step forward, two steps back.

Sounds like the Oakland Raiders.

After a 12-win season in 2016, the 2017 Raiders' pre-season Win Total was eight games. They won six. They turned to **Jon Gruden** on a ten-year, $100 million guaranteed contract along with a boatload of free agents and four top-100 picks. Projected to win eight games again last year, Oakland won four.

This offseason witnessed the Raiders again spend generously in free agency, and they made three first-round picks. One step forward, right? Sportsbook linemakers aren't buying it. This year's Raiders are projected at six wins. Two steps back.

I don't pretend to know what to make of this team, but I do know it has Gruden's fingerprints all over it. The 12-win 2016 Raiders' offensive spending ranked 15th in the league, and their defensive spending ranked tenth. Fast forward to 2019, and Oakland is allocating the NFL's fifth-most cap room to offense. Their defensive spending ranks dead last.

Last year's Raiders signed the second-most free agents in the league, targeting bargain-bin values and one-year, prove-it deals. Those players' agents should have thought twice before placing their clients in Gruden's hands in his first year as the Raiders' coach and de-facto GM.

In theory, at least, this year's spending spree was overseen by **Reggie McKenzie** replacement **Mike Mayock**. Yet how much power Mayock truly has is fair to question; Gruden is easily the most-powerful presence in the Raiders' organization and signs off on all moves made.

The 2019 Raiders dedicated the NFL's fourth-most cap room to free agent acquisitions, notably signing **Antonio Brown** to a three-year, $50.1 million contract revision, OT **Trent Brown** to a four-year, $66 million deal, WR **Tyrell Williams** for $44.4 million over four years, and

(cont'd - see OAK2)

Key Free Agents/ Trades Added

Player	AAV (MM)
Antonio Brown (WR)	Trade
LaMarcus Joyner (FS)	$10.
Mike Glennon (QB)	$2
Nevin Lawson (CB)	$3
Trenton Brown (RT)	$16.
Tyrell Williams (WR)	$11.
Vontaze Burfict (OLB)	$2

Drafted Players

Rd	Pk	Player (College)
1	4	DE - Clelin Ferrell (Clemson)
	24	RB - Josh Jacobs (Alabama)
	27	S - Johnathan Abram (Mississippi State)
2	40	CB - Trayvon Mullen (Clomoon)
4	106	DE - Maxx Crosby (Eastern Michigan)
	129	CB - Isaiah Johnson (Houston)
4*	137	TE - Foster Moreau (LSU)
5	149	WR - Hunter Renfrow (Clemson)
7	230	DE - Quinton Bell (Prairie View A&M)

Lineup & Cap Hits

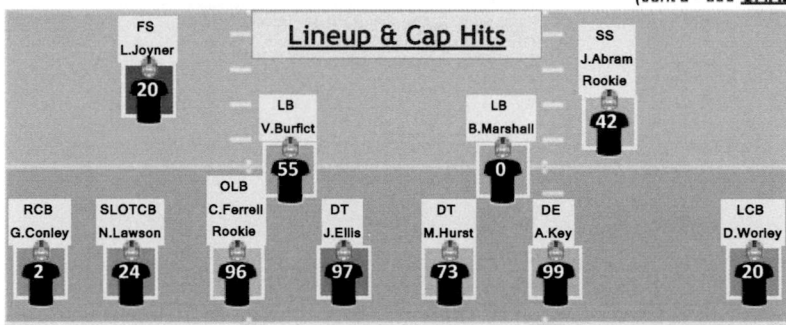

Defense:
FS - L.Joyner (20), SS - J.Abram Rookie (42)
LB - V.Burfict (55), LB - B.Marshall (0)
RCB - G.Conley (2), SLOTCB - N.Lawson (24), OLB C.Ferrell Rookie (96), DT - J.Ellis (97), DT - M.Hurst (73), DE - A.Key (99), LCB - D.Worley (20)

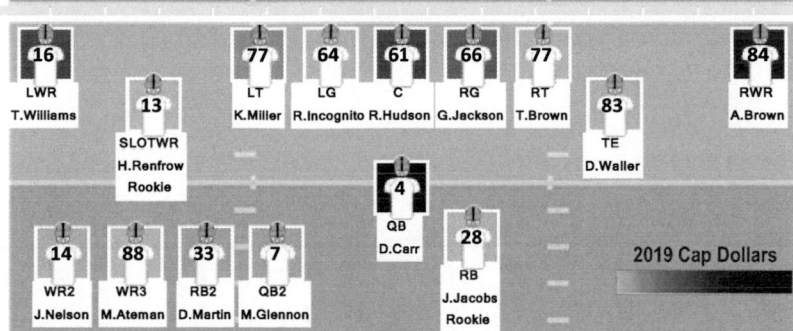

Offense:
LWR - T.Williams (16), SLOTWR - H.Renfrow Rookie (13), LT - K.Miller (77), LG - R.Incognito (64), C - R.Hudson (61), RG - G.Jackson (66), RT - T.Brown (77), TE - D.Waller (83), RWR - A.Brown (84)
QB - D.Carr (4), RB - J.Jacobs Rookie (28)
WR2 - J.Nelson (14), WR3 - M.Ateman (88), RB2 - D.Martin (33), QB2 - M.Glennon (7)

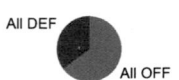

2019 Cap Dollars

2019 Unit Spending

All DEF / All OFF

Positional Spending

	Rank	Total	2017 Rk
All OFF	6	$111.80M	2
QB	12	$25.66M	6
OL	7	$43.16M	4
RB	21	$6.62M	12
WR	4	$32.22M	13
TE	30	$4.15M	6
All DEF	31	$60.49M	31
DL	28	$16.57M	27
LB	29	$12.51M	26
CB	25	$12.97M	22
S	6	$18.44M	14

193

FS **Lamarcus Joyner** to a four-year, $42 million pact. CB **Nevin Lawson**, LG **Richie Incognito**, WR **J.J. Nelson**, QB **Mike Glennon**, LB **Brandon Marshall**, LB **Vontaze Burfict**, and TE **Luke Willson** came aboard on cheaper, short-term deals.

Using the Brown trade, free agency, and the draft, Gruden replaced *all* of his skill-position starters at wide receiver, running back, and tight end.

That level of turnover is typically unwise, as is building through free agency in general. Unlike 2018's offseason plan – where the Raiders spent on over-the-hill free agents **Derrick Johnson**, **Jordy Nelson**, **Leon Hall**, **Breno Giacomini**, and **Shareece Wright** – 2019's strategy brought on younger talents with higher ceilings.

Question marks about this year's free agent class come less from dollars and more from the *types* of players Oakland welcomed into its locker room.

When Burfict came out of Arizona State in 2012, Mayock – then NFL Network's lead draft analyst – watched Burfict's tape and called him undraftable. Burfict indeed went undrafted but signed with the Bengals, whose defense was then coordinated by **Paul Guenther**, now the Raiders' defensive boss. Burfict has missed 37 games over the last five seasons due to injuries and suspensions. He was cut by the Bengals this offseason and reunited with Guenther the next day on a one-year, $5 million deal.

With Burfict on the Bengals and Brown on the division-rival Steelers, Burfict nearly decapitated A.B. with a head shot during a 2016 playoff game. In Cincinnati, Burfict's dirty plays were not isolated incidents. They were his standard, and Burfict is commonly viewed among his NFL peers as the dirtiest player in the sport.

The Raiders' Incognito signing also raised eyebrows around the league. Last with Buffalo, the Bills were compelled to heighten security at team headquarters after Incognito announced his retirement, unretired, then demanded his release.

Mayock defended the moves by stating the Raiders "can't have all boy scouts" on the team, and that is true. No one would confuse Incognito for a boy scout. Skipping over his assault charges and suspensions, Incognito's locker-room history and off-field incidents are more than a little concerning. Incognito harassed a female at a charity golf event, infamously hazed **Jonathan Martin** with the Dolphins, racially harassed a trainer, and used racial slurs against the Jaguars during the Bills' 2017 playoff game. Incognito assaulted a gym member with weights and was held for psychiatric evaluation. After the Vikings declined to sign Incognito before the 2018 season, he was arrested for an even more-concerning incident.

Two days after arguing with his 90-year-old grandmother, punching a hole in her wall and ripping a security unit out of it, Incognito was signing cremation papers for his deceased father. He rampaged around the funeral home, punching caskets and threatening to shoot employees. Incognito also stated he wanted to cut off his father's head for "research." When police arrived, they found two Glocks, a silencer, three rifles,

and multiple magazines in Incognito's car.

Because Incognito pleaded guilty to misdemeanor criminal damage and disorderly conduct, he will be subject to a suspension under the NFL's personal conduct policy.

Incognito has played well on the field, and the Raiders hope he received the help he clearly needed. But any team signing a player with Incognito's background smells of desperation for a team coming off a 4-12 season and relocating to Las Vegas next year. Signing Incognito could easily prove a move that causes Oakland to take two more steps back.

But most concerning for the Raiders' offensive line is position coach **Tom Cable**.

Walking through pass-protection rankings everywhere Cable has coached yields startling results. His 2016 Falcons line finished 31st in pass pro. *(cont'd - see OAK-3)*

2018 Passing Performance

QB	1st Dwn	2nd Dwn	3rd Dwn	
Derek Carr	55%	52%	35%	Success Rate
	6.9	8.0	6.9	YPA
	86.2	102.7	91.1	Rating
Pass Rate	53%	65%	83%	
NFL AVG	53%	47%	36%	Success Rate
	7.7	7.3	6.9	YPA
	95.1	93.7	87.1	Rating
Pass Rate	53%	62%	80%	

2018 Rushing Performance

Offense	1st Dwn	2nd Dwn	3rd Dwn	
OAK	51%	46%	49%	Success Rate
	4.5	3.9	2.5	YPC
Run Rate	47%	35%	17%	
NFL AVG	48%	46%	51%	Success Rate
	4.5	4.4	4.3	YPC
Run Rate	47%	38%	20%	

2018 Offensive Advanced Metrics

Rank values: EDSR Off 18, 30 & In Off 16, Red Zone Off 19, 3rd Down Off 23, YPPA Off 20, YPPT Off 2, Offensive Efficiency 25, Pass Efficiency Off 17, Pass Pro Efficiency Off 25, RB Pass Eff Off 9, Rush Efficiency Off 29, Explosive Pass Off 13, Explosive Run Off 2

2018 Defensive Advanced Metrics

Rank values: EDSR Def 21, 30 & In Def 30, Red Zone Def 30, 3rd Down Def 2, YPPA Def 2, YPPT Def 30, Defensive Efficiency 2, Pass Efficiency Def 2, Pass Pro Efficiency Def 9, RB Pass Eff Def 22, Rush Efficiency Def 21, Explosive Pass Def 13, Explosive Run Def

2018 Weekly EDSR & Season Trending Performance

	1	2	3	4	5	6	8	9	10	11	12	13	14	15	16	17	
WEEK	1	2	3	4	5	6	8	9	10	11	12	13	14	15	16	17	
RESULT	L	L	L	W	L	L	L	L	W	L	W	L	W	L	W	L	
OPP	LA	DEN	MIA	CLE	LAC	SEA	IND	SF	LAC	ARI	BAL	KC	PIT	CIN	DEN	KC	
SITE	H	A	A	H	A	N	H	A	H	A	A	H	H	A	H	A	
MARGIN	-20	-1	-8	3	-16	-24	-14	-31	-14	2	-17	-7	3	-14	13	-32	
PTS	13	19	20	45	10	3	28	3	6	23	17	33	24	16	27	3	
OPP PTS	33	20	28	42	26	27	42	34	20	21	34	40	21	30	14	35	

EDSR by Wk
W=Green
L=Red

OFF/DEF
EDSR
Blue=OFF
(high=good)
Red=DEF
(low=good)

2018 Close Game Records

All 2018 Wins: **4**
FG Games (<=3 pts) W-L: **3-1**
FG Games Win %: **75% (#7)**
FG Games Wins (% of Total Wins): **75% (#1)**
1 Score Games (<=8 pts) W-L: **3-3**
1 Score Games Win %: **50% (#15)**
1 Score Games Wins (% of Total Wins): **75% (#5)**

2018 Critical & Game-Deciding Stats

TO Margin	-7
TO Given	24
INT Given	10
FUM Given	14
TO Taken	17
INT Taken	14
FUM Taken	3
Sack Margin	-39
Sacks	13
Sacks Allow	52
Return TD Margin	-2
Ret TDs	2
Ret TDs Allow	4
Penalty Margin	+7
Penalties	110
Opponent Penalties	117

Oakland Raiders 2019 Strength of Schedule In Detail (compared to 2018)

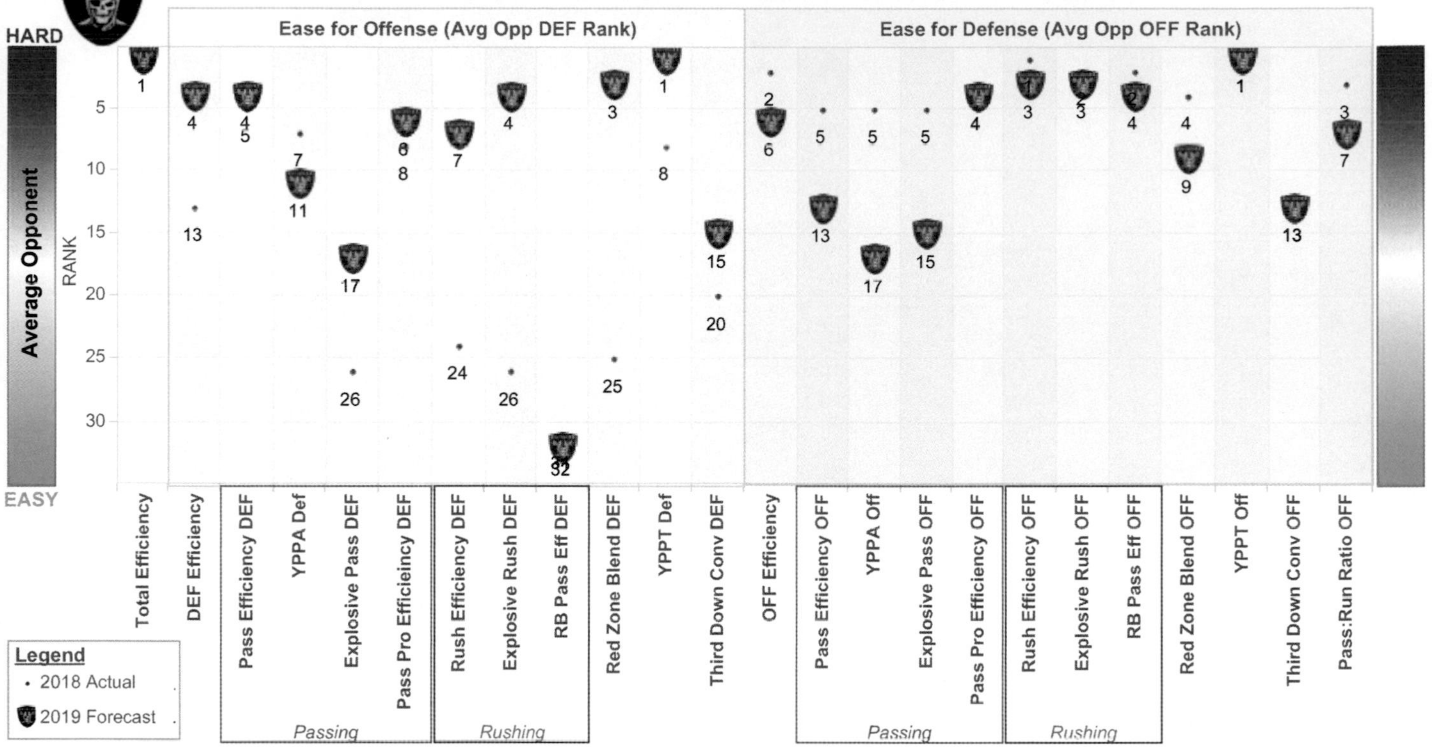

HARD ... **EASY**

Ease for Offense (Avg Opp DEF Rank)

Data points (2018 Actual) and 2019 Forecast by category:
- Total Efficiency: 1
- DEF Efficiency: 4, 13
- Pass Efficiency DEF: 4, 5
- YPPA Def: 7, 11
- Explosive Pass DEF: 17
- Pass Pro Efficiency DEF: 6, 8
- Rush Efficiency DEF: 7
- Explosive Rush DEF: 4
- RB Pass Eff DEF: 32
- Red Zone Blend DEF: 3
- YPPT Def: 1, 8
- Third Down Conv DEF: 15

Passing / Rushing

Ease for Defense (Avg Opp OFF Rank)

- OFF Efficiency: 2, 6
- Pass Efficiency OFF: 5, 13
- YPPA Off: 5, 17
- Explosive Pass OFF: 5, 15
- Pass Pro Efficiency OFF: 4
- Rush Efficiency OFF: 3
- Explosive Rush OFF: 3
- RB Pass Eff OFF: 2, 4
- Red Zone Blend OFF: 4, 9
- YPPT Off: 1
- Third Down Conv OFF: 13
- Pass:Run Ratio OFF: 3, 7

Passing / Rushing

Legend
- • 2018 Actual
- 🏴 2019 Forecast

2019 v 2018 Schedule Variances* (OFF=Rank of DEF faced, 2019 vs 2018)

Pass OFF Rank	Pass OFF Blend Rk	Rush OFF Rk	Rush OFF Blend Rk	Pass DEF Rk	Pass DEF Blend Rk	Rush DEF Rk	Rush DEF Blend Rk
13	14	4	3	25	26	17	17

* 1=Hardest Jump in 2019 schedule from 2018 (aka a much harder schedule in 2019), 32=Easiest Jump in 2019 schedule from 2018 (aka a much easier schedule in 2019);
Pass Blend *metric blends 4 metrics: Pass Efficiency, YPPA, Explosive Pass & Pass Rush;* **Rush Blend** *metric blends 3 metrics: Rush Efficiency, Explosive Rush & RB Targets*

Team Records & Trends

	2018	2017	2016
Average line	6.0	0.3	-1.2
Average O/U line	47.6	46.2	47.6
Straight Up Record	4-12	6-10	12-4
Against the Spread Record	6-10	5-9	10-6
Over/Under Record	6-9	5-11	11-5
ATS as Favorite	1-0	2-4	7-3
ATS as Underdog	5-10	3-5	3-3
Straight Up Home	3-4	4-3	6-2
ATS Home	4-3	3-3	3-4
Over/Under Home	3-4	3-4	6-1
ATS as Home Favorite	1-0	2-3	3-3
ATS as a Home Dog	3-3	1-0	0-1
Straight Up Away	1-7	2-6	6-2
ATS Away	2-6	2-5	6-2
Over/Under Away	3-4	2-6	4-4
ATS Away Favorite	0-0	0-1	3-0
ATS Away Dog	2-6	2-4	3-2
Six Point Teaser Record	9-7	10-6	13-3
Seven Point Teaser Record	9-7	11-5	13-3
Ten Point Teaser Record	10-6	11-5	13-3

OAK-3

His 2007-2010 Raiders lines ranked 27th, 30th, 31st, and 26th. In 2011, Cable inherited a Seahawks line that ranked 14th in pass protection the year before. His Seattle lines ranked 24th, 20th, 32nd, 24th, 30th, 25th, and 25th.

In the four years preceding Cable's hire, the Raiders' offensive line ranked third, fourth, first, and seventh in pass protection. They fell to 25th in Cable's first year.

13 years in the league, and Cable's offensive lines have ranked better than bottom ten *once* with an average ranking of 27th. With Incognito, **Rodney Hudson**, and **Gabe Jackson** manning Oakland's interior line and **Trent Brown** bookended by 2018 top-15 pick **Kolton Miller** at tackle, there are no excuses for Cable's unit to finish below average in pass protection this year.

Pass protection is of utmost 2019 importance after **Derek Carr** struggled mightily under pressure last year. He absorbed the league's fourth-highest sack rate and was one of the NFL's easiest quarterbacks to take down. Carr's passer rating when pressured ranked 30th among 39 QBs.
(cont'd - see OAK-4)

2019 Rest Analysis

Team More Rest	2
Opp More Rest	2
Net Rest Edge	0
Week 2 Edge	-1
Week 3 Edge	0
Week 4 Edge	0
Week 5 Edge	0
Week 7 Edge	8
Week 8 Edge	0
Week 9 Edge	0
Week 10 Edge	0
Week 11 Edge	3
Week 12 Edge	0
Week 13 Edge	-6
Week 14 Edge	0
Week 15 Edge	0
Week 16 Edge	0
Week 17 Edge	0

Health by Unit*

2018 Rk	19
2017 Rk	8
2018 v 2017 Rk	25
Off Rk	16
Def Rk	21
QB Rk	1
RB Rk	26
WR Rk	18
TE Rk	3
Oline Rk	21
Dline Rk	
LB Rk	1
DB Rk	10

*Based on the work of Football Outsiders

2018 Weekly Betting Lines (wks 1-16)

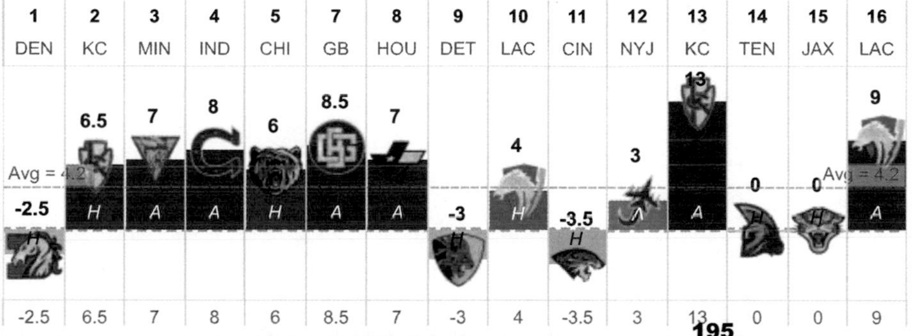

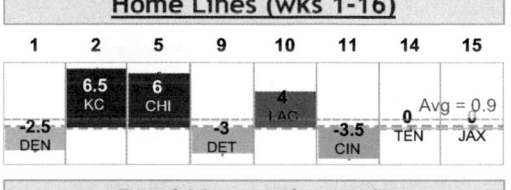

1	2	3	4	5	6	7	8	9	10	11	12	13	14	15	16
DEN	KC	MIN	IND	CHI	GB	HOU	DET	LAC	CIN	NYJ	KC	TEN	JAX	LAC	
-2.5	6.5	7	8	6	8.5	7	-3	4	-3.5	3	13	0	0	9	

Avg = 4.2

Home Lines (wks 1-16)

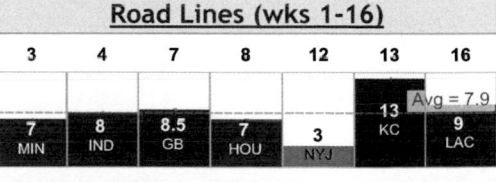

1	2	5	9	10	11	14	15
-2.5 DEN	6.5 KC	6 CHI	-3 DET	4 LAC	-3.5 CIN	0 TEN	0 JAX

Avg = 0.9

Road Lines (wks 1-16)

3	4	5	7	8	12	13	16
7 MIN	8 IND	8.5 GB	7 HOU		3 NYJ	13 KC	9 LAC

Avg = 7.9

Oakland Raiders
2018 Play Analysis

2018 Play Tendencies

All Pass %	61%
All Pass Rk	12
All Rush %	39%
All Rush Rk	21
1 Score Pass %	58%
1 Score Pass Rk	14
2017 1 Score Pass %	57%
2017 1 Score Pass Rk	17
2018 Pass Increase %	1%
Pass Increase Rk	15
1 Score Rush %	42%
1 Score Rush Rk	19
Up Pass %	49%
Up Pass Rk	19
Up Rush %	51%
Up Rush Rk	14
Down Pass %	67%
Down Pass Rk	13
Down Rush %	33%
Down Rush Rk	20

2018 Down & Distance Tendencies

Down	Distance	Total Plays	Pass Rate	Run Rate	Play Success %
1	Short (1-3)	5	40%	60%	40%
	Med (4-7)	13	54%	46%	54%
	Long (8-10)	295	47%	53%	55%
	XL (11+)	21	71%	29%	43%
2	Short (1-3)	57	32%	68%	54%
	Med (4-7)	79	61%	39%	59%
	Long (8-10)	87	68%	32%	48%
	XL (11+)	33	82%	18%	30%
3	Short (1-3)	48	63%	38%	56%
	Med (4-7)	43	95%	5%	37%
	Long (8-10)	32	91%	9%	34%
	XL (11+)	24	92%	8%	13%
4	Short (1-3)	6	50%	50%	50%
	Med (4-7)	1	0%	100%	100%

Shotgun %:

Under Center	Shotgun
40%	60%

37% AVG 63%

Run Rate:

Under Center	Shotgun
64%	24%

68% AVG 23%

Pass Rate:

Under Center	Shotgun
36%	76%

32% AVG 77%

Short Yardage Intelligence:

2nd and Short Run

Run Freq	Run Rk	NFL Run Freq Avg	Run 1D Rate	Run NFL 1D Avg
60%	24	65%	56%	68%

2nd and Short Pass

Pass Freq	Pass Rk	NFL Pass Freq Avg	Pass 1D Rate	Pass NFL 1D Avg
40%	9	35%	65%	56%

Most Frequent Play

Down	Distance	Play Type	Player	Total Plays	Play Success %
1	Short (1-3)	RUSH	Doug Martin	2	50%
	Med (4-7)	RUSH	Doug Martin	4	50%
	Long (8-10)	RUSH	Doug Martin	80	59%
	XL (11+)	PASS	Jalen Richard	3	67%
		RUSH	Doug Martin	3	33%
2	Short (1-3)	RUSH	Doug Martin	20	45%
	Med (4-7)	RUSH	Doug Martin	15	47%
	Long (8-10)	PASS	Jordy Nelson	11	64%
	XL (11+)	PASS	Doug Martin	5	20%
			Jared Cook	5	80%
3	Short (1-3)	RUSH	Doug Martin	9	67%
	Med (4-7)	PASS	Jared Cook	12	67%
	Long (8-10)	PASS	Jared Cook	5	40%
			Jordy Nelson	5	40%
	XL (11+)	PASS	Jalen Richard	4	25%

Most Successful Play*

Down	Distance	Play Type	Player	Total Plays	Play Success %
1	Long (8-10)	PASS	Lee Smith	5	80%
2	Short (1-3)	RUSH	Marshawn Lynch	11	64%
	Med (4-7)	PASS	Jordy Nelson	9	89%
	Long (8-10)	PASS	Seth Roberts	6	67%
	XL (11+)	PASS	Jared Cook	5	80%
3	Short (1-3)	PASS	Amari Cooper	5	80%
	Med (4-7)	PASS	Jared Cook	12	67%
	Long (8-10)	PASS	Jared Cook	5	40%
			Jordy Nelson	5	40%

*Minimum 5 plays to qualify

2018 Weekly Snap Rates

Wk	Opp	Score	Jordy Nelson	Jared Cook	Seth Roberts	Marcell Ateman	Doug Martin	Amari Cooper	Brandon LaFell	Martavis Bryant	Marshawn Lynch
1	LA	L 33-13	68 (97%)	64 (91%)	45 (64%)		9 (13%)	66 (94%)			24 (34%)
2	DEN	L 20-19	54 (83%)	52 (80%)	22 (34%)		16 (25%)	54 (83%)	7 (11%)	26 (40%)	42 (65%)
3	MIA	L 28-20	55 (72%)	62 (82%)			13 (17%)	60 (79%)	33 (43%)	35 (46%)	42 (55%)
4	CLE	W 45-42	80 (87%)	76 (83%)	30 (33%)		6 (7%)	80 (87%)		40 (43%)	50 (54%)
5	LAC	L 26-10	47 (89%)	48 (91%)	28 (53%)		6 (11%)	51 (96%)		13 (25%)	21 (40%)
6	SEA	L 27-3	57 (95%)	51 (85%)	44 (73%)		6 (10%)	12 (20%)		43 (72%)	30 (50%)
8	IND	L 42-28	45 (90%)	31 (62%)	30 (60%)		28 (56%)		46 (92%)	7 (14%)	
9	SF	L 34-3	43 (75%)	34 (60%)	32 (56%)		26 (46%)		53 (93%)	21 (37%)	
10	LAC	L 20-6	43 (68%)	37 (59%)	28 (44%)		30 (48%)		57 (90%)	35 (56%)	
11	ARI	W 23-21		39 (57%)	47 (69%)	65 (96%)	14 (21%)		37 (54%)		
12	BAL	L 34-17	52 (90%)	32 (55%)	39 (67%)	48 (83%)	28 (48%)				
13	KC	L 40-33	69 (91%)	55 (72%)	59 (78%)	62 (82%)	40 (53%)				
14	PIT	W 24-21	63 (94%)	57 (85%)	52 (78%)	50 (75%)	33 (49%)				
15	CIN	L 30-16	57 (97%)	52 (88%)	40 (68%)	49 (83%)	27 (46%)				
16	DEN	W 27-14	49 (79%)	34 (55%)	30 (48%)	47 (76%)	34 (55%)				
17	KC	L 35-3	59 (89%)	43 (65%)	43 (65%)	49 (74%)	43 (65%)				
	Grand Total		841 (86%)	767 (73%)	569 (59%)	370 (81%)	359 (36%)	323 (77%)	233 (64%)	220 (42%)	209 (50%)

Personnel Groupings

Personnel	Team %	NFL Avg	Succ. %
1-1 [3WR]	67%	65%	47%
1-2 [2WR]	12%	17%	57%
2-1 [2WR]	8%	8%	57%
2-2 [1WR]	7%	3%	38%
1-3 [1WR]	4%	3%	45%

Grouping Tendencies

Personnel	Pass Rate	Pass Succ. %	Run Succ. %
1-1 [3WR]	68%	45%	53%
1-2 [2WR]	67%	58%	55%
2-1 [2WR]	43%	65%	51%
2-2 [1WR]	12%	38%	39%
1-3 [1WR]	35%	57%	38%

Red Zone Targets (min 3)

Receiver	All	Inside 5	6-10	11-20
Jared Cook	10	2	6	2
Brandon LaFell	5	1	1	3
Jordy Nelson	5		3	2
Marshawn Lynch	5	1	3	1
Amari Cooper	4		3	1
Lee Smith	3	3		
Martavis Bryant	3		1	2

Red Zone Rushes (min 3)

Rusher	All	Inside 5	6-10	11-20
Doug Martin	31	11	6	14
Marshawn Lynch	15	3	5	7
Jalen Richard	8	2	1	5
DeAndre Washington	7	2	2	3

Early Down Target Rate

	RB	TE	WR
	29%	21%	50%
	23%	21%	56%
		NFL AVG	

Overall Target Success %

	RB	TE	WR
	50%	60%	55%
	#8	#6	#9

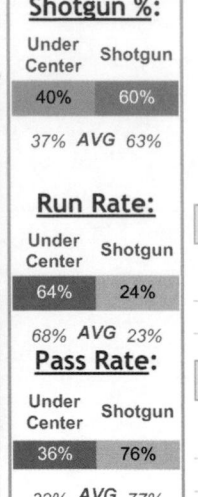

196

Oakland Raiders 2018 Passing Recap & 2019 Outlook

To add further context to **Derek Carr**'s solid first season under **Jon Gruden**, last year's Raiders faced the NFL's fifth-toughest schedule of pass defenses and fourth-hardest pass-rush slate. Carr played 11 games against top-13 pass defenses. But with the exception of outdueling **Hue Jackson**'s Browns last Week 4, the Raiders didn't win a single game when opponents scored over 21 points. And their 2019 schedule is chock full of high-scoring teams.

Looking at this chapter's final page, Carr was solid on first- and second-level throws, and he was solid with and without play action. He was solid against both man and zone coverages. But the Raiders now need Carr to take the step from acceptable and solid to game winner.

2018 Standard Passing Table

QB	Comp	Att	Comp %	Yds	YPA	TDs	INT	Sacks	Rating	Rk
Derek Carr	381	555	69%	4,043	7.3	19	10	49	94	22
NFL Avg			62%		7.0				87.5	

2018 Advanced Passing Table

QB	Success %	EDSR Passing Success %	20+ Yd Pass Gains	20+ Yd Pass %	30+ Yd Pass Gains	30+ Yd Pass %	Avg. Air Yds per Comp	Avg. YAC per Comp	20+ Air Yd Comp	20+ Air Yd %
Derek Carr	48%	54%	52	9.0%	20	4.0%	5.2	5.4	23	4%
NFL Avg	44%	48%	29.5	8.4%	12.5	3.7%	5.8	5.1	14.5	6%

Interception Rates by Down

Yards to Go	1st Dwn	2nd Dwn	3rd Dwn	4th Dwn	Total
1 & 2	33.3%	0.0%	0.0%	0.0%	2.5%
3, 4, 5	0.0%	6.8%	0.0%	0.0%	3.3%
6 - 9	0.0%	0.0%	0.0%	0.0%	0.0%
10 - 14	2.1%	2.9%	0.0%		2.1%
15+	0.0%	0.0%	0.0%		0.0%
Total	**2.3%**	**2.4%**	**0.0%**	**0.0%**	**1.7%**

3rd Down Passing - Short of Sticks Analysis

QB	Avg. Yds to Go	Avg. YIA (of Comp)	Avg Yds Short	Short of Sticks Rate	Short Rk
Derek Carr	7.9	5.3	-2.6	61%	34
NFL Avg	7.8	6.4	-1.4	60%	

Air Yds vs YAC

	Air Yds %	YAC %	Rk
	49%	51%	32
	53%	48%	

Derek Carr Rating All Downs

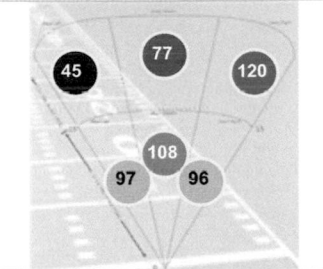

Derek Carr Rating Early Downs

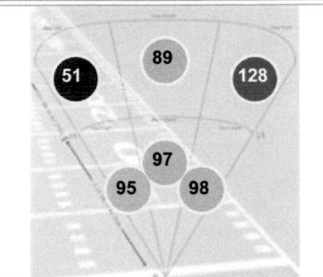

2018 Receiving Recap & 2019 Outlook

The Raiders' 2018 leading receiver was 31-year-old TE **Jared Cook**. Their second-leading receiver was **Jordy Nelson**, who retired after the season. It would be difficult for this year's Raiders to *not* outplay last year's skill-position corps. **Antonio Brown** gives Carr a Hall of Fame-caliber No. 1 receiver, and **Tyrell Williams** was underrated throughout his Chargers career. At tight end, I am intrigued by former Georgia Tech WR **Darren Waller**. Signed off the Ravens' practice squad after Thanksgiving last year, Waller caught all six of his targets. He is a freak athlete with 4.46 speed and a wide catching radius.

Player *Min 50 Targets	Targ	Comp %	YPA	Rating	Success %	Success Rk	Missed YPA Rk	YAS % Rk	YTS % Rk	TDs
Jared Cook	101	67%	8.9	98.5	57%	32	26	43	67	6
Amari Cooper	94	70%	9.5	116.2	59%	21	12	11	87	5
Jordy Nelson	88	72%	8.4	98.6	60%	14	72	36	77	2
Jalen Richard	81	84%	7.5	97.9	53%	52	15	123	26	0
Seth Roberts	65	69%	7.6	101.7	52%	59	48	106	38	2

Directional Passer Rating Delivered

Receiver	Short Left	Short Middle	Short Right	Deep Left	Deep Middle	Deep Right	Player Total
Jared Cook	122	127	70	80	96	114	98
Jordy Nelson	76	96	116	82	96	96	99
Jalen Richard	87	105	100	119		40	98
Seth Roberts	97	91	81	44	82	144	102
Amari Cooper	91	121	90	56		110	93
Marcell Ateman	82	66	78	74	40	96	74
Martavis Bryant	95	117	91	36	40	119	71
Doug Martin	91	59	84				85
Marshawn Lynch	91	60	77				85
Brandon LaFell	80	142	142	119		40	139
Lee Smith	127	119	120				134
Darren Waller	94	119	92				119
Team Total	96	110	96	45	79	123	99

2018 Rushing Recap & 2019 Outlook

First-round pick **Josh Jacobs** should be an immediate upgrade on **Doug Martin**, who returns in Oakland's No. 2 role. Jacobs gives the backfield explosiveness after Martin and **Marshawn Lynch** were deliberate and lacked suddenness as runners last year. Martin and Lynch did both finish top 20 in Success Rate, but Jacobs was one of college football's top tackle-breaking backs at Alabama, showing outstanding vision and punishing violence on the ground.

Player *Min 50 Rushes	Rushes	YPC	Success %	Success Rk	Missed YPA Rk	YTS % Rk	YAS % Rk	Early Down Success %	Early Down Success Rk	TDs
Doug Martin	172	4.2	52%	16	7	7	52	52%	17	4
Marshawn Lynch	90	4.2	53%	13	8	10	43	53%	12	3
Jalen Richard	55	4.7	42%	58	25	71	38	44%	52	1

Yards per Carry by Direction

7.6 | 3.8 | 4.1 | 3.7 | 3.5 | 5.0 | 3.7
LT | LG | C | RG | RT

Directional Run Frequency

8% | 14% | 15% | 37% | 9% | 12% | 4%
LT | LG | C | RG | RT

But when Carr was clean, his passer rating shot to 104.8 and he ranked No. 9 among qualified quarterbacks in accuracy. I project this year's Raiders to face the league's sixth-toughest schedule of opposing pass rushes.

Initial impressions of Carr and Gruden's relationship where highlighted by Gruden's sideline frustrations on Monday Night Football in Week 1 against the Rams. The next week, Carr bounced back. He became the NFL's first-ever quarterback to complete over 90% of his passes with at least 27 attempts, going 29-of-32 with 9.0 yards per attempt and a 73% Success Rate against Denver.

Examining the Raiders' Early Down Success Rate on page two of this chapter, Carr's game against the Broncos came in by-far Oakland's best performance of 2018. Unfortunately, the Raiders lost the game in the final seconds.

Carr's first season under Gruden still wasn't a failure, especially in context of the Raiders' sorry supporting cast. Gruden is a creative offensive mind who gets on players, and if Carr's skin is thick enough to hold up, this has the potential to be a successful marriage.

While I maintain doubts about Carr's worthiness of his five-year, $125 million contract, his cap hits from 2019 onward are more than palatable in this era of quarterback deals. He hits the 2020 cap for **Nick Foles-Alex Smith** money, and slightly north of **Andy Dalton** and **Joe Flacco**, who have the NFL's lowest starting-quarterback cap hits in 2020.

But the Raiders' biggest 2019 concern should *not* be their offense.

Their biggest concern is a defense that was

(cont'd - see OAK-5)

Oakland Raiders Fantasy Corner

A "trust the tape" prospect who never started at Alabama and became the first running back since 1998 to be drafted in the first round after never totaling 1,000 yards in a college season, **Josh Jacobs** indeed shined in his opportunities under **Nick Saban**, scoring 11 TDs on 120 carries as a 2018 junior and gaining a first down or hitting pay dirt on a nation-high 41% of his runs. Jacobs lacks homerun-hitting long speed (4.60/4.63) but runs with violence and quick feet between the tackles, drops hammers in the blitz-pickup game, and is a dangerous receiver. In Oakland, Jacobs offers immediate 300-touch potential as an RB2 pick with RB1 upside.

- Evan Silva

2018 Situational Usage by Player & Position

Usage Rate by Score

		Being Blown Out (14+)	Down Big (9-13)	One Score	Large Lead (9-13)	Blowout Lead (14+)
RUSH	Doug Martin	19%	13%	57%	9%	2%
	Jalen Richard	25%	13%	55%	5%	2%
	Marshawn Lynch	14%	1%	81%	3%	
	Jordy Nelson			100%		
	Seth Roberts		33%	67%		
	Amari Cooper			100%		
	DeAndre Washington	28%	21%	48%		3%
	Martavis Bryant			100%		
	Total	19%	10%	63%	6%	2%
PASS	Doug Martin	26%	13%	57%		4%
	Jalen Richard	28%	24%	43%	1%	3%
	Marshawn Lynch	29%	6%	65%		
	Jared Cook	24%	21%	55%		
	Jordy Nelson	19%	17%	52%	5%	6%
	Seth Roberts	33%	18%	43%		6%
	Amari Cooper	3%	3%	84%	10%	
	DeAndre Washington			100%		
	Martavis Bryant	21%	4%	75%		
	Brandon LaFell	19%	25%	56%		
	Johnny Holton		100%			
	Total	23%	17%	55%	2%	3%

Share of Offensive Plays by Type

	Doug Martin	Jalen Richard	Marshawn Lynch	Jared Cook	Jordy Nelson	Seth Roberts	Amari Cooper	DeAndre Washington	Martavis Bryant	Brandon LaFell	Johnny Holton
RUSH	49%	16%	25%		0%	1%	0%	8%	1%		
PASS	6%	19%	4%	21%	19%	13%	8%	0%	6%	4%	0%
ALL	26%	17%	14%	11%	10%	7%	4%	4%	4%	2%	0%

Positional Target Distribution vs NFL Average

		NFL Wide				Team Only			
		Left	Middle	Right	Total	Left	Middle	Right	Total
Deep	WR	33%	17%	31%	**81%**	32%	13%	26%	**71%**
	TE	5%	4%	7%	**15%**	7%	8%	11%	**26%**
	RB	1%	0%	2%	**3%**	1%		1%	**3%**
	All	39%	22%	39%	**100%**	40%	21%	39%	**100%**
Short	WR	20%	14%	21%	**55%**	21%	12%	16%	**48%**
	TE	6%	6%	8%	**20%**	6%	7%	11%	**24%**
	RB	10%	5%	10%	**25%**	12%	7%	9%	**28%**
	All	36%	25%	39%	**100%**	38%	26%	36%	**100%**
Total		37%	24%	39%	**100%**	39%	25%	36%	**100%**

Positional Success Rates vs NFL Average

		NFL Wide				Team Only			
		Left	Middle	Right	Total	Left	Middle	Right	Total
Deep	WR	40%	50%	40%	**42%**	35%	22%	58%	**41%**
	TE	44%	54%	41%	**45%**	40%	50%	63%	**53%**
	RB	36%	33%	43%	**40%**	100%		0%	**50%**
	All	40%	50%	40%	**42%**	38%	33%	57%	**44%**
Short	WR	55%	60%	52%	**55%**	58%	69%	55%	**59%**
	TE	55%	62%	54%	**57%**	73%	60%	55%	**61%**
	RB	46%	54%	45%	**47%**	49%	48%	51%	**50%**
	All	53%	59%	51%	**54%**	57%	61%	54%	**57%**
Total		50%	58%	49%	**51%**	55%	57%	55%	**55%**

Division History: Season Wins & 2019 Projection

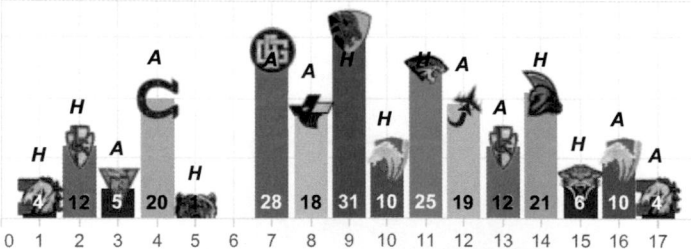

2015 Wins | 2016 Wins | 2017 Wins | 2018 Wins | Forecast 2019 Wins

Rank of 2019 Defensive Pass Efficiency Faced by Week

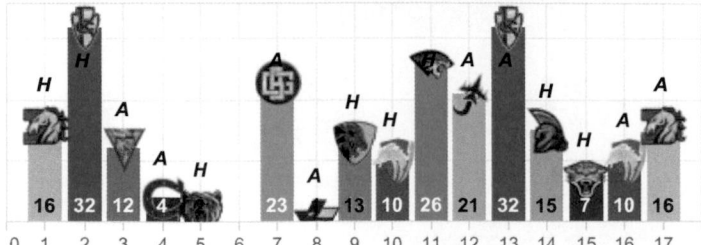

Rank of 2019 Defensive Rush Efficiency Faced by Week

2018 Detailed Analytics Summary
Success by Play Type & Primary Personnel Groupings

Type	1-1 [3WR]	1-2 [2WR]	2-1 [2WR]	2-2 [1WR]	1-3 [1WR]	1-0 [4WR]	0-1 [4WR]	2-3 [0WR]	2-0 [3WR]	0-0 [5WR]	ALL
PASS	45% (458)	58% (77)	65% (34)	38% (8)	57% (14)	43% (7)	25% (4)	50% (2)			48% (604)
RUSH	53% (211)	55% (38)	51% (45)	39% (57)	38% (26)	33% (3)		50% (2)	33% (3)	100% (1)	50% (386)
All	47% (669)	57% (115)	57% (79)	38% (65)	45% (40)	40% (10)	25% (4)	50% (4)	33% (3)	100% (1)	48% (990)

Format Success Rate (Total # of Plays)

Receiving Success by Top-4 Personnel Groupings
(Min 50 targets)

POS	Player	1-1 [3WR]	1-2 [2WR]	2-1 [2WR]	1-0 [4WR]	4 Grp Total
RB	Jalen Richard	48% (69) 6.9, 95.2	88% (8) 9.3, 105.2	100% (2) 15.0, 118.8	50% (2) 15.0, 118.8	53% (81) 7.5, 97.9
TE	Jared Cook	52% (77) 8.2, 90.4	69% (16) 9.9, 121.4	100% (3) 21.0, 118.8		56% (96) 8.9, 98.2
WR	Jordy Nelson	59% (68) 7.6, 101.2	75% (8) 8.6, 102.6	78% (9) 16.7, 118.8		62% (85) 8.7, 105.9
WR	Seth Roberts	54% (61) 8.0, 106.3	0% (1) 0.0, 39.6			53% (62) 7.8, 104.6
WR	Amari Cooper	74% (23) 10.3, 102.8	67% (6) 6.8, 86.1	0% (1) 3.0, 79.2		70% (30) 9.3, 99.3

Format Line 1: Success Rate (Total # of Plays) Line 2: YPA, Passer Rating

Rushing Success by Top-4 Personnel Groupings
(Min 25 carries)

Rusher (Last, First)	1-1 [3WR]	2-2 [1WR]	2-1 [2WR]	1-2 [2WR]	4 Grp Total
Martin Doug	55% (97) 4.6	42% (26) 3.0	56% (18) 5.7	67% (15) 4.1	54% (156) 4.4
Lynch Marshawn	60% (42) 5.6	50% (12) 1.3	50% (10) 3.1	54% (13) 4.3	56% (77) 4.4
Richard Jalen	47% (38) 5.0	0% (1) 0.0	56% (9) 5.6	20% (5) 0.8	45% (53) 4.6
Washington DeAndre	53% (17) 4.4	80% (5) 3.8	50% (6) 2.7	50% (2) 2.5	57% (30) 3.8

Format Line 1: Success Rate (Total # of Plays) Line 2: YPC

Passing by Coverage Scheme

Zone	54% (233) 7.5, 97.6
M2M	59% (215) 8.2, 97.9
Screen	50% (50) 5.6, 90.1
Combo	31% (13) 4.9, 61.1

Passing by Route

Curl	56% (71) 7.4, 98.4
Flat	52% (64) 5.2, 88.5
Screen	53% (53) 6.3, 93.1
Out	63% (51) 5.4, 91.5
Slant	72% (46) 10.0, 108.4
Dig	56% (27) 9.3, 112.0

Throw Types

Level 1	59% (381) 6.9, 99.8
Level 2	58% (84) 11.2, 125.2
Level 3	29% (41) 9.1, 33.5
Sidearm	30% (10) 5.8, 90.8
Shovel	29% (7) 4.0, 83.3

QB Drop Types

3 Step	51% (220) 7.5, 87.1
0/1 Step	56% (151) 7.3, 109.2
5 Step	63% (79) 10.4, 115.1
7 Step	58% (24) 7.3, 95.0
Basic Screen	39% (23) 5.6, 90.0
Designed Rollout Right	70% (20) 5.4, 95.4

QB State at Pass

Planted	58% (368) 8.2, 98.0
Shuffling	48% (69) 6.1, 101.0
Moving	51% (61) 5.5, 94.6

Play Action

	Play Action	No P/A
Under Center	64% (66) 7.9, 102.1	60% (58) 8.5, 106.5
Shotgun	64% (28) 7.3, 96.9	52% (374) 7.5, 97.2
ALL	64% (94) 7.7, 100.8	53% (432) 7.7, 98.5

Run Types

Outside Zone	44% (106) 4.0
Inside Zone	60% (105) 4.2
Lead	48% (42) 3.8
Power	53% (36) 3.1
Pitch	38% (16) 6.4
Stretch	67% (9) 6.3

OAK-5

historically awful last season, ranking dead last in pass rush and pass-defense efficiency. Managing a league-low 13 sacks, the Raiders sorely missed **Khalil Mack**. Which is ironic because Oakland received an award at this year's MIT Sloan Sports Analytics Conference for "best transaction" in pro sports for the Mack trade.

Yet the Mack deal caused the Raiders to field the league's worst pass rush and overall pass defense, playing a huge role in Oakland managing the fourth-worst record in the league. Yes, the Raiders received a 2019 first-rounder plus first- and third-round picks in 2020. But the Raiders used that initial first-rounder on – of all positions – a _running back_.

Now knowing a major part of Oakland's Mack compensation, I wonder if the analytics voters would take back the award. Analytics have definitively shown passing is many times more valuable than rushing. The Raiders sacrificed their pass defense for a running back.

Not even the Raiders believed they won the MIT analytics award. Called by Sloan Sports Conference director **Daryl Morey** to be informed of the accolade, the Raiders' team president hung up the phone believing he was being prank called. Somehow, the analytics voters deemed the trade "better" than the NBA champion Raptors' acquisition of **Kawhi Leonard**.

The Raiders' reach for DE **Clelin Ferrell** at No. 4 overall was egregious, but it certainly filled a need. I would have preferred a trade down to accumulate more draft capital. Gruden preferred making sure he got his guy. The Raiders did need a running back and got **Josh Jacobs**, and SS **Johnathan Abram** at No. 27 overall also addressed a glaring roster weakness. Talent wise, there is no question the Raiders' starting 22 is better now than it was to end last season.

Unfortunately, I project the Raiders to face the NFL's third-toughest 2019 schedule, including the league's fourth-toughest slate of opposing defenses and sixth-toughest schedule of enemy offenses. I don't believe Oakland's defense will be strong enough to deal with the offenses it will face, making it incumbent upon Gruden and Carr to outscore opponents.

Being featured on HBO's Hard Knocks with a volatile cast of personalities ensure it'll be a fascinating journey.

Philadelphia Eagles

Coaches (Prior Yrs)

Head Coach:
Doug Pederson (Calls Plays) (3 yrs)
Offensive Coordinator:
Mike Groh (1 yr)
Defensive Coordinator:
Jim Schwartz (2 yrs)

EASY   HARD

2019 Forecast

Wins	Div Rank
10	#1

Past Records

2018: 9-7
2017: 13-3
2016: 7-9

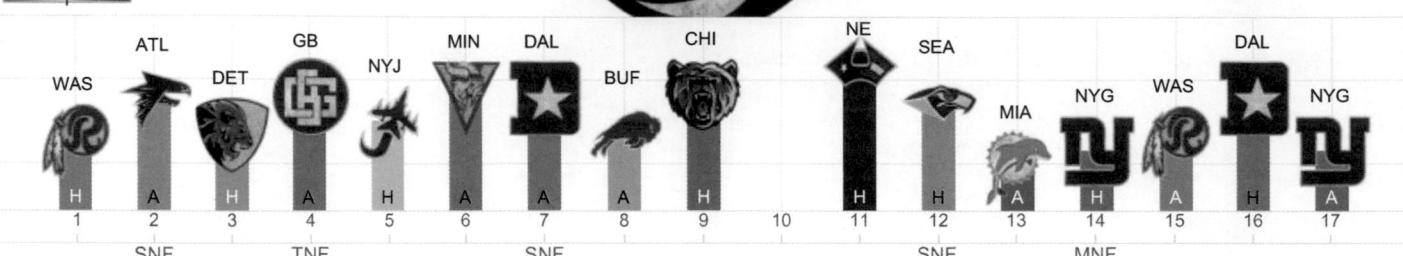

	WAS	ATL	DET	GB	NYJ	MIN	DAL	BUF	CHI		NE	SEA	MIA	NYG	WAS	DAL	NYG
	H	A	H	A	H	A	A	A	H		H	H	A	H	A	H	A
	1	2	3	4	5	6	7	8	9	10	11	12	13	14	15	16	17

SNF (2)   TNF (4)   SNF (7)   SNF (12)   MNF (14)

Key Players Lost

Player	New
Chris Long (DE)	Retired
D.J. Alexander (ILB)	JAC
Golden Tate (WR)	NYG
Haloti Ngata (DT)	Retired
Jordan Hicks (ILB)	ARI
Jordan Matthews (WR)	SF
Michael Bennett (DE)	NE
Nick Foles (QB)	JAC

Average Line	# Games Favored	# Games Underdog
-3.1	11	4

2019 Philadelphia Eagles Overview

For years, TV Networks have filled broadcasts with graphic packages illustrating third down conversion rates. Third downs are certainly important, but the only way to reach them is to fail on first and second down. Instead, I focused on creating an efficiency metric for early-down success rate, or EDSR.

I've found that EDSR was more valuable than I'd initially believed. Among all basic statistics, turnover differential correlates most strongly with wins and losses, with teams who finish with a 2+ turnover margin winning 87% of the time. But in games where neither team had a 2+ turnover margin and neither team was favored by 9 or more points, no statistic better correlates to wins and losses than EDSR.

There are many reasons why the Eagles have been great ever since a 7-9 finish in 2016, but the metric which they have most dominated is EDSR.

In 2017 they were one of two teams to rank top 10 both offensively and defensively on early-down efficiency. In games that **Carson Wentz** started in 2018, they also ranked in the top 10 on both offense and defense, something only two other teams accomplished.

In total EDSR (combining both offensive and defensive success rates), the Eagles are one of just six teams to finish both 2017 and 2018 in the top 10, along with the Rams, Patriots, Chargers, Steelers, and Ravens.

In total, the Eagles won the EDSR battle in ten of Carson Wentz's eleven starts,

*(cont'd - see **PHI2**)*

Key Free Agents/ Trades Added

Player	AAV (MM)
DeSean Jackson (WR)	Trade
Hassan Ridgeway (DE)	Trade
Jordan Howard (RB)	Trade
L.J. Fort (ILB)	$1.8
Malik Jackson (DT)	$10
Vinny Curry (DE)	$2.2

Drafted Players

Rd	Pk	Player (College)
1	22	OT - Andre Dillard (Washington State)
2	53	RB - Miles Sanders (Penn State)
	57	WR - JJ Arcega-Whiteside (Stanford)
4*	138	DE - Shareef Miller (Penn State)
5	167	QB - Clayton Thorson (Northwestern)

Regular Season Wins: Past & Current Proj

Forecast 2019 Wins	10
2018 Wins	9
Forecast 2018 Wins	10.5
2017 Wins	13
2016 Wins	7
2015 Wins	7

1 3 5 7 9 11 13 15

Lineup & Cap Hits

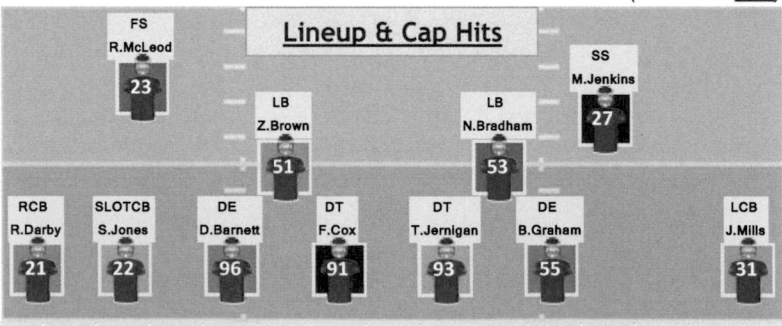

FS R.McLeod 23
SS M.Jenkins 27
LB Z.Brown 51
LB N.Bradham 53
RCB R.Darby 21
SLOTCB S.Jones 22
DE D.Barnett 96
DT F.Cox 91
DT T.Jernigan 93
DE B.Graham 55
LCB J.Mills 31

LWR A.Jeffery 17
SLOTWR N.Agholor 13
LT J.Peters 71
LG I.Seumalo 73
C J.Kelce 62
RG B.Brooks 79
RT L.Johnson 65
TE Z.Ertz 86
RWR D.Jackson 10
QB C.Wentz 11
RB M.Sanders 26 Rookie

TE2 D.Goedert 88
WR3 J.Arcega-Whiteside 19 Rookie
RB2 J.Howard 24
QB2 N.Sudfeld 7

2019 Cap Dollars

2019 Unit Spending

All DEF / All OFF

Positional Spending

	Rank	Total	2017 Rk
All OFF	13	$101.95M	12
QB	23	$12.08M	18
OL	9	$40.76M	7
RB	22	$6.06M	21
WR	3	$33.16M	17
TE	12	$9.89M	17
All DEF	21	$80.07M	18
DL	12	$36.40M	5
LB	28	$12.69M	30
CB	28	$10.55M	31
S	5	$20.44M	4

yet somehow managed to go just 5-5 in those ten games. How?

In Week 4, the Eagles squandered a 17-3 third-quarter lead over the Titans. In overtime, they received the ball first and kicked an opening-drive field goal, only for Tennessee to put together an 18-play game-winning drive where they convered on 4th-and-15, 4th-and-4, and 4th-and-2 to score a touchdown with five seconds remaining.

In Week 5, they gave up a 64-yard fumble return touchdown to a 330 pound defensive tackle and lost another fumble on 1st-and-goal from the 6.

Two weeks later, at home against the Panthers, they took a 17-0 lead into the fourth quarter before giving up 21 unanswered points and ending their day with a 4th-down sack in the red zone.

It was the second time in their first seven games that the Eagles lost a game where they led by at least 14 points in the second half and at least 7 points at the start of the 4th quarter, a feat that the rest of the league combined would only manage seven times all year.

They're the tenth team in the last thirty years with two such losses in a single season.

A fourth loss saw the Eagles win the EDSR battle, but self-distruct on third down: in a week 14 road match against the Cowboys, the Eagles were much better at avoiding third down, facing nine all game to eighteen for Dallas. The Eagles, however, went 1-of-9 on third down, the Cowboys went 9-of-18, and Dallas managed to win the game on the first possession of overtime.

Carson Wentz signed a contract at the beginning of June that included an NFL-record $107 million in guaranteed money.

This dominance on early downs often gets lost in discussions of whether Wentz deserved a contract of that magnitude.

Also lost is the fact that, despite being nine months removed from a torn ACL and LCL, playing on a team that was among the league leaders in

injuries to its running backs and wide receivers, and playing half of the season with an injured back, Wentz still put together one of the best seasons ever by a third-year quarterback.

In league history, only twelve quarterbacks have finished their third season with more pass attempts and a higher yard-per-attempt passing average than Wentz had in 2018. Adjusted yards per attempt, or AY/A, includes a bonus for touchdowns and a penalty for interceptions; the only third-year player with at least 400 pass attempts and a higher AY/A average than Wentz had in 2018 is classmate Jared Goff.

Wentz certainly wasn't perfect. He turned the ball over ten times

(cont'd - see PHI-3)

2018 Passing Performance

QB	1st Dwn	2nd Dwn	3rd Dwn	
Carson Wentz	56%	53%	37%	Success Rate
	8.2	7.6	6.3	YPA
	102.6	108.6	90.2	Rating
Pass Rate	57%	64%	78%	
NFL AVG	53%	47%	36%	Success Rate
	7.7	7.3	6.9	YPA
	95.1	93.7	87.1	Rating
Pass Rate	53%	62%	80%	

2018 Rushing Performance

Offense	1st Dwn	2nd Dwn	3rd Dwn	
PHI	47%	44%	49%	Success Rate
	3.9	3.6	4.5	YPC
Run Rate	43%	36%	22%	
NFL AVG	48%	46%	51%	Success Rate
	4.5	4.4	4.3	YPC
Run Rate	47%	38%	20%	

2018 Offensive Advanced Metrics

Rank (1 top to 30 bottom)

EDSR Off: 14
30 & In Off: 6
Red Zone Off: 7
3rd Down Off: 18
YPPA Off: 14
YPPT Off: 16
Offensive Efficiency: 16
Pass Efficiency Off: 11
Pass Pro Efficiency Off: 17
RB Pass Eff Off: 23
Rush Efficiency Off: 27
Explosive Pass Off: 21
Explosive Run Off: 17

2018 Defensive Advanced Metrics

Rank (1 top to 30 bottom)

EDSR Def: 5
30 & In Def: 18
Red Zone Def: 9
3rd Down Def: 11
YPPA Def: 14
YPPT Def: 16
Defensive Efficiency: 15
Pass Efficiency Def: 15
Pass Pro Efficiency Def: 26
RB Pass Eff Def: 12
Rush Efficiency Def: 9
Explosive Pass Def: 20
Explosive Run Def: 16

2018 Weekly EDSR & Season Trending Performance

	1	2	3	4	5	6	7	8	10	11	12	13	14	15	16	17	WEEK
	W	L	W	L	L	W	L	W	L	L	W	W	L	W	W	W	RESULT
	ATL	TB	IND	TEN	MIN	NYG	CAR	JAC	DAL	NO	NYG	WAS	DAL	LA	HOU	WAS	OPP
	H	A	H	A	H	A	H	N	H	A	H	H	A	A	H	A	SITE
	6	-6	4	-3	-2	21	-4	6	-7	-41	3	15	-6	7	2	24	MARGIN
	18	21	20	23	21	34	17	24	20	7	25	28	23	30	32	24	PTS
	12	27	16	26	23	13	21	18	27	48	22	13	29	23	30	0	OPP PTS

EDSR by Wk
W=Green
L=Red

OFF/DEF EDSR
Blue=OFF (high=good)
Red=DEF (low=good)

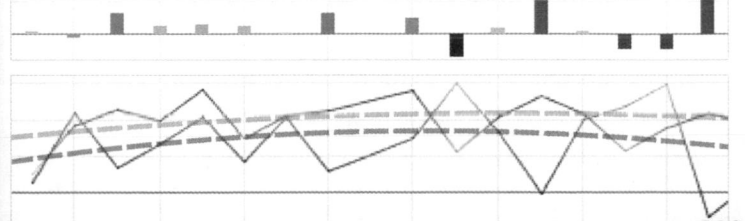

2018 Close Game Records

All 2018 Wins: **9**

FG Games (<=3 pts) W-L: **2-2**
FG Games Win %: **50% (#13)**
FG Games Wins (% of Total Wins): **22% (#21)**

1 Score Games (<=8 pts) W-L: **6-6**
1 Score Games Win %: **50% (#15)**
1 Score Games Wins (% of Total Wins): **67% (#8)**

2018 Critical & Game-Deciding Stats

TO Margin	-6
TO Given	23
INT Given	11
FUM Given	12
TO Taken	17
INT Taken	11
FUM Taken	6
Sack Margin	+3
Sacks	43
Sacks Allow	40
Return TD Margin	-1
Ret TDs	0
Ret TDs Allow	1
Penalty Margin	+15
Penalties	100
Opponent Penalties	115

Philadelphia Eagles 2019 Strength of Schedule In Detail (compared to 2018)

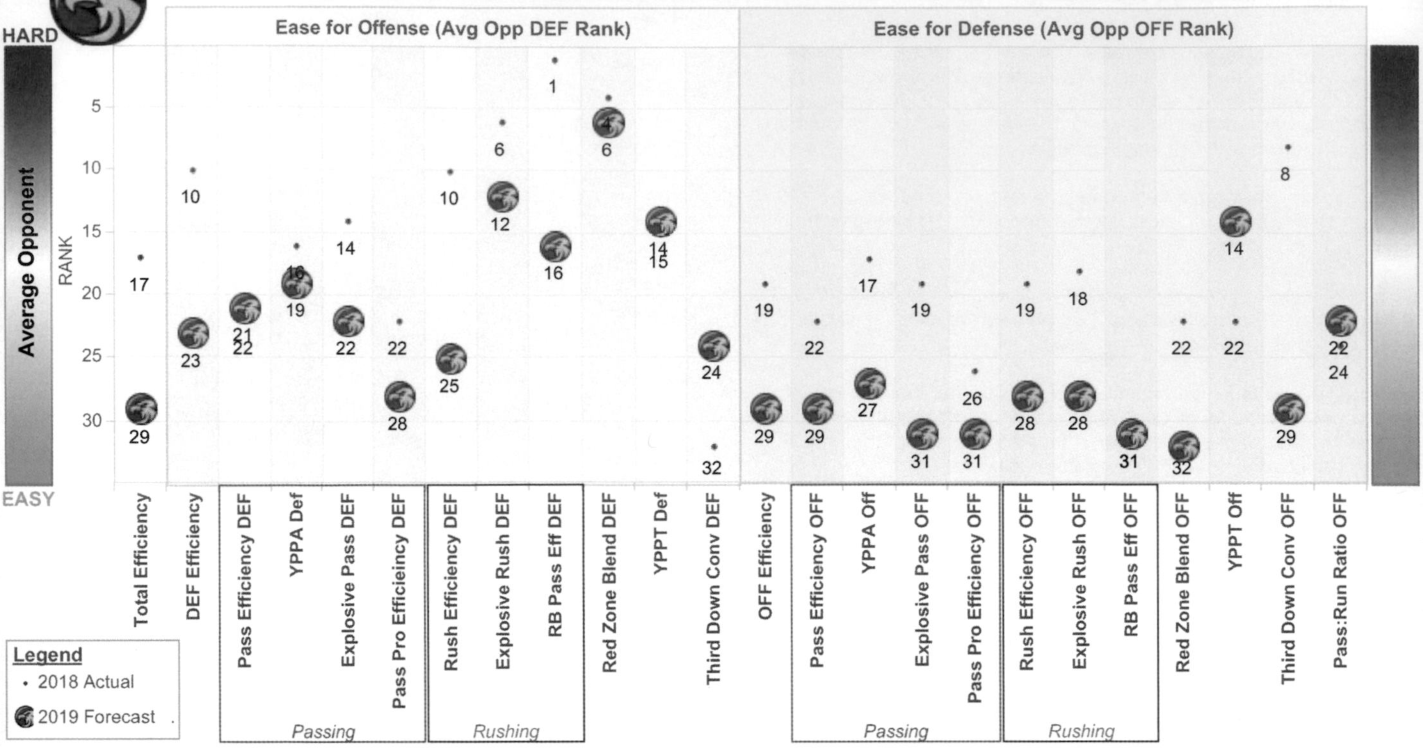

HARD / **EASY**

Ease for Offense (Avg Opp DEF Rank) | **Ease for Defense (Avg Opp OFF Rank)**

Average Opponent RANK

Data points (2019 Forecast / 2018 Actual) by category:

- Total Efficiency: 29 / 17
- DEF Efficiency: 23 / 10
- Pass Efficiency DEF: 21, 22 / 18, 19
- YPPA Def: 19 / 14
- Explosive Pass DEF: 22
- Pass Pro Efficieincy DEF: 28 / 22
- Rush Efficiency DEF: 25 / 10
- Explosive Rush DEF: 12 / 6
- RB Pass Eff DEF: 16
- Red Zone Blend DEF: 6 / 1
- YPPT Def: 14, 15
- Third Down Conv DEF: 24 / 32
- OFF Efficiency: 29 / 19
- Pass Efficiency OFF: 29 / 22
- YPPA Off: 27 / 17
- Explosive Pass OFF: 31 / 19
- Pass Pro Efficiency OFF: 31 / 26
- Rush Efficiency OFF: 28 / 19
- Explosive Rush OFF: 28 / 18
- RB Pass Eff OFF: 31
- Red Zone Blend OFF: 32 / 22
- YPPT Off: 14 / 22
- Third Down Conv OFF: 29 / 8
- Pass:Run Ratio OFF: 22, 24

Passing / *Rushing* (Offense); *Passing* / *Rushing* (Defense)

Legend
- 2018 Actual
- 2019 Forecast

2019 v 2018 Schedule Variances* (OFF=Rank of DEF faced, 2019 vs 2018)

Pass OFF Rank	Pass OFF Blend Rk	Rush OFF Rk	Rush OFF Blend Rk	Pass DEF Rk	Pass DEF Blend Rk	Rush DEF Rk	Rush DEF Blend Rk
13	21	30	31	23	28	26	27

** **1**=Hardest Jump in 2019 schedule from 2018 (aka a much harder schedule in 2019), **32**=Easiest Jump in 2019 schedule from 2018 (aka a much easier schedule in 2019);*
Pass Blend metric blends 4 metrics: Pass Efficiency, YPPA, Explosive Pass & Pass Rush; **Rush Blend** metric blends 3 metrics: Rush Efficiency, Explosive Rush & RB Targets

---

Team Records & Trends

	2018	2017	2016
Average line	-2.1	-4.1	0.7
Average O/U line	45.6	45.5	44.2
Straight Up Record	9-7	13-3	7-9
Against the Spread Record	6-9	10-6	8-8
Over/Under Record	6-9	7-8	8-7
ATS as Favorite	5-7	7-4	3-3
ATS as Underdog	1-2	2-2	4-5
Straight Up Home	5-3	7-1	6-2
ATS Home	2-5	5-3	6-2
Over/Under Home	2-6	3-5	2-6
ATS as Home Favorite	2-5	5-2	3-1
ATS as a Home Dog	0-0	0-1	2-1
Straight Up Away	3-4	6-2	1-7
ATS Away	3-4	5-3	2-6
Over/Under Away	4-2	4-3	6-1
ATS Away Favorite	2-2	2-2	0-2
ATS Away Dog	1-2	2-1	2-4
Six Point Teaser Record	11-4	15-1	13-3
Seven Point Teaser Record	12-4	15-1	13-3
Ten Point Teaser Record	14-2	15-1	13-2

PHI-3

when the score was within a touchdown. His red zone production was down significantly from his potential MVP campaign in 2017. His third-down production was down, as well.

But on early downs, Wentz showed substantial improvement despite the lack of a go-to wide receiver on the outside or any semblance of a running game.

In 2018, Wentz took major strides in early down passing. And he did so with no wide receiver catching over 65 passes & no running back averaging over 4.3 YPC. Wentz delivered a 105.3 rating on early downs (6th of 50 quarterbacks) and his 55 percent success rate ranked second best in the league behind only Drew Brees.

(cont'd - see PHI-4)

2019 Rest Analysis

Team More Rest	0
Opp More Rest	3
Net Rest Edge	-3
Week 2 Edge	0
Week 3 Edge	0
Week 4 Edge	0
Week 5 Edge	-4
Week 6 Edge	0
Week 7 Edge	0
Week 8 Edge	0
Week 9 Edge	0
Week 11 Edge	0
Week 12 Edge	-6
Week 13 Edge	0
Week 14 Edge	0
Week 15 Edge	-1
Week 16 Edge	0
Week 17 Edge	0

Health by Unit*

2018 Rk	
2017 Rk	13
2018 v 2017 Rk	
Off Rk	21
Def Rk	
QB Rk	
RB Rk	
WR Rk	25
TE Rk	1
Oline Rk	2
Dline Rk	
LB Rk	13
DB Rk	

*Based on the work of Football Outsiders

2018 Weekly Betting Lines (wks 1-16)

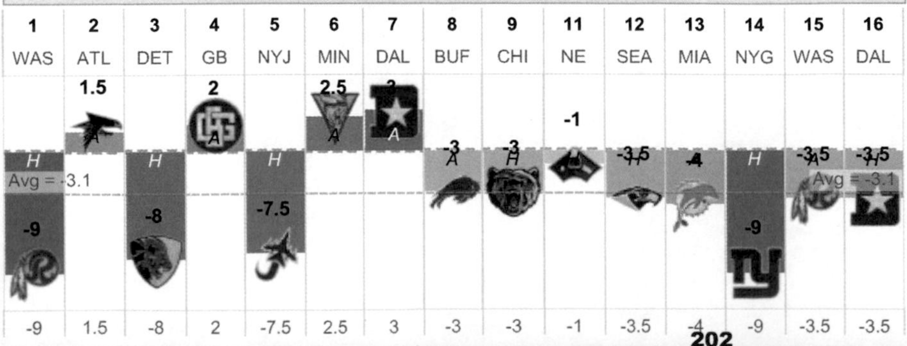

1	2	3	4	5	6	7	8	9	11	12	13	14	15	16
WAS	ATL	DET	GB	NYJ	MIN	DAL	BUF	CHI	NE	SEA	MIA	NYG	WAS	DAL
	1.5		2		2.5	3			-1					
H	*H*	*H*	*H*			*A*	-3	-3	-1	-3.5	-4	*H*	-3.5	-3.5
Avg = -3.1				-7.5			*A*	*H*					Avg = -3.1	
-9		-8										-9		
-9	1.5	-8	2	-7.5	2.5	-3	-3	-3	-1	-3.5	-4	-9	-3.5	-3.5

Home Lines (wks 1-16)

1	3	5	9	11	12	14	16
-9 WAS	-8 DET	-7.5 NYJ	-3 CHI	-1 NE	-3.5 SEA	-9 NYG	-3.5 DAL

Avg = -5.6

Road Lines (wks 1-16)

2	4	6	7	8	13	15
1.5 ATL	2 GB	2.5 MIN	3 DAL	-3 BUF	-4 MIA	-3.5 WAS

Avg = -0.2

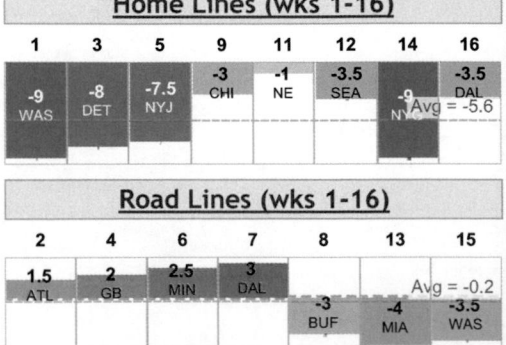

2018 Play Tendencies

All Pass %	62%
All Pass Rk	9
All Rush %	38%
All Rush Rk	24
1 Score Pass %	63%
1 Score Pass Rk	6
2017 1 Score Pass %	59%
2017 1 Score Pass Rk	12
2018 Pass Increase %	4%
Pass Increase Rk	12
1 Score Rush %	37%
1 Score Rush Rk	27
Up Pass %	56%
Up Pass Rk	5
Up Rush %	44%
Up Rush Rk	28
Down Pass %	66%
Down Pass Rk	18
Down Rush %	34%
Down Rush Rk	15

2018 Down & Distance Tendencies

Down	Distance	Total Plays	Pass Rate	Run Rate	Play Success %
1	Short (1-3)	6	83%	17%	33%
	Med (4-7)	12	42%	58%	42%
	Long (8-10)	356	54%	46%	53%
	XL (11+)	18	83%	17%	44%
2	Short (1-3)	44	41%	59%	52%
	Med (4-7)	93	62%	38%	47%
	Long (8-10)	94	66%	34%	44%
	XL (11+)	43	81%	19%	33%
3	Short (1-3)	45	44%	56%	58%
	Med (4-7)	58	88%	12%	50%
	Long (8-10)	32	97%	3%	34%
	XL (11+)	30	87%	13%	17%
		41	1	100%	0%	0%
4	Short (1-3)	13	31%	69%	77%
	Med (4-7)	3	100%	0%	33%

Shotgun %:

Under Center	Shotgun
21%	79%

37% AVG 63%

Run Rate:

Under Center	Shotgun
64%	30%

68% AVG 23%

Pass Rate:

Under Center	Shotgun
36%	70%

32% AVG 77%

Philadelphia Eagles 2018 Play Analysis

Short Yardage Intelligence:

2nd and Short Run

Run Freq	Run Rk	NFL Run Freq Avg	Run 1D Rate	Run NFL 1D Avg
67%	13	65%	67%	68%

2nd and Short Pass

Pass Freq	Pass Rk	NFL Pass Freq Avg	Pass 1D Rate	Pass NFL 1D Avg
33%	19	35%	58%	56%

Most Frequent Play

Down	Distance	Play Type	Player	Total Plays	Play Success %
1	Med (4-7)	RUSH	Darren Sproles	2	100%
	Long (8-10)	PASS	Zach Ertz	55	67%
	XL (11+)	PASS	Alshon Jeffery	4	25%
2	Short (1-3)	RUSH	Jay Ajayi	7	71%
	Med (4-7)	RUSH	Josh Adams	13	54%
	Long (8-10)	PASS	Zach Ertz	13	77%
	XL (11+)	PASS	Zach Ertz	8	25%
3	Short (1-3)	RUSH	Josh Adams	6	33%
	Med (4-7)	PASS	Alshon Jeffery	13	77%
	Long (8-10)	PASS	Zach Ertz	8	38%
			Golden Tate	8	25%
	XL (11+)	PASS	Nelson Agholor	4	0%

Most Successful Play*

Down	Distance	Play Type	Player	Total Plays	Play Success %
1	Long (8-10)	PASS	Alshon Jeffery	21	86%
2	Short (1-3)	RUSH	Jay Ajayi	7	71%
	Med (4-7)	RUSH	Wendell Smallwood	7	71%
	Long (8-10)	PASS	Zach Ertz	13	77%
	XL (11+)	PASS	Zach Ertz	8	25%
3	Short (1-3)	RUSH	Corey Clement	5	80%
	Med (4-7)	PASS	Alshon Jeffery	13	77%
	Long (8-10)	PASS	Zach Ertz	8	38%

*Minimum 5 plays to qualify

2018 Weekly Snap Rates

Wk	Opp	Score	Zach Ertz	Nelson Agholor	Alshon Jeffery	Dallas Goedert	Jordan Matthews	Golden Tate	Corey Clement	Mike Wallace
1	ATL	W 18-12	70 (97%)	68 (94%)		17 (24%)			13 (18%)	66 (92%)
2	TB	L 27-21	74 (94%)	72 (91%)		17 (22%)			33 (42%)	7 (9%)
3	IND	W 20-16	81 (99%)	80 (98%)		55 (67%)	33 (40%)		45 (55%)	
4	TEN	L 26-23	76 (97%)	72 (92%)	65 (83%)	32 (41%)	46 (59%)			
5	MIN	L 23-21	57 (97%)	52 (88%)	55 (93%)	34 (58%)	22 (37%)			
6	NYG	W 34-13	71 (100%)	64 (90%)	59 (83%)	32 (45%)	26 (37%)		26 (37%)	
7	CAR	L 21-17	65 (97%)	59 (88%)	64 (96%)	37 (55%)	29 (43%)		25 (37%)	
8	JAC	W 24-18	57 (92%)	57 (92%)	54 (87%)	30 (48%)	34 (55%)		13 (21%)	
10	DAL	L 27-20	62 (100%)	55 (89%)	60 (97%)	17 (27%)	38 (61%)	18 (29%)	18 (29%)	
11	NO	L 48-7	47 (92%)	44 (86%)	51 (100%)	16 (31%)	14 (27%)	36 (71%)	14 (27%)	
12	NYG	W 25-22	52 (80%)	47 (72%)	64 (98%)	36 (55%)	14 (22%)	39 (60%)	24 (37%)	
13	WAS	W 28-13	59 (79%)	65 (87%)	66 (88%)	39 (52%)	21 (28%)	36 (48%)	23 (31%)	
14	DAL	L 29-23	44 (85%)	49 (94%)	51 (98%)	31 (60%)	10 (19%)	20 (38%)	4 (8%)	
15	LA	W 30-23	59 (92%)	63 (98%)	64 (100%)	39 (61%)	5 (8%)	22 (34%)		
16	HOU	W 32-30	73 (89%)	74 (90%)	61 (74%)	48 (59%)	33 (40%)	29 (35%)		
17	WAS	W 24-0	53 (75%)	64 (90%)	57 (80%)	44 (62%)	19 (27%)	40 (56%)		
	Grand Total		1,000 (91%)	985 (90%)	771 (91%)	524 (48%)	344 (36%)	240 (47%)	238 (31%)	73 (50%)

Personnel Groupings

Personnel	Team %	NFL Avg	Succ. %
1-1 [3WR]	55%	65%	46%
1-2 [2WR]	36%	17%	51%
1-3 [1WR]	6%	3%	44%

Grouping Tendencies

Personnel	Pass Rate	Pass Succ. %	Run Succ. %
1-1 [3WR]	64%	46%	47%
1-2 [2WR]	61%	52%	50%
1-3 [1WR]	41%	59%	33%

Red Zone Targets (min 3)

Receiver	All	Inside 5	6-10	11-20
Zach Ertz	25	4	4	17
Alshon Jeffery	13	4	3	6
Nelson Agholor	13	2	4	7
Dallas Goedert	6	1	2	3
Golden Tate	6	1	2	3
Jordan Matthews	3	2		1
Wendell Smallwood	3		2	1

Red Zone Rushes (min 3)

Rusher	All	Inside 5	6-10	11-20
Josh Adams	18	5	8	5
Wendell Smallwood	17	3	3	11
Corey Clement	16	1	2	13
Jay Ajayi	11	4	3	4
Carson Wentz	5	3	1	1
Nick Foles	5	1	1	3

Early Down Target Rate

	RB	TE	WR
	18%	37%	45%
	23%	21%	56%
		NFL AVG	

Overall Target Success %

	RB	TE	WR
	45%	56%	50%
	#20	#13	#21

Philadelphia Eagles 2018 Passing Recap & 2019 Outlook

Carson Wentz ranked fourth in deep passing in 2017 before falling precipitously in 2018, so the addition of **DeSean Jackson** should allow him to return to his strengths. The offensive line in front of him is one of the better pass-blocking units in the league, finishing 11th-best in pressures allowed per attempt, and while Wentz was below-average at avoiding sacks when pressured in 2018, he was much better when fully healthy in 2017. Center **Jason Kelce** is the biggest star on the line, leading all centers in average distance from the quarterback on passing downs.

2018 Standard Passing Table

QB	Comp	Att	Comp %	Yds	YPA	TDs	INT	Sacks	Rating	Rk
Carson Wentz	279	402	69%	3,050	7.6	21	7	30	102	9
Nick Foles	184	266	69%	1,892	7.1	10	8	10	89	31
NFL Avg			62%		7.0				87.5	

2018 Advanced Passing Table

QB	Success %	EDSR Passing Success %	20+ Yd Pass Gains	20+ Yd Pass %	30+ Yd Pass Gains	30+ Yd Pass %	Avg. Air Yds per Comp	Avg. YAC per Comp	20+ Air Yd Comp	20+ Air Yd %
Carson Wentz	50%	55%	37	9.0%	16	4.0%	5.9	5.1	16	4%
Nick Foles	44%	44%	19	7.0%	12	5.0%	5.1	5.2	11	4%
NFL Avg	44%	48%	29.5	8.4%	12.5	3.7%	5.8	5.1	14.5	6%

Interception Rates by Down

Yards to Go	1st Dwn	2nd Dwn	3rd Dwn	4th Dwn	Total
1 & 2	0.0%	0.0%	0.0%	0.0%	0.0%
3, 4, 5	33.3%	0.0%	0.0%	0.0%	1.5%
6 - 9	0.0%	2.1%	0.0%	0.0%	1.2%
10 - 14	1.9%	2.0%	0.0%		1.8%
15+	0.0%	9.1%	0.0%		3.1%
Total	2.2%	2.1%	0.0%	0.0%	1.6%

3rd Down Passing - Short of Sticks Analysis

QB	Avg. Yds to Go	Avg. YIA (of Comp)	Avg Yds Short	Short of Sticks Rate	Short Rk
Carson Wentz	7.6	5.6	-1.9	66%	27
NFL Avg	7.8	6.4	-1.4	60%	

Air Yds vs YAC

Air Yds %	YAC %	Rk
53%	47%	24
53%	48%	

2018 Receiving Recap & 2019 Outlook

With 6'5" **Zach Ertz**, 6'4" **Dallas Goedert**, 6'3" **Alshon Jeffery**, and 6'3" **J.J. Arcega-Whiteside**, the Eagles have assembled one of the largest receiving corps in the NFL, which should help Wentz with his accuracy on third-down in the red zone, where he finished worst in the NFL in 2018. The addition of **DeSean Jackson**, again, adds a deep dimension that the Eagles offense has lacked for several years.

Player *Min 50 Targets	Targ	Comp %	YPA	Rating	Success %	Success Rk	Missed YPA Rk	YAS % Rk	YTS % Rk	TDs
Zach Ertz	171	74%	7.4	95.2	56%	37	45	80	59	7
Alshon Jeffery	109	70%	9.0	108.5	60%	14	20	56	59	5
Nelson Agholor	106	64%	7.4	91.0	45%	102	156	36	77	4
Golden Tate	69	64%	7.5	94.9	48%	93	102	126	26	5

Directional Passer Rating Delivered

Receiver	Short Left	Short Middle	Short Right	Deep Left	Deep Middle	Deep Right	Player Total
Zach Ertz	97	106	95	55	53	110	95
Alshon Jeffery	95	113	118	66	104	100	109
Nelson Agholor	110	83	96	88	79	32	91
Golden Tate	92	80	129	40	96	0	85
Dallas Goedert	102	133	120	135	0	65	125
Wendell Smallwood	119	50	105	119			100
Darren Sproles	68	56	130	119			107
Jordan Matthews	133	47	90	158	96	119	141
Corey Clement	105	99	100	40		40	99
Kamar Aiken	73		89		119		98
Jay Ajayi	83		56				81
Mike Wallace				40		40	40
Team Total	102	104	108	105	68	60	101

2018 Rushing Recap & 2019 Outlook

Jay Ajayi entered 2018 with momentum and a backfield ripe for the taking. He ended his season with a torn ACL in Week 5. In his absence, the Eagles rotated between undrafted rookie **Josh Adams**, undrafted sophomore **Corey Clement**, and former 5th-round pick **Wendell Smallwood**. This offseason, the team added **Jordan Howard** from the Bears and drafted **Miles Sanders** in the second round, giving them a pair of more potent challengers for playing time.

Player *Min 50 Rushes	Rushes	YPC	Success %	Success Rk	Missed YPA Rk	YTS % Rk	YAS % Rk	Early Down Success %	Early Down Success Rk	TDs
Josh Adams	121	4.2	50%	28	30	14	20	53%	12	3
Wendell Smallwood	105	4.0	49%	33	33	8	70	48%	29	3
Corey Clement	68	3.8	46%	43	67	20	25	41%	58	2

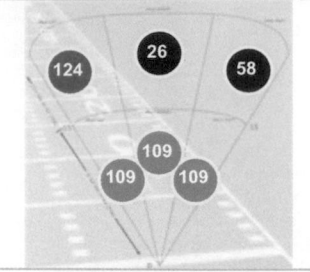

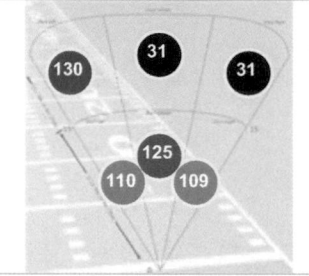

Yards per Carry by Direction

	LT	LG	C	RG	RT	
	3.8	1.9	4.6	4.2	3.5	3.8	4.9

Directional Run Frequency

	LT	LG	C	RG	RT	
	18%	9%	12%	30%	11%	8%	12%

These marks were dramatically better than his marks in 2017 (90.3 rating and 44 percent success).

Wentz is poised to continue his upward trajectory with the acquisition of **DeSean Jackson**, who excels on the routes that Wentz throws well and whose speed gives the offense the ability to dictate defensive coverages pre-snap.

While the offense will go as Wentz goes, Executive Vice President **Howie Roseman** has done a masterful job of acquiring additional talent over the last two years, who has excelled at manipulating the NFL's compensatory draft pick formula and moving in the draft to get his targets just before another team was reportedly set to take them, as was the case with **Dallas Goedert** and the Cowboys last year and **Andre Dillard** and the Texans this year.

Roseman also brought in DT **Malik Jackson** and bargain free agents **Vinny Curry** and **Zach Brown** to shore up their defensive front seven. They added **Jordan Howard** to boost their anemic running game, then doubled down by drafting rookie **Miles Sanders**, who excels at running out of shotgun formations.

The Eagles had the second-highest rate of shotgun snaps last season and the

(cont'd - see PHI-5)

Philadelphia Eagles Fantasy Corner

Miles Sanders exploded as Penn State's feature back once **Saquon Barkley** left, earning 18.8 touches per game and ranking eighth in the nation in yards after contact per carry (3.68) in 2018. At 5-foot-11, 211 with 4.49 speed and a twitchy 6.89 three-cone time, Sanders runs like a suped-up **Devonta Freeman** with a jump-cutting, energetic style. Sanders also shined as a pass blocker but had one of the highest fumble rates in this year's draft class. If he cleans up his ball security, Sanders has a chance to emerge as the Eagles' first true feature back since **LeSean McCoy**. **Jordan Howard** is a role player in a contract year, while Nos. 3-5 backs **Wendell Smallwood**, **Corey Clement**, and **Josh Adams** are battling for roster spots.

- Evan Silva

2018 Situational Usage by Player & Position

Usage Rate by Score

		Being Blown Out (14+)	Down Big (9-13)	One Score	Large Lead (9-13)	Blowout Lead (14+)
RUSH	Wendell Smallwood	3%	2%	64%	10%	22%
	Josh Adams	5%	3%	77%	11%	4%
	Nelson Agholor	25%		75%		
	Corey Clement	3%	10%	66%	7%	13%
	Darren Sproles			98%		2%
	Golden Tate	100%				
	Jay Ajayi	16%	11%	73%		
	Total	5%	5%	73%	7%	10%
PASS	Zach Ertz	5%	7%	77%	7%	5%
	Wendell Smallwood	3%	3%	89%	6%	
	Josh Adams	31%	8%	46%	15%	
	Nelson Agholor	3%	7%	81%	6%	3%
	Corey Clement	8%	16%	64%	4%	8%
	Alshon Jeffery	7%	1%	76%	7%	10%
	Darren Sproles			96%		4%
	Golden Tate	13%	6%	69%	9%	
	Jay Ajayi		20%	80%		
	Dallas Goedert	5%	3%	77%	15%	
	Jordan Matthews	11%		82%		7%
	Kamar Aiken	14%	14%	71%		
	Mike Wallace			100%		
	Richard Rodgers			100%		
	Total	6%	5%	77%	7%	5%

Share of Offensive Plays by Type

	Zach Ertz	Wendell Smallwood	Josh Adams	Nelson Agholor	Corey Clement	Alshon Jeffery	Darren Sproles	Golden Tate	Jay Ajayi	Dallas Goedert	Jordan Matthews	Kamar Aiken	Mike Wallace	Richard Rodgers
RUSH		27%	31%	1%	17%		12%	0%	12%					
PASS	26%	6%	2%	17%	4%	16%	5%	9%	1%	7%	5%	1%	1%	0%
ALL	16%	14%	14%	11%	10%	9%	7%	6%	5%	4%	3%	1%	0%	0%

Positional Target Distribution vs NFL Average

		NFL Wide				Team Only			
		Left	Middle	Right	Total	Left	Middle	Right	Total
Deep	WR	33%	17%	31%	81%	27%	15%	30%	72%
	TE	5%	4%	7%	15%	6%	7%	11%	24%
	RB	1%	0%	2%	3%	3%		1%	4%
	All	39%	22%	39%	100%	36%	22%	42%	100%
Short	WR	21%	14%	21%	55%	14%	9%	22%	45%
	TE	6%	6%	8%	20%	12%	9%	15%	36%
	RB	10%	5%	10%	25%	7%	2%	9%	18%
	All	36%	25%	39%	100%	33%	20%	47%	100%
Total		37%	24%	39%	100%	33%	20%	46%	100%

Positional Success Rates vs NFL Average

		NFL Wide				Team Only			
		Left	Middle	Right	Total	Left	Middle	Right	Total
Deep	WR	40%	49%	40%	42%	37%	47%	30%	36%
	TE	43%	54%	41%	45%	50%	43%	55%	50%
	RB	35%	33%	43%	40%	67%		0%	50%
	All	40%	50%	40%	42%	42%	45%	36%	40%
Short	WR	55%	61%	52%	55%	55%	49%	56%	55%
	TE	55%	62%	54%	57%	54%	70%	53%	58%
	RB	47%	54%	45%	48%	44%	60%	44%	46%
	All	53%	59%	51%	54%	53%	60%	53%	54%
Total		50%	58%	49%	52%	51%	57%	50%	52%

Division History: Season Wins & 2019 Projection

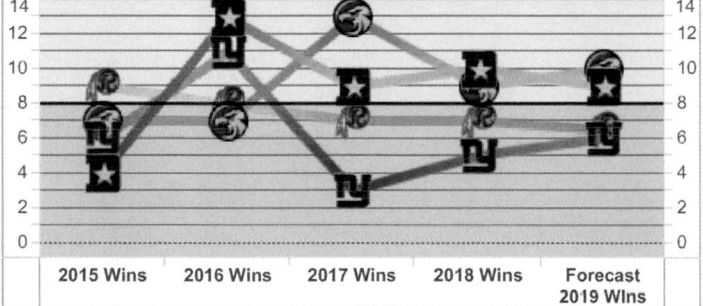

2015 Wins   2016 Wins   2017 Wins   2018 Wins   Forecast 2019 Wins

Rank of 2019 Defensive Pass Efficiency Faced by Week

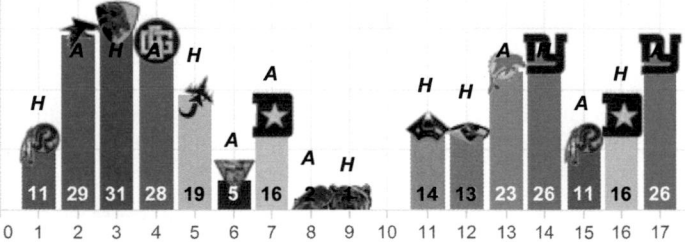

11   29   31   28   19   5   16   14   13   23   26   11   16   26

Rank of 2019 Defensive Rush Efficiency Faced by Week

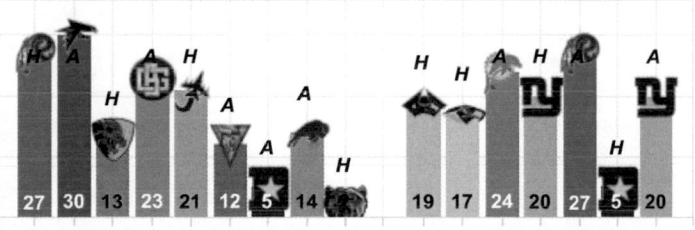

27   30   13   23   21   12   5   14   19   17   24   20   27   5   20

2018 Detailed Analytics Summary
Success by Play Type & Primary Personnel Groupings

Successful Play Rate 0% — 100%

Type	1-1 [3WR]	1-2 [2WR]	1-3 [1WR]	1-0 [4WR]	0-1 [4WR]	2-2 [1WR]	2-1 [2WR]	ALL
PASS	47% (415)	51% (251)	59% (27)	50% (4)	25% (4)	100% (1)	0% (2)	48% (704)
RUSH	46% (232)	49% (160)	32% (41)	0% (2)		0% (2)		45% (437)
All	46% (647)	50% (411)	43% (68)	33% (6)	25% (4)	33% (3)	0% (2)	47% (1,141)

Format   Success Rate (Total # of Plays)

Receiving Success by Top-4 Personnel Groupings
(Min 50 targets)

POS	Player	1-1 [3WR]	1-2 [2WR]	1-3 [1WR]	1-0 [4WR]	4 Grp Total
TE	Zach Ertz	58% (81) 7.5, 92.2	54% (74) 6.8, 98.1	80% (10) 11.2, 146.7	0% (2) 4.0, 83.3	57% (167) 7.4, 98.3
WR	Alshon Jeffery	59% (64) 8.9, 88.5	60% (43) 9.6, 140.7	50% (2) 3.5, 58.3		60% (109) 9.0, 108.5
	Nelson Agholor	41% (69) 7.2, 92.4	56% (34) 8.2, 82.8			46% (103) 7.5, 89.3
	Golden Tate	45% (53) 6.1, 87.1	0% (2) 3.0, 56.3		100% (1) 8.0, 100.0	45% (56) 6.0, 86.6

Format   Line 1: Success Rate (Total # of Plays)   Line 2: YPA, Passer Rating

Rushing Success by Top-4 Personnel Groupings
(Min 25 carries)

Rusher (Last, First)	1-1 [3WR]	1-2 [2WR]	2-2 [1WR]	4 Grp Total
Smallwood Wendell	40% (53) 3.7	56% (45) 4.1	0% (1) 1.0	46% (99) 3.8
Clement Corey	43% (35) 4.4	48% (25) 3.7		45% (60) 4.1
Sproles Darren	38% (34) 3.8	20% (10) 1.7		34% (44) 3.3
Ajayi Jay	42% (24) 3.3	58% (19) 5.1		49% (43) 4.0
Wentz Carson	60% (10) 4.6	57% (14) 4.1		58% (24) 4.3

Format   Line 1: Success Rate (Total # of Plays)   Line 2: YPC

Passing by Coverage Scheme

Zone	52% (263) 8.2, 97.4
M2M	54% (250) 7.9, 104.1
Screen	48% (79) 5.5, 102.2
Combo	12% (17) 1.6, 15.1

Passing by Route

Curl	63% (76) 7.3, 101.5
Screen	49% (74) 5.9, 104.7
Out	63% (62) 7.5, 107.5
Flat	41% (41) 5.2, 96.4
Slant	63% (41) 7.5, 90.4
Dig	54% (26) 7.0, 66.3

Throw Types

Level 1	55% (477) 6.7, 101.6
Level 2	50% (111) 9.9, 102.7
Level 3	34% (41) 13.3, 67.4
Sidearm	27% (11) 4.2, 84.1
Shovel	50% (6) 3.0, 79.2

QB Drop Types

0/1 Step	54% (265) 6.9, 92.8
3 Step	47% (184) 7.4, 88.3
5 Step	55% (74) 11.5, 133.5
Basic Screen	49% (43) 6.6, 102.0
Designed Rollout Right	63% (30) 9.5, 146.0
7 Step	40% (25) 6.0, 66.9

QB State at Pass

Planted	55% (421) 8.3, 104.6
Shuffling	43% (99) 5.8, 91.8
Moving	50% (72) 7.0, 101.7

Play Action

	Play Action	No P/A
Under Center	58% (57) 10.0, 122.8	67% (15) 12.7, 158.3
Shotgun	59% (134) 9.0, 110.4	48% (442) 6.7, 89.8
ALL	59% (191) 9.3, 114.1	49% (457) 6.9, 92.5

Run Types

Inside Zone	42% (113) 3.6
Outside Zone	48% (50) 3.6
Power	49% (37) 4.6
Stretch	26% (19) 3.3
Pitch	75% (12) 6.8
Lead	0% (1) 0.0

PHI-5

4th-highest run percentage when in shotgun.

Beyond general roster improvements, the Eagles also have the benefit of two divisional rivals who drafted quarterbacks in the first round of this year's draft and will presumably be turning to those rookie quarterbacks at some point during the season.

Facing the Giants at the very end of the season has its benefits. The likelihood that the Eagles will get to face **Daniel Jones** increases. Additionally, the amount of tape the Eagles will have on him by that point in time is an added benefit. Rookie QBs playing in Philadelphia the last five years (any week of the season) average a 53.2 percent completion rate, 6.6 YPA, an 8:5 TD:INT ratio and are sacked an average of 3 times per game.

Their last division rival is another matter entirely; the Eagles have not just lost three of their last four games against the Cowboys, they never led at any point during those losses.

Unless they can secure a first-round bye in the playoffs, the Eagles will also have the unfortunate distinction of being the only team in the league that won't play a single game in 2019 with a rest advantage over their opponent. The Eagles' opponent coming out of their bye is the New England Patriots, who will be coming off a bye of their own. Philadelphia will, however, play the Jets and Seahawks fresh off of their byes, and also has a one-day rest disadvantage against Washington in Week 15. Just as bad, two potential competitors for playoff seeding, the Vikings and the Rams, are the only two teams in the league to have five games with a rest advantage.

Still, despite the lack of help from the schedule makers, I project the Eagles to face the second-easiest schedule for this upcoming year. Carson Wentz will be another year removed from his torn ACL, the roster will be better and deeper, and the team is unlikely to rank worse than last year's 31st-place finish in overall health. The Eagles have put themselves in a great position heading into 2019, and now it's on them to deliver.

Pittsburgh Steelers

Coaches (Prior Yrs)

Head Coach:
Mike Tomlin (12 yrs)
Offensive Coordinator:
Randy Fichtner (1 yr)
Defensive Coordinator:
Keith Butler (3 yrs)

2019 Forecast

Wins	Div Rank
9	#2

Past Records
2018: 9-7
2017: 13-3
2016: 11-5

EASY → HARD

Schedule:
Wk	1	2	3	4	5	6	7	8	9	10	11	12	13	14	15	16	17
Opp	NE	SEA	SF	CIN	BAL	LAC		MIA	IND	LAR	CLE	CIN	CLE	ARI	BUF	NYJ	BAL
H/A	A	H	A	H	H	A		H	H	H	A	A	H	A	H	A	A

SNF (1), MNF (4), SNF (6), MNF (8), TNF (11)

Key Players Lost

Player	New
Antonio Brown (WR)	OAK
Jesse James (TE)	DET
L.J. Fort (ILB)	PHI
Le'Veon Bell (RB)	NYJ
Marcus Gilbert (RT)	ARI
Morgan Burnett (SS)	CLE

Average Line	# Games Favored	# Games Underdog
-2.2	10	3

2019 Pittsburgh Steelers Overview

Steelers Nation was uncomfortable when **Le'Veon Bell** didn't accept the five-year, $70 million contract he was offered last July. Apparently, Le'Veon had opted to play the 2018 season under the franchise tag before hitting free agency at age 27.

Reports soon emerged that Bell would skip training camp and return to the team by Week 1, as he had in 2017. As Labor Day approached, OC **Randy Fichtner** said he didn't expect Bell's workload to be limited to open the season.

But Bell didn't report on Labor Day. Or any day *near* Labor Day.

By Week 1, the Steelers stopped listing Bell on their depth chart. In late September, Pittsburgh reportedly began listening to trade offers for its disgruntled running-back star. Speculation continued as to when Bell would sign his franchise tender and report, but by the deadline in mid-November he still hadn't.

Instead, Bell sat out an *entire season* of his prime.

Surely a full season without the NFL's best running back would prove catastrophic for the Steelers. After all, Bell appeared in at least eight games three times from 2014 to 2017, and in those three seasons ranked 1st, 4th, and 7th in scrimmage yards per game. No other player even managed two seasons in the top 15.

Beyond Bell's offensive production, many spoke of the impact his presence had *on the defense.*

(cont'd - see PIT2)

Key Free Agents/ Trades Added

Player	AAV (MM)
Donte Moncrief (WR)	$4.5
Mark Barron (ILB)	$6
Steven Nelson (CB)	$8.5

Drafted Players

Rd	Pk	Player (College)
1	10	LB - Devin Bush (Michigan)
3	66	WR - Diontae Johnson (Toledo)
3	83	CB - Justin Layne (Michigan State)
4	122	RB - Benny Snell Jr. (Kentucky)
5	141	TE - Zach Gentry (Michigan)
6	175	DE - Sutton Smith (Northern Illinois)
6	192	DT - Isaiah Buggs (Alabama)
6*	207	LB - Ulysees Gilbert III (Akron)
7	219	OT - Derwin Gray (Maryland)

Regular Season Wins: Past & Current Proj

- Forecast 2019 Wins: 9
- 2018 Wins: 9
- Forecast 2018 Wins: 10.5
- 2017 Wins: 13
- 2016 Wins: 11
- 2015 Wins: 10

(scale: 1 3 5 7 9 11 13 15)

Lineup & Cap Hits

FS S.Davis 21
LB V.Williams 98
LB J.Bostic 51
SS T.Edmunds 34
RCB J.Haden 23
SLOTCB M.Hilton 28
OLB B.Dupree 48
DE C.Heyward 97
DE S.Tuitt 91
OLB T.Watt 90
LCB S.Nelson 20

LWR D.Moncrief 11
LT A.Villanueva 78
LG R.Foster 73
C M.Pouncey 53
RG D.DeCastro 66
RT M.Feiler 71
RWR J.Washington 13
SLOTWR J.Smith-Schuster 19
TE V.McDonald 81

QB B.Roethlisberger 7
RB J.Conner 30

WR2 E.Rogers 17
WR3 D.Johnson Rookie 82
RB2 J.Samuels 38
QB2 J.Dobbs 5

2019 Cap Dollars

2019 Unit Spending

All DEF / All OFF

Positional Spending

	Rank	Total	2017 Rk
All OFF	22	$91.90M	17
QB	7	$27.88M	9
OL	10	$39.55M	8
RB	32	$3.00M	32
WR	32	$10.32M	23
TE	8	$11.15M	20
All DEF	10	$94.74M	19
DL	11	$37.00M	21
LB	5	$28.62M	10
CB	16	$22.12M	15
S	28	$7.00M	22

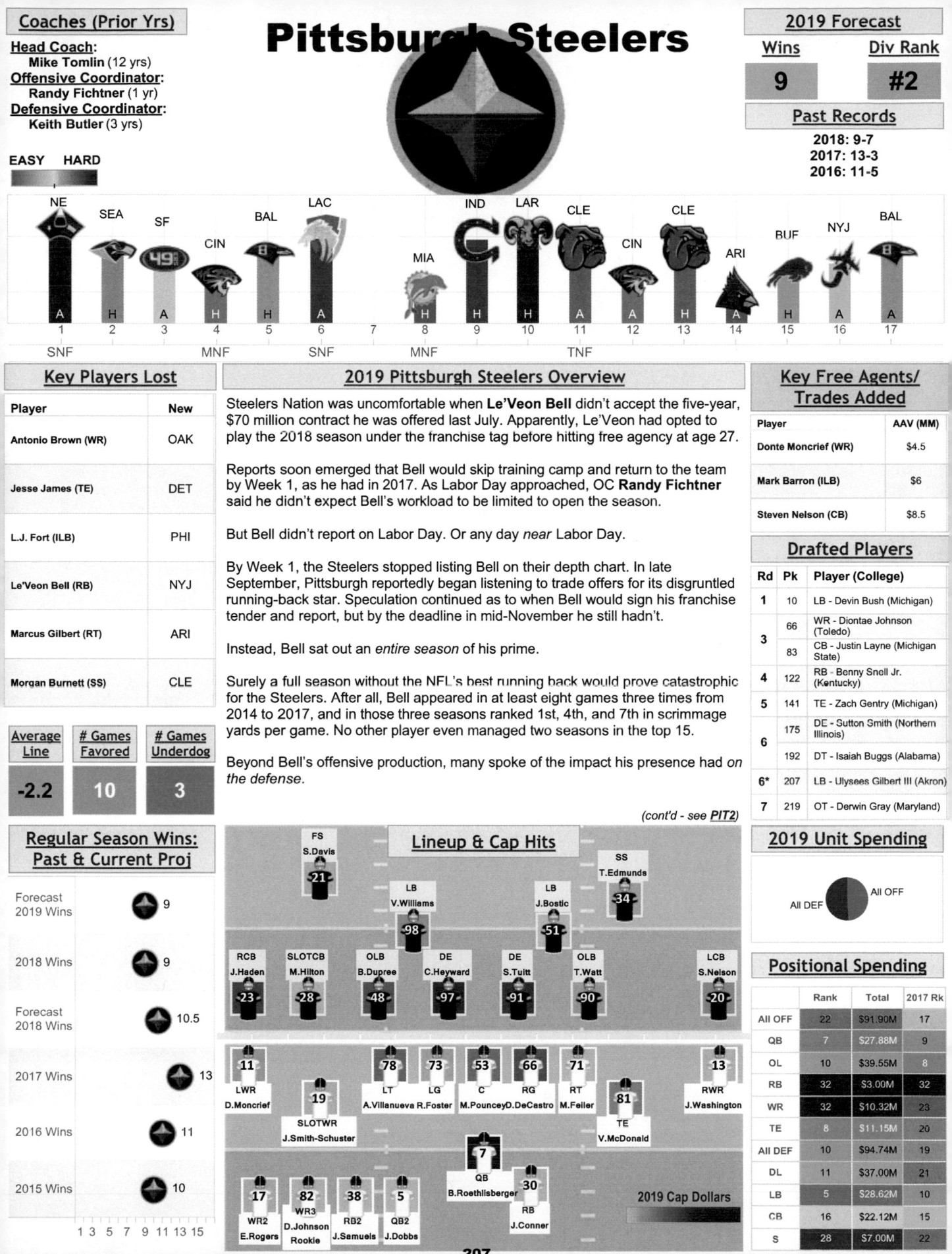

Apparently, those observers missed Pittsburgh's 2017 season. Despite Bell being fully healthy for the last four games of the season, the Steelers gave up 45 points to **Blake Bortles** and the Jaguars, 38 points to **Joe Flacco** and the Ravens, 28 to **Brett Hundley** and the Packers, and squandered an eight-point 4th-quarter lead to the Patriots. The Steelers' defense was perfectly capable of underperforming even with Bell playing on offense.

But the modern NFL is no longer a running league. Depending on how one looks at the problem, passing offense contributes *three to four times more* to winning football games than rushing offense. And running backs are among the most-injured players in the league.

In a salary-capped league, the amount of value a player provides is secondary to the amount of value he provides relative to his cost. From 2005 to 2017, the average running back on a Super Bowl roster counted $2.5 million against the cap. Most expensive was **Marshawn Lynch**, who cost $8.5 million for the 2013 Seahawks, a figure mitigated by the fact that their quarterback was a former third-round pick still on his rookie deal.

Perhaps the Steelers were actually *better off* not striking a long-term deal with Bell and devoting $13-15 million a year to a running back.

Indeed. Comparing the performance of replacement **James Conner** to Bell himself during the 2017 campaign, Conner averaged more yards per carry (4.5 to 4.0), more yards per target (7.0 vs. 6.2), and had an identical Success Rate (49%) to Le'Veon. Looking only at carries on first down, Conner averaged 5.0 yards with a 48% Success Rate compared to 3.7 and 45% respectively for Bell. Conner also had a higher Success Rate in the red zone, 56% to 49%.

While running backs have different attributes, abilities, and skills, no position's performance is as dependent on his teammates and scheme.

Bell might be more talented than Conner, but Le'Veon was still easily replaced.

2018 Passing Performance

QB	1st Dwn	2nd Dwn	3rd Dwn	
Ben Roethlisberger	53%	53%	42%	Success Rate
	7.5	7.9	7.2	YPA
	97.2	98.6	91.1	Rating
Pass Rate	62%	74%	88%	
NFL AVG	53%	47%	36%	Success Rate
	7.7	7.3	6.9	YPA
	95.1	93.7	87.1	Rating
Pass Rate	53%	62%	80%	

2018 Rushing Performance

Offense	1st Dwn	2nd Dwn	3rd Dwn	
PIT	47%	42%	65%	Success Rate
	4.3	4.0	4.3	YPC
Run Rate	38%	26%	12%	
NFL AVG	48%	46%	51%	Success Rate
	4.5	4.4	4.3	YPC
Run Rate	47%	38%	20%	

What about wide receivers? Just a year after losing one All-Pro on offense, the Steelers are saying goodbye to another after trading disgruntled **Antonio Brown** to the Raiders. Will Brown prove as replaceable as Bell? Probably not, but there is still reason for optimism.

Over the last ten years, no team has been better at drafting wide receivers than the Steelers. They have received the most wide receiver production per year, and the most value relative to draft capital spent. They have done this despite rarely devoting premium picks to the position; the team has taken just three receivers in the first 75 picks of the draft over that span. They are **JuJu Smith-Schuster**, **James Washington**, and rookie **Diontae Johnson**.

(cont'd - see PIT-3)

2018 Offensive Advanced Metrics

Rank — EDSR Off: 5, 30 & In Off: 8, Red Zone Off: 4, 3rd Down Off: 6, YPPA Off: 10, YPPT Off: 15, Offensive Efficiency: 6, Pass Efficiency Off: 8, Pass Pro Efficiency Off: 4, RB Pass Eff Off: 3, Rush Efficiency Off: 11, Explosive Pass Off: 18, Explosive Run Off: 15

2018 Defensive Advanced Metrics

Rank — EDSR Def: 15, 30 & In Def: 12, Red Zone Def: 15, 3rd Down Def: 7, YPPA Def: 6, YPPT Def: 24, Defensive Efficiency: 13, Pass Efficiency Def: 17, Pass Pro Efficiency Def: 1, RB Pass Eff Def: 6, Rush Efficiency Def: 8, Explosive Pass Def: 16, Explosive Run Def: 17

2018 Weekly EDSR & Season Trending Performance

WEEK	1	2	3	4	5	6	8	9	10	11	12	13	14	15	16	17
RESULT	T	L	W	L	W	W	W	W	W	W	L	L	L	W	L	W
OPP	CLE	KC	TB	BAL	ATL	CIN	CLE	BAL	CAR	JAC	DEN	LAC	OAK	NE	NO	CIN
SITE	A	H	A	H	H	A	H	A	H	A	H	A	H	H	A	H
MARGIN	0	-5	3	-12	24	7	15	7	31	4	-7	-3	-3	7	-3	3
PTS	21	37	30	14	41	28	33	23	52	20	17	30	21	17	28	16
OPP PTS	21	42	27	26	17	21	18	16	21	16	24	33	24	10	31	13

EDSR by Wk
W=Green
L=Red

OFF/DEF
EDSR
Blue=OFF
(high=good)
Red=DEF
(low=good)

2018 Close Game Records

All 2018 Wins: **9**
FG Games (<=3 pts) W-L: **2-3**
FG Games Win %: **40% (#18)**
FG Games Wins (% of Total Wins): **22% (#21)**
1 Score Games (<=8 pts) W-L: **6-5**
1 Score Games Win %: **55% (#13)**
1 Score Games Wins (% of Total Wins): **67% (#8)**

2018 Critical & Game-Deciding Stats

TO Margin	-11
TO Given	26
INT Given	17
FUM Given	9
TO Taken	15
INT Taken	8
FUM Taken	7
Sack Margin	+28
Sacks	52
Sacks Allow	24
Return TD Margin	+1
Ret TDs	3
Ret TDs Allow	2
Penalty Margin	+25
Penalties	111
Opponent Penalties	136

Pittsburgh Steelers 2019 Strength of Schedule In Detail (compared to 2018)

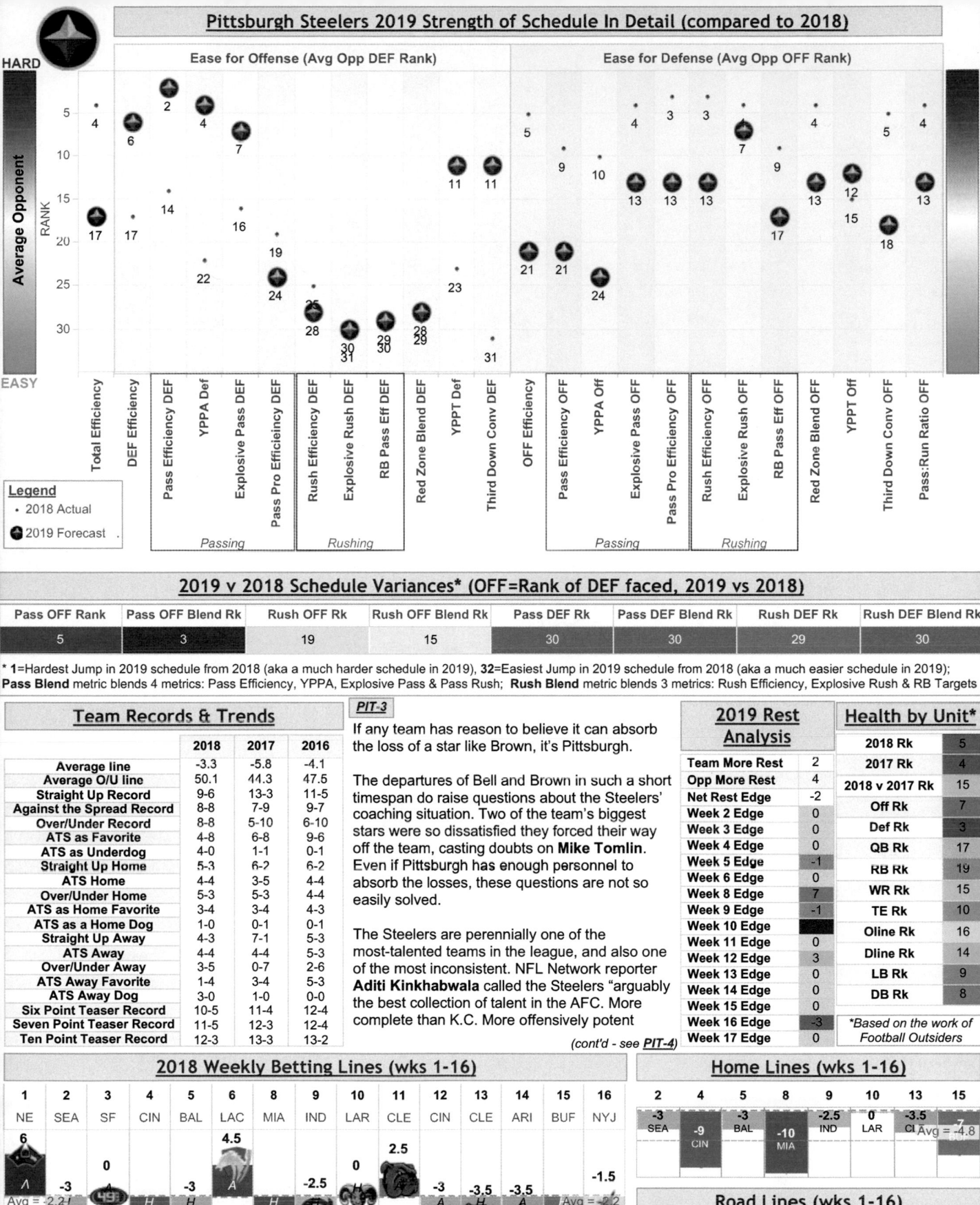

Ease for Offense (Avg Opp DEF Rank)

Metric	2018 Actual	2019 Forecast
Total Efficiency	—	17
DEF Efficiency	4	6
Pass Efficiency DEF	14	2
YPPA Def	22	4
Explosive Pass DEF	16	7
Pass Pro Efficieincy DEF	19	24
Rush Efficiency DEF	25	28
Explosive Rush DEF	31	30
RB Pass Eff DEF	30	29
Red Zone Blend DEF	29	28
YPPT Def	23	11
Third Down Conv DEF	31	11

Passing / Rushing

Ease for Defense (Avg Opp OFF Rank)

Metric	2018 Actual	2019 Forecast
OFF Efficiency	5	21
Pass Efficiency OFF	9	21
YPPA Off	10	24
Explosive Pass OFF	4	13
Pass Pro Efficiency OFF	3	13
Rush Efficiency OFF	3	13
Explosive Rush OFF	7	7
RB Pass Eff OFF	9	17
Red Zone Blend OFF	4	13
YPPT Off	12	15
Third Down Conv OFF	5	18
Pass:Run Ratio OFF	4	13

Passing / Rushing

Legend
- 2018 Actual
- 2019 Forecast

2019 v 2018 Schedule Variances* (OFF=Rank of DEF faced, 2019 vs 2018)

Pass OFF Rank	Pass OFF Blend Rk	Rush OFF Rk	Rush OFF Blend Rk	Pass DEF Rk	Pass DEF Blend Rk	Rush DEF Rk	Rush DEF Blend Rk
5	3	19	15	30	30	29	30

* **1**=Hardest Jump in 2019 schedule from 2018 (aka a much harder schedule in 2019), **32**=Easiest Jump in 2019 schedule from 2018 (aka a much easier schedule in 2019);
Pass Blend metric blends 4 metrics: Pass Efficiency, YPPA, Explosive Pass & Pass Rush; **Rush Blend** metric blends 3 metrics: Rush Efficiency, Explosive Rush & RB Targets

---

Team Records & Trends

	2018	2017	2016
Average line	-3.3	-5.8	-4.1
Average O/U line	50.1	44.3	47.5
Straight Up Record	9-6	13-3	11-5
Against the Spread Record	8-8	7-9	9-7
Over/Under Record	8-8	5-10	6-10
ATS as Favorite	4-8	6-8	9-6
ATS as Underdog	4-0	1-1	0-1
Straight Up Home	5-3	6-2	6-2
ATS Home	4-4	3-5	4-4
Over/Under Home	5-3	5-3	4-4
ATS as Home Favorite	3-4	3-4	4-3
ATS as a Home Dog	1-0	0-1	0-1
Straight Up Away	4-3	7-1	5-3
ATS Away	4-4	4-4	5-3
Over/Under Away	3-5	0-7	2-6
ATS Away Favorite	1-4	3-4	5-3
ATS Away Dog	3-0	1-0	0-0
Six Point Teaser Record	10-5	11-4	12-4
Seven Point Teaser Record	11-5	12-3	12-4
Ten Point Teaser Record	12-3	13-3	13-2

PIT-3

If any team has reason to believe it can absorb the loss of a star like Brown, it's Pittsburgh.

The departures of Bell and Brown in such a short timespan do raise questions about the Steelers' coaching situation. Two of the team's biggest stars were so dissatisfied they forced their way off the team, casting doubts on **Mike Tomlin**. Even if Pittsburgh has enough personnel to absorb the losses, these questions are not so easily solved.

The Steelers are perennially one of the most-talented teams in the league, and also one of the most inconsistent. NFL Network reporter **Aditi Kinkhabwala** called the Steelers "arguably the best collection of talent in the AFC. More complete than K.C. More offensively potent

(cont'd - see PIT-4)

2019 Rest Analysis

Team More Rest	2
Opp More Rest	4
Net Rest Edge	-2
Week 2 Edge	0
Week 3 Edge	0
Week 4 Edge	0
Week 5 Edge	-1
Week 6 Edge	0
Week 8 Edge	7
Week 9 Edge	-1
Week 10 Edge	
Week 11 Edge	0
Week 12 Edge	3
Week 13 Edge	0
Week 14 Edge	0
Week 15 Edge	0
Week 16 Edge	-3
Week 17 Edge	0

Health by Unit*

2018 Rk	5
2017 Rk	4
2018 v 2017 Rk	15
Off Rk	7
Def Rk	3
QB Rk	17
RB Rk	19
WR Rk	15
TE Rk	10
Oline Rk	16
Dline Rk	14
LB Rk	9
DB Rk	8

Based on the work of Football Outsiders

2018 Weekly Betting Lines (wks 1-16)

1	2	3	4	5	6	8	9	10	11	12	13	14	15	16
NE	SEA	SF	CIN	BAL	LAC	MIA	IND	LAR	CLE	CIN	CLE	ARI	BUF	NYJ
6	-3	0	-9	-3	4.5	-10	-2.5	0	2.5	-3	-3.5	-3.5	-7	-1.5

Avg = -2.2

| 6 | -3 | 0 | -9 | -3 | 4.5 | -10 | -2.5 | 0 | 2.5 | -3 | -3.5 | -3.5 | -7 | -1.5 |

Home Lines (wks 1-16)

2	4	5	8	9	10	13	15
-3 SEA	-9 CIN	-3 BAL	-10 MIA	-2.5 IND	0 LAR	-3.5 CLE	-7

Avg = -4.8

Road Lines (wks 1-16)

1	3	6	11	12	14	16
6 NE	0 SF	4.5 LAC	2.5 CLE	-3 CIN	-3.5 ARI	-1.5 NYJ

Avg = 0.7

2018 Play Tendencies

All Pass %	67%
All Pass Rk	2
All Rush %	33%
All Rush Rk	31
1 Score Pass %	66%
1 Score Pass Rk	1
2017 1 Score Pass %	60%
2017 1 Score Pass Rk	7
2018 Pass Increase %	7%
Pass Increase Rk	7
1 Score Rush %	34%
1 Score Rush Rk	32
Up Pass %	55%
Up Pass Rk	7
Up Rush %	45%
Up Rush Rk	26
Down Pass %	82%
Down Pass Rk	1
Down Rush %	18%
Down Rush Rk	32

2018 Down & Distance Tendencies

Down	Distance	Total Plays	Pass Rate	Run Rate	Play Success %
1	Short (1-3)	17	35%	65%	59%
	Med (4-7)	11	45%	55%	55%
	Long (8-10)	344	57%	43%	50%
	XL (11+)	7	100%	0%	43%
2	Short (1-3)	35	63%	37%	69%
	Med (4-7)	88	67%	33%	60%
	Long (8-10)	113	81%	19%	48%
	XL (11+)	26	81%	19%	23%
3	Short (1-3)	45	67%	33%	64%
	Med (4-7)	43	98%	2%	53%
	Long (8-10)	31	87%	13%	42%
	XL (11+)	23	100%	0%	26%
4	Short (1-3)	6	100%	0%	67%

Shotgun %:

Under Center	Shotgun
21%	79%

37% AVG 63%

Run Rate:

Under Center	Shotgun
73%	20%

68% AVG 23%

Pass Rate:

Under Center	Shotgun
27%	80%

32% AVG 77%

Short Yardage Intelligence:

2nd and Short Run

Run Freq	Run Rk	NFL Run Freq Avg	Run 1D Rate	Run NFL 1D Avg
31%	32	65%	90%	68%

2nd and Short Pass

Pass Freq	Pass Rk	NFL Pass Freq Avg	Pass 1D Rate	Pass NFL 1D Avg
69%	1	35%	59%	56%

Most Frequent Play

Down	Distance	Play Type	Player	Total Plays	Play Success %
1	Short (1-3)	RUSH	James Conner	8	63%
	Med (4-7)	RUSH	James Conner	4	50%
	Long (8-10)	RUSH	James Conner	99	48%
	XL (11+)	PASS	Juju Smith-Schuster	2	50%
2	Short (1-3)	RUSH	James Conner	9	89%
	Med (4-7)	RUSH	James Conner	20	50%
	Long (8-10)	PASS	Antonio Brown	17	71%
	XL (11+)	PASS	James Conner	4	25%
			Antonio Brown	4	25%
			Juju Smith-Schuster	4	75%
3	Short (1-3)	RUSH	James Conner	10	70%
	Med (4-7)	PASS	Vance McDonald	9	44%
	Long (8-10)	PASS	Vance McDonald	7	57%
	XL (11+)	PASS	Antonio Brown	7	29%

Most Successful Play*

Down	Distance	Play Type	Player	Total Plays	Play Success %
1	Short (1-3)	RUSH	James Conner	8	63%
	Long (8-10)	PASS	James Conner	19	63%
2	Short (1-3)	PASS	Juju Smith-Schuster	6	100%
	Med (4-7)	PASS	Juju Smith-Schuster	9	67%
	Long (8-10)	PASS	Vance McDonald	5	80%
3	Short (1-3)	PASS	Juju Smith-Schuster	7	71%
	Med (4-7)	PASS	Juju Smith-Schuster	6	67%
	Long (8-10)	PASS	Vance McDonald	7	57%
	XL (11+)	PASS	Vance McDonald	5	40%

Minimum 5 plays to qualify

2018 Weekly Snap Rates

Wk	Opp	Score	Antonio Brown	Juju Smith-Schuster	James Conner	Vance McDonald	Jesse James	James Washington	Ryan Switzer	Roosevelt Nix
1	CLE	T 21-21	83 (99%)	63 (75%)	77 (92%)		69 (82%)	11 (13%)	7 (8%)	19 (23%)
2	KC	L 42-37	77 (94%)	76 (93%)	72 (88%)	37 (45%)	45 (55%)	66 (80%)	13 (16%)	4 (5%)
3	TB	W 30-27	62 (94%)	55 (83%)	56 (85%)	32 (48%)	33 (50%)	40 (61%)	7 (11%)	11 (17%)
4	BAL	L 26-14	59 (95%)	60 (97%)	49 (79%)	39 (63%)	27 (44%)	47 (76%)	21 (34%)	1 (2%)
5	ATL	W 41-17	57 (93%)	50 (82%)	45 (74%)	37 (61%)	36 (59%)	35 (57%)	4 (7%)	8 (13%)
6	CIN	W 28-21	63 (86%)	50 (68%)	66 (90%)	51 (70%)	51 (70%)	16 (22%)	2 (3%)	17 (23%)
8	CLE	W 33-18	70 (99%)	56 (79%)	56 (79%)	27 (38%)	40 (56%)		19 (27%)	10 (14%)
9	BAL	W 23-16	81 (100%)	77 (95%)	68 (84%)	51 (63%)	35 (43%)	70 (86%)	13 (16%)	
10	CAR	W 52-21	51 (88%)	42 (72%)	23 (40%)	25 (43%)	34 (59%)	46 (79%)	8 (14%)	6 (10%)
11	JAC	W 20-16	64 (98%)	61 (94%)	58 (89%)	52 (80%)	16 (25%)	35 (54%)	24 (37%)	4 (6%)
12	DEN	L 24-17	72 (92%)	66 (85%)	67 (86%)	33 (42%)	50 (64%)	18 (23%)	52 (67%)	8 (10%)
13	LAC	L 33-30	67 (99%)	60 (88%)	49 (72%)	44 (65%)	33 (49%)		24 (35%)	3 (4%)
14	OAK	L 24-21	59 (98%)	52 (87%)		38 (63%)	31 (52%)	22 (37%)	28 (47%)	4 (7%)
15	NE	W 17-10	61 (95%)	60 (94%)		23 (36%)	22 (34%)	44 (69%)	21 (33%)	5 (8%)
16	NO	L 31-28	72 (96%)	69 (92%)		34 (45%)	17 (23%)	27 (36%)	35 (47%)	5 (7%)
17	CIN	W 16-13		63 (93%)	32 (47%)	41 (60%)	23 (34%)	49 (72%)	24 (35%)	5 (7%)
	Grand Total		998 (95%)	960 (86%)	718 (77%)	564 (55%)	562 (50%)	526 (55%)	302 (27%)	110 (10%)

Personnel Groupings

Personnel	Team %	NFL Avg	Succ. %
1-1 [3WR]	69%	65%	50%
1-2 [2WR]	9%	17%	51%
0-1 [4WR]	6%	1%	43%
2-2 [1WR]	6%	3%	39%
2-1 [2WR]	3%	8%	49%
0-0 [5WR]	3%	0%	73%
1-3 [1WR]	2%	3%	41%

Grouping Tendencies

Personnel	Pass Rate	Pass Succ. %	Run Succ. %
1-1 [3WR]	73%	50%	51%
1-2 [2WR]	53%	61%	40%
0-1 [4WR]	90%	43%	43%
2-2 [1WR]	25%	47%	36%
2-1 [2WR]	11%	25%	52%
0-0 [5WR]	90%	78%	33%
1-3 [1WR]	55%	50%	30%

Red Zone Targets (min 3)

Receiver	All	Inside 5	6-10	11-20
Juju Smith-Schuster	20	6	2	12
Antonio Brown	16	4	1	11
Vance McDonald	9	3	1	5
James Conner	7		3	4
Jaylen Samuels	6	1	2	3
Ryan Switzer	6	1	2	3
Jesse James	4	1	1	2

Red Zone Rushes (min 3)

Rusher	All	Inside 5	6-10	11-20
James Conner	34	17	6	11
Jaylen Samuels	7	2	2	3
Ben Roethlisberger	5	3		2
Stevan Ridley	4	2		2

Early Down Target Rate

RB	TE	WR
19%	17%	64%
23%	21%	56%
	NFL AVG	

Overall Target Success %

RB	TE	WR
54%	60%	51%
#3	#4	#16

Pittsburgh Steelers 2018 Passing Recap & 2019 Outlook

Ben Roethlisberger has one of the league's best offensive lines, but he needs to take better care of the football. Last season, Roethlisberger had six turnovers when games were within one score after halftime, second most in the league.

The team used more three- and four-receiver sets in 2018, flooding the field with wideouts, but Roethlisberger was much better passing out of traditional formations using two receivers and two tight ends. The Steelers should accommodate this more in 2018.

Even with **Le'Veon Bell** gone, Pittsburgh must do a better job of incorporating its running backs in the passing game. Despite the loss of Bell, Pittsburgh's Success Rate and passer rating on passes to backs were both up in 2018, even as their total passes to running backs were down.

2018 Standard Passing Table

QB	Comp	Att	Comp %	Yds	YPA	TDs	INT	Sacks	Rating	Rk
Ben Roethlisberger	452	675	67%	5,086	7.5	34	16	24	96	16
Joshua Dobbs	6	12	50%	43	3.6	0	1	0	24	58
NFL Avg			62%		7.0				87.5	

2018 Advanced Passing Table

QB	Success %	EDSR Passing Success %	20+ Yd Pass Gains	20+ Yd Pass %	30+ Yd Pass Gains	30+ Yd Pass %	Avg. Air Yds per Comp	Avg. YAC per Comp	20+ Air Yd Comp	20+ Air Yd %
Ben Roethlisberger	51%	53%	60	9.0%	23	3.0%	5.0	6.2	26	4%
Joshua Dobbs	33%	50%	1	8.0%			3.8	3.3	1	8%
NFL Avg	44%	48%	29.5	8.4%	12.5	3.7%	5.8	5.1	14.5	6%

Interception Rates by Down

Yards to Go	1st Dwn	2nd Dwn	3rd Dwn	4th Dwn	Total
1 & 2	0.0%	0.0%	4.0%	0.0%	1.8%
3, 4, 5	0.0%	0.0%	2.4%	0.0%	1.2%
6 - 9	0.0%	2.3%	3.8%	0.0%	2.8%
10 - 14	1.9%	3.6%	5.4%	0.0%	2.6%
15+	0.0%	0.0%	0.0%	0.0%	0.0%
Total	1.8%	2.1%	3.6%	0.0%	2.3%

3rd Down Passing - Short of Sticks Analysis

QB	Avg. Yds to Go	Avg. YIA (of Comp)	Avg Yds Short	Short of Sticks Rate	Short Rk
Ben Roethlisberger	7.3	5.4	-1.9	64%	25
NFL Avg	7.8	6.4	-1.4	60%	

Air Yds vs YAC

Air Yds %	YAC %	Rk
53%	56%	49
53%	48%	

2018 Receiving Recap & 2019 Outlook

JuJu Smith-Schuster has huge shoes to fill, but his performance to date creates plenty of optimism that he's up for the challenge. The question becomes how much less open will he be now that teams are no longer rolling coverage to **Antonio Brown**. Smith-Schuster can't do it all, though; second-year WR **James Washington** will be thrust into the spotlight, and the team could use production from rookie **Diontae Johnson** and enigmatic veteran **Donte Moncrief**.

Player *Min 50 Targets	Targ	Comp %	YPA	Rating	Success %	Success Rk	Missed YPA Rk	YAS % Rk	YTS % Rk	TDs
Antonio Brown	169	62%	7.7	87.8	49%	85	124	28	87	12
Juju Smith-Schuster	166	67%	8.3	96.5	57%	32	21	18	97	4
Vance McDonald	73	68%	8.4	106.5	55%	43	150	75	26	4
James Conner	71	77%	7.0	100.5	51%	64	28	127	38	1

Directional Passer Rating Delivered

Receiver	Short Left	Short Middle	Short Right	Deep Left	Deep Middle	Deep Right	Player Total
Antonio Brown	108	45	86	134	67	82	88
Juju Smith-Schuster	72	91	103	89	141	96	97
Vance McDonald	127	122	69			96	107
James Conner	75	120	90	40			100
Ryan Switzer	98	102	88	40	119		98
Jesse James	101	96	68	158	110	110	118
James Washington	86	124	57	40	40	60	70
Jaylen Samuels	93	128	139				130
Eli Rogers	88	102	70	40			90
Justin Hunter	56	40	78	40	40	40	40
Xavier Grimble	119	113	92	40			109
Team Total	96	97	92	118	87	89	97

2018 Rushing Recap & 2019 Outlook

The 2018 Steelers had things relatively easy, playing the 25th-ranked schedule of opposing run defenses. **James Conner** excelled against that lighter slate, but could he continue to replicate Bell's success against tougher opponents? Fortunately, the Steelers likely won't need to find out; their schedule is projected as fifth easiest in the league against the run. Things get especially easy after Pittsburgh's bye, so be looking to potentially snag Conner from impatient fantasy owners if he struggles at all early.

Player *Min 50 Rushes	Rushes	YPC	Success %	Success Rk	Missed YPA Rk	YTS % Rk	YAS % Rk	Early Down Success %	Early Down Success Rk	TDs
James Conner	215	4.5	49%	32	21	54	31	47%	34	12
Jaylen Samuels	56	4.6	52%	17	19	32	34	53%	12	0

Ben Roethlisberger Rating All Downs

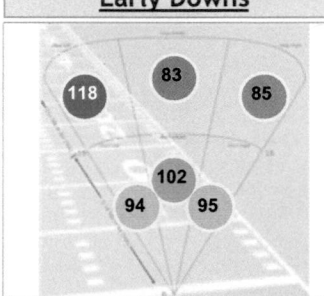

Ben Roethlisberger Rating Early Downs

Yards per Carry by Direction

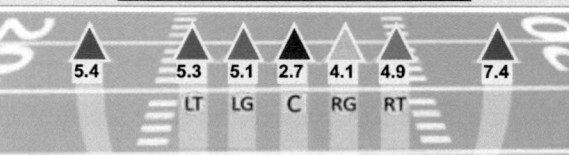

Directional Run Frequency

than Baltimore, more talented than New England. More battle tested than L.A. But **Mike Tomlin**'s laissez-faire approach let way too much distraction and BS fester. I felt he showed that he knows it."

Tomlin's staff has proven a mixed bag. From 2009 to 2013, Pittsburgh's offensive line was mediocre at best. Averaging their pass-blocking and run-blocking performances, they ranked 21st, 24th, 12th, 21st, and 19th during that span. Then Pittsburgh hired well-respected offensive line coach **Mike Munchak**, and in the five years since they ranked 10th, 8th, 4th, 4th, and 10th. This offseason, Munchak left in a lateral move to take over as Denver's offensive line coach.

Defensive coordinator **Keith Butler** has been a disaster. Butler was unprepared from his first game – on September 10, 2015 – when his team surrendered three touchdowns to tight end **Rob Gronkowski** of the Patriots. Gronkowski is undeniably a dominant talent, but it was just the fifth (and almost certainly the final) three-touchdown game of his career.

Butler's defenses consistently show embarrassing lapses in coverage which inevitably lead to long touchdowns. During last season, Butler himself discussed with the media how he was game planning to

(cont'd - see PIT-5)

Pittsburgh Steelers Fantasy Corner

JuJu Smith-Schuster belongs in this year's first tier of fantasy wide receivers along with **Odell Beckham**, **Davante Adams**, **Julio Jones**, **Michael Thomas**, and **DeAndre Hopkins**. Smith-Schuster finished fourth in the NFL in targets last season, and this year's Steelers are missing the NFL's fifth-most targets from last year's team. **Ben Roethlisberger** has a trust factor with Smith-Schuster from 2018, but lacks it with Pittsburgh's complementary weapons. If your league mates laugh at you for drafting JuJu in the second round because he's "going to get double teamed without **Antonio Brown**," remind them Smith-Schuster is now the No. 1 option on a Roethlisberger-quarterbacked team and will push to lead the NFL in targets.

- Evan Silva

2018 Situational Usage by Player & Position

Usage Rate by Score

		Being Blown Out (14+)	Down Big (9-13)	One Score	Large Lead (9-13)	Blowout Lead (14+)
RUSH	James Conner	3%	3%	74%	4%	16%
	Juju Smith-Schuster			100%		
	Jaylen Samuels			84%	4%	13%
	Ryan Switzer	33%		67%		
	Stevan Ridley			66%	3%	31%
	Eli Rogers			100%		
	Darrius Heyward-Bey			100%		
	Total	3%		75%	4%	16%
PASS	James Conner	2%	13%	77%	8%	
	Juju Smith-Schuster	6%	13%	71%	4%	6%
	Antonio Brown	6%	13%	70%	5%	6%
	Jaylen Samuels		9%	68%	5%	18%
	Vance McDonald	5%	10%	73%	3%	10%
	Ryan Switzer	6%	11%	69%	9%	6%
	Jesse James	9%	3%	76%	3%	9%
	Stevan Ridley			75%		25%
	Eli Rogers		7%	93%		
	Justin Hunter			85%	8%	8%
	Xavier Grimble		29%	71%		
	Darrius Heyward-Bey			50%		50%
	Total	5%	11%	72%	5%	7%

Share of Offensive Plays by Type

	James Conner	Juju Smith-Schuster	Antonio Brown	Jaylen Samuels	Vance McDonald	Ryan Switzer	Jesse James	Stevan Ridley	Eli Rogers	Justin Hunter	Xavier Grimble	Darrius Heyward-Bey
RUSH	70%	0%		18%		2%		9%	0%			0%
PASS	11%	26%	26%	4%	12%	7%	6%	1%	3%	2%	1%	0%
ALL	33%	17%	16%	9%	7%	5%	4%	4%	2%	2%	1%	0%

Positional Target Distribution vs NFL Average

		NFL Wide				Team Only			
		Left	Middle	Right	Total	Left	Middle	Right	Total
Deep	WR	33%	17%	31%	**81%**	39%	17%	33%	**90%**
	TE	5%	4%	7%	**16%**	3%	3%	4%	**10%**
	RB	1%	0%	2%	**4%**	1%			**1%**
	All	**39%**	**22%**	**39%**	**100%**	**43%**	**20%**	**37%**	**100%**
Short	WR	20%	13%	21%	**55%**	21%	21%	21%	**62%**
	TE	6%	6%	8%	**20%**	5%	8%	7%	**20%**
	RB	10%	5%	10%	**25%**	5%	6%	7%	**18%**
	All	**36%**	**24%**	**39%**	**100%**	**32%**	**34%**	**34%**	**100%**
Total		**37%**	**24%**	**39%**	**100%**	**34%**	**32%**	**34%**	**100%**

Positional Success Rates vs NFL Average

		NFL Wide				Team Only			
		Left	Middle	Right	Total	Left	Middle	Right	Total
Deep	WR	40%	50%	40%	**42%**	40%	35%	34%	**37%**
	TE	43%	53%	41%	**45%**	67%	67%	60%	**64%**
	RB	39%	33%	42%	**41%**	0%			**0%**
	All	**40%**	**50%**	**40%**	**42%**	**41%**	**39%**	**37%**	**39%**
Short	WR	55%	61%	52%	**55%**	55%	60%	50%	**55%**
	TE	55%	61%	55%	**57%**	62%	72%	43%	**60%**
	RB	47%	53%	45%	**47%**	43%	64%	56%	**55%**
	All	**53%**	**59%**	**51%**	**54%**	**54%**	**63%**	**50%**	**56%**
Total		**50%**	**58%**	**49%**	**52%**	**51%**	**61%**	**48%**	**53%**

Division History: Season Wins & 2019 Projection

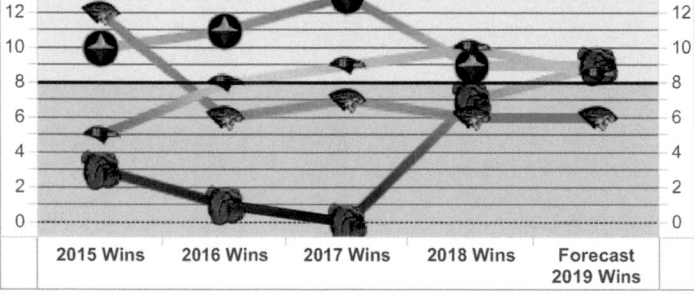

| 2015 Wins | 2016 Wins | 2017 Wins | 2018 Wins | Forecast 2019 Wins |

Rank of 2019 Defensive Pass Efficiency Faced by Week

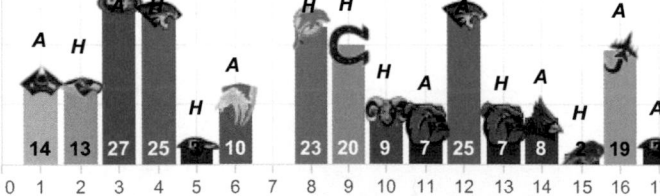

14 13 27 25 10 | 23 20 9 7 25 7 8 19

Rank of 2019 Defensive Rush Efficiency Faced by Week

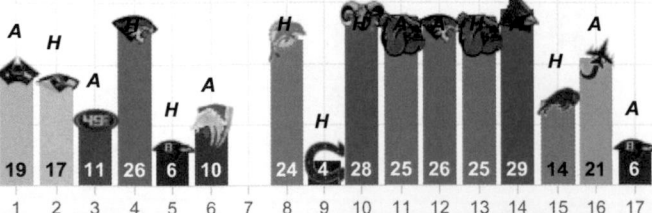

19 17 11 26 10 | 24 4 28 25 26 25 29 14 21 6

2018 Detailed Analytics Summary
Success by Play Type & Primary Personnel Groupings

Type	1-1 [3WR]	1-2 [2WR]	0-1 [4WR]	2-2 [1WR]	2-1 [2WR]	0-0 [5WR]	1-3 [1WR]	2-0 [3WR]	1-0 [4WR]	2-3 [0WR]	ALL
PASS	50% (534)	61% (51)	43% (61)	47% (15)	25% (4)	78% (27)	50% (12)		100% (1)		51% (705)
RUSH	51% (194)	40% (45)	43% (7)	36% (44)	52% (31)	33% (3)	30% (10)	25% (4)	50% (2)	67% (3)	47% (343)
All	50% (728)	51% (96)	43% (68)	39% (59)	49% (35)	73% (30)	41% (22)	25% (4)	67% (3)	67% (3)	50% (1,048)

Format   Success Rate (Total # of Plays)

Receiving Success by Top-4 Personnel Groupings
(Min 50 targets)

POS	Player	1-1 [3WR]	1-2 [2WR]	1-3 [1WR]	2-1 [2WR]	4 Grp Total
RB	James Conner	53% (59) 6.9, 100.9	50% (10) 8.0, 100.0		0% (1) 0.0, 39.6	51% (70) 6.9, 100.0
TE	Vance McDonald	53% (53) 8.8, 111.0	83% (6) 11.3, 113.9	67% (3) 6.0, 91.7		56% (62) 8.9, 111.8
WR	Antonio Brown	51% (124) 7.4, 91.4	60% (15) 9.9, 105.3	50% (2) 3.0, 56.3	0% (1) 0.0, 0.0	51% (142) 7.6, 91.7
	JuJu Smith-Schuster	56% (130) 7.9, 100.5	56% (9) 19.2, 97.9	0% (1) 0.0, 39.6		56% (140) 8.6, 101.0

Format   Line 1: Success Rate (Total # of Plays)   Line 2: YPA, Passer Rating

Rushing Success by Top-4 Personnel Groupings
(Min 25 carries)

Rusher (Last, First)	1-1 [3WR]	1-2 [2WR]	2-2 [1WR]	2-1 [2WR]	4 Grp Total
Conner James	50% (125) 4.9	33% (27) 3.1	60% (25) 5.2	52% (25) 4.6	49% (202) 4.7
Samuels Jaylen	51% (49) 4.8	60% (5) 4.2			52% (54) 4.7
Ridley Stevan	0% (6) 2.0	44% (9) 4.0	17% (6) 2.7	25% (4) 2.0	24% (25) 2.9
Roethlisberger Ben	92% (12) 7.5	50% (2) 0.5	0% (8) -1.1	100% (2) 2.0	58% (24) 3.6

Format   Line 1: Success Rate (Total # of Plays)   Line 2: YPC

Passing by Coverage Scheme

M2M	54% (271) 7.8, 101.2
Zone	57% (213) 8.6, 91.8
Screen	55% (84) 5.8, 110.7
Combo	47% (30) 7.3, 68.5

Passing by Route

Screen	55% (89) 6.0, 114.2
Curl	64% (75) 8.0, 87.8
Out	59% (66) 7.0, 106.9
Slant	61% (44) 9.1, 83.6
Flat	53% (40) 6.1, 108.8
Dig	68% (31) 8.0, 94.6

Throw Types

Level 1	60% (429) 7.1, 103.5
Level 2	48% (155) 7.8, 87.4
Level 3	28% (65) 11.9, 93.2
Sidearm	57% (14) 7.9, 69.9
Shovel	33% (3) 3.7, 72.9

QB Drop Types

3 Step	58% (292) 8.7, 101.7
0/1 Step	55% (216) 6.5, 99.0
5 Step	35% (57) 7.7, 85.5
Basic Screen	57% (47) 6.9, 102.6
7 Step	45% (31) 11.1, 86.1
Designed Rollout Right	64% (11) 6.3, 92.8

QB State at Pass

Planted	56% (423) 8.0, 103.7
Shuffling	54% (98) 6.7, 95.7
Moving	53% (47) 7.9, 82.7

Play Action

	Play Action	No P/A
Under Center	47% (36) 8.1, 86.6	41% (22) 12.3, 91.3
Shotgun	63% (43) 8.0, 115.6	54% (568) 7.5, 97.3
ALL	56% (79) 8.0, 104.1	53% (590) 7.7, 97.1

Run Types

Inside Zone	51% (74) 3.3
Power	46% (57) 5.0
Outside Zone	33% (49) 3.3
Lead	49% (41) 3.7
Pitch	73% (11) 7.6
Stretch	33% (3) 5.0

PIT-5

stop a player *who had been on injured reserve for months* (**Tyler Eifert**).

What should have been the final straw came against the Chargers last year. Pittsburgh missed out on the playoffs by one game, and this could have been the game. They were sitting at 7-3-1 at this point in the season. They were hosting the Chargers, who were playing without their starting running back, **Melvin Gordon**. Pittsburgh opened up a 23-7 halftime lead despite struggling at times against Los Angeles' top receiver, **Keenan Allen**, who inexplicably wound up drawing a linebacker in coverage throughout the game.

Rather than adjust, Butler continued to allow Allen to run free against much slower linebackers in the second half. Allen finished with 14 catches for 148 yards and a touchdown, while the Chargers scored 21 unanswered points and won 33-30.

Tomlin said after the game that his defense "ran out of smoke," citing the loss of sub-package DBs **Morgan Burnett** and **Cam Sutton** and crediting Chargers quarterback **Philip Rivers** with creating favorable matchups via good pre-snap reads.

But the Steelers *didn't actually run out of anything*; on the very first snap of the game, the Chargers lined up with just two wide receivers and still OLB **Brad Dupree** was left in man coverage on **Keenan Allen**. On the Chargers' second pass, Allen was covered by ILB **L.J. Fort**, a former undrafted free agent who had been cut by six teams since 2012 and was making his second career start. By the end of the game, no wide receiver received more targets in a game with a linebacker in coverage than Allen since *Next Gen Stats* began tracking data.

Pittsburgh should know the difference coaching and play calling makes. After firing Todd Haley, the Steelers posted the NFL's best conversion rate in the red zone (73 percent) since 2003. Coaching matters, and I'm concerned with the Steelers coaching. It hasn't been good enough to out-strategize opponents to win key games, especially in the playoffs, and it hasn't been good enough to avoid semi-frequent letdowns during the season to far more inferior opponents. The Steelers should again have more than enough talent to compete with any team in the NFL. But unless their coaching staff updates and accepts change, it likely won't make a difference.

San Francisco 49ers

Coaches (Prior Yrs)

Head Coach:
Kyle Shanahan (Calls Plays) (2 yrs)
Offensive Coordinator:
n/a ()
Defensive Coordinator:
Robert Saleh (1 yr)

EASY   HARD

2019 Forecast	
Wins	Div Rank
8	#3

Past Records

2018: 4-12
2017: 6-10
2016: 2-14

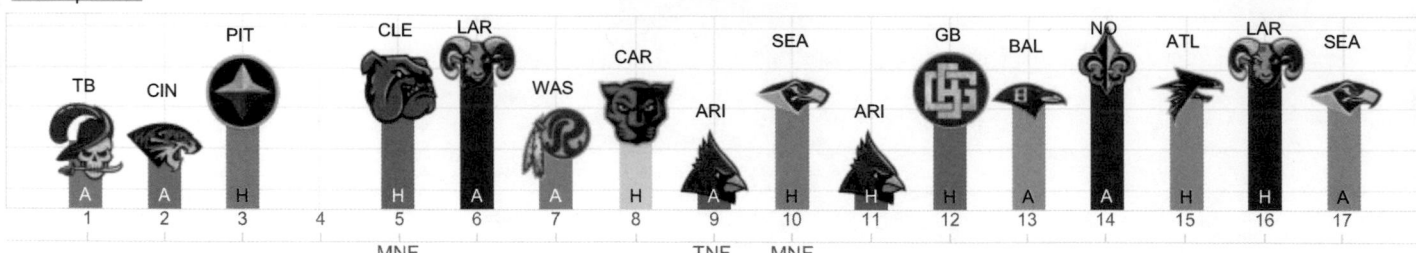

	TB	CIN	PIT		CLE	LAR	WAS	CAR	ARI	SEA	ARI	GB	BAL	NO	ATL	LAR	SEA
	A	A	H		H	A	A	H	A	H	H	H	A	A	H	H	A
	1	2	3	4	5	6	7	8	9	10	11	12	13	14	15	16	17

MNF (under 5) · TNF (under 9) · MNF (under 10)

Key Players Lost

Player	New
Bradley Pinion (P)	TB
Brock Coyle (OLB)	Retired
Cassius Marsh (OLB)	SEA
Dekoda Watson (LB)	DEN

Average Line	# Games Favored	# Games Underdog
0.4	6	6

Regular Season Wins: Past & Current Proj

Forecast 2019 Wins — 8
2018 Wins — 4
Forecast 2018 Wins — 8
2017 Wins — 6
2016 Wins — 2
2015 Wins — 5

1 3 5 7 9 11 13 15

2019 San Francisco 49ers Overview

The 2018 49ers were one of the best 4-12 teams in recent memory, but I would excuse you for having no memory of them at all. Both of their Sunday night games were flexed out, and their other two primetime appearances came without franchise quarterback **Jimmy Garoppolo**, who was lost for the season to a torn ACL in Week 3.

As the 49ers' luck would have it, they ended up as the fourth-most injured team in the NFL, and it didn't help that they played the league's seventh-toughest schedule.

But in terms of Early Down Success Rate -- my custom metric that identifies efficiency and correlates to wins and losses better than almost any statistic – last year's Niners were one of only two teams to rank top 10 both offensively and defensively. This comes in stark contrast to other popular advanced metrics: Football Outsiders' DVOA ranked the 49ers 30th overall, while Pro Football Focus graded them 28th.

A more basic metric also picks up on what EDSR is noticing, though, and that metric is net yards per play, in which San Francisco ranked eighth.

So how is it that a team so good at gaining yards and staying out of difficult third downs went 4-12, exactly?

Turnovers.

The only metric that correlates better to wins and losses than EDSR is turnovers, and the 49ers had a turnover margin of -25, worst in the NFL. To put that into context, the 49ers' -25 turnover margin was a margin of seven worse than the next-worst team and twice as many as the third worst. More than three-quarters of the league didn't even have 25 giveaways *total*, let alone a margin (offset by takeaways) of -25.

(cont'd - see SF2)

Key Free Agents/ Trades Added

Player	AAV (MM)
Dee Ford (OLB)	Trade
Jason Verrett (CB)	$3
Jordan Matthews (WR)	$1.8
Kwon Alexander (ILB)	$13.
Tevin Coleman (RB)	$4.2

Drafted Players

Rd	Pk	Player (College)
1	2	DE - Nick Bosa (Ohio State)
2	36	WR - Deebo Samuel (South Carolina)
3	67	WR - Jalen Hurd (Baylor)
4	110	P - Mitch Wishnowsky (Utah)
5	148	LB - Dre Greenlaw (Arkansas)
	176	TE - Kaden Smith (Stanford)
6	183	OT - Justin Skule (Vanderbilt)
	198	CB - Tim Harris (Virginia)

Lineup & Cap Hits

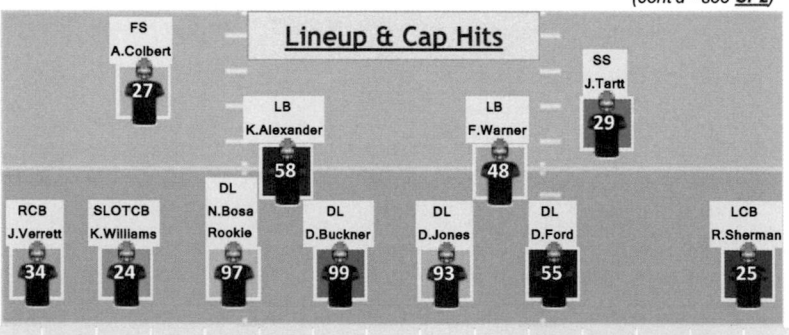

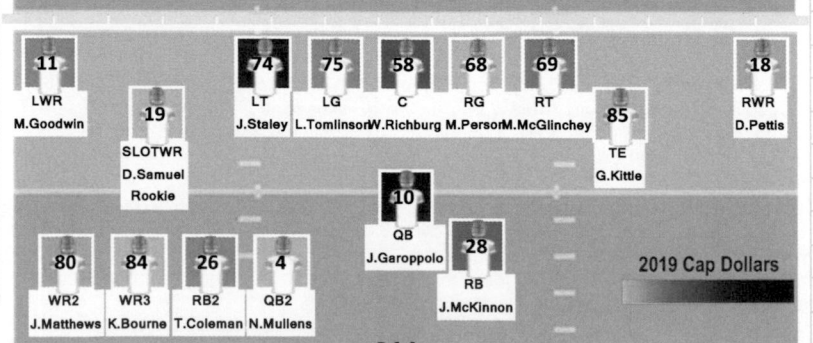

2019 Cap Dollars

2019 Unit Spending

All DEF / All OFF

Positional Spending

	Rank	Total	2017 Rk
All OFF	23	$91.67M	1
QB	16	$21.38M	1
OL	13	$38.90M	12
RB	2	$14.46M	7
WR	31	$11.90M	14
TE	27	$5.04M	27
All DEF	9	$94.83M	28
DL	6	$43.25M	14
LB	12	$23.25M	27
CB	19	$19.74M	12
S	21	$8.58M	29

The 49ers won the EDSR battle in nine games last year, but were -2 or worse in turnover margin in four of those games, losing all four. In the other five, they were between -1 to +1 in turnover margin and went 4-1.

They also went 0-3 in games where their EDSR was roughly neutral, owing to a combined -7 turnover differential.

Though it seems like oversimplification, the 49ers need to play as well as they did in 2018 while avoiding turnovers that plagued them. San Francisco was often able to bypass third down altogether due to its first-down explosiveness, joining the Patriots, Chargers, Chiefs and Bengals as the only five teams to rank in the top 10 in both explosive pass and rush rate on early downs.

A whopping 16 percent of San Francisco's first-down plays were explosive, which is roughly 45% above average. Tight end **George Kittle** ranked third in the league in explosive play rate on first downs, and running back **Matt Breida** was 10th. (Running back **Raheem Mostert** actually ranked No. 1, though it is unclear if he will have a role with the team in 2019 after complications resulting from a broken arm.)

After going 6-10 in Year 1 and 4-12 in Year 2, head coach **Kyle Shanahan** needs to turn things around to avoid the hot seat. Among the biggest reasons for the team's losing ways last season was a lack of production at the wide receiver position.

Only **Kendrick Bourne** compiled at least 50 targets and 30 receptions. "Why him?", you may ask. It's because he was seemingly the team's only wideout who didn't get hurt. The 49ers featured the NFL's sixth-most injured wide receiving corps, as **Dante Pettis** missed four games; **Marquise Goodwin**, five; and **Pierre Garcon**, eight.

Garcon is gone, but Goodwin will return, and the arrow is ticking up on Pettis entering Year 2. The team also drafted two wide receivers on Day 2 of the 2019 NFL Draft, nabbing speedy **Deebo Samuel** out of South Carolina in Round 2 before scooping up versatile **Jalen Hurd** out of Baylor in Round 3.

Pettis is locked in as the starting X receiver. At Z, the team will likely rely on a rotation of Goodwin and Samuel. In the lead for slot duties is third-year man **Trent Taylor**, but I suspect that could be an issue. 87% of Taylor's targets came out of the slot last season, and the results were abysmal: 36% Success Rate, 5.2 YPA, 0:2 TD:INT, 48.9 rating. The 49ers would be better off using the Pettis-Goodwin-Samuel trio in 11 personnel, as Pettis averaged 12.2 YPA and registered a 129 passer rating when targeted over the final five games of his rookie campaign.

With all of his team's injuries at wide receiver, Shanahan opted to employ heavy personnel at a high rate. He became the first coach I've

(cont'd - see SF-3)

2018 Passing Performance

QB	1st Dwn	2nd Dwn	3rd Dwn	
Jimmy Garoppolo	49%	55%	25%	Success Rate
	10.4	6.2	6.1	YPA
	99.6	105.7	48.1	Rating
Pass Rate	52%	65%	79%	
NFL AVG	53%	47%	36%	Success Rate
	7.7	7.3	6.9	YPA
	95.1	93.7	87.1	Rating
Pass Rate	53%	62%	80%	

2018 Rushing Performance

Offense	1st Dwn	2nd Dwn	3rd Dwn	
SF	45%	40%	52%	Success Rate
	5.0	3.5	4.2	YPC
Run Rate	48%	35%	21%	
NFL AVG	48%	46%	51%	Success Rate
	4.5	4.4	4.3	YPC
Run Rate	47%	38%	20%	

2018 Offensive Advanced Metrics

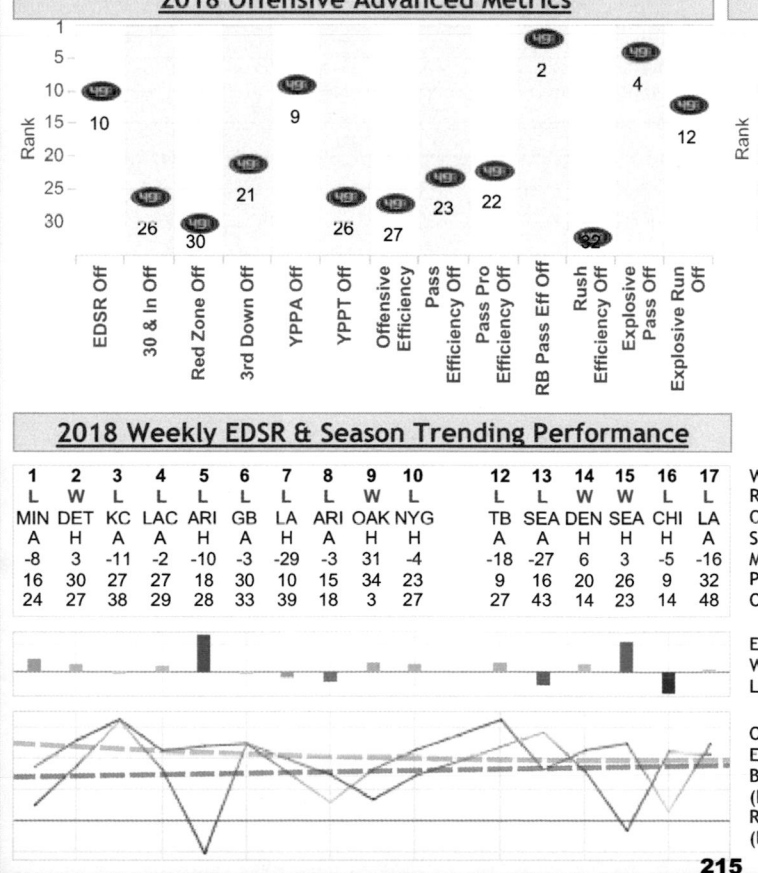

2018 Defensive Advanced Metrics

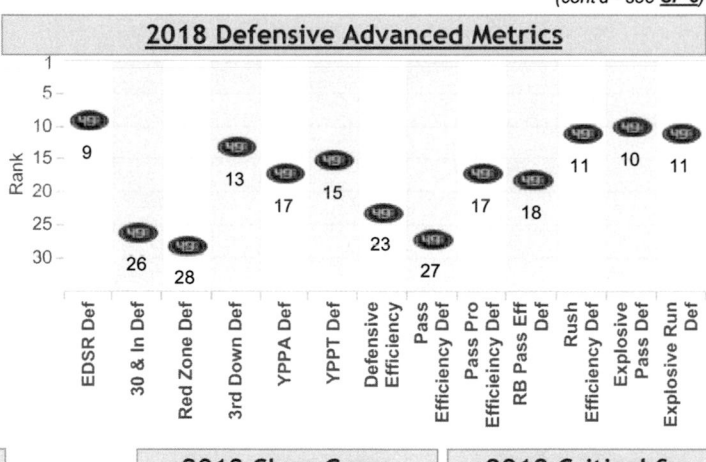

2018 Weekly EDSR & Season Trending Performance

	1	2	3	4	5	6	7	8	9	10		12	13	14	15	16	17	WEEK
	L	L	L	L	L	L	L	L	W	L		L	W	W	W	L	L	RESULT
	MIN	DET	KC	LAC	ARI	GB	LA	ARI	OAK	NYG		TB	SEA	DEN	SEA	CHI	LA	OPP
	A	H	A	A	H	A	H	A	H	H		A	A	H	H	H	A	SITE
	-8	3	-11	-2	-10	-3	-29	-3	31	-4		-18	-27	6	3	-5	-16	MARGIN
	16	30	27	27	18	30	10	15	34	23		9	16	20	26	9	32	PTS
	24	27	38	29	28	33	39	18	3	27		27	43	14	23	14	48	OPP PTS

EDSR by Wk
W=Green
L=Red

OFF/DEF
EDSR
Blue=OFF
(high=good)
Red=DEF
(low=good)

2018 Close Game Records

All 2018 Wins: **4**

FG Games (<=3 pts) W-L: **2-3**

FG Games Win %: **40% (#18)**

FG Games Wins (% of Total Wins): **50% (#3)**

1 Score Games (<=8 pts) W-L: **3-6**

1 Score Games Win %: **33% (#24)**

1 Score Games Wins (% of Total Wins): **75% (#5)**

2018 Critical & Game-Deciding Stats

TO Margin	-25
TO Given	32
INT Given	20
FUM Given	12
TO Taken	7
INT Taken	2
FUM Taken	5
Sack Margin	-10
Sacks	38
Sacks Allow	48
Return TD Margin	-2
Ret TDs	2
Ret TDs Allow	4
Penalty Margin	+5
Penalties	112
Opponent Penalties	117

San Francisco 49ers 2019 Strength of Schedule In Detail (compared to 2018)

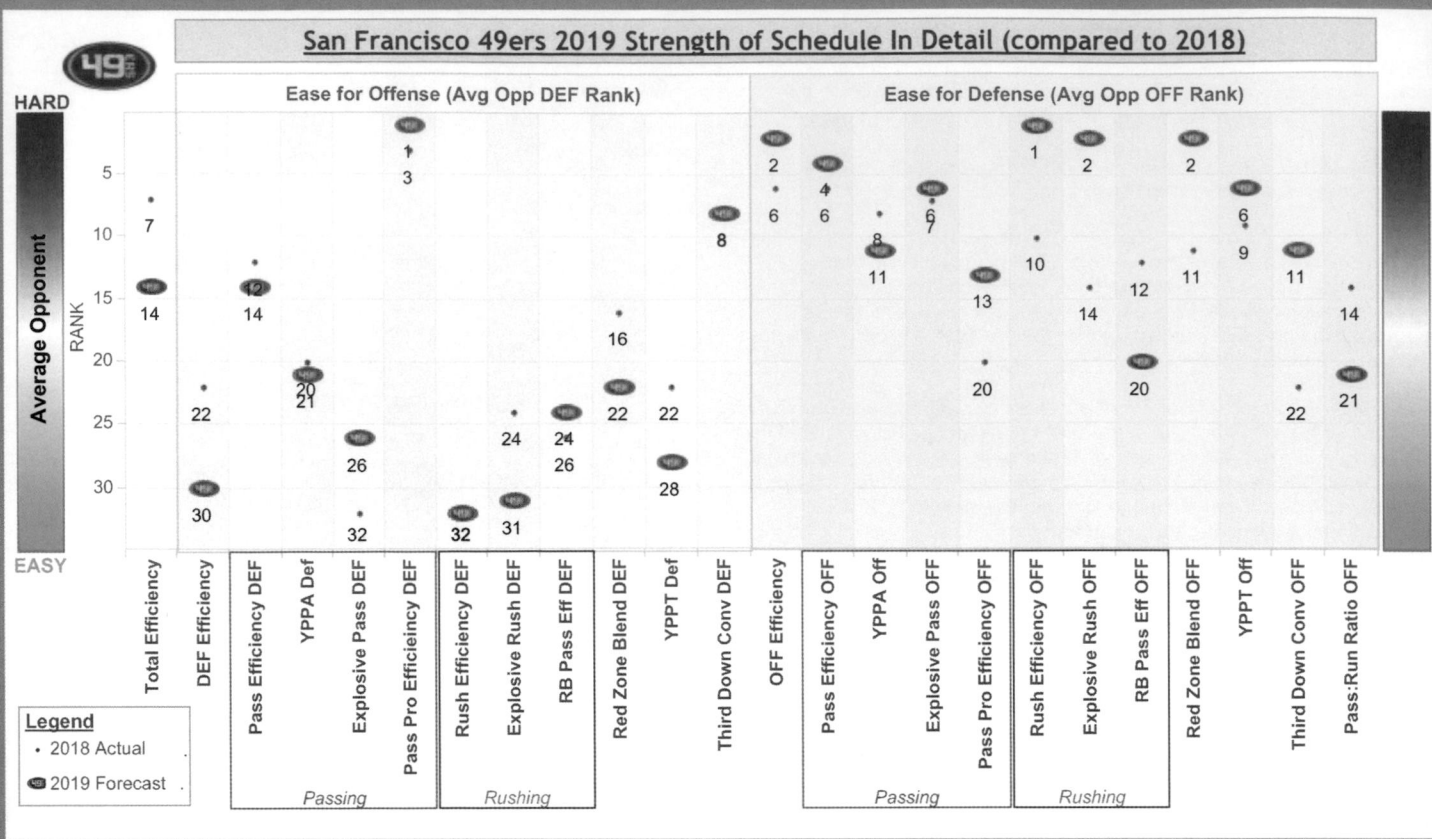

2019 v 2018 Schedule Variances* (OFF=Rank of DEF faced, 2019 vs 2018)

Pass OFF Rank	Pass OFF Blend Rk	Rush OFF Rk	Rush OFF Blend Rk	Pass DEF Rk	Pass DEF Blend Rk	Rush DEF Rk	Rush DEF Blend Rk
17	15	14	20	14	13	7	8

* **1**=Hardest Jump in 2019 schedule from 2018 (aka a much harder schedule in 2019), **32**=Easiest Jump in 2019 schedule from 2018 (aka a much easier schedule in 2019);
Pass Blend metric blends 4 metrics: Pass Efficiency, YPPA, Explosive Pass & Pass Rush; **Rush Blend** metric blends 3 metrics: Rush Efficiency, Explosive Rush & RB Targets

Team Records & Trends

	2018	2017	2016
Average line	3.8	4.4	6.7
Average O/U line	46.7	43.8	45.4
Straight Up Record	4-12	6-10	2-14
Against the Spread Record	5-11	9-6	5-10
Over/Under Record	9-7	8-8	10-6
ATS as Favorite	1-4	1-0	0-1
ATS as Underdog	4-7	8-6	5-7
Straight Up Home	4-4	3-5	1-7
ATS Home	3-5	3-4	2-5
Over/Under Home	4-4	5-3	4-4
ATS as Home Favorite	1-3	0-0	0-1
ATS as a Home Dog	2-2	3-4	2-3
Straight Up Away	0-8	3-5	1-7
ATS Away	2-6	6-2	3-5
Over/Under Away	5-3	3-5	6-2
ATS Away Favorite	0-1	1-0	0-0
ATS Away Dog	2-5	5-2	3-4
Six Point Teaser Record	11-5	12-4	7-8
Seven Point Teaser Record	11-4	12-4	8-8
Ten Point Teaser Record	12-4	13-2	11-5

SF-3

tracked since 2016 to use more 21 personnel (41%) than 11 personnel (39%) during a season. But it's a big credit to him that not only was he willing to adapt, but that he was able to do so effectively:

The 49ers recorded a 61% Success Rate, 11.9 YPA, 120.8 rating and 4:2 TD:INT ratio from 12 personnel and a 53% Success Rate, 8.3 YPA, 92.2 rating, and 9:5 TD:INT ratio from 21 personnel.

Meanwhile, they managed just a 39% Success Rate, 6.0 YPA, 67.9 rating, and 12:12 TD:INT ratio from 11 personnel.

Another example of Shanahan's expert adaptability on offense: He used the

(cont'd - see **SF-4**)

2019 Rest Analysis

Team More Rest	3
Opp More Rest	5
Net Rest Edge	-2
Week 2 Edge	0
Week 3 Edge	0
Week 5 Edge	7
Week 6 Edge	-4
Week 7 Edge	0
Week 8 Edge	
Week 9 Edge	0
Week 10 Edge	3
Week 11 Edge	-1
Week 12 Edge	
Week 13 Edge	1
Week 14 Edge	-3
Week 15 Edge	0
Week 16 Edge	0
Week 17 Edge	0

Health by Unit*

2018 Rk	
2017 Rk	23
2018 v 2017 Rk	17
Off Rk	
Def Rk	24
QB Rk	
RB Rk	
WR Rk	27
TE Rk	12
Oline Rk	3
Dline Rk	3
LB Rk	
DB Rk	27

*Based on the work of Football Outsiders

2018 Weekly Betting Lines (wks 1-16)

1	2	3	5	6	7	8	9	10	11	12	13	14	15	16
TB	CIN	PIT	CLE	LAR	WAS	CAR	ARI	SEA	ARI	GB	BAL	NO	ATL	LAR
1	0	0	-2.5	8.5	1	-2.5	-3	-1.5	-8.5	0	4	8.5	-1.5	2

Avg = 0.4

Home Lines (wks 1-16)

3	5	8	10	11	12	15	16
0	-2.5	-2.5	-1.5	-8.5	0	-1.5	2
PIT	CLE	CAR	SEA	ARI	GB	ATL	

Avg = -1.8

Road Lines (wks 1-16)

1	2	6	7	9	13	14
1	0	8.5	1	-3	4	8.5
TB	CIN	LAR	WAS	ARI	BAL	NO

Avg = 2.9

San Francisco 49ers 2018 Play Analysis

2018 Play Tendencies

All Pass %	58%
All Pass Rk	21
All Rush %	42%
All Rush Rk	12
1 Score Pass %	57%
1 Score Pass Rk	20
2017 1 Score Pass %	59%
2017 1 Score Pass Rk	10
2018 Pass Increase %	-3%
Pass Increase Rk	27
1 Score Rush %	43%
1 Score Rush Rk	13
Up Pass %	50%
Up Pass Rk	15
Up Rush %	50%
Up Rush Rk	18
Down Pass %	63%
Down Pass Rk	27
Down Rush %	37%
Down Rush Rk	6

2018 Down & Distance Tendencies

Down	Distance	Total Plays	Pass Rate	Run Rate	Play Success %
1	Short (1-3)	6	17%	83%	50%
	Med (4-7)	10	40%	60%	30%
	Long (8-10)	325	46%	54%	51%
	XL (11+)	14	43%	57%	21%
2	Short (1-3)	36	31%	69%	69%
	Med (4-7)	64	56%	44%	55%
	Long (8-10)	91	64%	36%	41%
	XL (11+)	44	84%	16%	20%
3	Short (1-3)	36	50%	50%	61%
	Med (4-7)	41	95%	5%	51%
	Long (8-10)	25	92%	8%	36%
	XL (11+)	35	74%	26%	9%
4	Short (1-3)	2	0%	100%	100%
	Med (4-7)	1	100%	0%	100%

Shotgun %:

Under Center	Shotgun
56%	44%

37% AVG 63%

Run Rate:

Under Center	Shotgun
61%	18%

68% AVG 23%

Pass Rate:

Under Center	Shotgun
39%	82%

32% AVG 77%

Short Yardage Intelligence:

2nd and Short Run

Run Freq	Run Rk	NFL Run Freq Avg	Run 1D Rate	Run NFL 1D Avg
62%	21	65%	56%	68%

2nd and Short Pass

Pass Freq	Pass Rk	NFL Pass Freq Avg	Pass 1D Rate	Pass NFL 1D Avg
38%	12	35%	82%	56%

Most Frequent Play

Down	Distance	Play Type	Player	Total Plays	Play Success %
1	Short (1-3)	RUSH	Alfred Morris	4	25%
	Med (4-7)	PASS	George Kittle	2	50%
		RUSH	Matt Breida	2	0%
			Kyle Juszczyk	2	0%
	Long (8-10)	RUSH	Matt Breida	75	49%
	XL (11+)	RUSH	Matt Breida	4	25%
2	Short (1-3)	RUSH	Matt Breida	11	73%
	Med (4-7)	RUSH	Matt Breida	14	43%
	Long (8-10)	PASS	George Kittle	17	59%
	XL (11+)	PASS	George Kittle	10	40%
3	Short (1-3)	PASS	George Kittle	6	50%
		RUSH	Alfred Morris	6	83%
	Med (4-7)	PASS	George Kittle	9	67%
	Long (8-10)	PASS	Trent Taylor	5	0%
	XL (11+)	PASS	George Kittle	5	0%
		RUSH	Matt Breida	5	0%

Most Successful Play*

Down	Distance	Play Type	Player	Total Plays	Play Success %
1	Long (8-10)	PASS	Kendrick Bourne	11	82%
2	Short (1-3)	RUSH	Matt Breida	11	73%
	Med (4-7)	PASS	Pierre Garcon	5	80%
	Long (8-10)	PASS	Matt Breida	6	83%
	XL (11+)	PASS	George Kittle	10	40%
3	Short (1-3)	RUSH	Alfred Morris	6	83%
	Med (4-7)	PASS	Marquise Goodwin	5	80%
	Long (8-10)	PASS	Trent Taylor	5	0%
	XL (11+)	PASS	George Kittle	5	0%
		RUSH	Matt Breida	5	0%

*Minimum 5 plays to qualify

2018 Weekly Snap Rates

Wk	Opp	Score	George Kittle	Kyle Juszczyk	Kendrick Bourne	Dante Pettis	Marquise Goodwin	Pierre Garcon	Matt Breida	Trent Taylor	Garrett Celek	Alfred Morris
1	MIN	L 24-16	51 (77%)	26 (39%)	8 (12%)	48 (73%)	17 (26%)	53 (80%)	30 (45%)	37 (56%)	23 (35%)	34 (52%)
2	DET	W 30-27	50 (78%)	40 (63%)	10 (16%)	56 (88%)		49 (77%)	25 (39%)	16 (25%)	30 (47%)	31 (48%)
3	KC	L 38-27	54 (79%)	53 (78%)	15 (22%)	25 (37%)	42 (62%)	52 (76%)	29 (43%)	25 (37%)	19 (28%)	23 (34%)
4	LAC	L 29-27	50 (83%)	37 (62%)	25 (42%)		37 (62%)	49 (82%)	38 (63%)	31 (52%)	17 (28%)	14 (23%)
5	ARI	L 28-18	87 (89%)	68 (69%)	42 (43%)			62 (63%)	13 (13%)	50 (51%)	26 (27%)	44 (45%)
6	GB	L 33-30	53 (93%)	39 (68%)	23 (40%)		54 (95%)	45 (79%)	27 (47%)		17 (30%)	1 (2%)
7	LA	L 39-10	52 (90%)	34 (59%)	26 (45%)		55 (95%)	32 (55%)	5 (9%)	20 (34%)	20 (34%)	20 (34%)
8	ARI	L 18-15	60 (91%)	47 (71%)	54 (82%)	7 (11%)	61 (92%)		31 (47%)	19 (29%)	23 (35%)	11 (17%)
9	OAK	W 34-3	33 (60%)	34 (62%)	12 (22%)	11 (20%)	40 (73%)	37 (67%)	27 (49%)		20 (36%)	10 (18%)
10	NYG	L 27-23	71 (97%)	46 (63%)	69 (95%)	41 (56%)	61 (84%)		44 (60%)	7 (10%)	6 (8%)	14 (19%)
12	TB	L 27-9	60 (94%)	38 (59%)	56 (88%)	58 (91%)			31 (48%)	9 (14%)	12 (19%)	
13	SEA	L 43-16	67 (88%)	39 (51%)	67 (88%)	71 (93%)		10 (13%)		23 (30%)	16 (21%)	
14	DEN	W 20-14	66 (92%)	42 (58%)	43 (60%)	61 (85%)	24 (33%)			23 (32%)	27 (38%)	4 (6%)
15	SEA	W 26-23	59 (95%)	46 (74%)	46 (74%)	57 (92%)	7 (11%)		45 (73%)	15 (24%)	17 (27%)	
16	CHI	L 14-9	54 (98%)	33 (60%)	52 (95%)	17 (31%)	38 (69%)		9 (16%)	26 (47%)	3 (5%)	
17	LA	L 48-32	61 (98%)	40 (65%)	58 (94%)					20 (32%)		44 (71%)
	Grand Total		928 (88%)	662 (63%)	606 (57%)	452 (61%)	436 (64%)	379 (72%)	364 (40%)	321 (34%)	276 (28%)	250 (31%)

Personnel Groupings

Personnel	Team %	NFL Avg	Succ. %
2-1 [2WR]	41%	8%	50%
1-1 [3WR]	39%	65%	38%
1-2 [2WR]	10%	17%	54%
2-2 [1WR]	7%	3%	42%

Grouping Tendencies

Personnel	Pass Rate	Pass Succ. %	Run Succ. %
2-1 [2WR]	45%	53%	48%
1-1 [3WR]	83%	39%	33%
1-2 [2WR]	41%	61%	49%
2-2 [1WR]	23%	50%	40%

Red Zone Targets (min 3)

Receiver	All	Inside 5	6-10	11-20
George Kittle	18	4	3	11
Kendrick Bourne	12	4	2	6
Kyle Juszczyk	5		1	4
Marquise Goodwin	5	1		4
Trent Taylor	5	1	1	3
Dante Pettis	4			4
Jeff Wilson	4	1		3
Pierre Garcon	3		1	2

Red Zone Rushes (min 3)

Rusher	All	Inside 5	6-10	11-20
Alfred Morris	26	10	4	12
Matt Breida	23	6	6	11
Jeff Wilson	11		2	9
Jimmy Garoppolo	5			5
C.J. Beathard	4	2	1	1
Kyle Juszczyk	3	1	1	1

Early Down Target Rate

RB	TE	WR
23%	29%	48%
23%	21%	56%
	NFL AVG	

Overall Target Success %

RB	TE	WR
54%	57%	49%
#2	#11	#24

San Francisco 49ers 2018 Passing Recap & 2019 Outlook

Jimmy Garoppolo remains on track for training camp, but he was limited to individual drills at minicamp, participating in seven-on-seven drills in May while sitting out all of the 11-on-11 sessions. This is entirely normal for ACL injuries, which typically take 9-12 months to heal from. Jimmy G tore his ACL on September 23, 2018, so June 23 would mark nine months.

It is hard to take too many positives from Garoppolo's 2.5-game stint in 2018, but there wasn't anything alarming to undo the promise he flashed in five starts at the end of 2017. The 49ers play a middle-of-the-road schedule of pass defenses in 2019, and with their own defense likely to struggle vs. the second-toughest schedule of offenses, Garoppolo is going to need to play like his 2017 self for his team to have a chance to win games. In the process, he will have to lean on Kittle just as Mullens and Beathard did, but also build on his blossoming connection with Goodwin while elevating unproven players in Pettis, Samuel, Taylor, and Hurd.

2018 Standard Passing Table

QB	Comp	Att	Comp %	Yds	YPA	TDs	INT	Sacks	Rating	Rk
Nick Mullens	175	273	64%	2,282	8.4	13	10	17	91	26
Jimmy Garoppolo	53	89	60%	718	8.1	5	3	13	90	29
NFL Avg			62%		7.0				87.5	

2018 Advanced Passing Table

QB	Success %	EDSR Passing Success %	20+ Yd Pass Gains	20+ Yd Pass %	30+ Yd Pass Gains	30+ Yd Pass %	Avg. Air Yds per Comp	Avg. YAC per Comp	20+ Air Yd Comp	20+ Air Yd %
Nick Mullens	48%	51%	35	13.0%	12	4.0%	6.0	7.0	8	3%
Jimmy Garoppolo	45%	51%	9	10.0%	5	6.0%	6.6	7.0	5	6%
NFL Avg	44%	48%	29.5	8.4%	12.5	3.7%	5.8	5.1	14.5	6%

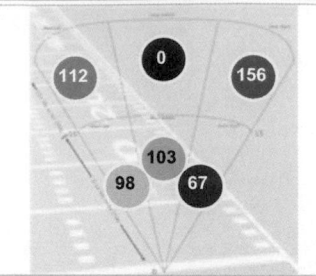

Jimmy Garoppolo Rating All Downs

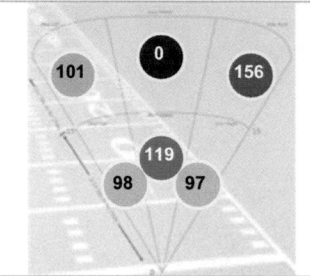

Jimmy Garoppolo Rating Early Downs

Interception Rates by Down

Yards to Go	1st Dwn	2nd Dwn	3rd Dwn	Total
1 & 2		0.0%	0.0%	0.0%
3, 4, 5	0.0%	0.0%	0.0%	0.0%
6 - 9		0.0%	10.0%	4.8%
10 - 14	2.3%	8.3%	0.0%	3.2%
15+	0.0%	0.0%	0.0%	0.0%
Total	2.2%	3.0%	4.2%	2.9%

3rd Down Passing - Short of Sticks Analysis

QB	Avg. Yds to Go	Avg. YIA (of Comp)	Avg Yds Short	Short of Sticks Rate	Short Rk
Nick Mullens	7.6	6.1	-1.5	63%	19
NFL Avg	7.8	6.4	-1.4	60%	

Air Yds vs YAC

Air Yds %	YAC %	Rk
48%	52%	35
53%	48%	

2018 Receiving Recap & 2019 Outlook

Kittle is a beastly treasure who can line up as an in-line tight end, out wide, in the slot, or even as a running back. He was at his best aligning as a tight end in 11 personnel, but a note for coach Shanahan, if I may: In 21 personnel, Kittle produced at a much better rate (64% Success Rate, 13.1 YPA, 143 rating) when aligned in the slot rather than in-line (46% Success Rate, 9.9 YPA, 86 rating). Samuel sat out minicamp with a hip injury, allowing Goodwin to take more first-team reps. The 49ers would get a big boost if Goodwin regained his form with Garoppolo from 2017 when Jimmy G started the final five games, in which Goodwin averaged 5.8 receptions on 8.6 targets for 76.8 yards.

Player *Min 50 Targets	Targ	Comp %	YPA	Rating	Success %	Success Rk	Missed YPA Rk	YAS % Rk	YTS % Rk	TDs
George Kittle	135	65%	10.2	105.1	57%	32	70	18	97	4
Kendrick Bourne	66	64%	7.4	93.4	55%	43	118	67	26	4

Directional Passer Rating Delivered

Receiver	Short Left	Short Middle	Short Right	Deep Left	Deep Middle	Deep Right	Player Total
George Kittle	115	111	94	54	119	96	105
Kendrick Bourne	93	141	36	110	117	55	93
Dante Pettis	70	84	134	156	149	19	114
Pierre Garcon	65	70	115	110	56	58	71
Marquise Goodwin	33	149	59	158	90	40	77
Kyle Juszczyk	95	96	76	119	40	158	107
Trent Taylor	52	44	118	92	0	40	66
Matt Breida	128	134	107	40			123
Alfred Morris	55	40	59				42
Garrett Celek	0	106	104		40	158	101
Team Total	86	110	92	131	90	96	96

2018 Rushing Recap & 2019 Outlook

If **Jerrick McKinnon** is healthy in 2019, I wouldn't be surprised if he ends up leading the backfield, but at worst, he should play a major part in the passing game. Coleman, signed to a two-year, $8.5 million deal, is an explosive player who has only missed one game over the past two seasons and will help take some of the burden off less-durable Breida and McKinnon. **Kyle Juszczyk** is also highly paid for a fullback and will likely continue to play a large role as a Swiss-army knife for Shanahan in 21 personnel. However the backfield rotation shakes out, I expect the 49ers' run game to have success this season against what I project to be the easiest schedule of run defenses in football.

Player *Min 50 Rushes	Rushes	YPC	Success %	Success Rk	Missed YPA Rk	YTS % Rk	YAS % Rk	Early Down Success %	Early Down Success Rk	TDs
Matt Breida	152	5.2	45%	45	61	68	9	46%	41	3
Alfred Morris	111	3.9	41%	59	56	50	27	38%	65	2
Jeff Wilson	66	4.0	48%	34	14	35	72	46%	41	0

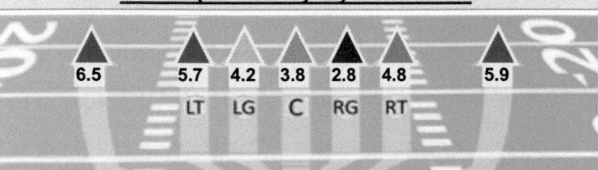

Yards per Carry by Direction

6.5 (LT) · 5.7 (LG) · 4.2 (C) · 3.8 / 2.8 (RG) · 4.8 (RT) · 5.9

Directional Run Frequency

11% (LT) · 16% (LG) · 9% (C) · 26% (RG) · 9% · 15% (RT) · 14%

fourth-highest play action rate with Garoppolo, but reduced play action dramatically when backups **C.J. Beathard** and **Nick Mullens** took over. Why this strategy? In 11 personnel, Garoppolo improved from 5.3 YPA and a 29% Success Rate without play action to 13.2 and a 70% Success Rate with play action.

But Beathard and Mullens were worse with play action from 11, so Shanahan rarely used it, reserving it mostly for 21 and 12 sets, in which both young quarterbacks felt most comfortable using play action.

The 49ers put a lot of work into the other side of the ball this offseason. They improved their front seven by acquiring pass rusher **Dee Ford** from the Chiefs and signing linebacker **Kwon Alexander** from the Buccaneers, as well as drafting defensive end **Nick Bosa** out of Ohio State with the No. 2 overall pick. San Francisco's pass rush ranked 17th last year but is certainly a candidate to be one of the NFL's most-improved units in 2019.

It's what's behind the front seven that could still be an issue. The 49ers finished 27th in pass-defense efficiency last season, and unfortunately, their only move of significance was adding oft-injured former Chargers cornerback **Jason Verrett**. He was outstanding in 2015, but injuries have

(cont'd - see SF-5)

San Francisco 49ers Fantasy Corner

Deebo Samuel was reported to be the No. 2 wide receiver on San Francisco's draft board behind **N'Keal Harry**. Dogged by injuries early in his South Carolina career, Samuel shook them off for a breakout redshirt senior year (62/882/11) in which he burned Clemson's National Championship secondary for 210 yards. He also returned four career kickoffs for TDs and tested as a 93rd-percentile athlete in Indy, blazing 4.48 at 5-foot-11, 214. Coach **Kyle Shanahan** has prioritized receivers capable of moving all around the formation, and Samuel perfectly fits the bill as a cross between **Golden Tate** and **Pierre Garcon**. Samuel is every bit as likely as **Dante Pettis** to emerge as the Niners' short- or even long-term No. 1 wideout.

- Evan Silva

2018 Situational Usage by Player & Position

Usage Rate by Score

		Being Blown Out (14+)	Down Big (9-13)	One Score	Large Lead (9-13)	Blowout Lead (14+)
RUSH	Matt Breida	9%	7%	76%	5%	3%
	George Kittle			100%		
	Alfred Morris	31%	4%	55%	3%	8%
	Jeff Wilson	15%	11%	58%	15%	2%
	Marquise Goodwin			100%		
	Raheem Mostert	18%		65%	3%	15%
	Dante Pettis			100%		
	Kyle Juszczyk	38%		38%	13%	13%
	Total	18%	6%	65%	6%	5%
PASS	Matt Breida	20%	3%	77%		
	George Kittle	31%	6%	59%	2%	3%
	Alfred Morris	25%		75%		
	Jeff Wilson	54%	15%	31%		
	Kendrick Bourne	25%	2%	71%		2%
	Marquise Goodwin	17%	5%	76%		2%
	Raheem Mostert	50%		50%		
	Dante Pettis	24%	11%	63%		3%
	Kyle Juszczyk	33%		60%	7%	
	Pierre Garcon	15%	3%	73%	6%	3%
	Trent Taylor	40%	17%	43%		
	Garrett Celek	29%		71%		
	Total	28%	6%	63%	1%	2%

Share of Offensive Plays by Type

	Matt Breida	George Kittle	Alfred Morris	Jeff Wilson	Kendrick Bourne	Marquise Goodwin	Raheem Mostert	Dante Pettis	Kyle Juszczyk	Pierre Garcon	Trent Taylor	Garrett Celek
RUSH	40%	0%	29%	18%		1%	9%	0%	2%			
PASS	7%	29%	2%	3%	13%	10%	1%	9%	7%	8%	7%	2%
ALL	23%	15%	15%	10%	7%	6%	5%	5%	5%	4%	4%	1%

Positional Target Distribution vs NFL Average

		NFL Wide				Team Only			
		Left	Middle	Right	Total	Left	Middle	Right	Total
Deep	WR	33%	17%	31%	81%	23%	24%	20%	66%
	TE	5%	4%	7%	15%	10%	3%	14%	27%
	RB	1%	0%	2%	3%	3%	1%	3%	7%
	All	39%	22%	39%	100%	35%	28%	37%	100%
Short	WR	20%	14%	21%	55%	18%	14%	17%	48%
	TE	6%	6%	8%	20%	12%	9%	11%	31%
	RB	10%	5%	10%	25%	10%	4%	7%	20%
	All	36%	25%	39%	100%	40%	26%	35%	100%
Total		37%	24%	39%	100%	39%	26%	35%	100%

Positional Success Rates vs NFL Average

		NFL Wide				Team Only			
		Left	Middle	Right	Total	Left	Middle	Right	Total
Deep	WR	39%	49%	40%	42%	75%	53%	21%	51%
	TE	44%	53%	41%	45%	29%	50%	60%	47%
	RB	40%	40%	41%	40%	0%	0%	100%	40%
	All	40%	50%	40%	42%	56%	50%	42%	49%
Short	WR	55%	61%	52%	56%	46%	52%	48%	48%
	TE	55%	62%	54%	57%	52%	71%	57%	59%
	RB	46%	53%	45%	47%	64%	64%	44%	58%
	All	53%	59%	51%	54%	52%	60%	50%	54%
Total		50%	58%	49%	52%	53%	58%	49%	53%

Division History: Season Wins & 2019 Projection

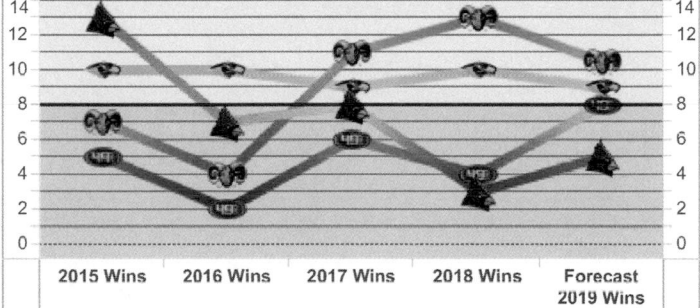

2015 Wins   2016 Wins   2017 Wins   2018 Wins   Forecast 2019 Wins

Rank of 2019 Defensive Pass Efficiency Faced by Week

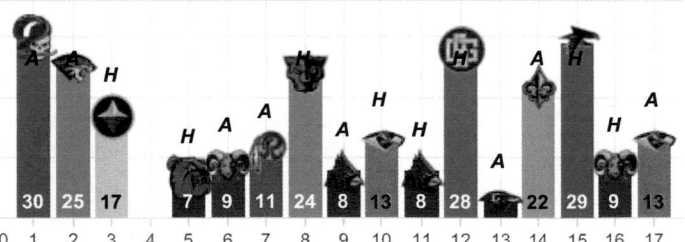

30 25 17 7 9 11 24 8 13 8 28 22 29 9 13

Rank of 2019 Defensive Rush Efficiency Faced by Week

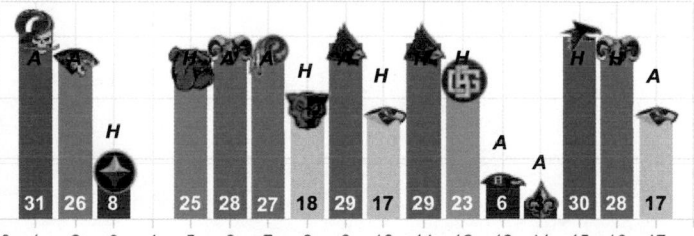

31 26 8 25 28 27 18 29 17 29 23 6 30 28 17

2018 Detailed Analytics Summary
Success by Play Type & Primary Personnel Groupings

Successful Play Rate 0% — 100%

Type	2-1 [2WR]	1-1 [3WR]	1-2 [2WR]	2-2 [1WR]	1-3 [1WR]	0-1 [4WR]	2-0 [3WR]	1-0 [4WR]	ALL
PASS	53% (188)	39% (320)	61% (41)	50% (16)	100% (1)	50% (8)	100% (2)	100% (1)	46% (577)
RUSH	48% (226)	33% (67)	49% (59)	40% (55)	56% (9)		50% (4)		45% (420)
All	50% (414)	38% (387)	54% (100)	42% (71)	60% (10)	50% (8)	67% (6)	100% (1)	46% (997)

Format — Success Rate (Total # of Plays)

Receiving Success by Top-4 Personnel Groupings
(Min 50 targets)

POS	Player	1-1 [3WR]	2-1 [2WR]	1-2 [2WR]	2-2 [1WR]	4 Grp Total
TE	George Kittle	62% (58) 9.0, 88.4	50% (54) 10.4, 100.8	63% (16) 15.0, 132.3	75% (4) 11.5, 112.5	58% (132) 10.4, 100.8
WR	Kendrik Bourne	46% (37) 6.6, 92.6	57% (21) 6.5, 76.7	100% (2) 16.0, 118.8	100% (1) 17.0, 118.8	52% (61) 7.0, 90.1
	Dante Pettis	30% (27) 8.4, 74.0	63% (16) 10.3, 123.2	100% (2) 38.0, 158.3		44% (45) 10.4, 113.8

Format — Line 1: Success Rate (Total # of Plays)   Line 2: YPA, Passer Rating

Rushing Success by Top-4 Personnel Groupings
(Min 25 carries)

Rusher (Last, First)	2-1 [2WR]	1-1 [3WR]	1-2 [2WR]	2-2 [1WR]	4 Grp Total
Breida Matt	48% (91) 5.4	29% (21) 4.7	50% (26) 6.5	45% (11) 3.0	46% (149) 5.3
Morris Alfred	43% (58) 4.4	17% (18) 2.2	53% (17) 5.1	50% (10) 2.6	41% (103) 3.9
Mostert Raheem	78% (18) 10.8	63% (8) 6.0	100% (2) 4.0	17% (6) 1.8	65% (34) 7.7

Format — Line 1: Success Rate (Total # of Plays)   Line 2: YPC

Passing by Coverage Scheme

Zone	52% (212) 8.3, 93.0
M2M	48% (206) 7.8, 82.3
Screen	63% (46) 7.9, 106.8
Combo	60% (10) 14.9, 106.3

Passing by Route

Curl	58% (59) 7.6, 87.3
Slant	52% (58) 7.7, 83.0
Out	52% (56) 6.9, 93.2
Dig	63% (52) 9.7, 73.1
Screen	64% (50) 8.0, 113.4
Flat	62% (26) 6.4, 89.6

Throw Types

Level 1	55% (341) 7.5, 93.8
Level 2	46% (99) 11.4, 96.6
Level 3	33% (24) 9.8, 75.3
Sidearm	56% (16) 8.3, 99.0
Shovel	83% (6) 8.5, 141.7

QB Drop Types

3 Step	55% (163) 9.3, 106.8
0/1 Step	50% (136) 6.5, 89.8
5 Step	41% (79) 7.5, 41.6
7 Step	60% (50) 11.9, 121.7
Basic Screen	64% (25) 9.6, 106.5
Designed Rollout Right	61% (23) 9.2, 94.8

QB State at Pass

Planted	51% (368) 8.0, 87.2
Shuffling	52% (56) 7.8, 104.5
Moving	55% (40) 8.5, 106.0

Play Action

	Play Action	No P/A
Under Center	56% (110) 9.8, 103.6	57% (82) 9.3, 98.6
Shotgun	60% (20) 13.2, 152.1	48% (281) 7.2, 82.8
ALL	57% (130) 10.3, 111.8	50% (363) 7.7, 86.4

Run Types

Outside Zone	40% (72) 4.0
Lead	57% (67) 6.3
Pitch	50% (52) 6.5
Inside Zone	49% (35) 3.6
Stretch	48% (29) 4.3
Power	41% (22) 4.8

SF-5

robbed Verrett of all but five games over the past three seasons. Heading into his age-28 season, there is no telling exactly how much of a toll those injuries have taken on Verrett.

The 49ers' 2019 schedule of opposing offenses is concerning. After facing the sixth-toughest schedule last season, I'm forecasting their defense to face the second-toughest overall, including most difficult vs. rush offenses and fourth toughest vs. pass offenses.

They also face the second-most brutal finish to the season, having to contend with the Packers, Ravens, Saints, Falcons, Rams, and Seahawks – all of which I'm projecting to be winning squads in 2019.

On top of that, the 49ers will be at a rest disadvantage in five games. They have to face a Rams team that will have had four extra days of rest, both the Panthers and Packers off of byes, and the Saints off of a mini-bye.

Still, I'm higher than most on the 49ers this season.

Most see the 4-12 record, chalk them up as a trash team, and end it at that, but I dug deeper into this supposed dumpster fire and came away with many things to like.

The 49ers will finally get the use of 2018 free-agent signing McKinnon, which should be music to Shanahan's ears. As soon as McKinnon became available in free agency, GM **John Lynch** overpaid him on a four-year, $30 million pact. While Breida had a splendid campaign that saw him rush for 5.2 yards per carry despite dealing with various ailments, he ranked just 45th in Success Rate.

The Niners face the NFL's easiest slate of run defenses, and their pass defense schedule (14th) is manageable, especially with Garoppolo back. Add in a high-upside group of pass catchers headed by a budding superstar in Kittle, as well as a talented stable of backs including Breida, **Tevin Coleman**, and **Jerick McKinnon**, and an improved front seven, and the 49ers could surprise in 2019.

Seattle Seahawks

2019 Forecast

Wins	Div Rank
9	#2

Past Records

2018: 10-6
2017: 9-7
2016: 10-5-1

EASY   HARD

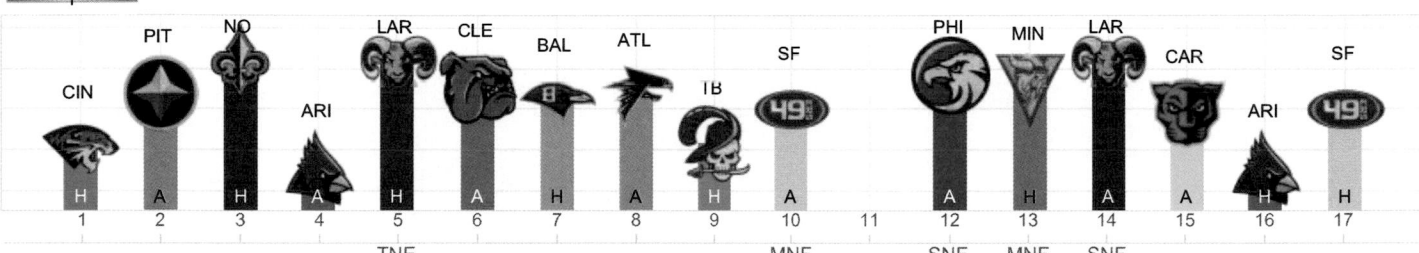

CIN	PIT	NO	ARI	LAR	CLE	BAL	ATL	TB	SF		PHI	MIN	LAR	CAR	ARI	SF	
H	A	H	A	H	A	H	A	H	A		A	H	A	A	H	H	
1	2	3	4	5	6	7	8	9	10	11	12	13	14	15	16	17	

TNF (week 5) · MNF (week 10) · SNF (week 12) · MNF (week 13) · SNF (week 14)

Key Players Lost

Player	New
Brett Hundley (QB)	ARI
Earl Thomas (FS)	BAL
Frank Clark (DE)	KC
J.R. Sweezy (G)	ARI
Justin Coleman (CB)	DET
Maurice Alexander (LB)	BUF
Mike Davis (RB)	CHI
Sebastian Janikowski (K)	Retired
Shamar Stephen (DT)	MIN

Average Line	# Games Favored	# Games Underdog
-1.4	7	7

2019 Seattle Seahawks Overview

The Seahawks *think* they are on the right track, given last year's 10-6 record and playoff berth.

But I've got some bad news. **Pete Carroll**'s team isn't nearly as far along as it thinks and is wasting time to become much better.

The Seahawks' game plan for their playoff loss to Dallas was always going to be problematic because of *the way they choose to play*. The 2018 Seahawks were the league's run-heaviest team, and the only club to pass on less than 52% of all plays. On first-half first downs, the league averages a 51% pass rate. Seattle passed at 40%. On all early downs, the Seahawks were the NFL's only team to pass at less than a 45% rate.

This is a losing strategy, and the results are irrefutable. This strategy decreases a team's odds of bypassing third downs altogether – see Seattle's No. 19 Early Down Success Rate ranking – and when faced with third downs, they have longer yards-to-go distances. Seattle also ranked 19th in yards to go on third downs. With the ease of passing – completion rates are at an all-time high, and league rules have all been tweaked to protect quarterbacks and pass catchers – Seattle's run-heavy strategy is archaic, and hurts more than it helps.

This strategy also lessens the impact of one of the NFL's best quarterbacks. The three nearest teams to Seattle in first-half early-down run rate were Buffalo, Jacksonville, and Tennessee. Those three teams field liabilities at quarterback.

Seattle's quarterback is six-time Pro Bowler and Super Bowl champion **Russell Wilson**, to whom the organization devoted a four-year, $140 million contract.

(cont'd - see SEA2)

Key Free Agents/ Trades Added

Player	AAV (MM)
Al Woods (DT)	$2.2
Cassius Marsh (OLB)	$1.8
Ezekiel Ansah (DE)	$9
Jacob Hollister (TE)	Trade
Jason Myers (K)	$3.8
Mike Iupati (G)	$2.7

Drafted Players

Rd	Pk	Player (College)
1	29	DE - L. J. Collier (TCU)
2	47	S - Marquise Blair (Utah)
2	64	WR - D. K. Metcalf (Ole Miss)
3	88	LB - Cody Barton (Utah)
4	120	WR - Gary Jennings Jr. (Wes..
4	124	G - Phil Haynes (Wake Forest)
4	132	S - Ugochukwu Amadi (Oreg..
5	142	LB - Ben Burr-Kirven (Washi..
6	204	RB - Travis Homer (Miami)
6ᴬ	209	DT - Demarcus Christmas (Fl..
7	236	WR - John Ursua (Hawaii)

Regular Season Wins: Past & Current Proj

	Wins
Forecast 2019 Wins	9
2018 Wins	10
Forecast 2018 Wins	9
2017 Wins	9
2016 Wins	10
2015 Wins	10

1 3 5 7 9 11 13 15

Lineup & Cap Hits

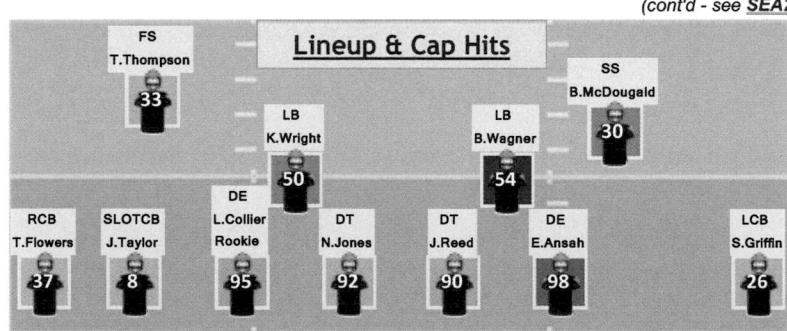

Defense:
- FS 33 T.Thompson
- SS 30 B.McDougald
- LB 50 K.Wright
- LB 54 B.Wagner
- RCB 37 T.Flowers
- SLOTCB 8 J.Taylor
- DE 95 L.Collier (Rookie)
- DT 92 N.Jones
- DT 90 J.Reed
- DE 98 E.Ansah
- LCB 26 S.Griffin

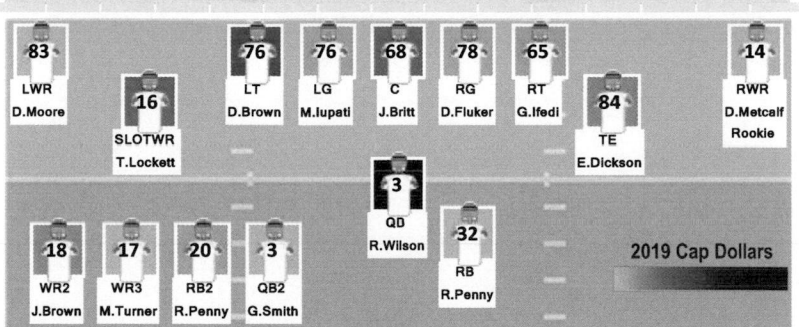

Offense:
- LWR 83 D.Moore
- SLOTWR 16 T.Lockett
- LT 76 D.Brown
- LG 76 M.Iupati
- C 68 J.Britt
- RG 78 D.Fluker
- RT 65 G.Ifedi
- TE 84 E.Dickson
- RWR 14 D.Metcalf (Rookie)
- QD 3 R.Wilson
- RB 32 R.Penny
- WR2 18 J.Brown
- WR3 17 M.Turner
- RB2 20 R.Penny
- QB2 3 G.Smith

2019 Cap Dollars

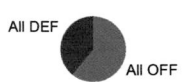

2019 Unit Spending

All DEF / All OFF

Positional Spending

	Rank	Total	2017 Rk
All OFF	21	$92.23M	20
QB	10	$26.93M	8
OL	20	$34.46M	26
RB	24	$5.55M	23
WR	25	$17.61M	11
TE	18	$7.89M	28
All DEF	32	$59.04M	17
DL	31	$11.17M	30
LB	4	$31.27M	8
CB	32	$5.72M	25
S	16	$10.89M	1

So *why in the hell* are the Seahawks trying to "hide" their best player? They hid Wilson more than the Jags hid **Blake Bortles**, more than the Bills hid **Josh Allen**, and more than the Titans hid **Marcus Mariota** and **Blaine Gabbert**.

It all set up for disaster against the Cowboys. Dallas entered the Wild Card Round ranked No. 5 against the run but No. 16 in pass-defense efficiency. The Seahawks knew this before kickoff, we must assume. But they didn't prepare differently. On first-half first downs, Seattle averaged 2.0 yards per carry and 12.4 yards per pass attempt. In the first half, Wilson averaged 8.8 yards per attempt on all downs, while Seahawks backs gained 19 yards on nine carries with a long run of five. Wilson was 7-of-8 for 12.1 YPA and a 117 passer rating on early-down throws.

Yet Seattle continued running on first downs in the second half as if it was still a good strategy. You want to talk about being stubborn. On the first drive out of the locker room and trailing on the scoreboard, the Seahawks ran the ball with a running back for a 1-yard gain and a three-yard gain, then called a predictable third-and-long pass, which was followed by a punt.

Trailing on every offensive play in the second half while knowing their running game had been a disaster – predictably so against the league's No. 5 run defense – the Seahawks called *six first-down running back runs and only one first-down pass* on their first four drives in the second half of the game. The running back runs averaged 3.9 yards with a 14% Success Rate. The lone pass went for a gain of nine.

It made no sense, and Seattle *didn't even consider* halftime adjustments. With running back runs gaining 2.1 yards per carry, the Seahawks called 11 running back runs on early downs. They recorded an 18% Success Rate and 3.5 yards per carry.

Ultimately, the Seahawks were more concerned with doing "what we do" than optimally game planning and calling plays. The fact that they did not adjust is even more infuriating, and reason to maintain skepticism about this year's team.

Just a few weeks prior, the Seahawks had begun incorporating some +EV game planning. They beat the Chiefs as **Russell Wilson** went 4-of-5 for 12.6 yards per attempt and a touchdown when passing on first downs in the second half. He drew two DPI penalties on first-half first-down throws. Seattle broke tendency and beat a Super Bowl contender with aggressive early-down passing.

But they learned *nothing* from it.

2018 Passing Performance

QB	1st Dwn	2nd Dwn	3rd Dwn	
Russell Wilson	51% 8.1 99.0	46% 8.4 114.4	32% 7.6 112.0	Success Rate YPA Rating
Pass Rate	38%	48%	75%	
NFL AVG	53% 7.7 95.1	47% 7.3 93.7	36% 6.9 87.1	Success Rate YPA Rating
Pass Rate	53%	62%	80%	

2018 Rushing Performance

Offense	1st Dwn	2nd Dwn	3rd Dwn	
SEA	47% 4.5	46% 4.8	54% 5.5	Success Rate YPC
Run Rate	62%	52%	25%	
NFL AVG	48% 4.5	46% 4.4	51% 4.3	Success Rate YPC
Run Rate	47%	38%	20%	

Let's take a more in-depth look at the totality of the Seahawks' 2018 season.

Turnovers matter in football, but to last year's Seahawks, their turnover margin didn't impact games as much as most.

Seattle was 1-2 when losing the takeaway battle, 1-2 when turnover margin was neutral, and 8-3 when winning the turnover margin, including their playoff loss to Dallas. When turnover margins were within one (-1 to +1), the Seahawks went 6-6. When they won the turnover battle by at least two, they were 4-1.

Thus, turnover margins did not drive the 2018 Seahawks' success or failure. Going 6-6 in one-turnover games is flipping coins, and the fact that Seattle

(cont'd - see SEA-3)

2018 Offensive Advanced Metrics

Rank (by category): EDSR Off 19, 30 & In Off 13, Red Zone Off 11, 3rd Down Off 17, YPPA Off 8, YPPT Off 3, Offensive Efficiency 9, Pass Efficiency Off 6, Pass Pro Efficiency Off 30, RB Pass Eff Off 15, Rush Efficiency Off 7, Explosive Pass Off 7, Explosive Run Off 28

2018 Defensive Advanced Metrics

Rank (by category): EDSR Def 24, 30 & In Def 7, Red Zone Def 6, 3rd Down Def 6, YPPA Def 20, YPPT Def 4, Defensive Efficiency 14, Pass Efficiency Def 13, Pass Pro Efficiency Def 14, RB Pass Eff Def 27, Rush Efficiency Def 17, Explosive Pass Def 5, Explosive Run Def 24

2018 Weekly EDSR & Season Trending Performance

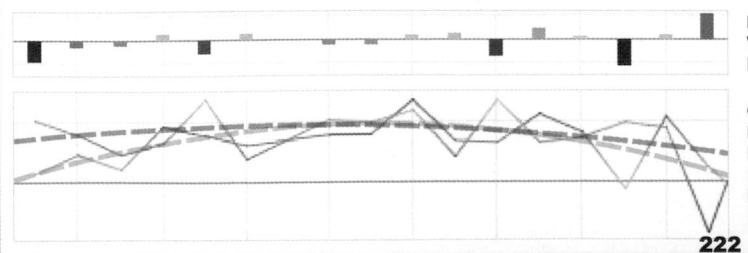

WEEK	1	2	3	4	5	6	8	9	10	11	12	13	14	15	16	17
RESULT	L	L	W	W	L	W	W	L	L	W	W	W	W	L	W	W
OPP	DEN	CHI	DAL	ARI	LA	OAK	DET	LAC	LA	GB	CAR	SF	MIN	SF	KC	ARI
SITE	A	A	H	A	H	N	A	H	A	H	A	H	H	A	H	H
MARGIN	-3	-7	11	3	-2	24	14	-8	-5	3	3	27	14	-3	7	3
PTS	24	17	24	20	31	27	28	17	31	27	30	43	21	23	38	27
OPP PTS	27	24	13	17	33	3	14	25	36	24	27	16	7	26	31	24

EDSR by Wk
W=Green
L=Red

OFF/DEF
EDSR
Blue=OFF
(high=good)
Red=DEF
(low=good)

2018 Close Game Records

All 2018 Wins: **10**
FG Games (<=3 pts) W-L: **4-3**
FG Games Win %: **57% (#12)**
FG Games Wins (% of Total Wins): **40% (#6)**
1 Score Games (<=8 pts) W-L: **5-6**
1 Score Games Win %: **45% (#20)**
1 Score Games Wins (% of Total Wins): **50% (#15)**

2018 Critical & Game-Deciding Stats

TO Margin	+15
TO Given	11
INT Given	7
FUM Given	4
TO Taken	26
INT Taken	12
FUM Taken	14
Sack Margin	-8
Sacks	43
Sacks Allow	51
Return TD Margin	-2
Ret TDs	2
Ret TDs Allow	4
Penalty Margin	-3
Penalties	111
Opponent Penalties	108

Seattle Seahawks 2019 Strength of Schedule In Detail (compared to 2018)

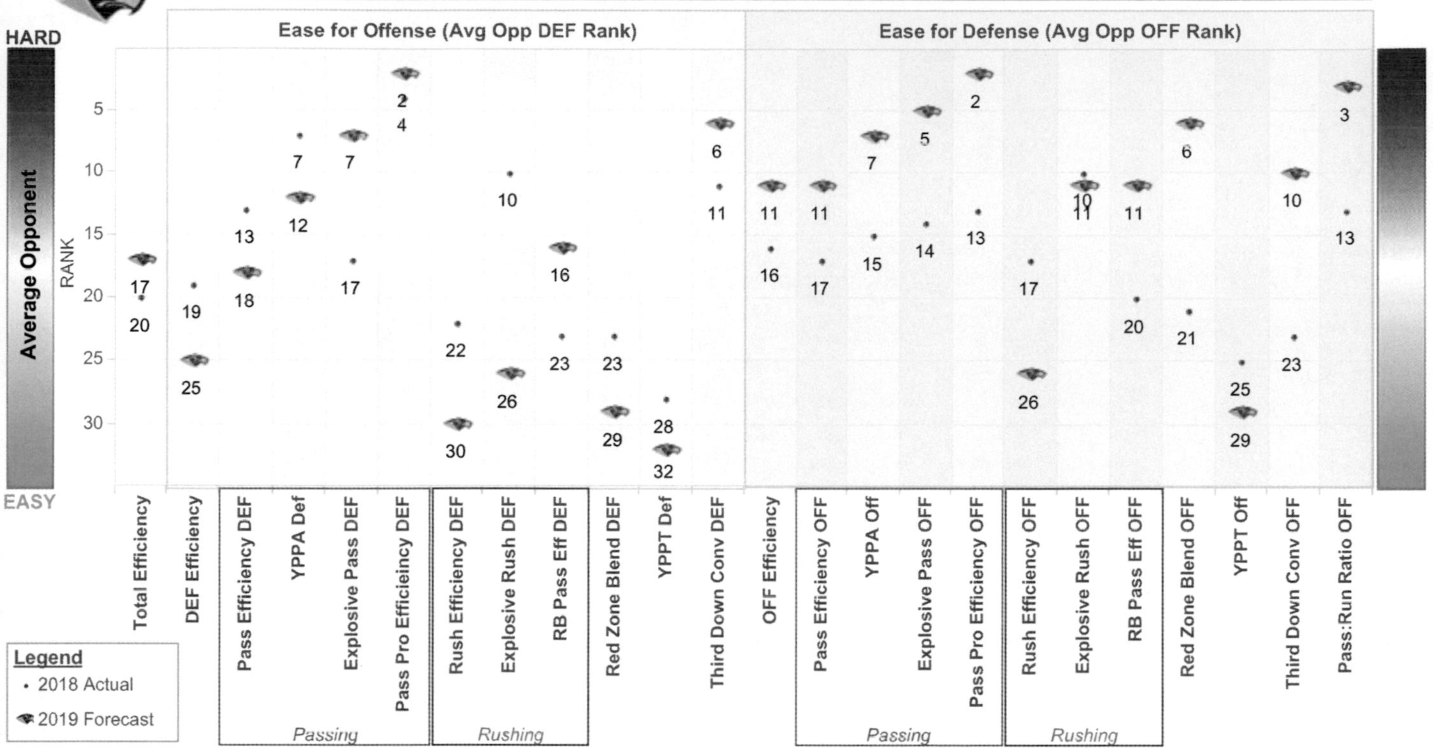

HARD · **EASY** (left axis gradient)

Average Opponent RANK (vertical axis label)

Ease for Offense (Avg Opp DEF Rank)

Category	2018 Actual	2019 Forecast
Total Efficiency	20	17
DEF Efficiency	19	25
Pass Efficiency DEF	13	18
YPPA Def	7	12
Explosive Pass DEF	7	17
Pass Pro Efficiency DEF	2	4
Rush Efficiency DEF	22	30
Explosive Rush DEF	10	26
RB Pass Eff DEF	23	16
Red Zone Blend DEF	23	29
YPPT Def	28	32
Third Down Conv DEF	6	11

Passing · *Rushing*

Ease for Defense (Avg Opp OFF Rank)

Category	2018 Actual	2019 Forecast
OFF Efficiency	16	11
Pass Efficiency OFF	11	17
YPPA Off	7	15
Explosive Pass OFF	2	5
Pass Pro Efficiency OFF	13	14
Rush Efficiency OFF	26	11
Explosive Rush OFF	19	11
RB Pass Eff OFF	11	20
Red Zone Blend OFF	6	21
YPPT Off	25	29
Third Down Conv OFF	23	10
Pass:Run Ratio OFF	3	13

Passing · *Rushing*

Legend
- 2018 Actual
- 2019 Forecast

2019 v 2018 Schedule Variances* (OFF=Rank of DEF faced, 2019 vs 2018)

Pass OFF Rank	Pass OFF Blend Rk	Rush OFF Rk	Rush OFF Blend Rk	Pass DEF Rk	Pass DEF Blend Rk	Rush DEF Rk	Rush DEF Blend Rk
22	17	26	25	9	6	26	13

** **1**=Hardest Jump in 2019 schedule from 2018 (aka a much harder schedule in 2019), **32**=Easiest Jump in 2019 schedule from 2018 (aka a much easier schedule in 2019);*
Pass Blend metric blends 4 metrics: Pass Efficiency, YPPA, Explosive Pass & Pass Rush; **Rush Blend** metric blends 3 metrics: Rush Efficiency, Explosive Rush & RB Targets

---

Team Records & Trends

	2018	2017	2016
Average line	-0.8	-3.3	-5.6
Average O/U line	46.0	44.0	44.0
Straight Up Record	10-6	9-7	10-5
Against the Spread Record	10-5	6-9	7-8
Over/Under Record	9-7	7-9	9-7
ATS as Favorite	5-4	3-6	5-8
ATS as Underdog	5-1	3-3	2-0
Straight Up Home	6-2	4-4	7-1
ATS Home	6-2	2-6	4-3
Over/Under Home	5-3	5-3	5-3
ATS as Home Favorite	4-2	1-6	4-3
ATS as a Home Dog	2-0	1-0	0-0
Straight Up Away	3-4	5-3	3-4
ATS Away	3-3	4-3	3-5
Over/Under Away	4-3	2-6	4-4
ATS Away Favorite	0-2	2-0	1-5
ATS Away Dog	3-1	2-3	2-0
Six Point Teaser Record	13-3	12-4	9-6
Seven Point Teaser Record	14-2	12-4	10-6
Ten Point Teaser Record	15-1	12-2	12-4

SEA-3

won 80% of games when up by two or more turnovers is consistent with league average.

The 2018 Seahawks' team health did improve from No. 22 to No. 10, the NFL's fifth-largest health improvement year to year. Seattle's offensive efficiency also jumped from No. 19 to No. 9. Their defensive efficiency rose from 26th to 14th, and their net turnover margin jumped from +8 to +15. Seattle's penalty margin catapulted from -46 to -3.

And I made an interesting discovery about field goals as they related to the 2017 and 2018 Seahawks.

In 2017, opponents made 89% of their field goals against the Seahawks, while Seattle made just 72% for a -17% deficit. But in 2018, Seattle's field-goal rate climbed to 80%, and opponents dipped to 77%. The Seahawks' year-to-year improvement of 19% was second best in the NFL.

(cont'd - see **SEA-4**)

2019 Rest Analysis

Team More Rest	2
Opp More Rest	3
Net Rest Edge	-1
Week 2 Edge	0
Week 3 Edge	0
Week 4 Edge	0
Week 5 Edge	0
Week 6 Edge	4
Week 7 Edge	0
Week 8 Edge	0
Week 9 Edge	0
Week 10 Edge	-3
Week 12 Edge	6
Week 13 Edge	0
Week 14 Edge	-1
Week 15 Edge	0
Week 16 Edge	0
Week 17 Edge	0

Health by Unit*

2018 Rk	10
2017 Rk	22
2018 v 2017 Rk	5
Off Rk	11
Def Rk	14
QB Rk	15
RB Rk	12
WR Rk	8
TE Rk	23
Oline Rk	9
Dline Rk	20
LB Rk	27
DB Rk	12

*Based on the work of Football Outsiders

2018 Weekly Betting Lines (wks 1-16)

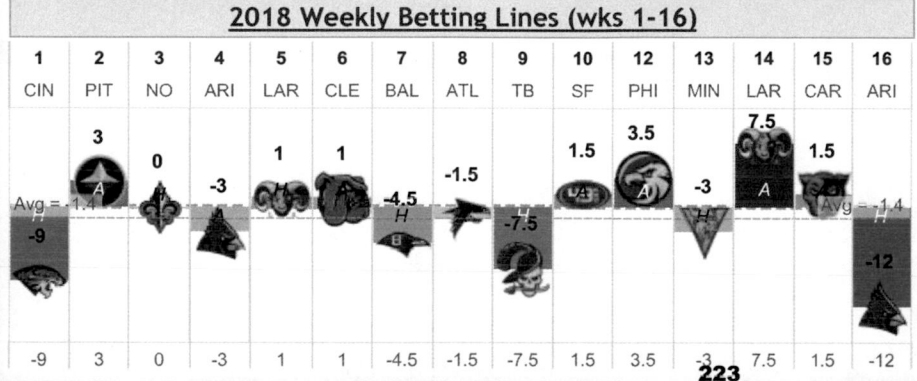

Wk	1	2	3	4	5	6	7	8	9	10	12	13	14	15	16
Opp	CIN	PIT	NO	ARI	LAR	CLE	BAL	ATL	TB	SF	PHI	MIN	LAR	CAR	ARI
Line	-9	3	0	-3	1	1	-4.5	-1.5	-7.5	1.5	3.5	-3	7.5	1.5	-12

Avg = -1.4

Home Lines (wks 1-16)

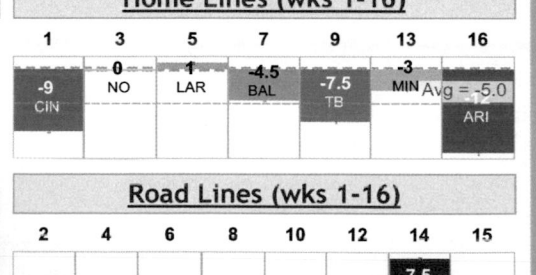

Wk	1	3	5	7	9	13	16
Opp	CIN	NO	LAR	BAL	TB	MIN	ARI
Line	-9	0	1	-4.5	-7.5	-3	

Avg = -5.0

Road Lines (wks 1-16)

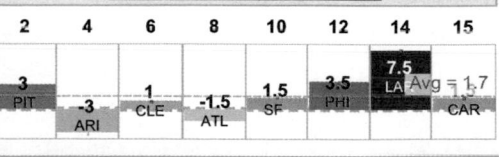

Wk	2	4	6	8	10	12	14	15
Opp	PIT	ARI	CLE	ATL	SF	PHI	LA	CAR
Line	3	-3	1	-1.5	1.5	3.5	7.5	

Avg = 1.7

Seattle Seahawks 2018 Play Analysis

2018 Play Tendencies

All Pass %	47%
All Pass Rk	32
All Rush %	53%
All Rush Rk	1
1 Score Pass %	47%
1 Score Pass Rk	32
2017 1 Score Pass %	59%
2017 1 Score Pass Rk	9
2018 Pass Increase %	-12%
Pass Increase Rk	32
1 Score Rush %	53%
1 Score Rush Rk	1
Up Pass %	40%
Up Pass Rk	31
Up Rush %	60%
Up Rush Rk	2
Down Pass %	57%
Down Pass Rk	32
Down Rush %	43%
Down Rush Rk	1

2018 Down & Distance Tendencies

Down	Distance	Total Plays	Pass Rate	Run Rate	Play Success %
1	Short (1-3)	7	14%	86%	57%
	Med (4-7)	12	8%	92%	33%
	Long (8-10)	301	36%	64%	52%
	XL (11+)	16	50%	50%	38%
2	Short (1-3)	31	23%	77%	61%
	Med (4-7)	97	43%	57%	56%
	Long (8-10)	87	41%	59%	34%
	XL (11+)	41	61%	39%	24%
3	Short (1-3)	39	44%	56%	64%
	Med (4-7)	61	93%	7%	44%
	Long (8-10)	32	88%	13%	31%
	XL (11+)	28	68%	32%	14%
4	Short (1-3)	6	50%	50%	67%
	Med (4-7)	1	100%	0%	100%

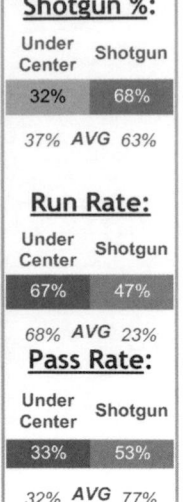

Shotgun %:

Under Center	Shotgun
32%	68%

37% AVG 63%

Run Rate:

Under Center	Shotgun
67%	47%

68% AVG 23%

Pass Rate:

Under Center	Shotgun
33%	53%

32% AVG 77%

Short Yardage Intelligence:

2nd and Short Run

Run Freq	Run Rk	NFL Run Freq Avg	Run 1D Rate	Run NFL 1D Avg
69%	11	65%	67%	68%

2nd and Short Pass

Pass Freq	Pass Rk	NFL Pass Freq Avg	Pass 1D Rate	Pass NFL 1D Avg
31%	21	35%	38%	56%

Most Frequent Play

Down	Distance	Play Type	Player	Total Plays	Play Success %
1	Short (1-3)	RUSH	Chris Carson	5	60%
	Med (4-7)	RUSH	Chris Carson	8	25%
	Long (8-10)	RUSH	Chris Carson	105	57%
	XL (11+)	RUSH	Chris Carson	4	50%
2	Short (1-3)	RUSH	Chris Carson	13	54%
	Med (4-7)	RUSH	Chris Carson	27	48%
	Long (8-10)	RUSH	Chris Carson	21	29%
	XL (11+)	RUSH	Chris Carson	8	13%
3	Short (1-3)	RUSH	Chris Carson	15	80%
	Med (4-7)	PASS	Tyler Lockett	9	56%
		PASS	Doug Baldwin	9	67%
	Long (8-10)	PASS	Tyler Lockett	4	50%
		RUSH	Russell Wilson	4	50%
	XL (11+)	PASS	David Moore	7	14%

Most Successful Play*

Down	Distance	Play Type	Player	Total Plays	Play Success %
1	Short (1-3)	RUSH	Chris Carson	5	60%
	Med (4-7)	RUSH	Chris Carson	8	25%
	Long (8-10)	PASS	Ed Dickson	5	100%
2	Short (1-3)	RUSH	Mike Davis	6	83%
	Med (4-7)	RUSH	Russell Wilson	5	100%
	Long (8-10)	PASS	Tyler Lockett	7	71%
	XL (11+)	PASS	Doug Baldwin	6	50%
3	Short (1-3)	RUSH	Mike Davis	5	100%
	Med (4-7)	PASS	David Moore	6	83%
	XL (11+)	PASS	David Moore	7	14%

*Minimum 5 plays to qualify

2018 Weekly Snap Rates

Wk	Opp	Score	Tyler Lockett	Doug Baldwin	David Moore	Chris Carson	Mike Davis	Ed Dickson	Jaron Brown	Brandon Marshall	J.D. McKissic
1	DEN	L 27-24	56 (98%)	11 (19%)	16 (28%)	25 (44%)			33 (58%)	37 (65%)	
2	CHI	L 24-17	60 (91%)		20 (30%)	19 (29%)	9 (14%)		47 (71%)	53 (80%)	
3	DAL	W 24-13	61 (88%)		23 (33%)	51 (74%)	8 (12%)		50 (72%)	43 (62%)	
4	ARI	W 20-17	62 (94%)	50 (76%)	43 (65%)		47 (71%)		15 (23%)	24 (36%)	
5	LA	L 33-31	52 (87%)	53 (88%)	31 (52%)	35 (58%)	25 (42%)		9 (15%)	7 (12%)	
6	OAK	W 27-3	51 (78%)	49 (75%)	30 (46%)	27 (42%)	24 (37%)		22 (34%)	25 (38%)	
8	DET	W 28-14	44 (70%)	54 (86%)	45 (71%)	42 (67%)	20 (32%)	20 (32%)	18 (29%)	2 (3%)	
9	LAC	L 25-17	68 (84%)	72 (89%)	63 (78%)	10 (12%)	59 (73%)	25 (31%)	19 (23%)		
10	LA	L 36-31	60 (88%)	67 (99%)	45 (66%)		39 (57%)	24 (35%)	9 (13%)		
11	GB	W 27-24	53 (76%)	62 (89%)	40 (57%)	30 (43%)	22 (31%)	29 (41%)	14 (20%)		
12	CAR	W 30-27	56 (90%)	56 (90%)	32 (52%)	32 (52%)	18 (29%)	44 (71%)	13 (21%)		
13	SF	W 43-16	40 (69%)	54 (93%)	28 (48%)	34 (59%)	10 (17%)	28 (48%)	15 (26%)		2 (3%)
14	MIN	W 21-7	56 (85%)		52 (79%)	35 (53%)	18 (27%)	36 (55%)	43 (65%)		1 (2%)
15	SF	L 26-23	68 (91%)	61 (81%)	58 (77%)	39 (52%)	33 (44%)	46 (61%)	12 (16%)		3 (4%)
16	KC	W 38-31	69 (86%)	65 (81%)	55 (69%)	43 (54%)	36 (45%)	64 (80%)	15 (19%)		2 (3%)
17	ARI	W 27-24	52 (83%)	56 (89%)	39 (62%)	32 (51%)	25 (40%)	48 (76%)	16 (25%)		1 (2%)
	Grand Total		908 (85%)	710 (81%)	620 (57%)	454 (49%)	393 (38%)	364 (53%)	350 (33%)	191 (42%)	9 (3%)

Personnel Groupings

Personnel	Team %	NFL Avg	Succ. %
1-1 [3WR]	73%	65%	45%
1-2 [2WR]	12%	17%	49%
1-0 [4WR]	7%	2%	58%
2-1 [2WR]	4%	8%	39%
2-2 [1WR]	2%	3%	38%

Grouping Tendencies

Personnel	Pass Rate	Pass Succ. %	Run Succ. %
1-1 [3WR]	52%	43%	48%
1-2 [2WR]	44%	45%	52%
1-0 [4WR]	24%	44%	63%
2-1 [2WR]	39%	35%	41%
2-2 [1WR]	19%	50%	35%

Red Zone Targets (min 3)

Receiver	All	Inside 5	6-10	11-20
Doug Baldwin	14	3	6	5
David Moore	8		3	5
Nick Vannett	7	2	2	3
Ed Dickson	6	1	2	3
Jaron Brown	6	2	2	2
Tyler Lockett	6		3	3
Brandon Marshall	3		1	2
J.D. McKissic	3		1	2

Red Zone Rushes (min 3)

Rusher	All	Inside 5	6-10	11-20
Chris Carson	44	17	13	14
Mike Davis	23	3	5	15
Russell Wilson	10	2	2	6
Rashaad Penny	9	1	1	7

Early Down Target Rate

RB	TE	WR
26%	17%	57%
23%	21%	56%
	NFL AVG	

Overall Target Success %

RB	TE	WR
46%	58%	51%
#17	#8	#14

Seattle Seahawks 2018 Passing Recap & 2019 Outlook

When the Seahawks record more sacks than they allow, they are 40-6 (87%) with **Russell Wilson** at quarterback. That's the second-best record in the league since 2012 behind only the Patriots (88%). Sacks are a proxy for pressure, but the way to minimize Wilson's sacks taken is not to throw the ball less. It's to *throw the ball smarter*.

Last year, Wilson absorbed a 14.6% sack rate on third-down passes, but only a 6.6% sack rate on early-down throws. The Seahawks need to let him throw more on early downs and eliminate situations that reduce the offense's efficiency. As Wilson's advanced metrics show he is only getting better as a quarterback, it's time for Seattle to start using him more, not less.

Russell Wilson Rating All Downs

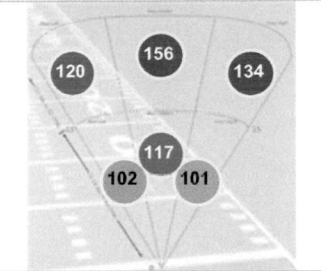

2018 Standard Passing Table

QB	Comp	Att	Comp %	Yds	YPA	TDs	INT	Sacks	Rating	Rk
Russell Wilson	297	453	66%	3,672	8.1	36	7	52	111	6
NFL Avg			62%		7.0				87.5	

2018 Advanced Passing Table

QB	Success %	EDSR Passing Success %	20+ Yd Pass Gains	20+ Yd Pass %	30+ Yd Pass Gains	30+ Yd Pass %	Avg. Air Yds per Comp	Avg. YAC per Comp	20+ Air Yd Comp	20+ Air Yd %
Russell Wilson	43%	48%	52	11.0%	24	5.0%	7.3	5.1	34	8%
NFL Avg	44%	48%	29.5	8.4%	12.5	3.7%	5.8	5.1	14.5	6%

Russell Wilson Rating Early Downs

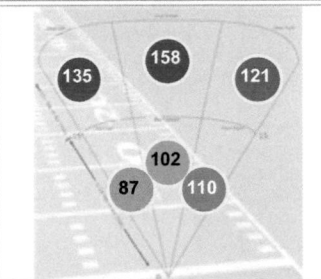

Interception Rates by Down

Yards to Go	1st Dwn	2nd Dwn	3rd Dwn	4th Dwn	Total
1 & 2	33.3%	0.0%	0.0%	0.0%	4.0%
3, 4, 5	0.0%	0.0%	2.3%	0.0%	1.6%
6 - 9	0.0%	1.5%	1.5%	0.0%	1.4%
10 - 14	1.4%	0.0%	0.0%	0.0%	0.9%
15+	0.0%	0.0%	6.7%		2.0%
Total	1.8%	0.6%	1.9%	0.0%	1.4%

3rd Down Passing - Short of Sticks Analysis

QB	Avg. Yds to Go	Avg. YIA (of Comp)	Avg Yds Short	Short of Sticks Rate	Short Rk
Russell Wilson	7.7	8.5	0.0	54%	4
NFL Avg	7.8	6.4	-1.4	60%	

Air Yds vs YAC

Air Yds %	YAC %	Rk
59%	41%	8
53%	48%	

2018 Receiving Recap & 2019 Outlook

Tyler Lockett was sensational last season both as a slot and perimeter receiver. Outside, he produced a 60% Success Rate, 15.7 yards per target, and a 149 passer rating when targeted. Inside, Lockett's Success Rate was 67% with 13.4 YPT and a 148 rating. Seattle primarily passed from 11 personnel last year. **David Moore's** 2018 inconsistency led Seattle to draft **D.K. Metcalf**. Moore recorded a 38% Success Rate and 7.6 yards per target on 45 targets in 11 personnel last season. TE **Ed Dickson** was particularly bad in the slot – 43% Success Rate, 4.7 yards per target – but excellent as an in-line tight end with 90% success and 14.4 YPT.

Player *Min 50 Targets	Targ	Comp %	YPA	Rating	Success %	Success Rk	Missed YPA Rk	YAS % Rk	YTS % Rk	TDs
Doug Baldwin	79	67%	8.2	108.1	52%	59	37	67	59	5
Tyler Lockett	77	79%	14.1	158.3	64%	2	25	4	129	9
David Moore	52	50%	8.6	95.4	38%	124	184	18	120	3

Directional Passer Rating Delivered

Receiver	Short Left	Short Middle	Short Right	Deep Left	Deep Middle	Deep Right	Player Total
Doug Baldwin	131	45	84	129	104	119	108
Tyler Lockett	103	130	108	156	158	151	158
David Moore	58	40	60	110	158	127	95
Nick Vannett	74	141	105	40		40	105
Mike Davis	90	96	105				97
Chris Carson	70	103	103				92
Brandon Marshall	32	57	83	40		158	63
Jaron Brown	134	96	136	25	156		114
Ed Dickson	143	142	101	119	119		149
J.D. McKissic	133	40	40				97
Team Total	100	117	103	120	158	137	120

2018 Rushing Recap & 2019 Outlook

Critical for Seattle is to run *when it's most efficient to run*. Don't just run to "control tempo" or win time of possession unless it's the fourth quarter. **Chris Carson** was much more successful than **Rashaad Penny** last season, but Penny has superior breakaway speed and finished sixth in explosive run rate. But his explosion waned as games progressed.

In fact, the Seahawks ran so often that their three primary backs were much better in first and third quarters than in the second and fourth. First quarter: 5.4 YPC, 53% success. Second quarter: 3.9 YPC, 36% success. Third quarter: 5.5 YPC, 48% success. Fourth quarter: 3.5 YPC, 43% success.

Player *Min 50 Rushes	Rushes	YPC	Success %	Success Rk	Missed YPA Rk	YTS % Rk	YAS % Rk	Early Down Success %	Early Down Success Rk	TDs
Chris Carson	260	4.5	50%	27	17	38	46	47%	34	9
Mike Davis	116	4.5	51%	21	58	44	65	52%	17	4
Rashaad Penny	89	5.0	40%	62	49	70	6	40%	62	2

Yards per Carry by Direction

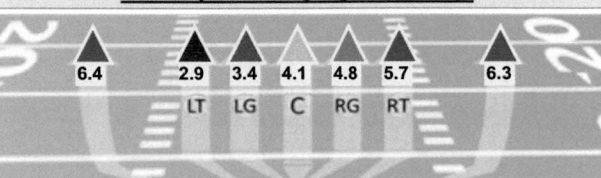

Directional Run Frequency

Based on this phenomenal improvement in a wide range of areas, one might expect 2018's team to do significantly better than 2017's version. It shouldn't have been close, right?

Yet last year's Seahawks still played 11 games that were decided by just one score, even more than their 2017 total of 10.

The 2018 Seahawks played in seven games decided by a field goal, two more than their previous-year sum.

And last year's Seahawks won just one more game (10-6) than the year before (9-7).

Ultimately, the biggest difference between the two teams was Early Down Success Rate, which was highly correlated to Seattle's success. The Seahawks went 7-1 when winning the EDSR Battle. When losing EDSR, they went 3-6, including their playoff loss.

The Seahawks' lone loss when winning EDSR was a game where Seattle was -1 in turnover margin and lost by five points to the Rams. They held leads in all four quarters and had the ball to drive for a go-ahead score in the middle of the fourth quarter. But they fumbled at their own nine-yard line, and the Rams scored a touchdown on the next play to seal the win.

How did ESDR compare between 2017 and 2018?

Therein lies the answer.

(cont'd - see SEA-5)

Seattle Seahawks Fantasy Corner

Seahawks rookie WR **D.K. Metcalf**'s limitations were apparent at both Ole Miss and the Combine. He lined up only on the left side of the formation and ran almost strictly go routes and screens, then bombed agility drills with 4.50 short-shuttle and 7.38 three-cone times. Metcalf runs 4.33 at 6-foot-3, 228, however, and no one in this entire draft has a quicker first step; Metcalf's 1.48 ten-yard split easily led all 2019 Combine invitees. In Seattle, Metcalf will be an absolute bear for secondaries to chase on **Russell Wilson**'s improvisational plays. Metcalf also has immediate opportunity as a probable day-one starter across from **Tyler Lockett**. My favorite pre-draft Metcalf comparison was **Martavis Bryant**, obviously without the off-field concerns.

- Evan Silva

2018 Situational Usage by Player & Position

Usage Rate by Score

	Being Blown Out (14+)	Down Big (9-13)	One Score	Large Lead (9-13)	Blowout Lead (14+)
PASS					
Chris Carson			81%		19%
Mike Davis	5%	19%	69%	2%	5%
Rashaad Penny	8%		83%		8%
Tyler Lockett	6%	7%	78%	3%	7%
Doug Baldwin		15%	68%	3%	14%
David Moore	2%	8%	85%		4%
Nick Vannett	12%	7%	68%	7%	5%
Brandon Marshall		9%	77%	5%	9%
Jaron Brown	10%		70%	10%	5%
Ed Dickson	6%	6%	83%		6%
J.D. McKissic		50%	25%		25%
C.J. Prosise	100%				
Total	5%	10%	74%	3%	9%
RUSH					
Chris Carson		2%	82%	7%	10%
Mike Davis	4%	9%	75%	3%	9%
Rashaad Penny	7%	6%	70%	4%	13%
Tyler Lockett			77%	8%	15%
David Moore			100%		
Ed Dickson			100%		
J.D. McKissic			100%		
C.J. Prosise			100%		
Total	2%	4%	78%	5%	11%

Share of Offensive Plays by Type

	Chris Carson	Mike Davis	Rashaad Penny	Tyler Lockett	Doug Baldwin	David Moore	Nick Vannett	Brandon Marshall	Jaron Brown	Ed Dickson	J.D. McKissic	C.J. Prosise
PASS	7%	11%	3%	19%	20%	12%	11%	6%	5%	5%	1%	1%
RUSH	54%	24%	18%	3%		0%				0%	1%	0%
ALL	33%	18%	12%	10%	9%	6%	5%	3%	2%	2%	1%	0%

Positional Target Distribution vs NFL Average

		NFL Wide				Team Only			
		Left	Middle	Right	Total	Left	Middle	Right	Total
Deep	WR	33%	17%	31%	81%	48%	14%	30%	92%
	TE	5%	4%	7%	16%	3%	1%	3%	8%
	RB	1%	0%	2%	4%				
	All	39%	22%	40%	100%	52%	15%	33%	100%
Short	WR	20%	14%	21%	55%	25%	9%	22%	57%
	TE	6%	6%	8%	20%	3%	6%	10%	19%
	RB	10%	5%	10%	25%	10%	7%	8%	25%
	All	36%	25%	39%	100%	38%	22%	40%	100%
Total		37%	24%	39%	100%	41%	20%	38%	100%

Positional Success Rates vs NFL Average

		NFL Wide				Team Only			
		Left	Middle	Right	Total	Left	Middle	Right	Total
Deep	WR	39%	49%	39%	41%	49%	77%	57%	56%
	TE	44%	53%	42%	46%	33%	100%	0%	29%
	RB	38%	33%	42%	40%				
	All	40%	49%	40%	42%	48%	79%	52%	54%
Short	WR	55%	61%	52%	56%	51%	41%	51%	49%
	TE	55%	62%	54%	57%	56%	78%	59%	64%
	RB	47%	53%	45%	47%	40%	67%	43%	49%
	All	53%	59%	51%	54%	48%	59%	51%	52%
Total		50%	58%	49%	52%	48%	63%	51%	52%

Division History: Season Wins & 2019 Projection

| 2015 Wins | 2016 Wins | 2017 Wins | 2018 Wins | Forecast 2019 Wins |

Rank of 2019 Defensive Pass Efficiency Faced by Week

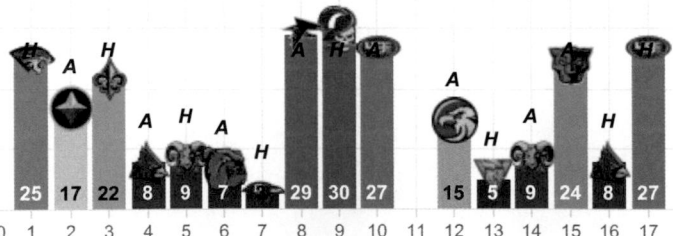

25 17 22 8 9 7 29 30 27 15 5 9 24 8 27

Rank of 2019 Defensive Rush Efficiency Faced by Week

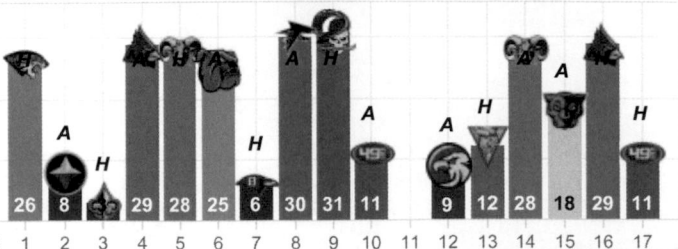

26 8 29 28 25 6 30 31 11 9 12 28 18 29 11

2018 Detailed Analytics Summary
Success by Play Type & Primary Personnel Groupings

Successful Play Rate 0% — 100%

Type	1-1 [3WR]	1-2 [2WR]	1-0 [4WR]	2-1 [2WR]	2-2 [1WR]	2-0 [3WR]	0-1 [4WR]	0-0 [5WR]	1-3 [1WR]	ALL
PASS	43% (401)	46% (57)	41% (17)	35% (17)	50% (4)	57% (7)	50% (2)			43% (505)
RUSH	47% (368)	52% (71)	58% (59)	41% (27)	35% (17)	58% (12)	0% (1)	100% (1)	0% (1)	48% (557)
All	45% (769)	49% (128)	54% (76)	39% (44)	38% (21)	58% (19)	33% (3)	100% (1)	0% (1)	46% (1,062)

Format Success Rate (Total # of Plays)

Receiving Success by Top-4 Personnel Groupings
(Min 50 targets)

POS	Player	1-1 [3WR]	1-2 [2WR]	1-0 [4WR]	2-1 [2WR]	4 Grp Total
WR	Doug Baldwin	48% (61) 7.3, 101.0	70% (10) 11.1, 112.9	50% (4) 4.3, 121.9	67% (3) 20.0, 109.7	51% (78) 8.2, 107.6
	Tyler Lockett	64% (59) 14.9, 158.3	75% (12) 15.5, 158.3	0% (3) 0.0, 70.1		64% (74) 14.4, 158.3
	David Moore	38% (47) 8.3, 101.2	0% (1) 0.0, 39.6	0% (1) 0.0, 39.6		37% (49) 8.0, 98.7

Format Line 1: Success Rate (Total # of Plays)   Line 2: YPA, Passer Rating

Rushing Success by Top-4 Personnel Groupings
(Min 25 carries)

Rusher (Last, First)	1-1 [3WR]	1-2 [2WR]	2-1 [2WR]	2-2 [1WR]	4 Grp Total
Carson Chris	47% (158) 4.8	57% (35) 5.5	46% (13) 3.7	44% (9) 1.3	48% (215) 4.7
Davis Mike	47% (93) 4.7	57% (7) 2.9	100% (1) 12.0	50% (2) 4.5	49% (103) 4.6
Penny Rashaad	34% (58) 4.7	47% (15) 6.8	33% (3) 2.7		37% (76) 5.0
Wilson Russell	66% (47) 6.8	22% (9) 5.2	29% (7) 3.7	0% (5) -1.0	51% (68) 5.7

Format Line 1: Success Rate (Total # of Plays)   Line 2: YPC

Passing by Coverage Scheme

M2M	49% (184) 7.8, 120.1
Zone	58% (166) 10.0, 119.0
Screen	42% (31) 5.2, 88.4
Combo	38% (8) 4.4, 62.0

Passing by Route

Curl	59% (59) 7.1, 97.8
Flat	52% (33) 5.3, 98.9
Screen	40% (25) 6.0, 91.8
Slant	54% (24) 6.6, 50.5
Out	50% (22) 7.1, 111.4
Dig	57% (7) 9.4, 128.6

Throw Types

Level 1	52% (229) 6.7, 106.4
Level 2	52% (130) 9.5, 123.6
Level 3	45% (47) 15.7, 122.1
Shovel	45% (11) 5.7, 90.5
Sidearm	33% (6) 2.0, 70.1

QB Drop Types

3 Step	49% (142) 9.4, 118.1
0/1 Step	44% (138) 5.9, 100.8
5 Step	55% (53) 10.1, 121.2
Designed Rollout Right	62% (42) 9.9, 131.5
7 Step	78% (18) 15.6, 155.8
Basic Screen	47% (17) 6.0, 91.7

QB State at Pass

Planted	51% (243) 8.9, 119.7
Moving	60% (106) 8.6, 132.9
Shuffling	38% (32) 6.2, 87.6

Play Action

	Play Action	No P/A
Under Center	65% (79) 11.6, 140.2	20% (15) 3.9, 68.5
Shotgun	56% (62) 9.4, 133.9	47% (267) 7.6, 110.2
ALL	61% (141) 10.6, 137.9	46% (282) 7.4, 108.0

Run Types

Inside Zone	48% (199) 4.7
Outside Zone	46% (118) 4.3
Power	44% (36) 4.3
Pitch	46% (28) 5.9
Lead	46% (26) 2.9
Stretch	90% (10) 6.5

SEA-5

The answer as to why the Seahawks failed to make a significant 2018 win-loss leap despite so much improvement.

Seattle's offense ranked 19th in EDSR in both 2017 and 2018, and their defense took a slight step back last season, falling from 20th to 24th. Overall, the Seahawks ranked No. 20 in EDSR in 2017 and No. 23 in EDSR last season.

Thanks to their run-heavy nature, there was absolutely no improvement in EDSR.

And thus, despite an improvement in so many other areas, the 2018 Seahawks were unable to take a significant leap forward. The 2019 Seahawks must do everything in their power to improve their early-down success.

But I'm concerned that won't happen. Because the Seahawks *think* they were successful last year, they may not self scout thoroughly enough. "We don't have to do much different, just reboot and roll," they may think. "We just got unlucky against Dallas in the playoffs." They may look at the Super Bowl Rams and say, "We were beating these guys entering the fourth quarter in both games we played last year. We're as good as any team in the NFC, and we'll take the next step in 2019."

The problem with this thinking is that Seattle had a significant amount of good fortune last year that may regress to the mean in 2019. And they didn't improve where it matters most (EDSR).

After a first-and-ten run with minimal to no gain, the Seahawks went run on second and long at a league-high 54% rate. (League average was 31%.) These Seattle runs gained 3.4 yards per carry with a 20% Success Rate. The Seahawks averaged a 57% Success Rate and 9.3 yards per attempt when using play action in three-receiver 11 personnel but managed 41% success and 6.4 YPA without play action in 11. Play action from 11 also dropped Seattle's sack rate from 10.4% to 6.3%. Yet Seattle used play action on only 17.9% of their 11-personnel pass attempts. The Super Bowl Rams used play action on 32% of 11-personnel plays.

The Seahawks must adapt to modern football or else they will continue to waste **Russell Wilson**'s prime. Losing pieces from Seattle's defense has badly hurt, so the burden will continue to fall on the offense. It's time for Wilson to be unleashed.

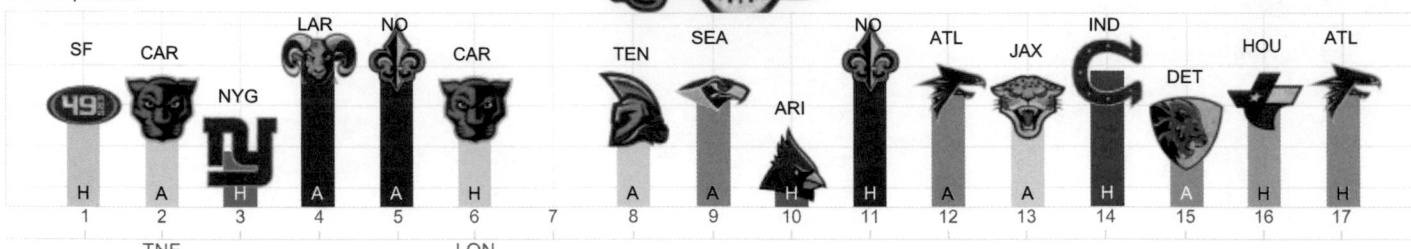

Coaches (Prior Yrs)

Head Coach:
Bruce Arians (ARI HC) (new)
Offensive Coordinator:
Byron Leftwich (ARI OC) (new)
Defensive Coordinator:
Todd Bowles (NYJ HC) (new)

EASY   HARD

SF	CAR	NYG	LAR	NO	CAR		TEN	SEA	ARI	NO	ATL	JAX	IND	DET	HOU	ATL
H	A	H	A	A	H		A	A	H	H	A	A	H	A	H	H
1	2	3	4	5	6	7	8	9	10	11	12	13	14	15	16	17

TNF   LON

2019 Forecast

Wins	Div Rank
6	#4

Past Records
2018: 5-11
2017: 5-11
2016: 9-7

Key Players Lost

Player	New
Adam Humphries (WR)	TEN
Adarius Taylor (ILB)	CLE
Andrew Adams (S)	DET
DeSean Jackson (WR)	PHI
Gerald McCoy (DT)	CAR
Javien Elliott (CB)	CAR
Josh Shaw (FS)	ARI
Kwon Alexander (ILB)	SF
Ryan Fitzpatrick (QB)	MIA
Vinny Curry (DE)	PHI

Average Line	# Games Favored	# Games Underdog
3.8	3	12

2019 Tampa Bay Buccaneers Overview

Bruce Arians is a beast.

When last saw Arians coach, he squeezed an 8-8 record out of a 2017 Cardinals team that lost virtually its entire offense to injury. Arians previously won two Super Bowls in Pittsburgh, where he was rudely dismissed by **Mike Tomlin** after the 2011 season for refusing to reconcile his aggressive pass-first approach with ownership's run-first edict.

Arians joined the 2012 Colts, focused on coordinating **Andrew Luck**'s offense as a rookie, and stood in while head coach **Chuck Pagano** battled leukemia. Arians' interim-coached Colts were so successful he earned AP NFL Coach of the Year, directing Indianapolis to a 9-3 finish before earning the Cardinals' head-coaching job in 2013.

Before Arians' arrival, the Cardinals went three straight years without a winning record. Arians engineered 10-, 11-, and 13-win seasons, reaching the NFC Championship Game in 2015 and earning his second AP Coach of the Year award.

Why did Arians' tenure end in Arizona? After that NFC Championship appearance in 2015, the Cardinals went 7-8-1, then 8-8. Arians got worried about his own health. He almost retired after a cancer scare in 2016, but he wanted to return and "not let cancer win."

Diagnosed with high blood pressure, however, Arians admitted there was "too much to live for to die on the sideline." So, he took the 2018 season off.

If you think Arians retired because his offensive philosophy wasn't working, you're sorely mistaken. But his players couldn't stay healthy. The 2016 Cardinals fielded the NFL's sixth most-injured offensive line, derailing Arians' deep-passing style. The 2016 Cardinals were also unfortunate to go 3-5 in one-score games.

2017 was more of the same. The Cardinals were the NFL's fifth most-injured team, including

*(cont'd - see **TB2**)*

Key Free Agents/ Trades Added

Player	AAV (MM)
Bradley Pinion (P)	$2.7
Breshad Perriman (WR)	$4
Deone Bucannon (ILB)	$2.5
Ndamukong Suh (DT)	$9.3
Shaquil Barrett (OLB)	$4

Drafted Players

Rd	Pk	Player (College)
1	5	LB - Devin White (LSU)
2	39	CB - Sean Murphy-Bunting (Central Michigan)
3	94	CB - Jamel Dean (Auburn)
3*	99	S - Mike Edwards (Kentucky)
4	107	DE - Anthony Nelson (Iowa)
5	145	K - Matt Gay (Utah)
6*	208	WR - Scott Miller (Bowling Green)
7	215	DT - Terry Beckner (Missouri)

Regular Season Wins: Past & Current Proj

Forecast 2019 Wins	6
2018 Wins	5
Forecast 2018 Wins	6.5
2017 Wins	5
2016 Wins	9
2015 Wins	6

1 3 5 7 9 11 13 15

Lineup & Cap Hits

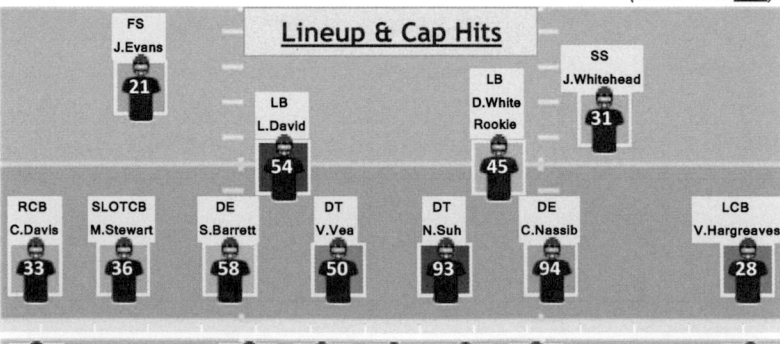

2019 Cap Dollars

2019 Unit Spending

All DEF   All OFF

Positional Spending

	Rank	Total	2017 Rk
All OFF	1	$118.29M	11
QB	14	$24.27M	22
OL	4	$47.22M	25
RB	23	$5.94M	25
WR	7	$28.75M	1
TE	7	$12.12M	10
All DEF	15	$87.22M	6
DL	2	$48.28M	1
LB	15	$21.21M	21
CB	26	$11.12M	18
S	31	$6.61M	26

the league's fourth most-injured offensive line. They lost **David Johnson** for the season in Week 1. **Carson Palmer** went out for the year in Week 7. **John Brown** could never get right. Out of sheer desperation, the Cards traded for aging **Adrian Peterson** midyear and watched as he too landed on injured reserve after six games.

Arians was never pleased with that 2017 team. Prior to the season, he ripped the receiver corps GM **Steve Keim** had assembled. Asked about his wide receiver group's terrible start to camp, Arians replied he "might have two" out of 12 who could even play in the NFL.

And the Cardinals couldn't run the ball without Johnson, falling to dead last in the NFL in both rushing efficiency and explosive runs.

Arians resorted to spreading out the field and dialing up a bevy of quick passes to try to keep backup quarterbacks **Drew Stanton** and **Blaine Gabbert** alive. Arians ran four-receiver sets on 271 pass plays, by far most in the NFL. Next closest were the Giants at 144 snaps of four-receiver formations. The NFL average was 31 four-wide passing snaps *per team*. The Cardinals went four wide on 42% of their 649 passing plays.

Even when games were within one score, the Cardinals went four-plus wide on 35% of their passing snaps. They ran 83 snaps of five-receiver "00" personnel. As the entire NFL totaled just 125 snaps of 00 personnel, the 2017 Cardinals accounted for 66% of five-wide plays across the entire league.

Before losing Palmer, Arizona stood at 3-3 and would have been 4-2 if not for a 20-point fourth-quarter meltdown against Detroit in Week 1. The rest of the way, the Cardinals played with the league's most-injured roster, and Gabbert or Stanton at quarterback. They still led entering fourth quarters in five of their final nine games. In only one game did the Cardinals trail by more than five points entering the fourth. They beat multiple playoff teams with a horrendous roster.

Arians *coached his butt off* to get that Cardinals team to 8-8.

When the Bucs needed a new head coach, they wondered if Arians' one-year hiatus was enough to rejuvenate him. But they didn't take chances. They ordered Arians to take a full physical and included his doctor as part of the interview process. Arians passed and signed a four-year deal. We should all be grateful for another chance to witness his great coaching.

The play caller-quarterback relationship is the most important in football, and Arians employs a "no risk it, no biscuit" approach. To hit pay dirt as a passing offense, Arians believes you've *got to* take chances. Arians' teachings are diametrically opposed to 2018 Bucs coach **Dirk Koetter**, who preached ball security to **Jameis Winston** above all else.

On the first episode of HBO's Hard Knocks in 2017, Koetter sat Winston down

in his office. "We have a great defense now," Koetter told Jameis. "We've got to cut our risk a bit."

The 2017 Bucs finished with the worst defense in the league.

Now entering his make-or-break contract year, Winston will not have Koetter as his head coach or offensive coordinator for the first time in his career. Jameis is moving from a coach who wanted to "cut risk" to a coach whose motto is literally to "risk it."

I remain skeptical of Winston long term based on his unreliable on-field decision making. But I have an open mind to what he could do with Arians, **Mike Evans**, **Chris Godwin**, and **O.J. Howard** in 2019.

Just two months after the Bucs exercised Winston's fifth-year option last April, Winston was suspended three games for allegedly groping *(cont'd - see TB-3)*

2018 Passing Performance

QB	1st Dwn	2nd Dwn	3rd Dwn	
Jameis Winston	56%	47%	44%	Success Rate
	7.9	8.0	8.0	YPA
	90.2	78.6	107.7	Rating
Pass Rate	57%	66%	82%	
NFL AVG	53%	47%	36%	Success Rate
	7.7	7.3	6.9	YPA
	95.1	93.7	87.1	Rating
Pass Rate	53%	62%	80%	

2018 Rushing Performance

Offense	1st Dwn	2nd Dwn	3rd Dwn	
TB	47%	34%	58%	Success Rate
	3.9	3.5	5.9	YPC
Run Rate	43%	34%	18%	
NFL AVG	48%	46%	51%	Success Rate
	4.5	4.4	4.3	YPC
Run Rate	47%	38%	20%	

2018 Offensive Advanced Metrics

Rank (y-axis, 1 at top to 30 at bottom)

Metric	Rank
EDSR Off	4
30 & In Off	21
Red Zone Off	10
3rd Down Off	2
YPPA Off	2
YPPT Off	31
Offensive Efficiency	12
Pass Efficiency Off	9
Pass Pro Efficiency Off	15
RB Pass Eff Off	27
Rush Efficiency Off	23
Explosive Pass Off	6
Explosive Run Off	27

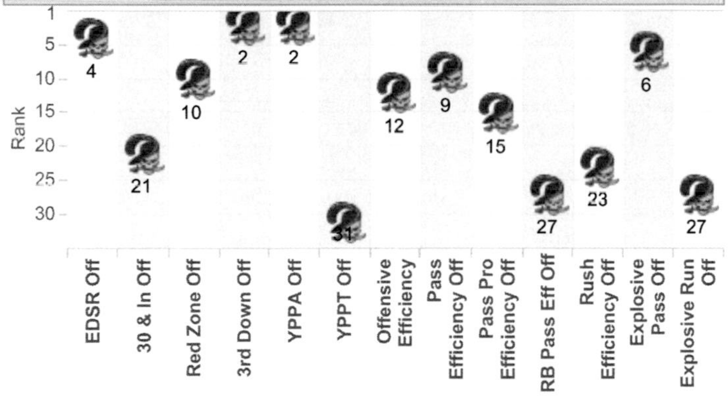

2018 Defensive Advanced Metrics

Rank (y-axis, 1 at top to 30 at bottom)

Metric	Rank
EDSR Def	30
30 & In Def	30
Red Zone Def	31
3rd Down Def	21
YPPA Def	30
YPPT Def	27
Defensive Efficiency	22
Pass Efficiency Def	30
Pass Pro Efficiency Def	8
RB Pass Eff Def	10
Rush Efficiency Def	31
Explosive Pass Def	23
Explosive Run Def	31

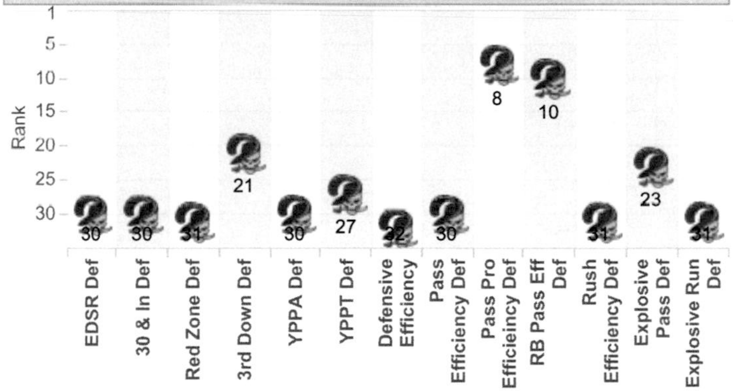

2018 Weekly EDSR & Season Trending Performance

	1	2	3	4	6	7	8	9	10	11	12	13	14	15	16	17	WEEK
RESULT	W	W	L	L	L	W	L	L	L	W	W	L	L	L	L	L	
OPP	NO	PHI	PIT	CHI	ATL	CLE	CIN	CAR	WAS	NYG	SF	CAR	NO	BAL	DAL	ATL	
SITE	A	H	H	A	A	H	A	A	H	A	H	H	H	A	A	H	
MARGIN	8	6	-3	-38	-5	3	-3	-14	-13	-3	18	7	-14	-8	-7	-2	
PTS	48	27	27	10	29	26	34	28	3	35	27	24	14	12	20	32	
OPP PTS	40	21	30	48	34	23	37	42	16	38	9	17	28	20	27	34	

EDSR by Wk
W=Green
L=Red

OFF/DEF
EDSR
Blue=OFF
(high=good)
Red=DEF
(low=good)

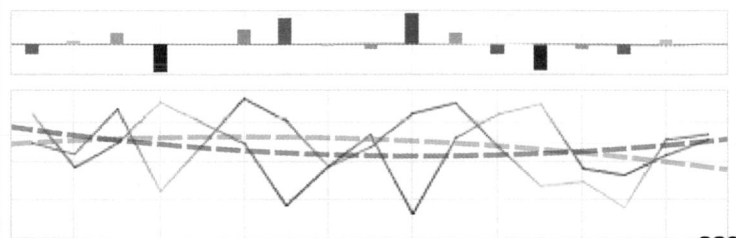

2018 Close Game Records

All 2018 Wins: **5**
FG Games (<=3 pts) W-L: **1-4**
FG Games Win %: **20% (#29)**
FG Games Wins (% of Total Wins): **20% (#23)**
1 Score Games (<=8 pts) W-L: **4-7**
1 Score Games Win %: **36% (#23)**
1 Score Games Wins (% of Total Wins): **80% (#3)**

2018 Critical & Game-Deciding Stats

TO Margin	-18
TO Given	35
INT Given	26
FUM Given	9
TO Taken	17
INT Taken	9
FUM Taken	8
Sack Margin	-3
Sacks	38
Sacks Allow	41
Return TD Margin	-2
Ret TDs	2
Ret TDs Allow	4
Penalty Margin	+10
Penalties	117
Opponent Penalties	127

Tampa Bay Buccaneers 2019 Strength of Schedule In Detail (compared to 2018)

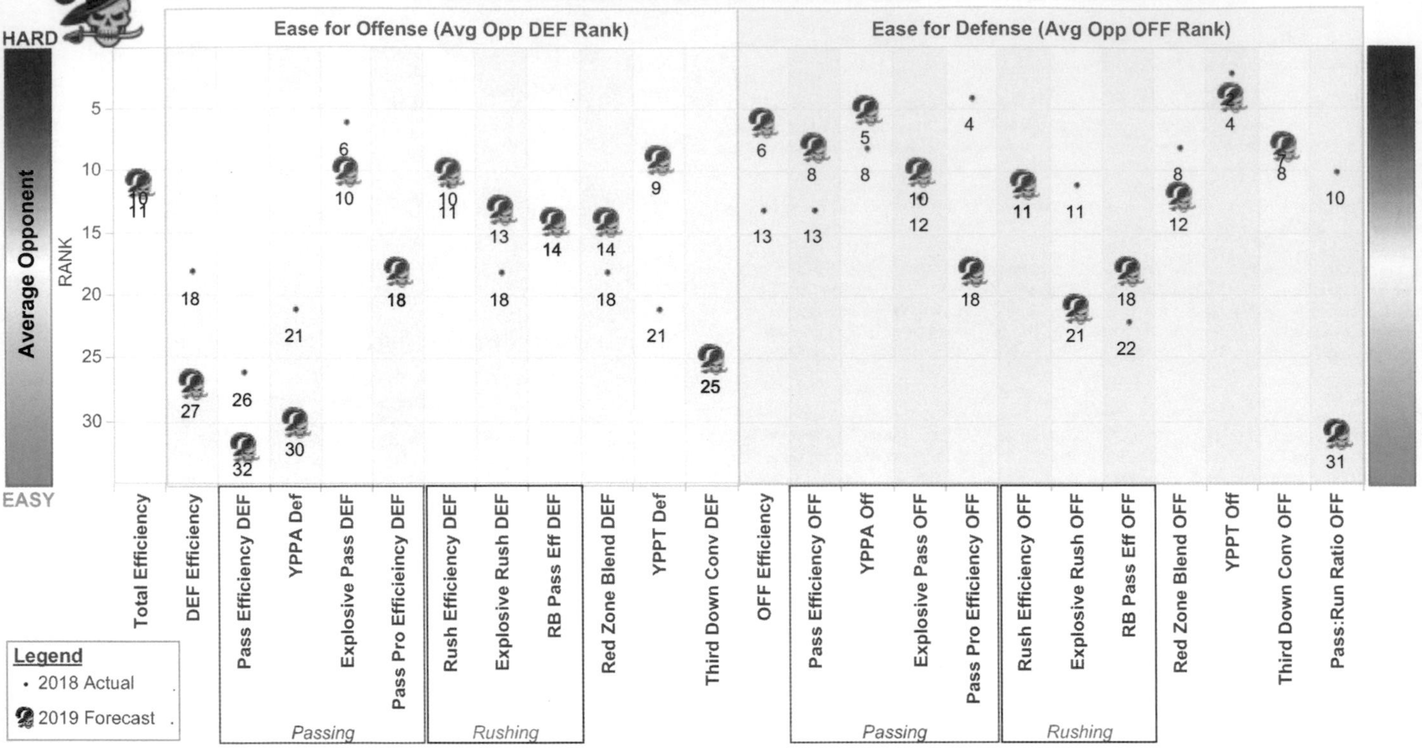

HARD (top) ... **EASY** (bottom)

Ease for Offense (Avg Opp DEF Rank)

Metrics (left to right): Total Efficiency, DEF Efficiency, Pass Efficiency DEF, YPPA Def, Explosive Pass DEF, Pass Pro Efficiency DEF, Rush Efficiency DEF, Explosive Rush DEF, RB Pass Eff DEF, Red Zone Blend DEF, YPPT Def, Third Down Conv Def

Passing (Pass Efficiency DEF, YPPA Def, Explosive Pass DEF, Pass Pro Efficiency DEF)
Rushing (Rush Efficiency DEF, Explosive Rush DEF, RB Pass Eff DEF)

2019 Forecast values: 11, 27, 32, 30, 6/10, 18, 10/11, 13, 14, 14, 9, 25
2018 Actual values: 19, 18, 26, 21, 18, 18, 21

Ease for Defense (Avg Opp OFF Rank)

Metrics (left to right): OFF Efficiency, Pass Efficiency OFF, YPPA Off, Explosive Pass OFF, Pass Pro Efficiency OFF, Rush Efficiency OFF, Explosive Rush OFF, RB Pass Eff OFF, Red Zone Blend OFF, YPPT Off, Third Down Conv OFF, Pass:Run Ratio OFF

Passing / *Rushing*

2019 Forecast values: 6, 8, 8/5, 10, 11, 11, 18, 21, 18, 8/12, 4, 8, 31
2018 Actual values: 13, 13, 4, 12, 22, 10

Legend
- 2018 Actual
- 2019 Forecast

2019 v 2018 Schedule Variances* (OFF=Rank of DEF faced, 2019 vs 2018)

Pass OFF Rank	Pass OFF Blend Rk	Rush OFF Rk	Rush OFF Blend Rk	Pass DEF Rk	Pass DEF Blend Rk	Rush DEF Rk	Rush DEF Blend Rk
23	24	10	10	10	16	14	19

* **1**=Hardest Jump in 2019 schedule from 2018 (aka a much harder schedule in 2019), **32**=Easiest Jump in 2019 schedule from 2018 (aka a much easier schedule in 2019);
Pass Blend metric blends 4 metrics: Pass Efficiency, YPPA, Explosive Pass & Pass Rush; **Rush Blend** metric blends 3 metrics: Rush Efficiency, Explosive Rush & RB Targets

---

Team Records & Trends

	2018	2017	2016
Average line	3.4	2.3	2.6
Average O/U line	51.8	46.3	47.0
Straight Up Record	5-11	5-11	9-7
Against the Spread Record	5-8	6-8	9-7
Over/Under Record	9-6	8-8	7-8
ATS as Favorite	1-2	2-4	1-2
ATS as Underdog	4-6	3-4	7-5
Straight Up Home	4-4	4-4	4-4
ATS Home	3-4	4-3	3-5
Over/Under Home	3-5	2-6	4-4
ATS as Home Favorite	1-2	1-2	1-2
ATS as a Home Dog	2-2	2-1	2-3
Straight Up Away	1-7	1-7	5-3
ATS Away	2-4	2-5	6-2
Over/Under Away	6-1	6-2	3-4
ATS Away Favorite	0-0	1-2	0-0
ATS Away Dog	2-4	1-3	5-2
Six Point Teaser Record	13-3	12-4	12-4
Seven Point Teaser Record	13-3	13-3	12-4
Ten Point Teaser Record	14-2	13-3	13-3

TB-3

a female Uber driver. **Ryan Fitzpatrick** started the year and played lights out during a 2-1 start. Winston was reinserted in Week 4, after Fitzpatrick melted down against the Bears. The Bucs emerged from their Week 5 bye with Winston starting, and he put up nearly 400 yards and four touchdowns in a Week 6 loss to the Falcons. Tampa Bay followed up with an overtime win, which seemingly went to Jameis' head.

The very next week in Cincinnati, Winston's stat line was repulsive. He went 18-of-35 passing with one touchdown, four picks, and a 47.7 passer rating, and was benched again.

Fitzpatrick started the next three games, losing them all.

At 3-7, the Bucs decided to let Jameis close out their lost season. Fitzpatrick didn't take another snap, and Winston wrapped up with a 2-5 record in the Bucs' final seven games.

(cont'd - see TB-4)

2019 Rest Analysis

Team More Rest	2
Opp More Rest	1
Net Rest Edge	1
Week 2 Edge	0
Week 3 Edge	3
Week 4 Edge	0
Week 5 Edge	0
Week 6 Edge	0
Week 8 Edge	7
Week 9 Edge	0
Week 10 Edge	-3
Week 11 Edge	0
Week 12 Edge	0
Week 13 Edge	0
Week 14 Edge	0
Week 15 Edge	0
Week 16 Edge	0
Week 17 Edge	0

Health by Unit*

	2018 Rk	
2017 Rk	18	
2018 v 2017 Rk		
Off Rk	5	
Def Rk		
QB Rk	12	
RB Rk	9	
WR Rk	12	
TE Rk	20	
Oline Rk	5	
Dline Rk	24	
LB Rk		
DB Rk		

*Based on the work of Football Outsiders

2018 Weekly Betting Lines (wks 1-16)

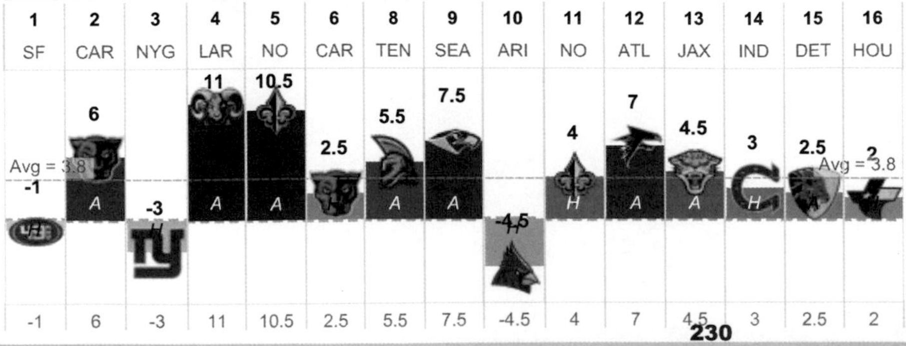

1	2	3	4	5	6	8	9	10	11	12	13	14	15	16
SF	CAR	NYG	LAR	NO	CAR	TEN	SEA	ARI	NO	ATL	JAX	IND	DET	HOU
-1	6	-3	11	10.5	2.5	5.5	7.5	-4.5	4	7	4.5	3	2.5	2

Avg = 3.8

Home / Away markers: A, A, A, A, A, A, A, H, A, A, H

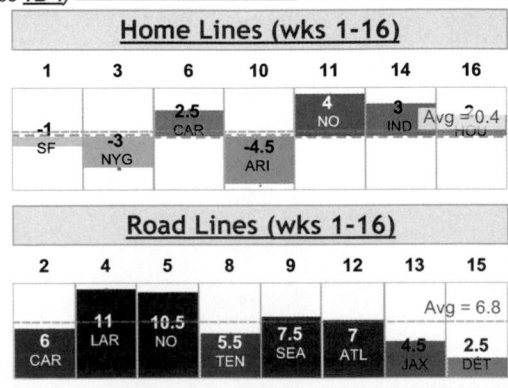

Home Lines (wks 1-16)

1	3	6	10	11	14	16
-1 SF	-3 NYG	2.5 CAR	-4.5 ARI	4 NO	3 IND	Avg = 0.4 HOU

Road Lines (wks 1-16)

2	4	5	8	9	12	13	15
6 CAR	11 LAR	10.5 NO	5.5 TEN	7.5 SEA	7 ATL	4.5 JAX	2.5 DET

Avg = 6.8

230

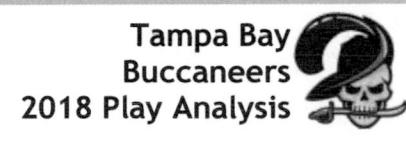

Tampa Bay Buccaneers 2018 Play Analysis

2018 Play Tendencies

All Pass %	63%
All Pass Rk	6
All Rush %	37%
All Rush Rk	27
1 Score Pass %	60%
1 Score Pass Rk	11
2017 1 Score Pass %	61%
2017 1 Score Pass Rk	3
2018 Pass Increase %	-1%
Pass Increase Rk	17
1 Score Rush %	40%
1 Score Rush Rk	22
Up Pass %	57%
Up Pass Rk	3
Up Rush %	43%
Up Rush Rk	30
Down Pass %	68%
Down Pass Rk	10
Down Rush %	32%
Down Rush Rk	23

2018 Down & Distance Tendencies

Down	Distance	Total Plays	Pass Rate	Run Rate	Play Success %
1	Short (1-3)	8	0%	100%	75%
	Med (4-7)	11	27%	73%	45%
	Long (8-10)	350	53%	47%	52%
	XL (11+)	19	68%	32%	26%
2	Short (1-3)	35	54%	46%	57%
	Med (4-7)	81	63%	37%	54%
	Long (8-10)	97	65%	35%	37%
	XL (11+)	48	73%	27%	17%
3	Short (1-3)	33	58%	42%	64%
	Med (4-7)	39	90%	10%	46%
	Long (8-10)	37	89%	11%	46%
	XL (11+)	33	94%	6%	30%
4	Short (1-3)	5	60%	40%	80%
	Med (4-7)	1	0%	100%	100%
	Long (8-10)	1	100%	0%	0%

Shotgun %:

Under Center	Shotgun
38%	62%

37% AVG 63%

Run Rate:

Under Center	Shotgun
62%	15%

68% AVG 23%

Pass Rate:

Under Center	Shotgun
38%	85%

32% AVG 77%

Short Yardage Intelligence:

2nd and Short Run

Run Freq	Run Rk	NFL Run Freq Avg	Run 1D Rate	Run NFL 1D Avg
64%	18	65%	44%	68%

2nd and Short Pass

Pass Freq	Pass Rk	NFL Pass Freq Avg	Pass 1D Rate	Pass NFL 1D Avg
36%	15	35%	56%	56%

Most Frequent Play

Down	Distance	Play Type	Player	Total Plays	Play Success %
1	Short (1-3)	RUSH	Peyton Barber	6	67%
	Med (4-7)	RUSH	Peyton Barber	6	50%
	Long (8-10)	RUSH	Peyton Barber	111	48%
	XL (11+)	PASS	Adam Humphries	3	67%
2	Short (1-3)	RUSH	Peyton Barber	11	55%
	Med (4-7)	RUSH	Peyton Barber	23	30%
	Long (8-10)	RUSH	Peyton Barber	23	30%
	XL (11+)	PASS	Chris Godwin	10	40%
3	Short (1-3)	RUSH	Peyton Barber	7	71%
	Med (4-7)	PASS	Adam Humphries	8	63%
	Long (8-10)	PASS	Mike Evans	11	64%
	XL (11+)	PASS	Adam Humphries	7	29%

Most Successful Play*

Down	Distance	Play Type	Player	Total Plays	Play Success %
1	Short (1-3)	RUSH	Peyton Barber	6	67%
	Med (4-7)	RUSH	Peyton Barber	6	50%
	Long (8-10)	PASS	Chris Godwin	20	80%
2	Short (1-3)	RUSH	Peyton Barber	11	55%
	Med (4-7)	PASS	Adam Humphries	11	82%
	Long (8-10)	PASS	Chris Godwin	8	75%
	XL (11+)	PASS	Chris Godwin	10	40%
3	Short (1-3)	RUSH	Peyton Barber	7	71%
	Med (4-7)	PASS	Adam Humphries	8	63%
	Long (8-10)	PASS	Mike Evans	11	64%
	XL (11+)	PASS	Chris Godwin	6	83%

*Minimum 5 plays to qualify

2018 Weekly Snap Rates

Wk	Opp	Score	Mike Evans	Adam Humphries	Chris Godwin	Peyton Barber	Cameron Brate	DeSean Jackson	O.J. Howard	Jacquizz Rodgers
1	NO	W 48-40	50 (76%)	44 (67%)	46 (70%)	48 (73%)	24 (36%)	20 (30%)	43 (65%)	15 (23%)
2	PHI	W 27-21	47 (81%)	29 (50%)	29 (50%)	36 (62%)	14 (24%)	34 (59%)	46 (79%)	18 (31%)
3	PIT	L 30-27	58 (79%)	53 (73%)	37 (51%)	44 (60%)	31 (42%)	42 (58%)	48 (66%)	25 (34%)
4	CHI	L 48-10	57 (90%)	49 (78%)	31 (49%)	31 (49%)	37 (59%)	39 (62%)	15 (24%)	11 (17%)
6	ATL	L 34-29	57 (86%)	51 (77%)	37 (56%)	41 (62%)	22 (33%)	34 (52%)	34 (52%)	10 (15%)
7	CLE	W 26-23	82 (86%)	57 (60%)	66 (69%)	35 (37%)	39 (41%)	43 (45%)	63 (66%)	30 (32%)
8	CIN	L 37-34	70 (80%)	62 (70%)	63 (72%)	43 (49%)	26 (30%)	46 (52%)	53 (60%)	33 (38%)
9	CAR	L 42-28	60 (90%)	55 (82%)	37 (55%)	35 (52%)	27 (40%)	32 (48%)	37 (55%)	26 (39%)
10	WAS	L 16-3	55 (80%)	54 (78%)	34 (49%)	33 (48%)	19 (28%)	44 (64%)	45 (65%)	26 (38%)
11	NYG	L 38-35	65 (92%)	49 (69%)	23 (32%)	48 (68%)	20 (28%)	53 (75%)	51 (72%)	23 (32%)
12	SF	W 27-9	58 (79%)	38 (52%)	49 (67%)	36 (49%)	51 (70%)	36 (49%)		34 (47%)
13	CAR	W 24-17	57 (88%)	41 (63%)	52 (80%)	40 (62%)	44 (68%)			15 (23%)
14	NO	L 28-14	61 (87%)	57 (81%)	60 (86%)	32 (46%)	46 (66%)			31 (44%)
15	BAL	L 20-12	45 (90%)	29 (58%)	41 (82%)	32 (64%)	41 (82%)			13 (26%)
16	DAL	L 27-20	66 (83%)	63 (79%)	61 (76%)	47 (59%)	57 (71%)	29 (36%)		32 (40%)
17	ATL	L 34-32	51 (84%)	50 (82%)	51 (84%)	35 (57%)	36 (59%)			25 (41%)
	Grand Total		939 (84%)	781 (70%)	717 (64%)	616 (56%)	534 (49%)	452 (52%)	435 (60%)	367 (32%)

Personnel Groupings

Personnel	Team %	NFL Avg	Succ. %
1-1 [3WR]	70%	65%	50%
1-2 [2WR]	17%	17%	47%
2-1 [2WR]	5%	8%	47%
1-0 [4WR]	3%	2%	50%
1-3 [1WR]	2%	3%	35%

Grouping Tendencies

Personnel	Pass Rate	Pass Succ. %	Run Succ. %
1-1 [3WR]	70%	51%	46%
1-2 [2WR]	48%	52%	42%
2-1 [2WR]	39%	58%	40%
1-0 [4WR]	83%	48%	60%
1-3 [1WR]	35%	38%	33%

Red Zone Targets (min 3)

Receiver	All	Inside 5	6-10	11-20
Chris Godwin	15	4	7	4
Mike Evans	14	2	4	8
Adam Humphries	12	4	1	7
Cameron Brate	10	2	1	7
O.J. Howard	7	2	2	3
Jacquizz Rodgers	6			6
DeSean Jackson	5		1	4

Red Zone Rushes (min 3)

Rusher	All	Inside 5	6-10	11-20
Peyton Barber	37	14	9	14
Ryan Fitzpatrick	12	3	4	5
Jameis Winston	8		3	5
Ronald Jones	5	2		3
Jacquizz Rodgers	4	1		3

Early Down Target Rate

	RB	TE	WR
	17%	17%	66%
NFL AVG	23%	21%	56%

Overall Target Success %

	RB	TE	WR
	41%	55%	57%
	#28	#16	#4

Tampa Bay Buccaneers 2018 Passing Recap & 2019 Outlook

Arians is going to ensure his passing game delivers. He'll squeeze out every drop. The Bucs' pass-catcher upside is sky high with **Mike Evans**, **Chris Godwin**, and **O.J. Howard**, and Arians hopes **Breshad Perriman** or rookie **Scott Miller** steps up as a downfield vertical presence.

Due to Tampa Bay's deficiencies in the secondary, much will be expected out of this passing offense. Combine the NFL's easiest schedule of opposing pass defenses with a need to pass due to the Bucs' poor defense, and **Jameis Winston** is theoretically set up for a career year.

Jameis Winston Rating All Downs

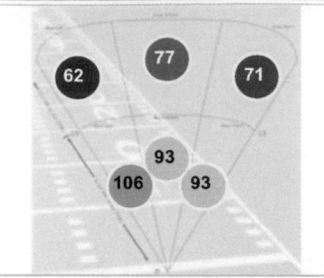

2018 Standard Passing Table

QB	Comp	Att	Comp %	Yds	YPA	TDs	INT	Sacks	Rating	Rk
Jameis Winston	244	378	65%	2,992	7.9	19	14	27	90	28
Ryan Fitzpatrick	164	246	67%	2,366	9.6	17	12	14	100	10
NFL Avg			62%		7.0				87.5	

2018 Advanced Passing Table

QB	Success %	EDSR Passing Success %	20+ Yd Pass Gains	20+ Yd Pass %	30+ Yd Pass Gains	30+ Yd Pass %	Avg. Air Yds per Comp	Avg. YAC per Comp	20+ Air Yd Comp	20+ Air Yd %
Ryan Fitzpatrick	51%	52%	37	15.0%	15	6.0%	9.0	5.5	16	7%
Jameis Winston	50%	52%	34	9.0%	11	3.0%	8.5	3.8	12	3%
NFL Avg	44%	48%	29.5	8.4%	12.5	3.7%	5.8	5.1	14.5	6%

Jameis Winston Rating Early Downs

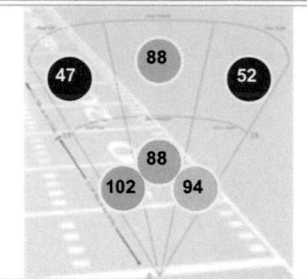

Interception Rates by Down

Yards to Go	1st Dwn	2nd Dwn	3rd Dwn	4th Dwn	Total
1 & 2		0.0%	0.0%	0.0%	0.0%
3, 4, 5	0.0%	4.5%	0.0%	0.0%	1.7%
6 - 9	0.0%	4.3%	0.0%		2.6%
10 - 14	4.3%	2.2%	7.1%		4.1%
15+	0.0%	14.3%	0.0%		5.9%
Total	4.0%	4.6%	1.0%	0.0%	3.5%

3rd Down Passing - Short of Sticks Analysis

QB	Avg. Yds to Go	Avg. YIA (of Comp)	Avg Yds Short	Short of Sticks Rate	Short Rk
Jameis Winston	8.0	10.2	0.0	36%	2
NFL Avg	7.8	6.4	-1.4	60%	

Air Yds vs YAC

Air Yds %	YAC %	Rk
69%	31%	1
53%	48%	

2018 Receiving Recap & 2019 Outlook

Mike Evans is coming off a career-high 1,524 receiving yards, joining **Randy Moss** and **A.J. Green** as the only three wide receivers in NFL history to begin their careers with five straight 1,000-yard seasons. Still only 25 years old, Evans hasn't touched his ceiling yet entering **Bruce Arians'** vertical attack. **O.J. Howard** was criminally underutilized by ex-coach **Dirk Koetter**, and Arians has talked up **Chris Godwin** as a slot-receiver solution in the same way Arians moving **Larry Fitzgerald**, **Reggie Wayne**, and **Hines Ward** inside maximized their careers.

Player *Min 50 Targets	Targ	Comp %	YPA	Rating	Success %	Success Rk	Missed YPA Rk	YAS % Rk	YTS % Rk	TDs
Mike Evans	139	62%	11.0	94.5	60%	14	58	5	113	8
Adam Humphries	104	73%	7.8	107.7	58%	27	78	97	18	5
Chris Godwin	95	62%	8.9	106.6	58%	27	18	67	18	7
DeSean Jackson	75	55%	10.3	69.5	51%	64	110	1	130	4

Directional Passer Rating Delivered

Receiver	Short Left	Short Middle	Short Right	Deep Left	Deep Middle	Deep Right	Player Total
Mike Evans	101	97	82	62	39	133	95
Adam Humphries	120	103	91	119	40	94	108
Chris Godwin	130	80	109	66	119	85	107
DeSean Jackson	53	40	74	28	104	72	70
Cameron Brate	110	93	68	81	138		100
O.J. Howard	148	145	99	54	70	96	110
Jacquizz Rodgers	61	102	86				86
Peyton Barber	52	109	88				84
Team Total	103	104	95	52	91	112	97

2018 Rushing Recap & 2019 Outlook

Arians spoke to the hearts of the analytics community when he essentially said, "running backs don't matter," and that teams must be careful to not overpay such a replaceable and injury-prone position. But don't conflate those statements with a refusal to run.

The Bucs need **Ronald Jones** to step up. Out of 56 qualified backs with at least 100 touches last year, **Peyton Barber** ranked 44th in yards per carry (3.7), 55th in yards per target (4.6), and 54th in yards per touch (3.8). Since Arians didn't draft Jones and inherited Barber, he will presumably approach them with an open mind. In fantasy football, Jones is currently being drafted as the RB37 in ADP. Barber is the RB52.

Player *Min 50 Rushes	Rushes	YPC	Success %	Success Rk	Missed YPA Rk	YTS % Rk	YAS % Rk	Early Down Success %	Early Down Success Rk	TDs
Peyton Barber	234	3.7	44%	54	48	16	44	43%	55	5

Yards per Carry by Direction

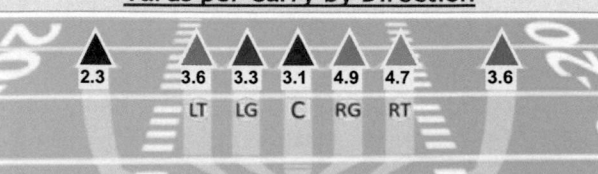

Directional Run Frequency

In Arians' final two seasons with the Cardinals, he ran 90% and 94% of plays from shotgun. Winston has historically struggled in the gun, managing a 47% Success Rate, 7.4 yards per attempt, and an 85 rating on shotgun passes. From under center, his Success Rate (54%), YPA (8.2), and rating (97) are all much higher.

Arians has devised outside-the-box ways to coach up Winston. He brought virtual reality to Tampa Bay after Palmer fell in love with it in Arizona. The STRIVR system allows quarterbacks to put on goggles and watch practice. Using virtual reality, quarterbacks can turn 360 degrees, see the coaches behind them, and see practice.

"It's not a video game," Arians insisted. "It's from our actual practice. **Carson Palmer** had it in his house and would study it every Thursday night. All the blitz pickups. You can see both receivers. You see everything."

Winston's box-score upside is immense in his first season under Arians with the weaponry in place. Arians' final two Cardinals teams ranked No. 2 and No. 5 in offensive plays per game, and I project this year's Bucs face the NFL's easiest schedule of opposing pass defenses.

Arians doesn't love Tampa Bay's schedule on the whole, however. The Bucs have back-to-back road games in Weeks 4 and 5 against the Super Bowl-contending Rams and Saints and lose a home game to play the Panthers in London in Week 6. Following their Week 7 bye, the Bucs travel to Tennessee, then visit Seattle. *Six straight weeks* without a game at their home field.

If it's any consolation, the Bucs are one of three teams (also Packers and Chiefs) to have a

(cont'd - see TB-5)

Tampa Bay Buccaneers Fantasy Corner

Chris Godwin is one of 2019's most-obvious breakout candidates moving into the slot, where far-inferior talent **Adam Humphries** caught 76 passes for the 2018 Bucs. On slot routes alone since entering the NFL, Godwin has caught 24-of-35 targets (69%) for 330 yards and a touchdown, averaging 1.90 yards per route run compared to Humphries' 1.69 YPRR clip. **Reggie Wayne** caught 106 balls when **Bruce Arians** moved him to the slot with the 2012 Colts, and **Larry Fitzgerald** topped 100 catches three times at slot receiver for Arians' Cardinals. Moving inside will allow Godwin to run higher-percentage routes and vacuum targets in a Bucs offense that projects to contend for the league lead in pass attempts.

- Evan Silva

2018 Situational Usage by Player & Position

Usage Rate by Score

		Being Blown Out (14+)	Down Big (9-13)	One Score	Large Lead (9-13)	Blowout Lead (14+)
RUSH	Peyton Barber	19%	5%	65%	5%	6%
	Adam Humphries	50%		50%		
	DeSean Jackson	17%	17%	67%		
	Jacquizz Rodgers	6%	9%	61%	9%	15%
	Ronald Jones	57%		43%		
	Total	20%	5%	63%	5%	6%
PASS	Peyton Barber	22%	19%	59%		
	Mike Evans	24%	10%	58%	6%	2%
	Adam Humphries	28%	15%	48%	5%	4%
	Chris Godwin	22%	12%	53%	11%	2%
	DeSean Jackson	25%	20%	48%	3%	4%
	Jacquizz Rodgers	30%	13%	50%	3%	5%
	O.J. Howard	35%	19%	44%		2%
	Cameron Brate	20%	11%	64%	2%	2%
	Ronald Jones	56%	11%	33%		
	Total	26%	14%	53%	4%	3%

Share of Offensive Plays by Type

	Peyton Barber	Mike Evans	Adam Humphries	Chris Godwin	DeSean Jackson	Jacquizz Rodgers	O.J. Howard	Cameron Brate	Ronald Jones
RUSH	79%		1%		2%	11%			8%
PASS	5%	24%	17%	15%	13%	7%	9%	8%	2%
ALL	30%	16%	11%	10%	9%	9%	6%	5%	4%

Positional Target Distribution vs NFL Average

		NFL Wide				Team Only			
		Left	Middle	Right	Total	Left	Middle	Right	Total
Deep	WR	33%	17%	31%	81%	31%	21%	31%	84%
	TE	5%	4%	7%	16%	3%	10%	4%	16%
	RB	1%	0%	2%	4%				
	All	39%	21%	40%	100%	34%	31%	35%	100%
Short	WR	20%	14%	21%	55%	29%	16%	22%	66%
	TE	6%	6%	8%	20%	5%	5%	6%	17%
	RB	10%	5%	10%	25%	6%	7%	4%	17%
	All	36%	25%	39%	100%	40%	28%	32%	100%
Total		37%	24%	39%	100%	39%	29%	33%	100%

Positional Success Rates vs NFL Average

		NFL Wide				Team Only			
		Left	Middle	Right	Total	Left	Middle	Right	Total
Deep	WR	40%	49%	39%	42%	37%	52%	50%	46%
	TE	43%	52%	41%	45%	50%	64%	50%	58%
	RB	38%	33%	42%	40%				
	All	40%	50%	40%	42%	38%	56%	50%	48%
Short	WR	55%	60%	52%	55%	65%	65%	57%	62%
	TE	55%	62%	55%	57%	59%	63%	44%	55%
	RB	47%	53%	45%	48%	28%	63%	42%	46%
	All	53%	59%	51%	54%	59%	64%	53%	58%
Total		50%	58%	49%	51%	54%	62%	52%	56%

Division History: Season Wins & 2019 Projection

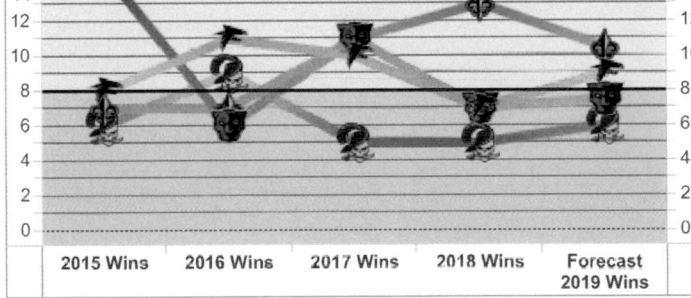

Rank of 2019 Defensive Pass Efficiency Faced by Week

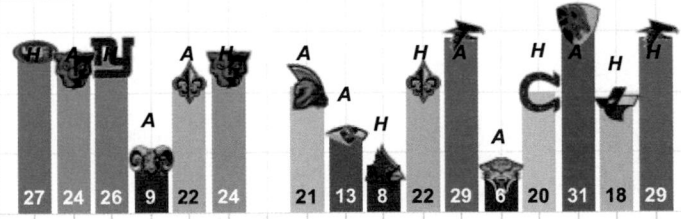

27	24	26	9	22	24		21	13	8	22	29	6	20	31	18	29

0 1 2 3 4 5 6 7 8 9 10 11 12 13 14 15 16 17

Rank of 2019 Defensive Rush Efficiency Faced by Week

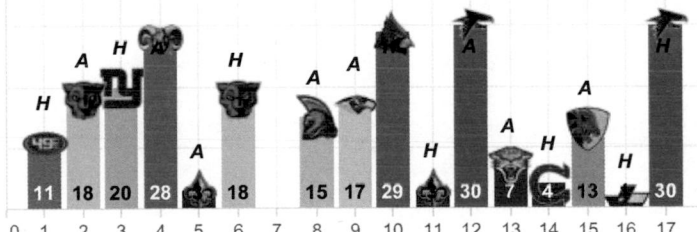

11	18	20	28		18		15	17	29		30	7	4	13		30

0 1 2 3 4 5 6 7 8 9 10 11 12 13 14 15 16 17

2018 Detailed Analytics Summary
Success by Play Type & Primary Personnel Groupings

Type	1-1 [3WR]	1-2 [2WR]	2-1 [2WR]	1-0 [4WR]	1-3 [1WR]	2-2 [1WR]	0-1 [4WR]	0-0 [5WR]	2-3 [0WR]	2-0 [3WR]	ALL
PASS	51% (512)	52% (85)	58% (19)	48% (25)	38% (8)	100% (2)	22% (9)	0% (1)			51% (661)
RUSH	46% (224)	42% (93)	40% (30)	60% (5)	33% (15)	18% (11)	100% (2)	0% (1)	0% (2)	100% (1)	44% (384)
All	50% (736)	47% (178)	47% (49)	50% (30)	35% (23)	31% (13)	36% (11)	0% (2)	0% (2)	100% (1)	48% (1,045)

Format   Success Rate (Total # of Plays)

Receiving Success by Top-4 Personnel Groupings
(Min 50 targets)

POS	Player	1-1 [3WR]	1-2 [2WR]	1-0 [4WR]	2-1 [2WR]	4 Grp Total
TE	Cameron Brate	45% (40) 5.9, 97.6	57% (7) 6.7, 50.0			47% (47) 6.0, 87.5
WR	Mike Evans	57% (97) 10.0, 90.3	63% (27) 8.9, 88.5	100% (5) 23.8, 118.8	100% (6) 18.8, 118.8	61% (135) 10.7, 96.7
	Adam Humphries	57% (93) 7.6, 108.9	0% (1) 2.0, 79.2	71% (7) 9.1, 99.7		57% (101) 7.6, 107.3
	Chris Godwin	62% (73) 9.1, 116.3	45% (11) 6.4, 66.5	100% (2) 24.0, 118.8	33% (3) 5.3, 52.1	60% (89) 8.9, 109.5
	DeSean Jackson	52% (63) 9.4, 63.9	33% (3) 20.0, 121.5	0% (2) 0.0, 39.6	75% (4) 27.3, 156.3	51% (72) 10.6, 74.9

Format   Line 1: Success Rate (Total # of Plays)   Line 2: YPA, Passer Rating

Rushing Success by Top-4 Personnel Groupings
(Min 25 carries)

Rusher (Last, First)	1-1 [3WR]	1-2 [2WR]	2-1 [2WR]	2-2 [1WR]	4 Grp Total
Barber Peyton	44% (116) 4.1	43% (74) 3.7	38% (24) 3.9	40% (5) 2.6	43% (219) 3.9
Winston Jameis	58% (36) 6.5	33% (6) 3.3	100% (2) 10.5	0% (2) -1.0	54% (46) 5.9
Rodgers Jacquizz	35% (23) 3.4	20% (5) 1.0	50% (2) 10.0		33% (30) 3.4
Fitzpatrick Ryan	50% (24) 5.0	50% (2) 2.5		0% (3) -0.7	45% (29) 4.2

Format   Line 1: Success Rate (Total # of Plays)   Line 2: YPC

Passing by Coverage Scheme

Zone	60% (285) 9.3, 100.4
M2M	53% (235) 8.5, 107.5
Screen	36% (39) 6.9, 95.3
Combo	43% (7) 6.1, 23.8

Passing by Route

Curl	68% (99) 7.7, 89.7
Out	59% (76) 6.4, 73.6
Dig	64% (58) 8.9, 77.9
Screen	33% (39) 6.7, 94.7
Flat	24% (38) 3.2, 81.0
Slant	57% (37) 9.4, 108.6

Throw Types

Level 1	57% (362) 7.1, 99.7
Level 2	59% (173) 10.4, 87.9
Level 3	35% (63) 13.4, 96.4
Sidearm	40% (10) 6.6, 87.9
Shovel	33% (3) 5.3, 79.9

QB Drop Types

3 Step	56% (285) 8.2, 93.9
0/1 Step	56% (127) 8.0, 93.2
5 Step	56% (121) 10.3, 94.8
7 Step	59% (39) 11.8, 113.2
Basic Screen	27% (15) 5.3, 88.9
Designed Rollout Right	45% (11) 3.8, 72.7

QB State at Pass

Planted	57% (449) 9.2, 100.7
Shuffling	43% (56) 5.7, 91.1
Moving	57% (54) 9.1, 136.6

Play Action

	Play Action	No P/A
Under Center	54% (76) 9.0, 106.5	60% (58) 10.2, 105.0
Shotgun	62% (26) 10.0, 104.8	54% (454) 8.3, 92.5
ALL	56% (102) 9.3, 106.0	55% (512) 8.5, 93.9

Run Types

Inside Zone	42% (93) 3.1
Outside Zone	44% (72) 4.6
Power	38% (37) 3.1
Lead	35% (26) 3.8
Pitch	38% (16) 3.6
Stretch	33% (15) 0.2

TB-5

better passing Success Rate, yards per attempt, passer rating, and explosive pass rate when playing on the road than at home.

Over the last ten years, teams playing the second leg of back-to-back road games are 51.4% against the spread as an average underdog of 2.4 points. They win 43% of these games outright. Compare this to teams playing the *first* leg of back-to-back road games, who cover only 49.7% of the time with a 41.5% outright win rate.

As dogs of over seven points – like the Bucs are Week 4 against the Rams and Week 5 against the Saints – teams are 45.7% against the spread in their first road game with just a 13.6% outright win rate, but 52.6% against the spread with a 16.7% win rate in the second road affair.

So, although it sounds detrimental, teams actually perform marginally *better* in their second straight road game. And the Bucs get clusters of home games before and after that stint. They start with two of their first three games at home and finish with five of their last eight games in Tampa Bay, including three of their final four.

The Bucs lost primary slot receiver **Adam Humphries** to Tampa Bay, but plan to replace him with **Chris Godwin**. I'll be fascinated to see how many three-receiver formations Arians uses in Tampa Bay. The Bucs have a much better pass-protecting offensive line than Arians' Arizona teams, and a far better tight end in **O.J. Howard**.

Losing **DeSean Jackson** in addition to Humphries, Tampa Bay went from an offense that could easily run four-receiver 10 personnel to a thinner passing game. I personally would like to see this year's Bucs run more two-tight end 12.

Last year, **Mike Evans** dominated in the slot in 12 personnel. While typical offenses align their No. 1 receiver outside, Evans produced 11.3 yards per target and an 80% Success Rate on slot targets in 12 personnel.

The Bucs' running back picture remains unsettled. **Peyton Barber** was highly inefficient last season, and **Ronald Jones** was a second-round flop. GM **Jason Licht** didn't address tailback in free agency or the draft, only somewhat-notably adding undrafted rookie **Bruce Anderson**.

Running backs still offer value in Arians' offense, especially if they can catch the ball. But Arians did say this offseason that he believes teams shouldn't overpay running backs, and that "you don't need a **David Johnson** or a **Todd Gurley**" for a successful rushing attack. This statement further fueled my admiration for Arians.

A much bigger concern than running back is the Bucs' defense. Tampa Bay ranked dead last in defensive efficiency in each of the last two years, albeit while fielding last season's most-injured defense in the league. But they're not 100% this year, either, as sack leader **Jason Pierre-Paul** is likely out (cont'd - see **Page 246**)

Head Coach:
Mike Vrabel (1 yr)
Offensive Coordinator:
Arthur Smith (TEN TE) (new)
Defensive Coordinator:
Dean Pees (1 yr)

EASY   HARD

Tennessee Titans

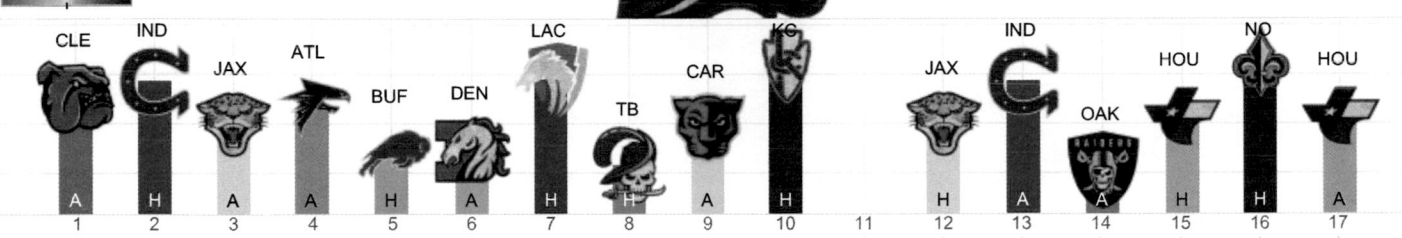

CLE	IND	JAX	ATL	BUF	DEN	LAC	TB	CAR	KC		IND	JAX	OAK	HOU	NO	HOU
A	H	A	A	H	A	H	H	A	H		H	A	A	H	H	A
1	2	3	4	5	6	7	8	9	10	11	12	13	14	15	16	17

TNF

2019 Forecast

Wins	Div Rank
8	#3

Past Records
2018: 9-7
2017: 9-7
2016: 9-7

Key Players Lost

Player	New
Blaine Gabbert (QB)	TB
Chris Johnson (RB)	Retired
Darius Kilgo (DT)	DET
Josh Kline (G)	MIN
Luke Stocker (TE)	ATL
Quinton Spain (G)	BUF

Average Line	# Games Favored	# Games Underdog
1.1	4	8

2019 Tennessee Titans Overview

Last offseason, Tennessee Titans fans were like children waiting for Christmas. After two seasons of **Mike Mularkey's** "exotic smashmouth" offense, new head coach **Mike Vrabel** hired offensive coordinator Matt LaFleur away from the Los Angeles, where the Rams had just undergone the largest year-over-year scoring increase since the 1950 New York Yanks.

If the beginning of the season was like Christmas, then the new offense Tennessee fans woke up to was a lump of coal. Instead of emphasizing the pass, the 2018 Titans ran more often on first down than their "smash mouth" predecessors, and were less successful on their first-down runs, to boot.

2016: 54% run rate on 1st down, 52% success rate.
2017: 51% run rate on 1st down, 45% success rate.
2018: 56% run rate on 1st down, 44% success rate.

Tennessee's run rate on 1st down was the second-highest in the NFL. On first down runs in the first half, when the offense is theoretically not constrained by score differential or time remaining, Tennessee ranks 29th in yards per carry. On passes in the same situation, the Titans were actually above league average in success rate.

Was this emphasis on an anemic running game a reaction to quarterback **Marcus Mariota's** nerve issues? Consider that in Week 1, before Mariota was injured, the Titans ran nine times on twelve first down attempts in the first half, averaging

*(cont'd - see **TEN2**)*

Key Free Agents/ Trades Added

Player	AAV (MM)
Adam Humphries (WR)	$9
Cameron Wake (DE)	$7.7
Rodger Saffold (G)	$11
Ryan Tannehill (QB)	Trade

Drafted Players

Rd	Pk	Player (College)
1	19	DT - Jeffery Simmons (Mississippi State)
2	51	WR - A. J. Brown (Ole Miss)
3	82	G - Nate Davis (Charlotte)
4	116	S - Amani Hooker (Iowa)
5	168	LB - D'Andre Walker (Georgia)
6	188	LB - David Long Jr. (West Virginia)

Regular Season Wins: Past & Current Proj

Forecast 2019 Wins — 8
2018 Wins — 9
Forecast 2018 Wins — 8
2017 Wins — 9
2016 Wins — 9
2015 Wins — 3

1 3 5 7 9 11 13 15

Lineup & Cap Hits

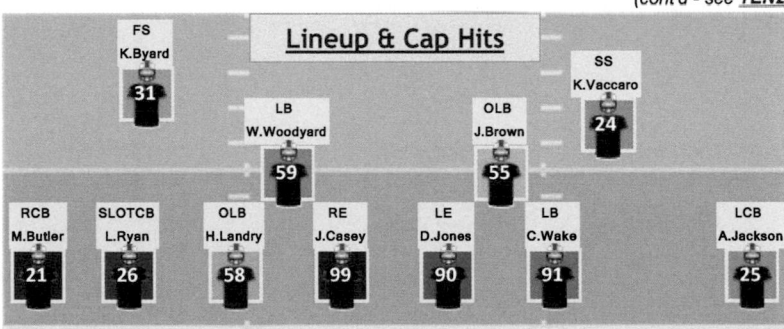

FS K.Byard 31
SS K.Vaccaro 24
LB W.Woodyard 59
OLB J.Brown 55
RCB M.Butler 21
SLOTCB L.Ryan 26
OLB H.Landry 58
RE J.Casey 99
LE D.Jones 90
LB C.Wake 91
LCB A.Jackson 25

LWR A.Brown Rookie 11
LT T.Lewan 77
LG R.Saffold 76
C B.Jones 60
RG N.Davis 64
RT J.Conklin 78
TE D.Walker 82
RWR C.Davis 84
SLOTWR A.Humphries 10

QB M.Mariota 8
RB D.Henry 22

WR2 T.Sharpe 19
WR3 T.Taylor 13
RB2 D.Lewis 33
QB2 R.Tannehill 17

2019 Cap Dollars

2019 Unit Spending

All DEF   All OFF

Positional Spending

	Rank	Total	2017 Rk
All OFF	11	$102.42M	25
QB	15	$23.29M	26
OL	8	$42.56M	11
RB	12	$9.58M	15
WR	24	$17.95M	31
TE	13	$9.03M	7
All DEF	16	$86.25M	4
DL	20	$26.45M	13
LB	13	$22.40M	4
CB	5	$29.93M	11
S	26	$7.46M	12

1.7 yards per carry with a 33% success rate.

On all first and second downs in the first half of that game, Tennessee called run plays 59% of the time, averaging 3.0 yards per carry with a 38% success rate. Passes in the same situation averaged 9.4 yards per attempt with a 56% success rate.

The 2018 Titans final record was closely aligned with what would be predicted by their early-down success rate (EDSR). When the team won the EDSR battle, the team went 7-0. When the team lost the EDSR battle, they went 2-7. The two wins were a 20-17 nail biter against the Houston Texans that featured a 66-yard touchdown pass on a fake punt and 26-23 overtime victory against the Eagles where they won with five seconds remaining after a drive that featured three conversions on fourth down.

A team that was heavily dependent on succeeding on early downs hired a rising star offensive coordinator coming from a team that had reversed its fortunes overnight with a creative passing game. That team jettisoned a run-heavy offense that ranked 9th in EDSR in 2017 for an even-more-run-heavy offense that ranked 23rd in EDSR in 2018.

Even when the Titans did pass, there were concerns. **Matt LaFleur** came from a system that emphasized "11 personnel" (formations with three wide receivers, one running back, and one tight end). In last year's Preview, I noted with concern how poorly Mariota had played in 11 personnel. In 2016, Mariota averaged 8.1 air yards per attempt with three wide receivers on the field. He had a 25:9 touchdown-to-interception ratio and a passer rating of 95. In 2017, those numbers fall to 6.7 air yards per attempt, 17:16 TD:INT, and 81 passer rating.

On first down, Mariota was even more of a disaster in that personnel grouping. He had a 46% success rate, averaged just 5.1 yards per attempt, threw two interceptions for every touchdown, and had a passer rating of 47. By contrast, on first-down plays with two or fewer wide receivers, Mariota had a 69% success rate, averaged 10.6 yards per attempt, threw 7 touchdowns against 3 interceptions, and had a passer rating of 121.

Given LaFleur came from an offense specializing in three-receiver sets, could he improve Mariota's efficiency from them? He certainly tried. The Titans increased their usage of 11 personnel from 44% in 2017 to 56% in 2018. On first down, their usage of the grouping rose from 59% in 2017 to 70% in 2018.

But that increase in usage didn't correspond to an improvement in results.

2018 Passing Performance

QB	1st Dwn	2nd Dwn	3rd Dwn	
Marcus Mariota	52% 8.6 84.2	47% 6.8 96.2	38% 7.4 93.8	Success Rate YPA Rating
Pass Rate	44%	52%	80%	
NFL AVG	53% 7.7 95.1	47% 7.3 93.7	36% 6.9 87.1	Success Rate YPA Rating
Pass Rate	53%	62%	80%	

2018 Rushing Performance

Offense	1st Dwn	2nd Dwn	3rd Dwn	
TEN	44% 4.5	44% 4.5	57% 4.3	Success Rate YPC
Run Rate	56%	48%	21%	
NFL AVG	48% 4.5	46% 4.4	51% 4.3	Success Rate YPC
Run Rate	47%	38%	20%	

In 2018, Mariota averaged 6.2 yards per attempt in 11 personnel with a 43% success rate, nine touchdowns against eight interceptions, and a passer rating of 74.9. In the Titan's second-most-common grouping (two wide receivers, two tight ends, and one running back), Mariota averaged 7.9 yards per attempt, had a 54% success rate, threw one touchdown against zero interceptions, and had a passer rating of 93.7.

Digging deeper into the splits, the primary problems in passing from 11 personnel came on passes to running backs. Here are the splits by position.

WRs: 51% success rate, 7.3 yards per attempt
TEs: 64% success rate, 7.5 yards per attempt
RBs: 30% success rate, 5.9 yards per attempt

(cont'd - see TEN-3)

2018 Offensive Advanced Metrics

Rank by category: EDSR Off (23), 30 & In Off (20), Red Zone Off (18), 3rd Down Off (11), YPPA Off (19), YPPT Off (17), Offensive Efficiency (22), Pass Efficiency Off (25), Pass Pro Efficiency Off (29), RB Pass Eff Off (26), Rush Efficiency Off (12), Explosive Pass Off (23), Explosive Run Off (11)

2018 Defensive Advanced Metrics

Rank by category: EDSR Def (12), 30 & In Def (11), Red Zone Def (1), 3rd Down Def (5), YPPA Def (8), YPPT Def (10), Defensive Efficiency (18), Pass Efficiency Def (21), Pass Pro Efficiency Def (22), RB Pass Eff Def (1), Rush Efficiency Def (15), Explosive Pass Def (13), Explosive Run Def (7)

2018 Weekly EDSR & Season Trending Performance

WEEK	1	2	3	4	5	6	7	9	10	11	12	13	14	15	16	17
RESULT	L	W	W	W	L	L	L	W	W	L	L	W	W	W	W	L
OPP	MIA	HOU	JAC	PHI	BUF	BAL	LAC	DAL	NE	IND	HOU	NYJ	JAC	NYG	WAS	IND
SITE	A	H	A	H	A	H	N	A	H	A	A	H	H	A	H	H
MARGIN	-7	3	3	3	-1	-21	-1	14	24	-28	-17	4	21	17	9	-16
PTS	20	20	9	26	12	0	19	28	34	10	17	26	30	17	25	17
OPP PTS	27	17	6	23	13	21	20	14	10	38	34	22	9	0	16	33

EDSR by Wk
W=Green
L=Red

OFF / DEF
EDSR
Blue=OFF
(high=good)
Red=DEF
(low=good)

2018 Close Game Records

All 2018 Wins: **9**
FG Games (<=3 pts) W-L: **3-2**
FG Games Win %: **60% (#11)**
FG Games Wins (% of Total Wins):
33% (#11)
1 Score Games (<=8 pts) W-L: **4-3**
1 Score Games Win %: **57% (#10)**
1 Score Games Wins (% of Total Wins): **44% (#22)**

2018 Critical & Game-Deciding Stats

TO Margin	-1
TO Given	18
INT Given	12
FUM Given	6
TO Taken	17
INT Taken	11
FUM Taken	6
Sack Margin	-8
Sacks	39
Sacks Allow	47
Return TD Margin	+1
Ret TDs	3
Ret TDs Allow	2
Penalty Margin	+38
Penalties	82
Opponent Penalties	120

Tennessee Titans 2019 Strength of Schedule In Detail (compared to 2018)

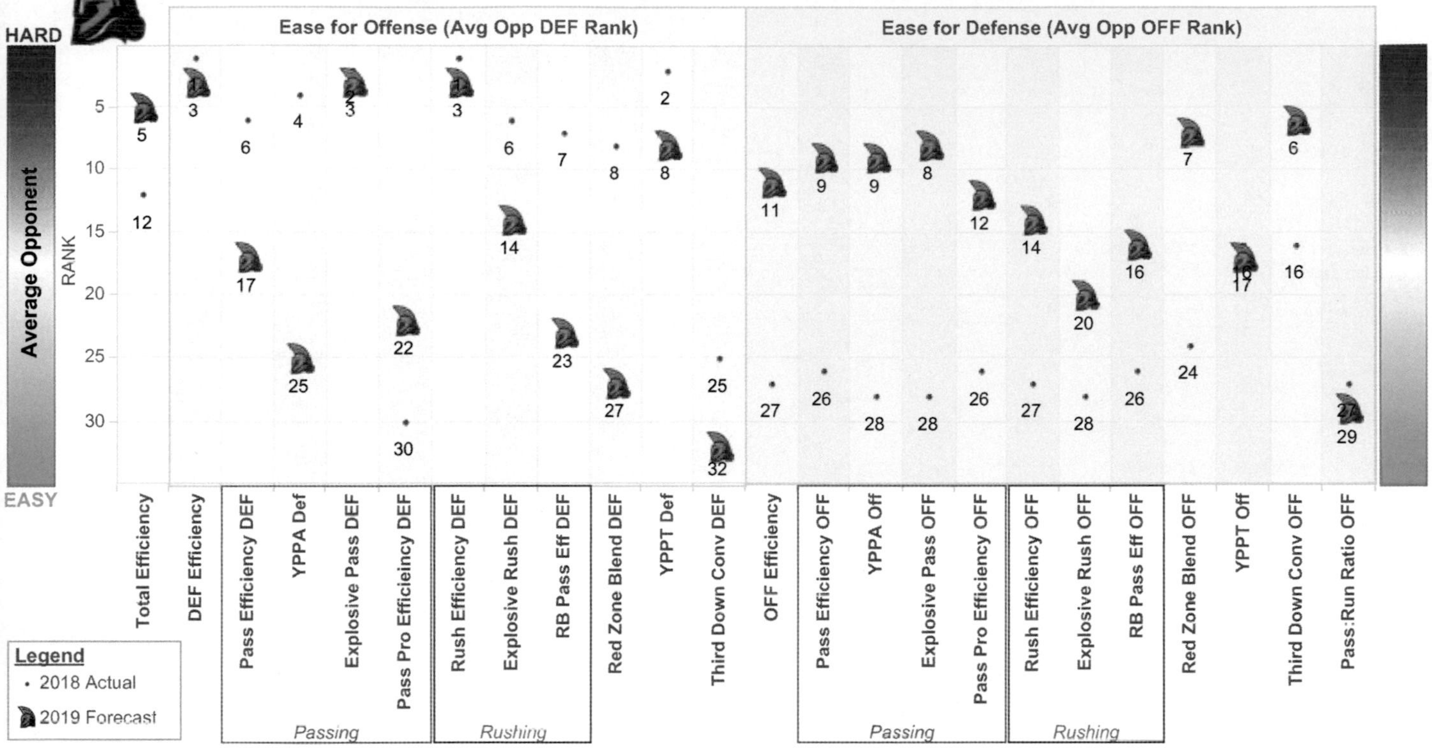

HARD

EASY

Average Opponent RANK

Ease for Offense (Avg Opp DEF Rank)

Total Efficiency	5, 12
DEF Efficiency	3, 6
Pass Efficiency DEF	4
YPPA Def	3
Explosive Pass DEF	17
Pass Pro Efficiency DEF	25, 22
Rush Efficiency DEF	3
Explosive Rush DEF	6, 14
RB Pass Eff DEF	7, 23
Red Zone Blend DEF	8
YPPT Def	2, 8, 25, 27
Third Down Conv DEF	30, 32

(Passing, Rushing)

Ease for Defense (Avg Opp OFF Rank)

OFF Efficiency	11, 27
Pass Efficiency OFF	9, 26
YPPA Off	9, 28
Explosive Pass OFF	8, 28
Pass Pro Efficiency OFF	12, 26
Rush Efficiency OFF	14, 27
Explosive Rush OFF	20, 28
RB Pass Eff OFF	16, 24, 26
Red Zone Blend OFF	7
YPPT Off	17, 17
Third Down Conv OFF	6, 16
Pass:Run Ratio OFF	27, 29

(Passing, Rushing)

Legend
- 2018 Actual
- 2019 Forecast

2019 v 2018 Schedule Variances* (OFF=Rank of DEF faced, 2019 vs 2018)

Pass OFF Rank	Pass OFF Blend Rk	Rush OFF Rk	Rush OFF Blend Rk	Pass DEF Rk	Pass DEF Blend Rk	Rush DEF Rk	Rush DEF Blend Rk
30	26	18	29	3	2	5	5

* **1**=Hardest Jump in 2019 schedule from 2018 (aka a much harder schedule in 2019), **32**=Easiest Jump in 2019 schedule from 2018 (aka a much easier schedule in 2019);
Pass Blend metric blends 4 metrics: Pass Efficiency, YPPA, Explosive Pass & Pass Rush; **Rush Blend** metric blends 3 metrics: Rush Efficiency, Explosive Rush & RB Targets

Team Records & Trends

	2018	2017	2016
Average line	1.2	-2.0	0.1
Average O/U line	42.3	43.9	45.0
Straight Up Record	9-7	9-7	9-7
Against the Spread Record	8-8	7-8	8-8
Over/Under Record	8-8	8-7	10-5
ATS as Favorite	2-3	6-6	4-3
ATS as Underdog	6-4	1-1	4-5
Straight Up Home	6-2	6-2	5-3
ATS Home	4-4	5-3	4-4
Over/Under Home	5-3	4-3	5-2
ATS as Home Favorite	1-2	4-3	3-2
ATS as a Home Dog	3-2	1-0	1-2
Straight Up Away	3-4	3-5	4-4
ATS Away	3-4	2-5	4-4
Over/Under Away	3-4	4-4	5-3
ATS Away Favorite	1-1	2-3	1-1
ATS Away Dog	2-2	0-1	3-3
Six Point Teaser Record	10-5	11-4	12-3
Seven Point Teaser Record	11-4	12-4	14-2
Ten Point Teaser Record	12-4	13-3	14-2

TEN-3

LaFleur came from an offense in Los Angeles that revolved heavily around passes to its running backs but maintaining that emphasis in Tennessee clearly hurt his team. In 2017, the Titans targeted their running backs on 12% of early-down passes. In 2018, that rate was doubled.

In addition to an undeserved emphasis on the run and inefficient passes to the running backs, the Titans also didn't run play action enough. While all those first-down runs would seemingly set the stage for some trickery, the Titans ran play action just 24% of the time on first down, despite Mariota averaging 10.0 yards per attempt, a 59% success rate, and a 105 passer rating on play-action passes (vs. 6.0 YPA, a 49% success rate, and a passer rating of 75 without play action).

Matt LaFleur has gone on to coach the Green Bay Packers, which means Mariota will enter his

(cont'd - see **TEN-4**)

2019 Rest Analysis

Team More Rest	3
Opp More Rest	2
Net Rest Edge	1
Week 2 Edge	0
Week 3 Edge	0
Week 4 Edge	3
Week 5 Edge	0
Week 6 Edge	0
Week 7 Edge	0
Week 8 Edge	
Week 9 Edge	0
Week 10 Edge	0
Week 12 Edge	7
Week 13 Edge	-3
Week 14 Edge	0
Week 15 Edge	0
Week 16 Edge	1
Week 17 Edge	0

Health by Unit*

2018 Rk	11
2017 Rk	3
2018 v 2017 Rk	26
Off Rk	10
Def Rk	19
QB Rk	21
RB Rk	1
WR Rk	6
TE Rk	27
Oline Rk	8
Dline Rk	8
LB Rk	23
DB Rk	23

Based on the work of Football Outsiders

2018 Weekly Betting Lines (wks 1-16)

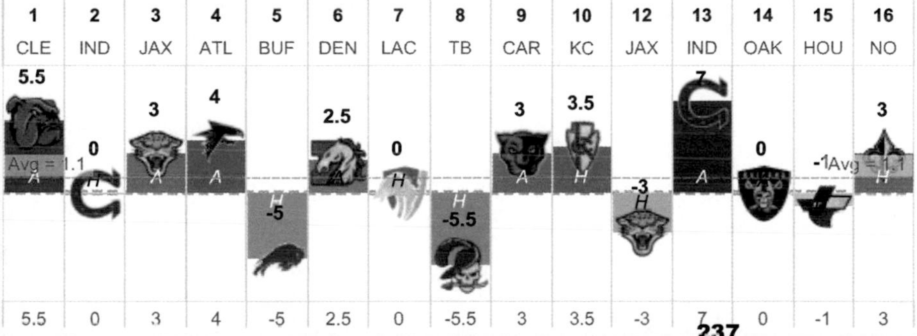

1	2	3	4	5	6	7	8	9	10	12	13	14	15	16
CLE	IND	JAX	ATL	BUF	DEN	LAC	TB	CAR	KC	JAX	IND	OAK	HOU	NO
5.5	0	3	4	-5	2.5	0	-5.5	3	3.5	-3	7	0	-1	3

Avg = 1.1

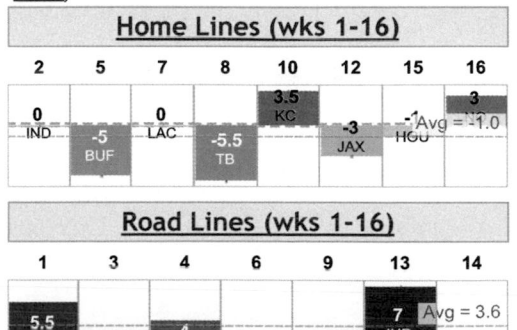

Home Lines (wks 1-16)

2	5	7	8	10	12	15	16
0 (IND)	-5 (BUF)	0 (LAC)	-5.5 (TB)	3.5 (KC)	-3 (JAX)	-1 (HOU)	3

Avg = -1.0

Road Lines (wks 1-16)

1	3	4	6	9	13	14
5.5 (CLE)	3 (JAX)	4 (ATL)	2.5 (DEN)	3 (CAR)	7 (IND)	0 (OAK)

Avg = 3.6

Tennessee Titans 2018 Play Analysis

2018 Play Tendencies

All Pass %	52%
All Pass Rk	31
All Rush %	48%
All Rush Rk	2
1 Score Pass %	50%
1 Score Pass Rk	30
2017 1 Score Pass %	54%
2017 1 Score Pass Rk	25
2018 Pass Increase %	-4%
Pass Increase Rk	28
1 Score Rush %	50%
1 Score Rush Rk	3
Up Pass %	41%
Up Pass Rk	30
Up Rush %	59%
Up Rush Rk	3
Down Pass %	58%
Down Pass Rk	31
Down Rush %	42%
Down Rush Rk	2

2018 Down & Distance Tendencies

Down	Distance	Total Plays	Pass Rate	Run Rate	Play Success %
1	Short (1-3)	7	0%	100%	100%
	Med (4-7)	6	33%	67%	67%
	Long (8-10)	276	42%	58%	47%
	XL (11+)	16	56%	44%	31%
2	Short (1-3)	30	33%	67%	67%
	Med (4-7)	73	44%	56%	48%
	Long (8-10)	79	48%	52%	42%
	XL (11+)	44	66%	34%	36%
3	Short (1-3)	40	53%	48%	63%
	Med (4-7)	54	93%	7%	33%
	Long (8-10)	27	96%	4%	41%
	XL (11+)	27	85%	15%	19%
4	Short (1-3)	5	40%	60%	60%
	Med (4-7)	1	100%	0%	100%
	XL (11+)	1	100%	0%	100%

Shotgun %:

Under Center	Shotgun
49%	51%

37% AVG 63%

Run Rate:

Under Center	Shotgun
71%	25%

68% AVG 23%

Pass Rate:

Under Center	Shotgun
29%	75%

32% AVG 77%

Short Yardage Intelligence:

2nd and Short Run

Run Freq	Run Rk	NFL Run Freq Avg	Run 1D Rate	Run NFL 1D Avg
73%	9	65%	63%	68%

2nd and Short Pass

Pass Freq	Pass Rk	NFL Pass Freq Avg	Pass 1D Rate	Pass NFL 1D Avg
27%	24	35%	71%	56%

Most Frequent Play

Down	Distance	Play Type	Player	Total Plays	Play Success %
1	Short (1-3)	RUSH	Derrick Henry	7	100%
	Med (4-7)	RUSH	Derrick Henry	4	100%
	Long (8-10)	RUSH	Derrick Henry	80	50%
	XL (11+)	PASS	Corey Davis	3	100%
		RUSH	Dion Lewis	3	0%
		RUSH	Marcus Mariota	3	0%
2	Short (1-3)	RUSH	Derrick Henry	10	70%
	Med (4-7)	RUSH	Derrick Henry	22	50%
	Long (8-10)	RUSH	Derrick Henry	18	39%
		RUSH	Dion Lewis	18	39%
	XL (11+)	RUSH	Dion Lewis	9	0%
3	Short (1-3)	RUSH	Marcus Mariota	10	80%
	Med (4-7)	PASS	Corey Davis	14	36%
	Long (8-10)	PASS	Corey Davis	5	80%
	XL (11+)	PASS	Corey Davis	4	50%

Most Successful Play*

Down	Distance	Play Type	Player	Total Plays	Play Success %
1	Short (1-3)	RUSH	Derrick Henry	7	100%
	Long (8-10)	PASS	Taywan Taylor	12	83%
2	Short (1-3)	RUSH	Derrick Henry	10	70%
	Med (4-7)	PASS	Tajae Sharpe	5	60%
	Long (8-10)	PASS	Corey Davis	5	40%
	XL (11+)	PASS	Corey Davis	7	57%
3	Short (1-3)	RUSH	Derrick Henry	5	80%
			Marcus Mariota	10	80%
	Med (4-7)	PASS	Corey Davis	14	36%
	Long (8-10)	PASS	Corey Davis	5	80%

*Minimum 5 plays to qualify

2018 Weekly Snap Rates

Wk	Opp	Score	Corey Davis	Jonnu Smith	Dion Lewis	Tajae Sharpe	Taywan Taylor	Derrick Henry	Delanie Walker
1	MIA	L 27-20	63 (91%)	40 (58%)	49 (71%)	58 (84%)	9 (13%)	20 (29%)	39 (57%)
2	HOU	W 20-17	48 (81%)	59 (100%)	34 (58%)	28 (47%)	24 (41%)	25 (42%)	
3	JAC	W 9-6	52 (84%)	57 (92%)	30 (48%)	24 (39%)	32 (52%)	32 (52%)	
4	PHI	W 26-23	60 (85%)	69 (97%)	48 (68%)	31 (44%)	45 (63%)	28 (39%)	
5	BUF	L 13-12	49 (91%)	42 (78%)	34 (63%)	33 (61%)	25 (46%)	21 (39%)	
6	BAL	L 21-0	38 (86%)	25 (57%)	32 (73%)	35 (80%)	33 (75%)	12 (27%)	
7	LAC	L 20-19	61 (86%)	56 (79%)	45 (63%)	56 (79%)	49 (69%)	24 (34%)	
9	DAL	W 28-14	65 (93%)	53 (76%)	59 (84%)	55 (79%)	18 (26%)	14 (20%)	
10	NE	W 34-10	59 (91%)	60 (92%)	49 (75%)	54 (83%)		15 (23%)	
11	IND	L 38-10	58 (92%)	42 (67%)	44 (70%)	58 (92%)		21 (33%)	
12	HOU	L 34-17	53 (96%)	42 (76%)	29 (53%)	38 (69%)		27 (49%)	
13	NYJ	W 26-22	65 (96%)	48 (71%)	40 (59%)	53 (78%)	29 (43%)	28 (41%)	
14	JAC	W 30-9	49 (82%)	17 (28%)	38 (63%)	20 (33%)	41 (68%)	24 (40%)	
15	NYG	W 17-0	65 (93%)		23 (33%)	39 (56%)	54 (77%)	49 (70%)	
16	WAS	W 25-16	49 (88%)		22 (39%)	3 (5%)	44 (79%)	35 (63%)	
17	IND	L 33-17	38 (78%)		24 (49%)	7 (14%)	41 (84%)	26 (53%)	
	Grand Total		872 (88%)	610 (75%)	600 (61%)	592 (59%)	444 (57%)	401 (41%)	39 (57%)

Personnel Groupings

Personnel	Team %	NFL Avg	Succ. %
1-1 [3WR]	56%	65%	44%
1-2 [2WR]	30%	17%	48%
1-3 [1WR]	11%	3%	40%
2-1 [2WR]	2%	8%	63%

Grouping Tendencies

Personnel	Pass Rate	Pass Succ. %	Run Succ. %
1-1 [3WR]	65%	40%	50%
1-2 [2WR]	38%	57%	42%
1-3 [1WR]	22%	57%	35%
2-1 [2WR]	53%	50%	78%

Red Zone Targets (min 3)

Receiver	All	Inside 5	6-10	11-20
Corey Davis	14	4	4	6
Tajae Sharpe	9	1	3	5
Dion Lewis	6		2	4
Jonnu Smith	5	2	3	
Anthony Firkser	4			4
Taywan Taylor	4			4
Derrick Henry	2			2

Red Zone Rushes (min 3)

Rusher	All	Inside 5	6-10	11-20
Derrick Henry	43	17	5	21
Dion Lewis	23	5	5	13
Marcus Mariota	12	6	1	5

Early Down Target Rate

RB	TE	WR
25%	22%	53%
23%	21%	56%
	NFL AVG	

Overall Target Success %

RB	TE	WR
41%	60%	51%
#27	#4	#17

Tennessee Titans 2018 Passing Recap & 2019 Outlook

It's a concerning indictment of Tennessee's player evaluations that that, of the four players who have been eligible for the team to exercise a fifth-year option on their contract, Mariota is the first player to actually receive one. Even in Mariota's case, Tennessee's seeming willingness to let their starting quarterback reach free agency speaks volumes about their belief in him. Nevertheless, their unwillingness to commit to mediocrity is laudable, as giving middling quarterbacks massive contracts is one of the most damaging moves a team can make. I wonder what Mariota could do if the team ever stopped trying to scheme around him and truly featured him, instead. Restricting him hasn't been in the team's best interest to this point; Mariota's 2018 success rate was still well below average and his early-down passer rating ranked 23rd out of 32 qualify quarterbacks. On the other hand, when Mariota trailed last year, his 77.5 passer rating ranked 37th out of 41 qualifying quarterbacks, and his two touchdowns to six interceptions was the worst ratio in the NFL, so perhaps keeping the game out of his hands is for the best.

Marcus Mariota Rating All Downs

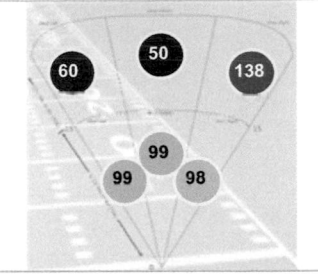

2018 Standard Passing Table

QB	Comp	Att	Comp %	Yds	YPA	TDs	INT	Sacks	Rating	Rk
Marcus Mariota	228	331	69%	2,528	7.6	11	8	42	92	23
Blaine Gabbert	61	101	60%	626	6.2	4	4	5	75	43
NFL Avg			62%		7.0				87.5	

Marcus Mariota Rating Early Downs

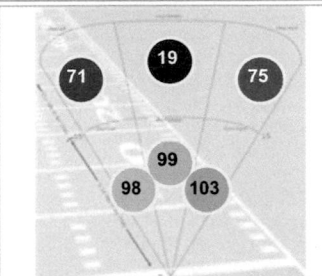

2018 Advanced Passing Table

QB	Success %	EDSR Passing Success %	20+ Yd Pass Gains	20+ Yd Pass %	30+ Yd Pass Gains	30+ Yd Pass %	Avg. Air Yds per Comp	Avg. YAC per Comp	20+ Air Yd Comp	20+ Air Yd %
Marcus Mariota	46%	49%	31	9.0%	8	2.0%	5.4	5.7	14	4%
Blaine Gabbert	40%	48%	4	4.0%	1	1.0%	5.2	5.0	3	3%
NFL Avg	44%	48%	29.5	8.4%	12.5	3.7%	5.8	5.1	14.5	6%

Interception Rates by Down

Yards to Go	1st Dwn	2nd Dwn	3rd Dwn	4th Dwn	Total
1 & 2		0.0%	0.0%	0.0%	0.0%
3, 4, 5	0.0%	0.0%	2.9%	0.0%	1.7%
6 - 9		2.3%	0.0%		1.2%
10 - 14	3.4%	0.0%	0.0%		2.2%
15+	11.1%	11.1%	0.0%	0.0%	7.7%
Total	3.8%	1.7%	0.8%	0.0%	2.1%

3rd Down Passing - Short of Sticks Analysis

QB	Avg. Yds to Go	Avg. YIA (of Comp)	Avg Yds Short	Short of Sticks Rate	Short Rk
Marcus Mariota	7.3	7.6	0.0	48%	8
NFL Avg	7.8	6.4	-1.4	60%	

Air Yds vs YAC

Air Yds %	YAC %	Rk
49%	51%	34
53%	48%	

2018 Receiving Recap & 2019 Outlook

Taking receiver **A.J. Brown** in the second round of the 2019 draft gives Mariota yet another talented young receiver to work with, but the team needs to target these receivers it is spending so much draft capital to acquire. Since Mariota was drafted in 2015, the Titans and the Pittsburgh Steelers are the only teams to use four picks in the first three rounds on wide receivers. The Steelers, however, have been the most pass-heavy team in the NFL during that span, passing the ball on 65% of offensive plays in the first half over the last three years, tops in the league. The Titans have thrown the ball just 53% of the time in the first half over that same span, last in the NFL. Once again, we can only hope that the Titans take their cues from the Steelers and act..

Player *Min 50 Targets	Targ	Comp %	YPA	Rating	Success %	Success Rk	Missed YPA Rk	YAS % Rk	YTS % Rk	TDs
Corey Davis	112	58%	8.0	91.8	51%	64	106	59	26	4
Dion Lewis	67	88%	6.0	90.3	42%	114	130	123	38	1
Taywan Taylor	56	66%	8.3	90.3	55%	43	125	43	87	1

Directional Passer Rating Delivered

Receiver	Short Left	Short Middle	Short Right	Deep Left	Deep Middle	Deep Right	Player Total
Corey Davis	69	83	97	136	67	116	92
Dion Lewis	84	90	99				90
Taywan Taylor	120	104	32	90	40	96	90
Tajae Sharpe	130	55	89	21	40	40	64
Jonnu Smith	73	104	136	56			83
Luke Stocker	133	103	95	73		40	126
Anthony Firkser	138	119	108			119	130
Derrick Henry	90	98	67				90
Delanie Walker	3	119	98				41
Team Total	100	94	93	60	45	105	92

2018 Rushing Recap & 2019 Outlook

Dion Lewis was a colossal disappointment in 2018. On the ground, his 33% success rate was nearly 20% worse than Derrick Henry's and ranked 73rd in the league. In the air, despite catching 88% of his targets, his 42% success rate ranked 114th in the NFL. A large part of the team's struggles from 11 personnel stemmed from Lewis catching 91% of his targets, but gaining enough yardage to count as a successful play just 34% of the time. As bad as that was, Lewis was even worse on 3rd-and-long, drawing a third-down target with five or more yards to go seven times without a single first down to show for it. Lewis played well for the Patriots but in his first year with the Titans, he was clearly holding the team back. Despite this, he received 50% more offensive snaps than fellow running back **Derrick Henry**. Lewis turns 29 years old in September.

Yards per Carry by Direction

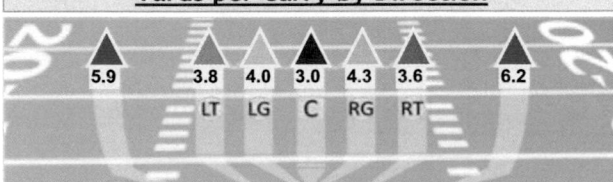

Player *Min 50 Rushes	Rushes	YPC	Success %	Success Rk	Missed YPA Rk	YTS % Rk	YAS % Rk	Early Down Success %	Early Down Success Rk	TDs
Derrick Henry	215	4.9	51%	20	15	47	29	51%	22	12
Dion Lewis	154	3.3	33%	73	70	41	62	33%	73	1

Directional Run Frequency

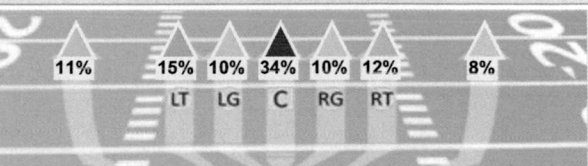

fifth season with his fourth different offensive coordinator (and fifth different play-caller). New OC **Arthur Smith** coached Tight Ends for the Titans last year and was hired in part to give Mariota a bit of stability. Smith has promised to keep terminology and many aspects of the offense the same from last year to allow Mariota to grow more comfortable with them.

But Smith predates LaFleur's tenure with the Titans; in fact, he has worked with Tennessee since 2011, starting as a quality control coach, moving to an assistant coach for the offensive line and tight ends, on to the tight ends coach, and now up to offensive coordinator.

Allowing Mariota to gain comfort in a system is a laudable goal, but hopefully (for Mariota's sake), the Titans don't hew too closely to last year's offense. Mariota has reportedly put on 12-13 pounds this offseason to help him withstand more hits, and he's entering the final year of his rookie contract, meaning he has a lot to prove this year with free agency potentially looming.

Mariota spoke this summer about the need to establish more consistency as a team. Last year's Titans beat the Patriots but lost to the Bills. They won by 24 one week, then lost by 28 the next. Consistency starts with a winning strategy, and a winning strategy starts with establishing a productive identity on early downs.

The Titans have also intimated they plan to give more work to running back **Derrick**

(cont'd - see TEN-5)

Tennessee Titans Fantasy Corner

A.J. Brown was one of my two highest-rated rookie receivers before April's draft after breaking Ole Miss' all-time records for receiving yards and 100-plus-yard games, then running 4.49 at 6-foot-1, 226 at the Combine. Brown reminded me of **JuJu Smith-Schuster** on college tape. But he couldn't have picked a worse fantasy landing spot. The Titans are committed to a run-first offense for the foreseeable future, and **Corey Davis** emerged as one of the NFL's premier target hogs in 2018. **Adam Humphries** and **Delanie Walker** will soak up action in the middle of the field, while Tennessee lacks long-term quarterback stability with both **Marcus Mariota** and **Ryan Tannehill** in contract years.

- Evan Silva

2018 Situational Usage by Player & Position

Usage Rate by Score

		Being Blown Out (14+)	Down Big (9-13)	One Score	Large Lead (9-13)	Blowout Lead (14+)
PASS	Derrick Henry	18%	12%	65%		6%
	Dion Lewis	12%	19%	67%		2%
	Corey Davis	12%	10%	72%	1%	6%
	Taywan Taylor	7%	9%	80%		5%
	Tajae Sharpe	21%	8%	67%		5%
	Jonnu Smith	24%	21%	52%	3%	
	Luke Stocker	11%	5%	84%		
	Delanie Walker		14%	86%		
	Rishard Matthews			83%		17%
	Total	13%	12%	70%	1%	4%
RUSH	Derrick Henry	13%	5%	70%	1%	12%
	Dion Lewis	5%	6%	72%		17%
	Corey Davis		17%	83%		
	Tajae Sharpe			100%		
	Luke Stocker			100%		
	Total	9%	6%	71%	1%	14%

Share of Offensive Plays by Type

	Derrick Henry	Dion Lewis	Corey Davis	Taywan Taylor	Tajae Sharpe	Jonnu Smith	Luke Stocker	Delanie Walker	Rishard Matthews
PASS	5%	18%	32%	14%	12%	9%	6%	2%	2%
RUSH	57%	41%	2%		0%		0%		
ALL	33%	30%	16%	6%	6%	4%	3%	1%	1%

Positional Target Distribution vs NFL Average

		NFL Wide				Team Only			
		Left	Middle	Right	Total	Left	Middle	Right	Total
Deep	WR	33%	17%	31%	81%	36%	19%	30%	85%
	TE	5%	4%	7%	16%	11%		4%	15%
	RB	1%	0%	2%	4%				
	All	39%	22%	39%	100%	47%	19%	34%	100%
Short	WR	20%	14%	21%	55%	13%	14%	17%	44%
	TE	6%	6%	8%	20%	10%	9%	7%	26%
	RB	10%	5%	10%	25%	13%	7%	9%	30%
	All	36%	25%	39%	100%	36%	30%	34%	100%
Total		37%	24%	39%	100%	38%	29%	34%	100%

Positional Success Rates vs NFL Average

		NFL Wide				Team Only			
		Left	Middle	Right	Total	Left	Middle	Right	Total
Deep	WR	40%	49%	40%	42%	47%	56%	43%	48%
	TE	44%	53%	41%	45%	40%		50%	43%
	RB	38%	33%	42%	40%				
	All	40%	50%	40%	42%	45%	56%	44%	47%
Short	WR	55%	61%	53%	56%	51%	54%	41%	48%
	TE	55%	62%	54%	57%	52%	72%	65%	63%
	RB	47%	54%	45%	48%	37%	43%	46%	41%
	All	53%	60%	51%	54%	46%	56%	47%	50%
Total		50%	58%	49%	52%	46%	56%	47%	49%

Division History: Season Wins & 2019 Projection

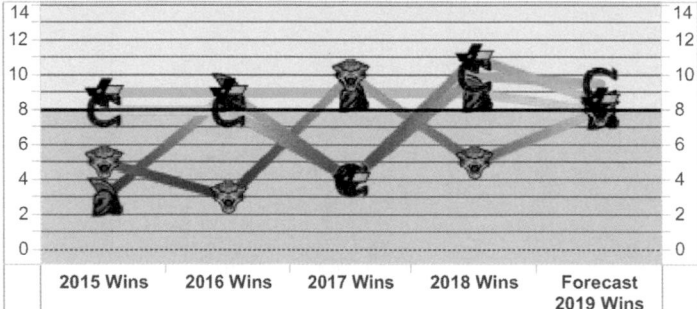

2015 Wins | 2016 Wins | 2017 Wins | 2018 Wins | Forecast 2019 Wins

Rank of 2019 Defensive Pass Efficiency Faced by Week

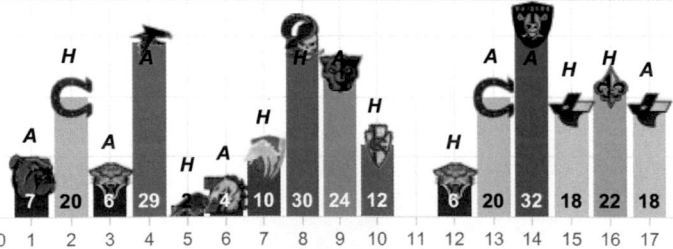

7 20 6 29 4 10 30 24 12 6 20 32 18 22 18

Rank of 2019 Defensive Rush Efficiency Faced by Week

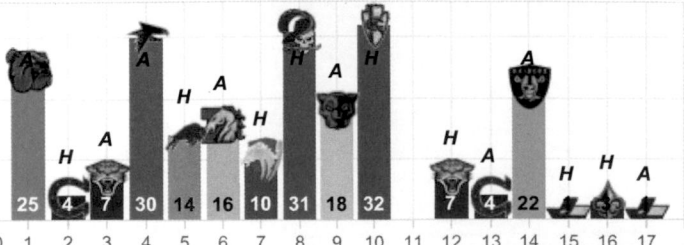

25 4 7 30 14 16 10 31 18 32 7 4 22

2018 Detailed Analytics Summary
Success by Play Type & Primary Personnel Groupings

Successful Play Rate 0% — 100%

Type	1-1 [3WR]	1-2 [2WR]	1-3 [1WR]	2-1 [2WR]	1-0 [4WR]	0-0 [5WR]	2-2 [1WR]	ALL
PASS	40% (339)	57% (105)	57% (23)	50% (10)	100% (2)	50% (2)		45% (481)
RUSH	50% (185)	42% (173)	35% (83)	78% (9)	0% (1)		100% (1)	45% (452)
All	44% (524)	48% (278)	40% (106)	63% (19)	67% (3)	50% (2)	100% (1)	45% (933)

Format Success Rate (Total # of Plays)

Receiving Success by Top-4 Personnel Groupings
(Min 50 targets)

POS	Player	1-1 [3WR]	1-2 [2WR]	2-1 [2WR]	1-0 [4WR]	4 Grp Total
RB	Dion Lewis	33% (45) 6.0, 89.6	53% (17) 5.9, 91.4	50% (4) 3.0, 77.1	100% (1) 9.0, 104.2	40% (67) 5.8, 89.7
WR	Corey Davis	46% (83) 7.0, 88.6	70% (23) 11.2, 106.6	50% (2) 12.0, 93.8		51% (108) 8.0, 92.5
	Taywan Taylor	56% (41) 7.6, 88.6	69% (13) 11.9, 109.5			59% (54) 8.6, 93.6

Format Line 1: Success Rate (Total # of Plays)   Line 2: YPA, Passer Rating

Rushing Success by Top-4 Personnel Groupings
(Min 25 carries)

Rusher (Last, First)	1-1 [3WR]	1-2 [2WR]	2-1 [2WR]	2-2 [1WR]	4 Grp Total
Henry Derrick	57% (74) 4.8	42% (88) 4.5	83% (6) 10.0	100% (1) 3.0	50% (169) 4.8
Lewis Dion	36% (70) 3.9	35% (60) 3.3	50% (2) 5.0		36% (132) 3.6
Mariota Marcus	61% (33) 6.5	60% (20) 6.6	100% (1) 7.0		61% (54) 6.5

Format Line 1: Success Rate (Total # of Plays)   Line 2: YPC

Passing by Coverage Scheme

Zone	52% (163) 8.5, 93.2
M2M	46% (139) 6.5, 77.6
Screen	54% (71) 5.5, 97.8
Combo	78% (9) 9.9, 107.9

Passing by Route

Screen	48% (64) 5.3, 92.5
Curl	63% (46) 7.7, 96.9
Out	62% (45) 7.7, 102.8
Dig	59% (27) 10.3, 91.4
Flat	58% (26) 5.8, 103.5
Slant	32% (22) 4.0, 34.1

Throw Types

Level 1	49% (233) 6.3, 86.7
Level 2	57% (116) 9.3, 93.9
Level 3	31% (36) 8.9, 80.8
Shovel	75% (12) 6.6, 121.9
Sidearm	67% (3) 5.0, 78.5

QB Drop Types

3 Step	50% (134) 7.3, 78.5
0/1 Step	52% (108) 6.7, 85.4
5 Step	45% (67) 8.9, 100.3
Basic Screen	52% (33) 5.2, 85.9
7 Step	65% (23) 10.5, 114.8
Designed Rollout Right	59% (17) 9.0, 118.0

QB State at Pass

Planted	51% (268) 7.5, 92.0
Shuffling	47% (58) 6.9, 93.9
Moving	49% (47) 5.8, 74.2

Play Action

	Play Action	No P/A
Under Center	61% (76) 9.0, 116.4	57% (35) 8.7, 116.7
Shotgun	53% (40) 8.8, 82.3	46% (250) 6.5, 78.9
ALL	58% (116) 8.9, 104.6	48% (285) 6.8, 83.5

Run Types

Inside Zone	45% (124) 3.9
Outside Zone	39% (107) 4.7
Lead	38% (40) 3.8
Stretch	40% (30) 4.7
Power	43% (28) 4.1
Pitch	54% (26) 4.8

TEN-5

Henry in 2019, a welcome change given how much more productive he was than **Dion Lewis**, the man he split time with last season.

Committing to Henry is one thing, but how the team uses him is as important as how often the team uses him. If Tennessee wants to make a playoff run in 2019, they'll need him healthy. Henry was most successful running from under center in 11 personnel (54% success rate, 4.8 yards per carry), but the team gave him nearly as many carries from 13 personnel (one receiver, one running back, three tight ends), and in that personnel grouping he averaged a 36% success rate and 3.4 yards per carry.

Henry excelled on inside zone runs (55% success rate), but the team called nearly as many outside zone runs for him, and while those runs did produce slightly more explosive plays, his success rate fell to 41%. On outside zone runs from 11 personnel, Henry averaged just 2.5 yards per carry with a 38% success rate. On early down runs from 13 personnel, Henry averaged 1.9 yards per carry with a 25% success rate.

Defensively, the Titans may have appeared to take a step forward in 2018, but much of that was paper gains as Tennessee faced the sixth-easiest schedule of opposing offenses. The Titans defense feasted on **Josh Allen, Eli Manning, Josh Johnson, Josh McCown, Blake Bortles, Joe Flacco, Kody Kessler,** and **Ryan Tannehill** last year; every other quarterback to face them had a passer rating of at least 99 with the exception of a legitimately tremendous performance against **Tom Brady** and the Patriots.

In 2019, the team can't rely on schedule luck to keep them afloat; this year's squad draws non-divisional games against **Patrick Mahomes, Drew Brees, Baker Mayfield, Philip Rivers**, and **Matt Ryan**.

It'll be interesting to see what changes Smith makes to the offense and interesting to see how Mariota responds. Mariota's play to date has been a cause for concern, and a commitment to "more of the same" from 2018 does nothing to assuage those concerns. The Titans need to remake their entire early-down philosophy to reach their ceiling, and I'm skeptical they will be willing to make those tough choices.

Washington Redskins

Coaches (Prior Yrs)

Head Coach:
  Jay Gruden (Calls Plays) (5 yrs)
Offensive Coordinator:
  Kevin O'Connell (WAS QB) (new)
Defensive Coordinator:
  Greg Manusky (2 yrs)

EASY   HARD

2019 Forecast

Wins	Div Rank
6.5	#3

Past Records

2018: 7-9
2017: 7-9
2016: 8-7-1

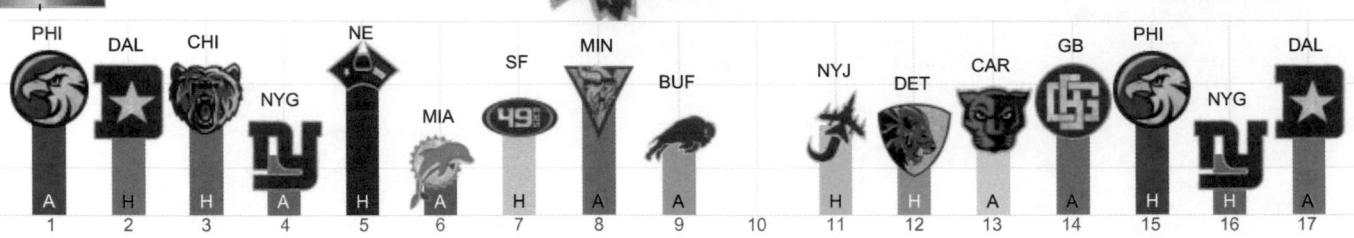

PHI	DAL	CHI	NYG	NE	MIA	SF	MIN	BUF		NYJ	DET	CAR	GB	PHI	NYG	DAL
A	H	H	A	H	A	H	A	A		H	H	A	H	A	H	A
1	2	3	4	5	6	7	8	9	10	11	12	13	14	15	16	17

MNF (under 3), TNF (under 7)

Key Players Lost

Player	New
HaHa Clinton-Dix (FS)	CHI
Jamison Crowder (WR)	NYJ
Maurice Harris (WR)	NE
Michael Floyd (WR)	BAL
Pernell McPhee (OLB)	BAL
Preston Smith (OLB)	GB
Ty Nsekhe (RT)	BUF
Zach Brown (ILB)	PHI

Average Line	# Games Favored	# Games Underdog
2.8	4	10

2019 Washington Redskins Overview

Alex Smith is the **Leroy Hoard** of quarterbacks.

Hoard, a 5-foot-11, 225-pound short-yardage/goal-line back for the Browns and Vikings in the early '90s, once said, "Coach, if you need 1 yard, I'll get you 3 yards. If you need 5 yards, I'll get you 3 yards."

Never were the similarities between Smith and Hoard more evident than in a 43-19 loss to the Saints on Monday Night Football last season. At one point, head coach **Jay Gruden** dialed up a deep shot on second-and-five, only to watch Smith check down to the underneath receiver for a 2-yard gain.

The Redskins may as well have had Hoard in on first downs in 2018, because they quite frequently gained no more than 3 yards and found themselves facing second-and-long. Gruden would later lament to the media that his team "had more second-and-long plays than maybe any NFL team in history."

I like to believe he said that with a straight face, as if he had no clue how or why it happened; as if some mysterious curse beset itself on his team – as if the Redskins were just innocently minding their business, and *boom! Another second-and-long.*

The warning signs were there. The Redskins were the third-most run-heavy team in the NFL on first downs in the first half in 2017, running on 62 percent of first-half plays. However, those runs produced a Success Rate of just 44 percent and gained just 3.4 yards per carry, fifth worst in the NFL. Meanwhile, when they passed on first down in the first half, they were 10 percent more successful and gained 8.1 yards per attempt. I wondered why a team would want to be so run-heavy in situations where they were so much more effective at passing, and I declared that the Redskins needed to overhaul

(cont'd - see WAS2)

Key Free Agents/ Trades Added

Player	AAV (MM)
Case Keenum (QB)	Trade
Ereck Flowers (RT)	$3.2
Landon Collins (FS)	$14

Drafted Players

Rd	Pk	Player (College)
1	15	QB - Dwayne Haskins (Ohio State)
	26	DE - Montez Sweat (Mississippi State)
3	76	WR - Terry McLaurin (Ohio State)
4	112	RB - Bryce Love (Stanford)
	131	G - Wes Martin (Indiana)
5	153	G - Ross Pierschbacher (Alabama)
5*	173	LB - Cole Holcomb (North Carolina)
6*	206	WR - Kelvin Harmon (NC State)
7	227	CB - Jimmy Moreland (James Madison)
7*	253	DE - Jordan Brailford (Oklahoma State)

Regular Season Wins: Past & Current Proj

Forecast 2019 Wins	6.5
2018 Wins	7
Forecast 2018 Wins	7
2017 Wins	7
2016 Wins	8
2015 Wins	9

1 3 5 7 9 11 13 15

Lineup & Cap Hits

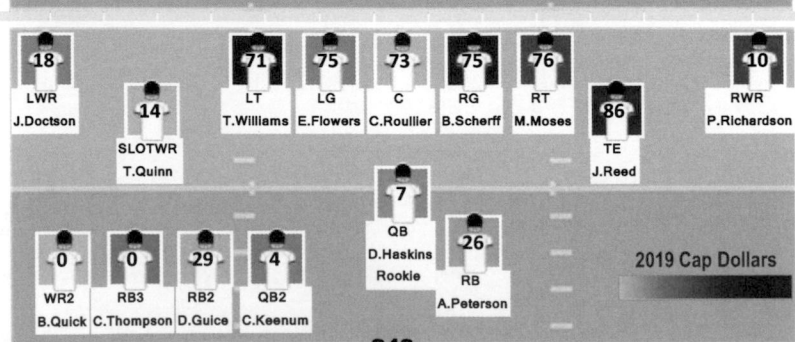

FS M.Nicholson 35
SS L.Collins 21
LB S.Hamilton 51
LB M.Foster 54
RCB J.Norman 24
SLOTCB F.Moreau 31
OLB M.Sweat Rookie 90
DL J.Allen 93
DL M.Ioannidis 98
OLB R.Kerrigan 91
LCB Q.Dunbar 23

LWR J.Doctson 18
SLOTWR T.Quinn 14
LT T.Williams 71
LG E.Flowers 75
C C.Roullier 73
RG B.Scherff 75
RT M.Moses 76
TE J.Reed 86
RWR P.Richardson 10

QB D.Haskins Rookie 7
RB A.Peterson 26
WR2 B.Quick 0
RB3 C.Thompson 0
RB2 D.Guice 29
QB2 C.Keenum 4

2019 Cap Dollars

2019 Unit Spending

All DEF / All OFF

Positional Spending

	Rank	Total	2017 Rk
All OFF	2	$117.73M	5
QB	4	$30.39M	14
OL	6	$44.28M	5
RB	13	$8.93M	18
WR	28	$15.87M	29
TE	1	$18.25M	2
All DEF	29	$69.19M	23
DL	30	$12.54M	29
LB	7	$26.15M	9
CB	15	$22.48M	10
S	23	$8.02M	28

their strategy on first down in order to be more successful on offense in 2018.

But on August 20, the Redskins signed **Adrian Peterson** after losing second-round draft pick **Derrius Guice** for the season with an ACL injury, and I immediately realized my level of concern was far too low. Smith starting at quarterback and Peterson starting at running back was a recipe for the perfect storm of inefficiency. Peterson was one of the worst backs in the NFL the prior two years on first-down runs in the first half, ranking 34th of 37 qualifier in yards per carry (3.48) and 32nd in Success Rate (39 percent).

With my forecasts calling for the Redskins to face the league's third-toughest schedule of run defenses but only the 13th-easiest pass defense slate, it would be even more imperative for Gruden to avoid running too often on first downs early in the game, but I knew it would be tough because Gruden has struggled in this regard for several years. Since he took over, the Redskins were in the top 10 in he NFL in first-down rushing rate in the first half despite averaging the third-worst production – all of this despite posting the fourth-best passing efficiency in such situations over that span.

Gruden again couldn't help himself in 2018. The Redskins were the fourth-most run-heavy team on first-half first downs, but those handoffs produced a Success Rate of just 39 percent, third-worst in the NFL, and gained only 4.1 yards per carry.

Compounding the problem was that this issue extended beyond the just first half, as Washington would end up running the ball at the third-highest rate in the league through three quarters. Those runs collectively produced the second-worst Success Rate in the NFL (40 percent) and gained only 3.9 yards a pop.

The Redskins ended up facing what was indeed a tough slate of run defenses (sixth-toughest), but an even more forgiving lineup of pass defenses (third-easiest) than I predicted, and yet Gruden rode right into the heart of the storm. It would be one thing if this were only an issue once Smith was lost to a gruesome leg injury in Week 11, but the Redskins were run-heavy and unproductive on first downs all year long and averaged 8.6 yards to go on second down, second-worst in the league, as a result.

Another issue with going run-heavy on first down was that it minimized the impact of tight end **Jordan Reed**, the team's best receiver. Looking only at the games that Smith played, it is clear that Reed was only effective on first down.

2018 Passing Performance

QB	1st Dwn	2nd Dwn	3rd Dwn	
Alex Smith	52%	42%	35%	Success Rate
	6.4	6.1	7.6	YPA
	86.6	87.5	88.4	Rating
Pass Rate	42%	65%	80%	
NFL AVG	53%	47%	36%	Success Rate
	7.7	7.3	6.9	YPA
	95.1	93.7	87.1	Rating
Pass Rate	53%	62%	80%	

2018 Rushing Performance

Offense	1st Dwn	2nd Dwn	3rd Dwn	
WAS	43%	53%	56%	Success Rate
	4.0	5.0	4.3	YPC
Run Rate	58%	35%	20%	
NFL AVG	48%	46%	51%	Success Rate
	4.5	4.4	4.3	YPC
Run Rate	47%	38%	20%	

- First down: 71 percent Success Rate, 7.1 yards per target
- Second down: 48 percent Success Rate, 6.9 yards per target
- Third down: 30 percent Success Rate, 6.1 yards per target

How could a player of Reed's caliber deliver such poor production on third down? By playing with the Leroy Hoard of quarterbacks, that's how. Starting around Week 6, Smith began primarily using Reed as a safety valve for third-down check downs that had no shot of picking up a first down. From Week 6 onward, only 19 percent of Reed's third-down targets ended up converting for a first down. The Redskins averaged a 9.7 yards to go on Reed's third-down targets, yet his average depth of target on those plays was 5.8 yards. We already knew Smith hates taking risks on third down and rarely throws beyond the sticks, but forcing a receiver already garnering the most

(cont'd - see WAS-3)

2018 Offensive Advanced Metrics

EDSR Off	30 & In Off	Red Zone Off	3rd Down Off	YPPA Off	YPPT Off	Offensive Efficiency	Pass Efficiency Off	Pass Pro Efficiency Off	RB Pass Eff Off	Rush Efficiency Off	Explosive Pass Off	Explosive Run Off
28	14	28	24	28	21	28	29	24	25	20	25	19

2018 Defensive Advanced Metrics

EDSR Def	30 & In Def	Red Zone Def	3rd Down Def	YPPA Def	YPPT Def	Defensive Efficiency	Pass Efficiency Def	Pass Pro Efficiency Def	RB Pass Eff Def	Rush Efficiency Def	Explosive Pass Def	Explosive Run Def
23	19	13	28	16	1	20	11	11	5	27	15	19

2018 Weekly EDSR & Season Trending Performance

	1	2	3		5	6	7	8	9	10	11	12	13	14	15	16	17	WEEK
	W	L	W		L	W	W	W	L	W	L	L	L	L	W	L	L	RESULT
	ARI	IND	GB		NO	CAR	DAL	NYG	ATL	TB	HOU	DAL	PHI	NYG	JAC	TEN	PHI	OPP
	A	H	H		A	H	H	H	A	H	A	H	A	A	H	A	H	SITE
	18	-12	14		-24	6	3	7	-24	13	-2	-8	-15	-24	3	-9	-24	MARGIN
	24	9	31		19	23	20	20	14	16	21	23	13	16	16	16	0	PTS
	6	21	17		43	17	17	13	38	3	23	31	28	40	13	25	24	OPP PTS

EDSR by Wk
W=Green
L=Red

OFF/DEF
EDSR
Blue=OFF
(high=good)
Red=DEF
(low=good)

2018 Close Game Records

All 2018 Wins: **7**
FG Games (<=3 pts) W-L: **2-1**
FG Games Win %: **67% (#8)**
FG Games Wins (% of Total Wins): **29% (#17)**
1 Score Games (<=8 pts) W-L: **4-2**
1 Score Games Win %: **67% (#6)**
1 Score Games Wins (% of Total Wins): **57% (#12)**

2018 Critical & Game-Deciding Stats

TO Margin	+7
TO Given	19
INT Given	15
FUM Given	4
TO Taken	26
INT Taken	15
FUM Taken	11
Sack Margin	+2
Sacks	46
Sacks Allow	44
Return TD Margin	-3
Ret TDs	1
Ret TDs Allow	4
Penalty Margin	-13
Penalties	115
Opponent Penalties	102

Washington Redskins 2019 Strength of Schedule In Detail (compared to 2018)

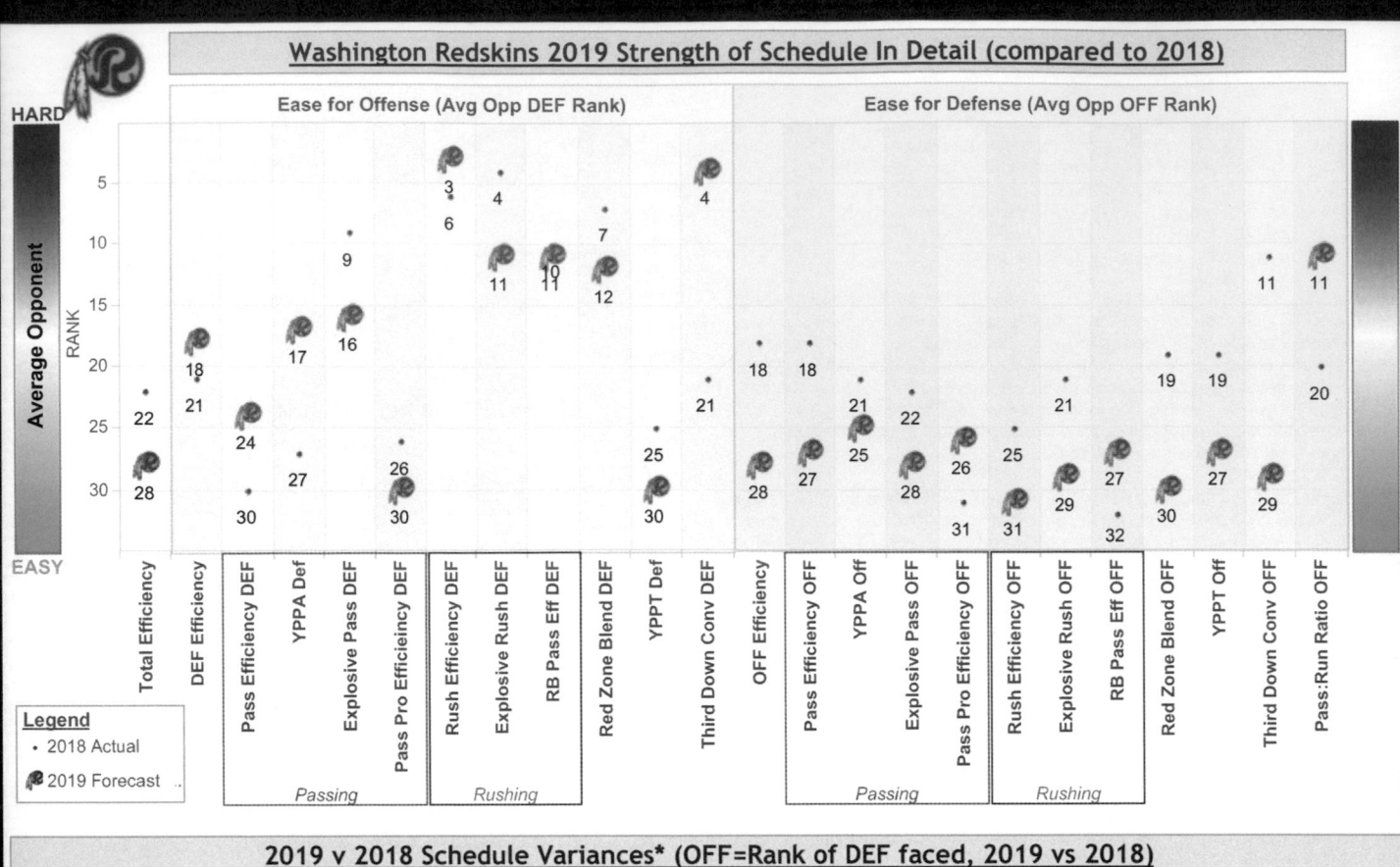

2019 v 2018 Schedule Variances* (OFF=Rank of DEF faced, 2019 vs 2018)

Pass OFF Rank	Pass OFF Blend Rk	Rush OFF Rk	Rush OFF Blend Rk	Pass DEF Rk	Pass DEF Blend Rk	Rush DEF Rk	Rush DEF Blend Rk
7	15	9	19	27	20	25	21

* **1**=Hardest Jump in 2019 schedule from 2018 (aka a much harder schedule in 2019), **32**=Easiest Jump in 2019 schedule from 2018 (aka a much easier schedule in 2019);
Pass Blend metric blends 4 metrics: Pass Efficiency, YPPA, Explosive Pass & Pass Rush; **Rush Blend** metric blends 3 metrics: Rush Efficiency, Explosive Rush & RB Targets

Team Records & Trends

	2018	2017	2016
Average line	2.8	1.2	-0.8
Average O/U line	43.9	46.2	47.8
Straight Up Record	7-9	7-9	8-7
Against the Spread Record	9-7	7-9	10-6
Over/Under Record	7-9	7-8	12-4
ATS as Favorite	2-2	3-2	5-3
ATS as Underdog	6-5	4-6	5-2
Straight Up Home	3-5	5-3	4-4
ATS Home	4-4	4-4	4-4
Over/Under Home	4-4	3-5	6-2
ATS as Home Favorite	1-2	3-1	3-3
ATS as a Home Dog	2-2	1-3	1-1
Straight Up Away	4-4	2-6	4-3
ATS Away	5-3	3-5	5-2
Over/Under Away	3-5	4-3	5-2
ATS Away Favorite	1-0	0-1	2-0
ATS Away Dog	4-3	3-3	3-1
Six Point Teaser Record	10-6	9-6	12-4
Seven Point Teaser Record	10-6	10-6	12-3
Ten Point Teaser Record	11-5	11-5	13-3

WAS-3

attention from opposing defenses to pick up nearly half of the necessary yardage for a first down on his own after the catch is simply not optimal.

Another issue that was impossible to understand was Reed's lack of red zone involvement. Reed is the most sure-handed Redskins receiver and was a mismatch for most defenders. Yet in Weeks 1-10, the Redskins ran 71 plays in the red zone, and Reed was targeted on just – all on third down. Meanwhile, Gruden seemingly thought it better to give a 33-year-old Peterson 23 carries in such situations, but they produced just a 35 percent success rate and 1.3 yards per tote. Sixteen of those carries came on first down, producing a drive-killing 31 percent Success Rate and 0.9 YPC.

The Redskins converted 52 percent of red zone trips into touchdowns through Week 10 and finished with that same rate over the full season, ranking 25th.

(cont'd - see WAS-4)

2019 Rest Analysis

Team More Rest	3
Opp More Rest	2
Net Rest Edge	1
Week 2 Edge	0
Week 3 Edge	0
Week 4 Edge	-1
Week 5 Edge	0
Week 6 Edge	
Week 7 Edge	0
Week 8 Edge	0
Week 9 Edge	3
Week 11 Edge	7
Week 12 Edge	0
Week 13 Edge	0
Week 14 Edge	0
Week 15 Edge	1
Week 16 Edge	0
Week 17 Edge	0

Health by Unit*

2018 Rk	24
2017 Rk	
2018 v 2017 Rk	6
Off Rk	
Def Rk	1
QB Rk	
RB Rk	
WR Rk	
TE Rk	14
Oline Rk	28
Dline Rk	7
LB Rk	4
DB Rk	5

*Based on the work of Football Outsiders

2018 Weekly Betting Lines (wks 1-16)

1	2	3	4	5	6	7	8	9	11	12	13	14	15	16
PHI	DAL	CHI	NYG	NE	MIA	SF	MIN	BUF	NYJ	DET	CAR	GB	PHI	NYG
9	0	2.5	3	6.5	1	-1	7.5	3.5	-2.5	-2	5	9	3.5	-3
A		A	H	A	A				H		A	H	H	

Avg = 2.8

Home Lines (wks 1-16)

2	3	5	7	11	12	15	16
DAL	CHI	NE	SF	NYJ	DET	PHI	NYG
0	2.5	6.5	-1	-2.5	-2	3.5	-3

Avg = 0.5

Road Lines (wks 1-16)

1	4	6	8	9	13	14
PHI	NYG	MIA	MIN	BUF	CAR	GB
9	3	1	7.5	3.5	5	9

Avg = 5.4

Washington Redskins 2018 Play Analysis

2018 Play Tendencies

All Pass %	57%
All Pass Rk	22
All Rush %	43%
All Rush Rk	11
1 Score Pass %	55%
1 Score Pass Rk	26
2017 1 Score Pass %	57%
2017 1 Score Pass Rk	18
2018 Pass Increase %	-2%
Pass Increase Rk	24
1 Score Rush %	45%
1 Score Rush Rk	7
Up Pass %	45%
Up Pass Rk	27
Up Rush %	55%
Up Rush Rk	6
Down Pass %	65%
Down Pass Rk	21
Down Rush %	35%
Down Rush Rk	12

2018 Down & Distance Tendencies

Down	Distance	Total Plays	Pass Rate	Run Rate	Play Success %
1	Short (1-3)	6	17%	83%	67%
	Med (4-7)	9	44%	56%	56%
	Long (8-10)	277	39%	61%	44%
	XL (11+)	17	65%	35%	41%
2	Short (1-3)	29	31%	69%	55%
	Med (4-7)	73	66%	34%	52%
	Long (8-10)	85	68%	32%	47%
	XL (11+)	52	77%	23%	21%
3	Short (1-3)	36	56%	44%	67%
	Med (4-7)	44	91%	9%	41%
	Long (8-10)	34	91%	9%	32%
	XL (11+)	36	86%	14%	8%
4	Short (1-3)	7	43%	57%	71%
	Med (4-7)	2	100%	0%	0%
	Long (8-10)	1	100%	0%	0%

Shotgun %:

Under Center	Shotgun
37%	63%

37% AVG 63%

Run Rate:

Under Center	Shotgun
73%	22%

68% AVG 23%

Pass Rate:

Under Center	Shotgun
27%	78%

32% AVG 77%

Short Yardage Intelligence:

2nd and Short Run

Run Freq	Run Rk	NFL Run Freq Avg	Run 1D Rate	Run NFL 1D Avg
53%	30	65%	75%	68%

2nd and Short Pass

Pass Freq	Pass Rk	NFL Pass Freq Avg	Pass 1D Rate	Pass NFL 1D Avg
47%	2	35%	43%	56%

Most Frequent Play

Down	Distance	Play Type	Player	Total Plays	Play Success %
1	Short (1-3)	RUSH	Adrian Peterson	2	100%
			Chris Thompson	2	0%
	Med (4-7)	RUSH	Adrian Peterson	5	80%
	Long (8-10)	RUSH	Adrian Peterson	127	37%
	XL (11+)	RUSH	Adrian Peterson	4	25%
2	Short (1-3)	RUSH	Adrian Peterson	12	75%
	Med (4-7)	RUSH	Adrian Peterson	14	29%
	Long (8-10)	PASS	Josh Doctson	11	45%
		RUSH	Adrian Peterson	11	64%
	XL (11+)	PASS	Jordan Reed	5	40%
		RUSH	Adrian Peterson	5	0%
3	Short (1-3)	RUSH	Adrian Peterson	9	78%
	Med (4-7)	PASS	Jordan Reed	8	63%
	Long (8-10)	PASS	Jordan Reed	6	33%
	XL (11+)	PASS	Jordan Reed	6	17%

Most Successful Play*

Down	Distance	Play Type	Player	Total Plays	Play Success %
1	Med (4-7)	RUSH	Adrian Peterson	5	80%
	Long (8-10)	PASS	Paul Richardson	6	83%
2	Short (1-3)	RUSH	Adrian Peterson	12	75%
	Med (4-7)	PASS	Jordan Reed	8	88%
	Long (8-10)	RUSH	Chris Thompson	6	67%
	XL (11+)	PASS	Jordan Reed	5	40%
3	Short (1-3)	RUSH	Adrian Peterson	9	78%
	Med (4-7)	PASS	Jordan Reed	8	63%
	Long (8-10)	PASS	Josh Doctson	5	40%
	XL (11+)	PASS	Josh Doctson	5	20%

Minimum 5 plays to qualify

2018 Weekly Snap Rates

Wk	Opp	Score	Josh Doctson	Jordan Reed	Maurice Harris	Vernon Davis	Jamison Crowder	Paul Richardson	Jeremy Sprinkle	Chris Thompson
1	ARI	W 24-6	70 (89%)	41 (52%)		47 (59%)	49 (62%)	61 (77%)	34 (43%)	33 (42%)
2	IND	L 21-9	71 (96%)	40 (54%)		27 (36%)	69 (93%)	68 (92%)	13 (18%)	50 (68%)
3	GB	W 31-17	47 (77%)	40 (66%)	9 (15%)	37 (61%)	37 (61%)	45 (74%)	24 (39%)	25 (41%)
5	NO	L 43-19		39 (64%)	49 (80%)	26 (43%)	52 (85%)	42 (69%)	11 (18%)	40 (66%)
6	CAR	W 23-17	59 (84%)	47 (67%)	44 (63%)	36 (51%)		52 (74%)	21 (30%)	
7	DAL	W 20-17	57 (95%)	41 (68%)	36 (60%)	27 (45%)			19 (32%)	
8	NYG	W 20-13	56 (82%)	53 (78%)	56 (82%)	33 (49%)		46 (68%)	19 (28%)	26 (38%)
9	ATL	L 38-14	68 (99%)	37 (54%)	60 (87%)	32 (46%)		54 (78%)	12 (17%)	
10	TB	W 16-3	45 (78%)	38 (66%)	38 (66%)	27 (47%)			26 (45%)	
11	HOU	L 23-21	64 (85%)	50 (67%)	41 (55%)	28 (37%)			27 (36%)	
12	DAL	L 31-23	59 (94%)	47 (75%)	36 (57%)	26 (41%)			10 (16%)	
13	PHI	L 28-13	43 (96%)	31 (69%)	28 (62%)	23 (51%)	29 (64%)		8 (18%)	29 (64%)
14	NYG	L 40-16	55 (89%)	7 (11%)	35 (56%)	49 (79%)	54 (87%)		16 (26%)	25 (40%)
15	JAC	W 16-13	56 (82%)		30 (44%)	30 (44%)	42 (62%)		41 (60%)	29 (43%)
16	TEN	L 25-16	55 (89%)				54 (87%)		46 (74%)	22 (35%)
17	PHI	L 24-0	41 (91%)				42 (93%)		36 (80%)	29 (64%)
	Grand Total		846 (88%)	511 (61%)	462 (61%)	448 (49%)	428 (77%)	368 (76%)	363 (36%)	308 (50%)

Personnel Groupings

Personnel	Team %	NFL Avg	Succ. %
1-1 [3WR]	71%	65%	44%
1-2 [2WR]	18%	17%	41%
1-3 [1WR]	7%	3%	51%

Grouping Tendencies

Personnel	Pass Rate	Pass Succ. %	Run Succ. %
1-1 [3WR]	63%	41%	49%
1-2 [2WR]	50%	39%	43%
1-3 [1WR]	34%	57%	48%

Red Zone Targets (min 3)

Receiver	All	Inside 5	6-10	11-20
Josh Doctson	8	2	2	4
Jordan Reed	7	1	4	2
Chris Thompson	4		1	3
Jamison Crowder	4		1	3
Jeremy Sprinkle	4		3	1
Maurice Harris	4	1		3
Adrian Peterson	3		2	1

Red Zone Rushes (min 3)

Rusher	All	Inside 5	6-10	11-20
Adrian Peterson	31	8	5	18
Alex Smith	10	1	1	8
Chris Thompson	3	2		1

Early Down Target Rate

	RB	TE	WR
	24%	26%	50%
	23%	21%	56%
		NFL AVG	

Overall Target Success %

	RB	TE	WR
	41%	50%	47%
	#26	#25	#27

Additional Team Analysis

From the Colts Chapter

But in 2018, Luck's deep-right YPA dropped to 10.7 with a 37% Success Rate.

Luck excelled on a variety of drops under Reich, his most frequent being three steps. But his Success Rates were also high at five and seven steps. Luck wasn't necessarily as reliant on play action as other quarterbacks are for success, but his 60% Success Rate and 9.3 yards per attempt were upper echelon on play-action throws.

2019 offers much hope for the Colts in Luck's second year removed from his injury and year two with Reich. Despite Luck's return for all 16 games, Indianapolis was the NFL's third most-injured team in 2018, particularly suffering casualties at defensive line and secondary. The Colts should experience positive regression there.

Noteworthy is Indianapolis' strength of schedule. The offense faces a softer slate of defenses, but last year's Colts' defense faced the NFL's easiest schedule of opposing offenses and will shift to a league-average SOS this year.

The ceiling is justifiably high for the Colts in 2019. The 2017 Colts led entering halftime in nine games and entering the fourth quarter in nine games. The 2018 Colts led entering halftime in nine games and entering the fourth quarter in nine games. The 2017 Colts went 2-7 and 4-5 respectively in those nine games, whereas the 2018 Colts went 8-1 in both situations. Coaching matters, as does a healthy quarterback.

I'm just wondering what the world will discuss this summer in the vacuum that is created from so much time spent speculating negatively on Luck's future last summer? Surely there will be something else to get mad about online. There always is.

From the Rams Chapter

At least this year's Rams face the NFL's seventh-softest schedule based on overall opponent strength, including just three top-ten foes. The 2018 Rams were even better in offensive Early Down Success Rate than 2017's club, and bring back all of their most critical pieces highlighted by the return of Cooper Kupp.

Last year's Rams dropped from No. 8 to No. 22 in Early Down Success Rate defense, however. There was a midyear stretch where the Rams covered the spread in just 1-of-8 games and lost the EDSR battle in five of six. Yet they won four of those five, albeit by five points or less. All told, the Rams went 6-1 in one-score games and 4-0 in games decided by a field goal or less.

The Rams have also been the NFL's healthiest team over the last three years. Some regression to those closely-decided wins and health normalcy is inevitable.

But McVay's scheme is still difficult to defend, and the Rams have enough pieces to capitalize. While I believe Goff's ceiling is lower than most do, this team remains poised for another title run. It helps that the Rams play a whopping five games with rest advantages on their opponents, including key tilts with the Saints, Browns, 49ers, Steelers, and Seahawks.

From the Buccaneers Chapter

until at least October after suffering a neck injury in a May 2 car accident.

Arians is justifiably excited about No. 5 overall pick Devin White. "People say we need a pass rusher," Arians stated after the White pick. "He's pretty good at that. And we do like to blitz up the middle, and quarterbacks don't like pressure up the middle." In a division with Alvin Kamara, Christian McCaffrey, and Devonta Freeman, White's 4.4 speed will be valuable in running back coverage.

The Bucs also lost DT Gerald McCoy, but Arians believes Ndamukong Suh is a better fit. The back half of the defense remains a problem, although the Bucs used second- and third-round picks on defensive backs. The good news is the defense can't possibly be worse than it was the last two years. Playing in the NFC South is always a major challenge for any defense, and Tampa Bay also must face non-division offenses including the Rams, Colts, and Texans, as well as 49ers and Cardinals offenses that will be better this year.

Washington Redskins 2018 Passing Recap & 2019 Outlook

Despite having **Dwayne Haskins** fall to them, the Redskins are in a tough situation at quarterbacks. Installing journeyman **Case Keenum** as the starter would be akin to entering quarterback purgatory. Keenum is a lot more likely to produce a win-loss record similar to his 26-28 career mark as a starter than his outlier 11-3 season in 2017 with the Vikings – especially since the Redskins' current crop of receivers are a far cry from **Adam Thielen** and **Stefon Diggs**. Haskins has franchise quarterback potential, but his draft day slide should be at least mildly concerning. Another concern is that Snyder will likely influence the decision of when he's ready to start more than Gruden will. I'm projecting the Redskins will face the ninth-easiest schedule of pass defenses this year, but whoever starts at quarterback likely won't have the benefit of a solid run game, as Washington comes up with the third-toughest schedule of run defenses in my projections. A lot of second-and-longs are likely in store for the Redskins offense, which will make it tough for their quarterbacks to have consistent success throwing the football.

2018 Standard Passing Table

QB	Comp	Att	Comp %	Yds	YPA	TDs	INT	Sacks	Rating	Rk
Alex Smith	205	328	63%	2,180	6.6	10	5	22	86	34
Colt McCoy	34	54	63%	372	6.9	3	3	6	79	41
NFL Avg			62%		7.0				87.5	

2018 Advanced Passing Table

QB	Success %	EDSR Passing Success %	20+ Yd Pass Gains	20+ Yd Pass %	30+ Yd Pass Gains	30+ Yd Pass %	Avg. Air Yds per Comp	Avg. YAC per Comp	20+ Air Yd Comp	20+ Air Yd %
Alex Smith	43%	47%	28	9.0%	7	2.0%	5.8	4.8	11	3%
Colt McCoy	45%	52%	4	7.0%	2	4.0%	6.4	4.5	1	2%
NFL Avg	44%	48%	29.5	8.4%	12.5	3.7%	5.8	5.1	14.5	6%

Interception Rates by Down

Yards to Go	1st Dwn	2nd Dwn	3rd Dwn	4th Dwn	Total
1 & 2	0.0%	0.0%	0.0%	50.0%	3.8%
3, 4, 5	0.0%	0.0%	4.2%	0.0%	2.1%
6 - 9	0.0%	0.0%	3.1%	0.0%	1.2%
10 - 14	2.2%	0.0%	0.0%	0.0%	1.3%
15+	0.0%	0.0%	0.0%		0.0%
Total	1.9%	0.0%	1.9%	12.5%	1.4%

3rd Down Passing - Short of Sticks Analysis

QB	Avg. Yds to Go	Avg. YIA (of Comp)	Avg Yds Short	Short of Sticks Rate	Short Rk
Alex Smith	8.0	6.8	-1.2	60%	15
NFL Avg	7.8	6.4	-1.4	60%	

Air Yds vs YAC

Air Yds %	YAC %	Rk
55%	45%	15
53%	48%	

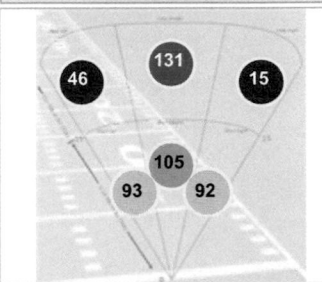

Alex Smith Rating All Downs

59	129	42
	102	
	85 · 91	

Alex Smith Rating Early Downs

46	131	15
	105	
	93 · 92	

2018 Receiving Recap & 2019 Outlook

Two notable contradictory headlines surrounding the team emerged during the 2019 offseason: "Washington passes on **Josh Doctson's** fifth-year option," and "Gruden is expecting big things from Josh Doctson this year." The latter would be highly optimistic for the former first-round pick that has thus far failed to meet expectations. Perimeter WRs should average much more than 7.0 YPA, but in each of the past two years, Doctson failed to exceed 6.8, catching just 50% of his targets with just 33 yards per game. 2018 signing **Paul Richardson** has missed 26 games over his five-year career and may not be able to stay healthy enough to maintain the role, while other options such as **Trey Quinn** and rookies **Terry McLaurin** and **Kelvin Harmon** lack experience.

Player *Min 50 Targets	Targ	Comp %	YPA	Rating	Success %	Success Rk	Missed YPA Rk	YAS % Rk	YTS % Rk	TDs
Jordan Reed	84	64%	6.7	81.5	49%	85	142	106	38	2
Josh Doctson	79	56%	6.7	58.6	51%	64	144	88	9	2
Chris Thompson	55	75%	4.8	90.3	40%	121	172	130	18	1
Jamison Crowder	50	58%	7.8	87.8	44%	110	155	113	38	1

Directional Passer Rating Delivered

Receiver	Short Left	Short Middle	Short Right	Deep Left	Deep Middle	Deep Right	Player Total
Jordan Reed	54	96	90	94	110		82
Josh Doctson	111	115	37	8	41	0	59
Chris Thompson	93	83	86				90
Jamison Crowder	67	119	77	76	96	52	88
Maurice Harris	94	88	21	61	42	58	52
Vernon Davis	100	109	98	127	129	39	109
Paul Richardson	69	125	88	63	105	117	100
Adrian Peterson	93	123	102				112
Michael Floyd	93	66	81	40	58	40	51
Kapri Bibbs	101	8	131				81
Samaje Perine	83		56				77
Brian Quick	92	92	92				92
Team Total	89	98	76	50	77	27	80

2018 Rushing Recap & 2019 Outlook

The big question in DC will be whether **Derrius Guice** is fully healed from his ACL injury and how effective he will be upon returning. I worry about Washington's offensive line more than its running backs. Last year the line ranked 28th in stuffed run rate and 26th in Adjusted Line Yards, per Football Outsiders. The Redskins could be without left tackle **Trent Williams**, who is currently at odds with the organization over an injury dispute. They also lost **Ty Nsekhe**, a very underrated tackle, to the Bills this offseason. Add that to the fact that Gruden tends to be too run-heavy, which causes the entire run game to operate less efficiently, and the fact that the Redskins will face third-toughest schedule of run defenses, and the Washington run game could struggle in 2019.

Player *Min 50 Rushes	Rushes	YPC	Success %	Success Rk	Missed YPA Rk	YTS % Rk	YAS % Rk	Early Down Success %	Early Down Success Rk	TDs
Adrian Peterson	251	4.2	47%	41	52	34	8	45%	46	7

Yards per Carry by Direction

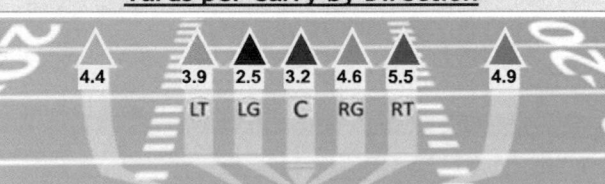

4.4		3.9	2.5	3.2	4.6	5.5		4.9
		LT	LG	C	RG	RT		

Directional Run Frequency

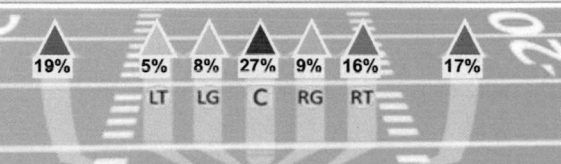

19%		5%	8%	27%	9%	16%		17%
		LT	LG	C	RG	RT		

Somehow, though, the Redskins sat at 6-3 through Week 10, making the situation ripe for a backwards, results-over-process mentality.

"The run game is backwards on first down."
"Who cares? They're 6-3."

"They're misusing their best receiver."
"Could be. But hey, they're 6-3."

"They're short-circuiting potential touchdown drives with fruitless handoffs to an over-the-hill running back." "I can't hear you, I'm too busy singing the Redskins fight song. Did you know that they're 6-3?"

Many of the Redskins' early-season wins were not sustainable. They should have lost to the Panthers in Week 6, when Carolina earned 22 first downs and was forced into third down only 10 times while Washington had as many first downs (18) as third-down attempts. But thanks to being +3 in the turnover department, Washington held on for a 23-17 victory. And thanks to more favorable turnover luck, the Redskins narrowly bested the Cowboys, 20-17, the next week despite seeing Dallas post a higher Success Rate.

Washington's Week 10 victory over Tampa Bay in Week 10 takes the cake, though. The Buccaneers thoroughly dominated the Redskins, besting them 501-286 in total yardage, 29-15 in first downs, and 5-2 in offensive red zone trips. But somehow, the Buccaneers could not convert on a single one of those red zone trips and

(cont'd - see WAS-5)

Washington Redskins Fantasy Corner

A plus-sized (6'3/231) pocket passer who started only one year at Ohio State but made the most of it, **Dwayne Haskins** earned 2018's Big Ten Offensive Player of the Year by averaging 9.14 yards per attempt with a 50:8 TD-to-INT ratio for the 13-1 Buckeyes. He lacks dual-threat capability with 5.04 "speed," however, and struggles when forced off his spot. Haskins' destination is also unideal based on Washington's weak pass-catcher corps and organizational dysfunction. Long term, Haskins best profiles as a fantasy QB2.

- Evan Silva

2018 Situational Usage by Player & Position

Usage Rate by Score

		Being Blown Out (14+)	Down Big (9-13)	One Score	Large Lead (9-13)	Blowout Lead (14+)
RUSH	Adrian Peterson	3%	6%	74%	11%	6%
	Chris Thompson	19%	9%	53%	12%	7%
	Maurice Harris			50%	50%	
	Jamison Crowder		25%	50%	25%	
	Kapri Bibbs	35%	10%	30%	20%	5%
	Paul Richardson			100%		
	Samaje Perine	63%		38%		
	Rob Kelley			75%		25%
	Total	9%	7%	67%	12%	6%
PASS	Adrian Peterson	4%	8%	76%		12%
	Chris Thompson	28%	30%	34%	4%	4%
	Jordan Reed	10%	18%	55%	11%	6%
	Josh Doctson	9%	15%	66%	4%	5%
	Maurice Harris	35%	13%	50%	2%	
	Jamison Crowder	23%	16%	49%	7%	5%
	Kapri Bibbs	6%	28%	61%		6%
	Paul Richardson	26%	11%	34%	9%	20%
	Vernon Davis	28%	3%	59%	9%	
	Michael Floyd	9%	5%	77%	9%	
	Samaje Perine	75%				25%
	Total	18%	15%	54%	6%	6%

Share of Offensive Plays by Type

	Adrian Peterson	Chris Thompson	Jordan Reed	Josh Doctson	Maurice Harris	Jamison Crowder	Kapri Bibbs	Paul Richardson	Vernon Davis	Michael Floyd	Samaje Perine	Byron Marshall	Rob Kelley	Brian Quick
RUSH	74%	13%			1%	1%	6%	1%			2%	1%	1%	
PASS	6%	11%	19%	17%	11%	10%	4%	8%	7%	5%	1%	1%		1%
ALL	36%	12%	11%	10%	6%	6%	5%	5%	4%	3%	2%	1%	1%	0%

Positional Target Distribution vs NFL Average

		NFL Wide				Team Only			
		Left	Middle	Right	Total	Left	Middle	Right	Total
Deep	WR	33%	17%	31%	**81%**	31%	21%	23%	**75%**
	TE	4%	4%	7%	**15%**	14%	5%	6%	**25%**
	RB	1%	0%	2%	**4%**				
	All	39%	22%	40%	**100%**	45%	26%	29%	**100%**
Short	WR	20%	14%	21%	**55%**	18%	13%	14%	**45%**
	TE	6%	6%	8%	**20%**	9%	10%	7%	**26%**
	RB	10%	5%	10%	**25%**	11%	8%	10%	**28%**
	All	36%	25%	39%	**100%**	38%	31%	31%	**100%**
Total		37%	24%	39%	**100%**	39%	30%	31%	**100%**

Positional Success Rates vs NFL Average

		NFL Wide				Team Only			
		Left	Middle	Right	Total	Left	Middle	Right	Total
Deep	WR	40%	50%	40%	**42%**	23%	35%	27%	**28%**
	TE	43%	53%	42%	**45%**	46%	60%	33%	**46%**
	RB	38%	33%	42%	**40%**				
	All	41%	50%	41%	**43%**	30%	40%	29%	**32%**
Short	WR	55%	61%	52%	**55%**	58%	53%	50%	**54%**
	TE	55%	62%	55%	**57%**	53%	57%	41%	**51%**
	RB	47%	54%	46%	**48%**	40%	50%	34%	**41%**
	All	53%	60%	51%	**54%**	52%	54%	43%	**50%**
Total		50%	58%	49%	**52%**	47%	51%	40%	**46%**

Division History: Season Wins & 2019 Projection

	2015 Wins	2016 Wins	2017 Wins	2018 Wins	Forecast 2019 Wins

Rank of 2019 Defensive Pass Efficiency Faced by Week

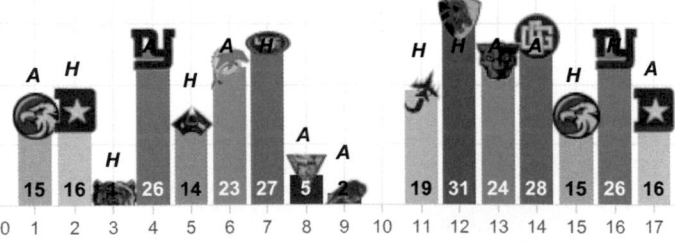

| 15 | 16 | | 26 | 14 | 23 | 27 | 5 | 2 | | 19 | 31 | 24 | 28 | 15 | 26 | 16 |

0 1 2 3 4 5 6 7 8 9 10 11 12 13 14 15 16 17

Rank of 2019 Defensive Rush Efficiency Faced by Week

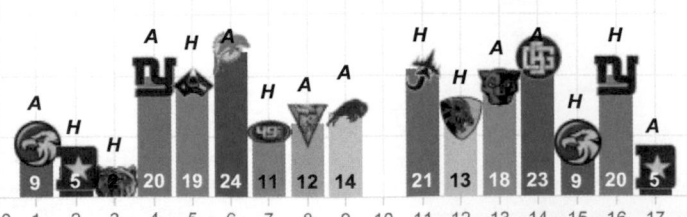

| 9 | 5 | 2 | 20 | 19 | 24 | 11 | 12 | 14 | | 21 | 13 | 18 | 23 | 9 | 20 | 5 |

0 1 2 3 4 5 6 7 8 9 10 11 12 13 14 15 16 17

2018 Detailed Analytics Summary
Success by Play Type & Primary Personnel Groupings

Successful Play Rate 0% ▬▬▬ 100%

Type	1-1 [3WR]	1-2 [2WR]	1-3 [1WR]	2-2 [1WR]	2-1 [2WR]	0-0 [5WR]	2-3 [0WR]	1-0 [4WR]	2-0 [3WR]	ALL
PASS	41% (434)	39% (87)	57% (23)		50% (2)	100% (2)		100% (1)	50% (2)	42% (551)
RUSH	49% (253)	43% (87)	48% (44)	50% (16)	20% (5)	0% (3)	100% (3)	0% (1)		47% (412)
All	44% (687)	41% (174)	51% (67)	50% (16)	29% (7)	40% (5)	100% (3)	50% (2)	50% (2)	44% (963)

Format   Success Rate (Total # of Plays)

Receiving Success by Top-4 Personnel Groupings
(Min 50 targets)

POS	Player	1-1 [3WR]	1-2 [2WR]	1-3 [1WR]	2-0 [3WR]	4 Grp Total
RB	Chris Thompson	41% (51) 5.1, 94.4	0% (1) 0.0, 39.6	50% (2) 2.5, 56.3		41% (54) 4.9, 91.9
TE	Jordan Reed	48% (56) 6.3, 94.0	41% (17) 6.2, 47.4	73% (11) 9.3, 101.3		50% (84) 6.7, 85.5
WR	Josh Doctson	47% (60) 6.2, 51.3	65% (17) 8.4, 100.9	0% (1) 0.0, 39.6	100% (1) 20.0, 118.8	51% (79) 6.7, 62.8
WR	Jamison Crowder	46% (46) 8.3, 92.7	100% (1) 8.0, 100.0			47% (47) 8.3, 93.2

Format   Line 1: Success Rate (Total # of Plays)   Line 2: YPA, Passer Rating

Rushing Success by Top-4 Personnel Groupings
(Min 25 carries)

Rusher (Last, First)	1-1 [3WR]	1-2 [2WR]	2-2 [1WR]	2-1 [2WR]	4 Grp Total
Peterson Adrian	46% (138) 4.4	41% (68) 3.5	63% (8) 2.5		45% (214) 4.0
Thompson Chris	26% (34) 4.2	33% (6) 3.2		50% (2) 2.5	29% (42) 4.0
Smith Alex	60% (20) 5.9	50% (8) 3.9	25% (4) -0.3	0% (1) 0.0	52% (33) 4.5

Format   Line 1: Success Rate (Total # of Plays)   Line 2: YPC

Passing by Coverage Scheme

Zone	49% (233) 6.5, 83.3
M2M	53% (154) 8.0, 89.7
Screen	27% (49) 5.3, 95.7
Combo	43% (7) 5.4, 72.3

Passing by Route

Curl	60% (85) 6.1, 91.1
Out	57% (58) 6.0, 79.0
Screen	29% (49) 5.4, 95.8
Slant	65% (43) 9.6, 102.1
Flat	60% (35) 7.6, 107.7
Dig	59% (29) 6.9, 114.2

Throw Types

Level 1	53% (299) 6.5, 94.9
Level 2	45% (134) 7.3, 69.7
Level 3	21% (39) 8.0, 56.1
Shovel	25% (4) 2.8, 77.1
Sidearm	100% (1) 23.0, 118.8

QB Drop Types

3 Step	50% (206) 7.3, 82.2
0/1 Step	59% (128) 7.3, 109.9
5 Step	34% (77) 5.1, 59.0
Basic Screen	21% (28) 4.5, 85.4
Designed Rollout Right	44% (16) 7.3, 39.6
7 Step	57% (14) 9.4, 64.9

QB State at Pass

Planted	53% (331) 7.2, 91.4
Shuffling	39% (54) 6.5, 104.4
Moving	29% (51) 5.4, 47.6

Play Action

	Play Action	No P/A
Under Center	44% (57) 7.7, 64.7	44% (16) 3.8, 93.8
Shotgun	54% (37) 8.8, 110.9	48% (370) 6.6, 83.2
ALL	48% (94) 8.1, 82.9	48% (386) 6.5, 84.6

Run Types

Outside Zone	37% (100) 3.1
Inside Zone	48% (85) 4.8
Power	52% (42) 5.2
Stretch	54% (24) 4.8
Pitch	38% (16) 3.9
Lead	29% (7) 2.7

WAS-5

were -4 in turnover differential, allowing Washington to escape with a 16-3 win.

I could have done minimal research for this chapter, chalking up the Redskins' 1-6 finish following a 6-3 start to losing their starting quarterback and having the most-injured offense in the league overall. I could have then written that they reason for optimism in 2019 after Ohio State quarterback **Dwayne Haskins** fell into their lap at No. 15 overall.

But I have chosen to take a much more pragmatic approach.

The Redskins' overly run-heavy tendencies on first down have not been addressed thus far, so why should we expect them to be with either a rookie quarterback or a veteran in his first year with the team under center?

Washington has the fifth-most difficult schedule of any team over the first five weeks of 2019, with games against the Eagles, Cowboys, Bears, and Patriots. Their schedule gets considerably easier after a Thursday night game in Minnesota in Week 8, but that should offer little reason for optimism given that it may already be too late: The team has lost more players to injury over the last five years than any team in the NFL, which hints at something more than just bad luck playing a role.

The Redskins have the second-most expensive offense in the NFL but calls plays like they have one of the cheapest.

Not that you would know this is an expensive offense from the players currently on the roster. Please don't defend Alex Smith's salary though confined to the bench: in 2018 Alex Smith faced the NFL's easiest schedule of pass defenses in his starts yet ranked 33/39 in YPA (6.6) & 31/34 in Success Rate (43%).

While I loved the top-half of their draft, the overall talent on offense is still lacking. And based on past history and current circumstance, we should have little confidence that Gruden will make the adjustments necessary to maximize his team's offensive potential and compliment what has become a solid defense.

This offseason, defensive tackle **Jonathan Allen** said, "We have a bunch of pieces, but pieces don't win games." Unfortunately, you could recycle this message virtually every year for the Redskins since **Daniel Snyder** bought the team in 1999.

44942928R00155

Made in the USA
Lexington, KY
14 July 2019